NEW! Entrepreneurs in Action Opening Vignettes

Each chapter opens with a real-world success story emphasizing timely ideas done well—such as Crocs, Spanx, Leatherman, infomercial entrepreneurs—or new ideas in the face of change—including Cryogenic rail cars, FaceBook, iModerate, FLIP camcorders, and more. These insightful examples enable students to see chapter concepts in the context of real-world marketing.

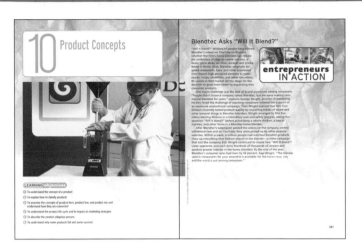

New! Responsible Marketing?

This insightful marginal feature presents a controversial marketing topic and then challenges students to contemplate the black, white, and gray area surrounding the marketing practice in question—giving students practice looking at all sides of today's marketing issues.

New! Illustrations and Examples

New advertisements from well-known organizations illustrate chapter topics, while experiences of real-world companies exemplify marketing concepts and strategies throughout.

globalEDGE™ Exercises

Provided by the Center for International Business Education and Research at Michigan State University (founders of the globalEDGE website), these hands-on applications invite students to look at the global economy and ways to market to it and from within it.

New! Developing Your Marketing Plan

Comprehensive end-of-chapter exercises tie chapter concepts into the overall marketing plan. Each exercise ends with a reference to Interactive Marketing Plan activity found at **www.cengage.com/ marketing/pride-ferrell**. Together, these two exercises can create a potential semester-long project on the marketing plan.

Strategic Cases

At the end of each part, a strategic case helps students apply the diverse concepts that have been discussed within the related chapters by focusing on companies like Reebok, XM Satellite Radio, and Texas Instruments.

End-of-Chapter Cases

Two in-depth cases end each chapter, allowing students to apply chapter concepts through real-world examples featuring such companies as Netflix, Method, SmartCar USA, Harley, and many more. The headlining video case is supported by company-specific video segments that can be viewed with the companion DVD or online with EduSpace.

Snapshot Features

All 20 Snapshot features are new and engage students by highlighting interesting, up-to-date statistics that link marketing theory to students' own world.

MARKETING

MARKETING

2010 EDITION

William M. Pride
Texas A & M University

O. C. Ferrell
University of New Mexico

Montante Family Library
D'Youville College

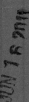

SOUTH-WESTERN
CENGAGE Learning™

Australia • Brazil • Japan • Korea • Mexico • Singapore • Spain • United Kingdom • United States

To Sherry McKenzie, Eric and Cathy McKenzie, Heather McKenzie, and Nancy and Peter Norris

To Linda Ferrell

Special Dedication
To Gwyneth Walters who has made a significant contribution to our book over the past 20 years.

SOUTH-WESTERN
CENGAGE Learning

Marketing, **2010 Edition**
William M. Pride
O. C. Ferrell

Vice President and Editorial Director:
Jack Calhoun
Editor in Chief: Melissa Acuña
Acquisitions Editors: Mike Schenk,
Mike Roche
Development Editor: Suzanna Bainbridge
Editorial Assistants: Matt DiGangi,
Shanna Shelton, Jill Clark
Senior Media Producer: Nancy Hiney
Media Editor: John Rich
Media Producer: John Farrell
Senior Content Manager:
Rachel D'Angelo Wimberly
Executive Marketing Manager:
Kimberly Kanakes
Marketing Communications Manager:
Sarah Greber
Senior Project Manager, Editorial
Production: Nancy Blodget
Senior Content Project Manager:
Cliff Kallemeyn
Creative Director: Rob Hugel
Art and Design Manager: Jill Haber
Senior Manufacturing Coordinator:
Diane Gibbons
Senior Rights Acquisition Account
Manager: Katie Huha
Permissions Editor: Karyn Morrison
Text Designer: Jerilyn Bockorick
Senior Photo Editor: Jennifer Meyer Dare
Photo Researcher: Susan Holtz
Copy Editor: Deborah Prato
Art Editor: Karen Lindsay
Illustrator: Pat Rossi
Composition Buyer: Chuck Dutton
Cover Design Manager: Anne S. Katzeff
Cover Designer: Walter Kopec
Cover Credits: © Rtimages/shutterstock,
© Carr Clifton/Minden Pictures
Compositor: Nesbitt Graphics, Inc.

For product information and technology assistance, contact us at
Cengage Learning Customer & Sales Support, 1-800-354-9706

For permission to use material from this text or product,
submit all requests online at **www.cengage.com/permissions**
Further permissions questions can be e-mailed to
permissionrequest@cengage.com.

Library of Congress Control Number: 2008928620

Library Edition ISBN-13: 978-0-547-16747-3

Library Edition ISBN-10: 0-547-16747-4

Looseleaf Edition ISBN-13: 978-0-547-16746-6

Looseleaf Edition ISBN-10: 0-547-16746-6

Instructor's Edition ISBN-13: 978-0-324-83429-1

Instructor's Edition ISBN-10: 0-324-83429-2

South-Western Cengage Learning
5191 Natorp Boulevard
Mason, OH 45040
USA

Cengage Learning products are represented in Canada by
Nelson Education, Ltd.

For your course and learning solutions, visit **www.cengage.com**
Purchase any of our products at your local college store or at our
preferred online store **www.ichapters.com.**

Printed in China by China Translation & Printing Services Limited
2 3 4 5 6 7 12 11 10 09

BRIEF CONTENTS

v

part **2**

Environmental Forces and Social and Ethical Responsibilities   61

3
The Marketing Environment   62

4
Social Responsibility and Ethics in Marketing 92

part 3

Using Information, Technology, and Target Market Analysis   127

5
Marketing Research and Information Systems 128

6

Target Markets: Segmentation, Evaluation, and Positioning   158

part 4

Customer Behavior   191

7

Consumer Buying Behavior   192

8
Business Markets and
Buying Behavior   222

9
Reaching
Global Markets   244

part 5

Product Decisions   279

10
Product Concepts 280

11
Developing and Managing Products 304

12 Branding and Packaging 326

13 Services Marketing 354

part 6

Distribution Decisions   385

14
Marketing Channels and Supply-Chain Management   386

15
Retailing, Direct Marketing, and Wholesaling   422

part 7

Promotion Decisions   457

16
Integrated Marketing Communications   458

17
Advertising and Public Relations   488

18
Personal Selling and Sales Promotion   516

part 8

Pricing Decisions   **549**

appendix **A**
Careers in Marketing   A-1

appendix **B**
Financial Analysis in Marketing   A-17

appendix **C**
Sample Marketing Plan   A-27

PREFACE

Marketing in a Changing World

Marketing excites students and interests them in business because of the need to adapt and respond to the changing world environment. *Marketing: Concepts and Strategies* leads the market with relevant foundational concepts and best practices that relate to the real world. This new edition has undergone the most extensive revision ever, resulting in the most up-to-date text possible. In reflecting the need for efficiency and learning, we have paid careful attention to maintaining all key concepts with a reduced number of chapters and shorter page count. In making this book more compact, we have carefully analyzed and rebuilt the content to be current and reflect important changes in the marketing environment.

As business has begun to recognize the importance of sustainability initiatives, we have incorporated a green theme throughout the book. We view green marketing as a strategic process involving stakeholder assessment in order to create meaningful long-term relationships with customers while maintaining, supporting, and enhancing the natural environment. Green marketing has become important to business because of the many challenges we face in maintaining a habitable world for generations to come. With carbon emissions becoming a focal point of most reports on how to minimize global warming, the need to reduce, reuse, and recycle has become a source of green initiatives for most businesses. There is a lot of room for growth in this area. Consider that the United States uses more than 100 billion plastic bags each year, with only 1 percent of these bags recycled, while the rest end up in landfills. Not only is going green popular, seeking sustainability can also help businesses save money and energy in the long run. Recycling just one aluminum can saves enough energy to keep a one-hundred-watt light bulb burning for four hours or to power a television for three hours. Facts like these are changing the way companies engage in marketing. With only 12 percent of electrical appliances being recycled, Dell was the first and is the only computer company to provide consumers free recycling of products from Dell and other manufacturers. This program keeps toxic waste out of landfills while giving the company a source for reusable materials. We believe that green marketing is not only good for the environment but can also provide a competitive advantage for business. Our book is printed on recycled paper, and everything we did in this revision considered ways to minimize negative impacts on the environment. Growing up around these topics, students understand and relate to creating a greener world.

Details of this extensive revision are available in the transition guide in the *Instructor's Resource Manual*. We have also made efforts to improve all teaching ancillaries and student learning tools. PowerPoints continue to be a very popular teaching device, and a special effort has been made to upgrade the PowerPoint program to enhance classroom teaching. The authors and publisher have worked together to provide a competent teaching package and ancillaries that are unsurpassed in the marketplace.

The authors have maintained a hands-on approach to teaching this material and revising the text and its ancillaries. This results in an integrated teaching package and approach that is accurate, sound, and successful in reaching students. The outcome of this involvement fosters trust and confidence in the teaching package and in student learning outcomes.

Keeping Pace with the Challenges and the Changing World

We believe that marketing students are changing as rapidly as the marketing environment. Today's students are looking for knowledge that is timely, relevant, and application oriented. We also know that a concise feature or application such as a box or exercise can enliven foundational marketing concepts. Therefore, in this edition we created three totally new boxed features and a new marginal feature that help to make the book engaging. Every chapter starts with an **Entrepreneurs in Action** feature. The opening vignette to each chapter provides an example of how an entrepreneur started a business that was based on a sound marketing decision. This feature provides an opportunity to discuss the role of entrepreneurship and marketing and the need for creativity in developing successful marketing strategies. Each chapter also contains an entertainment marketing feature—**E-ntertainment Marketing**—that highlights a highly visible example from the sports or entertainment industry, including widely publicized products that are often associated with mass media interest. This feature includes a number of very successful products associated with e-marketing and online services. In addition, each chapter has a **Green Marketing** box that relates marketing activities to sustainability and the natural environment. These features were carefully selected after examining key student interests and emerging marketing environment considerations. These three themes provide the opportunity to discuss the emerging marketing trends and practices in every chapter.

We continue to emphasize global marketing, ethics, and social responsibility as well through integrated concepts and examples in most of the chapters. The role of the United States and our world economy has become challenging and at times controversial. **Responsible Marketing?** is a new marginal feature that allows students to examine and debate ethical and other responsibility issues. And, with the economies of developing countries accelerating at a fast pace, global economic resources are under strain. Nearly every business decision has to consider global competition and environmental implications as they shape marketing strategies. The 2008–2009 downturn in the world economy created new marketing challenges that are reflected in this revision. We address these issues and provide examples to help students understand the marketing implications.

An introductory marketing text must be revised on a timely basis to remain up to date and to reflect current changes in marketing and the marketing environment. For example, we have included the American Marketing Association's new definition of marketing in Chapter 1 along with our definition so students can see how perceptions about marketing's role in business and society are changing. Throughout the text we have updated content with the most recent research that supports the frameworks and best practices for marketing.

Features of the Book

As with previous editions, this edition of the text provides a comprehensive and practical introduction to marketing that is both easy to teach and to learn. *Marketing: Concepts and Strategies* continues to be one of the most widely adopted introductory textbooks in the world. We appreciate the confidence that adopters have placed in our textbook and continue to work hard to make sure that, as in previous editions, this edition keeps pace with changes. The entire text is structured to excite students about the subject and to help them learn completely and efficiently.

- An *organizational model* at the beginning of each part provides a "road map" of the text and a visual tool for understanding the connection among various components.

- *Learning objectives* at the start of each chapter present concrete expectations about what students are to learn as they read the chapter.

■ Every chapter begins with an *Entrepreneurs in Action* opening vignette. This feature provides an example of how an entrepreneur started a business based on a sound marketing decision. It introduces the role of entrepreneurship in marketing and the need for creativity when developing successful marketing strategies. These vignettes feature such companies as Crocs, Wikipedia, Facebook, iModerate, FLIP camcorders, and TerraCycle.

■ *Key term definitions* appear in the margins to help students build their marketing vocabulary.

■ Figures, tables, photographs, advertisements, and snapshot features increase comprehension and stimulate interest.

■ Boxed features—*E-ntertainment Marketing* and *Green Marketing*—reinforce the focus of this edition on responsible marketing in a changing world by enhancing the chapter concepts with such examples as: Wii, Burning Man, Extreme Home Green Makeover, Skype, and Recycline.

■ A new *Responsible Marketing?* marginal feature discusses a controversial issue related to ethics and social responsibility.

■ A complete *chapter summary* reviews the major topics discussed, and the list of *important terms* provides another end-of-chapter study aid to expand students' marketing vocabulary.

■ *Discussion and review questions* at the end of each chapter encourage further study and exploration of chapter content, and *application questions* enhance students' comprehension of important topics.

■ An *Internet exercise* at the end of each chapter asks students to examine a website and assess one or more strategic issues associated with the site. This section also points students to the various learning tools that are available on the text's website.

■ *Developing Your Marketing Plan* ties the chapter concepts into an overall marketing plan that can be created by completing the Interactive Marketing Plan activity found at **www.cengage.com/marketing/pride-ferrell**. The *Developing Your Marketing Plan* feature allows students to explore each chapter topic in relation to developing and implementing a marketing campaign.

■ Two **globalEDGE™** exercises invite students to look at the global economy and ways to market to it and from within it. These exercises are provided by the Center for International Business Education and Research at Michigan State University (CIBER@MSU), the founders of the **globalEDGE** website. A knowledge web portal that connects international business professionals worldwide to a wealth of information, insights, and learning resources on global business activities, the site is the most comprehensive international business resource on the Internet and the world's leading online source in international business as ranked by Google, Yahoo!, MSN, and AOL.

■ Two *cases* at the end of each chapter help students understand the application of chapter concepts. One of the end-of-chapter cases is related to a video segment. Some examples of companies highlighted in the cases are Method, Numi Tea, Lonely Planet, Netflix, Vans Shoes, Washburn Guitars, and the Smart Car (Smart Car USA).

■ A *strategic case* at the end of each part helps students integrate the diverse concepts that have been discussed within the related chapters.

■ *Appendixes* discuss marketing career opportunities, explore financial analysis in marketing, and present a sample marketing plan.

■ A comprehensive *glossary* defines more than 625 important marketing terms.

Text Organization

We have organized the eight parts of *Marketing: Concepts and Strategies* to give students a theoretical and practical understanding of marketing decision making.

Part One   **Marketing Strategy and Customer Relationships**
Provides an overview of marketing, strategic marketing planning, and implementation

Part Two   **Environmental Forces and Social and Ethical Responsibilities**
Provides an overview of the marketing environmental concepts, influences, and trends within a responsible and ethical scope

Part Three **Using Information, Technology, and Target Market Analysis**
Examines how marketers use information and technology to better understand and reach customers

Part Four   **Customer Behavior**
Focuses on the development of the marketing strategy as it pertains to the customer

Part Five   **Product Decisions**
Discusses product concepts, developing and managing products, branding, packaging, and services marketing

Part Six   **Distribution Decisions**
Provides coverage of marketing channels, supply-chain management, wholesaling, physical distribution, retailing, and direct marketing

Part Seven **Promotion Decisions**
Focuses on integrated communications, advertising, public relations, personal selling, and sales promotion

Part Eight **Pricing Decisions**
Covers pricing concepts and the setting of prices in a dynamic marketing environment

What's New to This Edition?

This edition is revised and updated to address the dynamic issues emerging in the current environment, while continuing to stress the importance of traditional marketing issues. These revisions assist students in gaining a full understanding of marketing practices pertinent today and in helping them anticipate increasing future changes.

Overarching Content Changes

- *Extensive reorganization.* We revised this edition with a keen eye on the current marketing landscape. Upon analysis, we determined that a 20-chapter book fit the current market needs. With e-marketing as a fundamental activity in successful marketing strategy rather than simply a marketing trend, we removed the e-marketing chapter and thoroughly integrated e-marketing practices throughout the text through concept and example. In addition, to help students navigate through various distribution practices, we clearly defined these practices by consolidating the distribution activities into two chapters rather than three. We anticipate that the reorganization of the text to provide students with a clearer path to success and understanding of marketing.

- *Theme-related coverage.* We saw major marketing trends merging at a critical moment in global business when preparing for this revision—entrepreneurial marketing in the wake of growing "green" concerns within a highly cultural-driven marketplace. We combined all three themes in a comprehensive way. In addition to in-text examples, we start every chapter with an entrepreneurial vignette and included theme-specific boxes on green marketing and entertainment marketing throughout the chapter. To really bring the concept of responsible marketing to life, we present a controversial issue in our *Responsible Marketing?* feature and ask students to look at all angles of today's real world marketing environment.

Changes in Every Chapter

- *Opening vignettes.* All of the chapter-opening vignettes are new. They are written to introduce the theme of each chapter by focusing on actual entrepreneurial companies and how they deal with real-world situations.

- *Boxed features.* Each chapter includes two new boxed features that highlight green marketing and entertainment marketing. The majority of the boxed features are new to this edition; a few have been significantly updated and revised to fit the themes of this edition.

- *New Snapshot features.* All 20 Snapshot features are new and engage students by highlighting interesting, up-to-date statistics that link marketing theory to the real world.

- *New research.* Throughout the text we have updated content with the most recent research that supports the frameworks and best practices for marketing.

- *New illustrations and examples.* All new advertisements from well-known firms are employed to illustrate chapter topics. Experiences of real-world companies are used to exemplify marketing concepts and strategies throughout the text. Most examples are new or updated to include e-marketing concepts as well as several new green marketing and entertainment marketing concepts to support the focus of this revision.

- *End-of-chapter cases.* Each chapter contains two cases, including a video case, profiling firms to illustrate concrete application of marketing strategies and concepts. The vast majority of our video cases are new to this edition and supported by current and engaging video clips of exciting companies such as Netflix, Harley-Davidson, Lonely Planet, Washburn Guitars, and Smart Car USA.

- *Responsible Marketing?* This is an exciting feature that asks students to get involved with the current marketing landscape. It presents a controversial marketing concept that is going on within the business world and asks them to consider how they would handle the challenge as a marketer.

A Comprehensive Instructional Resource Package

For instructors, this edition of *Marketing* includes an exceptionally comprehensive package of teaching materials.

- *Instructor Companion Website.* Password protected, the instructor website includes valuable tools to help design and teach the course. Content includes files from the *Instructor's Manual,* the Ad Bank (in PowerPoint ®), premium Power-Point® slides, *CRS (Classroom Response System) Clicker Content,* access to the Interactive Marketing Plan, and more.

- *PowerPoint® slide presentations.* You can now enhance your lecture with a variety of PowerPoint options. Premium PowerPoint slides have been created to provide instructors with up-to-date unique content to increase student application and interest. The Premium PowerPoint slides offer such multimedia content as advertisements, video clips, web links, surveys and graphs, and important terms. An Ad Bank will contain a library of advertisements to further illustrate real-world examples of active marketing and will add a colorful enhancement to your day-to-day lectures.

■ *Classroom Management Systems.* With *Eduspace* powered by Blackboard and *Blackboard/WebCT* course management tools, instructors can create and customize online course materials to use in distance learning, distributed learning, or as a supplement to traditional classes. Each system includes a variety of study aids for instructors, including a gradebook, the Video Cases video footage, and test pools. Active links direct you to the *Instructor's Manual*, PowerPoint slides and Ad Bank, *Classroom Response System (CRS) Clicker Content*, and more.

■ *Computerized Test Bank.* The computerized test bank provides more than 4,000 test items including true/false, multiple-choice, and essay questions. Each objective test item is accompanied by the correct answer, question type and level of difficulty, main text page reference, and AACSB standard coding. Instructors are able to select, edit, and add questions, or generate randomly selected questions to produce a test master for easy duplication.

■ *Instructor's Manual.* The *Instructor's Manual* has been revamped to meet the standards of the text revision. Each chapter contains:

- Quick Reference Guide

- Purpose Statement

- Integrated Lecture Outline with features and multimedia (e.g. PowerPoint call-outs) incorporated

- Discussion Starter recommendations that encourage active exploration of the in-text examples

- Class Exercises, Semester Project Activities (tied to the Interactive Marketing Plan), and Chapter Quizzes

- Suggested Answers to end-of-chapter exercises, cases, and strategic cases

■ *CRS (Classroom Response System) Clicker Content.* CRS provides a convenient and inexpensive way to gauge student comprehension, deliver quizzes or exams, and provide "on-the-spot" assessment. As a testing platform, as an assessment tool, or simply as a way to increase interactivity in the classroom, a CRS provides the technology you need to transform a lecture into a dynamic learning environment.

■ *Marketing Video Case Series.* This series contains videos specifically tied to the end-of-chapter video cases. The vast majority of our video cases are new to this edition and supported by current and engaging video clips of exciting companies such as Netflix, Harley-Davidson, Lonely Planet, Washburn Guitars, and Smart Car USA.

A Format and Supplements to Meet Student Needs

Text Format

We have heard students' concerns about price. In response, we continue to offer all the benefits of a comprehensive textbook, but in the convenient, low-cost loose-leaf format. Students have told us they like this format—they can carry only those chapters they need, and it is available for about two-thirds the cost of a hardcover textbook. For professors or students who want a bound book, we do offer the traditional hardcover, Library version. We also offer a low-cost e-book version of the text. For more information about an e-book, contact your Cengage sales representative.

Supporting Supplements

The complete package available with *Marketing: Concepts and Strategies* includes support materials that facilitate student learning.

- *Companion Website* (**www.cengage.com/marketing/pride-ferrell**). The companion website provides students with learning objectives, chapter summaries, glossary terms, and other text-specific tools.

- *Course Management Systems Powered by Blackboard and WebCT.* Allow your students to take command of the content with such reinforcement activities as:

  - Games—Quiz Bowl and Beat the Clock

  - Interactive Quizzes and Audio Quizzes organized by Learning Objective

  - Audio Summaries

  - Interactive Marketing Plan supported by engaging and unique video

  - Key Term Flashcards

  - Marketing mini-cases and exercises and much more

- *Interactive Marketing Plan.* In this edition, the *Marketing Plan Worksheets* have been revamped and reproduced within an interactive and multimedia environment. A video program has been developed around the worksheets, allowing students to follow a company through the trials and tribulations of launching a new product. This video helps place the conceptual marketing plan into an applicable light and is supported by a summary of the specific stages of the marketing plan as well as a sample plan based on the events of the video. These elements act as the 1-2-3 punch supporting the student while completing his or her own plan, the last step of the *Interactive Marketing Plan. The Plan* is broken up into three functional sections that can either be completed in one simple project or carried over throughout the semester.

Your Comments and Suggestions Are Valued

As authors, our major focus has been on teaching and preparing learning material for introductory marketing students. We have both traveled extensively to work with students and understand the needs of professors of introductory marketing courses. We both teach this marketing course on a regular basis and test the materials included in the book, *Test Bank,* and other ancillary materials to make sure they are effective in the classroom.

Through the years, professors and students have sent us many helpful suggestions for improving the text and ancillary components. We invite your comments, questions, and criticisms. We want to do our best to provide materials that enhance the teaching and learning of marketing concepts and strategies. Your suggestions will be sincerely appreciated. Please write us, or e-mail us at **w-pride@tamu.edu** or **OCFerrell@mgt.unm.edu**, or call 979-845-5857 (Dr. Pride) or 505-277-3468 (Dr. Ferrell).

Acknowledgments

Like most textbooks, this one reflects the ideas of many academicians and practitioners who have contributed to the development of the marketing discipline. We appreciate the opportunity to present their ideas in this book.

A special faculty advisory board assisted us in making decisions during the development of the text and the instructional package. For being "on-call" and available to answer questions and make valuable suggestions, we are grateful to those who participated:

Sana Akili
Iowa State University

Kathleen Krentler
San Diego State University

Katrece Albert
Southern University

John Krupa Jr.
Johnson & Wales University

Frank Barber
Cuyahoga Community College

Marilyn L. Liebrenz-Himes
George Washington University

Nancy Bloom
Nassau Community College

Edna Ragins
North Carolina A&T State University

Peter Bortolotti
Johnson & Wales Uniiversity

Linda Rose
Westwood College Online

Sandra Coyne
Springfield College

Tom Rossi
Broome Community College

Tamara Davis
Davenport University

Don Roy
Middle Tennessee State University

Todd Donovan
Colorado State University

Catherine Ruggieri
St. John's University

Kent Drummond
University of Wyoming

Crina Tarasi
Central Michigan University

Robert Garrity
University of Hawaii

Ruth Taylor
Texas State University

John Hafer
University of Nebraska at Omaha

Janice Williams
University of Central Oklahoma

David Hansen
Texas Southern University

John Withey
Indiana University—South Bend

Tony Henthorne
University of Southern Mississippi

A number of individuals have made helpful comments and recommendations in their reviews of this and earlier editions. We appreciate the generous help of these reviewers:

Zafar U. Ahmed
Minot State University

Julie Baker
Texas Christian University

Thomas Ainscough
*University of Massachusetts—
Dartmouth*

Siva Balasubramanian
Southern Illinois University

Joe F. Alexander
University of Northern Colorado

Joseph Ballenger
Stephen F. Austin State University

Mark I. Alpert
University of Texas at Austin

Guy Banville
Creighton University

David M. Ambrose
University of Nebraska

Joseph Barr
Framingham State College

David Andrus
Kansas State University

Thomas E. Barry
Southern Methodist University

Linda K. Anglin
Minnesota State University

Charles A. Bearchell
*California State University—
Northridge*

George Avellano
Central State University

Richard C. Becherer
University of Tennessee—Chattanooga

Emin Babakus
University of Memphis

Walter H. Beck, Sr.
Reinhardt College

Russell Belk
University of Utah

John Bennett
University of Missouri—Columbia

W. R. Berdine
California State Polytechnic Institute

Karen Berger
Pace University

Bob Berl
University of Memphis

Stewart W. Bither
Pennsylvania State University

Roger Blackwell
Ohio State University

Peter Bloch
University of Missouri—Columbia

Wanda Blockhus
San Jose State University

Paul N. Bloom
University of North Carolina

James P. Boespflug
Arapahoe Community College

Joseph G. Bonnice
Manhattan College

John Boos
Ohio Wesleyan University

Jenell Bramlage
University of Northwestern Ohio

James Brock
Susquehanna College

John R. Brooks, Jr.
Houston Baptist University

William G. Browne
Oregon State University

John Buckley
Orange County Community College

Gul T. Butaney
Bentley College

James Cagley
University of Tulsa

Pat J. Calabros
University of Texas—Arlington

Linda Calderone
*State University of New York
College of Technology atFarmingdale*

Joseph Cangelosi
University of Central Arkansas

William J. Carner
University of Texas—Austin

James C. Carroll
University of Central Arkansas

Terry M. Chambers
Westminster College

Lawrence Chase
*Tompkins Cortland Community
College*

Larry Chonko
Baylor University

Barbara Coe
University of North Texas

Ernest F. Cooke
Loyola College—Baltimore

Robert Copley
University of Louisville

John I. Coppett
University of Houston—Clear Lake

Robert Corey
West Virginia University

Deborah L. Cowles
Virginia Commonwealth University

Melvin R. Crask
University of Georgia

William L. Cron
Texas Christian University

Gary Cutler
Dyersburg State Community College

Bernice N. Dandridge
Diablo Valley College

Lloyd M. DeBoer
George Mason University

Sally Dibb
University of Warwick

Ralph DiPietro
Montclair State University

Paul Dishman
Idaho State University

Suresh Divakar
*State University of New York—
Buffalo*

Casey L. Donoho
Northern Arizona University

Peter T. Doukas
Westchester Community College

Lee R. Duffus
Florida Gulf Coast University

Robert F. Dwyer
University of Cincinnati

Roland Eyears
Central Ohio Technical College

Thomas Falcone
Indiana University of Pennsylvania

James Finch
University of Wisconsin—La Crosse

Letty C. Fisher
*SUNY/Westchester Community
College*

Renée Florsheim
Loyola Marymount University

Charles W. Ford
Arkansas State University

John Fraedrich
*Southern Illinois University,
Carbondale*

David J. Fritzsche
University of Washington

Donald A. Fuller
University of Central Florida

Terry Gable
Truman State University

Ralph Gaedeke
*California State University,
Sacramento*

Cathy Goodwin
University of Manitoba

Geoffrey L. Gordon
Northern Illinois University

Robert Grafton-Small
University of Strathclyde

Harrison Grathwohl
California State University—Chico

Alan A. Greco
*North Carolina A&T State
University*

Blaine S. Greenfield
Bucks County Community College

Thomas V. Greer
University of Maryland

Sharon F. Gregg
Middle Tennessee University

Jim L. Grimm
Illinois State University

Charles Gross
University of New Hampshire

Joseph Guiltinan
University of Notre Dame

Richard C. Hansen
Ferris State University

Nancy Hanson-Rasmussen
University of Wisconsin—Eau Claire

Robert R. Harmon
Portland State University

Mary C. Harrison
Amber University

Lorraine Hartley
Franklin University

Michael Hartline
Florida State University

Timothy Hartman
Ohio University

Salah S. Hassan
George Washington University

Manoj Hastak
American University

Del I. Hawkins
University of Oregon

Dean Headley
Wichita State University

Esther Headley
Wichita State University

Debbora Heflin-Bullock
California State Polytechnic University—Pomona

Merlin Henry
Rancho Santiago College

Lois Herr
Elizabethtown College

Charles L. Hilton
Eastern Kentucky University

Elizabeth C. Hirschman
Rutgers, State University of New Jersey

George C. Hozier
University of New Mexico

John R. Huser
Illinois Central College

Joan M. Inzinga
Bay Path College

Deloris James

University of Maryland University College

Ron Johnson
Colorado Mountain College

Theodore F. Jula
Stonehill College

Peter F. Kaminski
Northern Illinois University

Yvonne Karsten
Minnesota State University

Jerome Katrichis
Temple University

Garland Keesling
Towson University

James Kellaris
University of Cincinnati

Alvin Kelly
Florida A&M University

Philip Kemp
DePaul University

Sylvia Keyes
Bridgewater State College

William M. Kincaid, Jr.
Oklahoma State University

Roy Klages
State University of New York at Albany

Hal Koenig
Oregon State University

Douglas Kornemann
Milwaukee Area Technical College

Barbara Lafferty
University of South Florida

Patricia Laidler
Massasoit Community College

Bernard LaLond
Ohio State University

Richard A. Lancioni
Temple University

Irene Lange
California State University— Fullerton

Geoffrey P. Lantos
Stonehill College

Charles L. Lapp
University of Texas—Dallas

Virginia Larson
San Jose State University

John Lavin
Waukesha County Technical Institute

Marilyn Lavin
University of Wisconsin— Whitewater

Hugh E. Law
East Tennessee University

Monle Lee
Indiana University—South Bend

Ron Lennon
Barry University

Richard C. Leventhal
Metropolitan State College

Marilyn Liebrenz-Himes
George Washington University

Jay D. Lindquist
Western Michigan University

Terry Loe
Kennesaw State University

Mary Logan
Southwestern Assemblies of God College

Paul Londrigan
Mott Community College

Anthony Lucas
Community College of Allegheny County

George Lucas
U.S. Learning, Inc.

William Lundstrom
Cleveland State University

Rhonda Mack
College of Charleston

Stan Madden
Baylor University

Patricia M. Manninen
North Shore Community College

Gerald L. Manning
Des Moines Area Community College

Lalita A. Manrai
University of Delaware

Franklyn Manu
Morgan State University

Allen S. Marber
University of Bridgeport

Gayle J. Marco
Robert Morris College

Carolyn A. Massiah
University of Central Florida

James McAlexander
Oregon State University

Donald McCartney
University of Wisconsin—Green Bay

Anthony McGann
University of Wyoming

Jack McNiff
State University of New York College of Technology at Farmington

Lee Meadow
Eastern Illinois University

Carla Meeske
University of Oregon

Jeffrey A. Meier
Fox Valley Technical College

James Meszaros
County College of Morris

Brain Meyer
Minnesota State University

Martin Meyers
University of Wisconsin—Stevens Point

Stephen J. Miller
Oklahoma State University

William Moller
University of Michigan

Kent B. Monroe
University of Illinois

Carlos W. Moore
Baylor University

Carol Morris-Calder
Loyola Marymount University

David Murphy
Madisonville Community College

Keith Murray
Bryant College

Sue Ellen Neeley
University of Houston—Clear Lake

Carolyn Y. Nicholson
Stetson University

Francis L. Notturno, Sr.
Owens Community College

Terrence V. O'Brien
Northern Illinois University

James R. Ogden
Kutztown University of Pennsylvania

Lois Bitner Olson
San Diego State University

Mike O'Neill
California State University—Chico

Robert S. Owen
State University of New York—Oswego

Allan Palmer
University of North Carolina at Charlotte

David P. Paul, III
Monmouth University

Terry Paul
Ohio State University

Teresa Pavia
University of Utah

John Perrachione
Truman State University

Michael Peters
Boston College

Linda Pettijohn
Missouri State University

Lana Podolak
Community College of Beaver County

Raymond E. Polchow
Muskingum Area Technical College

Thomas Ponzurick
West Virginia University

William Presutti
Duquesne University

Kathy Pullins
Columbus State Community College

Edna J. Ragins
North Carolina A&T State University

Daniel Rajaratnam
Baylor University

Mohammed Rawwas
University of Northern Iowa

James D. Reed
Louisiana State University—Shreveport

William Rhey
University of Tampa

Glen Riecken
East Tennessee State University

Winston Ring
University of Wisconsin—Milwaukee

Ed Riordan
Wayne State University

Bruce Robertson
San Francisco State University

Robert A. Robicheaux
University of Alabama—Birmingham

Bert Rosenbloom
Drexel University

Robert H. Ross
Wichita State University

Vicki Rostedt
The University of Akron

Michael L. Rothschild
University of Wisconsin—Madison

Kenneth L. Rowe
Arizona State University

Elise Sautter
New Mexico State University

Ronald Schill
Brigham Young University

Bodo Schlegelmilch
Vienna University of Economics and Business Administration

Edward Schmitt
Villanova University

Thomas Schori
Illinois State University

Donald Sciglimpaglia
San Diego State University

Stanley Scott
University of Alaska—Anchorage

Harold S. Sekiguchi
University of Nevada—Reno

Gilbert Seligman
Dutchess Community College

Richard J. Semenik
University of Utah

Beheruz N. Sethna
Lamar University

Morris A. Shapero
Schiller International University

Terence A. Shimp
University of South Carolina

Mark Siders
Southern Oregon University

Carolyn F. Siegel
Eastern Kentucky University

Dean C. Siewers
Rochester Institute of Technology

Lyndon Simkin
University of Warwick

Roberta Slater
Cedar Crest College

Paul J. Solomon
University of South Florida

Sheldon Somerstein
City University of New York

Eric R. Spangenberg
University of Mississippi

Rosann L. Spiro
Indiana University

William Staples
University of Houston—Clear Lake

Bruce Stern
Portland State University

Claire F. Sullivan
Metropolitan State University

Carmen Sunda
University of New Orleans

Robert Swerdlow
Lamar University

Steven A. Taylor
Illinois State University

Hal Teer
James Madison University

Ira Teich
Long Island University—C.W. Post

Debbie Thorne
Texas State University

Dillard Tinsley
Stephen F. Austin State University

Sharynn Tomlin
Angelo State University

Hale Tongren
George Mason University

James Underwood
*University of Southwest
Louisiana—Lafayette*

Barbara Unger
Western Washington University

Tinus Van Drunen
University Twente (Netherlands)

Dale Varble
Indiana State University

Bronis Verhage
Georgia State University

R. Vish Viswanathan
University of Northern Colorado

Charles Vitaska
Metropolitan State College

Kirk Wakefield
Baylor University

Harlan Wallingford
Pace University

Jacquelyn Warwick
Andrews University

James F. Wenthe
Georgia College

Sumner M. White
*Massachusetts Bay Community
College*

Alan R. Wiman
Rider College

Ken Wright
*West Australia College of Advanced
Education—Churchland Campus*

Tomas Hult, Michigan State University, completely revised the Supply-Chain Management and Marketing Channels chapter as well as the Retailing, Wholesaling, and Direct Marketing chapter. In addition, he assisted in providing the globalEDGE™ exercises at the end of each chapter in the book. He provided advice in helping to integrate the global dimension throughout the text.

We're grateful to Phyllis Mansfield for her work on the new feature, *Developing Your Marketing Plan*, and the test bank. In addition, we'd like to acknowledge Catherine Curran-Kelly for her diligence and attention to updating the *Instructor's Manual* and the PowerPoint program. Their work on our ancillary program met the demands and standards of this edition. We thank you.

Michael Hartline, Florida State University, helped in the development of the marketing plan outline and the sample marketing plan in Appendix C, as well as the career worksheets on the website. We also wish to thank John Drea, Western Illinois University, for developing the *Who Wants to Be an 'A' Student* game.

We deeply appreciate the assistance of Jennifer Jackson, Marian Wood, Clarissa Means, Saleha Amin, Brenda Lake, Jonathan Wickersham, Joshua Lake, Michelle Watkins, Alexi Sherrill, and Melanie Drever for providing editorial suggestions, technical assistance, and support.

We would like to extend a note of special gratitude to the work of Gwyneth Walters. Over the past 20 years, her dedication and commitment to excellence has enhanced our authoring experience time and again.

We express appreciation for the support and encouragement given to us by our colleagues at Texas A&M University and University of New Mexico. We are also grateful for the comments and suggestions we receive from our own students, student focus groups, and student correspondents who provide ongoing feedback through the website.

A number of talented professionals at Cengage Learning have contributed to the development of this book. We are especially grateful to Mike Roche, Suzanna Bainbridge, Susan Holtz, Jennifer Meyer-Dare, Craig Mertens, Nancy Blodget, Cliff Kallemeyn, Terry Wilton, Jill Haber, Anne Katzeff, Tippy McIntosh, Kimberly Kanakes, and Sarah Greber. Their inspiration, patience, support, and friendship are invaluable.

William M. Pride
O. C. Ferrell

About the Authors

William M. Pride is Professor of Marketing, Mays Business School, at Texas A&M University. He received his Ph.D. from Louisiana State University. He is the author of Houghton Mifflin Company's *Business* text, a market leader.

Dr. Pride's research interests are in advertising, promotion, and distribution channels. Dr. Pride's research articles have appeared in major journals in the fields of advertising and marketing such as the *Journal of Marketing, Journal of Marketing Research, Journal of the Academy of Marketing Science,* and *Journal of Advertising.*

Dr. Pride is a member of the American Marketing Association, Academy of Marketing Science, Association of Collegiate Marketing Educators, Society for Marketing Advances, and the Marketing Management Association.

Dr. Pride has taught principles of marketing and other marketing courses for more than 30 years at both the undergraduate and graduate levels.

O. C. Ferrell is Professor of Marketing and Creative Enterprise Scholar, Anderson Schools of Management, University of New Mexico. He recently served as the Bill Daniels Distinguished Professor of Business Ethics at the University of Wyoming and previously as Chair of the Colorado State University Marketing Department. He has also been on the faculties of University of Memphis, Texas A&M University, and Illinois State University. He received his Ph.D. in Marketing from Louisiana State University.

He is past president of the Academic Council of the American Marketing Association and chaired the American Marketing Association Ethics Committee. Under his leadership, the committee developed the AMA Code of Ethics and the AMA Code of Ethics for Marketing on the Internet. He is currently a member of the advisory committee for the AMA marketing certification program. In addition, he is a former member of the Academy of Marketing Science Board of Governors and is a Society of Marketing Advances and Southwestern Marketing Association Fellow. He is the Academy of Marketing Science's Vice President of Publications. He currently serves as Marketing Ethics and Social Issues Section Editor of the *Journal of Macromarketing.*

Dr. Ferrell is the co-author of 18 books and approximately 75 articles. His articles have been published in the *Journal of Marketing Research, Journal of Marketing, Journal of Business Ethics, Journal of Business Research, Journal of the Academy of Marketing Science, Journal of Public Policy Marketing,* as well as other journals.

part 1

Marketing Strategy and Customer Relationships

CHAPTERS

1 An Overview of Strategic Marketing

2 Planning, Implementing, and Controlling Marketing Strategies

Part One introduces the field of marketing and offers a broad perspective from which to explore and analyze various components of the marketing discipline. **Chapter 1** defines *marketing* and explores several key concepts, including customers and target markets, the marketing mix, relationship marketing, the marketing concept, and value-driven marketing. **Chapter 2** provides an overview of strategic marketing issues, such as the role of the mission statement; corporate, business-unit, and marketing strategies; and the creation of the marketing plan.

1 An Overview of Strategic Marketing

LEARNING objectives

1. To be able to define marketing as focused on customers

2. To identify some important marketing terms, including *target market, marketing mix, marketing exchanges,* and *marketing environment*

3. To become aware of the marketing concept and marketing orientation

4. To understand the importance of building customer relationships

5. To learn about the process of marketing management

6. To recognize the role of marketing in our society

Leatherman: a Knife, a Tool, a Marketing Concept

The idea for the Leatherman Pocket Survival Tool came from a routine car breakdown. Tim Leatherman and his wife spent nine months traveling around Europe and Asia in a used Fiat with leaky hoses and wiring that constantly failed. Leatherman's pocketknife was not especially helpful for repairing the car and getting it back on the road. "Why not just add pliers to a pocketknife?" he wondered. After they returned home, Tim decided to try to build such a tool himself. He expected it to take about

entrepreneurs IN ACTION

a month, but he ended up working on it for three years. When he took his prototype to a Portland knife business, they looked at it and said, "This is not a knife; it is a tool." When he brought it to tool companies, they considered it a knife. Leatherman tried to sell his invention to the U.S. Army and to AT&T, but they were not interested either.

At the time, a variety of Swiss Army knives and hand tools, such as files and pliers, were widely available, but Leatherman's tool fell into neither category. After discussing his invention with friends, Leatherman realized that he had to know more about his "target market"—the specific group of customers who would be interested in his product. He called his prototype the Pocket Survival Tool to make it sound attractive to the 20,000 survivalists who were gaining fame about that time. Finally, in 1983, two mail-order companies placed modest orders for Leatherman's tool. With his product available in catalogs, it was sure to find its way to the right market. One catalog featured the tool on the back page of its Christmas issue and had to reorder more of the tools several times. In 1984, Leatherman and his partner sold 30,000 tools, 69,000 in 1985, and over 1 million a year by 1993.

Once Leatherman had targeted his customer base, he was able to develop a strategy to ensure that the Personal Survival Tool would become a must-have for all outdoor enthusiasts. Today the Leatherman Tool Group, Inc., is a privately held corporation with more than 350 employees in its Portland, Oregon, headquarters. Tim Leatherman stepped down as CEO in early 2007, but he remains chairman of the board and majority shareholder. Because his name is stamped on every single product the company makes, he feels responsible for the quality of each one. Over the years, the tool has faced some stiff competition from less-expensive foreign imports, but Leatherman continues to have faith in the outstanding quality of his products. From its humble beginnings in the backwaters of Europe to a product now sold in more than 75 countries, Leatherman owes his success to determining his customers' needs and finding out how to reach them.[1]

L ike all organizations, the Leatherman Tool Group attempts to develop products that customers want, communicate useful information about them to excite interest, price them appropriately, and make them available when and where customers want to buy them. Even if an organization does all these things well, however, competition from marketers of similar products, economic conditions, and other factors can impact the company's success. Such factors influence the decisions that all organizations must make in strategic marketing.

This chapter introduces the strategic marketing concepts and decisions that will be discussed throughout the book. First, we develop a definition of *marketing* and explore each element of the definition in detail. Next, we introduce the marketing concept and consider several issues associated with implementing it. We also take a brief look at the management of customer relationships and then at the concept of value, which customers are demanding today more than ever before. We next explore the process of marketing management, which includes planning, organizing, implementing, and controlling marketing activities to encourage marketing exchanges. Finally, we examine the importance of marketing in our global society.

Defining *Marketing*

L O 1 To be able to define marketing as focused on customers

If you ask several people what *marketing* is, you are likely to hear a variety of definitions. Although many people think marketing is advertising or selling, marketing actually encompasses many more activities. In this book, we define **marketing** as the process of creating, distributing, promoting, and pricing goods, services, and ideas to facilitate satisfying exchange relationships with customers and develop and maintain favorable relationships with stakeholders in a dynamic environment. Our definition is consistent with the American Marketing Association (AMA), which defines marketing as "the activity, set of institutions, and processes for creating, communicating, delivering, and exchanging offerings that have value for customers, clients, partners, and society at large."[2] Let's take a closer look at the parts of our definition.

Marketing Focuses on Customers

As the purchasers of the products that organizations develop, promote, distribute, and price, **customers** are the focal point of all marketing activities (see Figure 1.1). Organizations must define their products not according to what they produce but according to how they satisfy customers. The Walt Disney Company, for example, is not in the business of establishing theme parks; it is in the business of making people happy. At Disney World, customers are the guests, the crowd is the audience, and the employees are the cast members. Customer satisfaction and enjoyment can come from anything experienced when buying and using a product.

The essence of marketing is to develop satisfying exchange relationships from which both customers and marketers benefit. The customer expects to gain a reward or benefit in excess of the costs incurred in a marketing transaction. The marketer expects to gain something of value in return—generally the price charged for the product. Through buyer-seller interactions, a customer develops expectations about the seller's future behavior. To fulfill these expectations, the marketer must deliver on promises made. Over time, this interaction results in interdependencies between the two parties. Fast-food restaurants such as Wendy's and Burger King depend on repeat purchases from satisfied customers, many of whom live or work a few miles from these restaurants, whereas customer expectations revolve around high-quality food, good value, and dependable service.

Organizations generally focus their marketing efforts on a specific group of customers, called a **target market.** Marketing managers may define a target market as a vast number of people or a relatively small group. Firefly Mobile, for example, targets its FlyPhone cellular phone at a small market: 13- to 17-year-olds who want a phone with which they can take photos, play MP3 tunes, and play games.[3] Other companies target multiple markets with different products, promotions, prices, and

marketing The process of creating, distributing, promoting, and pricing goods, services, and ideas to facilitate satisfying exchange relationships with customers and develop and maintain favorable relationships with stakeholders in a dynamic environment

customers The purchasers of organizations' products; the focal point of all marketing activities

target market The group of customers on which marketing efforts are focused

figure 1.1

COMPONENTS OF STRATEGIC MARKETING

distribution systems for each one. Nike uses this strategy, marketing different types of shoes and apparel to meet specific needs of cross-trainers, rock climbers, basketball players, aerobics enthusiasts, and other athletic shoe buyers. Nike has even developed an athletic shoe for a single ethnicity: the Air Native N7 for American Indians.[4] We explore the concept of target markets in more detail in Chapter 6.

Marketing Deals with Products, Distribution, Promotion, and Price

LO 2 To identify some important marketing terms, including *target market, marketing mix, marketing exchanges,* and *marketing environment*

Marketing is more than just advertising or selling a product; it involves developing and managing a product that will satisfy customer needs. It focuses on making the product available in the right place and at a price that buyers are willing to pay. It also requires communicating information that helps customers determine if the product will satisfy their needs. These activities are planned, organized, implemented, and controlled to meet the needs of customers within the target market. Marketers refer to these activities—product, distribution, promotion, and pricing— as the **marketing mix** because they decide what type of each element to use and in what amounts. A primary goal of a marketing manager is to create and maintain the right mix of these elements to satisfy customers' needs for a general product type. Note in Figure 1.1 that the marketing mix is built around the customer.

Marketing managers strive to develop a marketing mix that matches the needs of customers in the target market. The marketing mix for Nissan Rogue, for example, combines a crossover SUV with coordinated distribution, promotion, and price that

marketing mix Four marketing activities—product, distribution, promotion, and pricing—that a firm can control to meet the needs of customers within its target markets

E-ntertainment MARKETING

Wii Wins the Battle for New Customers

Just a few years ago, it seemed like "game over" for Nintendo's computer gaming business. The Japanese game maker was lagging behind newer, more powerful game systems from Sony and Microsoft. While the video game business grew into a $30 billion global industry, Nintendo watched its U.S. sales dwindle to half of what they had been 20 years before when its Nintendo Entertainment System was at the forefront of the modern video game age. Today, Nintendo is making a comeback in the gaming world. Instead of following Sony and Microsoft in the race to pack gaming consoles with as much power and high-performance graphics as possible, Nintendo introduced the Wii—a low-priced, motion-controlled machine that appeals to everyone from high-flying executives to grandparents and preschoolers. By targeting a broader demographic, Nintendo executives hoped to increase the number of people buying its hardware and ultimately increase the number of gamers as well.

The Wii's distinguishing feature is its wireless controller, the Wii remote, which can be used as a handheld pointing device and can detect motion and rotation in three dimensions. The controller enables players to curve the Wii remote to throw a football in Madden NFL, tilt it to steer off-road vehicles in Excite Truck, and swing it to play sports like Wii tennis and baseball. Nintendo's market tests showed that it was appealing enough to interest even nongamers and simple enough that newbies could quickly learn how to play. Another distinctive feature of the system is the WiiConnect24, which allows the console to receive messages and updates over the Internet while in standby mode. Even the system's name "Wii," with two lowercase "i" characters meant to resemble two people standing side by side, sets it apart by representing players gathering together. Indeed, it is no accident that "Wii" sounds like "we" and thus emphasizes that the console is for everyone. The name is recognizable all over the world, regardless of language—no confusion, no need to abbreviate, just *Wii*.

When Nintendo marketed the Wii, it used traditional television campaigns that targeted school kids, as well as television programs aimed at 25- to 49-year-olds. The company even put Wii ads in publications like *AARP* and *Reader's Digest.* To reach the under-25 audience, Nintendo pushed the message through online and social networking sites such as MySpace. However, Nintendo's most effective marketing technique was to give away the popular Wii Sports package—with tennis, baseball, golf, boxing, and bowling games— with every console sold. This worked mainly because Nintendo makes a $50 profit on each console sold, so it can afford to give away a game. Nintendo's strategy seems to have worked. The Wii has proven so popular that Nintendo has had difficulty keeping up with demand. The Wii consistently outsold Sony's PlayStation 3 and Microsoft's Xbox 360 during 2007, and it was profitable from the very beginning, whereas both Sony and Microsoft lost money on every game console they sold after expecting to make money selling high-margin games for their respective systems. Although the product is extremely successful, Nintendo's inability to keep up with demand may affect the Wii's long-term success.[a]

Great taste has its benefits.

Great taste + vitamins and minerals

Appealing to Target Markets

Diet Coke targets the health conscious while Pepsi appeals to a broader, less calorie-conscious market segment.

products Goods, services, or ideas

are appropriate for the target market of primarily men and women in their twenties and early thirties. The marketing mix for the Rogue includes an economical engine, stylish design, and performance handling; a price around $20,000; product placement and advertising during the hit show *Heroes*; and a five-car giveaway.[5]

Before marketers can develop a marketing mix, they must collect in-depth, up-to-date information about customer needs. Such information might include data about the age, income, ethnicity, gender, and educational level of people in the target market; their preferences for product features; their attitudes toward competitors' products; and the frequency with which they use the product. Procter & Gamble, for example, introduced Old Spice High Endurance Hair & Body Wash after viewing hours of videotape of men taking showers (wearing swimsuits!) and observing that many men used body wash to shampoo their hair.[6] In Chapter 5, we explore how organizations gather marketing research data. Armed with such data, marketing managers are better able to develop a marketing mix that satisfies a specific target market. Let's look more closely at the decisions and activities related to each marketing mix variable.

The Product Variable. Successful marketing efforts result in **products** that become a part of everyday life. Consider the satisfaction customers have had over the years from Coca-Cola, Levi's jeans, Visa credit cards, Tylenol pain relievers, and 3M Post-it Notes. The product variable of the marketing mix deals with researching customers' needs and wants and designing a product that satisfies them. A product can be a good, a service, or an idea. A good is a physical entity you can touch. A Toyota Yaris, an iPod, a Duracell battery, and a puppy available for adoption at an animal shelter are examples of goods. A service is the application of human and mechanical efforts to people or objects to provide intangible benefits to customers. Air travel, dry cleaning, hair cutting, banking, insurance, medical care, and day care are examples of services. Ideas include concepts, philosophies, images, and issues. For instance, a marriage counselor, for a fee, gives spouses ideas to help improve their relationship. Other marketers of ideas include political parties, churches, and schools. Note,

YOU'LL KNOW YOU'RE WEARING IT WHEN A ROCK FALLS ON YOUR HEAD.
OTHER THAN THAT, PROBABLY NOT.

PETZL
www.petzl.com

Product

Petzl's ad focuses on the quality, comfort, and reliability of its climbing helmet.

however, that the actual production of tangible goods is not a marketing activity.

The product variable also involves creating or modifying brand names and packaging, and it may also include decisions regarding warranty and repair services. Even one of the world's best soccer players is a global brand. David Beckham, who now plays for the Major League Soccer team, the Los Angeles Galaxy, has promoted or endorsed products from Adidas, ESPN, and Motorola, and his celebrity standing helps sell out soccer stadiums.[7]

Product variable decisions and related activities are important because they are directly involved in creating products that address customers' needs and wants. To maintain an assortment of products that helps an organization achieve its goals, marketers must develop new products, modify existing ones, and eliminate those that no longer satisfy enough buyers or that yield unacceptable profits. In the funeral home industry, for example, some companies have developed new products such as DVD memoirs, grave markers that display photos along with a soundtrack, and caskets with drawers to hold mementos from the bereaved. To appeal to the growing number of people who prefer to be cremated, other firms are offering more cremation and memorial services.[8] We will examine such product issues and many others in Chapters 10 through 13.

The Distribution Variable. To satisfy customers, products must be available at the right time and in convenient locations. Starbucks, for example, is opening outlets on college campuses, including student centers and libraries, to reach more customers in places where they might need a caffeine boost. In addition to its many locations in supermarkets, bookstores, and public libraries, the Seattle chain has opened 30 university library locations.[9] In dealing with the distribution variable, a marketing manager makes products available in the quantities desired to as many target market customers as possible, keeping total inventory, transportation, and storage costs as low as possible. A marketing manager may also select and motivate intermediaries (wholesalers and retailers), establish and maintain inventory control procedures, and develop and manage transportation and storage systems. The Internet and other technologies have also dramatically influenced the distribution variable. Companies can now make their products available throughout the world without maintaining facilities in each country. We examine distribution issues in Chapters 14 and 15.

The Promotion Variable. The promotion variable relates to activities used to inform individuals or groups about the organization and its products. Promotion can aim to increase public awareness of the organization and of new or existing products. Del Monte Foods, for example, used humorous television commercials, a traveling bus tour, and a new website (SmoochablePooch.com) to introduce its new Kibbles 'n Bits Brushing Bites dog treats, which keep dogs' teeth clean and their breath fresh.[10] Promotional activities can also educate customers about product features or urge people to take a particular stance on a political or social issue, such as smoking or drug abuse. For example, the Office of National Drug Control Policy launched a promotional campaign called "Above the Influence" that featured television and magazine ads, as well as an interactive website with games, quizzes, facts, and much more to help teens and young people recognize and resist the influences in their lives that could lead to alcohol and illegal drug use.[11] Promotion can also help sustain interest in established products that have been available for decades, such as Arm & Hammer baking soda or Ivory soap. Many companies are using the Internet to communicate information about themselves and their products. Ragu's website, for example, offers tips, recipes, and a sweepstakes, and Southwest Airlines' website enables customers to

Source: American Pet Product Manufacturers Association.

make flight reservations. In Chapters 16 through 18, we take a more detailed look at promotion activities.

The Price Variable. The price variable relates to decisions and actions associated with establishing pricing objectives and policies and determining product prices. Price is a critical component of the marketing mix because customers are concerned about the value obtained in an exchange. Consider the One Laptop Per Child (OLPC) project, which lets consumers support literacy and technology in Third World countries by buying a super-tough XO laptop for $400 so a second XO laptop can be donated to poor children in the world's least-developed countries. In addition to supporting global literacy, buyers can take a $200 tax write-off.[12] Price is often used as a competitive tool, and intense price competition sometimes leads to price wars. Airlines, for example, develop complex systems for determining the right price for each seat on a specific flight. High prices can be used competitively to establish a product's image. Waterman and Mont Blanc pens, for example, have an image of high quality and high price that has given them significant status. Likewise, specialty salts, which are marketed by color, grind, and source, can sell for as much as 50 times the typical supermarket brands.[13] We explore pricing decisions in Chapters 19 and 20.

The marketing mix variables are often viewed as controllable because they can be modified. However, there are limits to how much marketing managers can alter them. Economic conditions, competitive structure, or government regulations may prevent a manager from adjusting prices frequently or significantly. Making changes in the size, shape, and design of most tangible goods is expensive, so such product features cannot be altered very often. In addition, promotional campaigns and methods used to distribute products ordinarily cannot be rewritten or revamped overnight.

Marketing Builds Relationships with Customers and Other Stakeholders

Individuals and organizations engage in marketing to facilitate **exchanges**—the provision or transfer of goods, services, or ideas in return for something of value. Any product (good, service, or even idea) may be involved in a marketing exchange. We assume only that individuals and organizations expect to gain a reward in excess of the costs incurred.

For an exchange to take place, four conditions must exist. First, two or more individuals, groups, or organizations must participate, and each must possess something of value that the other party desires. Second, the exchange should provide a benefit or satisfaction to both parties in the transaction. Third, each party must have confidence in the promise of the "something of value" held by the other. If you go to a Coldplay concert, for example, you go with the expectation of a great performance. Finally, to build trust, the parties to the exchange must meet expectations.

Figure 1.2 depicts the exchange process. The arrows indicate that the parties communicate that each has something of value available to exchange. An exchange will not necessarily take place just because these conditions exist; marketing activities can occur even without an actual transaction or sale. You may see an ad for a plasma TV, for instance, but you may never buy the product. When an exchange occurs, products are traded for other products or for financial resources.

Marketing activities should attempt to create and maintain satisfying exchange relationships. To maintain an exchange relationship, buyers must be satisfied with the obtained good, service, or idea, and sellers must be satisfied with the financial

exchanges The provision or transfer of goods, services, or ideas in return for something of value

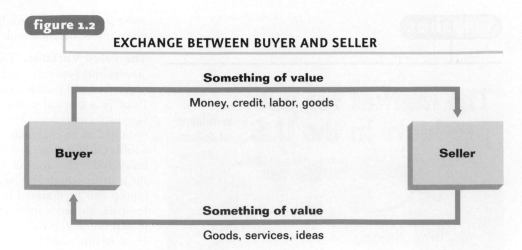

figure 1.2

EXCHANGE BETWEEN BUYER AND SELLER

Something of value

Money, credit, labor, goods

Buyer

Seller

Something of value

Goods, services, ideas

reward or something else of value received. A dissatisfied customer who lacks trust in the relationship often searches for alternative organizations or products.

Marketers are concerned with building relationships not only with customers but also with relevant stakeholders. **Stakeholders** include those constituents who have a "stake," or claim, in some aspect of a company's products, operations, markets, industry, and outcomes; stakeholders include customers, employees, investors and shareholders, suppliers, governments, communities, and many others. Stakeholders have the power to provide or withdraw needed resources or influence customer opinion about a firm's marketing strategy and products. Developing and maintaining favorable relations with stakeholders is crucial to the long-term growth of an organization and its products.

Marketing Occurs in a Dynamic Environment

Marketing activities do not take place in a vacuum. The **marketing environment,** which includes competitive, economic, political, legal and regulatory, technological, and sociocultural forces, surrounds the customer and affects the marketing mix (see Figure 1.1). The effects of these forces on buyers and sellers can be dramatic and difficult to predict. Consider that the feature that made rap music appealing to a large segment of the population—the power to say whatever one pleased—has now come under increasing criticism, even from within the hip-hop community. Rap music sales have fallen 44 percent since 2000 and now make up less than 10 percent of all music sales.[14] Environmental forces can create threats to marketers, but they can also generate opportunities for new products and new methods of reaching customers.

The forces of the marketing environment affect a marketer's ability to facilitate exchanges in three general ways. First, they influence customers by affecting their lifestyles, standards of living, and preferences and needs for products. Because a marketing manager tries to develop and adjust the marketing mix to satisfy customers, effects of environmental forces on customers also have an indirect impact on marketing mix components. For example, rising gasoline prices and declining sales of gas-guzzling models have led many automakers, including General Motors, Ford, and Chrysler, to make the improvement of vehicle fuel economy their highest priority. Likewise, Hertz introduced a new service called "Green Collection" that allows customers to rent more fuel-efficient vehicles.[15]

Second, marketing environment forces help determine whether and how a marketing manager can perform certain marketing activities. Finally, environmental forces may affect a marketing manager's decisions and actions by influencing buyers' reactions to the firm's marketing mix. Marketing environment forces can fluctuate quickly and dramatically, which is one reason that marketing is so interesting and challenging. Because these forces are closely interrelated, changes in one may cause changes in others. For example, evidence linking children's consumption of soft drinks and fast foods to health issues such as obesity, diabetes, and osteoporosis has exposed marketers of such products to negative publicity and generated calls

stakeholders Constituents who have a "stake," or claim, in some aspect of a company's products, operations, markets, industry, and outcomes

marketing environment The competitive, economic, political, legal and regulatory, technological, and sociocultural forces that surround the customer and affect the marketing mix

RESPONSIBLE marketing?

What does *sustainability* mean to marketers? Is it good business and marketing strategy, good shareholder relations, or the creation of sustainable competitive advantage? Would it surprise you to learn that many of the nation's largest companies have begun to work together to address global warming and other environmental sustainability issues? Ford, Wal-Mart, McDonald's, Time Inc., Walgreens, Dow, Anheuser-Busch, Kimberly-Clark, PG&E, BP, and Abbott all provided speakers at a Corporate Climate Response Conference to share information on their experiences with what works and what does not.

Some of the topics discussed at the conference were fundamentals of corporate climate change strategy, carbon footprint and life-cycle analysis, energy efficiency, waste management, fleet management, green power and RECs (Renewable Energy Certificate products), carbon offsetting and emissions trading, climate adaptation, and ways to engage consumers and the public in the dialogue on climate change. If you were an executive with one of these firms or a competing firm, would you feel at a competitive disadvantage sharing your personal experiences on successes and failures in this area? How would you defend involvement? If consumers want these initiatives, why would you not use sustainability as a key competitive advantage?[b]

Partnerships and Sustainability Strategies

ISSUE: Should companies partner in managing their environmental and social responsibility issues, or should they maintain independence, making this a competitive marketing strategy?

for legislation regulating the sale of soft drinks in public schools. Some companies have responded to these concerns by reformulating products to make them healthier or even introducing new products. Burger King, for example, revamped its menu to include healthier Kids Meals with fewer than 560 calories, less than 30 percent of calories from fat, and no added trans fats. It also pledged to restrict advertising to children under age 12 and use licensed characters to promote only products that meet health guidelines. Dunkin' Donuts likewise eliminated trans fats from all items on its menu.[16]

Changes in the marketing environment produce uncertainty for marketers and at times hurt marketing efforts, but they also create opportunities. Marketers who are alert to changes in environmental forces can adjust to and influence these changes and can capitalize on the opportunities such changes provide. Marketing mix elements—product, distribution, promotion, and price—are factors over which an organization has control; the forces of the environment, however, are more difficult to control. But even though marketers know they cannot predict changes in the marketing environment with certainty, they must nevertheless plan for them. Because these environmental forces have such a profound effect on marketing activities, we explore each of them in considerable depth in Chapter 3.

Understanding the Marketing Concept

L O 3 To become aware of the marketing concept and marketing orientation

marketing concept A philosophy that an organization should try to provide products that satisfy customers' needs through a coordinated set of activities that also allows the organization to achieve its goals

Some firms have sought success by buying land, building a factory, equipping it with people and machines, and then making a product they believe buyers want and need. However, these firms frequently fail to attract customers with what they have to offer because they defined their business as "making a product" rather than as "helping potential customers satisfy their needs and wants." For example, when compact discs became more popular than vinyl records, turntable manufacturers had an opportunity to develop new products to satisfy customers' needs for home entertainment. Companies that did not pursue this opportunity, such as Dual and Empire, are no longer in business. Such organizations failed to implement the marketing concept. Likewise, the growing popularity of MP3 technology has enabled firms such as Apple and Microsoft to develop products like the iPod and Zune to satisfy the consumer desire of being able to store customized music libraries. Instead of buying CDs, a consumer can download a song for 99 cents from Apple's iTunes.

According to the **marketing concept,** an organization should try to provide products that satisfy customers' needs through a coordinated set of activities that also allows the organization to achieve its goals. Customer satisfaction is the major focus of the marketing concept. To implement the marketing concept, an organization strives to determine what buyers want and uses this information to develop satisfying products. It focuses on customer analysis, competitor analysis, and integration of the firm's resources to provide customer value and satisfaction as well as generate long-term profits.[17] The firm must also continue to alter, adapt, and develop products to

The Marketing Concept

SSI understands the importance of a customer orientation by listening to customers and providing great service.

keep pace with customers' changing desires and preferences. Ben & Jerry's Homemade Ice Cream, for example, continuously assesses customer demand for ice cream and sorbet. On its website, it maintains a "flavor graveyard" that lists combinations that were tried and ultimately failed. It also lists its top ten flavors each month.

Ralph Lauren, whose name is well known throughout the world for designer clothing, is introducing for sale at JCPenney a new line of moderately priced apparel and home furnishings that will appeal to a broader target market. The new American Living line will not be identified with the Ralph Lauren name, but word-of-mouth promotion is expected to create an awareness of the line's designer and attract new customers.[18] Thus, the marketing concept emphasizes that marketing begins and ends with customers. Research has found a positive association between customer satisfaction and shareholder value,[19] and high levels of customer satisfaction also tend to attract and retain high-quality employees and managers.[20]

The marketing concept is not a second definition of *marketing*. It is a management philosophy that guides an organization's overall activities and affects all organizational activities, not just marketing. Production, finance, accounting, human resources, and marketing departments must work together.

The marketing concept is also not a philanthropic philosophy aimed at helping customers at the expense of the organization. A firm that adopts the marketing concept must satisfy not only its customers' objectives but also its own, or it will not stay in business long. The overall objectives of a business might relate to increasing profits, market share, sales, or a combination of the three. The marketing concept stresses that an organization can best achieve these objectives by being customer oriented. Thus, implementing the marketing concept should benefit the organization as well as its customers.

It is important for marketers to consider not only their current buyers' needs but also the long-term needs of society. Striving to satisfy customers' desires by sacrificing society's long-term welfare is unacceptable. For example, although many parents want disposable diapers that are comfortable, absorbent, and safe for their babies, society in general does not want nonbiodegradable disposable diapers that create tremendous landfill problems now and for the future. Marketers are expected to act in a socially responsible manner, an idea we discuss in more detail in Chapter 4.

Evolution of the Marketing Concept

The marketing concept may seem to be an obvious approach to running a business. However, businesspeople have not always believed that the best way to make sales and profits is to satisfy customers (see Figure 1.3).

The Production Orientation. During the second half of the nineteenth century, the Industrial Revolution was in full swing in the United States. Electricity, rail transportation, division of labor, assembly lines, and mass production made it possible to produce goods more efficiently. With new technology and new ways to use labor, products poured into the marketplace, where demand for manufactured goods was strong.

The Sales Orientation. In the 1920s, strong demand for products subsided, and businesses realized they would have to "sell" products to buyers. From the mid-1920s to the early 1950s, businesses viewed sales as the major means of increasing profits and came to adopt a sales orientation. Businesspeople believed the most

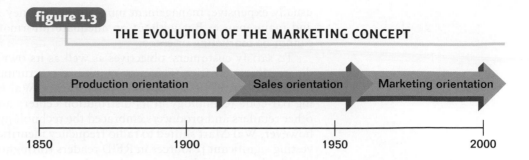

figure 1.3

THE EVOLUTION OF THE MARKETING CONCEPT

important marketing activities were personal selling, advertising, and distribution. Today some people incorrectly equate marketing with a sales orientation.

The Marketing Orientation. By the early 1950s, some businesspeople began to recognize that efficient production and extensive promotion did not guarantee that customers would buy products. These businesses, and many others since, found they must first determine what customers want and then produce these products, rather than make the products first and then try to convince customers they needed them. As more organizations realized the importance of satisfying customers' needs, U.S. businesses entered the marketing era, one of marketing orientation.

A **marketing orientation** requires the "organizationwide generation of market intelligence pertaining to current and future customer needs, dissemination of the intelligence across departments, and organizationwide responsiveness to it."[21] Marketing orientation is linked to new-product innovation by developing a strategic focus to explore and develop new products to serve target markets.[22] Top management, marketing managers, nonmarketing managers (those in production, finance, human resources, and so on), and customers are all important in developing and carrying out a marketing orientation. Trust, openness, honoring promises, respect, collaboration, and recognizing the market as the raison d'être are six values required by organizations that want to become more marketing oriented.[23] Unless marketing managers provide continuous customer-focused leadership with minimal interdepartmental conflict, achieving a marketing orientation will be difficult. Nonmarketing managers must share with marketing managers any information that is pertinent to understanding the customer. Finally, a marketing orientation involves being responsive to ever-changing customer needs and wants. For example, to accomplish this, Amazon.com follows buyers' online purchases and recommends related purchases. Trying to assess what customers want, a difficult task to begin with, is further complicated by the speed with which fashions and tastes can change. Today businesses want to satisfy customers and build meaningful, long-term buyer-seller relationships. Doing so helps a company boost its own financial value.[24]

Implementing the Marketing Concept

A philosophy may sound reasonable and look good on paper, but that does not mean it can be put into practice easily. To implement the marketing concept, a marketing-oriented organization must accept some general conditions and recognize and deal with several problems. Consequently, the marketing concept has yet to be fully accepted by all U.S. businesses. Management must first establish an information system to discover customers' real needs and then use the information to create satisfying products. Kimberly-Clark, for example, conducted intensive marketing research by observing moms struggling to hold on to their babies while changing their diapers or bathing them. As a result, the company made significant changes to the design of its Huggies Baby Wipes Travel Pack and Huggies Baby Wash products so they could be used with one hand.[25] This example illustrates one way marketers can obtain information about customers' desires and then use that information to forge a positive marketing relationship. An information system is

marketing orientation An organizationwide commitment to researching and responding to customer needs

usually expensive; management must commit money and time for its development and maintenance. But without an adequate information system, an organization cannot be marketing oriented.

To satisfy customers' objectives as well as its own, a company must also coordinate all its activities. This may require restructuring the internal operations and overall objectives of one or more departments. Wal-Mart, for example, began using bar-code technology in its distribution centers and stores in 1984, and many other retailers and producers embraced the technology within a few years. In 2003, however, Wal-Mart shifted to radio frequency identification (RFID) technology, investing significant resources in RFID readers throughout its system and demanding that its larger suppliers adopt the technology as well. After suppliers balked at RFID's cost and poor return on investment, Wal-Mart was forced drop the supplier initiative. Although Wal-Mart is renowned for its low prices, distribution efficiencies and technologies, and its strong relationships with some suppliers, today the company is struggling to maintain supplier relationships and to satisfy consumers who are increasingly demanding not only low prices but greater choices, fresher designs, and more current items. Procter & Gamble gets 15 percent of its revenues from Wal-Mart, down 3 percent from 2003. Some suppliers are finding they can get faster turnover and higher profits at Walgreens and CVS pharmacies.[26] If the head of the marketing unit is not a member of the organization's top-level management, a new technology may fail to sufficiently address actual customer needs and desires. Implementing the marketing concept demands the support not only of top management but also of managers and staff across all functions and levels of the organization.

Managing Customer Relationships

LO 4 To understand the importance of building customer relationships

Achieving the full profit potential of each customer relationship should be the fundamental goal of every marketing strategy. Marketing relationships with customers are the lifeblood of all businesses. At the most basic level, profits can be obtained through relationships by (1) acquiring new customers, (2) enhancing the profitability of existing customers, and (3) extending the duration of customer relationships. Implementing the marketing concept means optimizing the exchange relationship: the relationship between a company's investment in customer relationships and the return generated by customers' loyalty and retention.[27]

Maintaining positive relationships with customers is an important goal for marketers. The term **relationship marketing** refers to "long-term, mutually beneficial arrangements in which both the buyer and seller focus on value enhancement through the creation of more satisfying exchanges."[28] Relationship marketing continually deepens the buyer's trust in the company, which, as the customer's confidence grows, in turn increases the firm's understanding of the customer's needs. Successful marketers respond to customer needs and strive to increase value to buyers over time. Eventually this interaction becomes a solid relationship that allows for cooperation and mutual dependency.

Customer-centric marketing involves developing collaborative relationships with customers based on focusing on their individual needs and concerns. It adopts the view that customers buy offerings that provide value and prefer a relationship rather than a transactional orientation. The focus is on the individual. Collaborating with and learning from customers leads to a "sense-and-respond" approach rather than a produce-and-sell approach.[29] Best Buy has been a leader in "customer-centricity," or catering to customers based on their specific issues and needs. The company classified its most profitable customers into one of four typologies: Ray (price-conscious family guy), Buzz (young gadget fiend), Barry (affluent tech enthusiast), or Jill (busy suburban mom) and then began retooling each of its stores to target one or more of the typologies based on marketing research and demographics. Stores that target Jills, for example, include personal shopping assistants, whereas stores that target

relationship marketing
Establishing long-term, mutually satisfying buyer-seller relationships

customer-centric marketing
Developing collaborative relationships with customers based on focusing on their individual needs and concerns

Buzzes offer lots of video games. Best Buy stores that use the customer-centric model have enjoyed sales growth that is three times that of the conventional stores.[30]

To build long-term customer relationships, marketers are increasingly turning to marketing research and information technology. **Customer relationship management (CRM)** focuses on using information about customers to create marketing strategies that develop and sustain desirable customer relationships. By increasing customer value over time, organizations try to retain and increase long-term profitability through customer loyalty.[31] Chico's, a specialty women's retailer, offers a Passport Club that costs $500 to join but gives the club member such benefits as monthly coupons, free shipping, and 5 percent off all future purchases. Borders likewise offers Borders Rewards, a card-based system that provides incentives for frequent shoppers.[32] Such initiatives give stores the opportunity to acquire a greater share of each customer's business.

Managing customer relationships requires identifying patterns of buying behavior and then using that information to focus on the most promising and profitable customers. Companies must be sensitive to customers' requirements and desires, and establish communication to build customers' trust and loyalty. The lifetime value of a Lexus customer may be about 50 times that of a Taco Bell customer, but there are a lot more Taco Bell customers! For either organization, however, a customer is important. A customer's lifetime value results from his or her frequency of purchases, average value of purchases, and brand-switching patterns.[33] A customer's value over a lifetime represents an intangible asset to a marketer that can be augmented by addressing the customer's varying needs and preferences at different stages in his or her relationship with the firm.[34] Because the loss of a loyal, potential lifetime customer can result in lower profits, managing customer relationships has become a major focus of strategic marketing today.

Through the use of Internet-based marketing strategies (e-marketing), companies can personalize customer relationships on a nearly one-on-one basis. A wide range of products, such as computers, jeans, golf clubs, cosmetics, and greeting cards, can be tailored for specific customers. CRM provides a strategic bridge between information technology and marketing strategies aimed at long-term relationships with high-revenue customers.[35] Thus, information technology helps Amazon.com manage customer relationships to build value and increase sales and satisfaction.

Value-Driven Marketing

customer relationship management (CRM) Using information about customers to create marketing strategies that develop and sustain desirable customer relationships

value A customer's subjective assessment of benefits relative to costs in determining the worth of a product

Value is an important element of managing long-term customer relationships and implementing the marketing concept. We view **value** as a customer's subjective assessment of benefits relative to costs in determining the worth of a product (customer value = customer benefits – customer costs). Consumers develop a concept of value through the integration of their perceptions of product quality and financial sacrifice.[36] From a company's perspective, there is a tradeoff between increasing the value offered to a customer and maximizing the profits from a transaction.[37] Consider that General Electric is significantly cutting back its 128-year-old incandescent light bulb business in favor of expanding its compact fluorescent and other energy-efficient lighting products. In recent years, the incandescent lighting business accounted for less than 2 percent of GE's revenues as consumers shifted to compact fluorescents under the perception that they are a better value and are beneficial to the environment.[38]

Customer benefits include anything a buyer receives in an exchange. Hotels and motels, for example, basically provide a room with a bed and a bathroom, but each firm provides a different level of service, amenities, and atmosphere to satisfy its guests. Hampton Inns offers the minimum services necessary to maintain a quality, efficient, low-priced overnight accommodation. In contrast, the Ritz-Carlton provides every imaginable service a guest might desire and strives to ensure that all service is of the highest quality. Customers judge which type of accommodation offers

Strong on the first mile.   Strong on the last mile.

We consider endurance racing nothing less than the world's greatest test track for street tires. For the 9th consecutive year, the winner of the ultimate endurance race, the 24 Hours of Le Mans, rode on Michelin® tires. Not surprisingly, our street tires are just as remarkable. The Michelin® Pilot® Series tires have the highest combined levels of performance in the category? Go to michelinman.com/performance.

MICHELIN
a better way forward

Value-Driven Marketing

Michelin positions its tires as durable and efficient, driving customer value.

the best value according to the benefits they desire and their willingness and ability to pay for the costs associated with those benefits.

Customer costs include anything a buyer must give up to obtain the benefits the product provides. The most obvious cost is the monetary price of the product, but nonmonetary costs can be equally important in a customer's determination of value. Two nonmonetary costs are the time and effort customers expend to find and purchase desired products. To reduce time and effort, a company can increase product availability, thereby making it more convenient for buyers to purchase the firm's products. Another nonmonetary cost is risk, which can be reduced by offering good basic warranties or extended warranties for an additional charge.[39] Another risk reduction strategy is the offer of a 100 percent satisfaction guarantee. This strategy is increasingly popular in today's catalog/telephone/Internet shopping environment. L.L. Bean, for example, uses such a guarantee to reduce the risk involved in ordering merchandise from its catalogs and online store.

The process people use to determine the value of a product is not highly scientific. We all tend to get a feel for the worth of products based on our own expectations and previous experiences. We can, for example, compare the value of tires, batteries, and computers directly with the value of competing products. We evaluate movies, sporting events, and performances by entertainers on the more subjective basis of personal preferences and emotions. For most purchases, we do not consciously try to calculate the associated benefits and costs. It becomes an instinctive feeling that Kellogg's Corn Flakes are a good value or that McDonald's is a good place to take children for a quick lunch. The purchase of an automobile or a mountain bike may have emotional components, but more conscious decision making may also figure in the process of determining value.

In developing marketing activities, it is important to recognize that customers receive benefits based on their experiences. For example, many computer buyers consider services such as fast delivery, ease of installation, technical advice, and training assistance to be important elements of the product. Customers also derive benefits from the act of shopping and selecting products. These benefits can be affected by the atmosphere or environment of a store, such as Red Lobster's nautical theme. Even the ease of navigating a website can have a tremendous impact on perceived value. For this reason, General Motors has developed a user-friendly way to navigate its website for researching and pricing vehicles. Using the Internet to compare a Saturn with a Mercedes could result in different customers viewing each automobile as an excellent value. Owners have highly rated the Saturn as providing low-cost, reliable transportation and having dealers who provide outstanding service. A Mercedes may cost twice as much but has been rated as a better-engineered automobile that also has a higher social status than the Saturn. Different customers may view each car as being an exceptional value for their own personal satisfaction.

The marketing mix can be used to enhance perceptions of value. A product that demonstrates value usually has a feature or an enhancement that provides benefits. Promotional activities can also help create an image and prestige characteristics that customers consider in their assessment of a product's value. In some cases, value may simply be perceived as the lowest price. Many customers may not care about the quality of the paper towels they buy; they simply want the cheapest ones for use in cleaning up spills because they plan to throw them in the trash anyway. On the other hand, more people are looking for the fastest, most convenient way to achieve a certain goal and therefore become insensitive to pricing. For example, many busy customers are buying more prepared meals in supermarkets to take home and serve quickly, even though these meals cost considerably more than meals prepared from scratch. In such cases, the products with the greatest convenience may be perceived as having the greatest value. The availability or distribution of products can also enhance their value. Taco Bell, for example, wants to have its Mexican fast-food products available at any time and any place people are thinking about consuming food. It has therefore introduced Taco Bell products into supermarkets, vending machines, college campuses, and other convenient locations. Thus, the development of an effective marketing strategy requires understanding the needs and desires of customers and designing a marketing mix to satisfy them and provide the value they want.

Marketing Management

L O 5 To learn about the process of marketing management

Marketing management is the process of planning, organizing, implementing, and controlling marketing activities to facilitate exchanges effectively and efficiently. Effectiveness and efficiency are important dimensions of this definition. *Effectiveness* is the degree to which an exchange helps achieve an organization's objectives. *Efficiency* refers to minimizing the resources an organization must spend to achieve a specific level of desired exchanges. Thus, the overall goal of marketing management is to facilitate highly desirable exchanges and to minimize the costs of doing so.

Planning is a systematic process of assessing opportunities and resources, determining marketing objectives, and developing a marketing strategy and plans for implementation and control. Planning determines when and how marketing activities are performed and who performs them. It forces marketing managers to think ahead, establish objectives, and consider future marketing activities and their impact on society. Effective planning also reduces or eliminates daily crises.

Organizing marketing activities involves developing the internal structure of the marketing unit. The structure is the key to directing marketing activities. The marketing unit can be organized by functions, products, regions, types of customers, or a combination of all four. Proper implementation of marketing plans hinges on coordination of marketing activities, motivation of marketing personnel, and effective communication within the unit. Marketing managers must motivate marketing personnel, coordinate their activities, and integrate their activities both with those in other areas of the company and with the marketing efforts of personnel in external organizations, such as advertising agencies and research firms. If McDonald's runs a promotion advertising Big Macs for 99 cents, proper implementation of this plan requires that each of the company's restaurants has enough staff and product on hand to handle the increased demand. An organization's communication system must allow the marketing manager to stay in contact with high-level management, with managers of other functional areas within the firm, and with personnel involved in marketing activities both inside and outside the organization.

The marketing control process consists of establishing performance standards, comparing actual performance with established standards, and reducing the difference between desired and actual performance. An effective control process has four requirements. First, it should ensure a rate of information flow that allows the marketing manager to detect quickly any differences between actual and planned levels of performance. Second, it must accurately monitor various activities and be flexible enough to accommodate changes. Third, the costs of the control process must be low relative to costs that would arise without controls. Finally, the control process should be designed so that both managers and subordinates can understand it. We examine the development, organization, implementation, and controlling of marketing strategies in greater detail in the next chapter.

marketing management
The process of planning, organizing, implementing, and controlling marketing activities to facilitate exchanges effectively and efficiently

The Importance of Marketing in Our Global Economy

L O 6 To recognize the role of marketing in our society

Our definition of *marketing* and discussion of marketing activities reveal some of the obvious reasons the study of marketing is relevant in today's world. In this section, we look at how marketing affects us as individuals and at its role in our increasingly global society.

Marketing Costs Consume a Sizable Portion of Buyers' Dollars

Studying marketing will make you aware that many marketing activities are necessary to provide satisfying goods and services. Obviously these activities cost money. About one-half of a buyer's dollar goes toward marketing costs. If you spend $14 on a new CD, 50 to 60 percent goes toward marketing expenses, including promotion and distribution, as well as profit margin. The production (pressing) of the CD represents about $1, or 6.25 percent of its price. A family with a monthly income of $3,000 that allocates $600 to taxes and savings spends about $2,400 for goods and services. Of this amount, $1,200 goes for marketing activities. If marketing expenses consume that much of your dollar, you should know how this money is used.

Marketing Is Used in Nonprofit Organizations

Although the term *marketing* may bring to mind advertising for Burger King, Toyota, and Apple, marketing is also important in organizations working to achieve goals other than ordinary business objectives such as profit. Government agencies at the federal, state, and local levels engage in marketing activities to fulfill their mission and goals. The U.S. armed forces, for example, use promotion, including television advertisements and event sponsorships, to communicate the benefits of enlisting to potential recruits. The U.S. Agriculture Department launched a promotional website with games to help teach kids about eating right according to its revised "Food Pyramid."[40] Universities and colleges also engage in marketing activities to recruit new students as well as donations from alumni and businesses.

In the private sector, nonprofit organizations employ marketing activities to create, distribute, promote, and even price programs that benefit particular segments of society. Habitat for Humanity, for example, must promote its philosophy of low-income housing to the public to raise funds and donations of supplies to build or renovate housing for low-income families who contribute "sweat equity" to the construction of their own homes. In a recent year, such activities helped nonprofit organizations raise more than $292 billion in philanthropic contributions to assist them in fulfilling their missions.[41]

Marketing Is Important to Business and the Economy

Businesses must sell products to survive and grow, and marketing activities help sell their products. Financial resources generated from sales can be used to develop innovative products. New products allow a firm to better satisfy customers' changing needs, which in turn enables the firm to generate more profits. Even nonprofit businesses need to "sell" to survive.

Marketing activities help produce the profits that are essential not only to the survival of individual businesses but also to the health and ultimate survival of the global economy. Profits drive economic growth because without them businesses find it difficult, if not impossible, to buy more raw materials, hire more employees, attract more capital, and create additional products that in turn make more profits. Without profits, marketers cannot continue to provide jobs and contribute to social causes.

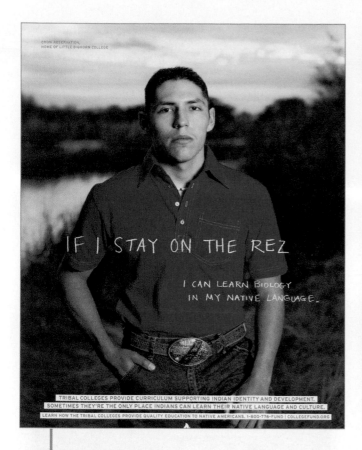

WE EXIST TO MAKE SURE IT DOESN'T

Multiple sclerosis interrupts the flow of information between the brain and the body and stops people from moving. With the help of people like you, the National MS Society addresses the challenges of each person whose life is affected by MS and helps them stay connected to the great big moving world.

JOIN THE MOVEMENT
jointhemovement.org

Carole, diagnosed in 2005
Geoffrey, diagnosed in 1987

Nonprofit Organizations

The American Indian College Fund and National Multiple Sclerosis Society use marketing to promote their causes.

Marketing Fuels Our Global Economy

Profits from marketing products contribute to the development of new products and technologies. Advances in technology, along with falling political and economic barriers and the universal desire for a higher standard of living, have made marketing across national borders commonplace while stimulating global economic growth. As a result of worldwide communications and increased international travel, many U.S. brands have achieved widespread acceptance around the world. At the same time, customers in the United States have greater choices among the products they buy as foreign brands such as Toyota (Japan), Bayer (Germany), and BP (Great Britain) now sell alongside U.S. brands such as Ford, Tylenol, and Chevron. People around the world watch CNN and MTV on Toshiba and Sony televisions they purchased at Wal-Mart. Some well-known brands have been sold to foreign companies: IBM's personal computer unit, for example, was purchased by Lenovo, a Chinese firm.[42] Electronic commerce via the Internet now enables businesses of all sizes to reach buyers worldwide. We explore the international markets and opportunities for global marketing in Chapter 9.

Marketing Knowledge Enhances Consumer Awareness

Besides contributing to the well-being of our economy, marketing activities improve the quality of our lives. Studying marketing allows us to assess a product's value and flaws and its marketing strategy more effectively. Consider that research suggests that low-fat nutrition claims for a food product can actually increase the intake of that product, thus countering the desired effects of consuming low-fact snacks to lose weight.[43] We can determine which marketing efforts need improvement and how to attain that goal. For example, an unsatisfactory experience with a warranty may make you wish for stricter law enforcement so sellers would fulfill their promises. You may also wish you had more accurate information about a product before you purchased it. Understanding marketing enables us to evaluate corrective measures (such as laws, regulations, and industry guidelines) that could stop unfair, damaging,

Marketing and the Growth of Technology

Apple and Sprint manage the development of technology to produce customer satisfaction and loyalty.

or unethical marketing practices. Thus, understanding how marketing activities work can help you be a better consumer.

Marketing Connects People Through Technology

Technology, especially computers and telecommunications, helps marketers understand and satisfy more customers than ever before. Over the phone and online, customers can provide feedback about their experiences with a company's products. Even products such as Dasani bottled water provide a customer service number and a website for questions or comments. This feedback helps marketers refine and improve their products to better satisfy customer needs. Today marketers must recognize the impact not only of websites but of instant messaging, blogs, online forums, online games, mailing lists, and wikis, as well as text messaging via cell phones and podcasts via MP3 players. Increasingly, these tools are facilitating marketing exchanges. Some restaurants, for example, are permitting customers to preorder their food and coffee products by sending text messages to the restaurants via their cell phones.

The Internet allows companies to provide tremendous amounts of information about their products to consumers and to interact with them through e-mail and websites. A consumer who is shopping for a new car, for example, can access automakers' webpages, configure an ideal vehicle, and get instant feedback on its price. They can visit Autobytel, Edmund's, and other websites to find professional reviews and obtain comparative pricing information on both new and used cars to help them find the best value. They can also visit a consumer opinion site, such as Epinions.com, to read other consumers' reviews of the products. They can then purchase a vehicle online or at a dealership. The Internet permits marketers to target and interact with consumers in unique ways, as through virtual environments such as Second Life, an online multi-player game. American Apparel, for example, opened a virtual retail store in Second Life where subscribers can dress their online characters, called avatars, to play in the alternate reality. Shoppers who buy virtual American Apparel products get coupons for 15 percent off the same item in the real world. Other companies also have a presence in Second Life, including Adidas, Coca-Cola, Wells Fargo, and ESPN.[44]

Marketers of everything from computers to travel reservations can now use the Internet for transactions. Southwest Airlines, for example, now books 74 percent of its passenger revenue online.[45] In fact, online sales now exceed $116 billion, accounting for more than 5 percent of all retail sales.[46] The Internet has also become a vital tool for marketing to other businesses. Successful companies are using technology in their marketing strategies to develop profitable relationships with these customers. Table 1.1 shows the most common online activities.

Socially Responsible Marketing: Promoting the Welfare of Customers and Society

The success of our economic system depends on marketers whose values promote trust and cooperative relationships in which customers are treated with respect. The public is increasingly insisting that social responsibility and ethical concerns be considered in planning and implementing marketing activities. Although some marketers' irresponsible or unethical activities end up on the front pages of *USA Today* or the *Wall Street Journal,* more firms are working to develop a responsible approach to developing long-term relationships with customers and other stakeholders. For example, Staples, the office supply superstore chain, has provided financial support and donated more than $400,000 worth of school supplies to the School, Home & Office Products Association (SHOPA) Kids in Need Foundation, which provides school supplies to needy children and teachers in low-income schools, through its Staples Foundation for Learning.[47]

table 1.1   LEADING INTERNET ACTIVITIES

Activity	Percent of U.S. Adults Who Have Engaged in Online Activity
Using e-mail	91
Using a search engine to find information	91
Searching for a map or driving directions	86
Looking for information on a hobby or interest	83
Looking for medical/health information	80
Researching products before making a purchase	78
Checking the weather	78
Getting travel information	73
Getting news	72
Making online purchases	71

Source: "Internet Activities," Pew Internet & Life Product, June 11, 2007, **www.pewinternet.org/trends/Internet_Activities_8.28.07.htm.**

green MARKETING

Building Green Buildings

Buildings in the United States account for 39 percent of the country's primary energy use, 70 percent of its resource consumption, 15 trillion gallons of water use, and 136 million tons of construction and demolition debris annually. Buildings are beginning to get more attention in the fight against global warming because carbon dioxide emissions could be cut by 6 million tons a year—the equivalent of taking 1 million cars off the road—if half the nation's new commercial buildings used 50 percent less energy. Increasingly, commercial tenants are demanding energy-efficient buildings, not only to be more environmentally responsible but also to save on energy costs. Residential buildings are coming under the same scrutiny: it has been estimated that about 10 percent of new homes will be "green"—built to more environmentally friendly standards—by 2010. The city of Austin, Texas, for example, plans to require homebuilders to increase the energy efficiency of new homes by 65 percent or more by 2015.

The National Association of Home Builders has developed guidelines for environmentally sound building practices, ranging from site design to materials used in construction. Companies that make building walls and roofs out of plant materials are slowly increasing their impact on the way buildings are constructed. G-Sky, for example, manufactures "green" wall panels and sky gardens that are safe to install on almost any structure. Green walls and roofs have many benefits, including heat island mitigation, storm water control, habitat restoration, and clean air and CO_2 fixation. Building owners also experience benefits such as energy savings, sound insulation, improved health and wellness for residents and tenants, and building protection. A ten-story office building in Los Angeles with a green roof and walls would save $141,000 annually on its electricity bill and extract 40 tons of carbon from the air.

Marketing these new green building products requires educating customers about the new technologies available, as well as demonstrating that the technology works and provides benefits to both customers and society as a whole. As technology advances, larger companies are joining the new green building revolution. The Gap retail chain installed a 69,000-square-foot green roof on its headquarters in San Bruno, California, and the Ford Motor Company installed green roofs on its corporate headquarters. Other green projects include the Church of Jesus Christ of Latter-Day Saints Conference Center in Salt Lake City, Utah, which installed 348,480 square feet of extensive and intensive green roof in 2000.

Some cities are encouraging their residents and developers to install green roof projects. The cities of Chicago and Portland have installed or are planning to install over 43 and 42 green roof projects, respectively. As customers and citizens become more aware of the potential benefits and savings of these products, they will demand that contractors and builders use them. The welfare of both customers and society will then improve through value-driven marketing.[c]

In the area of the natural environment, companies are increasingly embracing the notion of **green marketing,** which is a strategic process involving stakeholder assessment to create meaningful long-term relationships with customers while maintaining, supporting, and enhancing the natural environment. The multinational enterprise Unilever, for example, not only produces and markets a variety of food and personal care products around the world, but it also operates a free community laundry in São Paulo, funds a hospital that provides free medical care in Bangladesh, provides financing and educational materials to help suppliers around the world to convert to more environmentally friendly practices, and reports on its carbon dioxide and hazardous waste releases to interested stakeholders. Unilever's chief executive officer, Patrick Cescau, believes that such activities are necessary to remain competitive in future decades, declaring, "You cannot ignore the impact your company has on the community and environment."[48] Even Hollywood is "going green" with networks, television shows, and movies that are incorporating more green themes, like Homer and Marge Simpson tooling around in their biodiesel-fueled vehicle in *The Simpson's Movie* and *The Early Show*'s new "Going Green" segment.[49] By addressing concerns about the impact of marketing on society, a firm can protect the interests of the general public and the natural environment. We examine these issues and many others as we develop a framework for understanding more about marketing in the remainder of this book.

Marketing Offers Many Exciting Career Prospects

From 25 to 33 percent of all civilian workers in the United States perform marketing activities. The marketing field offers a variety of interesting and challenging career opportunities throughout the world, such as personal selling, advertising, packaging, transportation, storage, marketing research, product development, wholesaling, and retailing. In addition, many individuals working for nonbusiness organizations engage in marketing activities to promote political, educational, cultural, church, civic, and charitable activities. Whether a person earns a living through marketing activities or performs them voluntarily for a nonprofit group, marketing knowledge and skills are valuable personal and professional assets.

green marketing A strategic process involving stakeholder assessment to create meaningful long-term relationships with customers while maintaining, supporting, and enhancing the natural environment

SUMMARY

Marketing is the process of creating, distributing, promoting, and pricing goods, services, and ideas to facilitate satisfying exchange relationships with customers and develop and maintain favorable relationships with stakeholders in a dynamic environment. As the purchasers of the products that organizations develop, promote, distribute, and price, customers are the focal point of all marketing activities. The essence of marketing is to develop satisfying exchanges from which both customers and marketers benefit. Organizations generally focus their marketing efforts on a specific group of customers called a target market.

Marketing involves developing and managing a product that will satisfy customer needs, making the product available in the right place and at a price acceptable to customers, and communicating information that helps customers determine if the product will satisfy their needs. These activities—product, distribution, promotion, and pricing—are known as the marketing mix because marketing managers decide what type of each element to use and in what amounts. Marketing managers strive to develop a marketing mix that matches the needs of customers in the target market. Before marketers can develop a marketing mix, they must collect in-depth, up-to-date information about customer needs. The product variable of the marketing mix deals with researching customers' needs and wants and designing a product that satisfies them. A product can be a good, a service, or an idea. In dealing with the distribution variable, a marketing manager tries to make products available in the quantities desired to as many customers as possible. The promotion variable relates to activities used to inform individuals or groups about the organization and its products. The price variable involves decisions and actions associated with establishing pricing policies and determining product prices. These marketing mix variables are often viewed as controllable because they can be changed, but there are limits to how much they can be altered.

Individuals and organizations engage in marketing to facilitate exchanges—the provision or transfer of goods, services, and ideas in return for something of value. Four conditions must exist for an exchange to occur. First, two or more individuals, groups, or organizations must participate, and each must possess something of value that the other party desires. Second, the exchange should provide a benefit or satisfaction to both parties involved in the transaction. Third, each party must have confidence in the promise of the "something of value" held by the other. Finally, to build trust, the parties to the exchange must meet expectations. Marketing activities should attempt to create and maintain satisfying exchange relationships.

The marketing environment, which includes competitive, economic, political, legal and regulatory, technological, and sociocultural forces, surrounds the customer and the marketing mix. These forces can create threats to marketers, but they also generate opportunities for new products and new methods of reaching customers. These forces can fluctuate quickly and dramatically.

According to the marketing concept, an organization should try to provide products that satisfy customers' needs through a coordinated set of activities that also allows the organization to achieve its goals. Customer satisfaction is the marketing concept's major objective. The philosophy of the marketing concept emerged in the United States during the 1950s after the production and sales eras. Organizations that develop activities consistent with the marketing concept become marketing-oriented organizations. To implement the marketing concept, a marketing-oriented organization must establish an information system to discover customers' needs and use the information to create satisfying products. It must also coordinate all its activities and develop marketing mixes that create value for customers in order to satisfy their needs.

Relationship marketing involves establishing long-term, mutually satisfying buyer-seller relationships. Customer-centric marketing requires developing collaborative relationships with customers based on focusing on their individual needs and concerns. Customer relationship management (CRM) focuses on using information about customers to create marketing strategies that develop and sustain desirable customer relationships. Managing customer relationships requires identifying patterns of buying behavior and using that information to focus on the most promising and profitable customers.

Value is a customer's subjective assessment of benefits relative to costs in determining the worth of a product. Benefits include anything a buyer receives in an exchange; costs include anything a buyer must give up to obtain the benefits the product provides. The marketing mix can be used to enhance perceptions of value.

Marketing management is the process of planning, organizing, implementing, and controlling marketing activities to facilitate effective and efficient exchanges. Planning is a systematic process of assessing opportunities and resources, determining marketing objectives, developing a marketing strategy, and preparing for implementation and control. Organizing marketing activities involves developing the marketing unit's internal structure. Proper implementation of marketing plans depends on coordinating marketing activities, motivating marketing personnel, and communicating effectively within the unit. The marketing control process consists of establishing performance standards, comparing actual performance with established standards, and reducing the difference between desired and actual performance.

Marketing is important in our society in many ways. Marketing costs absorb about half of each buyer's dollar. Marketing activities are performed in both business and nonprofit organizations. Marketing activities help business organizations generate profits and help fuel the increasingly global economy. Knowledge of marketing enhances consumer awareness. New technology improves marketers' ability to connect with customers. Socially responsible marketing can promote the welfare of customers and society. Green marketing is a strategic process involving stakeholder assessment to create meaningful long-term relationships with customers while maintaining, supporting, and enhancing the natural environment. Finally, marketing offers many exciting career opportunities.

IMPORTANT TERMS

Marketing, 4
Customers, 4
Target market, 4
Marketing mix, 5
Products, 7
Exchanges, 9
Stakeholders, 10

Marketing environment,
   10
Marketing concept, 11
Marketing orientation, 13
Relationship marketing, 14

Customer-centric
   marketing, 14
Customer relationship
   management
   (CRM), 15

Value, 15
Marketing management,
   17
Green marketing, 23

DISCUSSION & REVIEW QUESTIONS

1. What is *marketing*? How did you define the term before you read this chapter?

2. What is the focus of all marketing activities? Why?

3. What are the four variables of the marketing mix? Why are these elements known as variables?

4. What conditions must exist before a marketing exchange can occur? Describe a recent exchange in which you participated.

5. What are the forces in the marketing environment? How much control does a marketing manager have over these forces?

6. Discuss the basic elements of the marketing concept. Which businesses in your area use this philosophy? Explain why.

7. How can an organization implement the marketing concept?

8. What is customer relationship management? Why is it so important to "manage" this relationship?

9. What is *value*? How can marketers use the marketing mix to enhance customers' perception of value?

10. What types of activities are involved in the marketing management process?

11. Why is marketing important in our society? Why should you study marketing?

APPLICATION QUESTIONS

1. Identify several businesses in your area that have *not* adopted the marketing concept. What characteristics of these organizations indicate nonacceptance of the marketing concept?

2. Identify possible target markets for the following products:
   a. Kellogg's Corn Flakes
   b. Wilson tennis rackets
   c. Disney World
   d. Diet Pepsi

3. Discuss the variables of the marketing mix (product, price, promotion, and distribution) as they might relate to each of the following:
   a. A trucking company
   b. A men's clothing store
   c. A skating rink
   d. A campus bookstore

INTERNET EXERCISE

Visit **www.cengage.com/marketing/pride-ferrell** for resources to help you master the material in this chapter, as well as materials that will help you expand your marketing knowledge, including Internet exercise updates, ACE Self-Tests, hotlinks to companies featured in this chapter, and much more.

The American Marketing Association

The American Marketing Association (AMA) is the marketing discipline's primary professional organization. In addition to sponsoring academic research, publishing marketing literature, and organizing meetings of local businesspeople with student members, it helps individual members find employment in member firms. To see what the AMA has to offer you, visit the AMA website at **www.marketingpower.com**.

1. What type of information is available on the AMA website to assist students in planning their careers and finding jobs?

2. If you joined a student chapter of the AMA, what benefits would you receive?

3. What marketing mix variable does the AMA's Internet marketing efforts exemplify?

developing your MARKETING PLAN

Successful companies develop strategies for marketing their products. The strategic plan guides the marketer as it makes decisions about the attributes of the product, its distribution, promotional activities, and pricing. A clear understanding of the foundations of marketing is essential in formulating a strategy and in the development of a specific marketing plan. To guide you in relating the information in this chapter to the development of your marketing plan, consider the following:

1. Discuss how the marketing concept contributes to a company's long-term success.

2. Describe the level of marketing orientation that currently exists in your company. How will a marketing orientation contribute to the success of your new product?

3. What benefits will your product provide to the customer? How will these benefits play a role in determining the customer value of your product?

The information obtained from these questions should assist you in developing various aspects of your marketing plan found in the *Interactive Marketing Plan* exercise at **www.cengage.com/marketing/pride-ferrell**.

globalEDGE

1. *Forbes* magazine publishes a composite ranking as a part of its Forbes Global 2000 based on four common business measures: sales, profit, assets, and market value. This information can be particularly useful if your firm intends to enter a new global market sector. Use the search term "composite ranking" at **http://globaledge.msu.edu/ibrd** to find the most recent Forbes 2000 ranking and then sort based on category. What are the top three semiconductor firms based on sales? In which country is each firm based?

2. Your firm is planning to develop a customer relationship management (CRM) initiative after it internationalizes. One way to understand the similarity or dissimilarity of markets and cultures is to use Hofstede's cultural dimensions, based on scores for 56 countries. Hofstede's cultural dimensions can be found using the search term "56 countries" at **http://globaledge.msu.edu/ibrd** to access the Geert Hofstede Resource Center and then the link called Hofstede Scores. The Power Distance Index (PDI) can be valuable in developing a CRM strategy. What are the five countries scoring lowest on Hofstede's PDI? Are these countries on the same continent? Are they geographically close?

video CASE 1.1

Method Cleans Up the Home Care Industry Using Green Marketing

"People against dirty" is the intriguing slogan of the San Francisco–based home and body care brand *Method*. The founders claim that they seek not only to clean our homes and bodies, but to remove harmful chemicals from our lives as well. All *Method* products are chemical-free and made with natural, safe ingredients. The company has embraced the marketing concepts, and its target market is receptive to a green marketing strategy. However, *Method* has not become one of the fastest-growing new brands in the United States (sold in more than 25,000 retail outlets) by focusing only on a green philosophy. The company has attracted customers through its cool brand with hip, eye-catching packaging, edgy marketing, and even a link to a blog about clean living on the company's website.

Method was founded in 2000 by former roommates and high school friends Adam Lowry, a chemical engineer who worked as a climatologist for the Carnegie Institute before becoming *Method's* "chief greens keeper," and Eric Ryan, a marketing expert with experience designing campaigns for Saturn and The Gap. Deciding to join forces to help wean people off of the harmful chemicals we use to clean our homes and bodies, Lowry and Ryan were able to combine their complementary skill sets to develop products that were not only effective and natural, but that looked great as well.

Method's concept is not new. Companies such as Seventh Generation and Ecover have been around for years, but they were never able to break into the mainstream. *Method*, however, looks like it will become a household name with annual revenues nearing $100 million. When choosing distribution channels, Lowry and Ryan decided to steer away from coops and health food stores and instead sought mass recognition and distribution at Target, Linens 'n Things, Amazon.com, and other large retailers. In order to make this possible, the founders knew that they could not charge the high prices established by other eco-friendly cleaner companies. They needed to compete head-on with the major cleaning brands. Although Lowry is dedicated to creating products that adhere to strict green standards, he and Ryan agreed from the beginning that taking the green slant would not be the best way to sell their products.

In order to literally stand out from the competition, they enlisted designer Karim Rashid (who also has designed for the likes of Prada and Dirt Devil) to design visually appealing packaging for their products. The result was affordable cleaning products contained in beautiful, standout bottles. In a highly competitive industry, the fight to get noticed on the shelf is fierce. Most large companies push the smaller brands out of the prime locations, but with *Method's* artistic packaging, people take notice even though it is a smaller company. Customers drawn to the product for its looks or the all-natural scents will be purchasing more non-polluting green products for their home without even knowing it. In the end, Lowry and Ryan hope that this approach does create a change in perspective among consumers previously uninterested in going green or unable to afford to do so.

As with any successful company, *Method* has had to be highly innovative. It has been ahead of the curve in developing new kinds of cleaning products. For example, *Method* was an industry leader when it created a triple-concentrated laundry detergent long before major companies began doing so. *Method* has also taken stock of competitive products on the market already, and continually works on making its own brand's versions more eco-friendly. Cases in point are dryer sheets and the Omop. Conventional dryer sheets are coated in beef fat in order to create soft clothing. Lowry found this disgusting and unacceptable. Looking for a vegetarian solution, the company developed dryer sheets coated with canola oil instead. The Omop, *Method's* answer to the Swiffer, is a stylish mop using cloths created from a corn-based plastic product. Unlike Swiffer's cloths, which are synthetic, the Omop's cloths are completely biodegradable.

Focusing on product quality, trends, price point, design, and accessibility have helped *Method* grow from a small, unknown company to one making a name for itself in mainstream media for its innovativeness and quality products. The company came in at number 16 on *Fast Company's* "World's Most Innovative Companies" 2008 list, and, through its high-profile distribution at major retail outlets, it is becoming increasingly popular among consumers.

Method may find that clever marketing and competitive pricing may, in the long run, be one of the best ways to help the environment. With these marketing techniques, they have given green products a competitive advantage in a large market segment. . .and they continue growing.[50]

Questions for Discussion

1. How has *Method* implemented the marketing concept?
2. Why is *Method* successful in a highly competitive industry?
3. Does the success of *Method* provide insights about the future of green marketing?

CASE 1.2

Danone Focuses on Health Nutrition

Groupe Danone, based in Paris, sells nearly $19 billion worth of dairy products and bottled water under such well-known brand names as Evian, Dannon, Stoneyfield Farm, Volvic, Frucor, Activia, and more. The company was created in 1966 when two glass companies, the French-owned Souchon-Neuvesel glassworks and Glaces de Boussois, merged to form BSN. The merger decision was partly in response to changing market trends toward "no-deposit, no-return" bottles. Soon thereafter, BSN took control of the Evian bottled water and Kronenbourg beer brands through its acquisition of the European Breweries Company. After reflecting on the future of the industry, BSN executives realized that although glass bottles would likely lose their monopoly in the beverage industry, they had no desire to produce plastic bottles. They did, however, find a better solution: to produce what went into their glass containers. Since BSN was already selling bottled water, they decided to sell baby food in glass jars. BSN became the leading manufacturer of beer, mineral waters, and baby food in glass bottle containers.

In 1973, BSN merged with Gervais Danone, creating the largest food group in France. The merger introduced BSN to new markets, making food products and beverages the core of the company's business. Executives then decided to refocus the company's strategy and concentrate essentially on selling food items. In the 1980s, BSN Gervais Danone recognized the potential of the growing European market and through acquisitions, partnerships, and takeovers, grew to become the third-largest food group in Europe. By 1997, the company had changed its name to Groupe Danone and implemented a new strategy: concentrating on the market sectors of fresh dairy products, beverages, and cookies and cereal products. In the following years, Groupe Danone increased its presence on the international market while focusing on its new strategy.

By 2007, Groupe Danone had become the world leader in the yogurt and fresh-dairy industries and number two in the packaged-water and cookie industries. That year, Groupe Danone sold its cookie division to Kraft Food Inc., for $7.4 billion and purchased Royal Dumico, a Dutch company that makes hospital meals and baby food, for $17.2 billion. This initiative was taken when the group decided to go even further with their strategy. The sale of the cookie division marked a turning point in Danone's history. With 98 percent of Danone sales in functional health and nutrition products, the company is now focusing on a marketing strategy that stresses health and wellness. Many consumers are aware of the importance of healthy lifestyles, but they are not willing to pay premium prices for healthier foods. Danone is depending on the trend that consumers are finally willing to purchase healthy products as well as bottled water.

Group Danone's new products include Activia, a yogurt that includes patented probiotic bacteria and aids digestion; it already accounts for almost $2 billion in sales worldwide. Danone is tailoring its products by mapping diet deficiencies by region and designing products that fit the requirements of children, adults, and senior citizens in that area. Although defining what is good for you is difficult, the market has become receptive to healthy brands. Other leading brands include Evian, DanActive, Volvic Revive, and Essensis. Evian, discovered in 1789, has become the world's number one water brand. DanActive, a liquid yogurt, helps strengthen the body's defense system. Volvic Revive is the new Danone "on-the-go" energy drink. Targeted toward active customers, Danone promotes Volvic Revive on the basis of its healthful plant extracts, such as ginseng and guarana. Danone Canada launched DHA-fortified children's yogurt to improve children's brain development through nutrition. Essensis, the latest yogurt product launched by Danone, is marketed in Europe and promoted for its ingredients that help the skin.

Groupe Danone filed 30 health-related patents last year and maintains a "biobank" with 3,000 strains of bacteria for research purposes. By founding 16 new Danone Institutes to study nutrition, the company has clearly established a strategic blueprint focused on consumer health. The marketing concept is being implemented at Danone by discovering what consumers want and developing products to serve those desires.[51]

Questions for Discussion

1. Describe Group Danone's target market for its probiotic yogurt products.
2. What forces from the marketing environment provide opportunities for Group Danone? Provide threats?
3. Does Group Danone appear to be implementing the marketing concept? Explain your answer.

2 Planning, Implementing, and Controlling Marketing Strategies

LEARNING objectives

1. To describe the strategic planning process

2. To explain how organizational resources and opportunities affect the planning process

3. To understand the role of the mission statement in strategic planning

4. To examine corporate, business-unit, and marketing strategies

5. To understand the process of creating the marketing plan

6. To describe the marketing implementation process and the major approaches to marketing implementation

Croc Attack

You have probably heard of Crocs. Maybe you already own a pair of these strange-looking plastic shoes. Have you ever wondered where they came from and how they became so popular? Crocs began when three friends from Boulder, Colorado, went sailing in the Caribbean. One of them brought along a pair of foam clogs he had purchased in Canada. The clogs, aided by the warmth of the Caribbean sun, inspired the trio to build their own business around a marketing opportunity. They purchased the Canadian company, Foam Creations, that produced the clogs and in 2002 began to market and distribute them in the United States under the Crocs brand. The shoes are made of Crosslite™, a proprietary closed-cell resin that makes them antimicrobial, lightweight, and odor resistant while providing flexibility and support. Despite a lack of funding and the derision of many (not everyone thinks they are fashionable), the multicolored Crocs—with their vent holes and lightweight, skid-resistant, nonmarking soles—quickly became a global phenomenon.

entrepreneurs IN ACTION

Crocs' initial target market was sailors and other water sports enthusiasts, but word of the shoes' comfort and functionality quickly spread, and it was quickly apparent that the shoes appealed to a much larger and more diverse group of consumers than the company's founders had anticipated. Soon, restaurant workers, doctors, nurses, and others who spend much of their time on their feet were sporting the colorful clogs in workplaces everywhere.

Crocs was able to make a name for itself by focusing on what it did well and by identifying and capitalizing on a combination of circumstances that helped the company reach many target markets. The company exploited its growing popularity by slowly introducing new and different types of shoes, such as the closed Crocs for hospital staff and even a Croc version of flip-flops. The Crocs line now includes more than 25 models in a wide variety of colors, color combinations, and patterns. The company is also diversifying into other products such as Crocs-branded apparel and accessories, which are intended to increase awareness of the brand and the product. The company is also growing through strategic acquisitions. Last year Crocs acquired Jibbitz, a company that specializes in accessories for Crocs footwear. The company now features more than 1,100 different products being sold through 4,000 retail outlets in the United States, Canada, Asia, and Europe. Crocs also bought Fury, a producer and distributor of hockey and lacrosse equipment for adults and children. Fury now produces products using Crocs' patented Crosslite™ material. Crocs then purchased the Exo Italia company, an Italian design house that has been instrumental in the development of cutting-edge footwear made with EVA (ethylene vinyl acetate). Exo has been collaborating with Crocs to design a new line of footwear for the company. The new YOU by Crocs™ line combines Crocs' legendary comfort with Italian design. Crocs also bought Ocean Minded, a designer and manufacturer of high-quality leather and EVA-based sandals for the beach, hiking, and action sports market. Crocs' newest acquisition is Bite Inc., a leader in comfortable and supportive performance shoes and sports sandals. This newest acquisition will help expand and complement Crocs RX™ medical line. By diversifying its product line and adding new companies to its existing portfolio, Crocs should be able to improve its overall image and build on its successful Crocs brand, applying strengths and competencies both from within and from its acquisitions.[1]

With competition increasing, Crocs and many other companies are spending more time and resources on strategic planning—that is, on determining how to use their resources and abilities to achieve their objectives and satisfy their customers. Although most of this book deals with specific marketing decisions and strategies, this chapter focuses on "the big picture": all the functional areas and activities—finance, production, human resources, and research and development, as well as marketing—that must be coordinated to reach organizational goals. To effectively implement the marketing concept of satisfying customers and achieving organizational goals, all organizations must engage in strategic planning.

We begin this chapter with an overview of the strategic planning process. Next, we examine how organizational resources and opportunities affect strategic planning and the role played by the organization's mission statement. After discussing the development of both corporate and business-unit strategy, we explore the nature of marketing strategy and the creation of the marketing plan. These elements provide a framework for the development and implementation of marketing strategies, as we will see throughout the remainder of this book.

Understanding the Strategic Planning Process

L O ❶ To describe the strategic planning process

Through the process of **strategic planning,** a firm establishes an organizational mission and formulates goals, corporate strategy, marketing objectives, marketing strategy, and, finally, a marketing plan.[2] A marketing orientation should guide the process of strategic planning to ensure that a concern for customer satisfaction is an integral part of the process. A marketing orientation is also important for the successful implementation of marketing strategies.[3] Figure 2.1 shows the components of strategic planning.

strategic planning The process of establishing an organizational mission and formulating goals, corporate strategy, marketing objectives, marketing strategy, and a marketing plan

figure 2.1

COMPONENTS OF STRATEGIC PLANNING

Analysis of organization's strengths and weaknesses
Identification of organization's opportunities and threats

↓

Organizational mission and goals

↓

Corporate and business-unit strategies

Marketing	**Production**	**Finance**	**Human Resources**
▸ Objectives	▸ Objectives	▸ Objectives	▸ Objectives
▸ Strategy	▸ Strategy	▸ Strategy	▸ Strategy
▸ Marketing plan	▸ Production plan	▸ Finance plan	▸ Human resources plan

Source: Figure adapted from *Marketing Strategy,* Third Edition, by O. C. Ferrell and Michael Hartline. Reprinted with permission of South-Western, a division of Thomson Learning: www .thomsonrights.com. Fax 800-730-2215.

Let's Cruise Tonight.

☐ Your Car
☐ Your Crew
☐ Your King

BK® Late-night. Open 'til midnight or later.*

™ & © 2007 Burger King Brands, Inc. All rights reserved.

The Marketing Strategy
Burger King targets the "late night" market by keeping some of its locations open until midnight and beyond.

The process begins with a detailed analysis of the organization's strengths and weaknesses and with identification of opportunities and threats within the marketing environment. Based on this analysis, the firm can establish or revise its mission and goals, and then develop corporate strategies to achieve those goals. Next, each functional area of the organization (marketing, production, finance, human resources, etc.) establishes its own objectives and develops strategies to achieve them.[4] The objectives and strategies of each functional area must support the organization's overall goals and mission, and should also be coordinated with a focus on marketing orientation.

Because our focus is marketing, we are, of course, most interested in the development of marketing objectives and strategies. Marketing objectives should be designed so their achievement will contribute to the corporate strategy and so they can be accomplished through efficient use of the firm's resources. To achieve its marketing objectives, an organization must develop a **marketing strategy,** which includes identifying and analyzing a target market and developing a marketing mix to meet the needs of individuals in that market. Thus, a marketing strategy includes a plan of action for developing, distributing, promoting, and pricing products that meet the needs of the target market. Marketing strategy is best formulated when it reflects the overall direction of the organization and is coordinated with all the firm's functional areas. When properly implemented and controlled, a marketing strategy will contribute to the achievement not only of marketing objectives but also of the organization's overall goals. Consider that Apple's successful marketing strategy for its iPod digital music player and iPhone smartphone helped revitalize the computer firm's reputation for excellent design, which may transfer to other Apple products.[5]

The strategic planning process ultimately yields a marketing strategy that is the framework for a **marketing plan,** a written document that specifies the activities to be performed to implement and control the organization's marketing activities. In the remainder of this chapter, we discuss the major components of the strategic planning process: organizational opportunities and resources, organizational mission and goals, corporate and business-unit strategy, marketing strategy, and the role of the marketing plan.

Assessing Organizational Resources and Opportunities

L O 2 To explain how organizational resources and opportunities affect the planning process

marketing strategy A plan of action for identifying and analyzing a target market and developing a marketing mix to meet the needs of that market

marketing plan A written document that specifies the activities to be performed to implement and control the organization's marketing activities

The strategic planning process begins with an analysis of the marketing environment. As we will see in Chapter 3, economic, competitive, political, legal and regulatory, sociocultural, and technological forces can threaten an organization and influence its overall goals; they also affect the amount and type of resources the firm can acquire. However, these environmental forces can create favorable opportunities as well—opportunities that can be translated into overall organizational goals and marketing objectives. Organizational culture and information use affect the extent to which managers perceive such opportunities as situations on which they can successfully capitalize.[6]

Any strategic planning effort must assess the organization's available financial and human resources and capabilities, as well as how the level of these factors is likely to change in the future, as additional resources may be needed to achieve the organization's goals and mission.[7] Resources indirectly affect marketing and financial performance by helping to create customer satisfaction and loyalty.[8] Resources can also include goodwill, reputation, and brand names. The reputation and well-known brand names of Rolex watches and Mercedes-Benz automobiles, for example, are resources that give these firms an advantage over their competitors. Such strengths

THE REST STOP ON THE CORPORATE LADDER.

Rated #1 International Business Class among U.S. airlines.

The climb up the corporate ladder can be steep. Luckily, BusinessFirst® is an excellent way to recharge. Even before stretching out in our extra-wide sleeper seats, you'll be relaxing preflight in our exclusive Presidents Club®, with free Wi-Fi, snacks and an open bar. And forget the hustle and bustle; you've got EliteAccess privileges like priority boarding and priority check-in to minimize wait times. Ready for the next step up? Fly BusinessFirst. For reservations and information, go to continental.com or call 1-800-523-FARE.

Conde Nast
Traveler

Continental Airlines

Work Hard.
Fly Right.

Market Opportunity
Appealing to the business traveler, Continental Airlines rated number one in business class service.

core competencies Things a firm does extremely well, which sometimes give it an advantage over its competition

market opportunity A combination of circumstances and timing that permits an organization to take action to reach a particular target market

strategic windows Temporary periods of optimal fit between the key requirements of a market and the particular capabilities of a firm competing in that market

also include **core competencies,** things a firm does extremely well—sometimes so well that they give the company an advantage over its competition. For example, Wal-Mart's core competency—efficiency in supply chain management—has enabled the discount chain to build a strong reputation for low prices and even to expand the number of generic medications eligible for its pharmacy's $4 prescription plan. Wal-Mart's ability to distribute its products so efficiently helped the firm's $4 prescription plan save Wal-Mart consumers $613 million last year.[9]

Analysis of the marketing environment involves not only an assessment of resources but also identification of opportunities in the marketplace. When the right combination of circumstances and timing permits an organization to take action to reach a particular target market, a **market opportunity** exists. For example, after consumers began to perceive bottled-water products as having a negative impact on the natural environment because of their plastic containers, Sigg USA recognized a market opportunity for its reusable aluminum water bottles. The bottles can be refilled with tap water and carried easily, making them both environmentally friendly and economical.[10] Such opportunities are often called **strategic windows,** temporary periods of optimal fit between the key requirements of a market and the particular capabilities of a firm competing in that market.[11]

E-ntertainment MARKETING

Reach Out and Twitter Someone

Twitter is a free social networking and "micro-blogging" service. Users can send "updates" about their comings and goings in the form of text-based posts, up to 140 characters long, via SMS, instant messaging, or e-mail to the Twitter website or to an application such as Twitterific. The updates are displayed on the user's profile page and simultaneously delivered to other users who have signed up to receive them. The sender can restrict delivery to certain people or send them to everyone who might want to view them. Twitter, according to its web-site, aims to be a global community of friends and strangers who answer the simple question "What are you doing?" For example, a post might say, "I'm in class now. . . . I hope the prof doesn't catch me txting!"

But do people *really* want to know what their friends and family members are doing 24 hours a day, or is Twitter just adding to the information overload in an information-hungry society? Some people who have tried the service say they were inundated with mundane and sometimes frustratingly boring snippets and details about other people's lives. Others complain that some of the newer members of the service seem to focus more on the quantity of messages than the quality. Some had to rethink their network plan after experiencing a "Twitter storm" and receiving 30 to 40 posts a day from one person with musings about what to have for dinner or TV commercials.

So what do the 100,000 Twitter users have in common? According to *Time*'s Anita Hamilton, they are, more often than not, simply killing time. Most people either love the free service or hate it, but in either case, they still blog, write, and, yes, even Twitter about it. No one, however, seems to be able to explain its rapidly growing success. According to *Wired*'s Clive Thompson, Twitter is experiential, and scrolling through random Twitter messages can't explain the appeal. You have to *do* it—and do it with friends rather than just strangers.

But will enough people "do it" and like it to satisfy Twitter's realized marketing strategy? As a free online service, it must attract enough users to gain online advertising revenue. With the next new thing just around the corner, will Twitter capture a lasting following, or will it become another Friendster? Facebook has already incorporated a "Status Bar" into its website that lets people know what *you* are doing *right now.* Is there a need for another tool that does the same thing? Only time will tell if Twitter is sticky with a marketable competitive advantage or just another "Twittering" fad.[a]

When a company matches a core competency to opportunities it has discovered in the marketplace, it is said to have a **competitive advantage.** In some cases, a company may possess manufacturing, technical, or marketing skills that it can match to market opportunities to create a competitive advantage. For example, eBay pioneered the online auction and built the premier site where 248 million users around the world buy and sell products. By analyzing its customer base, eBay found an opportunity to improve growth by targeting the nearly 23 million small businesses in the United States, many of which already use the auction site to buy and sell construction, restaurant, and other business equipment. To appeal to this important market, eBay sought ways to improve customers' online shopping experience.[12]

competitive advantage
The result of a company's matching a core competency to opportunities it has discovered in the marketplace

Competitive Advantage

Boca Burgers offer health benefits over traditional beef burgers.

SWOT Analysis

One tool marketers use to assess an organization's strengths, weaknesses, opportunities, and threats is the **SWOT analysis.** Strengths and weaknesses are internal factors that can influence an organization's ability to satisfy its target markets. Strengths refer to competitive advantages or core competencies that give the firm an advantage in meeting the needs of its target markets. John Deere, for example, promotes its service, experience, and reputation in the farm equipment business to emphasize the craftsmanship used in its lawn tractors and mowers for city dwellers. Weaknesses refer to any limitations a company faces in developing or implementing a marketing strategy. Consider that AOL, once the leading Internet service provider, watched its customer base shrivel as they departed for low-price and free Internet service providers. Both strengths and weaknesses should be examined from a customer perspective because they are meaningful only when they help or hinder the firm in meeting customer needs. Only those strengths that relate to satisfying customers should be considered true competitive advantages. Likewise, weaknesses that directly affect customer satisfaction should be considered competitive disadvantages. To boost profits, AOL has altered its marketing model, effectively ending paid subscribership in favor of advertising-driven revenues. To achieve its goals, the Internet provider will make much of its content, including e-mail, free.[13]

Opportunities and threats exist independently of the firm and therefore represent issues to be considered by all organizations, even those that do not compete with the firm. *Opportunities* refer to favorable conditions in the environment that could produce rewards for the organization if acted on properly. That is, opportunities are situations that exist but must be exploited for the firm to benefit from them. *Threats,* on the other hand, refer to conditions or barriers that may prevent the firm from reaching its objectives. For example, although Chrysler has improved the quality of its vehicles in recent years, it continues to face the threat of consumer perceptions that its vehicles are not as reliable as import brands such as Toyota and Lexus.[14] Threats must be acted upon to prevent them from limiting the organization's capabilities.

SWOT analysis Assessment of an organization's strengths, weaknesses, opportunities, and threats

figure 2.2

THE FOUR-CELL SWOT MATRIX

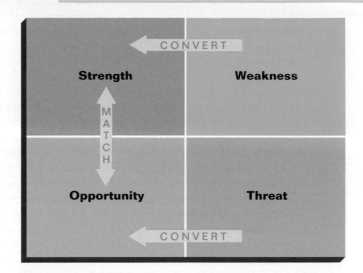

Source: Adapted from Nigel F. Piercy, *Market-Led Strategic Change.* Copyright © 1992 Butterworth-Heinemann Ltd., p. 371. Reprinted with permission.

To counter this particular problem, Chrysler launched an initiative to clarify the Chrysler marquee's premium identity. Along with new promotional campaigns, the company is spending more resources to identify, via feedback from dealers and customers, ways to make its cars more appealing to import buyers.[15] Opportunities and threats can stem from many sources within the environment. When a competitor's introduction of a new product threatens a firm, a defensive strategy may be required. If the firm can develop and launch a new product that meets or exceeds the competition's offering, it can transform the threat into an opportunity.[16]

Figure 2.2 depicts a four-cell SWOT matrix that can help managers in the planning process. When an organization matches internal strengths to external opportunities, it creates competitive advantages in meeting the needs of its customers. In addition, an organization should act to convert internal weaknesses into strengths and external threats into opportunities. Procter & Gamble, for instance, converted the weaknesses of not having competitive advantages in five areas that are essential to succeeding in consumer products—consumer understanding, brand-building, innovation, go-to-market capability, and scale—into strengths by investing billions of dollars into areas such as marketing research and supply-chain management. Indeed, the company's research and development program has become a core competency that fosters significant innovation in areas such as enzymes, perfumes, flavors, polymers, substrates, and surfactants.[17] A firm that lacks adequate marketing skills can hire outside consultants to help convert a weakness into a strength.

Establishing an Organizational Mission and Goals

L O 3 To understand the role of the mission statement in strategic planning

Once an organization has assessed its resources and opportunities, it can begin to establish goals and strategies to take advantage of those opportunities. The goals of any organization should derive from its **mission statement,** a long-term view, or vision, of what the organization wants to become. Herbal tea marketer Celestial Seasonings, for example, says that its mission is "to create and sell healthful, naturally oriented products that nurture people's bodies and uplift their souls."[18]

When an organization decides on its mission, it really answers two questions: Who are our customers? and What is our core competency? Although these questions appear very simple, they are two of the most important questions any firm must answer. Defining customers' needs and wants gives direction to what the company must do to satisfy them.

mission statement A long-term view, or vision, of what the organization wants to become

Companies try to develop and manage their *corporate identity*—their unique symbols, personalities, and philosophies—to support all corporate activities, including marketing. Managing identity requires broadcasting mission goals and values, sending a consistent image, and implementing visual identity with stakeholders. Mission statements, goals, and objectives must be properly implemented to achieve the desired corporate identity.[19] Johnson Controls, for example, has developed a new mission—"a more comfortable, safe and sustainable world"—to highlight its focus on helping customers add value to their daily lives by using its diverse industrial products. The industrial conglomerate also revamped its corporate logo and introduced a new slogan, "Ingenuity Welcome." In addition to a new advertising campaign, the firm will add the new corporate logo to a number of the company's well-known brands, including HomeLink (garage door openers), York (air-conditioning and heating products), Optima (batteries), and Varta (auto batteries).[20]

An organization's goals and objectives, derived from its mission statement, guide the remainder of its planning efforts. Goals focus on the end results the organization seeks. Starbucks' mission statement, for example, incorporates the company's goals of striving for a high-quality product, a sound financial position, and community responsibility

A **marketing objective** states what is to be accomplished through marketing activities. A marketing objective of Ritz-Carlton hotels, for example, is to have more than 90 percent of its customers indicate they had a memorable experience at the hotel. Marketing objectives should be based on a careful study of the SWOT analysis and should relate to matching strengths to opportunities and/or converting weaknesses or threats. These objectives can be stated in terms of product introduction, product improvement or innovation, sales volume, profitability, market share, pricing, distribution, advertising, or employee training activities. With nearly one out of four consumer airline flights delayed, making significant improvements in on-time performance—such as having 90 percent on-time arrivals—would be a good marketing objective for an airline.

Marketing objectives should possess certain characteristics. First, a marketing objective should be expressed in clear, simple terms so all marketing personnel understand exactly what they are trying to achieve. Second, an objective should be written so it can be measured accurately. This allows the organization to determine if and when the objective has been achieved. If an objective is to increase market share by 10 percent, the firm should be able to measure market share changes accurately. Third, a marketing objective should specify a time frame for its accomplishment. A firm that sets an objective of introducing a new product should state the time period in which to do this. Finally, a marketing objective should be consistent with both business-unit and corporate strategy. This ensures that the firm's mission is carried out at all levels of the organization.

Developing Corporate, Business-Unit, and Marketing Strategies

L O 4 To examine corporate, business-unit, and marketing strategies

In any organization, strategic planning begins at the corporate level and proceeds downward to the business-unit and marketing levels. Corporate strategy is the broadest of these three levels and should be developed with the organization's overall mission in mind. Business-unit strategy should be consistent with the corporate strategy, and marketing strategy should be consistent with both the business-unit and corporate strategies. Figure 2.3 shows the relationships among these planning levels.

Corporate Strategy

marketing objective A statement of what is to be accomplished through marketing activities

corporate strategy A strategy that determines the means for utilizing resources in the various functional areas to reach the organization's goals

Corporate strategy determines the means for utilizing resources in the functional areas of marketing, production, finance, research and development, and human resources to reach the organization's goals. A corporate strategy determines not only the scope of the business but also its resource deployment, competitive advantages, and overall coordination of functional areas. In particular, top management's marketing expertise and deployment of resources for addressing markets contribute to sales growth and profitability.[21] Corporate strategy addresses the two questions

figure 2.3

LEVELS OF STRATEGIC PLANNING

Mission statement

↓

Corporate strategy

↓

Business-unit strategy

↓

Marketing strategy

↓

Marketing mix elements
- ▸ Product
- ▸ Distribution
- ▸ Promotion
- ▸ Pricing

posed in the organization's mission statement: Who are our customers? and What is our core competency? The term *corporate* in this context does not apply solely to corporations; corporate strategy is used by all organizations, from the smallest sole proprietorship to the largest multinational corporation.

Corporate strategy planners are concerned with broad issues such as corporate culture, competition, differentiation, diversification, interrelationships among business units, and environmental and social issues. They attempt to match the resources of the organization with the opportunities and threats in the environment. Cell phone maker Nokia, for example, purchased Navteq, a producer of digital mapping and navigational software, for $8.1 billion after recognizing the opportunity to incorporate more satellite-based location services onto its phones.[22] Corporate strategy planners are also concerned with defining the scope and role of the firm's business units so the units are coordinated to reach the ends desired. A firm's corporate strategy may affect its technological competence and ability to innovate.[23]

Business-Unit Strategy

After analyzing corporate operations and performance, the next step in strategic planning is to determine future business directions and develop strategies for individual business units. A **strategic business unit (SBU)** is a division, product line, or other profit center within the parent company. Borden's strategic business units, for example, consist of dairy products, snacks, pasta, niche grocery products like ReaLemon juice and Cremora coffee creamer, and other units such as glue and paints. Each of these units sells a distinct set of products to an identifiable group of customers, and each competes with a well-defined set of competitors. The revenues, costs, investments, and strategic plans of each SBU can be separated from those of the parent company and evaluated. SBUs operate in a variety of markets, all with differing growth rates, opportunities, degrees of competition, and profit-making potential. Business strategy is fundamentally focused on the measures required to create value for the firm's target markets and achieve greater performance. Marketing research suggests that this requires implementing appropriate strategic actions and targeting appropriate market segments.[24]

strategic business unit (SBU) A division, product line, or other profit center within the parent company

Corporate Strategy
Boeing continues to excel in producing innovative new jetliners such as the Dream Liner.

market A group of individuals and/or organizations that have needs for products in a product class and have the ability, willingness, and authority to purchase those products

market share The percentage of a market that actually buys a specific product from a particular company

market growth/market share matrix A helpful business tool, based on the philosophy that a product's market growth rate and its market share are important considerations in determining its marketing strategy

Strategic planners should recognize the strategic performance capabilities of each SBU and carefully allocate scarce resources among those divisions. This requires market-focused flexibility in considering changes in the environment.[25] Several tools allow a firm's portfolio of strategic business units, or even individual products, to be classified and visually displayed according to the attractiveness of various markets and the business's relative market share within those markets. A **market** is a group of individuals and/or organizations that have needs for products in a product class and have the ability, willingness, and authority to purchase those products. The percentage of a market that actually buys a specific product from a particular company is referred to as that product's (or business unit's) **market share.** Apple, for example, controls 81 percent of the market for digital music players in the United States with its iPod line, and SanDisk and Microsoft command 5.8 percent and 4.4 percent, respectively.[26] Product quality, order of entry into the market, and market share have been associated with SBU success.[27]

One of the most helpful tools is the **market growth/market share matrix,** the Boston Consulting Group (BCG) approach, which is based on the philosophy that a product's market growth rate and its market share are important considerations in determining its marketing strategy. All the firm's SBUs and products should be integrated into a single, overall matrix and evaluated to determine appropriate strategies for individual products and overall portfolio strategies. Managers can use this model to determine and classify each product's expected future cash contributions and future cash requirements. The BCG analytical approach is more of a diagnostic tool than a guide for making strategy prescriptions.

Figure 2.4, which is based on work by the BCG, enables the strategic planner to classify a firm's products into four basic types: stars, cash cows, dogs, and question marks.[28] *Stars* are products with a dominant share of the market and good prospects for growth. However, they use more cash than they generate to finance growth, add capacity, and increase market share. An example of a star might be Sony's Wii video game system or Tesla Motors' $100,000 electric roadster. *Cash cows* have a dominant share of the market but low prospects for growth; typically they generate more cash than is required to maintain market share. Bounty, the best-selling paper towels in the United States, represents a cash cow for Procter & Gamble. *Dogs* have a subordinate share of the market and low prospects for growth; these products are often found in established markets. Conventional cathode-ray tube televisions (CRTs) may be considered dogs at Sony, Toshiba, and Panasonic; the increasing popularity of

figure 2.4

GROWTH SHARE MATRIX DEVELOPED BY THE BOSTON CONSULTING GROUP

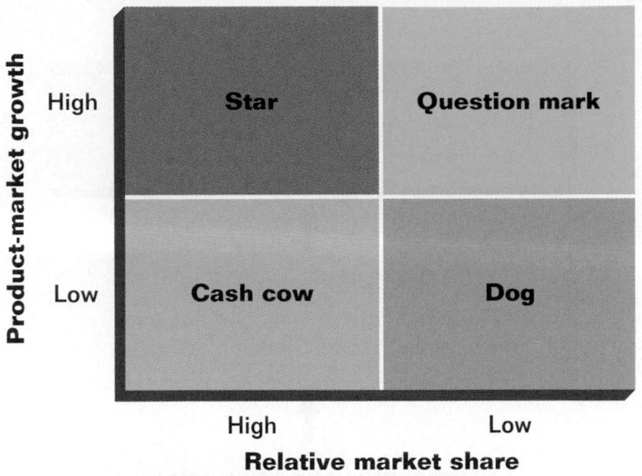

Source: *Perspectives,* No. 66, "The Product Portfolio." Reprinted by permission from The Boston Consulting Group, Inc., Boston, MA. Copyright © 1970.

flat-screen plasma and LCD televisions, especially high-definition televisions, has resulted in plummeting profits and market share for CRTs, and many manufacturers are phasing them out. *Question marks,* sometimes called "problem children," have a small share of a growing market and generally require a large amount of cash to build market share. Mercedes carbon racing bikes, for example, are a question mark relative to Mercedes's automobile products.

The long-term health of an organization depends on having some products that generate cash (and provide acceptable profits) and others that use cash to support growth. In the 1990s, recognizing this fact, Procter & Gamble implemented business strategies intended to reduce its reliance on two SBUs that accounted for 85 percent of the value it created during the 1990s. Today, the multinational corporation's portfolio is spread across 22 categories to balance fast-growing, high-margin businesses, such as home care and beauty products, with foundation businesses including baby care and laundry products (see Figure 2.5).[29] Among the indicators of overall health are the size and vulnerability of the cash cows; the prospects for the stars, if any; and the number of question marks and dogs. Particular attention should be paid to those products with large cash appetites. Unless the company has an abundant cash flow, it cannot afford to sponsor many such products at one time. If resources, including debt capacity, are spread too thin, the company will end up with too many marginal products and will be unable to finance promising new-product entries or acquisitions in the future.

Marketing Strategy

The next phase in strategic planning is the development of sound strategies for each functional area of the organization, including marketing. Corporate strategy and marketing strategy must balance and synchronize the organization's mission and goals with stakeholder relationships. This means that marketing must deliver value and be responsible in facilitating effective relationships with all relevant stakeholders.[30] Consider that customers depend on the Coca-Cola Company to provide a standardized, reliable, satisfying soft drink or beverage anyplace in the world. Due to its efforts to expand distribution to every possible location, Coca-Cola sells 33 percent of its volume in Europe and the Middle East, 31 percent in North America, 22 percent in the Asian/Pacific region, 10 percent in Latin America, and 5 percent in Africa.[31] The company continues to introduce new products, expand distribution, and maintain a high-quality product. Coca-Cola is also a good "corporate citizen," donating millions of dollars to education, health and human services, and disaster-plagued regions each year. An effective marketing strategy must gain the support of key stakeholders including employees, investors, and communities, as well as channel members. The complexity of marketing strategy decisions requires the identification of key

figure 2.5

DEVELOPING STRATEGIC BUSINESS UNITS FOR PERFORMANCE AT PROCTER & GAMBLE

Source: Adapted from "Designed to Grow," 2007 Annual Report, Procter & Gamble, p. 5.

stakeholders and their support or reaction to marketing activities.[32] There is a need in marketing to develop more of a stakeholder orientation to go beyond markets, competitors, and channel members to understand and address all stakeholder concerns.[33]

Within the marketing area, a strategy is typically designed around two components: the selection of a target market and the creation of a marketing mix that will satisfy the needs of the chosen target market. A marketing strategy articulates the best use of the firm's resources and tactics to achieve its marketing objectives. It should also match customers' desire for value with the organization's distinctive capabilities. Internal capabilities should be used to maximize external opportunities. The planning process should be guided by a marketing-oriented organizational culture and processes.[34] A comprehensive strategy involves a thorough search for information, the analysis of many potential courses of action, and the use of specific criteria for making decisions regarding strategy development and implementation.[35] When properly implemented, a sound marketing strategy enables a company to achieve its business-unit and corporate objectives. Although corporate, business-unit, and marketing strategies all overlap to some extent, the marketing strategy is the most detailed and specific of the three.

Target Market Selection. Selecting an appropriate target market may be the most important decision a company must make in the planning process because the target market must be chosen before the organization can adapt its marketing mix to meet this market's needs and preferences. Defining the target market and developing an appropriate marketing mix are the keys to strategic success. Toyota, for example, designed its Yaris sedan to appeal to 18- to 34-year-olds by giving the compact cars a "mischievous" personality to complement their quirky styling and then promoting them where Generation Y consumers were likely to be: MySpace and Facebook, a user-generated-content website, "mobisodes" (short mobile-phone episodes) of the television show *Prison Break*, and events such as the South X Southwest Music

JUST ADD WILDERNESS

These handcrafted hikers feature a rugged new Vibram® outsole for extra traction wherever you go. And a waterproof, breathable Gore-Tex® liner for maximum comfort under any conditions. So now when you hear the call of the wild, you can answer it - in comfort. **L.L.Bean**

Gore-Tex Mountain Tread Hikers from $119

FOR A FREE CATALOG CALL 800·917·2326 or SHOP ONLINE AT llbean.com

©2007 L.L.Bean, Inc.

Target Marketing Selection

L.L.Bean targets the outdoor enthusiast with many of its products.

Festival and the Evolution Fighting Championships for video games.[36] If a company selects the wrong target market, all other marketing decisions will be made in vain.

Accurate target market selection is crucial to productive marketing efforts. Products and even companies sometimes fail because marketers do not identify appropriate customer groups at whom to aim their efforts. Organizations that try to be all things to all people rarely satisfy the needs of any customer group very well. An organization's management therefore should designate which customer groups the firm is trying to serve and gather adequate information about those customers. Identification and analysis of a target market provide a foundation on which the firm can develop a marketing mix.

When exploring possible target markets, marketing managers try to evaluate how entering them would affect the company's sales, costs, and profits. Marketing information should be organized to facilitate a focus on the chosen target customers. Accounting and information systems, for example, can be used to track revenues and costs by customer (or group of customers). In addition, managers and employees need to be rewarded for focusing on profitable customers. Teamwork skills can be developed with organizational structures that promote a customer orientation that allows quick responses to changes in the marketing environment.[37]

Marketers should also assess whether the company has the resources to develop the right mix of product, price, promotion, and distribution to meet the needs of a particular target market. In addition, they should determine if satisfying those needs is consistent with the firm's overall objectives and mission. When Amazon.com, the number one Internet bookseller, began selling electronics on its website, it made the decision with the belief that efforts to target this market would increase profits and be consistent with its objective to be the largest online retailer. The size and number of competitors already marketing products in potential target markets are concerns as well.

Creating the Marketing Mix. The selection of a target market serves as the basis for creating a marketing mix to satisfy the needs of that market. The decisions made in creating a marketing mix are only as good as the organization's understanding of its target market. This understanding typically comes from careful, in-depth research into the characteristics of the target market. Thus, although demographic information is important, the organization should also analyze customer needs, preferences, and behaviors with respect to product design, pricing, distribution, and promotion. For example, Kimberly-Clark's marketing researchers found that younger, design-conscious consumers so disliked the packaging of its Kleenex tissues that they would not even put them on top of the toilet. So Kimberly-Clark introduced Kleenex Oval Expressions tissues that are packaged in a contemporary oval box with bright colors and patterns that is stylish enough to be seen in any room in the home.[38]

Sustainable Competitive Advantage
Southwest Airlines has maintained a loyal customer base as a result of its low fares and routing.

Marketing mix decisions should have two additional characteristics: consistency and flexibility. All marketing mix decisions should be consistent with the business-unit and corporate strategies. Such consistency allows the organization to achieve its objectives on all three levels of planning. Flexibility, on the other hand, permits the organization to alter the marketing mix in response to changes in market conditions, competition, and customer needs. Marketing strategy flexibility has a positive influence on organizational performance. Marketing orientation and strategic flexibility complement each other to help the organization manage varying environmental conditions.[39]

The concept of the four marketing mix variables has stood the test of time, providing marketers with a rich set of questions for the four most important decisions in strategic marketing. Consider the efforts of Harley-Davidson to improve its competitive position. The company worked to improve its product by eliminating oil leaks and other problems, and set prices that customers consider fair. The firm used promotional tools to build a community of Harley riders renowned for their camaraderie. Harley-Davidson also fostered strong relationships with the dealers that distribute the company's motorcycles and related products and that reinforce the firm's promotional messages.[40]

At the marketing mix level, a firm can detail how it will achieve a competitive advantage. To gain an advantage, the firm must do something better than its competition. In other words, its products must be of higher quality, its prices must be consistent with the level of quality (value), its distribution methods must be efficient and cost as little as possible, and its promotion must be more effective than the competition's. It is also important that the firm attempt to make these advantages sustainable. A **sustainable competitive advantage** is one that the competition cannot copy. Wal-Mart, for example, maintains a sustainable competitive advantage in groceries over supermarkets because of its highly efficient and low-cost distribution system. This advantage allows Wal-Mart to offer lower prices and helps it gain the largest share of the supermarket business. Maintaining a sustainable competitive advantage requires flexibility in the marketing mix when facing uncertain competitive environments.[41]

sustainable competitive advantage An advantage that the competition cannot copy

Creating the Marketing Plan

L O 5 To understand the process of creating the marketing plan

A major concern in the strategic planning process is **marketing planning,** the systematic process of assessing marketing opportunities and resources, determining marketing objectives, defining marketing strategies, and establishing guidelines for implementation and control of the marketing program. The outcome of marketing planning is the development of a marketing plan. As noted earlier, a marketing plan is a written document that outlines and explains all the activities necessary to implement marketing strategies. It describes the firm's current position or situation, establishes marketing objectives for the product or product group, and specifies how the organization will attempt to achieve those objectives. For example, Flexpetz's "time-share pet" marketing plan for targeting dog lovers who do not have enough time to care for a pet full time includes rental and registration fees of $120 per month, and part-time owners can book their time with "their" pet online or by telephone. Each dog has an embedded GPS chip in case it strays and brings its own leash, chew toys, bed, bowls, and dog food to the customer's home. Customers are required to attend an hour-long training session and to rent their dog at least twice a month. The company's

marketing planning The systematic process of assessing marketing opportunities and resources, determining marketing objectives, defining marketing strategies, and establishing guidelines for implementation and control of the marketing program

table 2.1	COMPONENTS OF THE MARKETING PLAN	
Plan Component	**Component Summary**	**Highlights**
Executive Summary	One- to two-page synopsis of the entire marketing plan	
Environmental Analysis	Information about the company's current situation with respect to the marketing environment	1. Assessment of marketing environment factors 2. Assessment of target market(s) 3. Assessment of current marketing objectives and performance
SWOT Analysis	Assessment of the organization's strengths, weaknesses, opportunities, and threats	1. Strengths 2. Weaknesses 3. Opportunities 4. Threats
Marketing Objectives	Specification of the firm's marketing objectives	Qualitative measures of what is to be accomplished
Marketing Strategies	Outline of how the firm will achieve its objectives	1. Target market(s) 2. Marketing mix
Marketing Implementation	Outline of how the firm will implement its marketing strategies	1. Marketing organization 2. Activities and responsibilities 3. Implementation timetable
Evaluation and Control	Explanation of how the firm will measure and evaluate the results of the implemented plan	1. Performance standards 2. Financial controls 3. Monitoring procedures (audits)

objectives also include expansion from San Diego and Los Angeles to 50 more cities and $6 million in annual revenues.[42]

Developing a clear, well-written marketing plan, though time consuming, is important. The plan is the basis for internal communication among employees. It covers the assignment of responsibilities and tasks, as well as schedules for implementation. It presents objectives and specifies how resources are to be allocated to achieve those objectives. Finally, it helps marketing managers monitor and evaluate the performance of a marketing strategy.

Marketing planning and implementation are inextricably linked in successful companies. The marketing plan provides a framework to stimulate thinking and provide strategic direction, whereas implementation occurs as an adaptive response to day-to-day issues, opportunities, and unanticipated situations—for example, increasing interest rates or an economic slowdown—that cannot be incorporated into marketing plans. Implementation-related adaptations directly affect an organization's marketing orientation, rate of growth, and strategic effectiveness.[43]

Organizations use many different formats when devising marketing plans. Plans may be written for strategic business units, product lines, individual products or brands, or specific markets. Most plans share some common ground, however, by including many of the same components. Table 2.1 describes the major parts of a typical marketing plan.

marketing implementation
The process of putting marketing strategies into action

Implementing Marketing Strategies

L O 6 To describe the marketing implementation process and the major approaches to marketing implementation

Marketing implementation is the process of putting marketing strategies into action. Although implementation is often neglected in favor of strategic planning, the implementation process itself can determine whether a marketing strategy succeeds. It is also important to recognize that marketing strategies almost always turn out differently than expected. In essence, all organizations have two types of strategy: intended strategy and realized strategy.[44] The **intended strategy** is the strategy the organization decides on during the planning phase and wants to use, whereas the **realized strategy** is the strategy that actually takes place. The difference between the two is often the result of how the intended strategy is implemented. For example, when Japanese fast-food restaurants were first introduced, they were generally located in food courts to offer menu diversity. However, Japanese- and Asian-fare fast-food chains such as Yoshinoya and Hibachi-San Japanese Grill are growing at three times the rate of other fast-food restaurants in the United States. Yoshinoya has plans to double its number of locations by 2010 by providing low-fat fast-food options at reasonable prices.[45] The realized strategy, though not necessarily any better or worse than the intended strategy, often does not live up to planners' expectations.

intended strategy The strategy the organization decides on during the planning phase and wants to use

realized strategy The strategy that actually takes place

green MARKETING

Spudware ... Not Just for Potato Heads

In the United States, approximately 39 billion pieces of plastic cutlery are used every year. Many West Coast cities, however, are voting them out of existence because polystyrene containers and plastic cutlery are not recyclable and do not biodegrade. Portland, Oakland, Santa Monica, and San Francisco have already banned the products, and other cities are considering bans. This is great news for a company called Excellent Packaging & Supply (EPS), which makes and markets bioplastics—tableware derived from corn and sugar, and Spud-Ware, cutlery made from potato starch and soybean oil. The three-year-old company, based in Richmond, California, is already profitable and has seen growth of 40 percent a year for the past two years. The company specializes in environmentally sustainable packaging, offering compostable, biodegradable, and recyclable product lines.

EPS sells dinner plates and coffee cups that are made from sugar cane residue, plus drinking straws and take-out boxes made from cornstarch, and its famous SpudWare silverware, made from 80 percent potato starch or cornstarch and 20 percent soy or other vegetable oils. These new products are giving restaurant owners more legal and environmentally friendly choices than ever before. EPS is one of the few distributors in the country that offers restaurants a complete line of biodegradable or compostable items, not just one or two products.

SpudWare made its debut at ESPN's X Games, where thousands of attendees used plates and bowls made from sugar cane, clear cups and food containers made from corn, and, of course, Spud-Ware cutlery. All of the products were gathered after use in compostable garbage can liners so they could be composted locally after the event.

Excellent Packaging & Supply did not initially intend to focus on environmentally friendly products. Although the firm sells many other items, its eco-friendly products have become its core competency and thus its realized strategy rather than its intended one. Before developing its SpudWare line, the company tried marketing utensils made from corn, but consumers complained that those products melted. So far, the company has not had any complaints about the SpudWare products in high-heat situations—even if they are used for soup. Only if the utensils are left soaking in water overnight do they become slightly "tacky." Spud-Ware was a major breakthrough in the search for a functional and green alternative to plastic cutlery. It is manufactured in China by several vendors that market them under different names. The new move toward environmentally friendly products enables companies to profit from new products that replace older, more harmful ones, which is especially useful when legal and consumer preference changes create a new niche in this new marketing opportunity.[b]

Approaches to Marketing Implementation

Just as organizations can achieve their goals by using different marketing strategies, they can also implement their marketing strategies by using different approaches. In this section, we discuss three general approaches to marketing implementation: customer relationship management, internal marketing, and total quality management. Each approach represents a mindset that marketing managers may adopt when organizing and planning marketing activities. These approaches are not mutually exclusive; indeed, many companies adopt more than one when designing marketing activities.

Customer Relationship Management. As we saw in Chapter 1, customer relationship management (CRM) focuses on using information about customers to create marketing strategies that develop and sustain desirable long-term customer relationships. The Philadelphia Eagles, for example, had developed relationships with fans and sponsors based on the team's long history, but it wasn't able to translate that into profits from its online presence. The football team contracted with a third-party e-commerce expert that redesigned the team's website, which generated a 100 percent increase in user satisfaction, traffic, and frequency, all of which improved the team's relationship with its fans.[46] Relationship-building efforts have been shown to increase customer value.[47]

CRM strives to build satisfying exchange relationships between buyers and sellers by gathering useful data at all customer-contact points—telephone, fax, Internet, and personal—and analyzing those data to better understand customers' needs, desires, and habits. It focuses on analyzing and using databases and leveraging technologies to identify strategies and methods that will maximize the lifetime value of each desirable customer to the firm.[48] It is imperative that marketers educate themselves about their customers' expectations if they are to satisfy their needs; customer dissatisfaction will only lead to defection.[49]

CRM technologies help marketers to identify specific customers, establish interactive dialogues with them to learn about their needs, and combine this information with their purchase histories to customize products to meet those needs. Like many online retailers, Amazon.com stores and analyzes purchase data to understand each customer's interests. This information helps the retailer improve its ability to satisfy individual customers and thereby increase sales of books, music, movies, and other products to each customer. The ability to identify individual customers allows marketers to shift their focus from targeting groups of similar customers to increasing their share of an individual customer's purchases. Thus, the emphasis shifts from *share of market* to *share of customer*.

Focusing on share of customer requires recognizing that all customers have different needs and that not all customers weigh the value of a firm equally. CRM technologies help marketers analyze individual customers' purchases and identify the most profitable and loyal customers. The most basic application of this idea is the 80/20 rule: 80 percent of business profits come from 20 percent of customers. The goal is to assess the worth of individual customers and thus estimate their lifetime value to the firm. The concept of *customer lifetime value* (CLV) may include not only an individual's propensity to engage in purchases but also his or her strong word-of-mouth communication about the firm's products.[50] Some customers—those who require considerable hand-holding or who return products frequently—may simply be too expensive to retain due to the low level of profits they generate. Companies can discourage these unprofitable customers by requiring them to pay higher fees for additional services.

CLV is a key measurement that forecasts a customer's lifetime economic contribution based on continued relationship marketing efforts. It can be calculated by taking the sum of the customer's present value contributions to profit margins over a specific time frame. For example, the lifetime value of a Lexus customer could be predicted by how many new automobiles Lexus could sell the customer over a period of years and a summation of the contribution to margins across the time period. Although this is not an exact science, knowing a customer's potential lifetime value can help marketers determine how best to allocate resources to marketing strategies to sustain that customer over a lifetime.

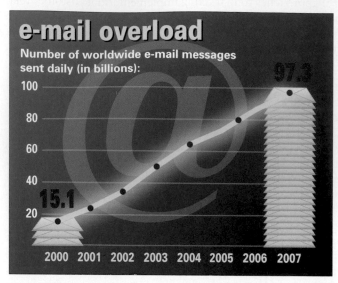

snapshot

e-mail overload

Number of worldwide e-mail messages sent daily (in billions):

Source: IDC.

external customers Individuals who patronize a business—the familiar definition of "customers"

internal customers The company's employees

internal marketing A management philosophy that coordinates internal exchanges between the organization and its employees to achieve successful external exchanges between the organization and its customers

total quality management (TQM) A philosophy that uniform commitment to quality in all areas of the organization will promote a culture that meets customers' perceptions of quality

Internal Marketing. **External customers** are the individuals who patronize a business—the familiar definition of "customers"—whereas **internal customers** are the company's employees. For implementation to succeed, the needs of both groups of customers must be met. If internal customers are not satisfied, it is likely that external customers will not be satisfied either. Thus, in addition to targeting marketing activities at external customers, a firm uses internal marketing to attract, motivate, and retain qualified internal customers by designing internal products (jobs) that satisfy their wants and needs. **Internal marketing** is a management philosophy that coordinates internal exchanges between the organization and its employees to achieve successful external exchanges between the organization and its customers.[51]

Generally speaking, internal marketing refers to the managerial actions necessary to make all members of the marketing organization understand and accept their respective roles in implementing the marketing strategy. Thus, marketing managers need to focus internally on employees as well as externally on customers.[52] This means that all internal customers, from the president of the company down to the hourly workers on the shop floor, must understand the roles they play in carrying out their jobs and implementing the marketing strategy. At Starbucks, all employees receive training and support, including health-care benefits, which fosters an organizational culture founded on product quality and environmental concern. In short, anyone invested in the firm, both marketers and those who perform other functions, must recognize the tenet of customer orientation and service that underlies the marketing concept.

Like external marketing activities, internal marketing may involve all the elements of the marketing mix: product, price, promotion, and distribution. For instance, an organization may sponsor sales contests to inspire sales personnel to boost their selling efforts. Motorola, for example, took its MotoZone mobile consumer promotional tour to eight corporate campuses to permit employees to tour the demo areas, experience the products, and play games for prizes.[53] Some companies are implementing "e-mail-free Fridays," not only to combat e-mail overload but to foster more direct, free-flowing communication through telephone and face-to-face meetings.[54] Such efforts help employees (and ultimately the company) understand customers' needs and problems, foster communication between employees and management, teach valuable new skills, and heighten the employees' enthusiasm for their jobs. In addition, many companies use planning sessions, websites, e-mail, workshops, letters, formal reports, and personal conversations to ensure that employees comprehend the corporate mission, the organization's goals, and the marketing strategy. The ultimate results are more satisfied employees and improved customer relations.

Total Quality Management. Quality has become a major concern in many organizations, particularly in light of intense foreign competition, more demanding customers, and poorer profit performance owing to reduced market share and higher costs. To regain a competitive edge, a number of firms have adopted a total quality management approach. **Total quality management (TQM)** is a philosophy that uniform commitment to quality in all areas of the organization will promote a culture that meets customers' perceptions of quality. Indeed, research has shown that quality orientation and marketing orientation are complementary and together are sources of superior performance.[55] TQM involves coordinating efforts to improve customer satisfaction, increasing employee participation and empowerment, forming and strengthening supplier partnerships, and facilitating an organizational culture of continuous quality improvement. It requires continuous quality improvement and employee empowerment.

imagine a revolutionary black screen
designed to enhance beauty.

Experience the latest HDTV innovation from Samsung. Its
revolutionary super clear panel gives you blacker blacks, which
makes colors appear richer and truer, for the ultimate TV
experience. With the uncompromising design and technology of
the new Samsung full HD LCD TV, it's not that hard to imagine. To
learn more, visit www.samsung.com/hdtv

Samsung full HD LCD TV
with super clear panel.

Available at these and other fine retailers:

Total Quality Management

Samsung utilizes total quality management in the production of its consumer electronics.

benchmarking Comparing the quality of the firm's goods, services, or processes with that of its best-performing competitors

empowerment Giving customer-contact employees authority and responsibility to make marketing decisions without seeking approval of their supervisors

Continuous improvement of an organization's goods and services is built around the notion that quality is free; in contrast, *not* having high-quality goods and services can be very expensive, especially in terms of dissatisfied customers.[56] A primary tool of the continuous improvement process is **benchmarking**, comparing the quality of the organization's goods, services, or processes with that of the best-performing companies in the industry.[57] Benchmarking fosters organizational "learning" by helping firms identify and enhance valuable marketing capabilities.[58] Benchmarking lets the organization assess where it stands competitively in its industry, thus giving it a goal to aim for over time.

Ultimately TQM succeeds or fails because of the efforts of the organization's employees. Thus, employee recruitment, selection, and training are critical to the success of marketing implementation. **Empowerment** gives customer-contact employees the authority and responsibility to make marketing decisions without seeking the approval of their supervisors.[59] Although employees at any level in an organization can be empowered to make decisions, empowerment is used most often at the frontline, where employees interact daily with customers.

One characteristic of empowerment is that employees can perform their jobs the way they see fit, as long as their methods and outcomes are consistent with the organization's mission. However, empowering employees is successful only if the organization is guided by an overall corporate vision, shared goals, and a culture that supports the TQM effort.[60] For example, Ritz-Carlton hotels give each customer-contact employee permission to take care of customer needs as he or she observes issues. A great deal of time, effort, and patience is needed to develop and sustain a quality-oriented culture in an organization.

Organizing Marketing Activities

The structure and relationships of a marketing unit, including lines of authority and responsibility that connect and coordinate individuals, strongly affect marketing activities. Firms that truly adopt the marketing concept develop a distinct organizational culture: a culture based on a shared set of beliefs that makes the customer's needs the pivotal point of the firm's decisions about strategy and operations.[61] Instead of developing products in a vacuum and then trying to persuade customers to purchase them, companies that use the marketing concept begin with an orientation toward their customers' needs and desires. Recreational Equipment, Inc. (REI), for example, gives customers a chance to try out sporting goods in conditions that approximate how the products will actually be used. Customers can try out hiking boots on a simulated hiking path with a variety of trail surfaces and inclines or test climbing gear on an indoor climbing wall. In addition, REI offers clinics to customers, such as "Rock Climbing Basics," "Basic Backpacking," and "REI's Outdoor School."

If the marketing concept serves as a guiding philosophy, the marketing unit will be closely coordinated with other functional areas such as production, finance, and human resources. Marketing must interact with other departments in a number of key areas. It needs to work with manufacturing in determining the volume and variety of the company's products. Those in charge of production rely on marketers for accurate sales forecasts. Research and development departments depend heavily on

RESPONSIBLE marketing?

McDonald's: The Case for Customization of Corporate Social Responsibility Around the World

ISSUE: Which stakeholders' interests should dominate in determining CSR focus: local or global interests?

When McDonald's evaluated its approach to green marketing, it was attempting to develop a plan that would encompass over 31,000 restaurants operating in 118 countries. What McDonald's learned in the process was that a wide variety of environmental interests existed around the world. Whereas McDonald's has centralized many of its strategic decisions to provide consistency, guidance, and some level of control, the decision with respect to green marketing was to decentralize the decision process as much as possible. This strategic decision would allow greater customization of the initiatives to each market and allow for greater "buy-in" among franchisees and corporate-owned restaurants.

McDonald's has moved forward with implementing this strategy on a local basis. In Japan, which has a high population density, waste and recycling are significant concerns. In Australia, water conservation is a major issue. In Pensacola, Florida, one restaurant is digging fifty-five 350-foot-deep holes to heat and cool the new location, using geothermal energy. Bob Langert, vice president of Corporate Social Responsibility, notes that restaurants in these markets are functioning as "laboratories of green experimentation." In addition, as part of its global commitment to CSR, McDonald's is working to manage and reduce energy consumption in its restaurants around the world. McDonalds's earned an "A" for the quality of its voluntary reporting on environmental and social issues from the Roberts Environmental Center at Claremont McKenna College, the only company in its sector to do so.^c

centralized organization
A structure in which top-level managers delegate little authority to lower levels

decentralized organization
A structure in which decision-making authority is delegated as far down the chain of command as possible

information gathered by marketers about product features and benefits consumers desire. Decisions made by the physical distribution department hinge on information about the urgency of delivery schedules and cost/service tradeoffs.

How effectively a firm's marketing management can plan and implement marketing strategies also depends on how the marketing unit is organized. Organizing marketing activities in ways that mesh with a firm's strategic marketing approach enhances performance.[62] Effective organizational planning can give the firm a competitive advantage. The organizational structure of a marketing department establishes the authority relationships among marketing personnel and specifies who is responsible for making certain decisions and performing particular activities. This internal structure helps direct marketing activities.

One crucial decision regarding structural authority is centralization versus decentralization. In a **centralized organization,** top-level managers delegate little authority to lower levels. In a **decentralized organization,** decision-making authority is delegated as far down the chain of command as possible. The decision to centralize or decentralize the organization directly affects marketing. Most traditional organizations are highly centralized. In these organizations, most, if not all, marketing decisions are made at the top levels. However, as organizations become more marketing oriented, centralized decision making proves somewhat ineffective. In these organizations, decentralized authority allows the company to respond to customer needs more quickly.

No single approach to organizing a marketing unit works equally well in all businesses. The best approach or approaches depend on the number and diversity of the firm's products, the characteristics and needs of the people in the target market, and many other factors. A marketing unit can be organized according to (1) functions, (2) products, (3) regions, or (4) types of customers. Firms often use some combination of these organizational approaches. Product features may dictate that the marketing unit be structured by products, whereas customer characteristics may require that it be organized by geographic region or by types of customers. By using more than one type of structure, a flexible marketing unit can develop and implement marketing plans to match customers' needs precisely.

Organizing by Functions. Some marketing departments are organized by general marketing functions, such as marketing research, product development, distribution, sales, advertising, and customer relations. The personnel who direct these functions report directly to the top-level marketing executive. This structure is fairly common because it works well for some businesses with centralized marketing operations, such as Ford and General Motors. In more decentralized firms, such as grocery store chains, functional organization can cause serious coordination problems. However, the functional approach may suit a large, centralized company whose products and customers are neither numerous nor diverse.

Organizing by Products. An organization that produces and markets diverse products may find the functional approach inadequate. The decisions and problems related to a single marketing function for one product may be quite different from those related to the same marketing function for another product. As a result, businesses that produce diverse products sometimes organize their marketing units according to product groups. Organizing by product groups gives a firm the flexibility to develop special marketing mixes for different products. Procter & Gamble, like many firms in the consumer packaged goods industry, is organized by product group. Although organizing by products allows a company to remain flexible, this approach can be rather expensive unless efficient categories of products are grouped together to reduce duplication and improve coordination of product management.

Organizing by Regions. A large company that markets products nationally (or internationally) may organize its marketing activities by geographic regions. Managers of marketing functions for each region report to their regional marketing manager; all the regional marketing managers report directly to the executive marketing manager. Frito-Lay, for example, is organized into four regional divisions, allowing the company to get closer to its customers and respond more quickly and efficiently to regional competitors. This form of organization is especially effective for a firm whose customers' characteristics and needs vary greatly from one region to another. Firms that try to penetrate the national market intensively may divide regions into subregions.

Organizing by Types of Customers. Sometimes a company's marketing unit is organized according to types of customers. This form of internal organization works well for a firm that has several groups of customers whose needs and problems differ significantly. For example, Home Depot targets home builders and contractors as well as do-it-yourself customers and consumers who desire installation and service. Retailers may want more rapid delivery of small shipments and more personal selling by the producer than do either wholesalers or institutional buyers. Because the marketing decisions and activities required for these two groups of customers differ considerably, the company may find it efficient to organize its marketing unit by types of customers.

Controlling Marketing Activities

To achieve both marketing and general organizational objectives, marketing managers must effectively control marketing efforts. The **marketing control process** consists of establishing performance standards, evaluating actual performance by comparing it with established standards, and reducing the differences between desired and actual performance.

Although the control function is a fundamental management activity, it has received little attention in marketing. Organizations have both formal and informal control systems. The formal marketing control process, as mentioned earlier, involves performance standards, evaluation of actual performance, and corrective action to remedy shortfalls (see Figure 2.6). The informal control process involves self-control, social or group control, and cultural control through acceptance of the firm's value system. Which type of control system dominates depends on the environmental context of the firm.[63] We now discuss these steps in the formal control process and consider the major problems they involve.

Establishing Performance Standards. Planning and controlling are closely linked because plans include statements about what is to be accomplished. For purposes of control, these statements function as performance standards. A **performance standard** is an expected level of performance against which actual performance can be compared. A performance standard might be a 20 percent reduction in customer complaints, a monthly sales quota of $150,000, or a 10 percent increase per month in new-customer accounts. Toyota, for example, had a goal of selling 9.85 million vehicles worldwide in 2008, allowing it to surpass General Motors as the world's number one automaker.[64] As stated earlier, performance standards should be tied to organizational goals.

Evaluating Actual Performance. To compare actual performance with performance standards, marketing managers must know what employees within the

marketing control process Establishing performance standards, evaluating actual performance by comparing it with established standards, and reducing the differences between desired and actual performance

performance standard An expected level of performance against which actual performance can be compared

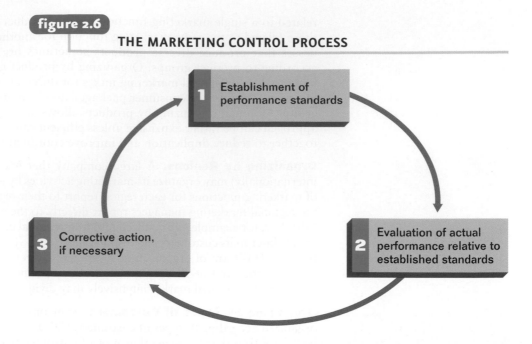

figure 2.6

THE MARKETING CONTROL PROCESS

1 Establishment of performance standards

2 Evaluation of actual performance relative to established standards

3 Corrective action, if necessary

company are doing and have information about the activities of external organizations that provide the firm with marketing assistance. For example, Cadillac, like many automakers, uses many measures to evaluate its product and service levels, including how well it ranks on the J. D. Power & Associates Customer Service Index. In 2007, Cadillac ranked number three and tied with Lexus among all automakers, behind only Jaguar and Buick.[65] Records of actual performance are compared with performance standards to determine whether and how much of a discrepancy exists. For example, if Toyota determines that only 9.6 million vehicles were sold in 2008, a discrepancy would have existed because its goal was 9.85 million vehicles.

Taking Corrective Action. Marketing managers have several options for reducing a discrepancy between established performance standards and actual performance. They can take steps to improve actual performance, reduce or totally change the performance standard, or do both. For example, facing intense competition and tight profit margins, HDTV makers have begun to add new features, such as LED backlighting, 120-hertz screen refresh (to prevent motion blur in sporting events), proprietary color-processing technology, and easier connections, to engage customers.[66] To improve actual performance, the marketing manager may have to use better methods of motivating marketing personnel or find more effective techniques for coordinating marketing efforts.

Problems in Controlling Marketing Activities. In their efforts to control marketing activities, marketing managers frequently run into several problems. Often the information required to control marketing activities is unavailable or is available only at a high cost. Although marketing controls should be flexible enough to allow for environmental changes, the frequency, intensity, and unpredictability of such changes may hamper control. In addition, the time lag between marketing activities and their results limits a marketing manager's ability to measure the effectiveness of specific marketing activities. This is especially true for all advertising activities.

Because marketing and other business activities overlap, marketing managers cannot determine the precise costs of marketing activities. Without an accurate measure of marketing costs, it is difficult to know if the outcome of marketing activities is worth the expense. Finally, marketing control may be difficult because it is very hard to develop exact performance standards for marketing personnel.

SUMMARY

Through the process of strategic planning, a firm identifies or establishes an organizational mission and goals, corporate strategy, marketing goals and objectives, marketing strategy, and a marketing plan. To achieve its marketing objectives, an organization must develop a marketing strategy, which includes identifying a target market and developing a plan of action for developing, distributing, promoting, and pricing products that meet the needs of customers in that target market. The strategic planning process ultimately yields the framework for a marketing plan, a written document that specifies the activities to be performed for implementing and controlling an organization's marketing activities.

The marketing environment, including economic, competitive, political, legal and regulatory, sociocultural, and technological forces, can affect the resources a firm can acquire and create favorable opportunities. Resources may include core competencies, which are things that a firm does extremely well, sometimes so well that it gives the company an advantage over its competition. When the right combination of circumstances and timing permits an organization to take action toward reaching a particular target market, a market opportunity exists. Strategic windows are temporary periods of optimal fit between the key requirements of a market and the particular capabilities of a firm competing in that market. When a company matches a core competency to opportunities it has discovered in the marketplace, it is said to have a competitive advantage.

An organization's goals should be derived from its mission statement, a long-term view, or vision, of what the organization wants to become. A well-formulated mission statement helps give an organization a clear purpose and direction, distinguish it from competitors, provide direction for strategic planning, and foster a focus on customers. An organization's goals and objectives, which focus on the end results sought, guide the remainder of its planning efforts.

Corporate strategy determines the means for utilizing resources in the areas of production, finance, research and development, human resources, and marketing to reach the organization's goals. Business-unit strategy focuses on strategic business units (SBUs)—divisions, product lines, or other profit centers within the parent company used to define areas for consideration in a specific strategic market plan. The Boston Consulting Group's market growth/market share matrix integrates a firm's products or SBUs into a single, overall matrix for evaluation to determine appropriate strategies for individual products and business units. Marketing strategies, the most detailed and specific of the three levels of strategy, are composed of two elements: the selection of a target market and the creation of a marketing mix that will satisfy the needs of the chosen target market. The selection of a target market serves as the basis for the creation of the marketing mix to satisfy the needs of that market. Marketing mix decisions should also be consistent with business-unit and corporate strategies and be flexible enough to respond to changes in market conditions, competition, and customer needs. Different elements of the marketing mix can be changed to accommodate different marketing strategies.

The outcome of marketing planning is the development of a marketing plan, which outlines all the activities necessary to implement marketing strategies. The plan fosters communication among employees, assigns responsibilities and schedules, specifies how resources are to be allocated to achieve objectives, and helps marketing managers monitor and evaluate the performance of a marketing strategy.

Marketing implementation is the process of executing marketing strategies. Marketing strategies do not always turn out as expected. Realized marketing strategies often differ from the intended strategies because of issues related to implementation. Proper implementation requires efficient organizational structures and effective control and evaluation.

One major approach to marketing implementation is customer relationship management (CRM), which focuses on using information about customers to create marketing strategies that develop and sustain desirable long-term customer relationships. CRM employs database marketing techniques to identify different types of customers and develop specific strategies for interacting with each customer. Another approach is internal marketing, a management philosophy that coordinates internal exchanges between the organization and its employees to achieve successful external exchanges between the organization and its customers. For strategy implementation to be successful, the needs of both internal and external customers must be met. Still another approach is total quality management (TQM), which relies heavily on the talents of employees to continually improve the quality of the organization's goods and services.

The organization of marketing activities involves the development of an internal structure for the marketing unit. In a centralized organization, top-level managers delegate very little authority to lower levels, whereas in decentralized organizations, decision-making authority is delegated as far down the chain of command as possible. The marketing unit can be organized by functions, products, regions, or types of customers, or some combination of those elements.

The marketing control process consists of establishing performance standards, evaluating actual performance by comparing it with established standards, and reducing the discrepancy between desired and actual performance. When actual performance is compared with performance standards, marketers must determine whether a discrepancy exists and, if so, whether it requires corrective action, such as changing the performance standard or improving actual performance. Problems encountered in controlling marketing activities include lack of information, environmental changes, time lags between marketing activities and their effects, and difficulty in determining the costs of marketing activities.

IMPORTANT TERMS

Strategic planning, 32
Marketing strategy, 33
Marketing plan, 33
Core competencies, 34
Market opportunity, 34
Strategic windows, 34
Competitive advantage, 35
SWOT analysis, 36
Mission statement, 37
Marketing objective, 38

Corporate strategy, 38
Strategic business unit
   (SBU), 39
Market, 40
Market share, 40
Market growth/market
   share matrix, 40
Sustainable competitive
   advantage, 44
Marketing planning, 44

Marketing implementa-
   tion, 45
Intended strategy, 46
Realized strategy, 46
External customers, 48
Internal customers, 48
Internal marketing, 48
Total quality manage-
   ment (TQM), 48
Benchmarking, 49

Empowerment, 49
Centralized organization,
   50
Decentralized organiza-
   tion, 50
Marketing control process,
   51
Performance standard, 51

DISCUSSION & REVIEW QUESTIONS

1. Identify the major components of strategic planning, and explain how they are interrelated.

2. What are the two major parts of a marketing strategy?

3. What are some issues to consider in analyzing a firm's resources and opportunities? How do these issues affect marketing objectives and marketing strategy?

4. How important is the SWOT analysis to the marketing planning process?

5. How should organizations set marketing objectives?

6. Explain how an organization can create a competitive advantage at the corporate, business-unit, and marketing strategy levels.

7. Refer to question 6. How can an organization make its competitive advantages sustainable over time? How difficult is it to create sustainable competitive advantages?

8. What benefits do marketing managers gain from planning? Is planning necessary for long-run survival? Why or why not?

9. Why does an organization's intended strategy often differ from its realized strategy?

10. Why might an organization use multiple bases for organizing its marketing unit?

11. What are the major steps of the marketing control process?

APPLICATION QUESTIONS

1. Contact three organizations that appear to be successful. Ask one of the company's managers or executives if he or she would share with you the company's mission statement or organizational goals. Obtain as much information as possible about the statement and organizational goals. Discuss how the statement matches the criteria outlined in the text.

2. Assume you own a new, family-style restaurant that will open for business in the coming year. Formulate a long-term goal for the company, and then develop short-term goals to help you achieve the long-term goal.

3. **Amazon.com** identified an opportunity to capitalize on a desire of many consumers to shop at home. This strategic window gave **Amazon.com** a very competitive position in a new market. Consider the opportunities that may be present in your city, your

region, or the United States as a whole. Identify a strategic window, and discuss how a company could take advantage of this opportunity. What types of core competencies are necessary?

4. Marketing units may be organized according to functions, products, regions, or types of customers. Describe how you would organize the marketing units for the following:

   a. A toothpaste with whitener; a toothpaste with extra-strong nicotine cleaners; a toothpaste with bubble gum flavor

   b. A national line offering all types of winter and summer sports clothing for men and women

   c. A life insurance company that provides life, health, and disability insurance

INTERNET EXERCISE

Visit **www.cengage.com/marketing/pride-ferrell** for resources to help you master the material in this chapter, plus materials that will help you expand your marketing knowledge, including Internet exercise updates, ACE Self-Tests, hotlinks to companies featured in this chapter, and much more.

Sony

Internet analysts have praised Sony's website as one of the best organized and most informative on the Internet. See why by accessing **www.sony.com.**

1. Based on the information provided on the website, describe Sony's SBUs.

2. Based on your existing knowledge of Sony as an innovative leader in the consumer electronics industry, describe the company's primary competitive advantage. How does Sony's website support this competitive advantage?

3. Assess the quality and effectiveness of Sony's website. Specifically, perform a preliminary SWOT analysis comparing Sony's website with other high-quality websites you have visited.

developing your MARKETING PLAN

One of the foundations of a successful marketing strategy is a thorough analysis of your company. To make the best decisions about what products to offer, which markets to target, and how to reach those targets, you must recognize your company's strengths and weaknesses. The information collected in this analysis should be referenced when making many of the decisions in your marketing plan. While writing the beginning of your plan, the information in this chapter can help you with the following issues:

1. Can you identify the core competencies of your company? Do they currently contribute to a competitive advantage? If not, what changes could your company make to establish a competitive advantage?

2. Conduct a SWOT analysis of your company to identify its strengths and weaknesses. Continue your analysis to include the business environment, discovering any opportunities that exist or threats that may impact your company.

3. Using the information from your SWOT analysis, have you identified any opportunities that are a good match with your company's core competencies? Likewise, have you discovered any weaknesses that could be converted to strengths through careful marketing planning?

The information obtained from these questions should assist you in developing various aspects of your marketing plan found in the *Interactive Marketing Plan* exercise at **www.cengage.com/marketing/pride-ferrell.**

globalEDGE

1. Rankings of the world's largest manufacturing companies provide a variety of data. Rankings by industry can be found using the search term "largest manufacturing companies" at **http://globaledge.msu.edu/ibrd** to access *IndustryWeek*'s IW 1000 ranking. Perform a SWOT (i.e., strengths, weaknesses, opportunities, and threats) analysis of the top five firms in the apparel industry. From the information included, which firm has the strongest market position? Analyze all firms in the apparel industry. Which five firms have the weakest positions?

2. Your firm is currently developing a marketing strategy based on the expected age of both the Canadian and U.S. populations for the foreseeable future. By analyzing the population pyramids provided in the International Data Base (IDB) by the U.S. Census Bureau, you can better understand the estimated demographic shifts from 2000 to 2025 and 2050 for both countries. The population pyramids can be found using the search term "international data base" at **http://globaledge.msu.edu/ibrd** to reach the U.S. Census Bureau's International Data Base (IDB), and then choosing the Population Pyramid link. Provide a summary of your findings.

Green Mountain Coffee Roasters Brews Up the Best Market Strategy

Green Mountain Coffee Roasters, Inc., is a leader in the specialty coffee industry. Founded in 1981 as a small café in Waitsfield, Vermont, Green Mountain quickly gained a reputation for its high quality, and demand for its freshly roasted coffee grew among local restaurants and inns. Incorporated in 1993, the firm today markets more than $342 million worth of coffee and related products through a coordinated multichannel distribution network with both wholesale and direct-to-consumer operations. This distribution network is designed to maximize brand recognition and product availability.

Green Mountain derives the majority of its revenue from more than 8,000 wholesale customer accounts located primarily in the eastern United States. The wholesale operation serves customers such as supermarkets, specialty food stores, convenience stores, food service companies, hotels, restaurants, universities, and office coffee services. Many of these wholesale customers then resell the coffee in whole bean or ground form for home consumption or brew and sell coffee beverages at their places of business.

Green Mountain Coffee roasts 100 varieties of high-quality Arabica coffee beans and offers more than 100 selections of coffee such as single-origin, estate, and certified organic coffee, as well as proprietary blends and flavored coffees sold under the Green Mountain Coffee Roasters and Newman's Own Organics brand names. It has made a point of marketing certified Fair Trade™ coffees that help struggling coffee farmers earn fair market value for their efforts. It carefully selects its coffee beans and then roasts them to maximize their taste and flavor differences. Green Mountain Coffee is delivered in a variety of packages, including whole bean, fractional packages, and premium one-cup coffee pods.

Green Mountain's objective is to be the leading specialty coffee company. It aims to achieve the highest market share in its target markets while maximizing company values. To meet these objectives, Green Mountain differentiates and reinforces the Green Mountain Coffee brand by distributing only the highest-quality products,

providing superior customer service and distribution, stressing corporate governance and employee development, and implementing socially responsible business practices. Through these strategies, Green Mountain believes it engenders a high degree of customer loyalty.

The company employs 849 people but has a flat organizational structure, which makes all employees responsible for implementation. Although it has functional departments that vary across the company, there are typically about four layers of hierarchy in each department. There is openness in all aspects of communication that allows employees to have regular access to all levels of the organization, including CEO Bob Stiller. The company urges each employee to voice his or her opinions and ideas. This encourages passion and commitment so employees can get to the heart of issues and challenges instead of playing office politics. In this way, Green Mountain has fostered a culture that involves its workers in decision making and challenges them to find solutions to problems. Empowering employees to this degree means that the company may sometimes appear chaotic, but the communication across channels in what is sometimes termed a "constellation of communication" ensures the collaborative nature of getting things done.

In addition to growing sales and a reputation for quality, Green Mountain Coffee Roasters has been ranked among *Forbes* magazine's list of 200 Best Small Companies in America for seven out of eight years. The company's commitment to social responsibility—not only to secure fair trade prices for coffee growers but also its support of social and environmental programs in coffee-growing regions—earned it a first place on *Business Ethics* magazine's annual list of 100 Best Corporate Citizens in 2007 for the second year in a row.[67]

Questions for Discussion

1. Describe Green Mountain's marketing strategy.
2. How does Green Mountain use implementation to achieve success in a very competitive market?
3. How does empowerment work at Green Mountain?

CASE 2.2

A Turnaround King Helps Burger King Recover

Burger King, founded in Miami in 1954 by James McLamore and David Edgerton, serves almost 12 million customers a day at more than 11,200 restaurants in 69 countries. However, in the early 1990s the profits and success of Burger King restaurants steadily declined, while rivals McDonald's and Wendy's grabbed its market share. Ten CEOs passed through Burger King in 14 years, but CEO number 11, Greg Brenneman, finally turned things around. This charismatic, driven CEO has implemented new strategies that have boosted sales 6.8 percent in restaurants open more than a year—the largest increase in more than ten years. The company's market share is also expected to show improvement this year after falling since 1999.

Brenneman certainly has experience with corporate turnarounds. Before taking the lead at Burger King, he helped turn around PwC Consulting and helped facilitate that company's merger with IBM Global Services. This merger earned the title of "deal of the year" from *Institutional Investor* magazine. Prior to that, Brenneman spent six years at the helm of Continental Airlines, helping to return the company to profitability after 16 years of losses. Although Brenneman has an MBA from Harvard Business School, he attributes much of his success to growing up on a Kansas farm, where days began at 6 a.m. and ended late in the evening, and where he developed a strong work ethic. His early jobs included manicuring golf courses and working at a furniture warehouse. Those who work with him view him as intelligent, aggressive, and quick. Even Edgerton feels Brenneman is the first CEO in a long time who listens to *everyone*.

To approach the issues facing Burger King, Brenneman took a simple path and initiated the "Go Forward Plan," which required a single sheet of paper to articulate. He set straightforward goals for the company: to earn money, bring in more customers/build enthusiasm in existing customers, and motivate BK employees. To reach those goals, he first slashed the costs of building new Burger King restaurants from $1.3 million to $970,000 by recommending making new stores smaller. His idea was supported by research that suggested that most customers currently order food to go, so the new Burger King prototype (one of which is already open in Miami) has about half the previous number of seats. The kitchens of these new stores are also smaller to make preparation more efficient. In addition, Brenneman wants the new stores built with materials readily available at Home Depot. Doing all of this may save up to 50 percent on the price of land, which should enable franchisees to achieve profits more quickly. In addition to reducing the size of the new restaurants, the company has introduced a new "industrial chic" decoration scheme, which executives believe will be a major draw for customers. When Brenneman took the reins at Burger King, the company had just one project idea on the table. To take the company forward, he is determined that now there will always be at least 30 project ideas in the works. His first project was the Enormous Omelet Sandwich, which raised breakfast profits 20 percent.

One of Brenneman's biggest challenges is soothing franchisees, who are vital to the firm's continuing success. In particular, one group of franchisees is unhappy that a recent $340 million ad campaign targets teenage males at the expense of other market segments, especially women. Although some franchisees worry that the advertising focus is too narrow, a spokeswoman for Burger King says that sales—the only way to measure success—have been up since the campaign began. Other issues of concern to franchisees relate to new menu items, pricing, and hours of operations. Given that 90 percent of Burger King restaurants are franchised, Brenneman clearly has work to do to settle these issues.

Despite these issues, Brenneman is optimistic about Burger King's future. There are signs to support his optimism. For example, customer satisfaction is at an all-time high according to the University of Michigan's American Customer Satisfaction Index, at a time when McDonald's has seen customer satisfaction decline. In 2006 Burger King opened 25 more restaurants than it closed—a first since the 1990s. The company is also opening new restaurants overseas, with new locations in Brazil and China. All told, the company opened 441 international locations in 2006.

Even given the challenges to be faced, employees and franchisees alike are rooting for Brenneman and the success of Burger King. The company still has a ways to go to return to the successful levels of the early 1990s, but Brenneman is certainly laying solid groundwork for success. In 2006 he prepared the company for a successful public offering of its stock and then hired a new CEO, John W. Chidsey, to carry on his ideas for building a successful strategy for Burger King. It is now the second-largest hamburger fast-food chain in the world, behind McDonald's, which has 31,000 restaurants.[68]

Questions for Discussion

1. Briefly describe the target market and marketing mix used by Burger King.
2. Do you believe that targeting teenage males at the expense of other markets, especially women, is an appropriate strategy?
3. Have Burger King's strategic marketing planning efforts been successful? Why or why not?

strategic CASE 1

FedEx Packages Marketing for Overnight Success

In 1973, Frederick W. Smith founded Federal Express Corporation with part of an $8 million inheritance. At the time, the U.S. Postal Service and United Parcel Service (UPS) provided the only means of delivering packages, and they often took several days or more to get packages to their destinations. While a student at Yale in 1965, Smith studied topology, a mathematical discipline dedicated to geometric configurations. He applied these principles to a business plan and envisioned a hub system from which packages could be delivered across the globe. Smith wrote a paper proposing an independent overnight delivery service. Although he received a "C" on the paper, Smith never lost sight of his vision. He believed many businesses would be willing to pay more to get letters, documents, and packages delivered overnight. He was right.

Federal Express began shipping packages overnight from Memphis, Tennessee, on April 17, 1973. On that first night of operations, the company handled six packages, one of which was a birthday present sent by Smith himself. Today FedEx Corporation handles more than 6.5 million shipments a day around the world, including the hot markets of India, China, and Brazil. FedEx controls more than 50 percent of the overnight delivery market, with an astounding $35.2 billion in total revenue. FedEx does not view itself as being in the package and document transport business, but rather it describes its business as delivering "certainty." FedEx delivers this certainty by connecting the global economy with a wide range of transportation, information, and supply-chain services.

FedEx Express and FedEx Ground provide the bulk of the company's business, offering valuable services to anyone who needs to deliver letters, documents, and packages. Whether it is dropped off at one of nearly 42,000 drop boxes or 718 world service centers or picked up by a FedEx courier, each package is taken to a local FedEx office, where it is trucked to the nearest airport. The package is flown to one of the company's distribution "hubs" for sorting and then flown to the airport nearest its destination. The package is then trucked to another FedEx office, where a courier picks it up and hand-delivers it to the correct recipient. All of this takes place overnight, with many packages delivered before 8:00 a.m. the following day. FedEx confirms that roughly 99 percent of its deliveries are made on time.

To achieve this highly successful delivery rate, FedEx maintains an impressive infrastructure of equipment and processes. The company owns more than 75,000 vehicles, and its 669 aircraft fly more than 500,000 miles every day. FedEx operates its own weather forecasting service, ensuring that most of its flights arrive within 15 minutes of schedule. The hub envisioned by Smith in college is located in Memphis, Tennessee. FedEx takes over control of Memphis International Airport at roughly 11:00 each night. For an hour every night, FedEx planes begin to arrive in Memphis and land side by side on parallel runways every minute. After the packages are sorted, all FedEx planes take off in time to reach their destinations. Beginning at 2:48 a.m. every Monday through Friday, FedEx dispatches eight to twelve aircraft every six minutes. By 4:12 a.m., FedEx has launched about 150 aircraft to over 136 domestic and international destinations. Not all packages, however, are shipped via air; whenever possible, FedEx uses ground transportation to save on expenses. For international deliveries, FedEx uses a combination of direct services and independent contractors. To handle the logistics of its large number of planes, FedEx relies on high-tech software originally developed by NASA. The program displays real-time maps of the airport layout, runways, aircraft, taxiways, and gates. With a single click of the mouse, the operator can receive detailed information about an individual airplane's arrival and departure times.

Growth and Flexibility

FedEx has been expanding its reach by merging with Kinko's, partnering with its former competitor. FedEx purchased Kinko's in 2004 to provide new business services and expand FedEx shipping options at Kinko's nationwide stores. The purchase followed rival UPS's acquisition of 3,000 Mail Boxes Etc. stores. Renamed as the UPS Stores, that acquisition put UPS closer to small and medium-size customers and high-profit, infrequent shippers. FedEx's purchase of Kinko's, which operates in 11 countries, is expected to help the company reach new customers and expand in Asia and Europe.

In 2001, FedEx Express expanded its reach further with the announcement of two seven-year service agreements with the U.S. Postal Service. In the first agreement, FedEx Express provides air transportation for certain postal services, including Priority Mail. The second agreement gives FedEx Express the option to place a drop box in every U.S. post office. FedEx did not get the exclusive rights to drop boxes, which left open the potential for UPS to negotiate its own agreement with the postal service. Both FedEx and the postal service operate competitively and maintain separate services in all other categories.

One of the most important keys to success for FedEx is its flexibility. FedEx must always be ready to deal with the unexpected or the uncontrollable. "That's the nature of the business," says Dave Bronczek, the head of FedEx's Express division. Natural disasters are a natural obstacle in the shipping business. In 2004 and 2005, FedEx had to rely on contingency plans to successfully navigate the 57 tropical storms that threatened to interrupt its business. "We're used to dealing with crisis," says Bronczek. When television reporters covered the inability of FEMA workers and Army personnel to communicate during post–Hurricane Katrina rescue operations, FedEx came to the rescue. The company contacted FEMA and offered use of its intact radio network to aid rescue workers. Every day, some part of the globe visited by FedEx is experiencing some type of political or natural unrest. This is the reason FedEx has implemented disaster drills covering everything from bioterrorism to typhoons. Each night eight planes sit in Memphis with fuel, supplies, and communications gear ready to deploy to a FedEx facility in need. Also, five cargoless planes roam the skies, ready to help out in cases of unexpected volume, air emergencies, or broken-down planes.

FedEx Relies Heavily on Information Technology

Despite its tremendous successes, FedEx has faced some difficult times in its efforts to grow and compete against strong rivals. The overnight delivery market matured very rapidly as intense competition from the U.S. Postal Service, UPS, Emery, DHL, RPS, and electronic document delivery (i.e., fax machines and e-mail) forced FedEx to search for viable means of expansion. In 1984, facing a growing threat from electronic document delivery, FedEx introduced its ZapMail service for customers who could not afford expensive fax machines. For $35, FedEx would fax up to 10 pages of text to any FedEx site around the world. The document was then hand-delivered to its recipient. Soon after the service was introduced, the price of fax machines plummeted, ultimately forcing FedEx to drop ZapMail after losing close to $200 million.

Many analysts still argue that the overnight delivery market could eventually lose as much as 30 percent of its letter business to electronic document delivery, especially e-mail. This trend may be balanced by the enormous growth of online businesses that rely on shipping services to deliver merchandise. This boom of clicking, buying, and shipping led to a record-breaking holiday season for FedEx recently. The company experienced all-time highs in business and broke its own records with 9 million packages handled in a single day.

FedEx constantly strives to improve its services by enhancing its distribution networks, transportation infrastructure, information technology, and employee performance. FedEx also continues to invest heavily in information technology by installing computer terminals at customers' offices and giving away its proprietary tracking software. Today the vast majority of FedEx customers—more than 70 percent—electronically generate their own pickup and delivery requests. FedEx has also moved more aggressively into e-commerce with respect to order fulfillment for business-to-business and business-to-consumer merchants. For example, FedEx's Home Delivery network has grown rapidly and now reaches virtually every U.S. residential address.

FedEx offers several electronic tools, applications, and online interfaces for customers to integrate into their processes to shorten response time, reduce inventory costs, generate better returns, and simplify their shipping. FedEx InSight was the first online application to offer proactive, real-time status information on inbound, outbound, and third-party shipments. It enables customers to identify issues instantly and address them before they become problems. In addition, FedEx InSight allows customers to see the progress of their shipments without requiring a tracking number, giving them convenient and unprecedented data visibility critical to effective management of their supply-chain systems. FedEx technology enables customers, couriers, and contract delivery personnel to access the company's information systems networks by wireless technology anytime, anywhere. In fact, FedEx was the first transportation company to embrace wireless technology—more than two decades ago—and continues to be a leader in the use of innovative wireless solutions.

Why Is FedEx Successful?

As FedEx moves ahead, the company has a lot going for it. No other carrier can match FedEx's global capabilities or one-stop shopping—at least not yet. To increase its competitiveness, FedEx is focusing on increasing revenue and reducing costs through tighter integration and consolidation, improved productivity, and reduced capital expenditures.

FedEx has been successful for many reasons. First, FedEx tries to stay focused on its mission statement:

> FedEx will produce superior financial returns for share-owners by providing high-value-added supply chain, transportation, business, and related information services through focused operating companies. Customer requirements will be met in the highest-quality manner appropriate to each market segment served. FedEx will strive to develop mutually rewarding relationships with its employees, partners, and suppliers. Safety will be the first consideration in all operations. Corporate activities will be conducted to the highest ethical and professional standards.

A second reason is the company's enviable corporate culture and workforce. Because employees are critical to the company's success, FedEx strives to hire the best people and offers them the best training and compensation in the industry. FedEx employees are loyal, highly efficient, and extremely effective in delivering good service. In fact, FedEx employees claim to have "purple blood" to match the company's official color. It is not surprising that FedEx has been named one of the "100 Best Companies to Work For" for nine consecutive years.

A third reason for FedEx's success is its technology and customer relationship management. The company's focus on "delivering certainty" has allowed it to concentrate on opportunities that give FedEx additional capabilities in innovative information technology solutions.

And a final reason for FedEx's success is its highly effective marketing. FedEx is a master at recognizing untapped customer needs and building relationships. FedEx is also never content to sit on its laurels as it constantly strives to improve service and offer more options to its customers. After 30 years of success, there is little doubt that Fred Smith's "C" paper has become an indispensable part of the business world.[69]

Questions for Discussion

1. Which three environmental forces are likely to have the greatest effects on FedEx? Explain your answer.
2. What are the major strengths, weaknesses, opportunities, and threats (SWOT) associated with FedEx?
3. Is there evidence that FedEx has attempted to adopt and use the marketing concept? Explain.
4. Evaluate FedEx's mission statement. Explain the major strengths and weaknesses of this mission statement.

part 2

Environmental Forces and Social and Ethical Responsibilities

Part Two deals with the marketing environment, examining concepts, influences, and trends both in the United States and abroad. **Chapter 3** examines competitive, economic, political, legal and regulatory, technological, and sociocultural forces in the marketing environment, which can have profound effects on marketing strategies. **Chapter 4** explores the role of social responsibility and ethical issues in marketing decisions.

3 The Marketing Environment

LEARNING objectives

1 To recognize the importance of environmental scanning and analysis

2 To understand how competitive and economic factors affect an organization's ability to compete and a customer's ability and willingness to buy products

3 To identify the types of political forces in the marketing environment

4 To understand how laws, government regulations, and self-regulatory agencies affect marketing activities

5 To explore the effects of new technology on society and on marketing activities

6 To analyze sociocultural issues marketers must deal with as they make decisions

Developing a Wiki World for Profit

Almost everyone has consulted Wikipedia at one time or another. Wikipedia, the multilingual, free, web-based encyclopedia, is written collaboratively by volunteers from all over the world, and its articles can be edited by anyone with access to the Internet. Wikipedia is a wiki, an interface that enables any user to add or edit the site content, including other users' contributions, using a regular web browser. A wiki site operates on a principle of collaborative trust. The word *wiki* comes from "wikiwiki," the Hawaiian word for "fast." Since its creation in 2001 as a nonprofit organization based on user donations, Wikipedia has grown rapidly into one of the largest reference websites in the world. It has more than 8.2 million articles in 253 languages, with the English-language edition having more than 2 million articles. It has likewise been growing in popularity and currently ranks among the top ten most-visited websites worldwide, with more than 160 million monthly first-time visitors—a number that increases daily.

Although Wikipedia was launched long before the better-known MySpace and YouTube websites, its creators made no attempt to capitalize on its success. As a nonprofit with no advertising, it missed out on potentially hundreds of millions of dollars of revenue. Now Wikipedia's founder, Jimmy Wales, is hoping to use the wiki concept—and replicate its success—to build a new ad-supported for-profit company. Wikia, which Wales launched in 2004, lets users build wikis around their favorite obsession and then looks for ways to increase user traffic. Thus far, Wookieepedia is the Wikia's largest wiki, with more than 53,000 pages on everything *Star Wars*. Wikia itself is generating about 2.5 million page views a day, and that rate is rising faster than Wikipedia's early growth. Some of Wales's admirers include Amazon.com founder Jeff Bezos, who described Wikipedia as the site that "cracked the code for user-generated content." Bezos now admits that he wishes he had designed Amazon with user reviews of books and CDs like the collaborative wiki pages. One of Wales's key rules for success is to be frugal, like Craig Newmark, who founded Craigslist.

Jimmy Wales's success as an entrepreneur is based on his grasp of the rapid changes in the marketing environment and using emerging technologies to develop new products. He has made transparency a core principle; his collaborative products capture social networking and the desire to make information accessible in an efficient and inexpensive way. To be successful in the long run, Wales must always monitor the competition and recognize that technology products are easily duplicated.[1]

ompanies like Wikia are modifying marketing strategies in response to changes in the marketing environment. Because recognizing and addressing such changes in the marketing environment are crucial to marketing success, we will focus in detail on the forces that contribute to these changes.

This chapter explores the competitive, economic, political, legal and regulatory, technological, and sociocultural forces that constitute the marketing environment. First, we define the marketing environment and consider why it is critical to scan and analyze it. Next, we discuss the effects of competitive forces and explore the influence of general economic conditions: prosperity, recession, depression, and recovery. We also examine buying power and look at the forces that influence consumers' willingness to spend. We then discuss the political forces that generate government actions that affect marketing activities and examine the effects of laws and regulatory agencies on these activities. After analyzing the major dimensions of the technological forces in the environment, we consider the impact of sociocultural forces on marketing efforts.

Examining and Responding to the Marketing Environment

L O 1 To recognize the importance of environmental scanning and analysis

The marketing environment consists of external forces that directly or indirectly influence an organization's acquisition of inputs (human, financial, natural resources and raw materials, and information) and creation of outputs (goods, services, or ideas). As we saw in Chapter 1, the marketing environment includes six such forces: competitive, economic, political, legal and regulatory, technological, and sociocultural.

Whether fluctuating rapidly or slowly, environmental forces are always dynamic. Changes in the marketing environment create uncertainty, threats, and opportunities for marketers. Consider that after uncertainty in the Middle East and the effects of Hurricanes Katrina and Rita led to escalating fuel costs, many automakers saw sales of their gas-guzzling sport utility vehicles plummet. For some firms, though, the situation proved fortuitous, as Honda, Nissan, and Toyota gained sales when many consumers switched to more fuel-efficient vehicles, like the Toyota Prius.[2] Although the future is not very predictable, marketers try to forecast what may happen. We can say with certainty that marketers continue to modify their marketing strategies and plans in response to dynamic environmental forces. Consider how technological changes have affected the products offered by computer companies and how the public's growing concern with health and fitness has influenced the products of clothing, food, exercise equipment, and health-care companies. Marketing managers who fail to recognize changes in environmental forces leave their firms unprepared to capitalize on marketing opportunities or to cope with threats created by those changes. Monitoring the environment is crucial to an organization's survival and to the long-term achievement of its goals.

Environmental Scanning and Analysis

To monitor changes in the marketing environment effectively, marketers engage in environmental scanning and analysis. **Environmental scanning** is the process of collecting information about forces in the marketing environment. Scanning involves observation; secondary sources such as business, trade, government, and general-interest publications; and marketing research. The Internet has become a popular scanning tool because it makes data more accessible and allows companies to gather needed information quickly. Environmental scanning gives companies an edge over competitors in allowing them to take advantage of current trends. However, simply gathering information about competitors and customers is not enough; companies must know *how* to use that information in the strategic planning process. Managers must be careful not to gather so much information that sheer volume makes analysis impossible.

Environmental analysis is the process of assessing and interpreting the information gathered through environmental scanning. A manager evaluates the information for accuracy, tries to resolve inconsistencies in the data, and, if warranted, assigns significance to the findings. Evaluating this information should enable the manager to identify potential threats and opportunities linked to environmental changes.

environmental scanning
The process of collecting information about forces in the marketing environment

environmental analysis
The process of assessing and interpreting the information gathered through environmental scanning

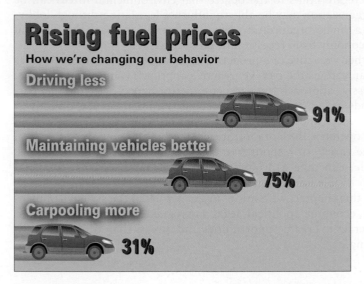

Rising fuel prices
How we're changing our behavior

Driving less — 91%

Maintaining vehicles better — 75%

Carpooling more — 31%

Source: AAIA Survey.

Understanding the current state of the marketing environment and recognizing threats and opportunities that might arise from changes within it help companies in their strategic planning. In particular, it can help marketing managers assess the performance of current marketing efforts and develop future marketing strategies.

Responding to Environmental Forces

Marketing managers take two general approaches to environmental forces: accepting them as uncontrollable or attempting to influence and shape them. An organization that views environmental forces as uncontrollable remains passive and reactive toward the environment. Instead of trying to influence forces in the environment, its marketing managers adjust current marketing strategies to environmental changes. They approach with caution market opportunities discovered through environmental scanning and analysis. On the other hand, marketing managers who believe environmental forces can be shaped adopt a more proactive approach. For example, if a market is blocked by traditional environmental constraints, proactive marketing managers may apply economic, psychological, political, and promotional skills to gain access to and operate within it. Once they identify what is constraining a market opportunity, they assess the power of the various parties involved and develop strategies to overcome the obstructing environmental forces. Microsoft, Intel, and Google, for example, have responded to political, legal, and regulatory concerns about their power in the computer industry by communicating the value of their competitive approaches to various publics. The computer giants contend that their competitive success results in superior products for their customers.

A proactive approach can be constructive and bring desired results. To influence environmental forces, marketing managers seek to identify market opportunities or to extract greater benefits relative to costs from existing market opportunities. For example, a firm that is losing sales to competitors with lower-priced products develops a technology that makes its production processes more efficient, thus allowing it to

Responding to Environmental Forces

Subaru and Honda respond to consumer demand for environmentally friendly and technologically advanced automobiles.

lower the prices of its own products. Political action is another way to affect environmental forces. The pharmaceutical industry, for example, has lobbied very effectively for fewer restrictions on prescription drug marketing. However, managers must recognize that there are limits to the degree that environmental forces can be shaped. Although an organization may be able to influence legislation through lobbying, it is unlikely that a single organization can significantly increase the national birthrate or move the economy from recession to prosperity.

We cannot say whether a reactive or a proactive approach to environmental forces is better. For some organizations the passive, reactive approach is more appropriate, but for others the aggressive approach leads to better performance. Selection of a particular approach depends on an organization's managerial philosophies, objectives, financial resources, customers, and human skills, as well as on the environment within which the organization operates. Both organizational factors and managers' personal characteristics affect the variety of responses to changing environmental conditions. Microsoft, for example, can take a proactive approach because of its financial resources and the highly visible image of its founder, Bill Gates.

In the remainder of this chapter, we explore in greater detail the six environmental forces—competitive, economic, political, legal and regulatory, technological, and sociocultural—that interact to create opportunities and threats that must be considered in strategic planning.

Competitive Forces

LO 2 To understand how competitive and economic factors affect an organization's ability to compete and a customer's ability and willingness to buy products

competition Other organizations that market products that are similar to or can be substituted for a marketer's products in the same geographic area

brand competitors Firms that market products with similar features and benefits to the same customers at similar prices

product competitors Firms that compete in the same product class but market products with different features, benefits, and prices

generic competitors Firms that provide very different products that solve the same problem or satisfy the same basic customer need

total budget competitors Firms that compete for the limited financial resources of the same customers

Few firms, if any, operate free of competition. In fact, for most goods and services, customers have many alternatives from which to choose. For example, although the five best-selling soft drinks are Coke Classic, Pepsi-Cola, Diet Coke, Mountain Dew, and Diet Pepsi, soft-drink sales in general have flattened as consumers have turned to alternatives such as bottled water, flavored water, fruit juice, and iced tea products.[3] Thus, when marketing managers define the target market(s) their firm will serve, they simultaneously establish a set of competitors.[4] In addition, marketing managers must consider the type of competitive structure in which the firm operates. In this section, we examine types of competition and competitive structures, as well as the importance of monitoring competitors' actions.

Types of Competitors

Broadly speaking, all firms compete with one another for customers' dollars. More practically, however, a marketer generally defines **competition** as other firms that market products that are similar to or can be substituted for its products in the same geographic area. These competitors can be classified into one of four types. **Brand competitors** market products with similar features and benefits to the same customers at similar prices. For example, a thirsty, calorie-conscious customer may choose a diet soda such as Diet Coke or Diet Pepsi from the soda machine. However, these sodas face competition from other types of beverages. **Product competitors** compete in the same product class but market products with different features, benefits, and prices. The thirsty dieter, for instance, might purchase iced tea, juice, mineral water, or bottled water instead of a soda. Jamba Juice is testing new breakfast menu items that would enable the firm to offer products that will compete with McDonald's, Burger King's, and Dunkin Donuts' breakfast products.[5]

Generic competitors provide very different products that solve the same problem or satisfy the same basic customer need. Our dieter, for example, might simply have a glass of water from the kitchen tap to satisfy her thirst. **Total budget competitors** compete for the limited financial resources of the same customers.[6] Total budget competitors for Diet Coke, for example, might include gum, a newspaper, and bananas. Although all four types of competition can affect a firm's marketing performance, brand competitors are the most significant because buyers typically see the

Brand and Product Competition

IKEA and Lowe's compete in the kitchen remodeling market.

different products of these firms as direct substitutes for one another. Consequently marketers tend to concentrate environmental analyses on brand competitors.

Types of Competitive Structures

The number of firms that supply a product may affect the strength of competitors. When just one or a few firms control supply, competitive factors exert a different form of influence on marketing activities than when many competitors exist. Table 3.1 presents four general types of competitive structures: monopoly, oligopoly, monopolistic competition, and pure competition.

A **monopoly** exists when an organization offers a product that has no close substitutes, making that organization the sole source of supply. Because the organization has no competitors, it controls the supply of the product completely and, as a single seller, can erect barriers to potential competitors. In reality, most monopolies surviving today are local utilities, which are heavily regulated by local, state, or federal agencies. These

monopoly A competitive structure in which an organization offers a product that has no close substitutes, making that organization the sole source of supply

table 3.1	SELECTED CHARACTERISTICS OF COMPETITIVE STRUCTURES			
Type of Structure	**Number of Competitors**	**Ease of Entry into Market**	**Product**	**Example**
Monopoly	One	Many barriers	Almost no substitutes	Fort Collins (Colorado) Water Utilities
Oligopoly	Few	Some barriers	Homogeneous or differentiated (with real or perceived differences)	General Motors (autos)
Monopolistic competition	Many	Few barriers	Product differentiation, with many substitutes	Levi Strauss (jeans)
Pure competition	Unlimited	No barriers	Homogeneous products	Vegetable farm (sweet corn)

E-ntertainment MARKETING

Barbie Gets a Virtual Facelift

Barbie, a best-selling fashion doll produced by Mattel, Inc., was launched in 1959. She was based on an adult German doll called Bild Lilli at a time when most dolls for little girls were infants. Over the last 50 years, Barbie has become a cultural icon and has earned honors that are rare in the toy world. By 2001, however, Barbie faced her first serious competition in the fashion doll market when MGA Entertainment introduced the Bratz line of dolls. Within a few years, Bratz dolls were outselling Barbie dolls in the United Kingdom. Sales of Barbie dolls fell by 30 percent in the United States from their peak sales, and by 18 percent worldwide, with much of the drop being attributed to the popularity of the Bratz dolls. However, Mattel maintained that in terms of numbers of dolls, clothes, and accessories, Barbie remained the leading brand.

In 2007 Mattel initiated a new strategy to revive Barbie's flagging sales. The latest Barbie doll isn't actually a doll at all: it's a four-and-a-half-inch-long $60 device that connects girls to the website BarbieGirls.com via personal computer. Through the virtual world of Barbie-Girls.com, girls can create a character they can name, dress, and customize by skin tone, hair color, style, and expression. They can shop for clothes and furniture in a virtual mall using "B-bucks" that are earned by playing games and watching promotional videos. Girls can also chat with friends on the site, with real-life friends' dolls being recognized as friends once they are plugged into the users' computers. Security software monitors exchanges to ensure that girls don't give out personally identifying information such as names or addresses. The device also functions as an MP3 player, so consumers can listen to music when not online.

Mattel hopes that the new product will invigorate the brand and serve as a case study in how a 1950s-era business finds its place in the digital age. Its target market for the device is 6- to 11-year-old girls, many of whom are now embarrassed to admit they still play with a doll. According to Mediamark Research, more than half of American 6- to 11-year-olds have gone online in the past 30 days. Rather than charging real money for virtual clothes and accessories, Mattel will sell snap-on accessories to dress up the Barbie Girls device, just as people decorate and accessorize their iPods and cell phones. Mattel hopes that the more girls interact with their brand, the more dolls and accessories it can sell.

Mattel's foray into the online world is not unique: other doll manufacturers are close behind, with Bratz starting its own online world called Be-bratz.com. Both the Bratz and Barbie websites provide a nearly identical virtual experience for children to build and furnish their own rooms, have pets, and interact with friends. As Barbie approaches her fiftieth birthday, will she be able to continue to reinvent herself, or will competitors, like the upstart Bratz, continue to make inroads into the appeal of today's young girls?[a]

monopolies are tolerated because of the tremendous financial resources needed to develop and operate them. For example, few organizations can obtain the financial or political resources to mount any competition against a local water supplier. On the other hand, competition is increasing in the electric and cable television industries.

An **oligopoly** exists when a few sellers control the supply of a large proportion of a product. In this case, each seller considers the reactions of other sellers to changes in marketing activities. Products facing oligopolistic competition may be homogeneous, such as aluminum, or differentiated, such as automobiles. Usually barriers of some sort make it difficult to enter the market and compete with oligopolies. For

oligopoly A competitive structure in which a few sellers control the supply of a large proportion of a product

example, because of the enormous financial outlay required, few companies or individuals could afford to enter the oil-refining or steel-producing industry. Moreover, some industries demand special technical or marketing skills, a qualification that deters entry of many potential competitors.

Monopolistic competition exists when a firm with many potential competitors attempts to develop a marketing strategy to differentiate its product. For example, Levi Strauss has established an advantage for its blue jeans through a well-known trademark, design, advertising, and a reputation for quality. Although many competing brands of blue jeans are available, this firm has carved out a market niche by emphasizing differences in its products.

Pure competition, if it existed at all, would entail a large number of sellers, none of which could significantly influence price or supply. Products would be homogeneous, and entry into the market would be easy. The closest thing to an example of pure competition is an unregulated farmers' market, where local growers gather to sell their produce.

Pure competition is an ideal at one end of the continuum, and a monopoly is at the other end. Most marketers function in a competitive environment somewhere between these two extremes.

Monitoring Competition

Marketers need to monitor the actions of major competitors to determine what specific strategies competitors are using and how those strategies affect their own. Competitive intensity influences a firm's strategic approach to markets.[7] Price is one marketing strategy variable that most competitors monitor. When AirTran or Southwest Airlines lowers its fare on a route, most major airlines attempt to match the price. Monitoring guides marketers in developing competitive advantages and in adjusting current marketing strategies and planning new ones.

In monitoring competition, it is not enough to analyze available information; the firm must develop a system for gathering ongoing information about competitors and potential competitors. Understanding the market and what customers want, as well as what the competition is providing, will help the firm maintain a marketing orientation.[8] Information about competitors allows marketing managers to assess the performance of their own marketing efforts and to recognize the strengths and weaknesses in their own marketing strategies. In addition, organizations are rewarded for taking risks and dealing with the uncertainty created by inadequate information.[9] Data about market shares, product movement, sales volume, and expenditure levels can be useful. However, accurate information on these matters is often difficult to obtain.

monopolistic competition A competitive structure in which a firm has many potential competitors and tries to develop a marketing strategy to differentiate its product

pure competition A market structure characterized by an extremely large number of sellers, none strong enough to significantly influence price or supply

Economic Forces

Economic forces in the marketing environment influence both marketers' and customers' decisions and activities. In this section, we examine the effects of general economic conditions as well as buying power and the factors that affect people's willingness to spend.

Economic Conditions

The overall state of the economy fluctuates in all countries. Changes in general economic conditions affect (and are affected by) supply and demand, buying power, willingness to spend, consumer expenditure levels, and intensity of competitive behavior. Therefore, current economic conditions and changes in the economy have a broad impact on the success of organizations' marketing strategies.

Fluctuations in the economy follow a general pattern, often referred to as the **business cycle.** In the traditional view, the business cycle consists of four stages: prosperity, recession, depression, and recovery. From a global perspective, different regions of the world may be in different stages of the business cycle during the same period. Throughout much of the last decade, for example, the United States experienced booming growth (prosperity). The U.S. economy began to slow in 2000, with a brief

business cycle A pattern of economic fluctuations that has four stages: prosperity, recession, depression, and recovery

recession, especially in high-technology industries, in 2001. Japan, however, endured a recession during most of the last decade and into the early 2000s. Economic variation in the global marketplace creates a planning challenge for firms that sell products in multiple markets around the world. In 2008, the United States experienced an economic downturn due to higher energy prices, falling home values, increasing unemployment, the financial crisis in the banking industry, and fluctuating currency values.

During **prosperity,** unemployment is low and total income is relatively high. Assuming a low inflation rate, this combination ensures high buying power. If the economic outlook remains prosperous, consumers generally are willing to buy. In the prosperity stage, marketers often expand their product offerings to take advantage of increased buying power. They can sometimes capture a larger market share by intensifying distribution and promotion efforts.

Because unemployment rises during a **recession,** total buying power declines. These factors, usually accompanied by consumer pessimism, often stifle both consumer and business spending. As buying power decreases, many customers may become more price and value conscious, and look for basic, functional products. During a recession, some firms make the mistake of drastically reducing their marketing efforts, thus damaging their ability to survive. Obviously, however, marketers should consider some revision of their marketing activities during a recessionary period. Because consumers are more concerned about the functional value of products, a company should focus its marketing research on determining precisely what functions buyers want and make sure those functions become part of its products. Promotional efforts should emphasize value and utility.

A prolonged recession may become a **depression,** a period in which unemployment is extremely high, wages are very low, total disposable income is at a minimum, and consumers lack confidence in the economy. A depression usually lasts for an extended period, often years, and has been experienced by Russia, Mexico, and Brazil in the last decade. Although evidence supports maintaining or even increasing spending during economic slowdowns, marketing budgets are more likely to be cut in the face of an economic downturn.

During **recovery,** the economy moves from recession or depression toward prosperity. During this period, high unemployment begins to decline, total disposable income increases, and the economic gloom that reduced consumers' willingness to buy subsides. Both the ability and the willingness to buy rise. Marketers face some problems during recovery; for example, it is difficult to ascertain how quickly and to what level prosperity will return. In this stage, marketers should maintain as much flexibility in their marketing strategies as possible so they can make the needed adjustments.

Buying Power

The strength of a person's **buying power** depends on economic conditions and the size of the resources—money, goods, and services that can be traded in an exchange—that enable the individual to make purchases. The major financial sources of buying power are income, credit, and wealth. For an individual, **income** is the amount of money received through wages, rents, investments, pensions, and subsidy payments for a given period, such as a month or a year. Normally this money is allocated among taxes, spending for goods and services, and savings. The median annual household income in the United States is approximately $48,200.[10] However, because of differences in people's educational levels, abilities, occupations, and wealth, income is not equally distributed in this country.

Marketers are most interested in the amount of money left after payment of taxes because this **disposable income** is used for spending or saving. Because disposable income is a ready source of buying power, the total amount available in a nation is important to marketers. Several factors determine the size of total disposable income. One is the total amount of income, which is affected by wage levels, the rate of unemployment, interest rates, and dividend rates. Because disposable income is income left after taxes are paid, the number and amount of taxes directly affect the size of total disposable income. When taxes rise, disposable income declines; when taxes fall, disposable income increases.

prosperity A stage of the business cycle characterized by low unemployment and relatively high total income, which together ensure high buying power (provided the inflation rate stays low)

recession A stage of the business cycle during which unemployment rises and total buying power declines, stifling both consumer and business spending

depression A stage of the business cycle when unemployment is extremely high, wages are very low, total disposable income is at a minimum, and consumers lack confidence in the economy

recovery A stage of the business cycle in which the economy moves from recession or depression toward prosperity

buying power Resources, such as money, goods, and services, that can be traded in an exchange

income For an individual, the amount of money received through wages, rents, investments, pensions, and subsidy payments for a given period

disposable income After-tax income

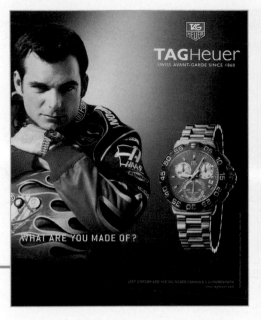 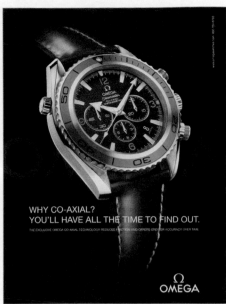

Economic Forces

Tag Heuer and Omega rely on consumers with significant discretionary income to purchase their watches.

Disposable income that is available for spending and saving after an individual has purchased the basic necessities of food, clothing, and shelter is called **discretionary income.** People use discretionary income to purchase entertainment, vacations, automobiles, education, pets, furniture, appliances, and so on. Changes in total discretionary income affect sales of these products, especially automobiles, furniture, large appliances, and other costly durable goods.

Credit enables people to spend future income now or in the near future. However, credit increases current buying power at the expense of future buying power. Several factors determine whether people use or forgo credit. First, credit must be available. Interest rates also affect buyers' decisions to use credit, especially for expensive purchases such as homes, appliances, and automobiles. When interest rates are low, the total cost of automobiles and houses becomes more affordable. In the United States, low interest rates over the past ten years induced many buyers to take on the high level of debt necessary to own a home, fueling a tremendous boom in the construction of new homes and the sale of older homes. In contrast, when interest rates are high, consumers are more likely to delay buying such expensive items. Use of credit is also affected by credit terms, such as size of the down payment and amount and number of monthly payments.

Wealth is the accumulation of past income, natural resources, and financial resources. It exists in many forms, including cash, securities, savings accounts, jewelry, and real estate. Global wealth is increasing, with 9.5 million millionaires worldwide, double the number ten years ago.[11] Like income, wealth is unevenly distributed. A person can have a high income and very little wealth. It is also possible, but not likely, for a person to have great wealth but little income. The significance of wealth to marketers is that as people become wealthier, they gain buying power in three ways: they can use their wealth to make current purchases, to generate income, and to acquire large amounts of credit.

Income, credit, and wealth equip consumers with buying power to purchase goods and services. Marketing managers must be aware of current levels and expected changes in buying power in their own markets because buying power directly affects the types and quantities of goods and services customers purchase. Information about buying power is available from government sources, trade associations, and research agencies. One of the most current and comprehensive sources of buying power data is the *Sales & Marketing Management Survey of Buying Power,* published annually by *Sales & Marketing Management* magazine. Having buying power, however, does not mean consumers will buy. They must also be willing to use their buying power.

discretionary income Disposable income available for spending and saving after an individual has purchased the basic necessities of food, clothing, and shelter

wealth The accumulation of past income, natural resources, and financial resources

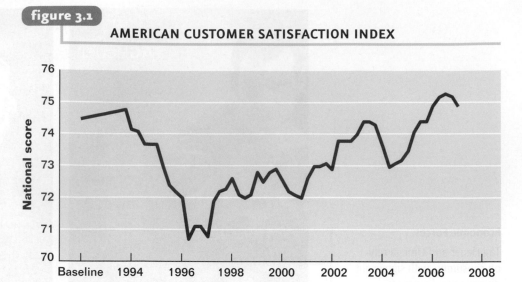

figure 3.1

AMERICAN CUSTOMER SATISFACTION INDEX

Source: "National Quarterly Scores," American Customer Satisfaction Index, University of Michigan Business School, www.theacsi.org/index.php?option=com_content&task=view&id=31&Itemid=35 (accessed Jan. 8, 2008).

Willingness to Spend

People's **willingness to spend**—their inclination to buy because of expected satisfaction from a product—is, to some degree, related to their ability to buy. That is, people are sometimes more willing to buy if they have the buying power. However, a number of other elements also influence willingness to spend. Some elements affect specific products; others influence spending in general. A product's price and value influence almost all of us. Cross pens, for example, appeal to customers who are willing to spend more for fine writing instruments even when lower-priced pens are readily available. Increasingly, middle-class consumers seem more willing to spend on high-price luxury products, such as Coach purses, BMW automobiles, and spa vacations, although they may shop for discounted groceries and other basic products at Wal-Mart and Target in order to afford the upscale products.[12] The amount of satisfaction received from a product already owned may also influence customers' desire to buy other products. Satisfaction depends not only on the quality of the currently owned product but also on numerous psychological and social forces. The American Customer Satisfaction Index, computed by the National Quality Research Center at the University of Michigan (see Figure 3.1), offers an indicator of customer satisfaction with a wide variety of businesses.

Factors that affect consumers' general willingness to spend are expectations about future employment, income levels, prices, family size, and general economic conditions. Willingness to spend ordinarily declines if people are unsure whether or how long they will be employed, and it usually increases if people are reasonably certain of higher incomes in the future. Expectations of rising prices in the near future may also increase willingness to spend in the present. For a given level of buying power, the larger the family, the greater the willingness to spend. One reason for this relationship is that as the size of a family increases, more dollars must be spent to provide the basic necessities to sustain family members.

willingness to spend An inclination to buy because of expected satisfaction from a product, influenced by the ability to buy and numerous psychological and social forces

Political Forces

L O 3 To identify the types of political forces in the marketing environment

Political, legal, and regulatory forces of the marketing environment are closely interrelated. Legislation is enacted, legal decisions are interpreted by courts, and regulatory agencies are created and operated, for the most part, by elected or appointed officials. Legislation and regulations (or their lack) reflect the current political outlook. For example, after several *E. coli* scares, the U.S. Department of Agriculture modified regulations to speed up meat recalls when contaminated meat is discovered. Evidence suggests that some U.S. meat-processing plants are not meeting food safety regulations, which may have contributed to the rise in *E. coli*–contamination cases.[13]

RESPONSIBLE marketing?

Dyson's Airblade: Out with the Old and in with the New

ISSUE: When should organizations abandon existing technology in light of new, more energy-efficient options?

James Dyson has built a career on making everyday products work better. His line of vacuum cleaners has taken a unique market position by providing greater suction and cleaning ability than major competitors. One of Dyson's latest innovations is the Airblade. The Airblade is a hand dryer like the ones you see in public and corporate restrooms that blows filtered, unheated air through a narrow opening the width of an eyelash at 400 miles per hour. Your hands are dried in just 12 seconds, and the Airblade uses 80 percent less energy than conventional dryers. The downside, if there is any, is that each unit costs $1,400—about three times as much as traditional hand dryers.

Dyson admits to the unique challenge in marketing the Airblade. If you want a better vacuum cleaner, for example, you go out and buy one. But what business wants to remove perfectly adequate, functioning technology in their restrooms and replace them with "superior" technology? To spur interest and create some buzz about the product, Dyson gave away 1,000 machines (costing $840 each to manufacture). These giveaways were placed in high-traffic locations, such as the London Eye, a popular tourist spot. Current Airblade customers include the Le Parker Meridien New York Hotels; Advocate Lutheran General Hospital in Park Ridge, Illinois; and AMC movie theaters. The National Sanitation Foundation called the Airblade the world's first "hygienic hand dryer," thanks to its Hepa filter. The hard part is selling your better, cleaner product at a higher price when capital expenditures on such an item are not necessary. Should companies feel pressured to innovate in this way?[b]

Consequently the political forces of the marketing environment have the potential to influence marketing decisions and strategies.

Marketing organizations strive to maintain good relations with elected and appointed political officials for several reasons. Political officials well disposed toward particular firms or industries are less likely to create or enforce laws and regulations unfavorable to those companies. For example, political officials who believe oil companies are making honest efforts to control pollution are unlikely to create and enforce highly restrictive pollution-control laws. In addition, governments are big buyers, and political officials can influence how much a government agency purchases and from whom. Finally, political officials can play key roles in helping organizations secure foreign markets.

Many marketers view political forces as beyond their control and simply adjust to conditions that arise from those forces. Some firms, however, seek to influence the political process. In some cases, organizations publicly protest the actions of legislative bodies. More often, organizations help elect to political offices individuals who regard them positively. Much of this help is in the form of campaign contributions.

Although laws limit corporate contributions to campaign funds for specific candidates, it is legal for businesses and other organizations to contribute to political parties. Some companies even choose to donate to more than one party. These donations are made in the form of "soft money," which refers to money that is donated to a political party with no specification on how the money will be spent. For instance, over the last 18 years AT&T has made corporate donations in excess of $38 million.[14] Marketers can also influence the political process through political action committees (PACs) that solicit donations from individuals and then contribute those funds to candidates who are running for political office. Companies are barred by federal law from donating directly to candidates for federal offices or to PACs, but they can organize PACs to which their executives, employees, and stockholders can make significant donations as individuals. Companies can also participate in the political process through lobbying to persuade public and/or government officials to favor a particular position in decision making. Many organizations concerned about the threat of legislation or regulation that may negatively affect their operations employ lobbyists to communicate their concerns to elected officials. Marketers of cigarettes, for example, spent millions on lobbyists to persuade state and local officials that their governments should not increase taxes on cigarettes, effectively raising their price.[15]

Legal and Regulatory Forces

L O ④ To understand how laws, government regulations, and self-regulatory agencies affect marketing activities

A number of federal laws influence marketing decisions and activities. Table 3.2 lists some of the most important laws. In addition to discussing these laws, which deal with competition and consumer protection, this section examines the effects of regulatory agencies and self-regulatory forces on marketing efforts.

table 3.2 · MAJOR FEDERAL LAWS THAT AFFECT MARKETING DECISIONS

Name and Date Enacted	Purpose
Sherman Antitrust Act (1890)	Prohibits contracts, combinations, or conspiracies to restrain trade; establishes as a misdemeanor monopolizing or attempting to monopolize
Clayton Act (1914)	Prohibits specific practices such as price discrimination, exclusive-dealer arrangements, and stock acquisitions whose effect may noticeably lessen competition or tend to create a monopoly
Federal Trade Commission Act (1914)	Created the Federal Trade Commission; also gives the FTC investigatory powers to be used in preventing unfair methods of competition
Robinson-Patman Act (1936)	Prohibits price discrimination that lessens competition among wholesalers or retailers; prohibits producers from giving disproportionate services or facilities to large buyers
Wheeler-Lea Act (1938)	Prohibits unfair and deceptive acts and practices regardless of whether competition is injured; places advertising of foods and drugs under the jurisdiction of the FTC
Lanham Act (1946)	Provides protections for and regulation of brand names, brand marks, trade names, and trademarks
Celler-Kefauver Act (1950)	Prohibits any corporation engaged in commerce from acquiring the whole or any part of the stock or other share of the capital assets of another corporation when the effect would substantially lessen competition or tend to create a monopoly
Fair Packaging and Labeling Act (1966)	Prohibits unfair or deceptive packaging or labeling of consumer products
Magnuson-Moss Warranty (FTC) Act (1975)	Provides for minimum disclosure standards for written consumer product warranties; defines minimum consent standards for written warranties; allows the FTC to prescribe interpretive rules in policy statements regarding unfair or deceptive practices
Consumer Goods Pricing Act (1975)	Prohibits the use of price maintenance agreements among manufacturers and resellers in interstate commerce
Trademark Counterfeiting Act (1980)	Imposes civil and criminal penalties against those who deal in counterfeit consumer goods or any counterfeit goods that can threaten health or safety
Trademark Law Revision Act (1988)	Amends the Lanham Act to allow brands not yet introduced to be protected through registration with the Patent and Trademark Office
Nutrition Labeling and Education Act (1990)	Prohibits exaggerated health claims; requires all processed foods to contain labels with nutritional information
Telephone Consumer Protection Act (1991)	Establishes procedures to avoid unwanted telephone solicitations; prohibits marketers from using an automated telephone dialing system or an artificial or prerecorded voice to certain telephone lines
Federal Trademark Dilution Act (1995)	Grants trademark owners the right to protect trademarks and requires relinquishment of names that match or parallel existing trademarks
Digital Millennium Copyright Act (1996)	Refined copyright laws to protect digital versions of copyrighted materials, including music and movies
Children's Online Privacy Protection Act (2000)	Regulates the collection of personally identifiable information (name, address, e-mail address, hobbies, interests, or information collected through cookies) online from children under age 13
Do Not Call Implementation Act (2003)	Directs the FCC and FTC to coordinate so their rules are consistent regarding telemarketing call practices including the Do Not Call Registry and other lists, as well as call abandonment

Procompetitive Legislation

Procompetitive laws are designed to preserve competition. Most of these laws were enacted to end various antitrade practices deemed unacceptable by society. The Sherman Antitrust Act, for example, was passed in 1890 to prevent businesses from restraining trade and monopolizing markets. Examples of illegal anticompetitive practices include stealing trade secrets or obtaining other confidential information from a competitor's employees, trademark and copyright infringement, price fixing, false advertising, and deceptive selling methods such as "bait and switch" and false representation of products. For example, the Lanham Act (1946) and the Federal Trademark Dilution Act (1995) help companies protect their trademarks (brand names, logos, and other registered symbols) against infringement. The latter also requires users of names that match or parallel existing trademarks to relinquish them to prevent confusion among consumers. Antitrust laws also authorize the government to punish companies that engage in such anticompetitive practices. For example, British Airways and Korean Air Lines each paid a $300 million criminal fine for participating in conspiracies to fix the prices of passenger and cargo flights.[16]

Consumer Protection Legislation

Consumer protection legislation is not a recent development. During the mid-1800s, lawmakers in many states passed laws to prohibit adulteration of food and drugs. However, consumer protection laws at the federal level mushroomed in the mid-1960s and early 1970s. A number of them deal with consumer safety, such as the food and drug acts, and are designed to protect people from actual and potential physical harm caused by adulteration or mislabeling. Other laws prohibit the sale of various hazardous products, such as flammable fabrics and toys that may injure children. Others concern automobile safety. Congress has also passed several laws concerning information disclosure. Some require that information about specific products, such as textiles, furs, cigarettes, and automobiles, be provided on labels. Other laws focus on particular marketing activities: product development and testing, packaging, labeling, advertising, and consumer financing. For example, concerns about companies' online collection and use of personal information, especially about children, resulted in the passage of the Children's Online Privacy Protection Act, which prohibits websites and Internet providers from seeking personal information from children under age 13 without parental consent. An example of more recent consumer protection legislation is the Mortgage Debt Relief Act of 2007, which attempts to reduce the number of home foreclosures by allowing vulnerable homeowners to renegotiate the terms of their home mortgages.[17] The legislation was enacted because some mortgage companies made loans to consumers who could no longer afford those loans when interest rates rose.

Encouraging Compliance with Laws and Regulations

Marketing activities are sometimes at the forefront of organizational misconduct, with fraud and antitrust violations the most frequently sentenced organizational crimes. Legal violations usually begin when marketers develop programs that unwittingly overstep legal bounds. Many marketers lack experience in dealing with complex legal actions and decisions. Some test the limits of certain laws by operating in a legally questionable way to see how far they can get with certain practices

Consumer Protections Legislation

Tobacco labeling and packaging have been impacted by consumer protection legislation through disclosures and warnings.

before being prosecuted. Other marketers interpret regulations and statutes very strictly to avoid violating a vague law. When marketers interpret laws in relation to specific marketing practices, they often analyze recent court decisions both to better understand what the law is intended to do and to predict future court interpretations.

The current trend is away from legally based organizational compliance programs to providing incentives that foster a culture of ethics and responsibility that encourages compliance with laws and regulations. Developing best practices and voluntary compliance creates rules and principles that guide decision making. Many companies are encouraging their employees to take responsibility for avoiding legal misconduct themselves. The New York Stock Exchange, for example, requires all member companies to have a code of ethics, and some firms try to go beyond what is required by the law. For example, many firms are seeking out and implementing alternative energy solutions before stricter laws are enacted to protect the environment.

Regulatory Agencies

Federal regulatory agencies influence many marketing activities, including product development, pricing, packaging, advertising, personal selling, and distribution. Usually these bodies have the power to enforce specific laws, as well as some discretion in establishing operating rules and regulations to guide certain types of industry practices. Because of this discretion and overlapping areas of responsibility, confusion or conflict regarding which agencies have jurisdiction over which marketing activities is common.

Of all the federal regulatory units, the **Federal Trade Commission (FTC)** most heavily influences marketing activities. Although the FTC regulates a variety of business practices, it allocates a large portion of resources to curbing false advertising, misleading pricing, and deceptive packaging and labeling. When it has reason to believe a firm is violating a law, the commission typically issues a complaint stating that the business is in violation and takes appropriate action. For example, the FTC settled charges against Smart Inventions, Inc.; John Nokes; and Darrell Stoddard for making deceptive claims in an infomercial that their Biotape adhesive pain-relief product provides significant and permanent relief from pain and that their product is superior to other pain relievers. The settlement includes approximately $2.5 million for consumer refunds; the parties also agreed to make no more unsubstantiated claims about the product.[18] If, after it is issued a complaint, a company continues the questionable practice, the FTC can issue a cease-and-desist order demanding that the business stop doing whatever caused the complaint. The firm can appeal to the federal courts to have the order rescinded. However, the FTC can seek civil penalties in court, up to a maximum penalty of $10,000 a day for each infraction if a cease-and-desist order is violated.

The commission can require companies to run corrective advertising in response to previous ads deemed misleading (see Figure 3.2). For example, after it settled charges that it had engaged in deceptive practices associated with marketing its gift cards, the FTC required Darden Restaurants, Inc., which owns the Olive Garden and Red Lobster restaurant chains, to restore fees deducted from consumer gift cards and to prominently disclose fees and expiration dates in all advertising for future gift card offers. "The FTC works to make sure consumers have the facts they need to make smart decisions, no matter what they're buying," said Lydia Parnes, director of the FTC's Bureau of Consumer Protection.[19]

The FTC also assists businesses in complying with laws and evaluates new marketing methods every year. For example, the agency has held hearings to help firms establish guidelines for avoiding charges of price fixing, deceptive advertising, and questionable telemarketing practices. It has also held conferences and hearings on electronic (Internet) commerce, identity theft, and childhood obesity. When general sets of guidelines are needed to improve business practices in a particular industry, the FTC sometimes encourages firms within that industry to establish a set of trade practices voluntarily. The FTC may even sponsor a conference that brings together industry leaders and consumers for this purpose.

Unlike the FTC, other regulatory units are limited to dealing with specific products, services, or business activities. For example, the Food and Drug Administration

Federal Trade Commission (FTC) An agency that regulates a variety of business practices and curbs false advertising, misleading pricing, and deceptive packaging and labeling

figure 3.2

FEDERAL TRADE COMMISSION ENFORCEMENT TOOLS

Cease-and-desist order	Consent decree	Redress	Corrective advertising	Civil penalties
A court order to a business to stop engaging in an illegal practice	An order for a business to stop engaging in questionable activities to avoid prosecution (In 2005, 10,021 were issued)	Money paid to customer to settle or resolve a complaint	A requirement that a business make new advertisement to correct misinformation	Court-ordered civil fines for up to $10,000 per day for violating a cease-and-desist order

Source: www.ftc.gov.

(FDA) enforces regulations that prohibit the sale and distribution of adulterated, misbranded, or hazardous food and drug products. Table 3.3 outlines the areas of responsibility of six federal regulatory agencies.

In addition, all states, as well as many cities and towns, have regulatory agencies that enforce laws and regulations regarding marketing practices within their states or municipalities. State and local regulatory agencies try not to establish regulations that conflict with those of federal regulatory agencies. They generally enforce laws dealing with the production and sale of particular goods and services. The utility, insurance, financial, and liquor industries are commonly regulated by state agencies. Among these agencies' targets are misleading advertising and pricing. Recent legal actions suggest that states are taking a firmer stance against perceived deceptive pricing practices and are using basic consumer research to define deceptive pricing.

table 3.3   MAJOR FEDERAL REGULATORY AGENCIES

Agency	Major Areas of Responsibility
Federal Trade Commission (FTC)	Enforces laws and guidelines regarding business practices; takes action to stop false and deceptive advertising, pricing, packaging, and labeling
Food and Drug Administration (FDA)	Enforces laws and regulations to prevent distribution of adulterated or misbranded foods, drugs, medical devices, cosmetics, veterinary products, and potentially hazardous consumer products
Consumer Product Safety Commission (CPSC)	Ensures compliance with the Consumer Product Safety Act; protects the public from unreasonable risk of injury from any consumer product not covered by other regulatory agencies
Federal Communications Commission (FCC)	Regulates communication by wire, radio, and television in interstate and foreign commerce
Environmental Protection Agency (EPA)	Develops and enforces environmental protection standards and conducts research into the adverse effects of pollution
Federal Power Commission (FPC)	Regulates rates and sales of natural gas producers, thereby affecting the supply and price of gas available to consumers; also regulates wholesale rates for electricity and gas, pipeline construction, and U.S. imports and exports of natural gas and electricity

Self-Regulatory Forces

The Sustainable Forest Initiative is proactive in protecting our forests and wildlife.

State consumer protection laws offer an opportunity for state attorneys general to deal with marketing issues related to fraud and deception. Most states have consumer protection laws that are very general in nature and provide enforcement when new schemes evolve that injure consumers. For example, the New York Consumer Protection Board is very proactive in monitoring consumer protection and providing consumer education. New York also became the first state to implement an airline passenger rights law in 2008.

Self-Regulatory Forces

In an attempt to be good corporate citizens and prevent government intervention, some businesses try to regulate themselves. Kraft Foods, for example, stopped advertising sugary snacks and cereals to children under 12 in response to growing concerns about childhood obesity and its effects on children's long-term health. Although some competitors were astonished by the decision, Kraft executives recognized that if food product marketers did not begin to police themselves, the government could impose restrictions on advertising to children and the industry could face potential lawsuits.[20] Similarly, a number of trade associations have developed self-regulatory programs. Though these programs are not a direct outgrowth of laws, many were established to stop or stall the development of laws and governmental regulatory groups that would regulate the associations' marketing practices. Sometimes trade associations establish ethics codes by which their members must abide or risk censure or exclusion from the association. For example, the Pharmaceutical Research and Manufacturers of America released its "Guiding Principles" to function as a set of voluntary industry rules for drug companies to follow when advertising directly to consumers. Some of the key guidelines are explained in detail in Table 3.4.[21]

Perhaps the best-known self-regulatory group is the **Better Business Bureau (BBB),** which is a system of nongovernmental, independent, local regulatory agencies

Better Business Bureau (BBB) A system of non-governmental, independent, local regulatory agencies supported by local businesses that helps settle problems between customers and specific business firms

table 3.4	SELECTED DIRECT-TO-CONSUMER PHARMACEUTICAL GUIDELINES
Doctor information	Doctors must be informed about a product before it is marketed to consumers.
Schedule of advertisements	Advertisements must be aired at times for age-appropriate viewers. (Ads for Viagra and similar medications, for example, must appear at later hours.)
Identification of health condition	Advertisements must include the health condition the drug treats and include more than only the product name.
Advertisement review by FDA	All new television advertising must be submitted to the FDA before being broadcast.
Suggestions of other positive health-related actions	Advertisements must include other positive health-related behaviors.

that are supported by local businesses. More than 150 bureaus help settle problems between consumers and specific business firms. Each bureau also acts to preserve good business practices in a locality, although it usually lacks strong enforcement tools for dealing with firms that employ questionable practices. When a firm continues to violate what the Better Business Bureau believes to be good business practices, the bureau warns consumers through local newspapers or broadcast media. If the offending organization is a BBB member, it may be expelled from the local bureau. For example, the Better Business Bureau of Upstate New York expelled two building contractors for having too many unresolved complaints on file.[22]

The Council of Better Business Bureaus is a national organization composed of all local Better Business Bureaus. The National Advertising Division (NAD) of the Council operates a self-regulatory program that investigates claims regarding alleged deceptive advertising. For example, after NAD investigated a complaint from Procter & Gamble, it recommended that McNeil-PPC modify the advertising for its Tylenol Cold Multi-Symptom Nighttime cold medicine to avoid misleading consumers about its effectiveness relative to Procter & Gamble's Nyquil Multi-Symptom Cold/Flu Relief medicine after both firms reformulated their products.[23]

Another self-regulatory entity, the **National Advertising Review Board (NARB)**, considers cases in which an advertiser challenges issues raised by the NAD about an advertisement. Cases are reviewed by panels drawn from NARB members that represent advertisers, agencies, and the public. For example, General Mills appealed to the NARB about an NAD order to abandon its claim "Betcha Can't Taste the Difference" between its Malt-O-Meal cereal and those of other manufacturers because the NAD said the claim couldn't be substantiated. The NARB concurred with the NAD on the issue.[24] The NARB, sponsored by the Council of Better Business Bureaus and three advertising trade organizations, has no official enforcement powers. However, if a firm refuses to comply with its decision, the NARB may publicize the questionable practice and file a complaint with the FTC.

Self-regulatory programs have several advantages over governmental laws and regulatory agencies. Establishment and implementation are usually less expensive, and guidelines are generally more realistic and operational. In addition, effective self-regulatory programs reduce the need to expand government bureaucracy. However, these programs have several limitations. When a trade association creates a set of industry guidelines for its members, nonmember firms do not have to abide by them. Furthermore, many self-regulatory programs lack the tools or authority to enforce guidelines. Finally, guidelines in self-regulatory programs are often less strict than those established by government agencies.

Technological Forces

L O 5 To explore the effects of new technology on society and on marketing activities

National Advertising Review Board (NARB) A self-regulatory unit that considers challenges to issues raised by the National Advertising Division (an arm of the Council of Better Business Bureaus) about an advertisement

technology The application of knowledge and tools to solve problems and perform tasks more efficiently

The word *technology* brings to mind scientific advances such as information technology and biotechnology, which have resulted in the Internet, cell phones, cloning, stem-cell research, pharmaceutical products, lasers, and more. Technology has revolutionized the products created and offered by marketers and the channels by which they communicate about those products. However, even though these innovations are outgrowths of technology, none of them *are* technology. **Technology** is the application of knowledge and tools to solve problems and perform tasks more efficiently. Technology grows out of research performed by businesses, universities, government agencies, and nonprofit organizations. More than half of this research is paid for by the federal government, which supports research in such diverse areas as health, defense, agriculture, energy, and pollution.

The rapid technological growth of the last several decades is expected to accelerate. It has transformed the U.S. economy into the most productive in the world and provided Americans with an ever-higher standard of living and tremendous opportunities for sustained business expansion. Technology and technological advancements clearly influence buyers' and marketers' decisions, so let's take a closer look at the impact of technology and its use in the marketplace.

48 miles per kernel.

How much ethanol can a company extract from corn? Today, BASF helps increase both the quality and quantity of corn that farmers can grow. So it is now possible to improve corn supplies for ethanol production without reducing the crops intended for the kitchen table. And with more BASF agricultural innovations on the way, there's no telling how much mileage our efforts may yield down the road. Learn more at basf.com/stories

Helping Make
Products Better™

■■BASF
The Chemical Company

Impact of Technology

The use of corn ethanol is having an impact on many industries and companies such as BASF.

Impact of Technology

Technology determines how we, as members of society, satisfy our physiological needs. In various ways and to varying degrees, eating and drinking habits, sleeping patterns, sexual activities, health care, and work performance are all influenced by both existing technology and changes in technology. Because of the technological revolution in communications, for example, marketers can now reach vast numbers of people more efficiently through a variety of media. E-mail, voice mail, cell phones, pagers, and PDAs help marketers stay in touch with clients, make appointments, and handle last-minute orders or cancellations. Some companies, including Ford Motor, are even abandoning the use of traditional wired telephones in favor of exclusive use of cell phones in the workplace.[25] A growing number of U.S. households have given up their "land lines" in favor of using cell phones as their primary phones, and growth in wireless subscriptions is expected to continue at a compounded 2.9 percent through 2010.[26] The proliferation of cell phones, most with text message capabilities, have led experts to project that 89 percent of brands will employ text and multimedia messaging on cell phones to reach their target markets. Restaurants, for example, can send their lunch specials to subscribers' cell phones.[27] Increasingly, they can also accept customers' take-out orders via cell phone text messaging as well. Indeed, Papa John's Pizza projects that text ordering will soon rival ordering online, which currently is about 20 percent of the pizza chain's sales.[28]

Personal computers are now in three-quarters of U.S. consumers' homes, and most of them include broadband or modems for accessing the Internet. The Internet has become a major tool in most households for communicating, researching, shopping, and entertaining. The use of video online, especially through websites such as YouTube, has exploded from 7 percent of all Internet traffic in 2005 to 18 percent in 2007, and it is expected to grow tenfold by 2011.[29] Although we enjoy the benefits of communicating through the Internet, we are increasingly concerned about protecting our privacy and intellectual property. Likewise, although research done in the areas of health and medicine has led to the creation of new drugs that save lives, cloning and genetically modified foods have become controversial issues in many segments of society. In various ways and to varying degrees, home environments, health care, leisure, and work performance are all influenced by both current technology and advances in technology.[30]

The effects of technology relate to such characteristics as dynamics, reach, and the self-sustaining nature of technological progress. The *dynamics* of technology involve the constant change that often challenges the structures of social institutions, including social relationships, the legal system, religion, education, business, and leisure. *Reach* refers to the broad nature of technology as it moves through society. Consider the impact of cell phones. The ability to call from almost any location has many benefits, but it also has negative side effects, including increases in traffic accidents, increased noise pollution, and fears about potential health risks.[31]

The *self-sustaining* nature of technology relates to the fact that technology acts as a catalyst to spur even faster development. As new innovations are introduced, they stimulate the need for more advancements to facilitate further development. For example, the Internet has created the need for ever-faster transmission of signals through broadband connections such as high-speed phone lines (DSL), satellites, and cable. Technology initiates a change process that creates new opportunities for new technologies in every industry segment or personal life experience that it touches. At some point, there is a multiplier effect that causes still greater demand for more change to improve performance.[32]

The expanding opportunities for e-commerce, the sharing of business information, and the ability to maintain business relationships and conduct business transactions via telecommunications networks are already changing the relationship between businesses and consumers.[33] More and more people are turning to the Internet to purchase computers and related peripherals, software, books, music, and even furniture. Consumers are increasingly using the Internet to book travel reservations, transact banking business, and trade securities. The forces unleashed by the Internet are particularly important in business-to-business relationships, where uncertainties are being reduced by improving the quantity, reliability, and timeliness of information.

Adoption and Use of Technology

Many companies lose their status as market leaders because they fail to keep up with technological changes. It is important for firms to determine when a technology is changing the industry and to define the strategic influence of the new technology. For example, wireless devices in use today include radios, cell phones, laptop computers, TVs, pagers, and car keys. To remain competitive, companies today must keep up with and adapt to technological advances.

The extent to which a firm can protect inventions that stem from research also influences its use of technology. How secure a product is from imitation depends on how easily others can copy it without violating its patent. If groundbreaking products and processes cannot be protected through patents, a company is less likely to market them and make the benefits of its research available to competitors.

Through a procedure known as *technology assessment,* managers try to foresee the effects of new products and processes on their firm's operations, on other business organizations, and on society in general. With information obtained through a technology assessment, management tries to estimate whether benefits of adopting a specific technology outweigh costs to the firm and to society at large. The degree to which a business is technologically based also influences its managers' response to technology.

Sociocultural Forces

L O 6 To analyze sociocultural issues marketers must deal with as they make decisions

Sociocultural forces are the influences in a society and its culture(s) that bring about changes in people's attitudes, beliefs, norms, customs, and lifestyles. Profoundly affecting how people live, these forces help determine what, where, how, and when people buy products. Like the other environmental forces, sociocultural forces present marketers with both challenges and opportunities. For a closer look at sociocultural forces, we examine three major issues: demographic and diversity characteristics, cultural values, and consumerism.

Demographic and Diversity Characteristics

Changes in a population's demographic characteristics—age, gender, race, ethnicity, marital and parental status, income, and education—have a significant bearing on relationships and individual behavior. These shifts lead to changes in how people live and ultimately in their consumption of such products as food, clothing, housing, transportation, communication, recreation, education, and health services. We look at a few of the changes in demographics and diversity that are affecting marketing activities.

One demographic change that is affecting the marketplace is the increasing proportion of older consumers. According to the U.S. Bureau of the Census, the number

sociocultural forces The influences in a society and its culture(s) that change people's attitudes, beliefs, norms, customs, and lifestyles

Demographic Changes

With more ownership of pets, spending on pet food and pet-care products has grown significantly.

of people age 65 and older is expected to more than double by the year 2050, reaching 87 million.[34] Consequently, marketers can expect significant increases in the demand for health-care services, recreation, tourism, retirement housing, and selected skin-care products. Del Webb Development Company is one firm taking advantage of this opportunity by creating several Sun City retirement communities for mature adults. In addition to providing housing, facilities, and activities designed for older residents, Del Webb's developments are typically situated to take advantage of a location's moderate climate, outdoor opportunities, and proximity to nearby cultural events. To reach older customers effectively, of course, marketers must understand the diversity within the mature market with respect to geographic location, income, marital status, and limitations in mobility and self-care.

The number of singles is also on the rise. Nearly 41 percent of U.S. adults are single, and many plan to remain that way. Moreover, single men who live alone comprise 11 percent of all households (up from 3.5 percent in 1970), and single women who live alone make up nearly 15 percent (up from 7.3 percent in 1970).[35] Single people have quite different spending patterns than couples and families with children. They are less likely to own homes and thus buy less furniture and fewer appliances. They spend more heavily on convenience foods, restaurants, travel, entertainment, and recreation. In addition, they tend to prefer smaller packages, whereas families often buy bulk goods and products packaged in multiple servings.

The United States is entering another baby boom, with nearly 82 million Americans age 19 or younger. The new baby boom represents 27.6 percent of the total population; the original baby boomers, born between 1946 and 1964, account for nearly 25 percent.[36] The children of the original baby boomers differ from one another radically in terms of race, living arrangements, and socioeconomic status. Thus, the newest baby boom is much more diverse than in previous generations.

Another noteworthy population trend is the increasingly multicultural nature of U.S. society. The number of immigrants into the United States has steadily risen during the last 40 years. In the 1960s, 3.3 million people immigrated to the United States; in the 1970s, 4.4 million came here; in the 1980s, 7.3 million arrived; in the 1990s, the United States received 9.1 million immigrants; and thus far in the 2000s, more than 6 million people have immigrated to the United States.[37] In contrast to earlier immigrants, very few recent ones are of European origin. Another reason for the increasing cultural diversification of the United States is that most recent immigrants are relatively young, whereas U.S. citizens of European origin are growing older.

figure 3.3

U.S. POPULATION PROJECTIONS BY RACE

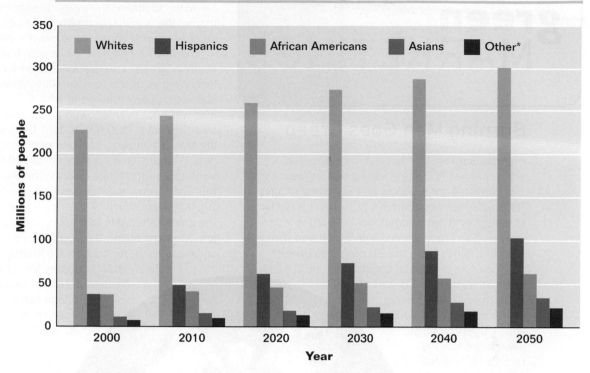

*Includes American Indian, Alaska Native, Native Hawaiian, Other Pacific Islander, and Two or More Races

Source: U.S. Census Bureau, "U.S. Interim Projections by Age, Sex, Race, and Hispanic Origin," Mar. 18, 2004, www.census.gov/ipc/www/usinterimproj/natprojtab01a.pdf.

These younger immigrants tend to have more children than their older counterparts, further shifting the population balance. By the turn of the twentieth century, the U.S. population had shifted from one dominated by whites to one consisting largely of three racial and ethnic groups: whites, blacks, and Hispanics. The U.S. government projects that by the year 2050, more than 102 million Hispanics, 61 million blacks, and 33 million Asians will call the United States home.[38] Figure 3.3 depicts how experts believe the U.S. population will change over the next 50 years.

Marketers recognize that these profound changes in the U.S. population bring unique problems and opportunities. Hispanics, for example, wield about $862 billion in annual buying power, and experts project that figure will grow to $1.2 trillion by 2012.[39] But a diverse population means a more diverse customer base, and marketing practices must be modified—and diversified—to meet its changing needs. The California Milk Processor Board, for example, has been targeting Latinos with Spanish-language campaigns designed to resonate among the diverse Hispanic market, which includes Mexican Americans, Cuban Americans, Puerto Ricans, Dominicans, Salvadorans, and more Hispanic subcultures. The industry group recently moved away from its long-running campaign "Familia, Amor y Leche" ("Family, Love, and Milk") to a more dynamic campaign themed "Toma Leche" ("Drink Milk") to promote the health benefits to younger Latinos.[40]

Cultural Values

Changes in cultural values have dramatically influenced people's needs and desires for products. Although cultural values do not shift overnight, they do change at varying speeds. Marketers try to monitor these changes, knowing this information can equip them to predict changes in consumers' needs for products at least in the near future.

green MARKETING

Burning Man Goes Green

The Burning Man project illustrates the changes in cultural values that influence preferences for products and company images. The first event occurred in 1986 when Larry Harvey and his friend Jerry James built a giant wooden man on San Francisco's Baker Beach and then set it on fire. Since then, the Burning Man project has grown to an annual counterculture gathering in the desert of more than 44,000 people with a budget of $10 million. The Burning Man experience has fostered a unique culture that has led to people banding together nationwide and putting on their own events in an attempt to rekindle the magic the Burning Man community offers.

Each year's Burning Man event follows a different theme chosen by Harvey. In 2007, the theme was "The Green Man," which came out of the festival organizers' desire to offset the 28,000 tons of carbon they estimate the event generates—including from the long flights and drives people make to attend the event. In keeping with the theme, the organization switched to biodiesel generators to provide most of the event's electricity.

The 2007 event also broke with tradition by inviting "green" corporations to exhibit their clean technologies at the festival—but without their logos and without any marketing whatsoever. The companies were not even allowed to demonstrate their own products. They had to turn them over to Burning Man organizers, who demonstrated the products in whatever ways they chose. MMA Renewable Ventures, which funds clean technologies around the world, provided the event's Black Rock City with 270 kilowatts worth of solar cells—enough to light the giant flammable Man itself and power the pavilion. After the event, the company reinstalled the solar panels, at no cost, in the nearby town of Gerlach. MMA's rebates from the state of Nevada were not enough to cover its $1.5 million tab, but the publicity it received more than made up for the difference.

Although the companies were not allowed to market their products at Burning Man, it turns out that letting the products speak for themselves worked for Current TV, Google, and the other companies that were confident their products could market themselves. The companies that took part in the festival demonstrated their recognition that current sociocultural forces highlight consumers' concerned about the future of the world and the importance of the natural environment.[c]

Starting in the late 1980s, issues of health, nutrition, and exercise grew in importance. People today are more concerned about the foods they eat and thus are choosing healthier products. Compared to those in the previous two decades, Americans today are more likely to favor smoke-free environments and to consume less alcohol. They have also altered their sexual behavior to reduce the risk of contracting sexually transmitted diseases. Marketers have responded with a proliferation of foods, beverages, and exercise products that fit this new lifestyle, as well as with programs to help people quit smoking and contraceptives that are safer and more effective. Americans are also becoming increasingly open to alternative medicines and nutritionally improved foods. As a result, sales of organic foods, herbs and herbal remedies, vitamins, and dietary supplements have escalated. In addition to the proliferation of new organic brands, such as Earthbound Farm, Horizon Dairy, and Whole Foods' 365, many conventional marketers have introduced organic versions of their products, including Orville Redenbacher, Heinz, and even Wal-Mart.

The major source of cultural values is the family. For years, when asked about the most important aspects of their lives, adults specified family issues and a happy marriage. Today, however, only one out of three marriages is predicted to last. Values regarding the permanence of marriage are changing. Because a happy marriage is prized so highly, more people are willing to give up an unhappy one and seek a different marriage partner or opt to stay single. Children remain important, however. Marketers have responded with safer, upscale baby gear and supplies, children's electronics, and family entertainment products. Marketers are also aiming more marketing efforts directly at children because children often play pivotal roles in purchasing decisions.

Children and family values are also factors in the trend toward more eat-out and take-out meals. Busy families in which both parents work generally want to spend less time in the kitchen and more time together enjoying themselves. Beneficiaries of this trend have primarily been fast-food and casual restaurants like McDonald's, Taco Bell, and Applebee's, but most supermarkets have added more ready-to-cook and ready-to-serve meal components to meet the needs of busy customers. Some also offer dine-in cafés.

Green marketing helps establish long-term consumer relationships by maintaining, supporting, and enhancing the natural environment. One of society's environmental hurdles is proper disposal of waste, especially of nondegradable materials such as disposable diapers and polystyrene packaging. Companies have responded by developing more environmentally sensitive products and packaging. Procter & Gamble, for example, uses recycled materials in some of its packaging and sells environment-friendly refills. Raytheon has developed a new Amana refrigerator that does not use chlorofluorocarbons (CFCs), which harm the earth's ozone layer. A number of marketers sponsor recycling programs and encourage their customers to take part in them. Many organizations, including America's Electric Utility Companies and Phillips Petroleum, take pride in their efforts to protect the environment.

Consumerism

Consumerism involves organized efforts by individuals, groups, and organizations to protect consumers' rights. The movement's major forces are individual consumer advocates, consumer organizations and other interest groups, consumer education, and consumer laws.

To achieve their objectives, consumers and their advocates write letters or send e-mails to companies, lobby government agencies, broadcast public service announcements, and boycott companies whose activities they deem irresponsible. Consider that most consumers would like to eliminate telemarketing and e-mail spam, and many have joined organizations and groups attempting to stop these activities. Companies that consistently and willfully ignore society's wishes on these issues fuel public desire for a regulatory response.[41] For example, several organizations evaluate children's products for safety, often announcing dangerous products before Christmas so parents can avoid them. Other actions by the consumer movement have resulted in seat belts and air bags in automobiles, dolphin-free tuna, the banning of unsafe three-wheel motorized vehicles, and numerous laws regulating product safety and information. We take a closer look at consumerism in the next chapter.

consumerism Organized efforts by individuals, groups, and organizations to protect consumers' rights

SUMMARY

The marketing environment consists of external forces that directly or indirectly influence an organization's acquisition of inputs (personnel, financial resources, raw materials, and information) and generation of outputs (goods, services, and ideas). The marketing environment includes competitive, economic, political, legal and regulatory, technological, and sociocultural forces.

Environmental scanning is the process of collecting information about forces in the marketing environment; environmental analysis is the process of assessing and interpreting information obtained in scanning. This information helps marketing managers predict opportunities and threats associated with environmental fluctuation. Marketing managers may assume either a passive, reactive approach or a proactive, aggressive approach in responding to these environmental fluctuations. The choice depends on the organization's structures and needs and on the composition of environmental forces that affect it.

All businesses compete for customers' dollars. A marketer, however, generally defines *competition* as other firms that market products that are similar to or can be substituted for its products in the same geographic area. These competitors can be classified into one of four types: brand competitors, product competitors, generic competitors, and total budget competitors. The number of firms controlling the supply of a product may affect the strength of competitors. The four general types of competitive structures are monopoly, oligopoly, monopolistic competition, and pure competition. Marketers monitor what competitors are currently doing and assess changes occurring in the competitive environment.

General economic conditions, buying power, and willingness to spend can strongly influence marketing decisions and activities. The overall state of the economy fluctuates in a general pattern known as the business cycle, which consists of four stages: prosperity, recession, depression, and recovery. Consumers' goods, services, and financial holdings make up their buying power, or ability to purchase. Financial sources of buying power are income, credit, and wealth. After-tax income used for spending or saving is disposable income. Disposable income left after an individual has purchased the basic necessities of food, clothes, and shelter is discretionary income. Factors affecting buyers' willingness to spend include product price; level of satisfaction obtained from currently used products; family size; and expectations about future employment, income, prices, and general economic conditions.

The political, legal, and regulatory forces of the marketing environment are closely interrelated. The political

environment may determine what laws and regulations affecting specific marketers are enacted and how much the government purchases and from which suppliers. It can also be important in helping organizations secure foreign markets.

Federal legislation affecting marketing activities can be divided into procompetitive legislation—laws designed to preserve and encourage competition—and consumer protection laws, which generally relate to product safety and information disclosure. Actual effects of legislation are determined by how marketers and courts interpret the laws. Federal guidelines for sentencing violations of these laws represent an attempt to force marketers to comply with the laws.

Federal, state, and local regulatory agencies usually have power to enforce specific laws and some discretion in establishing operating rules and drawing up regulations to guide certain types of industry practices. Industry self-regulation represents another regulatory force; marketers view this type of regulation more favorably than government action because they have more opportunity to take part in creating guidelines. Self-regulation may be less expensive than government regulation, and its guidelines are generally more realistic. However, such regulation generally cannot ensure compliance as effectively as government agencies.

Technology is the application of knowledge and tools to solve problems and perform tasks more efficiently. Consumer demand, product development, packaging, promotion, prices, and distribution systems are all influenced directly by technology.

Sociocultural forces are the influences in a society and its culture that result in changes in attitudes, beliefs, norms, customs, and lifestyles. Major sociocultural issues directly affecting marketers include demographic and diversity characteristics, cultural values, and consumerism.

Changes in a population's demographic characteristics, such as age, income, race, and ethnicity, can lead to changes in that population's consumption of products. Changes in cultural values, such as those relating to health, nutrition, family, and the natural environment, have had striking effects on people's needs for products and therefore are closely monitored by marketers. Consumerism involves the efforts of individuals, groups, and organizations to protect consumers' rights. Consumer rights organizations inform and organize other consumers, raise issues, help businesses develop consumer-oriented programs, and pressure lawmakers to enact consumer protection laws.

IMPORTANT TERMS

Environmental
 scanning, 64
Environmental
 analysis, 64
Competition, 66
Brand competitors, 66
Product competitors, 66
Generic competitors, 66
Total budget
 competitors, 66

Monopoly, 67
Oligopoly, 68
Monopolistic
 competition, 69
Pure competition, 69
Business cycle, 69
Prosperity, 70
Recession, 70
Depression, 70
Recovery, 70

Buying power, 70
Income, 70
Disposable income, 70
Discretionary
 income, 71
Wealth, 71
Willingness to
 spend, 72
Federal Trade Commission
 (FTC), 76

Better Business Bureau
 (BBB), 78
National Advertising
 Review Board
 (NARB), 79
Technology, 79
Sociocultural
 forces, 81
Consumerism, 85

DISCUSSION & REVIEW QUESTIONS

1. Why are environmental scanning and analysis important to marketers?

2. What are the four types of competition? Which is most important to marketers?

3. In what ways can each of the business cycle stages affect consumers' reactions to marketing strategies?

4. What business cycle stage are we experiencing currently? How is this stage affecting business firms in your area?

5. Define *income, disposable income,* and *discretionary income.* How does each type of income affect consumer buying power?

6. How do wealth and consumer credit affect consumer buying power?

7. What factors influence a buyer's willingness to spend?

8. Describe marketers' attempts to influence political forces.

9. What types of problems do marketers experience as they interpret legislation?

10. What are the goals of the Federal Trade Commission? List the ways in which the FTC affects marketing activities. Do you think a single regulatory agency should have such broad jurisdiction over so many marketing practices? Why or why not?

11. Name several nongovernmental regulatory forces. Do you believe self-regulation is more or less effective than governmental regulatory agencies? Why?

12. What does the term *technology* mean to you? Do the benefits of technology outweigh its costs and potential dangers? Defend your answer.

13. Discuss the impact of technology on marketing activities.

14. What factors determine whether a business organization adopts and uses technology?

15. What evidence exists that cultural diversity is increasing in the United States?

16. In what ways are cultural values changing? How are marketers responding to these changes?

17. Describe consumerism. Analyze some active consumer forces in your area.

APPLICATION QUESTIONS

1. Assume you are opening one of the following retail stores. Identify publications at the library or online that provide information about the environmental forces likely to affect the store. Briefly summarize the information each source provides.

   a. Convenience store

   b. Women's clothing store

   c. Grocery store

   d. Fast-food restaurant

   e. Furniture store

2. For each of the following products, identify brand competitors, product competitors, generic competitors, and total budget competitors.

   a. Dodge Caravan minivan

   b. Levi's jeans

   c. America Online

3. Technological advances and sociocultural forces have a great impact on marketers. Identify at least one technological advance and one sociocultural change that has affected you as a consumer. Explain the impact of each change on your needs as a customer.

INTERNET EXERCISE

Visit **www.cengage.com/marketing/pride-ferrell** for resources to help you master the material in this chapter, plus materials that will help you expand your marketing knowledge, including Internet exercise updates, ACE Self-Tests, hotlinks to companies featured in this chapter, and much more.

The Federal Trade Commission

To learn more about the Federal Trade Commission and its functions, look at the FTC's website at **www.ftc.gov.**

1. Based on information on the website, describe the FTC's impact on marketing.

2. Examine the sections entitled Newsroom and Formal Actions. Describe three recent incidents of illegal or inappropriate marketing activities and the FTC's response to those actions.

3. How could the FTC's website assist a company in avoiding misconduct?

developing your MARKETING PLAN

A marketing strategy is dynamic. Companies must constantly monitor the marketing environment not only to create their marketing strategy but to revise it if necessary. Information about various forces in the marketplace is collected, analyzed, and used as a foundation for several marketing plan decisions. The following questions will help you to understand how the information in this chapter contributes to the development of your marketing plan.

1. Describe the current competitive market for your product. Can you identify the number of brands or market share they hold? Expand your analysis to include other products that are similar or could be substituted for yours.

2. Using the business cycle pattern, in which of the four stages is the current state of the economy? Can you identify any changes in consumer buying power that would affect the sale and use of your product?

3. Referring to Tables 3.2 and 3.3, do you recognize any laws or regulatory agencies that would have jurisdiction over your type of product?

4. Conduct a brief technology assessment, determining the impact that technology has on your product, its sale, or use.

5. Discuss how your product could be affected by changes in social attitudes, demographic characteristics, or lifestyles.

The information obtained from these questions should assist you in developing various aspects of your marketing plan found in the *Interactive Marketing Plan* exercise at **www.cengage.com/marketing/pride-ferrell.**

globalEDGE

1. Free trade influences the global marketing environment in many ways. Though contingent on the by-laws of a specific free trade agreement, such contracts between countries typically increase the number of competitors from abroad contending with current players in the market. The Free Trade Area of the Americas (FTAA) is one such example. More information about this trade agreement can be found using the search term "FTAA" at **http://globaledge.msu.edu/ibrd** to access the FTAA. How many FTAA members are there? Besides the United States, which are the most prominent members? Are there any countries that are conspicuously absent?

2. Globalization is a phenomenon that is affecting many countries. As a result, your firm is attempting to define its own role in a globalizing environment with a particular focus on western Europe. Public opinion regarding the globalization trend is likely to influence many competitive and market forces worldwide for a prolonged period of time. To gain valuable information about attitudes toward globalization in western European countries, use the search term "public opinion analysis" at **http://globaledge.msu.edu/ibrd** to access the Eurobarometer website and follow the Globalization link. To help your firm develop its European marketing strategy, identify the top two markets that support globalization and the top four markets that oppose globalization. From these results, what conclusions do you draw in your effort to enter these markets?

Organic Valley Responds to a Changing Environment

Founded in 1988, Organic Valley is one of the nation's largest organic dairy cooperatives with 1,266 farm families in 28 states. Organic Valley works with small, independent organic dairy farmers, ensuring a high standard of quality and a fair price for farmer output.

Paul Deutsch of Sweet Ridge Organic Dairy Farm is one of these farmers. After working for some time at a conventional commercial dairy farm, Deutsch became fed up over the miserable conditions of the animals, the drugs administered to animals, and the huge amount of pollution that the factory farms caused. And, ultimately, he determined that large conventional farms produced an inferior product with less taste and less nutritional value. Deutsch purchased his own land so he could work on his own terms—cultivating healthier land and happier, healthier, more productive cows. By the late 1990s he was certified organic and soon after became a member of the Organic Valley co-op. Deutsch now benefits from the good reputation and extensive distribution channels of Organic Valley as well as the large network of knowledge and support of fellow organic farmers.

While the life of an organic farmer is not an easy one—keeping plants and animals healthy without resorting to chemicals can be labor intensive and complicated—marketing and selling organic products is growing easier by the day. Changing consumer attitudes toward organic products profoundly affect how, when, where, and what people purchase. As more news comes out about salmonella-tainted vegetables, infected meat, and the harmful environmental effects of conventional farming, more and more people are going organic. The media coverage of the potential harm of conventionally grown foods has acted like an endorsement of organic products as the safer, more nutritious, and more environmentally friendly alternative. In fact, the entire organic industry has enjoyed 20 percent annual growth rates for over a decade, while organic dairy has exceeded that with 27 percent annual growth. Farmers' markets have never been so popular. Organic grocers, like Whole Foods, are as large as and more profitable than conventional supermarkets. Organic food brands, once available only in specialty shops and health food stores, are showing up in all supermarkets. Also, the farmers often benefit from higher profit margins and healthier, chemical-free work environments.

While organic has not caught on in all parts of the country, it is a growing trend that has afforded the likes of Paul Deutsch a means of doing what he loves while supplying the marketplace with nutritious, safe products. Consumer demand is driving the expansion of the organic industry and providing brands like Organic Valley with increased distribution opportunities. Because Organic Valley is a cooperative, as it expands and takes on new members, farmers like Deutsch can directly benefit from growth of Organic Valley as well as the industry at large. The cooperative model also encourages collaboration, not competition, between other members of the co-op. For example, to learn from each other, Deutsch and other farmers in the region get together periodically to share advice, knowledge, and methods so that they can all benefit from the best practices of their peers.

Organic Valley and other co-ops like it are concerned not only about the health of the cows and the environment but also with the well-being of small farmers and their communities. To meet these means, the Organic Valley cooperative has developed a profit-sharing model wherein farmers and employees each receive 45 percent of the profits and their communities receive the remaining 10 percent. This model not only builds loyal producers; it also encourages a growing base of loyal consumers as more people recognize the health benefits of organic and the good things the company does for small farming communities. These current sociocultural trends are providing opportunities for Organic Valley and all of its co-op members.

As more news emerges daily about food-related health scares, diminished nutritional value of conventionally produced foods, environmental damage wrought by pesticides, and other dire topics, Paul Deutsch and company are able to look forward to using organic dairy products as a competitive advantage.[42]

Questions for Discussion

1. Has Organic Valley differentiated its product offerings from traditional dairies?
2. How has Organic Valley benefited from changing attitudes of the health-conscious consumer toward food products?
3. Why do you think a growing market segment of consumers is willing to pay more for organic foods?

CASE 3.2

First Solar Turns Sunshine into Profits

With skyrocketing oil prices that reached new highs, and the world recognizing that alternative energy has become a responsible and economical alternative to fossil fuels, 2007 was a watershed year for First Solar, which designs, manufactures, and markets solar energy products. From its inception in 1999, the Phoenix-based company was funded by the Walton family of Wal-Mart fame, which still owns a majority of the firm's stock. First Solar has taken advantage of environmental opportunities to harness the sun to provide alternative energy, in the form of cadmium telluride solar cells and panels, allowing it to lock in more than $6 billion worth of contracts over the next five years. The company's profits jumped from $4.3 million in 2006 to $46 million in 2007, and its stock likewise accelerated almost 1,000 percent in value. This success comes from being in tune with changes in both the physical and social environment. The opportunity for making a profit with alternative energy has arrived around the world.

First Solar is committed to improving the global natural environment, as well as the health and safety of employees, customers, and communities. By marketing cost-efficient solar energy solutions, the company helps reduce our dependence on fossil fuels and other conventional energy solutions drawn from raw materials. The company produces a perpetually renewable energy resource that reduces harmful air emissions and removes solid waste from the environment. It also engages in continuous improvement in the environmental quality of its products, processes, and services.

Among First Solar's products are modules designed for use in large-scale, grid-connected solar power plants that are sold to leading solar project developers for use in commercial projects. First Solar engineers therefore work closely with the firm's project development partners to design the optimal balance of systems and solutions that can produce solar energy efficiently. The foundation of First Solar's main product is a crystalline thin-film structure that employs a cadmium telluride semiconductor material to convert sunlight into electrical energy. Because this product is not dependent on the silicon wafers used by most of the solar industry, First Solar is well positioned ahead of its competition because silicon is in short supply and quite expensive, creating a bottleneck for the rest of the industry. This advantage enables the company to move aggressively forward with its production capabilities and to serve markets that are undersupplied.

First Solar is growing rapidly because it is now targeting the U.S. utility market, where solar products that are installed on commercial and residential rooftops are in high demand. To that end, First Solar recently purchased Turner Renewable Energy LLC, which markets solar systems to utility companies, thereby opening up the consumer utility market for First Solar. This move brings solar energy into the mainstream of helping to generate electricity that can reach everyone, not just those individuals and businesses that have their own solar generators.

Until recently, First Solar's primary market production was in Germany. Europe remains slightly ahead of the United States in concern for renewable energy alternatives and recognition of the need to reduce pollution associated with fossil fuels. Today, the company operates production facilities in the United States, Germany,

and Malaysia. By maintaining a global perspective, the company can take advantage of both marketing and production opportunities to achieve maximum efficiency and market penetration. First Solar is strategically positioned to use technology associated with its cadmium telluride cells and market knowledge to become a market leader in the emerging alternative energy industry. In the future, the company will have to maintain environmental assessments related to competition, fossil fuel prices, new solar technology innovations, and the willingness of businesses and consumers to adopt renewable energy practices that will contribute to the world's concern for a clean and healthful environment. If the trend continues, First Solar will be a name that everyone will recognize.[43]

Questions for Discussion

1. Which marketing environment forces are likely to have the greatest impact on First Solar?
2. What types of organizations are most likely to exert the strongest competitive forces on First Solar?
3. How did technology affect First Solar's responses to the changes in the marketing environment? How can it continue to maintain its technological edge in its industry?

4 Social Responsibility and Ethics in Marketing

Entrepreneurs Fight Hunger with Plumpy'nut

More than 850 million people live in a state of hunger today, and malnutrition kills more people annually than AIDS, malaria, and tuberculosis combined. The majority of malnourished people live in the developing world, especially India, and sub-Saharan Africa. Nutriset, a French private company founded by former African aid worker Michel Lescanne, has been selling food products to combat hunger and malnutrition since 1986. The firm's mandate is to make products accessible and available to enhance the nutritional status of children and other vulnerable people. In 1998 the company launched "Plumpy'nut," a true revolution in the management of severe malnutrition.

Plumpy'nut is a thick, brown paste made from ground peanuts, sugar, and powdered milk and is fortified with vitamins. It is similar to Nutella, the chocolate-hazelnut spread that is popular in Europe. One 3-ounce packet of Plumpy'nut delivers 500 calories, so severely malnourished children can thrive on just three or four packets a day. It does not require clean water for dilution and can easily be consumed by a child without assistance from her mother or aid workers. Plumpy'nut isn't perishable, it does not require refrigeration, and its small size and weight make it is easy to transport.

Niger has become Plumpy'nut's proving ground. A day's worth of product costs about $1, and Nutriset has partnered with local entrepreneurs to make the product locally, even using local ingredients when possible. The nonprofit organization Doctors Without Borders helps distribute Plumpy'nut to the children who need it. The organization can distribute a week's supply of Plumpy'nut to mothers, who can then serve it to their children at home. Mothers and caregivers come every week to get another week's supply, and the children are weighed. The program's success rate has been significant, with hospitals that previously had more patients than beds now reporting empty beds. But Plumpy'nut can help only if children get it early enough. Unfortunately, children are still dying of malnutrition when parents wait too long before bringing their children into the hospitals. According to Doctors Without Borders' Dr. Milton Tectonidis, if the United States and the European Union were willing to spend part of their food aid on Plumpy'nut, more companies would be willing to make it. Tectonidis believes that just a minuscule portion of the global food aid budget would have a huge impact.

Nutriset reinvests 80 percent of its profit—about $2.5 million last year—into developing new products. The company is partnering with entrepreneurs in the Democratic Republic of Congo, Ethiopia, Malawi, and Niger to produce Plumpy'nut locally. These nonprofit African entities will serve as franchisees that will use less-expensive local ingredients for their Plumpy'nut recipe. Nutriset has found a way to combine entrepreneurship and social responsibility to earn profits.[1]

Most marketers operate responsibly and within the limits of the law, and some, like Nutriset, attempt to go beyond society's expectations for a for-profit business. Some companies, however, engage in activities that customers, other marketers, and society in general deem unacceptable. Such activities include questionable selling practices, bribery, price discrimination, deceptive advertising, misleading packaging, and marketing defective products. Deceptive advertising in particular causes consumers to become defensive toward all promotional messages and distrustful of all advertising, so it hurts not only the consumers but the marketers as well.[2] Practices of this kind raise questions about marketers' obligations to society. Inherent in these questions are the issues of social responsibility and marketing ethics.

Because social responsibility and ethics often have profound impacts on the success of marketing strategies, we devote this chapter to their role in marketing decision making. We begin by defining social responsibility and exploring its dimensions. We then discuss social responsibility issues, such as the natural environment and the marketer's role as a member of the community. Next, we define and examine the role of ethics in marketing decisions. We consider ethical issues in marketing, the ethical decision-making process, and ways to improve ethical conduct in marketing. Finally, we incorporate social responsibility and ethics into strategic market planning.

The Nature of Social Responsibility

L O 1 To understand the concept and dimensions of social responsibility

social responsibility An organization's obligation to maximize its positive impact and minimize its negative impact on society

In marketing, **social responsibility** refers to an organization's obligation to maximize its positive impact and minimize its negative impact on society. Social responsibility thus deals with the total effect of all marketing decisions on society. In marketing, social responsibility includes the managerial processes needed to monitor, satisfy, and even exceed stakeholder expectations and needs.[3] Remember from Chapter 1 that stakeholders are groups that have a "stake," or claim, in some aspect of a company's products, operations, markets, industry, and outcomes. CEOs such as Indra Nooyi, chairman and CEO of PepsiCo, are increasingly recognizing that in the future companies will have to "do better by doing better." She says, in harmony with "employees, regulators, consumers, customers, communities, and many other stakeholders, it will leave no doubt that performance without purpose is not a long-term sustainable formula."[4]

Ample evidence demonstrates that ignoring stakeholders' demands for responsible marketing can destroy customers' trust and even prompt government regulations. Irresponsible actions that anger customers, employees, or competitors may not only jeopardize a marketer's financial standing but have legal repercussions as well. For instance, Purdue Pharma, the marketer of the painkiller OxyContin®, and three executives pled guilty to criminal charges of misleading consumers and physicians after the company aggressively promoted the painkiller as being less likely to be abused than traditional narcotic medicines because of its time-release formulation. However, the drug quickly became a highly abused narcotic, and the prosecutors in the case blamed Purdue Pharma's marketing practices for rising crime rates, teen drug addiction, deaths, and other problems. The company paid $600 million in criminal fines, and the three executives paid a total of $34.5 million in fines. The company had already spent years and hundreds of millions of dollars fighting lawsuits from addicted patients.[5] In contrast, socially responsible activities can generate positive publicity and boost sales. The Breast Cancer Awareness Crusade sponsored by Avon Products, for example, has helped raise nearly $450 million to fund

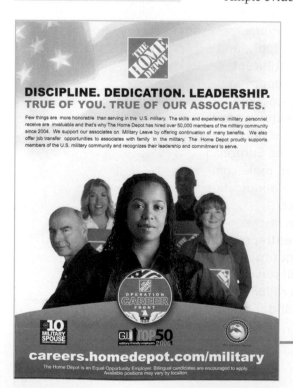

The Nature of Social Responsibility
The Home Depot recognizes its social responsibility in hiring over 50,000 members of the military community over the past several years.

community-based breast cancer education and early-detection services. Within the first few years of the Awareness Crusade, hundreds of stories about Avon's efforts appeared in major media, which contributed to an increase in company sales. Avon, a marketer of women's cosmetics, is also known for employing a large number of women and promoting them to top management; the firm has more female top managers (86 percent) than any other Fortune 500 company.[6]

Socially responsible efforts like Avon's and Nutriset's have a positive impact on local communities; at the same time, they indirectly help the sponsoring organization by attracting goodwill, publicity, and potential customers and employees. Thus, although social responsibility is certainly a positive concept in itself, most organizations embrace it in the expectation of indirect long-term benefits. Our own research suggests that an organizational culture that is conducive to social responsibility engenders greater employee commitment and improved business performance.[7] Table 4.1 provides a sampling of companies that have chosen to make social responsibility a strategic long-term objective.

table 4.1	BUSINESS ETHICS' BEST CORPORATE CITIZENS 2007
1	Green Mountain Coffee Roasters, Inc.
2	Advanced Micro Devices, Inc.
3	NIKE, Inc.
4	Motorola, Inc.
5	Intel Corporation
6	IBM
7	Agilent Technologies, Inc.
8	Timberland Company (The)
9	Starbucks Corporation
10	General Mills Incorporated
11	Salesforce.com, Inc.
12	Applied Materials, Inc.
13	Texas Instruments Incorporated
14	Hermand Miller, Inc.
15	Rockwell Collins
16	Interface, Inc.
17	Steelcase, Inc.
18	Dell, Inc.
19	Cisco Systems, Inc.
20	Lam Research Corporation

Source: From "100 Best Corporate Citizens 2007" in CRO Magazine, February 14, 2007. Reprinted by permission of the publisher, Crossing Media LL, via Forster Reprints.

figure 4.1

THE PYRAMID OF CORPORATE SOCIAL RESPONSIBILITY

RESPONSIBILITIES

Philanthropic
Be a good corporate citizen
▶ Contribute resources to the community; improve quality of life

Ethical
Be ethical
▶ Obligation to do what is right, just, and fair
▶ Avoid harm

Legal
Obey the law
▶ Law is society's codification of right and wrong
▶ Play by the rules of the game

Economic
Be profitable
▶ The foundation upon which all others rest

The Dimensions of Social Responsibility

Socially responsible organizations strive for **marketing citizenship** by adopting a strategic focus for fulfilling the economic, legal, ethical, and philanthropic social responsibilities that their stakeholders expect of them. Companies that consider the diverse perspectives of stakeholders in their daily operations and strategic planning are said to have a *stakeholder orientation,* an important element of social responsibility.[8] A stakeholder orientation in marketing goes beyond customers, competitors, and regulators to include understanding and addressing the needs of all stakeholders, including communities and special-interest groups. As a result, organizations are now under pressure to undertake initiatives that demonstrate a balanced perspective on stakeholder interests.[9] Pfizer, for example, has secured stakeholder input on a number of issues including rising health-care costs and health-care reform.[10] As Figure 4.1 shows, the economic, legal, ethical, and philanthropic dimensions of social responsibility can be viewed as a pyramid.[11] The economic and legal aspects have long been acknowledged, whereas ethical and philanthropic issues have gained recognition more recently.

At the most basic level, all companies have an economic responsibility to be profitable so they can provide a return on investment to their owners and investors, create jobs for the community, and contribute goods and services to the economy. How organizations relate to shareholders, employees, competitors, customers, the community, and the natural environment affects the economy. When economic downturns or poor decisions lead companies to lay off employees, communities often suffer as they attempt to absorb the displaced employees. Customers may experience diminished levels of service as a result of fewer experienced employees. Stock prices often decline when layoffs are announced, reducing the value of shareholders' investment portfolios. Moreover, stressed-out employees facing demands to reduce expenses may make poor decisions that affect the natural environment, product quality, employee rights, and customer service. An organization's sense of economic responsibility is especially significant for employees, raising such issues as equal job opportunities, workplace diversity, job safety, health, and employee privacy. Economic

marketing citizenship The adoption of a strategic focus for fulfilling the economic, legal, ethical, and philanthropic social responsibilities expected by stakeholders

DON'T THROW ANYTHING AWAY.
THERE IS NO AWAY.

The Dimensions of Social Responsibility

Shell recognizes its environmental responsibilities through recycling programs and efforts to reduce greenhouse gases.

marketing ethics Principles and standards that define acceptable marketing conduct as determined by various stakeholders

responsibilities require finding a balance between society's demand for social responsibility and investors' desire for profits.

Marketers also have an economic responsibility to compete fairly. Size frequently gives companies an advantage over rivals. Large firms can often generate economies of scale that allow them to put smaller firms out of business. Consequently small companies and even whole communities may resist the efforts of firms like Wal-Mart, Home Depot, and Best Buy to open stores in their vicinity. These firms are able to operate at such low costs that small, local firms find it difficult to compete. Though consumers appreciate lower prices, the failure of small businesses creates unemployment for some members of the community. Such issues create concerns about social responsibility for organizations, communities, and consumers.

Marketers are also expected, of course, to obey laws and regulations. The efforts of elected representatives and special-interest groups to promote responsible corporate behavior have resulted in laws and regulations designed to keep U.S. companies' actions within the range of acceptable conduct. When marketers engage in deceptive practices to advance their own interests over those of others, charges of fraud may result. In general, fraud is any purposeful communication that deceives, manipulates, or conceals facts to create a false impression. It is considered a crime, and convictions may result in fines, imprisonment, or both. Fraud costs U.S. companies more than $600 billion a year; the average company loses about 6 percent of total revenues to fraud and abuses committed by its own employees.[12]

When customers, interest groups, or businesses become outraged over what they perceive as irresponsibility on the part of a marketing organization, they may urge their legislators to draft new legislation to regulate the behavior or engage in litigation to force the organization to "play by the rules." Procter & Gamble, for example, filed a lawsuit against Blue Cross Laboratories, accusing the smaller firm of copying the packaging of its Herbal Essences shampoos and conditioners and mimicking its brand name with Blue Cross's brand name, Herbal Passion. The suit seeks to have Blue Cross cease distribution of its product, recall existing inventory from store shelves, and destroy its bottle molds to avoid packaging that too closely resembles Herbal Essences'.[13]

Economic and legal responsibilities are the most basic levels of social responsibility for a good reason: failure to consider them may mean that a marketer is not around long enough to engage in ethical or philanthropic activities. Beyond these dimensions is **marketing ethics,** principles and standards that define acceptable conduct in marketing as determined by various stakeholders, including the public, government regulators, private-interest groups, consumers, industry, and the organization itself. The most basic of these principles have been codified as laws and regulations to encourage marketers to conform to society's expectations for conduct. However, marketing ethics goes beyond legal issues. Ethical marketing decisions foster trust, which helps build long-term marketing relationships. We take a more detailed look at the ethical dimension of social responsibility later in this chapter.

At the top of the pyramid of corporate responsibility (see Figure 4.1) are philanthropic responsibilities. These responsibilities, which go beyond marketing ethics, are not required of a company, but they promote human welfare or goodwill, as do the economic, legal, and ethical dimensions of social responsibility. That many companies have demonstrated philanthropic responsibility is evidenced by the nearly $13 billion in annual corporate donations and contributions to environmental and social causes.[14] After natural disasters such as Hurricane Katrina and the California wildfires, for example, many corporations—including Anheuser-Busch, BP, Capitol One, AT&T, DuPont, General Motors, Lowe's, Office Depot, Toyota, and Wal-Mart—have donated millions of dollars in cash, supplies, equipment, food, and medicine to help victims. Even small companies participate in philanthropy through donations

RESPONSIBLE marketing?

Many companies today engage in significant social responsibility activities. Avon raises money for breast cancer research, many homebuilders work with Habitat for Humanity (donating materials and employee time), Starbucks invests in fair trade activities, and other companies transfer significant corporate dollars to social activities with little concern for shareholders' interests. If foundational economists were to discuss the positives and negatives of these CSR activities, they would weigh heavily on the negative side, noting that this raises the cost of doing business and lowers corporate productivity. On the positive side, billions of dollars are being allocated to worthy social causes, impacting the greater overall good of our society.

Should consumers be allowed to buy products that are devoid of a heavy social cost and make decisions to give on an individual basis? Massachusetts gave taxpayers the option of donating to social services by simply checking a box on their tax return. The message that came back was clear: $100 million was generated for social services. What if Dell sold one notebook computer for $1,000 and the same computer for $1,150, with the notation that the purchase of this computer would support the fight against AIDS around the world? Dell and Microsoft recently created products for the Product (Red) campaign, joining other large corporate companies such as The Gap, Apple, and Motorola in support of The Global Fund, an international organization devoted to fighting AIDS, tuberculosis, and malaria. How many consumers do you think would support the companies' AIDS donation from their product purchases? How many would prefer to purchase a less-expensive product and just donate the money themselves? Should consumers have the right to decide if they support the social causes of a company, or should companies assume that many consumers are not as charitable as they could be and make these decisions for them?[a]

Who Pays for Corporate Social Responsibility Activities: The Economic Issue

ISSUE: Who should pay for corporate social responsibility activities?

and volunteer support of local causes and national charities, such as the Red Cross and the United Way. Boston-based Dancing Deer Baking, for example, uses environmentally friendly packaging for its scones, cookies, brownies, and cakes, and it donates 35 percent of the profits from its Sweet Home cakes to Boston nonprofits that help homeless people find jobs and housing.[15]

More companies than ever are adopting a strategic approach to corporate philanthropy. Many firms link their products to a particular social cause on an ongoing or short-term basis, a practice known as **cause-related marketing**. The Campbell Soup Company, for example, temporarily changed the iconic red and white labels on its best-selling chicken noodle and tomato soups to pink and white to support National Breast Cancer Awareness Month. The company donated $300,000 to the several charities that support breast cancer research and awareness initiatives.[16] Such cause-related programs tend to appeal to consumers because they provide an additional reason to "feel good" about a particular purchase. Marketers like the programs because well-designed ones increase sales and create feelings of respect and admiration for the companies involved. Indeed, research suggests that such corporate support of causes generates trust in a company for 80 percent of those surveyed.[17]

Some companies are beginning to extend the concept of corporate philanthropy beyond financial contributions by adopting a **strategic philanthropy** approach, the synergistic use of organizational core competencies and resources to address key stakeholders' interests and achieve both organizational and social benefits. Strategic philanthropy involves employees, organizational resources and expertise, and the ability to link those assets to the concerns of key stakeholders, including employees, customers, suppliers, and social needs. Strategic philanthropy involves both financial and nonfinancial contributions to stakeholders (employee time, goods and services, and company technology and equipment, as well as facilities), but it also benefits the company.[18] Home Depot, for example, has been progressive in aligning its expertise and resources to address community needs. Its relationship with Habitat for Humanity gives employees a chance to improve their skills and bring direct knowledge back into the workplace to benefit customers. It also enhances Home Depot's image of expertise as the "do-it-yourself" center. Home Depot also responds to customers' needs during disasters such as hurricanes. During natural disasters, some homebuilding supply and hardware stores have taken advantage of customers by inflating prices on emergency materials, but Home Depot opens its stores 24 hours a day and makes materials available at reduced costs to help customers survive the disaster.[19]

Social Responsibility Issues

Although social responsibility may seem to be an abstract ideal, managers make decisions related to social responsibility every day. To be successful, a business must

cause-related marketing
The practice of linking products to a particular social cause on an ongoing or short-term basis

strategic philanthropy The synergistic use of organizational core competencies and resources to address key stakeholders' interests and achieve both organizational and social benefits

table 4.2   SOCIAL RESPONSIBILITY ISSUES

Issue	Description	Major Social Concerns
Natural environment	Consumers insisting not only on a good quality of life but on a healthful environment so they can maintain a high standard of living during their lifetimes	Conservation Water pollution Air pollution Land pollution
Consumerism	Activities undertaken by independent individuals, groups, and organizations to protect their rights as consumers	The right to safety The right to be informed The right to choose The right to be heard
Community relations	Society eager to have marketers contribute to its well-being, wishing to know what marketers do to help solve social problems	Equality issues Disadvantaged members of society Safety and health Education and general welfare

determine what customers, government regulators, and competitors, as well as society in general, want or expect in terms of social responsibility. Table 4.2 summarizes three major categories of social responsibility issues: the natural environment, consumerism, and community relations.

The Natural Environment. One of the more common ways marketers demonstrate social responsibility is through programs designed to protect and preserve the natural environment. Many companies are making contributions to environmental protection organizations, sponsoring and participating in cleanup events, promoting recycling, retooling manufacturing processes to minimize waste and pollution, and generally reevaluating the effects of their products on the natural environment. Procter & Gamble, for example, uses recycled materials in some of its packaging and sells refills for some products, which reduces packaging waste. Wal-Mart provides on-site recycling for customers and encourages its suppliers to reduce wasteful packaging. It has also opened "green" prototype stores in McKinney, Texas, and Aurora, Colorado, that use wind power to generate electricity, harvest rainwater, and offer many other environmentally friendly and energy-saving features. The company has also pledged to sharply reduce its energy use, emissions, and waste; encourage its suppliers to offer more eco-friendly products and packaging; and encourage consumers to buy greener products such as compact fluorescent lightbulbs.[20] Such efforts generate positive publicity and often increase sales for the companies involved.

Green marketing is a strategic process involving stakeholder assessment to create meaningful long-term relationships with customers while maintaining, supporting, and enhancing the natural environment. Toyota, Honda, and Ford, for example, have succeeded in marketing "hybrid" cars that use electric motors to augment their internal-combustion engines, improving the vehicles' fuel economy without reducing their power. Benjamin Moore & Co. has introduced a new line of paint called Aura that emits only about one-third as much in harmful volatile organic compounds (VOCs) as regular paint does.[21] New Leaf Paper has taken a leadership role in the paper-production industry, producing paper made from 50–100 percent postconsumer waste instead of virgin tree pulp. The small firm's success has forced many larger competitors to introduce their own sustainable paper products. The growing trend of recycled papers is saving trees and reducing the amount of solid waste going into landfills.[22]

Many products have been certified as "green" by environmental organizations such as Green Seal and carry a special logo identifying their organization as green marketers. Lumber products at Home Depot, for example, may carry a seal from the Forest Stewardship Council to indicate they were harvested from sustainable forests using environmentally friendly methods.[23] Likewise, most Chiquita bananas are certified through the Rainforest Alliance's Better Banana Project as having been

green marketing A strategic process involving stakeholder assessment to create meaningful long-term relationships with customers while maintaining, supporting, and enhancing the natural environment

green MARKETING

Levi's Blue Jeans Go Green

Levi Strauss & Co. has long been known for its 501 jeans and affordable prices. Recently, the venerable company has moved into the premium denim market—dominated by brands such as Earl Jeans, Seven for All Mankind, Citizens for Humanity, and True Religion—by launching its Premium collection. Now, in an attempt to exploit yet another strategic window and hot market, Levi's is going green as part of an eco-friendly marketing campaign.

Thanks in part to the popularity of Al Gore's documentary *An Inconvenient Truth*, consumers are more determined than ever before to go green. According to the research group Mintel, about 35 million people in the United States regularly purchase eco-friendly products. Consumers also seem more willing to pay more for earth-friendly products and services. As a result, a growing number of companies are going to great lengths to demonstrate that they are part of the green movement. Many are switching to earth-friendly packaging and/or new production processes that conserve energy and resources. Following this environmentally friendly marketing strategy, Levi's is producing 100 percent organic cotton jeans.

These new jeans, priced at $250 each (or $125 a leg), are made with 100 percent organic cotton, natural dyes, and even recycled rivets to hold the jeans together. Even the signature-attached tags are made from recycled paper and soy ink. The company is also introducing less-expensive lines that include some organic and recycled materials.

Although many of us might be willing to switch to "green" jeans, the price may be harder to take. This is due to the organic cotton that is used to make the jeans. Because the demand for organic cotton is greater than the supply, procuring organic cotton for jeans is expensive. To be certified as "organic," cotton cannot be genetically modified, and it must be pesticide and fungicide free. However, more than 50 percent of cotton grown in the United States is genetically modified. Many companies are getting their organic cotton from overseas farmers, but certification in other countries can be challenging. As of 2007, organic cotton comprised less than 1 percent of the world's cotton supply. For now, Levi's can produce only a limited number of green jeans with a hefty price tag.

However, the very issue that drives up prices can be used as a marketing strategy. Many buyers are willing to pay more to support farmers who are committed to harvesting through organic methods. In fact, at the 2007 Cannes Lions International Advertising Festival, "eco-marketing" was an extremely popular topic. Consumers are excited about eco-friendly products, and companies are spending a lot of their promotion budgets to tout their stances on the natural environment. According to TNS Media Intelligence, marketers spent $18 million on eco-focused television advertising in one three-month time span.

Although eco-responsible marketing is a hot topic, it seems likely to gain more and more traction. According to the Organic Trade Association, U.S. organic retail sales have grown between 20 to 24 percent annually since 1990. Levi's is giving consumers what they want, and consumers are willing to pay the price. The green jeans are satisfying a unique but growing market demand.[b]

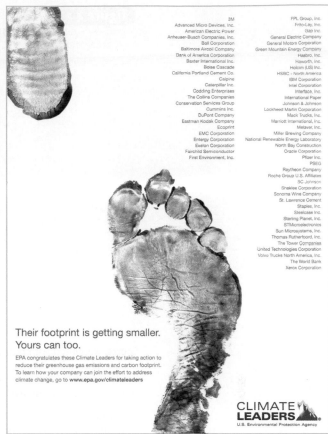

Green Marketing

Hertz offers hybrid automobiles in its rental car fleet as part of its "Green Collection."

The EPA recognizes companies as "Climate Leaders" who reduce their carbon footprint and control greenhouse gas emissions.

grown with more environmentally and labor-friendly practices.[24] In Europe, companies can voluntarily apply for the European Eco-label to indicate that their products are less harmful to the environment than competing products, based on scientifically determined criteria (see Figure 4.2).

Although demand for economic, legal, and ethical solutions to environmental problems is widespread, the environmental movement in marketing includes many different groups whose values and goals often conflict. Some environmentalists and marketers believe companies should work to protect and preserve the natural environment by implementing the following goals:

1. *Eliminate the concept of waste.* Recognizing that pollution and waste usually stem from inefficiency, the question is not what to do with waste but how to make things without waste.

2. *Reinvent the concept of a product.* Products should be reduced to only three types and eventually just two. The first type is consumables, which are eaten or, when placed in the ground, turn into soil with few harmful side effects. The second type is durable goods—such as cars, televisions, computers, and refrigerators—that should be made, used, and returned to the manufacturer within a closed-loop system. Such products should be designed for disassembly and recycling. The third category is unsalables and includes such products as radioactive materials, heavy metals, and toxins. These products should always belong to the original makers, who should be responsible for the products and their full life

| figure 4.2 | THE EUROPEAN ECO-LABEL |

Source: Reprinted with permission of European Eco-label.

cycle effects. Reclassifying products in this way encourages manufacturers to design products more efficiently.

3. *Make prices reflect the cost.* Every product should reflect or at least approximate its actual cost—not only the direct cost of production but also the cost of air, water, and soil. For example, the cost of a gallon of gasoline, according to the World Resources Institute in Washington, D.C., is significantly more when pollution, waste disposal, health effects, and defense expenditures like those of the Persian Gulf and Iraq wars are factored in.

4. *Make environmentalism profitable.* Consumers are beginning to recognize that competition in the marketplace should not occur between companies that are harming the environment and those that are trying to save it.[25]

Consumerism. Another significant issue in socially responsible marketing is consumerism, which we defined in Chapter 3 as the efforts of independent individuals, groups, and organizations to protect the rights of consumers. A number of interest groups and individuals have taken action against companies they consider irresponsible by lobbying government officials and agencies, engaging in letter-writing campaigns and boycotts, and making public-service announcements. Some consumers choose to boycott firms and products out of a desire to support a cause and make a difference.[26] How a firm handles customer complaints affects consumer evaluations and in turn customer satisfaction and loyalty.[27] The consumer movement has been helped by news-format television programs, such as *Dateline, 60 Minutes,* and *Prime Time Live,* as well as by 24-hour news coverage from CNN and MSNBC. The Internet too has changed the way consumers obtain information about companies' goods, services, and activities. Consumers can share their opinions about goods and services and about companies they see as irresponsible at consumer-oriented websites, such as epinions.com and ConsumerReview.com, and through blogs.

Ralph Nader, one of the best-known consumer activists, continues to crusade for consumer rights. Consumer activism by Nader and others has resulted in legislation requiring many features that make cars safer: seat belts, air bags, padded dashboards, stronger door latches, head restraints, shatterproof windshields, and collapsible steering columns. Activists' efforts have also facilitated the passage of several consumer protection laws, including the Wholesome Meat Act of 1967, the Radiation Control for Health and Safety Act of 1968, the Clean Water Act of 1972, and the Toxic Substance Act of 1976.

Extreme Makeover Gets a Makeover

Extreme Makeover: Home Edition is an Emmy award–winning reality TV series on ABC that remodels a needy family's home, including all the rooms and even the landscaping, while the family goes away on vacation. Most of the families' homes are demolished, and an entirely new replacement home is constructed within a few weeks. Hosted by popular carpenter Ty Pennington, the show went "green" in 2007 to illustrate how homes can be remodeled to be environmentally and socially responsible. The first green house makeover was for the Yazzie family, who had been living in poor conditions on a Navajo reservation. The construction of the new home incorporated the Navajo principles of living off the land, not wasting anything, and recycling everything the earth has to offer.

More than 50 percent of the materials used in incorporating eco-friendly, low-energy, and recyclable resources were taken from a landfill within 500 miles from the building site. All wood products were from forests certified by the Forest Stewardship Council. Light sensors, fluorescent bulbs, and many of the windows were installed to enhance the Yazzies' lighting system. The home was also designed to collect rainwater for irrigation for a vegetable and herb garden. Solar panels were used for water heating, and interior temperatures were boosted by terminal heaters—rather than large gas or electric tanks—through heated coils installed in air ducts. Grapevines were used to cover walls to stop the sun from hitting the building directly, thus saving energy. All appliances in the show are Energy Star rated for efficiency, and Sears' (the show's sponsor) Kenmore appliance brands are featured in every episode. The family will even have a "utilize energy block" to help them track their energy consumption.

The Yazzies' new home features a green roof with plants such as prairie grass to reduce heating and air-conditioning costs by 10 percent or more, as well as rainwater runoff. Green roofs are becoming more popular, with 2.5 million square feet of downtown-Chicago roof space covered with hardy plants. Green roofs are not only energy efficient but reduce the need for roof repairs and give the house a unique and attractive appearance that is appropriate for homes on the Navajo reservation.

Both *Extreme Makeover: Home Edition* and ABC are promoting green housing that will conserve resources and limit harm to the natural environment. With houses being a major source of energy use and pollution, this program serves as an example of how all homeowners can learn to make their homes more eco-responsible. As individuals become more focused on socially responsible housing, the market for wind and solar energy, recycled and biodegradable products, and energy-efficient appliances and lighting will grow rapidly. Firms that supply construction products will have an incentive to innovate and develop products that can be used to construct these energy-efficient houses of the future.[c]

Also of great importance to the consumer movement are four basic rights spelled out in a consumer "bill of rights" that was drafted by President John F. Kennedy. These rights include the right to safety, the right to be informed, the right to choose, and the right to be heard.

Ensuring consumers' *right to safety* means marketers are obligated not to market a product that they know could harm consumers. This right can be extended to imply that all products must be safe for their intended use, include thorough and explicit instructions for proper and safe use, and have been tested to ensure reliability and quality.

Consumers' *right to be informed* means consumers should have access to and the opportunity to review all relevant information about a product before buying it. Many laws require specific labeling on product packaging to satisfy this right.

In addition, labels on alcoholic and tobacco products must inform consumers that these products may cause illness and other problems.

The *right to choose* means consumers should have access to a variety of products and services at competitive prices. They should also be assured of satisfactory quality and service at a fair price. Activities that reduce competition among businesses in an industry might jeopardize this right.

The *right to be heard* ensures that consumers' interests will receive full and sympathetic consideration in the formulation of government policy. The right to be heard also promises consumers fair treatment when they complain to marketers about products. This right benefits marketers too because when consumers complain about a product, the manufacturer can use this information to modify the product and make it more satisfying.

The Federal Trade Commission provides a wealth of consumer information at its website (**www.ftc.gov/bcp/consumer.shtm**) on a variety of topics ranging from automobiles and the Internet to diet, health, and fitness to identity theft.

Community Relations. Social responsibility also extends to marketers' roles as community members. Individual communities expect marketers to make philanthropic contributions to civic projects and institutions and to be "good corporate citizens." The Weaver Street Market Cooperative in Carrboro, North Carolina, for example, serves as a community hub and live music venue, as well as a farmers' market and food store that emphasize sustainable and local food products. It has also used its resources to support a community radio station, affordable housing, and a satellite market to serve consumers nearby.[28]

Although most charitable donations come from individuals, corporate philanthropy is on the rise. Target, for example, contributes significant resources to education, including fundraising and scholarship programs that assist teachers and students, as well as direct donations of more than $200 million to schools. Through the retailer's Take Charge of Education program, customers who use a Target Guest Card can designate a specific school to which Target donates 1 percent of their total purchase. This program is designed to make customers feel that their purchases are benefiting their community while increasing the use of Target Guest Cards.[29]

Smaller firms can also make positive contributions to their communities. For example, Colorado-based New Belgium Brewing Company donates $1 for every barrel of beer brewed to charities within the markets it serves. The brewery divides the funds among states in proportion to interests and needs, considering environmental, human services, drug and alcohol awareness, and cultural issues.[30] From a positive perspective, a marketer can significantly improve its community's quality of life through employment opportunities, economic development, and financial contributions to educational, health, cultural, and recreational causes.[31]

Marketing Ethics

LO 2 To define and describe the importance of marketing ethics

As noted earlier, marketing ethics is a dimension of social responsibility that involves principles and standards that define acceptable conduct in marketing. Acceptable standards of conduct in making individual and group decisions in marketing are determined by various stakeholders and by an organization's ethical climate.

Marketers should be aware of ethical standards for acceptable conduct from several viewpoints: company, industry, government, customers, special-interest groups, and society at large. When marketing activities deviate from accepted standards, the exchange process can break down, resulting in customer dissatisfaction, lack of trust, and lawsuits. In recent years, a number of ethical scandals have resulted in a massive loss of confidence in the integrity of U.S. businesses.[32] In fact, 73 percent of consumers say they would boycott the products of a socially irresponsible company, and 90 percent would consider switching to a competitor's products.[33] Sony BMG Music Entertainment, for example, was sharply criticized for including copy-protection software on millions of CDs. Although most marketers of music have sought innovative ways to stifle rampant CD piracy, many consumers felt that Sony's copy-protection software went too far because it could potentially disable computers or enable a hacker to unleash a virus if the CD was played on a Windows-based computer. Sony ultimately recalled an estimated 4.7 million CDs, at a projected cost of $2 to $4 million, but not before generating considerable consumer anger and confusion over the technology as well as at least one class-action lawsuit. The company later settled charges by the Texas and California attorneys general that the copy-protection software violated the states' antispyware laws.[34] When marketers engage in activities that deviate from accepted principles, continued marketing exchanges become difficult, if not impossible. The best time to deal with such problems is during the strategic planning process, not after major problems materialize.

As we already noted, marketing ethics goes beyond legal issues. Marketing decisions based on ethical considerations foster mutual trust in marketing relationships. Although we often try to draw a boundary between legal and ethical issues, the distinction between the two is frequently blurred in decision making. Marketers operate in an environment in which overlapping legal and ethical issues color many decisions. To separate legal and ethical decisions, one must assume that marketing managers can instinctively differentiate legal and ethical issues. However, although the legal ramifications of some issues and problems may be very obvious, others are not. Questionable decisions and actions often result in disputes that must be resolved through litigation. The legal system therefore provides a formal venue for marketers to resolve ethical disputes as well as legal ones. For example, Tropicana Entertainment, which owns the Tropicana hotel and casino chain, filed suit against a Newport, Rhode Island, restaurateur for using the Tropicana name and logo on his restaurant, right down to the Las Vegas Tropicana's gold, triangular, pointed block letters. The suit asks the restaurant to cease using the Tropicana name and logo and to pay damages for and profits from using the name.[35] Indeed, most ethical disputes reported in the media involve the legal system at some level. In many cases, however, settlements are reached without requiring the decision of a judge or jury.

Before we proceed with our discussion of ethics in marketing, it is important to state that it is not our purpose to question anyone's ethical beliefs or personal convictions. Nor is it our purpose to examine the conduct of consumers, although some do behave unethically (engaging, for instance, in coupon fraud, shoplifting, returning clothing after wearing it, and other abuses). Instead, our goal here is to underscore the importance of resolving ethical issues in marketing and to help you learn about marketing ethics.

Ethical Issues in Marketing

An **ethical issue** is an identifiable problem, situation, or opportunity that requires an individual or organization to choose from among several actions that must be evaluated as right or wrong, ethical or unethical. Any time an activity causes marketing managers or customers in their target market to feel manipulated or cheated, a marketing ethical issue exists, regardless of the legality of that activity. For example, a Los Angeles consumer filed a lawsuit against Kraft Foods after noticing on the label on their guacamole that the dip did not contain a significant quantity of avocadoes. Although most consumers assume that Kraft's top-selling guacamole dip is made mostly of avocadoes, the product primarily consists of modified food starch, coconut and soybean oils, food coloring, and less than 2 percent avocado. Although Kraft quickly changed the labeling to read "guacamole-flavored" dip, the California Avocado Commission expressed dismay at the dearth of avocado in the dip and asked its own lawyers to look at the suit.[36]

Regardless of the reasons behind specific ethical issues, marketers must be able to identify those issues and decide how to resolve them. Doing so requires familiarity with the many kinds of ethical issues that may arise in marketing. Research suggests that the greater the consequences associated with an issue, the more likely it will be recognized as an ethics issue and the more important it will be to making an ethical decision.[37] Some examples of ethical issues related to product, promotion, price, and distribution (the marketing mix) appear in Table 4.3.

ethical issue An identifiable problem, situation, or opportunity requiring a choice among several actions that must be evaluated as right or wrong, ethical or unethical

table 4.3	SAMPLE ETHICAL ISSUES RELATED TO THE MARKETING MIX
Product Issue *Product information*	Covering up defects that could cause harm to a consumer; withholding critical performance information that could affect a purchase decision.
Distribution Issue *Counterfeiting*	Counterfeit products are widespread, especially in the areas of computer software, clothing, and audio and video products. The Internet has facilitated the distribution of counterfeit products.
Promotion Issue *Advertising*	Deceptive advertising or withholding important product information in a personal selling situation.
Pricing Issue *Pricing*	Indicating that an advertised sale price is a reduction below the regular price when in fact that is not the case.

Product-related ethical issues generally arise when marketers fail to disclose risks associated with a product or information regarding the function, value, or use of a product. Most automobile and many toy companies have experienced negative publicity associated with design or safety issues that resulted in a government-required recall of specific models. Pressures can build to substitute inferior materials or product components to reduce costs. Ethical issues also arise when marketers fail to inform customers about existing conditions or changes in product quality; such failure is a form of dishonesty about the nature of the product. Consider the introduction of a new size of candy bar, labeled with a banner touting its "new larger size." However, when placed in vending machines alongside older candy bars of the same brand, it was apparent that the product was actually slightly *smaller* than the candy bar it replaced. Although this could have been a mistake, the firm still has to defend and deal with the consequences of its actions.

Promotion can create ethical issues in a variety of ways, among them false or misleading advertising and manipulative or deceptive sales promotions, tactics, and publicity. One controversial issue in the area of promotion is the promotion of pharmaceuticals that require a doctor's prescription directly to consumers. Proponents of the practice argue that it arms consumers with more information about products that may be beneficial for their conditions. Critics worry about the potential for overtreatment and have called for tighter guidelines on the promotion of drugs. With new studies suggesting that pharmaceutical ads are strongly influencing both doctors and consumers and consumers growing wary of the ads, the Pharmaceutical Researchers and Manufacturers of America announced plans to release voluntary guidelines to better self-regulate the industry.[38] Another major ethical issue in promotion pertains to the marketing of video games that allegedly promote violence and weapons to children. Many other ethical issues are linked to promotion, including the use of bribery in personal selling situations. Even a bribe that is offered to benefit the organization is usually considered unethical. Because it jeopardizes trust and fairness, it hurts the organization in the long run.

In pricing, common ethical issues are price fixing, predatory pricing, and failure to disclose the full price of a purchase. The emotional and subjective nature of price creates many situations in which misunderstandings between the seller and buyer cause ethical problems. Marketers have the right to price their products to earn a reasonable profit, but ethical issues may crop up when a company seeks to earn high profits at the expense of its customers. Some pharmaceutical companies, for example, have been accused of pricing products at exorbitant levels and taking advantage of customers who must purchase the medicine to survive or to maintain their quality of life. Another issue relates to quantity surcharges that occur when consumers are effectively overcharged for buying a larger package size of the same grocery product.[39]

Ethical issues in distribution involve relationships among producers and marketing middlemen. Marketing middlemen, or intermediaries (wholesalers and retailers),

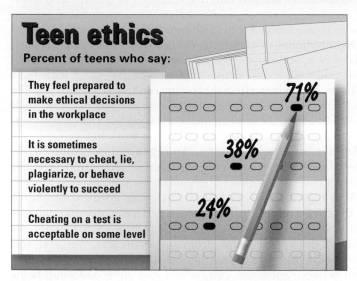

Teen ethics

Percent of teens who say:

They feel prepared to make ethical decisions in the workplace — 71%

It is sometimes necessary to cheat, lie, plagiarize, or behave violently to succeed — 38%

Cheating on a test is acceptable on some level — 24%

Source: Data from Junior Achievement/Deloitte Teen Ethics Survey.

facilitate the flow of products from the producer to the ultimate customer. Each intermediary performs a different role and agrees to certain rights, responsibilities, and rewards associated with that role. For example, producers expect wholesalers and retailers to honor agreements and keep them informed of inventory needs. Other serious ethical issues with regard to distribution include manipulating a product's availability for purposes of exploitation and using coercion to force intermediaries to behave in a specific manner. Several companies have been accused of channel stuffing, which involves shipping surplus inventory to wholesalers and retailers at an excessive rate, typically before the end of a quarter. The practice may conceal declining demand for a product or inflate financial statement earnings, misleading investors.[40]

The Nature of Marketing Ethics

To grasp the significance of ethics in marketing decision making, it is helpful to examine the factors that influence the ethical decision-making process. As Figure 4.3 shows, individual factors, organizational relationships, and opportunity interact to determine ethical decisions in marketing.

Individual Factors. When people need to resolve ethical conflicts in their daily lives, they often base their decisions on their own values and principles of right or wrong. For example, a study by the Josephson Institute of Ethics reported that 60 percent of students admitted to cheating on a test at least once in the past year, and 81 percent admitted to lying to their parents in the past year. One out of three students confessed to plagiarizing documents from the Internet in the same period.[41] People learn values and principles through socialization by family members, social groups, religion, and formal education. In the workplace, however, research has established that an organization's values often have more influence on marketing decisions than do a person's own values.[42]

Organizational Relationships. Although people can and do make ethical choices pertaining to marketing decisions, no one operates in a vacuum.[43] Ethical choices in marketing are most often made jointly, in work groups and committees or in conversations and discussions with coworkers. Marketing employees resolve ethical issues based not only on what they learned from their own backgrounds but also on what they learn from others in the organization. The outcome of this learning process depends on the strength of each individual's personal values, opportunity for unethical

figure 4.3

FACTORS THAT INFLUENCE THE ETHICAL DECISION-MAKING PROCESS IN MARKETING

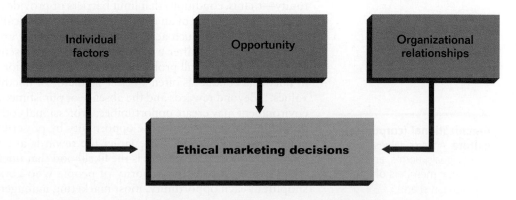

We get asked all the time if hemp is the same thing as marijuana.

I mean, really, if the hemp we use in our shoes got you high, don't you think we'd have enough money to hire some models for our ads?

We're committed to making our shoes 100% sustainable. We make ecoSNEAKS™ with materials like:

Hemp   Recycled Tires   organic cotton

Simple
a nice little shoe company™
shoes for a happy planet™

available at select **URBAN OUTFITTERS** and www.simpleshoes.com

Organizational Culture

Urban Outfitters' corporate culture supports making sustainable products available to consumers.

behavior, and exposure to others who behave ethically or unethically. Superiors, peers, and subordinates in the organization influence the ethical decision-making process. Although people outside the organization, such as family members and friends, also influence decision makers, organizational culture and structure operate through organizational relationships to influence ethical decisions.

Organizational, or corporate, culture is a set of values, beliefs, goals, norms, and rituals that members of an organization share. These values also help shape employees' satisfaction with their employer, which may affect the quality of the service they provide to customers. A firm's culture may be expressed formally through codes of conduct, memos, manuals, dress codes, and ceremonies, but it is also conveyed informally through work habits, extracurricular activities, and anecdotes. An organization's culture gives its members meaning and suggests rules for how to behave and deal with problems within the organization.

With regard to organizational structure, most experts agree that the chief executive officer or vice president of marketing sets the ethical tone for the entire marketing organization. Lower-level managers obtain their cues from top managers, but they too impose some of their personal values on the company. This interaction between corporate culture and executive leadership helps determine the firm's ethical value system.

Coworkers' influence on an individual's ethical choices depends on the person's exposure to unethical behavior. Especially in gray areas, the more a person is exposed to unethical activity by others in the organizational environment, the more likely he or she is to behave unethically. Most marketing employees take their cues from coworkers in learning how to solve problems, including ethical problems.[44] For example, the 2007 National Business Ethics Survey (NBES) found that 56 percent of employees had observed at least one type of misconduct in the past year; nearly one-half of them (42 percent) had chosen not to report the misconduct to management.[45] Figure 4.4 lists some commonly observed types of observed misconduct. Moreover, research suggests that marketing employees who perceive their work environment as ethical experience less role conflict and ambiguity, are more satisfied with their jobs, and are more committed to their employer.[46]

Organizational pressure plays a key role in creating ethical issues. For example, because of pressure to meet a schedule, a superior may ask a salesperson to lie to a customer over the phone about a late product shipment. Similarly, pressure to meet a sales quota may result in overly aggressive sales tactics. Research in this area indicates that superiors and coworkers can generate organizational pressure, which plays a key role in creating ethical issues. Nearly all marketers face difficult issues whose solutions are not obvious or that present conflicts between organizational objectives and personal ethics.

Opportunity. Another factor that may shape ethical decisions in marketing is opportunity—that is, conditions that limit barriers or provide rewards. A marketing employee who takes advantage of an opportunity to act unethically and is rewarded or suffers no penalty may repeat such acts as other opportunities arise. For example, a salesperson who receives a raise after using a deceptive sales presentation to increase sales is being rewarded and thus will probably continue the behavior. Indeed, opportunity to engage in unethical conduct is often a better predictor of unethical activities than are personal values.[47] Beyond rewards and the absence of punishment, other elements in the business environment may create opportunities. Professional codes of conduct and ethics-related corporate policy also influence opportunity by prescribing what behaviors are acceptable, as we will see later. The larger the rewards and the milder the punishment for unethical conduct, the greater is the likelihood that unethical behavior will occur.

However, just as the majority of people who go into retail stores do not try to shoplift at each opportunity, most marketing managers do not try to take advantage

organizational (corporate) culture A set of values, beliefs, goals, norms, and rituals that members of an organization share

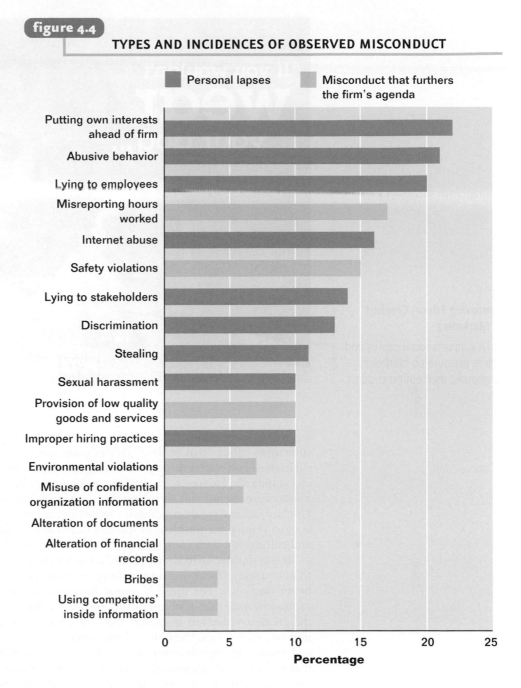

figure 4.4

TYPES AND INCIDENCES OF OBSERVED MISCONDUCT

■ Personal lapses   ■ Misconduct that furthers the firm's agenda

(Horizontal bar chart showing percentages from 0 to 25)

- Putting own interests ahead of firm
- Abusive behavior
- Lying to employees
- Misreporting hours worked
- Internet abuse
- Safety violations
- Lying to stakeholders
- Discrimination
- Stealing
- Sexual harassment
- Provision of low quality goods and services
- Improper hiring practices
- Environmental violations
- Misuse of confidential organization information
- Alteration of documents
- Alteration of financial records
- Bribes
- Using competitors' inside information

Percentage

of every opportunity for unethical behavior in their organizations. Although marketing managers often perceive many opportunities to engage in unethical conduct in their companies and industries, research suggests that most refrain from taking advantage of such opportunities. Moreover, most marketing managers do not believe that unethical conduct in general results in success.[48] Individual factors as well as organizational culture may influence whether an individual becomes opportunistic and tries to take advantage of situations unethically.

Improving Ethical Conduct in Marketing

It is possible to improve ethical conduct in an organization by hiring ethical employees and eliminating unethical ones, and by improving the organization's ethical standards. One way to approach improvement of an organization's ethical standards is to use a "bad apple–bad barrel" analogy. Some people always do things in their own

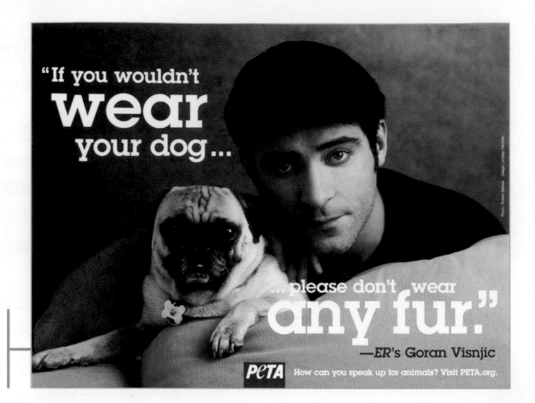

Improving Ethical Conduct in Marketing

PETA supports social causes and places pressure on marketers to improve their ethical conduct.

self-interest, regardless of organizational goals or accepted moral standards; they are sometimes called "bad apples." To eliminate unethical conduct, an organization must rid itself of bad apples through screening techniques and enforcement of the firm's ethical standards. However, organizations sometimes become "bad barrels" themselves, not because the individuals within them are unethical but because the pressures to survive and succeed create conditions (opportunities) that reward unethical behavior. One way to resolve the problem of the bad barrel is to redesign the organization's image and culture so that it conforms to industry and societal norms of ethical conduct.[49]

If top management develops and enforces ethical and legal compliance programs to encourage ethical decision making, it becomes a force to help individuals make better decisions. The 2007 National Business Ethics Survey found that well-implemented formal ethics and compliance programs and a strong corporate culture result in the greatest reduction in ethical risks for an organization. Companies that wish to improve their ethics, then, should implement a strong ethics and compliance program and encourage organizationwide commitment to an ethical culture.[50] Ethics programs that include written standards of conduct, ethics training, ethics advice lines or offices, and systems for anonymous reporting increase the likelihood that employees will report misconduct observed in the workplace. When top managers talk about the importance of ethics, inform employees, keep promises, and model ethical behavior, employees observe significantly fewer instances of unethical conduct. When marketers understand the policies and requirements for ethical conduct, they can more easily resolve ethical conflicts. However, marketers can never fully abdicate their personal ethical responsibility in making decisions. Claiming to be an agent of the business ("the company told me to do it") is unacceptable as a legal excuse and is even less defensible from an ethical perspective.[51] According to the 2007 NBES, most employees (54 percent) who failed to report misconduct they had witnessed claimed they were skeptical that their reporting would make a difference, and 36 percent of the nonreporters feared retaliation for reporting misconduct.[52] Table 4.4 lists some of the types of misconduct that employees are unlikely to report.

Codes of Conduct. Without compliance programs and uniform standards and policies regarding conduct, it is hard for employees to determine what conduct is

table 4.4	**TYPES OF MISCONDUCT *LEAST* LIKELY TO BE REPORTED WHEN OBSERVED**

Improper hiring practices

Discrimination

Giving or accepting bribes, kickbacks, or inappropriate gifts

E-mail or Internet abuse

Lying to employees, customers, vendors, or the public

Source: National Business Ethics Survey, "The Ethics Resource Center's 2007 *National Business Ethics Survey: An Inside View of Private Sector Ethics.*" Ethics Resource Center 2007, p. 17. © Ethics Resource Center, Washington, DC.

acceptable within the company. In the absence of such programs and standards, employees will generally make decisions based on their observations of how coworkers and superiors behave. To improve ethics, many organizations have developed **codes of conduct** (also called *codes of ethics*) that consist of formalized rules and standards that describe what the company expects of its employees. Most large corporations have formal codes of conduct. Tyco, for example, established a Guide to Ethical Conduct as part of a major corporate overhaul that involved forcing out nearly 300 managers, dramatic changes in reporting relationships, and many more initiatives to ensure that Tyco developed an ethical corporate culture.[53]

Codes of conduct promote ethical behavior by reducing opportunities for unethical behavior; employees know both what is expected of them and what kind of punishment they face if they violate the rules. Codes help marketers deal with ethical issues or dilemmas that develop in daily operations by prescribing or limiting specific activities. At Hospital Corporation of America (HCA), for example, the code of conduct specifies that any violation of the code may trigger an oral warning, written warning, written reprimand, suspension, termination, and/or restitution, depending on the nature, severity, and frequency of the violation.[54] Codes of conduct have also made companies that subcontract manufacturing operations abroad more aware of the ethical issues associated with supporting facilities that underpay and even abuse their workforce. The American Apparel & Footwear Association, for example, has endorsed the principles and certification program of Worldwide Responsible Apparel Production (WRAP), a nonprofit organization dedicated to promoting and certifying "lawful, humane, and ethical manufacturing throughout the world." Companies that endorse the principles are expected to allow independent monitoring to ensure that their contractors are complying with the principles.[55]

Codes of conduct do not have to be so detailed that they take every situation into account, but they should provide guidelines that enable employees to achieve organizational objectives in an ethical, acceptable manner. The American Marketing Association Code of Ethics, reprinted in Table 4.5, does not cover every possible ethical issue, but it provides a useful overview of what marketers believe are sound principles for guiding marketing activities. This code serves as a helpful model for structuring an organization's code of conduct.

Ethics Officers. Organizational compliance programs must also have oversight by high-ranking persons in the organization who are known to respect legal and ethical standards. Ethics officers are typically responsible for creating and distributing a code of conduct, enforcing the code, and meeting with organizational members to discuss or provide advice about ethical issues. Many firms have created ethics officer positions, including the New York Stock Exchange, Marsh & McLennan, Nortel Networks, and Computer Associates International.[56] At Tyco, for example, senior vice president of corporate governance Eric Pillmore is in the process of revamping the firm's ethics program. In addition to revising the company's code of conduct, Pillmore, who reports directly to Tyco's board of directors, is responsible for providing ethics training.[57]

Many ethics officers also employ toll-free telephone "hotlines" to provide advice, anonymously when desired, to employees who believe they face an ethical issue. Since the passage of the 2002 Sarbanes-Oxley Act, more companies have implemented anonymous hotlines for employees to report misconduct; many companies, including Halliburton and Coca-Cola, have contracted the operation of these hotlines to third parties, such as EthicsPoint, Global Compliance Services, National Hotline Services, and Pinkerton Consulting & Investigations.

codes of conduct Formalized rules and standards that describe what the company expects of its employees

table 4.5   CODE OF ETHICS OF THE AMERICAN MARKETING ASSOCIATION

Ethical Norms and Values for Marketers

Preamble

The American Marketing Association commits itself to promoting the highest standard of professional ethical norms and values for its members. Norms are established standards of conduct expected and maintained by society and/or professional organizations. Values represent the collective conception of what people find desirable, important, and morally proper. Values serve as the criteria for evaluating the actions of others. Marketing practitioners must recognize that they serve not only their enterprises but also act as stewards of society in creating, facilitating, and executing the efficient and effective transactions that are part of the greater economy. In this role, marketers should embrace the highest ethical norms of practicing professionals as well as the ethical values implied by their responsibility toward stakeholders (e.g., customers, employees, investors, channel members, regulators, and the host community).

General Norms

1. Marketers must first do no harm. This means doing work for which they are appropriately trained or experienced so they can actively add value to their organizations and customers. It also means adhering to all applicable laws and regulations, as well as embodying high ethical standards in the choices they make.

2. Marketers must foster trust in the marketing system. This means that products are appropriate for their intended and promoted uses. It requires that marketing communications about goods and services are not intentionally deceptive or misleading. It suggests building relationships that provide for the equitable adjustment and/or redress of customer grievances. It implies striving for good faith and fair dealing so as to contribute toward the efficacy of the exchange process.

3. Marketers should embrace, communicate, and practice the fundamental ethical values that will improve consumer confidence in the integrity of the marketing exchange system. These basic values are intentionally aspirational and include: Honesty, Responsibility, Fairness, Respect, Openness, and Citizenship.

Ethical Values

Honesty—this means being truthful and forthright in our dealings with customers and stakeholders.

We will tell the truth in all situations and at all times.

We will offer products of value that do what we claim in our communications.

We will stand behind our products if they fail to deliver their claimed benefits.

We will honor our explicit and implicit commitments and promises.

Responsibility—this involves accepting the consequences of our marketing decisions and strategies.

We will make strenuous efforts to serve the needs of our customers.

We will avoid using coercion with all stakeholders.

We will acknowledge the social obligations to stakeholders that come with increased marketing and economic power.

We will recognize our special commitments to economically vulnerable segments of the market such as children, the elderly, and others who may be substantially disadvantaged.

Fairness—this has to do with justly trying to balance the needs of the buyer with the interests of the seller.

We will clearly represent our products in selling, advertising, and other forms of communication; this includes the avoidance of false, misleading, and deceptive promotion.

We will reject manipulations and sales tactics that harm customer trust.

We will not engage in price fixing, predatory pricing, price gouging, or "bait and switch" tactics.

We will not knowingly participate in material conflicts of interest.

Respect—this addresses the basic human dignity of all stakeholders.

We will value individual differences even as we avoid customer stereotyping or depicting demographic groups (e.g., gender, race, sexual) in a negative or dehumanizing way in our promotions.

We will listen to the needs of our customers and make all reasonable efforts to monitor and improve their satisfaction on an ongoing basis.

We will make a special effort to understand suppliers, intermediaries, and distributors from other cultures.

(continued)

table 4.5   CODE OF ETHICS OF THE AMERICAN MARKETING ASSOCIATION (*continued*)

We will appropriately acknowledge the contributions of others, such as consultants, employees, and coworkers, to our marketing endeavors.

Openness—this focuses on creating transparency in our marketing operations.

We will strive to communicate clearly with all our constituencies.

We will accept constructive criticism from our customers and other stakeholders.

We will explain significant product or service risks, component substitutions, or other foreseeable eventualities affecting the customer or their perception of the purchase decision.

We will fully disclose list prices and terms of financing as well as available price deals and adjustments.

Citizenship—this involves a strategic focus on fulfilling the economic, legal, philanthropic, and societal responsibilities that serve stakeholders.

We will strive to protect the natural environment in the execution of marketing campaigns.

We will give back to the community through volunteerism and charitable donations.

We will work to contribute to the overall betterment of marketing and its reputation.

We will encourage supply-chain members to ensure that trade is fair for all participants, including producers in developing countries.

Implementation

Finally, we recognize that every industry sector and marketing subdiscipline (e.g., marketing research, e-commerce, direct selling, direct marketing, advertising, etc.) has its own specific ethical issues that require policies and commentary. An array of such codes can be accessed via links on the AMA website. We encourage all such groups to develop and/or refine their industry and discipline-specific codes of ethics in order to supplement these general norms and values.

Source: Copyright © 2004 by the American Marketing Association.

LO 3 To become familiar with ways to improve ethical decisions in marketing

Implementing Ethical and Legal Compliance Programs. To nurture ethical conduct in marketing, open communication and coaching on ethical issues are essential. This requires providing employees with ethics training, clear channels of communication, and follow-up support throughout the organization.

It is important that companies consistently enforce standards and impose penalties or punishment on those who violate codes of conduct and ethics policies. Clear Channel Communications, for example, fired two executives and disciplined other employees for violating the firm's policies on "payola," the illegal practice of accepting payment for playing songs on the air without divulging such deals. The firm, which owns approximately 1,200 radio stations, also required station managers and programming personnel to undergo additional training on its policies.[58] In addition, companies must take reasonable steps in response to violations of standards and, as appropriate, revise their compliance programs to diminish the likelihood of future misconduct. To succeed, a compliance program must be viewed as a part of the overall marketing strategy implementation. If ethics officers and other executives are not committed to the principles and initiatives of marketing ethics and social responsibility, the program's effectiveness will be in question.

Although the virtues of honesty, fairness, and openness are often assumed to be self-evident and universally accepted, marketing strategy decisions involve complex and detailed matters in which correctness may not be so clear-cut. A high level of personal morality may not be sufficient to prevent an individual from violating the law in an organizational context in which even experienced lawyers debate the exact meaning of the law. Because it is impossible to train all members of an organization as lawyers, the identification of ethical issues and implementation of compliance programs and codes of conduct that incorporate both legal and ethical concerns constitute the best approach to preventing violations and avoiding litigation. Codifying ethical standards into meaningful policies that spell out what is and is not acceptable gives marketers an opportunity to reduce the probability of behavior that could create legal problems. Without proper ethical training and guidance, it is impossible for the average marketing manager to understand the exact boundaries of illegality in the areas of price fixing, copyright violations, fraud, export/import violations, and so on. A corporate focus on ethics helps create a buffer zone around issues that could trigger serious legal complications for the company.

Incorporating Social Responsibility and Ethics into Strategic Planning

L O 4 To understand the role of social responsibility and ethics in improving market performance

Although the concepts of marketing ethics and social responsibility are often used interchangeably, it is important to distinguish between them. *Ethics* relates to individual and group decisions—judgments about what is right or wrong in a particular decision-making situation—whereas *social responsibility* deals with the total effect of marketing decisions on society. The two concepts are interrelated because a company that supports socially responsible decisions and adheres to a code of conduct is likely to have a positive effect on society. Because ethics and social responsibility programs can be profitable as well, an increasing number of companies are incorporating them into their overall strategic market planning.

As we have emphasized throughout this chapter, ethics is one dimension of social responsibility. Being socially responsible relates to doing what is economically sound, legal, ethical, and socially conscious. One way to evaluate whether a specific activity is ethical and socially responsible is to ask other members of the organization if they approve of it. Contact with concerned consumer groups and industry or government regulatory groups may be helpful. A check to see whether there is a specific company policy about an activity may help resolve ethical questions. If other organizational members approve of the activity and it is legal and customary within the industry, chances are the activity is acceptable from both an ethical and a social responsibility perspective. Table 4.6 provides an audit of mechanisms to help control ethics and social responsibility in marketing.

A rule of thumb for resolving ethical and social responsibility issues is that if an issue can withstand open discussion that results in agreement or limited debate, an acceptable solution may exist. Nevertheless, even after a final decision is reached, different viewpoints on the issue may remain. Openness is not the end-all solution to the ethics problem. However, it creates trust and facilitates learning relationships.[59]

Incorporating Social Responsibility and Ethics

Companies such as Yoplait and others support fundraising for breast cancer research and the goal of finding a cure.

We can live without our hair.
We can live without our breasts.
WE CANNOT LIVE WITHOUT OUR HOPE FOR A CURE.

The Challenge of Ethical and Socially Responsible Behavior

To promote socially responsible and ethical behavior while achieving organizational goals, marketers must monitor changes and trends in society's values. Consider that as aging baby boomers face increased rates of obesity, diabetes, heart conditions, and other chronic illnesses, many companies in the food industry are responding by introducing or adapting products to address their needs. Their approaches range from special brands and labels to introducing low-fat, low-sugar, whole-grain, and other specialty-food requirements to maintaining separate shelf space for products that target these conditions. Developing a more user-friendly grocery store for these consumers is both socially responsible and lucrative.[60] An organization's top management must assume some responsibility for employees' conduct by establishing and enforcing policies that address society's desires.

After determining what society wants, marketers must attempt to predict the long-term effects of decisions pertaining to those wants. Specialists outside the company, such as doctors,

table 4.6	ORGANIZATIONAL AUDIT OF SOCIAL RESPONSIBILITY AND ETHICS CONTROL MECHANISMS

Answer True or False for each statement

T	F	1. No mechanism exists for top management to detect social responsibility and ethical issues relating to employees, customers, the community, and society.
T	F	2. There is no formal or informal communication within the organization about procedures and activities that are considered acceptable behavior.
T	F	3. The organization fails to communicate its ethical standards to suppliers, customers, and groups that have a relationship with the organization.
T	F	4. There is an environment of deception, repression, and cover-ups concerning events that could be embarrassing to the company.
T	F	5. Compensation systems are totally dependent on economic performance.
T	F	6. The only concerns about environmental impact are those that are legally required.
T	F	7. Concern for the ethical value systems of the community with regard to the firm's activities is absent.
T	F	8. Products are described in a misleading manner, with no information on negative impact or limitations communicated to customers.

True answers indicate a lack of control mechanisms, which, if implemented, could improve ethics and social responsibility.

lawyers, and scientists, are often consulted, but sometimes there is a lack of agreement within a discipline as to what is an acceptable marketing decision. Forty years ago, for example, tobacco marketers promoted cigarettes as being good for one's health. Today, years after the discovery that cigarette smoking is linked to cancer and other medical problems, society's attitude toward smoking has changed, and marketers face new social responsibilities, such as providing a smoke-free atmosphere for customers. Most major hotel chains allocate at least some of their rooms to nonsmokers, many rental car companies provide smoke-free cars, and most other businesses within the food, travel, and entertainment industries provide smoke-free environments or sections.

Many of society's demands impose costs. For example, society wants a cleaner environment and the preservation of wildlife and their habitats, but it also wants low-priced products. Consider the plight of the gas station owner who asked his customers if they would be willing to spend an additional 1 cent per gallon if he instituted an air filtration system to eliminate harmful fumes. The majority indicated they supported his plan. However, when the system was installed and the price increased, many customers switched to a lower-cost competitor across the street. Thus, companies must carefully balance the costs of providing low-priced products against the costs of manufacturing, packaging, and distributing their products in an environmentally responsible manner.

In trying to satisfy the desires of one group, marketers may dissatisfy others. Regarding the smoking debate, for example, marketers must balance nonsmokers' desire for a smoke-free environment against smokers' desire, or need, to continue to smoke. Some antitobacco crusaders call for the complete elimination of tobacco products to ensure a smoke-free world. However, this attitude fails to consider the difficulty smokers have in quitting (now that tobacco marketers have admitted their product is addictive) and the impact on U.S. communities and states that depend on tobacco crops for their economic survival. Thus, this issue, like most ethical and social responsibility issues, cannot be viewed in black and white.

Balancing society's demands to satisfy all members of society is difficult, if not impossible. Marketers must evaluate the extent to which members of society are willing to pay for what they want. For instance, customers may want more information

Pros Magaga and her daughter tend their newly-expanded shop in Kampala, Uganda

An elegant solution to global poverty turns small loans into big changes

There is no better word to describe a solution to poverty that uses small loans to create big changes. That combines the power of compassion with economic common sense. That makes impoverished communities blossom through the promise of their own entrepreneurs. Help us launch 100,000 Village Banks by 2010, because hope and opportunity make the world a better place for us all.

Find out more at *www.VillageBanking.org*

GIVE A LITTLE · CHANGE A LOT

VillageBanking.org

VISA

VISA is a proud sponsor of The Village Banking Campaign of FINCA International
1101 14th Street, NW, Washington, DC 20005 / Phone: 202.682.1510
Visit myspace.com/villagebanking featuring Ambassador of Hope Natalie Portman

FINCA

Social Responsibility Improves Marketing Performance

VISA's social responsibility program strives to lessen the impact of global poverty and create a more significant relationship with its customers.

about a product but be unwilling to pay the costs the firm incurs in providing the data. Marketers who want to make socially responsible decisions may find the task a challenge because, ultimately, they must ensure their economic survival.

Social Responsibility and Ethics Improve Marketing Performance

Do not think, however, that the challenge is not worth the effort. On the contrary, increasing evidence indicates that being socially responsible and ethical pays off. Research suggests that a relationship exists between a marketing orientation and an organizational climate that supports marketing ethics and social responsibility. This relationship implies that being ethically and socially concerned is consistent with meeting the demands of customers and other stakeholders. By encouraging employees to understand their markets, companies can help them respond to stakeholders' demands.[61]

A direct association exists between corporate social responsibility and customer satisfaction, profits, and market value.[62] In a survey of consumers, nearly 86 percent indicated that when quality and price are similar among competitors, they would be more likely to buy from the company associated with a particular cause. In addition, young adults age 18–25 are especially likely to take a company's citizenship efforts into account when making not only purchasing but also employment and investment decisions.[63]

Thus, recognition is growing that the long-term value of conducting business in a socially responsible manner far outweighs short-term costs.[64] Companies that fail to develop strategies and programs to incorporate ethics and social responsibility into their organizational culture may pay the price with poor marketing performance and the potential costs of legal violations, civil litigation, and damaging publicity when questionable activities are made public. Because marketing ethics and social responsibility are not always viewed as organizational performance issues, many managers do not believe they need to consider them in the strategic planning process. Individuals also have different ideas as to what is ethical or unethical, leading them to confuse the need for workplace ethics and the right to maintain their own personal values and ethics. Although the concepts are undoubtedly controversial, it is possible—and desirable—to incorporate ethics and social responsibility into the planning process.

SUMMARY

Social responsibility refers to an organization's obligation to maximize its positive impact and minimize its negative impact on society. It deals with the total effect of all marketing decisions on society. Although social responsibility is a positive concept, most organizations embrace it in the expectation of indirect long-term benefits.

Marketing citizenship involves adopting a strategic focus for fulfilling the economic, legal, ethical, and philanthropic social responsibilities expected of organizations by their stakeholders, those constituents who have a stake, or claim, in some aspect of the company's products, operations, markets, industry, and outcomes. At the most basic level, companies have an economic responsibility to be profitable so they can provide a return on investment to their stockholders, create jobs for the community, and contribute goods and services to the economy. Marketers are also expected to obey laws and regulations. Marketing ethics refers to principles and standards that define acceptable conduct in marketing as determined by various stakeholders, including the public, government regulators, private-interest groups, industry, and the organization itself. Philanthropic responsibilities go beyond marketing ethics; they are not required of a company, but they promote human welfare or goodwill. Many firms use cause-related marketing, the practice of linking products to a social cause on an ongoing or short-term basis. Strategic philanthropy is the synergistic use of organizational core competencies and resources to address key stakeholders' interests and achieve both organizational and social benefits.

Three major categories of social responsibility issues are the natural environment, consumerism, and community relations. One of the more common ways marketers demonstrate social responsibility is through programs designed to protect and preserve the natural environment. Green marketing refers to the specific development, pricing, promotion, and distribution of products that do not harm the environment. Consumerism consists of the efforts of independent individuals, groups, and organizations to protect the rights of consumers. Consumers expect to have the right to safety, the right to be informed, the right to choose, and the right to be heard. Many marketers view social responsibility as including contributions of resources (money, products, and time) to community causes such as the natural environment, arts and recreation, disadvantaged members of the community, and education.

Whereas social responsibility is achieved by balancing the interests of all stakeholders in the organization, ethics relates to acceptable standards of conduct in making individual and group decisions. Marketing ethics goes beyond legal issues. Ethical marketing decisions foster mutual trust in marketing relationships.

An ethical issue is an identifiable problem, situation, or opportunity requiring an individual or organization to choose from among several actions that must be evaluated as right or wrong, ethical or unethical. A number of ethical issues relate to the marketing mix (product, promotion, price, and distribution).

Individual factors, organizational relationships, and opportunity interact to determine ethical decisions in marketing. Individuals often base their decisions on their own values and principles of right or wrong. However, ethical choices in marketing are most often made jointly, in work groups and committees or in conversations and discussions with coworkers. Organizational culture and structure operate through organizational relationships (with superiors, peers, and subordinates) to influence ethical decisions. Organizational, or corporate, culture is a set of values, beliefs, goals, norms, and rituals that members of an organization share. The more a person is exposed to unethical activity by others in the organizational environment, the more likely he or she is to behave unethically. Organizational pressure plays a key role in creating ethical issues, as does opportunity, conditions that limit barriers or provide rewards.

It is possible to improve ethical behavior in an organization by hiring ethical employees and eliminating unethical ones, and by improving the organization's ethical standards. If top management develops and enforces ethics and legal compliance programs to encourage ethical decision making, it becomes a force to help individuals make better decisions. To improve company ethics, many organizations have developed codes of conduct, formalized rules and standards that describe what the company expects of its employees. A marketing compliance program must have oversight by a high-ranking organizational member known to abide by legal and common ethical standards; this person is usually called an ethics officer. To nurture ethical conduct in marketing, open communication and coaching on ethical issues are essential. This requires providing employees with ethics training, clear channels of communication, and follow-up support throughout the organization. Companies must consistently enforce standards and impose penalties or punishment on those who violate codes of conduct.

An increasing number of companies are incorporating ethics and social responsibility programs into their overall strategic market planning. To promote socially responsible and ethical behavior while achieving organizational goals, marketers must monitor changes and trends in society's values. They must determine what society wants and attempt to predict the long-term effects of their decisions. Costs are associated with many of society's demands, and balancing those demands to satisfy all of society is difficult. However, increasing evidence indicates that being socially responsible and ethical results in valuable benefits: an enhanced public reputation (which can increase market share), costs savings, and profits.

IMPORTANT TERMS

Social responsibility, 94
Marketing citizenship, 96
Marketing ethics, 97

Cause-related marketing, 98
Strategic philanthropy, 98
Green marketing, 99

Ethical issue, 105
Organizational (corporate) culture, 108

Codes of conduct, 111

DISCUSSION & REVIEW QUESTIONS

1. What is social responsibility? Why is it important?

2. What are stakeholders? What role do they play in strategic marketing decisions?

3. What are four dimensions of social responsibility? What impact do they have on marketing decisions?

4. What is strategic philanthropy? How does it differ from more traditional philanthropic efforts?

5. What are some major social responsibility issues? Give an example of each.

6. What is the difference between ethics and social responsibility?

7. Why is ethics an important consideration in marketing decisions?

8. How do the factors that influence ethical or unethical decisions interact?

9. What ethical conflicts may exist if business employees fly on certain airlines just to receive benefits for their personal "frequent flier" programs?

10. Give an example of how ethical issues can affect each component of the marketing mix.

11. How can the ethical decisions involved in marketing be improved?

12. How can people with different personal values work together to make ethical decisions in organizations?

13. What tradeoffs might a company have to make to be socially responsible and responsive to society's demands?

14. What evidence exists that being socially responsible and ethical is worthwhile?

APPLICATION QUESTIONS

1. Some organizations promote their social responsibility. These companies often claim that being ethical is good business and that it pays to be a "good corporate citizen." Identify an organization in your community that has a reputation for being ethical and socially responsible. What activities account for this image? Is the company successful? Why or why not?

2. If you had to conduct a social audit of your organization's ethics and social responsibility, what information would most interest you? What key stakeholders would you want to communicate with? How could such an audit assist the company in improving its ethics and social responsibility?

3. Suppose that in your job you face situations that require you to make decisions about what is right or wrong and then act on these decisions. Describe such a situation. Without disclosing your actual decision, explain what you based it on. What and whom did you think of when you were considering what to do? Why did you consider them?

4. Consumers interact with many businesses daily and weekly. Not only do companies in an industry acquire a reputation for being ethical or unethical; entire industries also become known as ethical or unethical. Identify two types of businesses with which you or others you know have had the most conflict involving ethical issues. Describe those ethical issues.

INTERNET EXERCISE

Visit **www.cengage.com/marketing/pride-ferrell** for resources to help you master the material in this chapter, plus materials that will help you expand your marketing knowledge, including Internet exercise updates, ACE Self-Tests, hotlinks to companies featured in this chapter, and much more.

Business for Social Responsibility

Business for Social Responsibility (BSR) is a nonprofit organization for companies who want to operate responsibly and demonstrate respect for ethical values, people, communities, and the natural environment. Founded in 1992, BSR offers members practical information, research, educational programs, and technical assistance, as well as the opportunity to network with peers on current social responsibility issues. To learn more about this organization and access its many resources, visit **www.bsr.org**.

1. What types of businesses join BSR, and why?

2. Describe the services available to member companies. How can these services help companies improve their performances?

3. Peruse the "CRS Issue Areas and Information Links" and find the reports on ethics codes and training. Using these reports, list some examples of corporate codes of ethics and training.

developing your MARKETING PLAN

When developing a marketing strategy, companies must consider that their decisions affect not only their own company but also society in general. Many socially responsible and ethical companies identify their intentions as part of their mission statement, which serves as a guide for making all decisions about the company, including those in the marketing plan. To assist you in relating the information in this chapter to the development of your marketing plan, consider the following.

1. Determine the level of importance that marketing citizenship holds in your company. Identify the various stakeholders who would be affected by your strategic decisions.
2. Referring to Table 4.2 as a guide, discuss how the negative impact of your product's production and use could be minimized.
3. Using Table 4.3, identify additional issues related to your product for each of the 4Ps.

   The information obtained from these questions should assist you in developing various aspects of your marketing plan found in the *Interactive Marketing Plan* exercise at **www.cengage.com/marketing/pride-ferrell.**

globalEDGE

1. Corporate social responsibility is an emerging area of interest for firms. As such, many companies have conducted research and developed reports on corporate social responsibility. One such report is the KPMG International Survey of Corporate Responsibility Reporting. This report can be accessed using the search term "international survey" at **http://globaledge.msu.edu/ibrd.** In the most recent report, which category of corporate social responsibility was most widely reported, and what does it say?
2. The use of bribery in the business setting is an important ethical dilemma that many companies face both domestically and globally. Although bribery is illegal for U.S. companies to use as a business strategy, there are still industries and countries in which it is perceived as acceptable. Transparency International's Bribe Payers Index, which assesses the perceived level of bribery in each country, can be found using the search term "bribe payers" at **http://globaledge.msu.edu/ibrd.** Using the most recent index, find the three industries in which bribery is perceived to be least prevalent. How does this compare with the three industries thought to have the largest problems with bribery?

video CASE 4.1

Ben & Jerry's Makes Ethics and Social Responsibility Tasty and Profitable

Ben Cohen and Jerry Greenfield opened their first ice cream shop on May 5, 1978, in a converted gas station in Burlington, Vermont. Armed with nothing more than $12,000 worth of secondhand equipment, their hippie spirit, and the knowledge gained from a $5 correspondence course in ice cream making, they launched what was to become one of the most successful, and ethical, ice cream companies around. In addition to international distribution, Ben & Jerry's now has 450 franchise "scoop shops" in North America and 240 in other parts of the world.

From the beginning, Cohen and Greenfield made social responsibility a key concern—responsibility to key stakeholders including their employees, consumers, the community, and the world at large. Interestingly,

Ben & Jerry's has three integrated mission statements focused on the product, the economy, and society. According to the company, their success expands from their belief that all stakeholders must flourish equally in a way that commands respect for all individuals and supports local communities. Even after Unilever's purchase of the company in 2000, Ben & Jerry's has fought to maintain these missions.

Many Ben & Jerry's consumers, stakeholders, and employees remain loyal to the company because of its ethical reputation. For example, the Ben & Jerry's Foundation is dedicated to encouraging social change through the donation of 7.5 percent of the company's pretax profits. The company contributes a minimum of $1.1 million in corporate philanthropy annually, most of which is employee led. Ben & Jerry's has also been a leader in the evolution of environmentally conscious businesses. In 2001, Ben & Jerry's debuted the "Eco-Pint" container, a more environmentally friendly, unbleached, paperboard pint that does not use the chemicals required in traditional paper processing. To reduce its carbon footprint, the company purchases carbon offsets from NativeEnergy, a turbine wind power project developed by the Rosebud St. Francis tribe of South Dakota, and reduced overall CO_2 output by 32 percent between 2002 and 2007.

Ben & Jerry's social concern is also reflected in its products. For example, ONE Cheesecake Brownie ice cream emerged out of a partnership with Google, and profits are donated to the grassroots ONE campaign to fight extreme poverty around the world. Likewise, profits from Willie Nelson's Country Peach Cobbler ice cream are donated to Farm Aid. Ben & Jerry's also uses sustainably harvested inputs whenever possible, such as Fair Trade certified ingredients, eggs from cage-free chickens, and hormone-free milk.

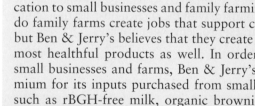

Always cognizant of its hippie roots, Ben & Jerry's further displays its social commitment through a dedication to small businesses and family farming. Not only do family farms create jobs that support communities, but Ben & Jerry's believes that they create the best and most healthful products as well. In order to support small businesses and farms, Ben & Jerry's pays a premium for its inputs purchased from small operations, such as rBGH-free milk, organic brownies, and Fair Trade rainforest nuts.

Ben & Jerry's even gears its promotional efforts toward its social mission by choosing to advertise through events such as music and arts festivals, including the Newport Folk Festival, Farm Aid, and its own One World, One Heart festival. By doing so, the company promotes itself as a socially responsible business while simultaneously drawing attention to the efforts that it supports. Even a buyout by one of the world's largest MNCs has not weakened Ben & Jerry's vision. Unilever purchased the company in 2000, but insisted upon a special arrangement wherein Ben & Jerry's would maintain its operational independence from Unilever's other ice cream business. It has also maintained a separate board of directors. In this way, Ben & Jerry's has managed to maintain a level of autonomy that preserves both its social mission and its brand integrity. When you enjoy Ben & Jerry's ice creams and sorbets, you not only know that they taste great, but you can rest easy knowing that you are buying something that was produced with an eye toward being green, ethical, and socially responsible—and that is good for small businesses.[65]

Questions for Discussion

1. How has Ben & Jerry's appealed to its target markets using social responsibility in their marketing?
2. Could all companies adopt Ben & Jerry's business model and relate it to their stakeholders?
3. How has Ben & Jerry's maintained its philosophy of social responsibility, even after being sold to industry giant Unilever?

CASE 4.2

PETCO: Putting Pets First Earns Loyal Customers

PETCO Animal Supplies is the nation's number two specialty pet supply retailer, with more than 850 stores in 49 states and the District of Columbia. Its pet-related products include pet food, pet supplies, grooming products, toys, novelty items, vitamins, veterinary supplies, and small pets such as fish, birds, and hamsters. It does not sell cats or dogs. PETCO strives to offer customers a complete assortment of pet-related products and services at competitive prices at convenient locations and through its website, **www.petco.com**, with a high level of customer service.

Most PETCO stores are 12,000 to 15,000 square feet and conveniently located near local neighborhood shopping destinations, such as supermarkets, bookstores, coffee shops, dry cleaners, and video stores, where its target customers make regular weekly shopping trips. PETCO executives believe the company is well positioned, in terms of both product offerings and location, to benefit from favorable long-term demographic trends: a growing pet population and an increasing willingness of "pet parents" to spend on their pets. Indeed, the U.S. pet population has now reached 378 million companion animals, including 143 million cats and dogs. An estimated 62 percent of all U.S. households own at least one pet, and three-quarters of those households have two or more pets. The trend to have more pets and the number of pet-owning households will continue to grow, driven by an increasing number of children under 18 as well as a growing population of empty nesters whose pets become their new children. U.S. retail sales of pet food, supplies, small animals (excluding cats and dogs), and services grew to approximately $34 billion in 2004.

PETCO was founded on the principle of "connecting with the community." One of its most important missions is to promote the health, well-being, and humane treatment of animals. It strives to carry out this mission through vendor-selection programs, pet-adoption programs, and partnerships with animal welfare organizations. The company is involved every year in a number of programs to raise money for local communities and local animal initiatives.

Recognizing that between 5 and 10 million pets are euthanized in the United States every year, PETCO launched an annual "Spay Today" initiative in 2000 to address the growing problem of pet overpopulation in the United States. The "Spay Today" funds come from customer donations at PETCO stores, where customers are encouraged to round up their purchases to the nearest dollar or more. In 2005, PETCO launched the "Think Adoption First" program, which supports and promotes the human-animal bond. It is a program that sets the standard for responsibility and community involvement for the industry. The "Spring a Pet" fundraiser encourages pet lovers to donate $1, $5, $10, or $20 to animal welfare causes. Donors received a personalized cutout bunny as a reminder of their generosity. In 2007, $1.7 million was raised, and each PETCO store selected an animal welfare organization to be the recipient of the money raised at its location. The Tree of Hope program encourages customers to think of animals during the Christmas season. Customers who visit PETCO during the Christmas season can purchase card ornaments, the proceeds of which go to animal welfare charities. The PETCO Foundation also sponsors "Kind News," a Humane Education Program that educates children about humane treatment of companion animals and fellow human beings. It features stories about responsible pet environmental concerns and issues as well as information on all types of animals.

Like all companies, PETCO operates in an environment in which a single negative incident can influence customers' perceptions of a firm's image and reputation instantly and potentially for years afterward. Because pets engender such strong emotional attachments, it is especially important for companies that sell pets and pet products to provide a rapid response to justify or to correct activities that may arouse potentially negative perceptions. The focus should be on a commitment to make correct decisions and to continually assess and address the risks of operating the business.

All retailers are subject to criticisms and must remain vigilant to maintain internal controls that provide assurance that employees and other partners follow ethical codes. PETCO accomplishes this through an ethics office and by developing an ethical corporate culture. PETCO has also developed and implemented a comprehensive code of ethics, which addresses all areas of organizational risk associated with human resources, conflicts of interests, and appropriate behavior in the workplace. The code's primary emphasis is that animals always come first. PETCO insists that the well-being of animals in its care is of paramount importance. In the case of PETCO, a desire to do the right thing and to train all organizational members to make ethical decisions ensures not only success in the marketplace but a significant contribution to society.[66]

Questions for Discussion

1. How does PETCO's ethics program help manage the risks associated with the pet industry?
2. How can PETCO's social responsibility programs advance its marketing strategy?
3. Why is it important for PETCO to train all of its employees to understand and implement its ethical policies?

strategic CASE 2

Texas Instruments

Introduction

Texas Instruments (TI) strives to develop the most effective organizational ethics and compliance program possible. The company knows it is vital to identify potential risks and uncover the existence of activities or events that relate to misconduct. It also understands that it must have the infrastructure and a plan in place to deal with unethical issues or events, which must include a rapid-response system. Through explicit codes of conduct and statements of values and ethics documented in organizational communication, TI must maintain the values, the culture, and the expectations for conduct that employees hold about daily life within the firm. This same goal is also accomplished implicitly through stories about ethical decisions, by treatment of customer and employee complaints, and by the way that meetings are conducted. Another way employees learn a company's code of conduct is by noticing which behaviors and accomplishments get rewarded and recognized and which behaviors are criticized, ignored, or punished.

Texas Instruments Incorporated (NYSE: TXN) is headquartered in Dallas, Texas, and has manufacturing, design, or sales operations in more than 25 countries. It has three separate business segments: (1) Semiconductor, which accounts for about 85 percent of its revenue; (2) Sensors & Controls, which accounts for about 10 percent of its revenue; and (3) Educational & Productivity Solutions, which accounts for about 5 percent of its revenue. Its largest geographic sources of revenue, in order, are Asia (excluding Japan), Europe, the United States, and Japan. The company's vision is world leadership in digital solutions for the networked society. It wants to accomplish this with excellence in everything it does, by producing products and technologies that make them and its customers substantially different from the competition, by competing in high-growth markets, and by providing consistently good financial performance.

Background and History

The company was founded in 1930 as Geophysical Service Inc. (GSI), a pioneering provider of seismic exploration services. In December 1941, four GSI managers purchased the company, as the United States entered World War II. During the war, the company began manufacturing submarine detection equipment for the U.S. Navy, and following the war, it became a supplier of defense systems and launched a strategy that would completely change the company. In 1951, the company changed its name to Texas Instruments (TI) to reflect the change in its business strategy, and it entered the semiconductor business in 1952.

TI designed the first transistor radio in 1954, the handheld calculator in 1967, and the single-chip microcomputer in 1971. It was assigned the first patent on a single-chip microprocessor in 1973. TI is usually given credit with Intel for the almost simultaneous invention of the microprocessor.

TI also created the first commercial silicon transistor and invented the integrated circuit. It continued to manufacture equipment for use in the seismic industry, as well as providing seismic services. TI sold its GSI subsidiary to Halliburton in 1988 and in the early 1990s began a strategic process of focusing on its semiconductor business, primarily digital signal processors and analog semiconductors. Few companies can match the 75-year record of innovations from TI. Today TI continues to work in processing and interpreting signals, and its products are used in many things that are an integral part of our daily lives—from the single-chip mobile-phone solution to cable modems, home theaters, wireless Internet, digital cameras, and advanced automotive systems. TI is also working on new signal-processing innovations that will help create cars that drive themselves and allow the blind to see, as well as much more.

The Business of TI

Semiconductors are the electronic building blocks used to create modern electronic systems and equipment. Semiconductors come in two basic forms: individual transistors and integrated circuits (generally known as "chips") that combine different transistors on a single piece of material to form a complete electronic circuit. TI's Semiconductor segment designs, manufactures, and sells integrated circuits.

The global semiconductor market is characterized by constant, though generally incremental, advances in product designs and manufacturing methods. Typically, new chips are produced in limited quantities at first and then are ramped up to high-volume production over time. Chip prices and manufacturing costs tend to decline over time as manufacturing methods and product life cycles mature.

The "semiconductor cycle" is an important concept that refers to the ebb and flow of supply and demand. The semiconductor market is characterized by periods of tight supply caused by strong demand and/or insufficient manufacturing capacity, followed by periods of surplus products caused by declining demand and/or excess manufacturing capacity. This cycle is affected by the significant time and capital required to build and maintain semiconductor manufacturing facilities.

TI was the world's third-largest semiconductor company in 2004 in terms of revenue. Historically, its Semiconductor segment averages a significantly higher growth rate than its other two business segments. About 75 percent of Semiconductor revenue comes from its core products, which are analog semiconductors and digital signal processors, or DSPs. These products enhance, and often make possible, a variety of applications that serve the communications, computer, consumer, automotive, and industrial markets. The company believes that virtually all of today's digital electronic equipment requires some form of analog or digital signal processing.

TI also designs and manufactures other types of semiconductors, such as Digital Light Processing™ devices that enable exceptionally clear video and microprocessors that serve as the brains of high-end computer servers. Knowledge about the systems its products go into is becoming increasingly important because it enables TI to differentiate its product offerings for its customers. Where a customer may have previously required multiple chips for a system to operate, TI now uses its system-level knowledge to integrate the functionality of those multiple chips onto fewer chips. A recent example is its single-chip cell phone, which combines the functionality of many separate chips onto a single chip. The digitization of electronics also requires more high-performance analog functionality. With expertise in both digital signal processing and analog at the system level, TI believes it is one of a very few semiconductor companies capable of integrating both technologies onto a single chip.

In addition, TI enables its customers, particularly original design manufacturers (ODMs), to take advantage of its system-level knowledge. This speeds its customers' time to market by making available to them standard chipsets and reference designs. Reference designs are technical blueprints that contain all the essential elements in a system. Customers using its reference designs, such as cell phone ODMs, may enhance or modify the design as required. TI's ability to deliver integrated solutions and system-level knowledge allows its customers to create more advanced systems and products.

In each of its product categories, TI faces significant competition. TI believes that competitive performance in the semiconductor market depends upon several factors, including the breadth of a company's product line as well as technological innovation, quality, reliability, price, customer service, technical support, and scale.

Employee Stakeholders

TI employs approximately 30,000 people worldwide, with about 15,000 in the United States. During the last year, TI's job growth was −6 percent, or a reduction of 1,076 people, while its voluntary turnover was 5 percent. TI's workforce is made up of 34 percent minorities and 25 percent women. The company supports diversity through 30 employee-networking groups. Among them are the "lesbian and gay employee network," "Christian Values Initiative," and "Muslim Initiative." TI has also been mentioned as one of nine companies that have a "Best 401k Match": it offers a 100 percent match up to 4 percent of total compensation. In addition to financial incentives, Texas Instruments offers employees ancillary benefits such as flexible work options, an employee trip–reduction program, an onsite concierge, a day spa, elder care, a summer camp for kids, and even special-interest clubs such as a flying club.

TI's flexible work arrangements include flextime, part time, compressed workweek schedules, and telecommuting. It has New Mothers Rooms for nursing mothers in all major facilities and an online parents' network for employees to share information on issues related to children and parenting. Onsite seminars on topics such as parenting, child care, elder care, and other work-life balance issues are yet another benefit. TI also has corporate wellness programs, services, and recreation associations, which include a child-care room at the onsite Dallas fitness center. Its wellness programs include tobacco-cessation programs, travel-well programs for worldwide employees, and immunizations and preventive screenings for TI employees. TI also provides onsite walking and weight management programs, as well as nutrition resources to ensure that its employees are as healthy as possible. Its benefits include discount programs at daycare centers, education assistance, adoption benefits, life insurance options, pretax reimbursement accounts for dependent care and health care, and an employee assistance program that offers confidential counseling for TI employees and their family members. TI also offers a time bank program that allows accrued time off to be used for any reason.

Not only has TI been on the 2005 list of Best Employers for Healthy Lifestyles, from the National Business Group on Health's Institute on the Costs and Health Effects of Obesity, it was also listed on the 2005 Healthcare Heroes Award in the *Dallas Business Journal*. In 1998 it also received the C. Everett Koop National Health Award for excellence in health-risk reduction and cost-reduction programs, which is part of The Health Project at the University of Stanford.

TI ranked eighty-third on the Fortune list of "100 Best Companies to Work For" in 2006, up from eighty-sixth in 2005. In 2008, it ranked 100, down from 87 in 2007. The year 2008 marks the ninth time that TI has been on the list. This list is based on two criteria: an evaluation of the policies and culture of each company and the opinions of the company's employees. The opinions of employees are given a weight of two-thirds of the total score and are based on responses to a 57-question survey of 350 randomly selected employees. The remaining one-third of the score is based on an evaluation of each company's demographic makeup, pay, and benefits programs and culture. Companies are scored in four areas: credibility (communication to employees), respect (opportunities and benefits), fairness (compensation, diversity), and pride/camaraderie (philanthropy, celebrations).

TI also ranked thirteenth on *Business Ethics* magazine's "100 Best Corporate Citizens" in 2007, up from fiftieth in 2005. The aim of the list is to identify firms that excel at serving a variety of stakeholders with excellence and integrity. For each company the list rates eight categories: shareholders, community, minorities and women, employees, environment, human rights, customers, and governance. For each area, strengths and concerns are matched against each other to arrive at the final score. TI is also a member of the Domini 400 Social Index and has won numerous awards for corporate citizenship and ethics as well as for being a good employer and for its diversity.

TI is also concerned with the environment, safety, and health. It is a "Sony Green Partner" for supplying components, devices, and materials to ensure the production of environmentally friendly products. TI is also building a "green" chip factory in Richardson, near Dallas. Although China, Taiwan, and Singapore were all tempting alternatives, TI proposed a challenge to the design team: if the TI design team and community leaders could find a way to build the new factory for $180 million less than the last Dallas factory built in the late 1990s, then TI would locate in Dallas. The design team did it. Instead of three floors, the new design has just two, and it is expected to cut utility costs by 20 percent and water usage by 35 percent. Creative design and engineering will eliminate waste and reduce energy usage. Almost all the waste from the building construction is being recycled and all the urinals are waterless.

TI Ethics Program

TI has always been concerned about ethics in its company. The company believes that maintaining the highest ethical standards requires a partnership between employees and employers. It proactively supports employees by communicating values and giving individual guidance, while empowered employees participate actively in problem solving. In 1987, TI decided to actively support employees by establishing a TI ethics office and appointing a TI ethics director. The TI Ethics Office has three primary functions:

To ensure that business policies and practices continue to be aligned with ethical principles.
To clearly communicate ethical expectations.
To provide multiple channels for feedback through which people can ask questions, voice concerns, and seek resolution to ethical issues.

TI has strong documented requirements for ethical business practices. These include the TI Standard Policies and Procedures, the TI Commitment, and "The Values and Ethics of TI" booklet. The TI Values and Principles are:

Integrity—respect and value people; be honest.
Innovation—learn and create; act boldly.
Commitment—take responsibility; commit to win.

The Ethics quick test is also an integral part of everything TI does. It is included in the Code of Ethics booklet as a punch-out card to put in a wallet or purse, and it is printed on the TI mouse pads given to employees.

The TI Ethics Quick Test:
Is the action legal?
Does it comply with our values?
If you do it, will you feel bad?
How will it look in the newspaper?
If you know it's wrong, don't do it!
If you're not sure, ask.
Keep asking until you get an answer.

There are many resources and alternative communication channels available to help ensure compliance—whether as an individual or as a company. These are the compliance procedures.

Take Direct Action. The best and most effective approach is to fix problems on the spot. If employees are considering an action or see a proposed action that raises ethical concerns, they should raise the ethical concerns right away. Frequently—perhaps usually—merely highlighting and discussing the issue will result in actions that achieve the desired goal in full compliance with TI's Values and Ethics Statement and the Code of Business Conduct. Employees should use available resources, including the Code of Ethics, the Values and Ethics Statement, the Code of Business Conduct, the Ethics Quick Test, Policies, Business Rules, Chart of Accounts, and other guidance.

Consult Your Supervisor. TI supervisors know employees' assignments and circumstances better than anyone else. TI supervisors can often help employees find answers and solutions if the one that is being tried just doesn't seem to fit.

Talk with Human Resources. If for any reason employees cannot communicate with a supervisor or local managers, they should contact the site Human Resources. The TI HR staff is there to help employees resolve many issues. Employees may counsel with them at any time.

Call the TI Law Department. For questions regarding contracts, pricing practices, or anything with a legal orientation, the TI Law Department can help employees find the answers. There are attorneys assigned to assist each business group, as well as attorneys who specialize in the areas of law that TI most frequently encounters.

Get Online. TI is an information-rich company. There are many sites on its intranet, where TI-specific information can be found.

Contact the TI Ethics Office. At any time, for any reason, employees can contact the TI Ethics Office for answers to questions, including any concerns about accounting, internal accounting controls, or auditing matters. They may even remain anonymous.[67]

Questions for Discussion

1. How effectively has TI managed the ethical and legal environment?
2. What are the ethical and legal risks associated with competing in TI's industries?
3. How would you describe TI's organizational culture?
4. Is there room for improvement in TI's ethics program?

part

3

Using Information, Technology, and Target Market Analysis

CHAPTERS

5 Marketing Research and Information Systems

6 Target Markets: Segmentation, Evaluation, and Positioning

Part Three examines how marketers use information and technology to better understand and reach customers. **Chapter 5** provides a foundation for analyzing buyers through a discussion of marketing information systems and the basic steps in the marketing research process. Understanding elements that affect buying decisions enables marketers to better analyze customers' needs and to evaluate how specific marketing strategies can satisfy those needs. **Chapter 6** deals with selecting and analyzing target markets, which is one of the major steps in marketing strategy development.

5 Marketing Research and Information Systems

LEARNING objectives

1. To describe the basic steps in conducting marketing research

2. To explore the fundamental methods of gathering data for marketing research

3. To describe the nature and role of information systems in marketing decision making

4. To understand how such tools as databases, decision support systems, and the Internet facilitate marketing research

5. To identify key ethical and international considerations in marketing research

iModerate Uses Text Messaging to Research Consumer Feelings

Marketing research serves as the eyes and ears of decision makers when it comes to planning and implementing marketing strategies. Researchers may use online questionnaires to reach respondents who have previously agreed to be contacted and have provided their e-mail addresses. The problem with online surveys, however, is that they provide only one-way communication without offering any insight into the respondent's personal feelings and attitudes. iModerate LLC, a new marketing research company, is attempting to deal with this issue. Carl Rosso, who cofounded the company with Joel Bensensen after working in polling for the administration of President Bill Clinton, observed that something seemed to be missing when surveys were done via the Internet. The surveys just did not provide *enough* information from each respondent, so he created a company to develop a new methodology to address this issue. Although it is not this company's intent to replace traditional marketing research companies, it is becoming an important add-on product to enhance efficient information gathering. Some of the clients that use the iMpact system include Coors, MTV, and the National Basketball Association.

iModerate's new methodology, iMpact, intercepts respondents for qualitative interviews. Participants are interviewed online via instant messaging, just like the instant messaging they already use at home and in the office. iModerate can use the online interviews to test reactions to advertisements in any medium, gain feedback on new-product names, and assess customer satisfaction as well as most other marketing research activities. The interactive online questionnaire creates sessions that expose feelings, uncover connections, and enhance survey data.

A team of 23 trained moderators at iModerate's office interact with one client at a time in up to two interviews simultaneously connected to the instant-messaging technology. The sessions created by the moderators can do just about anything except let respondents reach into the screen and grab a product. Moderators decipher if and how previous thoughts have changed and distinguish the respondents' points of view going forward. There is the opportunity for "tip-of-the-tongue" statements, preferences, and motivations, and the moderator can get a complete picture of the participants' thought processes that can add life to the research results.

The field of marketing research is changing very rapidly based on Internet research opportunities related to web-based forums, blogs, and news groups used to identify trends of interest and consumption patterns. iModerate is an example of using evolving technology and the Internet to allow for considerable flexibility in designing online questionnaires.[1]

Moderate and other marketing research firms enable marketers to implement the marketing concept by helping them acquire information about whether and how their goods and services satisfy the desires of target market customers. When used effectively, such information facilitates relationship marketing by helping marketers focus their efforts on meeting and even anticipating the needs of their customers. Marketing research and information systems that can provide practical and objective information to help firms develop and implement marketing strategies therefore are essential to effective marketing.

In this chapter, we focus on how marketers gather information needed to make marketing decisions. First, we define marketing research and examine the individual steps of the marketing research process, including various methods of collecting data. Next, we look at how technology aids in collecting, organizing, and interpreting marketing research data. Finally, we consider ethical and international issues in marketing research.

The Importance of Marketing Research

Marketing research is the systematic design, collection, interpretation, and reporting of information to help marketers solve specific marketing problems or take advantage of marketing opportunities. As the word *research* implies, it is a process for gathering information that is not currently available to decision makers. The purpose of marketing research is to inform an organization about customers' needs and desires, marketing opportunities for particular goods and services, and changing attitudes and purchase patterns of customers. Market information increases marketers' ability to respond to customer needs, which leads to improved organizational performance.[2] Detecting shifts in buyers' behaviors and attitudes helps companies stay in touch with the ever-changing marketplace. Coffee marketers, for example, would be very interested to know that demand for supermarket brands such as Folger's and Maxwell House is declining, whereas on-the-go brands such as Starbucks, Dunkin' Donuts, and McDonald's are growing at a compounded annual rate of 15 percent. Moreover, just 37 percent of 18- to 24-year-olds drink coffee today compared with 60 percent of those between 40 and 59 years of age.[3] Strategic planning requires marketing research to facilitate the process of assessing such opportunities or threats.

marketing research The systematic design, collection, interpretation, and reporting of information to help marketers solve specific marketing problems or take advantage of marketing opportunities

Marketing research can help a firm better understand market opportunities, ascertain the potential for success for new products, and determine the feasibility of a particular marketing strategy. JCPenney, for example, conducted extensive research to learn more about a core segment of shoppers who weren't being adequately reached by department stores: middle-income mothers between the ages of 35 and 54. The research involved asking 900 women about their casual clothes preferences. Later, the firm conducted in-depth interviews with 30 women about their clothing needs, feelings about fashion, and shopping experiences. The research helped the company recognize that this "missing middle" segment of shoppers was frustrated with the choices and quality of clothing available in their price range and stressed out by the experience of shopping for clothes for themselves. Armed with this information, Penney launched two new lines of moderately priced, quality casual women's clothing, including one by designer Nicole Miller.[4] A study by SPSS Inc. found that the most common reasons for conducting marketing research surveys included determining satisfaction (43 percent); product development (29 percent); branding (23 percent); segmentation (18 percent); awareness, trend tracking, and concept testing (18 percent); and business markets (11 percent).[5]

All sorts of organizations use marketing research to help them develop marketing mixes to match the needs of customers. Supermarkets, for example, have learned

Source: Data from National Coffee Association.

Value of Marketing Research

Irwin provides services to help companies better understand their customers' needs.

from marketing research that roughly half of all Americans prefer to have their dinners ready in 15 to 30 minutes. Such information highlights a tremendous opportunity for supermarkets to offer high-quality "heat and eat" meals to satisfy this growing segment of the food market. Political candidates also depend on marketing research to understand the scope of issues their constituents view as important. National political candidates may spend millions surveying voters to better understand issues and craft their images accordingly.

The real value of marketing research is measured by improvements in a marketer's ability to make decisions. Marketing research conducted for OfficeMax, for example, highlighted problems with store layouts that customers found confusing and supplied executives with ideas on how to improve the layouts. As a result, OfficeMax is replacing gridlike aisles with a less-cluttered "racetrack" layout that gives shoppers a clear view all the way to the back wall and invites them to peruse expensive electronics showcased inside a main aisle that loops inside each store.[6] Marketers should treat information the same way they use other resources, and they must weigh the costs of obtaining information against the benefits. Information should be judged worthwhile if it results in marketing activities that better satisfy the firm's target customers, lead to increased sales and profits, or help the firm achieve some other goal.

The Marketing Research Process

LO 1 To describe the basic steps in conducting marketing research

To maintain the control needed to obtain accurate information, marketers approach marketing research as a process with logical steps: (1) locating and defining problems or issues, (2) designing the research project, (3) collecting data, (4) interpreting research findings, and (5) reporting research findings (see Figure 5.1). These steps should be viewed as an overall approach to conducting research rather than as a rigid set of rules to be followed in each project. In planning research projects, marketers must consider each step carefully and determine how they can best adapt the steps to resolve the particular issues at hand.

Locating and Defining Problems or Research Issues

The first step in launching a research study is problem or issue definition, which focuses on uncovering the nature and boundaries of a situation or question related to marketing strategy or implementation. The first sign of a problem is typically a departure from some normal function, such as failure to attain objectives. If a corporation's objective is a 12 percent sales increase and the current marketing strategy resulted in a 6 percent increase, this discrepancy should be analyzed to help guide future marketing strategies. Declining sales, increasing expenses, and decreasing profits also signal problems. Customer relationship management (CRM) is frequently based on analysis of existing customers. However, research indicates that this information could be biased and therefore misleading when making decisions related to identifying and acquiring new customers.[7] Armed with this knowledge, a firm could define a problem as finding a way to adjust for biases stemming from existing customers when gathering data or to develop methods for gathering information to help find new customers. Conversely, when an organization experiences a dramatic rise in sales or some other positive event, it may conduct marketing research to discover the reasons and maximize the opportunities stemming from them.

Marketing research often focuses on identifying and defining market opportunities or changes in the environment. When a firm discovers a market opportunity, it may need to conduct research to understand the situation more precisely so it can craft an appropriate marketing strategy. For example, when General Motors saw that 42 percent of Hummer H3 buyers were women (compared to 26.3 percent of H2 buyers), it recognized an opportunity to position the smaller sport utility vehicle to appeal to women buyers.[8]

To pin down the specific boundaries of a problem or an issue through research, marketers must define the nature and scope of the situation in a way that requires probing beneath the superficial symptoms. The interaction between the marketing manager and the marketing researcher should yield a clear definition of the research need. Researchers and decision makers should remain in the problem or issue definition stage until they have determined precisely what they want from marketing research and how they will use it. Deciding how to refine a broad, indefinite problem or issue into a precise, researchable statement is a prerequisite for the next step in the research process.

Designing the Research Project

Once the problem or issue has been defined, the next step is to create a **research design,** an overall plan for obtaining the information needed to address it. This step requires formulating a hypothesis and determining what type of research is most appropriate for testing the hypothesis to ensure the results are reliable and valid.

Developing a Hypothesis. The objective statement of a marketing research project should include hypotheses based on both previous research and expected research findings. A **hypothesis** is an informed guess or assumption about a certain problem or set of circumstances. It is based on all the insight and knowledge available about the problem or circumstances from previous research studies and other sources. As information is gathered, the researcher can test the hypothesis. For example, a food marketer such as H. J. Heinz might propose the hypothesis that children today have considerable influence on their families' buying decisions regarding ketchup and other grocery products. A marketing researcher would then gather data, perhaps through surveys of children and their parents, and draw conclusions as to whether the hypothesis is correct. Movie theater, sports arena, and concert venue owners who may be wondering why sales are down sharply have hypothesized that consumers are

research design An overall plan for obtaining the information needed to address a research problem or issue

hypothesis An informed guess or assumption about a certain problem or set of circumstances

figure 5.1

THE FIVE STEPS OF THE MARKETING RESEARCH PROCESS

| 1 Locating and defining issues or problems | 2 Designing the research project | 3 Collecting data | 4 Interpreting research findings | 5 Reporting research findings |

E-ntertainment MARKETING

Pirated Music Provides Research for Radio Playlists

Although many in the music industry blame illegal song downloading for the current decline in music sales, data about file sharing are actually helping the radio industry boost its bottom line. BigChampagne LLC is a marketing research company that collects data about popular media and the tens of millions of people who get their music, movies, games, and other entertainment online. The company started out in 2000 focusing on the original Napster, but today it also incorporates information about a wide variety of legal and illegal downloading and "streaming" of music and video online, traditional radio, as well as information on traditional "bricks and mortar" sales and online sales. It collects information about how and where people enjoy popular music, movies, and other media and then analyzes the information to help clients learn what titles are most popular, who is interested, and, most important, why.

Radio networks such as Clear Channel Communications have used data on the most popular downloads from illegal file-sharing networks to help their radio stations shape their playlists. The theory is that the songs that attract the most downloads will also be popular on radio stations, which will attract listeners and therefore help stations sell advertising. The increased advertising and playing of songs will also come full circle and help the record labels as well because radio play is still the biggest factor influencing record sales.

However, some people are doubtful that using data about pirated music to help mold playlists will have any effect. The London-based IFPI music trade group believes that illegal file sharing has contributed to the continuing decline in music sales, which were down 7 percent last year after a 3 percent decline the year before. BigChampagne, however, contends that ignoring the illegal music downloads is the same as ignoring a fact of life. Joe Fleischer, BigChampagne's vice president for sales and marketing, says that the legality of downloading music is a completely separate issue from the insight into people's tastes that download information offers. Fleischer points out that his company does not rely solely on illegal downloads for its data; it also incorporates data from legal downloads such as from Apple's iTunes, although they represent only a tiny fraction of all downloads.

Although data from BigChampagne have been influencing a small number of radio stations' playlists, more traditional marketing research methods are still used in conjunction with the download data. Although some remain skeptical about the use of illegal download data to influence radio playlists, BigChampagne remains certain that it is going to be big. It has already surpassed its target of signing up 100 radio stations this year.[a]

staying home more because of rising event prices, widespread availability of home theater systems and broadband Internet access, and families' increasingly busy schedules.[9] Marketers could test these hypotheses by manipulating prices or offering strong incentives for consumers to return. Sometimes several hypotheses are developed during an actual research project; the hypotheses that are accepted or rejected become the study's chief conclusions.

Types of Research. The nature and type of research vary based on the research design and the hypotheses under investigation. Marketers may elect to conduct either exploratory research or conclusive research. Although each has a distinct purpose, the major differences between them are formalization and flexibility rather than the specific research methods used. Table 5.1 summarizes the differences.

Exploratory Research. When marketers need more information about a problem or want to make a tentative hypothesis more specific, they may conduct **exploratory research.** The main purpose of exploratory research is to better understand a problem or situation and/or to help identify additional data needs or decision alternatives.[10]

exploratory research
Research conducted to gather more information about a problem or to make a tentative hypothesis more specific

| table 5.1 | DIFFERENCES BETWEEN EXPLORATORY AND CONCLUSIVE RESEARCH | |

Research Project Components	Exploratory Research	Conclusive Research
Research purpose	General: to generate insights about a situation	Specific: to verify insights and aid in selecting a course of action
Data needs	Vague	Clear
Data sources	Ill defined	Well defined
Data collection form	Open-ended, rough	Usually structured
Sample	Relatively small; subjectively selected to maximize generalization of insights	Relatively large; objectively selected to permit generalization of findings
Data collection	Flexible; no set procedure	Rigid; well-laid-out procedure
Data analysis	Informal; typically nonquantitative	Formal; typically quantitative
Inferences/ recommendations	More tentative than final	More final than tentative

Source: A. Parasuraman, Dhruv Grewal, and R. Krishnan, *Marketing Research,* p. 64. Copyright © 2004 by Houghton Mifflin Company. Used by permission.

Consider that until recently, there was no research available to help marketers understand how consumers perceive the terms *clearance* versus *sale* in describing a discounted price event. An exploratory study asked one group of 80 consumers to write down their thoughts about a store window sign that said "sale" and another group of 80 consumers about a store window sign that read "clearance." The results revealed that consumers expected deeper discounts when the term *clearance* was used, and they expected the quality of the clearance products to be lower than that of products on sale.[11] This exploratory research helped marketers better understand how consumers view these terms and opened up the opportunity for additional research hypotheses about decision alternatives for retail pricing.

Conclusive Research. **Conclusive research** is designed to verify insights through an objective procedure to help marketers make decisions. It is used when the marketer has one or more alternatives in mind and needs assistance in the final stages of decision making.[12] For example, exploratory research revealed that the terms *clearance* and *sale* send different signals to consumers, but to make a decision, a well-defined and structured research project could be used to help marketers decide which approach is best for a specific set of products and target consumers. The study would be specific to selecting a course of action and typically quantitative, using methods that can be verified. Two types of conclusive research are descriptive and experimental research.

If marketers need to understand the characteristics of certain phenomena to solve a particular problem, **descriptive research** can aid them. Descriptive studies may range from general surveys of customers' educations, occupations, or ages to specifics on how often teenagers consume sports drinks or how often customers buy new pairs of athletic shoes. For example, if Nike and Reebok want to target more young women, they might ask 15- to 35-year-old females how often they work out, how frequently they wear athletic shoes for casual use, and how many pairs of athletic shoes they buy in a year. Such descriptive research can be used to develop specific marketing strategies

conclusive research
Research designed to verify insights through objective procedures and to help marketers in making decisions

descriptive research
Research conducted to clarify the characteristics of certain phenomena to solve a particular problem

Primary Data Collection

M/A/R/C works with multinational companies to collect primary data to maintain strong brand equity.

experimental research
Research that allows marketers to make causal inferences about relationships

reliability A condition that exists when a research technique produces almost identical results in repeated trials

validity A condition that exists when a research method measures what it is supposed to measure

L O 2 To explore the fundamental methods of gathering data for marketing research

primary data Data observed and recorded or collected directly from respondents

secondary data Data compiled both inside and outside the organization for some purpose other than the current investigation

for the athletic-shoe market. Descriptive studies generally demand much prior knowledge and assume that the problem or issue is clearly defined. For example, a survey of automobile buyers found that those who use the Internet to search for vehicles are more likely to be younger and more educated and to spend more time searching in general.[13] Some descriptive studies require statistical analysis and predictive tools. The marketer's major task is to choose adequate methods for collecting and measuring data.

Descriptive research is limited in providing evidence necessary to make causal inferences (i.e., that variable X causes a variable Y). **Experimental research** allows marketers to make causal deductions about relationships.[14] Such experimentation requires that an independent variable (one not influenced by or dependent on other variables) be manipulated and the resulting changes in a dependent variable (one contingent on, or restricted to, one value or set of values assumed by the independent variable) be measured. For example, when Coca-Cola introduced Dasani flavored waters, managers needed to estimate sales at various potential price points. In some markets, Dasani was introduced at $6.99 per six pack. By holding variables such as advertising and shelf position constant, Coca-Cola could manipulate the price variable to study its effect on sales. If sales increased 40 percent when the price was reduced by $2, then managers could make an informed decision about the effect of price on sales. Coca-Cola could also use experimental research to manipulate other variables such as advertising or in-store shelf position to determine their effect on sales. Manipulation of the causal variable and control of other variables are what make experimental research unique. As a result, they can provide much stronger evidence of cause and effect than data collected through descriptive research.

Research Reliability and Validity. In designing research, marketing researchers must ensure that research techniques are both reliable and valid. A research technique has **reliability** if it produces almost identical results in repeated trials. However, a reliable technique is not necessarily valid. To have **validity,** the research method must measure what it is supposed to measure, not something else. For example, although a group of customers may express the same level of satisfaction based on a rating scale, as individuals they may not exhibit the same repurchase behavior because of different personal characteristics. This result may cause the researcher to question the validity of the satisfaction scale if the purpose of rating satisfaction was to estimate potential repurchase behavior.[15] A study to measure the effect of advertising on sales would be valid if advertising could be isolated from other factors or variables that affect sales. The study would be reliable if replications of it produced the same results.

Collecting Data

The next step in the marketing research process is collecting data to help prove (or disprove) the research hypothesis. The research design must specify what types of data to collect and how they will be collected.

Types of Data. Marketing researchers have two types of data at their disposal. **Primary data** are observed and recorded or collected directly from respondents. This type of data must be gathered by observing phenomena or surveying people of interest. **Secondary data** are compiled both inside and outside the organization for some purpose other than the current investigation. Secondary data include general reports supplied to an enterprise by various data services and internal and online databases. Such reports might concern market share, retail inventory levels, and customers' buying behavior. Commonly, secondary data are already available in private or public reports or have been collected and stored by the organization itself. Due to the opportunity to obtain data via the Internet, more than half of all marketing research now comes from secondary sources.

green MARKETING

Message in a Bottle: Secondary Data Provide Recycling Lessons

Many marketing problems can be analyzed through secondary data. Information compiled inside and outside the organization for some purpose other than current decision making can provide data to indicate challenges that need attention. An example of current data related to social responsibility and environmental challenges is beverage companies' reaction to the branded-water market. Leading companies such as Coca-Cola, Nestlé, and PepsiCo are gathering information on the current impact of discarded plastic bottles on the environment.

The Beverage Container Recycling Report, compiled by As You Sow and the Container Recycling Institute, provided current data on beverage companies' recycling efforts for consumers and other stakeholders. The report identifies efforts by beverage producers to use more recycled content in their containers, increase recovery in recycling, and reduce material use. The report evaluated 12 beverage companies by using publicly available information from websites and annual reports and on the basis of survey responses. According to the study, PepsiCo leads the surveyed beverage companies in container recycling with a grade of C. Slightly behind PepsiCo in total score but also earning a C is Coca-Cola, which is on par with PepsiCo on most recycling issues, with the exception that it

is not using 10 percent recycled content in its plastic bottles in North America.

The Coca-Cola Company, which has a 36 percent share of the $106-billion-a-year nonalcoholic ready-to-drink beverage business, plans to build a plant that will be able to recycle 2 billion 20-ounce bottles annually. PepsiCo is looking for ways to boost consumer interest in recycling. Although both Coke and Pepsi have traditionally contested efforts to enact laws mandating deposits on bottles and cans, some beverage companies are looking more positively toward financial incentives for recycling.

Last year more than 5 billion pounds of polyethylene terephthalate (PET) was used in plastic containers, and of that only about 1 billion pounds were recycled. At salvage prices that range as high as 25 cents per pound, the remaining 4 billion pounds represent the equivalent of sending 1 billion $1 bills to landfills. Although beverage makers have shrunk the weight of their PET bottles, recycling rates have slowed. Recycling efforts in the United States are falling behind; in 1995 the country used about 2 billion pounds of "virgin" PET resin and recycled approximately 775 million pounds. Every day in the United States more than 60 million plastic water bottles are thrown away. Most end up in landfills or incinerators, but millions litter America's streets, parks, and waterways.

Beverage companies must rethink and develop new strategies to deal with the problem that their products are creating. In this case secondary data are providing information about the issues associated with plastic beverage bottles, not only to beverage companies but to consumer groups, regulatory officials, and other stakeholders concerned with ecology and the environment. With PET container-recycling rates decreasing in the United States, it is important for bottlers to get the message and reduce the weight of their bottles, facilitate recycling, and increase the amount of recycled material in their bottles.[b]

Sources of Secondary Data. Marketers often begin the data-collection phase of the marketing research process by gathering secondary data. They may use available reports and other information from both internal and external sources to study a marketing problem.

Internal sources of secondary data can contribute tremendously to research. An organization's own database may contain information about past marketing activities, such as sales records and research reports, that can be used to test hypotheses and pinpoint problems. From sales reports, for example, a firm may be able to determine not only which product sold best at certain times of the year but also which colors and sizes customers preferred. Such information may have been gathered using customer-relationship management tools for marketing, management, or financial purposes.

Accounting records are also an excellent source of data but, surprisingly, are often overlooked. The large volume of data an accounting department collects does not automatically flow to other departments. As a result, detailed information about costs, sales, customer accounts, or profits by product category may not be easily accessible to the marketing area. This condition develops particularly in organizations that do not store marketing information on a systematic basis. A third source of internal secondary data is competitive information gathered by the sales force.

External sources of secondary data include trade associations, periodicals, government publications, unpublished sources, and online databases. Trade associations such as the American Marketing Association offer guides and directories that are rife with information. Periodicals such as *Business Week,* the *Wall Street Journal, Sales & Marketing Management, Advertising Age, Marketing Research,* and *Industrial Marketing* publish general information that can help marketers define problems and develop hypotheses. *Survey of Buying Power,* an annual supplement to *Sales & Marketing Management,* contains sales data for major industries on a county-by-county basis. Many marketers also consult federal government publications such as the *Statistical Abstract of the United States,* the *Census of Business,* the *Census of Agriculture,* and the *Census of Population;* most of these government publications are available online. Although the government still conducts its primary census every ten years, it now surveys 250,000 households every month, providing marketers with a more up-to-date demographic picture of the nation's population every year. Target executives, for example, use such data to make merchandising and marketing decisions and to identify promising locations for new Target stores.[16]

In addition, companies may subscribe to services, such as ACNielsen or Information Resources, Inc. (IRI), that track retail sales and other information. For example, IRI tracks consumer purchases using in-store, scanner-based technology. Marketing firms can purchase information from IRI about a product category, such as frozen orange juice, as secondary data.[17] Small businesses may be unable to afford such services, but they can still find a wealth of information through industry publications and trade associations.[18]

The Internet can be especially useful to marketing researchers. Search engines such as Google can help marketers locate many types of secondary data or to research topics of interest. Of course, companies can mine their own websites for useful information by using CRM tools. Amazon.com, for example, has built a relationship with its customers by tracking the types of books, music, and other products they purchase. Each time a customer logs on to the website, the company can offer recommendations based on the customer's previous purchases. Such a marketing system helps the company track the changing desires and buying habits of its most valued customers. And marketing researchers are increasingly monitoring blogs to discover what consumers are saying about their products—both positive and negative. Some, including yogurt maker Stonyfield Farms, have even established their own blogs as a way to monitor consumer dialog on issues of their choice. Table 5.2 lists the reasons people blog, and Table 5.3 summarizes the external sources of secondary data, excluding syndicated services.

Methods of Collecting Primary Data. Collecting primary data is a lengthier, more expensive, and more complex process than collecting secondary data. To gather

table 5.2 WHY PEOPLE CHOOSE TO BLOG	
Why People Choose to Blog	**Percent Who Cite as Primary Reason**
To express themselves creatively	52
To document their personal experiences and/or share them with others	50
To keep in touch with friends and family	37
To share their practical knowledge or skills with others	34
To motivate other people to action	29
To entertain other people	28
To store resources or information that is important to them	28
To influence the way other people think	27
To network or to meet new people	16
To make money	7

Source: "Bloggers: A Portrait of the Internet's New Storytellers," Pew/Internet & American Life Project, July 19, 2006, www.pewinternet.org/pdfs/PIP%20Bloggers%20Report%20July%2019%202006.pdf.

primary data, researchers use sampling procedures, survey methods, and observation. These efforts can be handled in-house by the firm's own research department or contracted to a private research firm such as ACNielsen; Information Resources, Inc.; or IMS International.

Sampling. Because the time and resources available for research are limited, it is almost impossible to investigate all the members of a target market or other population. A **population,** or "universe," includes all the elements, units, or individuals of interest to researchers for a specific study. For example, for a Gallup poll designed to predict the results of a presidential election, all registered voters in the United States would constitute the population. By systematically choosing a limited number of units—a **sample**—to represent the characteristics of a total population, researchers can project the reactions of a total market or market segment. (In the case of the presidential poll, a representative national sample of several thousand registered voters would be selected and surveyed to project the probable voting outcome.) **Sampling** in marketing research, therefore, is the process of selecting representative units from a total population. Sampling techniques allow marketers to predict buying behavior fairly accurately on the basis of the responses from a representative portion of the population of interest. Most types of marketing research employ sampling techniques.

There are two basic types of sampling: probability sampling and nonprobability sampling. With **probability sampling,** every element in the population being studied has a known chance of being selected for study. Random sampling is a form of probability sampling. When marketers employ **random sampling,** all the units in a population have an equal chance of appearing in the sample. The various events that can occur have an equal or known chance of taking place. For example, a specific card in a regulation deck should have a 1/52 probability of being drawn at any one time. Sample units are ordinarily chosen by selecting from a table of random numbers statistically generated so that each digit, 0 through 9, will have an equal probability of occurring in each position in the sequence. The sequentially numbered elements of a population are sampled randomly by selecting the units whose numbers appear in the table of random numbers.

population All the elements, units, or individuals of interest to researchers for a specific study

sample A limited number of units chosen to represent the characteristics of a total population

sampling The process of selecting representative units from a total population

probability sampling A type of sampling in which every element in the population being studied has a known chance of being selected for study

random sampling A form of probability sampling in which all units in a population have an equal chance of appearing in the sample, and the various events that can occur have an equal or known chance of taking place

table 5.3   EXTERNAL SOURCES OF SECONDARY DATA

Government Sources

Economic Census	www.census.gov/econ/census02/index.html
Export.gov—country and industry market research	www.export.gov/mrktresearch/index.asp
National Technical Information Services	www.ntis.gov/
STAT-USA	www.stat-usa.gov/
Strategis—Canadian trade	http://strategis.ic.gc.ca/engdoc/main.html

Trade Associations and Shows

American Society of Association Executives	www.asaecenter.org/peoplegroups/content.cfm?ItemNumber=16433&navItemNumber=14962
Directory of Associations	www.marketingsource.com/associations/
Trade Show News Network	www.tsnn.com/
Tradeshow Week	www.tradeshowweek.com/

Magazines, Newspapers, Video, Audio News Programming

Blinkx	www.blinkx.com/home?safefilter=off
FindArticles.com	www.directcontactpr.com/jumpstation/
Google Video Search	http://video.google.com/
Media Jumpstation	www.directcontactpr.com/jumpstation/
News Directory	www.newsdirectory.com/magazine.php?cat=3&sub=&c=
Yahoo Video Search	http://video.search.yahoo.com/

Corporate Information

Annual Report Service	www.annualreportservice.com/
Bitpipe	http://www.bitpipe.com/
Business Wire—press releases	http://home.businesswire.com/portal/site/home/index.jsp?front_door=true
Hoover's Online	www.hoovers.com/free/
Open Directory Project	http://dmoz.org/
PR Newswire—press releases (Jan. 11, 2008)	www.prnewswire.com/

Collecting Data Through Surveys

Infosurv assists clients in the development and execution of online surveys.

stratified sampling A type of probability sampling in which the population is divided into groups with a common attribute and a random sample is chosen within each group

nonprobability sampling A sampling technique in which there is no way to calculate the likelihood that a specific element of the population being studied will be chosen

quota sampling A nonprobability sampling technique in which researchers divide the population into groups and then arbitrarily choose participants from each group

Another type of probability sampling is **stratified sampling,** in which the population of interest is divided into groups according to a common attribute, and a random sample is then chosen within each group. The stratified sample may reduce some of the error that could occur in a simple random sample. By ensuring that each major group or segment of the population receives its proportionate share of sample units, investigators avoid including too many or too few sample units from each group. Samples are usually stratified when researchers believe there may be variations among different types of respondents. For example, many political opinion surveys are stratified by gender, race, age, and/or geographic location.

The second type of sampling, **nonprobability sampling,** is more subjective than probability sampling because there is no way to calculate the likelihood that a specific element of the population being studied will be chosen. Quota sampling, for example, is highly judgmental because the final choice of participants is left to the researchers. In **quota sampling,** researchers divide the population into groups and then arbitrarily choose participants from each group. In quota sampling, there are some controls—usually limited to two or three variables, such as age, gender, or race—over the selection of participants. The controls attempt to ensure that representative categories of respondents are interviewed. A study of people who wear eyeglasses, for example, may be conducted by interviewing equal numbers of men and women who wear eyeglasses. Because quota samples are not probability samples, not everyone has an equal chance of being selected, and sampling error therefore cannot be measured statistically. Quota samples are used most often in exploratory studies, when hypotheses are being developed. Often a small quota sample will not be projected to the total population, although the findings may provide valuable insights into a problem. Quota samples are useful when people with some common characteristic are found and questioned about the topic of interest. A probability sample used to study people who are allergic to cats, for example, would be highly inefficient.

Survey Methods. Marketing researchers often employ sampling to collect primary data through mail, telephone, online, or personal interview surveys. The results of such surveys are used to describe and analyze buying behavior. The survey method chosen depends on the nature of the problem or issue; the data needed to test the hypothesis; and the resources, such as funding and personnel, available to the researcher. Marketers may employ more than one survey method depending on the goals of the research. The SPSS Inc. survey of American Marketing Association members found that 43.8 percent use telephone surveys; 39.3 percent, web-based surveys; 36.8 percent, focus groups; 19 percent, mail surveys; 11.8 percent, e-mail surveys; and 9.6 percent, in-person interviews.[19] Surveys can be quite expensive (Procter & Gamble spends about $200 million to have 600 organizations conduct surveys around the world),[20] but small businesses can turn to sites such as SurveyMonkey.com and zoomerang.com for inexpensive or even free online surveys. Table 5.4 summarizes and compares the advantages of the various survey methods.

table 5.4 COMPARISON OF THE FOUR BASIC SURVEY METHODS

	Mail Surveys	Telephone Surveys	Online Surveys	Personal Interview Surveys
Economy	Potentially lower in cost per interview than telephone or personal surveys if there is an adequate response rate.	Avoids interviewers' travel expenses; less expensive than in-home interviews.	The least expensive method if there is an adequate response rate.	The most expensive survey method; shopping mall and focus-group interviews have lower costs than in-home interviews.
Flexibility	Inflexible; questionnaire must be short and easy for respondents to complete.	Flexible because interviewers can ask probing questions, but observations are impossible.	Less flexible; survey must be easy for online users to receive and return; short, dichotomous, or multiple-choice questions work best.	Most flexible method; respondents can react to visual materials; demographic data are more accurate; in-depth probes are possible.
Interviewer bias	Interviewer bias is eliminated; questionnaires can be returned anonymously.	Some anonymity; may be hard to develop trust in respondents.	Interviewer bias is eliminated, but e-mail address on the return eliminates anonymity.	Interviewers' personal characteristics or inability to maintain objectivity may result in bias.
Sampling and respondents' cooperation	Obtaining a complete mailing list is difficult; nonresponse is a major disadvantage.	Sample limited to respondents with telephones; devices that screen calls, busy signals, and refusals are a problem.	Sample limited to respondents with computer access; the available e-mail address list may not be a representative sample for some purposes.	Not-at-homes are a problem, which may be overcome by focus-group and shopping mall interviewing.

Gathering information through surveys is becoming increasingly difficult because fewer people are willing to participate.[21] Many people believe responding to surveys takes up too much scarce personal time, especially as surveys become longer and more detailed. Others have concerns about how much information marketers are gathering and whether their privacy is being invaded. The unethical use of selling techniques disguised as marketing surveys has also led to decreased cooperation. These factors contribute to nonresponse rates for any type of survey.

In a **mail survey,** questionnaires are sent to respondents, who are encouraged to complete and return them. Mail surveys are used most often when the individuals in the sample are spread over a wide area and funds for the survey are limited. A mail survey is less expensive than a telephone or personal interview survey as long as the response rate is high enough to produce reliable results. The main disadvantages of this method are the possibility of a low response rate and of misleading results if respondents differ significantly from the population being sampled. One method of improving response rates involves attaching a brief note with a personal message on a Post-it® Note to the survey packet. Response rates to these surveys are higher, and the quality and timeliness of the responses are also improved.[22] As a result of these issues, companies are increasingly moving to Internet surveys and automated telephone surveys.

Premiums or incentives that encourage respondents to return questionnaires have been effective in developing panels of respondents who are interviewed regularly by mail. Such mail panels, selected to represent a target market or market segment, are especially useful in evaluating new products and providing general information about customers, as well as records of their purchases (in the form of purchase diaries). Mail panels and purchase diaries are much more widely used than custom mail surveys, but both panels and purchase diaries have shortcomings. People who take the time to fill out a diary may differ from the general population based on income, education, or behavior, such as the time available for shopping activities.

In a **telephone survey,** an interviewer records respondents' answers to a questionnaire over a phone line. A telephone survey has some advantages over a mail survey. The rate of response is higher because it takes less effort to answer the telephone and talk than to fill out and return a questionnaire. If enough interviewers are available, a telephone survey can be conducted very quickly. Thus, political candidates or organizations that want an immediate reaction to an event may choose this method. In addition, a telephone survey permits interviewers to gain rapport with respondents and ask probing questions. Automated telephone surveys, also known as interactive voice response or "robosurveys," rely on a recorded voice to ask the questions while a computer program records respondents' answers. The primary benefit of automated surveys is the elimination of any "bias" that might be introduced by a live researcher.

However, only a small proportion of the population likes to participate in telephone surveys. Just one-third of Americans are willing to participate in telephone interviews, down from two-thirds 20 years ago.[23] This poor image can significantly limit participation and distort representation in a telephone survey. Moreover, telephone surveys are limited to oral communication; visual aids or observation cannot be included. Interpreters of results must make adjustments for individuals who are not at home or do not have telephones. Many households are excluded from telephone directories by choice (unlisted numbers) or because the residents moved after the directory was published. Potential respondents often use telephone answering machines, voice mail, or caller ID to screen or block calls; millions have signed up for "Do Not Call Lists." Moreover, an increasing number of younger Americans are giving up their fixed telephone lines in favor of cellular or wireless phones.[24] These issues have serious implications for the use of telephone samples in conducting surveys. Some adjustment must be made for groups of respondents that may be undersampled because of a smaller-than-average incidence of telephone listings. Nondirectory telephone samples can overcome such bias. Various methods are available, including random-digit dialing (adding random numbers to the telephone prefix) and plus-one telephone sampling (increasing the last digit of a directory number by 1). These methods make it feasible to dial any working number, whether or not

mail survey A research method in which respondents answer a questionnaire sent through the mail

telephone survey A research method in which respondents' answers to a questionnaire are recorded by an interviewer on the phone

it is listed in a directory. However, these methods do not address the fact that younger Americans are increasingly favoring their cell phones, which marketing researchers may not call.[25]

Online surveys are evolving as an alternative to telephone surveys. In an **online survey,** questionnaires can be transmitted to respondents who have agreed to be contacted and have provided their e-mail addresses. Because e-mail is semi-interactive, recipients can ask for clarification of specific questions or pose questions of their own. The potential advantages of e-mail surveys are quick response and lower cost than traditional mail, telephone, and personal interview surveys if the response rate is adequate. In addition, more firms are using their websites to conduct surveys. Online surveys can also use online communities—such as chat rooms, web-based forums, blogs, and newsgroups—to identify trends in interests and consumption patterns. Movies, consumer electronics, food, and computers are popular topics in many online communities.[26] Indeed, by "listening in" on these ongoing conversations, marketers may be able to identify new product opportunities and consumer needs. Moreover, this type of online data can be gathered at little incremental cost compared to alternative data sources.[27] Evolving technology and the interactive nature of the Internet allow for considerable flexibility in designing online questionnaires.

Given the growing number of households that have computers with Internet access, marketing research is likely to rely heavily on online surveys in the future. Furthermore, as negative attitudes toward telephone surveys render that technique less representative and more expensive, the integration of e-mail, fax, and voice mail functions into one computer-based system provides a promising alternative for survey research. E-mail surveys have especially strong potential within organizations whose employees are networked and for associations that publish members' e-mail addresses. However, there are some ethical issues to consider when using e-mail for marketing research, such as unsolicited e-mail, which could be viewed as "spam," and privacy, as some potential survey respondents fear their personal information will be given or sold to third parties without their knowledge or permission.

In a **personal interview survey,** participants respond to questions face-to-face. Various audiovisual aids—pictures, products, diagrams, or prerecorded advertising copy—can be incorporated into a personal interview. Rapport gained through direct interaction usually permits more in-depth interviewing, including probes, follow-up questions, or psychological tests. In addition, because personal interviews can be longer, they may yield more information. Finally, respondents can be selected more carefully, and reasons for nonresponse can be explored.

One such research technique is the **in-home (door-to-door) interview.** The in-home interview offers a clear advantage when thoroughness of self-disclosure and elimination of group influence are important. In an in-depth interview of 45 to 90 minutes, respondents can be probed to reveal their real motivations, feelings, behaviors, and aspirations.

The object of a **focus-group interview** is to observe group interaction when members are exposed to an idea or a concept. General Motors, for example, used focus groups comprised of celebrity athletes, actors, and musicians, including XZibit, as part of its effort to redesign the Cadillac Escalade SUV and CTS sedan.[28] Focus-group interviews are often conducted informally, without a structured questionnaire, in small groups of 8 to 12 people. They allow customer attitudes, behaviors, lifestyles, needs, and desires to be explored in a flexible and creative manner. Questions are open-ended and stimulate respondents to answer in their own words. Researchers can ask probing questions to clarify something they do not fully understand or something unexpected and interesting that may help explain buying behavior. For example, Ford may use focus groups to determine whether to change its advertising to emphasize a vehicle's safety features rather than its style and performance. On the other hand, focus-group participants do not always tell the truth. Some participants may be less than honest in an effort to be sociable or to receive money and/or food in exchange for their participation.[29] However, they generally provide only qualitative, not quantitative data, and are thus best used to uncover issues that can then be explored using quantifiable marketing research techniques.

online survey A research method in which respondents answer a questionnaire via e-mail or on a website

personal interview survey A research method in which participants respond to survey questions face-to-face

in-home (door-to-door) interview A personal interview that takes place in the respondent's home

focus-group interview An interview that is often conducted informally, without a structured questionnaire, in small groups of 8 to 12 people, to observe interaction when members are exposed to an idea or a concept

More organizations are starting **customer advisory boards,** which are small groups of actual customers who serve as sounding boards for new-product ideas and offer insights into their feelings and attitudes toward a firm's products, promotion, pricing, and other elements of marketing strategy. While these advisory boards help companies maintain strong relationships with valuable customers, they can also provide great insight into marketing research questions.[30] YUM Brands' KFC, for example, formed the KFC Moms Matter! Advisory Board to obtain insight and recommendations from mothers about its brand and products.[31]

Still another option is the **telephone depth interview,** which combines the traditional focus group's ability to probe with the confidentiality provided by a telephone survey. This type of interview is most appropriate for qualitative research projects among a small targeted group that is difficult to bring together for a traditional focus group because of members' professions, locations, or lifestyles. Respondents can choose the time and day for the interview. Although this method is difficult to implement, it can yield revealing information from respondents who otherwise would be unwilling to participate in marketing research.[32] Similar efforts can be conducted online through WebEx meetings.

The nature of personal interviews has changed. In the past, most personal interviews, which were based on random sampling or prearranged appointments, were conducted in the respondent's home. Today most personal interviews are conducted in shopping malls. **Shopping mall intercept interviews** involve interviewing a percentage of individuals who pass by an "intercept" point in a mall. Like any face-to-face interviewing method, mall intercept interviewing has many advantages. The interviewer is in a position to recognize and react to respondents' nonverbal indications of confusion. Respondents can be shown product prototypes, videotapes of commercials, and the like, and asked for their reactions. The mall environment lets the researcher deal with complex situations. For example, in taste tests, researchers know that all the respondents are reacting to the same product, which can be prepared and monitored from the mall test kitchen. In addition to the ability to conduct tests requiring bulky equipment, lower cost and greater control make shopping mall intercept interviews popular.

An **on-site computer interview** is a variation of the shopping mall intercept interview in which respondents complete a self-administered questionnaire displayed on a computer monitor. A computer software package can be used to conduct such interviews in shopping malls. After a brief lesson on how to operate the software, respondents can proceed through the survey at their own pace. Questionnaires can be adapted so that respondents see only those items (usually a subset of an entire scale) that may provide useful information about their attitudes.[33]

Questionnaire Construction. A carefully constructed questionnaire is essential to the success of any survey. Questions must be clear, easy to understand, and directed toward a specific objective; that is, they must be designed to elicit information that meets the study's data requirements. Researchers need to define the objective before trying to develop a questionnaire because the objective determines the substance of the questions and the amount of detail. A common mistake in constructing questionnaires is to ask questions that interest the researchers but do not yield information useful in deciding whether to accept or reject a hypothesis. Finally, the most important rule in composing questions is to maintain impartiality.

The questions are usually of three kinds: open-ended, dichotomous, and multiple-choice.

Open-Ended Question
How do you feel about broadband Internet access for your computer?

_____

_____

_____

Dichotomous Question
Do you presently have broadband access at home, work, or school?
Yes _____ No _____

---

customer advisory boards
Small groups of actual customers who serve as sounding boards for new-product ideas and offer insights into their feelings and attitudes toward a firm's products and other elements of marketing strategy

telephone depth interview
An interview that combines the traditional focus group's ability to probe with the confidentiality provided by telephone surveys

shopping mall intercept interviews A research method that involves interviewing a percentage of individuals passing by "intercept" points in a mall

on-site computer interview
A variation of the shopping mall intercept interview in which respondents complete a self-administered questionnaire displayed on a computer monitor

Multiple-Choice Question

What age group are you in?

Under 20 _____

20–29 _____

30–39 _____

40–49 _____

50–59 _____

60 and over _____

Problems may develop in the analysis of dichotomous or multiple-choice questions which responses for one outcome outnumber others. For example, a dichotomous question that asks respondents to choose between "buy" or "not buy" might require additional sampling from the disproportionately smaller group if there were not enough responses to analyze.[34]

Researchers must also be very careful about questions that a respondent might consider too personal or that might require an admission of activities that other people are likely to condemn. Questions of this type should be worded to make them less offensive.

Observation Methods. In using observation methods, researchers record individuals' overt behavior, taking note of physical conditions and events. Direct contact with them is avoided; instead, their actions are examined and noted systematically. For instance, researchers might use observation methods to answer the question "How long does the average McDonald's restaurant customer have to wait in line before being served?" Observation may include the use of ethnographic techniques, such as watching customers interact with a product in a real-world environment.

Microsoft employed ethnographic techniques when it sent researchers into 50 consumers' homes to observe and videotape how the entire family used the firm's Vista operating system software, which had not yet been released for sale to the public. Based on their observations and interactions with the households, Microsoft made a number of changes to improve the software, including correcting about 1,000 problems identified by the observed households.[35]

Observation may also be combined with interviews. For example, during a personal interview, the condition of a respondent's home or other possessions may be observed and recorded. The interviewer can also directly observe and confirm such demographic information as race, approximate age, and gender.

Data gathered through observation can sometimes be biased if the person is aware of the observation process. However, an observer can be placed in a natural market environment, such as a grocery store, without influencing shoppers' actions. If the presence of a human observer is likely to bias the outcome or if human sensory abilities are inadequate, mechanical means may be used to record behavior. Mechanical observation devices include cameras, recorders, counting machines, scanners, and equipment that records physiological changes. A special camera can be used to record the eye movements of people as they look at an advertisement; the camera detects the sequence of reading and the parts of the advertisement that receive greatest attention. The electronic scanners used in supermarkets are very useful in marketing research: they provide accurate data on sales and customers' purchase patterns, and marketing researchers may buy such data from the supermarkets.

Observation is straightforward and avoids a central problem of survey methods: motivating respondents to state their true feelings or opinions. However, observation tends to be descriptive. When it is the only method of data collection, it may not provide insights into causal relationships. Another drawback is that analyses based on observation are subject to the observer's biases or the limitations of the mechanical device.

Interpreting Research Findings

After collecting data to test their hypotheses, marketers need to interpret the research findings. Interpretation of the data is easier if marketers carefully plan their data

Interpreting Research
Companies like Market Strategies can help interpret the data collected from market research and offer insights into the areas investigated.

analysis methods early in the research process. They should also allow for continual evaluation of the data during the entire collection period. They can then gain valuable insights into areas that should be probed during the formal interpretation.

The first step in drawing conclusions from most research is to display the data in table format. If marketers intend to apply the results to individual categories of the things or people being studied, cross-tabulation may be useful, especially in tabulating joint occurrences. For example, using the two variables of gender and purchase rates of automobile tires, a cross-tabulation could show how men and women differ in purchasing automobile tires.

After the data are tabulated, they must be analyzed. **Statistical interpretation** focuses on what is typical and what deviates from the average. It indicates how widely responses vary and how they are distributed in relation to the variable being measured. When marketers interpret statistics, they must take into account estimates of expected error or deviation from the true values of the population. The analysis of data may lead researchers to accept or reject the hypothesis being studied. Data require careful interpretation by the marketer. If the results of a study are valid, the decision maker should take action; if a question has been incorrectly or poorly worded, however, the results may produce poor decisions. Consider the research conducted for a food marketer that asked respondents to rate a product on criteria such as "hearty flavor," as well as how important each criterion was to the respondent. Although such results may have had utility for advertising purposes, they were less helpful in product development because it was not possible to discern respondents' meaning of "hearty flavor."[36] Managers must understand the research results and relate them to a context that permits effective decision making.

Reporting Research Findings

The final step in the marketing research process is to report the research findings. Before preparing the report, the marketer must take a clear, objective look at the findings to see how well the gathered facts answer the research question or support or negate the initial hypotheses. In most cases, it is extremely doubtful that the study can provide everything needed to answer the research question. Thus, the researcher must point out the deficiencies, and the reasons for them, in the report.

The report of research results is usually a formal, written document. Researchers must allow time for the writing task when they plan and schedule the project.

statistical interpretation
Analysis of what is typical and what deviates from the average

Because the report is a means of communicating with the decision makers who will use the research findings, researchers need to determine beforehand how much detail and supporting data to include. They should keep in mind that corporate executives prefer reports that are short, clear, and simply expressed. Researchers often give their summary and recommendations first, especially if decision makers do not have time to study how the results were obtained. A technical report allows its users to analyze data and interpret recommendations because it describes the research methods and procedures and the most important data gathered. Thus, researchers must recognize the needs and expectations of the report user and adapt to them.

Bias and distortion can be a major problem if the researcher is intent on obtaining favorable results. For example, research analyzing consumers' reports of their frequency of using long-distance telephone calls, letters, cards, and visits for personal communication found that some groups underreport their usage, whereas other groups overreport it. In particular, researchers found that consumers underestimate the duration of lengthy telephone calls but overestimate the length of short ones; in general, people tend to overestimate both the frequency and duration of their telephone calls. Without this information, companies relying on survey results may get a distorted view of the market for long-distance telephone services by mistakenly judging it to be larger and more homogeneous than it really is.[37]

Marketing researchers want to know about behavior and opinions, and they want accurate data to help them in making decisions. Careful wording of questions is very important because a biased or emotional word can dramatically change the results. Marketing research and marketing information systems can provide an organization with accurate and reliable customer feedback, which a marketer must have to understand the dynamics of the marketplace. As managers recognize the benefits of marketing research, they assign it a much larger role in decision making.

Using Technology to Improve Marketing Information Gathering and Analysis

Technology is making information for marketing decisions increasingly accessible. The ability of marketers to track customer buying behavior and to better discern what buyers want is changing the nature of marketing. Customer relationship management is being enhanced by integrating data from all customer contacts and combining that

Using Technology

Re Rez uses some of the most advanced marketing research technology to assist clients.

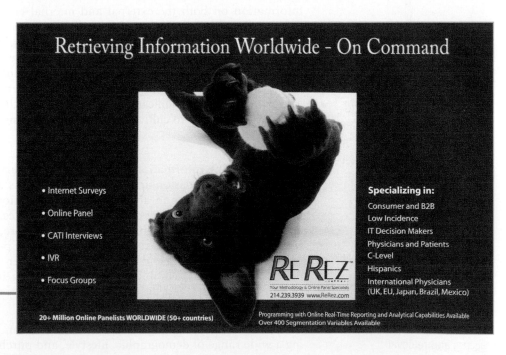

information to improve customer retention. Information technology permits internal research and quick information gathering to help marketers better understand and satisfy customers. For example, company responses to e-mail complaints as well as to communications through mail, telephone, and personal contact can be used to improve customer satisfaction, retention, and value.[38] Armed with such information, marketers can fine-tune marketing mixes to satisfy their customers' needs.

The integration of telecommunications and computer technologies is allowing marketers to access a growing array of valuable information sources related to industry forecasts, business trends, and customer buying behavior. Electronic communication tools can be effectively used to gain accurate information with minimal customer interaction. Most marketing researchers have e-mail, voice mail, teleconferencing, and fax machines at their disposal. In fact, many firms use marketing information systems and customer relationship management technologies to network all these technologies and organize all the marketing data available to them. In this section, we look at marketing information systems and specific technologies that are helping marketing researchers obtain and manage marketing research data.

Marketing Information Systems

A **marketing information system (MIS)** is a framework for the day-to-day management and structuring of information gathered regularly from sources both inside and outside the organization. As such, an MIS provides a continuous flow of information about prices, advertising expenditures, sales, competition, and distribution expenses. Anheuser-Busch, for example, uses a system called BudNet that compiles information about past sales at individual stores, inventory, competitors' displays and prices, and a host of other information collected by distributors' sales representatives on handheld computers. BudNet allows managers to respond quickly to changes in competitors' strategies with an appropriate promotional message, package, display, or discount.[39]

The main focus of the MIS is on data storage and retrieval, as well as on computer capabilities and management's information requirements. Regular reports of sales by product or market categories, data on inventory levels, and records of salespeople's activities are examples of information that is useful in making decisions. In the MIS, the means of gathering data receive less attention than do the procedures for expediting the flow of information.

An effective MIS starts by determining the objective of the information—that is, by identifying decision needs that require certain information. The firm can then specify an information system for continuous monitoring to provide regular, pertinent information on both the external and internal environment. Federal Express, for example, has developed interactive marketing systems to provide instantaneous communication between the company and its customers. Via either telephone or the Internet, customers can track their packages and receive immediate feedback concerning delivery. The company's website provides valuable information about customer usage and allows customers to express directly what they think about company services. The evolving telecommunications and computer technologies are allowing marketing information systems to cultivate one-to-one relationships with customers.

Databases

Most marketing information systems include internal databases. A **database** is a collection of information arranged for easy access and retrieval. Databases allow marketers to tap into an abundance of information useful in making marketing decisions: internal sales reports, newspaper articles, company news releases, government economic reports, bibliographies, and more, often accessed through a computer system. Information technology has made it possible to develop databases to guide strategic planning and help improve customer services. Customer relationship management (CRM) employs database marketing techniques to identify different types of customers and develop specific strategies for interacting with each customer. It incorporates these three elements:

1. Identifying and building a database of current and potential consumers, including a wide range of demographic, lifestyle, and purchase information

---

LO 3 To describe the nature and role of information systems in marketing decision making

LO 4 To understand how such tools as databases, decision support systems, and the Internet facilitate marketing research

marketing information system (MIS) A framework for managing and structuring information gathered regularly from sources inside and outside the organization

database A collection of information arranged for easy access and retrieval

Internet Research

Western Wats provides its customers with research delivered by a readily available online panel.

single-source data Information provided by a single marketing research firm

marketing decision support system (MDSS) Customized computer software that aids marketing managers in decision making

2. Delivering differential messages according to each consumer's preferences and characteristics through established and new media channels

3. Tracking customer relationships to monitor the costs of retaining individual customers and the lifetime value of their purchases[40]

It is important for marketers to distinguish *active* customers—those who are likely to continue buying from the firm—from *inactive* customers—those who are likely to defect and those who have already defected. This information should help to (1) identify profitable inactive customers who can be reactivated; (2) remove inactive, unprofitable customers from the customer database; and (3) identify active customers who should be targeted with regular marketing activities.[41]

When Pulte Homes, the nation's top homebuilder, analyzed information in its database, it realized that 80 percent of its home buyers were selecting the same countertops, carpet, fixtures, lighting, and so on. The company used that information to streamline its 2,000 floor plans and reduce the number of fixtures and other home features to better match customer desires and to improve overall efficiency and decision making.[42] Many commercial websites require consumers to register and provide personal information to access the site or to make a purchase. Frequent-flier programs permit airlines to ask loyal customers to participate in surveys about their needs and desires, and to track their best customers' flight patterns by time of day, week, month, and year. Supermarkets gain a significant amount of data through checkout scanners tied to store discount cards. In fact, one of the best ways to predict market behavior is the use of database information gathered through loyalty programs or other transaction-based processes.[43]

Marketing researchers can also use commercial databases developed by information research firms, such as Lexis-Nexis, to obtain useful information for marketing decisions. Many of these commercial databases are accessible online for a fee. They can also be obtained in printed form or on computer compact discs (CD-ROMs). With most commercial databases, the user typically conducts a computer search by keyword, topic, or company, and the database service generates abstracts, articles, or reports that can then be printed out. Accessing multiple reports or a complete article may cost extra.

Information provided by a single firm on household demographics, purchases, television viewing behavior, and responses to promotions such as coupons and free samples is called **single-source data.**[44] For example, Behavior Scan, offered by Information Resources, Inc., screens about 60,000 households in 26 U.S. markets. This single-source information service monitors consumer household televisions and records the programs and commercials watched. When buyers from these households shop in stores equipped with scanning registers, they present Hotline cards (similar to credit cards) to cashiers. This enables each customer's identification to be electronically coded so the firm can track each product purchased and store the information in a database. It is important to gather longitudinal (long-term) information on customers to maximize the usefulness of single-source data.[45]

Marketing Decision Support Systems

A **marketing decision support system (MDSS)** is customized computer software that aids marketing managers in decision making by helping them anticipate the effects of certain decisions. Some decision support systems have a broader range and offer greater computational and modeling capabilities than spreadsheets; they let managers explore a greater number of alternatives. For example, an MDSS can determine how sales and profits might be affected by higher or lower interest rates or how sales forecasts, advertising expenditures, production levels, and the like might affect overall profits. For this reason, MDSS software is often a major component of a company's marketing information system. Customized decision support systems can support a customer orientation and customer satisfaction in business marketing.[46] Some decision support systems incorporate artificial intelligence and other advanced computer technologies.

Issues in Marketing Research

L O 5 To identify key ethical and international considerations in marketing research

The Importance of Ethical Marketing Research

Marketing managers and other professionals are relying more and more on marketing research, marketing information systems, and new technologies to make better decisions. It is therefore essential that professional standards be established by which to judge the reliability of marketing research. Such standards are necessary because of the ethical and legal issues that develop in gathering marketing research data. In the area of online interaction, for example, consumers remain wary of how the personal information collected by marketers will be used, especially whether it will be sold to third parties. In addition, the relationships between research suppliers, such as marketing research agencies, and the marketing managers who make strategy decisions require ethical behavior. Organizations such as the Marketing Research Association have developed codes of conduct and guidelines to promote ethical marketing research. To be effective, such guidelines must instruct marketing researchers on how to avoid misconduct. Here are nine guidelines interviewers should follow when introducing a questionnaire.[47]

1. Allow interviewers to introduce themselves by name.

2. State the name of the research company.

3. Indicate this is a marketing research project.

4. Explain there will be no sales involved.

5. Note the general topic of discussion (if this is a problem in a "blind" study, a statement such as "consumer opinion" is acceptable).

6. State the likely duration of the interview.

7. Assure the anonymity of the respondent and confidentiality of all answers.

8. State the honorarium if applicable (for many business-to-business and medical studies, this is done up front for both qualitative and quantitative studies).

9. Reassure the respondent with a statement such as "There are no right or wrong answers, so please give thoughtful and honest answers to each question" (recommended by many clients).

International Issues in Marketing Research

As we shall see in Chapter 9, sociocultural, economic, political, legal, and technological forces vary in different regions of the world. These variations create challenges for the organizations that are attempting to understand foreign customers through marketing research. The marketing research process we describe in this chapter is used globally, but to ensure the research is valid and reliable, data-gathering methods may have to be modified to allow for regional differences. For example, experts have found that Latin Americans do not respond well to focus groups or in-depth interviews that are longer than 90 minutes. Researchers therefore need to adjust their tactics to generate information that is useful for marketing products in Latin America.[48]

RESPONSIBLE marketing?

Marketing Research to Measure Business Ethics

ISSUE: Can you measure marketing ethics?

*E*thisphere magazine conducts marketing research to measure the world's most ethical companies. The editors and writers for the magazine try to distinguish absolute behaviors that can be used to differentiate one organization from another. The magazine also attempts to examine companies to make certain their claims are translated into actions. The methodology for this research involves an eight-step process of collecting and screening information. Nine criteria are explored in this research: litigation and controversy/conflict analysis; ethical tone analysis; innovation and industry leadership analysis; corporate citizenship analysis; industry effort and participation analysis; governance and transparency analysis; public and trade partner perception analysis; and ethics/compliance program system analysis. Companies highlighted in the study included Alcoa, Eaton Corporation, Kiplingers, GE, Kellogg's, and John Deere.

Fortune magazine conducts research to find the Most Admired Companies. The Hay Group assists the magazine in assessing companies based on nine criteria: attraction and retention of talent; corporate culture; leadership development; performance measurement; strategy implementation; responses to economic uncertainty; innovation; effectiveness of managing globally; and board governance and effectiveness. Some of *Fortune's* Most Admired Companies include Apple, Berkshire Hathaway, GE, Google, Toyota, Starbucks, Federal Express, P&G, Johnson & Johnson, Goldman Sachs, Target, and Southwest Airlines. Admiration is a function of effectively managing your risks and relating to consumers and the public. Which measurement approach do you feel generates the greatest accuracy in measuring organizational ethics related to marketing?ᶜ

To ensure that global and regional differences are satisfactorily addressed, many companies retain a research firm with experience in the country of interest. Most of the largest marketing research firms derive a significant share of their revenues from research conducted outside the United States. As Table 5.5 indicates, the Nielsen Company, the largest marketing research firm in the world, received nearly half of its revenues from outside the United States.[49]

Experts recommend a two-pronged approach to international marketing research. The first phase involves a detailed search for and analysis of secondary data to gain greater understanding of a particular marketing environment and to pinpoint issues that must be taken into account in gathering primary research data. Secondary data can be particularly helpful in building a general understanding of the market, including economic, legal, cultural, and demographic issues, as well as in assessing the risks of doing business in that market and in forecasting demand.[50] Marketing researchers often begin by studying country trade reports from the U.S. Department of Commerce, as well as country-specific information from local sources, such as a country's website, and trade and general business publications such as the *Wall Street Journal.* These sources can offer insights into the marketing environment in a particular country and can even indicate untapped market opportunities abroad.

The second phase involves field research using many of the methods described earlier, including focus groups and telephone surveys, to refine a firm's understanding of specific customer needs and preferences. Specific differences among countries can have a profound influence on data gathering. For example, in-home (door-to-door)

table 5.5	TOP GLOBAL MARKETING RESEARCH FIRMS	
Company	**Global Revenues (millions U.S. dollars)**	**Percent of Revenues from Outside the U.S.**
1. The Nielsen Co.	3,696	46.7
2. IMS Health, Inc.	1,959	63.4
3. Taylor Nelson Sofres	1,851	85.0
4. The Kantar Group	1,401	77.2
5. GfK AG	1,397	75.8

Source: "Top 25 Global Research Organizations," *Marketing News,* Aug. 15, 2007, p. H4.

interviews are illegal in some countries. In China, few people have regular telephone lines, making telephone surveys both impractical and nonrepresentative of the total population. Primary data gathering may have a greater chance of success if the firm employs local researchers who better understand how to approach potential respondents and can do so in their own language.[51] Regardless of the specific methods used to gather primary data, whether in the United States or abroad, the goal is to better understand the needs of specific target markets to craft the best marketing strategy to satisfy the needs of customers in each market, as we will see in the next chapter.

SUMMARY

Marketing research is the systematic design, collection, interpretation, and reporting of information to help marketers solve specific marketing problems or take advantage of marketing opportunities. It is a process for gathering information not currently available to decision makers. Marketing research can help a firm better understand market opportunities, ascertain the potential for success for new products, and determine the feasibility of a particular marketing strategy. The value of marketing research is measured by improvements in a marketer's ability to make decisions.

To maintain the control needed to obtain accurate information, marketers approach marketing research as a process with logical steps: (1) locating and defining problems or issues, (2) designing the research project, (3) collecting data, (4) interpreting research findings, and (5) reporting research findings.

The first step in launching a research study, problem or issue definition, focuses on uncovering the nature and boundaries of a situation or question related to marketing strategy or implementation. When a firm discovers a market opportunity, it may need to conduct research to understand the situation more precisely so it can craft an appropriate marketing strategy.

In the second step, marketing researchers design a research project to obtain the information needed to address it. This step requires formulating a hypothesis and determining what type of research to employ to test the hypothesis so the results are reliable and valid. A hypothesis is an informed guess or assumption about a problem or set of circumstances. Marketers conduct exploratory research when they need more information about a problem or want to make a tentative hypothesis more specific; they use conclusive research to verify insights through an objective procedure. Research is considered reliable if it produces almost identical results in repeated trials; it is valid if it measures what it is supposed to measure.

For the third step of the research process, collecting data, two types of data are available. Primary data are observed and recorded or collected directly from respondents; secondary data are compiled inside or outside the organization for some purpose other than the current investigation. Sources of secondary data include an organization's own database and other internal sources, periodicals,

government publications, unpublished sources, and online databases. Methods of collecting primary data include sampling, surveys, observation, and experimentation. Sampling involves selecting representative units from a total population. In probability sampling, every element in the population being studied has a known chance of being selected for study. Nonprobability sampling is more subjective than probability sampling because there is no way to calculate the likelihood that a specific element of the population being studied will be chosen. Marketing researchers employ sampling to collect primary data through mail, telephone, online, or personal interview surveys. A carefully constructed questionnaire is essential to the success of any survey. In using observation methods, researchers record respondents' overt behavior and take note of physical conditions and events. In an experiment, marketing researchers attempt to maintain certain variables while measuring the effects of experimental variables.

To apply research data to decision making, marketers must interpret and report their findings properly—the final two steps in the marketing research process. Statistical interpretation focuses on what is typical or what deviates from the average. After interpreting the research findings, the researchers must prepare a report on the findings that the decision makers can understand and use. Researchers must also take care to avoid bias and distortion.

Many firms use computer technology to create a marketing information system (MIS), a framework for managing and structuring information gathered regularly from sources both inside and outside the organization. A database is a collection of information arranged for easy access and retrieval. A marketing decision support system (MDSS) is customized computer software that aids marketing managers in decision making by helping them anticipate the effects of certain decisions. Online information services and the Internet also enable marketers to communicate with customers and obtain information.

Eliminating unethical marketing research practices and establishing generally acceptable procedures for conducting research are important goals of marketing research. Both domestic and international marketing use the same marketing research process, but international marketing may require modifying data-gathering methods to address regional differences.

IMPORTANT TERMS

Marketing research, 130
Research design, 132
Hypothesis, 132
Exploratory research, 133
Conclusive research, 134
Descriptive research, 134
Experimental research, 135
Reliability, 135
Validity, 135
Primary data, 135
Secondary data, 135

Population, 138
Sample, 138
Sampling, 138
Probability sampling, 138
Random sampling, 138
Stratified sampling, 140
Nonprobability sampling, 140
Quota sampling, 140
Mail survey, 142
Telephone survey, 142
Online survey, 143

Personal interview survey, 143
In-home (door-to-door) interview, 143
Focus-group interview, 143
Customer advisory boards, 144
Telephone depth interview, 144
Shopping mall intercept interview, 144

On-site computer interview, 144
Statistical interpretation, 146
Marketing information system (MIS), 148
Database, 148
Single-source data, 149
Marketing decision support system (MDSS), 149

DISCUSSION & REVIEW QUESTIONS

1. What is marketing research? Why is it important?
2. Describe the five steps in the marketing research process.
3. What is the difference between defining a research problem and developing a hypothesis?
4. Describe the different types of approaches to marketing research, and indicate when each should be used.
5. Where are data for marketing research obtained? Give examples of internal and external data.
6. What is the difference between probability sampling and nonprobability sampling? In what situation would random sampling be best? Stratified sampling? Quota sampling?
7. Suggest some ways to encourage respondents to cooperate in mail surveys.
8. If a survey of all homes with listed telephone numbers is to be conducted, what sampling design should be used?
9. Describe some marketing problems that could be solved through information gained from observation.
10. What is a marketing information system, and what should it provide?
11. Define a database. What is its purpose, and what does it include?
12. How can marketers use online services and the Internet to obtain information for decision making?
13. What role does ethics play in marketing research? Why is it important that marketing researchers be ethical?
14. How does marketing research in other countries differ from marketing research in the United States?

APPLICATION QUESTIONS

1. After observing customers' traffic patterns, Bashas' Markets repositioned the greeting card section in its stores, and card sales increased substantially. To increase sales for the following types of companies, what information might marketing researchers want to gather from customers?
   a. Furniture stores
   b. Gasoline outlets/service stations
   c. Investment companies
   d. Medical clinics

2. When a company wants to conduct research, it must first identify a problem or possible opportunity to market its goods or services. Choose a company in your city that you think might benefit from a research project. Develop a research question and outline a method to approach this question. Explain why you think the research question is relevant to the organization and why the particular methodology is suited to the question and the company.

3. Input for marketing information systems can come from internal or external sources. ACNielsen Corporation is the largest provider of single-source marketing research in the world. Identify two firms in your city that might benefit from internal sources and two that might benefit from external sources. Explain why these sources would be useful to these companies. Suggest the type of information each company should gather.

4. Suppose you are opening a health insurance brokerage firm and want to market your services to small businesses with fewer than 50 employees. Determine which database for marketing information you will use in your marketing efforts, and explain why you will use it.

INTERNET EXERCISE

Visit **www.cengage.com/marketing/pride-ferrell** for resources to help you master the material in this chapter, plus materials that will help you expand your marketing knowledge, including Internet exercise updates, ACE Self-Tests, hotlinks to companies featured in this chapter, and much more.

World Association of Opinion and Marketing Research Professionals

The World Association of Opinion and Marketing Research Professionals (ESOMAR, founded as the European Society for Opinion and Marketing Research in 1948) is a nonprofit association for marketing research professionals. ESOMAR promotes the use of opinion and marketing research to improve marketing decisions in companies worldwide and works to protect personal privacy in the research process. Visit the association's website at **www.esomar.org**.

1. How can ESOMAR help marketing professionals conduct research to guide marketing strategy?

2. How can ESOMAR help marketers protect the privacy of research subjects when conducting marketing research in other countries?

3. ESOMAR introduced the first professional code of conduct for marketing research professionals in 1948. The association continues to update the document to address new technology and other changes in the marketing environment. According to ESOMAR's code, what are the specific professional responsibilities of marketing researchers?

developing your MARKETING PLAN

Decisions about which market opportunities to pursue, what customer needs to satisfy, and how to reach potential customers are not made in a vacuum. The information provided by marketing research activities is essential in developing both the strategic plan and the specific marketing mix. Focus on the following issues as you relate the concepts in this chapter to the development of your marketing plan.

1. Define the nature and scope of the questions you must answer with regard to your market. Identify the types of information you will need about the market to answer those questions. For example, do you need to know about the buying habits, household income levels, or attitudes of potential customers?

2. Determine whether or not this information can be obtained from secondary sources. Visit the websites provided in Table 5.3 as possible resources for the secondary data.

3. Using Table 5.4, choose the appropriate survey method(s) you would use to collect primary data for one of your information needs. What sampling method would you use?

The information obtained from these questions should assist you in developing various aspects of your marketing plan found in the *Interactive Marketing Plan* exercise at **www.cengage.com/marketing/pride-ferrell.**

globalEDGE

1. Your firm is considering entering the Japanese information technology market, and you have been asked to analyze the top ten Japanese companies in this industry. One way to begin your research on this market segment is to access *BusinessWeek's* Global 1,000 firms by using the search term "top global companies" at **http://globaledge.msu.edu/ibrd** (and check the box "Resource Desk Only"). Once there, click on the Country-by-Country scoreboard to find the best document for analysis. Considering the criteria given, prepare a summary that includes the largest and smallest firms. In addition, describe which firms are the most and least healthy.

2. For a marketing research company, an important element in gathering data for a market is the level of information technology (IT) infrastructure that exists. NationMaster.com's website offers a subcategory of Personal Computers (PCs) that can provide insight on the level of personal computer (PC) usage in a country. Use the search term "compare various statistics" at **http://globaledge.msu.edu/ibrd** (and check the box "Resource Desk Only") to reach NationMaster.com. Select the Media category and then the subcategory of Personal Computers (PCs). Give a summary of the top 15 countries as ranked by the number of PCs used. From this specified list of markets, include an assessment of the three countries with the most and least access to PCs. What conclusions can you make?

video CASE 5.1

Getting to the Heart of the Matter: Research Design at LSPMA

Lake Research Partners, previously known as Lake, Snell, Perry, Mermin & Associates, Inc. (LSPMA), is a national public opinion and political strategy research firm. Its expertise lies in conducting objective opinion polls to assess the attitudes and behaviors of important target groups that concern its clients. The Washington, D.C.–based firm is nationally recognized for its knowledge of women's issues, children's and youth's concerns, and environmental political issues. Among the company's clients are the Democratic National Committee, the Democratic Governor's Association, Sierra Club, Planned Parenthood, Human Rights Campaign, Emily's List, and the Kaiser Foundation. LSPMA also conducts regular polls for *U.S. News & World Report,* and with the Terrance Group it conducts the Battleground Poll, which surveys the year's political landscape and draws attention to critical issues that Washington insiders can't afford to ignore. In 2005 LPSMA acquired the Washington- and San Diego–based polling firm Decision Research, giving it even greater capacity to conduct research for both business and political clients.

LSPMA's primary goal is to discover what the public thinks for people who want to know. Its staff serves as among the Democratic Party's leading strategists, acting as tacticians and senior advisers to dozens of political incumbents and challengers at all levels of the electoral process, as well as to a wide range of advocacy organizations, nonprofit organizations, and foundations. Its client base is split evenly among three groups: political candidates such as senators and governors; progressive issue organizations that want research on social issues such as poverty, education, health care, and teen pregnancy; and foundations or major institutions such as the American Cancer Society.

Through research techniques, including reconnaissance and espionage, LSPMA gathers and presents hard data regarding what specific segments of the public think about certain issues or candidates. LSPMA's work helps clients identify potential problems or opportunities and determine what strategies and messages would best help them achieve their goals and reach their target audiences. It is important to know what different segments of the population think, feel, and need so that advertising can then be targeted at the people who organizations want to reach. LSPMA uses a variety of methods, including telephone interviews, online polls, and focus groups, to create portraits of groups of people, such as "soccer moms," "waitress moms," or "NASCAR dads," so its clients can understand these segments and recognize important trends.

Research allows LSPMA's clients to know what Americans are thinking and helps them determine how to target those segments of the population who are likely to think their firm has the right product or the right candidate. It allows clients to understand where they are most vulnerable and where they have the greatest opportunities to gain more support. By knowing which people feel strongly, which are sitting on the fence, and which are capable of changing their opinions, it is possible to segment people according to what they think and how they act and behave. Once organizations know whom to target and which issues are most important to those they wish to target, they can narrow their approaches to accomplish their goals in the most cost-efficient way.

There are many reasons to segment the public. Since people are different, segmentation enables marketers and pollsters to cluster together like-minded people to better understand who they are. It is then possible to craft a message that precisely targets a particular audience. Markets can be segmented by age, gender, education, geographic region, income, or race to create new ways of looking at a group that tends to behave similarly.

There are pitfalls to segmentation, however. It can sometimes make people seem more diverse than they actually are. For example, women hold similar views on 80 percent of political issues. Segmentation can help

an individual or organization only so much; the rest depends on the hottest new trends. Few groups are static or truly homogeneous, which means that continuous research is necessary to remain up to date with changes in attitudes and behaviors and to ensure that messages still reach their target audiences.

Like all marketing research firms, LSPMA plans its marketing research strategy well in advance, including such details as deciding what questions to ask, which audience to target, in what setting to target them, what time frame to use, and how to manage costs. It enables the firm to know what it has to do and how to do it. All research firms, regardless of their clients, create information for more informed understanding and decisions.[52]

Questions for Discussion

1. Why do political organizations need marketing research conducted by LSPMA?
2. What is the relationship between marketing research conducted by LSPMA and identifying the needs and wants of specific market segments?
3. Why would a business rely on a marketing research firm that is heavily into political polling?

CASE 5.2

Best Buy Uncovers Angels in the Market

Best Buy Company, Inc., is a retailer of consumer electronics, home-office products, entertainment software, appliances, and related services. One of the company's goals is to make life easier and more fun for consumers. To meet that objective, the company's retail environment focuses on educating customers on the features and benefits of technology and entertainment products. The Minneapolis-based firm operates more than 1,200 retail stores across the United States and in Canada under the names Best Buy, Future Shop, GeekSquad, and Magnolia Audio Video, as well as an outlet store on eBay.

Best Buy operates in the highly competitive consumer electronics retail industry and must compete against other electronics retailers, specialty home-office retailers, mass merchants, home improvement superstores, and a growing number of direct-to-consumer alternatives. It also competes against independent dealers, regional chain discount stores, wholesale clubs, video rental stores, and other specialty retail stores. There is also increasing pressure from online sites, which offer entertainment as downloads, as well as pay-per-view cable television companies.

Best Buy collects data on nearly every transaction made, rain check issued, and call-center problem resolved for 75 million customers. To discover what its customers want and need, the company developed a database that incorporated information from 19 customer touch points including point of sale, and enhanced it with Experian's INSOURCE℠ consumer marketing data to develop a complete picture of its customers. It gained further insight by using purchase histories to study its customers' current as well as their future needs through segmentation analysis. This allowed Best Buy to develop and identify new-customer segments, to better understand existing customers, to more precisely target promotions, and to identify key locations for expansion.

Best Buy collects data from its transactions and from mailing lists; it also has demographic information from local census numbers, surveys of customers, and targeted focus groups. In 2004 it launched a customer loyalty program called Reward Zone, which today has more than 24 million members from whom the company hopes to gain valuable insights. Best Buy retains Larry Selden, a professor at Columbia University's

Graduate Schools of Business, as a consultant. Selden argued that losses produced by what he calls "devil" customers can wipe out profits generated by "angels." Through its consultation with Selden and its data analysis with Experian, Best Buy identified its angel and devil customers. The angels were customers who bought high-definition TVs, portable electronics, and newly released DVDs without waiting for markdowns or rebates. The devils bought products, applied for their rebates, and then returned the products and bought them back again at returned-merchandise discounts. Best Buy then categorized its angel customers into these five segments:

- The Small Business customer ("BBfB"): These customers use Best Buy's products and services to enhance the profitability of their businesses.
- The Young Entertainment Enthusiast ("Buzz"): These are active younger men who want the latest technology and entertainment. They are early adopters who are interested in buying and showing off the latest gadgets.
- The Affluent Professional ("Barry"): These customers want the best technology and entertainment experience, and they do not mind spending to get the best, regardless of the cost. They are enthusiasts of action movies and cameras.
- The Busy Suburban Mom ("Jill"): These customers want to enrich their children's lives with technology and entertainment. They are busy but willing to talk about helping their families. They are smart and affluent but usually avoid electronics stores because the products intimidate them. "Jills" are typically the main shopper for the family and will make purchases based on staff recommendations.
- The Tech-Savvy Family Man ("Ray"): These are family men who want technology to improve their lives. They are practical adopters of technology and entertainment.

Best Buy's new "customer-centric" operating model focuses on these five key segments. The company launched the initiative with 67 stores, each of which would analyze the demographics of its local market and then choose one or two of these groups to be their focus. Each store would then stock merchandise for and include elements designed to appeal to the targeted segments. Executives believe that this model offers customers a richer in-store experience, including better shopping assistance, and also provides more of the goods and services that they want. It also empowers employees to recognize unique sets of customers and to build offerings and experiences to meet their needs.

In fact, employees receive training in how to differentiate the customer types and how to help each.

To encourage its angel customers, Best Buy sends out associates with pink umbrellas to escort the Jills to and from their cars on rainy days. Personal Shopping Assistants have been provided to help Jills from the moment they enter the stores till they leave via the express checkout. For Barrys, there are comfortable couches for watching large TVs hooked up to high-end sound systems; even popcorn is included to add to the atmosphere. Magnolia Home Theatre specialists provide personalized expert advice. For Buzzes, Best Buy has set up video game areas with leather chairs and game players hooked to mammoth plasma-screen TVs, and TVs and games just a short walk from the area.

To discourage the undesirable devil customers, Best Buy is cutting back on promotions and sales tactics that tend to attract them, and it is also removing many of them from mailing lists. The company is also enforcing a 15 percent restocking fee on returned merchandise to discourage customers who return items with the intention of repurchasing them at "open-box" discounts. Best Buy is experimenting with reselling returned merchandise over the Internet, so the products do not reappear in the store where they were originally purchased.

Best Buy has already converted 85 stores to the new customer-centered model and plans to convert all of its U.S. Best Buy stores within three years. The 67 stores that underwent conversion in 2005 have reported a sales increase of 8.2 percent for the portion of the year in which they operated under the customer centricity model. Compared to an average store sales gain of 1.9 percent at other U.S. Best Buy stores, this is a considerable gain. However, due to onetime conversion costs and a higher expense structure, the selling, general, and administrative expenses for the converted stores were higher than for that of other U.S. Best Buy stores for the same period. Nonetheless, Best Buy believes that the profitability of stores operating under the customer-centered platform will improve over time, which is similar to its historical experience with new-store openings.[53]

Questions for Discussion

1. From what internal and secondary sources did Best Buy acquire the data that helped it develop its customer centricity initiative?
2. How did Best Buy employ database marketing to better satisfy its customers?
3. How are the data gathered by Best Buy useful in customer relationship management?

6

Target Markets: Segmentation, Evaluation, and Positioning

LEARNING objectives

1. To learn what a *market* is

2. To understand the differences among general targeting strategies

3. To become familiar with the major segmentation variables

4. To know what segment profiles are and how they are used

5. To understand how to evaluate market segments

6. To identify the factors that influence the selection of specific market segments for use as target markets

7. To understand positioning

8. To become familiar with sales forecasting methods

Tasty Bite Tempts Adventurous Tastebuds with Quick, Exotic Meals

Start with authentic Indian recipes, stir in all-natural ingredients, add a generous dash of convenience, and place the foods on U.S. supermarket shelves—that's how Ashok Vasudevan and his wife, Meera, built the Tasty Bite brand into a $15 million business. Vasudevan discovered Tasty Bite's heat-and-eat meals, prepared and packaged in Pune, India, when he was in the area on assignment for PepsiCo. In addition to the rich flavors and all-natural ingredients, he was particularly impressed that Tasty Bite's foods needed no refrigeration and were ready to eat from the pouch after a minute or two of boiling or microwaving.

entrepreneurs IN ACTION

Knowing that many U.S. families are pressed for time, desire variety, and want to eat healthier, Vasudevan envisioned a place for Indian convenience foods on U.S. supermarket shelves—and dinner tables. When he couldn't convince Pepsi to acquire the company, he and his wife bought it and cooked up a strategy for entering the U.S. market. Their first step was to rename the dishes. For example, they changed the name of "Palak Paneer" to "Kashmir Spinach"—"to give it a certain romance," says Vasudevan. They also packaged their products in colorful boxes to attract consumers' attention in stores.

By playing up Tasty Bite's natural ingredients, the new owners got placement in specialty stores like Whole Foods and Trader Joe's. To change the misperception that Indian food is overly spicy, they held hundreds of in-store taste demonstrations. The results: 40 percent of the shoppers who took a bite of Tasty Bite immediately bought a box to take home. This proof of Tasty Bite's sales potential soon persuaded bigger supermarket chains to stock the product line. Now the company is expanding into Thai foods and other ethnic specialties as it pushes to have its products carried by more U.S. supermarkets. What market will Tasty Bite target next?[1]

Like most organizations that are trying to compete effectively, Tasty Bite has identified specific customer groups toward which it will direct its marketing efforts. Any organization that wants to succeed must identify its customers and develop and maintain marketing mixes that satisfy the needs of those customers.

In this chapter, we explore markets and market segmentation. Initially we define the term *market* and discuss the major requirements of a market. Then we examine the steps in the target market selection process, including identifying the appropriate targeting strategy, determining which variables to use for segmenting consumer and business markets, developing market segment profiles, evaluating relevant market segments, and selecting target markets. Then we examine the concept of positioning products in customers' minds. Finally, we discuss various methods for developing sales forecasts.

What Are Markets?

LO 1 To learn what a *market* is

In Chapter 2 we defined a *market* as a group of people who, as individuals or as organizations, have needs for products in a product class and have the ability, willingness, and authority to purchase such products. Students, for example, are part of the market for textbooks, as well as for computers, clothes, food, music, and other products. Individuals can have the desire, the buying power, and the willingness to purchase certain products, but may not have the authority to do so. For example, teenagers may have the desire, the money, and the willingness to buy liquor, but a liquor producer does not consider them a market because teenagers are prohibited by law from buying alcoholic beverages. A group of people that lacks any one of the four requirements thus does not constitute a market.

Markets fall into one of two categories: consumer markets and business markets. These categories are based on the characteristics of the individuals and groups that make up a specific market and the purposes for which they buy products. A **consumer market** consists of purchasers and household members who intend to consume or benefit from the purchased products and do not buy products for the main purpose of making a profit. Consumer markets are sometimes also referred to as *business-to-consumer (B2C) markets*. Each of us belongs to numerous consumer markets. The millions of individuals with the ability, willingness, and authority to buy make up a multitude of consumer markets for products such as housing, food, clothing, vehicles, personal services, appliances, furniture, recreational equipment, and so on, as we shall see in Chapter 7.

A **business market** consists of individuals or groups that purchase a specific kind of product for one of three purposes: resale, direct use in producing other products, or use in general daily operations. For example, a lamp producer that buys electrical wire to use in the production of lamps is part of a business market for electrical wire. This same firm purchases dust mops to clean its office areas. Although the mops are not used in the direct production of lamps, they are used in the operations of the firm; thus, this manufacturer is part of a business market for dust mops. Business markets also may be called *business-to-business (B2B), industrial,* or *organizational markets*. They also can be classified into producer, reseller, government, and institutional markets, as we shall see in Chapter 8.

consumer market Purchasers and household members who intend to consume or benefit from the purchased products and do not buy products to make profits

business market Individuals or groups that purchase a specific kind of product for resale, direct use in producing other products, or use in general daily operations

Target Market Selection Process

In Chapter 1, we pointed out that the first of two major components of developing a marketing strategy is to select a target market. Although marketers may employ several methods for target market selection, generally they use a five-step process. This process is shown in Figure 6.1, and we discuss it in the following sections.

figure 6.1

TARGET MARKET SELECTION PROCESS

| 1 Identify the appropriate targeting strategy | 2 Determine which segmentation variables to use | 3 Develop market segment profiles | 4 Evaluate relevant market segments | 5 Select specific target markets |

Step 1: Identify the Appropriate Targeting Strategy

LO 2 To understand the differences among general targeting strategies

Recall from Chapter 1 that a target market is a group of people or organizations for which a business creates and maintains a marketing mix specifically designed to satisfy the needs of group members. The strategy used to select a target market is affected by target market characteristics, product attributes, and the organization's objectives and resources. Figure 6.2 illustrates the three basic targeting strategies: undifferentiated, concentrated, and differentiated.

Undifferentiated Targeting Strategy

An organization sometimes defines an entire market for a particular product as its target market. When a company designs a single marketing mix and directs it at the entire market for a particular product, it is using an **undifferentiated targeting strategy**. As Figure 6.2 shows, the strategy assumes that all customers in the target market for a specific kind of product have similar needs, and thus the organization can satisfy most customers with a single marketing mix. This mix consists of one type of product with little or no variation, one price, one promotional program aimed at everybody, and one distribution system to reach most customers in the total market. Products marketed successfully through the undifferentiated strategy include commodities and staple food items, such as sugar and salt, and certain kinds of farm produce.

The undifferentiated targeting strategy is effective under two conditions. First, a large proportion of customers in a total market must have similar needs for the product, a situation termed a **homogeneous market.** A marketer using a single marketing mix for a total market of customers with a variety of needs would find that the marketing mix satisfies very few people. A "universal car" meant to suit everyone would fulfill very few customers' needs for cars because it would not provide the specific combination of attributes sought by a particular person. Second, the organization must be able to develop and maintain a single marketing mix that satisfies customers' needs. The company must be able to identify a set of needs common to most customers in a total market and have the resources and managerial skills to reach a sizable portion of that market.

The reality is that although customers may have similar needs for a few products, for most products their needs decidedly differ. In such instances, a company should use a concentrated or a differentiated strategy.

Concentrated Targeting Strategy Through Market Segmentation

A market made up of individuals or organizations with diverse product needs is called a **heterogeneous market.** Not everyone wants the same type of car, furniture, or clothes. For example, some individuals want an economical car, whereas others desire a status symbol, and still others seek a roomy and comfortable or fuel-efficient vehicle. The automobile market thus is heterogeneous.

For such heterogeneous markets, market segmentation is appropriate. **Market segmentation** is the process of dividing a total market into groups, or segments, that

undifferentiated targeting strategy A strategy in which an organization designs a single marketing mix and directs it at the entire market for a particular product

homogeneous market A market in which a large proportion of customers have similar needs for a product

heterogeneous market A market made up of individuals or organizations with diverse needs for products in a specific product class

market segmentation The process of dividing a total market into groups with relatively similar product needs to design a marketing mix that matches those needs

figure 6.2

TARGETING STRATEGIES

Undifferentiated strategy

Organization — Single marketing mix (Product, Price, Distribution, Promotion) — Target market

Concentrated strategy

Organization — Single marketing mix (Product, Price, Distribution, Promotion) — Target market

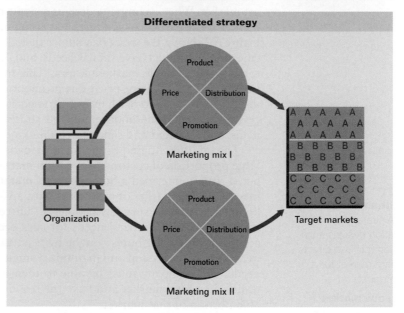

Differentiated strategy

Organization — Marketing mix I (Product, Price, Distribution, Promotion) — Target markets

Marketing mix II (Product, Price, Distribution, Promotion)

The letters in each target market represent potential customers. Customers with the same letters have similar characteristics and similar product needs.

consist of people or organizations with relatively similar product needs. The purpose is to enable a marketer to design a marketing mix that more precisely matches the needs of customers in the selected market segment. A **market segment** consists of individuals, groups, or organizations that share one or more similar characteristics that cause them to have relatively similar product needs. The automobile market is divided into many different market segments. Toyota, for instance, aims its subcompact Yaris at the economy market segment rather than all car buyers.[2] The main rationale for segmenting heterogeneous markets is that a company is better able to develop a satisfying marketing mix for a relatively small portion of a total market than to develop a mix that meets the needs of all people. Market segmentation is widely used. Fast-food chains, soft-drink companies, magazine publishers, hospitals, and banks are just a few types of organizations that employ market segmentation.

market segment Individuals, groups, or organizations sharing one or more similar characteristics that cause them to have similar product needs

For market segmentation to succeed, five conditions must exist. First, customers' needs for the product must be heterogeneous; otherwise, there is little reason to segment the market. Second, segments must be identifiable and divisible. The company must find a characteristic or variable for effectively separating individuals in a total market into groups containing people with relatively uniform needs for the product. Third, the total market should be divided so segments can be compared with respect to estimated sales potential, costs, and profits. Fourth, at least one segment must have enough profit potential to justify developing and maintaining a special marketing mix for that segment. Finally, the company must be able to reach the chosen segment with a particular marketing mix. Some market segments may be difficult or impossible to reach because of legal, social, or distribution constraints. For instance, marketers of Cuban rum and cigars cannot market to U.S. consumers because of political and trade restrictions.

When an organization directs its marketing efforts toward a single market segment using one marketing mix, it is employing a **concentrated targeting strategy.** Porsche focuses on the luxury sports car segment and directs all its marketing efforts toward high-income individuals who want to own high-performance sports cars. Captrust Financial Advisors targets its money and asset management services at professional and retired athletes who may need to make a few years' worth of earnings last a lifetime or fund new business ventures after their retirement from sports. With several former football players turned financial advisers on staff, Captrust is uniquely positioned to build successful relationships with professional athletes who need its financial services.[3] Notice in Figure 6.2 that the organization that is using the concentrated strategy is aiming its marketing mix only at "B" customers.

The chief advantage of the concentrated strategy is that it allows a firm to specialize. The firm analyzes characteristics and needs of a distinct customer group and then focuses all its energies on satisfying that group's needs. A firm may generate a large sales volume by reaching a single segment. Also, concentrating on a single segment permits a firm with limited resources to compete with larger organizations that may have overlooked smaller segments.

Specialization, however, means that a company puts all its eggs in one basket, which can be hazardous. If a company's sales depend on a single segment and the segment's demand for the product declines, the company's financial strength also deteriorates. Moreover, when a firm penetrates one segment and becomes well entrenched, its popularity may keep it from moving into other segments. For example, it is very unlikely that Mont Blanc could or would want to compete with Bic in the low-end, disposable-pen market segment.

Differentiated Targeting Strategy Through Market Segmentation

With a **differentiated targeting strategy,** an organization directs its marketing efforts at two or more segments by developing a marketing mix for each segment (refer to Figure 6.2). After a firm uses a concentrated strategy successfully in one market segment, it sometimes expands its efforts to include additional segments. For example, Fruit of the Loom underwear has traditionally been aimed at one segment: men. However, the company now markets underwear for women and children as well. Marketing mixes for a differentiated strategy may vary as to product features, distribution methods, promotion methods, and prices.

A firm may increase sales in the aggregate market through a differentiated strategy because its marketing mixes are aimed at more people. For example, Neiman Marcus, which established its retail apparel reputation by targeting wealthy people in their fifties with luxurious environments, is now experimenting with several boutiques geared toward other age groups. One experimental concept is Cusp, a casual boutique chain that is targeted at young women. The stores, which do not reference Neiman Marcus in any way, carry designer jeans, T-shirts, short dresses, and other casual attire.[4] A company with excess production capacity may find a differentiated strategy advantageous because the sale of products to additional segments may absorb excess capacity. On the other hand, a differentiated strategy often demands more production processes, materials, and people. Thus, production costs may be higher than with a concentrated strategy.

concentrated targeting strategy A market segmentation strategy in which an organization targets a single market segment using one marketing mix

differentiated targeting strategy A strategy in which an organization targets two or more segments by developing a marketing mix for each segment

Differentiated Targeting

Many companies employ the differentiated targeting strategy by focusing on more than one market segment, using multiple marketing mixes. VISA offers a variety of products and targets them at different market segments.

Step 2: Determine Which Segmentation Variables to Use

L○❸ To become familiar with the major segmentation variables

Segmentation variables are the characteristics of individuals, groups, or organizations used to divide a market into segments. For example, location, age, gender, and rate of product usage can all be bases for segmenting markets. Most marketers use several variables in combination. Haggar Clothing, for example, is targeting slacks at men (gender) between the ages of 30 and 45 (age) with new products and lighthearted advertisements that feature older male models.[5] To select a segmentation variable, several factors are considered. The segmentation variable should relate to customers' needs for, uses of, or behavior toward the product. Television marketers might segment the television market based on income and age but not on religion because people's television needs do not differ due to religion. Furthermore, if individuals or organizations in a total market are to be classified accurately, the segmentation variable must be measurable. Age, location, and gender are measurable because such information can be obtained through observation or questioning. In contrast, segmenting a market on the basis of, say, intelligence is extremely difficult because this attribute is harder to measure accurately.

A company's resources and capabilities affect the number and size of segment variables used. The type of product and degree of variation in customers' needs also dictate the number and size of segments targeted. In short, there is no best way to segment markets.

Choosing one or more segmentation variables is a critical step in targeting a market. Selecting an inappropriate variable limits the chances of developing a successful marketing strategy. To help you better understand potential segmentation variables,

segmentation variables
Characteristics of individuals, groups, or organizations used to divide a market into segments

figure 6.3

SEGMENTATION VARIABLES FOR CONSUMER MARKETS

Demographic variables
- Age
- Gender
- Race
- Ethnicity
- Income
- Education
- Occupation
- Family size
- Family life cycle
- Religion
- Social class

Geographic variables
- Region
- Urban, suburban, rural
- City size
- County size
- State size
- Market density
- Climate
- Terrain

Psychographic variables
- Personality attributes
- Motives
- Lifestyles

Behavioristic variables
- Volume usage
- End use
- Benefit expectations
- Brand loyalty
- Price sensitivity

we next examine the major types of variables used to segment consumer markets and the types used to segment business markets.

Variables for Segmenting Consumer Markets

A marketer that is using segmentation to reach a consumer market can choose one or several variables from an assortment of possibilities. As Figure 6.3 shows, segmentation variables can be grouped into four categories: demographic, geographic, psychographic, and behavioristic.

Demographic Variables. Demographers study aggregate population characteristics such as the distribution of age and gender, fertility rates, migration patterns, and mortality rates. Demographic characteristics that marketers commonly use in segmenting

Gender-Based Segmentation

These companies use gender-based market segmentation. Old Spice body wash is aimed at men, and Dove body wash is aimed at women.

markets include age, gender, race, ethnicity, income, education, occupation, family size, family life cycle, religion, and social class. Marketers rely on these demographic characteristics because they are often closely linked to customers' needs and purchasing behaviors and can be readily measured. Like demographers, a few marketers even use mortality rates. Service Corporation International (SCI), the largest U.S. funeral services company, attempts to locate its facilities in higher-income suburban areas with high mortality rates. SCI operates more than 2,000 funeral service locations, cemeteries, and crematoriums.[6]

Age is a commonly used variable for segmentation purposes. A trip to the shopping mall highlights the fact that many retailers, including Abercrombie & Fitch, Aeropostale, and American Eagle Outfitters, target teens and very young adults. Some of these retailers are now looking to create new marketing mixes for their customers as they age by opening new concept stores targeted at 25- to 40-year-olds, such as Ruehl No. 925, Metropark, and Martin + Osa, which offer more work clothes.[7] Marketers need to be aware of age distribution and how that distribution is changing. All age groups under 55 are expected to decrease by the year 2025, whereas all age categories 55 and older are expected to increase. In 1970, the average age of a U.S. citizen was 27.9; currently it is about 36.2.[8] As Figure 6.4 shows, Americans 65 and older spend as much or more on food, housing, and health care compared to Americans in the two younger age groups.

Many marketers recognize the purchase influence of children and are targeting more marketing efforts at them. Kimberly-Clark, for example, introduced a toilet paper product, Cottonelle Kids, that helps children learn not to waste toilet paper.[9] As a group, parents of children ages 4 to 12 have annual incomes in excess of $40 billion. Numerous products are aimed specifically at children—toys, clothing, food and beverages, and entertainment such as movies and TV cable channels. In addition, children in this age group influence $500 billion of parental spending yearly.[10] In households with only one parent or those in which both parents work, children often take on additional responsibilities such as cooking, cleaning, and grocery shopping, and thus influence the types of products and brands these households purchase.

Gender is another demographic variable that is commonly used to segment markets, including the markets for clothing, soft drinks, nonprescription medications, toiletries, magazines, and even cigarettes. The U.S. Census Bureau reports that girls and women account for 50.7 percent and boys and men for 49.3 percent of the total

Age-Based Segmentation

These companies are aiming products at specific age groups.

figure 6.4

SPENDING LEVELS OF THREE AGE GROUPS FOR SELECTED PRODUCT CATEGORIES

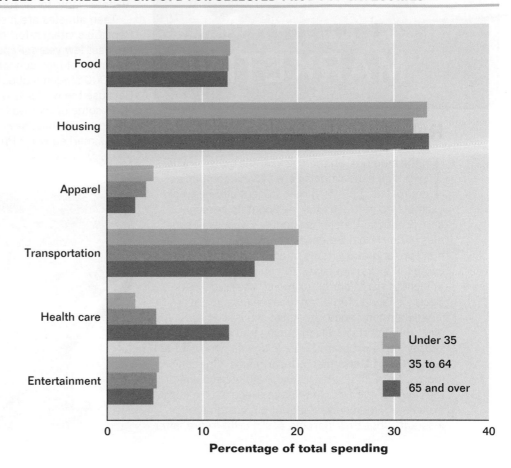

Source: "Table 3: Reference Person: Average Annual Expenditures and Characteristics, Consumer Expenditure Survey 2005," U.S. Department of Labor, Bureau of Labor Statistics, 2005, www.bls.gov/cex/2005/Standard/age.pdf.

U.S. population.[11] Some deodorant marketers use gender segmentation: Secret and Soft & Dri are targeted specifically at women, whereas Degree and Mitchum are directed toward men. Food and beverage companies are paying close attention to women and have determined that all important food marketing trends are partially the result of women's influence in the home.[12]

Marketers also use race and ethnicity as variables for segmenting markets for such products as food, music, clothing, and cosmetics and for services such as banking and insurance. The U.S. Hispanic population illustrates the importance of ethnicity as a segmentation variable. This ethnic group is growing five times faster than the general population. Consequently, Campbell Soup, Procter & Gamble, and other companies are targeting Hispanic consumers, viewing this segment as attractive because of its size and growth potential. Kmart, for example, launched an initiative to stock more multicultural dolls in all of its 1,400 stores, not just those located in predominantly minority neighborhoods. Designed to appeal to Asian Americans, African Americans, and Hispanics, the four dozen types of dolls—including Dora the Explorer and Baby Abuelita—are supported with an advertising campaign in the stores' weekly circulars.[13]

Because income strongly influences people's product needs, it often provides a way to divide markets. Income affects people's ability to buy and their desires for certain lifestyles. Product markets segmented by income include sporting goods, housing, furniture, cosmetics, clothing, jewelry, home appliances, automobiles, and electronics. Although many retailers choose to target consumers with upscale

E-ntertainment MARKETING

Rah, Rah, Varsity Marketing!

In the stadium, on the track, at the gym, or wherever high school sports are played, companies are reaching out to target student athletes. For example, to get teens talking about its personal care products, Procter & Gamble gives away samples of its Herbal Essences shampoo, Cover Girl makeup, and other items at cheerleader training camps. It's "a unique way to get involved with an influential set of our consumers," observes P&G Beauty's teen external relations manager.

Allstate Insurance, an active sponsor of NASCAR and other sports, is also jumping into high school sports with a program for local agents who want to support teams or athletic departments. "In many, many communities, high school athletics is one of the premier events," an Allstate executive explains. "Teenagers themselves are not big customers for insurance, but their parents are." Furthermore, after students graduate and need car or home insurance, Allstate wants to be sure its brand is in the game.

Teen athletes are a sizable target market for PepsiCo's vitamin-fortified Propel fitness water. In the past few years, Pepsi has held workshops at hundreds of high school sports events and taught 500,000 students about nutrition and water. Because the workshops are educational, the teens "lose some of that wall they put up" against mainstream marketing, says the senior vice president of sports marketing for Propel.[a]

incomes, some marketers are instead going after lower-income consumers with new products ranging from prepaid cell phones and debit cards to budget paper towels.[14]

Among the factors that influence household income and product needs are marital status and the presence and age of children. These characteristics, often combined and called the *family life cycle*, affect needs for housing, appliances, food and beverages, automobiles, and recreational equipment.

Marketers also use many other demographic variables. For instance, dictionary publishing companies segment markets by education level. Some insurance companies segment markets using occupation, targeting health insurance at college students and young workers with employers that do not provide health coverage. Family life cycles can be broken down in various ways. Figure 6.5 shows a breakdown into nine categories. The composition of the U.S. household in relation to the family life cycle has changed considerably over the last several decades.

Single-parent families are on the rise, meaning that the "typical" family no longer consists of a married couple with children. Since 1970, the number of households headed by a single mother increased from 12 percent to 26 percent of total family households, and that number grew from 1 percent to 6 percent for families headed by a single father. Another factor that influences the family life cycle is that the increase in median marrying age for women has increased from 20.8 years to 25.3 years since 1970, while for men it increased from 23.2 years to 27.1 years. Additionally, the proportion of women ages 20 to 24 who have never been married has more than doubled over this time, and for women ages 30 to 34 this number has nearly tripled. Other important changes in the family life cycle include the rise in the

figure 6.5   FAMILY LIFE CYCLE STAGES AS A PERCENTAGE OF ALL HOUSEHOLDS

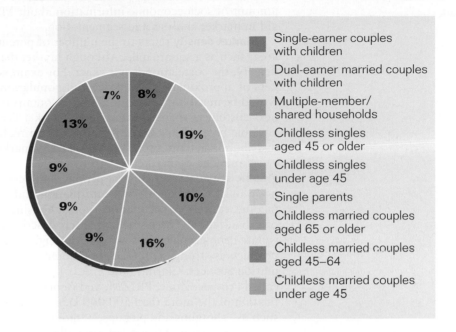

- Single-earner couples with children
- Dual-earner married couples with children
- Multiple-member/ shared households
- Childless singles aged 45 or older
- Childless singles under age 45
- Single parents
- Childless married couples aged 65 or older
- Childless married couples aged 45–64
- Childless married couples under age 45

Source: U.S. Bureau of the Census, *Current Population Survey.*

number of people living alone and the number of unmarried couples living together.[15] Tracking these changes helps marketers satisfy the needs of particular target markets through new marketing mixes. For example, MicroMarketing, Inc., helps companies target customers through what it calls Lifestage Marketing. MicroMarketing can create a direct-mail campaign aimed at groups such as people who recently moved, soon-to-be newlyweds, recent high school and college graduates, and expectant parents.[16]

Geographic Variables. Geographic variables—climate, terrain, city size, population density, and urban/rural areas—also influence consumer product needs. Markets may be divided into regions because one or more geographic variables can cause customers to differ from one region to another. Consumers in the South, for instance, rarely have need for snow tires. A company that sells products to a national market might divide the United States into the following regions: Pacific, Southwest, Central, Midwest, Southeast, Middle Atlantic, and New England. A firm that is operating in one or several states might regionalize its market by counties, cities, zip code areas, or other units.

City size can be an important segmentation variable. Some marketers focus efforts on cities of a certain size. For example, one franchised restaurant organization will not locate in cities of fewer than 200,000 people. It concluded that a smaller population base would result in inadequate profits. Other firms actively seek opportunities in smaller towns. A classic example is Wal-Mart, which initially was located only in small towns.

Because cities often cut across political boundaries, the U.S. Census Bureau developed a system to classify metropolitan areas (any area with a city or urbanized area with a population of at least 50,000 and a total metropolitan population of at least 100,000). Metropolitan areas are categorized as one of the following: a metropolitan statistical area (MSA), a primary metropolitan statistical area (PMSA), or a consolidated metropolitan statistical area (CMSA). An MSA is an urbanized area encircled by nonmetropolitan counties and is neither socially nor economically dependent on any other metropolitan area. A metropolitan area within a complex of at least 1 million inhabitants can elect to be named a PMSA. A CMSA is a metropolitan area of at least 1 million that has two or more PMSAs. Of the 20 CMSAs, the 5 largest— New York, Los Angeles, Chicago, San Francisco, and Philadelphia—account for 20 percent of the U.S. population. The federal government provides a considerable amount of socioeconomic information about MSAs, PMSAs, and CMSAs that can aid in market analysis and segmentation.

Market density refers to the number of potential customers within a unit of land area, such as a square mile. Although market density relates generally to population density, the correlation is not exact. For example, in two different geographic markets of approximately equal size and population, market density for office supplies would be much higher in one area if it contained a much greater proportion of business customers than the other area. Market density may be a useful segmentation variable because low-density markets often require different sales, advertising, and distribution activities than do high-density markets.

A number of marketers are using geodemographic segmentation. **Geodemographic segmentation** clusters people in zip code areas and even smaller neighborhood units based on lifestyle information and especially demographic data such as income, education, occupation, type of housing, ethnicity, family life cycle, and level of urbanization. These small, precisely described population clusters help marketers isolate demographic units as small as neighborhoods where the demand for specific products is strongest. Information companies such as Donnelley Marketing Information Services, Claritas, and C.A.C.I., Inc., provide geodemographic data services called Prospect Zone, PRIZM, and Acorn, respectively. PRIZM is based on a classification of the more than 500,000 U.S. neighborhoods into one of 40 cluster types, such as "shotguns and pickups," "money and brains," and "gray power."

Geodemographic segmentation allows marketers to engage in micromarketing. **Micromarketing** is the focusing of precise marketing efforts on very small geographic markets, such as community and even neighborhood markets. Providers of financial and health-care services, retailers, and consumer products companies use micromarketing. Special advertising campaigns, promotions, retail site location analyses, special pricing, and unique retail product offerings are a few examples of micromarketing facilitated through geodemographic segmentation. Many retailers use micromarketing to determine the merchandise mix for individual stores. Wal-Mart is joining the micromarketing bandwagon by experimenting with tailored marketing mixes for six demographic groups: African American, affluent, empty-nesters, Hispanics, suburbanites, and rural residents. The product mix for its affluent stores, for example, includes a 1,000-bottle wine department, double the organic products of its traditional stores, and an expanded home fitness equipment area in place of a gun department.[17]

Climate is commonly used as a geographic segmentation variable because of its broad impact on people's behavior and product needs. Product markets affected by climate include air-conditioning and heating equipment, fireplace accessories, clothing, gardening equipment, recreational products, and building materials.

Psychographic Variables. Marketers sometimes use psychographic variables, such as personality characteristics, motives, and lifestyles, to segment markets. A psychographic dimension can be used by itself to segment a market or it can be combined with other types of segmentation variables.

Personality characteristics can be useful for segmentation when a product resembles many competing products and consumers' needs are not significantly related to other segmentation variables. However, segmenting a market according to personality traits can be risky. Although marketing practitioners have long believed consumer choice and product use vary with personality, until recently marketing research had indicated only weak relationships. It is hard to measure personality traits accurately, especially since most personality tests were developed for clinical use, not for segmentation purposes.

When appealing to a personality characteristic, a marketer almost always selects one that many people view positively. Individuals with this characteristic, as well as those who would like to have it, may be influenced to buy that marketer's brand.

market density The number of potential customers within a unit of land area

geodemographic segmentation A method of market segmentation that clusters people in zip code areas and smaller neighborhood units based on lifestyle and demographic information

micromarketing An approach to market segmentation in which organizations focus precise marketing efforts on very small geographic markets

Marketers taking this approach do not worry about measuring how many people have the positively valued characteristic; they assume a sizable proportion of people in the target market either have it or want to have it.

When motives are used to segment a market, the market is divided according to consumers' reasons for making a purchase. Personal appearance, affiliation, status, safety, and health are examples of motives affecting the types of products purchased and the choice of stores in which they are bought. Marketing efforts based on health and fitness motives can be a point of competitive advantage. For example, Taco Bell, Jack in the Box, and Starbucks each introduced new "light" products at the beginning of the year to target consumers who overindulged during the holidays or set weight-loss resolutions. Jack in the Box launched a 300-calorie chicken fajita pita and grilled chicken strips with a teriyaki dipping sauce. Taco Bell introduced a "Fresco menu" with nine items with 350 or fewer calories.[18]

Lifestyle segmentation groups individuals according to how they spend their time, the importance of things in their surroundings (homes or jobs, for example), beliefs about themselves and broad issues, and some demographic characteristics, such as income and education.[19] Lifestyle analysis provides a broad view of buyers because it encompasses numerous characteristics related to people's activities (work, hobbies, entertainment, sports), interests (family, home, fashion, food, technology), and opinions (politics, social issues, education, the future).

One of the most popular consumer frameworks is VALS™ from SRI Consulting Business Intelligence. VALS classifies consumers based on psychological characteristics (personality characteristics) that are correlated with purchase behavior and key demographics. The VALS classification questionnaire, which is used to determine a consumers' VALS type, can be integrated into larger questionnaires to find out about consumers' lifestyle choices. Figure 6.6 is an example of VALS data that shows the proportion of each VALS group that purchased a mountain bike, purchased golf clubs, owns a fishing rod, and goes hunting. VALS research is also used to create new products as well as to segment existing markets. VALS systems have been developed for the United States, Japan, and the United Kingdom.[20] Many other lifestyle classification systems exist. Several companies, such as Hesperian's Behavior Bank, collect lifestyle data on millions of consumers.

Behavioristic Variables. Firms can divide a market according to some feature of consumer behavior toward a product, commonly involving some aspect of product use. For example, a market may be separated into users—classified as heavy, moderate, or light—and nonusers. To satisfy a specific group, such as heavy users, marketers may create a distinctive product, set special prices, or initiate special promotion and distribution activities. Per capita consumption data help identify different levels of usage. For example, the global per capita consumption of electricity varies from 26,102 kWh (kilowatt-hours) in Iceland to 8.7 kWh in Cambodia. Per capita consumption of electricity in the United States is 12,343 kWh; in China and India it is 1,887 kWh and 520 kWh, respectively.[21]

How customers use or apply products may also determine the method of segmentation. To satisfy customers who use a product in a certain way, some feature—say, packaging, size, texture, or color—may be designed precisely to make the product easier to use, safer, or more convenient.

Benefit segmentation is the division of a market according to benefits that consumers want from the product. Although most types of market segmentation assume a relationship between the variable and customers' needs, benefit segmentation differs in that the benefits customers

benefit segmentation The division of a market according to benefits that consumers want from the product

Lifestyle Segmentation

In this advertisement, Garmin GPS targets people who enjoy an outdoors lifestyle.

Where do you go to rock n' roll?

The Colorado™ 400t, with its unique Rock 'n Roller™ one-handed thumbwheel operation, is designed for people who are serious about getting out there, finding adventure and then making their way back home safely.

Scroll through preloaded detailed U.S. TOPO maps with 3D elevation viewed on a huge 3-inch color display. Rugged and waterproof to IPX7 standards, the Colorado features a high-sensitivity GPS receiver, barometric altimeter, electronic compass, and the ability to wirelessly exchange user routes, tracks, waypoints and geocaches with other select Garmin devices. Additional mapping sold separately on plug-in SD cards. So, where will you go to rock 'n roll? With four Colorado models to choose from, anywhere you want to.

To pull up more, go to www.garmin.com.

GARMIN.

figure 6.6

VALS™ TYPES AND SPORTS PREFERENCES

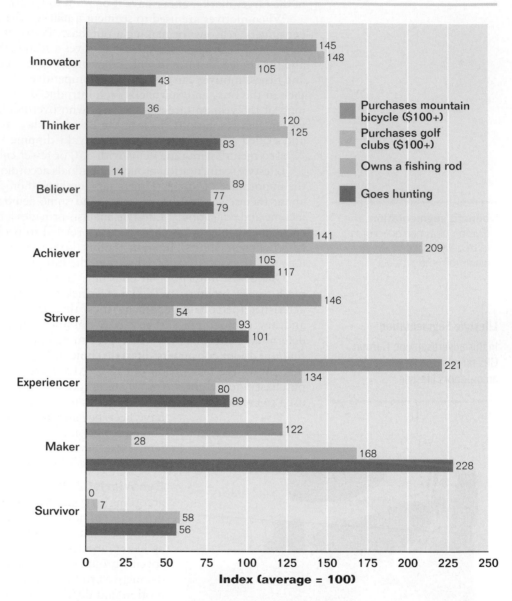

seek *are* their product needs. Consider that a customer who purchases over-the-counter cold relief medication may be specifically interested in two benefits: stopping a runny nose and relieving chest congestion. Thus, individuals are segmented directly according to their needs. By determining the desired benefits, marketers may be able to divide people into groups seeking certain sets of benefits. Dannon, for example, is targeting people who want to lose weight with its Light & Fit Crave Control probiotic yogurt.[22] The effectiveness of such segmentation depends on three conditions: (1) the benefits sought must be identifiable; (2) using these benefits, marketers must be able to divide people into recognizable segments; and (3) one or more of the resulting segments must be accessible to the firm's marketing efforts. Both Timberland and Avia, for example, segment the foot apparel market based on benefits sought.

As this discussion shows, consumer markets can be divided according to numerous characteristics. Business markets are segmented using different variables, as we will see in the following section.

green MARKETING

The Three Shades of "Green"

One shade of green does *not* fit all. Actually, marketers who position their products as eco-friendly should look for three shades of green when they segment their markets. "True Green" consumers—12 percent of the U.S. population, according to one survey—buy green products regularly. "Light Green" consumers (68 percent of the population) sometimes buy green, particularly when the products are easily available. "Never Green" consumers, who make up 20 percent of the population, never buy green.

Fairmont Resort Hotels has been seeing shades of green since 1990, when it repositioned itself on the basis of commitment to environmental sustainability. "It really has become a point of differentiation for us," says Fairmont's director of environmental affairs. The company also positions its conference facilities as green by offering earth-friendly conference meals.

Packaging can support a product's green positioning, as well. Unilever is a case in point. A 32-ounce container of its new "Small & Mighty" concentrated All laundry detergent cleans the same amount of clothing as a 100-ounce container of the old version. Yet, the "Small & Mighty" container requires half as much plastic as the older container, which saves 150 million pounds of plastic and millions of gallons of oil each year—an important selling point for green consumers.[b]

Variables for Segmenting Business Markets

Like consumer markets, business markets are frequently segmented, often by multiple variables in combination. Marketers segment business markets according to geographic location, type of organization, customer size, and product use.

Geographic Location. Earlier we noted that the demand for some consumer products can vary considerably among geographic areas because of differences in climate, terrain, customer preferences, and similar factors. Demand for business products also varies according to geographic location. For example, producers of certain types of lumber divide their markets geographically because their customers' needs vary from region to region. Geographic segmentation may be especially appropriate for reaching industries concentrated in certain locations. Furniture and textile producers, for example, are concentrated in the Southeast.

Type of Organization. A company sometimes segments a market by types of organizations within that market. Different types of organizations often require different product features, distribution systems, price structures, and selling strategies. Given these variations, a firm may either concentrate on a single segment with one marketing mix (a concentration targeting strategy) or focus on several groups with multiple mixes (a differentiated targeting strategy). A carpet producer, for example, could segment potential customers into several groups, such as automobile makers, commercial carpet contractors (firms that carpet large commercial buildings), apartment complex developers, carpet wholesalers, and large retail carpet outlets.

Customer Size. An organization's size may affect its purchasing procedures and the types and quantities of products it wants. Size can thus be an effective variable for segmenting a business market. To reach a segment of a particular size, marketers may have to adjust one or more marketing mix components. For example, customers who buy in extremely large quantities are sometimes offered discounts. In addition, marketers often must expand personal selling efforts to serve large organizational buyers properly. Because the needs of large and small buyers tend to be quite distinct, marketers frequently use different marketing practices to reach various customer groups.

Product Use. Certain products, especially basic raw materials like steel, petroleum, plastics, and lumber, are used in numerous ways. How a company uses products affects the types and amounts of products purchased, as well as the purchasing method. For example, computers are used for engineering purposes, basic scientific research, and business operations such as word processing, accounting, and telecommunications. A computer maker therefore may segment the computer market by types of use because organizations' needs for computer hardware and software depend on the purpose for which products are purchased.

Step 3: Develop Market Segment Profiles

L O 4 To know what segment profiles are and how they are used

A market segment profile describes the similarities among potential customers within a segment and explains the differences among people and organizations in different segments. A profile may cover such aspects as demographic characteristics, geographic factors, product benefits sought, lifestyles, brand preferences, and usage rates. Individuals and organizations within segments should be relatively similar with respect to several characteristics and product needs, and differ considerably from those within other market segments. Marketers use market segment profiles to assess the degree to which their possible products can match or fit potential customers' product needs. Market segment profiles help marketers understand how a business can use its capabilities to serve potential customer groups.

The use of market segment profiles benefits marketers in several ways. Such profiles help a marketer determine which segment or segments are most attractive to the organization relative to the firm's strengths, weaknesses, objectives, and resources. Although marketers may initially believe certain segments are quite attractive, development of market segment profiles may yield information that indicates the opposite. For the market segment or segments chosen by the organization, the information included in market segment profiles can be highly useful in making marketing decisions.

Step 4: Evaluate Relevant Market Segments

L O 5 To understand how to evaluate market segments

After analyzing the market segment profiles, a marketer is likely to identify several relevant market segments that require further analysis and eliminate certain segments from consideration. To further assess relevant market segments, several important factors, including sales estimates, competition, and estimated costs associated with each segment, should be analyzed.

Sales Estimates

Potential sales for a market segment can be measured along several dimensions, including product level, geographic area, time, and level of competition.[23] With respect to product level, potential sales can be estimated for a specific product item (for example, Diet Coke) or an entire product line (Coca-Cola Classic, Caffeine-Free Coke, Diet Coke, Caffeine-Free Diet Coke, Vanilla Coke, Diet Vanilla Coke, Cherry Coca-Cola, and Diet Cherry Coca-Cola comprise one product line). A manager must also determine the geographic area to include in the estimate. In relation to time, sales estimates can be short range (one year or less), medium range (one to five years), or long range (longer than five years). The competitive level specifies whether sales are being estimated for a single firm or for an entire industry.

Market potential is the total amount of a product that customers will purchase within a specified period at a specific level of industrywide marketing activity. Market potential can be stated in terms of dollars or units. A segment's market potential is affected by economic, sociocultural, and other environmental forces. Marketers must assume a certain general level of marketing effort in the industry when they estimate market potential. The specific level of marketing effort varies from one firm to another, but the sum of all firms' marketing activities equals industrywide marketing efforts. A marketing manager must also consider whether and to what extent industry marketing efforts will change.

Company sales potential is the maximum percentage of market potential that an individual firm within an industry can expect to obtain for a specific product. Several factors influence company sales potential for a market segment. First, the market potential places absolute limits on the size of the company's sales potential. Second, the magnitude of industrywide marketing activities has an indirect but definite impact on the company's sales potential. Those activities have a direct bearing on the size of the market potential. When Domino's Pizza advertises home-delivered pizza, for example, it indirectly promotes pizza in general; its commercials may indirectly help sell Pizza Hut's and other competitors' home-delivered pizza. Third, the intensity and effectiveness of a company's marketing activities relative to competitors' affect the size of the company's sales potential. If a company spends twice as much as any of its competitors on marketing efforts and if each dollar spent is more effective in generating sales, the firm's sales potential will be quite high compared to competitors'.

Two general approaches that measure company sales potential are breakdown and buildup. In the **breakdown approach,** the marketing manager first develops a general economic forecast for a specific time period. Next, the manager estimates market potential based on this economic forecast. Then the manager derives the company's sales potential from the general economic forecast and estimate of market potential. In the **buildup approach,** the marketing manager begins by estimating how much of a product a potential buyer in a specific geographic area, such as a sales territory, will purchase in a given period. The manager then multiplies that amount by the total number of potential buyers in that area. The manager performs the same calculation for each geographic area in which the firm sells products and then adds the totals for each area to calculate market potential. To determine company sales potential, the manager must estimate, based on planned levels of company marketing activities, the proportion of the total market potential the company can obtain.

Competitive Assessment

Besides obtaining sales estimates, it is crucial to assess competitors that are already operating in the segments being considered. Without competitive information, sales estimates may be misleading. A market segment that initially seems attractive based on sales estimates may turn out to be much less so after a competitive assessment. Such an assessment should ask several questions about competitors: How many exist? What are their strengths and weaknesses? Do several competitors have major market shares and together dominate the segment? Can our company create a marketing mix to compete effectively against competitors' marketing mixes? Is it likely that new competitors will enter this segment? If so, how will they affect our firm's ability to compete successfully? Answers to such questions are important for proper assessment of the competition in potential market segments.

The actions of a national food company that considered entering the dog food market illustrate the importance of competitive assessment. Through a segmentation study, the company determined that dog owners could be divided into three segments according to how they viewed their dogs and dog foods. One group treated their dogs as companions and family members. These individuals were willing to pay relatively high prices for dog foods and wanted a variety of types and flavors so their dogs would not get bored. The second group saw their dogs as performing a definite utilitarian function, such as protecting family members, playing with children, guarding the property,

market potential The total amount of a product that customers will purchase within a specified period at a specific level of industrywide marketing activity

company sales potential The maximum percentage of market potential that an individual firm within an industry can expect to obtain for a specific product

breakdown approach Measuring company sales potential based on a general economic forecast for a specific period and the market potential derived from it

buildup approach Measuring company sales potential by estimating how much of a product a potential buyer in a specific geographic area will purchase in a given period, multiplying the estimate by the number of potential buyers, and adding the totals of all the geographic areas considered

or herding farm animals. These people wanted a low-priced, nutritious dog food and were not interested in a wide variety of flavors. Dog owners in the third segment were found to actually hate their dogs. These people wanted the cheapest dog food they could buy and were not concerned with nutrition, flavor, or variety. The food company examined the extent to which competitive brands were serving all these dog owners and found that each segment contained at least three well-entrenched competing brands, which together dominated the segment. The company's management decided not to enter the dog food market because of the strength of the competing brands.

Cost Estimates

To fulfill the needs of a target segment, an organization must develop and maintain a marketing mix that precisely meets the wants and needs of individuals and organizations in that segment. Developing and maintaining such a mix can be expensive. Distinctive product features, attractive package design, generous product warranties, extensive advertising, attractive promotional offers, competitive prices, and high-quality personal service consume considerable organizational resources. Indeed, to reach certain segments, the costs may be so high that a marketer concludes the segment is inaccessible. Another cost consideration is whether the organization can effectively reach a segment at costs equal to or below competitors' costs. If the firm's costs are likely to be higher, it will be unable to compete in that segment in the long run.

Step 5: Select Specific Target Markets

L O 6 To identify the factors that influence the selection of specific market segments for use as target markets

An important initial consideration in selecting a target market is whether customers' needs differ enough to warrant the use of market segmentation. If segmentation analysis shows customer needs to be fairly homogeneous, the firm's management may decide to use the undifferentiated approach, discussed earlier. However, if customer needs are heterogeneous, which is much more likely, one or more target markets must be selected. On the other hand, marketers may decide not to enter and compete in any of the segments.

Assuming one or more segments offer significant opportunities to achieve organizational objectives, marketers must decide in which segments to participate. Ordinarily information gathered in the previous step—about sales estimates, competitors, and cost estimates—requires careful consideration in this final step to determine long-term profit opportunities. Also, the firm's management must investigate whether the organization has the financial resources, managerial skills, employee expertise, and facilities to enter and compete effectively in selected segments. Furthermore, the requirements of some market segments may be at odds with the firm's overall objectives, and the possibility of legal problems, conflicts with interest groups, and technological advancements could make certain segments unattractive. In addition, when prospects for long-term growth are taken into account, some segments may appear very attractive and others less desirable.

Selecting appropriate target markets is important to an organization's adoption and use of the marketing concept philosophy. Identifying the right target market is the key to implementing a successful marketing strategy, whereas failure to do so can lead to low sales, high costs, and severe financial losses. A careful target market analysis places an organization in a better position to both serve customers' needs and achieve its objectives.

product positioning Creating and maintaining a certain concept of a product in customers' minds

Product Positioning and Repositioning

L O 7 To understand positioning

Once a target market is selected, a firm must consider how to position its product. **Product positioning** refers to the decisions and activities intended to create and maintain a certain concept of the firm's product (relative to competitive brands) in customers' minds. When marketers introduce a product, they try to

RESPONSIBLE marketing?

Cigarettes' Smoking Markets

ISSUE: Do cigarette makers target minors?

Tobacco companies are believed to spend substantial promotional dollars to recruit "replacement smokers." This target market of replacements consists mostly of 14- to 20-year-olds. In a recent decision, Judge Gladys Kessler released her opinion on the government's case against tobacco companies, stating, "The defendants [tobacco companies] spent enormous resources tracking the preferences and behaviors of youth under 21 . . . to start young people smoking and keep them smoking." Although the tobacco companies claim they do not intentionally market their products to minors, they continue to advertise in ways that reach this vulnerable age group. Almost 90 percent of all smokers begin before age 18. Thus, without this young market, the tobacco companies' sales would significantly decline. Each day, about 4,000 kids try smoking for the first time.

One of the major reasons that teens begin smoking is to look more mature. Some tobacco critics point out that tobacco companies promote their products to young adults (over 21) to reach teens. Do you believe that cigarette makers use advertisements aimed at young adults to reach teens that are under 18? Short of banning all cigarette advertising, how can government regulators deal with this type of advertising that may encourage teens to start smoking?ᶜ

position it so that it appears to have the characteristics that the target market most desires. PepsiCo positioned its new Fuelosophy protein drinks as being from a small entrepreneurial company so they would better appeal to shoppers at Whole Foods, where the new drinks are sold. The drinks' packaging and website bear no hint as to their corporate parentage.[24] This projected image is crucial. Crest is positioned as a fluoride toothpaste that fights cavities, whereas Close-Up is positioned as a whitening toothpaste that enhances the user's sex appeal, as shown in Figure 6.7.

Perceptual Mapping

A product's position is the result of customers' perceptions of the product's attributes relative to those of competitive brands. Buyers make numerous purchase decisions on a regular basis. To avoid a continuous reevaluation of numerous products, buyers tend to group, or "position," products in their minds to simplify buying decisions. Rather than allowing customers to position products independently, marketers often try to influence and shape consumers' concepts or perceptions of products through advertising. Marketers

figure 6.7

TOOTHPASTE PRODUCT POSITIONS

Brand	Product position
Colgate Total	Fights full range of oral health problems
Close-Up	Sexy, whitener, great breath for kissing
Crest	Powerful fluoride cavity fighter
Aim	Milder taste than other brands, kid-friendly
Arm & Hammer	Popular baking soda mixed with toothpaste
AquaFresh	Kills germs, for young adults
Biotene	Reduces bacteria and germs in mouth
Oral-B	High quality, dentist approved
Rembrandt	Higher-quality whitening
Sensodyne	Especially for sensitive teeth
Mentadent	Baking soda and peroxide for fresh breath
Ultrabrite	Low-priced whitener, removes stains

sometimes analyze product positions by developing perceptual maps, as shown in Figure 6.8. Perceptual maps are created by questioning a sample of consumers about their perceptions of products, brands, and organizations with respect to two or more dimensions. To develop a perceptual map like the one in Figure 6.8, respondents would be asked how they perceive selected pain relievers in regard to price and type of pain for which the products are used. Also, respondents would be asked about their preferences for product features to establish "ideal points" or "ideal clusters," which represent a consensus about what a specific group of customers desires in terms of product features. Then marketers can compare how their brand is perceived compared with the ideal points.

Product Positioning

The maker of Dockers positions its products as being comfortable, flexible, and a reasonable value.

Bases for Positioning

Marketers can use several bases for product positioning. A common basis for positioning products is to use competitors. A firm can position a product to compete head-on with another brand, as PepsiCo has done against Coca-Cola, or to avoid competition, as 7Up has done relative to other soft-drink producers. Head-to-head competition may be a marketer's positioning objective if the product's performance

figure 6.8

HYPOTHETICAL PERCEPTUAL MAP FOR PAIN RELIEVERS

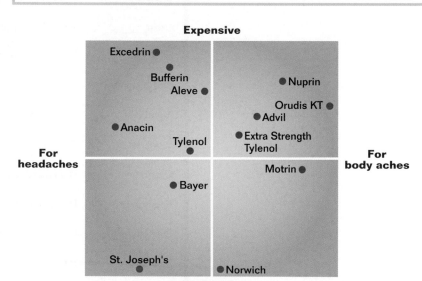

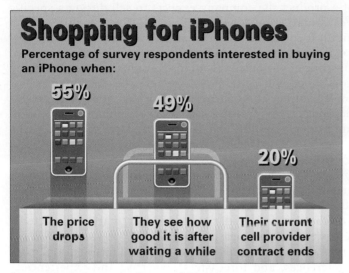

Shopping for iPhones

Percentage of survey respondents interested in buying an iPhone when:

55%

49%

20%

| The price drops | They see how good it is after waiting a while | Their current cell provider contract ends |

Source: Harris Interactive Survey of 10,410 respondents aged 13 to 64.

characteristics are at least equal to those of competitive brands and if the product is priced lower. Head-to-head positioning may be appropriate even when the price is higher if the product's performance characteristics are superior. For example, Ford has positioned its Fusion sedan head to head against the Honda Accord and Toyota Camry through advertisements that highlight the results of a *Car and Driver* magazine driving challenge in which the Fusion earned the top ratings.[25] Conversely, positioning to avoid competition may be best when the product's performance characteristics do not differ significantly from competing brands. Moreover, positioning a brand to avoid competition may be appropriate when that brand has unique characteristics that are important to some buyers. Volvo, for example, has for years positioned itself away from competitors by focusing on the safety characteristics of its cars. Whereas some auto companies mention safety issues in their advertisements, many are more likely to focus on style, fuel efficiency, performance, or terms of sale. Avoiding competition is critical when a firm introduces a brand into a market in which the company already has one or more brands. Marketers usually want to avoid cannibalizing sales of their existing brands, unless the new brand generates substantially larger profits.

A product's position can be based on specific product attributes or features. For example, Apple's iPhone is positioned based on product attributes such as its unique shape, easy-to-use touchscreen, and its access to iTunes' music store. If a product has been planned properly, its features will give it the distinct appeal needed. Style, shape, construction, and color help create the image and the appeal. If buyers can easily identify the benefits, they are, of course, more likely to purchase the product. When the new product does not offer certain preferred attributes, there is room for another new product.

Other bases for product positioning include price, quality level, and benefits provided by the product. For example, Era detergent provides stain treatment and stain removal. Also, a positioning basis employed by some marketers is the target market. This type of positioning relies heavily on promoting the types of people who use the product.

Repositioning

Positioning decisions are not just for new products. Evaluating the positions of existing products is important because a brand's market share and profitability may be strengthened by product repositioning. For example, several years ago Kraft was on the verge of discontinuing Cheez Whiz because its sales had declined considerably. After Kraft marketers repositioned Cheez Whiz as a fast, convenient, microwavable cheese sauce, its sales rebounded and achieved new heights. When introducing a new product into a product line, one or more existing brands may have to be repositioned to minimize cannibalization of established brands and ensure a favorable position for the new brand.

Repositioning can be accomplished by physically changing the product, its price, or its distribution. Rather than making any of these changes, marketers sometimes reposition a product by changing its image through promotional efforts. Burgerville USA, for example, repositioned itself as being an environmentally friendly and more healthful alternative to McDonald's and Wendy's. The chain, which has half of its 40 stores in Portland, Oregon, heavily promoted its corporate citizenship, sustainable agriculture, and healthy food.[26] Finally, a marketer may reposition a product by aiming it at a completely different target market.

Developing Sales Forecasts

LO 8 To become familiar with sales forecasting methods

Forecasting

The maker of Reese's candy relies on seasonal forecasts for certain products as well as long-term forecasts.

WE FEEL SORRY FOR THE CHOCOLATE BUNNIES. THEY'RE JUST SO EMPTY INSIDE.

Reese's   *perfectly easter*

sales forecast The amount of a product a company expects to sell during a specific period at a specified level of marketing activities

executive judgment A sales forecasting method based on the intuition of one or more executives

customer forecasting survey A survey of customers regarding the types and quantities of products they intend to buy during a specific period

After a company targets its market and positions its product, it needs a **sales forecast**—the amount of a product the company expects to sell during a specific period at a specified level of marketing activities. The sales forecast differs from the company sales potential. It concentrates on what actual sales will be at a certain level of company marketing effort, whereas the company sales potential assesses what sales are possible at various levels of marketing activities, assuming certain environmental conditions will exist. Businesses use the sales forecast for planning, organizing, implementing, and controlling their activities. The success of numerous activities depends on this forecast's accuracy. Common problems in failing companies are improper planning and lack of realistic sales forecasts. Overly ambitious sales forecasts can lead to overbuying, over investment, and higher costs.

To forecast sales, a marketer can choose from a number of forecasting methods, some arbitrary and others more scientific, complex, and time consuming. A firm's choice of method or methods depends on the costs involved, type of product, market characteristics, time span of the forecast, purposes of the forecast, stability of the historical sales data, availability of required information, managerial preferences, and forecasters' expertise and experience.[27] Common forecasting techniques fall into five categories: executive judgment, surveys, time series analysis, regression analysis, and market tests.

Executive Judgment

At times, a company forecasts sales chiefly on the basis of **executive judgment:** the intuition of one or more executives. This approach is unscientific but expedient and inexpensive. Executive judgment may work reasonably well when product demand is relatively stable and the forecaster has years of market-related experience. However, because intuition is swayed most heavily by recent experience, the forecast may be overly optimistic or overly pessimistic. Another drawback to intuition is that the forecaster has only past experience as a guide for deciding where to go in the future.

Surveys

Another way to forecast sales is to question customers, sales personnel, or experts regarding their expectations about future purchases. In a **customer forecasting survey,** marketers ask customers what types and quantities of products they intend to buy during a specific period. This approach may be useful to a business with relatively few customers. For example, Intel, which markets to a limited number of companies (primarily computer manufacturers), could conduct customer forecasting surveys effectively. PepsiCo, in contrast, has millions of customers and could not feasibly use a customer survey to forecast future sales.

Customer surveys have several drawbacks. Customers must be able and willing to make accurate estimates of future product requirements. Although some organizational buyers can estimate their anticipated purchases accurately from historical buying data and their own sales forecasts, many cannot make such estimates. In addition, customers may not want to take part in a survey. Occasionally a few respondents give answers they know are incorrect, making survey results inaccurate. Moreover, customer surveys reflect buying intentions rather than actual purchases. Customers' intentions may not be well formulated, and even when potential purchasers have definite buying intentions, they do not necessarily follow through on them. Finally, customer surveys consume much time and money.

In a **sales force forecasting survey,** the firm's salespeople estimate anticipated sales in their territories for a specified period. The forecaster combines these territorial estimates to arrive at a tentative forecast. A marketer may survey the sales staff for several reasons. The most important is that the sales staff is closer to customers on a daily basis than other company personnel and therefore should know more about customers' future product needs. Moreover, when sales representatives assist in developing the forecast, they are more likely to work toward its achievement. In addition, forecasts can be prepared for single territories, divisions consisting of several territories, regions made up of multiple divisions, and the total geographic market. Thus, the method provides sales forecasts from the smallest geographic sales unit to the largest.

A sales force survey also has limitations. Salespeople may be too optimistic or pessimistic due to recent experiences. In addition, salespeople tend to underestimate sales potential in their territories when they believe their sales goals will be determined by their forecasts. They also dislike paperwork because it takes up time that could be spent selling. If preparation of a territorial sales forecast is time consuming, the sales staff may not do the job adequately.

Nonetheless, sales force surveys can be effective under certain conditions. The salespeople as a group must be accurate, or at least consistent, estimators. If the aggregate forecast is consistently over or under actual sales, the individual who develops the final forecast can make the necessary adjustments. Assuming the survey is well administered, the sales force can have the satisfaction of helping to establish reasonable sales goals and the assurance that its forecasts are not being used to set sales quotas.

When a company wants an **expert forecasting survey,** it hires professionals to help prepare the sales forecast. These experts are usually economists, management consultants, advertising executives, college professors, or other individuals outside the firm with solid experience in a specific market. Drawing on this experience and their analyses of available information about the company and the market, experts prepare and present forecasts or answer questions regarding a forecast. Using experts is expedient and relatively inexpensive. However, because they work outside the firm, these forecasters may be less motivated than company personnel to do an effective job.

A more complex form of the expert forecasting survey incorporates the Delphi technique. In the **Delphi technique,** experts create initial forecasts, submit them to the company for averaging, and have the results returned to them so they can make individual refined forecasts. The premise is that the experts will use the averaged results when making refined forecasts and these forecasts will be in a narrower range. The procedure may be repeated several times until the experts, each working separately, reach a consensus on the forecasts. The ultimate goal in using the Delphi technique is to develop a highly accurate sales forecast.

Time Series Analysis

With **time series analysis,** the forecaster uses the firm's historical sales data to discover a pattern or patterns in the firm's sales over time. If a pattern is found, it can be used to forecast sales. This forecasting method assumes that past sales patterns will continue in the future. The accuracy, and thus usefulness, of time series analysis hinges on the validity of this assumption.

In a time series analysis, a forecaster usually performs four types of analyses: trend, cycle, seasonal, and random factor. **Trend analysis** focuses on aggregate sales data, such as the company's annual sales figures, covering a period of many years to determine whether annual sales are generally rising, falling, or staying about the same. Through **cycle analysis,** a forecaster analyzes sales figures (often monthly sales data) from a period of three to five years to ascertain whether sales fluctuate in a consistent, periodic manner. When performing a **seasonal analysis,** the analyst studies daily, weekly, or monthly sales figures to evaluate the degree to which seasonal factors, such as climate and holiday activities, influence sales. In a **random factor analysis,** the forecaster attempts to attribute erratic sales variations to random, nonrecurrent events, such as a regional power failure, a natural disaster, or political

---

sales force forecasting survey A survey of a firm's sales force regarding anticipated sales in their territories for a specified period

expert forecasting survey Sales forecasts prepared by experts outside the firm, such as economists, management consultants, advertising executives, or college professors

Delphi technique A procedure in which experts create initial forecasts, submit them to the company for averaging, and then refine the forecasts

time series analysis A forecasting method that uses historical sales data to discover patterns in the firm's sales over time and generally involves trend, cycle, seasonal, and random factor analyses

trend analysis An analysis that focuses on aggregate sales data over a period of many years to determine general trends in annual sales

cycle analysis An analysis of sales figures for a period of three to five years to ascertain whether sales fluctuate in a consistent, periodic manner

seasonal analysis An analysis of daily, weekly, or monthly sales figures to evaluate the degree to which seasonal factors influence sales

random factor analysis An analysis attempting to attribute erratic sales variations to random, nonrecurrent events

unrest in a foreign market. After performing each of these analyses, the forecaster combines the results to develop the sales forecast. Time series analysis is an effective forecasting method for products with reasonably stable demand, but not for products with highly erratic demand.

Regression Analysis

Like time series analysis, regression analysis requires the use of historical sales data. In **regression analysis,** the forecaster seeks to find a relationship between past sales (the dependent variable) and one or more independent variables, such as population, per capita income, or gross domestic product. Simple regression analysis uses one independent variable, whereas multiple regression analysis includes two or more independent variables. The objective of regression analysis is to develop a mathematical formula that accurately describes a relationship between the firm's sales and one or more variables; however, the formula indicates only an association, not a causal relationship. Once an accurate formula is established, the analyst plugs the necessary information into the formula to derive the sales forecast.

Regression analysis is useful when a precise association can be established. However, a forecaster seldom finds a perfect correlation. Furthermore, this method can be used only when available historical sales data are extensive. Thus, regression analysis is futile for forecasting sales of new products.

Market Tests

A **market test** involves making a product available to buyers in one or more test areas and measuring purchases and consumer responses to distribution, promotion, and price. Test areas are often cities with populations of 200,000 to 500,000, but they can be larger metropolitan areas or towns with populations of 50,000 to 200,000. For example, ACNielsen Market Decisions, a marketing research firm, conducts market tests for client firms in Boise, Tucson, Colorado Springs, Peoria, Evansville, Charleston, and Portland, in addition to custom test markets in cities chosen by clients.[28] A market test provides information about consumers' actual rather than intended purchases. In addition, purchase volume can be evaluated in relation to the intensity of other marketing activities such as advertising, in-store promotions, pricing, packaging, and distribution. Procter & Gamble conducted market tests for new concentrated versions of its Tide, Gain, Dreft, Cheer, and Era laundry detergents in Cedar Rapids, Iowa. The company, which planned to replace its current detergents with the new, more environmentally friendly products, needed to assess consumer reaction to the products, their price, and TV, in-store, and online promotional efforts.[29] Forecasters base their sales estimates for larger geographic units on customer response in test areas.

Because it does not require historical sales data, a market test is effective for forecasting sales of new products or sales of existing products in new geographic areas. A market test also gives a marketer an opportunity to test various elements of the marketing mix. However, these tests are often time consuming and expensive. In addition, a marketer cannot be certain that consumer response during a market test represents the total market response or that such a response will continue in the future.

Using Multiple Forecasting Methods

Although some businesses depend on a single sales forecasting method, most firms use several techniques. Sometimes a company is forced to use multiple methods when marketing diverse product lines, but even a single product line may require several forecasts, especially when the product is sold to different market segments. Thus, a producer of automobile tires may rely on one technique to forecast tire sales for new cars and on another to forecast sales of replacement tires. Variation in the length of needed forecasts may call for several forecasting methods. A firm that employs one method for a short-range forecast may find it inappropriate for long-range forecasting. Sometimes a marketer verifies results of one method by using one or more other methods and comparing outcomes.

regression analysis A method of predicting sales based on finding a relationship between past sales and one or more independent variables, such as population or income

market test Making a product available to buyers in one or more test areas and measuring purchases and consumer responses to marketing efforts

SUMMARY

A market is a group of people who, as individuals or as organizations, have needs for products in a product class and have the ability, willingness, and authority to purchase such products. Markets can be categorized as consumer markets or business markets based on the characteristics of the individuals and groups that make up a specific market and the purposes for which they buy products. A consumer market, also known as a *business-to-consumer (B2C) market,* consists of purchasers and household members who intend to consume or benefit from the purchased products and do not buy products for the main purpose of making a profit. A business market, also known as *business-to-business (B2B), industrial,* or *organizational market,* consists of individuals or groups that purchase a specific kind of product for one of three purposes: resale, direct use in producing other products, or use in general daily operations.

In general, marketers employ a five-step process when selecting a target market. Step 1 is to identify the appropriate targeting strategy. When a company designs a single marketing mix and directs it at the entire market for a particular product, it is using an undifferentiated targeting strategy. The undifferentiated strategy is effective in a homogeneous market, whereas a heterogeneous market needs to be segmented through a concentrated targeting strategy or a differentiated targeting strategy. Both these strategies divide markets into segments consisting of individuals, groups, or organizations that have one or more similar characteristics and thus can be linked to similar product needs. When using a concentrated strategy, an organization directs marketing efforts toward a single market segment through one marketing mix. With a differentiated targeting strategy, an organization directs customized marketing efforts at two or more segments.

Certain conditions must exist for effective market segmentation. First, customers' needs for the product should be heterogeneous. Second, the segments of the market should be identifiable and divisible. Third, the total market should be divided so segments can be compared with respect to estimated sales, costs, and profits. Fourth, at least one segment must have enough profit potential to justify developing and maintaining a special marketing mix for that segment. Fifth, the firm must be able to reach the chosen segment with a particular marketing mix.

Step 2 is determining which segmentation variables to use. Segmentation variables are the characteristics of individuals, groups, or organizations used to divide a total market into segments. The segmentation variable should relate to customers' needs for, uses of, or behavior toward the product. Segmentation variables for consumer markets can be grouped into four categories: demographic (e.g., age, gender, income, ethnicity, family life cycle), geographic (population, market density, climate), psychographic (personality traits, motives, lifestyles), and behavioristic (volume usage, end use, expected benefits, brand loyalty, price sensitivity). Variables for segmenting business markets include geographic location, type of organization, customer size, and product use.

Step 3 in the target market selection process is to develop market segment profiles. Such profiles describe the similarities among potential customers within a segment and explain the differences among people and organizations in different market segments. Step 4 is evaluating relevant market segments, which requires that several important factors—including sales estimates, competition, and estimated costs associated with each segment—be determined and analyzed. Step 5 involves the actual selection of specific target markets. In this final step, the company considers whether customers' needs differ enough to warrant segmentation and which segments to target.

Product positioning relates to the decisions and activities that create and maintain a certain concept of the firm's product in customers' minds. It plays a role in market segmentation. Organizations can position a product to compete head to head with another brand or to avoid competition. Repositioning by making physical changes in the product, changing its price or distribution, or changing its image can boost a brand's market share and profitability.

A sales forecast is the amount of a product the company actually expects to sell during a specific period at a specified level of marketing activities. To forecast sales, marketers can choose from a number of methods. The choice depends on various factors, including the costs involved, type of product, market characteristics, and time span and purposes of the forecast. There are five categories of forecasting techniques: executive judgment, surveys, time series analysis, regression analysis, and market tests. Executive judgment is based on the intuition of one or more executives. Surveys include customer, sales force, and expert forecasting surveys. Time series analysis uses the firm's historical sales data to discover patterns in the firm's sales over time and employs four major types of analyses: trend, cycle, seasonal, and random factor. With regression analysis, forecasters attempt to find a relationship between past sales and one or more independent variables. Market testing involves making a product available to buyers in one or more test areas and measuring purchases and consumer responses to distribution, promotion, and price. Many companies employ multiple forecasting methods.

IMPORTANT TERMS

Consumer market, 160
Business market, 160
Undifferentiated targeting
strategy, 161
Homogeneous
market, 161
Heterogeneous market, 161
Market segmentation, 161
Market segment, 162
Concentrated targeting
strategy, 163

Differentiated targeting
strategy, 163
Segmentation
variables, 164
Market density, 170
Geodemographic
segmentation, 170
Micromarketing, 170
Benefit segmentation,
171
Market potential, 175

Company sales
potential, 175
Breakdown approach, 175
Buildup approach, 175
Product positioning, 176
Sales forecast, 180
Executive judgment, 180
Customer forecasting
survey, 180
Sales force forecasting
survey, 181

Expert forecasting
survey, 181
Delphi technique, 181
Time series analysis, 181
Trend analysis, 181
Cycle analysis, 181
Seasonal analysis, 181
Random factor
analysis, 181
Regression analysis, 182
Market test, 182

DISCUSSION & REVIEW QUESTIONS

1. What is a market? What are the requirements for a market?

2. In your local area, identify a group of people with unsatisfied product needs who represent a market. Could this market be reached by a business organization? Why or why not?

3. Outline the five major steps in the target market selection process.

4. What is an undifferentiated strategy? Under what conditions is it most useful? Describe a present market situation in which a company is using an undifferentiated strategy. Is the business successful? Why or why not?

5. What is market segmentation? Describe the basic conditions required for effective segmentation. Identify several firms that use market segmentation.

6. List the differences between concentrated and differentiated strategies, and describe the advantages and disadvantages of each.

7. Identify and describe four major categories of variables that can be used to segment consumer markets. Give examples of product markets that are segmented by variables in each category.

8. What dimensions are used to segment business markets?

9. Define *geodemographic segmentation*. Identify several types of firms that might employ this type of market segmentation, and explain why.

10. What is a market segment profile? Why is it an important step in the target market selection process?

11. Describe the important factors that marketers should analyze to evaluate market segments.

12. Why is a marketer concerned about sales potential when trying to select a target market?

13. Why is selecting appropriate target markets important for an organization that wants to adopt the marketing concept philosophy?

14. What is product positioning? Under what conditions would head-to-head product positioning be appropriate? When should head-to-head positioning be avoided?

15. What is a sales forecast? Why is it important?

16. What are the two primary types of surveys a company might use to forecast sales? Why would a company use an outside expert forecasting survey?

17. Under what conditions are market tests useful for sales forecasting? What are the advantages and disadvantages of market tests?

18. Under what conditions might a firm use multiple forecasting methods?

APPLICATION QUESTIONS

1. MTV Latino targets the growing Hispanic market in the United States. Identify another product marketed to a distinct target market. Describe the target market, and explain how the marketing mix appeals specifically to that group.

2. Generally marketers use one of three basic targeting strategies to focus on a target market: undifferentiated, concentrated, or differentiated. Locate an article that discusses the target market for a specific product. Describe the target market, and explain the targeting strategy used to reach that target market.

3. The stereo market may be segmented according to income and age. Discuss two ways the market for each of the following products might be segmented.

a. Candy bars

b. Travel agency services

c. Bicycles

d. Hair spray

4. Product positioning aims to create a certain concept of a product in consumers' minds relative to its competition. For example, Pepsi is positioned in direct competition with Coca-Cola, whereas Volvo has traditionally positioned itself away from competitors by emphasizing its cars' safety features. Following are several distinct positions in which an organization may place its product. Identify a product that would fit into each position.

a. High price/high quality

b. Low price

c. Convenience

d. Uniqueness

5. If you were using a time series analysis to forecast sales for your company for the next year, how would you use the following sets of sales figures?

a. 2000 $145,000

   2001 $144,000

   2002 $147,000

   2003 $145,000

   2004 $148,000

   2005 $149,000

   2006 $148,000

   2007 $180,000

   2008 $191,000

   2009 $227,000

b.

	2007	2008	2009
Jan.	$12,000	$14,000	$16,000
Feb.	$13,000	$14,000	$15,500
Mar.	$12,000	$14,000	$17,000
Apr.	$13,000	$15,000	$17,000
May	$15,000	$17,000	$20,000
June	$18,000	$18,000	$21,000
July	$18,500	$18,000	$21,500
Aug.	$18,500	$19,000	$22,000
Sep.	$17,000	$18,000	$21,000
Oct.	$16,000	$15,000	$19,000
Nov.	$13,000	$14,000	$19,000
Dec.	$14,000	$15,000	$18,000

c. 2007 sales increased 21.2 percent (opened an additional store in 2007)

   2008 sales increased 18.8 percent (opened another store in 2008)

INTERNET EXERCISE

Visit **www.cengage.com/marketing/pride-ferrell** for resources to help you master the material in this chapter, as well as materials that will help you expand your marketing knowledge, including Internet exercise updates, ACE Self-Tests, hotlinks to companies featured in this chapter, and much more.

iExplore

iExplore is an Internet company that offers a variety of travel and adventure products. Learn more about its goods, services, and travel advice through its website at **www.iexplore.com.**

1. Based on the information provided at the website, what are some of iExplore's basic products?

2. What market segments does iExplore appear to be targeting with its website? What segmentation variables is the company using to segment these markets?

3. How does iExplore appeal to comparison shoppers?

developing your MARKETING PLAN

Identifying and analyzing a target market is a major component of formulating a marketing strategy. A clear understanding and explanation of a product's target market is crucial to developing a useful marketing plan. References to various dimensions of a target market are likely to appear in several locations in a marketing plan. To assist you in understanding how information in this chapter relates to the creation of your marketing plan, focus on the following considerations:

1. What type of targeting strategy is being used for your product? Should a different targeting strategy be employed?

2. Select and justify the segmentation variables that are most appropriate for segmenting the market for your product. If your product is a consumer product, use Figure 6.3 for ideas regarding the most appropriate segmentation variables. If your marketing plan focuses on a business product, review the information in the section entitled "Variables for Segmenting Business Markets."

3. Using Figure 6.7 as a guide, discuss how your product should be positioned in the minds of customers in the target market relative to the product positions of competitors.

The decisions and discussions of these dimensions should help you to answer some of the questions that are a part of the online interactive marketing plan.

globalEDGE

1. One approach for marketers to evaluate the level of expectations among consumers is to analyze a city's standard of living. A comparison of the overall quality of life across a variety of cities can be accomplished by analyzing Mercer's "Top 50 Rankings for Quality of Living." This ranking can be accessed by using the search term "overall quality of life" at **http://globaledge.msu.edu/ibrd** (and check the box "Resource Desk only"). In addition to the likelihood that market offerings may be more expensive in certain cities, marketers may determine which cities have higher expectations of product and service quality. What are the top five cities in the United States? What cities rank in the top five worldwide? Can the locations of these cities complicate or simplify a differentiated marketing strategy campaign?

2. The level of a country's urbanization can have profound implications for marketers. Although a variety of resources may provide insight on this topic, data from the Population Reference Bureau's website may be useful. This data can be found by using the search term "data query tool" at **http://globaledge.msu.edu/ibrd** (and check the box "Resource Desk only"). Once you get to the Population Reference Bureau website, the level of urban population statistic can be found under the All Variables category. What is the level of urbanization of the United States? Choose four additional countries and compare your results with the United States. What particular challenges might you need to consider in markets with higher or lower levels of urbanization?

Video CASE 6.1

Jordan's Furniture: Shoppertaining Its Target Market

Samuel Tatelman began selling furniture out of the back of his truck in Waltham, Massachusetts, in 1918. Today, Jordan's Furniture sells more furniture per square foot than any other furniture retailer in the country and attracts record numbers of guests each week. With just four stores, Jordan's Furniture has grown from 15 employees 25 years ago to more than 1,000 today. Jordan's Furniture is also in the process of a massive expansion and plans to double its number of both stores and employees in the next few years.

The company has broken just about all industry standards. Inventory turns over at a rate of 13 times a year, compared to an average of 1 to 2 times a year in most furniture stores. Advertising expenditures are 2 percent, whereas the industry average is 7 percent.

Sales per square foot are $950, whereas most furniture stores average $150 in sales per square foot.

When Samuel Tatelman's grandsons took over the business in 1973, they decided to focus their efforts on the 18- to 34-year-old market segment. Whereas most furniture stores do not target specific customers, the Tatelmans felt that people with first homes or new families would need furniture more. To bring customers, even those not currently shopping for furniture, into the stores (particularly young families), the brothers invented what they call "shoppertainment" and created stores that were imaginative, fun, and a little Disney-like. Their "shoppertainment" concept paid off because the stores now host more than 4,000 visitors on an average weekend.

When customers walk into a Jordan's Furniture store, they might be greeted with a welcome map, offered freshly baked chocolate chip cookies, or receive a hearty greeting from an animatronic Elvis. "We've taken furniture shopping and given it new life by making it more of a fun experience rather than this 'God, I have to go furniture shopping' [experience]," says Eliot. "Beantown," a recreation of Boston made of 25 million jelly beans, stands next to an ice cream stand. Indoor fireworks and jazz music enliven a re-creation of New Orleans's famous Bourbon Street, complete with amusement rides for kids, animated characters, and snack stands. Jordan's Furniture also offers a flight simulator and trapeze lessons to adventurous customers. A 300-seat IMAX theater brings customers in for a movie, but they leave the store by walking through showrooms of furniture.

The stores are strategically laid out to make the shopping experience not only fun but easy. Instead of arranging furniture by manufacturer, Jordan's Furniture puts all of its categories together so customers can see all of their offerings at the same time. "If you came in looking for a bedroom set, we'll make it easy to see every bedroom set we carry," says Eliot. The stores are also equipped with Dell workstations so employees can quickly look up product details and pricing. Their Sleep Lab (complete with white-coated "Sleep Technicians") offers a questionnaire that helps customers find a mattress suited for maximum personal comfort. The showrooms are also equipped with low-level lighting that dim when customers lie down on a mattress.

With so many families making Jordan's Furniture a weekend outing and school groups visiting the IMAX on field trips, Jordan's Furniture has expanded its product mix to include nursery and children's furniture. The playful displays of hanging basketballs and soccer balls are designed especially to appeal to young tastes. The youth department uses painted murals to create a fun atmosphere. A safari-themed room showcases bunk beds and lofts.

Jordan's Furniture has also added an infants' section with soft-white track lights. Since each department at Jordan's Furniture has its own theme music to set the tone, soft lullabies can be heard in the nursery section. Because of the high volume of families visiting the stores, Jordan's Furniture nursery products have been successful based on word of mouth alone.

By taking the focus off furniture and putting it on people, Jordan's Furniture has pulled ahead of its competitors. "A lot of people look at their business strictly from the cash register's point of view. I can stand outside and watch people leaving and coming in and see smiles on their faces. When they're walking out smiling, happy, and having a good time," says Tatelman, "I know the cash register is going to be ringing."[30]

Questions for Discussion

1. What type of targeting strategy is Jordan's Furniture using?
2. Describe and evaluate the company's target market.
3. Discuss the positioning of Jordan's Furniture's bedding products.

CASE 6.2

Global Hyatt Goes After the Global Travel Market

Whether travelers want stylish rooms, more entertainment choices, or round-the-clock room service, Global Hyatt has a hotel to fit their needs. Now more than 50 years old, Global Hyatt has expanded to more than 735 properties in 44 nations by carefully positioning each of its brands to appeal to a particular segment of the travel market.

Hyatt Place hotels, one of the company's newer brands, targets business travelers in their thirties and forties, particularly women, who visit smaller cities such as Cincinnati or busy suburban areas like Lombard, Illinois. These travelers "grew up in an era of independence and mobility, so there's a lot more travel consumption and different expectations," notes a Hyatt senior vice president. "Business and leisure travel are blending. What we discovered was not so much a demographic but a mind-set."

Through research, the company learned that many of these business travelers were uncomfortable sitting alone in a lobby bar, but they did not like to feel "trapped" in their rooms. Hyatt Place created a lobby area "not to replicate the home or office but the so-called third place that is a blend of both," the Hyatt executive explains. The lobby includes an entertainment nook with a big-screen television and easy chair, a wine and coffee bar for socializing, and a casual dining area where guests can order meals and use their laptops. The guest rooms are also geared to the target segment's interests and behavior, with a flat-panel television and a plush sofa for relaxing. Wireless Internet access is available throughout the hotel so guests can check e-mail or surf the Web at any time.

The brand that put Hyatt in the public eye is Hyatt Regency. Famous for their dramatic atrium lobbies, Hyatt Regency hotels in major cities provide a full array of services, including restaurants, meeting facilities, and business centers. The premium Park Hyatt hotels, located in prestigious neighborhoods in cities such as Tokyo and Toronto, target upscale travelers who value personalized service and luxurious touches like special room décor. Grand Hyatt hotels in major cities like Seoul and Seattle are larger and have a full range of amenities for vacationers and business travelers, including hundreds of guest rooms and suites, on-site restaurants and cafés, exercise facilities, and ballrooms and meeting rooms for business and social functions.

Hyatt Summerfield Suites cater to families or business travelers who spend a lot of time away from home or want more room to spread out. In addition to a bedroom, each suite has a living room and kitchen plus free Internet service so guests can stay connected. What's more, these hotels provide free breakfast and host a reception every evening so guests of all ages can chat while nibbling appetizers. Hyatt Resorts emphasize extras such as spa facilities, golfing, and skiing for travelers who like a choice of activities when they take time off.

The newest Global Hyatt brand is Andaz, created to appeal to travelers with a sense of style who seek out luxurious boutique lodgings with local flair instead of more anonymous, chain-style, cookie-cutter hotels. Because each Andaz hotel reflects its city's personality and heritage, in keeping with the targeted segment's sense of individuality and lifestyle, no two properties—whether in New York or London—look exactly alike. The Andaz positioning extends to environmentally friendly features such as energy-efficient buildings and organically grown foods.

Other hotel companies are targeting specific segments, often overlapping those targeted by Global Hyatt. Marriott International, for instance, has repositioned its SpringHill Suites for price-conscious, tech-savvy travelers who want to combine business and pleasure. As Global Hyatt expands its brands, therefore, it will have to deal with fiercer competition and stay in touch with each segment's changing needs and characteristics.[31]

Questions for Discussion

1. Of the four types of segmentation variables for consumer markets, which are being applied by Global Hyatt? Why are these appropriate?
2. According to the Global Hyatt executive, "Business and leisure travel are blending. What we discovered was not so much a demographic but a mind-set." What are the implications for Hyatt Place's segmentation and targeting?
3. What combination of techniques might Global Hyatt use to forecast sales for its newest hotel brand, Andaz?

strategic CASE 3

Reebok Races into the Urban Market

Reebok wants to give front-runner Nike a run for its money in the race for market share in athletic footwear, apparel, and equipment. Reebok, based in Canton, Massachusetts, gained speed from the 1980s into the early 1990s by marketing special aerobics shoes for women. Then Nike pulled way ahead with new clothing and equipment endorsed by high-profile athletes such as Michael Jordan and Tiger Woods. Nike has remained the market leader, completely outdistancing all competitors to dominate the industry with $10.7 billion in annual sales and a 35 percent share of the U.S. sportswear market. In contrast, Reebok's U.S. market share is about one-half that of Nike, and its $3.5 billion in annual sales is about one-third of Nike's. Now Reebok is seeking to close the distance by changing its selection of target markets. In the process, it is aiming to change consumers' perceptions of and attitudes toward its brand and its products with the objective of boosting both sales and profits.

Breaking Tradition with Hip-Hop

Traditionally sneaker manufacturers have captured market attention by signing successful or fast-rising sports stars to promote their shoes. Reebok still likes to link its brand to popular sports. The fierce rivalry with Nike continues on the playing field. Reebok has lucrative contracts to make branded hats for the National Basketball Association and to supply the National Football League with uniforms and equipment. Nike has an exclusive contract to provide performance apparel to all 30 major league baseball teams.

Looking beyond sports, Reebok's marketers investigated the urban market, where fashion rather than performance is the deciding factor in buying decisions. Urban teens tend to be extremely style conscious, buying as many as ten pairs of athletic-style shoes a year so they can be seen in the very latest thing. Many are also fans of hip-hop music and buy clothing designed by hip-hop celebrities such as Jay-Z, Sean "P. Diddy" Combs, and Russell Simmons.

Reebok's marketing research confirmed this market's considerable buying power and the influence of hip-hop artists. To effectively reach this market, Reebok needed a new brand, new products, and new promotional efforts. First, the company took the focus off its mainstream Reebok brand by creating Rbk as a new brand specifically for the urban market. Next, it partnered with hip-hop artists such as Jay-Z and 50 Cent to develop special footwear collections, backed by targeted promotional efforts emphasizing style with attitude.

Reebok Races into the Urban Market

New Street Credibility

Reebok found it was tapping into a significant market opportunity. Right after Reebok introduced soft-leather, flat-soled S. Carter shoes (after Jay-Z's original name, Shawn Carter), the line sold out. Demand for the $100 shoes quickly spiked so high that eager buyers bid up to $250 for one pair on the eBay auction site. Within eight months, the company had shipped 500,000 pairs to retailers around the country and was preparing to launch a second S. Carter shoe.

On the heels of this success, Reebok introduced G-unit footwear, named after a hit song by the rapper 50 Cent, who says, "Reebok's Rbk Collection is the real thing when it comes to connecting with the street and hip-hop culture." Hip-hop's Eve was also asked to design a shoe. "She is one of the first artists in the campaign who has male and female appeal, urban and suburban," observes Reebok's director of global advertising. "She is as much a fashion icon as a music icon."

Moreover, the company found a way to bring sports and hip-hop together by launching the 13 Collection line of shoes by basketball star Allen Iverson. Iverson promoted the line by appearing in a series of fast-paced commercials filmed in rap-video style. Although he was shown playing basketball for a second or two, the commercials focused more on his off-court style than on his on-court technique.

Despite the added credibility that such celebrities bring to the Rbk brand, the strategy entails some risks. Fads in street fashion and music can come and go at a dizzying pace, which means a shoe that is red hot one day may be ice cold the next. Moreover, Reebok might feel the repercussions if one of its celebrities gets into trouble. Still, the company's chief marketing officer is committed to the strategy. "With athletes, they wear the shoes for the length of a basketball season," he comments. "With hip-hop, the publicity is intense but short, just like movies." The advantage, he says, is that "you'll know very quickly whether you hit or miss."

Targeting Urban Markets in China

In pursuit of growth, Reebok is also targeting promising global markets. China is high on its list of priorities. Interest in sports is skyrocketing there, thanks in part to Chinese basketball star Yao Ming's move to the NBA. According to company research, 93 percent of Chinese males ages 13 to 25—a prime market for athletic shoes— watch NBA broadcasts on a regular basis. Reebok's Asia Pacific general manager cites one projection showing 50 percent annual growth in footwear sales. His prediction: "It's hard to say what the [actual sales] numbers are going to be, but they are going to be huge."

To make the most of this opportunity, Reebok has set up "Yao's House" basketball courts around central Shanghai. Each features the Reebok trademark and a giant *Sports Illustrated* cover showing the basketball star. By giving teens and young adults a place to hone their slam dunks, Reebok hopes to shape their attitudes toward its products. "The trends are made in the urban areas and on street basketball courts, just like in the United States," says one Reebok executive.

Reebok is not the only athletic-shoe manufacturer entering this market. Nike sponsors a basketball court in Beijing, New Balance is building awareness of its shoes, and Pony is selling sneakers in Beijing, Shanghai, and Guandong.

Reebok's New Vector

Nike has its Swoosh, one of the most recognized trademarks in the world. Now Reebok has its Vector, a streamlined trademark designed to communicate the brand's attributes in a fast, fun way. The idea is to make the Vector synonymous with Reebok, just as the Swoosh is synonymous with Nike. "Our research suggests that consumers react better to logos than words, and it's a very effective marketing tool," stresses Reebok's head of marketing.

In addition, the company is giving its brand a touch of glamour with showcase stores in major U.S. cities. In New York City, for example, Reebok opened a new men's store right next to its women's store. Both feature footwear, apparel, and accessories, and both share the building with the Reebok Sport Club/NY. The displays are as stylish as the products, showing a mix of cashmere sweaters, varsity jackets, wristwatches, and sunglasses, along with shoes. "We want people to say, 'I didn't know Reebok made that,'" notes Reebok's vice president of retail. CEO Paul Fireman sums things up as follows: "The ultimate thing we are striving for is not brand recognition but how people perceive us."[32]

Questions for Discussion

1. What segmentation variables is Reebok using for its products? Why are these variables appropriate?
2. Which of the three targeting strategies is Reebok applying? Explain.
3. What influences on the consumer buying decision process appear to have the most impact on Reebok's customers' purchase decisions?
4. In terms of segmentation and buying behavior, explain the meaning of this statement by a Reebok executive: "The trends are made in the urban areas and on street basketball courts, just like in the United States."

part 4

Customer Behavior

CHAPTERS

7 Consumer Buying Behavior

8 Business Markets and Buying Behavior

9 Reaching Global Markets

Part Four focuses on the buyer. The development of a marketing strategy begins with the customer. Understanding elements that affect buying decisions enables marketers to better analyze customers' needs and evaluate how specific marketing strategies can satisfy those needs. **Chapter 7** examines consumer buying decision processes and factors that influence buying decisions. **Chapter 8** explores business markets, business customers, the buying center, and the business buying decision process. **Chapter 9** focuses on the actions, involvement, and strategies of marketers that serve international customers.

7 Consumer Buying Behavior

LEARNING objectives

1 To understand consumers' level of involvement with a product and describe the types of consumer problem-solving processes

2 To recognize the stages of the consumer buying decision process

3 To explore how situational influences may affect the consumer buying decision process

4 To understand the psychological influences that may affect the consumer buying decision process

5 To examine the social influences that may affect the consumer buying decision process

The Facebook Phenomenon

Are you one of the 40 million people who can't go a day—or an hour—without checking Facebook? Then you're exactly the kind of user founder Mark Zuckerberg wants to attract. He started Facebook in 2004 as an online directory for Harvard students. Two weeks after the site went live, more than 4,000 Harvard students, alumni, and faculty members had posted their profiles and were logging on to see who else had joined. As word spread, Zuckerberg created versions for Yale, Columbia, and Stanford universities. Within a few months, Facebook had become a full-blown social networking phenomenon that connected friends with uploaded photos, videos, graphics, notes, and messages.

entrepreneurs IN ACTION

Today Facebook has moved beyond the campus crowd into the mainstream, and its user network is growing at the rate of 3 percent per week. Because users update their pages all the time and check back frequently for news about friends and colleagues, the site draws lots of eyeballs. As a result, Facebook is profiting by selling advertising that is targeted to certain interests or demographics.

The company also invites developers to create specialized software that is tailored to the attitudes, activities, and actions of Facebook users. One example is iLike, a tool that allows Facebook users to post brief clips of their favorite music. Another is Super Wall, an expanded version of the Facebook Wall where visitors to a user's profile page can post photos, messages, or videos. These tools help users make the most of Facebook while providing an opportunity for the developers to test and distribute all kinds of software in record time.

Despite Facebook's popularity, it still has formidable competitors like MySpace, Linked-In, and other social networking sites. Its ad revenues are increasing as more people join and encourage their friends to join. Yet, just as Facebook became an overnight success by making itself a "must-visit" site, it could run into trouble almost as quickly if users click away.[1]

Both online and traditional marketers go to great lengths to understand their customers' needs and gain a better grasp of customers' **buying behavior:** the decision processes and actions of people involved in buying and using products. **Consumer buying behavior** refers to the buying behavior of ultimate consumers—those who purchase products for personal or household use and not for business purposes. Marketers attempt to understand buying behavior for several reasons. First, customers' reactions to a firm's marketing strategy have a great impact on the firm's success. Second, as we saw in Chapter 1, the marketing concept stresses that a firm should create a marketing mix that satisfies customers. To find out what satisfies buyers, marketers must examine the main influences on what, where, when, and how consumers buy. Third, by gaining a deeper understanding of the factors that affect buying behavior, marketers are in a better position to predict how consumers will respond to marketing strategies.

We begin this chapter by examining how a customer's level of involvement with a product affects the type of problem solving employed and by discussing the types of consumer problem-solving processes. Then we analyze the major stages of the consumer buying decision process, beginning with problem recognition, information search, and evaluation of alternatives and proceeding through purchase and postpurchase evaluation. Next, we examine situational influences—surroundings, time, purchase reason, and buyer's mood and condition—that affect purchasing decisions. We go on to consider psychological influences on purchasing decisions: perception, motives, learning, attitudes, personality and self-concept, and lifestyles. We conclude with a discussion of social influences that affect buying behavior, including roles, family, reference groups and opinion leaders, electronic networks, social classes, and culture and subcultures.

Level of Involvement and Consumer Problem-Solving Processes

L O 1 To understand consumers' level of involvement with a product and describe the types of consumer problem-solving processes

To acquire and maintain products that satisfy their current and future needs, consumers engage in problem solving. People engage in different types of problem-solving processes depending on the nature of the products involved. The amount of effort, both mental and physical, that buyers expend in solving problems also varies considerably. A major determinant of the type of problem-solving process employed depends on the customer's **level of involvement:** the degree of interest in a product and the importance the individual places on that product. High-involvement products tend to be those that are visible to others (such as clothing, furniture, or automobiles) and are expensive. High-importance issues, such as health care, are also associated with high levels of involvement. Low-involvement products tend to be less expensive and have less associated social risk, such as many grocery items. A person's interest in a product or product category that is ongoing and long term is referred to as *enduring involvement*. For example, a consumer who is interested in technology might always have the most advanced electronic devices, read electronics magazines, and work in a related field. However, most consumers have an enduring involvement with only a very few activities or items. In contrast, *situational involvement* is temporary and dynamic, and it results from a particular set of circumstances, such as the need to buy a new car after being involved in an accident. For a short time period, the consumer will visit car dealerships, visit a car company's website, or even purchase automotive-related magazines or books. However, once the car purchase is made, the consumer's interest and involvement taper off. Consumer involvement may be attached to product categories (such as sports), loyalty to a specific brand, interest in a specific advertisement (e.g., a funny commercial) or a medium (such as a particular television show), or to certain decisions and behaviors (e.g., a love of shopping). On the other hand, a consumer may find a particular advertisement entertaining but still not get involved with the brand advertised because of loyalty to another brand.[2] Involvement level, as well as other factors, affects a person's selection of one of three types of consumer problem solving: routinized response behavior, limited problem solving, or extended problem solving (Table 7.1).

buying behavior The decision processes and actions of people involved in buying and using products

consumer buying behavior The decision processes and purchasing activities of people who purchase products for personal or household use and not for business purposes

level of involvement An individual's degree of interest in a product and the importance of the product for that person

table 7.1	**CONSUMER PROBLEM SOLVING**		
	Routinized Response	**Limited**	**Extended**
Product cost	Low	Low to moderate	High
Search effort	Little	Little to moderate	Extensive
Time spent	Short	Short to medium	Lengthy
Brand preference	More than one is acceptable, although one may be preferred	Several	Varies; usually many

routinized response behavior A consumer problem-solving process used when buying frequently purchased, low-cost items that require very little search-and-decision effort

limited problem solving A consumer problem-solving process used when purchasing products occasionally or needing information about an unfamiliar brand in a familiar product category

extended problem solving A consumer problem-solving process employed when purchasing unfamiliar, expensive, or infrequently bought products

impulse buying An unplanned buying behavior resulting from a powerful urge to buy something immediately

consumer buying decision process A five-stage purchase decision process that includes problem recognition, information search, evaluation of alternatives, purchase, and postpurchase evaluation

A consumer uses **routinized response behavior** when buying frequently purchased, low-cost items that require very little search-and-decision effort. When buying such items, a consumer may prefer a particular brand but is familiar with several brands in the product class and views more than one as acceptable. Typically, low-involvement products are bought through routinized response behavior—that is, almost automatically. For example, most buyers spend little time or effort selecting soft drinks or cereals.

Buyers engage in **limited problem solving** when they buy products occasionally or when they need to obtain information about an unfamiliar brand in a familiar product category. This type of problem solving requires a moderate amount of time for information gathering and deliberation. For example, if Procter & Gamble introduces an improved Tide laundry detergent, interested buyers will seek additional information about the new product, perhaps by asking a friend who has used it, watching a commercial about it, or visiting the company's website, before making a trial purchase.

The most complex type of problem solving, **extended problem solving,** occurs when purchasing unfamiliar, expensive, or infrequently bought products—for instance, a car, home, or college education. The buyer uses many criteria to evaluate alternative brands or choices and spends much time seeking information and deciding on the purchase. Extended problem solving is frequently used for purchasing high-involvement products.

Purchase of a particular product does not always elicit the same type of problem-solving process. In some instances, we engage in extended problem solving the first time we buy a certain product but find that limited problem solving suffices when we buy it again. If a routinely purchased, formerly satisfying brand no longer satisfies us, we may use limited or extended problem solving to switch to a new brand. Thus, if we notice that the brand of pain reliever we normally buy is no longer working, we may seek out a different brand through limited problem solving. Most consumers occasionally make purchases solely on impulse and not on the basis of any of these three problem-solving processes. **Impulse buying** involves no conscious planning but results from a powerful urge to buy something immediately.

Consumer Buying Decision Process

LO 2 To recognize the stages of the consumer buying decision process

The **consumer buying decision process,** shown in Figure 7.1, includes five stages: problem recognition, information search, evaluation of alternatives, purchase, and postpurchase evaluation. Before we examine each stage, consider these important points. First, the actual act of purchasing is just one stage in the process and usually not the first stage. Second, even though we indicate that a purchase occurs, not all decision processes lead to a purchase; individuals may end the process at any stage. Finally, not all consumer decisions include all five stages. People who are engaged in extended problem solving usually go through all stages of this decision process, whereas those who are engaged in limited problem solving and routinized response behavior may omit some stages.

figure 7.1

CONSUMER BUYING DECISION PROCESS AND POSSIBLE INFLUENCES ON THE PROCESS

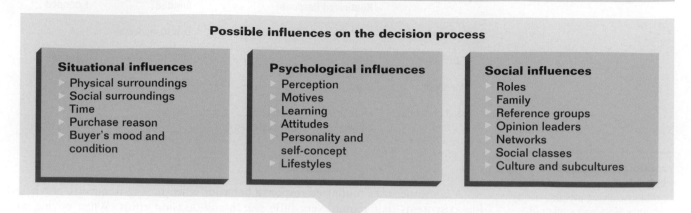

Possible influences on the decision process

Situational influences
- Physical surroundings
- Social surroundings
- Time
- Purchase reason
- Buyer's mood and condition

Psychological influences
- Perception
- Motives
- Learning
- Attitudes
- Personality and self-concept
- Lifestyles

Social influences
- Roles
- Family
- Reference groups
- Opinion leaders
- Networks
- Social classes
- Culture and subcultures

Consumer buying decision process

Problem recognition → Information search → Evaluation of alternatives → Purchase → Postpurchase evaluation

Problem Recognition

Problem recognition is the first stage of the consumer buying decision process. In this advertisement, the maker of Ban deodorant is attempting to stimulate problem recognition.

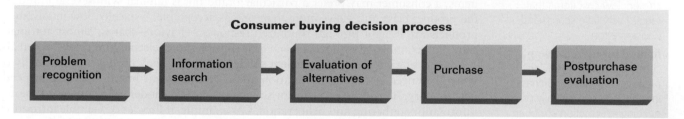

Ban Self-Doubt

BAN ODOR BETTER.
BAN SOLIDS KEEP YOU UP TO **3X FRESHER** THAN SECRET OR DOVE SOLIDS WHEN YOU'RE STRESSED.*

internal search An information search in which buyers search their memories for information about products that might solve their problem

Problem Recognition

Problem recognition occurs when a buyer becomes aware of a difference between a desired state and an actual condition. Consider a student who owns a nonprogrammable calculator and learns she needs a programmable one for her math course. She recognizes that a difference exists between the desired state—having a programmable calculator— and her actual condition. She therefore decides to buy a new calculator.

The speed of consumer problem recognition can be quite rapid or rather slow. Sometimes a person has a problem or need but is unaware of it. Marketers use sales personnel, advertising, and packaging to help trigger recognition of such needs or problems. For example, a university bookstore may advertise programmable calculators in the school newspaper at the beginning of the term. Students who see the advertisement may recognize that they need these calculators for their course work.

Information Search

After recognizing the problem or need, a buyer (if continuing the decision process) searches for product information that will help resolve the problem or satisfy the need. For example, after recognizing her need for a programmable calculator, the student may search for information about different types and brands of calculators. She acquires information over time from her surroundings. However, the information's impact depends on how she interprets it.

An information search has two aspects. In an **internal search,** buyers search their memories for information about products that might solve their problem. If they cannot retrieve enough information from memory to make a decision, they seek additional

SAVE ON EVERY RENTAL

SKIP THE LINES

DEDICATED ACCOUNT SERVICE

E-RECEIPTS

ELECTRONIC TOLL PASSES AND MORE

And a tidy sum of cash back every year.

All premium car companies have a great fleet and services. So do we. But we're the only company that offers cash back on every qualifying rental day and up to 25% off your rental.* It can add up to thousands of dollars in savings.

Sign up today at budget.com/bizprogram or call 1-800-822-7379.

Budget Business
It all adds up.

Up to 25% off applies to Time and Mileage charges only. Up to 25% off and $2 cash back only apply when renting a car on the Budget Business Program. Additional Terms and Conditions apply. See budget.com/bizprogram for details. Budget features Ford and Lincoln Mercury vehicles. To bypass the lines at more than 500 worldwide locations requires enrollment in Fastbreak. Fastbreak service is complimentary.

Budget features Ford and Lincoln Mercury vehicles.   © 2007 Budget Rent A Car System, Inc. A global system of corporate and licensee-owned locations.

Framing Product Attributes

Budget Rent-a-Car frames product attributes that include savings on every rental, no waiting at the rent-a-car counter, dedicated account services, e-receipts, electronic toll passes, and cash back.

external search An information search in which buyers seek information from sources other than their memories

consideration set A group of brands within a product category that a buyer views as alternatives for possible purchase

evaluative criteria Objective and subjective product characteristics that are important to a buyer

information from outside sources in an **external search.** The external search may focus on communication with friends or relatives, comparison of available brands and prices, marketer-dominated sources, and/or public sources. An individual's personal contacts—friends, relatives, and coworkers—often are influential sources of information because the person trusts and respects them. However, research suggests that consumers may overestimate friends' knowledge about products and their ability to evaluate them.[3] Using marketer-dominated sources of information, such as salespeople, advertising, websites, package labeling, and in-store demonstrations and displays, typically requires little effort on the consumer's part. Indeed, the Internet has become a major information source during the consumer buying decision process, especially for product and pricing information. Buyers also obtain information from independent sources—for instance, government reports, news presentations, publications such as *Consumer Reports*, and reports from product-testing organizations. Consumers frequently view information from these sources as highly credible because of their factual and unbiased nature.

Repetition, a technique well known to advertisers, increases consumers' learning of information. When they see or hear an advertising message for the first time, recipients may not grasp all its important details, but they learn more details as the message is repeated. Nevertheless, even when commercials are initially effective, repetition eventually may cause wear-out, meaning consumers pay less attention to the commercial and respond to it less favorably than they did at first. Information can be presented verbally, numerically, or visually. Marketers pay great attention to the visual components of their advertising materials.

Evaluation of Alternatives

A successful information search within a product category yields a group of brands that a buyer views as possible alternatives. This group of brands is sometimes called a **consideration set** (also called an *evoked set*). For example, a consideration set of programmable calculators might include those made by Texas Instruments, Hewlett-Packard, Sharp, and Canon. Research suggests that consumers assign a greater value to a brand they have heard of than to one they have not—even when they do not know anything else about the brand. Thus, when attempting to choose between two airlines for an emergency trip, most consumers will choose the one they have heard of over an unfamiliar name.[4]

To assess the products in a consideration set, the buyer uses **evaluative criteria:** objective characteristics (such as the size of a calculator) and subjective characteristics (such as style) that are important to him or her. For example, one calculator buyer may want a rechargeable unit with a large display and large buttons, whereas another may have no size preferences but dislikes rechargeable calculators. The buyer also assigns a certain level of importance to each criterion: some features and characteristics carry more weight than others. Using the criteria, the buyer rates and eventually ranks brands in the consideration set. The evaluation stage may yield no brand the buyer is willing to purchase. In that case, a further information search may be necessary.

Marketers may influence consumers' evaluations by *framing* the alternatives—that is, describing the alternatives and their attributes in a certain manner. Framing can make a characteristic seem more important to a consumer and facilitate its recall from memory. For example, by stressing a car's superior comfort and safety features over those of a competitor's, a carmaker can direct consumers' attention toward these points of superiority. Framing probably influences the decision processes of inexperienced buyers more than those of experienced ones. If the evaluation of alternatives yields one or more brands the consumer is willing to buy, he or she is ready to move on to the next stage of the decision process: the purchase.

Purchase

In the purchase stage, the consumer chooses the product or brand to be bought. Selection is based on the outcome of the evaluation stage and on other dimensions. Product availability may influence which brand is purchased. For example, if the brand that ranked highest in evaluation is unavailable, the buyer may purchase the brand that ranked second. If a consumer wants a pair of black Nikes and cannot find them in his size, he may buy a pair of black Reeboks.

During this stage, buyers also pick the seller from which they will buy the product. The choice of seller may affect final product selection and therefore the terms of sale, which, if negotiable, are determined at this stage. Other issues, such as price, delivery, warranties, maintenance agreements, installation, and credit arrangements, are also settled. Finally, the actual purchase takes place during this stage, unless the consumer decides to terminate the buying decision process.

Postpurchase Evaluation

After the purchase, the buyer begins evaluating the product to ascertain if its actual performance meets expected levels. Many criteria used in evaluating alternatives are applied again during postpurchase evaluation. The outcome of this stage is either satisfaction or dissatisfaction, which influences whether the consumer complains, communicates with other possible buyers, and repurchases the brand or product.

Shortly after purchase of an expensive product, evaluation may result in **cognitive dissonance,** doubts in the buyer's mind about whether purchasing the product was the right decision. For example, after buying a $399 iPhone, the consumer may feel guilty about the purchase or wonder whether she purchased the right brand and quality. Cognitive dissonance is most likely to arise when a person has recently bought an expensive, high-involvement product that lacks some of the desirable features of competing brands. A buyer who is experiencing cognitive dissonance may attempt to return the product or seek positive information about it to justify choosing it. Marketers sometimes attempt to reduce cognitive dissonance by having salespeople telephone recent purchasers to make sure they are satisfied with their new purchases. At times, recent buyers are sent results of studies showing that other consumers are very satisfied with the brand.

As Figure 7.1 shows, three major categories of influences are believed to affect the consumer buying decision process: situational, psychological, and social. In the remainder of this chapter, we focus on these influences. Although we discuss each major influence separately, their effects on the consumer decision process are interrelated.

Marketers employ a number of marketing research techniques (some of which will be discussed in Chapter 9) to better understand their customers' buying decision processes and factors that influence those buying decision processes. Both conventional and unconventional marketing research methods are used.

cognitive dissonance A buyer's doubts shortly after a purchase about whether the decision was the right one

situational influences Influences that result from circumstances, time, and location that affect the consumer buying decision process

Situational Influences on the Buying Decision Process

LO 3 To explore how situational influences may affect the consumer buying decision process

Situational influences result from circumstances, time, and location that affect the consumer buying decision process. For example, buying an automobile tire after noticing, while washing your car, that the tire is badly worn is a different experience from buying a tire right after a blowout on the highway spoils your vacation. Situational factors can influence the buyer during any stage of the consumer buying decision process and may cause the individual to shorten, lengthen, or terminate the process. Situational factors can be classified into five categories: physical surroundings, social surroundings, time perspective, reason for purchase, and the buyer's momentary mood and condition.[5]

Physical surroundings include location, store atmosphere, aromas, sounds, lighting, weather, and other factors in the physical environment in which the decision process occurs. Research suggests that retail store chains should design their store environment to make browsing as easy as possible to increase shoppers' willingness to choose and eventually make purchases.[6] Marketers at banks, department stores, and specialty stores go to considerable effort and expense to create physical settings that are conducive to making purchase decisions. Most restaurant chains, such as Olive Garden and Chili's, invest heavily in facilities, often building from the ground up, to provide special surroundings that enhance customers' dining experiences. In some settings, dimensions such as weather, traffic sounds, and odors are clearly beyond the marketers' control; instead, marketers must try to make customers more comfortable. General climatic conditions, for example, may influence a customer's decision to buy a specific type of vehicle (such as an SUV) and certain accessories (such as four-wheel drive). Current weather conditions, depending on whether they are favorable or unfavorable, may be either encouraging or discouraging to consumers when they are deciding whether to go shopping to seek out specific products.

Social surroundings include characteristics and interactions of others who are present during a purchase decision, such as friends, relatives, salespeople, and other customers. Buyers may feel pressured to behave in a certain way because they are in a public place such as a restaurant, store, or sports arena. Thoughts about who will be around when the product is used or consumed are another dimension of the social setting. An overcrowded store or an argument between a customer and a salesperson may cause consumers to leave the store.

The time dimension, too, influences the buying decision process in several ways, such as the amount of time required to become knowledgeable about a product, to search for it, and to buy and use it. For instance, more men are buying diamond engagement rings online partly to make an informed decision at their own convenience. An online jeweler like Blue Nile features a comfortable, anonymous, easy-to-use website to help men educate themselves about diamonds and then select a unique combination from its large inventory of diamonds and settings.[7] Time plays a major role in that the buyer considers the possible frequency of product use, the length of time required to use the product, and the length of the overall product life. Other time dimensions that influence purchases include time of day, day of the week or month, seasons, and holidays. The amount of time pressure a consumer is under affects how much time is devoted to purchase decisions. A customer under severe time constraints is likely to either make a quick purchase decision or delay a decision.

The purchase reason raises the questions of what exactly the product purchase should accomplish and for whom. Generally, consumers purchase an item for their own use, for household use, or as a gift. For example, people who are buying a gift may buy a different product from one they would buy for themselves. If you own a Cross pen, for example, it is unlikely that you bought it for yourself.

The buyer's momentary moods (such as anger, anxiety, contentment) or momentary conditions (fatigue, illness, being flush with cash) may have a bearing on the consumer buying decision process. These moods or conditions immediately precede the current situation and are not chronic. Any of these moods or conditions can affect a person's ability and desire to search for information, receive information, or seek and evaluate alternatives. Research suggests that sad buyers are more inclined to take risks, whereas happy buyers are more likely to be risk averse when making buying decisions.[8] They can also significantly influence a consumer's postpurchase evaluation.

psychological influences
Factors that in part determine people's general behavior, thus influencing their behavior as consumers

Psychological Influences on the Buying Decision Process

L O 4 To understand the psychological influences that may affect the consumer buying decision process

Psychological influences partly determine people's general behavior and thus influence their behavior as consumers. Primary psychological influences on consumer behavior are perception, motives, learning, attitudes, personality and self-concept, and lifestyles. Even though these psychological factors operate internally, they are very much affected by social forces outside the individual.

Fish or Fowl?

Do you see fish or birds?
Source: p. 128: M. C. Escher's
"Sky and Water I" © 2006 The
M. C. Escher Company – Baarn –
Holland. All Rights Reserved. Used
by permission.

perception The process of
selecting, organizing, and
interpreting information inputs
to produce meaning

information inputs Sensations received through sight,
taste, hearing, smell, and touch

selective exposure The
process by which some inputs
are selected to reach awareness and others are not

selective distortion An individual's changing or twisting
of information that is inconsistent with personal feelings or
beliefs

selective retention Remembering information inputs that
support personal feelings and
beliefs and forgetting inputs
that do not

Perception

Different people perceive the same thing at the same time in different ways. When you first look at the illustration on the left, do
you see fish or birds? Similarly, an individual may perceive the
same item in a number of ways at different times. **Perception** is the
process of selecting, organizing, and interpreting information
inputs to produce meaning. **Information inputs** are sensations
received through sight, taste, hearing, smell, and touch. When we
hear an advertisement, see a friend, smell food cooking at a nearby
restaurant, or touch a product, we receive information inputs.
Marketers are increasingly using scent to help attract consumers
who may be in the problem recognition or information search
stages of the buying decision process. Some Westin Hotels, for
example, use a fragrance that blends green tea, geranium, green
ivy, black cedar, and freesia to evoke a sense of serenity and tran-
quility in their lobbies, and Sony uses an orange-vanilla-cedar-
wood scent in some SonyStyle stores to make women shoppers feel
more comfortable.[9]

As the definition indicates, perception is a three-step process.
Although we receive numerous pieces of information at once, only
a few reach our awareness. We select some inputs and ignore others because we cannot be conscious of all inputs at one time. This
process is called **selective exposure** because an individual selects
which inputs will reach awareness. If you are concentrating on this
paragraph, you probably are not aware that cars outside are making noise, that the
room light is on, that a song is playing on your MP3 player, or that you are touching this page. Even though you receive these inputs, they do not reach your awareness until they are pointed out.

An individual's current set of needs affects selective exposure. Information inputs
that relate to one's strongest needs at a given time are more likely to be selected to
reach awareness. It is not by random chance that many fast-food commercials are
aired near mealtimes. Customers are more likely to tune in to these advertisements
at these times.

The selective nature of perception may result not only in selective exposure but also
in two other conditions: selective distortion and selective retention. **Selective distortion**
is changing or twisting currently received information; it occurs when a person receives
information inconsistent with personal feelings or beliefs. For example, on seeing an
advertisement promoting a disliked brand, a viewer may distort the information to
make it more consistent with prior views. This distortion substantially lessens the effect
of the advertisement on the individual. In **selective retention,** a person remembers
information inputs that support personal feelings and beliefs and forgets inputs that do
not. After hearing a sales presentation and leaving a store, for example, a customer
may forget many selling points if they contradict personal beliefs.

The second step in the process of perception is perceptual organization. Information inputs that reach awareness are not received in an organized form. To produce meaning, an individual must mentally organize and integrate new information
with what is already stored in memory. People use several methods to organize. One
method, called *closure*, occurs when a person mentally fills in missing elements in a
pattern or statement. In an attempt to draw attention to its brand, an advertiser will
capitalize on closure by using incomplete images, sounds, or statements in its advertisements.

Interpretation, the third step in the perceptual process, is the assignment of meaning to what has been organized. A person bases interpretation on what he or she
expects or what is familiar. For this reason, a manufacturer that changes a product or
its package faces a major problem: when people are looking for the old, familiar product or package, they may not recognize the new one. For instance, when Smucker's
redesigned its packaging, marketers told designers that although they wanted a more

contemporary package design, they also wanted a classic look so customers would perceive the products to be the familiar ones they had been buying for years. Unless a product or package change is accompanied by a promotional program that makes people aware of the change, an organization may suffer a sales decline.

Although marketers cannot control buyers' perceptions, they often try to influence them through information. Several problems may arise from such attempts, however. First, a consumer's perceptual process may operate such that a seller's information never reaches that person. For example, a buyer may block out a salesperson's presentation. Second, a buyer may receive a seller's information but perceive it differently than was intended. For example, when a toothpaste producer advertises that "35 percent of the people who use this toothpaste have fewer cavities," a customer might infer that 65 percent of users have more cavities. Third, a buyer who perceives information inputs to be inconsistent with prior beliefs is likely to forget the information quickly.

Motives

A **motive** is an internal energizing force that directs a person's activities toward satisfying needs or achieving goals. Buyers' actions are affected by a set of motives rather than by just one motive. At a single point in time, some of a person's motives are stronger than others. For example, a person's motives for having a cup of coffee are much stronger right after waking up than just before going to bed. Motives also affect the direction and intensity of behavior. Some motives may help an individual achieve his or her goals, whereas others create barriers to goal achievement. Research indicates that for consumers who are trying to avoid impulsive eating behaviors, self-distracting, substitution, and reframing the tempting food item in a less attractive manner are all motivational strategies that can be used to correct inappropriate impulsive behaviors.[10]

Abraham Maslow, an American psychologist, conceived a theory of motivation based on a hierarchy of needs. According to Maslow, humans seek to satisfy five levels of needs, from most important to least important, as shown in Figure 7.2. This sequence is known as **Maslow's hierarchy of needs.** Once needs at one level are met, humans seek to fulfill needs at the next level up in the hierarchy.

At the most basic level are *physiological needs,* requirements for survival such as food, water, sex, clothing, and shelter, which people try to satisfy first. Food and beverage marketers often appeal to physiological needs. Marketers of whitening toothpastes such as Ultrabrite sometimes promote their brands based on sex appeal.

At the next level are *safety needs,* which include security and freedom from physical and emotional pain and suffering. Life insurance, automobile air bags, carbon

motive An internal energizing force that directs a person's behavior toward satisfying needs or achieving goals

Maslow's hierarchy of needs The five levels of needs that humans seek to satisfy, from most to least important

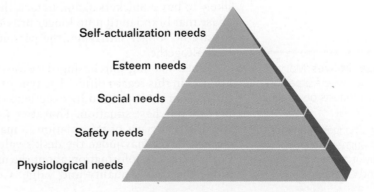

figure 7.2

MASLOW'S HIERARCHY OF NEEDS

- Self-actualization needs
- Esteem needs
- Social needs
- Safety needs
- Physiological needs

Maslow believed that people seek to fulfill five categories of needs.

RESPONSIBLE marketing?

Banks in Credit Trouble

ISSUE: Should banks be allowed on college campuses to solicit applications for credit cards?

From the moment college students step on campus, they are bombarded by credit card companies that want to give them airline miles and free T-shirts if they apply for a credit card. The average student racks up over $1,500 by the end of his or her freshman year. Many activists stress that the major banks are poaching a vulnerable market of teens that are unlikely to be able to pay their balance on time. They believe it is unethical for companies to be on campus. Other activists aim to educate students on how to effectively manage their credit rather than discouraging them from having a card at all.

Many credit card companies are being charged with using overly complex charging systems and fee assessment. In a recent study, a usability consultant for the Government Accountability Office (GAO) found that many disclosures in the customer solicitation materials and card-member agreements were too complicated for many consumers to understand. Some of the more confusing issues were higher rates used after a late payment and the different rates used for different types of purchases. Critics argue that it is assuming too much for college students to really know what they are getting into when they swipe that card. Should credit card companies be allowed on college campuses? Are they taking advantage of a vulnerable market, or are they simply offering a service to new customers?[a]

monoxide detectors, vitamins, and decay-fighting toothpastes are products that consumers purchase to meet safety needs.

Next are *social needs:* the human requirements for love and affection and a sense of belonging. Advertisements frequently appeal to social needs. Ads for cosmetics and other beauty products, jewelry, and even cars often suggest that purchasing these products will bring love. Certain types of trendy clothing, such as Abercrombie jeans, Nike athletic shoes, or T-shirts imprinted with logos or slogans, appeal to the customer's need to belong.

At the level of *esteem needs,* people require respect and recognition from others as well as self-esteem, a sense of one's own worth. Owning a Lexus automobile, having a beauty makeover, or flying first class can satisfy esteem needs.

At the top of the hierarchy are *self-actualization needs.* These refer to people's need to grow and develop and to become all they are capable of becoming. Some products that satisfy these needs include fitness center memberships, education, self-improvement workshops, and skiing lessons. In its recruiting advertisements, the U.S. Army told potential enlistees to "be all that you can be in the Army," a message that implies that people can reach their full potential by enlisting in the U.S. Army.

Motives that influence where a person purchases products on a regular basis are called **patronage motives.** A buyer may shop at a specific store because of such patronage motives as price, service, location, product variety, or friendliness of salespeople. To capitalize on patronage motives, marketers try to determine why regular customers patronize a particular store and to emphasize these characteristics in the store's marketing mix.

Learning

Learning refers to changes in a person's thought processes and behavior caused by information and experience. Consequences of behavior strongly influence the learning process. Behaviors that result in satisfying consequences tend to be repeated. For example, a consumer who buys a Snickers candy bar and enjoys the taste is more likely to buy a Snickers again. In fact, the individual will probably continue to purchase that brand until it no longer provides satisfaction. When effects of the behavior are no longer satisfying, the person may switch brands or stop eating candy bars altogether.

When making purchasing decisions, buyers process information. Individuals' abilities in this regard differ. The type of information inexperienced buyers use may differ from the type used by experienced shoppers who are familiar with the product and purchase situation. Thus, two potential purchasers of an antique desk may use different types of information in making their purchase decisions. The inexperienced buyer may judge the desk's value by price, whereas the more experienced buyer may seek information about the manufacturer, period, and place of origin to judge the desk's quality and value. Consumers who lack experience may seek

patronage motives Motives that influence where a person purchases products on a regular basis

learning Changes in an individual's thought processes and behavior caused by information and experience

Your food + Our shakes

This is the weight loss
Combine your food with our shakes to help you
lose the weight that's right for you. It's weight loss
you can live with. Weight loss for the real world.

FIND YOUR SLIM. FIND OUT HOW.
SLIM-FAST.COM

SlimFast optimum

Learning
Changing thought processes and
behaviors is challenging. In this
advertisement the maker of Slim
Fast is attempting to change
thought processes and behaviors
toward food choices and fitness.

attitude An individual's
enduring evaluation of feelings about and behavioral
tendencies toward an object
or idea

information from others when making a purchase
and even take along an informed "purchase pal."
More experienced buyers have greater self-
confidence and more knowledge about the product
and can recognize which product features are reliable cues to product quality.

Marketers help customers learn about their
products by helping them gain experience with
them. Free samples, sometimes coupled with
coupons, can successfully encourage trial and
reduce purchase risk. For example, because some
consumers may be wary of exotic menu items,
restaurants sometimes offer free samples. In-store
demonstrations foster knowledge of product uses.
A software producer may use point-of-sale product
demonstrations to introduce a new product. Test
drives give potential new-car purchasers some
experience with the automobile's features.

Consumers also learn by experiencing products
indirectly through information from salespeople,
advertisements, websites, friends, and relatives.
Through sales personnel and advertisements, marketers offer information before (and sometimes
after) purchases to influence what consumers learn
and to create more favorable attitudes toward the
product. However, their efforts are seldom fully
successful. Marketers encounter problems in attracting and holding consumers' attention, providing
consumers with important information for making
purchase decisions, and convincing them to try the
product.

Attitudes

An **attitude** is an individual's enduring evaluation
of feelings about and behavioral tendencies toward an object or idea. The objects
toward which we have attitudes may be tangible or intangible, living or nonliving.
For example, we have attitudes toward sex, religion, politics, and music, just as we
do toward cars, football, and breakfast cereals. Although attitudes can change, they
generally tend to remain stable and do not vary from moment to moment. However,
all of a person's attitudes do not have equal impact at any one time; some are
stronger than others. Individuals acquire attitudes through experience and interaction with other people.

An attitude consists of three major components: cognitive, affective, and behavioral. The cognitive component is the person's knowledge and information about the
object or idea. The affective component comprises the individual's feelings and emotions toward the object or idea. The behavioral component manifests itself in the person's actions regarding the object or idea. Changes in one of these components may
or may not alter the other components. Thus, a consumer may become more knowledgeable about a specific brand without changing the affective or behavioral components of his or her attitude toward that brand.

Consumer attitudes toward a company and its products greatly influence success
or failure of the firm's marketing strategy. When consumers have strong negative
attitudes toward one or more aspects of a firm's marketing practices, they may not
only stop using its products but also urge relatives and friends to do likewise.

Because attitudes play such an important part in determining consumer behavior, marketers should measure consumer attitudes toward prices, package designs,
brand names, advertisements, salespeople, repair services, store locations, features of

One day, you may have to tell your grandchildren stories about places like this.

Experts predict that within 100 years, natural lands and water resources will become scarce. Climate change will irreversibly alter the planet. And the habitats that support all life could be lost forever.

Support our mission to protect the future of our natural world. To make a difference that lasts, join The Nature Conservancy.

Log onto **www.nature.org** today or call **(800) 842-8905.**

The Nature Conservancy
Protecting nature. Preserving life.

Iguazu National Park, Parana State, Brazil. Image © Scott Warren

Attempting to Change Attitudes

Major Conservancy attempts to change peoples' attitudes regarding conservation and to encourage them to support its organization.

attitude scale A means of measuring consumer attitudes by gauging the intensity of individuals' reactions to adjectives, phrases, or sentences about an object

personality A set of internal traits and distinct behavioral tendencies that result in consistent patterns of behavior in certain situations

existing or proposed products, and social responsibility efforts. Several methods help marketers gauge these attitudes. One of the simplest ways is to question people directly. Hampton Hotels, for example, asked travelers about their attitudes toward hotel cleaning smells. Most travelers (86 percent) reported that they found the smell of fresh air and linens most indicative of a clean hotel room, whereas only 14 percent said the smell of cleaning products indicate a clean room. The research helped the hotel chain refine its cleaning practices and use of cleaning products to leave rooms smelling of fresh air and linens—and nothing else.[11] Marketers also evaluate attitudes through attitude scales. An **attitude scale** usually consists of a series of adjectives, phrases, or sentences about an object. Respondents indicate the intensity of their feelings toward the object by reacting to the adjectives, phrases, or sentences in a certain way. For example, a marketer that is measuring people's attitudes toward shopping might ask respondents to indicate the extent to which they agree or disagree with a number of statements, such as "Shopping is more fun than watching television." By using an attitude scale, a marketing research company was able to identify and classify six major types of clothing purchasers. The scale was based on such attributes as demographics, media use, and purchase behavior.

When marketers determine that a significant number of consumers have negative attitudes toward an aspect of a marketing mix, they may try to change those attitudes to make them more favorable. This task is generally lengthy, expensive, and difficult, and may require extensive promotional efforts. For example, the California Prune Growers, an organization of prune producers, has tried to use advertising to change consumers' attitudes toward prunes by presenting them as a nutritious snack high in potassium and fiber. To alter consumers' responses so more of them buy a given brand, a firm might launch an information-focused campaign to change the cognitive component of a consumer's attitude or a persuasive (emotional) campaign to influence the affective component. Distributing free samples might help change the behavioral component. Both business and nonbusiness organizations try to change people's attitudes about many things, from health and safety to prices and product features.

Personality and Self-Concept

Personality is a set of internal traits and distinct behavioral tendencies that result in consistent patterns of behavior in certain situations. An individual's personality arises from hereditary characteristics and personal experiences that make the person unique. Personalities typically are described as having one or more characteristics, such as compulsiveness, ambition, gregariousness, dogmatism, authoritarianism, introversion, extroversion, and competitiveness. Marketing researchers look for relationships between such characteristics and buying behavior. Even though a few links between several personality traits and buyer behavior have been determined, results of many studies have been inconclusive. The weak association between personality and buying behavior may be the result of unreliable measures rather than a lack of a relationship. A number of marketers are convinced that consumers'

Land's End | Cabo San Lucas | 22° 52' 33.16" N by 109° 53' 33.16" W

sperrytopsider.com

GET WET.

SPERRY
TOP-SIDER

Cabo Collection | Inspired by life on the water | Available at Bass Pro Shops

Lifestyles

Sperry Top-Siders promotes a particular type of lifestyle in this advertisement.

self-concept A perception or view of oneself

lifestyle An individual's pattern of living expressed through activities, interests, and opinions

personalities do influence types and brands of products purchased. For example, the type of clothing, jewelry, or automobile a person buys may reflect one or more personality characteristics. The VALS™ program is one consumer framework, based on individual personality differences, that is successful. (See Lifestyles section.)

At times, marketers aim advertising at certain types of personalities. For example, ads for certain cigarette brands are directed toward specific personality types. Marketers focus on positively valued personality characteristics, such as security consciousness, sociability, independence, or competitiveness, rather than on negatively valued ones, such as insensitivity or timidity.

A person's self-concept is closely linked to personality. **Self-concept** (sometimes called *self-image*) is a perception or view of oneself. Individuals develop and alter their self-concepts based on an interaction between psychological and social dimensions. Research shows that buyers purchase products that reflect and enhance their self-concepts and that purchase decisions are important to the development and maintenance of a stable self-concept. Consumers' self-concepts may influence whether they buy a product in a specific product category and may affect brand selection as well as where they buy. For example, home improvement retailer Lowe's is targeting women—who make 90 percent of household decisions about home décor and home improvement—using self-concept as the basis of its advertising message. "Only Lowe's has everything and everyone to help your house tell the story about who you really are," says the company's advertising tag line.[12]

Lifestyles

As we saw in Chapter 6, many marketers attempt to segment markets by lifestyle. A **lifestyle** is an individual's pattern of living expressed through activities, interests, and opinions. Lifestyle patterns include the ways people spend time, the extent of their interaction with others, and their general outlook on life and living. People partially determine their own lifestyles, but the pattern is also affected by personality and by demographic factors such as age, education, income, and social class. Lifestyles are measured through a lengthy series of questions.

Lifestyles have a strong impact on many aspects of the consumer buying decision process, from problem recognition to postpurchase evaluation. Lifestyles influence consumers' product needs, brand preferences, types of media used, and how and where they shop.

One of the most popular frameworks for exploring consumer lifestyles is a survey from SRI Consulting Business Intelligence. The company's VALS Program uses a short questionnaire to help classify consumers into eight basic groups: Innovators, Thinkers, Achievers, Experiencers, Believers, Strivers, Makers, and Survivors (see Figure 7.3). The segmentation is based on psychological characteristics that are correlated with purchase behavior and four key demographics. This VALS questionnaire is then attached to larger surveys that focus on particular products, services, leisure activities, or media preferences to learn about the lifestyles of the eight groups.[13] VALS is a framework that links personality with consumers' lifestyles.

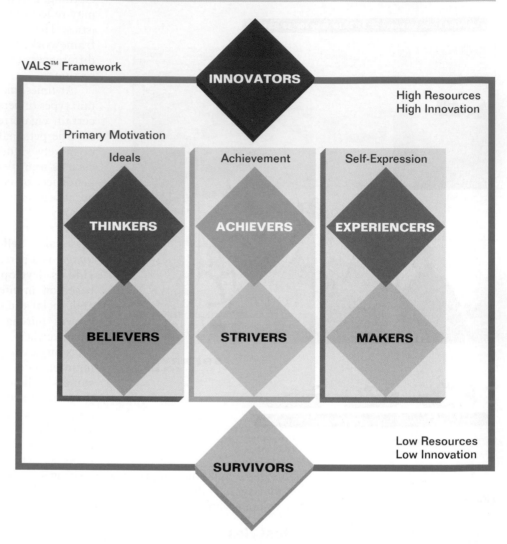

figure 7.3
VALS TYPES

VALS™ Framework

Primary Motivation

INNOVATORS

High Resources
High Innovation

Ideals — THINKERS / BELIEVERS

Achievement — ACHIEVERS / STRIVERS

Self-Expression — EXPERIENCERS / MAKERS

Low Resources
Low Innovation

SURVIVORS

Source: VALS™ Program. SRI Consulting Business Intelligence (SRIC-BI), www.sric-bi.com/VALS/types.shtml. Reprinted with permission.

Social Influences on the Buying Decision Process

LO 5 To examine the social influences that may affect the consumer buying decision process

Forces that other people exert on buying behavior are called **social influences.** As Figure 7.1 shows, they are grouped into five major areas: roles, family, reference groups and opinion leaders, digital networks, social classes, and culture and subcultures.

Roles

All of us occupy positions within groups, organizations, and institutions. Associated with each position is a **role:** a set of actions and activities a person in a particular position is supposed to perform based on expectations of both the individual and surrounding persons. Because people occupy numerous positions, they have many roles. For example, a man may perform the roles of son, husband, father, employee or employer, church member, civic organization member, and student in an evening college class. Thus, multiple sets of expectations are placed on each person's behavior.

An individual's roles influence both general behavior and buying behavior. The demands of a person's many roles may be diverse and even inconsistent. Consider the various types of clothes that you buy and wear depending on whether you are going

social influences The forces other people exert on one's buying behavior

role Actions and activities that a person in a particular position is supposed to perform based on expectations of the individual and surrounding persons

green MARKETING

Toyota's Prius Heads the Hybrid Pack

With 1 million Prius vehicles sold worldwide—more than 400,000 in the United States alone—Toyota is far and away the hybrid leader. A major reason for its success is fuel efficiency. On the highway, the Prius's hybrid gas-electric motor delivers a whopping 48 miles per gallon. Another reason is that the Prius is considerably more eco-friendly than ordinary cars, leaving only a tiny trail of smog-forming emissions. But the main reason many owners buy a Prius, according to a recent study, is that it "makes a statement about me." In other words, they're proud to be driving an icon of green.

The Prius is hardly the only hybrid on the road. In fact, Toyota also makes a Camry Hybrid sedan and a Highlander Hybrid SUV. Rivals like Honda, Ford, and General Motors are driving deeper into hybrid territory with models of their own. Still, the Prius is a very distinctive car, with a clean, spare silhouette that is unmistakable—on purpose. Instead of grafting a hybrid motor onto an existing car model, Toyota built the Prius from scratch so it looks like nothing else on the road.

And that's where "makes a statement about me" comes in: onlookers who spot a Prius know immediately that the owner cares about environmental issues. In the words of Prius owner Dan Becker, who heads the Sierra Club's global warming program, "The Prius allowed you to make a green statement with a car for the first time ever."[b]

to class, to work, to a party, or to the gym. You and others involved in these settings have expectations about what is acceptable clothing for these events. Thus, the expectations of those around us affect our purchases of clothing and many other products.

Family Influences

Family influences have a very direct impact on the consumer buying decision process. Parents teach children how to cope with a variety of problems, including those dealing with purchase decisions. **Consumer socialization** is the process through which a person acquires the knowledge and skills to function as a consumer. Often children gain this knowledge and set of skills by observing parents and older siblings in purchase situations, as well as through their own purchase experiences. Children observe brand preferences and buying practices in their families and, as adults, retain some of these brand preferences and buying practices as they establish and raise their own families. Buying decisions made by a family are a combination of group and individual decision making.

The extent to which family members take part in family decision making varies among families and product categories. Traditionally, family decision-making processes have been grouped into four categories: autonomic, husband dominant, wife dominant, and syncratic, as shown in Table 7.2. Although female roles continue to change, women still make buying decisions related to most household items, including health-care products, laundry supplies, paper products, and foods. Indeed, research indicates that women are the primary decision makers for 80 to 85 percent of all consumer buying decisions.[14] Spouses participate jointly in the purchase of a variety of products, especially durable goods. Due to changes in men's roles, a significant proportion of men are major grocery shoppers.

consumer socialization
The process through which a person acquires the knowledge and skills to function as a consumer

table 7.2   TYPES OF FAMILY DECISION MAKING

Decision-Making Type	Decision Maker	Types of Products
Husband dominant	Male head of household	Lawn mowers, hardware and tools, stereos, refrigerators, washer and dryer
Wife dominant	Female head of household	Children's clothing, women's clothing, groceries, pots and pans, toiletries, home decoration
Autonomic	Equally likely to be made by the husband or wife, but not by both	Men's clothing, luggage, toys and games, sporting equipment, cameras
Syncratic	Made jointly by husband and wife	Vacations, TVs, living room furniture, carpets, financial planning services, family cars

The family life cycle stage affects individual and joint needs of family members. (Family life cycle stages are discussed in Chapter 6.) For example, consider how the car needs of recently married "twenty-somethings" differ from those of the same couple when they are "forty-somethings" with a 13-year-old daughter and a 17-year-old son. Family life cycle changes can affect which family members are involved in purchase decisions and the types of products purchased. Children make many purchase decisions and influence numerous household purchase decisions.

When two or more family members participate in a purchase, their roles may dictate that each is responsible for performing certain purchase-related tasks, such as initiating the idea, gathering information, determining if the product is affordable, deciding whether to buy the product, or selecting the specific brand. The specific purchase tasks performed depend on the types of products being considered, the kind of family purchase decision process typically employed, and the amount of influence children have in the decision process. Thus, different family members may play different roles in the family buying process.

Within a household, an individual may perform one or more roles related to making buying decisions. The gatekeeper is the household member who collects and controls information. This may include price and quality comparisons, locations of sellers, and assessment of which brand best suits the family's needs. For example, if a family is planning a summer vacation, the gatekeeper might compare prices for hotels and airfare. The influencer is a family member who expresses his or her opinions and tries to influence buying decisions. In the vacation example, an influencer might be a child who wants to go to Disney World or a teenager who wants only to go snowboarding. The decider is a member who makes the buying choice. This role switches based on the type and expense of the product being purchased. In the case of a vacation, the decider will more likely be the adults, who use a combination of information, influences, and their own preferences. The buyer is a member who actually makes the purchase. After the family has decided to go to Disney World, the buyer will make all of the actual travel purchases. The user is a household member who consumes or uses the product. In this Disney World example, all members of the family would be users.

Reference Groups

A **reference group** is a group that a person identifies with so strongly that he or she adopts the values, attitudes, and behavior of group members. Reference groups can be large or small. Most people have several reference groups, such as families, work-related groups, fraternities or sororities, civic clubs, professional organizations, or church-related groups.

reference group A group that a person identifies with so strongly that he or she adopts the values, attitudes, and behavior of group members

E-ntertainment MARKETING

High School Musical: **The Hit**

From Memphis to Moscow, Boston to Bangalore, teen and tween fans in 100 countries have made Disney's *High School Musical* a mega-hit. The original Disney Channel cable TV movie, which cost just $4.2 million, was seen by 200 million viewers worldwide and prompted a $500 million consumer shopping spree.

Millions bought the DVD or the CD (or both) so they and their friends could sing and dance along with Troy, Gabriella, Sharpay, and Ryan, their aspirational reference group. The movie quickly became a marketing springboard for Disney to launch a successful concert tour, a stage musical, and sales of branded items like dolls, novels, and stationery. To keep the excitement going, the movie's website posted behind-the-scenes interviews, quizzes, downloadable posters, and party-planning ideas.

Eighteen months later, the Disney Channel became the leading basic-cable channel in prime time among preteens and young teens after a record 17 million viewers tuned in to the premiere of *High School Musical 2.* Now Disney has put the movie brand on cosmetics, clothing, iPod gadgets, and even an ice-skating show, while marketing partners like Dannon, Honda, and Wal-Mart created tie-in promotions for kids and their parents. Even before the third movie debuted, Disney had earned $100 million in profits from the *High School Musical* brand by understanding the behavior of its audience.[c]

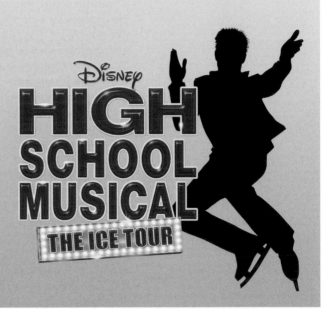

In general, there are three major types of reference groups: membership, aspirational, and disassociative. A membership reference group is one to which an individual actually belongs; the individual identifies with group members strongly enough to take on the values, attitudes, and behaviors of people in that group. An aspirational reference group is a group to which a person aspires to belong; the individual desires to be like those group members. A group that a person does not wish to be associated with is a disassociative or negative reference group; the individual does not want to take on the values, attitudes, and behavior of group members.

A reference group may serve as an individual's point of comparison and source of information. A customer's behavior may change to be more in line with actions and beliefs of group members. For example, a person may stop buying one brand of shirts and switch to another based on reference group members' advice. An individual may also seek information from the reference group about other factors regarding a prospective purchase, such as where to buy a certain product.

The extent to which a reference group affects a purchase decision depends on the product's conspicuousness and on the individual's susceptibility to reference group influence. Generally, the more conspicuous a product, the more likely that the purchase decision will be influenced by reference groups. A product's conspicuousness is determined by whether others can see it and whether it can attract attention. Reference groups can affect whether a person does or does not buy a product at all, buys a type of product within a product category, or buys a specific brand. One way that reference groups may influence behavior is by ridiculing people who violate group norms; research has identified this practice among adolescents who admonish, haze, or even shun peers who deviate from group norms.[15]

A marketer sometimes tries to use reference group influence in advertisements by suggesting that people in a specific group buy a product and are highly satisfied with it. In this type of appeal, the advertiser hopes that many people will accept the suggested group as a reference group and buy (or react more favorably to) the product. Whether this kind of advertising succeeds depends on three factors: how effectively the advertisement communicates the message, the type of product, and the individual's susceptibility to reference group influence.

Opinion Leaders

An **opinion leader** is a member of an informal group who provides information about a specific topic, like software, to other group members who seek that information. He or she is in a position or has knowledge or expertise that makes him or her a credible source of information about a few topics. Opinion leaders are easily accessible, and they are viewed by other group members as being well informed about a particular topic. Opinion leaders are not the foremost authority on all topics, but because such individuals know they are opinion leaders, they feel a responsibility to remain informed about a topic and thus seek out advertisements, manufacturers' brochures, salespeople, and other sources of information.

An opinion leader is likely to be most influential when consumers have high product involvement but low product knowledge, when they share the opinion leader's values and attitudes, and when the product details are numerous or complicated. Possible opinion leaders and topics are shown in Table 7.3.

Digital Networks

Although consumers often rely on the recommendations and suggestions from friends and family when making purchasing decisions, they are increasingly turning to electronic network sources during the decision-making process for consumer products. Some websites, such as CNET.com and consumerreports.org, have established themselves as reliable sources of information for consumers because of their unbiased product comparisons and stringent testing procedures. However, many lesser-known consumer advocate sites and even many individuals are exerting a stronger influence on consumers who are turning to the Internet for product reviews.

Consumers' reliance on the Internet for assistance during the decision-making process can be seen in the proliferation of blogs, social networking sites, online forums, mailing lists, and wikis, as well as text messaging via cell phones and podcasts via MP3 players. **Blogs** (short for "weblogs") are web-based journals in which writers can editorialize and interact with other Internet users, and **wikis** are software that create an interface that enables users to add or edit the content of some types of websites (also called wikipages). One of the best-known wikis is Wikipedia.com, an online

opinion leader A member of an informal group who provides information about a specific topic to other group members

blogs Web-based journals in which people can editorialize and interact with other Internet users

wikis Software that create an interface that enables users to add or edit the content of some types of websites (also called wikipages)

table 7.3	EXAMPLES OF OPINION LEADERS AND TOPICS
Opinion Leader	**Possible Topics**
Local religious leader	Charities to support, political ideas, lifestyle choices
Sorority president	Clothing and shoe purchases, hair styles, nail and hair salons
"Movie buff" friend	Movies to see in theater or rent, DVDs to buy, television programs to watch
Family doctor	Prescription drugs, vitamins, health products
"Techie" acquaintance	Computer and other electronics purchases, software purchases, Internet service choices, video game purchases

Social Networks

In this advertisement, myspace.com promotes the idea of its social network.

social networks Web-based services that allow members to share personal profiles that include blogs, pictures, audios, and videos

social class An open group of individuals with similar social rank

encyclopedia. **Social networks,** such as Facebook, MySpace, CarSpace, livejournal, or Slashdot, allow members to share personal profiles that include blogs, pictures, audios, and videos. For example, after Jeff Jarvis had an unhappy experience with Dell's ineffective attempts to resolve problems with his new laptop, he wrote about it on his blog. Within days, his blog became one of the most-visited websites, and it triggered a surge of Dell horror stories across the Web. Soon after, when people typed "Dell" into search engines, Jarvis's blog and websites with unflattering names would appear on the first listings page.[16]

Another way consumers share information is through video sites such as YouTube, where they can post videos they make, perhaps of themselves using a particular product. Companies can also post videos about their products and their use on their own websites or on third-party video sites.

Social Classes

In all societies, people rank others into higher or lower positions of respect. This ranking process, called social stratification, results in social classes. A **social class** is an open aggregate of people with similar social rank. A class is referred to as *open* because people can move into and out of it. Criteria for grouping people into classes vary from one society to another. In the United States, we take into account many factors, including occupation, education, income, wealth, race, ethnic group, and possessions. A person who is ranking someone does not necessarily apply all of a society's criteria. Sometimes, too, the role of income tends to be overemphasized in social class determination. Although income does help determine social class, the other factors also play a role. Within social classes, both incomes and spending habits differ significantly among members.

Analyses of social class in the United States commonly divide people into three to seven categories. Social scientist Richard P. Coleman suggests that for purposes of consumer analysis the population is divided into the four major status groups shown in Table 7.4. However, he cautions marketers that considerable diversity exists in people's life situations within each status group.

To some degree, individuals within social classes develop and assume common behavioral patterns. They may have similar attitudes, values, language patterns, and possessions. Social class influences many aspects of people's lives. Because people have the most frequent interaction with people from within their own social class, most people are more likely to be influenced by others within their own class than by those in other classes. For example, it affects their chances of having children and their children's chances of surviving infancy. It influences their childhood training, choice of religion, financial planning decisions, access to higher education, selection of occupation, and leisure time activities. Because social class has a bearing on so many aspects of a person's life, it also affects buying decisions.

Social class influences people's spending, saving, and credit practices. It determines to some extent the type, quality, and quantity of products a person buys and uses. For example, it affects purchases of clothing, foods, financial and health-care

table 7.4   SOCIAL CLASS BEHAVIORAL TRAITS AND PURCHASING CHARACTERISTICS

Class (Percent of Population)	Behavioral Traits	Buying Characteristics
Upper Americans		
Upper-Upper (0.5)	Social elite Of aristocratic, prominent families Inherited their position in society	Children attend private preparatory schools and best colleges Do not consume ostentatiously Spend money on private clubs, various causes, and the arts
Lower-Upper (3.8)	Newer social elite Successful professionals earning very high incomes Earned their position in society	Purchase material symbols of their status, such as large, suburban houses and expensive automobiles Provide a substantial market for luxury product offerings Visit museums and attend live theater Spend money on skiing, golf, swimming, and tennis
Upper-Middle (13.8)	Career-oriented, professional degree holders Demand educational attainment of their children	Provide a substantial market for quality product offerings Family lifestyle characterized as gracious yet careful Spend money on movies, gardening, and photography
Middle Americans		
Middle Class (32.8)	"Typical" Americans Work conscientiously and adhere to culturally defined standards Average-pay white-collar workers Attend church and obey the law Often very involved in children's school and sports activities	Greatly value living in a respected neighborhood and keep their homes well furnished Generally price sensitive Adopt conventional consumption tastes and consult category experts Spend on family-oriented, physical activities, such as fishing, camping, boating, and hunting
Working Class (32.3)	Average-pay blue-collar workers Live a routine life with unchanging day-to-day activities Hold jobs that entail manual labor and moderate skills Some are union members Socially not involved in civic or church activities; limit social interaction to close neighbors and relatives	Reside in small houses/apartments in depressed areas Impulsive as consumers yet display high loyalty to national brands Seek best bargains Enjoy leisure activities like local travel and recreational parks
Lower Americans		
Upper-Lower (9.5)	Low-income individuals who generally fail to rise above this class Reject middle-class morality	Living standard is just above poverty Seek pleasure whenever possible, especially through impulse purchases Frequently purchase on credit
Lower-Lower (7.3)	Some are on welfare and may be homeless Poverty stricken Some have strong religious beliefs Some are unemployed In spite of their problems, often good-hearted toward others May be forced to live in less desirable neighborhoods	Spend on products needed for survival Able to convert discarded goods into usable items

Source: Roger D. Blackwell, Paul W. Miniard, and James F. Engel, *Consumer Behavior,* 10th Ed. (Mason, OH: South-western, 2005); "The Continuing Significance of Social Class Marketing," *Journal of Consumer Research* 10 (Dec. 1983): 265–280; Eugene Sivadas, George Mathew, and David J. Curry, "A Preliminary Examination of the Continued Significance of Social Class in Marketing," *Journal of Consumer Marketing* 14 (No. 6, 1997): 463–469.

services, travel, recreation, entertainment, and home furnishings. The behaviors of people in one class can influence consumers in others. Most common is the "trickle-down" effect in which members of lower classes attempt to emulate members of higher social classes, such as purchasing expensive automobiles, homes, appliances, and other status symbols. For example, couture fashions designed for the upper class influence the clothing sold in department stores frequented by the middle class, which eventually influences the working class who shop at discount clothing stores. Less often, status float will occur, when a product that is traditionally associated with a lower class gains status and usage among upper classes. Blue jeans, for example, were originally worn exclusively by the working class. Youth of the 1950s began wearing them as a symbol of rebellion against their parents. By the 1970s and 1980s, jeans had also been adopted by upper-class youth when they began to acquire designer labels. Today, blue jeans are acceptable attire for all social classes and cost anywhere from $9.99 to $4,000.

Social class also affects an individual's shopping patterns and types of stores patronized. In some instances, marketers attempt to focus on certain social classes through store location and interior design, product design and features, pricing strategies, personal sales efforts, and advertising. Many companies focus on the middle and working classes because they account for such a large portion of the population. Outside the United States, the middle class is growing in India, China, Mexico, and other countries, making these consumers increasingly desirable to marketers as well. Some firms target different classes with different products. BMW, for example, introduced several models priced in the mid $20,000 range to target middle-class consumers, although it usually targets upper-class customers with more expensive vehicles.

culture The accumulation of values, knowledge, beliefs, customs, objects, and concepts of a society

Subcultures

This Scifen advertisement is aimed at a specific subculture

O.C THE PHENOMENON
"HIDDEN GEMS"
WWW.NEXTMILLENT.COM
WWW.SCIFEN.COM

Culture and Subcultures

Culture is the accumulation of values, knowledge, beliefs, customs, objects, and concepts that a society uses to cope with its environment and passes on to future generations. Examples of objects are foods, furniture, buildings, clothing, and tools. Concepts include education, welfare, and laws. Culture also includes core values and the degree of acceptability of a wide range of behaviors in a specific society. For example, in U.S. culture, customers as well as businesspeople are expected to behave ethically.

Culture influences buying behavior because it permeates our daily lives. Our culture determines what we wear and eat and where we reside and travel. Society's interest in the healthfulness of food affects food companies' approaches to developing and promoting their products. Culture also influences how we buy and use products and our satisfaction from them. In the U.S. culture, makers of furniture, cars, and clothing strive to understand how people's color preferences are changing.

Because culture determines product purchases and uses to some degree, cultural changes affect product development, promotion, distribution, and pricing. Food marketers, for example, have made a multitude of changes in their marketing efforts. Thirty years ago, most U.S. families ate at least two meals a day together, and the

Growing minority buying power

Buying power in billions of dollars:

☐ 1990 ☐ 2007 ☐ 2012* (*projected)

All Americans

1990	4,300
2007	10,000
2012*	13,000
(*projected)	

Asian Americans
116 459 670

Hispanic Americans
212 862 1,200

African Americans
318 845 1,100

Source: Jeffrey M. Humphreys, "The Multicultural Economy 2007," *Georgia Business and Economic Conditions* 67 (Third Quarter 2007), www.selig.uga.edu/forecast/GBEC/GBEC0703Q.pdf.

subculture A group of individuals whose characteristics, values, and behavioral patterns are similar within the group and different from those of people in the surrounding culture

mother spent four to six hours a day preparing those meals. Today more than 75 percent of women between ages 25 and 54 work outside the home, and average family incomes have risen considerably. These shifts, along with scarcity of time, have resulted in dramatic changes in the national per capita consumption of certain food products, such as take-out foods, frozen dinners, and shelf-stable foods.

When U.S. marketers sell products in other countries, they realize the tremendous impact those cultures have on product purchases and use. Global marketers find that people in other regions of the world have different attitudes, values, and needs, which call for different methods of doing business as well as different types of marketing mixes. Some international marketers fail because they do not or cannot adjust to cultural differences.

A culture consists of various subcultures. A **subculture** is a group of individuals whose characteristics, values, and behavioral patterns are similar within the group and different from those of people in the surrounding culture. Subcultural boundaries are usually based on geographic designations and demographic characteristics, such as age, religion, race, and ethnicity. U.S. culture is marked by many different subcultures. Among them are West Coast, teenage, Asian American, and college students. Within subcultures, greater similarities exist in people's attitudes, values, and actions than within the broader culture. Relative to other subcultures, individuals in one subculture may have stronger preferences for specific types of clothing, furniture, or foods. Research has shown that subcultures can play a significant role in how people respond to advertisements, particularly when pressured to make a snap judgment.[17] It is important to understand that a person can be a member of more than one subculture and that the behavioral patterns and values attributed to specific subcultures do not necessarily apply to all group members.

The percentage of the U.S. population consisting of ethnic and racial subcultures is expected to grow. By 2050, about one-half of the U.S. population will be members of racial and ethnic minorities. The U.S. Census Bureau reports that the three largest and fastest-growing ethnic U.S. subcultures are African Americans, Hispanics, and Asians. The population growth of these subcultures interests marketers. Businesses recognize that to succeed, their marketing strategies will have to take into account the values, needs, interests, shopping patterns, and buying habits of various subcultures.

African American Subculture. In the United States, the African American subculture represents 12.4 percent of the population.[18] Like all subcultures, African American consumers possess distinct buying patterns. For example, African American consumers spend more money on utilities, footwear, children's apparel, groceries, and housing than do white consumers.[19] The combined buying power of African American consumers is projected to reach $1.1 trillion by 2012.

Like many companies, Procter & Gamble Company has hiked its marketing initiatives that are aimed at the African American community, spending $52.5 million last year.[20] By including African American actors in its ads, the company believes it can encourage a positive response to its products, increasing sales among African American consumers while still maintaining ties with white consumers. Many other corporations are reaching out to the African American community with targeted efforts. Wal-Mart, for example, has adjusted the merchandising of 1,500 stores located in areas with large black populations to include more products favored by African American customers, such as ethnic hair-care products and large selections of more urban music offerings. The retailer has also included more African American actors in its advertising campaigns.[21] Another retailer, Target, launched a yearlong campaign called "Dream in Color" to celebrate diversity. The campaign included numerous Martin Luther King Day events, guest appearances by poet Dr. Maya Angelou, free posters for schools, and a unique online curriculum to provide access to historical and contemporary African American poets.[22] McDonald's launched 365BLACK, a program that celebrates Black History all year-round. The following year, it introduced 365BLACK Awards, which honor African Americans for their outstanding achievements.

Hispanic Subculture. Hispanics represent nearly 15 percent of the U.S. population, and their buying power is expected to reach $1.2 trillion by 2012.[23] When considering the buying behavior of Hispanics, marketers must keep in mind that this subculture is really composed of nearly two dozen nationalities, including Cuban, Mexican, Puerto Rican, Caribbean, Spanish, and Dominican. Each has its own history and unique culture that affect consumer preferences and buying behavior. They should also recognize that the terms *Hispanic* and *Latino* refer to an ethnic category rather than a racial distinction. Because of the group's growth and purchasing power, understanding the Hispanic subculture is critical to marketers. Like African American consumers, Hispanics spend more on housing, groceries, telephone services, and children's apparel and shoes. But they also spend more on men's apparel and appliances, while they spend less than average on health care, entertainment, and education.[24]

To attract this powerful subculture, marketers are taking Hispanic values and preferences into account when developing products and creating advertising and promotions. For example, a growing number of retailers, including Wal-Mart, are promoting the Hispanic holiday of Three Kings Day on January 6 in markets with a significant concentration of Latino consumers.[25] American Airlines has launched a Spanish-language advertising campaign to encourage more Latinos to fly across the country during the holiday. The *destino* campaign, which includes ads on television, radio, online, and out-of-home, includes vignettes showing Latinos' lives to illustrate how the airline can help them fulfill their destinies.[26]

Asian American Subculture. The term *Asian American* includes people from more than 15 ethnic groups, including Filipinos, Chinese, Japanese, Asian Indians, Koreans, and Vietnamese, and this group represents 4.4 percent of the U.S. population. The individual language, religion, and value system of each group influences its members' purchasing decisions. Some traits of this subculture, however, carry across ethnic divisions, including an emphasis on hard work, strong family ties, and a high value placed on education.[27] Asian Americans are the fastest-growing U.S. subculture. They also have the most money, the best education, and the largest percentage of professionals and managers of all U.S. minorities, and they are expected to wield $670 billion in buying power by 2012.

Marketers are targeting the diverse Asian American market in many ways. Kraft, for example, learned from marketing research that its Asian American customers were not interested in having "Asian" products from Kraft but rather in learning how to use well-known Kraft brands to create healthy Western-style dishes. Targeting immigrant mothers trying to balance between Eastern and Western cultures, the company therefore launched a new ad campaign in Chinese and Mandarin—the two most commonly spoken Asian dialects—and offered samples and demonstrations in Chinese as well as a website with recipes and healthy tips. Retailer JCPenney likewise used an advertising campaign to tout its competitive prices to Chinese and Vietnamese women, particularly during cultural holidays.[28]

SUMMARY

Buying behavior consists of the decision processes and acts of people involved in buying and using products. Consumer buying behavior is the buying behavior of ultimate consumers.

An individual's level of involvement—the importance and intensity of interest in a product in a particular situation—affects the type of problem-solving process used. Enduring involvement is an ongoing interest in a product class because of personal relevance, whereas situational involvement is a temporary interest that stems from the particular circumstance or environment in which buyers find themselves. There are three kinds of consumer problem solving: routinized response behavior, limited problem solving, and extended problem solving. Consumers rely on routinized response behavior when buying frequently purchased, low-cost items requiring little search-and-decision effort. Limited problem solving is used for products purchased occasionally or when buyers need to acquire information about an unfamiliar brand in a familiar product category. Consumers engage in extended problem solving when purchasing an unfamiliar, expensive, or infrequently bought product. Purchase of a certain product does not always elicit the same type of decision making. Impulse buying is not a consciously planned buying behavior but involves a powerful urge to buy something immediately.

The consumer buying decision process includes five stages: problem recognition, information search, evaluation of alternatives, purchase, and postpurchase evaluation. Not all decision processes culminate in a purchase, nor do all consumer decisions include all five stages. Problem recognition occurs when buyers become aware of a difference between a desired state and an actual condition. After recognizing the problem or need, buyers search for information about products to help resolve the problem or satisfy the need. In the internal search, buyers search their memories for information about products that might solve the problem. If they cannot retrieve from memory enough information for a decision, they seek additional information through an external search. A successful search yields a group of brands, called a consideration set, that a buyer views as possible alternatives. To evaluate the products in the consideration set, the buyer establishes certain criteria by which to compare, rate, and rank different products. Marketers can influence consumers' evaluations by framing alternatives.

In the purchase stage, consumers select products or brands on the basis of results from the evaluation stage and on other dimensions. Buyers also choose the seller from whom they will buy the product. After the purchase, buyers evaluate the product to determine if its actual performance meets expected levels. Shortly after the purchase of an expensive product, for example, the postpurchase evaluation may result in cognitive dissonance, dissatisfaction brought on by the consumer's doubts as to whether he or she should have bought the product in the first place or would have been better off buying another desirable brand.

Three major categories of influences affect the consumer buying decision process: situational, psychological, and social. Situational influences are external circumstances or conditions existing when a consumer makes a purchase decision. Situational influences include surroundings, time, reason for purchase, and the buyer's mood and condition.

Psychological influences partly determine people's general behavior, thus influencing their behavior as consumers. The primary psychological influences on consumer behavior are perception, motives, learning, attitudes, personality and self-concept, and lifestyles. Perception is the process of selecting, organizing, and interpreting information inputs (sensations received through sight, taste, hearing, smell, and touch) to produce meaning. The three steps in the perceptual process are selection, organization, and interpretation. Individuals have numerous perceptions of packages, products, brands, and organizations that affect their buying decision processes. A motive is an internal energizing force that orients a person's activities toward satisfying needs or achieving goals. Learning refers to changes in a person's thought processes and behavior caused by information and experience. Marketers try to shape what consumers learn to influence what they buy. An attitude is an individual's enduring evaluation, feelings, and behavioral tendencies toward an object or idea and consists of three major components: cognitive, affective, and behavioral. Personality is the set of traits and behaviors that make a person unique. Self-concept, closely linked to personality, is one's perception or view of oneself. Research indicates that buyers purchase products that reflect and enhance their self-concepts. Lifestyle is an individual's pattern of living expressed through activities, interests, and opinions. Lifestyles influence consumers' needs, brand preferences, and how and where they shop.

Social influences are forces that other people exert on buying behavior. They include roles, family, reference groups and opinion leaders, electronic networks, social class, and culture and subcultures. Everyone occupies positions within groups, organizations, and institutions, and each position has a role, a set of actions and activities that a person in a particular position is supposed to perform based on expectations of both the individual and surrounding persons. In a family, children learn from parents and older siblings how to make decisions, such as purchase decisions. Consumer socialization is the process through which a person acquires the knowledge and skills to function as a consumer. The consumer socialization process is partially accomplished through family influences. A reference group is a group that a person identifies with so strongly that he or she adopts the values, attitudes, and behavior of group members. The three major types of reference groups are membership, aspirational, and disassociative. An opinion leader is a member of an informal group who provides information about a specific topic to other group members. Consumers may turn to Internet networks—especially blogs, wikis, and social networks—for information to aid them in buying decisions. A social class is an open group of individuals with similar social rank. Social class influences people's spending, saving, and credit practices. Culture is the accumulation of values, knowledge, beliefs, customs, objects, and concepts that a society uses to cope with its environment and passes on to future generations. A culture is made up of subcultures, groups of individuals whose characteristic values and behavior patterns are similar but different from those of the surrounding culture. U.S. marketers focus on three major ethnic subcultures: African American, Hispanic, and Asian American.

IMPORTANT TERMS

Buying behavior, 194
Consumer buying
   behavior, 194
Level of involvement, 194
Routinized response
   behavior, 195
Limited problem
   solving, 195
Extended problem
   solving, 195
Impulse buying,
   195

Consumer buying decision
   process, 195
Internal search, 196
External search, 197
Consideration set, 197
Evaluative criteria, 197
Cognitive dissonance, 198
Situational influences, 198
Psychological
   influences, 199
Perception, 200
Information inputs, 200

Selective exposure, 200
Selective distortion, 200
Selective retention, 200
Motive, 201
Maslow's hierarchy of
   needs, 201
Patronage motives, 202
Learning, 202
Attitude, 203
Attitude scale, 204
Personality, 204
Self-concept, 205

Lifestyle, 205
Social influences, 206
Role, 206
Consumer socialization, 207
Reference group, 208
Opinion leader, 210
Blogs, 210
Wikis, 210
Social networks, 211
Social class, 211
Culture, 213
Subculture, 214

DISCUSSION & REVIEW QUESTIONS

1. How does a consumer's level of involvement affect his or her choice of problem-solving process?

2. Name the types of consumer problem-solving processes. List some products you have bought using each type. Have you ever bought a product on impulse? If so, describe the circumstances.

3. What are the major stages in the consumer buying decision process? Are all these stages used in all consumer purchase decisions? Why or why not?

4. What are the categories of situational factors that influence consumer buying behavior? Explain how each of these factors influences buyers' decisions.

5. What is selective exposure? Why do people engage in it?

6. How do marketers attempt to shape consumers' learning?

7. Why are marketers concerned about consumer attitudes?

8. In what ways do lifestyles affect the consumer buying decision process?

9. How do roles affect a person's buying behavior? Provide examples.

10. What are family influences, and how do they affect buying behavior?

11. What are reference groups? How do they influence buying behavior? Name some of your own reference groups.

12. How does an opinion leader influence the buying decision process of reference group members?

13. How might consumer behavior be influenced by digital networks?

14. In what ways does social class affect a person's purchase decisions?

15. What is culture? How does it affect a person's buying behavior?

16. Describe the subcultures to which you belong. Identify buying behavior that is unique to one of your subcultures.

APPLICATION QUESTIONS

1. Consumers use one of three problem-solving processes when purchasing goods or services: routinized response behavior, limited problem solving, or extended problem solving. Describe three buying experiences you have had (one for each type of problem solving), and identify which problem-solving type you used. Discuss why that particular process was appropriate.

2. The consumer buying process consists of five stages: problem recognition, information search, evaluation of alternatives, purchase, and postpurchase evaluation. Not every buying decision goes through all five stages, and the process does not necessarily conclude in a purchase. Interview a classmate about the last purchase he or she made. Report the stages used and those skipped, if any.

3. Attitudes toward products or companies often affect consumer behavior. The three components of an attitude are cognitive, affective, and behavioral. Briefly describe how a beer company might alter the cognitive and affective components of consumer attitudes toward beer products and toward the company.

4. An individual's roles influence that person's buying behavior. Identify two of your roles, and give an example of how they have influenced your buying decisions.

5. Select five brands of toothpaste and explain how the appeals used in advertising these brands relate to Maslow's hierarchy of needs.

INTERNET EXERCISE

Amazon.com

Visit **www.cengage.com/marketing/pride-ferrell** for resources to help you master the material in this chapter, plus materials that will help you expand your marketing knowledge, including Internet exercise updates, ACE Self-Tests, hotlinks to companies featured in this chapter, and much more.

Some mass-market e-commerce sites, such as **Amazon.com,** have extended the concept of customization to their customer base. **Amazon.com** has created an affinity group by drawing on certain users' likes and dislikes to make product recommendations to other users. Check out this pioneering online retailer at **www.amazon.com.**

1. What might motivate some consumers to read a "Top Selling" list?

2. Is the consumer's level of involvement with an online book purchase likely to be high or low?

3. Discuss the consumer buying decision process as it relates to a decision to purchase from **Amazon.com.**

Developing Your MARKETING PLAN

Understanding the process an individual consumer goes through when purchasing a product is essential for developing marketing strategy. Knowledge about the potential customers' buying behavior will become the basis for many of the decisions in the specific marketing plan. Using the information from this chapter, you should be able to determine the following:

1. What type of problem solving are your customers likely to use when purchasing your product (see Table 7.1)?

2. Determine the evaluative criteria that your target market(s) would use when choosing between alternative brands.

3. Using Table 7.2, what types of family decision making, if any, would your target market(s) use?

4. Identify the reference groups or subcultures that may influence your target market's product selection.

The information obtained from these questions should assist you in developing various aspects of your marketing plan found in the *Interactive Marketing Plan* exercise at **www.cengage.com/marketing/pride-ferrell.**

globalEDGE

1. Marketers may define subcultures by a variety of demographic characteristics, including ethnicity, income, or social class. Another attribute that can define a subculture is religion. To find information about religion in the United States and other countries, use the search term "world factbook" at **http://globaledge.msu.edu/ibrd** (and check the box "Resource Desk only") and choose a resource published by an agency of the United States government. Using this information, how might you segment the U.S. population according to religion? Are there any defining characteristics that marketers may use for the U.S. religions listed? Choose four other countries and report any commonalities or differences. Are there any differences in your sample of five countries that might be important to marketers?

2. Your firm is currently designing the next generation of mountain-climbing accessories and footwear. To understand the needs and behaviors of this distinctive global market segment, you must perform market research in a variety of countries. From your own knowledge on the subject, you know that the number of Mt. Everest ascents per capita, developed by NationMaster.com, is an excellent measure of moun- tain climbing's popularity. To access this information, use the search term "compare various statistics" at **http://globaledge.msu.edu/ibrd** (and check the box "Resource Desk only"). Choose "Sports" under "Facts and Statistics" to find Mt. Everest ascents. Determine the top five countries in mountain-climbing popularity. In which three countries would you con- duct focus groups to develop your new product line?

video **CASE 7.1**

Click to Get Away with Travelocity

When Travelocity began in 1996, it was one of the first Internet travel websites offering air- line and hotel reservations, cruises, vacation packages, and car rentals. Today, Travelocity offers consumers a choice of more than 70,000 hotels, 50 car rental companies, 6,000 travel packages, and flights on dozens of airlines worldwide. Its total travel bookings exceed more than $7 billion annually.

Although it helped pioneer the online travel busi- ness, Travelocity faces intense competition from Expe- dia, Orbitz, and other popular travel websites. That's why its marketers decided several years ago to make the company stand out by standing behind travelers every step of the way. The result is the unique four-point Travelocity Guarantee.

First, Travelocity guarantees its low price. If, within 24 hours, consumers find a lower price for travel they have booked through Travelocity, the company will refund the difference and add a $50 credit toward future travel. Second, Travelocity allows cus- tomers to change passenger names, flight dates, and flight times without paying extra if they make the change within 24 hours of booking their travel. Third, Travelocity pledges to alert customers in advance to any issues that might negatively affect their travel arrangements, such as hotel construction, and work with its trusted partners to fix the problem by switching hotels or making other changes. Fourth, if something goes wrong during a customer's travels, Travelocity will work with its partners to put things right. For example, if a customer books a hotel with a swimming pool but finds that the swimming pool is closed on arrival, Travelocity will, at its own expense, find a comparable or better-quality hotel and move the customer there. Travelocity main- tains a 24-hour hotline open seven days a week to ensure that customers get what they want.

The Travelocity Guarantee allays the concerns of customers who may be worried about booking online. One time the company made a pricing mistake and, despite the cost, stood by its guarantee and wound up selling $0 tickets to Fiji for a short time.

The company has promoted the guarantee with a "Roaming Gnome Enforcer of the Travelocity Guarantee" advertising campaign. The distinctive Roaming Gnome humanized the brand, embodied the joy of travel, and symbolized seeing the world with new eyes. The adver- tising campaign created a tremendous buzz about Trav- elocity and boosted revenues by 37 percent. Based on customer reaction to the campaign, Travelocity opened an online store to sell mugs, magnets, tote bags, and other items featuring the Roaming Gnome, who even has his own page on MySpace.com.

Over time, Travelocity has acquired a number of travel sites to broaden its offerings. When it purchased Site59, for example, Travel- ocity solidified its position as a major player in the last-minute travel busi- ness. Now customers who feel the urge to travel can get special deals by booking no more than 14 days before they want to leave. The savings are even bigger when cus- tomers book a vacation package just a few days in advance. To find out about special deals to favorite destinations, customers simply subscribe to Travelocity's Easy Escapes e-mail newsletter.

Travelocity regularly tests its website for ease of use. It has seven testers clicking all over its website to determine what customers might find confusing and how to make the site faster and more convenient. One lesson Travelocity learned was that customers don't always remember their passwords. To counteract this problem, Travelocity changed the system so that customers could reenter an address or e-mail address and use those details to access their personal profile rather than relying on a password. Thanks to this change, revenues quickly rose by 10 percent. Watch for more changes ahead as Travelocity finds new ways to satisfy its customers and new places for its Gnome to visit.[29]

Questions for Discussion

1. How does the Travelocity Guarantee give Travelocity a competitive advantage in various stages of the consumer buying decision process?
2. What is Travelocity doing to influence consumer perceptions of and attitudes toward its product offerings?
3. What are the major situational influences that affect Travelocity customers' buying decisions? Explain.

CASE 7.2

AutoTrader.com Fuels Online Auto Buying

AutoTrader.com operates the largest virtual used-car lot in the United States. Founded in 1997, this fast-growing company has accelerated beyond competitors eBay and **cars.com** to capture a dominant share of the online used-car market. At any one time, the Auto Trader website (**www.autotrader.com**) features classified ads for more than 3 million cars, both new and used. Buyers and sellers make contact through the site to negotiate the final terms for purchases. Today Auto Trader's customers can choose from vehicles offered by 40,000 dealers and 250,000 individuals across the United States.

When Auto Trader first opened its online business, few people had ever bought or sold a vehicle on the Internet. Therefore, the company's initial challenge was to change the habits of consumers and dealers who were accustomed to using newspaper classified advertising for used-car transactions. Instead of charging dealers for every listing, as newspapers did, Auto Trader decided to set a flat monthly fee for posting any number of descriptions and photos. Because dealers did not have to pay separately for every car listed, they could afford to post information about every vehicle in their inventories.

As more dealers signed up and listed cars for sale, the website became more attractive to consumers who wanted to choose from a large selection of vehicles. However, the company still had to educate its primary target market, 25- to 49-year-old men, about an unfamiliar buying process. Auto Trader's solution was to run informative television commercials showing step by step how to use its site. Its policy of charging buyers no fee to browse or buy was a plus. Soon the site was drawing more than 5.5 million visitors every month.

Next, Auto Trader targeted a slightly younger segment of 18- to 24-year-olds because research showed that these first-time buyers account for a significant percentage of used-car purchasers. The company hired a video game specialist to adapt the look of its fast-paced television commercials to an online promotion titled "Slide into Your Ride." Players earned prizes for correctly lining up three cars by matching their colors and were entered in a sweepstakes to win a $25,000 Auto Trader shopping spree and other prizes.

Knowing that students typically search for used cars before heading off for college in the fall, Auto Trader scheduled this promotional game for August and September. The company placed banner ads on popular websites and sent e-mail announcements to its online newsletter subscribers, as well as to people on a *Sports Illustrated* list. Although this promotion cost $1 million, it was a good investment because it raised brand awareness and drew an additional 500,000 visitors to the site during the first month alone.

More than half the visitors who played the game were women, and about one-third of the players were in the 18- to 24-year-old age group. More than 60 percent of the players signed up to receive Auto Trader's monthly online newsletter, enabling the company to continue building relationships with these potential buyers. Equally important, several hundred thousand players searched for used cars on the Auto Trader site during the promotional period.

Meanwhile, Auto Trader noticed that online auctions were becoming more popular. At one time it cooperated with eBay, the world's best-known auction site, to link the two sites so consumers could search for cars on either one. After monitoring buyer behavior for two years, Auto Trader ended the agreement and created its own vehicle auction operation, going into direct competition with eBay. "We did a lot of research and studied very closely the behavior of auction style users on our site," says Chip Perry, Auto Trader's CEO. He acknowledges that eBay is the "current major player in an extremely small niche segment of the car business." At the same time, he sees plenty of room for Auto Trader to profitably serve customers in this $2 billion market segment.

As its annual vehicle sales accelerate past $100 million, Auto Trader is not putting on the brakes. The company continues to reinforce brand recognition through television advertising, especially during the weeks leading up to the busy fall buying season. And it constantly introduces new features to draw new visitors and serve the

nearly 10 million qualified buyers who use the site every month to check the listings, compare prices, and buy or bid on vehicles. The firm's success can be measured in part by its number 1 rank in J. D. Powers & Associates satisfaction survey of new- and used-vehicle dealers.[30]

Questions for Discussion

1. In what ways has Auto Trader helped potential car buyers learn how to buy cars online?
2. In which stage of the consumer buying decision process would Auto Trader's television commercials be most likely to influence potential car buyers to use Auto Trader's website? Why?
3. Why is it important for Auto Trader to influence first-time buyers' perceptions of its site through online promotions such as "Slide into Your Ride"?

8

Business Markets and Buying Behavior

LEARNING objectives

1. To be able to distinguish among the various types of business markets

2. To identify the major characteristics of business customers and transactions

3. To understand several attributes of demand for business products

4. To become familiar with the major components of a buying center

5. To understand the stages of the business buying decision process and the factors that affect this process

6. To describe industrial classification systems and explain how they can be used to identify and analyze business markets

Steelcase Helps Businesses Race Ahead

Steelcase knows that business customers, like consumers, are always looking for innovative new products that solve problems. Michigan-based Steelcase received its first patent in 1914 for a steel wastebasket, marketed as a solution to the common business problem of straw wastebaskets that could catch on fire. Today, Steelcase has 13,000 employees worldwide and sells its chairs, desks, filing systems, office partitions, and other office furnishings through 800 dealers in dozens of nations.

entrepreneurs IN ACTION

One of Steelcase's strengths is its ability to understand and find solutions for the problems that business customers face in creating office environments that help employees to be as efficient and effective as possible. For example, knowing that employee health is a growing concern for many business employers, Steelcase's marketing experts worked with a doctor at Mayo Clinic to develop a line of office furniture that helps office workers get (or stay) in shape. The Walkstation consists of an adjustable desk and computer workstation attached to a treadmill that can be set for a one- or two-mile walking pace (the matching chair is optional). "The idea isn't to force people to walk and work," the doctor explains. "The idea is to give people a choice, because they've never had it before."

Another Steelcase feature designed to enhance employee health is the Airtouch mechanism, which lets users raise or lower the desk area on workstation desks by simply pressing a handle. The idea for this feature came from a Steelcase employee who was advised to change his position regularly during the workday to avoid back pain. With the Airtouch, office workers can quickly adjust their desks as they switch from standing to sitting and back again. Steelcase's CEO asks one key question over and over as he talks with his marketing experts about the new goods and services they're developing: "What's the user insight that led to this product?"[1]

Serving business markets effectively requires understanding those markets. Marketers at Steelcase go to considerable lengths to understand their customers so they can provide better goods and develop and maintain long-term customer relationships. Like consumer marketers, business marketers are concerned about satisfying their customers.

In this chapter, we look at business markets and business buying decision processes. We first discuss various kinds of business markets and the types of buyers that comprise those markets. Next, we explore several dimensions of business buying, such as characteristics of transactions, attributes and concerns of buyers, methods of buying, and distinctive features of demand for products sold to business purchasers. We then examine how business buying decisions are made and who makes the purchases. Finally, we consider how business markets are analyzed.

Business Markets

LO 1 To be able to distinguish among the various types of business markets

As defined in Chapter 6, a **business market** (also called a *business-to-business market* or *B2B market*) consists of individuals, organizations, or groups that purchase a specific kind of product for one of three purposes: resale, direct use in producing other products, or use in general daily operations. Marketing to businesses employs the same concepts as marketing to ultimate consumers, such as defining target markets, understanding buying behavior, and developing effective marketing mixes, but we devote a complete chapter to business marketing because there are structural and behavioral differences in business markets. A company that markets to another company must understand how its product will affect other firms in the marketing channel, such as resellers and other manufacturers. Business products can also be technically complex, and the market often consists of sophisticated buyers.

Because the business market consists of relatively smaller customer populations, a segment of the market could be as small as a few customers.[2] The market for railway equipment in the United States, for example, is limited to a few major carriers. On the other hand, a business product can be a commodity, such as corn or a bolt or screw, but the quantity purchased and the buying methods differ significantly from the consumer market. Business marketing is often based on long-term mutually profitable relationships across members of the marketing channel. Networks of suppliers and customers recognize the importance of building strong alliances based on cooperation, trust, and collaboration.[3] Manufacturers may even codevelop new products, with business customers sharing marketing research, production, scheduling, inventory management, and information systems. For example, when the largest distributor for independent book publishers, Consortium Book & Sales Distribution Inc., discovered its information technology system was obsolete, the firm partnered with Integrated Knowledge Systems, Inc., for a solution. Together they developed a new database to track book sales in real time to let publishers know which titles sell well and which should be eliminated. In this case, the marketer custom-designed IT solutions with the customer to resolve its operational services and efficiency concerns.[4] Although business marketing can be based on collaborative long-term buyer-seller relationships, there are also transactions based on timely exchanges of basic products at highly competitive market prices. For most business marketers, the goal is understanding customer needs and providing a value-added exchange that shifts from attracting customers to keeping customers and developing relationships.[5]

The four categories of business markets are producer, reseller, government, and institutional. In the remainder of this section, we discuss each of these types of markets.

business market Individuals, organizations, or groups that purchase a specific kind of product for resale, direct use in producing other products, or use in general daily operations

producer markets Individuals and business organizations that purchase products to make profits by using them to produce other products or using them in their operations

Producer Markets

Individuals and business organizations that purchase products for the purpose of making a profit by using them to produce other products or using them in their operations are classified as producer markets. **Producer markets** include buyers of raw materials, as well as purchasers of semifinished and finished items, used to produce

table 8.1 NUMBER OF ESTABLISHMENTS IN INDUSTRY GROUPS

Industry	Number of Establishments
Agriculture, forestry, fishing and hunting	25,500
Mining	23,800
Construction	760,400
Manufacturing	334,100
Transportation, warehousing, utilities	224,600
Finance, insurance, real estate	819,300
Other services	3,418,500

Source: U.S. Bureau of the Census, *Statistical Abstract of the United States, 2008* (Washington, DC: Government Printing Office, 2007), p. 497.

other products. For example, manufacturers buy raw materials and component parts for direct use in product production. Grocery stores and supermarkets are part of producer markets for numerous support products such as paper and plastic bags, shelves, counters, and scanners. Farmers are part of producer markets for farm machinery, fertilizer, seed, and livestock. Producer markets include a broad array of industries ranging from agriculture, forestry, fisheries, and mining to construction, transportation, communications, and utilities. As Table 8.1 indicates, the number of business establishments in national producer markets is enormous.

Manufacturers are geographically concentrated. More than half are located in just seven states: New York, California, Pennsylvania, Illinois, Ohio, New Jersey, and Michigan. This concentration sometimes enables businesses that sell to producer markets to serve them more efficiently. Within certain states, production in a specific industry may account for a sizable proportion of that industry's total production.

Reseller Markets

Reseller markets consist of intermediaries, such as wholesalers and retailers, that buy finished goods and resell them for a profit. Aside from making minor alterations, resellers do not change the physical characteristics of the products they handle. Except for items producers sell directly to consumers, all products sold to consumer markets are first sold to reseller markets.

Wholesalers purchase products for resale to retailers, to other wholesalers, and to producers, governments, and institutions. Arrow Electronics, for example, buys computer chips and other electronics components and resells them to producers of subsystems for cell phones, computers, and automobiles. Of the 429,489 wholesalers in the United States, a large number are located in New York, California, Illinois, Texas, Ohio, Pennsylvania, and Florida.[6] Although some products are sold directly to end users, many manufacturers sell their products to wholesalers, which in turn sell the products to other firms in the distribution system. Thus, wholesalers are very important in helping producers get products to customers. Professional buyers and buying committees make wholesalers' initial purchase decisions. Reordering is often automated.

Retailers purchase products and resell them to final consumers. There are approximately 1.1 million retailers in the United States, employing more than 15 million people and generating nearly $4 trillion in annual sales.[7] Some retailers—Home Depot, PetSmart, and Staples, for example—carry a large number of items.

reseller markets Intermediaries that buy finished goods and resell them for a profit

RESPONSIBLE marketing?

When Outsourcing Goes Bad

ISSUE: Who should be held responsible?

Over the last decade, many U.S. manufacturers have joined the widely publicized trend of outsourcing to foreign countries for cheaper products to cut their costs, particularly in China. Many of the products made in China have an acceptable quality level, but some products do not and may even be unsafe. Can the country to which work is outsourced influence the consumers' ultimate purchasing decision?

During the summer of 2007, Mattel Toys had to recall nearly 1 million toys because the products were covered in paint that contained lead, a potential health hazard. Once the news hit the media, Mattel had to make countless public relations moves to try and maintain consumer confidence in its products. The products were made in factories in China, and public opinion regarding Chinese products has become rather shaky after several product recalls.

When manufacturing is outsourced to producers in another country, who should take responsibility? Should the Chinese or U.S. government share some of the blame? How much is the cost of losing a good reputation worth to companies that want to cut costs through outsourcing? Can the cost of a tarnished reputation more than offset the cost savings associated with outsourcing production?[a]

Take a closer look inside your medicine cabinet, and it's likely you'll find time-release or sustained-release pills. It's a concept that seemed unimaginable not too many years ago. BASF advances in bioavailability help pharmaceutical companies ensure that the medicine inside each pill is delivered precisely when you need it. And when it comes to caring for patients of today and tomorrow, precision is everything. Learn more at basf.com/stories

Helping Make Products Better™

□·BASF
The Chemical Company

Focused on Producer Market

Some business marketers focus on producer markets. BASF aims the products discussed in the advertisement at manufacturers of pharmaceutical products.

government markets
Federal, state, county, or local governments that buy goods and services to support their internal operations and provide products to their constituencies

Supermarkets may handle as many as 50,000 different products. In small, individually owned retail stores, owners or managers make purchasing decisions. In chain stores, a central office buyer or buying committee frequently decides whether a product will be made available for selection by store managers. For most products, however, local managers make the actual buying decisions for a particular store.

When making purchase decisions, resellers consider several factors. They evaluate the level of demand for a product to determine in what quantity and at what prices the product can be resold. Retailers assess the amount of space required to handle a product relative to its potential profit, sometimes on the basis of sales per square foot of selling area. Because customers often depend on resellers to have products available when needed, resellers typically appraise a supplier's ability to provide adequate quantities when and where wanted. Resellers also take into account the ease of placing orders and the availability of technical assistance and training programs from producers. When resellers consider buying a product not previously carried, they try to determine whether the product competes with or complements products they currently handle. These types of concerns distinguish reseller markets from other markets.

Government Markets

Federal, state, county, and local governments make up **government markets.** These markets spend billions of dollars annually for a variety of goods and services, ranging from office supplies and health-care services to vehicles, heavy equipment, and weapons, to support their internal operations and provide citizens with such products as highways, education, water, energy, and national defense. The federal government spends more than $570 billion annually on national defense alone. Government expenditures annually account for about 20 percent of the U.S. gross domestic product.[8] Besides the federal government, there are 50 state governments, 3,034 county governments, and 84,491 local governments.[9] The amount spent by federal, state, and local units during the last 30 years has increased rapidly because the total number of government units and the services they provide have both increased. Costs of providing these services have also risen.

The types and quantities of products bought by government markets reflect social demands on various government agencies. As citizens' needs for government services change, so does demand for products by government markets. For example, the U.S. Department of State granted Identix a contract to supply large-scale facial recognition systems for visa processing, a capability that has become increasingly important in today's world.[10] Although it is common to hear of large corporations being awarded government contracts, in fact businesses of all sizes market to government agencies.

Because government agencies spend public funds to buy the products needed to provide services, they are accountable to the public. This accountability explains their relatively complex set of buying procedures. Some firms do not even try to sell to government buyers because they want to avoid the tangle of red tape. However, many marketers have learned to deal efficiently with government procedures and do not find them to be a stumbling block. For certain products, such as defense-related items, the government may be the only customer. The U.S. Government Printing Office publishes and distributes several documents that explain buying procedures and describe the types of products various federal agencies purchase.

Governments make purchases through bids or negotiated contracts. Although companies may be reluctant to approach government markets because of the complicated bidding process, once they understand the rules of this process, some firms routinely penetrate government markets. To make a sale under the bid system, firms must apply and be approved for placement on a list of qualified bidders. When a government unit wants to buy, it sends out a detailed description of the products to qualified bidders.

Businesses that want to sell such products submit bids. The government unit is usually required to accept the lowest bid.

When buying nonstandard or highly complex products, a government unit often uses a negotiated contract. Under this procedure, the government unit selects only a few firms and then negotiates specifications and terms; it eventually awards the contract to one of the negotiating firms. Most large defense-related contracts, once held by such companies as McDonnell Douglas and General Dynamics, traditionally were negotiated in this fashion. However, as the number and size of such contracts have declined, these companies have had to strengthen their marketing efforts and look to other markets. Although government markets can impose intimidating requirements, they can also be very lucrative.

Institutional Markets

Organizations with charitable, educational, community, or other nonbusiness goals constitute **institutional markets.** Members of institutional markets include churches, some hospitals, fraternities and sororities, charitable organizations, and private colleges. Institutions purchase millions of dollars' worth of products annually to provide goods, services, and ideas to congregations, students, patients, and others. Because institutions often have different goals and fewer resources than other types of organizations, marketers may use special marketing efforts to serve them. For example, Hussey Seating in Maine sells stadium seating to schools, colleges, churches, and other institutions, as well as to sports arenas around the world. The family-owned business shows its support for institutional customers through assistance with school funding and reduced-cost construction of local economic development projects.

Dimensions of Marketing to Business Customers

LO 2 To identify the major characteristics of business customers and transactions

Now that we have considered different types of business customers, we look at several dimensions of marketing to them, including transaction characteristics, attributes of business customers and some of their primary concerns, buying methods, major types of purchases, and the characteristics of demand for business products (see Figure 8.1).

figure 8.1

DIMENSIONS OF MARKETING TO BUSINESS CUSTOMERS

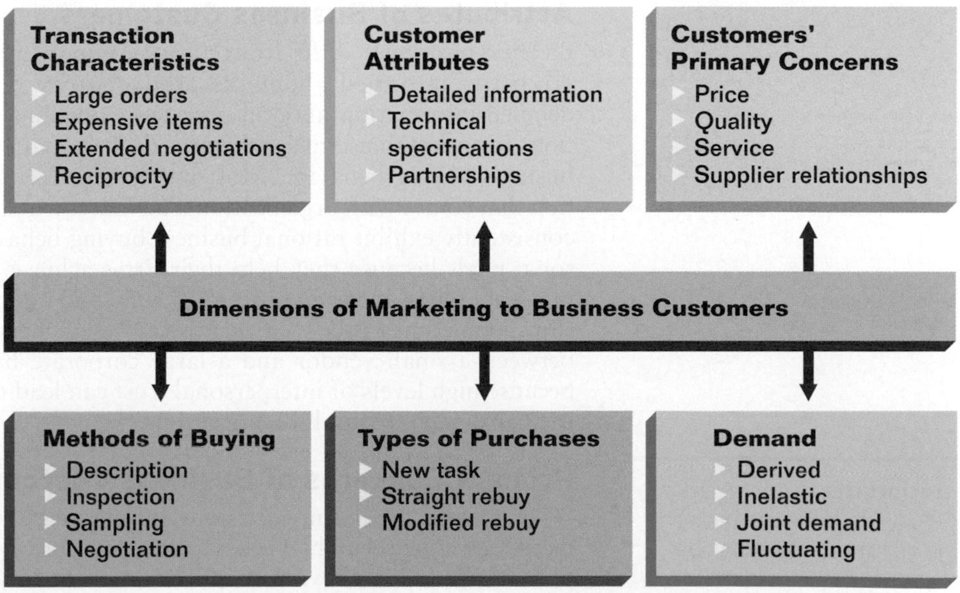

Transaction Characteristics	**Customer Attributes**	**Customers' Primary Concerns**
▸ Large orders	▸ Detailed information	▸ Price
▸ Expensive items	▸ Technical specifications	▸ Quality
▸ Extended negotiations	▸ Partnerships	▸ Service
▸ Reciprocity		▸ Supplier relationships

Dimensions of Marketing to Business Customers

Methods of Buying	**Types of Purchases**	**Demand**
▸ Description	▸ New task	▸ Derived
▸ Inspection	▸ Straight rebuy	▸ Inelastic
▸ Sampling	▸ Modified rebuy	▸ Joint demand
▸ Negotiation		▸ Fluctuating

institutional markets Organizations with charitable, educational, community, or other nonbusiness goals

Are small-business marketing costs questionable?

Survey respondents who reported seeing a corresponding upsurge in business/sales when they spent money on marketing:

No 45%

Yes 46%

Don't know 9%

Source: Data from American Express Fall Small Business Monitor survey of 627 small-business owners/managers of companies with fewer than 100 employees. Margin of error: ±4 percentage points.

Characteristics of Transactions with Business Customers

Transactions between businesses differ from consumer sales in several ways. Orders by business customers tend to be much larger than individual consumer sales. Consider that Fiji's Air Pacific placed an order for three Boeing 787-9 Dreamliner passenger jet aircraft at an estimated cost of $580 million. Combined with a recent order of five Dreamliner aircraft, Air Pacific's total Boeing order amounts to $1.5 billion, the largest transaction ever undertaken by a Fijian company. Suppliers often must sell products in large quantities to make profits; consequently they prefer not to sell to customers who place small orders. For example, Airborne Express competes successfully against FedEx and UPS by providing low-cost overnight delivery services primarily to businesses that buy such services in high volume.

Some business purchases involve expensive items, such as computer systems. Other products, such as raw materials and component items, are used continuously in production, and their supply may need frequent replenishing. The contract regarding terms of sale of these items is likely to be a long-term agreement.

Discussions and negotiations associated with business purchases can require considerable marketing time and selling effort. Purchasing decisions are often made by committee, orders are frequently large and expensive, and products may be custom built. Several people or departments in the purchasing organization are often involved. For example, one department expresses a need for a product, a second department develops the specifications, a third stipulates maximum expenditures, and a fourth places the order.

One practice unique to business markets is **reciprocity**, an arrangement in which two organizations agree to buy from each other. Reciprocal agreements that threaten competition are illegal. The Federal Trade Commission and the Justice Department take actions to stop anticompetitive reciprocal practices. Nonetheless, a certain amount of reciprocal activity occurs among small businesses and, to a lesser extent, among larger companies. Because reciprocity influences purchasing agents to deal only with certain suppliers, it can lower morale among agents and lead to less than optimal purchases.

Attributes of Business Customers

Business customers differ from consumers in their purchasing behavior because they are better informed about the products they purchase. They typically demand detailed information about a product's functional features and technical specifications to ensure that it meets their needs. Personal goals, however, may also influence business buying behavior. Most purchasing agents seek the psychological satisfaction that comes with organizational advancement and financial rewards. Agents who consistently exhibit rational business buying behavior are likely to attain these personal goals because they help their firms achieve organizational objectives. Today many suppliers and their customers build and maintain mutually beneficial relationships, sometimes called *partnerships*. Researchers find that even in a partnership between a small vendor and a large corporate buyer, a strong partnership exists because high levels of interpersonal trust can lead to higher levels of commitment to the partnership by both organizations.[11]

Primary Concerns of Business Customers

When making purchasing decisions, business customers take into account a variety of factors. Among their chief considerations are price, product quality, service, and supplier relationships. Obviously, price matters greatly to business customers because it

reciprocity An arrangement unique to business marketing in which two organizations agree to buy from each other

Concerns of Business Customers

In this advertisement, CDW promises excellent and timely service, one of the primary concerns of business customers.

influences operating costs and costs of goods sold, which in turn affect selling price, profit margin, and ultimately the ability to compete. When purchasing major equipment, a business customer views price as the amount of investment necessary to obtain a certain level of return or savings. A business customer is likely to compare the price of a product with the benefits the product will yield to the organization, often over a period of years.

Most business customers try to achieve and maintain a specific level of quality in the products they buy. To achieve this goal, most firms establish standards (usually stated as a percentage of defects allowed) for these products and buy them on the basis of a set of expressed characteristics, commonly called *specifications*. A customer evaluates the quality of the products being considered to determine whether they meet specifications. If a product fails to meet specifications or malfunctions for the ultimate consumer, the customer may drop that product's supplier and switch to a different one. On the other hand, customers are ordinarily cautious about buying products that exceed specifications because such products often cost more, thus increasing the organization's overall costs. Specifications are designed to meet a customer's wants, and anything that does not contribute to meeting those wants may be considered wasteful.

Business buyers value service. Services offered by suppliers directly and indirectly influence customers' costs, sales, and profits. In some instances, the mix of customer services is the major means by which marketers gain a competitive advantage. Procter & Gamble, for example, provided Wendy's International with customized videos and laminated guides to show Wendy's employees how to use its industrial cleaning supplies to clean every part of each restaurant. Typical services customers desire are market information, inventory maintenance, on-time delivery, and repair services. Business buyers are likely to need technical product information, data regarding demand, information about general economic conditions, or supply and delivery information. Maintaining adequate inventory is critical because it helps make products accessible when a customer needs them and reduces the customer's inventory requirements and costs. Because business customers are usually responsible for ensuring that products are on hand and ready for use when needed, on-time delivery is crucial. Furthermore, reliable, on-time delivery saves business customers money because it enables them to carry less inventory. Purchasers of machinery are especially concerned about obtaining repair services and replacement parts quickly because inoperable equipment is costly. Caterpillar Inc., manufacturer of earth-moving, construction, and materials-handling machinery, has built an international reputation, as well as a competitive advantage, by providing prompt service and replacement parts for its products around the world. Business customers are likely to resist a supplier's effort to implement a new technology if there are questions about the technology's compatibility, reliability, or other factors that could cause the supplier to fail to deliver on promises.[12]

Quality of service is a critical issue because customer expectations about service have broadened. Using traditional service quality standards based only on traditional manufacturing and accounting systems is not enough. Communication channels that allow customers to ask questions, voice complaints, submit orders, and trace shipments are indispensable components of service. Marketers should strive for uniformity of service, simplicity, truthfulness, and accuracy. They should also develop customer service objectives and monitor customer service programs. Firms can monitor service by formally surveying customers or informally calling on customers and asking questions about the service they receive. Expending the time and effort to ensure that customers are happy can greatly benefit marketers by increasing customer retention.

Finally, business customers are concerned about the costs of developing and maintaining relationships with their suppliers. By developing relationships and building trust with a particular supplier, buyers can reduce their search efforts and uncertainty

Business Travelers Want to "Fly Greener"

Fly faster, fly cheaper, fly greener? Business travelers are demanding customers—and now they have something else to be demanding about. A growing number of corporate travel coordinators are checking into airlines' environmental activities. Which airlines have a recycling program? What are airlines doing to reduce pollution and conserve natural resources?

When American Airlines began fielding inquiries about its environmental policies, it took the questions a step further and asked its own suppliers about *their* environmental policies. As a result, American's business travelers are actually putting green pressure on all the suppliers as well as the airline itself. And flying greener will make the carrier's bottom line greener by cutting waste and shaving costs.

Other airlines are also taking action to *fly greener*. British Airways, for example, has set a goal of recycling or reusing 40 percent of the solid waste generated per passenger (such as paper, bottles, and cans) by the end of this decade. Knowing that passengers are concerned about air quality and global warming, the airline put a carbon dioxide calculator on its website. Now passengers can determine the carbon dioxide emissions for their flights and, if they choose, make a donation to offset those emissions by investing in cleaner energy initiatives.[b]

about monetary prices. Research also demonstrates that satisfaction and perceived product quality in B2B relationships foster loyalty and future purchase intentions. Business customers have to keep in mind the overall fit of a purchase, including its potential to reduce inventory and carrying costs, as well as to increase inventory turnover and ability to move the right products to the right place at the right time. The entire business can be damaged by a single supplier's failure to be a good partner.[13]

Methods of Business Buying

Although no two business buyers do their jobs the same way, most use one or more of the following purchase methods: *description, inspection, sampling,* and *negotiation.* When products are standardized according to certain characteristics (such as size, shape, weight, and color) and graded using such standards, a business buyer may be able to purchase simply by describing or specifying quantity, grade, and other attributes. Agricultural products often fall into this category. Sometimes buyers specify a particular brand or its equivalent when describing the desired product. Purchases on the basis of description are especially common between a buyer and seller with an ongoing relationship built on trust.

Certain products, such as industrial equipment, used vehicles, and buildings, have unique characteristics and may vary with regard to condition. For example, a particular used truck may have a bad transmission. Consequently, business buyers of such products must base purchase decisions on inspection.

Sampling entails taking a specimen of the product from the lot and evaluating it on the assumption that its characteristics represent the entire lot. This method is appropriate when the product is homogeneous—for instance, grain—and examining the entire lot is not physically or economically feasible.

Some purchases by businesses are based on negotiated contracts. In certain instances, buyers describe exactly what they need and ask sellers to submit bids. They then negotiate with the suppliers that submit the most attractive bids. This approach may be used when acquiring commercial vehicles, for example. In other cases, the buyer may be unable to identify specifically what is to be purchased and can provide only a general description, as might be the case for a piece of custom-made equipment.

Method of Business Buying

Purchases of heavy equipment are likely to occur through negotiated contracts.

A buyer and seller might negotiate a contract that specifies a base price and provides for the payment of additional costs and fees. These contracts are most commonly used for onetime projects such as buildings, capital equipment, and special projects.

Types of Business Purchases

Most business purchases are one of three types: new-task, straight rebuy, or modified rebuy purchase. Each type is subject to different influences and thus requires business marketers to modify their selling approaches appropriately.[14] In a **new-task purchase,** an organization makes an initial purchase of an item to be used to perform a new job or solve a new problem. A new-task purchase may require development of product specifications, vendor specifications, and procedures for future purchases of that product. To make the initial purchase, the business buyer usually needs much information. New-task purchases are important to suppliers because if business buyers are satisfied with the products, suppliers may be able to sell buyers large quantities of them for many years.

A **straight rebuy purchase** occurs when buyers purchase the same products routinely under approximately the same terms of sale. Buyers require little information for these routine purchase decisions and tend to use familiar suppliers that have provided satisfactory service and products in the past. These marketers try to set up automatic reordering systems to make reordering easy and convenient for business buyers. A supplier may even monitor the business buyer's inventories and indicate to the buyer what should be ordered and when. For example, Degussa Construction Chemicals Operations, Inc., a chemical manufacturer, contracts with freight carrier Dist-Tech to manage and deliver its products with real-time shipment tracking.[15] Such a contract represents a straight rebuy purchase because the contract implies an understanding of a continued service.

In a **modified rebuy purchase,** a new-task purchase is changed the second or third time it is ordered, or requirements associated with a straight rebuy purchase are modified. A business buyer might seek faster delivery, lower prices, or a different quality level of product specifications. A modified rebuy situation may cause regular suppliers to become more competitive to keep the account since other suppliers could obtain the business. When a firm changes the terms of a service contract, such as for telecommunication services, it has made a modified purchase. Gateway Computer Systems is expanding its commercial business by focusing on small businesses by offering on-site help and online educational resources. This effort may give Gateway a competitive advantage in serving small firms making modified rebuy purchases.[16]

new-task purchase An initial purchase by an organization of an item to be used to perform a new job or solve a new problem

straight rebuy purchase A routine purchase of the same products under approximately the same terms of sale by a business buyer

modified rebuy purchase A new-task purchase that is changed on subsequent orders or when the requirements of a straight rebuy purchase are modified

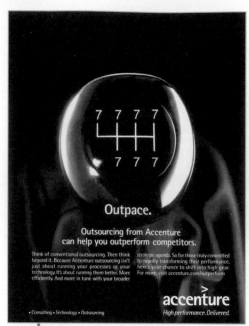

Types of Business Purchases

The purchase of consulting services is likely to be a new-task purchase.

L O ❸ To understand several attributes of demand for business products

derived demand Demand for industrial products that stems from demand for consumer products

inelastic demand Demand that is not significantly altered by a price increase or decrease

joint demand Demand involving the use of two or more items in combination to produce a product

Demand for Business Products

Unlike consumer demand, demand for business products (also called *industrial demand*) can be characterized as (1) derived, (2) inelastic, (3) joint, or (4) fluctuating.

Derived Demand. Because business customers, especially producers, buy products for direct or indirect use in the production of goods and services to satisfy consumers' needs, the demand for business products derives from the demand for consumer products; it is therefore called **derived demand.** In the long run, no demand for business products is totally unrelated to the demand for consumer products. The derived nature of demand is usually multilevel. Business marketers at different levels are affected by a change in consumer demand for a particular product. For instance, consumers have become concerned with health and good nutrition and, as a result, are purchasing more products with less fat, cholesterol, and sodium. When consumers reduced their purchases of high-fat foods, a change occurred in the demand for products marketed by food processors, equipment manufacturers, and suppliers of raw materials associated with these products. Change in consumer demand for a product affects demand for all firms involved in the production of that product.

Inelastic Demand. With **inelastic demand,** a price increase or decrease will not significantly alter demand for a business product. Because some business products contain a number of parts, price increases that affect only one or two parts may yield only a slightly higher per-unit production cost. When a sizable price increase for a component represents a large proportion of the product's cost, demand may become more elastic because the price increase in the component causes the price at the consumer level to rise sharply. For example, if aircraft engine manufacturers substantially increase the price of engines, forcing Boeing to raise the prices of the aircraft it manufactures, the demand for airliners may become more elastic as airlines reconsider whether they can afford to buy new aircraft. An increase in the price of windshields, however, is unlikely to greatly affect either the price of or the demand for airliners.

Inelasticity applies only to industry demand for business products, not to the demand an individual firm faces. Suppose a spark plug producer increases the price of spark plugs sold to small-engine manufacturers, but its competitors continue to maintain lower prices. The spark plug company will probably experience reduced unit sales because most small-engine producers will switch to lower-priced brands. A specific firm is vulnerable to elastic demand, even if industry demand for a specific business product is inelastic. We will take another look at price elasticity in Chapter 19.

Joint Demand. Demand for certain business products, especially raw materials and components, is subject to joint demand. **Joint demand** occurs when two or more items are used in combination to produce a product. For example, a firm that manufactures axes needs the same number of ax handles as it does ax blades. These two products thus are demanded jointly. If a shortage of ax handles exists, the producer buys fewer ax blades. Understanding the effects of joint demand is particularly important for a marketer that sells multiple jointly demanded items. Such a marketer realizes that when a customer begins purchasing one of the jointly demanded items, a good opportunity exists to sell related products.

Fluctuating Demand. Because the demand for business products is derived from consumer demand, it may fluctuate enormously. In general, when particular consumer products are in high demand, their producers buy large quantities of raw materials and components to ensure meeting long-run production requirements. In addition, these producers may expand production capacity, which entails acquiring new equipment and machinery, more workers, and more raw materials and component parts. Conversely, a decline in demand for certain consumer goods significantly reduces demand for business products used to produce those goods.

Marketers of business products may notice changes in demand when customers alter inventory policies, perhaps because of expectations about future demand. For

FAST, FASTER, QUAD-CORE.

INTRODUCING THE WORLD'S FIRST QUAD-CORE
PROCESSOR FOR MAINSTREAM SERVERS.

Derived Demand

The demand for Intel Quad-Core processors derives from the sales to end users of computing equipment containing these processors. In this ad message Intel advertises directly to computing equipment users, not to manufacturers of the equipment.

example, if several dishwasher manufacturers that buy timers from one producer increase their inventory of timers from a two-week to a one-month supply, the timer producer will have a significant, immediate increase in demand.

Sometimes price changes lead to surprising temporary changes in demand. A price increase for a business product may initially cause business customers to buy more of the item because they expect the price to rise further. Similarly, demand for a business product may decrease significantly following a price cut because buyers are waiting for further price reductions. Fluctuations in demand can be substantial in industries in which prices change frequently.

Business Buying Decisions

LO 4 To become familiar with the major components of a buying center

Business (organizational) buying behavior refers to the purchase behavior of producers, government units, institutions, and resellers. Although several factors that affect consumer buying behavior (discussed in the previous chapter) also influence business buying behavior, a number of factors are unique to the latter. In this section, we first analyze the buying center to learn who participates in business purchase decisions. Then we focus on the stages of the buying decision process and the factors that affect it.

The Buying Center

Relatively few business purchase decisions are made by just one person; often they are made through a buying center. The **buying center** is the group of people within the organization who make business purchase decisions. They include users, influencers, buyers, deciders, and gatekeepers.[17] One person may perform several roles. These participants share some goals and risks associated with their decisions.

Users are the organizational members who actually use the product being acquired. They frequently initiate the purchase process and/or generate purchase specifications. After the purchase, they evaluate product performance relative to the specifications.

Influencers are often technical personnel, such as engineers, who help develop the specifications and evaluate alternative products. Technical personnel are especially important influencers when the products being considered involve new, advanced technology.

Buyers select suppliers and negotiate terms of purchase. They may also become involved in developing specifications. Buyers are sometimes called purchasing agents or purchasing managers. Their choices of vendors and products, especially for new-task purchases, are heavily influenced by people occupying other roles in the buying center. For straight rebuy purchases, the buyer plays a major role in vendor selection and negotiations.

Deciders actually choose the products. Although buyers may be deciders, it is not unusual for different people to occupy these roles. For routinely purchased items, buyers are commonly deciders. However, a buyer may not be authorized to make purchases that exceed a certain dollar limit, in which case higher-level management personnel are deciders.

Finally, gatekeepers, such as secretaries and technical personnel, control the flow of information to and among people who occupy other roles in the buying center. Buyers

business (organizational) buying behavior The purchase behavior of producers, government units, institutions, and resellers

buying center The people within an organization who make business purchase decisions

who deal directly with vendors also may be gatekeepers because they can control information flows. The flow of information from a supplier's sales representatives to users and influencers is often controlled by personnel in the purchasing department.

The number and structure of an organization's buying centers are affected by the organization's size and market position, the volume and types of products being purchased, and the firm's overall managerial philosophy regarding exactly who should be involved in purchase decisions. The size of a buying center is influenced by the stage of the buying decision process and by the type of purchase. The size of the buying center likely would be larger for a new-task purchase than for a straight rebuy. Varying goals among members of a buying center can have both positive and negative effects on the purchasing process.

A marketer attempting to sell to a business customer should determine who is in the buying center, the types of decisions each individual makes, and which individuals are most influential in the decision process. Because in some instances many people make up the buying center, marketers cannot feasibly contact all participants. Instead, they must be certain to contact a few of the most influential.

L O 5 To understand the stages of the business buying decision process and the factors that affect this process

Stages of the Business Buying Decision Process

Like consumers, businesses follow a buying decision process. This process is summarized in the lower portion of Figure 8.2. In the first stage, one or more individuals recognize that a problem or need exists. Problem recognition may arise under a variety of circumstances—for instance, when machines malfunction or a firm modifies an existing product or introduces a new one. Individuals in the buying center, such as users, influencers, or buyers, may be involved in problem recognition, but it may be stimulated by external sources, such as sales representatives or advertisements.

The second stage of the process, development of product specifications, requires that buying center participants assess the problem or need and determine what is necessary to resolve or satisfy it. During this stage, users and influencers, such as engineers, often provide information and advice for developing product specifications. By assessing and describing needs, the organization should be able to establish product specifications.

figure 8.2 BUSINESS (ORGANIZATIONAL) BUYING DECISION PROCESS AND FACTORS THAT MAY INFLUENCE IT

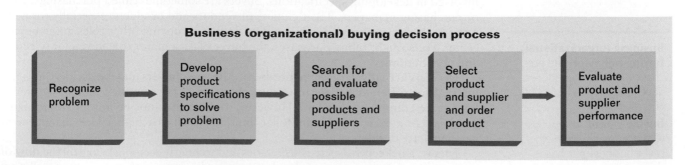

Possible influences on the decision process

Environmental
- Competitive factors
- Economic factors
- Political forces
- Legal and regulatory forces
- Technological changes
- Sociocultural issues

Organizational
- Objectives
- Purchasing policies
- Resources
- Buying center structure

Interpersonal
- Cooperation
- Conflict
- Power relationships

Individual
- Age
- Education level
- Personality
- Tenure
- Position in organization

Business (organizational) buying decision process

Recognize problem → Develop product specifications to solve problem → Search for and evaluate possible products and suppliers → Select product and supplier and order product → Evaluate product and supplier performance

Tired of paying for incoming calls?

Sprint Free Incoming Call Plans give you free incoming calls from all phones, all networks, all the time. AT&T plans don't. So your small business can cut wireless costs and still take every client's call. It's another reason why twice as many businesses choose Sprint over AT&T for their wireless needs.

1-8SPRINT-BIZ   sprint.com/business   Sprint **POWER UP**
Together with NEXTEL

Nationwide Sprint PCS and Nextel National Networks reach over 263 and 274 million people, respectively. Sprint Mobile Broadband Network reaches over 200 million people. Coverage not available everywhere – see sprint.com/coverage for details. Not available in all markets/retail locations. Subject to credit approval. "Twice as many businesses" claim based on a survey of corporate-liable users. Free Incoming Plans: Free incoming applies to calls received in the US. Additional restrictions and server/license fees apply. ©2007 Sprint Nextel. All rights reserved. Sprint, the "Going Forward" logo and other trademarks are trademarks of Sprint Nextel.

Problem Recognition

Sprint tries to help owners of small businesses recognize that they may have a problem—paying for incoming calls.

value analysis An evaluation of each component of a potential purchase

vendor analysis A formal, systematic evaluation of current and potential vendors

multiple sourcing An organization's decision to use several suppliers

sole sourcing An organization's decision to use only one supplier

Searching for and evaluating potential products and suppliers is the third stage in the decision process. Search activities may involve looking in company files and trade directories; contacting suppliers for information; soliciting proposals from known vendors; and examining websites, catalogs, and trade publications. To facilitate a vendor search, some organizations, such as Wal-Mart, advertise their desire to build partnerships with specific types of vendors, such as those owned by women or by minorities. During this stage, some organizations engage in **value analysis**, an evaluation of each component of a potential purchase. Value analysis examines quality, design, materials, and possibly item reduction or deletion to acquire the product in the most cost-effective way. Some vendors may be deemed unacceptable because they are not large enough to supply needed quantities; others may be excluded because of poor delivery and service records. Sometimes the product is not available from any existing vendor and the buyer must find a company known for its innovation, such as 3M, to design and make it. Products are evaluated to make sure they meet or exceed product specifications developed in the second stage. Usually suppliers are judged according to multiple criteria. A number of firms employ **vendor analysis,** a formal, systematic evaluation of current and potential vendors, focusing on such characteristics as price, product quality, delivery service, product availability, and overall reliability.

Results of deliberations and assessments in the third stage are used during the fourth stage to select the product to be purchased and the supplier from which to buy it. In some cases, the buyer selects and uses several suppliers, a process known as **multiple sourcing.** In others, only one supplier is selected, a situation called **sole sourcing.** For example, Best Buy and UPS agreed to an exclusive shipping relationship that resulted in greater savings, efficiencies, and customer loyalty for both companies.[18] Firms with federal government contracts are required to have several sources for an item. Sole sourcing has traditionally been discouraged except when a product is available from only one company. Sole sourcing is much more common today, however, partly because such an arrangement means better communications between buyer and supplier, stability and higher profits for suppliers, and often lower prices for buyers. However, many organizations still prefer multiple sourcing because this approach lessens the possibility of disruption caused by strikes, shortages, or bankruptcies. The actual product is ordered in this fourth stage, and specific details regarding terms, credit arrangements, delivery dates and methods, and technical assistance are finalized.

During the fifth stage, the product's performance is evaluated by comparing it with specifications. Sometimes the product meets the specifications, but its performance fails to adequately solve the problem or satisfy the need recognized in the first stage. In that case, product specifications must be adjusted. The supplier's performance is also evaluated during this stage. If supplier performance is inadequate, the business purchaser seeks corrective action from the supplier or searches for a new one. Results of the evaluation become feedback for the other stages in future business purchase decisions.

This business buying decision process is used in its entirety primarily for new-task purchases. Several stages, but not necessarily all, are used for modified rebuy and straight rebuy situations.

Influences on the Business Buying Decision Process

Figure 8.2 also lists four major categories of factors that influence business buying decisions: environmental, organizational, interpersonal, and individual. Environmental factors include competitive and economic factors, political forces, legal and regulatory forces, technological changes, and sociocultural issues. These factors generate considerable uncertainty for an organization, which can make individuals in the buying center apprehensive about certain types of purchases. Changes in one or more environmental forces can create new purchasing opportunities and threats. For example, changes in competition and technology can make buying decisions difficult for products such as software, computers, and telecommunications equipment. On the other hand, many business marketers believe the Internet can reduce their customer service costs and allow firms to improve relationships with business customers.[19]

Organizational factors that influence the buying decision process include the company's objectives, purchasing policies, and resources, as well as the size and composition of its buying center. An organization may have certain buying policies to which buying center participants must conform. For instance, a firm's policies may mandate unusually long- or short-term contracts, perhaps longer or shorter than most sellers desire. General Motors, for example, limits technology contracts to five years, even though the industry standard is seven- or ten-year contracts. The company has also imposed strict standardized sets of operating rules governing its awarding of contracts. These rules give GM greater flexibility and control but create additional challenges for firms marketing to the auto giant.[20] An organization's financial resources may require special credit arrangements. Any of these conditions could affect purchase decisions.

Interpersonal factors are the relationships among people in the buying center. Trust among all members of collaborative partnerships is crucial, particularly in purchases involving customized products.[21] The use of power and the level of conflict among buying center participants influence business buying decisions. Certain individuals in

Virtual Marketing, B2B Style

More business buyers are mousing around to find virtual product demonstrations or visit virtual trade shows as they search for goods and services to solve problems or satisfy business needs. It is not surprising that virtual marketing is a key activity for many companies that want an easy way to reach business buyers across the country or around the world.

IBM is using virtual marketing to sell sophisticated information technology systems. "As we looked at our market segmentation, we knew that 30 to 60 percent of the purchase decision is based on buzz," explains Sandy Carter, vice president for Service Oriented Architecture and WebSphere Marketing. To create buzz, Carter and her team used virtual marketing to help "reach an audience we hadn't reached before and help us reach it in a very effective way."

First they posted a product demonstration on Yahoo! Video, which proved so popular that the team planned a 30-minute movie about Service Oriented Architecture, promoted by trailers uploaded to YouTube and Yahoo! Video. IBM invited prospects to screenings around the world and then posted the movie online for buyers to watch at their convenience. The result: tens of thousands of new sales leads for IBM.

Virtual marketing isn't just for the tech trade. For example, businesses that buy marble and other stone materials can visit "The Virtual Stone Show" and examine suppliers' wares both day and night. Thanks to virtual marketing, the search for suppliers can click along quickly.[c]

the buying center may be better communicators and more persuasive than others. Often these interpersonal dynamics are hidden, making them difficult for marketers to assess.

Individual factors are personal characteristics of participants in the buying center, such as age, education level, personality, and tenure and position in the organization. For example, a 55-year-old manager who has been in the organization for 25 years may affect decisions made by the buying center differently than a 30-year-old person employed only two years. How influential these factors are depends on the buying situation; the type of product being purchased; and whether the purchase is new-task, modified rebuy, or straight rebuy. Negotiating styles of people vary within an organization and from one organization to another. To be effective, marketers must know customers well enough to be aware of these individual factors and their potential effects on purchase decisions.

Using Industrial Classification Systems

L O 6 To describe industrial classification systems and explain how they can be used to identify and analyze business markets

Marketers have access to a considerable amount of information about potential business customers, since much of this information is available through government and industry publications and websites. Marketers use this information to identify potential business customers and to estimate their purchase potential.

Identifying Potential Business Customers

Much information about business customers is based on industrial classification systems. In the United States, marketers traditionally have relied on the *Standard Industrial Classification (SIC) system,* which the federal government developed to classify selected economic characteristics of industrial, commercial, financial, and service organizations. However, the SIC system has been replaced by a new industry classification system called the **North American Industry Classification System (NAICS).** NAICS is a single industry classification system used by the United States, Canada, and Mexico to generate comparable statistics among the three partners of the North American Free Trade Agreement (NAFTA). The NAICS classification is based on the types of production activities performed. NAICS is similar to the International Standard Industrial Classification (ISIC) system used in Europe and many other parts of the world. Whereas the SIC system divided industrial activity into ten divisions, NAICS divides it into 20 sectors. NAICS contains 1,172 industry classifications, compared with 1,004 in the SIC system. NAICS is more comprehensive and up to date, and it provides considerably more information about service industries and high-tech products.[22] Table 8.2 shows some NAICS codes for Apple, Inc., and AT&T, Inc. Over the next few years, all three NAFTA countries will convert from previously used industrial classification systems to NAICS.

Industrial classification systems are ready-made tools that enable marketers to categorize organizations into groups based mainly on the types of goods and services provided. Although an industrial classification system is a vehicle for segmentation, it is most appropriately used in conjunction with other types of data to determine exactly how many and which customers a marketer can reach.

Input-output analysis works well in conjunction with an industrial classification system. This type of analysis is based on the assumption that the output, or sales, of one industry are the input, or purchases, of other industries. **Input-output data** identify what types of industries purchase the products of a particular industry. A major source of national input-output data is the *Survey of Current Business,* published by the Office of Business Economics, U.S. Department of Commerce. After learning which industries purchase the major portion of an industry's output, the next step is to find the industrial classification numbers for those industries. Because firms are grouped differently in input-output tables and industrial classification systems, ascertaining industrial classification numbers can be difficult. However, the Office of Business Economics provides some limited conversion tables with input-output data. These tables can help marketers assign classification numbers to industry categories used in input-output analysis.

North American Industry Classification System (NAICS) An industry classification system that generates comparable statistics among the United States, Canada, and Mexico

input-output data Information that identifies what types of industries purchase the products of a particular industry

table 8.2 EXAMPLES OF NAICS CLASSIFICATION

NAICS Hierarchy for AT&T, Inc.		NAICS Hierarchy for Apple, Inc.	
Sector 51	Information	Sector 31–33	Manufacturing
Subsector 517	Telecommunications	Subsector 334	Computer and Electronic Manufacturing
Industry Group 5171 Industry Group 5172	Wired Telecommunication Carriers Wireless Telecommunications Carriers	Industry Group 3341	Computer and Peripheral Equipment Manufacturing
Industry 51711 Industry 51721	Wired Telecommunication Carriers Wireless Telecommunications Carriers	Industry 33411	Computer and Peripheral Equipment Manufacturing
Industry 517110 Industry 517210	Wired Telecommunication Carriers Wireless Telecommunications Carriers	U.S. Industry 334111	Electronic Computer Manufacturing

Source: www.census.gov/epcd/ec97/industry/E3341.HTM, www.census.gov/econ/census02/naics/sector51/517110.htm, and www.census.gov/naics/2007/def/ND517210.HTM#N517210.

After determining the classification numbers of industries that buy the firm's output, a marketer is in a position to ascertain the number of organizations that are potential buyers. Government sources, such as the *Census of Business,* the *Census of Manufacturers,* and *County Business Patterns,* report the number of establishments, the value of industry shipments, the number of employees, the percentage of imports and exports, and industry growth rates within classifications. Commercial sources also provide information about organizations categorized by industrial classifications.

A marketer can take several approaches to determine the identities and locations of organizations in specific groups. One approach is to use state directories or commercial industrial directories, such as *Standard & Poor's Register* and Dun & Bradstreet's *Million Dollar Directory.* These sources contain such information about a firm as its name, industrial classification, address, phone number, and annual sales. By referring to one or more of these sources, marketers isolate business customers with industrial classification numbers, determine their locations, and develop lists of potential customers by desired geographic area. A more expedient, although more expensive, approach is to use a commercial data service. Dun & Bradstreet, for example, can provide a list of organizations that fall into a particular industrial classification group. For each company on the list, Dun & Bradstreet gives the name, location, sales volume, number of employees, type of products handled, names of chief executives, and other pertinent information. Either method can effectively identify and locate a group of potential customers. However, a marketer probably cannot pursue all organizations on the list. Because some companies have greater purchasing potential than others, marketers must determine which customer or customer group to pursue.

Estimating Purchase Potential

To estimate the purchase potential of business customers or groups of customers, a marketer must find a relationship between the size of potential customers' purchases and a variable available in industrial classification data, such as the number of employees. For example, a paint manufacturer might attempt to determine the average number of gallons purchased by a specific type of potential customer relative to the number of employees. A marketer with no previous experience in this market segment will probably have to survey a random sample of potential customers to establish a relationship between purchase sizes and numbers of employees. Once this relationship is established, it can be applied to customer groups to estimate their potential purchases. After deriving these estimates, the marketer is in a position to select the customer groups with the most sales and profit potential.

Despite their usefulness, industrial classification data pose several problems. First, a few industries do not have specific designations. Second, because a transfer of products from one establishment to another is counted as a part of total shipments, double counting may occur when products are shipped between two establishments within the same firm. Third, because the Census Bureau is prohibited from providing data that identify specific business organizations, some data, such as value of total shipments, may be understated. Finally, because government agencies provide industrial classification data, a significant lag usually exists between data-collection time and the time the information is released.

SUMMARY

Business (B2B) markets consist of individuals, organizations, and groups that purchase a specific kind of product for resale, direct use in producing other products, or use in day-to-day operations. Producer markets include those individuals and business organizations that purchase products for the purpose of making a profit by using them to produce other products or as part of their operations. Intermediaries that buy finished products and resell them to make a profit are classified as reseller markets. Government markets consist of federal, state, county, and local governments, which spend billions of dollars annually for goods and services to support internal operations and to provide citizens with needed services. Organizations with charitable, educational, community, or other nonprofit goals constitute institutional markets.

Transactions that involve business customers differ from consumer transactions in several ways. Such transactions tend to be larger, and negotiations occur less frequently, though they are often lengthy. They frequently involve more than one person or department in the purchasing organization. They may also involve reciprocity, an arrangement in which two organizations agree to buy from each other. Business customers are usually better informed than ultimate consumers and more likely to seek information about a product's features and technical specifications.

When purchasing products, business customers are particularly concerned about quality, service, price, and supplier relationships. Quality is important because it directly affects the quality of products the buyer's firm produces. To achieve an exact level of quality, organizations often buy products on the basis of a set of expressed characteristics, called specifications. Because services have such a direct influence on a firm's costs, sales, and profits, factors such as market information, on-time delivery, and availability of parts are crucial to a business buyer. Although business customers do not depend solely on price to decide which products to buy, price is of primary concern because it directly influences profitability.

Business buyers use several purchasing methods, including description, inspection, sampling, and negotiation. Most organizational purchases are new-task, straight rebuy, or modified rebuy. In a new-task purchase, an organization makes an initial purchase of items to be used to perform new jobs or solve new problems. In a modified rebuy purchase, a new-task purchase is changed the second or third time it is ordered or requirements associated with

a straight rebuy purchase are modified. A straight rebuy purchase occurs when a buyer purchases the same products routinely under approximately the same terms of sale.

Industrial demand differs from consumer demand along several dimensions. Industrial demand derives from demand for consumer products. At the industry level, industrial demand is inelastic. If an industrial item's price changes, product demand will not change as much proportionally. Some industrial products are subject to joint demand, which occurs when two or more items are used in combination to make a product. Finally, because organizational demand derives from consumer demand, the demand for business products can fluctuate widely.

Business (or organizational) buying behavior refers to the purchase behavior of producers, resellers, government units, and institutions. Business purchase decisions are made through a buying center, the group of people involved in making such purchase decisions. Users are those in the organization who actually use the product. Influencers help develop specifications and evaluate alternative products for possible use. Buyers select suppliers and negotiate purchase terms. Deciders choose the products. Gatekeepers control the flow of information to and among individuals occupying other roles in the buying center.

The stages of the business buying decision process are problem recognition, development of product specifications to solve problems, search for and evaluation of products and suppliers, selection and ordering of the most appropriate product, and evaluation of the product's and supplier's performance.

Four categories of factors influence business buying decisions: environmental, organizational, interpersonal, and individual. Environmental factors include competitive forces, economic conditions, political forces, laws and regulations, technological changes, and sociocultural factors. Business factors include the company's objectives, purchasing policies, and resources, as well as the size and composition of its buying center. Interpersonal factors are the relationships among people in the buying center. Individual factors are personal characteristics of members of the buying center, such as age, education level, personality, and tenure and position in the organization.

Business marketers have a considerable amount of information available for use in planning marketing strategies. Much of this information is based on an industrial classification system, which categorizes businesses into major industry groups, industry subgroups, and detailed industry categories. An industrial classification system—like the North American Industry Classification System (NAICS) used by the United States, Canada, and Mexico—provides marketers with information needed to identify business customer groups. It can best be used for this purpose in conjunction with other information, such as input-output data. After identifying target industries, a marketer can obtain the names and locations of potential customers by using government and commercial data sources. Marketers then must estimate potential purchases of business customers by finding a relationship between a potential customer's purchases and a variable available in industrial classification data.

IMPORTANT TERMS

Business market, 224
Producer markets, 224
Reseller markets, 225
Government markets, 226
Institutional markets, 227
Reciprocity, 228
New-task purchase, 231

Straight rebuy purchase, 231
Modified rebuy purchase, 232
Derived demand, 232
Inelastic demand, 232
Joint demand, 232

Business (organizational) buying behavior, 233
Buying center, 233
Value analysis, 235
Vendor analysis, 235
Multiple sourcing, 235
Sole sourcing, 235

North American Industry Classification System (NAICS), 237
Input-output data, 237

DISCUSSION & REVIEW QUESTIONS

1. Identify, describe, and give examples of the four major types of business markets.

2. Why might business customers generally be considered more rational in their purchasing behavior than ultimate consumers?

3. What are the primary concerns of business customers?

4. List several characteristics that differentiate transactions involving business customers from consumer transactions.

5. What are the commonly used methods of business buying?

6. Why do buyers involved in straight rebuy purchases require less information than those making new-task purchases?

7. How does demand for business products differ from consumer demand?

8. What are the major components of a firm's buying center?

9. Identify the stages of the business buying decision process. How is this decision process used when making straight rebuys?

10. How do environmental, business, interpersonal, and individual factors affect business purchases?

11. What function does an industrial classification system help marketers perform?

12. List some sources that a business marketer can use to determine the names and addresses of potential customers.

APPLICATION QUESTIONS

1. Identify organizations in your area that fit each business market category: producer, reseller, government, and institutional. Explain your classifications.

2. Indicate the method of buying (description, inspection, sampling, or negotiation) an organization would be most likely to use when purchasing each of the following items. Defend your selections.

   a. A building for the home office of a light bulb manufacturer

   b. Wool for a clothing manufacturer

   c. An Alaskan cruise for a company retreat, assuming a regular travel agency is used

   d. One-inch nails for a building contractor

3. Purchases by businesses may be described as new-task, modified rebuy, or straight rebuy. Categorize the following purchase decisions and explain your choices.

   a. Bob has purchased toothpicks from Smith Restaurant Supply for 25 years and recently placed an order for yellow toothpicks rather than the usual white ones.

   b. Jill's investment company has been purchasing envelopes from AAA Office Supply for a year and now needs to purchase boxes to mail year-end portfolio summaries to clients. Jill calls AAA to purchase these boxes.

   c. Reliance Insurance has been supplying its salespeople with small personal computers to assist in their sales efforts. The company recently agreed to begin supplying them with faster, more sophisticated computers.

4. Identifying qualified customers is important to the survival of any organization. NAICS provides helpful information about many different businesses. Find the NAICS manual at the library and identify the NAICS code for the following items.

a. Chocolate candy bars
b. Automobile tires
c. Men's running shoes

INTERNET EXERCISE

Visit **www.cengage.com/marketing/pride-ferrell** for resources to help you master the material in this chapter, plus materials that will help you expand your marketing knowledge, including Internet exercise updates, ACE Self-Tests, hotlinks to companies featured in this chapter, and much more.

Boeing

Boeing is the world's leading aerospace corporation and largest manufacturer of commercial and military aircraft.

Visit the company at **www.boeing.com.**

1. At what types of business markets are Boeing's products targeted?
2. How does Boeing address some of the concerns of business customers?
3. What environmental factors do you think affect demand for Boeing products?

developing your MARKETING PLAN

When developing a marketing strategy for business customers it is essential to understand the process the business goes through when making a buying decision. Knowledge of business buying behavior is important when developing several aspects of the marketing plan. To assist you in relating the information in this chapter to the creation of a marketing plan for business customers, consider the following issues:

1. What are the primary concerns of business customers? Could any of these concerns be addressed with strengths of your company?

2. Determine the type of business purchase your customer will likely be using when purchasing your product. How would this impact the level of information required by the business when moving through the buying decision process?

3. Discuss the different types of demand that the business customer will experience when purchasing your product.

The information obtained from these questions should assist you in developing various aspects of your marketing plan found in the *Interactive Marketing Plan exercise* at **www.cengage.com/marketing/pride-ferrell.**

globalEDGE

1. The world market for steel plays a vital role on projects that involve the construction of bridges, buildings, automobiles, and aircraft. After attending a conference sponsored by the International Iron and Steel Institute (IISI), you learn that the "World Steel in Figures" report can help your firm reassess its strategy for sourcing steel on the global market to be a better arbiter for clients. To access this report, use the search term "IISI" at **http://globaledge.msu.edu/ibrd.** Currently, your sourcing strategy is similar to typical North American companies. As such, from which regions does your company source steel? In which countries might your firm aim to find new sources for steel?

2. Part of your firm's evaluation of a supplier's performance is based on the degree to which it seamlessly

delivers goods and materials. A recent concern of global suppliers is an initiative to enhance shipping container security for international trade and transport. A report concerning container security for international trade and transportation can be found using the search term "international trade and transport" at **http://globaledge.msu.edu/ibrd.** At the United Nations Conference on Trade and Development (UNCTAD) website, click on the Transport & Trade Logistics link, go to the Documents section, and look for a report on Container Security. What are the four parts of this program? Based on this, do you think your firm should change its evaluation of supplier performance?

video CASE 8.1

Numi Tea Brews Up Business Relationships

Tea, one of the oldest beverages in the world, is a growth industry these days. Served hot or cold, brewed in bags or using loose leaves, tea accounts for $10 billion in U.S. sales every year. Although the business is dominated by corporate giants such as Lipton, companies with unique tea products can compete quite effectively by connecting with key resellers.

Numi Tea of Oakland, California, is riding the wave of tea popularity in just this way. Founded in 1999 by the brother-and-sister team Ahmed and Reem Rahim, Numi markets only organic full-leaf teas. Many of its teas are Fair Trade certified, which means the growers in India, China, and South Africa are paid more than the usual market rate for their leaves. For environmental sustainability, Numi's gift boxes and store displays are made from fast-growing bamboo.

Numi's product offerings include tea bags, tea leaf mixtures, herbal teas, and accessories such as teapots and filters. One of its most unusual products is flowering tea. When a hand-sewn bundle of these black, white, or green tea leaves is dropped into boiling water, it releases its fragrant flavor as it expands into a pretty blossom shape. In addition, Numi runs a Tea Garden in downtown Oakland, furnished with eco-friendly materials and featuring Numi's organic teas plus an assortment of cheeses, fruits, and bakery items.

How did Numi bring its sales to a multimillion-dollar boil in only a few years? From the start, the Rahims recognized that their company's growth depended on building long-term relationships with good wholesalers and retailers. Numi needed to educate resellers (and help them educate their customers) about the advantages of Numi's tea products. To do this, it created training materials for reseller employees and a series of informational tea cards for resellers to give to customers. It also developed colorful product highlight cards and displays for store shelves and restaurant tables, plus eye-catching posters and banners showcasing the brand.

Service is another important element of Numi's marketing strategy. The company has a brand ambassador who visits restaurants, wholesalers, and retailers to introduce new products and promotions, discuss point-of-purchase displays, conduct product demonstrations, and identify new sales opportunities. It also sends out newsletters and e-mails with product and promotion updates.

Rather than using a "one-size-fits-all" approach, Numi adapts its service to the differing needs of its various resellers. For example, to help upscale restaurants make a good impression on their patrons, Numi provides handsome bamboo tea chests and boxes in which to present tea choices at table-side. Numi also makes glossy presentation folders in which luxury hotels can leave Numi tea bags in guest rooms as a special amenity.

For the convenience of its resellers, Numi offers a number of ordering options. Depending on the size of their order and where they are located, retailers can buy through a local wholesaler, through Numi's website, or through the wholesaler WorldPantry.com. To make it easy for consumers to find Numi retailers in the United States and Canada, the company's website includes a store locator function.

Careful attention to reseller relationships has helped Numi increase revenues by more than 500 percent in the past five years. No wonder it was recently named one of the San Francisco area's fastest-growing, privately owned businesses. More growth is ahead as the company expands distribution by intensifying its marketing to gourmet grocery stores, quality restaurants, and upscale hotels across North America.[23]

Questions for Discussion

1. What important concerns might retailers and wholesalers have when making decisions about buying from Numi?
2. During vendor analysis, how much weight do you think a buyer for a high-end restaurant is likely to give Numi's service capabilities? Why?
3. How might local wholesalers react to the policy of allowing retailers to order directly from Numi's website?

CASE 8.2

Target Commercial Interiors Hit a Home Run

"Is the stadium going to look like their stores?" That's what the president of the Arizona Diamondbacks baseball team wondered when its executive vice president of business operations suggested that Target Commercial Interiors (TCI) redo Chase Field in Phoenix. Although TCI isn't well known, its success in business-to-business marketing has enhanced the sales and profits of Target Stores for some time. TCI began life as part of the furniture department at Minneapolis-based Dayton's department stores, Target's original parent company. After the department stores were sold and the company took the Target name, the commercial interiors business became Target Commercial Interiors.

During more than 50 years of operation, TCI has designed and decorated a wide variety of business facilities and commercial spaces. A few years ago, the company worked on offices in the General Mills headquarters building and provided stylish furnishings for a Starwood hotel in Minneapolis. It recently remodeled the American Lung Association's offices in St. Paul to make the building healthier and more energy efficient. And it designed interiors for new Chip Ganassi Racing facilities in North Carolina and Indiana (Target sponsors three Chip Ganassi Racing drivers).

Because the Diamondbacks' executive vice president worked for Chip Ganassi before joining the baseball team, he knew TCI's commitment to quality and cost containment. Still, the team's owners wondered whether a design company owned by the retailer famous for its red bull's-eye was the right choice for redoing their ten-year-old baseball stadium. "Is it going to look cheap?" the owners asked, concerned about what TCI could do on a budget of less than $7 million. Ultimately, TCI got the job because its experts demonstrated their ability to create interior designs that were creative and fashionable as well as functional.

TCI's careful planning saved the team so much money that "we were able to add things that we had not planned to do, such as redoing the bathrooms and replacing condiment carts," says the executive vice president. For example, the Diamondbacks' new branding strategy called for replacing the rainbow of colors used throughout the stadium with one signature color: Sedona red. Instead of buying everything new,

TCI applied heavy-duty Sedona red adhesive paper to many of the fixtures and signs. TCI also used its parent company's supplier connections and buying power to acquire eye-catching items (such as a large conference table for the team's boardroom) at reasonable prices.

The Diamondbacks organization appreciates TCI's work and its budget-conscious methods. "Now, I don't know what I like better, the job they did or what they charged us," comments the team's CEO. The Diamondbacks were so satisfied that they have hired TCI to work on several other stadium areas, including renovating the ticket sales office and the upscale Strike Zone Lounge located behind home plate.

When the law firm of Winthrop & Weinstine hired TCI to decorate its Minneapolis offices, the challenge was to find top-quality wood furniture that fit with the firm's other wood furnishings. Its designers managed to locate office furniture with the look but not the price tag of custom-made pieces. "Although Target is a discount store, this division is pretty high-end yet affordable," notes the law firm's executive director. "Architects are not always practical and functional. Target was both, and helped us come in under budget."

To reach business customers, TCI maintains showrooms and sales offices in Minnesota, Wisconsin, and Illinois. Its store in Bloomington, Minnesota, features professional office furniture, desk lamps, wall art, and related merchandise. In addition, TCI sells pictures, mirrors, and other accent items through its TCI Art website. TCI's president observes that having Target as a parent is a valuable asset: "With the Target name, the world is your oyster."[24]

Questions for Discussion

1. In which stage of the decision process is the Target name likely to be an especially important factor for business buyers who want to hire an interior design firm? Why?

2. How does derived demand apply to the demand for interior design services such as those Target provided for Chase Field?

3. When the Diamondbacks hired TCI to handle additional stadium renovations, was this a new-task, straight rebuy, or modified rebuy purchase? Explain your answer.

9 Reaching Global Markets

LEARNING objectives

1 To understand the nature of global marketing strategy

2 To analyze the environmental forces that affect international marketing efforts

3 To understand several important international trade agreements

4 To identify methods of international market entry

5 To examine various forms of global organizational structures

6 To examine the use of the marketing mix internationally

Entrepreneurs Take on Chinese Piracy: The Story of BraBaby

entrepreneurs IN ACTION

Even inexpensive household products face competitive challenges in global markets. When Robert and Laura Engel began their foray into entrepreneurship, they were developing household products such as key chain racks and gardening tools that were mainly sold through mail-order catalogs. Little did they know that they were about to hit a gold mine when Laura came up with the idea of the "BraBaby," a plastic device used for laundering bras, preserving and extending their wear. The Engels have sold as many as 10,000 units a week with the support of television personalities Rachael Ray and Tony Danza. However, the joy of success was tempered by the complexities of international marketing when the Engels realized that their product was being copied and made available all over the world without their permission, partnership, licensing, or compensation. "You think the hard part is coming up with a great product, but then you find out that the hard work has just begun," says Robert Engel, who has compared his attempts to deal with knockoffs like the game Whac-A-Mole, where you close down one company only to find another one has popped up.

With just eight additional employees, Angel Sales, the Engels' small Chicago-based firm, does not have the resources to police international piracy of their product the way large multinational firms such as Pfizer, Nike, or Walt Disney do. When his son asked Robert what he was doing on the computer one day, he replied, "Playing a new computer game: BraBaby Pirate Brigade." The Engels have been going online and finding companies not only using their product names but using taglines such as "as seen on TV" and showing official pictures from the Engels' website. The couple has seen their knockoffs selling for as little as 38 cents as compared to their $1.25 wholesale cost.

Through his online sleuthing and with the help of legal counsel, the Engels have sent out 71 cease-and-desist orders to Chinese companies. Thus far, however, only a few companies have stopped pirating their product. At a Chinese trade show, Robert Engel found a company called Ningbo Foreign Trading Company selling tens of thousands of the knockoffs for as little as 45 cents each. Engel took this information to the Intellectual Property Complaints Office, where he was told nothing could be done because he did not have the proper identification. When Engel registered BraBaby in China, the lawyer there told him his application was in a pipeline of applications, and it could take years for the application to be registered. The Engels have already spent nearly $125,000 registering, patenting, and copyrighting the trademark in the United States, Europe, Australia, New Zealand, Taiwan, Hong Kong, and China.

On a more positive note, the Engels have signed a licensing deal with oneCARE of Alpharetta, Georgia, which plans to brand the product with Procter & Gamble's Tide detergent and sell it through large retailers such as Target, Wal-Mart, and Bed, Bath & Beyond. The Engels have learned a valuable lesson about the challenges and futility in thinking you can control your brand name and image in global markets with intellectual property standards that are not enforced or culturally accepted.[1]

Technological advances and rapidly changing political and economic conditions are making it easier than ever for companies like Angel Sales to market their products overseas as well as at home. With most of the world's population and two-thirds of total purchasing power outside the United States, international markets represent tremendous opportunities for growth. Accessing these markets can promote innovation, while intensifying global competition can spur companies to market better, less-expensive products. MTV, for example, reaches 500 million people worldwide through 100 MTV, VH1, BET, and Nickelodeon channels. The company tailors the content of each channel to match the local language and culture. MTV Arabia, for example, has a regular call to prayer for its Muslim viewers, whereas MTV in Japan is very edgy and technology oriented. Only 26 percent of MTV Network viewers live in the United States.[2]

In deference to the increasingly global nature of marketing, we devote this chapter to the unique features of global markets and international marketing. We begin by considering the nature of global marketing strategy and the environmental forces that create opportunities and threats for international marketers. Next, we consider several regional trade alliances, markets, and agreements. Then we examine the modes of entry into international marketing and companies' degree of involvement in it, as well as some of the structures that can be used to organize multinational enterprises. Finally, we examine how firms may alter their marketing mixes when engaging in international marketing efforts. All of these factors must be considered in any marketing plan that includes an international component.

international marketing
Developing and performing marketing activities across national boundaries

The Nature of Global Marketing Strategy

LO ❶ To understand the nature of global marketing strategy

International marketing involves developing and performing marketing activities across national boundaries. For example, Wal-Mart has more than 1.9 million employees and operates more than 7,000 stores in 14 countries, including the United States, Brazil, and China, and Starbucks serves tens of millions of customers a week at more than 14,000 shops in 42 countries.[3] Even American icon Jack Daniels now sells more cases of whiskey abroad than it does in its own backyard.[4]

Firms are finding that international markets provide tremendous opportunities for growth. At the same time, governments and industry leaders often argue that too few firms take full advantage of international opportunities. To counter these dilemmas, many countries offer significant practical assistance and valuable benchmarking research that will help their domestic firms become more competitive globally. One example is the benchmarking of best international practices that is conducted by the network of CIBERs—Centers for International Business Education and Research—at leading business schools in the United States. These 31 CIBERs are funded by the U.S. government to help U.S. firms become more competitive globally.[5] A major element of the assistance that these governmental organizations can provide firms (especially small and medium-sized firms) is knowledge of the internationalization process of firms.

Traditionally, most companies—including McDonald's and KFC—have entered the global marketplace incrementally as they gained knowledge about various markets and opportunities. Beginning in the 1990s, however, some

International Marketing
This Latin American ad for Oreos is part of an extensive international marketing program.

firms—such as eBay, Google, and Logitech—were founded with the knowledge and resources to expedite their commitment and investment in the global marketplace. These "born globals"—typically small technology-based firms earning as much as 70 percent of their sales outside the domestic home market—export their products almost immediately after being established in market niches in which they compete with larger, more established firms.[6] Whether the traditional approach, the born global approach, or an approach that merges attributes of both approaches is adopted to market the firm's products and services, international marketing strategy is a critical element of a firm's global operations. Today, global competition in most industries is intense and becoming increasingly fierce with the addition of newly emerging markets and firms.

Environmental Forces in Global Markets

LO 2 To analyze the environmental forces that affect international marketing efforts

Firms that enter international markets often find they must make significant adjustments in their marketing strategies. The environmental forces that affect foreign markets may differ dramatically from those that affect domestic markets. Consider that McDonald's would like to expand in Russia, where its restaurants serve about 850,000 diners a year—or twice the store traffic in other markets. However, opening a new restaurant can require as many as 200 signatures from local officials, and land prices are high and growing in Russia's big cities, whereas unemployment is low, making it difficult to recruit employees for each new store. As a result, the firm is proceeding cautiously.[7] Thus, a successful international marketing strategy requires a careful environmental analysis. Conducting research to understand the needs and desires of international customers is crucial to global marketing success. Many firms have demonstrated that such efforts can generate tremendous financial rewards, increase market share, and heighten customer awareness of their products around the world. In this section, we explore how differences in the sociocultural; economic; political, legal, and regulatory; social and ethical; competitive; and technological forces in other countries can profoundly affect marketing activities.

Sociocultural Forces

Cultural Differences
Dentyne Ice gum is marketed in the United States to the Latino market.

Cultural and social differences among nations can have significant effects on marketing activities. Because marketing activities are primarily social in purpose, they are influenced by beliefs and values regarding family, religion, education, health, and recreation. By identifying major sociocultural deviations among countries, marketers lay groundwork for an effective adaptation of marketing strategy. In India, for instance, three-quarters of McDonald's menu was created to appeal to Indian tastes, including many vegetarian items, and it does not include pork or beef products at all. In China, however, the fast-food giant has made fewer menu adjustments and even promotes its beef burgers in a sexy ad campaign.[8]

Although football is a popular sport in the United States and a major opportunity for many television advertisers, soccer is the most popular televised sport in Europe and Latin America. And, of course, marketing communications often must be translated into other languages. Sometimes, however, the true meaning of translated messages can be misinterpreted or lost. Consider some translations that

Cuando te acercas es más interesante.   Dito de cerca.

went awry in foreign markets: KFC's long-running slogan "Finger lickin' good" was translated into Spanish as "Eat your fingers off," and Coors's "Turn it loose" campaign was translated into Spanish as "Drink Coors and get diarrhea."[9]

It can be difficult to transfer marketing symbols, trademarks, logos, and even products to international markets, especially if these are associated with objects that have profound religious or cultural significance in a particular culture. For example, when Big Boy opened a new restaurant in Bangkok, it quickly became popular with European and American tourists, but the local Thais refused to eat there. Instead, they placed gifts of rice and incense at the feet of the Big Boy statue—a chubby boy holding a hamburger—which reminded them of Buddha.[10]

Cultural differences may also affect marketing negotiations and decision-making behavior. Although U.S. and Taiwanese sales agents are equally sensitive to customer interests, research suggests that the Taiwanese are more sensitive to the interests of their companies and competitors and less attuned to the interests of colleagues. Identifying such differences in work-related values of employees across different nationalities helps companies design more effective sales management practices.[11] However, the use of U.S. sales management techniques among Polish retail salespeople has been successful despite many cultural, economic, and political differences in the environments.[12] Cultural differences in the emphasis placed on personal relationships, status, and decision-making styles have been known to complicate dealings between Americans and businesspeople from other countries. In the Far East, a gift may be considered a necessary introduction before negotiation, whereas in the United States or Canada, a gift may be misconstrued as an illegal bribe.

Buyers' perceptions of other countries can influence product adoption and use. Multiple research studies have found that consumer preferences for products depend on both the country of origin and the product category of competing products.[13] When people are unfamiliar with products from another country, their perceptions of the country itself may affect their attitude toward the product and influence whether they will buy it. If a country has a reputation for producing quality products and therefore has a positive image in consumers' minds, marketers of products from that country will want to make the country of origin well known. For example, a generally favorable image of Western computer technology has fueled sales of U.S.-made personal computers by Dell and Apple and Microsoft software in Japan. On the other hand, marketers may want to dissociate themselves from a particular country. Because the world has not always viewed Mexico as producing quality products, Volkswagen may not want to advertise that some of the models it sells in the United States, including the Beetle, are made in Mexico. The extent to which a product's brand image and country of origin influence purchases is subject to considerable variation based on national culture characteristics.[14]

When products are introduced from one nation into another, acceptance is far more likely if similarities exist between the two cultures. In fact, many similar cultural characteristics exist across countries. For international marketers, cultural differences have implications for product development, advertising, packaging, and pricing. Starbucks, for example, has found it difficult to sell coffee products in China, a nation of tea drinkers, but it has been successful in targeting China's younger generations, who like the chain's made-to-order drinks, personal service, and original music. To appeal to China's "little emperors," the generation of children who resulted from China's strict one-child-per-family policy, Starbucks offers formal coffee tastings, generous samples, helpful brochures, and a comfortable informal gathering place.[15]

Economic Forces

Global marketers need to understand the international trade system, particularly the economic stability of individual nations, as well as trade barriers that may stifle marketing efforts. Economic differences among nations—differences in standards of living, credit, buying power, income distribution, national resources, exchange rates, and the like—dictate many of the adjustments firms must make in marketing internationally.

The United States and western Europe are more stable economically than many other regions of the world. However, even these economies have downturns in regular cycles. In recent years, a number of countries, including Korea, Russia, Singapore, and

Thailand, have experienced economic problems such as depressions, high unemployment, corporate bankruptcies, instability in currency markets, trade imbalances, and financial systems that need major reforms. Even more stable developing countries, such as Mexico and Brazil, tend to have greater fluctuations in their business cycles than the United States does. Economic instability can disrupt the markets for U.S. products in places that otherwise might be excellent marketing opportunities. On the other hand, competition from the sustained economic growth of countries such as China and India can disrupt markets for U.S. products.

In terms of the value of all products produced by a nation, the United States has the largest gross domestic product in the world, nearly $14 trillion in 2007.[16] **Gross domestic product (GDP)** is an overall measure of a nation's economic standing; it is the market value of a nation's total output of goods and services for a given period. However, it does not take into account the concept of GDP in relation to population (GDP per capita). The United States has a GDP per capita of $46,000. Switzerland is roughly 230 times smaller than the United States—a little larger than the state of Maryland—but its population density is six times greater than that of the United States. Although Switzerland's GDP is about one-forty-sixth the size of the United States' GDP, its GDP per capita is only a little lower. Even Canada, which is comparable in size to the United States, has a lower GDP and GDP per capita.[17] Table 9.1

table 9.1   COMPARATIVE ANALYSIS OF SELECTED COUNTRIES

Country	Population (in Millions)	GDP (U.S.$ in Billions)	Exports (U.S.$ in Billions)	Imports (U.S.$ in Billions)	Internet Users (in Millions)	Cell Phones (in Millions)	Broadcast Television Stations
Brazil	190	1,840	159.2	115.6	42.6	99.9	138
Canada	33.4	1,270	440.1	394.4	22	17	80
China	1,322	7,040	1,220	917.4	137	461	3,240
Honduras	7.5	24.69	3.9	6.8	0.34	2.2	11
India	1.130	2,970	140.8	224.1	60	166	562
Japan	127.4	4,310	665.7	571.1	87.5	101.7	211
Jordan	6	28.18	6	11.1	0.80	4.3	20
Kenya	37	57.65	3.8	7.6	2.8	6.5	8
Mexico	108.7	1,350	267.5	279.3	22	57	236
Russia	141.3	2,080	348.9	226.5	25.7	120	7,306
South Africa	44	467.6	71.5	76.6	5.1	34	556
Switzerland	7.5	300.9	201	189.6	4.4	7.4	115
Turkey	71	667.7	110.5	156.9	12.3	43.6	635
Thailand	65	519.9	143.1	121.9	8.5	40.8	111
U.S.	301	1,386	1,100	2,000	208	233	2,218

Source: CIA, *The World Fact Book*, https://cia.gov/library/publications/the-world-factbook/index.html (Jan. 28, 2008); "Global Online Populations" CLickZ Stats, www.clickz.com/showPage.html?page=151151 (accessed Jan. 21, 2008).

gross domestic product (GDP) The market value of a nation's total output of goods and services for a given period; an overall measure of economic standing

provides a comparative economic analysis of 15 countries, including the United States. Knowledge about per capita income, credit, and the distribution of income provides general insights into market potential.

Opportunities for international trade are not limited to countries with the highest incomes. Some nations are progressing at a much faster rate than they were a few years ago, and these countries—especially in Latin America, Africa, eastern Europe, and the Middle East—have great market potential. Consider the market potential for bubble gum, sales of which are growing rapidly across the developing world while remaining flat in the United States. In India, for example, sales are growing between 10 and 15 percent a year. Cadbury Schweppes is capitalizing on the market potential for bubble gum in India by introducing Bubbaloo, which has a squirt of liquid in the center, using the same distribution system employed to sell its chocolate bars. Bubbaloo is also competing with Wm Wrigley Jr. Company's Boomer gum and Perfetti Vann Mellee SpA's Bib Babol gum.[18] Marketers must, however, understand the political and legal environments before they can convert buying power of customers in these countries into actual demand for specific products.

Political, Legal, and Regulatory Forces

The political, legal, and regulatory forces of the environment are closely intertwined in the United States. To a large degree, the same is true in many countries internationally. Typically, legislation is enacted, legal decisions are interpreted, and regulatory agencies are operated by elected or appointed officials. A country's legal and regulatory infrastructure is a direct reflection of the political climate in the country. In some countries, this political climate is determined by the people via elections, whereas in other countries leaders are appointed or have assumed leadership based on certain powers. Although laws and regulations have direct effects on a firm's operations in a country, political forces are indirect and often not clearly known in all countries. For example, the need to work with the government of China to enter and establish operations in the country has been a highly political process since the advent of Communist rule.

The political climate in a country or region, political officials in a country, and political officials in charge of trade agreements directly affect the legislation and regulations (or lack thereof). Within industries, elected or appointed officials of influential industry associations also set the tone for the regulatory environment that guides operations in a particular industry. For example, the American Marketing Association—one of the largest professional associations for marketers with 38,000 members worldwide in every area of marketing—has established Ethical Norms and Values for Marketers that guide the marketing profession in the United States.[19]

A nation's political system, laws, regulatory bodies, special-interest groups, and courts all have great impact on international marketing. A government's policies toward public and private enterprise, consumers, and foreign firms influence marketing across national boundaries. Some countries have established import barriers, such as tariffs. An **import tariff** is any duty levied by a nation on goods bought outside its borders and brought into the country. Because they raise the prices of foreign goods, tariffs impede free trade between nations. Tariffs are usually designed either to raise revenue for a country or to protect domestic products. In the United States, tariff revenues account for less than 2 percent of total federal revenues, down from about 50 percent of total federal revenues in the early 1900s.[20]

Nontariff trade restrictions include quotas and embargoes. A **quota** is a limit on the amount of goods an importing country will accept for certain product categories in a specific period of time. An **embargo** is a government's suspension of trade in a particular product or with a given country. Embargoes are generally directed at specific goods or countries and are established for political, health, or religious reasons. For example, the United States forbids the importation of uncertified Iberian ham, absinthe, and any product that contains dog or cat fur.[21] Laws regarding pricing policies may also serve as trade barriers. Great Britain, for example, has weaker antitrust laws than the United States and is generally more accepting of price collusion. Consequently many products cost more in Britain than in the United States. Because customers may be unable to afford the higher prices of imported products, such policies effectively create barriers to foreign trade.

import tariff A duty levied by a nation on goods bought outside its borders and brought into the country

quota A limit on the amount of goods an importing country will accept for certain product categories in a specific period of time

embargo A government's suspension of trade in a particular product or with a given country

exchange controls Government restrictions on the amount of a particular currency that can be bought or sold

balance of trade The difference in value between a nation's exports and its imports

Exchange controls, government restrictions on the amount of a particular currency that can be bought or sold, may also limit international trade. They can force businesspeople to buy and sell foreign products through a central agency, such as a central bank. On the other hand, to promote international trade, some countries have joined to form free trade zones, multinational economic communities that eliminate tariffs and other trade barriers. Such regional trade alliances are discussed later in the chapter. Foreign currency exchange rates also affect the prices marketers can charge in foreign markets. Fluctuations in the international monetary market can change the prices charged across national boundaries on a daily basis. Thus, these fluctuations must be considered in any international marketing strategy.

Countries may limit imports to maintain a favorable balance of trade. The **balance of trade** is the difference in value between a nation's exports and its imports. When a nation exports more products than it imports, a favorable balance of trade exists because money is flowing into the country. The United States has a negative balance of trade for goods and services of $759 billion.[22] A negative balance of trade is considered harmful because it means U.S. dollars are supporting foreign economies at the expense of U.S. companies and workers. At the same time, U.S. citizens benefit from the assortment of imported products and their typically lower prices.

Many nontariff barriers, such as quotas and minimum price levels set on imports, port-of-entry taxes, and stringent health and safety requirements, still make it difficult for U.S. companies to export their products. For example, the collectivistic nature of Japanese culture and the high-context nature of Japanese communication make some types of direct marketing messages less effective and may predispose many Japanese to support greater regulation of direct marketing practices.[23] A government's attitude toward importers has a direct impact on the economic feasibility of exporting to that country.

Global Diversity

Cargill recognizes the value of diversity and how it supports global competitiveness.

What does the provider of a good idea look like?
Maybe not always what we assume.
Maybe it's someone who doesn't look like us.
Someone with a totally unique perspective,
whose eyes and mind see things differently,
because they haven't viewed the same things as us.
Great companies know that ideas have many sources,
and working with diverse suppliers helps them succeed.
We're reminded of the lesson each day in 61 countries.

To learn more about Cargill's Supplier Diversity Initiative, go to www.cargillsupplierdiversity.com

www.cargill.com

Cargill
Nourishing Ideas. Nourishing People.

Ethical and Social Responsibility Forces

Differences in national standards are illustrated by what the Mexicans call *la mordida:* "the bite." The use of payoffs and bribes is deeply entrenched in many governments. Because U.S. trade and corporate policy, as well as U.S. law, prohibits direct involvement in payoffs and bribes, U.S. companies may have a hard time competing with foreign firms that engage in these practices. Some U.S. businesses that refuse to make payoffs are forced to hire local consultants, public relations firms, or advertising agencies, which results in indirect payoffs. The ultimate decision about whether to give small tips or gifts where they are customary must be based on a company's code of ethics. However, under the Foreign Corrupt Practices Act of 1977, it is illegal for U.S. firms to attempt to make large payments or bribes to influence policy decisions of foreign governments. Nevertheless, facilitating payments, or small payments to support the performance of standard tasks, are often acceptable. The Foreign Corrupt Practices Act also subjects all publicly held U.S. corporations to rigorous internal controls and record-keeping requirements for their overseas operations. Many other countries have also outlawed bribery.

Differences in ethical standards can also affect marketing efforts. In China and Vietnam, for example, standards regarding intellectual property differ dramatically from those in the United States, creating potential conflicts for marketers of computer software,

table 9.2   PERCEPTIONS OF THE LEAST AND MOST CORRUPT COUNTRIES

Least Corrupt	Most Corrupt
1. New Zealand	1. Somalia
2. Denmark	2. Myanmar
3. Finland	3. Iraq
4. Singapore	4. Haiti
5. Sweden	5. Uzbekistan
6. Iceland	6. Tonga
7. Netherlands	7. Afghanistan
8. Switzerland	8. Sudan
9. Norway	9. Chad
10. Canada	10. Laos
11. Australia	11. Equatorial Guinea
12. Luxembourg	12. Guinea
13. United Kingdom	13. Congo, Democratic Republic

* The United States is tied for twentieth least-corrupt nation.

Source: "Transparency International Corruption Perceptions Index 2007," Transparency International, Sept. 26, 2007, www.transparency.org/news_room/latest_news/press_releases/2007/2007_09_26_cpi_2007_en.

music, and books. In fact, the World Customs Organization estimates that pirated and counterfeit goods comprise as much as 5 to 7 percent of worldwide merchandise trade, particularly in China, resulting in lost sales of $512 billion a year. Among the products routinely counterfeited are consumer electronics, pharmaceuticals, cell phones, cigarettes, watches, shoes, motorcycles, and automobiles.[24] For example, several U.S. film studios—Disney, Twentieth Century Fox, Paramount Pictures, Universal Studios, and Columbia Pictures—teamed up to file a lawsuit in China against Beijing Shiji Haihong Commerce and Trade Company for allegedly selling counterfeit movies distributed by the studios.[25]

When marketers do business abroad, they sometimes perceive that other business cultures have different modes of operation.[26] This uneasiness is especially pronounced for marketers who have not traveled extensively or interacted much with foreigners in business or social settings. For example, a perception exists among many in the United States that U.S. firms are often different from those in other countries. This implied perspective of "us" versus "them" is also common in other countries. Table 9.2 indicates the countries that businesspeople, risk analysts, and the general public perceived as the most and least corrupt. In business, the idea that "we" differ from "them" is called the self-reference criterion (SRC). The SRC is the unconscious reference to one's own cultural values, experiences, and knowledge. When confronted with a situation, we react on the basis of knowledge we have accumulated over a lifetime, which is usually grounded in our culture of origin (and often rooted in our religious beliefs). Our reactions are based on meanings, values, and symbols that relate to our culture but may not have the same relevance to people of other cultures.

However, many businesspeople adopt the principle of "When in Rome, do as the Romans do." These businesspeople adapt to the cultural practices of the country they are in and use the host country's cultural practices as the rationalization for sometimes straying from their own ethical values when doing business internationally. For example, by defending the payment of bribes or "greasing the wheels of business" and other questionable practices in this fashion, some businesspeople are resorting to **cultural relativism**—the concept that morality varies from one culture to another and that business practices are therefore differentially defined as right or wrong by particular cultures.

Because of differences in cultural and ethical standards, many companies are working both individually and collectively to establish ethics programs and standards for international business conduct.[27] Levi Strauss's code of ethics, for example, bars the firm from manufacturing in countries where workers are known to be abused. Starbucks's global code of ethics strives to protect agricultural workers who harvest coffee beans. Many other firms, including Texas Instruments, Coca-Cola, Du Pont, Hewlett-Packard, Levi Strauss & Company, Texaco, and Wal-Mart, endorse following responsible business practices internationally. These companies support a globally based resource system called Business for Social Responsibility (BSR). BSR tracks emerging issues and trends, provides information on corporate leadership and best practices, conducts educational workshops and training, and assists organizations in developing practical business ethics tools. It addresses such issues as community investment,

cultural relativism The concept that morality varies from one culture to another and that business practices are therefore differentially defined as right or wrong by particular cultures

RESPONSIBLE marketing?

Would You Like Paper . . . or Paper?: The Worldwide Debate on Paper Versus Plastic Bags

ISSUE: Should plastic bags be banned globally?

What started in London as a Parliamentary bill to ban free plastic bags among retailers has sweeping implications throughout the world. The capital of Bangladesh was an innovator in 2002 when it banned plastic bags, but the world market has been slow to follow—until now. San Francisco has banned plastic bags, Ireland is now charging a nationwide tax of 15 cents on all supermarket shopping bags, and Australia and China are planning a similar program. Whole Foods, the United States' leading natural and organic supermarket, ended its use of plastic bags on Earth Day 2008. Whole Foods estimates this move will keep 150 million new plastic grocery bags out of the environment each year. Annual usage of plastic bags worldwide is estimated to be between 500 billion to 1 trillion.

Why are disposable plastic bags under fire? First, they do not disintegrate for more than 1,000 years, contributing to our landfill crisis, "rivaling the cockroach for indestructibility." The bags also contribute to a throw-away mentality, not a recycling one. The bags pose a serious threat to wildlife, particularly birds, turtles, and other sea creatures. According to the World Wildlife Fund, nearly 200 different species of sea life die after consuming plastic bags they thought were food. Plastic bags make up 10 percent of all debris on U.S. coastlines.

With the plastic bag industry facing scrutiny and abandonment, new technologies are coming into play to manufacture environmentally friendly plastic bags. Symphony Environmental Technologies in the United Kingdom has produced an additive that makes plastic bags break down in only two years. Diamant Film produces a plastic that biodegrades into nothing but carbon dioxide, water, and biomass. Should retailers continue to use plastic bags if they can be produced in an eco-friendly way?[a]

corporate social responsibility, the environment, governance, and accountability. BSR has also established formal partnerships with other organizations that focus on corporate responsibility in Brazil, Israel, the United Kingdom, Chile, and Panama.[28]

Competitive Forces

Competition is often viewed as a staple of the global marketplace. Customers thrive on the choices offered by competition, and firms constantly seek opportunities to outmaneuver their competition to gain customers' loyalty. Firms typically identify their competition when they establish target markets worldwide. Customers who are seeking alternative solutions to their product needs find the firms that can solve those needs. However, the increasingly interconnected international marketplace and advances in technology have resulted in competitive forces that are unique to the international marketplace.

Beyond the types of competition (i.e., brand, product, generic, and total budget competition) and types of competitive structures (i.e., monopoly, oligopoly, monopolistic competition, and pure competition), which are discussed in Chapter 3, firms that operate internationally must do the following:

- Be aware of the competitive forces in the countries they target
- Identify the interdependence of countries and the global competitors in those markets
- Be mindful of a new breed of customers: the global customer

Each country has unique competitive aspects—often founded in the other environmental forces (i.e., sociocultural, technological, political, legal, regulatory, and economic forces)—that are often independent of the competitors in that market. The most globally competitive countries are listed in Table 9.3. Although competitors drive competition, nations establish the infrastructure and the rules for the types of competition that can take place. For example, Microsoft's almost monopolistic dominance in many countries' markets led the United Nations' European Commission to a long-standing legal battle over the firm's marketing and competitive practices related to its bundling of a media player with its Windows computer operating system. Microsoft ultimately lost the battle as well as an appeal to the Court of First Instance and likely will pay fines and penalties in excess of $2.77 billion.[29] Like the United States, other countries allow some monopoly structures to exist. For example, most alcohol sales in Sweden are made through the governmental store Systembolaget, which is legally supported by the Swedish Alcohol Retail Monopoly. According to Systembolaget, the Swedish Alcohol Retail Monopoly exists for one reason: "to minimize alcohol-related problems by selling alcohol in a responsible way, without profit motive."[30]

A new breed of customer—the global customer—has changed the landscape of international competition drastically. Firms used to simply produce goods or services and provide local markets with information about the features and uses of their goods and services. Customers seldom had opportunities to compare products from competitors, know details about the competing products' features, and compare

table 9.3 RANKING OF THE MOST COMPETITIVE COUNTRIES IN THE WORLD

1. United States	11. Korea, Rep.
2. Switzerland	12. Hong Kong SAR
3. Denmark	13. Canada
4. Sweden	14. Taiwan, China
5. Germany	15. Austria
6. Finland	16. Norway
7. Singapore	17. Israel
8. Japan	18. France
9. United Kingdom	19. Australia
10. Netherlands	20. Belgium

Source: From Porter/Sala-i-Martin/Shwab, *The Global Competitiveness Report 2007–2008,* World Economic Forum (Palgrave Macmillan), www.weforum.org/en/initiatives/gcp/Global%20Competitiveness%20Report/index.htm.

other options beyond the local (country or region) markets. However, not only do customers who travel the globe expect to be able to buy the same product in most of the world's more than 200 countries, but they also expect that the product they buy in their local store in Miami will have the same features as similar products sold in London or even in Beijing. If the quality of the product or its features are more advanced in an international market, customers will soon demand that their local markets offer the same product at the same or lower prices.

Technological Forces

Advances in technology have made international marketing much easier. Interactive web systems, instant messaging, and podcast downloads (along with the traditional vehicles of voice mail, e-mail, fax, and cell phones) make international marketing activities more affordable and convenient. Internet use has accelerated dramatically within the United States and abroad. In Japan, 87.5 million have Internet access, and more than 25 million Russians, 60 million Indians, and 137 million Chinese are logging on to the Internet (see Table 9.1).[31] The majority of young adults (age 16 to 24) in Europe prefer advertisements on the Web over any other media vehicle; these ads are more directly targeting their needs.[32]

In many developing countries that lack the level of technological infrastructure found in the United States and Japan, marketers are beginning to capitalize on opportunities to leapfrog existing technology. For example, cellular and wireless phone technology is reaching many countries at a more affordable rate than traditional hard-wired telephone systems. Consequently opportunities for growth in the cell phone market remain strong in Southeast Asia, Africa, and the Middle East. One opportunity created by the rapid growth in cell phone service contracts in China is the *shouji jiayouzhan,* or "cell phone gas station," which allows consumers to recharge their phone, camera, and PDA batteries quickly for the equivalent of 12 cents, and they can watch commercials during the ten-minute charging session.[33] Hewlett-Packard also hopes to bring new technologies to less-developed countries. The company has launched World e-Inclusion, an economic development initiative that seeks to apply technology-based solutions to empower people in developing countries. Pilot programs for the initiative have already yielded high-speed Internet connections for remote villages in Central America and specialized software for coffee growers in Sumatra.[34]

Staying Ahead of the Competition
Verizon offers a BlackBerry World Edition to maintain a competitive advantage.

green MARKETING

Long-Distance Wi-Fi

Advances in technology are a key force in facilitating international marketing. Wireless technology is not only allowing people to access e-mail and instant messaging services, it is also helping Third World communities provide better health-care facilities in areas that are far from mainstream technology and transportation systems. This is all possible through a new product developed by Eric Brewer, a professor at the University of California–Berkeley, and his graduate students. They developed a wireless networking system they called Wildnet ("Wild" is short for "Wi-Fi over long distance"). Wildnet extends the range of Wi-Fi technology 100 times further than an airport "hot spot," up to a distance of 60 miles.

Relatively inexpensive to install, Wildnet uses the publicly available radio spectrum and the free Linux operating system on an inexpensive Intel computer board with off-the-shelf Wi-Fi radio chips. One router costs less than $400 and uses just 8 watts of power; it can even be run off a solar panel. The project currently has several deployments in India, Ghana, Guinea Bissau, and the Philippines. Several American Indian reservations and rural communities in Virginia have also expressed an interest.

Wildnet's most dramatic impact to date has been in southern India, where the high-speed links are bringing better eye care to poor villagers. Some of the local communities' clinics have set up links to regional hospitals to enable local residents to link to doctors without having to travel great distances. The Aravind Eye Hospital is a regional hospital that treats 1,400 new patients a month at five remote vision centers that are connected via Wildnet.

Brewer says, "Existing Western technologies are rarely a good fit. They are either too expensive or too complex" to work in poorer countries, particularly in low-density rural areas. Wildnet is proving to be cheaper and faster than satellite dishes, which can cost $10,000. Brewer doesn't believe that Wildnet will eliminate satellite, cellular broadband, Wi-Fi, or WiMax but is rather a complement to these—a "grassroots solution" for rural areas.

Wildnet opens up the opportunity for advancing economic development and the well-being of people in developing countries. These advances will create more educated and economically productive members of the global economy.[b]

Regional Trade Alliances, Markets, and Agreements

LO 3 To understand several important international trade agreements

Although many more firms are beginning to view the world as one huge marketplace, various regional trade alliances and specific markets affect companies engaging in international marketing; some create opportunities, and others impose constraints. In fact, while trade agreements in various forms have been around for centuries, the last century can be classified as the trade agreement period in the world's international development. Today, there are about 180 trade agreements around the world compared with only a select handful in the early 1960s. In this section, we examine several of the more critical regional trade alliances, markets, and changing conditions affecting markets. These include the North American Free Trade Agreement, the European Union, the Common Market of the Southern Cone, Asia-Pacific Economic Cooperation, and the World Trade Organization.

The North American Free Trade Agreement (NAFTA)

The **North American Free Trade Agreement (NAFTA),** implemented in 1994, effectively merged Canada, Mexico, and the United States into one market of nearly 440 million consumers. NAFTA will eliminate virtually all tariffs on goods produced and traded among Canada, Mexico, and the United States to create a free trade area by 2009. The estimated annual output for this trade alliance is more than $14 trillion.[35]

NAFTA makes it easier for U.S. businesses to invest in Mexico and Canada; provides protection for intellectual property (of special interest to high-technology and entertainment industries); expands trade by requiring equal treatment of U.S. firms in both countries; and simplifies country-of-origin rules, hindering Japan's use of Mexico as a staging ground for further penetration into U.S. markets. Although most tariffs on products coming to the United States will be lifted, duties on more sensitive products, such as household glassware, footwear, and some fruits and vegetables, will be phased out over a 15-year period.

Canada's 33.4 million consumers are relatively affluent, with a per capita GDP of $38,200.[36] Trade between the United States and Canada totals approximately $532 billion.[37] Currently exports to Canada support approximately 1.5 million U.S. jobs. Canadian investments in U.S. companies are also increasing, and various markets, including air travel, are opening as regulatory barriers dissolve.[38] In fact, Canada is the single largest trading partner of the United States.[39]

With a per capita GDP of $12,500, Mexico's 108.7 million consumers are less affluent than Canadian consumers. However, they bought more than $134 billion worth of U.S. products last year.[40] Many U.S. companies, including Hewlett-Packard, IBM, and General Motors, have taken advantage of Mexico's low labor costs and close proximity to the United States to set up production facilities, sometimes called *maquiladoras*. Production at the *maquiladoras*, especially in the automotive, electronics, and apparel industries, has grown rapidly as companies as diverse as Ford, John Deere, Motorola, Sara Lee, Kimberly-Clark, and VF Corporation set up facilities in north-central Mexican states. With the *maquiladoras* accounting for roughly half of Mexico's exports, Mexico has risen to become the world's twelfth-largest economy.[41] Although Mexico experienced financial instability throughout the 1990s, privatization of some government-owned firms and other measures instituted by the Mexican government and businesses, along with a booming U.S. economy, have helped Mexico's economy. Moreover, increasing trade between the United States and Canada constitutes a strong base of support for the ultimate success of NAFTA.

Mexico's membership in NAFTA links the United States and Canada with other Latin American countries, providing additional opportunities to integrate trade among all the nations in the Western Hemisphere. Indeed, efforts to create a free trade agreement among the 34 nations of North and South America are under way. Like NAFTA, the *Free Trade Area of the Americas (FTAA)* will progressively eliminate trade barriers and create the world's largest free trade zone, with 800 million people. However, the negotiations to complete the agreement have been contentious, and the agreement itself has become a lightning rod for antiglobalization activists. A related trade agreement—the *Dominican Republic–Central American Free Trade Agreement (DR-CAFTA)*—among Costa Rica, the Dominican Republic, El Salvador, Guatemala, Honduras, Nicaragua, and the United States has also been ratified in all those countries except Costa Rica. The United States has already begun implementing the provisions of the agreement with the countries that have ratified it. When these agreements are fully implemented, they will have great influences on trade in the region.

Despite its benefits, NAFTA has been controversial, and disputes continue to arise over its implementation. Exxon Mobil, for example, filed a lawsuit against the Canadian government for damages resulting from Canada's imposition of new costs on offshore petroleum projects, which the company believes violates the provisions of NAFTA.[42] Although many Americans feared the agreement would erase jobs in the United States, Mexicans have been disappointed that it failed to create more jobs. Although NAFTA has been controversial, it has become a positive factor for U.S.

North American Free Trade Agreement (NAFTA) An alliance that merges Canada, Mexico, and the United States into a single market

firms that want to engage in international marketing. Because licensing requirements have been relaxed under the pact, smaller businesses that previously could not afford to invest in Mexico and Canada will be able to do business in those markets without having to locate there. NAFTA's long phase-in period provides ample time for adjustment for those firms affected by reduced tariffs on imports. Furthermore, increased competition should lead to a more efficient market, and the long-term prospects of including most Western Hemisphere countries in the alliance promise additional opportunities for U.S. marketers.

The European Union (EU)

The **European Union (EU),** sometimes also referred to as the *European Community* or *Common Market,* was established in 1958 to promote trade among its members, which initially included Belgium, France, Italy, West Germany, Luxembourg, and the Netherlands. In 1991 East and West Germany united, and by 2007 the United Kingdom, Spain, Denmark, Greece, Portugal, Ireland, Austria, Finland, Sweden, Cyprus, Poland, Hungary, the Czech Republic, Slovenia, Estonia, Latvia, Lithuania, Slovakia, Malta, Romania, and Bulgaria had joined as well. (Croatia and Turkey have requested membership as well.)[43]

Until 1993 each nation functioned as a separate market, but in that year the members officially unified into one of the largest single world markets, which today includes nearly half a billion consumers with a combined GDP of more than $12 trillion.[44] The EU is a relatively diverse set of democratic European countries. It is not a state that is intended to replace existing country states, nor is it an organization for international cooperation. Instead, its member states have common institutions to which they delegate some of their sovereignty to allow specific matters of joint interest to be decided at the European level. The primary goals of the EU are to establish European citizenship; ensure freedom, security, and justice; promote economic and social progress; and assert Europe's role in world trade.[45]

To facilitate free trade among members, the EU is working toward standardizing business regulations and requirements, import duties, and value-added taxes; eliminating customs checks; and creating a standardized currency for use by all members. Many European nations (Austria, Belgium, Finland, France, Germany, Ireland, Italy, Luxembourg, the Netherlands, Portugal, and Spain) are linked to a common currency, the *euro,* but several EU members have rejected the euro in their countries (e.g., Denmark, Sweden, and the United Kingdom). Although the common currency may necessitate that marketers modify their pricing strategies and it subjects them to increased competition, it also frees companies that sell products among European countries from the complexities of exchange rates. The long-term goals are to eliminate all trade barriers within the EU, improve the economic efficiency of the EU nations, and stimulate economic growth, thus making the union's economy more competitive in global markets, particularly against Japan and other Pacific Rim nations, and North America.

As the EU nations attempt to function as one large market, consumers in the EU may become more homogeneous in their needs and wants. Marketers should be aware, however, that cultural differences among the nations may require modifications in the marketing mix for customers in each nation. Differences in tastes and preferences in these diverse markets are significant for international marketers. But there is evidence that such differences may be diminishing, especially within the younger population that includes teenagers and young professionals. Gathering information about these distinct tastes and preferences is likely to remain a very important factor in developing marketing mixes that satisfy the needs of European customers.

The Common Market of the Southern Cone (MERCOSUR)

The **Common Market of the Southern Cone (MERCOSUR)** was established in 1991 under the Treaty of Asunción to unite Argentina, Brazil, Paraguay, and Uruguay as a free trade alliance. Venezuela joined in 2006. Currently, Bolivia, Chile, Colombia, Ecuador, and Peru are associate members. The alliance represents two-thirds of South

European Union (EU) An alliance that promotes trade among its member countries in Europe

Common Market of the Southern Cone (MERCO-SUR) An alliance that promotes the free circulation of goods, services, and production factors, and has a common external tariff and commercial policy among member nations in South America

America's population and has a combined GDP of more than $1.1 trillion, making it the third-largest trading bloc behind NAFTA and the EU. Like NAFTA, MERCOSUR promotes "the free circulation of goods, services, and production factors among the countries" and establishes a common external tariff and commercial policy.[46]

The Asia-Pacific Economic Cooperation (APEC)

The **Asia-Pacific Economic Cooperation (APEC),** established in 1989, promotes open trade and economic and technical cooperation among member nations, which initially included Australia, Brunei Darussalam, Canada, Indonesia, Japan, Korea, Malaysia, New Zealand, the Philippines, Singapore, Thailand, and the United States. Since then the alliance has grown to include China, Hong Kong, Taiwan, Mexico, Papua New Guinea, Chile, Peru, Russia, and Vietnam. The 21-member alliance represents 2.6 billion consumers, has a combined GDP of $19 trillion, and accounts for nearly 49 percent of global trade. APEC differs from other international trade alliances in its commitment to facilitating business and its practice of allowing the business/private sector to participate in a wide range of APEC activities.[47]

Despite economic turmoil and a recession in Asia in recent years, companies of the APEC have become increasingly competitive and sophisticated in global business in the last two decades. Moreover, the markets of the APEC offer tremendous opportunities to marketers who understand them. In fact, the APEC region has consistently been the most economically dynamic part of the world. In its first decade, the APEC countries generated almost 70 percent of worldwide economic growth and the APEC region consistently outperformed the rest of the world.[48]

Japanese firms in particular have made tremendous inroads on world markets for automobiles, motorcycles, watches, cameras, and audio and video equipment. Products from Sony, Sanyo, Toyota, Mitsubishi, Canon, Suzuki, and Toshiba are sold all over the world and have set standards of quality by which other products are often judged. Sony is often viewed as the benchmark of the global company. Despite the high volume of trade between the United States and Japan, the two economies are less integrated than the U.S. economy is with Canada and western Europe. If Japan imported goods at the same rate as other major nations, the United States would sell billions of dollars more each year to Japan.

The most important emerging economic power is China, which has become one of the most productive manufacturing nations. China, which is now the United

Asia-Pacific Economic Cooperation (APEC) An alliance that promotes open trade and economic and technical cooperation among member nations throughout the world

Asia-Pacific Economic Cooperation (APEC)

The "China 8" team makes and sells the world's first container ads. Erudite, the advertiser, specializes in tracking and security technology for containers.

States' second-largest trading partner, has initiated economic reforms to stimulate its economy by privatizing many industries, restructuring its banking system, and increasing public spending on infrastructure. As a result, China has become a manufacturing powerhouse, with an economy growing at a rate of 11 percent a year.[49] Many foreign companies, including Nike and Adidas, are opening factories in China to take advantage of its low labor costs, and China has become a major producer of compact disc players, cell phones, portable stereos, and personal computers. The potential of China's consumer market is so vast that it is almost impossible to measure, but doing business in China also entails many risks. Political and economic instability—especially inflation, corruption, and erratic policy shifts—has undercut marketers' efforts to stake a claim in what could become the world's largest market. Moreover, piracy is a major issue, and protecting a brand name in China is difficult. Because copying is a tradition in China and laws that protect copyrights and intellectual property are weak and minimally enforced, the country is flooded with counterfeit videos, movies, compact discs, computer software, furniture, and clothing.

Pacific Rim regions such as South Korea, Thailand, Singapore, Taiwan, and Hong Kong have become major manufacturing and financial centers. Even before Korean brand names such as Samsung, Daewoo, and Hyundai became household words, these products prospered under U.S. company labels, including GE, GTE, RCA, and JCPenney. Singapore boasts huge global markets for rubber goods and pharmaceuticals. Hong Kong is still a strong commercial center after being transferred to Chinese control. Vietnam is becoming one of Asia's fastest-growing markets for U.S. businesses, but Taiwan may have the most promising future of all the Pacific Rim nations as a strong local economy and low import barriers draw increasing imports. Firms from Thailand and Malaysia are also thriving, carving out niches in the world markets for a variety of products from toys to automobile parts.

The markets of APEC offer tremendous opportunities to marketers who understand them. For example, YUM! Brands, the number two fast-food chain after McDonald's, opened its first KFC fast-food restaurant in China in 1987 and has since opened 2,000 KFC and Pizza Hut outlets in China, as well as a new concept store called East Dawning, which serves Chinese fast food. China accounts for about 16 percent of the company's profits.[50]

The World Trade Organization (WTO)

The **World Trade Organization (WTO)** is a global trade association that promotes free trade among 149 member nations. The WTO is the successor to the **General Agreement on Tariffs and Trade (GATT),** which was originally signed by 23 nations in 1947 to provide a forum for tariff negotiations and a place where international trade problems could be discussed and resolved. Rounds of GATT negotiations reduced trade barriers for most products and established rules to guide international commerce, such as rules to prevent **dumping:** the selling of products at unfairly low prices.

The WTO came into being in 1995 as a result of the Uruguay Round (1988–1994) of GATT negotiations. Broadly, WTO is the main worldwide organization that deals with the rules of trade between nations; its main function is to ensure that trade flows as smoothly, predictably, and freely as possible between nations. In 2006, 149 nations were members of the WTO.[51]

Fulfilling the purpose of the WTO requires eliminating trade barriers; educating individuals, companies, and governments about trade rules around the world; and assuring global markets that no sudden changes of policy will occur. At the heart of the WTO are agreements that provide legal ground rules for international commerce and trade policy. Based in Geneva, Switzerland, the WTO also serves as a forum for dispute resolution.[52] For example, the United States, Canada, and the European Union complained to the WTO that new WTO member China levies tariffs on imported car parts as if they were complete vehicles, putting foreign manufacturers of auto parts at a distinct disadvantage in China. After attempts to resolve the dispute failed, the nations asked the WTO to mediate and rule on whether China's actions are lawful.[53]

World Trade Organization (WTO) An entity that promotes free trade among member nations by eliminating trade barriers and educating individuals, companies, and governments about trade rules around the world

General Agreement on Tariffs and Trade (GATT) An agreement among nations to reduce worldwide tariffs and increase international trade

dumping Selling products at unfairly low prices

Modes of Entry Into International Markets

L O 4 To identify methods of international market entry

Marketers enter international markets and continue to engage in marketing activities at several levels of international involvement. Traditionally, firms have adopted one of four different modes of entering an international market; each successive "stage" represents different degrees of international involvement.

- Stage 1: No regular export activities
- Stage 2: Export via independent representatives (agents)
- Stage 3: Establishment of one or more sales subsidiaries internationally
- Stage 4: Establishment of international production/manufacturing facilities[54]

As Figure 9.1 shows, companies' international involvement today covers a wide spectrum, from purely domestic marketing to global marketing. Domestic marketing involves marketing strategies aimed at markets within the home country; at the other extreme, global marketing entails developing marketing strategies for the entire world (or at least more than one major region of the world). Many firms with an international presence start out as small companies serving local and regional domestic markets and expand to national markets before considering opportunities in foreign markets (the born global firm, described earlier, is one exception to this internationalization process). Limited exporting may occur even if a firm makes little or no effort to obtain foreign sales. Foreign buyers may seek out the company and/or its products, or a distributor may discover the firm's products and export them. The level of commitment to international marketing is a major variable in global marketing strategies. In this section,

figure 9.1

LEVELS OF INVOLVEMENT IN GLOBAL MARKETING

Globalized marketing
Marketing strategies are developed for the entire world (or more than one major region), with the focus on the similarities across regions and country markets.

Regional marketing
Marketing strategies are developed for each major region, with the countries in the region being marketed to in the same way based on similarities across the region's country markets.

Multinational marketing
International markets are a consideration in the marketing strategy, with customization for the country markets based on critical differences across regions and country markets.

Limited exporting
The firm develops no international marketing strategies, but international distributors, foreign firms, or selected customers purchase some of its products.

Domestic marketing
All marketing strategies focus on the market in the country of origin.

As a matter of fact, the water you drink does make a difference.

- Matt Damon

Over one billion people around the world lack clean water. Join me in my partnership with Ethos Water and H2O Africa and make a difference in the world water crisis. Every time you buy a bottle of Ethos, money goes to help provide children with the access to clean water they need. So if you choose to drink bottled water, please choose to make a difference. To learn more, **visit ethoswater.com.**

Every Bottle Makes a Difference."

Ethos is a proud supporter of "Running The Sahara." In theaters this spring.

A donation of $0.05 is made for every bottle of Ethos sold toward the Ethos Water Fund goal of donating $10 million by 2010.

Business Across Borders

Ethos Water supports a cause and exports resources to provide clean water for children in Africa.

importing The purchase of products from a foreign source

exporting The sale of products to foreign markets

trading company A company that links buyers and sellers in different countries

we examine importing and exporting, trading companies, licensing and franchising, contract manufacturing, joint ventures, direct ownership, and some of the other approaches to international involvement.

Importing and Exporting

Importing and exporting require the least amount of effort and commitment of resources. **Importing** is the purchase of products from a foreign source. **Exporting,** the sale of products to foreign markets, enables firms of all sizes to participate in global business. A firm may find an exporting intermediary to take over most marketing functions associated with marketing to other countries. This approach entails minimal effort and cost. Modifications in packaging, labeling, style, or color may be the major expenses in adapting a product for the foreign market

Export agents bring together buyers and sellers from different countries and collect a commission for arranging sales. Export houses and export merchants purchase products from different companies and then sell them abroad. They are specialists at understanding customers' needs in global markets. Using exporting intermediaries involves limited risk because no foreign direct investment is required.

Buyers from foreign companies and governments provide a direct method of exporting and eliminate the need for an intermediary. These buyers encourage international exchange by contacting overseas firms about their needs and the opportunities available in exporting to them. Indeed, research suggests that many small firms tend to rely heavily on such native contacts, especially in developed markets, and remain production oriented rather than marketing oriented in their approach to international marketing.[55] Domestic firms that want to export with minimal effort and investment should seek out export intermediaries. Once a company becomes involved in exporting, it usually develops more knowledge of the country and becomes more confident in its competitiveness.[56]

Trading Companies

Marketers sometimes employ a **trading company,** which links buyers and sellers in different countries but is not involved in manufacturing and does not own assets related to manufacturing. Trading companies buy products in one country at the lowest price consistent with quality and sell them to buyers in another country. For instance, SCiNet offers a 24-hour-per-day online world trade system that connects 17 million companies in 245 countries, offering more than 50 million products and services. The SCiNet system offers online payments and handles customs, tariffs, and inspections of goods for their clients. A trading company acts like a wholesaler, taking on much of the responsibility of finding markets while facilitating all marketing aspects of a transaction. An important function of trading companies is taking title to products and performing all the activities necessary to move the products to the targeted foreign country. For example, large grain-trading companies that operate out of home offices in both the United States and overseas control a major portion of the world's trade in basic food commodities. These trading companies sell homogeneous agricultural commodities that can be stored and moved rapidly in response to market conditions.

Trading companies reduce risk for firms that want to get involved in international marketing. A trading company provides producers with information about

Top 10 global franchises

1. **Subway**
2. **KFC Corp.**
3. **McDonald's**
4. **Dunkin' Donuts**
5. **Domino's Pizza LLC**
6. **Curves**
7. **RE/MAX International, Inc.**
8. **Sonic Drive-In Restaurants**
9. **Pizza Hut**
10. **UPS Store/Mail Boxes Etc.**

Source: "2008 Top Global Franchises," *Entrepreneur,* http://www .entrepreneur.com/topglobal/reprinted with permission of Entrepreneur.com, Inc. © 2008 by Entrepreneur.com, Inc. All rights reserved.

licensing An alternative to direct investment that requires a licensee to pay commissions or royalties on sales or supplies used in manufacturing

franchising A form of licensing in which a franchiser, in exchange for a financial commitment, grants a franchisee the right to market its product in accordance with the franchiser's standards

contract manufacturing The practice of hiring a foreign firm to produce a designated volume of the domestic firm's product or a component of it to specification; the final product carries the domestic firm's name

products that meet quality and price expectations in domestic and international markets. Additional services a trading company may provide include consulting, marketing research, advertising, insurance, product research and design, legal assistance, warehousing, and foreign exchange.

Licensing and Franchising

When potential markets are found across national boundaries, and when production, technical assistance, or marketing know-how is required, **licensing** is an alternative to direct investment. The licensee (the owner of the foreign operation) pays commissions or royalties on sales or supplies used in manufacturing. The licensee may also pay an initial down payment or fee when the licensing agreement is signed. Exchanges of management techniques or technical assistance are primary reasons for licensing agreements. Yoplait, for example, is a French yogurt that is licensed for production in the United States; the Yoplait brand tries to maintain a French image. Similarly, sports organizations such as the International Olympic Committee (IOC), which is responsible for the Olympic Games, typically concentrate on organizing their sporting events while licensing the merchandise and other products that are sold.

Licensing is an attractive alternative when resources are unavailable for direct investment or when the core competencies of the firm or organization are not related to the product being sold (such as in the case of Olympics merchandise). Licensing can also be a viable alternative when the political stability of a foreign country is in doubt. In addition, licensing is especially advantageous for small manufacturers wanting to launch a well-known brand internationally. For example, Questor Corporation owns the Spalding name but produces not a single golf club or tennis ball itself; all Spalding sporting products are licensed worldwide.

Franchising is a form of licensing in which a company (the franchiser) grants a franchisee the right to market its product, using its name, logo, methods of operation, advertising, products, and other elements associated with the franchiser's business, in return for a financial commitment and an agreement to conduct business in accordance with the franchiser's standard of operations. This arrangement allows franchisers to minimize the risks of international marketing in four ways: (1) the franchiser does not have to put up a large capital investment; (2) the franchiser's revenue stream is fairly consistent because franchisees pay a fixed fee and royalties; (3) the franchiser retains control of its name and increases global penetration of its product; and (4) franchise agreements ensure a certain standard of behavior from franchisees, which protects the franchise name.[57] Subway, Pizza Hut, and KFC are among the "top ten" franchisers in the world; other well-known franchisers with international visibility include Holiday Inn, Marriott, McDonald's, and Wendy's.

Contract Manufacturing

Contract manufacturing occurs when a company hires a foreign firm to produce a designated volume of the firm's product (or a component of a product) to specification and the final product carries the domestic firm's name. The Gap, for example, relies on contract manufacturing for some of its apparel; Reebok uses Korean contract manufacturers to produce many of its athletic shoes. Marketing may be handled by the contract manufacturer or by the contracting company.

Three specific forms of contract manufacturing have become popular in the last decade: outsourcing, offshoring, and offshore outsourcing. **Outsourcing** is defined as the contracting of noncore operations or jobs from internal production within a business to an external entity that specializes in that operation. For example, outsourcing certain elements of a firm's operations to China and Mexico has become popular. The majority of all footwear is now produced in China, regardless of the brand name on the shoe you wear. Services can also be outsourced. Tribune, which owns daily newspapers such as *Newsday* and the *Chicago Tribune,* outsourced its customer service operations to a firm in the Philippines, in an effort to improve efficiency and boost customer service at the newspaper chain.[58] **Offshoring** is defined as moving a business process that was done domestically at the local factory to a foreign country, regardless of whether the production accomplished in the foreign country is performed by the local company (e.g., in a wholly owned subsidiary) or a third party (e.g., subcontractor). Typically, the production is moved to reap the advantages of lower cost of operations in the foreign location. **Offshore outsourcing** is the practice of contracting with an organization to perform some or all business functions in a country other than the country in which the product or service will be sold.

Joint Ventures

In international marketing, a **joint venture** is a partnership between a domestic firm and a foreign firm or government. Joint ventures are especially popular in industries that require large investments, such as natural resources extraction or automobile manufacturing. Control of the joint venture may be split equally, or one party may control decision making. Joint ventures are often a political necessity because of nationalism and government restrictions on foreign ownership. eBay, for example, shuttered its troubled online auction site in China and instead entered into a joint venture with a knowledgeable Chinese firm, Tom Online Inc.[59] Joint ventures may also occur when acquisition or internal development is not feasible or when the risks and constraints leave no other alternative. They also provide legitimacy in the eyes of the host country's citizens. Local partners have firsthand knowledge of the economic and sociopolitical environment and the workings of available distribution networks, and they may have privileged access to local resources (raw materials, labor management, and so on). However, joint venture relationships require trust throughout the relationship to provide a foreign partner with a ready means of implementing its own marketing strategy.[60] Joint ventures are assuming greater global importance because of cost advantages and the number of inexperienced firms that are entering foreign markets. They may be the result of a tradeoff between a firm's desire for completely unambiguous control of an enterprise and its quest for additional resources.

Strategic alliances are partnerships formed to create competitive advantage on a worldwide basis. They are very similar to joint ventures, but while joint ventures are defined in scope, strategic alliances are typically represented by an agreement to work together (which can ultimately mean more involvement than a joint venture). In an international strategic alliance, the firms in the alliance may have been traditional rivals competing for the same market. They may also be competing in certain markets while working together in other markets where it is beneficial for both parties. One such collaboration is the Sky Team Alliance—involving Northwest Airlines, KLM, Aero Mexico, Air France, Alitalia, Continental Airlines, TSA Czech Airlines, Delta, and Korean Air—which is designed to improve customer service among the nine firms. Another example of such an alliance is New United Motor Manufacturing, Inc. (NUMMI), formed by Toyota and General Motors to make automobiles for both firms. This alliance united the quality engineering of Japanese cars with the marketing expertise and market access of General Motors. Today NUMMI manufactures the popular Toyota Tacoma compact pickup truck, as well as the Toyota Corolla and the Pontiac Vibe.[61] Whereas joint ventures are formed to create a new identity, partners in international strategic alliances often retain their distinct identities, with each partner bringing a core competency to the union.

outsourcing The practice of contracting noncore operations with an organization that specializes in that operation

offshoring The practice of moving a business process that was done domestically at the local factory to a foreign country, regardless of whether the production accomplished in the foreign country is performed by the local company (e.g., in a wholly owned subsidiary) or a third party (e.g., subcontractor)

offshore outsourcing The practice of contracting with an organization to perform some or all business functions in a country other than the country in which the product or service will be sold

joint venture A partnership between a domestic firm and a foreign firm or government

strategic alliances A partnership that is formed to create a competitive advantage on a worldwide basis

E-ntertainment MARKETING

Skype Joins the Mobile World

Joint ventures are especially popular in industries that require large investments, such as information technology. Skype, using voiceover Internet protocol (VoIP) technology, has partnered with a company called 3 Mobile, a wireless carrier in Europe, Asia, and Australia. 3 Mobile, owned by Hong Kong's Hutchison Whampoa, will work with Skype to develop a global net phone service using a handset that is code-named "the white phone." Although there currently are no plans to bring the white phone to North America, the two companies will try to license it to other carriers and sell "unlocked versions" directly to consumers to use on other networks. This partnership was developed to create a competitive advantage in an area of emerging information technology.

Skype is a software program that allows users to make telephone calls from their computers to other Skype users free of charge or to landlines and cell phones for a fee. Acquired by eBay in 2005, Skype now has more than 246 million unique user accounts, and up to 10.1 million concurrent Skype users may be online at any one time. However, use of Skype's VoIP technology has shown a significant decrease in growth, so eBay must improve Skype's profitability. Currently only one-quarter to one-third of Skype customers are regular users, and the vast majority of their calls are free.

Skype's joint venture is developing a handset that can make long-distance international calls available free to other Skype users and for only a few cents per minute to non-Skype landlines and cell phones. The 3 Mobile phone uses software, called iSkoot, that provides multimedia web capabilities and web browsing, but like Apple's iPhone, it will be easy to use with a large button above the keypad to activate Skype's service for long-distance and international calls.

Joint ventures are gaining greater global importance because of cost advantage and the need for combining technologies to have market success. Combining the cell phone with the Skype VoIP technology is a great example of the sum being greater than its parts. Competition in the information technology industry is so fierce and the costs of competing on a global basis are so high that few companies can succeed without the help of partners. If the white phone is successful, however, competitors will throng to the market or try to emulate the success of this joint venture.[c]

The success rate of international alliances could be higher if a better fit between the companies existed. A strategic alliance should focus on a joint market opportunity from which all partners can benefit.[62] In the automobile, computer, and airline industries, strategic alliances are becoming the predominant means of competing internationally. Competition in these industries is so fierce and the costs of competing on a global basis are so high that few firms have all the resources needed to do it alone. Firms that lack the internal resources essential for international success may seek to collaborate with other companies. A shared mode of leadership among partner corporations combines joint abilities and allows collaboration from a distance. Focusing on customer value and implementing innovative ways to compete create a winning strategy.[63]

Direct Ownership

Once a company makes a long-term commitment to marketing in a foreign country that has a promising market as well as a suitable political and economic environment, **direct ownership** of a foreign subsidiary or division is a possibility. Liz Claiborne Inc., for example, is opening 24 Juicy Couture retail stores and 23 Juicy Couture shops within other retail stores in China, Taiwan, Hong Kong, and throughout southeast Asia after recognizing a favorable attitude toward U.S. fashion labels and haute couture in general.[64] Most foreign investment covers only manufacturing equipment or personnel because the expenses of developing a separate foreign distribution system can be tremendous. The opening of retail stores in Europe, Canada, or Mexico can require a staggering financial investment in facilities, research, and management.

The term **multinational enterprise,** sometimes called multinational corporation, refers to a firm that has operations or subsidiaries in many countries. Often the parent company is based in one country and carries on production, management, and marketing activities in other countries. The firm's subsidiaries may be autonomous so they can respond to the needs of individual international markets, or they may be part of a global network that is led by the headquarters' operations.

At the same time, a wholly owned foreign subsidiary may be allowed to operate independently of the parent company to give its management more freedom to adjust to the local environment. Cooperative arrangements are developed to assist in marketing efforts, production, and management. A wholly owned foreign subsidiary may export products to the home country, its market may serve as a test market for the firm's global products, or it may be a component of the firm's globalization efforts. Some U.S. automobile manufacturers, for example, import cars built by their foreign subsidiaries. A foreign subsidiary offers important tax, tariff, and other operating advantages. Table 9.4 lists the ten largest global corporations.

One of the greatest advantages of a multinational enterprise is the cross-cultural approach. A subsidiary usually operates under foreign management so it can develop a local identity. In particular, the firm (i.e., seller) is often expected to adapt, if needed,

direct ownership A situation in which a company owns subsidiaries or other facilities overseas

multinational enterprise A firm that has operations or subsidiaries in many countries

table 9.4   THE TEN LARGEST GLOBAL CORPORATIONS

Rank	Company	Country	Industry	Revenues (in millions)
1	Wal-Mart Stores	U.S.	General merchandiser	$351,139
2	Exxon Mobil	U.S.	Petroleum refining	$347,254
3	Royal Dutch/ Shell Group	Netherlands/ Britain	Petroleum refining	$318,845
4	BP	Britain	Petroleum refining	$274,316
5	General Motors	U.S.	Motor vehicles and parts	$207,349
6	Toyota Motor	Japan	Motor vehicles and parts	$204,746.4
7	Chevron	U.S.	Petroleum refining	$200,567
8	DaimlerChrysler	Germany	Motor vehicles and parts	$190,191.4
9	ConocoPhillips	U.S.	Petroleum refining	$172,451
10	Total	France	Petroleum refining	$168,356.7

Source: "Global 500: 2007," *Fortune,* http://money.cnn.com/magazines/fortune/global500/2007/ (accessed Jan. 21, 2008).

to the buyer's culture. Interestingly, the cultural values of customers in the younger age group (30 years and younger) is becoming increasingly similar around the world. Today, a 20-year-old in Russia is increasingly similar in mindset to a 20-year-old in China and a 20-year-old in the United States, especially with regard to their tastes in music, clothes, and cosmetics. This makes marketing goods and services to the younger population easier today than it was only ten years ago. Nevertheless, there is still great danger involved in having a wholly owned subsidiary in some parts of the world due to political uncertainty, terrorism threats, and economic instability.

Global Organizational Structures

LO 5 To examine various forms of global organizational structures

Firms develop their international marketing strategies and manage their marketing mixes (i.e., product, distribution, promotion, and price) by developing and maintaining an organizational structure that best leverages their resources and core competencies. This organizational structure is defined as the way a firm divides its operations into separate functions and/or value-adding units and coordinates its activities. Most firms undergo a step-by-step development in their internationalization efforts of the firm's people, processes, functions, culture, and structure.[65] The pyramid in Figure 9.2 symbolizes how deeply rooted the international operations and values are in the firm, with the base of the pyramid—structure—being the most difficult to change (especially in the short term). Three basic structures of international organizations exist: export departments, international divisions, and internationally integrated structures (e.g., product division structures, geographic area structures, and matrix structures). The existing structure of the firm, or the structure that the firm chooses to adopt, has implications for international marketing strategy.

Export Departments

For most firms, the early stages of international development are often informal and not fully planned. During this early stage, sales opportunities in the global marketplace

figure 9.2

ORGANIZATIONAL ARCHITECTURE

People

Processes
How global decisions are made and how work gets done

Functions
Business functions such as finance, HR, production, marketing, and accounting

Culture
The norms, values, beliefs, and artifacts that are shared among the people throughout the global organization

Structure
Export departments, international divisions, and internationally integrated organizations

motivate a company to engage internationally. For example, born global firms make exporting a primary objective from their inceptions. For most firms, however, very minimal, if any, organizational adjustments take place to accommodate international sales. Foreign sales are typically so small that many firms cannot justify allocating structural or other resources to the internationalization effort in the infancy of internationalization. Exporting, licensing, and using trading companies are preferred modes of international market entry for firms with an export department structure.

Some firms develop an export department as a subunit of the marketing department, whereas others organize it as a department that structurally coexists at an equal level with the other functional units. Clipsal, the Australian maker of more than 20,000 different lines of electrical accessories, has taken its number one position in Australia and achieved international success led by its high-quality products and operations of its export department. Clipsal's "Export Department offers global support in many areas and this has resulted in a level of teamwork that has significantly strengthened the Clipsal brand throughout the world."[66]

Another unique case of developing a successful export operation early after its inception is the born global firm of Logitech International. Logitech, founded in 1981, is a Swiss company that designs personal computer peripherals that enable people to effectively work, play, and communicate in the digital world. Its products include webcams, mice, trackballs, keyboards, speakers, headsets, interactive gaming devices, digital pens, and advanced universal remote controls.

As demand for a firm's goods and services grows or its commitments increase due to its internationalization efforts, it develops an international structure. Many firms evolve from using their export department structure to forming an international division.

International Divisions

A company's international division centralizes all of the responsibility for international operations (and in many cases, all international activities also become centralized in the international division). The typical international division concentrates human resources (i.e., international expertise) into one unit and serves as the central point for all information flow related to international operations (e.g., international market opportunities, international research and development). At the same time, firms with an international division structure take advantage of economies of scale by keeping manufacturing and related functions within the domestic divisions. Firms may develop international divisions at a relatively early as well as a rather mature stage of their international development. As such, these firms use exporting, licensing and franchising, trading companies, contract manufacturing, and joint ventures as possible modes of international market entry.

This international division structure illustrates the importance of coordination and cooperation among domestic and international operations. Frequent interaction and strategic planning meetings are required to make this structure work effectively. In particular, firms that use an international division structure are often organized domestically on the basis of functions or product divisions, whereas the international division is organized on the basis of geography. This means that coordination and strategic alignment across domestic divisions and the international division are critical to success. At the same time, lack of coordination between domestic and international operations is commonly the most significant flaw in the international division structure.

An example of a firm that has used the international division structure to achieve worldwide success is Abbott Laboratories, a $22 billion diversified health-care company that develops products and services that span prevention and diagnosis to treatment and cure. As international sales grew in the late 1960s, the firm added an international division to its structure. This international division structure has benefits and drawbacks for Abbott, as it does for other firms that use it.

Some argue that to offset the natural "isolation" that may result between domestic and international operations in this structure, the international division structure should be used only when a company (1) intends to market only a small assortment of goods or services internationally and (2) when foreign sales account for only a small portion of total sales. When the product assortment increases or the percentage of foreign sales becomes significant, an internationally integrated structure may be more appropriate.

Internationally Integrated Structures

A number of different internationally integrated structures have been developed and implemented by firms in their quest to achieve global success. The three most common structures are the product division structure, the geographic area structure, and the global matrix structure. Firms with these varied structures have multiple choices for international market entry similar to international divisions (e.g., exporting, licensing and franchising, trading companies, contract manufacturing, and joint ventures). However, firms that have internationally integrated structures are the most likely to engage in direct ownership activities internationally.

The product division structure is the form used by the majority of multinational enterprises. This structure lends itself well to firms that are diversified, often driven by their current domestic operations. Each division is a self-contained entity with responsibility for its own operations, whether it is based on a country or regional structure. However, the worldwide headquarters maintains the overall responsibility for the strategic direction of the firm, whereas the product division is in charge of implementation. Procter & Gamble has a long-standing tradition of operating as a product division structure, with leading brands such as Pampers, Tide, Ariel, Always, Pantene, Bounty, Folgers, Pringles, Charmin, Downy, Crest, and Olay.

The geographic area structure lends itself well to firms with a low degree of diversification. Under this domestically influenced functional structure, the world is divided into logical geographical areas based on the firms' operations and the customers' characteristics. Accenture, a global management consulting firm, operates worldwide largely based on a geographic area structure. Each area tends to be relatively self-contained, and integration across areas is typically via the worldwide or the regional headquarters. This structure facilitates local responsiveness, but it is not ideal for reducing global costs and transferring core knowledge across the firm's geographic units. A key issue in geographic area structures, as in almost all multinational corporations, is the need to become more regionally and globally integrated.

The global matrix structure was designed to achieve both global integration and local responsiveness. Asea Brown Boveri (ABB), a Swedish-Swiss engineering multinational, is the best-known firm to implement a global matrix structure. ABB is an international leader in power and automation technologies that enable customers to improve their performance while lowering environmental impact. Global matrix structures theoretically facilitate a simultaneous focus on realizing local responsiveness, cost efficiencies, and knowledge transfers. However, few firms can operate a global matrix well, since the structure is based on, for example, product and geographic divisions simultaneously (or a combination of any two traditional structures). This means that employees belong to two divisions and often report to two managers throughout the hierarchies of the firm. An effectively implemented global matrix structure has the benefit of being global in scope while also being nimble and responsive locally. However, a poorly implemented global matrix structure results in added bureaucracy and indecisiveness in leadership and implementation.

Customization Versus Globalization of International Marketing Mixes

L O 6 To examine the use of the marketing mix internationally

Like domestic marketers, international marketers develop marketing strategies to serve specific target markets. Traditionally international marketing strategies have customized marketing mixes according to cultural, regional, and national differences. Table 9.5 provides a sample of international issues related to product, distribution, promotion, and price. For example, many soap and detergent manufacturers adapt their products to local water conditions, equipment, and washing habits.

table 9.5   MARKETING MIX ISSUES INTERNATIONALLY

Sample International Issues

Product Element

Core Product	Is there a commonality of the customer's needs across countries? What will the product be used for and in what context?
Product Adoption	How is awareness created for the product in the various country markets? How and where is the product typically bought?
Managing Products	How are truly new products managed in the country markets vis-à-vis existing products or products that have been modified slightly?
Branding	Is the brand accepted widely around the world? Does the home country help or hurt the brand perception of the consumer?

Distribution Element

Marketing Channels	What is the role of the channel intermediaries internationally? Where is value created beyond the domestic borders of the firm?
Physical Distribution	Is the movement of products the most efficient from the home country to the foreign market or to a regional warehouse?
Retail Stores	What is the availability of different types of retail stores in the various country markets?
Retailing Strategy	Where do customers typically shop in the targeted countries—downtown, in suburbs, or in malls?

Promotion Element

Advertising	Some countries' customers prefer firm-specific advertising instead of product-specific advertising. How does this affect advertising?
Public Relations	How is public relations used to manage the stakeholders' interests internationally? Are the stakeholders' interests different worldwide?
Personal Selling	What product types require personal selling internationally? Does it differ from how those products are sold domestically?
Sales Promotion	Is coupon usage a widespread activity in the targeted international markets? What other forms of sales promotion should be used?

Pricing Element

Core Price	Is price a critical component of the value equation of the product in the targeted country markets?
Analysis of Demand	Is the demand curve similar internationally as it is domestically? Will a change in price drastically change demand?
Demand, Cost, and Profit Relationships	What are the fixed and variable costs when marketing the product internationally? Are they similar to the domestic setting?
Determination of Price	How does the pricing strategy, environmental forces, business practices, and cultural values affect price?

Globalization

Although offering some modifications in packaging, Pepsi treats the world as one market.

Colgate-Palmolive even devised an inexpensive, plastic, hand-powered washing machine for use in households that have no electricity in less-developed countries. Coca-Cola markets distinct versions of its soft drinks for the tastes of different regions of the world; it also customizes promotion to feature local people, humor, and sports teams in its advertising. Realizing that both similarities and differences exist across countries is a critical first step to developing the appropriate marketing strategy effort targeted to particular international markets. Today, many firms strive to build their marketing strategies around similarities that exist instead of customizing around differences.

For many firms, **globalization** of marketing is the goal; it involves developing marketing strategies as though the entire world (or its major regions) were a single entity: a globalized firm markets standardized products in the same way everywhere.[67] Nike and Adidas shoes, for example, are standardized worldwide. Other examples of globalized products include electronic communications equipment, Western U.S. clothing, movies, soft drinks, rock and alternative music, cosmetics, and toothpaste. Sony televisions, Starbucks coffee, and U.S. cigarette brands post year-to-year gains in the world market.

For many years, organizations have attempted to globalize their marketing mixes as much as possible by employing standardized products, promotion campaigns, prices, and distribution channels for all markets. The economic and competitive payoffs for globalized marketing strategies are certainly great. Brand name, product characteristics, packaging, and labeling are among the easiest marketing mix variables to standardize; media allocation, retail outlets, and price may be more difficult. In the end, the degree of similarity among the various environmental and market conditions determines the feasibility and degree of globalization. A successful globalization strategy often depends on the extent to which a firm is able to implement the idea of "think globally, act locally."[68] Even take-out food lends itself to globalization: McDonald's, KFC, and Taco Bell restaurants satisfy hungry customers in both hemispheres, although menus may be altered slightly to satisfy local tastes. When Dunkin' Donuts entered the Chinese market, it served coffee, tea, donuts, and bagels, just as it does in the United States, but in China, the donut case also includes items like green tea and honeydew melon donuts and mochi rings, which are like traditional donuts but made with regionally popular rice flour.[69]

International marketing demands some strategic planning if a firm is to incorporate foreign sales into its overall marketing strategy. International marketing activities often require customized marketing mixes to achieve the firm's goals. Globalization

globalization The development of marketing strategies that treat the entire world (or its major regions) as a single entity requires a total commitment to the world, regions, or multinational areas as an integral part of the firm's markets; world or regional markets become as important as domestic ones. Regardless of the extent to which a firm chooses to globalize its marketing strategy, extensive environmental analysis and marketing research are necessary to understand the needs and desires of the target market(s) and successfully implement the chosen marketing strategy. A global presence does not automatically result in a global competitive advantage. However, a global presence generates five opportunities for creating value: (1) to adapt to local market differences, (2) to exploit economies of global scale, (3) to exploit economies of global scope, (4) to mine optimal locations for activities and resources, and (5) to maximize the transfer of knowledge across locations.[70] To exploit these opportunities, marketers need to conduct marketing research and work within the constraints of the international environment and regional trade alliances, markets, and agreements.

SUMMARY

International marketing involves developing and performing marketing activities across national boundaries. International markets can provide tremendous opportunities for growth and renewed opportunity for the firm.

A detailed analysis of the environment is essential before a company enters an international market. Environmental aspects of special importance include sociocultural; economic, political, legal, and regulatory; social and ethical; competitive; and technological forces. Because marketing activities are primarily social in purpose, they are influenced by beliefs and values regarding family, religion, education, health, and recreation. Cultural differences may affect marketing negotiations, decision-making behavior, and product adoption and use. A nation's economic stability and trade barriers can affect marketing efforts. Significant trade barriers include import tariffs, quotas, embargoes, and exchange controls. Gross domestic product (GDP) and GDP per capita are common measures of a nation's economic standing. Political and legal forces include a nation's political system, laws, regulatory bodies, special-interest groups, and courts. In the area of ethics, cultural relativism is the concept that morality varies from one culture to another and that business practices are therefore differentially defined as right or wrong by particular cultures. In addition to considering the types of competition and the types of competitive structures that exist in other countries, marketers also need to consider the competitive forces at work and recognize the importance of the global customer who is well informed about product choices from around the world. Advances in technology have greatly facilitated international marketing.

Various regional trade alliances and specific markets create both opportunities and constraints for companies engaged in international marketing. These include the North American Free Trade Agreement, the European Union, the Common Market of the Southern Cone, the Asia-Pacific Economic Cooperation, and the World Trade Organization.

There are several ways to enter international marketing. Importing (the purchase of products from a foreign source) and exporting (the sale of products to foreign markets) are the easiest and most flexible methods. Marketers may employ a trading company, which links buyers and sellers in different countries but is not involved in manufacturing and does not own assets related to manufacturing. Licensing and franchising are arrangements whereby one firm pays fees to another for the use of its name, expertise, and supplies. Contract manufacturing occurs when a company hires a foreign firm to produce a designated volume of the domestic firm's product to specification, and the final product carries the domestic firm's name. Joint ventures are partnerships between a domestic firm and a foreign firm or government. Strategic alliances are partnerships formed to create competitive advantage on a worldwide basis. Finally, a firm can build its own marketing or production facilities overseas. When companies have direct ownership of facilities in many countries, they may be considered multinational enterprises.

Firms develop their international marketing strategies and manage their marketing mixes by developing and maintaining an organizational structure that best leverages their resources and core competencies. Three basic structures of international organizations include export departments, international divisions, and internationally integrated structures (e.g., product division structures, geographic area structures, and matrix structures).

Although most firms adjust their marketing mixes for differences in target markets, some firms standardize their marketing efforts worldwide. Traditional full-scale international marketing involvement is based on products customized according to cultural, regional, and national differences. Globalization, however, involves developing marketing strategies as if the entire world (or regions of it) were a single entity; a globalized firm markets standardized products in the same way everywhere. International marketing demands some strategic planning if a firm is to incorporate foreign sales into its overall marketing strategy.

IMPORTANT TERMS

International marketing, 246

Gross domestic product (GDP), 249

Import tariff, 250

Quota, 250

Embargo, 250

Exchange controls, 251

Balance of trade, 251

Cultural relativism, 252

North American Free Trade Agreement (NAFTA), 256

European Union (EU), 257

Common Market of the Southern Cone (MERCOSUR), 257

Asia-Pacific Economic Cooperation (APEC), 258

World Trade Organization (WTO), 259

General Agreement on Tariffs and Trade (GATT), 259

Dumping, 259

Importing, 261

Exporting, 261

Trading company, 261

Licensing, 262

Franchising, 262

Contract manufacturing, 262

Outsourcing, 262

Offshoring, 263

Offshore outsourcing, 263

Joint venture, 263

Strategic alliances, 264

Direct ownership, 265

Multinational enterprise, 265

Globalization, 270

DISCUSSION & REVIEW QUESTIONS

1. How does international marketing differ from domestic marketing?

2. What factors must marketers consider as they decide whether to engage in international marketing?

3. Why are the largest industrial corporations in the United States so committed to international marketing?

4. Why do you think this chapter focuses on an analysis of the international marketing environment?

5. If you were asked to provide a small tip (or bribe) to have a document approved in a foreign nation where this practice is customary, what would you do?

6. How will NAFTA affect marketing opportunities for U.S. products in North America (the United States, Mexico, and Canada)?

7. What should marketers consider as they decide whether to license or enter into a joint venture in a foreign nation?

8. Discuss the impact of strategic alliances on international marketing strategies.

9. Contrast globalization with customization of marketing strategies. Is one practice better than the other?

10. What are some of the product issues that you need to consider when marketing luxury automobiles in Australia, Brazil, Singapore, South Africa, and Sweden?

APPLICATION QUESTIONS

1. To successfully implement marketing strategies in the international marketplace, a marketer must understand the complexities of the global marketing environment. Which environmental forces (sociocultural, economic, political/legal/regulatory, ethical, competitive, or technological) might a marketer need to consider when marketing the following products in the international marketplace, and why?
   a. Barbie dolls
   b. Beer
   c. Financial services
   d. Television sets

2. Many firms, including Procter & Gamble, FedEx, and Occidental Petroleum, wish to do business in eastern Europe and in the countries that were once part of the former Soviet Union. What events could occur that would make marketing in these countries more difficult? What events might make it easier?

3. This chapter discusses various organizational approaches to international marketing. Which would be the best arrangements for international marketing of the following products, and why?
   a. Construction equipment
   b. Cosmetics
   c. Automobiles

4. Procter & Gamble has made a substantial commitment to foreign markets, especially in Latin America. Its actions may be described as a "globalization of marketing." Describe how a shoe manufacturer (e.g., Wolverine World Wide) would go from domestic marketing to limited exporting, to international marketing, and finally to a globalization of marketing. Give examples of some activities that might be involved in this process.

INTERNET EXERCISE

Visit **www.cengage.com/marketing/pride-ferrell** for resources to help you master the material in this chapter, plus materials that will help you expand your marketing knowledge, including Internet exercise updates, ACE Self-Tests, hotlinks to companies featured in this chapter, and much more. The globalEDGE web portal (**http://globaledge.msu.edu/ibrd**)—the world's leading website on international business and trade (as ranked by all major search engines) and is developed and maintained by the Center for International Business Education and Research at Michigan State University—can also help you learn more about the concepts in this chapter, as well as provide up-to-date information about international marketing.

FTD

Founded in 1910 as Florists' Telegraph Delivery, FTD was the first company to offer a "flowers-by-wire" service.

FTD does not deliver flowers itself, but it depends on local florists to do it. In 1994, FTD expanded its toll-free telephone-ordering service by establishing a website. Visit the site at **www.ftd.com,** and answer the following:

1. Click on "International." Select a country to which you would like to send flowers. Summarize the delivery and pricing information that would apply to that country.

2. Determine the cost of sending fresh-cut seasonal flowers to Germany.

3. What are the benefits of this global distribution system for sending flowers worldwide? What other consumer products could be distributed globally through the Internet?

developing your MARKETING PLAN

When formulating marketing strategy, one of the issues a company must consider is whether or not to pursue international markets. Although international markets present increased marketing opportunities, they also require more complex decisions when formulating marketing plans. To assist you in relating the information in this chapter to the development of your marketing plan, focus on the following:

1. Review the environmental analysis that was completed in Chapter 3. Extend the analysis for each of the seven factors to include global markets.

2. Using Figure 9.1 as a guide, determine the degree of international involvement that is appropriate for your product and your company.

3. Discuss the concepts of customization and globalization for your product when moving to international markets. Refer to Table 9.5 for guidance in your discussion.

The information obtained from these questions should assist you in developing various aspects of your marketing plan found in the *Interactive Marketing Plan* exercise at **www.cengage.com/marketing/pride-ferrell.**

globalEDGE

1. Tariffs play a significant role in global markets. Sometimes designed to protect industries from excessive foreign competition, tariffs may be imposed by countries for political, economic, or legal reasons. Find data that pertains to the Free Trade Area of America (FTAA) in the Trade and Tariff Database by using the search term "FTAA" at **http://globaledge.msu.edu/ibrd.** From the Trade and Tariff Database in the FTAA website, open the HTML version and then click on the Tariffs link, then the Tariffs button, and then choose "Tariffs" to Imports. Next, click on the Ranking button. Determine the top five industries in the United States benefiting from tariffs. Compare this list to the top five industries with tariffs in Mexico. Are there any differences or similarities that you notice?

2. An important element in designing your firm's internationalization strategy is identifying the markets that are most similar and most different culturally. Because your firm is based in the United States, one approach to determine this is to calculate the average difference in scores from the United States for each country based on Hofstede's five cultural dimensions for 56 countries. Hofstede's cultural dimensions can be found using the search term "56 countries" at **http://globaledge.msu.edu/ibrd.** At the Geert Hofstede Resource Center, you will see a link called "Hofstede Scores." Which five countries are the most similar to the United States? Which five countries are the least similar?

Lonely Planet Provides Guidance to Global Explorers

Lonely Planet has been global since before it was even a company—in its audience, its scope, and its foundation. The now ubiquitous guidebook brand got its start in 1973 when Brit Tony Wheeler and his wife, Maureen, holed up in Australia to write a pamphlet on their experiences traveling in Asia. The couple had met in their native Britain, found that they shared a love of adventure, and gotten married soon thereafter. For their honeymoon they chose to make a trip that no one at the time believed was possible—a journey from Britain across Europe and Asia via land all the way to Australia. They made it, but were stuck in Australia with 27 cents between the two of them. Tony made the best of the situation by writing the 94-page *Across Asia on the Cheap*, which sold 8,500 copies. From this suitably adventurous start, Lonely Planet ballooned into one of the powerhouses of the growing guidebook and phrasebook industry, with around 500 titles on 118 countries. Lonely Planet now represents one quarter of all English-language guidebooks sold in the world and has annual revenues in excess of $75 million.

The company has offices in London and Oakland, with its headquarters in Melbourne. It employs 500 office staff and around 300 on-the-road contributors. Thanks to these contributors from dozens of different countries, the company has a global scope and a global perspective, which helps the company successfully market worldwide. The huge diversity of languages, cultures, and interests across their consumer base makes marketing and developing a coherent brand image difficult. To cope with these hurdles, Lonely Planet works on maintaining a balance between consistency in branding and customizing marketing to suit specific target markets.

In 2007, the Wheelers finally relinquished control of the company when they sold it to BBC Worldwide, which is the commercial branch of the British Broadcasting Company. The addition of the BBC's extensive network of distribution channels has helped Lonely Planet to market itself more successfully, and to branch into complementary business areas such as Lonely

Planet Images, Lonely Planet Television, Lonely Planet Foreign Rights Team, Lonely Planet Business Solutions unit, and Lonely Planet Foundation (which contributes 5% of all profits to international charities and has established a carbon offset program for printing and the travels of all employees). From the start, one of the fundamental tenets of the Lonely Planet brand has been that travel can truly change the world and make it a better place. Through the Lonely Planet Foundation, the Wheelers have tried to make profound differences in the places they visit. Their far-reaching message is being heard loud and clear as evidenced by the 4.3 million unique visitors clicking on **lonelyplanet.com** each month.

This marketing strategy of selective customization combined with relentless fact checking and updating, and a focus on hiring the best and most knowledgeable travel writers, has earned Lonely Planet a reputation for quality. Lonely Planet books are not only popular; they are considered by many to be the definitive guidebooks. In fact, Jay Garner, the first American administrator in Iraq, considers Lonely Planet such an authority on global travel that he used the book *Lonely Planet Iraq* to develop a list of historical sites worth saving. Another nod to the success of the brand is the fact that in Asia, imitation Lonely Planet guidebooks are now sold alongside imitation Gucci and Chanel handbags and Rolex watches.

No matter what criticisms people may have of Lonely Planet, this single guidebook brand has been responsible for the soaring popularity of adventure tourism worldwide. Because of Lonely Planet, there are surf camps in El Salvador, foreign-owned luxury resorts in Nicaragua, and remote villages in the heights of the Himalayas with economies based around tourism—monuments to the success of their marketing strategy.

Lonely Planet continues its trek toward boundless success, due largely to the organization's clear vision of its target market. The Lonely Planet traveler is willing to embrace foreign food and culture, but still wants to do it comfortably and cheaply, if possible. The company reaches its market through smart marketing and promotion strategies that balance a recognizable brand with customization to accommodate local tastes. Lonely Planet has never forgotten that there really is no such thing as global—that the world consists of thousands of different local populations. And Lonely Planet, by knowing clearly who comprises its market and by smart marketing strategies, has grown from a pamphlet written in a cheap hostel to a huge global brand loved by millions of travelers the world over.[71]

Questions for Discussion

1. Why is Lonely Planet a global success?
2. How has Lonely Planet been able to provide and market guidebooks that are useful across languages and cultures?
3. How could Lonely Planet guidebooks help marketers to develop effective marketing strategies in targeted foreign markets?

CASE 9.2

Gillette: One of Procter & Gamble's Best Brands

For those of you who have ever used a wet razor, whether it was for shaving your face, legs, head, or other body parts, chances are you used a Gillette brand razor. After all, the Gillette Company, which also makes the popular Duracell battery, owns over 70 percent of the $1.7 billion men's razor market in the United States, and the company has a dominant share of the worldwide razor market as well. And the international marketplace is changing, at least for Gillette's competitors.

On October 1, 2005, the merger of the Gillette Company and the Procter & Gamble Company was completed. This merger stands to profoundly affect the international marketplace. It represents a powerful merger of two giants spanning several global industries and centuries of experience and success (P&G was founded in 1837 and Gillette was founded in 1901).

Founded by King C. Gillette, the Gillette Company was one of the first great multinational organizations and, some would say, a marvel of marketing effectiveness—a trait that has also been synonymous with P&G. Just four years after founding Gillette in Boston, King Gillette opened a branch office in London, and the company quickly gained sales and profits throughout western Europe. About 20 years later, Gillette said of his safety razor, "There is no other article for individual use so universally known or widely distributed. In my travels, I have found it in the most northern town in Norway and in the heart of the Sahara Desert." From the beginning, Gillette set out to offer consumers high-quality shaving products that would satisfy their basic grooming needs at a fair price. Having gained more than half of the entire razor and blades market, Gillette's manufacturing efficiency allowed it to implement marketing programs on a large scale, which helped the company gain both profits and market leadership.

Today the Gillette Company is the world leader in male grooming products, a category that includes blades, razors, and shaving preparations, and in selected female grooming products, such as wet-shaving products and hair removal devices. In addition, the company holds the number 1 position worldwide in alkaline batteries and in manual and power toothbrushes. Gillette's manufacturing operations are conducted at 32 facilities in 15 countries, and products are distributed through wholesalers, retailers, and agents in more than 200 countries and territories.

Gillette's Mach3 and Mach3 Turbo shaving systems, which reap $2 billion in sales annually, remain the best-selling men's shavers, and its line of Venus razors leads the women's shaver market. "Gillette's blade and razor business is the single most valuable franchise in the household products and cosmetics industries," said William H. Steele, an analyst at Bank of America Securities. The blade and razor segment accounts for roughly 40 percent of Gillette's sales and more than 70 percent of the company's profits. Sales in this segment have more than doubled in the last decade, and the outlook for this segment is promising as the shaving population increases, particularly in such locations as Asia, eastern Europe, and Latin America. The company's progress in its principal line of business reflects the success of its technologically advanced products, including the Mach3 system.

The worldwide success of the Mach3 was not a simple task, however. It took ten years, 35 patents, $200 million in research and development, $550 million in capital investments, and $300 million in marketing efforts to make Mach3 successful. And all of these resources were spent on an item that costs roughly $6.50 to consumers. The promotional campaign for Mach3 is a fascinating one. Specifically, Gillette's goal for Mach3 was a worldwide product launch, not just a domestic one. As such, the company needed to ensure that it had enough Mach3 products in the global supply chain to satisfy the likely strong global demand. Any stockouts would be very costly to Gillette's market position and image and endanger its aggressive product launch. Mostly successful in its launch, the Mach3 razor set the tone for the marketplace and for how to launch such a product globally. Much of the launch success of the Venus razor for women is owed to the carefully delineated process of the Mach3 razor. Gillette used largely the same strategy for the Venus as it did for Mach3.

Gillette's current strategy in the personal-care market is to focus resources on core grooming products such as deodorants/antiperspirants and shaving preparations while providing supporting products in key markets. The premier brand in this product mix is the Gillette Series, which includes shaving gels and foams, as well as Gillette Series antiperspirants and deodorants. The personal-care segment also includes many of Gillette's best-known and most respected brands, including Foamy shaving cream and Right Guard, Soft & Dri, and Dry Idea deodorants/antiperspirants.

The Gillette Company also owns Braun, which turned in a record performance in 1997 but has since struggled to contribute profits. As a result, Braun is no longer considered one of the company's primary business segments. However, Gillette still values Braun's shaving products, oral-care products, and hair removal (epilation) devices, which fit well with the company's emphasis on product innovation and with its other business segments. Other Braun products—namely, kitchen appliances, personal-care products, and health-care instruments—do not fit as well with Gillette's focus. As a result, the company has contemplated selling most of the Braun line but keeping the key products in shaving, oral care, and hair removal.

Another brand in Gillette's stable is Oral-B, which develops and markets a broad range of superior oral-care products worldwide in a strong and well-established partnership with dental professionals. Led by toothbrushes, the Oral-B line also includes interdental products, specialty toothpastes, mouth rinses, and professional dental products. Sales and profits continue to increase in this segment as a function of technological developments and product innovations. For example, the Oral-B Triumph toothbrush features innovative technology with a Floss Action brushhead for superior cleaning.

With the acquisition of Duracell International, Gillette instantly achieved worldwide leadership in the alkaline battery market. Duracell leads this market with approximately a 40 percent share. This segment is key to Gillette's portfolio and complements P&G's portfolio well. Duracell products generate sizable sales and profits. Also, Duracell and Gillette share many characteristics, including global brand franchises, common distribution channels, and geographic expansion potential. With the company's backing, Duracell enjoys significant economies of scale and greater market penetration through P&G's worldwide distribution network.

Each day around the world, more than 1 billion people interact with Gillette products, while 2 billion times a day customers interact with P&G brands. Both Gillette and P&G have gained leadership positions through their strategies of managing their businesses with long-term, global perspectives. This ability to generate long-term, profitable growth in a changing global marketplace rests on several fundamental strengths, including a constantly increasing accumulation of scientific knowledge; innovative products that embody meaningful technological advances; and an immense manufacturing capability to produce billions of products every year reliably, efficiently, and cost effectively. Gillette's and P&G's strengths have created strong and enduring consumer brand loyalty around the world. Now, what can these firms do together? One prediction is that the merger between Gillette and Procter & Gamble will make consumers' brand loyalty even stronger—could this be the case?[72]

Questions for Discussion

1. What environmental factors have contributed to Gillette's success in global markets? What forces may have created challenges for the company?
2. What strategy does Gillette appear to have adopted for international marketing?
3. How can Gillette continue to compete effectively in the battery and grooming markets after the merger with Procter & Gamble?

strategic CASE 4

McDonald's Marketing Serves Up Global and Local Profits

Serving 52 million people in 32,000 locations worldwide may be a tall order, but it's just an ordinary day in the fast-paced world of fast-food giant McDonald's. A master marketer, McDonald's has increased annual revenues to $22 billion by understanding what, when, where, why, and how customers want to eat. It even targets corporations that like to reward employees or promote products by buying and giving away prepaid cards good for McDonald's purchases. Facing intense competition from traditional fast-food rivals like Burger King and KFC and casual dining chains like Panera's, McDonald's never stops looking for new ways to reinforce customer loyalty and build profits.

What's in Store?

One key to McDonald's success is its ever-changing menu that is adapted to local tastes. In Moscow, consumers who are too rushed to eat a traditional ham-and-egg breakfast at home have made Fresh McMuffin sausage sandwiches a top-selling morning item. In Argentina, the Ranchero hamburger sandwich, with special salsa sauce, is a particular customer favorite. In France, the Croque McDo is McDonald's version of the popular croque monsieur hot ham-and-cheese sandwich.

Although McDonald's built its reputation on burgers and fries, its marketers recognize that many consumers have become more health conscious in recent years. That's why McDonald's has developed lighter fast-food fare for adults and children alike, including new salads, wrap sandwiches, and apple slices snacks. The company now posts nutrition information online for consumers to check and has cooked up special french fry recipes for cities like New York that ban certain types of fats.

Ready for Customers Early, Late, and on the Go

Another way McDonald's has built sales and profits is by opening stores early to serve the breakfast crowd and then keeping selected stores open until midnight or later for night owls. Some of its units operate 24 hours a day, with the drive-through lanes doing a brisk business as commuters, carpoolers, and others buy meals or coffee to go.

In China, where McDonald's will soon have 1,000 outlets, late-night hours are a special draw and have helped the company significantly increase revenues. Also, McDonald's sees drive-through lanes as an important competitive element in China, where car ownership is growing fast and competitors like KFC have few drive-through locations. Now half of the new stores McDonald's opens in China are equipped for drive-through operations. Under an agreement with state-owned Sinopec, McDonald's is adding drive-through outlets at Sinopec gas stations all around China.

Dealing with the Dollar Menu

Knowing that many customers are eating out on a budget, McDonald's outlets often offer a Dollar Menu, with selected sandwiches priced at about $1 each. The idea is to "bring in consumers who are looking for ways to stretch their wallets," explains the company's president. In fact, the Dollar Menu accounts for more than 20 percent of overall sales in U.S. restaurants.

However, with food prices rising and other costs inching upward, some McDonald's franchisees complain that they are earning fairly low profit margins on Dollar Menu items. Under the terms of their franchise agreements with McDonald's, franchisees are free to charge more (or less) than the corporation's official Dollar Menu price. Therefore, some stores in high-cost markets are charging $1.29 or $1.39 for the Double Cheeseburger that franchisees in other areas sell for $1 on the Dollar Menu.

Rising costs are another problem for McDonald's stores outside the United States. In Russia, for example, McDonald's boosts menu prices up to four times a year to cope with the ongoing inflationary cycle that has driven food costs higher and higher. The company increases the price of less-expensive menu items by about half the inflation rate but increases the price of premium menu items by a bit more than the inflation rate because, according to one executive, "We still have a huge amount of people who are price sensitive." Despite the price hikes, the McDonald's in Moscow's Pushkin Square remains the busiest McDonald's on the planet, with 26 cash registers and seating for 900.

Social Responsibility on the Menu

Ronald McDonald is one of the world's most recognizable brand mascots. Not only does he appear in McDonald's marketing communications, but he also headlines the company's Ronald McDonald House Charities, which provide accommodations for families while their critically ill children are treated in hospitals far from home. The nonprofit group, now more than two decades old, operates 271 houses in 30 nations. Local McDonald's outlets support neighborhood charities and community causes, as well.

Prodded, in part, by animal activists, the company has established animal-handling standards for its meat suppliers. It's also going green by using paper and cardboard packaging made from recycled materials.

To showcase its charitable and environmental activities, the company issues a yearly corporate responsibility report and publicizes achievements such as raising millions of dollars on World Children's Day.

However, not all of McDonald's community activities are well received. For instance, McDonald's restaurants in Seminole County, Florida, arranged to give Happy Meals to local elementary school students as rewards for good grades and attendance. But some parents and child advocates raised concerns when students brought home report card jackets with a picture of Ronald McDonald on them. "It's a terribly troubling trend because it really, clearly links doing well in school with getting a Happy Meal," the head of the Campaign for a Commercial-Free Childhood told the *New York Times*.

Blogging About Beef

McDonald's has a strong presence on the Internet, with a corporate website, product and nutrition websites, and individual websites geared to each country where it does business. To generate grassroots word-of-mouth communications about food and service quality, it has enlisted six Mom's Quality Correspondents to go behind the scenes at headquarters, suppliers' facilities, and individual McDonald's stores. The moms are free to look around, ask questions, videotape what they see, and then blog about their experiences, including video snippets.

These bloggers can say whatever they like because, says a McDonald's marketing official, "if moms were out there speaking to their communities and online communities unedited, it would get us far more credibility than just posting an article or doing website copy." For example, after the moms traveled to a McDonald's beef supplier in Oklahoma City, one wrote on the blog, "Hey, moms across America—it is really 100% beef!"

McDonald's also maintains a corporate social responsibility blog where its managers post informal notes about issues such as environmental programs, healthy lifestyles, and responsible purchasing. When consumers post comments in response to these blogs, the resulting dialogue helps McDonald's to better understand public sentiment surrounding such issues and to plan appropriate actions and communications.

Selling the Arch Card

Although McDonald's has sold gift certificates for many years, it now has a corporate sales division that targets businesses that want to give small incentives to employees or customers. The incentive that McDonald's offers is its Arch Card, a prepaid gift card issued in the amount of $5, $10, $25, or $50. Businesses can buy up to 25 Arch Cards through local McDonald's outlets. The corporate sales division handles bulk purchases and gives business customers a discount if they buy $10,000 worth of Arch Cards. After recipients spend the initial gift amount, they can pay to reload up to $110 on each card. The next time they visit a McDonald's restaurant, they'll be ready to grab and go with just a swipe of plastic.[73]

Questions for Discussion

1. What role do opinion leaders play in McDonald's marketing?
2. How is McDonald's using marketing to spark learning and positive attitudes toward its brand and offerings?
3. Why would McDonald's select businesses as a target market for its Arch Cards?
4. What environmental forces have created challenges for McDonald's in global markets? What forces have created opportunities in global markets?

part 5

Product Decisions

We are now prepared to analyze the decisions and activities associated with developing and maintaining effective marketing mixes. In Parts Five through Eight, we focus on the major components of the marketing mix: product, distribution, promotion, and price. **Part Five** explores the product component of the marketing mix. **Chapter 10** introduces basic concepts and relationships that must be understood to make effective product decisions. **Chapter 11** analyzes a variety of dimensions regarding product management, including line extensions and product modification, new-product development, and product deletions. **Chapter 12** discusses branding, packaging, and labeling. **Chapter 13** explores the nature, importance, and characteristics of services.

10 Product Concepts

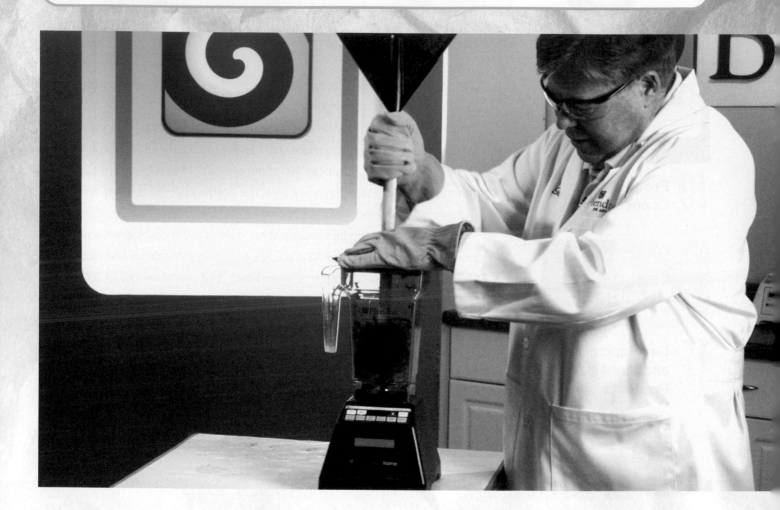

LEARNING objectives

1 To understand the concept of a product

2 To explain how to classify products

3 To examine the concepts of product item, product line, and product mix and understand how they are connected

4 To understand the product life cycle and its impact on marketing strategies

5 To describe the product adoption process

6 To understand why some products fail and some succeed

Blendtec Asks "Will It Blend?"

"Will it blend?" Millions of people have viewed Blendtec's videos on YouTube to find out whether the firm's home blenders can reduce the unlikeliest of objects—some marbles, a dozen glow sticks, an iPod—to dust and smoke. Based in Orem, Utah, Blendtec originally targeted restaurants, bars, and other businesses that require high-powered blenders to make sauces, soups, smoothies, and other specialties. Its success in that market set the stage for the decision to grow even faster by expanding into consumer products.

entrepreneurs
IN ACTION

One major challenge was the lack of brand awareness among consumers. "People didn't know a company called Blendtec, but we were making commercial blenders for years," explains George Wright, director of marketing. He also faced the challenge of reaching consumers without the support of an expensive promotional campaign. Then Wright learned that CEO Tom Dickson routinely tested product quality by crunching blocks of wood and other unusual things in Blendtec blenders. Wright arranged to film five videos starring Dickson in a laboratory coat and safety goggles, asking the question "Will it blend?" before pulverizing a whole chicken, a bag of marbles, and other items in a Blendtec home blender.

After Blendtec's webmaster posted the videos on the company-owned willitblend.com and on YouTube, they were picked up by other popular websites. Within a week, 6 million people had watched Blendtec products chew up everything that Dickson placed in the blender—a video campaign that cost the company $50. Wright continued to create new "Will it blend?" video segments, and each drew hundreds of thousands of viewers and sparked greater interest in the home blenders. By the end of the year, Blendtec's consumer sales had risen by 43 percent. Says Wright, "The blender used in restaurants for your smoothie is available for the home now, too, and the word is out among consumers."[1]

The product is an important variable in the marketing mix. Products such as the Blendtec home blender can be a firm's most important asset. If a company's products do not meet customers' desires and needs, the firm will fail unless it is willing to make adjustments. Developing successful products such as the Blendtec blender requires knowledge of fundamental marketing and product concepts.

In this chapter, we first define *product* and discuss how buyers view products. Next, we examine the concepts of product line and product mix. We then explore the stages of the product life cycle and the effect of each life cycle stage on marketing strategies. Then we outline the product adoption process. Finally, we discuss the factors that contribute to a product's failure or success.

What Is a Product?

L O 1 To understand the concept of a product

good A tangible physical entity

service An intangible result of the application of human and mechanical efforts to people or objects

idea A concept, philosophy, image, or issue

As defined in Chapter 1, a *product* is a good, a service, or an idea received in an exchange. It can be either tangible or intangible and includes functional, social, and psychological utilities or benefits. It also includes supporting services, such as installation, guarantees, product information, and promises of repair or maintenance. Thus, the four-year/50,000-mile warranty that covers most new automobiles is part of the product itself. A **good** is a tangible physical entity, such as an iPod Nano music player or a Subway sandwich. A **service,** in contrast, is intangible; it is the result of the application of human and mechanical efforts to people or objects. Examples of services include a performance by Alicia Keyes, online travel agency bookings, medical examinations, child day care, real estate services, and martial arts lessons. (Chapter 13 provides a detailed discussion of services.) An **idea** is a concept, philosophy, image, or issue. Ideas provide the psychological stimulation that aids in solving problems or adjusting to the environment. For example, MADD (Mothers Against Drunk Driving) promotes safe consumption of alcohol and stricter enforcement of laws against drunk driving.

It is helpful to think of a total product offering as having a combination of three interdependent elements: the core product itself, its supplemental features, and its symbolic or experiential value (Figure 10.1). Consider that some people buy new tires for their basic utility (e.g., Sears's Guardsman III), whereas some look for safety (e.g., Michelin), and others buy on the basis of brand name or exemplary performance (e.g., Pirelli).

The core product consists of a product's fundamental utility or main benefit. Broadband Internet services, for instance, offer speedy Internet access, but some buyers want additional features such as wireless connectivity anywhere they go. The core product usually addresses a fundamental need of the consumer. When you buy bottled water, you can buy name brands such as Dasani and Aquafina or more exclusive brands like Fiji or Evian. Regardless of price, each alternative will quench your thirst. Retailers such as Target and Wal-Mart specialize in offering core products of a generally acceptable quality level at competitive prices. Hotels such as Clarion and the Hampton Inn specialize in providing quality services at affordable prices.

A product's supplemental features provide added value or attributes in addition to its core utility or benefit. Supplemental products can also provide installation, delivery, training, and

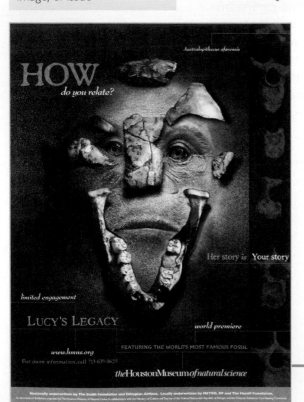

What Is a Product?

A product can be a service, an idea, goods, or a combination of these. The Houston Museum of Natural Science provides a service.

figure 10.1

THE TOTAL PRODUCT

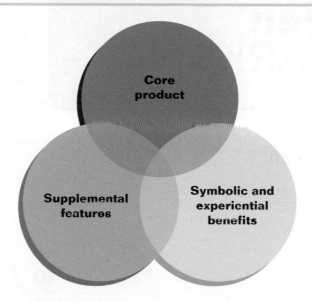

financing. These supplemental attributes are not required to make the core product function effectively, but they help differentiate one product brand from another. The Starwood Hotel chain, for example, introduced a new concept called Aloft that offers well-appointed "loftlike" guest rooms that appeal to business travelers at a midlevel price range. Hyatt offers a hotel concept that features larger rooms and work areas, free high-speed Internet, large flat-screen TVs, CD and DVD players, and cordless phones.[2] These supplemental features add real value to the core product of overnight hotel stays.

Finally, customers also receive benefits based on their experiences with the product. In addition, many products have symbolic meaning for buyers. For some consumers, the simple act of shopping gives symbolic value and improves their attitudes. Some stores capitalize on this value by striving to create a special experience for customers. For example, you can buy stuffed toys at many retailers, but at Build-A-Bear, you can choose the type of animal, stuff it yourself, give it a heart, create a name complete with a birth certificate, as well as give the toy a bath and clothe and accessorize it. The atmosphere and décor of a retail store, the variety and depth of product choices, the customer support, even the sounds and smells all contribute to the experiential element. When you check into a Hotel Monaco, not only do you get a great room with down comforters, bed toppers, and pillows, but you can also "check out" a fish as your companion during your stay. Customers credit the Hotel Monaco with providing a differentiated, enjoyable stay and become loyal customers. These symbolic and experiential features are all part of the Hotel Monaco total product.

Thus, when buyers purchase a product, they are really buying the benefits and satisfaction they think the product will provide. A Rolex watch, for example, is purchased to make a statement of success, not just for telling time. Services in particular are purchased on the basis of expectations. Expectations, suggested by images, promises, and symbols, as well as processes and delivery, help consumers make judgments about tangible and intangible products. Products are formed by the activities and processes that help satisfy expectations. Starbucks, for example, did not invent the coffee shop, but it did make high-quality coffee beverages readily available around the world with standardized service and in stylish, comfortable stores. Often symbols and cues are used to make intangible products more tangible, or real, to the consumer. Allstate Insurance Company, for example, uses giant hands to symbolize security, strength, and friendliness.

green MARKETING

What Makes a Product "Green"?

Is a chainsaw "green" when it runs on electricity instead of gasoline? What about a toothpaste that contains natural mint and green tea extract or a paintbrush with a plastic handle? This is a red-hot issue as sales of green products rise, and both marketers and consumers try to determine what, exactly, makes a product green.

Consider what happened when Home Depot invited suppliers to nominate green products for special attention in its Eco Options promotional campaign. The retailer suddenly discovered that of the 176,000 items carried in its stores, suppliers believed more than 60,000 to be worthy of the "green" designation. "In somebody's mind, the products they were selling us were environmentally friendly," remembers Ron Jarvis, the executive in charge of the Eco Options campaign. He adds, "If they say their product makes the sky bluer and the grass greener, that's just not good enough."

After screening the products using standards such as the Environmental Protection Agency's Energy Star designation, Jarvis allowed only 2,500 of them into the Eco Options program, including items such as solar-powered lawn lights and energy-efficient washing machines. To promote the program, the company gave away 1 million free compact fluorescent light bulbs and set up a website where customers can read about the products and see their environmental impact. And shoppers are responding: within three months, sales of Eco Options products were, on average, 10 percent higher than before the program began.[a]

Classifying Products

L O 2 To explain how to classify products

consumer products Products purchased to satisfy personal and family needs

business products Products bought to use in a firm's operations, to resell, or to make other products

Products fall into one of two general categories. Products that are purchased to satisfy personal and family needs are **consumer products.** Products bought to use in a firm's operations, to resell, or to make other products are **business products.** Consumers buy products to satisfy their personal wants, whereas business buyers seek to satisfy the goals of their organizations.

The same item can be classified as both a consumer product and a business product. For example, when a person buys a 100-watt light bulb for lighting a home closet, it is classified as a consumer product. However, when an organization purchases a 100-watt light bulb for lighting a reception area, it is considered a business product because it is used in daily operations. Thus, the buyer's intent—or the ultimate use of the product—determines whether an item is classified as a consumer or business product.

Product classifications are important because classes of products are aimed at particular target markets, which affects distribution, promotion, and pricing decisions. Furthermore, appropriate marketing strategies vary among the classes of consumer and business products. In short, how a product is classified can affect the entire marketing mix. In this section, we examine the characteristics of consumer and business products and explore the marketing activities associated with some of these products.

snapshot

Online product reviews

62% of Americans say they read consumer-written product reviews online when researching products. Percent who report being influenced by consumer reviews by product category:

Kitchen appliances	20%
Toys and games	22%
Personal electronics	39%
Home electronics	45%

Source: Deloitte & Touche. Margin of error ± 3%. As seen in *USA Today Snapshot* on Nov. 7, 2007, p. B1.

convenience products Relatively inexpensive, frequently purchased items for which buyers exert minimal purchasing effort

Consumer Products

The most widely accepted approach to classifying consumer products is based on characteristics of consumer buying behavior. It divides products into four categories: convenience, shopping, specialty, and unsought products. However, not all buyers behave in the same way when purchasing a specific type of product. Thus, a single product can fit into several categories. To minimize this problem, marketers think in terms of how buyers *generally* behave when purchasing a specific item. In addition, they recognize that the "correct" classification can be determined only by considering a particular firm's intended target market. Examining the four traditional categories of consumer products can provide further insight.

Convenience Products. **Convenience products** are relatively inexpensive, frequently purchased items for which buyers exert only minimal purchasing effort. They range from bread, soft drinks, and chewing gum to gasoline and newspapers. The buyer spends little time planning the purchase or comparing available brands or sellers. Today time has become one of our most precious assets, and many consumers therefore buy products at the closest location to preserve time for other activities. Even a buyer who prefers a specific brand will readily choose a substitute if the preferred brand is not conveniently available.

Classifying a product as a convenience product has several implications for a firm's marketing strategy. A convenience product is normally marketed through many retail outlets. Examples of typical outlets include 7-Eleven, Exxon Mobil, and Starbucks. Starbucks coffee, for example, is available in airports, hotels, and grocery stores, and many of the Starbucks company-owned stores now have drive-through lanes to ensure that customers can get coffee whenever or wherever the desire strikes.[3] Because sellers experience high inventory turnover, per-unit gross margins can be relatively low. Producers of convenience products, such as Altoid mints, expect little promotional effort at the retail level and thus must provide it themselves with advertising and sales promotion. Packaging is also an important element of the marketing

Convenience Product and Shopping Product

An ice cream bar is a convenience product, and hotels are shopping products.

mix for convenience products. The package may have to sell the product because many convenience items are available only on a self-service basis at the retail level.

Shopping Products. **Shopping products** are items for which buyers are willing to expend considerable effort in planning and making the purchase. Buyers spend much time comparing stores and brands with respect to prices, product features, qualities, services, and perhaps warranties. Shoppers may compare products at a number of outlets such as Best Buy, Circuit City, Sears, or Home Depot. Appliances, bicycles, furniture, stereos, cameras, and shoes exemplify shopping products. These products are expected to last a fairly long time and thus are purchased less frequently than convenience items. Although shopping products are more expensive than convenience products, few buyers of shopping products are particularly brand loyal. Most consumers, for example, are not brand loyal for computers and clothing. If they were, they would be unwilling to shop and compare among brands. Even when they are brand loyal, they may still spend considerable time comparing the features of different models of a brand. A consumer who is looking for a new Maytag washing machine, for example, may explore the company's website to compare the features of different washers before visiting a store and talking to a salesperson. Regardless of the number of brands of interest, buyers may also consult buying guides such as *Consumer Reports* or visit consumer information websites such as **www.epinions.com** to view others' opinions or ratings of brands and models before making an actual purchase.

To market a shopping product effectively, a marketer considers several key issues. Shopping products require fewer retail outlets than convenience products. Because shopping products are purchased less frequently, inventory turnover is lower, and marketing channel members expect to receive higher gross margins. Although large sums of money may be required to advertise shopping products, an even larger percentage of resources is likely to be used for personal selling. Usually the producer and the marketing channel members expect some cooperation from one another with respect to providing parts and repair services and performing promotional activities. In certain situations, both shopping products and convenience products may be marketed in the same location. H-E-B, a privately held Texas grocery chain, introduced a new store concept called H-E-B Plus, which carries everything from toys and home entertainment products to area rugs and high-end televisions, as well as the traditional groceries and ethnic foods in which H-E-B excels.[4]

Specialty Products. **Specialty products** possess one or more unique characteristics, and generally buyers are willing to expend considerable effort to obtain them. Buyers actually plan the purchase of a specialty product; they know exactly what they want and will not accept a substitute. Examples of specialty products include a Mont Blanc pen and a one-of-a-kind piece of baseball memorabilia, such as a ball signed by Babe Ruth. When searching for specialty products, buyers do not compare alternatives; they are concerned primarily with finding an outlet that has the preselected product available. Tag Heuer, for example, issued a special Indy 500 watch designed especially for racing fans.

shopping products Items for which buyers are willing to expend considerable effort in planning and making purchases

specialty products Items with unique characteristics that buyers are willing to expend considerable effort to obtain

RESPONSIBLE marketing?

Digital Rights Management Changing the Convenience Levels When Shopping for Music

ISSUE: Is Digital Rights Management (DRM) technology violating fair use rights in the entertainment industry?

Digital Rights Management, or DRM, refers to a number of ways to restrict the free use and transfer of digital content. With piracy becoming a big problem in media distribution by cutting into profits and sales, companies have started using DRM technology on their media to limit the ability of users to copy and distribute the data.

Critics of DRM argue that the use of digital technology should be unabated and that shifting the control of sharing to producers could ultimately hurt creative expression and damage consumer rights. Advocates for civil liberties make the case that while most music is protected by copyright, consumers have some flexibility under fair use clauses. However, DRM technologies makes no concessions and thus restricts the legal use of the content.

The digital media platform iTunes is making millions of dollars a day in sales, while the overall music industry's numbers are declining. Most DRM-protected media that is purchased outside iTunes is not technically compatible with the highly used iPod (which dominates over 70 percent of the MP3 player market), so users are forced to find ways around purchasing and sharing DRM-protected media to get music on their MP3 players. Steve Jobs, Apple's CEO, has said he would like the music companies to sell their music without DRM. "DRM restrictions only hurt people purchasing music legally, and . . . DRM only encourages users to obtain music illegally," he explains. Does DRM help or hurt the music industry's interests? Are there other avenues the music companies can take besides using DRM to protect their digital media from pirating? Do you think DRM violates the fair use of digital content?[b]

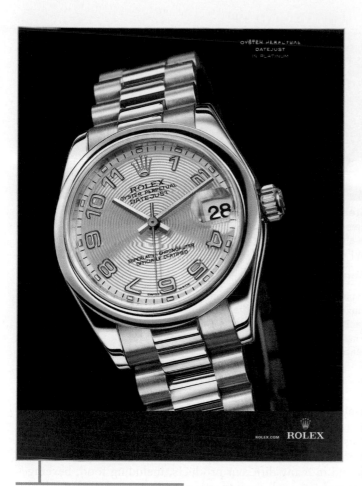

Speciality Product

Rolex's high price and exclusive distribution make it a specialty product.

unsought products Products purchased to solve a sudden problem, products of which customers are unaware, and products that people do not necessarily think of buying

installations Facilities and nonportable major equipment

accessory equipment Equipment that does not become part of the final physical product but is used in production or office activities

The fact that an item is a specialty product can affect a firm's marketing efforts in several ways. Specialty products are often distributed through a limited number of retail outlets. Like shopping products, they are purchased infrequently, causing lower inventory turnover and thus requiring relatively high gross margins.

Unsought Products. **Unsought products** are products purchased when a sudden problem must be solved, products of which customers are unaware, and products that people do not necessarily think of purchasing. Emergency medical services and automobile repairs are examples of products needed quickly to solve a problem. A consumer who is sick or injured has little time to plan to go to an emergency medical center or a hospital. Likewise, in the event of a broken fan belt on the highway, a consumer will likely seek out the nearest auto repair facility to get back on the road as quickly as possible. Computer users must purchase antivirus and spyware detection software to protect their computers even though they may not want to make such purchases. In such cases, speed and problem resolution are far more important than price and other features buyers might consider if they had more time for decision making. Companies such as ServiceMaster, which markets emergency services such as disaster recovery and plumbing repair, are making the purchases of these unsought products more bearable by building trust with consumers through recognizable brands (ServiceMaster Clean and Rescue Rooter) and superior functional performance.

Business Products

Business products are usually purchased on the basis of an organization's goals and objectives. Generally the functional aspects of the product are more important than the psychological rewards sometimes associated with consumer products. Business products can be classified into seven categories according to their characteristics and intended uses: installations, accessory equipment, raw materials, component parts, process materials, MRO supplies, and business services.

Installations. **Installations** include facilities, such as office buildings, factories, and warehouses, and major equipment that are nonportable, such as production lines and very large machines. Major equipment is normally used for production purposes. Some major equipment is custom made to perform specific functions for a particular organization; other items are standardized and perform similar tasks for many types of firms. Normally installations are expensive and intended to be used for a considerable length of time. Because they are so expensive and typically involve a long-term investment of capital, purchase decisions are often made by high-level management. Marketers of installations frequently must provide a variety of services, including training, repairs, maintenance assistance, and even financial assistance.

Accessory Equipment. **Accessory equipment** does not become a part of the final physical product but is used in production or office activities. Examples include file cabinets, fractional-horsepower motors, calculators, and tools. Compared with major equipment, accessory items are usually much cheaper, purchased routinely with less negotiation, and treated as expense items rather than capital items because they are not expected to last as long. Accessory products are standardized items that can be used in several aspects of a firm's operations. More outlets are required for distributing accessory equipment than for installations, but sellers do not have to provide the numerous services expected of installations marketers.

New Holland Skid Steers are built with you in mind, designed for productivity and profitability. Our skid steers feature a new deluxe cab that leads the industry in dimension, visibility and ease of operation. These workhorses are designed to lift heavier loads and place them higher and farther forward.

The Features You Want

- **Superior all-around visibility** - enhanced downward sight lines and frame-free rear view
- **Excellent reach at maximum lift height** - patented Super Boom® lift linkage
- **Outstanding lift capacity and stability** - longer wheelbase and low center of gravity
- **Faster cycle times** - fast hydraulics and ground speeds
- **More versatility** - over 55 hardworking attachments

Business Product

New Holland equipment is a business product designed for use by business customers.

raw materials Basic natural materials that become part of a physical product

component parts Items that become part of the physical product and are either finished items ready for assembly or items that need little processing before assembly

process materials Materials that are used directly in the production of other products but are not readily identifiable

MRO supplies Maintenance, repair, and operating items that facilitate production and operations but do not become part of the finished product

Raw Materials. **Raw materials** are the basic natural materials that actually become part of a physical product. They include minerals, chemicals, agricultural products, and materials from forests and oceans. They are usually bought and sold according to grades and specifications, and in relatively large quantities. Corn, for example, is a raw material that is found in many different products, including food, beverages (as corn syrup), and even fuel (ethanol). Indeed, the growing popularity of ethanol as an alternative fuel has caused corn prices to soar.[5]

Component Parts. **Component parts** become part of the physical product and are either finished items ready for assembly or products that need little processing before assembly. Although they become part of a larger product, component parts often can be easily identified and distinguished. Spark plugs, tires, clocks, brakes, and switches are all component parts of an automobile. German-based Robert Bosch GmbH, the world's largest auto parts maker, supplies 30 percent of the 46 million antilock brakes installed in vehicles worldwide.[6] Buyers purchase such items according to their own specifications or industry standards. They expect the parts to be of specified quality and delivered on time so that production is not slowed or stopped. Producers that are primarily assemblers, such as most lawn mower and computer manufacturers, depend heavily on suppliers of component parts.

Process Materials. **Process materials** are used directly in the production of other products. Unlike component parts, however, process materials are not readily identifiable. For example, a salad dressing manufacturer includes vinegar in its salad dressing. The vinegar is a process material because it is included in the salad dressing but is not identifiable. As with component parts, process materials are purchased according to industry standards or the purchaser's specifications.

MRO Supplies. **MRO supplies** are maintenance, repair, and operating items that facilitate production and operations but do not become part of the finished product. Paper, pencils, oils, cleaning agents, and paints are in this category. Although you might be familiar with Tide, Downy, and Febreze as consumer products, to restaurants and hotels, they are MRO supplies they require to wash dishes and launder sheets and towels. Procter & Gamble is increasingly targeting business customers in the $3.2 billion market for janitorial and housekeeping products.[7] MRO supplies are commonly sold through numerous outlets and are purchased routinely. To ensure supplies are available when needed, buyers often deal with more than one seller.

Business Services. **Business services** are the intangible products that many organizations use in their operations. They include financial, legal, marketing research, information technology, and janitorial services. Firms must decide whether to provide their own services internally or obtain them from outside the organization. This decision depends on the costs associated with each alternative and how frequently the services are needed. For example, few firms have the resources to provide global overnight delivery services efficiently, so most companies rely on FedEx, UPS, DHL, and other service providers.

Product Line and Product Mix

L O 3 To examine the concepts of product item, product line, and product mix and understand how they are connected

business services Intangible products that many organizations use in their operations

product item A specific version of a product that can be designated as a distinct offering among a firm's products

product line A group of closely related product items viewed as a unit because of marketing, technical, or end-use considerations

Marketers must understand the relationships among all the products of their organization to coordinate the marketing of the total group of products. The following concepts help describe the relationships among an organization's products.

A **product item** is a specific version of a product that can be designated as a distinct offering among an organization's products. An L.L. Bean flannel shirt represents a product item. A **product line** is a group of closely related product items that are considered to be a unit because of marketing, technical, or end-use considerations. For example, Reebok launched a new line of athletic shoes that have the fruity aroma of Kool-Aid flavors. The first shoes in the line, which get their smell from scent-infused sock liners, come in grape, cherry, and strawberry "flavors."[8] The exact boundaries of a product line (although sometimes blurred) are usually indicated by using descriptive terms such as "frozen dessert" product line or "shampoo" product line. To develop the optimal product line, marketers must understand buyers' goals. In the personal computer industry, for example, companies are likely to expand their product lines when industry barriers are low or perceived market opportunities exist. Firms with high market share are likely to expand their product lines aggressively, as are marketers with relatively high prices or limited product lines.[9] Specific product items in a product line usually reflect the desires of different target markets or the different needs of consumers.

Product Line and Product Mix
Mad Rock advertises its line of climbing accessories. It markets other product lines, too. The Hilton ad shows Hilton's entire product offering.

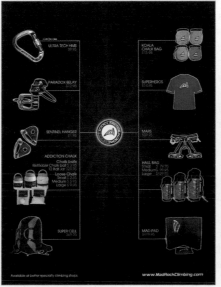

E-ntertainment MARKETING

Meet the Webkinz

The stuffed toy business is going to the dogs—and cats, cows, and avatars. Just ask Ganz, the company that sold 2 million Webkinz in the product line's first two years. The plush animals are cute and cuddly, but they also have an interactive element that children find irresistible. Each Webkinz comes with a secret code that allows the owner to log on to the Webkinz World site, adopt and name the animal, and then play with its virtual counterpart. Owners can make online playdates with friends' Webkinz and text-chat with other owners (with parents' consent). Indeed, experts project that 10 million children will be members of branded virtual worlds like Webkinz by 2011.

The initial purchase price buys a year's access to Webkinz World plus $2,000 in KinzCash for buying virtual extras like pet toys. Ganz wants Webkinz owners to visit often, so it awards KinzCash for entering contests or answering trivia questions.

In all, nearly 3 million users log on to Webkinz World every month. After the first year, however, the only way to gain entry is to get a new secret code by buying another Webkinz.

Without advertising, how did Webkinz get launched? "Most of our success comes from word of mouth," says a Ganz spokesperson. "We say it spreads from playground to playground." Word of mouth makes Webkinz especially appealing, confirms Professor Lisa Bolton of Wharton. "The kids have discovered it for themselves; they haven't had it pushed on them by a parent or a marketer."[c]

---

product mix The composite, or total, group of products that an organization makes available to customers

width of product mix The number of product lines a company offers

depth of product mix The average number of different products offered in each product line

product life cycle The progression of a product through four stages: introduction, growth, maturity, and decline

A **product mix** is the composite, or total, group of products that an organization makes available to customers. For example, all the health-care, beauty-care, laundry and cleaning, food and beverage, paper, cosmetic, and fragrance products that Procter & Gamble manufactures constitute its product mix. The **width of product mix** is measured by the number of product lines a company offers. Robert Bosch GmbH, for example, offers multiple product lines, including automotive technology components such as brakes and stability control systems, consumer products such as household appliances, and business products such as packaging machines.[10] The **depth of product mix** is the average number of different products offered in each product line. Figure 10.2 shows the width and depth of a part of Procter & Gamble's product mix. Procter & Gamble is known for using distinctive branding, packaging, and consumer advertising to promote individual items in its detergent product line. Tide, Bold, Gain, Cheer, and Era—all Procter & Gamble detergents—share the same distribution channels and similar manufacturing facilities, but each is promoted as a distinctive product, adding depth to the product line.

Product Life Cycles and Marketing Strategies

LO 4 To understand the product life cycle and its impact on marketing strategies

Just as biological cycles progress from birth through growth and decline, so do product life cycles. As Figure 10.3 shows, a **product life cycle** has four major stages: introduction, growth, maturity, and decline. As a product moves through its life cycle, the strategies that relate to competition, promotion, distribution, pricing, and market information

figure 10.2   **THE CONCEPTS OF PRODUCT MIX WIDTH AND DEPTH APPLIED TO U.S. PROCTER & GAMBLE PRODUCTS**

Reprinted by permission of Procter & Gamble Company.

Laundry detergents	Toothpastes	Bar soaps	Deodorants	Shampoos	Tissue/Towel
Ivory Snow 1930	Gleem 1952	Ivory 1879	Old Spice 1948	Pantene 1947	Charmin 1928
Dreft 1933	Crest 1955	Camay 1926	Secret 1956	Head & Shoulders 1961	Puffs 1960
Tide 1946		Zest 1952	Sure 1972	Vidal Sassoon 1974	Bounty 1965
Cheer 1950		Oufoguard 1967		Pert Plus 1979	
Bold 1965		Oil of Olay 1993		Ivory 1983	
Gain 1966				Infusium 23 1986	
Era 1972				Physique 2000	
Febreze Clean Wash 2000				Herbal Essence 2001	

Depth (vertical axis) — *Width* (horizontal axis)

must be periodically evaluated and possibly changed. Astute marketing managers use the life cycle concept to make sure the introduction, alteration, and termination of a product are timed and executed properly. By understanding the typical life cycle pattern, marketers are better able to maintain profitable products and drop unprofitable ones.

Introduction

The **introduction stage** of the product life cycle begins at a product's first appearance in the marketplace, when sales start at zero and profits are negative. Profits are below zero because initial revenues are low, and the company generally must cover large expenses for promotion and distribution. Notice in Figure 10.3 how sales should move upward from zero, and profits should also move upward from a position in which they are negative because of high expenses.

figure 10.3

THE FOUR STAGES OF THE PRODUCT LIFE CYCLE

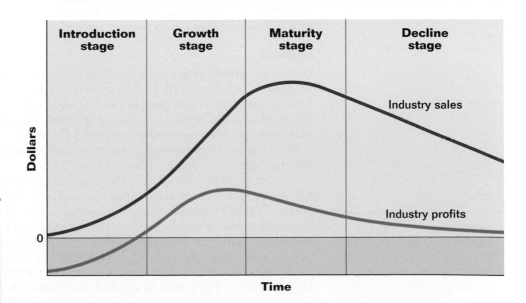

introduction stage The initial stage of a product's life cycle; its first appearance in the marketplace when sales start at zero and profits are negative

Thinnovation.

The world's thinnest notebook. 13.3-inch widescreen display. Full-size keyboard. **◆ MacBook** Air

Product Life Cycle

Notebook computers are in the maturity stage of the product life cycle.

Developing and introducing a new product can mean an outlay of $100 million or more. Cadbury Schweppes, for example, spent two years and millions of dollars to develop Trident Splash, a sugar-free gum with a candy shell and a liquid center, which it markets to adults for 99 cents a package.[11] And although the importance of new products is significant, the risk of new-product failure is quite high, depending on the industry. Although LeapFrog introduced the LeapPad educational reading toy with tremendous success, the company has since struggled to find a successful follow-up, and declining sales have left the company operating in the red for several years. The company has now staked its hopes on the Tag, a product that makes traditional printed books an interactive experience complete with word definitions and character voices. To thrive, LeapFrog must adapt to changing expectations from both children and their parents with new products.[12] Because of high risks and costs, few product introductions represent revolutionary inventions. More typically, product introductions involve a new packaged convenience food, a new model of automobile, or a new fashion in clothing rather than a major product innovation. Birds Eye, for example, introduced a new line of Steamfresh frozen foods, which includes frozen vegetables that are steamed in the microwave oven using a new process.[13] The more marketing oriented the firm, the more likely it will be to launch innovative, new-to-the-market products.[14]

Potential buyers must be made aware of the new product's features, uses, and advantages. Efforts to highlight a new product's value can create a foundation for building brand loyalty and customer relationships.[15] Two difficulties may arise at this point. First, sellers may lack the resources, technological knowledge, and marketing know-how to launch the product successfully. Firms without large budgets can still attract attention by giving away free samples, as Essence of Vali did with its aromatherapy products. Another small-budget tactic is to gain visibility through media appearances. Dave Dettman, a.k.a. Dr. Gadget, specializes in promoting new products on television news and talk programs. Companies such as Sony, Disney, Warner Brothers, and others have hired Dr. Gadget to help with the introduction of new products.[16] Second, the initial product price may have to be high to recoup expensive marketing research or development costs. Given these difficulties, it is not surprising that many products never get beyond the introduction stage.

Most new products start off slowly and seldom generate enough sales to bring immediate profits. As buyers learn about the new product, marketers should be alert for product weaknesses and make corrections quickly to prevent the product's early demise. Marketing strategy should be designed to attract the segment that is most interested in the product and has the fewest objections. As the sales curve moves upward and the break-even point is reached, the growth stage begins.

Growth

During the **growth stage,** sales rise rapidly, profits reach a peak, and then they start to decline (see Figure 10.3). The growth stage is critical to a product's survival because competitive reactions to the product's success during this period will affect the product's life expectancy. When Splenda, a sugar substitute, was introduced, sales rose quickly as consumers switched from other low-calorie sweeteners. Sales rose even more quickly when restaurants such as McDonald's and Starbucks began offering Splenda in single-serving packets.[17]

Profits begin to decline late in the growth stage as more competitors enter the market, driving prices down and creating the need for heavy promotional expenses. At this point, a typical marketing strategy encourages strong brand loyalty and competes with aggressive emulators of the product. During the growth stage, the organization tries to strengthen its market share and develop a competitive niche by emphasizing the product's benefits. Aggressive pricing, including price cuts, is also typical during this stage.

As sales increase, management must support the momentum by adjusting the marketing strategy. The goal is to establish and fortify the product's market position by

growth stage The product life cycle stage when sales rise rapidly, profits reach a peak, and then they start to decline

encouraging brand loyalty. To achieve greater market penetration, segmentation may have to be used more intensely. That would require developing product variations to satisfy the needs of people in several different market segments. Apple, for example, introduced more variations on its wildly popular iPod MP3 player, including the affordable iPod shuffle, the smaller iPod nano, and the iPod touch with a touch-screen interface, all of which helped expand Apple's market penetration in the competitive MP3 player industry. Marketers should also analyze competing brands' product positions relative to their own brands and take corrective actions.

Gaps in geographic market coverage should be filled during the growth period. As a product gains market acceptance, new distribution outlets usually become easier to obtain. Marketers sometimes move from an exclusive or a selective exposure to a more intensive network of dealers to achieve greater market penetration. Marketers must also make sure the physical distribution system is running efficiently so that customers' orders are processed accurately and delivered on time.

Promotion expenditures may be slightly lower than during the introductory stage but are still quite substantial. As sales increase, promotion costs should drop as a percentage of total sales. A falling ratio between promotion expenditures and sales should contribute significantly to increased profits. The advertising messages should stress brand benefits. Coupons and samples may be used to increase market share.

After recovering development costs, a business may be able to lower prices. As sales volume increases, efficiencies in production can result in lower costs. These savings may be passed on to buyers. For example, when flat-screen televisions were initially introduced, the price was $5,000 or more. As demand soared, manufacturers of both LCD and plasma technologies were able to take advantage of economies of scale to reduce production costs and lower prices to less than $1,000 within several years. If demand remains strong and there are few competitive threats, prices tend to remain stable. If price cuts are feasible, they can help a brand gain market share and discourage new competitors from entering the market.

Maturity

During the **maturity stage,** the sales curve peaks and starts to decline and profits continue to fall (see Figure 10.3). This stage is characterized by intense competition because many brands are now in the market. Competitors emphasize improvements and differences in their versions of the product. As a result, during the maturity stage, weaker competitors are squeezed out or lose interest in the product.

During the maturity phase, the producers who remain in the market are likely to change their promotional and distribution efforts. Advertising and dealer-oriented promotions are typical during this stage of the product life cycle. Marketers must also take into account that as the product reaches maturity, buyers' knowledge of it attains a high level. Consumers of the product are no longer inexperienced generalists; instead they are experienced specialists. Marketers of mature products sometimes expand distribution into global markets. Often the products have to be adapted to more precisely fit differing needs of global customers.

Because many products are in the maturity stage of their life cycles, marketers must know how to deal with these products and be prepared to adjust their marketing strategies. As Table 10.1 shows, there are many approaches to altering marketing strategies during the maturity stage. As noted in the table, to increase the sales of mature products, marketers may suggest new uses for them. Arm & Hammer has boosted demand for its baking soda with this method. As customers become more experienced and knowledgeable about products during the maturity stage (particularly about business products), the benefits they seek may change as well, necessitating product modifications. Consider that traditional truck-based sport utility vehicles, such as the Ford Explorer and GMC Tahoe, have reached maturity and their sales are beginning to decline. Facing rising gasoline costs, consumers seem more interested in "crossovers": car-based utility vehicles like the Honda Pilot, BMW X3, Porsche Cayenne, and Saturn Vue. Automakers responded to this interest with more models and features. With their improved ride, handling, and fuel economy, crossovers are in a rapid sales growth stage at the expense of traditional SUVs.[18]

maturity stage The stage of a product's life cycle when the sales curve peaks and starts to decline, and profits continue to fall

table 10.1   SELECTED APPROACHES FOR MANAGING PRODUCTS IN THE MATURITY STAGE

Approach	Examples
Develop new product uses	Knox gelatin used as a plant food Arm & Hammer baking soda marketed as a refrigerator and cat litter deodorant Cheez Whiz promoted as a microwavable cheese sauce
Increase product usage among current users	Multiple packaging used for products in which a larger supply at the point of consumption actually increases consumption (such as for soft drinks or beer)
Increase number of users	Global markets or small niches in domestic markets pursued
Add product features	Traditional SUVs slowly replaced by crossover vehicles Satellite radio and MP3 systems in automobiles
Change package sizes	Single-serving sizes introduced Travel-size packages of personal-care products introduced
Increase product quality	Life of light bulbs increased Reliability and durability of U.S.-made automobiles increased
Change nonproduct marketing mix variables—promotion, price, distribution	Focus of Dr Pepper advertisements shifted from teenagers to people ages 18 to 54 A package of dishwasher detergent containing one-third more product offered for the same price Computer hardware marketed through mail-order outlets

Three general objectives can be pursued during the maturity stage:

1. *Generate cash flow.* This is essential for recouping the initial investment and generating excess cash to support new products.

2. *Maintain share of market.* Companies with marginal market share must decide whether they have a reasonable chance to improve their position or whether they should drop out.

3. *Increase share of customer.* Whereas *market share* refers to the percentage of total customers a firm holds, *share of customer* relates to the percentage of each customer's needs that the firm is meeting. For example, many banks have added new services (brokerage, financial planning, auto leasing, etc.) to gain more of each customer's financial services business. Likewise, many supermarkets are seeking to increase share of customer by adding services such as restaurants, movie rentals, and dry cleaning to provide one-stop shopping for their customers' household needs.[19]

During the maturity stage, marketers actively encourage dealers to support the product. Dealers may be offered promotional assistance in lowering their inventory costs. In general, marketers go to great lengths to serve dealers and provide incentives for selling their brands.

Maintaining market share during the maturity stage requires moderate, and sometimes large, promotion expenditures. Advertising messages focus on differentiating a brand from the field of competitors, and sales promotion efforts are aimed at both consumers and resellers.

A greater mixture of pricing strategies is used during the maturity stage. Strong price competition is likely and may ignite price wars. Firms also compete in ways other than price, such as through product quality or service. In addition, marketers develop price flexibility to differentiate offerings in product lines. Markdowns and price incentives are common. Prices may have to be increased, however, if distribution and production costs rise.

Decline

During the **decline stage,** sales fall rapidly (refer to Figure 10.3). When this happens, the marketer considers pruning items from the product line to eliminate those that are no longer earning a profit. The marketer may also cut promotion efforts, eliminate marginal distributors, and, finally, plan to phase out the product. For example, Coca-Cola spent two years developing Coke Blak, an eight-ounce soft drink "with an adult cola taste" that was targeted at the over-30 crowd, but the beverage never developed a significant following. Although the company planned to continue selling the $1.99 drink in some overseas markets, it will stop marketing the cola in the United States when bottlers' concentrate supplies run out.[20] An organization can justify maintaining a product only as long as the product contributes to profits or enhances the overall effectiveness of a product mix. Kodak, after spending $1 billion over eight years to develop its Advantix photography system, pulled the plug after sales declined by 75 percent.[21]

In this stage, marketers must determine whether to eliminate the product or try to reposition it to extend its life. Usually a declining product has lost its distinctiveness because similar competing products have been introduced. Competition engenders increased substitution and brand switching as buyers become insensitive to minor product differences. For these reasons, marketers do little to change a product's style, design, or other attributes during its decline. New technology or social trends, product substitutes, or environmental considerations may also indicate that the time has come to delete the product. Consider the lowly incandescent light bulb. As consumers switch to "greener" compact fluorescent bulbs and LED lighting—increasingly prompted by government bans on incandescent bulbs—manufacturers are beginning to implement plans to phase them out of their product mixes.

During a product's decline, outlets with strong sales volumes are maintained and unprofitable outlets are weeded out. An entire marketing channel may be eliminated if it does not contribute adequately to profits. An outlet that was not previously used, such as a factory outlet or Internet retailer, is sometimes used to liquidate remaining inventory of an obsolete product. As sales decline, the product becomes more inaccessible, but loyal buyers seek out dealers who still carry it.

Spending on promotion efforts is usually reduced considerably. Advertising of special offers may slow the rate of decline. Sales promotions, such as coupons and premiums, may temporarily recapture buyers' attention. As the product continues to decline, the sales staff shifts its emphasis to more profitable products.

The marketing manager has two options during the decline stage: attempt to postpone the decline or accept its inevitability. Many firms lack the resources to renew a product's demand and are forced to consider harvesting or divesting the product or the strategic business unit (SBU). The *harvesting* approach employs a gradual reduction in marketing expenditures and a less resource-intensive marketing mix. A company adopting the *divesting* approach withdraws all marketing support from the declining product or SBU. It may continue to sell the product until losses are sustained or arrange for another firm to acquire the product. For example, although Procter & Gamble's Sure deodorant had been around for nearly three decades, sharply declining sales led the company to sell the well-known brand to Innovative Brands LLC, which had earlier purchased P&G's Pert shampoo brand.[22]

Because most businesses have a product mix that consists of multiple products, a firm's destiny is rarely tied to one product. A composite of life cycle patterns forms when various products in the mix are at different cycle stages: as one product is declining, other products are in the introduction, growth, or maturity stage. Marketers must deal with the dual problem of prolonging the lives of existing products and introducing new products to meet organizational sales goals.

decline stage The stage of a product's life cycle when sales fall rapidly

The Product Adoption Process

L O 5 To describe the product adoption process

Acceptance of new products—especially new-to-the-world products—usually doesn't happen overnight. In fact, it can take a very long time. People are sometimes cautious or even skeptical about adopting new products, as indicated by some of the remarks quoted in Table 10.2. Customers who eventually accept a new product do so through an adoption process. The stages of the **product adoption process** are as follows:

1. *Awareness.* The buyer becomes aware of the product.

2. *Interest.* The buyer seeks information and is receptive to learning about the product.

3. *Evaluation.* The buyer considers the product's benefits and decides whether to try it.

4. *Trial.* The buyer examines, tests, or tries the product to determine if it meets his or her needs.

5. *Adoption.* The buyer purchases the product and can be expected to use it again whenever the need for this general type of product arises.[23]

product adoption process
The five-stage process of buyer acceptance of a product: awareness, interest, evaluation, trial, and adoption

In the first stage, when individuals become aware that the product exists, they have little information about it and are not concerned about obtaining more. Consumers enter the interest stage when they are motivated to get information about the product's features, uses, advantages, disadvantages, price, or location. During the

table 10.2   MOST NEW IDEAS HAVE THEIR SKEPTICS

"I think there is a world market for maybe five computers."

—Thomas Watson, chairman of IBM, 1943

"This 'telephone' has too many shortcomings to be seriously considered as a means of communication. The device is inherently of no value to us."

—Western Union internal memo, 1876

"The wireless music box has no imaginable commercial value. Who would pay for a message sent to nobody in particular?"

—David Sarnoff's associates in response to his urgings for investment in the radio in the 1920s

"The concept is interesting and well-formed, but in order to earn better than a 'C,' the idea must be feasible."

—A Yale University management professor in response to Fred Smith's paper proposing reliable overnight delivery service (Smith went on to found Federal Express Corporation)

"Who the hell wants to hear actors talk?"

—H. M. Warner, Warner Brothers, 1927

"A cookie store is a bad idea. Besides, the market research reports say America likes crispy cookies, not soft and chewy cookies like you make."

—Banker's response to Debbie Fields's idea of starting Mrs. Fields' Cookies

"We don't like their sound, and guitar music is on the way out."

—Decca Recording Company rejecting the Beatles, 1962

evaluation stage, individuals consider whether the product will satisfy certain criteria that are crucial to meeting their specific needs. In the trial stage, they use or experience the product for the first time, possibly by purchasing a small quantity, taking advantage of free samples, or borrowing the product from someone. Supermarkets, for instance, frequently offer special promotions to encourage consumers to taste products. During this stage, potential adopters determine the usefulness of the product under the specific conditions for which they need it.

Individuals move into the adoption stage by choosing a specific product when they need a product of that general type. However, entering the adoption process does not mean the person will eventually adopt the new product. Rejection may occur at any stage, including the adoption stage. Both product adoption and product rejection can be temporary or permanent. This adoption model has several implications when launching a new product. First, the company must promote the product to create widespread awareness of its existence and its benefits. Samples or simulated trials should be arranged to help buyers make initial purchase decisions. At the same time, marketers should emphasize quality control and provide solid guarantees to reinforce buyer opinion during the evaluation stage. Finally, production and physical distribution must be linked to patterns of adoption and repeat purchases.

When an organization introduces a new product, people do not begin the adoption process at the same time, nor do they move through the process at the same speed. Of those who eventually adopt the product, some enter the adoption process rather quickly, whereas others start considerably later. For most products, there is also a group of nonadopters who never begin the process. For business marketers, success in managing production innovation, diffusion, and adoption requires great adaptability and significant effort in understanding customers.[24]

Depending on the length of time it takes them to adopt a new product, consumers fall into one of five major adopter categories: innovators, early adopters, early majority, late majority, and laggards.[25] Figure 10.4 illustrates each adopter category and the percentage of total adopters it typically represents. **Innovators** are the first to adopt a new product; they enjoy trying new products and tend to be venturesome. **Early adopters** choose new products carefully and are viewed as "the people to check with" by those in the remaining adopter categories. People in the **early majority** adopt a new product just prior to the average person; they are deliberate and cautious in trying new products. Individuals in the **late majority** are quite skeptical of new products but eventually adopt them because of economic necessity or social pressure. **Laggards,** the last to adopt a new product, are oriented toward the past. They are suspicious of new products, and when they finally adopt the innovation, it may already have been replaced by a new product.

innovators First adopters of new products

early adopters People who adopt new products early, choose new products carefully, and are viewed as "the people to check with" by later adopters

early majority Individuals who adopt a new product just prior to the average person

late majority Skeptics who adopt new products when they feel it is necessary

laggards The last adopters, who distrust new products

Source: Adapted with permission of The Free Press, a division of Simon & Schuster Adult Publishing Group, from *Diffusion of Innovations,* Fourth Edition, by Everett M. Rogers. Copyright © 1995 by Everett M. Rogers. Copyright © 1962, 1971, 1983 by The Free Press. All rights reserved.

figure 10.4

DISTRIBUTION OF PRODUCT ADOPTER CATEGORIES

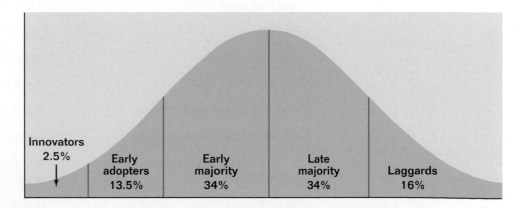

Innovators
2.5%

Early adopters
13.5%

Early majority
34%

Late majority
34%

Laggards
16%

Why Some Products Fail and Others Succeed

L O G To understand why some products fail and some succeed

Thousands of new products are introduced annually, and many fail. Statistical bureaus, consulting firms, and trade publications estimate that one out of every three new products fails each year; others report an annual new-product failure rate as high as 80 to 90 percent. The annual cost of product failures to U.S. firms can reach $100 billion. Failure and success rates vary from organization to organization, but in general consumer products fail more often than business products. Being one of the first brands launched in a product category is no guarantee of success. Table 10.3 shows examples of recent product successes and failures.

Products fail for many reasons. One of the most common reasons is the company's failure to match product offerings to customer needs. When products do not offer value and lack the features customers want, they fail in the marketplace. For example, Coca-Cola's C2 and PepsiCo's Pepsi Edge, both targeted at low-carbohydrate dieters with their midrange calorie count, ultimately garnered just 1 percent share of the market together because low-carb dieters generally avoid products with any refined sugar.[26] Ineffective or inconsistent branding has also been blamed for product failures. Examples of products that failed due to failure to convey the right message or image include Gerber Singles (gourmet food for adults packaged in baby food jars), Microsoft's Bob (a "social interface" cartoon character that many users perceived as juvenile), and Gillette's For Oily Hair Only shampoo.[27] Other reasons cited for new-product failure include technical or design problems, poor timing, overestimation of market size, ineffective promotion, and insufficient distribution.

When examining the problem of product failure, it is important to distinguish the degree of failure. Absolute failure occurs when an organization loses money on a new product because it is unable to recover development, production, and marketing costs. This product usually is deleted from the product mix. Relative product failure occurs when a product returns a profit but does not meet a company's profit or market share objectives. If a company repositions or improves a relative product failure, that product may become a successful member of the product line. Some products experience relative product failure after years of success. Campbell Soup, for example, has been growing slowly for many years. The company continues to focus on its condensed-soup product line but has done little to improve packaging, promotion, or distribution. This leaves Campbell Soup with a core product whose market share has fallen 21 percent during a recent four-year period.[28]

In contrast to this gloomy picture of new-product failure, some new products are very successful. Perhaps the most important ingredient for success is the product's

table 10.3 **PRODUCT SUCCESSES AND FAILURES**

Successes	Failures
Smith Kline Beecham Nicoderm CQ	R. J. Reynolds Premier smokeless cigarettes
Canon Elph digital camera	Cadillac Allante luxury cars
Palm PDAs	Apple Lisa personal computer
Coca-Cola Dasani water	Heinz Ketch Salsa
Starbucks coffee shops	Nestlé Panache coffee
Procter & Gamble Pantene shampoos	Gillette For Oily Hair Only shampoo
Tide High Efficiency laundry detergent	Drel Home Dry Cleaning Kits
Procter & Gamble Swiffer mop and dusting cloths	S. C. Johnson Allercare aerosol spray, carpet powder, and dust mite powder
Bacardi Breezers	Bud and Michelob Dry Beer

ability to provide a significant and perceivable benefit to a sizable number of customers. New products with an observable advantage over similar available products, such as more features, ease of operation, or improved technology, have a greater chance to succeed. Sometimes a product is simply in touch with consumers' feelings and taste. Consider the Whoopie Pie, a Maine product similar to the Moon Pie sold in the South. Critical to launching a product that will achieve market success is effective planning and management. Companies that follow a systematic, customer-focused plan for new-product development, such as Procter & Gamble and 3M, are well positioned to launch successful products.

SUMMARY

A product is a good, a service, or an idea received in an exchange. It can be either tangible or intangible and includes functional, social, and psychological utilities or benefits. When consumers purchase a product, they are buying the benefits and satisfaction they think the product will provide.

Products can be classified on the basis of the buyer's intentions. Consumer products are those purchased to satisfy personal and family needs. Business products are purchased for use in a firm's operations, to resell, or to make other products. Consumer products can be subdivided into convenience, shopping, specialty, and unsought products. Business products can be classified as installations, accessory equipment, raw materials, component parts, process materials, MRO supplies, or business services.

A product item is a specific version of a product that can be designated as a distinct offering among an organization's products. A product line is a group of closely related product items that are viewed as a unit because of marketing, technical, or end-use considerations. The product mix is the composite, or total, group of products that an organization makes available to customers. The width of the product mix is measured by the number of product lines the company offers. The depth of the product mix is the average number of different products offered in each product line.

The product life cycle describes how product items in an industry move through four stages: introduction, growth, maturity, and decline. The life cycle concept is used to ensure that the introduction, alteration, and termination of a product are timed and executed properly. The sales curve is at zero at introduction, rises at an increasing rate during growth, peaks at maturity, and

then declines. Profits peak toward the end of the growth stage of the product life cycle. The life expectancy of a product is based on buyers' wants, the availability of competing products, and other environmental conditions. Most businesses have a composite of life cycle patterns for various products. It is important to manage existing products and develop new ones to keep the overall sales performance at a desired level.

When customers accept a new product, they usually do so through a five-stage adoption process. The first stage is awareness, when buyers become aware that a product exists. Interest, the second stage, occurs when buyers seek information about the product. In the third stage, evaluation, buyers consider the product's benefits and decide whether to try it. The fourth stage is trial, when buyers examine, test, or try the product to determine if it meets their needs. The last stage is adoption, when buyers actually purchase the product and use it whenever a need for this general type of product arises.

Of the thousands of new products introduced every year, many fail. Absolute failure occurs when an organization loses money on a new product. Absolute failures are usually removed from the product mix. Relative failure occurs when a product returns a profit but fails to meet a company's objectives. Reasons for product failure include failure to match product offerings to customer needs, poor timing, and ineffective or inconsistent branding. New products that succeed provide significant and observable benefits to customers. Products that have perceivable advantages over similar products also have a better chance to succeed. Effective marketing planning and product management are important factors in a new product's chances of success.

IMPORTANT TERMS

DISCUSSION & REVIEW QUESTIONS

1. List the tangible and intangible attributes of a pair of Nike athletic shoes. Compare its benefits with those of an intangible product such as a hairstyling in a salon.

2. A product has been referred to as a "psychological bundle of satisfaction." Is this a good definition of a product? Why or why not?

3. Is a personal computer sold at a retail store a consumer product or a business product? Defend your answer.

4. How do convenience products and shopping products differ? What are the distinguishing characteristics of each type of product?

5. In the category of business products, how do component parts differ from process materials?

6. How does an organization's product mix relate to its development of a product line? When should an enterprise add depth to its product lines rather than width to its product mix?

7. How do industry profits change as a product moves through the four stages of its life cycle?

8. What is the relationship between the concepts of product mix and product life cycle?

9. What are the stages in the product adoption process, and how do they affect the commercialization phase?

10. What are the five major adopter categories describing the length of time required for a consumer to adopt a new product, and what are the characteristics of each?

11. In what ways does the marketing strategy for a mature product differ from the marketing strategy for a growth product?

12. What are the major reasons for new-product failure?

APPLICATION QUESTIONS

1. Choose a familiar clothing store. Describe its product mix, including its depth and width. Evaluate the mix and make suggestions to the owner.

2. Tabasco pepper sauce is a product that has entered the maturity stage of the product life cycle. Name products that would fit into each of the four stages: introduction, growth, maturity, and decline. Describe each product and explain why it fits in that stage.

3. Generally buyers go through a product adoption process before becoming loyal customers. Describe your experience in adopting a product you now use consistently. Did you go through all the stages of the process?

4. Identify and describe a friend or family member who fits into each of the following adopter categories. How would you use this information if you were product manager for a fashion-oriented, medium-priced clothing retailer such as J. Crew or JCPenney?

   a. Innovator

   b. Early adopter

   c. Early majority

   d. Late majority

   e. Laggard

INTERNET EXERCISE

Visit **www.cengage.com/marketing/pride-ferrell** for resources to help you master the material in this chapter, plus materials that will help you expand your marketing knowledge, including Internet exercise updates, ACE Self-Tests, hotlinks to companies featured in this chapter, and much more.

Goodyear Tire & Rubber Company

In addition to providing information about the company's products, Goodyear's website helps consumers find the exact products they want and will even direct them to the nearest Goodyear retailer. Visit the Goodyear site at **www.goodyear.com.**

1. How does Goodyear use its website to communicate information about the quality of its tires?

2. How does Goodyear's website demonstrate product design and features?

3. Based on what you learned at the website, describe what Goodyear has done to position its tires.

developing your **MARKETING PLAN**

Identifying the needs of consumer groups and developing products that satisfy those needs are essential when creating a marketing strategy. Successful product development begins with a clear understanding of fundamental product concepts. The product concept is the basis on which many of the marketing plan decisions are made. When relating the information in this chapter to the development of your marketing plan, consider the following:

1. Using Figure 10.2 as a guide, create a matrix of the current product mix for your company.

2. Discuss how the profitability of your product will change as it moves through each of the phases of the product life cycle.

3. Create a brief profile of the type of consumer who is likely to represent each of the product adopter categories for your product.

4. Discuss the factors that could contribute to the failure of your product. How will you define product failure?

The information obtained from these questions should assist you in developing various aspects of your marketing plan found in the *Interactive Marketing Plan* exercise at **www.cengage.com/marketing/pride-ferrell.**

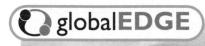

1. A firm's ability to innovate and develop new-product concepts is usually determined by the level of inventiveness and adeptness to adjust to market demands. As a result, successful firms generally benefit from an increase in revenue and publicity in magazines devoted to business innovation. *Business 2.0* annually ranks the fastest-growing companies, which often have the greatest rates of innovation. The ranking can be accessed by using the search term "business innovation" at **http://globaledge.msu.edu/ibrd.** Once you reach the *Business 2.0* website, click on "Small Business," and then choose the "FSB 100" option from the drop-down list. Based on the *Fortune* magazine list of Fastest-Growing Small Public Companies, what are the top ten fastest-growing companies? Which industry appears currently to have the most

successful commercial innovativeness? Why do you think this industry is thriving?

2. The development of concepts for new products requires a firm to devote resources to research and development (R&D). Although insight on different firms' R&D strategies and expenditures may be readily available in annual reports, *Technology Review,* a magazine of innovation, can consolidate this data in its Corporate R&D Scorecard to yield a more comprehensive analysis. The report can be accessed by using the search term "magazine of innovation" at **http://globaledge.msu.edu/ibrd.** Which three industries in a recent report devote the most resources to R&D? Which three industries allocate the least? What does this allow you to conclude about the characteristics of each industry?

video **CASE 10.1**

There's No Place Like . . . Starbucks

Starbucks was founded in 1971 by three partners in Seattle's renowned open-air Pike Place Market. In 1982, after returning from a trip to coffee-bar haven Milan, Italy, Howard Schultz saw an opportunity to develop a similar coffee-bar culture in Seattle and joined the company as director of Retail Operations and Marketing. Three years later, the company

tested the first downtown Seattle coffeehouse, served the first Starbucks Café latte, and introduced its now famous Christmas blend.

Today Starbucks operates more than 14,000 locations in 42 countries. In addition to buying and roasting high-quality whole coffee beans for resale, the company offers fresh-brewed coffees, Italian-style espresso beverages, cold-blended beverages, bottled water, some food items, coffee-related accessories and equipment, and premium teas through its retail stores. Starbucks also sells coffee and tea products and licenses its trademark through other channels and, with partners, markets bottled Frappuccino coffee drinks, DoubleShot espresso drinks, and a line of super-premium ice cream.

Starbucks makes a point of introducing new drinks with each season to boost revenues and provide customers with more choices. During the year, it constantly updates its product lines to stay ahead of changes in customer wants and needs. For example, to satisfy the needs of weight-conscious customers, it created a low-calorie version of its popular Frappuccino. However, not all new products are as successful as the low-cal Frappuccino has been. Starbucks recently discontinued Chantico, its "drinkable dessert," a thick, sweet hot-chocolate beverage that was available only in a six-ounce size. The size limitation proved to be a problem because it ran counter to what customers expect at Star-bucks. Customers are used to dictating not only the size of their drinks but also details such as whether they want regular or decaf coffee; non-fat, whole, or soy milk; sugar-free or regular flavor shots; and extras like whipped cream and caramel. The company also abandoned breakfast sandwiches in 2008 to focus on developing healthier alternatives.

Competition is growing as other companies see profit potential in the kinds of products that Starbucks has popularized. For instance, Coca-Cola has partnered with the Italian coffee company Illycaffe to launch a ready-to-drink coffee beverage that directly competes with the bottled coffee beverages marketed by Starbucks in its joint venture with Pepsi. Another new competitor, McDonald's, is adding coffee stations complete with baristas to make a limited selection of upscale lattes at 800 restaurants and already plans to expand the program. Because the $10 billion market for ready-to-drink coffee beverages is growing at about 10 percent annually, Starbucks can

expect more challengers to turn up the competitive heat in the coming years.

The company has also diversified beyond drinks and food items into entertainment products. Customers can buy compact discs by selected artists or pay to download individual songs they hear in the store via Wi-Fi Internet access. "For the customer, it's an instant gratification," says the head of Starbucks Entertainment. Customers who use iPhones or iPod touch devices can tap to download a song and put the 99-cent cost on their phone bills.

Starbucks has also built an excellent reputation for social responsibility and business ethics. It pays premium prices for top-quality coffee, helping growers make profits and support their families. It also invests in social development programs that build schools, health clinics, and other projects that benefit coffee-growing communities. Through the Farmer Support Center in Costa Rica, the company provides growers with the technical support and training they need to produce high-quality beans in an eco-friendly way. By buying Fair Trade Certified, shade-grown, and certified organic coffees, Starbucks does its part to promote responsible environmental and economic efforts. Another socially responsible product available at Starbucks outlets is Ethos Water, which helps raise money to pay for safe-water initiatives in developing countries. In 2007 Starbucks ranked ninth on *Business Ethics's* "100 Best Corporate Citizens" list, up from its 2006 position of seventeenth. Both social responsibility and care for the environment are part of the total product that the company markets to consumers who are concerned about such issues.[29]

Questions for Discussion

1. What is the total product that Starbucks markets?
2. What is the role of the development of new products in Starbucks's success?
3. Why do you think some new Starbucks products succeed and others, like Chantico, fail?

CASE 10.2

Dell Goes Back to Its PC Roots

Dell, based in Round Rock, Texas, originally made its name selling personal computers directly to customers through its website, catalogs, and phone orders. Over the years, it has expanded into related product lines while battling aggressive rivals such as Hewlett-Packard and Apple. A few years ago, Dell decided to enter the lucrative $100 billion world of consumer electronics, hoping to derive an ever-larger portion of revenues and profits from a wider mix of products for use beyond the home office.

With a long history of marketing technology-based products, Dell has become a well-known U.S. brand. Management saw the brand as a strength to exploit in marketing new flat-screen televisions, tiny digital music players, and other noncomputer products. "We've come out of nowhere to be the number three consumer brand in the United States in less than five years, while Coca-Cola has been doing it for 100 years," said Dell's general manager of consumer business for the United States. "We're not in this to be number three. Number one is the only target around here."

Despite considerable research and marketing investment, Dell's consumer electronics strategy did not succeed. In fact, it wasn't long before the company reversed course, pulling back from diversification to refocus on its core computer expertise. What happened? First, Dell launched its consumer electronics items just as major technological developments were roiling the industry and changing how consumers buy and use such products. Dell's affordable handheld computers initially touched off a flurry of customer interest and then sparked a price war with Hewlett-Packard as the two fought for market share. However, when Apple, Nokia, and others began marketing new-generation cell phones with built-in computer capabilities and multiple entertainment functions, customers found those offerings more appealing than the kind of stand-alone handhelds that Dell offered.

Second, Dell was caught in the crossfire of intense competition. At the start of its consumer electronics initiative, the company introduced the Dell Digital Jukebox and the Dell Music Store, putting it on a competitive collision course with Apple's popular iPods and iTunes store. In the end, Apple had so much momentum that Dell discontinued its own brand of music players and has been reselling products made by Samsung and other manufacturers. This allows Dell to satisfy customer demand for certain consumer electronics items but without the expense of researching, developing, manufacturing, and marketing the products under the Dell name.

Today Dell has gone back to its PC roots, emphasizing computers and laptops, inkjet and laser printers, networking equipment, and related products for home and office use. The company is not looking to pioneer revolutionary new lines for early adopters. Instead it adds new features to products with a proven market, finds ways to make production more cost effective, and seeks to distribute both Dell and non-Dell products as efficiently as possible. Moving away from its traditional policy of only selling directly to customers, Dell recently began distributing its brand of computers, monitors, printers, and accessories through Wal-Mart, Staples office supply stores, and other retailers around the world.

The company is also shining up its brand by improving customer service, an especially important step as PC sales grow more slowly throughout the industry and competitors dig in to defend market share. Dell's relentless cost cutting hurt its ability to handle technical questions and complaints, which in turn hurt customer satisfaction scores. Dell is rebuilding relationships by increasing its service budget and encouraging customers to have their say. "By listening to our customers, that is actually the most perfect form of marketing you could have," says Dell's chief marketing officer.[30]

Questions for Discussion

1. Why would Dell not pioneer revolutionary new products for innovators and early adopters the way its competitor Apple does?
2. In what stage of the product life cycle do personal computers appear to be? How does this explain Dell's attempt to expand into consumer electronics?
3. How far can Dell widen its product mix without hurting the company's credibility? For example, what might be the impact of new products such as Dell motorcycles or Dell frozen pastries?

11 Developing and Managing Products

Flip Brings New Fun to Camcorders

entrepreneurs IN ACTION

The camcorder was already well into its life cycle when Pure Digital Technologies introduced the Flip. Based in San Francisco, Pure Digital originally made small, one-time-use digital photo and video cameras. What they kept hearing from customers, however, was that they wanted a more permanent, shoot and share video camera that was fun and easy to use," according to the company's founder and CEO. Based on this feedback, the founder challenged his product design team to create a small, lightweight, basic camcorder without all the fuss and features that can confuse new users.

To ensure that the Flip camcorder would always be ready to record, the designers included digital storage for up to 60 minutes of video. Instead of having to insert or change a memory card, users just turn the Flip on and can see exactly how many minutes of video time they have left to shoot. For point-and-shoot operation, the designers created a big red button to start or stop recording. The Flip runs on just two AA batteries and includes editing software plus a flip-out USB connection for uploading videos to a computer. From there, videos can be e-mailed to others or posted on sites such as YouTube.

With 1 million sold in its first year, the Flip was an instant hit and allowed Pure Digital to capture 13 percent of the camcorder market. Despite intense competition from corporate giants such as Sony, Pure Digital is aiming to increase its market share with a series of new models. Although future Flips will take better-quality videos, they will not have fancy frills. "Most companies have a tendency to throw more and more in the product for new versions," says the founder, "and then it gets more complicated. I'm proud of our discipline."[1]

To compete effectively and achieve their goals, organizations like Pure Digital Technologies must be able to adjust their products' features in response to changes in customers' needs. To provide products that satisfy target markets and achieve the firm's objectives, a marketer must develop, alter, and maintain an effective product mix. An organization's product mix may require adjustment for a variety of reasons. Because customers' attitudes and product preferences change over time, their desire for certain products may wane. Coca-Cola, for example, has seen sales of carbonated drinks decline as consumers seek alternatives such as bottled water. The decline is particularly worrisome given that the cola giant gets 82 percent of its sales from soft drinks. Thus, the company has introduced thousands of new products, including Diet Coke with Splenda, flavored Dasani water, and the low-calorie Powerade sports drink. Coke also plans to introduce new juice, water, coffee, and iced-tea products over the next few years.[2] In some cases, a company needs to alter its product mix for competitive reasons. A marketer may have to delete a product from the mix because a competitor dominates the market for that product. Similarly, a firm may have to introduce a new product or modify an existing one to compete more effectively. A marketer may expand the firm's product mix to take advantage of excess marketing and production capacity.

In this chapter, we examine several ways to improve an organization's product mix. First, we discuss managing existing products through effective line extension and product modification. Next, we examine the stages of new-product development, including idea generation, screening, concept testing, business analysis, product development, test marketing, and commercialization. Then we look at how companies differentiate their products in the marketplace through quality, design, and support services. Next, we examine the importance of deleting weak products and the methods companies use to eliminate them. Finally, we look at the organizational structures used to manage products.

Managing Existing Products

LO 1 To understand how companies manage existing products through line extensions and product modifications

A company can benefit by capitalizing on its existing products. By assessing the composition of the current product mix, a marketer can identify weaknesses and gaps. This analysis can then lead to improvement of the product mix through line extension and product modification.

Line Extensions

A **line extension** is the development of a product that is closely related to one or more products in the existing product line but designed specifically to meet somewhat different customer needs. Procter & Gamble, for example, created several line extensions for its Febreze deodorizer, including candles and a travel-size version that fits in a purse or luggage.[3]

Many of the so-called new products introduced each year are in fact line extensions. Line extensions are more common than new products because they are a less-expensive, lower-risk alternative for increasing sales. A line extension may focus on a different market segment or be an attempt to increase sales within the same market segment by more precisely satisfying the needs of people in that segment. Hormel, for example, extended the Spam line of processed meat with new flavors like Stinky French Garlic and single-serve packets.[4] Line extensions are also used to take market share from competitors. Nestlé, the category leader in bottled waters, introduced a four-flavor line of water called Pure Life Splash in direct response to Coca-Cola's and Pepsi's latest line extensions.[5] However, one side effect of employing a line extension is that it may result in a more negative evaluation of the core product.[6]

Product Modifications

Product modification means changing one or more characteristics of a product. A product modification differs from a line extension in that the original product does

line extension Development of a product that is closely related to existing products in the line but is designed specifically to meet different customer needs

product modification Changes in one or more characteristics of a product

The responsible adult in you will want to read the bag.

The chocolate lover in you will have already torn it to shreds.

Chocolate Chex Mix. In Turtle and Peanut Butter.

Line Extension

Chocolate-flavored Chex Mix is a line extension.

not remain in the line. For example, U.S. automakers use product modifications annually when they create new models of the same brand. Once the new models are introduced, the manufacturers stop producing last year's model. Like line extensions, product modifications entail less risk than developing new products.

Product modification can indeed improve a firm's product mix but only under certain conditions. First, the product must be modifiable. Second, customers must be able to perceive that a modification has been made. Third, the modification should make the product more consistent with customers' desires so it provides greater satisfaction. One drawback to modifying a successful product is that the consumer who had experience with the original version of the product may view a modified version as a riskier purchase.[7] There are three major ways to modify products: quality, functional, and aesthetic modifications.

Quality Modifications. **Quality modifications** are changes relating to a product's dependability and durability. The changes usually are executed by altering the materials or the production process. For example, Energizer increased its product's durability by using better materials—a larger cathode and anode interface—that make batteries last longer. For a service, such as a sporting event or air travel, quality modifications may involve enhancing the emotional experience that makes the consumer passionate and loyal to the brand.

Reducing a product's quality may allow an organization to lower its price and direct the item at a different target market. In contrast, increasing the quality of a product may give a firm an advantage over competing brands. Higher quality may enable a company to charge a higher price by creating customer loyalty and lowering customer sensitivity to price. However, higher quality may require the use of

quality modifications
Changes relating to a product's dependability and durability

Refined, naturally.

If there's one thing that almost 70 years of climbing over boulders, crawling across scree and other grin-inducing Trail Rated® 4x4 fun has taught us, it's the value of a comfortable ride. Take a look inside the 2008 new all Jeep Liberty and you may be surprised at all the creature comforts. The spacious, durable interior with available heated leather-trimmed seats welcomes in dirt, mud, and – if you're lucky – fish scales. There's even more rear legroom for any long-legged friends you might take along the way. The rain-sensing wipers* smell the storm before you do and clear away the first drop as soon as it falls. If the weather outside changes, the Automatic Temperature Control* keeps the cabin nice and cool – or warm and toasty. As the 3.7-litre power plant purrs down the road, the howls of the MyGIG™ Multimedia Infotainment System** with Navigation will carry a tune no matter how far out there you go. So satisfy your natural curiosity about the outdoors and head out in our great indoors. Jeep.com/sessions

The new all Jeep Liberty. Have fun out there. Jeep

†No deductible. See dealer for a copy of limited warranty and details. Non-Transferable. Not available on certain fleet vehicles.

Product Modification

Automakers rely heavily on product modifications.

functional modifications
Changes affecting a product's versatility, effectiveness, convenience, or safety

---

more expensive components and processes, thus forcing the organization to cut costs in other areas. Some firms, such as Caterpillar, are finding ways to increase quality while reducing costs.

Functional Modifications. Changes that affect a product's versatility, effectiveness, convenience, or safety are called **functional modifications;** they usually require redesign of the product. Product categories that have undergone considerable functional modification include office and farm equipment, appliances, cleaning products, and telecommunications services. For example, Lexus introduced the LS 460 sedan with an Advanced Parking Guidance System that essentially parallel-parks the vehicle with little effort by the driver. The parking system comes as part of an options package that includes a navigation system, voice-activated Bluetooth, and XM satellite radio.[8]

Functional modifications can make a product useful to more people and thus enlarge its market. Research in Motion, for example, added GPS chips and navigation features to its BlackBerry smart phones.[9] They can place a product in a favorable competitive position by providing benefits that competing brands do not offer. They can also help an organization achieve and maintain a progressive image. Finally, functional modifications are sometimes made to reduce the possibility of product liability lawsuits.

Aesthetic Modifications. **Aesthetic modifications** change the sensory appeal of a product by altering its taste, texture, sound, smell, or appearance. A buyer making a purchase decision is swayed by how a product looks, smells, tastes, feels, or sounds. Thus, an aesthetic modification may strongly affect purchases. For years, automobile makers have relied on quality and aesthetic modifications. For example, the Acura MDX sport utility vehicle was redesigned to give it a sportier and more stylish look.[10]

Aesthetic modifications can help a firm differentiate its product from competing brands and thus gain a sizable market share. Eastern Spice & Flavors, for example, localizes its spice blends to match the tastes of various regional markets around the world.[11] The major drawback in using aesthetic modifications is that their value is determined subjectively. Although a firm may strive to improve the product's sensory appeal, customers may actually find the modified product less attractive.

Developing New Products

LO 2 To describe how businesses develop a product idea into a commercial product

A firm develops new products as a means of enhancing its product mix and adding depth to a product line. However, developing and introducing new products is frequently expensive and risky. For example, Hormel's management pulled the plug on the four ethnic-themed varieties of its Refrigerated Entrees line after just two years on the market after finally recognizing that most consumers were dubious that the producer of Spam could produce restaurant-quality ethnic meals.[12] As we discussed in the previous chapter, new-product failures occur frequently and can create major financial problems for organizations, sometimes even causing them to go out of business.

Failure to introduce new products is also risky. Both Ford Motor and General Motors have lost market share to Japanese and Korean automakers in recent years as sales of some of their most profitable models have declined. Chrysler, however, has maintained market share with successful new products.[13]

aesthetic modifications
Changes relating to the sensory appeal of a product

The term *new product* can have more than one meaning. A genuinely new product offers innovative benefits. Envigo, a green tea product offered by a joint venture of Coca-Cola and Nestlé, purports to be "calorie deficient" to help consumers burn fewer calories.[14] However, products that are different and distinctly better are often viewed as new. Cascade Lacrosse, for example, introduced a new sports helmet that reduces shock to the skull by 40 percent. Since 40 percent of pro hockey players get at least one concussion a year, this represents a significant new product.[15] Some product innovations of the last 30 years include Post-it Notes, cell phones, personal computers, PDAs, digital music players, satellite radio, and digital video recorders. Thus, a new product can be an innovative product that has never been sold by any organization, such as the digital camera was when introduced for the first time. A radically new product involves a complex developmental process, including an extensive business analysis to determine the potential for success.[16] It can also be a product that a given firm has not marketed previously, although similar products have been available from other companies, such as Crayola School Glue. Eddie Bauer, best known for its rugged outdoor apparel, extended this image with the introduction of a new line of baby products including diaper bags and car seats. Finally, a product can be viewed as new when it is brought to one or more markets from another market. For example, making the Saturn VUE SUV available in Japan was viewed as a new-product introduction in Japan.

Before a product is introduced, it goes through the seven phases of the **new-product development process** shown in Figure 11.1: (1) idea generation, (2) screening, (3) concept testing, (4) business analysis, (5) product development, (6) test marketing, and (7) commercialization. A product may be dropped (and many are) at any stage of development. In this section, we look at the process through which products are developed, from idea inception to fully commercialized product.

new-product development process A seven-phase process for introducing products: idea generation, screening, concept testing, business analysis, product development, test marketing, and commercialization

figure 11.1

PHASES OF NEW-PRODUCT DEVELOPMENT

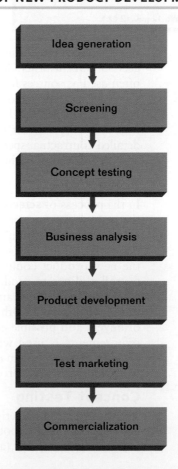

Idea generation

Screening

Concept testing

Business analysis

Product development

Test marketing

Commercialization

NO OILS • LOW CALORIES • FAT FREE   ALL NATURAL • NO PRESERVATIVES

ONLY 2 INGREDIENTS! FRESH POTATOES AND SEA SALT

ALL-NATURAL

NEW! POTATO
with a hint of Sea Salt

crisps

Better than "baked"
...Much better than "fried"...
IT'S A REVOLUTION!

100% FAT FREE

ORIGINAL

1/2 Cup   Net Wt. 12 g (0.42 oz.)

Example of a New Product?

Some marketers would consider this to be a new product, while others would view it as a line extension.

idea generation Seeking product ideas to achieve organizational objectives

screening Selecting the ideas with the greatest potential for further review

concept testing Seeking a sample of potential buyers' responses to a product idea

Idea Generation

Businesses and other organizations seek product ideas that will help them achieve their objectives. This activity is **idea generation.** The fact that only a few ideas are good enough to be commercially successful underscores the challenge of the task.

Although some organizations get their ideas almost by chance, firms that try to manage their product mixes effectively usually develop systematic approaches for generating new-product ideas. Indeed, in organizations there is a relationship between the amount of market information gathered and the number of ideas generated by work groups.[17] At the heart of innovation is a purposeful, focused effort to identify new ways to serve a market.

New-product ideas can come from several sources. They may stem from internal sources: marketing managers, researchers, sales personnel, engineers, or other organizational personnel. Brainstorming and incentives or rewards for good ideas are typical intrafirm devices for stimulating development of ideas. For example, the idea for 3M Post-it adhesive-backed notes came from an employee. As a church choir member, he used slips of paper to mark songs in his hymnal. Because the pieces of paper kept falling out, he suggested developing an adhesive-backed note.

In the restaurant industry, ideas may come from franchisees. At McDonald's, for example, franchise owners invented the Big Mac and the Egg McMuffin. Today, new McDonald's product ideas often come from corporate chef Dan Coudreaut, who developed the fast-food giant's new snack wrap.[18]

New-product ideas may also arise from sources outside the firm, such as customers, competitors, advertising agencies, management consultants, and private research organizations. Procter & Gamble gets 35 percent of its ideas from inventors and outside consultants.[19] Consultants are often used as sources for stimulating new-product ideas. For example, Fahrenheit 212 serves as an "idea factory" that provides ready-to-go product ideas, including market potential analysis.[20] When outsourcing new-product development activities to outside organizations, the best results are achieved from spelling out the specific tasks with detailed contractual specifications.[21] Asking customers what they want from products and organizations has helped many firms become successful and remain competitive.

Screening

In the process of **screening,** the ideas with the greatest potential are selected for further review. During screening, product ideas are analyzed to determine whether they match the organization's objectives and resources. If a product idea results in a product similar to the firm's existing offerings, marketers must assess the degree to which the new product could cannibalize the sales of current products. The company's overall abilities to produce and market the product are also analyzed. Keeping the product idea in focus and on track by understanding consumer needs and wants is the key to success.[22] Other aspects of an idea to be weighed are the nature and wants of buyers and possible environmental changes. At times a checklist of new-product requirements is used when making screening decisions. This practice encourages evaluators to be systematic and thus reduces the chances of overlooking some pertinent fact. Most new-product ideas are rejected during the screening phase.

Concept Testing

To evaluate ideas properly, it may be necessary to test product concepts. In **concept testing,** a small sample of potential buyers is presented with a product idea through a written or oral description (and perhaps a few drawings) to determine their attitudes and initial buying intentions regarding the product. For a single product idea, an organization can test one or several concepts of the same product. Concept testing is a low-cost procedure that allows a company to determine customers' initial reactions to a product idea before it invests considerable resources in research and development. Input from online communities may also be beneficial in the product development process.[23] The results of concept testing can help product development personnel better understand which product attributes and benefits are most important to potential customers.

Figure 11.2 shows a concept test for a proposed tick and flea control product. Notice that the concept is briefly described and then a series of questions is presented. The questions vary considerably depending on the type of product being tested. Typical questions are: In general, do you find this proposed product attractive? Which benefits are especially attractive to you? Which features are of little or no interest to you? Do you feel this proposed product would work better for you than the product you currently use? Compared with your current product, what are the primary advantages of the proposed product? If this product were available at an appropriate price, would you buy it? How often would you buy this product? How could this proposed product be improved?

Business Analysis

During the **business analysis** stage, the product idea is evaluated to determine its potential contribution to the firm's sales, costs, and profits. In the course of a business analysis, evaluators ask a variety of questions: Does the product fit in with the organization's existing product mix? Is demand strong enough to justify entering the

 figure 11.2

CONCEPT TEST FOR A TICK AND FLEA CONTROL PRODUCT

Product description

An insecticide company is considering the development and introduction of a new tick and flea control product for pets. This product would consist of insecticide and a liquid-dispensing brush for applying the insecticide to dogs and cats. The insecticide is in a cartridge that is installed in the handle of the brush. The insecticide is dispensed through the tips of the bristles when they touch the pet's skin (which is where most ticks and fleas are found). The actual dispensing works very much like a felt-tip pen. Only a small amount of insecticide actually is dispensed on the pet because of this unique dispensing feature. Thus, the amount of insecticide that is placed on your pet is minimal compared to conventional methods of applying a tick and flea control product. One application of insecticide will keep your pet free from ticks and fleas for fourteen days.

Please answer the following questions:

1. In general, how do you feel about using this type of product on your pet?

2. What are the major advantages of this product compared with the existing product that you are currently using to control ticks and fleas on your pet?

3. What characteristics of this product do you especially like?

4. What suggestions do you have for improving this product?

5. If it is available at an appropriate price, how likely are you to buy this product?

   Very likely   Semi-likely   Not likely

6. Assuming that a single purchase would provide 30 applications for an average-size dog or 48 applications for an average-size cat, approximately how much would you pay for this product?

business analysis Evaluating the potential impact of a product idea on the firm's sales, costs, and profits

market, and will the demand endure? What types of environmental and competitive changes can be expected, and how will these changes affect the product's future sales, costs, and profits? Are the organization's research, development, engineering, and production capabilities adequate to develop the product? If new facilities must be constructed, how quickly can they be built and how much will they cost? Is the necessary financing for development and commercialization on hand or obtainable at terms consistent with a favorable return on investment?

In the business analysis stage, firms seek market information. The results of customer surveys, along with secondary data, supply the specifics needed to estimate potential sales, costs, and profits.

For many products in this stage (when they are still just product ideas), forecasting sales accurately is difficult. This is especially true for innovative and completely new products. Organizations sometimes employ break-even analysis to determine how many units they would have to sell to begin making a profit. At times an organization also uses payback analysis, in which marketers compute the time period required to recover the funds that would be invested in developing the new product. Because break-even and payback analyses are based on estimates, they are usually viewed as useful but not particularly precise during this stage.

Product Development

Product development is the phase in which the organization determines if it is technically feasible to produce the product and if it can be produced at costs low enough to make the final price reasonable. To test its acceptability, the idea or concept is converted into a prototype, or working model. The prototype should reveal tangible and intangible attributes associated with the product in consumers' minds. The product's design, mechanical features, and intangible aspects must be linked to wants in the marketplace. Through marketing research and concept testing, product attributes important to buyers are identified. These characteristics must be communicated to customers through the design of the product. Honda Motor, for example, developed a prototype minivan that targets Japan's growing population of pet owners with pet-friendly features such as paneled floors and seats that convert to a holding pen. Displayed at the Tokyo Auto Show, the prototype helped Honda assess interest in the concept.[24]

After a prototype is developed, its overall functioning must be tested. Its performance, safety, convenience, and other functional qualities are tested both in a laboratory and in the field. Functional testing should be rigorous and lengthy enough to test the product thoroughly. Manufacturing issues that come to light at this stage may require adjustments. When Cadbury Schweppes was developing its new Trident Splash gum, production problems necessitated changes in the ingredients. One combination resulted in a too-soft gum that jammed machines; another combination resulted in the gum's liquid center leaking during trial deliveries. Finding just the right recipe required months.[25]

A crucial question that arises during product development is how much quality to build into the product. For example, a major dimension of quality is durability. Higher quality often calls for better materials and more expensive processing, which increase production costs and, ultimately, the product's price. In determining the specific level of quality, a marketer must ascertain approximately what price the target market views as acceptable. In addition, a marketer usually tries to set a quality level consistent with that of the firm's other products. Obviously the quality of competing brands is also a consideration.

The development phase of a new product is frequently lengthy and expensive; thus, a relatively small number of product ideas are put into development. If the product appears sufficiently successful during this stage to merit test marketing, then, during the latter part of the development stage, marketers begin to make decisions regarding branding, packaging, labeling, pricing, and promotion for use in the test marketing stage.

Test Marketing

Test marketing is a limited introduction of a product in geographic areas chosen to represent the intended market. Procter & Gamble, for example, test marketed Align,

product development
Determining if producing a product is technically feasible and cost effective

test marketing A limited introduction of a product in geographic areas chosen to represent the intended market

table 11.1 POPULAR TEST MARKETS IN THE UNITED STATES

Rank	City
1	Albany, NY
2	Rochester, NY
3	Greensboro, NC
4	Birmingham, AL
5	Syracuse, NY
6	Charlotte, NC
7	Nashville, TN
8	Eugene, OR
9	Wichita, KS
10	Richmond, VA

Source: "Which American City Provides the Best Consumer Test Market?" *Business Wire,* May 24, 2004.

a probiotic dietary supplement, in Cincinnati, Dallas, and St. Louis for two years before rolling out the product.[26] The aim of test marketing is to determine the extent to which potential customers will buy the product. It is not an extension of the development stage but a sample launching of the entire marketing mix. Test marketing should be conducted only after the product has gone through development and initial plans have been made regarding the other marketing mix variables. Companies use test marketing to lessen the risk of product failure. The dangers of introducing an untested product include undercutting already profitable products and, should the new product fail, loss of credibility with distributors and customers.

Test marketing provides several benefits. It lets marketers expose a product in a natural marketing environment to measure its sales performance. The company can strive to identify weaknesses in the product or in other parts of the marketing mix. A product weakness discovered after a nationwide introduction can be expensive to correct. Moreover, if consumers' early reactions are negative, marketers may be unable to persuade consumers to try the product again. Thus, making adjustments after test marketing can be crucial to the success of a new product. On the other hand, test marketing results may be positive enough to warrant accelerating the product's introduction. Test marketing also allows marketers to experiment with variations in advertising, pricing, and packaging in different test areas and to measure the extent of brand awareness, brand switching, and repeat purchases resulting from these alterations in the marketing mix.

Selection of appropriate test areas is very important because the validity of test marketing results depends heavily on selecting test sites that provide accurate representation of the intended target market. Table 11.1 lists some of the most popular test market cities. The criteria used for choosing test market cities depend on the product's attributes, the target market's characteristics, and the firm's objectives and resources.

Test marketing is not without risks. It is expensive, and competitors may try to interfere. A competitor may attempt to "jam" the test program by increasing its own advertising or promotions, lowering prices, and offering special incentives, all to combat recognition and purchase of the new brand. Any such tactics can invalidate test results. Sometimes, too, competitors copy the product in the testing stage and rush to introduce a similar product. This is the time to conduct research to identify issues that might drive potential customers to market-leading competitors instead.[27] It is therefore desirable to move to the commercialization phase as soon as possible after successful testing. On the other hand, some firms have been known to heavily promote new products long before they are ready for the market to discourage competitors from developing similar new products.

Because of these risks, many companies use alternative methods to measure customer preferences. One such method is simulated test marketing. Typically consumers at shopping centers are asked to view an advertisement for a new product and are given a free sample to take home. These consumers are subsequently interviewed over the phone and asked to rate the product. The major advantages of simulated test marketing are greater speed, lower costs, and tighter security, which reduce the flow of information to competitors and reduce jamming. Gillette's Personal Care Division, for example, spends less than $200,000 for a simulated test that lasts three to

E-ntertainment MARKETING

Marketers to Pirates: "Walk the Plank"

To fight pirates, marketers are changing the way they plan the launch of entertainment products such as movies and music. One threat is the speed with which unauthorized copies can circulate through underground websites and stores that illegally sell or swap bootlegged DVDs and CDs. Sony Pictures is dealing with this threat in two ways. First, it has guards patrol sneak previews and premieres to prevent attendees from using camera phones and camcorders to record bootleg versions. Second, it arranges for movie reels to arrive at theaters in more than one shipment, ideally at the last minute. "That way, no one has an entire print until opening day," explains Sony's head of worldwide marketing and distribution. As a result, Sony blockbusters like *Spider-Man 3* have enjoyed early box-office success before piracy can start to siphon off profits.

Another threat is that fake or real snippets of entertainment products will find their way to mainstream websites like YouTube and My Space or onto specialized music and movie sites. For example, more than a month before Britney Spears's *Blackout* album was to be introduced, counterfeit artwork and leaked songs from the album popped up on the Internet. Jive Records chose to blunt the effect and meet demand by releasing *Blackout* two weeks earlier than originally planned. Finally, YouTube and other major websites have joined the fight by testing special software to identify and remove illegally posted entertainment content as quickly as possible.[a]

five months. A live test market costs Gillette $2 million, counting promotion and distribution, and takes one to two years to complete. Several marketing research firms, such as ACNielsen Company, offer test marketing services to provide independent assessment of proposed products.

Clearly not all products that are test-marketed are launched. At times, problems discovered during test marketing cannot be resolved. Procter & Gamble, for example, test-marketed a new plastic wrap product called Impress in Grand Junction, Colorado, but decided not to launch the brand nationally based on the results of test marketing.[28]

Commercialization

During the **commercialization** phase, plans for full-scale manufacturing and marketing must be refined and finalized and budgets for the project prepared. Early in the commercialization phase, marketing management analyzes the results of test marketing to find out what changes in the marketing mix are needed before introducing the product. The results of test marketing may tell marketers to change one or more of the product's physical attributes, modify the distribution plans to include more retail outlets, alter promotional efforts, or change the product's price. However, as more and more changes are made based on test marketing findings, the test marketing projections may become less valid.

During the early part of this stage, marketers must not only gear up for larger-scale production but also make decisions about warranties, repairs, and replacement parts. The type of warranty a firm provides can be a critical issue for buyers, especially when expensive, technically complex goods such as appliances are involved. Maytag, for

commercialization Refining and finalizing plans and budgets for full-scale manufacturing and marketing of a product

snapshot

Reading the fine print

While making a purchase, percentage of Americans admitting they don't read:

29%
return/exchange policies

42%
extended warranties

46%
service contracts

Source: Kelton Research survey for the Better Business Bureau.

example, provides a money-back guarantee on its refrigerators. Establishing an effective system for providing repair services and replacement parts is necessary to maintain favorable customer relationships. Although the producer may furnish these services directly to buyers, it is more common for the producer to provide such services through regional service centers. Regardless of how services are provided, it is important to customers that they be performed quickly and correctly.

The product enters the market during the commercialization phase. When introducing a product, a firm may spend enormous sums for advertising, personal selling, and other types of promotion, as well as for more manufacturing facilities and equipment. Such expenditures may not be recovered for several years. Smaller firms may find this process difficult, but even so they may use press releases, blogs, podcasts, and other tools to capture quick feedback as well as promote the new product. Another low-cost promotional tool is product reviews in newspapers and magazines, which can be especially helpful when they are positive and target the same customers.

Usually products are not launched nationwide overnight but are introduced through a process called a *roll-out*. With a roll-out, a product is introduced in stages, starting in one set of geographic areas and gradually expanding into adjacent areas. It may take several years to market the product nationally. Sometimes the test cities are used as initial marketing areas, and the introduction of the product becomes a natural extension of test marketing. A product test-marketed in Sacramento, Fort Collins, Abilene, Springfield, and Jacksonville, as the map in Figure 11.3 shows, could be introduced first in those cities. After the stage 1 introduction is complete, stage 2 could include market coverage of the states where the test cities are located. In stage 3, marketing efforts might be extended into adjacent states. All remaining states would then be covered in stage 4.

figure 11.3   STAGES OF EXPANSION INTO A NATIONAL MARKET DURING COMMERCIALIZATION

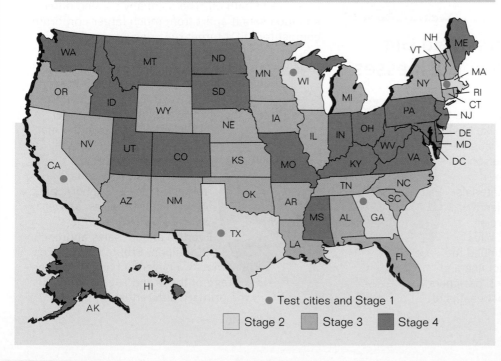

● Test cities and Stage 1   ☐ Stage 2   ☐ Stage 3   ■ Stage 4

Gradual product introductions do not always occur state by state; other geographic combinations, such as groups of counties that overlap across state borders, are sometimes used. Products destined for multinational markets may also be rolled out one country or region at a time. For example, after Heineken test-marketed its Heineken Premium Light beer in several cities in the United States, it gradually rolled out the product's distribution nationally.[29] Gradual product introduction is desirable for several reasons. First, it reduces the risks of introducing a new product. If the product fails, the firm will experience smaller losses if it introduced the item in only a few geographic areas than if it marketed the product nationally. Second, a company cannot introduce a product nationwide overnight because a system of wholesalers and retailers to distribute the product cannot be established so quickly; developing a distribution network may take considerable time. Third, if the product is successful, the number of units needed to satisfy nationwide demand for it may be too large for the firm to produce in a short time. Finally, it allows for fine-tuning of the marketing mix to better satisfy target customers. Procter & Gamble, for example, originally conceived of Febreze deodorizer as a fabric-care product, but over time, the company's view of the highly successful brand evolved into an air-freshening line because that's how consumers indicated they were using it.[30]

Despite the good reasons for introducing a product gradually, marketers realize this approach creates some competitive problems. A gradual introduction allows competitors to observe what the firm is doing and to monitor results just as the firm's own marketers are doing. If competitors see that the newly introduced product is successful, they may quickly enter the same target market with similar products. In addition, as a product is introduced region by region, competitors may expand their marketing efforts to offset promotion of the new product.

product differentiation
Creating and designing products so that customers perceive them as different from competing products

Product Differentiation Through Quality, Design, and Support Services

L O 3 To understand the importance of product differentiation and the elements that differentiate one product from another

Some of the most important characteristics of products are the elements that distinguish them from one another. **Product differentiation** is the process of creating and designing products so customers perceive them as different from competing products. Customer perception is critical in differentiating products. Perceived differences might include quality, features, styling, price, or image. A crucial element used to differentiate one product from another is the brand, discussed in the next chapter. In this

green MARKETING

Green Products Yield Big Profits for Small Businesses

Differentiating products as "green" has generated big profits for small businesses like New Leaf Paper and Carol's Daughter. Entrepreneur Jeff Mendelsohn founded New Leaf Paper in 1998 to turn recycled materials into high-quality, eco-friendly paper stock for commercial use. Although first-year sales were $1 million, he continued to expand his green product line and educate both printers and designers about the environmental benefits of

New Leaf Paper. Within eight years, Mendelsohn had increased annual sales to $19 million on the basis of the firm's green differentiation. "We have a unique product line and story to tell in the paper industry," he says.

Carol's Daughter specializes in all-natural personal-care products such as shampoo, skin cream, and bath oil. The company's green differentiation sets it apart from much larger corporate competitors that target the consumer cosmetics market. Lisa Price founded Carol's Daughter in 1994 when she began making beauty products in her kitchen, using fresh, natural ingredients. With investments from celebrities like Will Smith and his wife, Jada Pinkett Smith, plus the marketing savvy of Steve Stoute, Carol's Daughter's has expanded and now sells through Macy's, Sephora, and other major retailers, as well as in its own store outlets. Even as annual sales approach $30 million, Stoute emphasizes that "we haven't changed the heritage of the brand"—green remains the primary differentiation.[b]

1998
2008
A DECADE OF ACHIEVEMENT

FROM IDEA TO ICON IN TEN YEARS

Vertu was born from an idea. To create the finest phones for the most discerning individuals. Phones that combine craftsmanship and technology in pioneering new ways. That blend sapphire crystal and space age ceramic with leather and gold. That are hand-built in England, one at a time. That redefine personal service by offering global concierge assistance at the touch of a button. Ten years since its foundation, Vertu is an icon, recognised as the pinnacle of mobile phone excellence worldwide. This has been Vertu's decade of achievement. This is your phone.

VERTU

VERTU BOUTIQUE | THE PLAZA, 768 FIFTH AVENUE, NEW YORK. + 1 212 371 8701 | WYNN LAS VEGAS, 3131 LAS VEGAS BLVD SO., LAS VEGAS. + 1 702 650 57
FOR MORE ON VERTU'S DECADE OF ACHIEVEMENT VISIT VERTU.COM

Product Quality

Vertu phones are promoted as being high-quality products.

quality The overall characteristics of a product that allow it to perform as expected in satisfying customer needs

level of quality The amount of quality a product possesses

consistency of quality The degree to which a product has the same level of quality over time

product design How a product is conceived, planned, and produced

section, we examine three aspects of product differentiation that companies must consider when creating and offering products for sale: product quality, product design and features, and product support services. These aspects involve the company's attempt to create real differences among products.

Product Quality

Quality refers to the overall characteristics of a product that allow it to perform as expected in satisfying customer needs. The words *as expected* are very important to this definition because quality usually means different things to different customers. For some, durability signifies quality. Among the most durable products on the market today is the Craftsman line of tools at Sears; indeed, Sears provides a lifetime guarantee on the durability of its tools. For other consumers, a product's ease of use may indicate quality.

The concept of quality also varies between consumer and business markets. Consumers consider high-quality products to be reliable, durable, and easy to maintain. For business markets, technical suitability, ease of repair, and company reputation are important characteristics. Unlike consumers, most organizations place far less emphasis on price than on product quality.

One important dimension of quality is **level of quality:** the amount of quality a product possesses. The concept is a relative one; that is, the quality level of one product is difficult to describe unless it is compared with that of other products. For example, Burger King had suffered years of declining quality perceptions relative to other hamburger chains. After a new CEO instituted a number of changes, Burger King's customer satisfaction is at an all-time high according to the University of Michigan's American Customer Satisfaction Index, whereas rival McDonald's has seen its customer satisfaction decline.[31] How high should the level of quality be? It depends on the product and the costs and consequences of a product failure.

A second important dimension is consistency. **Consistency of quality** refers to the degree to which a product has the same level of quality over time. Consistency means giving consumers the quality they expect every time they purchase the product. Like level of quality, consistency is a relative concept; however, it implies a quality comparison within the same brand over time. The quality level of McDonald's french fries is generally consistent from one location to another. If FedEx delivers more than 99 percent of overnight packages on time, its service has consistent quality.

The consistency of product quality can also be compared across competing products. It is at this stage that consistency becomes critical to a company's success. Companies that can provide quality on a consistent basis have a major competitive advantage over rivals. FedEx, for example, is viewed as more consistent in delivery schedules than the U.S. Postal Service. In simple terms, no company has ever succeeded by creating and marketing low-quality products. Many companies have taken major steps, such as implementing total quality management (TQM), to improve the quality of their products.

By and large, higher product quality means marketers will charge a higher price for the product. This fact forces marketers to consider quality carefully in their product-planning efforts. Not all customers want or can afford the highest-quality products available. Thus, some companies offer products with moderate quality.

Product Design and Features

Product design refers to how a product is conceived, planned, and produced. Design is a very complex topic because it involves the total sum of all the product's physical characteristics. Many companies are known for the outstanding designs of their products:

RESPONSIBLE marketing?

Airborne's Lofty Advertising

ISSUE: Can drug companies get away with false advertising?

Recently, the makers of the herbal supplement Airborne agreed to pay a $23.3 million class-action lawsuit over claims of false advertising. The company first claimed that their product could ward off colds. Airborne later backed off and changed its campaign to claim the product helped "boost your immune system." In fact, Airborne had no evidence to support either claim. Although Airborne has agreed to refund the purchase price to consumers, they will not admit to false advertising.

Even though the class-action lawsuit was successful, Airborne is still available over the counter to anyone who wants to buy it. Ten years of advertising, although promoting false claims, still reside in the minds of many uninformed consumers who want to stay healthy this cold and flu season. In essence, Airborne has settled its lawsuit involving the false claims, but the public opinion on the product is still up in the air.

Should Airborne be forced to produce corrective advertising? If Airborne cannot prove to their customers that its product is beneficial, should it even be allowed on the shelves? Could the tests that show Airborne to be ineffective be wrong?[c]

Sony for personal electronics, Hewlett-Packard for printers, Apple for computers and music players, and JanSport for backpacks. Good design is one of the best competitive advantages any brand can possess.

One component of design is **styling**, or the physical appearance of the product. The style of a product is one design feature that can allow certain products to sell very rapidly. Good design, however, means more than just appearance; it also involves a product's functioning and usefulness. For example, a pair of jeans may look great, but if they fall apart after three washes, clearly the design was poor. Most consumers seek out products that both look good and function well.

Product features are specific design characteristics that allow a product to perform certain tasks. By adding or subtracting features, a company can differentiate its products from those of the competition. Chrysler promotes its line of minivans as having more features related to passenger safety—dual air bags, steel-reinforced doors, 180-degree swivel seats, and integrated child safety seats—than any other auto company. Product features can also be used to differentiate products within the same company. For example, Nike offers both a walking shoe and a run-walk shoe for specific consumer needs. In these cases, the company's products are sold with a wide range of features, from low-priced "base" or "stripped-down" versions to high-priced, prestigious "feature-packed" ones. The automotive industry regularly sells products with a wide range of features. In general, the more features a product has, the higher its price and, often, the higher its perceived quality.

For a brand to have a sustainable competitive advantage, marketers must determine the product designs and features that customers desire. Information from marketing research efforts and from databases can help in assessing customers' product design and feature preferences. Being able to meet customers' desires for product design and features at prices they can afford is crucial to a product's long-term success. Marketers must be careful not to misrepresent or overpromise regarding product features or product performance.

Product Support Services

Many companies differentiate their product offerings by providing support services. Usually referred to as **customer services**, these services include any human or mechanical efforts or activities a company provides that add value to a product.[32] Examples of customer services include delivery and installation, financing arrangements, customer training, warranties and guarantees, repairs, layaway plans, convenient hours of operation, adequate parking, and information through toll-free numbers and websites. For example, Zappos, an online shoe retailer, has earned a reputation for excellent customer service, in part due to its 24-hour service and free, fast returns.[33]

Whether as a major or minor part of the total product offering, all marketers of goods sell customer services. Providing good customer service may be the only way a company can differentiate its products when all products in a market have essentially the same quality, design, and features. This is especially true in the computer industry. When buying a laptop computer, for example, consumers shop more for fast delivery, technical support, warranties, and price than for product quality and design. Through research, a company can discover the types of services customers want and need. For example, some customers are more interested in financing, whereas others are more concerned with installation and training. The level of cus-

styling The physical appearance of a product

product features Specific design characteristics that allow a product to perform certain tasks

customer services Human or mechanical efforts or activities that add value to a product

Product Support Services

Cort Furniture provides product support services that some other office furniture manufacturers do not.

L O 4 To examine how product deletion is used to improve product mixes

product deletion Eliminating a product from the product mix when it no longer satisfies a sufficient number of customers

tomer service a company provides can profoundly affect customer satisfaction. The American Customer Satisfaction Index, compiled by the National Quality Research Center at the University of Michigan, ranks customer satisfaction among a wide variety of businesses. Dissatisfied customers may curtail their overall spending, which could stifle economic growth.

Product Deletion

Generally a product cannot satisfy target market customers and contribute to the achievement of the organization's overall goals indefinitely. **Product deletion** is the process of eliminating a product from the product mix, usually because it no longer satisfies a sufficient number of customers. Condé Naste, for example, discontinued its century-old *House & Garden* magazine after years of declining ad revenues, due in part to intense competition from other home décor and home life magazines.[34] A declining product reduces an organization's profitability and drains resources that could be used to modify other products or develop new ones. A marginal product may require shorter production runs, which can increase per-unit production costs. Finally, when a dying product completely loses favor with customers, the negative feelings may transfer to some of the company's other products.

Most organizations find it difficult to delete a product. A decision to drop a product may be opposed by managers and other employees who believe the product is necessary to the product mix. Salespeople who still have some loyal customers are especially upset when a product is dropped. In such cases, companies may spend considerable resources and effort to change a slipping product's marketing mix to improve its sales and thus avoid having to eliminate it.

Some organizations delete products only after the products have become heavy financial burdens. A better approach is some form of systematic review in which each product is evaluated periodically to determine its impact on the overall effectiveness of the firm's product mix. Such a review should analyze the product's contribution to the firm's sales for a given period, as well as estimate future sales, costs, and profits associated with the product. It should also gauge the value of making changes in the marketing strategy to improve the product's performance. A systematic review allows an organization to improve product performance and ascertain when to delete products. M&M Mars, for example, discontinued all but one variety of its M-Azing candy bar with embedded M&M candies after two years of disappointing performance. However, the company intends to rebrand the remaining M-Azing Crunchy Singles bar.[35]

Basically a product can be deleted in three ways: phase it out, run it out, or drop it immediately (see Figure 11.4). A *phase-out* allows the product to decline without a change in the marketing strategy; no attempt is made to give the product new life. A *run-out* exploits any strengths left in the product. Intensifying marketing efforts in core markets or eliminating some marketing expenditures, such as advertising, may cause a sudden jump in profits. This approach is commonly taken for technologically obsolete products, such as older models of computers and calculators. Often the price is reduced to generate a sales spurt. The third alternative, an *immediate drop* of an unprofitable product, is the best strategy when losses are too great to prolong the product's life.

figure 11.4

PRODUCT DELETION PROCESS

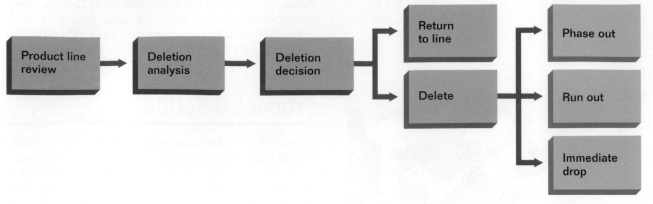

Source: Martin L. Bell, *Marketing: Concepts and Strategy,* 3rd ed., p. 267; Copyright © 1979, Houghton Mifflin Company. Reprinted by permission of Mrs. Martin L. Bell.

Organizing to Develop and Manage Products

L O 5 To describe organizational structures used for managing products

product manager The person within an organization who is responsible for a product, a product line, or several distinct products that make up a group

brand manager The person responsible for a single brand

market manager The person responsible for managing the marketing activities that serve a particular group of customers

venture team A cross-functional group that creates entirely new products that may be aimed at new markets

After reviewing the concepts of product line and mix and life cycles, it should be obvious that managing products is a complex task. Often the traditional functional form of organization, in which managers specialize in such business functions as advertising, sales, and distribution, does not fit a company's needs. In this case, management must find an organizational approach that accomplishes the tasks necessary to develop and manage products. Alternatives to functional organization include the product or brand manager approach, the market manager approach, and the venture team approach.

A **product manager** is responsible for a product, a product line, or several distinct products that make up an interrelated group within a multiproduct organization. A **brand manager** is responsible for a single brand. General Foods, for example, has one brand manager for Maxim coffee and one for Maxwell House coffee. Both product and brand managers operate cross-functionally to coordinate the activities, information, and strategies involved in marketing an assigned product. Product managers and brand managers plan marketing activities to achieve objectives by coordinating a mix of distribution, promotion (especially sales promotion and advertising), and price. They must consider packaging and branding decisions and work closely with personnel in research and development, engineering, and production. Marketing research helps product managers understand consumers and find target markets. Because luxury brands such as Mercedes-Benz and Jaguar can have their brand image reduced by association with their producers' other mass-market brands, brand managers must balance their brands' independent image with associated brands of the firm.[36] The product or brand manager approach to organization is used by many large, multiple-product companies.

A **market manager** is responsible for managing the marketing activities that serve a particular group of customers. This organizational approach is particularly effective when a firm engages in different types of marketing activities to provide products to diverse customer groups. A company might have one market manager for business markets and another for consumer markets. These broad market categories might be broken down into more limited market responsibilities.

A **venture team** creates entirely new products that may be aimed at new markets. Unlike a product or market manager, a venture team is responsible for all aspects of developing a product: research and development, production and engineering, finance and accounting, and marketing. Venture team members are brought together from different functional areas of the organization. In working outside established divisions, venture teams have greater flexibility to apply inventive approaches to develop new products that can take advantage of opportunities in highly segmented markets. Companies are increasingly using such cross-functional teams for product development in an effort to boost product quality. Quality may be positively related to information integration within the team, customers' influence on the product development process, and a quality orientation within the firm.[37] When a new product has demonstrated commercial potential, team members may return to their functional areas, or they may join a new or existing division to manage the product.

SUMMARY

Organizations must be able to adjust their product mixes to compete effectively and achieve their goals. A product mix can be improved through line extension and product modification. A line extension is the development of a product closely related to one or more products in the existing line but designed specifically to meet different customer needs. Product modification is the changing of one or more characteristics of a product. This approach can be effective when the product is modifiable, when customers can perceive the change, and when customers want the modification. Quality modifications relate to a product's dependability and durability. Functional modifications affect a product's versatility, effectiveness, convenience, or safety. Aesthetic modifications change the sensory appeal of a product.

Developing new products can enhance a firm's product mix and add depth to the product line. A new product may be an innovation that has never been sold by any organization; a product that a given firm has not marketed previously, although similar products have been available from other organizations; or a product brought from one market to another.

Before a product is introduced, it goes through a seven-phase new-product development process. In the idea generation phase, new-product ideas may come from internal or external sources. In the process of screening, ideas are evaluated to determine whether they are consistent with the firm's overall objectives and resources. Concept testing, the third phase, involves having a small sample of potential customers review a brief description of the product idea to determine their initial perceptions of the proposed product and their early buying intentions. During the business analysis stage, the product idea is evaluated to determine its potential contribution to the firm's sales, costs, and profits. In the product development stage, the organization determines if it is technically feasible to produce the product and if it can be produced at a cost low enough to make the final price reasonable. Test marketing is a limited introduction of a product in areas chosen to represent the intended market. Finally, in the commercialization phase, full-scale production of the product begins and a complete marketing strategy is developed.

Product differentiation is the process of creating and designing products so that customers perceive them as different from competing products. Product quality, product design and features, and product support services are three aspects of product differentiation that companies consider when creating and marketing products. Product quality includes the overall characteristics of a product that allow it to perform as expected in satisfying customer needs. The level of quality is the amount of quality a product possesses. Consistency of quality is the degree to which a product has the same level of quality over time. Product design refers to how a product is conceived, planned, and produced. Components of product design include styling (the physical appearance of the product) and product features (the specific design characteristics that allow a product to perform certain tasks). Companies often differentiate their products by providing support services, usually called customer services. Customer services are human or mechanical efforts or activities that add value to a product.

Product deletion is the process of eliminating a product that no longer satisfies a sufficient number of customers. Although a firm's personnel may oppose product deletion, weak products are unprofitable, consume too much time and effort, may require shorter production runs, and can create an unfavorable impression of the firm's other products. A product mix should be systematically reviewed to determine when to delete products. Products to be deleted can be phased out, run out, or dropped immediately.

Often the traditional functional form of organization does not lend itself to the complex task of developing and managing products. Alternative organizational forms include the product or brand manager approach, the market manager approach, and the venture team approach. A product manager is responsible for a product, a product line, or several distinct products that make up an interrelated group within a multiproduct organization. A brand manager is responsible for a single brand. A market manager is responsible for managing the marketing activities that serve a particular group or class of customers. A venture team is sometimes used to create entirely new products that may be aimed at new markets.

IMPORTANT TERMS

Line extension, 306
Product modification, 306
Quality modifications, 307
Functional modifications, 308
Aesthetic modifications, 308

New-product development process, 309
Idea generation, 310
Screening, 310
Concept testing, 310
Business analysis, 311
Product development, 312
Test marketing, 312

Commercialization, 314
Product differentiation, 316
Quality, 317
Level of quality, 317
Consistency of quality, 317
Product design, 317

Styling, 318
Product features, 318
Customer services, 318
Product deletion, 319
Product manager, 320
Brand manager, 320
Market manager, 320
Venture team, 320

DISCUSSION & REVIEW QUESTIONS

1. What is a line extension, and how does it differ from a product modification?

2. Compare and contrast the three major approaches to modifying a product.

3. Identify and briefly explain the seven major phases of the new-product development process.

4. Do small companies that manufacture just a few products need to be concerned about developing and managing products? Why or why not?

5. Why is product development a cross-functional activity—involving finance, engineering, manufacturing, and other functional areas—within an organization?

6. What is the major purpose of concept testing, and how is it accomplished?

7. What are the benefits and disadvantages of test marketing?

8. Why can the process of commercialization take a considerable amount of time?

9. What is product differentiation, and how can it be achieved?

10. Explain how the term *quality* has been used to differentiate products in the automobile industry in recent years. What are some makes and models of automobiles that come to mind when you hear the terms *high quality* and *poor quality*?

11. What types of problems does a weak product cause in a product mix? Describe the most effective approach for avoiding such problems.

12. What type of organization might use a venture team to develop new products? What are the advantages and disadvantages of such a team?

APPLICATION QUESTIONS

1. When developing a new product, a company often test-markets the proposed product in a specific area or location. Suppose you wish to test-market your new, revolutionary SuperWax car wax, which requires only one application for a lifetime finish. Where and how would you test-market your new product?

2. A product manager may make quality, functional, or aesthetic modifications when modifying a product. Identify a familiar product that recently was modified, categorize the modification (quality, functional, or aesthetic), and describe how you would have modified it differently.

3. Phasing out a product from the product mix often is difficult for an organization. Visit a retail store in your area, and ask the manager what products he or she has had to discontinue in the recent past. Find out what factors influenced the decision to delete the product and who was involved in the decision. Ask the manager to identify any products that should be but have not been deleted, and try to ascertain the reason.

INTERNET EXERCISE

Visit **www.cengage.com/marketing/pride-ferrell** for resources to help you master the material in this chapter, plus materials that will help you expand your marketing knowledge, including Internet exercise updates, ACE Self-Tests, hotlinks to companies featured in this chapter, and much more.

Merck & Company

Merck, a leading global pharmaceutical company, develops, manufactures, and markets a broad range of health-care products. In addition, the firm's Merck-Medco Managed Care Division manages pharmacy benefits for more than 40 million Americans. The company has established a website to serve as an educational and informational resource for Internet users around the world. To learn more about the company and its research, visit its award-winning site at **www.merck.com.**

1. What products has Merck developed and introduced recently?

2. What role does research play in Merck's success? How does research facilitate new-product development at Merck?

3. Find Merck's mission statement. Is Merck's focus on research consistent with the firm's mission and values?

developing your MARKETING PLAN

A company's marketing strategy may be revised to include new products as it considers its SWOT analysis and the impact of environmental factors on its product mix. When developing a marketing plan, the company must decide whether new products are to be added to the product mix or if existing ones should be modified. The information in this chapter will assist you in the creation of your marketing plan as you consider the following:

1. Identify whether your product will be the modification of an existing one in your product mix or the development of a new product.

2. If the product is an extension of one in your current product mix, determine the type(s) of modifications that will be performed.

3. Using Figure 11.1 as a guide, discuss how your product idea would move through the stages of new-product development. Examine the idea, using the tests and analyses included in the new-product development process.

4. Discuss how the management of this product will fit into your current organizational structure.

The information obtained from these questions should assist you in developing various aspects of your marketing plan found in the *Interactive Marketing Plan* exercise at **www.cengage.com/marketing/pride-ferrell.**

globalEDGE

1. A part of developing and managing new or existing products is to understand more about the competitive environment in which your firm's innovations may be commercialized. You are attempting to define the type of competitive structure of the future industry of the new product currently under development. The Industry Research Desk's website has developed 18 steps to assist in this process. The information can be accessed by using the search term "18 steps" at **http://globaledge.msu.edu/ibrd.** Once you reach the Industry Research Desk website, scroll down to Step 11 for the website's definitions of each of the following four types of competitive structure (note that this site uses the term *types of competition*): monopoly, oligopoly, monopolistic competition, and pure competition. How many different types of competition does your resource list? What are the differences between these different types of competition? Can you give examples of each type?

2. Before your firm decides to develop a new product for a specific industry, you have been asked to survey the level and quality of innovation in the biotechnology, computer software, and semiconductor industries. *Technology Review,* a magazine of innovation, can help you identify the firms with the highest and lowest levels of innovation in each industry. Access this journal by using the search term "magazine of innovation" at **http://globaledge .msu.edu/ibrd,** and then click on the pdf link in the first sentence of the welcome page to download the report. What are considered the top companies' core competencies? Given this information, what do you think may be important in the coming years in each industry?

Harley-Davidson: More Than Just a Motorcycle

Harley-Davidson's customers can spot each other instantly by the iconic black, white, and orange logo on their motorcycles, clothing, and saddlebags. More than a century after the first Harley-Davidson motorcycle hit the road, the company's annual worldwide sales have zoomed past $5 billion. Harley-Davidson dominates the U.S. motorcycle market, and sales are also strong in Japan and Europe. Its annual output of 300,000 motorcycles covers 31 models in five product lines (Sportster, Dyna, Softail, VRSA, and Touring).

Although Harley-Davidson teetered on the brink of bankruptcy in the 1980s, it has roared back by limiting production to focus on a consistently high level of quality. Many of its newer products marry the brand's image of freedom and individuality to motorcycles with styling, performance, and features that appeal to younger buyers and women buyers. To attract first-time buyers as well as experienced riders trading up to better bikes, Harley-Davidson prices its motorcycles starting at $6,695 and offers financing and insurance, as well. Each model's price depends on its specific combination of features and styling.

Buyers can also order limited-edition motorcycles custom built with distinctive paint designs and accessories. Customers see their bikes as a way of expressing their individuality. However, Harley-Davidson selects only a small number of orders annually for custom-built bikes. Not surprisingly, these custom products are in high demand.

To encourage the next generation of biking enthusiasts to learn to drive a motorcycle and then buy the Harley-Davidson bike of their dreams, many of the company's dealers offer the Rider's Edge driving course. Since 2000, when the course was first offered,

nearly 140,000 people have graduated and earned a motorcycle license. The Rider's Edge also helps experienced riders to hone their driving skills and learn special techniques for riding in groups.

Group riding is such an important part of the overall product experience that the company founded the Harley Owners Group (HOG) to foster a sense of community among its customers. Today, the 1+ million HOG members enjoy benefits such as access to dozens of exclusive group rides, a special customer service hotline, and a members-only website. They also receive two magazines: *Hog Tales,* with articles about members and member events, and *Enthusiast,* with articles about Harley-Davidson's goods and services. In addition, customers can use the Harley-Davidson website to plan travel, book hotels, rent bikes, or ship their bikes for their next riding adventure.

Knowing that customers are passionate about motorcycles and about Harley-Davidson in particular, the company arranges tours at four of its factories in Wisconsin, Pennsylvania, and Missouri. It recently opened the Harley-Davidson Museum in Milwaukee, Wisconsin, home of its headquarters, with 130,000 square feet of exhibits. Many of the exhibits feature products from Harley-Davidson's past, including a sample of the bikes, boats, golf carts, and snowmobiles the company once manufactured. Museumgoers can get a taste of the Harley experience by climbing onto one of the company's current bikes for a virtual ride through beautiful country scenery projected on a big screen.

The museum also looks ahead by highlighting Harley-Davidson's latest technology, its newest engines, and the inner workings of its new-product development process. One exhibit shows how a new motorcycle starts life as a sketch, is transformed into a clay model, becomes a testable prototype, and ultimately enters full production. "In creating this museum, we wanted to make sure that it told an evolving story," says the museum director. "We have a rich heritage, but we also have an exciting future."[38]

Questions for Discussion

1. Why would Harley-Davidson put as much emphasis on consistency of quality as it does on level of quality?
2. How does Harley-Davidson use customer services to differentiate its motorcycle products?
3. What role do you think the Harley-Davidson Museum might play in influencing how consumers perceive the company and its products?

CASE 11.2

Pepsi Sales Bubble with Limited-Edition Soft Drinks

Cucumber, berry, and cinnamon soft drinks may come and go in Japan, but colas are seemingly forever—at least in Pepsi's product lineup. The company and its local partner, Suntory, are using limited-edition soft drinks to boost market share in the $30 billion Japanese beverage market and keep sales bubbling despite a cola war with rival Coca-Cola and fierce competition for space on store shelves.

No new product is a sure thing, but the Japanese market is particularly challenging. Of the 1,500 beverages launched there every year, only the tiniest percentage survives the introductory period. Why? First, because Japanese convenience stores are small, they make room only for products that sell quickly. New drinks that don't gain a following soon after they're introduced are pulled from store shelves in a hurry and replaced by the next new thing. Second, despite intense brand loyalty, many Japanese consumers crave novelty and go out of their way to hunt down limited-edition products made for specific seasons, regions, or reasons. Nestlé has been effective in using a limited-edition strategy to drive sales of seasonal treats like melon-filled KitKat chocolate bars. Similarly, the Japanese division of Mars has attracted customers by offering limited-edition M&M candies linked to the local release of major Hollywood movies.

When Pepsi and Suntory set out to tap this widespread interest in variety by marketing limited-edition soft drinks, they started with berry-flavored Pepsi Blue. In the United States, Pepsi Blue remained on the market for two years. In Japan, however, the entire production run of 1.7 million bottles sold out within a few weeks. That experience led Pepsi and Suntory to plan the short-and-sweet life of Pepsi Red, Carnival, and other limited-edition soft drinks based on Pepsi drinks that are available in other countries.

Now the two companies were ready to plan for the development and introduction of a blockbuster limited-edition summer soft drink. After testing 60 possibilities, they chose a cucumber-melon flavor, created samples, and asked for feedback from focus-group participants. The positive reaction prompted Pepsi and Suntory to produce 4.8 million bottles of Ice Cucumber soft drink.

As with the previous limited-edition soft drinks, the entire production run sold out within a few weeks, fueled largely by word of mouth and YouTube clips showing fans gulping down bottle after bottle. Yet even though demand remained high, both scarcity and seasonality added to the appeal, which is why the partners decided not to produce more Ice Cucumber. "We didn't want it on the market past the summer," a Suntory marketer said at the time. "The value of Ice Cucumber is that it's gone already."

These limited-edition successes have also raised the profile of other Pepsi drinks, particularly Nex, a no-calorie soft drink available only in Japan. Backed by more advertising and expanded production capacity, Suntory aims to increase sales of Nex by more than 20 percent per year. Meanwhile, Coca-Cola launches 100 new beverages in Japan every year and has forged partnerships with firms like Italy's Illycaffe to create inventive new drinks that will grab the public imagination and keep customers coming back for more.

Given the competitive environment, the pressure from retailers to make new products perform, the speed with which consumer tastes change, and the cost of launching a new soft drink, Pepsi and Suntory are being careful not to overuse their limited-edition strategy. To make each new product stand out, they plan no more than four limited-edition introductions a year. If all goes according to plan, consumers will be primed for the introduction of the next new taste treat and will recognize that they have to buy quickly before that flavor disappears.[39]

Questions for Discussion

1. Pepsi and Suntory cap their limited-edition soft drink introductions at four per year. What effect is this cap likely to have on the new-product development process?
2. How important is product quality when a limited-edition soft drink like Ice Cucumber sells out in a matter of weeks?
3. What criteria would you suggest that Pepsi and Suntory use when screening ideas for new limited-edition soft drinks?

12 Branding and Packaging

Spanx Puts Its Best Foot Forward for Success

A last-minute change to the brand name added just the right touch of personality to get Spanx off on the right foot for fast growth. It all started when founder Sara Blakely wanted to wear control-top pantyhose for a smooth line under tight-fitting pants while leaving her feet bare for open-toed shoes. Not able to find the right kind of hosiery or undergarment, she resorted to cutting the feet off ordinary pantyhose.

entrepreneurs IN ACTION

Blakely's entrepreneurial instincts kicked in when she realized that other women were probably seeking solutions to the same problem. She quickly went online to start the lengthy process of patenting her innovative footless pantyhose. Then she went from manufacturer to manufacturer until she found one willing to create prototypes.

Now she needed a brand name to embody the confident, spunky attitude she wanted her product to project. As a former stand-up comic, Blakely knew that words with the letter "k" tend to make people laugh. She initially chose "Spanks," but at the last minute, she substituted "Spanx" after hearing that made-up words are more appealing than real words for brand names and are more easily trademarked, too!

With product samples in hand, Blakely made an important breakthrough when she persuaded Neiman Marcus to place a small initial order. Her next big breakthrough came when Oprah Winfrey touted the product on her talk show. Suddenly women all over the United States were looking for Spanx, and retailers eagerly stocked their shelves with the product. Within seven years, Spanx was making more than 100 products including a step-in hosiery comfort bra under the "Bra-llelujah" brand. Spanx now has annual sales in excess of $150 million. Today Blakely has become a celebrity through appearances on the reality shows *The Rebel Billionaire* and *American Inventor,* bringing her brand even more fame.[1]

Brands, components of brands, packages, and labels are all part of a product's tangible features, the verbal and physical cues that help customers identify the products they want and influence their choices when they are unsure. As such, branding and packaging play an important role in marketing strategy. A successful brand like Spanx is distinct and memorable; without one, a firm could not differentiate its products, and shoppers' choices would essentially be arbitrary. A good package design is cost effective, safe, environmentally responsible, and valuable as a promotional tool.

In this chapter, we first discuss branding, its value to customers and marketers, brand loyalty, and brand equity. Next, we examine the various types of brands. We then consider how companies choose and protect brands, the various branding policies employed, co-branding, and brand licensing. We look at packaging's critical role as part of the product. Next, we explore the functions of packaging, issues to consider in packaging design, how the package can be a major element in marketing strategy, and packaging criticisms. Finally, we discuss the functions of labeling and relevant legal issues.

Branding

LO 1 To explain the value of branding

Marketers must make many decisions about products, including choices about brands, brand names, brand marks, trademarks, and trade names. A **brand** is a name, term, design, symbol, or any other feature that identifies one marketer's product as distinct from those of other marketers. A brand may identify a single item, a family of items, or all of a seller's items.[2] Some have defined a brand as not just the physical good, name, color, logo, or ad campaign but everything associated with the product, including its symbolism and experiences.[3] For example, Hearts on Fire has branded a particular hearts and arrows cut for its diamonds, which maximizes their brilliance and fire—and allows Hearts on Fire diamonds to command a 15 to 20 percent premium over traditional diamonds.[4] A **brand name** is the part of a brand that can be spoken—including letters, words, and numbers—such as 7Up. A brand name is often a product's only distinguishing characteristic. Without the brand name, a firm could not differentiate its products. To consumers, a brand name is as fundamental as the product itself. Indeed, many brand names have become synonymous with the product, such as Scotch Tape and Xerox copiers. Through promotional activities, the owners of these brand names try to protect them from being used as generic names for tape and photocopiers, respectively.

The element of a brand that is not made up of words—often a symbol or design—is a **brand mark**. Examples of brand marks include McDonald's Golden Arches, Nike's "swoosh," and the stylized silhouette of Apple's iPod. A **trademark** is a legal designation indicating that the owner has exclusive use of a brand or a part of a brand and others are prohibited by law from using it. To protect a brand name or brand mark in the United States, an organization must register it as a trademark with the U.S. Patent and Trademark Office. The Patent and Trademark Office registers about 150,000 new trademarks a year.[5] Finally, a **trade name** is the full legal name of an organization, such as Ford Motor Company, rather than the name of a specific product.

Value of Branding

Both buyers and sellers benefit from branding. Brands help customers identify specific products that they do and do not like, which in turn facilitates the purchase of items that satisfy their needs and reduces the time required to purchase the product. Without brands, product selection would be quite random because buyers would have no assurance they were purchasing what they preferred. The purchase of certain brands can be a form of self-expression. For example, clothing brand names are important to many consumers; names such as Tommy Hilfiger, Polo, Champion, Guess, and Nike give manufacturers an advantage in the marketplace. A brand also helps buyers evaluate the quality of products, especially when they are unable to judge a product's characteristics; that is, a brand may symbolize a certain quality

brand A name, term, design, symbol, or other feature that identifies one marketer's product as distinct from those of other marketers

brand name The part of a brand that can be spoken, including letters, words, and numbers

brand mark The part of a brand that is not made up of words, such as a symbol or design

trademark A legal designation of exclusive use of a brand

trade name The full legal name of an organization

Brand Mark

The red and white target is the brand mark for Target Stores.

level to a customer, and in turn the person lets that perception of quality represent the quality of the item. A brand helps reduce a buyer's perceived risk of purchase. In addition, a psychological reward may come from owning a brand that symbolizes status. The Mercedes-Benz brand in the United States is an example.

Sellers benefit from branding because each company's brands identify its products, which makes repeat purchasing easier for customers. Branding helps a firm to introduce a new product that carries the name of one or more of its existing products because buyers are already familiar with those brands. It also facilitates promotional efforts because the promotion of each branded product indirectly promotes all other similarly branded products. Branding also fosters brand loyalty. To the extent that buyers become loyal to a specific brand, the company's market share for that product achieves a certain level of stability, allowing the firm to use its resources more efficiently. Once a firm develops some degree of customer loyalty for a brand, it can maintain a fairly consistent price rather than continually cutting the price to attract customers. A brand is as much of an asset as the company's building or machinery. When marketers increase their brand's value, they also raise the total asset value of the organization. Companies often spend significant resources to boost their brands' value. Bank of America, for example, sought to boost its brand value during the holidays by opening a Gift on Fifth store in a New York City shopping area with gift-wrapping services, children's activities, coffee and hot chocolate—and the opportunity to sign up for a new BoA Visa card.[6] (We discuss brand value in more detail later in this chapter.) At times, marketers must decide whether to change a brand name. This is a difficult decision because the value in the existing brand name must be given up to gain the potential to build a higher value in a new brand name.

GETTING SEXY UNDERARMS IS
NO SWEAT.

Secret FLAWLESS.

NEW **5** facets *of FLAWLESS PERFORMANCE*

because you're hot

1 Strong odor & wetness protection

2 Goes on clear

3 Smooth lightweight formula

4 Self-renewing fragrances

5 Skin-nurturing conditioners

Brand Insistence

Some consumers are brand insistent about their deodorant. When they find just the right brand that works with their body chemistry, they keep buying the same brand.

brand loyalty A customer's favorable attitude toward a specific brand

brand recognition The degree of brand loyalty in which a customer is aware that a brand exists and views the brand as an alternative purchase if their preferred brand is unavailable

brand preference The degree of brand loyalty in which a customer prefers one brand over competitive offerings

brand insistence The degree of brand loyalty in which a customer strongly prefers a specific brand and will accept no substitute

There is a cultural dimension to branding. Most brand experiences are individual, and each consumer confers his or her own social meaning onto brands. A brand's appeal is largely at an emotional level based on its symbolic image and key associations.[7] For some brands, such as Harley-Davidson, Google, and Apple, this can result in an almost cultlike following. These brands often develop a community of loyal customers that communicate through get-togethers, online forums, blogs, podcasts, and other means. These brands may even help consumers develop their identities and self-concepts and serve as forms of self-expression. In fact, the term *cultural branding* has been used to explain how a brand conveys a powerful myth that consumers find useful in cementing their identities.[8] It is also important to recognize that because a brand exists independently in the consumer's mind, it is not directly controlled by the marketer. Every aspect of a brand is subject to a consumer's emotional involvement, interpretation, and memory. By understanding how branding influences purchases, marketers can foster customer loyalty.[9]

Brand Loyalty

As we just noted, creating and maintaining customer loyalty toward a brand are two of the benefits of branding. **Brand loyalty** is a customer's favorable attitude toward a specific brand. If brand loyalty is strong enough, customers may consistently purchase this brand when they need a product in that product category. Customer satisfaction with a brand is the most common reason for loyalty to that brand.[10] Although brand loyalty may not result in a customer purchasing a specific brand all the time, the brand is at least viewed as a potentially viable choice in the variety of brands being considered for purchase. Development of brand loyalty in a customer reduces his or her risks and shortens the time spent buying the product. However, the degree of brand loyalty for products varies from one product category to another. For example, it is challenging to develop brand loyalty for most products because customers can usually judge a product's quality and do not need to refer to a brand as an indicator of quality. Brand loyalty also varies by country. Customers in France, Germany, and the United Kingdom tend to be less brand loyal than U.S. customers.

Three degrees of brand loyalty exist: recognition, preference, and insistence. **Brand recognition** occurs when a customer is aware that the brand exists and views it as an alternative purchase if the preferred brand is unavailable or if the other available brands are unfamiliar. This is the mildest form of brand loyalty. The term *loyalty* clearly is used very loosely here. One of the initial objectives when introducing a new brand is to create widespread awareness of the brand to generate brand recognition.

Brand preference is a stronger degree of brand loyalty: a customer definitely prefers one brand over competitive offerings and will purchase this brand if available. However, if the brand is not available, the customer will accept a substitute brand rather than expending additional effort finding and purchasing the preferred brand. A marketer is likely to be able to compete effectively in a market when a number of customers have developed brand preference for its specific brand.

When **brand insistence** occurs, a customer strongly prefers a specific brand, will accept no substitute, and is willing to spend a great deal of time and effort to acquire that brand. If a brand-insistent customer goes to a store and finds the brand unavailable, he or she will seek the brand elsewhere rather than purchase a substitute brand. Brand insistence can also apply to service products such as Hilton Hotels or sports teams such as the Chicago Bears or the Dallas Cowboys. Brand insistence is

LO 2 To understand brand loyalty

LO 3 To analyze the major components of brand equity

the strongest degree of brand loyalty—a brander's dream. However, it is the least-common type of brand loyalty. Customers vary considerably regarding the product categories for which they may be brand insistent. Can you think of products for which you are brand insistent? Perhaps it's a brand of deodorant, soft drink, jeans, or even pet food (if your pet is brand insistent).

Building brand loyalty is a major challenge for many marketers. Brand loyalty in general seems to be declining, partly because of marketers' increased reliance on sales, coupons, and other short-term promotions and partly because of the sometimes overwhelming array of similar new products from which customers can choose. Thus, it is an extremely important issue. The creation of brand loyalty significantly contributes to an organization's ability to achieve a sustainable competitive advantage.

Brand Equity

A well-managed brand is an asset to an organization. The value of this asset is often referred to as brand equity. **Brand equity** is the marketing and financial value associated with a brand's strength in a market. Besides the actual proprietary brand assets, such as patents and trademarks, four major elements underlie brand equity: brand name awareness, brand loyalty, perceived brand quality, and brand associations (see Figure 12.1).[11]

Recognition of a brand leads to brand familiarity, which in turn results in a level of comfort with the brand. A familiar brand is more likely to be selected than an unfamiliar brand because the familiar brand is often viewed as more reliable and of more acceptable quality. The familiar brand is likely to be in a customer's consideration set, whereas the unfamiliar brand is not.

Brand loyalty is an important component of brand equity because it reduces a brand's vulnerability to competitors' actions. Brand loyalty allows an organization to keep its existing customers and avoid spending an enormous amount of resources gaining new ones. Loyal customers provide brand visibility and reassurance to potential new customers. Because customers expect their brands to be available when and where they shop, retailers strive to carry the brands known for their strong customer following.

Customers associate a particular brand with a certain level of overall quality. A brand name may be used as a substitute for judgment of quality. In many cases, customers can't actually judge the quality of the product for themselves and instead must rely on the brand as a quality indicator. Perceived high brand quality helps support a premium price, allowing a marketer to avoid severe price competition. Also, favorable perceived brand quality can ease the introduction of brand extensions, since the high regard for the brand will likely translate into high regard for the related products.

The set of associations linked to a brand is another key component of brand equity. At times, a marketer works to connect a particular lifestyle or, in some instances, a certain personality type with a specific brand. For example, customers associate

brand equity The marketing and financial value associated with a brand's strength in a market

Source: Adapted with the permission of The Free Press, a division of Simon & Schuster Adult Publishing Group, from *Managing Brand Equity: Capitalizing on the Value of a Brand Name* by David A. Aaker. Copyright © 1991 by David A. Aaker. All rights reserved.

figure 12.1

MAJOR ELEMENTS OF BRAND EQUITY

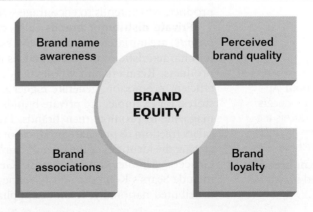

SEIZE THE MOMENT.
AND THE LAST CHICKEN WING.

SPEEDY

ALKA
SELTZER

For complete relief from headache, indigestion, heartburn and upset stomach.

GOOD TIMES. SPEEDY ALKA-SELTZER IS THERE.

Enjoy good times responsibly.

Stimulating Brand Association
The maker of Alka Seltzer uses its trade character, Speedy, to stimulate favorable brand associations.

L O 4 To recognize the types of brands and their benefits

manufacturer brand A brand initiated by producers to ensure that producers are identified with their products at the point of purchase

private distributor brand A brand initiated and owned by a reseller

Michelin tires with protecting family members; a De Beers diamond with a loving, long-lasting relationship ("A Diamond Is Forever"); and Dr Pepper with a unique taste. These types of brand associations contribute significantly to the brand's equity. Brand associations are sometimes facilitated by using trade characters, such as the Jolly Green Giant, the Pillsbury Dough Boy, and the Monster.com Monster. Placing these trade characters in advertisements and on packages helps consumers link the ads and packages to the brands.

Although difficult to measure, brand equity represents the value of a brand to an organization. An organization may buy a brand from another company at a premium price because outright brand purchase may be less expensive and less risky than creating and developing a brand from scratch. For example, Innovative Brands LLC purchased Procter & Gamble's Sure deodorant and Pert Plus shampoo brands after P&G decided they no longer fit with P&G's global strategies.[12] Brand equity helps give a brand the power to capture and maintain a consistent market share, which provides stability to the organization's sales volume.

Table 12.1 lists the ten global brands with the greatest economic value, as compiled by Interbrand, a consulting firm. Interbrand's top 100 brands account for nearly 30 percent of the market value of the firms that own them. The Coca-Cola brand, for example, represents two-thirds of the Coca-Cola Company's market capitalization.[13] Any company that owns a brand listed in Table 12.1 would agree that the economic value of that brand is likely to be the greatest single asset the organization possesses. A brand's overall economic value rises and falls with the brand's profitability, brand awareness, brand loyalty, and perceived brand quality and with the strength of positive brand associations.

Types of Brands

Brands come in three categories: manufacturer, private distributor, and generic. **Manufacturer brands** are initiated by producers and ensure that producers are identified with their products at the point of purchase—for example, Green Giant, Compaq Computer, and Levi's jeans. A manufacturer brand usually requires a producer to become involved in distribution, promotion, and, to some extent, pricing decisions. Brand loyalty is encouraged by promotion, quality control, and guarantees; it is a valuable asset to a manufacturer. The producer tries to stimulate demand for the product, which tends to encourage sellers and resellers to make the product available.

Private distributor brands (also called *private brands, store brands,* or *dealer brands*) are initiated and owned by resellers—that is, wholesalers or retailers. The major characteristic of private brands is that the manufacturers are not identified on the products. Retailers and wholesalers use private distributor brands to develop more efficient promotion, generate higher gross margins, and change store image. Safeway stores, for example, use private brands to compete against deep discounters and have a magazine to promote their brands. Private distributor brands give retailers or wholesalers freedom to purchase products of a specified quality at the lowest cost without disclosing the identities of the manufacturers. Wholesaler brands include IGA (Independent Grocers' Alliance) and Topmost (General Grocer). Familiar retailer brand names include Sears's Kenmore and JCPenney's Arizona. Many successful private brands are distributed nationally. Kenmore appliances are as well known as most manufacturer

Private Brand

Banana Republic has initiated and developed many private branded products including eyewear.

INTRODUCING

BANANA REPUBLIC

EYEWEAR

Brand	Brand Value (in Billions of $)
table 12.1	**THE WORLD'S MOST VALUABLE BRANDS**
Coca-Cola	65.3
Microsoft	58.7
IBM	57.1
GE	51.6
Nokia	33.7
Toyota	32.1
Intel	31.0
McDonald's	29.4
Disney	29.2
Mercedes	23.6

Source: From "All Brands Are Not Created Equal: Best Global Brands, 2007," Interbrand, www.ourfishbowl.com/images/surveys/Interbrand_BGB_2007.pdf (accessed Feb. 1, 2008).

brands. Sometimes retailers with successful private distributor brands start manufacturing their own products to gain more control over product costs, quality, and design in the hope of increasing profits. Sales of private labels now account for one out of every five product items sold in supermarkets, drugstores, and mass merchandisers, totaling some $65 billion of retail business.[14] Some private brands have even gone upscale, such as Whole Foods's 365 line of organic goods and Safeway's Rancher's Reserve premium beef.[15] Supermarket private brands are popular globally, too.

Competition between manufacturer brands and private distributor brands (sometimes called "the battle of the brands") is ongoing. To compete against manufacturer brands, retailers have tried to strengthen consumer confidence in private brands. Results of a recent study on consumer perceptions of private and manufacturer brands appear in Figure 12.2. For manufacturers, developing multiple manufacturer brands and distribution systems has been an effective means of combating the increased competition from private brands. By developing a new brand name, a producer can adjust various elements of its marketing mix to appeal to a different target market.

The growth of private brands has been steady. One reason for this is that retailers advertise the manufacturer brands, which brings customers to their stores, but sell the private brands, especially to price-sensitive customers. Another reason is that retailers with private labels negotiate better prices from producers of manufacturer brands.[16] To compete against private brands, some manufacturer brand makers have stopped increasing prices or even have cut their prices, which has narrowed the price gap—the major advantage of buying a private brand. Traditionally private brands have appeared in packaging that directly imitates the packaging of competing manufacturers' brands without significant legal ramifications. However, the legal risks of using look-alike packaging are increasing for private branders.

Some private distributor brands are produced by companies that specialize in making only private distributor brands; others are made by producers of manufacturer brands. At times, producers of both types of brands find it difficult to ignore

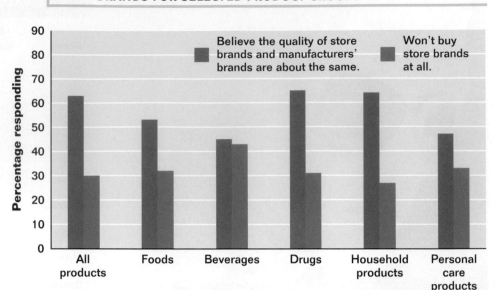

figure 12.2 CONSUMERS' PERCEPTIONS OF STORE AND MANUFACTURERS' BRANDS FOR SELECTED PRODUCT GROUPS

Source: "Store Brands at the Turning Point," Consumer Research Network, 3624 Market Street, Philadelphia, PA.

the opportunities that arise from producing private distributor brands. If a producer decides not to produce a private brand for a reseller, a competitor probably will. Moreover, the production of private distributor brands allows the producer to use excess capacity during periods when its own brands are at nonpeak production. The ultimate decision of whether to produce a private or a manufacturer brand depends on a company's resources, production capabilities, and goals.

Some marketers of traditionally branded products have embarked on a policy of not branding, often called *generic branding*. **Generic brands** indicate only the product category (such as aluminum foil) and do not include the company name or other identifying terms. Generic brands are usually sold at lower prices than comparable branded items. Although at one time generic brands may have represented as much as 10 percent of all retail grocery sales, today they account for less than half of 1 percent. One exception to this trend is generic prescription medications, which have grown to account for 56 percent of all prescriptions dispensed in the United States, largely due to the fact that they cost 30 to 80 percent less than branded prescription medications.[17]

Selecting a Brand Name

Marketers consider a number of factors when selecting a brand name. First, the name should be easy for customers (including foreign buyers, if the firm intends to market its products in other countries) to say, spell, and recall. Short, one-syllable names, such as Cheer, often satisfy this requirement. Second, the brand name should indicate the product's major benefits and, if possible, suggest in a positive way the product's uses and special characteristics; negative or offensive references should be avoided. For example, the brand names of such household cleaning products as Ajax dishwashing liquid, Vanish toilet bowl cleaner, Formula 409 multipurpose cleaner, Cascade dishwasher detergent, and Wisk laundry detergent connote strength and effectiveness. Research suggests that consumers are more likely to recall and to evaluate favorably names that convey positive attributes or benefits.[18] Third, to set it apart from competing brands, the brand should be distinctive. AT&T, for example, renamed its Cingular wireless service AT&T so all the company's products would have the same brand name.[19] If a marketer intends to use a brand for a product line, that brand must be compatible with all products in the line. Finally, a brand should be designed so that it can be used and recognized in all types of media. Finding the right brand name has become a challenging task because many obvious product names have already been used. After acquiring the AmeriSuites hotel chain, Hyatt changed

To understand how to select and protect brands

generic brand A brand indicating only the product category the brand name to Hyatt Place not only to emphasize the new chain's revamped interiors and exteriors but also to capitalize on its own more recognizable name.[20]

How are brand names devised? Brand names can be created from single or multiple words—for example, Bic or Dodge Nitro. Letters and numbers are used to create such brands as Volvo's S60 sedan or RIM's BlackBerry 8100. Words, numbers, and letters are combined to yield brand names such as Motorola's RAZR V3 phone or BMW's Z4 Roadster. To avoid terms that have negative connotations, marketers sometimes use fabricated words that have absolutely no meaning when created—for example, Kodak and Exxon. Starwood Hotels & Resorts named its new Westin extended-stay suite hotels ELEMENT after months of brainstorming among employees. The company wanted the new chain brand to have a simple, modern name that would stand out against competitors' names.[21] Occasionally a brand is simply brought out of storage and used as is or modified. Firms often maintain banks of registered brands, some of which may have been used in the past. Cadillac, for example, has a bank of approximately 360 registered trademarks. The LaSalle brand, used in the 1920s and 1930s, could be called up for a new Cadillac model in the future. Possible brand names sometimes are tested in focus groups or other settings to assess customers' reactions.

Who actually creates brand names? Brand names can be created internally by the organization. At Del Monte, a team of executives brainstormed 27 ideas for new cat food offerings with names like "pate," "souffle," and "crème brulee."[22] Sometimes a name is suggested by individuals who are close to the product's development. Some organizations have committees that participate in brand name creation and approval. Large companies that introduce numerous new products annually are likely to have a department that develops brand names. At times, outside consultants and companies that specialize in brand name development are used.

Although most of the important branding considerations apply to both goods and services, branding a service has some additional dimensions. The service brand is usually the same as the company name. Financial companies, such as Fidelity Investments and Charles Schwab Discount Brokerage, have established strong brand recognition. These companies have used their names to create an image of value and friendly, timely, responsible, accurate, and knowledgeable customer assistance. Service providers (such as United Airlines) are perceived by customers as having one brand name, even though they offer multiple products (first class, business class, and coach). Because the service brand name and company name are so closely interrelated, a service brand name must be flexible enough to encompass a variety of current services, as well as new ones the company may offer in the future. Geographical references such as *western* and descriptive terms such as *trucking* limit the scope of possible associations with the brand name. Because Southwest Airlines now flies to many parts of the country, its name has become too limited in its scope of associations. *Humana*, with its connotations of kindness and compassion, is flexible enough to encompass all services that a hospital, insurance plan, or health-care facility offers. Frequently a service marketer employs a symbol along with its brand name to make the brand distinctive and communicate a certain image.

Protecting a Brand

A marketer should also design a brand so that it can be protected easily through registration. A series of court decisions has created a broad hierarchy of protection based on brand type. From most protectable to least protectable, these brand types are fanciful (Exxon), arbitrary (Dr Pepper), suggestive (Spray 'n Wash), descriptive (Minute Rice), and generic (aluminum foil). Generic brands are not protectable. Surnames and descriptive, geographic, or functional names are difficult to protect.[23] Because of their designs, some brands can be legally infringed on more easily than others. Although registration protects trademarks domestically for ten years and trademarks can be renewed indefinitely, a firm should develop a system for ensuring that its trademarks are renewed as needed.

To protect its exclusive rights to a brand, a company must ensure that the brand is not likely to be considered an infringement on any brand already registered with the U.S. Patent and Trademark Office. This task may be complex because infringement

Protecting a Brand

Companies try to protect their brands by using certain phrases and symbols in their advertisements. Note the term "brand" after Ziploc, and the use of the ® symbol.

is determined by the courts, which base their decisions on whether a brand causes consumers to be confused, mistaken, or deceived about the source of the product. McDonald's is one company that aggressively protects its trademarks against infringement; it has brought charges against a number of companies with *Mc* names because it fears that the use of that prefix will give consumers the impression that these companies are associated with or owned by McDonald's. Auto Shack changed its name to AutoZone when faced with legal action from Tandy Corporation, owner of Radio Shack. Tandy maintained that it owned the name *Shack*. After research showed that virtually every auto supply store in the country used *auto* in its name, *zone* was deemed the best word to pair with *auto*.

A marketer should guard against allowing a brand name to become a generic term used to refer to a general product category. Generic terms cannot be protected as exclusive brand names. For example, *aspirin, escalator,* and *shredded wheat*—all brand names at one time—eventually were declared generic terms that refer to product classes. Thus, they could no longer be protected. To keep a brand name from becoming a generic term, the firm should spell the name with a capital letter and use it as an adjective to modify the name of the general product class, as in Kool-Aid Brand Soft Drink Mix.[24] Including the word *brand* just after the brand name is also helpful. An organization can deal with this problem directly by advertising that its brand is a trademark and should not be used generically. The firm can also indicate that the brand is a registered trademark by using the symbol®.

In the interest of strengthening trademark protection, Congress enacted the Trademark Law Revision Act in 1988, the only major federal trademark legislation since the Lanham Act of 1946. The purpose of this more recent legislation is to increase the value of the federal registration system for U.S. firms relative to foreign competitors and to better protect the public from counterfeiting, confusion, and deception.

A U.S. firm that tries to protect a brand in a foreign country frequently encounters problems. In many countries, brand registration is not possible; the first firm to use a brand in such a country automatically has the rights to it. In some instances, U.S. companies actually have had to buy their own brand rights from a firm in a foreign country because the foreign firm was the first user in that country. Consider the decade-long dispute over Havana Club rum, which is marketed in 183 countries by

Pernod Ricard, a French company, in a joint venture with the Cuban government, which nationalized the brand in 1960. However, Bacardi purchased the rights and original recipe from the brand's Cuban originators with the intention of producing it for distribution in the United States. Pernod Ricard sued Bacardi for violating its agreement, but Bacardi insisted that the Cuban registration of the trademark in the United States is no longer valid. The dispute has involved both U.S. courts and the World Trade Organization.[25]

Marketers that are trying to protect their brands must also contend with brand counterfeiting. In the United States, for instance, one can purchase counterfeit General Motors parts, Cartier watches, Louis Vuitton handbags, Walt Disney character dolls, Warner Bros. clothing, Mont Blanc pens, and a host of other products illegally marketed by manufacturers that do not own the brands. Annual losses caused by counterfeit products are estimated at between $250 billion and $350 billion. Many counterfeit products are manufactured overseas—in Turkey, China, Thailand, Italy, and Colombia, for example—but some are counterfeited in the United States. Counterfeit products are often hard to distinguish from the real brands. Products most likely to be counterfeited are well-known brands that appeal to a mass market and products whose physical materials are inexpensive relative to the products' prices. Microsoft estimates that its revenues would double if counterfeiting of its brand name products were eliminated. Some $40 billion a year are lost in the computer software business because of counterfeit and pirated products. Brand fraud results not only in lost revenue for the brand's owner; it also results in a low-quality product for customers, distorts competition, affects investment levels, reduces tax revenues and legitimate employment, creates safety risks, and affects international relations. It also likely affects customers' perceptions of the brand due to the counterfeit product's inferior quality.

Branding Policies

L O 6 To examine three types of branding policies

Before establishing branding policies, a firm must decide whether to brand its products at all. If a company's product is homogeneous and similar to competitors' products, it may be difficult to brand. Raw materials such as coal, sand, and farm produce are hard to brand because of the homogeneity and physical characteristics of such products.

If a firm chooses to brand its products, it may opt for one or more of the following branding policies: individual, family, or brand extension branding. **Individual branding** is a policy of giving each product a different name. Sara Lee uses individual branding among its many divisions, which include Hanes underwear, L'eggs pantyhose, Champion sportswear, Jimmy Dean, Bali, Ball Park, and other vastly diverse brands. A major advantage of individual branding is that if an organization introduces a poor product, the negative images associated with it do not contaminate the company's other products. An individual branding policy may also facilitate market segmentation when a firm wishes to enter many segments of the same market. Separate, unrelated names can be used and each brand aimed at a specific segment.

In **family branding**, all of a firm's products are branded with the same name or part of the name, such as Kellogg's Frosted Flakes, Kellogg's Rice Krispies, and Kellogg's Corn Flakes. In some cases, a company's name is combined with other words to brand items. Arm & Hammer uses its name on all its products, along with a generic description of the item, such as Arm & Hammer Heavy Duty Detergent, Arm & Hammer Pure Baking Soda, and Arm & Hammer Carpet Deodorizer. Unlike individual branding, family branding means that the promotion of one item with the family brand promotes the firm's other products. Other major companies that use family branding include Mitsubishi, Kodak, and Fisher-Price.

A **brand extension** occurs when a firm uses one of its existing brands to brand a new product in a different product category. For example, Kellogg employed a brand extension when it gave its Special K cereal brand name to a new protein water product and a calorie-counting watch.[26] Another example is when Bic, the maker of disposable pens, introduced Bic disposable razors and Bic lighters. A brand extension should not be confused with a line extension, which involves using an existing brand on a new product in the same product category, such as new flavors or sizes. For example, when the maker of Tylenol, McNeil Consumer Products, introduced Extra

individual branding A branding policy in which each product is given a different name

family branding Branding all of a firm's products with the same name or part of the name

brand extension An organization uses one of its existing brands to brand a new product in a different product category

Strength Tylenol P.M., the new product was a line extension because it was in the same category. Researchers have found that there may be an opportunity to charge a premium price relative to comparable products when extending a strong brand into a new-product category because of consumers' perceptions of lower risk associated with a known brand name.[27]

Marketers share a common concern that if a brand is extended too many times or extended too far outside its original product category, the brand can be significantly weakened. For example, Miller Brewing Company has extended its brand to Miller Lite, Genuine Draft, Draft Lite, Ice, Ice Lite, Milwaukee's Best, Ice House, and Red Dog, but so many extensions may confuse customers and encourage them to engage in considerable brand switching. The Nabisco Snackwell brand initially appeared only on crackers, cookies, and snack bars, all of which fall into the baked snack category. However, extending the brand to yogurts and gelatin mixes goes further afield. Although some experts might caution Nabisco against extending the Snackwell brand to this degree, some evidence suggests that brands can be successfully extended to less closely related product categories through the use of advertisements that extend customers' perceptions of the original product category. For example, Waterford, an upscale Irish brand of crystal, extended its name to writing instruments when seeking sales growth beyond closely related product categories such as china, cutlery, and table linens.[28] Research has found that a line extension into premium categories can be an effective strategy to revitalize a brand, but the line extension needs to be closely linked to the core brand.[29] Other research, however, suggests that diluting a brand by extending it into dissimilar product categories could have the potential to suppress consumer consideration and choice for the original brand.[30]

An organization is not limited to a single branding policy. A company that uses primarily individual branding for many of its products may also use brand extensions. Branding policy is influenced by the number of products and product lines the company produces, the characteristics of its target markets, the number and types of competing products available, and the size of the firm's resources.

Co-Branding

L O 7 To understand co-branding and brand licensing

Co-branding is the use of two or more brands on one product. Marketers employ co-branding to capitalize on the brand equity of multiple brands. It is popular in a number of processed food categories and in the credit card industry. The brands used for co-branding can be owned by the same company. For example, Kraft's Lunchables product teams the Kraft cheese brand with Oscar Mayer lunchmeats, another Kraft-owned brand. The brands may also be owned by different companies. Credit card companies such as American Express, Visa, and MasterCard, for instance, team up with other brands such as General Motors, AT&T, and many airlines.

Effective co-branding capitalizes on the trust and confidence customers have in the brands involved. The brands should not lose their identities, and it should be clear to customers which brand is the main brand. For example, it is fairly obvious that Kellogg owns the brand and is the main brander of Kellogg's Healthy Choice Cereal. (The Healthy Choice brand is owned by ConAgra.) It is important for marketers to understand that when a co-branded product is unsuccessful, both brands are implicated in the product failure. To gain customer acceptance, the brands involved must represent a complementary fit in the minds of buyers. Trying to link a brand like Harley-Davidson with a brand like Healthy Choice will not achieve co-branding objectives because customers are not likely to perceive these brands as compatible.

Co-branding can help an organization differentiate its products from those of competitors. By using the product development skills of a co-branding partner, an organization can create a distinctive product. For example, cell phone provider T-Mobile and fashion designer Diane von Furstenberg teamed up to produce a limited-edition Sidekick 3 phone, with the designer's trademark hot-pink lips, that retails for $350.[31] Co-branding can also allow the partners to take advantage of each other's distribution capabilities.

Although co-branding has been used for a number of years, it began to grow in popularity in the 1980s when Monsanto aggressively promoted its NutraSweet product as

co-branding Using two or more brands on one product

Co-Branding

Lunchables is a co-branded item consisting of Oscar Mayer and Kraft products.

an ingredient in such well-known brands as Diet Coke. Later a rival sweetner, Splenda, was co-branded with Diet Coke, Starbucks, and many other brands. Intel, too, has capitalized on ingredient co-branding through its "Intel Inside" program. The effectiveness of ingredient co-branding relies heavily on continued promotional efforts by the ingredient's producer.

Brand Licensing

A popular branding strategy involves **brand licensing,** an agreement in which a company permits another organization to use its brand on other products for a licensing fee. Royalties may be as low as 2 percent of wholesale revenues or higher than 10 percent. Kohl's, for example, licensed the Tony Hawk brand for use on a line of casual footwear.[32] The licensee is responsible for all manufacturing, selling, and advertising functions, and bears the costs if the licensed product fails. Not long ago only a few firms licensed their corporate trademarks, but today licensing is a multi-billion-dollar business. The top U.S. licensing company is Walt Disney Company. The NFL, the NCAA, NASCAR, and Major League Baseball are all leaders in the retail sales of licensed products.

The advantages of licensing range from extra revenues and low-cost or free publicity to new images and trademark protection. For example, Coca-Cola has licensed its trademark for use on glassware, radios, trucks, and clothing in the hope of protecting its trademark. However, brand licensing has drawbacks. The major disadvantages are a lack of manufacturing control, which could hurt the company's name, and bombarding consumers with too many unrelated products bearing the same name. Licensing arrangements can also fail because of poor timing, inappropriate distribution channels, or mismatching of product and name.

brand licensing An agreement whereby a company permits another organization to use its brand on other products for a licensing fee

Packaging

L O 8 To describe the major packaging functions and design considerations and how packaging is used in marketing strategies

Packaging involves the development of a container and a graphic design for a product. A package can be a vital part of a product, making it more versatile, safer, and easier to use. Like a brand name, a package can influence customers' attitudes toward a product and thus affect their purchase decisions. For example, several producers of jellies,

E-ntertainment MARKETING

Major League Baseball Licensing Yields a Home Run

Major League Baseball (MLB) has hit a grand-slam home run with its lucrative brand-licensing deals. The total annual revenue from all officially licensed baseball merchandise is nearing $4 billion. Names, mascots, colors, and logos of MLB's 30 teams are emblazoned on everything from sweatshirts and snow globes to bobblehead dolls and bottle openers. Companies can also license current and vintage MLB brand marks to produce merchandise linked to the World Series and other special baseball events.

Not just anyone can become a licensee. "We look for the best of breed in whatever business we go into," explains MLB's senior vice president of licensing. Once a company has been chosen, each product that bears the licensed brand must be reviewed and approved. MLB even examines the way licensed merchandise will be displayed before granting final approval. In addition, every licensed item must carry a label or sticker with the MLB hologram and a code that identifies the licensee.

Because licensing is big business, MLB carefully polices the use of its brands. Its representatives team up with law enforcement officials to scout stores and streets around baseball stadiums and seize counterfeit merchandise. MLB is also a member of the Coalition to Advance the Protection of Sports, an industry group that fights the illegal use of sports brands. "The sign of a popular brand is that someone is trying to steal it," comments an MLB official. Stealing home may be an old baseball tradition, but stealing a baseball brand is simply theft.[a]

sauces, and ketchups have packaged their products in squeezable containers to make use and storage more convenient, and some paint manufacturers have introduced easy-to-open and -pour paint cans. Package characteristics help shape buyers' impressions of a product at the time of purchase or during use. In this section, we examine the main functions of packaging and consider several major packaging decisions.

Packaging Functions

Effective packaging involves more than simply putting products in containers and covering them with wrappers. First, packaging materials serve the basic purpose of protecting the product and maintaining its functional form. Fluids such as milk, orange juice, and hair spray need packages that preserve and protect them. The packaging should prevent damage that could affect the product's usefulness and thus lead to higher costs. Because product tampering has become a problem, several packaging techniques have been developed to counter this danger. Some packages are also designed to deter shoplifting.

Another function of packaging is to offer convenience to consumers. For example, small aseptic packages—individual-size boxes or plastic bags that contain liquids and do not require refrigeration—strongly appeal to children and young adults with active lifestyles. The size or shape of a package may relate to the product's storage, convenience of use, or replacement rate. Small, single-serving cans of vegetables, for instance, may prevent waste and make storage easier.

A third function of packaging is to promote a product by communicating its features, uses, benefits, and image. Sometimes a reusable package is developed to make the product more desirable. For example, the Cool Whip package doubles as a food storage container.

Finally, packaging can be used to communicate symbolically the quality or premium nature of a product. It can also evoke an emotional response. Packaging has been a major force in bath and body products, especially those associated with the spa industry. The goal is to communicate what the product stands for and trigger an expected experience.[33]

Major Packaging Considerations

In developing packages, marketers must take many factors into account. Obviously one major consideration is cost. Although a variety of packaging materials, processes, and designs are available, costs vary greatly. In recent years, buyers have shown a willingness to pay more for improved packaging, but there are limits. Marketers should conduct research to determine exactly how much customers are willing to pay for effective and efficient package designs.

As already mentioned, developing tamper-resistant packaging is very important for certain products. Although no package is tamperproof, marketers can develop packages that are difficult to contaminate. At a minimum, all packaging must comply with the Food and Drug Administration's packaging regulations. However, packaging should also make any product tampering evident to resellers and consumers. Although effective tamper-resistant packaging may be expensive to develop, when balanced against the costs of lost sales, loss of consumer confidence and company reputation, and potentially expensive product liability lawsuits, the costs of ensuring consumer safety are minimal.

Marketers should also consider how much consistency is desirable among an organization's package designs. No consistency may be the best policy, especially if a firm's products are unrelated or aimed at vastly different target markets. To promote an overall company image, a firm may decide that all packages should be similar or include one major element of the design. This approach is called **family packaging**. Sometimes it is used only for lines of products, such as Campbell's soups, Weight Watchers' foods, and Planter's nuts.

A package's promotional role is an important consideration. Through verbal and nonverbal symbols, the package can inform potential buyers about the product's content, features, uses, advantages, and hazards. A firm can create desirable images and associations by its choice of color, design, shape, and texture. Many cosmetics manufacturers, for example, design their packages to create impressions of richness, luxury, and exclusivity. A package performs a promotional function when it is designed to be safer or more convenient to use if such characteristics help stimulate demand.

To develop a package that has a definite promotional value, a designer must consider size, shape, texture, color, and graphics. Beyond the obvious limitation that the package must be large enough to hold the product, a package can be designed to appear taller or shorter. Light-colored packaging may make a package appear larger, whereas darker colors may minimize the perceived size.

Colors on packages are often chosen to attract attention, and color can positively influence customers' emotions. People associate specific colors with certain feelings and experiences. Here are some examples:

- Blue is soothing; it is also associated with wealth, trust, and security.

- Gray is associated with strength, exclusivity, and success.

- Orange often signifies low cost.

- Red connotes excitement and stimulation.

- Purple is associated with dignity and stateliness.

- Yellow connotes cheerfulness and joy.

- Black is associated with being strong and masterful.[34]

family packaging Using similar packaging for all of a firm's products or packaging that has one common design element

RESPONSIBLE marketing?

Is Look-Alike Packaging OK?

ISSUE: Should a retailer be allowed to design its private branded package to look like the leading manufacturers' brand?

Discount stores, super-markets, and drugstores like CVS and Walgreens sometimes design the packages for their private brands to look very similar to packaging used for leading manufacturers' brands. At times, a retailer will place its "look-alike" private brand right next to the leading manufacturers' brand on the shelf. The retailer may defend this type of action on the basis that the colors and color combinations used to package the leading manufacturers' brand are actually used by consumers to identify the product category. For example, a number of private branded soups are packaged in red and white because the color combination identifies the canned soup product category, even though a leading manufacturer's brand, Campbell's, popularized red and white as the major color combination for packaging soup. The producer of the manufacturers' brand accuses the retailers' private brand package design of infringing on its brand. Also, some critics of this practice indicate that it leads to consumer confusion regarding the source of the product.

Is the leading manufacturer's brand affected by the presence of a private brand that is packaged to look like the leading brand? If so, in what ways are consumers confused by this practice on the part of retailers that engage in this type of private branding practice? Is it fair for a retailer to use a "look-alike" package design for its private brand?

When opting for color on packaging, marketers must judge whether a particular color will evoke positive or negative feelings when linked to a specific product. Rarely, for example, do processors package meat or bread in green materials because customers may associate green with mold. Marketers must also determine whether a specific target market will respond favorably or unfavorably to a particular color. Cosmetics for women are more likely to be sold in pastel packaging than are personal-care products for men. Packages designed to appeal to children often use primary colors and bold designs. A relatively recent trend in packaging is colorless packages. Clear products and packaging connote a pure, natural product.

Packaging must also meet the needs of resellers. Wholesalers and retailers consider whether a package facilitates transportation, storage, and handling. Concentrated versions of laundry detergents and fabric softeners, for example, enable retailers to offer more product diversity within the existing shelf space. Resellers may refuse to carry certain products if their packages are cumbersome.

A final consideration is whether to develop packages that are environmentally responsible. Nearly one-half of all garbage consists of discarded plastic packaging, such as polystyrene containers, plastic soft-drink bottles, and carryout bags. Plastic packaging material does not biodegrade, and paper requires the destruction of valuable forests. Consequently many companies have changed to environmentally sensitive packaging; they are also recycling more materials. Procter & Gamble markets several cleaning products and laundry detergents in a concentrated form, which requires less packaging than the ready-to-use version. H. J. Heinz is looking for alternatives to its plastic ketchup squeeze bottles. Other companies are also searching for alternatives to environmentally harmful packaging. In some instances, however, customers have objected to such switches because the newer environmentally responsible packaging may be less effective or more inconvenient. Therefore, marketers must carefully balance society's desire to preserve the environment against customers' desire for convenience.

Packaging and Marketing Strategies

Packaging can be a major component of a marketing strategy. A new cap or closure, a better box or wrapper, or a more convenient container may give a product a competitive advantage. The right type of package for a new product can help it gain market recognition very quickly. Sunsweet Growers, for example, had this in mind when it introduced New Ones dried prunes, targeted at consumers who wanted healthier snacks. Sold in transparent canisters containing 20 individually wrapped pitted prune snacks that look rather like candy, the package protects the product and makes it portable enough for the lunchbox or desk.[35] In the case of existing brands, marketers should reevaluate packages periodically. Marketers should view packaging as a major strategic tool, especially for consumer convenience products. For instance, in the food industry, jumbo and large package sizes for such products as hot dogs, pizzas, English muffins, frozen dinners, and biscuits have been very successful. When considering the

Convenience Packaging

Traditional ketchup packaging has not been convenient. Heinz's "top-down" ketchup package is designed for convenient use.

strategic uses of packaging, marketers must also analyze the cost of packaging and package changes. Table 12.2 lists the biggest packaging spenders. In this section, we examine several ways to use packaging strategically.

Altering the Package. At times, a marketer changes a package because the existing design is no longer in style, especially when compared with the packaging of com petitive products. Arm & Hammer now markets a refillable plastic shaker for its baking soda. Quaker Oats hired a package design company to redesign its Rice-A-Roni package to give the product the appearance of having evolved with the times while retaining its traditional taste appeal. Rice-A-Roni had been experiencing a lag in sales because of increased competition. An overhaul of the product packaging to a refreshing and more up-to-date look was credited with a 20 percent increase in sales over the previous year. Similarly, Del Monte introduced a contemporary look for its tomato products and experienced a double-digit gain in the first year.

A package may be redesigned because new product features need to be highlighted or because new packaging materials have become available. An organization may decide to change a product's packaging to reposition the product or to make the product safer or more convenient to use. Oscar Mayer introduced sliced bacon in a redesigned "Stay-Fresh Reclosable Tray" to address consumer complaints that traditional bacon packaging is sometimes messy and can't be sealed to ensure freshness through multiple servings. Developed in cooperation with packaging company Bemis Co., the new package represents the most significant change in bacon packaging since the 1920s.[36]

table 12.2	COMPANIES THAT SPEND THE MOST ON PACKAGING	
Anheuser-Busch	Kraft General Foods	
Campbell Soup	Kraft USA	
Coca-Cola	Miller Brewing	
Coca-Cola Foods	PepsiCo	
General Mills	Procter & Gamble	

Secondary-Use Packaging. A secondary-use package can be reused for purposes other than its initial function. For example, a margarine container can be reused to store leftovers, and a jelly container can serve as a drinking glass. Customers often view secondary-use packaging as adding value to products, in which case its use should stimulate unit sales.

Category-Consistent Packaging. With category-consistent packaging, the product is packaged in line with the packaging practices associated with a particular product category. Some product categories—for example, mayonnaise, mustard, ketchup, and peanut butter—have traditional package shapes. Other product categories are characterized by recognizable color combinations, such as red and white for soup and red, white, and blue for Ritz-like crackers. When an organization introduces a brand in one of these product categories, marketers will often use traditional package shapes and color combinations to ensure that customers will recognize the new product as being in that specific product category.

Innovative Packaging. Sometimes a marketer employs a unique cap, design, applicator, or other feature to make a product distinctive. Such packaging can be effective when the innovation makes the product safer or easier to use, or provides better protection for the product. Nestlé, for example, introduced its new Country Creamery ice cream in an innovative package that included a plastic lid that's easy to remove, even when the product is frozen, and ribbed carton corners that make it easier to grip while scooping.[37] In some instances, marketers use innovative or unique packages that are inconsistent with traditional packaging practices to make the brand stand out from competitors. To distinguish their products, marketers in the beverage industry have long used innovative shapes and packaging materials. Unusual packaging sometimes requires expending considerable resources, not only on package design but also on making customers aware of the unique package and its benefit. Research suggests that uniquely shaped packages that attract attention are more likely to be perceived as containing a higher volume of product.[38]

Multiple Packaging. Rather than packaging a single unit of a product, marketers sometimes use twin packs, tri-packs, six-packs, or other forms of multiple packaging. For certain types of products, multiple packaging may increase demand because it increases the amount of the product available at the point of consumption (in one's house, for example). It may also increase consumer acceptance of the product by encouraging the buyer to try the product several times. Multiple packaging can make products easier to handle and store, as in the case of six-packs for soft drinks; it can also facilitate special price offers, such as two-for-one sales. However, multiple packaging does not work for all types of products. One would not use additional table salt, for example, simply because an extra box is in the pantry.

Handling-Improved Packaging. A product's packaging may be changed to make it easier to handle in the distribution channel—for example, by changing the outer carton or using special bundling, shrink-wrapping, or pallets. In some cases, the shape of the package is changed. An ice cream producer, for instance, may change from a cylindrical package to a rectangular one to facilitate handling. In addition, at the retail level, the ice cream producer may be able to get more shelf facings with a rectangular package than with a round one. Outer containers for products are sometimes changed so they will proceed more easily through automated warehousing systems.

Criticisms of Packaging

The last several decades have brought a number of improvements in packaging. However, some packaging problems still need to be resolved. Some packages suffer from functional problems in that they simply do not work well. The packaging for flour and sugar is, at best, poor. Both grocers and consumers are very much aware that these packages leak and tear easily. Can anyone open and close a bag of flour without spilling at least a little bit? Certain packages, such as refrigerated biscuit cans, milk cartons with fold-out spouts, and potato chip bags, are frequently difficult to open. Research by Nestlé reveals that hard-to-open packages are among consumers' top complaints.[39] The traditional shapes of packages for products such as ketchup and salad dressing make the product inconvenient to use. Have you ever wondered when tapping on a ketchup bottle why the producer didn't put the ketchup in a mayonnaise jar?

Although many steps have been taken to make packaging safer, critics still focus on the safety issues. Containers with sharp edges and breakable glass bottles are sometimes viewed as a threat to safety. Certain types of plastic packaging and aerosol containers represent possible health hazards.

At times, packaging is viewed as deceptive. Package shape, graphic design, and certain colors may be used to make a product appear larger than it actually is. The inconsistent use of certain size designations, such as giant, economy, family, king, and super, can lead to customer confusion.

Finally, although customers in the United States traditionally prefer attractive, effective, convenient packaging, the cost of such packaging is high.

Labeling

L O 9 To examine the functions of labeling and describe some legal issues pertaining to labeling

labeling Providing identifying, promotional, or other information on package labels

universal product code (UPC) A series of electronically readable lines identifying a product and containing inventory and pricing information

Labeling is very closely interrelated with packaging and is used for identification, promotional, informational, and legal purposes. Labels can be small or large relative to the size of the product and carry varying amounts of information. The sticker on a Chiquita banana, for example, is quite small and displays only the brand name of the fruit and perhaps a stock-keeping unit number. A label can be part of the package itself or a separate feature attached to the package. The label on a can of Coke is actually part of the can, whereas the label on a two-liter bottle of Coke is separate and can be removed. Information presented on a label may include the brand name and mark, the registered trademark symbol, package size and content, product features, nutritional information, potential presence of allergens, type and style of the product, number of servings, care instructions, directions for use and safety precautions, the name and address of the manufacturer, expiration dates, seals of approval, and other facts.

For many products, the label includes a **universal product code (UPC),** a series of electronically readable lines identifying the product and providing inventory and pricing information for producers and resellers. The UPC is electronically read at the retail checkout counter.

Labels can facilitate the identification of a product by displaying the brand name in combination with a unique graphic design. For example, Heinz ketchup is easy to identify on a supermarket shelf because the brand name is easy to read and the label has a distinctive crownlike shape. By drawing attention to products and their benefits, labels can strengthen an organization's promotional efforts. Labels may contain such promotional messages as the offer of a discount or a larger package size at the same price, or information about a new or improved product feature.

A number of federal laws and regulations specify information that must be included on the labels of certain products. Garments must be labeled with the name of the manufacturer, country of manufacture, fabric content, and cleaning instructions. Labels on nonedible items such as shampoos and detergents must include both safety precautions and directions for use. In 1966, Congress passed the Fair Packaging and Labeling Act, one of the most comprehensive pieces of labeling and packaging legislation. This law focuses on mandatory labeling requirements, voluntary adoption of packaging standards by firms within industries, and the provision of power to the Federal Trade Commission and the Food and Drug Administration to establish and enforce packaging regulations.

The Nutrition Labeling Act of 1990 requires the FDA to review food labeling and packaging, focusing on nutrition content, label format, ingredient labeling, food descriptions, and health messages. This act regulates much of the labeling on more than 250,000 products made by some 17,000 U.S. companies. Any food

snapshot

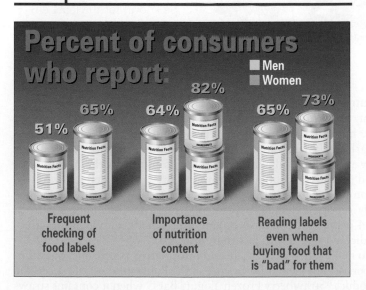

Percent of consumers who report:

■ Men
■ Women

51% 65% 64% 82% 65% 73%

Frequent checking of food labels

Importance of nutrition content

Reading labels even when buying food that is "bad" for them

Source: AP-Ipsos.

green MARKETING

How Green Are Timberland's Shoes? Check the Label!

Just as food containers have nutrition labels and major appliances have energy efficiency labels, many Timberland shoe products now have labels that show their environmental impact. Socially responsible Timberland, based in Stratham, New Hampshire, markets shoes, boots, clothing, and outdoor gear. Its "green index tags" rate each product in terms of greenhouse gas emissions; use of chemicals; and use of organic, renewable, or recycled materials. The lower the score, the more earth-friendly the product.

According to Timberland CEO Jeffrey B. Swartz, the idea is to help consumers "make value judgments at the point of sale." However, the labeling project has been challenging because the company had to "go back to the cow" to assess the environmental effects of raw materials provided by suppliers, as well as manufacturing, transportation, and storage activities.

As more shoe companies follow Timberland's lead and add such labeling, "it will become automatic for shoppers to compare green tags among brands, just like they compare price and color," says Swartz. Because consumers will come to expect environmental impact data on product labels, companies that lag behind will feel more pressure to participate as time goes on. "When that happens, we'll all be fighting to have the best tag. . . . No shoe company will want to be known for the least environmentally friendly shoes," he adds.[b]

product for which a nutritional claim is made must have nutrition labeling that follows a standard format. Food product labels must state the number of servings per container, serving size, number of calories per serving, number of calories derived from fat, number of carbohydrates, and amounts of specific nutrients such as vitamins. In addition, new nutritional labeling requirements focus on the amounts of trans-fatty acids in food products. Although consumers have responded favorably to this type of information on labels, evidence as to whether they actually use it has been mixed. One study reported that 80 percent of American consumers claim to read food labels, yet 44 percent admitted to buying a product even when the information on the label indicated that it was less than healthy.[40]

Despite legislation to make labels as accurate and informative as possible, questionable labeling practices persist. The Center for Science in the Public Interest questions the practice of naming a product "Strawberry Frozen Yogurt Bars" when it contains strawberry flavoring but no strawberries, or of calling a breakfast cereal "lightly sweetened"

table 12.3	PERCEIVED QUALITY AND VALUE OF PRODUCTS BASED ON COUNTRY OF ORIGIN*							
	"Made in U.S.A."		"Made in Japan"		"Made in Korea"		"Made in China"	
	Value	Quality	Value	Quality	Value	Quality	Value	Quality
U.S. adults	4.0	4.2	3.2	3.2	2.6	2.4	2.8	2.4
Western Europeans	3.3	3.4	3.5	3.5	2.8	2.4	2.9	2.4

Source: "American Demographics 2006 Consumer Perception Survey," *Advertising Age,* Jan. 2, 2006, p. 9. Data by Synovate.
*On a scale of 1 (low) to 5 (high).

when sugar makes up 22 percent of its ingredients. Many labels on vegetable oils say "no cholesterol," but many of these oils contain saturated fats that can raise cholesterol levels. The Food and Drug Administration amended its regulations to forbid producers of vegetable oil from making "no cholesterol" claims on their labels.

Another area of concern is "green labeling." Consumers who are committed to making environmentally responsible or natural purchasing decisions are sometimes fooled by labels that claim a product is environmentally friendly or organic. The U.S. Public Interest Research Group accused several manufacturers of "greenwashing" customers: using misleading claims to sell products by playing on customers' concern for the environment. For example, some manufacturers put a recycling symbol on labels for products made of polyvinyl chloride plastic, which cannot be recycled in the vast majority of U.S. communities.

Of concern to many manufacturers are the Federal Trade Commission's guidelines regarding "Made in U.S.A." labels, a growing problem due to the increasingly global nature of manufacturing. The FTC requires that "all or virtually all" of a product's components be made in the United States if the label says "Made in U.S.A." Although the FTC recently considered changing its guidelines to read "substantially all," it rejected this idea and maintains the "all or virtually all" standard. In light of this decision, the FTC ordered New Balance to stop using the "Made in U.S.A." claim on its athletic-shoe labels because some components (rubber soles) are made in China. The "Made in U.S.A." labeling issue has not been totally resolved. The FTC criteria for using "Made in U.S.A." are likely to be challenged and subsequently changed.[41] Table 12.3 provides insight into just how important the "Made in U.S.A." label can be for both Americans and western Europeans. It includes assessments of both quality and value for U.S.A.-, Japan-, Korea-, and Chinese-origin labels.

SUMMARY

A brand is a name, term, design, symbol, or any other feature that identifies one seller's good or service and distinguishes it from those of other sellers. A brand name is the part of a brand that can be spoken. A brand mark is the element not made up of words. A trademark is a legal designation indicating that the owner has exclusive use of the brand or part of the brand and others are prohibited by law from using it. A trade name is the legal name of an

organization. Branding helps buyers identify and evaluate products, helps sellers facilitate product introduction and repeat purchasing, and fosters brand loyalty.

Brand loyalty is a customer's favorable attitude toward a specific brand. If brand loyalty is strong enough, customers may consistently purchase a particular brand when they need a product in this product category. The three degrees of brand loyalty are brand recognition, brand preference, and brand insistence. Brand recognition occurs when a customer is aware that the brand exists and views it as an alternative purchase if the preferred brand is unavailable. With brand preference, a customer prefers one brand over competing brands and will purchase it if available. Brand insistence occurs when a customer will accept no substitute.

Brand equity is the marketing and financial value associated with a brand's strength. It represents the value of a brand to an organization. The four major elements underlying brand equity include brand-name awareness, brand loyalty, perceived brand quality, and brand associations.

A manufacturer brand, initiated by the producer, ensures that the firm is associated with its products at the point of purchase. A private distributor brand is initiated and owned by a reseller, sometimes taking on the name of the store or distributor. Manufacturers combat growing competition from private distributor brands by developing multiple brands. A generic brand indicates only the product category and does not include the company name or other identifying terms.

When selecting a brand name, a marketer should choose one that is easy to say, spell, and recall and that alludes to the product's uses, benefits, or special characteristics. Brand names can be devised from words, letters, numbers, nonsense words, or a combination of these. Brand names are created inside an organization by individuals, committees, or branding departments and by outside consultants. Services as well as products are branded, often with the company name and an accompanying symbol that makes the brand distinctive or conveys a desired image.

Producers protect ownership of their brands through registration with the U.S. Patent and Trademark Office. A company must make certain the brand name it selects does not infringe on an already registered brand by confusing or deceiving consumers about the source of the product. In most foreign countries, brand registration is on a first-come, first-serve basis, making protection more difficult. Brand counterfeiting is becoming increasingly common and can undermine consumers' confidence in a brand.

Companies brand their products in several ways. Individual branding designates a unique name for each of a company's products, family branding identifies all of a firm's products with a single name, and brand extension branding applies an existing name to a new product in a different product category. Co-branding is the use of two or more brands on one product. Effective co-branding profits from the trust and confidence customers have in the brands involved. Finally, through a licensing agreement and for a licensing fee, a firm may permit another organization to use its brand on other products. Brand licensing enables producers to earn extra revenue, receive low-cost or free publicity, and protect their trademarks.

Packaging involves development of a container and a graphic design for a product. Effective packaging offers protection, economy, safety, and convenience. It can influence a customer's purchase decision by promoting features, uses, benefits, and image. When developing a package, marketers must consider the value to the customer of efficient and effective packaging, offset by the price the customer is willing to pay. Other considerations include making the package tamper resistant, whether to use multiple packaging and family packaging, how to design the package as an effective promotional tool, how best to accommodate resellers, and whether to develop environmentally responsible packaging. Firms choose particular colors, designs, shapes, and textures to create desirable images and associations. Packaging can be an important part of an overall marketing strategy and can be used to target certain market segments. Modifications in packaging can revive a mature product and extend its product life cycle. Producers alter packages to convey new features or to make them safer or more convenient. If a package has a secondary use, the product's value to the consumer may increase. Category-consistent packaging makes products more easily recognizable to consumers. Innovative packaging enhances a product's distinctiveness. Consumers may criticize packaging that does not work well, poses health or safety problems, is deceptive in some way, or is not biodegradable or recyclable.

Labeling is closely interrelated with packaging and is used for identification, promotional, informational, and legal purposes. The labels of many products include a universal product code, a series of electronically readable lines identifying a product and containing inventory and pricing information. Various federal laws and regulations require that certain products be labeled or marked with warnings, instructions, nutritional information, manufacturer's identification, and the like. Despite legislation, questionable labeling practices persist, including misleading information about fat content and cholesterol, freshness, and "greenness" of packaging.

IMPORTANT TERMS

Brand, 328
Brand name, 328
Brand mark, 328
Trademark, 328
Trade name, 328
Brand loyalty, 330

Brand recognition, 330
Brand preference, 330
Brand insistence, 330
Brand equity, 331
Manufacturer
 brand, 332

Private distributor brand, 332
Generic brand, 334
Individual branding, 337
Family branding, 337
Brand extension, 337

Co-branding, 338
Brand licensing, 339
Family packaging, 341
Labeling, 345
Universal product
 code (UPC), 345

DISCUSSION & REVIEW QUESTIONS

1. What is the difference between a brand and a brand name? Compare and contrast a brand mark and a trademark.

2. How does branding benefit consumers and marketers?

3. What are the three major degrees of brand loyalty?

4. What is brand equity? Identify and explain the major elements of brand equity.

5. Compare and contrast manufacturer brands, private distributor brands, and generic brands.

6. Identify the factors a marketer should consider in selecting a brand name.

7. The brand name Xerox is sometimes used generically to refer to photocopiers, and Kleenex is used to refer to facial tissues. How can the manufacturers protect their brand names, and why would they want to do so?

8. What is co-branding? What major issues should be considered when using co-branding?

9. What are the major advantages and disadvantages of brand licensing?

10. Describe the functions a package can perform. Which function is most important? Why?

11. What are the main factors a marketer should consider when developing a package?

12. In what ways can packaging be used as a strategic tool?

13. What are the major criticisms of packaging?

14. What are the major functions of labeling?

15. In what ways do regulations and legislation affect labeling?

APPLICATION QUESTIONS

1. Identify two brands for which you are brand insistent. How did you begin using these brands? Why do you no longer use other brands?

2. General Motors introduced the subcompact Geo with a name that appeals to a world market. Invent a brand name for a line of luxury sports cars that also would appeal to an international market. Suggest a name that implies quality, luxury, and value.

3. When a firm decides to brand its products, it may choose one of several strategies. Name one company that uses each of the following strategies. How does each strategy help the company?
   a. Individual branding
   b. Family branding
   c. Brand extension

4. For each of the following product categories, choose an existing brand. Then, for each selected brand, suggest a co-brand and explain why the co-brand would be effective.
   a. Cookies
   b. Pizza
   c. Long-distance telephone service
   d. A sports drink

5. Packaging provides product protection; customer convenience; and promotion of image, key features, and benefits. Identify a product that uses packaging in each of these ways, and evaluate the effectiveness of the package for that function.

6. Identify a package that you believe is inferior. Explain why you think the package is inferior, and discuss your recommendations for improving it.

INTERNET EXERCISE

Visit **www.cengage.com/marketing/pride-ferrell** for resources to help you master the material in this chapter, plus materials that will help you expand your marketing knowledge, including Internet exercise updates, ACE Self-Tests, hotlinks to companies featured in this chapter, and much more.

Pillsbury

Like other marketers of consumer products, Pillsbury has set up a website to inform and entertain consumers.

Catering to the appeal of its most popular product spokesperson, Pillsbury has given its Dough Boy his own site. Visit him at **www.doughboy.com.**

1. What branding policy does Pillsbury seem to be using with regard to the products it presents on this site?

2. How does this Pillsbury website promote brand loyalty?

3. What degree of consistency exists in Pillsbury's packaging of its products displayed on the website?

developing your MARKETING PLAN

The selection and protection of the appropriate brand name is an important part of formulating a marketing strategy. A clear understanding of how branding and packaging decisions influence a customer's choice of products is essential when developing the marketing plan. The brand name and its packaging will influence several other marketing plan decisions. Relating to the information provided in this chapter, focus on the following issues:

1. Discuss the level of brand equity your company's products currently have in the marketplace. How will brand equity affect your branding strategy?

2. Which type of branding policy is most appropriate for your new-product idea?

3. Do any strategic opportunities exist from co-branding your new product with existing brands in your company's product mix or with other company's brands? You may want to refer to your SWOT analysis in Chapter 2.

4. Discuss the style, color, and labeling options for your product. Consider your target market's needs and your branding policy in this discussion.

The information obtained from these questions should assist you in developing various aspects of your marketing plan found in the *Interactive Marketing Plan* exercise at **www.cengage.com/marketing/pride-ferrell.**

globalEDGE

1. Brands are no longer a domestic phenomenon. In fact, many consumers now associate global brands with higher degrees of quality or prestige than more localized or even regionalized brands. Find data on this topic at *BusinessWeek*'s Global Brands section by using the search term "global brands" at **http://globaledge.msu.edu/ibrd.** What are the top ten brands worldwide? Which countries are represented? Which brands from the overall study are from Germany? Summarize three German brands and compare each with a competing brand.

2. To understand which brands are currently in the market your firm is hoping to enter, you have been asked to collect market data on specific brands and models. Given that you are aware of the Industry Research Desk's resources on 18 steps to assist in understanding the development and management of products, you can address this issue effectively. Use the search term "18 steps" at **http://globaledge.msu.edu/ibrd** to reach the Industry Research Desk's 18 steps, and then scroll down to Step 9 for information concerning collectors of market data on specific brands and models. What are the two main information providers that may assist in your assessment of the marketplace?

video CASE 12.1

Brand-Building at New Belgium Brewing Company

The idea for New Belgium Brewing Company (NBB) began with a bicycling trip through Belgium, where some of the world's finest ales have been brewed for centuries. As Jeff Lebesch, a U.S. electrical engineer, cruised around the country on a fat-tired mountain bike, he wondered if he could produce such high-quality ales in his home state of Colorado. After returning home, Lebesch began to experiment in his Fort Collins basement. When his home-brewed experiments earned rave reviews from friends, Lebesch and his wife, Kim Jordan, decided to open the New Belgium Brewing Company in 1991. They named their first brew Fat Tire Amber Ale in honor of Lebesch's Belgian biking adventure.

Today New Belgium markets a variety of permanent and seasonal ales and pilsners. The standard line includes Sunshine Wheat, Blue Paddle Pilsner, Abbey Ale, Trippel Ale, and 1554 Black Ale, as well as the firm's number 1 seller, the original Fat Tire Amber Ale. NBB also markets seasonal beers, such as Frambozen and Abbey Grand Cru, released at Thanksgiving and Christmas, and Farmhouse Ale, sold during the early fall months. The firm also occasionally offers one-time-only brews—such as LaFolie, a wood-aged beer—that are sold only until the batch runs out. Bottle label designs employ "good ol' days" nostalgia. The Fat Tire label, for example, features an old-style cruiser bike with wide tires, a padded seat, and a basket hanging from the handlebars. All the label and packaging designs were created by the same watercolor artist, Jeff Lebesch's next-door neighbor.

New Belgium beers are priced to reflect their quality at about $7 per six-pack. This pricing strategy conveys the message that the products are special and of consistently higher quality than macrobrews, such as Budweiser and Coors, but also keeps them competitive with other microbrews, such as Pete's Wicked Ale, Pyramid Pale Ale, and Sierra Nevada. To demonstrate its appreciation for its retailers and business partners, New Belgium does not sell beer to consumers on-site at the brewhouse for less than the retailers charge.

Although Fat Tire was initially sold only in Fort Collins, distribution quickly expanded throughout the rest of Colorado. Customers can now find Fat Tire and other New Belgium offerings in 15 western states, including Washington, Montana, Texas, New Mexico, and Arizona. The brewery regularly receives e-mails and telephone inquiries as to when New Belgium beers will be available elsewhere.

Since its founding, NBB's most effective promotion has been via word-of-mouth advertising by customers devoted to the brand. The company initially avoided mass advertising, relying instead on small-scale, local promotions, such as print advertisements in alternative magazines, participation in local festivals, and sponsorship of alternative sports events. Through event sponsorships, such as the Tour de Fat and Ride the Rockies, NBB has raised thousands of dollars for various environmental, social, and cycling nonprofit organizations.

With expanding distribution, however, the brewery recognized a need to increase its opportunities for reaching its far-flung customers. It consulted with Dr. David Holt, an Oxford professor and branding expert. After studying the young company, Holt, together with marketing director Greg Owsley, drafted a 70-page "manifesto" describing the brand's attributes, character, cultural relevancy, and promise. In particular, Holt identified in New Belgium an ethos of pursuing creative activities simply for the joy of doing them well and in harmony with the natural environment. With the brand thus defined, New Belgium went in search of an advertising agency to help communicate that brand identity; it

soon found Amalgamated, an equally young, independent New York advertising agency. Amalgamated created a $10 million advertising campaign for New Belgium that targets high-end beer drinkers, men ages 25 to 44, and highlights the brewery's image as being down to earth. The grainy ads focus on a man rebuilding a cruiser bike out of used parts and then riding it along pastoral country roads. The product appears in just five seconds of each ad between the tag lines, "Follow Your Folly . . . Ours Is Beer." The ads helped position the growing brand as whimsical, thoughtful, and reflective. In addition to the ad campaign, the company maintained its strategy of promotion through event sponsorships.

NBB is using aluminum cans for some of its Fat Tire beer. Not only are aluminum cans more convenient for customers because they can be taken to places glass cannot, like baseball parks and other outdoor venues, but they are environmentally friendly as well. Aluminum cans are 100 percent recyclable into new cans, and recycling 40 aluminum beverage cans saves energy equivalent to one gallon of gasoline, according to the Aluminum Association, Inc.

NBB's marketing strategy has always involved pairing the brand with a concern for how the company's activities affect the natural environment. The brewery looks for cost-efficient, energy-saving alternatives to conducting business and reducing its impact on the environment. Thus, the company's employee-owners unanimously agreed to invest in a wind turbine, making NBB the first fully wind-powered brewery in the United States. The company further reduces its energy use with a steam condenser that captures and reuses the hot water from boiling the barley and hops in the production process to start the next brew; the steam is redirected to heat the floor tiles and de-ice the loading docks in cold weather. NBB also strives to recycle as many supplies as possible, including cardboard boxes, keg caps, office materials, and the amber glass used in bottling. The brewery stores spent barley and hop grains in an on-premise silo and invites local farmers to pick up the grains, free of charge, to feed their pigs. Another way NBB conserves energy is through the use of "sun tubes," which provide natural daytime lighting throughout the brewhouse all year long. NBB also encourages employees to reduce air pollution through alternative transportation. As an incentive, NBB gives each employee a "cruiser bike"—just like the one on the Fat Tire Amber Ale label and in the television ads—after one year of employment to encourage biking to work.

Beyond its use of environment-friendly technologies and innovations, New Belgium Brewing Company strives to improve communities and enhance lives through corporate giving, event sponsorship, and philanthropic involvement. The company donates $1 per barrel of beer sold to various cultural, social, environmental, and drug and alcohol awareness programs across the 15 western states in which it distributes beer. Typical grants range from $2,500 to $5,000. Involvement is spread equally among the 15 states, unless a special need requires greater participation or funding. The brewhouse also maintains a community board where organizations can post community involvement activities and proposals. This board allows tourists and employees to see opportunities to help out the community and provides nonprofit organizations with a forum for making their needs known. Organizations can also apply for grants through the New Belgium Brewing Company website, which has a link designated for this purpose.

New Belgium's commitment to quality, the environment, and its employees and customers is clearly expressed in its stated purpose: "To operate a profitable brewery which makes our love and talent manifest." This dedication has been well rewarded with loyal customers and industry awards. From cutting-edge environmental programs and high-tech industry advancements

to employee-ownership programs and a strong belief in giving back to the community, New Belgium demonstrates its desire to create a living, learning community. According to David Edgar, director of the Institute for Brewing Studies, "They've created a very positive image for their company in the beer-consuming public with smart decision making." Although some members of society do not believe a brewery can be socially responsible, New Belgium has set out to prove that for those who make the choice to drink responsibly, the company can do everything possible to contribute to society.[42]

Questions for Discussion

1. How does New Belgium Brewing Company's social responsibility initiatives help build its brand?
2. Describe New Belgium's branding policy. How does it use packaging to further its brand image?
3. Assess New Belgium's brand equity.

CASE 12.2

The Brand's the Thing for Iconix

The Iconix Brand Group, founded by Neil Cole in 2004, is all about brands—and nothing but brands. With $81 million in annual revenues, fast-growing Iconix has thrived by buying well-known consumer brands that need a boost and then licensing them to manufacturers and retailers. Each licensee pays royalties of up to 10 percent on sales of merchandise marketed under an Iconix-owned brand. Although its licensees invest to build the brands, Iconix enjoys sizable profit margins without the cost and risk of actually designing, manufacturing, and distributing products on its own.

The first brand to get the Iconix touch was Candie's, which shot to fame in the 1980s with a fashionable line of young, flirty shoes for women. Despite its previous success, Candie's was losing money when Iconix arranged an exclusive U.S. license for Kohl's department store. The deal, said Kohl's president, was "based on the appeal of a brand with very high consumer awareness." Soon Kohl's was selling $300 million worth of Candie's-branded shoes and apparel every year and sending Iconix sizable royalty checks.

Joe Boxer is another 1980s brand brought back to life by an Iconix licensing arrangement. Founded as a fun, feisty underwear brand, Joe Boxer now appears on sleepwear, casual clothing, accessories, and even pillows marketed by the U.S. licensee Sears Holdings through its two store chains, Sears and Kmart. In

Canada, the licensee is a manufacturer that distributes a higher-priced line of Joe Boxer apparel through specialty and department stores.

Danskin, originally targeted toward dancers, is the oldest brand owned by Iconix. Although the company paid $70 million for it, the long-term payback looks quite promising because of high brand name awareness and positive brand associations. Already licensees have put the Danskin brand on a wide range of clothing items for active girls and women, including sweatshirts, legwear, and skirts.

Retailers see particular value in attracting shoppers and reinforcing customer loyalty by licensing Iconix brands that have a strong following. For example, Target has licensed Iconix's Mossimo brand for clothing. Meanwhile, its rival Wal-Mart has licensed Ocean Pacific, Iconix's surfing lifestyle brand, for apparel marketed through its stores in the United States, Brazil, China, and India.

Iconix prefers to arrange exclusive licenses area by area, which means each brand has multiple licensees. For example, Joe Boxer has different licensees in the United States, Canada, and the Middle East. In fact, Iconix sees so much growth opportunity in developing countries that it is aggressively signing licensees in China, Mexico, and other areas. In one recent deal, Iconix licensed the London Fog outerwear brand to a

Chinese real estate developer, which will make branded clothing and open dozens of branded stores in Beijing, Shanghai, and other major cities across China.

Other fashion brands in the Iconix portfolio are Mudd (aimed at teenagers), Rocawear (an urban lifestyle brand), Badgley Mischka (upscale evening wear), Bongo (a California lifestyle brand), and Rampage (stylish women's wear). The company has begun diversifying into non-fashion brands, as well. Not long ago, it paid $231 million to acquire Official Pillowtex, bringing it the widely recognized houseware brands Cannon, Royal Velvet, and Fieldcrest.

Iconix has only 65 employees, but its brands generate $5 billion in total sales for licensees all over the world. The CEO continues to seek out solid brands that need a boost and is willing to pay millions of dollars so Iconix can award brand licenses country by country and receive royalties for decades to come.[43]

Questions for Discussion

1. What questions should Iconix ask of an apparel manufacturer that wants to license the company's Danskin brand for a new line of women's casual clothing?

2. If Kohl's is the only U.S. licensee allowed to market Candie's products, can that brand be considered a private distributor brand? Explain your answer.

3. For Iconix, what are the advantages and disadvantages of having multiple licensees for a single brand?

13 Services Marketing

Service Lights Up Cirque du Soleil

entrepreneurs IN ACTION

Cirque du Soleil, the "circus of the sun," does not clown around with service. The winning combination of creativity and careful attention to detail has propelled this Montreal-based company into the top ranks of international entertainment. By making every show a special audience-pleasing experience, Cirque has grown into a $620 million global business that draws 10 million people every year.

When Guy Laliberté founded Cirque in 1984, his goal was to reinvent the circus. Originally, he worked with only a handful of street performers. Today Cirque employs 3,800 performers, choreographers, artists, trainers, and other professionals who plan and stage 14 distinctly different shows every year, each unique in theme. For example, *Dralion* incorporates Chinese circus tradition, and *Love* revolves around Beatles songs.

Clearly, costumes, music, lighting, props, and other theatrical elements are vital to the audience experience. Yet what happens behind the scenes—even before the audience arrives—is just as important. Cirque's scouts travel the world searching for extraordinary gymnasts, acrobats, musicians, and other performers to fill the roles for each show. Then cast members receive months of training to fine-tune every aspect of their performance before they appear in front of audiences.

Meanwhile, Cirque's marketing experts consider the image they want each show to project as they plan its marketing mix, including print ads and merchandise. These tangible elements help convey Cirque's innovative approach to the circus concept and hint at the memorable experiences that await audience members at every performance. Looking ahead, Cirque plans to have 22 shows running by 2010, each with its own theme but presented with the same high-quality service for which the company has been known for more than two decades.[1]

The products offered by Cirque du Soleil—namely, types of entertainment—are services rather than tangible goods. This chapter explores concepts that apply specifically to products that are services. The organizations that market service products include for-profit firms, such as those offering financial, personal, and professional services, and nonprofit organizations, such as educational institutions, churches, charities, and governments.

We begin this chapter with a focus on the growing importance of service industries in our economy. We then address the unique characteristics of services. Next, we deal with the challenges these characteristics pose in developing and managing marketing mixes for services. We then discuss customers' judgment of service quality and the importance of delivering high-quality services. Finally, we define nonprofit marketing and examine the development of nonprofit marketing strategies.

The Nature and Importance of Services

L O 1 To understand the nature and importance of services

All products, whether goods, services, or ideas, are intangible to some extent. We previously defined a service as an intangible product that involves a deed, a performance, or an effort that cannot be physically possessed.[2] Services are usually provided through the application of human and/or mechanical efforts that are directed at people or objects. For example, a service such as education involves the efforts of service providers (teachers) that are directed at people (students), whereas janitorial and interior decorating services direct their efforts at objects. Services can also involve the use of mechanical efforts directed at people (air transportation) or objects (freight transportation). A wide variety of services, such as health care and landscaping, involve both human and mechanical efforts. Although many services entail the use of tangibles such as tools and machinery, the primary difference between a service and a good is that a service is dominated by the intangible portion of the total product.

Services as products should not be confused with the related topic of customer services. Customer service involves any human or mechanical activity that adds value to the product.[3] Although the core product may be a good, complementary services help create the total product, and although customer service is a part of the marketing of goods, service marketers also provide customer services. For example, many service companies offer guarantees to their customers in an effort to increase value. Hampton Inn, a national chain of midprice hotels, gives its guests a free night if they are not 100 percent satisfied with their stay (fewer than one-half of 1 percent of Hampton customers ask for a refund). In some cases, a 100 percent satisfaction guarantee or similar service commitment may motivate employees to provide high-quality service, not because failure to do so leads to personal penalties but because they are proud to be part of an organization that is so committed to good service.

The increasing importance of services in the U.S. economy has led many people to call the United States the world's first service economy. In most developed countries, including Germany, Japan, Australia, and Canada, services account for about 70 percent of the gross domestic product (GDP). More than one-half of new businesses are service businesses, and service employment is expected to continue to grow. These industries have absorbed much of the influx of women and minorities into the workforce. In the United States, some customer-contact jobs, especially call centers, have been outsourced—into the homes of U.S. workers, especially women. Jet Blue, for example, has 1,400 reservation agents who work from their homes.[4]

One major catalyst in the growth of consumer services has been long-term economic growth (slowed only by a few recessions) in the United States, which has led to increased interest in financial services, travel, entertainment, and personal care. Lifestyle changes have similarly encouraged expansion of the service sector. The need for child care, domestic services, online dating services, and other time-saving services has increased, and many consumers want to avoid such tasks as meal preparation, house cleaning, yard maintenance, and tax preparation. Consequently, franchise service operations such as Subway, Merry Maids, Jiffy Lube, ChemLawn, and H&R

Block have experienced rapid growth. Also, because Americans have become more health, fitness, and recreation oriented, the demand for exercise and recreational facilities has escalated. In terms of demographics, the U.S. population is growing older, a fact that has spurred tremendous expansion of health-care services. Finally, the increasing number and complexity of high-tech goods have spurred demand for support services. Indeed, the services sector has been enhanced by dramatic changes in information technology. Entrepreneurs have emerged taking advantage of inexpensive computer hardware, free software, and broadband Internet access to launch new service-oriented businesses or to transform existing businesses to focus on services.[5] Consider service companies such as Google, eBay, and Amazon.com, which use technology to provide services to challenge and change traditional ways of conducting business.

Business services have prospered as well. Business services include support and maintenance, consulting, installation, equipment leasing, marketing research, advertising, temporary office personnel, and janitorial services. Expenditures for business services have risen even faster than expenditures for consumer services. The growth in business services has been attributed to the increasingly complex, specialized, and competitive business environment. IBM, for example, has shifted from a focus on computer hardware to consulting services and software applications.

One way to view services is from a theater framework with production elements such as actors, audience, a setting, and a performance. The actors (service workers) create a service (performance) for the audience (customers) in a setting (service environment) where the performance unfolds. Costumes (uniforms), props (devices,

E-ntertainment MARKETING

Merlin Makes Theme Park Magic

Magic Kingdom, move over: Merlin Entertainments Group, based in the United Kingdom, is making magic in theme parks all over the world. Merlin owns such well-known attractions as the Legoland and Sea Life parks, Madame Tussaud's wax museums, and the London Eye Ferris wheel. Not long ago, it acquired the Gardaland theme park and resort in Italy to extend its customer base by "attracting high volumes of young adults and teens, as well as our traditional family market," says

the CEO. In all, more than 16 million customers visit Merlin's 37 theme parks every year.

Bringing in new customers and encouraging repeat visits are important when the cost of a new theme park tops $300 million and competition is fierce. Just as Disney and Universal never stop adding new attractions in their theme parks, Merlin is constantly refreshing and expanding its attractions. For example, adding 15 new exhibits to Legoland in Carlsbad, California, including the popular Pirates Shores, drove peak-season attendance higher by 20 percent. Merlin has also opened the Land of Adventure and the Lost Kingdom Adventure inside that Legoland.

Most important, Merlin is combining its brands to create entertainment destinations that draw families for multiday stays. Next to Legoland in California, Merlin is building Sea Life Legoland to showcase underwater creatures that are native to local waters plus submarines and divers made entirely out of Lego building blocks. Watch for more theme-park magic as Merlin makes the most of its service brands.[a]

music, machines), and the setting (face-to-face or indirect through telephone or Internet) help complete the theatrical metaphor.[6] At Disney World, for example, all employees wear costumes, there is an entertainment setting, and most service contact with employees involves playing roles and engaging in planned skits. But the theatrical components are also visible in a Subway fast-food restaurant or on an airline flight. In addition, a performance involves a "script," a chronologically ordered representation of the steps that comprise the service performance from the customer's perspective.[7] Even sports events such as football, basketball, and hockey have sequences of events and rules that standardize the performance, even if the outcome depends on the performance itself.

Characteristics of Services

L O 2 To identify the characteristics of services that differentiate them from goods

The issues associated with marketing service products differ somewhat from those associated with marketing goods. To understand these differences, we need to look at the distinguishing characteristics of services. Services have six basic characteristics: intangibility, inseparability of production and consumption, perishability, heterogeneity, client-based relationships, and customer contact.[8]

Intangibility

As already noted, the major characteristic that distinguishes a service from a good is intangibility. **Intangibility** means a service is not physical and therefore cannot be perceived by the senses. For example, it is impossible to touch the education that students derive from attending classes; the intangible benefit is becoming more knowledgeable. In addition, services cannot be physically possessed. Students obviously cannot physically possess knowledge as they can an iPod or a car. There is a direct relationship between the level of intangibility and consumers' use of brands as a cue to the nature and quality of the service. This means that brand name is more important for financial services than for a cell phone.[9]

Figure 13.1 depicts a tangibility continuum from pure goods (tangible) to pure services (intangible). Pure goods, if they exist at all, are rare because practically all marketers of goods also provide customer services. Even a tangible product such as sugar must be delivered to the store, priced, and placed on a shelf before a customer

intangibility The characteristic that a service is not physical and cannot be perceived by the senses

figure 13.1

THE TANGIBILITY CONTINUUM

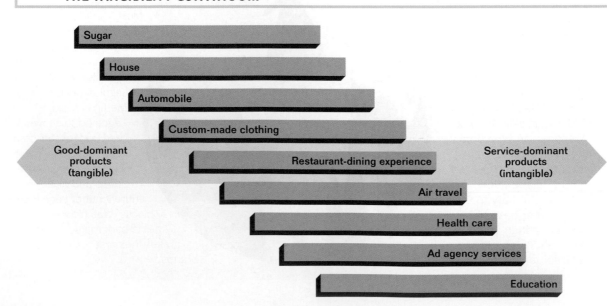

can purchase it. Intangible, service-dominant products such as education or health care are clearly service products. But what about products near the center of the continuum? Is a restaurant such as Chili's a goods marketer or a service marketer? Services like airline flights have something tangible to offer, such as seats and drinks. An Internet search engine such as Google or a news site such as CNN or MSNBC is service dominant. Knowing where the product lies on the continuum is important in creating marketing strategies for service-dominant products.

Inseparability of Production and Consumption

Another important characteristic of services that creates challenges for marketers is **inseparability**, which refers to the fact that the production of a service cannot be separated from its consumption by customers. For example, air passenger service is produced and consumed simultaneously—that is, services are often produced, sold, and consumed at the same time. In goods marketing, a customer can purchase a good, take it home, and store it until ready to use it. The manufacturer of the good may never see an actual customer. Customers, however, often must be present at the production of a service (such as investment consulting or surgery) and cannot take the service home. Indeed, both the service provider and the customer must work together to provide the service's full value.[10] Because of inseparability, customers not only want a specific type of service but expect it to be provided in a specific way by a specific individual. For example, the production and consumption of a medical exam occur simultaneously, and the patient knows in advance who the physician is and generally understands how the exam will be conducted. Inseparability implies a shared responsibility between the customer and service provider. As a

inseparability The quality of being produced and consumed at the same time

Some airlines run ads that talk to business travelers.
We're running an ad that says

WE LISTEN

to them.

1. **INTRODUCING A WHOLE NEW, BETTER BOARDING PROCESS**
   It's a calmer, more relaxed way to board. There is no need to line up early because your boarding pass number holds your place in line. So you are free to work, relax, or do whatever.

2. **INTRODUCING SOUTHWEST AIRLINES' BUSINESS SELECT**
   You deserve Southwest Airlines Business Select. For just a little extra, you can be part of the select group that's guaranteed to be one of the first to board and get a free drink and extra Rapid Rewards® credit. Plus, your fare is fully refundable.

3. **INTRODUCING MORE NONSTOP FLIGHTS FOR YOUR NONSTOP BUSINESS**
   Fly long without the stops. Southwest offers over 3,400 daily nonstop flights, which lets you fly nonstop to more places you do business.

SOUTHWEST.COM®

Inseparability

An airline flight is characterized by inseparability. Production and consumption occur simultaneously.

result, training programs for employees should stress the customer's role in the service experience to elevate their perceptions of shared responsibility and positive feelings.[11]

Perishability

Services are characterized by **perishability** in that the unused service capacity of one time period cannot be stored for future use. For example, empty seats on an airline flight today cannot be stored and sold to passengers at a later date. Other examples of service perishability include unsold basketball tickets, unscheduled dentists' appointment times, and empty hotel rooms. Although some goods, such as meat, milk, and produce, are perishable, goods generally are less perishable than services. If a pair of jeans has been sitting on a department store shelf for a week, someone can still buy them the next day. Goods marketers can handle the supply-demand problem through production scheduling and inventory techniques. Service marketers do not have the same advantage and face several hurdles in trying to balance supply and demand. They can, however, plan for demand that fluctuates according to day of the week, time of day, or season.

Heterogeneity

Services delivered by people are susceptible to **heterogeneity,** or variation in quality. Quality of manufactured goods is easier to control with standardized procedures, and mistakes are easier to isolate and correct. Because of the nature of human behavior, however, it is very difficult for service providers to maintain a consistent quality of service delivery. This variation in quality can occur from one organization to another, from one service person to another within the same service facility, and from one service facility to another within the same organization. For example, one bank may provide more convenient hours and charge fewer fees than the one next door, or the retail clerks in one bookstore may be more knowledgeable and therefore more helpful than those in another bookstore owned by the same chain. In addition, the service a single employee provides can vary from customer to customer, day to day, or even hour to hour. Although many service problems are onetime events that cannot be predicted or controlled ahead of time, training and establishment of standard procedures can help increase consistency and reliability. Because research suggests that service employees with greater sensitivity toward people of different countries and cultures are more attentive and have better interpersonal skills, job satisfaction, and social satisfaction, training that improves cultural sensitivity should improve consistency of service quality in cross-cultural environments.[12]

Heterogeneity usually increases as the degree of labor intensiveness increases. Many services, such as auto repair, education, and hairstyling, rely heavily on human labor. Other services, such as telecommunications, health clubs, grocery delivery, and public transportation, are more equipment intensive. People-based services are often prone to fluctuations in quality from one time period to the next. For example, the fact that a hairstylist gives a customer a good haircut today does not guarantee that customer a haircut of equal quality from the same hairstylist at a later date or even a later hour. A morning customer may receive a better haircut than an end-of-the-day customer from the same stylist. Equipment-based services suffer from this problem to a lesser degree than people-based services. For instance, automated teller machines have reduced inconsistency in the quality of teller services at banks, and bar-code scanning has improved the accuracy of service at checkout counters in grocery stores.

Client-Based Relationships

The success of many services depends on creating and maintaining **client-based relationships:** interactions that result in satisfied customers who use a service repeatedly over time.[13] In fact, some service providers, such as lawyers, accountants, and financial advisers, call their customers *clients* and often develop and maintain close, long-term relationships with them. For such service providers, it is not enough to attract customers. They are successful only to the degree to which they can maintain a group of

perishability The inability of unused service capacity to be stored for future use

heterogeneity Variation in quality

client-based relationships Interactions that result in satisfied customers who use a service repeatedly over time

welcome to **YOU**banking

You
should be banking on a
much more personal level.

You should have your own personal banker who's dedicated to your financial success. You
should have a skilled professional who will help make your day-to-day banking effortless. You
should have a financial ally who can leverage Union Bank's global resources on your behalf.
You deserve the exclusive personal financial services of Priority Banking.

**Call 1-888-818-6060 to schedule an appointment with a
Priority Banker.**

Invest in you

UNION
BANK OF
CALIFORNIA

unionbank.com/priority

The Priority Banking program offers a range of Union Bank products and services to individuals and businesses that maintain combined balances of $100,000 or more in
qualifying accounts. Terms and conditions of the Priority Banking program are subject to change. You may be assigned to another program or product if you no longer
meet the minimum balance requirement of Priority Banking. See our All About Personal, or All About Business, Accounts & Services Disclosure and Agreement for details.

©2008 Union Bank of California, N.A. Member FDIC.

Client-Based Relationships

Union Bank of California promotes the importance of having a
"personal banker," indicating that
this organization relies heavily on
client-based relationships.

customer contact The level
of interaction between
provider and customer
needed to deliver the service

clients who use their services on an ongoing basis. For
example, an accountant may serve a family in his or her
area for decades. If the members of this family like the
quality of the accountant's services, they are likely to
recommend the accountant to other families. If several
families repeat this positive word-of-mouth communication, the accountant will likely acquire a long list of
satisfied clients before long. Indeed, research has found
that word-of-mouth communication plays a key role in
services, particularly for consumers with innovative
personalities.[14] This process is the key to creating and
maintaining client-based relationships. To ensure that it
actually occurs, the service provider must take steps to
build trust, demonstrate customer commitment, and
satisfy customers so well that they become very loyal to
the provider and unlikely to switch to competitors.

Customer Contact

Not all services require a high degree of customer contact, but many do. **Customer contact** refers to the level
of interaction between the service provider and the customer necessary to deliver the service. High-contact services include health care, real estate, and legal and spa
services. Examples of low-contact services are tax
preparation, auto repair, travel reservations, and dry
cleaning. Some service-oriented businesses are reducing
their level of customer contact through technology.
Alamo Rent-A-Car, for example, introduced self-service check-in kiosks where customers can print out their
rental agreement and then head straight to the rental
vehicle.[15] Note that high-contact services generally involve actions directed toward
people, who must be present during production. A hairstylist's customer, for example, must be present during the styling process. Because the customer must be present,
the process of production may be just as important as its final outcome. Although it
is sometimes possible for the service provider to go to the customer, high-contact services typically require that the customer go to the production facility. Thus, the physical appearance of the facility may be a major component of the customer's overall
evaluation of the service. For example, when the physical setting fosters customer-to-
customer interactions, it can lead to greater loyalty to an establishment and positive
word-of-mouth communications.[16] Although low-contact services do not require the
customer's physical presence during delivery, the customer will likely need to be present
to initiate and terminate the service. For example, customers of auto-repair services
must bring in the vehicle and describe its symptoms, but often do not remain during
the repair process.

Employees of high-contact service providers are a crucial ingredient in creating
satisfied customers. A fundamental precept of customer contact is that satisfied
employees lead to satisfied customers. In fact, employee satisfaction is the single most
important factor in providing high-service quality. Thus, to minimize the problems
customer contact can create, service organizations must take steps to understand
and meet the needs of employees by adequately training them, empowering them to
make more decisions, and rewarding them for customer-oriented behavior.[17] To
provide the quality of customer service that has made it the fastest-growing coffee
retailer in the world, Starbucks provides extensive employee training. Employees
receive about 24 hours of initial training, which includes memorizing recipes and
learning the differences among a variety of coffees, proper coffee-making techniques, and many other skills that stress Starbucks's dedication to customer service.
Starbucks has approximately 14,000 coffee shops and about 150,000 employees
worldwide.[18]

Level of Customer Contact

There is a high level of customer contact associated with medical services.

Developing and Managing Marketing Mixes for Services

L O 3 To describe how the characteristics of services influence the development of marketing mixes for services

The characteristics of services discussed in the previous section create a number of challenges for service marketers (see Table 13.1). These challenges are especially evident in the development and management of marketing mixes for services. Although such mixes contain the four major marketing mix variables—product, distribution, promotion, and price—the characteristics of services require that marketers consider additional issues.

Development of Services

A service offered by an organization generally is a package, or bundle, of services consisting of a core service and one or more supplementary services. A core service is the basic service experience or commodity that a customer expects to receive. A supplementary service is a supportive one related to the core service and is used to differentiate the service bundle from competitors'. For example, Progressive provides auto insurance as a core service. Bundled with the insurance are such supplementary services as collision coverage for family pets injured in an auto accident. The $500 benefit, which does not require a premium increase, helps Progressive differentiate its service from rivals among the owners of the nation's 150 million pets.[19]

As discussed earlier, heterogeneity results in variability in service quality and makes it difficult to standardize service delivery. However, heterogeneity provides one advantage to service marketers: it allows them to customize their services to match the specific needs of individual customers. Customization plays a key role in providing competitive advantage for the service provider. Being able to personalize the service to fit the exact needs of the customer accommodates individual needs, wants, or desires.[20] Subway, for example, tries to let each customer participate in developing his or her own customized sandwich. IBM determines a business's needs and then develops information technology services to provide a customized application. Health care

table 13.1   SERVICE CHARACTERISTICS AND MARKETING CHALLENGES

Service Characteristics	Resulting Marketing Challenges
Intangibility	Difficult for customer to evaluate. Customer does not take physical possession. Difficult to advertise and display. Difficult to set and justify prices. Service process is usually not protectable by patents.
Inseparability of production and consumption	Service provider cannot mass produce services. Customer must participate in production. Other consumers affect service outcomes. Services are difficult to distribute.
Perishability	Services cannot be stored. Balancing supply and demand is very difficult. Unused capacity is lost forever. Demand may be very time sensitive.
Heterogeneity	Service quality is difficult to control. Service delivery is difficult to standardize.
Client-based relationships	Success depends on satisfying and keeping customers over the long term. Generating repeat business is challenging. Relationship marketing becomes critical.
Customer contact	Service providers are critical to delivery. Requires high levels of service employee training and motivation. Changing a high-contact service into a low-contact service to achieve lower costs is difficult to achieve without reducing customer satisfaction.

Sources: K. Douglas Hoffman and John E. G. Bateson, *Services Marketing: Concepts, Strategies, and Cases,* 3rd ed. (Cincinnati: Thomson/South-Western, 2006); Valarie A. Zeithaml, A. Parasuraman, and Leonard L. Berry, *Delivering Quality Service: Balancing Customer Perceptions and Expectations* (New York: Free Press, 1990); Leonard L. Berry and A. Parasuraman, *Marketing Services: Competing through Quality* (New York: Free Press, 1991), p. 5.

is an example of an extremely customized service; the services provided differ from one patient to the next.

Such customized services can be expensive for both provider and customer, and some service marketers therefore face a dilemma: how to provide service at an acceptable level of quality in an efficient and economic manner and still satisfy individual customer needs. To cope with this problem, some service marketers offer standardized packages. For example, a spa may provide a number of treatments such as hair styling, facials, and massages for one price. When service bundles are standardized, the specific actions and activities of the service provider usually are highly specified. Automobile quick-lube providers frequently offer a service bundle for a single price; the specific work to be done on a customer's car is spelled out in detail. Various other equipment-based services are also often standardized into packages. For instance, cable television providers frequently offer several packages, such as "Basic," "Standard," and "Premier."

The characteristic of intangibility makes it difficult for customers to evaluate a service prior to purchase. A customer who is shopping for a pair of jeans can try them on before buying them, but how does she or he evaluate legal advice before receiving the service? Intangibility requires service marketers such as attorneys to market promises to customers. The customer is forced to place some degree of trust in the service provider to perform the service in a manner that meets or exceeds those promises. Service marketers must guard against making promises that raise customer expectations beyond what they can provide.

To cope with the problem of intangibility, marketers employ tangible cues, such as well-groomed, professional-appearing contact personnel and clean, attractive physical facilities, to help assure customers about the quality of the service. Most service providers uniform at least some of their high-contact employees. Uniforms help make the service experience more tangible and serve as physical evidence to signal quality, create consistency, and send cues to suggest a desired image.[21] Consider the professionalism, experience, and competence conveyed by an airline pilot's uniform. Life insurance companies sometimes try to make the quality of their policies more tangible by printing them on premium-quality paper and enclosing them in leather sheaths. Because customers often rely on brand names as an indicator of product quality, service marketers at organizations whose names are the same as their service brand names should strive to build a strong national image for their companies. For example, American Express, McDonald's, eBay, American Life, and America Online try to maintain strong, positive national company images because these names are the brand names of the services they provide.

The inseparability of production and consumption and the level of customer contact also influence the development and management of services. The fact that customers take part in the production of a service means other customers can affect the outcome of the service. For instance, if a nonsmoker dines in a restaurant without a no-smoking section, the overall quality of service experienced by the nonsmoking customer declines. For this reason, many restaurants have no-smoking sections and some prohibit smoking anywhere on their premises. Service marketers can reduce these problems by encouraging customers to share the responsibility of maintaining an environment that allows all participants to receive the intended benefits of the service. Delta Airlines has attempted to address this issue by creating a series of humorous videos called "Planeguage" to help passengers deal with awkward social situations in the air, like a fellow passenger who hogs the armrest or an unruly child. The 25 videos help shape public expectations about what to expect and how to be a good travel companion when traveling by air.[22]

Distribution of Services

Marketers deliver services in a variety of ways. In some instances, customers go to a service provider's facility. For example, most health-care, dry-cleaning, and spa services are delivered at the provider's facilities. Some services are provided at the customer's home or business. Lawn care, air conditioning and heating repair, and carpet cleaning are examples. Other services are delivered primarily at "arm's length," meaning no face-to-face contact occurs between the customer and the service provider. A number of equipment-based services are delivered at arm's length, including electric, online, cable television, and telephone services. Providing high-quality customer service at arm's length can be costly but essential in keeping customers satisfied and maintaining market share. For example, many airlines, although trying to cut costs, are also increasing spending on overhauling their websites to make them more user-friendly and thus serve customers better.

Marketing channels for services are usually short and direct, meaning the producer delivers the service directly to the end user. Some services, however, use intermediaries. For example, travel agents facilitate the delivery of airline services, independent insurance agents participate in the marketing of a variety of insurance policies, and financial planners market investment services.

Service marketers are less concerned with warehousing and transportation than are goods marketers. They are, however, very concerned about inventory management, especially balancing supply and demand for services. The service characteristics of inseparability and level of customer contact contribute to the challenges of demand management. In some instances, service marketers use appointments and reservations as approaches for scheduling delivery of services. Health-care providers,

Looks like it's going to be one of those days? We can help with that.

The UPS Store ups

Small business solutions from The UPS Store® are designed to help you hold on no matter what the day brings.

Whether you've got a color presentation to print, copy, collate and bind, or need someone to sign for your packages, The UPS Store will get it done right. Let's face it—you've got enough excitement in your life.

PACKING · SHIPPING · DOCUMENT SERVICES · MAILBOX & POSTAL SERVICES · MOVING SUPPLIES · 4,200 LOCATIONS

www.theupsstore.com

The UPS Store centers are independently owned and operated by licensed franchisees of Mail Boxes Etc., Inc, an indirect subsidiary of United Parcel Service of America, Inc., a Delaware corporation. Services and hours of operation may vary by location. Copyright ©2007 Mail Boxes Etc., Inc.

Distribution

UPS provides some of its services through retail stores.

attorneys, accountants, auto mechanics, and restaurants often use appointments or reservations to plan and pace delivery of their services. DayJet, a new air taxi service for businesspeople, uses sophisticated computer systems, software, and mathematical algorithms to develop efficient routes and schedules for its custom flights, which carry a maximum of three passengers.[23] To increase the supply of a service, marketers use multiple service sites and also increase the number of contact service providers at each site. National and regional eye-care and hair-care services are examples.

To make delivery more accessible to customers and increase the supply of a service, as well as reduce labor costs, some service providers have replaced some contact personnel with equipment. In other words, they have changed a high-contact service into a low-contact one. The banking industry is an example. By installing ATMs, banks have increased production capacity and reduced customer contact. In addition, a number of automated banking services are now available by telephone 24 hours a day. ATMs and online banking have helped lower costs by reducing the need for customer service representatives. Changing the delivery of services from human to equipment has created some problems, however. Some customers complain that automated services are less personal. When designing service delivery, marketers must pay attention to the degree of personalization customers desire.

Promotion of Services

The intangibility of services results in several promotion-related challenges to service marketers. Because it may not be possible to depict the actual performance of a service in an advertisement or display it in a store, explaining a service to customers can be a difficult task. Promotion of services typically includes tangible cues that symbolize the service. For example, Trans America uses its pyramid-shaped building to symbolize strength, security, and reliability, important features associated with insurance and other financial services. Similarly, the cupped hands Allstate uses in its ads symbolize personalized service and trustworthy, caring representatives. Although these symbols have nothing to do with the actual services, they make it much easier for customers to understand the intangible attributes associated with insurance services. To make a service more tangible, advertisements for services often show pictures of facilities, equipment, and service personnel. Marketers may also promote their services as a tangible expression of consumers' lifestyles. Ameriprise, for example, featured *Easy Rider* actor Dennis Hopper in commercials for retirement financial services targeted at baby boomers nearing retirement age. The company chose Hopper for his "great antihero hero image" to provide an emotional appeal for baby boomers who may not desire a conventional retirement on the golf course.[24]

Compared with goods marketers, service providers are more likely to promote price, guarantees, performance documentation, availability, and training and certification of contact personnel. The International Smart Tan Network, a trade association for indoor tanning salons, offers a certification course in professional standards for tanning facility operators. The association encourages salons to promote their "Smart Tan Certification" in advertising and throughout the salon as a measure of quality training.[25] When preparing advertisements, service marketers are careful to use concrete, specific language to help make services more tangible in customers' minds. Bear Stearns, for

Promotion of Services

Verizon Wireless promotes an offer for customers to "test drive" its services.

example, advertises that it was voted "America's most admired securities company." Service companies are also careful not to promise too much regarding their services so that customer expectations do not rise to unattainable levels.

Through their actions, service contact personnel can be directly or indirectly involved in the personal selling of services. Personal selling is often important because personal influence can help the customer visualize the benefits of a given service. Because service contact personnel may engage in personal selling, some companies invest heavily in training. Best Buy, for example, spends 5 percent of its payroll on employee training. On a salesperson's first day on the job, he or she gets a four-hour classroom session that covers topics like how to fit into the company's sales force and the basics for providing customer satisfaction.[26]

As noted earlier, intangibility makes experiencing a service prior to purchase difficult, if not impossible in some cases. A car can be test-driven, a snack food can be sampled in a supermarket, and a new brand of bar soap can be mailed to customers as a free sample. Some services also can be offered on a trial basis at little or no risk to the customer, but a number of services cannot be sampled before purchase. Promotional programs that encourage trial use of insurance, health care, or auto repair are difficult to design because even after purchase of such services, assessing their quality may require a considerable length of time. For example, an individual may purchase auto insurance from the same provider for ten years before filing a claim, but the quality of the coverage is based primarily on how the customer is treated and protected when a claim is made.

Because of the heterogeneity and intangibility of services, word-of-mouth communication is particularly important in service promotion. What other people say about a service provider can have a tremendous impact on whether an individual decides to use that provider. Some service marketers attempt to stimulate positive word-of-mouth communication by asking satisfied customers to tell their friends and associates about the service and may even provide incentives for doing so.

Pricing of Services

Services should be priced with consumer price sensitivity, the nature of the transaction, and its costs in mind.[27] Prices for services can be established on several different bases. The prices of pest control services, dry cleaning, carpet cleaning, and health consultations are usually based on the performance of specific tasks. Other service prices are based on time. For example, attorneys, consultants, counselors, piano teachers, and plumbers often charge by the hour or day.

Some services use demand-based pricing. When demand for a service is high, the price also is high; when demand for a service is low, so is the price. The perishability of services means that when demand is low, the unused capacity cannot be stored and therefore is lost forever. Every empty seat on an airline flight or in a movie theater represents lost revenue. Some services are very time sensitive in that a significant number of customers desire the service at a particular time. This point in time is called *peak demand*. A provider of time-sensitive services brings in most of its revenue during peak demand. For an airline, peak demand is usually early and late

Pricing of Services

Service providers sometimes employ price competition. Who are FTD.com's direct competitors?

service quality Customers' perception of how well a service meets or exceeds their expectations

in the day; for cruise lines, peak demand occurs in the winter for Caribbean cruises and in the summer for Alaskan cruises. Providers of time-sensitive services often use demand-based pricing to manage the problem of balancing supply and demand. They charge top prices during peak demand and lower prices during off-peak demand to encourage more customers to use the service. This is why the price of a matinee movie is often half the price of the same movie shown at night. Major airlines maintain sophisticated databases to help them adjust ticket prices to fill as many seats as possible on every flight. On a single day, each airline makes thousands of fare changes to maximize the use of its seating capacity and thus maximize its revenues. To accomplish this objective, many airlines have to overbook flights and discount fares. However, research suggests that overbooking as a revenue management tool can cause dissatisfied customers to take their business elsewhere in the future, and customers who are "bumped up" or upgraded as a result of the overbooking may not exhibit particularly positive responses to the upgrade.[28]

When services are offered to customers in a bundle, marketers must decide whether to offer the services at one price, price them separately, or use a combination of the two methods. For example, some hotels offer a package of services at one price, whereas others charge separately for the room, phone service, breakfast, and even in-room safes. Some service providers offer a one-price option for a specific bundle of services and make add-on bundles available at additional charges. For example, a number of cable television companies offer a standard package of channels for one price and offer add-on channel packages for additional charges. Telephone services, such as call waiting and caller ID, are frequently bundled and sold as a package for one price.

Because of the intangible nature of services, customers sometimes rely heavily on price as an indicator of quality. If customers perceive the available services in a service category as being similar in quality, and if the quality of such services is difficult to judge even after these services are purchased, customers may seek out the lowest-priced provider. For example, many customers seek auto insurance providers with the lowest rates. If the quality of different service providers is likely to vary, customers may rely heavily on the price-quality association. For example, if you have to have an appendectomy, will you choose the surgeon who charges an average price of $1,500 or the surgeon who will take your appendix out for $399?

For certain types of services, market conditions may limit how much can be charged for a specific service, especially if the services in this category are perceived as generic in nature. For example, the prices charged by a self-serve laundromat are likely to be limited by the going price for laundromat services in a given community. Also, state and local government regulations may reduce price flexibility. Such regulations may substantially control the prices charged for auto insurance, utilities, cable television service, and even housing rentals.

Service Quality

L O 4 To understand the importance of service quality and explain how to deliver exceptional service quality

Delivery of high-quality services is one of the most important and most difficult tasks any service organization faces. Because of their characteristics, services are very difficult to evaluate. Hence customers must look closely at service quality when comparing services. **Service quality** is defined as customers' perceptions of how well a service meets or exceeds their expectations.[29] A survey by Customer Care Alliance and Arizona State University found that 70 percent of consumers that responded had

LET AN AGENT INSTALL YOUR WIRELESS NETWORK

IT'S SIMPLER FOR YOU AND WEIRDLY FUN FOR US

Geek Squad
24 HOUR COMPUTER SUPPORT TASK FORCE

1 800 GEEK SQUAD

UNITED FOR **WIRELESS INDEPENDENCE** ★ ★ ★

Quality of Service

This ad indirectly communicates about the quality of service provided by the Geek Squad.

search qualities Tangible attributes that can be judged before the purchase of a product

experience qualities Attributes that can be assessed only during purchase and consumption of a service

credence qualities Attributes that customers may be unable to evaluate even after purchasing and consuming a service

experienced "customer rage," indicating they were "extremely" or "very" upset about a negative service experience. More than 33 percent indicated they had raised their voices, and 3 percent admitted to using profanity when interacting with customer service representatives. Although 75 percent of respondents wanted an explanation of why the problem occurred, only 18 percent got an explanation, and only 25 percent heard "I'm sorry" from a customer service representative.[30] Note that customers, not the organization, evaluate service quality. This distinction is critical because it forces service marketers to examine quality from the customer's viewpoint. Thus, it is important for service organizations to determine what customers expect and then develop service products that meet or exceed those expectations. Research has identified a direct relationship among consumers' personality orientation, their emotional characteristics, and their self-reported satisfaction with the service experience.[31]

Customer Evaluation of Service Quality

The biggest obstacle for customers in evaluating service quality is the intangible nature of the service. How can customers evaluate something they cannot see, feel, taste, smell, or hear? Evaluation of a good is much easier because all goods possess **search qualities,** tangible attributes such as color, style, size, feel, or fit that can be evaluated prior to purchase. Trying on a new coat and taking a car for a test drive are examples of how customers evaluate search qualities. Services, on the other hand, have very few search qualities; instead, they abound in experience and credence qualities. **Experience qualities** are attributes, such as taste, satisfaction, or pleasure, that can be assessed only during the purchase and consumption of a service.[32] Restaurants and vacations are examples of services high in experience qualities. **Credence qualities** are attributes that customers may be unable to evaluate even after the purchase and consumption of the service. Examples of services high in credence qualities are surgical operations, automobile repairs, and legal representation. Most consumers lack the knowledge or skills to evaluate the quality of these types of services. Consequently they must place a great deal of faith in the integrity and competence of the service provider.

Despite the difficulties in evaluating quality, service quality may be the only way customers can choose one service over another. For this reason, service marketers live or die by understanding how consumers judge service quality. Table 13.2 defines five dimensions consumers use when evaluating service quality: tangibles, reliability, responsiveness, assurance, and empathy. Note that all of these dimensions have links to employee performance. Of the five, reliability is the most important in determining customer evaluations of service quality.[33]

Service marketers pay a great deal of attention to the tangibles of service quality. For example, at FreshDirect, an online grocery delivery service in the New York City area, every grocery item is scanned at least three times before it is loaded into a truck for delivery to reduce the potential for mistakes.[34] Tangible elements, such as the appearance of facilities and employees, are often the only aspects of a service that can

table 13.2   DIMENSIONS OF SERVICE QUALITY

Dimension	Evaluation Criteria	Examples
Tangibles: Physical evidence of the service	Appearance of physical facilities Appearance of service personnel Tools or equipment used to provide the service	A clean and professional-looking doctor's office A clean and neatly attired repairperson The freshness of food in a restaurant The equipment used in a medical exam
Reliability: Consistency and dependability in performing the service	Accuracy of billing or recordkeeping Performing services when promised	An accurate bank statement A confirmed hotel reservation An airline flight departing and arriving on time
Responsiveness: Willingness or readiness of employees to provide the service	Returning customer phone calls Providing prompt service Handling urgent requests	A server refilling a customer's cup of tea without being asked An ambulance arriving within three minutes
Assurance: Knowledge/competence of employees and ability to convey trust and confidence	Knowledge and skills of employees Company name and reputation Personal characteristics of employees	A highly trained financial adviser A known and respected service provider A doctor's bedside manner
Empathy: Caring and individual attention provided by employees	Listening to customer needs Caring about customers' interests Providing personalized attention	A store employee listening to and trying to understand a customer's complaint A nurse counseling a heart patient

Sources: Adapted from Leonard L. Berry and A. Parasuraman, *Marketing Services: Competing through Quality* (New York: Free Press, 1991); Valarie A. Zeithaml, A. Parasuraman, and Leonard L. Berry, *Delivering Quality Service: Balancing Customer Perceptions and Expectations* (New York: Free Press, 1990); A. Parasuraman, Leonard L. Berry, and Valarie A. Zeithaml, "An Empirical Examination of Relationships in an Extended Service Quality Model," *Marketing Science Institute Working Paper Series*, Report no. 90–112 (Cambridge, MA: Marketing Science Institute, 1990), p. 29.

be viewed before purchase and consumption. Indeed, research has found that a service provider's physical facilities have a very strong influence on customers' perceptions of quality.[35] Therefore, service marketers must ensure that these tangible elements are consistent with the overall image of the service.

Except for the tangibles dimension, the criteria customers use to judge service quality are intangible. For instance, how does a customer judge reliability? Since dimensions such as reliability cannot be examined with the senses, customers must rely on other ways of judging service. One of the most important factors in customer judgments of service quality is service expectations. Service expectations are influenced by past experiences with the service, word-of-mouth communication from other customers, and the service company's own advertising. For example, customers are usually eager to try a new restaurant, especially when friends recommend it. These same customers may have also seen advertisements placed by the restaurant. As a result, they have an idea of what to expect when they visit the restaurant for the first time. When they finally dine there, the quality they experience will change the expectations they have for their next visit. That is why providing consistently high service quality is important. If the quality of a restaurant, or of any service, begins to deteriorate, customers will alter their own expectations and change their word-of-mouth communication to others accordingly.

Delivering Exceptional Service Quality

Providing high-quality service on a consistent basis is very difficult. All consumers have experienced examples of poor service: late flight departures and arrivals, inattentive restaurant servers, rude bank employees, long lines. Obviously it is impossible for a service organization to ensure exceptional service quality 100 percent of the time.

RESPONSIBLE marketing?

Cell Phone Companies' Customer Service Temporarily out of Order

ISSUE: Does the quality of customer service affect consumer trust and selection of cell phone service providers?

The Better Business Bureau (BBB) recently commissioned a survey that focuses on consumer trust of businesses. Cell phone companies ranked as one of the least-trusted industries in the United States. The survey results showed that 26 percent of consumers said that customer service is a core component of trust in companies. On the other side of the coin, 30 percent of consumers said that high charges and fees, like those used by cellular phone service providers, are the largest factors in creating distrust in companies.

It's no secret that many cell phone companies don't always make their customers happy. In 2005 and 2006, cellular telephone companies ranked highest in the total number of complaints received by the Better Business Bureau. Steven Cole, president and CEO of the BBB, stated, "Earning consumers' trust isn't simply the result of good ethics or even low prices. . . . If they don't provide quality customer service and deliver on promises, they won't be trusted." Interestingly, the number of cell phone users continues to rise. Do the cell phone service providers' long-term contracts (12 to 24 months) lead to inferior customer service? Does the lack of service translate into a general distrust in cell phone service companies?[b]

However, an organization can take many steps to increase the likelihood of providing high-quality service. First, though, the service company must consider the four factors that affect service quality: (1) analysis of customer expectations, (2) service quality specifications, (3) employee performance, and (4) management of service expectations (see Figure 13.2).[36]

Analysis of Customer Expectations. Providers need to understand customer expectations when designing a service to meet or exceed those expectations. Only then can they deliver good service. Customers usually have two levels of expectations: desired and acceptable. The desired level of expectations is what the customer really wants. If this level of expectations is provided, the customer will be very satisfied. The acceptable level of expectations is what the customer views as adequate. The difference between these two levels of expectations is called the customer's *zone of tolerance.*[37]

Service companies sometimes use marketing research, such as surveys and focus groups, to discover customer needs and expectations. For instance, the All England Lawn Tennis and Croquet Club faces many challenges in hosting the annual Wimbledon Lawn Tennis Championships every year. The club surveys attendees during the event, and executives examine the data immediately after each year's event to identify areas that require improvement. Those areas then become a planning focus for the next year's event. The feedback and painstaking planning help the club

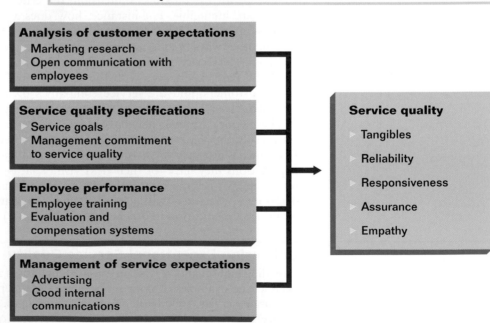

figure 13.2

SERVICE QUALITY MODEL

Analysis of customer expectations
▸ Marketing research
▸ Open communication with employees

Service quality specifications
▸ Service goals
▸ Management commitment to service quality

Employee performance
▸ Employee training
▸ Evaluation and compensation systems

Management of service expectations
▸ Advertising
▸ Good internal communications

Service quality
▸ Tangibles
▸ Reliability
▸ Responsiveness
▸ Assurance
▸ Empathy

Source: Adapted from A. Parasuraman, Leonard L. Berry, and Valarie A. Zeithaml, "An Empirical Examination of Relationships in an Extended Service Quality Model," *Marketing Science Institute Working Paper Series,* Report no. 90–112, 1990. Reprinted by permission of Marketing Science Institute, and the authors.

Who has the best customer service?

1. *USAA*
2. *Four Seasons Hotels and Resorts*
3. *Cadillac*
4. *Nordstrom*
5. *Wegmans Food Markets*

Source: Business Week.

Need a new battery?
We'll come to you!

Whether you're at home, work or around town, AAA Battery Service provides you with an easy and convenient mobile battery testing and replacement service to get you back on the road quickly.

- Free, accurate battery testing* and professional on-scene installation
- Exclusive AAA Member discount on a AAA Battery
- A high-quality AAA Battery that meets or exceeds your vehicle's original specifications
- A 36-month free replacement period, 72-month limited warranty
- A free Roadside Assistance call with the purchase of a AAA Battery

It's Easy! Call the Auto Club today at 800.560.6499.

We're always with you.®

| CALL: 1.800.560.6499 | CLICK: AAA.com/battery | VISIT: Your Local Auto Club Office |

maintain Wimbledon's reputation as a genteel sporting event.[38] Other service marketers, especially restaurants, use comment cards on which customers can complain or provide suggestions. Still another approach is to ask employees. Because customer contact employees interact daily with customers, they are in good positions to know what customers want from the company. Service managers should regularly interact with their employees by asking their opinions on the best way to serve customers.

Service Quality Specifications. Once an organization understands its customers' needs, it must establish goals to help ensure good service delivery. These goals, or service specifications, are typically set in terms of employee or machine performance. For example, a bank may require its employees to conform to a dress code. Likewise, the bank may require that all incoming phone calls be answered by the third ring. Specifications such as these can be very important in providing quality service as long as they are tied to the needs expressed by customers.

Perhaps the most critical aspect of service quality specifications is managers' commitment to service quality. Service managers who are committed to quality become role models for all employees in the organization. Such commitment motivates customer contact employees to comply with service specifications. It is crucial that all managers within the organization embrace this commitment, especially frontline managers, who are much closer to customers than higher-level managers.

Employee Performance. Once an organization sets service quality standards and managers are committed to them, the firm must find ways to ensure that customer contact employees perform their jobs well. Contact employees in most service industries (bank tellers, flight attendants, servers, sales clerks, etc.) are often the least-trained and lowest-paid members of the organization. Service organizations must realize that contact employees are the most important link to the customer, and thus their performance is critical to customer perceptions of service quality. The way to ensure that employees perform well is to train them well so they understand how to do their jobs. Providing information about customers, service specifications, and the organization itself during the training promotes this understanding.

Service Expectations
AAA Battery Service in this advertisement sets forth service expectations.

The evaluation and compensation system the organization uses also plays a part in employee performance. Many service employees are evaluated and rewarded on the basis of output measures, such as sales volume (automobile salespeople) or a low error rate (bank tellers). But systems using output measures overlook other major aspects of job performance, including friendliness, teamwork, effort, and customer satisfaction. These customer-oriented measures of performance may be a better basis for evaluation and reward. In fact, a number of service marketers use customer satisfaction ratings to determine a portion of service employee compensation.

Management of Service Expectations. Because expectations are so significant in customer evaluations of service quality, service companies recognize they must set realistic expectations about the service they can provide. They can set these expectations through advertising and good internal communication. In their advertisements, service companies make promises about the kind of service they will deliver. As

green MARKETING

Turning Over a New Business Leaf: The Eco-Conscious Resort

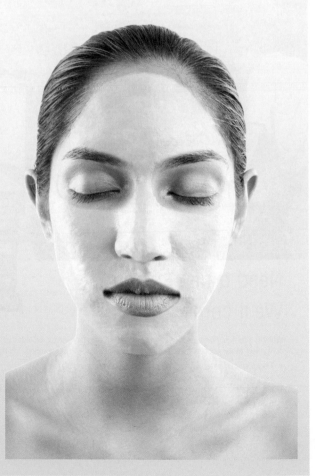

Can an upscale resort be both luxurious and eco-conscious? Although resort guests have traditionally appreciated personalized services and fine furnishings, many "are becoming eco-friendly and eco-fixated," says the general manager of a Phoenix-area resort. Yet a resort that cultivates a green image may face resistance if its environmental initiatives conflict with the top-notch pampering that guests expect.

For example, the King Pacific Lodge, a deluxe floating spa off the British Columbian coast, has been working hard to reduce energy consumption and environmental emissions. Now that it has outfitted all fishing boats to use less fuel, the trip to salmon-filled waters takes a few minutes longer—which sometimes annoys the high-powered guests. "We're asking our guests to make these sacrifices in hopes that a little bit will do a lot for us," notes the president of King Pacific. "But I can't guarantee that all the guests will understand that."

Bangkok-based Six Senses Resorts & Spas faces a similar dilemma as it goes green. Some changes, such as using cooking oil mixed with conventional fuel to power the resort's generators, are invisible

to guests. However, the firm will soon install a system in its Maldives resort that shuts off the air-conditioning system if a guest-room door is open for longer than a minute. Knowing that this may spark complaints, the resort's plan is to start educating guests about the environmental benefits— and keep going green.[c]

already noted, a service company is forced to make promises because the intangibility of services prevents the organization from showing the benefits in the advertisement. However, the advertiser should not promise more than it can deliver. Doing so will likely mean disappointed customers.

To deliver on promises made, a company needs to have thorough internal communication among its departments, especially management, advertising, and store operations. Assume, for example, that a restaurant's radio advertisements guarantee service within five minutes, or the meal is free. If top management or the advertising department fails to inform store operations about the five-minute guarantee, the restaurant will very likely fail to meet its customers' service expectations. Even though customers might appreciate a free meal, the restaurant will lose some credibility as well as revenue.

As mentioned earlier, word-of-mouth communication from other customers also shapes customer expectations. However, service companies cannot manage this "advertising" directly. The best way to ensure positive word-of-mouth communication is to provide exceptional service quality. It has been estimated that customers tell four times as many people about bad service as they do about good service.

Nonprofit Marketing

L O 5 To explore the nature of nonprofit marketing

Nonprofit marketing refers to marketing activities that are conducted by individuals and organizations to achieve some goal other than ordinary business goals such as profit, market share, or return on investment. Nonprofit marketing is divided into two categories: nonprofit-organization marketing and social marketing. Nonprofit-organization marketing is the use of marketing concepts and techniques by organizations whose goals do not include making profits. Social marketing promotes social causes, such as AIDS research and recycling.

Most of the previously discussed concepts and approaches to service products also apply to nonprofit organizations. Indeed, many nonprofit organizations provide mainly service products. In this section, we examine the concept of nonprofit marketing to determine how it differs from marketing activities in for-profit business organizations. We also explore the marketing objectives of nonprofit organizations and the development of their product strategies.

How Is Nonprofit Marketing Different?

Many nonprofit organizations strive for effective marketing activities. Charitable organizations and supporters of social causes are major nonprofit marketers in this country. Political parties, unions, religious sects, and fraternal organizations also perform marketing activities, but they are not considered businesses. Whereas the chief beneficiary of a business enterprise is whoever owns or holds stock in it, in theory the only beneficiaries of a nonprofit organization are its clients, its members, or the public at large. The American Museum of Natural History, for example, is a nonprofit service organization.

Nonprofit organizations have greater opportunities for creativity than most for-profit business organizations, but trustees or board members of nonprofit organizations are likely to have difficulty judging the performance of the trained professionals they oversee. It is harder for administrators to evaluate the performance of professors or social workers than it is for sales managers to evaluate the performance of salespeople in a for-profit organization.

Another way nonprofit marketing differs from for-profit marketing is that nonprofit marketing is sometimes quite controversial. Nonprofit organizations such as Greenpeace, the National Rifle Association, and the National Organization for Women spend lavishly on lobbying efforts to persuade Congress, the White House, and even the courts to support their interests, in part because not all of society agrees with their aims. However, marketing as a field of study does not attempt to state

nonprofit marketing Marketing activities conducted to achieve some goal other than ordinary business goals such as profit, market share, or return on investment

Marketing in Nonprofit Organizations

Some nonprofit marketers use advertising to explain their objectives and to seek support.

what an organization's goals should be or to debate the issue of nonprofit versus for-profit business goals. Marketing tries only to provide a body of knowledge and concepts to help further an organization's goals. Individuals must decide whether they approve or disapprove of a particular organization's goal orientation. Most marketers would agree that profit and consumer satisfaction are appropriate goals for business enterprises, but would probably disagree considerably about the goals of a controversial nonprofit organization.

Nonprofit Marketing Objectives

The basic aim of nonprofit organizations is to obtain a desired response from a target market. The response could be a change in values, a financial contribution, the donation of services, or some other type of exchange. For example, the primary objective of the nonprofit organization Declare Yourself is to register 300,000 18- to 25-year-olds to vote in the next presidential election. To help achieve its goal, the organization is using a website, celebrities who appeal to young people, mobile and Internet technologies, and viral videos.[39] Nonprofit marketing objectives are shaped by the nature of the exchange and the goals of the organization. These objectives should state the rationale for the organization's existence. An organization that defines its marketing objective as providing a product can be left without a purpose if the product becomes obsolete. However, servicing and adapting to the perceived needs and wants of a target public, or market, enhances an organization's chance to survive and achieve its goals.

Developing Nonprofit Marketing Strategies

Nonprofit organizations develop marketing strategies by defining and analyzing a target market and creating and maintaining a total marketing mix that appeals to that market.

Target Markets. We must revise the concept of target markets slightly to apply it to nonprofit organizations. Whereas a business seeks out target groups that are potential purchasers of its product, a nonprofit organization may attempt to serve many diverse groups. For our purposes, a **target public** is a collective of individuals who have an interest in or a concern about an organization, a product, or a social cause. The terms *target market* and *target public* are difficult to distinguish for many

target public A collective of individuals who have an interest in or concern about an organization, product, or social cause

nonproduct or social cause profit organizations. The target public of the Partnership for a Drug Free America consists of parents, adults, and concerned teenagers. However, the target market for the organization's advertisements consists of potential and current drug users. When an organization is concerned about changing values or obtaining a response from the public, it views the public as a market.[40]

In nonprofit marketing, direct consumers of the product are called **client publics** and indirect consumers are called **general publics.**[41] For example, the client public for a university is its student body, and its general public includes parents, alumni, and trustees. The client public usually receives most of the attention when an organization develops a marketing strategy.

Developing Marketing Mixes. A marketing mix strategy limits alternatives and directs marketing activities toward achieving organizational goals. The strategy should include a blueprint for making decisions about product, distribution, promotion, and price. These decision variables should be blended to serve the target market.

In developing the product, nonprofit organizations usually deal with ideas and services. Problems may evolve when an organization fails to define what it is providing. What product, for example, does the Peace Corps provide? Its services include vocational training, health services, nutritional assistance, and community development. It also markets the ideas of international cooperation and the implementation of U.S. foreign policy. The product of the Peace Corps is more difficult to define than the average business product. As indicated in the first part of this chapter, services are intangible and therefore need special marketing efforts. The marketing of ideas and concepts is likewise more abstract than the marketing of tangibles, and much effort is required to present benefits.

Distribution decisions in nonprofit organizations relate to how ideas and services will be made available to clients. If the product is an idea, selecting the right media to communicate the idea will facilitate distribution. By nature, services consist of assistance, convenience, and availability. Availability is thus part of the total service. Making a product such as health services available calls for knowledge of such retailing concepts as site location analysis.

Developing a channel of distribution to coordinate and facilitate the flow of nonprofit products to clients is a necessary task, but in a nonprofit setting the traditional concept of the marketing channel may need to be revised. The independent wholesalers available to a business enterprise do not exist in most nonprofit situations. Instead, a very short channel—nonprofit organization to client—is the norm because production and consumption of ideas and services are often simultaneous.

Making promotional decisions may be the first sign that a nonprofit organization is performing marketing activities. Nonprofit organizations use advertising and publicity to communicate with clients and the public. The March of Dimes, for example, launched a promotional campaign using television, radio, and print advertising in the form of public-service announcements to raise awareness of its public health programs for expectant mothers.[42] Direct mail remains the primary means of fundraising for social services, such as those provided by the Red Cross and Special Olympics. Environmentally focused organizations face a unique challenge in promotional materials: how to communicate using environmentally friendly products such as recycled paper and environmentally sensitive inks. The Nature Conservancy, for example, uses paper products that have been certified by the Forest Stewardship Council as having come from well-managed forests.[43] Increasingly, nonprofits are using the Internet to reach fundraising and promotional goals through e-mail, websites, and software that permits accepting online gifts.

Many nonprofit organizations also use personal selling, although they may call it by another name. Churches and charities rely on personal selling when they send volunteers to recruit new members or request donations. The U.S. Army uses personal selling when its recruiting officers attempt to persuade men and women to enlist. Special events to obtain funds, communicate ideas, or provide services are also effective promotional activities. Amnesty International, for example, has held worldwide concert tours featuring well-known musical artists to raise funds and increase public awareness of political prisoners around the world.

client publics Direct consumers of a product of a nonbusiness organization

general publics Indirect consumers of a product of a nonbusiness organization

Although product and promotional techniques may require only slight modification when applied to nonprofit organizations, pricing is generally quite different and decision making is more complex. The different pricing concepts the nonprofit organization faces include pricing in user and donor markets. Two types of monetary pricing exist: *fixed* and *variable*. There may be a fixed fee for users, or the price may vary depending on the user's ability to pay. When a donation-seeking organization will accept a contribution of any size, it is using variable pricing.

The broadest definition of price (valuation) must be used to develop nonprofit marketing strategies. Financial price, an exact dollar value, may or may not be charged for a nonprofit product. Economists recognize the giving up of alternatives as a cost. **Opportunity cost** is the value of the benefit given up by selecting one alternative over another. According to this traditional economic view of price, if a nonprofit organization persuades someone to donate time to a cause or to change his or her behavior, the alternatives given up are a cost to (or a price paid by) the individual. Volunteers who answer phones for a university counseling service or a suicide hotline, for example, give up the time they could spend studying or doing other things and the income they might earn from working at a for-profit business organization.

For other nonprofit organizations, financial price is an important part of the marketing mix. Nonprofit organizations today are raising money by increasing the prices of their services or are starting to charge for services if they have not done so before. They are using marketing research to determine what kinds of products people will pay for. Pricing strategies of nonprofit organizations often stress public and client welfare over equalization of costs and revenues. If additional funds are needed to cover costs, the organization may solicit donations, contributions, or grants.

opportunity cost The value of the benefit given up by choosing one alternative over another

SUMMARY

Services are intangible products that involve deeds, performances, or efforts that cannot be physically possessed. They are the result of applying human or mechanical efforts to people or objects. Services are a growing part of the U.S. economy. They have six fundamental characteristics: intangibility, inseparability of production and consumption, perishability, heterogeneity, client-based relationships, and customer contact. Intangibility means that a service cannot be seen, touched, tasted, or smelled. Inseparability refers to the fact that the production of a service cannot be separated from its consumption by customers. Perishability means unused service capacity of one time period cannot be stored for future use. Heterogeneity is variation in service quality. Client-based relationships are interactions with customers that lead to the repeated use of a service over time. Customer contact is the interaction between providers and customers needed to deliver a service.

Core services are the basic service experiences customers expect; supplementary services are those that relate to and support core services. Because of the characteristics of services, service marketers face several challenges in developing and managing marketing mixes. To address the problem of intangibility, marketers use cues that help assure customers about the quality of their services. The development and management of service products are also influenced by the service characteristics of inseparability and level of customer contact. Some services require that customers come to the service provider's facility; others are delivered with no face-to-face contact. Marketing channels for services are usually short and direct, but some services employ intermediaries. Service marketers are less concerned with warehousing and transportation than are goods marketers, but inventory management and balancing supply and demand for services are important issues. The intangibility of services poses several promotion-related challenges. Advertisements with tangible cues that symbolize the service and depict facilities, equipment, and personnel help address these challenges. Service providers are likely to promote price, guarantees, performance documentation, availability, and training and certification of contact personnel. Through their actions, service personnel can be involved directly or indirectly in the personal selling of services.

Intangibility makes it difficult to experience a service before purchasing it. Heterogeneity and intangibility make word-of-mouth communication an important means of promotion. The prices of services are based on task performance, time required, or demand. Perishability creates difficulties in balancing supply and demand because unused capacity cannot be stored. The point in time when a significant number of customers desire a service is called peak demand; demand-based pricing results in higher prices charged for services during peak demand. When services are offered in a bundle, marketers must decide whether to offer them at one price, price them separately, or use a combination of the two methods. Because services are intangible, customers may rely on price as a sign of quality. For some services, market conditions may dictate the price; for others, state and local government regulations may limit price flexibility.

Service quality is customers' perception of how well a service meets or exceeds their expectations. Although one of the most important aspects of service marketing, service quality is very difficult for customers to evaluate because the nature of services renders benefits impossible to assess before actual purchase and consumption. These benefits include experience qualities, such as taste, satisfaction, or pleasure, and credence qualities, which customers may be unable to evaluate even after consumption. When competing services are very similar, service quality may be the only way for customers to distinguish among them. Service marketers can increase the quality of their services by following the four-step process of understanding customer expectations, setting service specifications, ensuring good employee performance, and managing customers' service expectations.

Nonprofit marketing is marketing aimed at nonbusiness goals, including social causes. It uses most of the same concepts and approaches that apply to business situations. Whereas the chief beneficiary of a business enterprise is whoever owns or holds stock in it, the beneficiary of a nonprofit enterprise should be its clients, its members, or its public at large. The goals of a nonprofit organization reflect its unique philosophy or mission. Some nonprofit organizations have very controversial goals, but many organizations exist to further generally accepted social causes.

The marketing objective of nonprofit organizations is to obtain a desired response from a target market. Developing a nonprofit marketing strategy consists of defining and analyzing a target market and creating and maintaining a marketing mix. In nonprofit marketing, the product is usually an idea or a service. Distribution is aimed at the communication of ideas and the delivery of services. The result is a very short marketing channel. Promotion is very important to nonprofit marketing. Nonprofit organizations use advertising, publicity, and personal selling to communicate with clients and the public. Direct mail remains the primary means of fundraising for social services, but some nonprofits use the Internet for fundraising and promotional activities. Price is more difficult to define in nonprofit marketing because of opportunity costs and the difficulty of quantifying the values exchanged.

IMPORTANT TERMS

Intangibility, 358
Inseparability, 359
Perishability, 360
Heterogeneity, 360

Client-based relationships, 360
Customer contact, 361
Service quality, 367

Search qualities, 368
Experience qualities, 368
Credence qualities, 368
Nonprofit marketing, 373

Target public, 374
Client publics, 375
General publics, 375
Opportunity cost, 376

DISCUSSION & REVIEW QUESTIONS

1. How important are services in the U.S. economy?

2. Identify and discuss the major characteristics of services.

3. For each marketing mix element, which service characteristics are most likely to have an impact? Explain.

4. What is service quality? Why do customers find it difficult to judge service quality?

5. Identify and discuss the five components of service quality. How do customers evaluate these components?

6. What is the significance of tangibles in service marketing?

7. How do search, experience, and credence qualities affect the way customers view and evaluate services?

8. What steps should a service company take to provide exceptional service quality?

9. How does nonprofit marketing differ from marketing in for-profit organizations?

10. What are the differences among clients, publics, and customers? What is the difference between a target public and target market?

11. Discuss the development of a marketing strategy for a university. What marketing decisions must be made as the strategy is developed?

APPLICATION QUESTIONS

1. Imagine you are the owner of a new service business. What is your service? Be creative. What are some of the most important considerations in developing the service, training salespeople, and communicating about your service to potential customers?

2. As discussed in this chapter, the characteristics of services affect the development of marketing mixes for services. Choose a specific service and explain how each marketing mix element could be affected by these service characteristics.

3. In advertising services, a company must often use symbols to represent the offered product. Identify three service organizations you have seen in outdoor, television, or magazine advertising. What symbols do these organizations use to represent their services? What message do the symbols convey to potential customers?

4. Delivering consistently high-quality service is difficult for service marketers. Describe an instance when you received high-quality service and an instance when you experienced low-quality service. What contributed to your perception of high quality? Of low quality?

INTERNET EXERCISE

Visit **www.cengage.com/marketing/pride-ferrell** for resources to help you master the material in this chapter, plus materials that will help you expand your marketing knowledge, including Internet exercise updates, ACE Self-Tests, hotlinks to companies featured in this chapter, and much more.

Matchmaker.com

The Internet abounds with dating sites, but few offer as much information about their members as Matchmaker.com. Matchmaker profiles are gleaned from a survey of some 60 question and essay responses. Check out the site at **www.matchmaker.com**.

1. Classify Matchmaker.com's product in terms of its position on the service continuum.

2. How does Matchmaker.com enhance customer service and foster better client-based relationships through its Internet marketing efforts?

3. Discuss the degree to which experience and credence qualities exist in the services offered by Matchmaker.com and other dating websites.

developing your MARKETING PLAN

Products that are services rather than tangible goods present unique challenges to companies when they formulate marketing strategy. A clear comprehension of the concepts that apply specifically to service products is essential when developing the marketing plan. These concepts will form the basis for decisions in several plan areas. To assist you in relating the information in this chapter to the development of your marketing plan for a service product, focus on the following:

1. Using Figure 13.1, determine your product's degree of tangibility. If your product lies close to the tangible end of the continuum, then you may proceed to the questions in the next chapter. If your product is more intangible, then continue with this chapter's issues.

2. Discuss your product with regard to the six service characteristics. To what degree does it possess the qualities that make up each of these characteristics?

3. Using Table 13.1 as a guide, discuss the marketing challenges you are likely to experience.

4. Determine the search, experience, and credence qualities that customers are likely to use when evaluating your service product.

5. Consider how your service product relates to each of the dimension of service quality. Using Table 13.2 as a guide, develop the evaluation criteria and examples that are appropriate for your product.

The information obtained from these questions should assist you in developing various aspects of your marketing plan found in the *Interactive Marketing Plan* exercise at **www.cengage.com/marketing/pride-ferrell**.

globalEDGE

1. Service marketing is sometimes associated with franchise chains that deliver products to fulfill a global need in the marketplace. Though there are magazines that rank the leading franchisers, an examination of the top 50 gives the analyst information for understanding the nature of franchising. Prepare a brief report based on information from the *Entrepreneur* Top Global Franchises. This ranking can be accessed by using the search term "top 200 franchisers" at **http://globaledge.msu.edu/ibrd.** In particular, which company has the highest startup costs? Given what you know, do you think the startup costs required for this company are justifiable?

2. To be a better "social enterprise" and deliver quality services, firms must better understand, communicate, and respond to customers. However, sometimes companies fail to interact with and help improve the communities they service. According to a report titled "The Three Ds of Customer Experience" by the Harvard Business School (HBS), as firms grow larger, they sometimes fall into a dominance trap. This research can be accessed by using the search term "social enterprise" at **http://globaledge.msu.edu/ibrd.** Once you reach the HBS website, use the search term "The Three 'Ds' of Customer Experience" to find the relevant research paper with the same name. Based on this paper, define the concept of a dominance trap. Also, define and present three imperatives that may prevent this from occurring in a firm.

video CASE 13.1

Southwest Airlines: High-Flying Services Marketing

Southwest Airlines has risen to the top of the airline industry by making top-quality customer service and no-frills prices its highest priorities. Founded in 1971 as a regional airline flying three planes between Dallas, Houston, and San Antonio, Southwest has grown into a national carrier with 35,000 employees nationwide and $10 billion in annual revenue. Its stock symbol is LUV, which also sums up the airline's service attitude toward customers.

From the start, Southwest set its airfares low and its service standards high. The airline sees every flight as an opportunity to reinforce its reputation for friendly, attentive service in the sky and on the ground. In recognition of Southwest's financial and service successes, *Fortune* magazine regularly ranks it among the top 20 most admired U.S. companies.

Maintaining a consistently high level of customer service is an ongoing challenge as Southwest adds new destinations and expands its flight schedule year after year. Southwest starts by carefully screening job applicants in order to hire people who enjoy customer interaction, have good communication skills, and can work cooperatively with colleagues. The airline provides extensive training and allows customer contact personnel to take the initiative by resolving complaints and service problems on the spot.

Southwest employees, especially those who deal directly with customers, are required to look and behave professionally. They're also encouraged to add a bit of fun to the flying experience, a key element that differentiates Southwest from competitors. For instance, some crew members coax smiles from seat-belted passengers by leading toilet paper games or enlivening routine announcements with gentle humor. Delivering service with a smile shows that Southwest genuinely cares about its customers.

Just as important, Southwest keeps the service spirit alive through a culture committee at headquarters and similar committees in each of its airport and maintenance facilities across the country. These committees celebrate the achievements of employees who provide outstanding service. They also plan customer and employee appreciation events around the country, such as surprising incoming flight passengers and crew members with cookies and milk.

Thanks in part to its service spirit, Southwest has remained at cruising altitude for decades, despite some periods of turbulence. Not long ago, the airline was criticized and fined for continuing to fly 46 jets that were overdue for a federally mandated fuselage safety inspection. When questioned by officials, Southwest grounded the jets, completed the inspections, and quickly resumed regular flights. The airline also conducted an internal investigation and reassured customers by pointing to its long-standing safety record and its rigorous equipment maintenance schedule.

When the price of jet fuel reached sky-high levels recently, some large carriers began cutting back on flights, parking planes, and withdrawing from certain destinations to save money. Not Southwest. Because of smart negotiating, Southwest had its fuel costs under control and actually expanded to new cities while competitors were shrinking their schedules.

To offset higher fuel costs, other airlines have been unbundling services and tacking on extra fees for checking baggage and other services that used to be bundled with the ticket price. Southwest has differentiated itself by sticking with its bundle of services and promoting itself as the "no-fee airline." In fact, the airline has created a new "Business Select" airfare for business travelers, bundling priority boarding and a free drink at a slightly higher price. The fare is fully refundable if the traveler is unable to fly as scheduled—another feature that makes the Business Select bundle particularly appealing to businesspeople.

To keep growing, Southwest will soon link with another airline to offer international service. Although running an airline is serious business, Southwest's spirited approach to service keeps customers smiling—and keeps them coming back for more LUV.[44]

Questions for Discussion

1. As a high-contact service provider, how does Southwest Airlines ensure that its employees satisfy customers?
2. What experience qualities might weigh most heavily in customers' evaluations of the services delivered by Southwest Airlines? What are the implications for the airline's services marketing efforts?
3. What is Southwest Airlines doing to manage customers' service expectations?

CASE 13.2

Allstate: We Are All in Good Hands

Customers value high-quality service and the service companies that provide it. The Allstate Corporation, the largest public personal insurance company in the United States, is one such service provider. The company offers 13 lines of insurance, including auto, property, life, and business. It also offers retirement, investment, and banking services. Allstate serves 17 million households, with offices in 49 U.S. states and in Canada. The company prides itself on delivering great service that customers value and doing more than is expected of it, especially in the areas of customer relationships and social responsibility.

Allstate works hard to bring value to customers and all other stakeholders. The company has a strong commitment to high ethical standards. In today's climate of corporate scandal, this is a valuable asset for the company and builds strong long-term relationships with shareholders. The company has also managed and invested its capital in an ethical manner, thereby providing shareholders with long-term financial stability. Allstate is also focusing on building long-term customers.

One way the company works to satisfy and retain customers is by offering excellent claim management services. Currently it is investing $100 million to create a new computerized claims-processing system. The goal is to strengthen the connection between the company and its customers (customers know they are in good hands) and simultaneously improve efficiency. Allstate also focuses on streamlining its relationships with all individuals working with the company—employees and independent agents alike—so they can then better help customers.

Allstate invests in municipal bonds and low-interest loans to support and grow urban neighborhoods. Moreover, the company is committed to protecting the natural environment. It's changed the lighting inside and outside the headquarters building to reduce energy consumption and it participates in the Climate Resolve initiative to reduce greenhouse gas intensity. Employees who use public transportation are rewarded with subsidized tickets and complimentary shuttles to train stations.

The company is also committed to giving back to individuals and communities. For example, contributions from its subsidiaries fund an independent charity— the Allstate Foundation—which donates millions of dollars each year to causes that focus on three specific areas: economic empowerment; tolerance, inclusion, and diversity; and safe and vital communities. The foundation also makes an annual donation of $1 million to nonprofit organizations through Agency Hands in the Community grants. In all, the Allstate Foundation contributes more than $17 million to nonprofit groups every year, including $400,000 in school scholarships.

Both the foundation and parent company regularly send aid to areas devastated by natural disasters such as hurricanes and tsunamis. With its emphasis on responsive service, Allstate works hard to help customers who are affected by such disasters. When a series of wildfires destroyed homes in southern California, for example, Allstate sent a special squad of employees to evacuation centers to help property owners file claims. It also brought in hundreds of Allstate claims adjusters from California and neighboring states to process the fire claims as quickly as possible. Then, to honor those who battled the flames, it donated $50,000 to the San Diego Fire-Rescue Department.

Allstate's chairman summarizes the company's commitment to its communities this way: "One of the most rewarding aspects of working at Allstate is seeing the way our employees and agencies help others in a time of crisis. I know it is what we do as a business, but it is more than a business for Allstaters." This commitment rings true not only in times of disaster but in the company's day-to-day workings and its relationships with its customers and shareholders.[45]

Questions for Discussion

1. Classify Allstate's product in terms of its position on the service continuum.
2. Describe Allstate's primary products, using the six basic characteristics of services.
3. Discuss the degree to which experience and credence qualities exist in Allstate's services.

strategic CASE 5

Shutterfly Seeks Picture-Perfect Profits

Picture this: Just ten years ago, digital cameras were high-end products owned only by tech-savvy photo buffs, and most consumers who surfed the Internet used slow dial-up connections. The idea of uploading digital images to order prints from a web-based company was new even to people who enjoyed speedy broadband connections. Yet when Shutterfly started offering photo-printing services on the Internet late in 1999, it was entering a market that was already teeming with competition. Today, digital photography has moved into the mainstream, and Shutterfly has become a major force in the online photo-printing industry, introducing dozens of new products every year for consumers to embellish with their favorite photos.

Keeping Quality in Focus

Early on, Shutterfly, which is based in Redwood City, California, offered free prints to induce customers to try its photo-printing services, a technique used by many competitors, then and now. In all, Shutterfly gave away more than 80 percent of its prints during its first six months, part of a plan to showcase Shutterfly's high-quality printing. The company invested in special printing equipment at the outset so it would have full control over quality rather than outsource some or all of its orders to an outside photo-processing firm. Shutterfly's goal was to ensure that the customer photos it printed would always come out clear, crisp, and colorful. Its site also included photo-enhancement functions so customers could add special borders, eliminate the red-eye effect, and make other improvements before ordering prints.

Another way Shutterfly distinguished itself was by inviting consumers to upload and store their photos on its website without charge. Unlike some competitors, Shutterfly promised never to delete any photos, no matter how many had been uploaded or how long they had been stored—a feature highly valued by the company's fast-growing customer base. Photo sharing was also a key feature: Shutterfly made it easy for customers to let friends and family members view and order their photos online.

Staying Ahead of the Shakeout

To stay ahead of competitors, Shutterfly introduced a never-ending parade of new products for photo personalization, from calendars and cards to mugs and magnets. Meanwhile, intense competition and a prolonged price war resulted in an industry shakeout that drove many smaller firms out of business. Some of the

stronger firms were acquired by big corporations. Kodak bought Ofoto and rebranded the business as the Kodak Gallery; Hewlett-Packard bought Snapfish and kept the site's catchy brand. Shutterfly survived all of this industry turmoil and, by continuing to build on its high-quality reputation, became profitable in 2003.

In 2005 a new CEO, Jeff Housenbold, broadened the company's mission. Thinking about the lifestyle aspects of how consumers take, use, and share photos, Housenbold launched what he called "a next-generation personal publishing platform that would enable our customers to be more creative." In preparation, Shutterfly surveyed its customers to learn more about their needs and preferences. It also invested heavily in additional production capacity, buying sophisticated industrial printers that can each turn out 20,000 photos per hour.

Shutterfly sought to escape the print price war by diversifying its product mix beyond standard 4 × 6 photos. Adding higher-margin items such as customizable T-shirts, jewelry boxes, and tote bags helped the firm to expand its appeal and gave current customers more reasons to log on, upload new photos, and buy from Shutterfly again and again. The company also negotiated to license well-known characters such as Clifford the Big Red Dog and, later, SpongeBob SquarePants and other popular Nickelodeon characters for use on personalized photo greeting cards, photo albums, and other products. Shutterfly marketers introduced the new offerings with a multimedia campaign that included print ads in various parenting magazines and women's magazines and commercials on the Home Shopping Network.

Digital Imaging Goes Mainstream

By now, millions of U.S. consumers have made the transition from film-based cameras to digital cameras. Many cell phones are equipped with digital cameras, as well, which only adds to the market potential. So many people are busy snapping so many photos, but Shutterfly's analysis revealed that women accounted for 70 percent of its customer base. Why? "Women often are the people who take on the role of family historian or chief memory officer," the CEO explains. Not only are women taking photos (or taking charge of photos taken by other family members), but they are making key decisions about which photos to print, which printing service to use, and what kinds of prints and personalized products to buy. For this reason, much of Shutterfly's promotion budget is devoted to media that reach women.

The biggest surge in buying occurs in the last three months of the year. On the day after Halloween, for instance, Shutterfly's site is inundated by 3 million photos of costumed kids of all ages. On that day alone, customers order a total of 1.2 million prints—and the holiday rush is just beginning. "From Halloween, it is straight on to Thanksgiving, holiday cards, and calendars," says Housenbold, "and our lab is running 24 hours a day, seven days a week."

The Shutterfly of Tomorrow

To date, Shutterfly has sold 400 million prints and is storing at least 1 billion images for its customers.

Sales have increased 670 percent in the last five years to nearly $100 million, but profits still depend largely on the all-important year-end holiday season. The company's reputation for quality and responsive service has helped it maintain an enviably high customer-retention rate. For example, it originally operated one printing facility—in Hayward, California—and then added a second printing facility in Charlotte, North Carolina. Having facilities on both coasts means that customers receive their orders one day faster than before.

More innovations are ahead as Shutterfly's marketers act on their insights about the strong emotions that photos evoke. "People have an intrinsic desire for social expression: to capture and share their experiences, to relive special moments, and to communicate their memories," the CEO notes. A Shutterfly senior vice president adds, "Prints are great, and that is one way to tell a story. But there is another way—books, collages, and other products. You will see a lot more of that. That's the area where we are proud to have put up the flag and to be a leader."[46]

Questions for Discussion

1. What is Shutterfly doing to manage the marketing challenges of heterogeneity?
2. How has Shutterfly used marketing to draw customers through the product adoption process?
3. What has Shutterfly done to add supplemental features as well as symbolic and experiential benefits to its offerings?
4. Why would Shutterfly negotiate to license Nickelodeon characters for personalized photo products?

part 6

Distribution Decisions

CHAPTERS

14 Marketing Channels and Supply-Chain Management

15 Retailing, Direct Marketing, and Wholesaling

Developing products that satisfy customers is important, but it is not enough to guarantee successful marketing strategies. Products must also be available in adequate quantities in accessible locations at the times when customers desire them. Part 6 deals with the distribution of products and the marketing channels and institutions that help to make products available. **Chapter 14** discusses supply-chain management, marketing channels, and the decisions and activities associated with the physical distribution of products, such as order processing, materials handling, warehousing, inventory management, and transportation. **Chapter 15** explores retailing, and wholesaling, including types of retailers and wholesalers, direct marketing and selling, and strategic retailing issues.

14 Marketing Channels and Supply-Chain Management

LEARNING objectives

1. To describe the foundations of supply-chain management

2. To explore the role and significance of marketing channels and supply chains

3. To identify types of marketing channels

4. To understand factors that influence marketing channel selection

5. To identify the intensity of market coverage

6. To examine strategic issues in marketing channels, including leadership, cooperation, and conflict

7. To examine physical distribution as a part of supply-chain management

8. To explore legal issues in channel management

Using Rail to Take French Fries Back to the Future

entrepreneurs IN ACTION

When you order McDonald's french fries to go with your burger, do you ever think about how the fries got there? All goods must be moved from the point of production to the final point of consumption. To assemble all the supplies needed to operate a restaurant and satisfy its customers, many transportation activities are outsourced to the most efficient operators. Planning an efficient physical distribution system is crucial to developing an effective marketing strategy because it can decrease costs and increase value. One example of using transportation to reduce costs comes from Martin-Brower Company, a food distributor in Manassas, Virginia. Martin-Brower operates a food distribution network for 600 McDonald's restaurants in the mid-Atlantic region. The company operates 14 locations in the United States and Canada and employs 190 people at its Manassas facility, which operates around the clock.

Martin-Brower had been shipping all of its frozen potato products from Manitoba, Canada, to its Virginia location by truck. Facing escalating transportation costs, the company loading docks were always backed up because so many trucks were waiting to unload. Martin-Brower decided to go back to the future by shifting 100 percent of the company's frozen potato products to rail transportation. Converting to rail would alleviate significant congestion at the company docks, while decreasing transportation costs. At first not many rail companies thought it was possible to ship potatoes on refrigerated rail cars from Canada to Virginia. Cryo-Trans, a logistics and transportation provider, offered a solution. This company converted all shipments of Martin-Brower's frozen potatoes to rail transportation, saving the company millions in annual transportation costs. The task was challenging because at the time few U.S. or Canadian railroads offered refrigerated service. Cryo-Trans, which builds and leases mechanically refrigerated rail cars, secured support from rail carriers Canadian Pacific Railway and Norfolk Southern.

Today Martin-Brower receives about two rail cars of potatoes a day and moves pallets of them into a freezer until it is time to ship them to stores. It is especially noteworthy that every rail car leased provides tracking capabilities, making Martin-Brower's inventory visible during the entire shipping process so the company can carefully observe the product moving through the system. Now refrigerated rail shipping is almost seamless for both suppliers and customers. Today Martin-Brower is one of the few companies to ship 100 percent of frozen products through refrigerated rail service.[1]

Decisions like those made by Martin-Brower relate to the **distribution** component of the marketing mix, which focuses on the decisions and activities involved in making products available to customers when and where they want to purchase them. Choosing which channels of distribution to use is a major decision in the development of marketing strategies.

In this chapter, we focus on marketing channels and supply-chain management. First, we explore the concept of the supply chain and its various activities. Second, we elaborate on marketing channels and the need for intermediaries and then analyze the primary functions they perform. Next, we outline the types and characteristics of marketing channels, discuss how they are selected, and explore how marketers determine the appropriate intensity of market coverage for a product. We examine the strategic channel issues of leadership, cooperation, and conflict. We also look at the role of physical distribution within the supply chain, including its objectives and basic functions. Finally, we look at several legal issues that affect channel management.

distribution The decisions and activities that make products available to customers when and where they want to purchase them

Foundations of the Supply Chain

L O 1 To describe the foundations of supply-chain management

supply chain All the activities associated with the flow and transformation of products from raw materials through to the end customer

operations management The total set of managerial activities used by an organization to transform resource inputs into products

logistics management Planning, implementing, and controlling the efficient and effective flow and storage of products and information from the point of origin to consumption to meet customers' needs and wants

supply management In its broadest form, refers to the processes that enable the progress of value from raw material to final customer and back to redesign and final disposition

supply-chain management A set of approaches used to integrate the functions of operations management, logistics management, supply management, and marketing channel management so products are produced and distributed in the right quantities, to the right locations, and at the right time

An important function of distribution is the joint effort of all involved organizations to be part of creating an effective **supply chain,** which refers to all the activities associated with the flow and transformation of products from raw materials through to the end customer. This results in a total distribution system that involves firms that are both "upstream" in the supply chain (e.g., suppliers) and "downstream" (e.g., wholesalers, retailers) to serve customers and generate competitive advantage. Historically, marketing focused on only certain downstream activities of supply chains, but today marketing professionals are recognizing that important marketplace advantages can be secured by effectively integrating important activities in the supply chain. These include operations, logistics, sourcing, and marketing channels. Integrating these activities requires marketing managers to work with their counterparts in operations management, logistics management, and supply management.[2] **Operations management** is the total set of managerial activities used by an organization to transform resource inputs into products.[3] **Logistics management** involves planning, implementing, and controlling the efficient and effective flow and storage of products and information from the point of origin to consumption to meet customers' needs and wants. **Supply management** (e.g., purchasing, procurement, sourcing) in its broadest form refers to the processes that enable the progress of value from raw material to final customer and back to redesign and final disposition.

Supply-chain management (SCM) is therefore a set of approaches used to integrate the functions of operations management, logistics management, supply management, and marketing channel management so products are produced and distributed in the right quantities, to the right locations, and at the right time. It includes activities such as manufacturing, research, sales, advertising, shipping, and most of all, cooperating and understanding of tradeoffs throughout the whole chain to achieve optimal levels of efficiency and service. Table 14.1 outlines the key tasks involved in supply-chain management. It also includes suppliers of raw materials and other components to make goods and services, logistics and transportation firms, communication firms, and other firms that indirectly take part in marketing exchanges. Thus, the supply chain includes all entities that facilitate product distribution and benefit from cooperative efforts. Consider that Intel, the computer chip maker, spends $3 billion to build a new semiconductor facility, and it loses $1 million a day if an assembly line goes down due to system failures or part shortages. Consequently, Intel requires its equipment suppliers to respond to failures within 15 minutes.[4] Worldwide spending on supply-chain management systems is more than $22 billion.[5]

Technology has improved supply-chain management capabilities on a global basis. Information technology in particular has created an almost seamless distribution process for matching inventory needs to manufacturer requirements in the

table 14.1	KEY TASKS IN SUPPLY-CHAIN MANAGEMENT
Operations management	Organizational and systemwide coordination of operations and partnerships to meet customers' product needs
Supply management	Sourcing of necessary resources, products, and services from suppliers to support all supply-chain members
Logistics management	All activities designed to move the product through the marketing channel to the end user, including warehousing and inventory management
Channel management	All activities related to selling, service, and the development of long-term customer relationships

upstream portion of the supply chain and to customers' requirements in the downstream portion of the chain. With integrated information sharing among chain members, costs can be reduced, service can be improved, and increased value can be provided to the end customer. Indeed, information is crucial in operating supply chains efficiently and effectively.

As demand for innovative goods and services has escalated in recent years, marketers have had to increase their flexibility and responsiveness to develop new products and modify existing ones to meet the ever-changing needs of customers. Suppliers now provide material and service inputs to meet customer needs in the upstream portion of the supply chain. Customers are increasingly a knowledge source in developing the right product in the downstream portion of the supply chain. This means that the entire supply chain is critically important in ensuring that customers get the products when, where, and how they want them.

Firms must therefore be involved in the management of their own supply chains in partnership with the network of upstream and downstream organizations in the supply chain. Upstream firms provide direct or indirect input to make the product. Downstream firms are responsible for delivery of the product and after-market services to the end customers. The management of the upstream and downstream in the supply-chain activities is what is involved in managing supply chains.

Effective supply-chain management is closely linked to a marketing orientation. All functional areas of business (marketing, management, production, finance, and information systems) are involved in executing a customer orientation and supply-chain

**Technology Facilitates
Supply-Chain Management**

Technology-based tools help supply-chain managers improve efficiency and effectiveness.

management. Both of these activities overlap with operations management, logistics management, and supply management. If a firm has established a marketing strategy based on continuous customer-focused leadership, then supply-chain management will be driven by cooperation and strategic coordination to ensure customer satisfaction. Managers should recognize that supply-chain management is critical to fulfilling customer requirements and requires coordination with all areas of the business. This logical association between marketing orientation and supply-chain management should lead to increased firm performance.[6]

The Role of Marketing Channels in Supply Chains

LO 2 To explore the role and significance of marketing channels and supply chains

A **marketing channel** (also called a *channel of distribution* or *distribution channel*) is a group of individuals and organizations that direct the flow of products from producers to customers within the supply chain. The major role of marketing channels—in concert with operations management, logistics management, and supply management—is to make products available at the right time at the right place in the right quantities. Providing customer satisfaction should be the driving force behind marketing channel decisions. Buyers' needs and behavior are therefore important concerns of channel members.

Some marketing channels are direct, meaning that the product goes directly from the producer to the customer. For example, when a customer orders food online from Omaha Steaks (**www.omahasteaks.com**), the product is sent from the manufacturer to the customer. Most channels, however, have one or more **marketing intermediaries** that link producers to other intermediaries or to ultimate consumers through contractual arrangements or through the purchase and reselling of products. Marketing intermediaries perform the activities described in Table 14.2. They also play key roles in customer relationship management, not only through their distribution activities but also by maintaining databases and information systems to help all members of the marketing channel maintain effective customer relationships. For example, eBay serves as a marketing intermediary between Internet sellers and buyers. eBay not only provides a forum for these exchanges but also helps facilitate relationships among eBay channel members and eases payment issues through its PayPal subsidiary.

marketing channel A group of individuals and organizations that direct the flow of products from producers to customers within the supply chain

marketing intermediaries Middlemen that link producers to other intermediaries or ultimate consumers through contractual arrangements or through the purchase and resale of products

table 14.2 MARKETING CHANNEL ACTIVITIES PERFORMED BY INTERMEDIARIES

Marketing Activities	Sample Activities
Marketing information	Analyze sales data and other information in databases and information systems. Perform or commission marketing research.
Marketing management	Establish strategic and tactical plans for developing customer relationships and organizational productivity.
Facilitating exchanges	Choose product assortments that match the needs of customers. Cooperate with channel members to develop partnerships.
Promotion	Set promotional objectives. Coordinate advertising, personal selling, sales promotion, publicity, and packaging.
Price	Establish pricing policies and terms of sales.
Physical distribution	Manage transportation, warehousing, materials handling, inventory control, and communication.

Wholesalers and retailers are examples of intermediaries. Wholesalers buy and resell products to other wholesalers, to retailers, and to industrial customers. Retailers purchase products and resell them to the end consumers. For example, your local supermarket probably purchased the Tylenol or Advil on its shelves from a wholesaler, which purchased that pain medicine, along with other over-the-counter and prescription drugs, from manufacturers such as McNeil Consumer Labs and Whitehall-Robins. Chapter 15 discusses the functions of wholesalers and retailers in marketing channels in greater detail.

Supply chains start with the customer and require the cooperation of channel members to satisfy customer requirements. All members should focus on cooperation to reduce the costs of all channel members and thereby improve profits. When the buyer, the seller, marketing intermediaries, and facilitating agencies work together, the cooperative relationship results in compromise and adjustments that meet customers' needs regarding delivery, scheduling, packaging, or other requirements.

Each supply-chain member requires information from other channel members. For example, suppliers need order and forecast information from the manufacturer; they also may need availability information from their own suppliers. Customer relationship management (CRM) systems exploit the information from supply-chain partners' information systems to help all channel members make marketing strategy decisions that develop and sustain desirable customer relationships. Thus, managing relationships with supply-chain partners is crucial to satisfying customers. CRM is gaining popularity, with companies such as Hewlett-Packard and Amazon.com spending large sums of money on implementation and support for data mining and CRM analytical applications.

The Significance of Marketing Channels

Although marketing channel decisions do not have to precede other marketing decisions, they are a powerful influence on the rest of the marketing mix (i.e., product, promotion, and pricing). Channel decisions are critical because they determine a product's market presence and buyers' accessibility to the product. Without effective marketing channel operations, even the best goods and services will not be successful. Consider that small businesses are more likely to purchase computers from chain specialty stores such as Best Buy and Office Depot, putting computer companies without distribution through these outlets at a disadvantage. In fact, even Dell—which pioneered the direct-sales model in the computer industry—is now selling its computers at Best Buy. The option of buying Dell systems directly from Dell or in retail stores such as Best Buy means that customers can purchase what they need when and where they want while also allowing customers to "test drive" a computer system of their choice.

Marketing channel decisions have additional strategic significance because they generally entail long-term commitments among a variety of firms (e.g., suppliers, logistics providers, and operations firms). It is usually easier to change prices or promotional strategies than to change marketing channels. Marketing channels also serve many functions, including creating utility and facilitating exchange efficiencies. Although some of these functions may be performed by a single channel member, most functions are accomplished through both independent and joint efforts of channel members.

Marketing Channels Create Utility. Marketing channels create four types of utility: time, place, possession, and form. *Time utility* is having products available when the customer wants them. *Place utility* is created by making products available in locations where customers wish to purchase them. *Possession utility* means that the customer has access to the

Facilitating and Creating Utility

Organizations like Lynden provide transportation solutions for customers.

LYNDEN

When you need to talk to a freight...

Expert!

LYNDEN INTERNATIONAL

" When you need assistance with your shipping, call a freight expert at Lynden. Whether you need to find the fastest or the least expensive way to move a shipment, a Lynden freight expert can assist you with finding out all your options. "

www.shiplynden.com
1-888-596-3361

The Lynden Family of Companies **L**
Innovative Transportation Solutions

product to use or to store for future use. Possession utility can occur through ownership or through arrangements that give the customer the right to use the product, such as a lease or rental agreement. Channel members sometimes create *form utility* by assembling, preparing, or otherwise refining the product to suit individual customer needs.

Marketing Channels Facilitate Exchange Efficiencies. Marketing intermediaries can reduce the costs of exchanges by performing certain services or functions efficiently. Even if producers and buyers are located in the same city, there are costs associated with exchanges. As Figure 14.1 shows, when four buyers seek products from four producers, 16 transactions are possible. If one intermediary serves both producers and buyers, the number of transactions can be reduced to 8. Intermediaries are specialists in facilitating exchanges. They provide valuable assistance because of their access to and control over important resources used in the proper functioning of marketing channels.

Nevertheless, the press, consumers, public officials, and even other marketers freely criticize intermediaries, especially wholesalers. Critics accuse wholesalers of being inefficient and parasitic. Buyers often wish to make the distribution channel as short as possible, assuming the fewer the intermediaries, the lower the price will be.

Critics who suggest that eliminating wholesalers would lower customer prices fail to recognize that this would not eliminate the need for the services the wholesalers provide. Although wholesalers can be eliminated, their functions cannot. Other channel members would have to perform those functions, and customers still would have to pay for them. In addition, all producers would have to deal directly with retailers or customers, meaning that every producer would have to keep voluminous records and hire enough personnel to deal with a multitude of customers. Customers might end up paying a great deal more for products because prices would reflect the costs of less-efficient channel members.

figure 14.1

EFFICIENCY IN EXCHANGES PROVIDED BY AN INTERMEDIARY

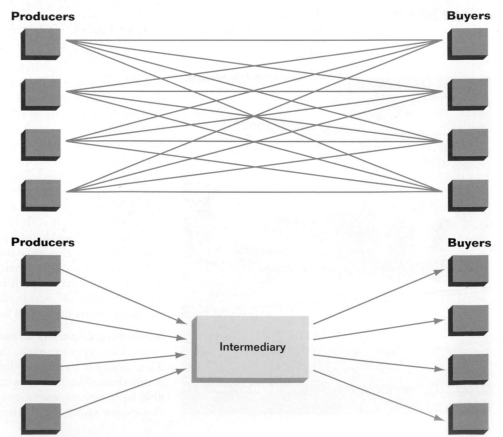

Because suggestions to eliminate wholesalers come from both ends of the marketing channel, wholesalers must be careful to perform only those marketing activities that are truly desired. To survive, they must be more efficient and more customer focused than other marketing institutions. Indeed, research suggests that lower wholesale prices may result in higher sales volume when combined with low retailing costs at discount firms such as Wal-Mart.[7]

Types of Marketing Channels

LO 3 To identify types of marketing channels

Because marketing channels that are appropriate for one product may be less suitable for others, many different distribution paths have been developed. The various marketing channels can be classified generally as channels for consumer products and channels for business products.

Channels for Consumer Products.   Figure 14.2 illustrates several channels used in the distribution of consumer products. Channel A depicts the direct movement of products from producer to consumers. For example, the legal advice given by attorneys moves through channel A. Producers that sell products directly from their factories to end users use direct marketing channels, as do companies that sell their own products via the Internet, such as Omaha Steaks. Direct marketing via the Internet has become a critically important part of some companies' distribution strategies, often as a complement to their products being sold in traditional retail stores. Faced with the strategic choice of going directly to the customer or using intermediaries, a firm must evaluate the benefits of going direct versus the transaction costs involved in using intermediaries.

Channel B, which moves goods from the producer to a retailer and then to customers, is a frequent choice of large retailers because it allows them to buy in quantity from manufacturers. Retailers such as Kmart and Wal-Mart sell clothing, stereos, and many other items purchased directly from producers. New automobiles and new college textbooks are also sold through this type of marketing channel. Primarily nonstore retailers, such as L.L. Bean and J. Crew, also use this type of channel.

Channel C represents a long-standing distribution channel, especially for consumer products. It takes goods from the producer to a wholesaler, then to a retailer, and finally to consumers. It is a practical option for producers that sell to hundreds of thousands of customers through thousands of retailers. Consider the number of retailers marketing Wrigley's chewing gum. It would be extremely difficult, if not

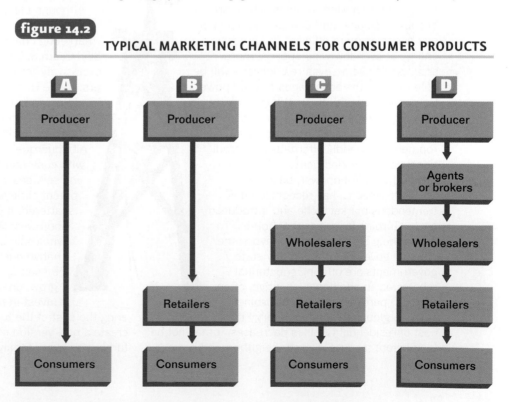

figure 14.2

TYPICAL MARKETING CHANNELS FOR CONSUMER PRODUCTS

impossible, for Wrigley to deal directly with each retailer that sells its brand of gum. Manufacturers of tobacco products, some home appliances, hardware, and many convenience goods sell their products to wholesalers, which then sell to retailers, which in turn do business with individual consumers.

Channel D, through which goods pass from producer to agents to wholesalers to retailers and then to consumers, is used frequently for products intended for mass distribution, such as processed foods. For example, to place its cracker line in specific retail outlets, a food processor may hire an agent (or a food broker) to sell the crackers to wholesalers. Wholesalers then sell the crackers to supermarkets, vending machine operators, and other retail outlets.

Contrary to popular opinion, a long channel may be the most efficient distribution channel for some consumer goods. When several channel intermediaries perform specialized functions, costs may be lower than when one channel member tries to perform them all. In essence, this logic is similar to outsourcing part of the production to firms in low-cost countries. For the marketing channel, it means that firms

green MARKETING

Wind Power Home Edition

Marketing channels for some products can gain incredible efficiency if the source of production can be at the point of consumption. One such case is electricity that is generated from one's own wind turbines, which are becoming smaller and cheaper. As technology becomes more efficient at harnessing energy at even low wind speeds, more small-scale users—even residences—will be able to enjoy the advantages of wind power. Companies around the world are already jumping on the renewable energy bandwagon, as consumers are demanding environmentally friendly alternatives to traditional coal-fired electricity.

Southwest Windpower, based in Flagstaff, Arizona, has recognized this tremendous market niche and introduced a wind turbine for residential homes. To further help Southwest's endeavors, the national government and many state governments are offering substantial rebates as an additional incentive, often up to 30 percent of the wind turbines' cost. As global demand for energy increases and the cost of residential turbines decreases, it may not be long before a house in every neighborhood has one.

The Skystream 3.7 is the newest creation from Southwest to hit the markets. Ranging between 34 and 70 feet tall with 12-foot rotors, the Skystream 3.7 can generate enough electricity to power a house, and any extra electricity produced can, in some areas, be sold back to power companies. The Skystream 3.7 is designed for very low winds; it begins producing power in an 8-mph breeze and achieves maximum output at 23 mph. Because costs per turbine range from $12,000 to $15,000, the current market for the product is not the average consumer. However, depending on installation costs, wind-speed average, rebates, and local electricity costs, the Skystream 3.7 can pay for itself in as quickly as five years.

Although electricity may thus be supplied at the point of consumption, consumers find a marketing channel or supply chain to obtain a Skystream 3.7. Southwest Windpower sells exclusively through its global network of dealers. In the United States, for example, Conergy and Sunwise are regional wholesalers who make the 3.7 turbines available to local dealers. Local dealers such as Affordable Solar in Albuquerque, New Mexico, work directly with customers, selling the units and offering services such as delivery. Because potential buyers of wind turbines are so scattered, it is much more efficient for Southwest Windpower to depend on wholesalers and dealers to sell its alternative energy products. If demand for these residential turbines continues to grow, one or more companies may invest in mass production, further lowering the cost of the turbine. This in turn could create a new version of Henry Ford's vision: a wind turbine for every family.[a]

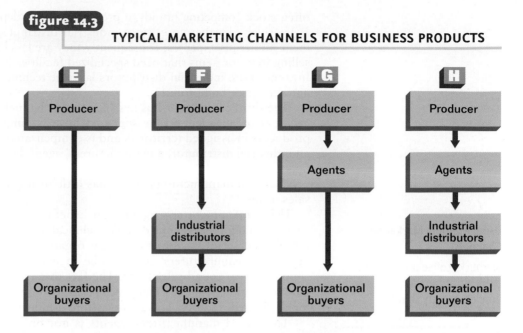

figure 14.3

TYPICAL MARKETING CHANNELS FOR BUSINESS PRODUCTS

that specialize in certain elements of producing a product or moving it through the channel are more effective and efficient at performing specialized tasks than the manufacturer. This results in cost efficiencies and added value to customers.

Channels for Business Products. Figure 14.3 shows four of the most common channels for business products. As with consumer products, manufacturers of business products sometimes work with more than one level of wholesalers.

Channel E illustrates the direct channel for business products. In contrast to consumer goods, more than half of all business products, especially expensive equipment, are sold through direct channels. Business customers prefer to communicate directly with producers, especially when expensive or technically complex products are involved. For example, buyers prefer to purchase expensive and highly complex SQL server computers directly from Dell. Similarly, Intel has established direct marketing channels for selling its microprocessor chips to computer manufacturers. In these circumstances, a customer wants the technical assistance and personal assurances that only a producer can provide.

In channel F, an industrial distributor facilitates exchanges between the producer and the customer. An **industrial distributor** is an independent business that takes title to products and carries inventories. Industrial distributors usually sell standardized items such as maintenance supplies, production tools, and small operating equipment. Some industrial distributors carry a wide variety of product lines. W.W. Grainger, for example, sells more than $6 billion of power and hand tools, pumps, janitorial supplies, and many other products to producer, government, and institutional markets around the world.[8] Other industrial distributors specialize in one or a small number of lines. Industrial distributors are carrying an increasing percentage of business products. Overall, these distributors can be most effectively used when a product has broad market appeal, is easily stocked and serviced, is sold in small quantities, and is needed on demand to avoid high losses.

Industrial distributors offer sellers several advantages. They can perform the needed selling activities in local markets at a relatively low cost to a manufacturer and reduce a producer's financial burden by providing customers with credit services. Also, because industrial distributors usually maintain close relationships with their customers, they are aware of local needs and can pass on market information to producers. By holding adequate inventories in their local markets, industrial distributors reduce producers' capital requirements.

Using industrial distributors has several disadvantages, however. Industrial distributors may be difficult to control since they are independent firms. Because they

industrial distributor An independent business organization that takes title to industrial products and carries inventories

often stock competing brands, a producer cannot depend on them to sell its brand aggressively. Furthermore, since industrial distributors maintain inventories, they incur numerous expenses; consequently they are less likely to handle bulky or slow-selling items or items that need specialized facilities or extraordinary selling efforts. In some cases, industrial distributors lack the technical knowledge necessary to sell and service certain products.

The third channel for business products, channel G, employs a *manufacturers' agent,* an independent businessperson who sells complementary products of several producers in assigned territories and is compensated through commissions. Unlike an industrial distributor, a manufacturers' agent does not acquire title to the products and usually does not take possession. Acting as a salesperson on behalf of the producers, a manufacturers' agent has little or no latitude in negotiating prices or sales terms.

Using manufacturers' agents can benefit an organizational marketer. These agents usually possess considerable technical and market information and have an established set of customers. For an organizational seller with highly seasonal demand, a manufacturers' agent can be an asset because the seller does not have to support a year-round sales force. The fact that manufacturers' agents are typically paid on a commission basis may also be an economical alternative for a firm that has highly limited resources and cannot afford a full-time sales force.

The use of manufacturers' agents is not problem free. Even though straight commissions may be more financially viable, the seller may have little control over manufacturers' agents. Because of the compensation method, manufacturers' agents generally prefer to concentrate on their larger accounts. They are often reluctant to spend time following up sales, putting forth special selling efforts, or providing sellers with market information when such activities reduce the amount of productive selling time. Because they rarely maintain inventories, manufacturers' agents have a limited ability to provide customers with parts or repair services quickly.

Finally, channel H includes both a manufacturers' agent and an industrial distributor. This channel may be appropriate when the producer wishes to cover a large geographic area but maintains no sales force due to highly seasonal demand or because it cannot afford a sales force. This type of channel can also be useful for a business marketer that wants to enter a new geographic market without expanding its existing sales force.

Multiple Marketing Channels and Channel Alliances.

To reach diverse target markets, manufacturers may use several marketing channels simultaneously, with each channel involving a different group of intermediaries. In particular, a manufacturer often uses multiple channels when the same

Using Multiple Marketing Channels

Starbucks coffee products are available at company stores and in select grocery stores.

product is directed to both consumers and business customers. For example, when Del Monte markets ketchup for household use, the product is sold to supermarkets through grocery wholesalers or, in some cases, directly to retailers, whereas ketchup being sold to restaurants or institutions follows a different distribution channel.

In some instances, a producer may prefer **dual distribution,** the use of two or more marketing channels to distribute the same products to the same target market. For example, Kellogg sells its cereals directly to large retail grocery chains (channel B) and to food wholesalers that, in turn, sell them to retailers (channel C). Another example of dual distribution is a firm that sells products through retail outlets and its own mail-order catalog or website. Dual distribution, however, can cause dissatisfaction among wholesalers and smaller retailers when they must compete with large retail grocery chains that make direct purchases from manufacturers such as Kellogg. Another example is State Farm Insurance, which has decided to maintain its "old" business model of using agents as the primary vehicle for customer interaction, potentially losing sales to other insurance companies by not offering insurance policies online as others, such as Progressive, do.

A **strategic channel alliance** exists when the products of one organization are distributed through the marketing channels of another. The products of the two firms are often similar with respect to target markets or uses, but they are not direct competitors. A brand of bottled water might be distributed through a marketing channel for soft drinks, or a domestic cereal producer might form a strategic channel alliance with a European food processor. Ocean Spray and PepsiCo formed such an alliance in which Pepsi manufactured, bottled, and distributed single-serve cranberry juice products under the Ocean Spray name.[9] Such alliances can provide benefits for both the organization that owns the marketing channel and the company whose brand is being distributed through the channel.

Selecting Marketing Channels

Selecting appropriate marketing channels is important. Although the process varies across organizations, channel selection decisions usually are significantly affected by one or more of the following factors: customer characteristics, product attributes, type of organization, competition, marketing environmental forces, and characteristics of intermediaries (see Figure 14.4).

Customer Characteristics. Marketing managers must consider the characteristics of target-market members in channel selection. As we have already seen, the channels that are appropriate for consumers are different from those for business customers. A different marketing channel will be required for business customers purchasing carpet for commercial buildings compared with consumers purchasing carpet for their homes. Business customers often prefer to deal directly with producers (or very knowledgeable channel intermediaries such as industrial distributors), especially for highly technical or expensive products such as mainframe computers, jet airplanes, and large mining machines. Moreover, business customers are more likely to buy complex products that require strict specifications and technical assistance or to buy in considerable quantities.

Consumers, on the other hand, generally buy limited quantities of a product, purchase from retailers, and often do not mind limited customer service. Additionally, when customers are concentrated in a small geographic area, a more direct channel may be ideal, but when many customers are spread across an entire state or nation, distribution through multiple intermediaries is likely to be more efficient.

Product Attributes. The attributes of the product can have a strong influence on the choice of marketing channels. Marketers of complex and expensive products such as automobiles likely will employ short channels, as will marketers of perishable products such as dairy and produce. Less-expensive, more standardized products such as soft drinks and canned goods can employ longer channels with many intermediaries. In addition, channel decisions may be affected by a product's sturdiness: fragile products that require special handling are more likely to be distributed through shorter channels to minimize the risk of damage. Firms

L O 4 To understand factors that influence marketing channel selection

dual distribution The use of two or more marketing channels to distribute the same products to the same target market

strategic channel alliance An agreement whereby the products of one organization are distributed through the marketing channels of another

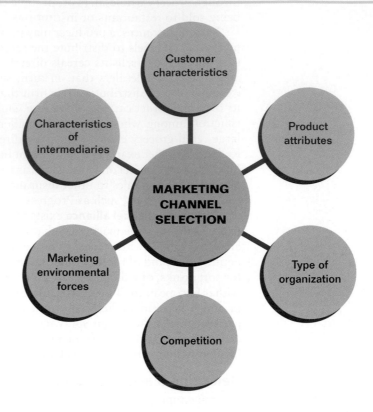

figure 14.4

SELECTING MARKETING CHANNELS

that desire to convey an exclusive image for their products may wish to limit the number of outlets available.

Type of Organization. Clearly, the characteristics of the organization will have a great impact on the distribution channels chosen. Owing to their sheer size, larger firms may be better able to negotiate better deals with vendors or other channel members. Compared with small firms, they may be in better positions to have more distribution centers, which may reduce delivery times to customers. A smaller regional company that uses regional or local channel members may be in a position to better serve customers in that region compared with a larger, less-flexible organization. Compared with smaller organizations, large companies can use an extensive product mix as a competitive tool. Smaller firms may not have the resources to develop their own sales force, to ship their products long distances, to store or own products, or to extend credit. In such cases, they may have to include other channel members that have the resources to provide these services to customers efficiently and cost effectively.

Competition. Competition is another important factor for supply-chain managers to consider. The success or failure of a competitor's marketing channel may encourage or dissuade an organization from considering a similar approach. A firm also may be forced to adopt a similar strategy to remain competitive. In a

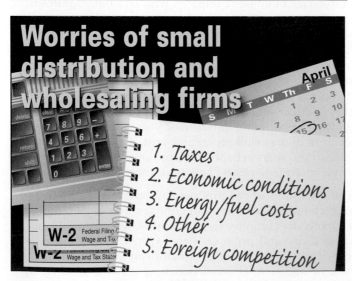

Worries of small distribution and wholesaling firms

1. Taxes
2. Economic conditions
3. Energy/fuel costs
4. Other
5. Foreign competition

Source: Small Business Research Board Study, in "Top 5 Business Concerns," *Inbound Logistics,* Sept. 2007, p. 20.

RESPONSIBLE marketing?

Duke Power Tries to Come Clean

ISSUE: Reducing carbons or greenwashing?

Duke Power is the third-largest corporate emitter of carbon dioxide (after American Electric Power and Southern Companies) in the United States. Utility companies are good examples of vertically integrated supply chains and marketing channels because they control most production and deliver energy to final customers. Therefore, utility companies have the potential to improve their environmental impacts through all levels of the marketing channel. Charlotte, North Carolina–based Duke Power is facing the possibility that they may have to start paying for CO_2 emissions if government regulators put a tax on greenhouse gases. Therefore, Duke is proactively going green with 500,000 solar panels on rooftops in a five-state territory. The utility is also installing a $1 billion communication network to optimize the flow of electricity through the grid. Duke built low-cost coal plants in the 1960s and 1970s when cheap, secure power supplies were the main concern. With current concerns about global warming, the firm has to reduce some of the 100,000 tons of CO_2 (27 million tons of carbon) in its supply chain. The firm is looking to nuclear plants and a Save-A-Watt program to encourage customer to use less energy. The company believes that conservation is the best and cheapest zero-emission power plant. Duke claims that not even plastering wind turbines all across the outer banks of North Carolina would produce enough electricity for the growing needs of customers in the Carolinas.

Yet Duke still has its hands full defending its emissions-reduction plan to environmentalists such as the Southern Alliance for Clean Energy. Environmentalists are concerned that the company is merely greenwashing, or "creating a positive association with environmental issues for an unsustainable product, service, or practice." Critics also raise questions about Duke's Save-A-Watt program, which is designed as an alternative revenue stream for the company. Duke will earn money for the power customers save by proportionately raising rates for the power they use. Even while preaching conservation as a solution, Duke plans to invest $23 billion in the next five years to build new coal and gas plants.[b]

highly competitive market, it is important for a company to keep its costs low so it can underprice its competitors if necessary.

Environmental Forces. Environmental forces also can play a role in channel selection. Adverse economic conditions might force an organization to use a low-cost channel, even though customer satisfaction is reduced. In contrast, a booming economy might allow a company to choose a channel that previously had been too costly to consider. The introduction of new technology might cause an organization to add or modify its channel strategy. For instance, as the Internet became a powerful marketing communication tool, many companies were forced to go online to remain competitive. Government regulations also can affect channel selection. As new labor and environmental regulations are passed, an organization may be forced to modify its existing distribution channel structure. Firms may choose to make the changes before regulations are passed to appear compliant or to avoid legal issues. Governmental regulations also can include trade agreements with other countries that complicate the supply chain.

Characteristics of Intermediaries. When an organization believes that a current intermediary is not promoting the organization's products adequately, it may reconsider its channel choices. In these instances the company may choose another channel member to handle its products, or it may choose to eliminate intermediaries altogether and perform the eliminated intermediaries' functions itself. Alternatively, an existing intermediary may not offer an appropriate mix of services, forcing an organization to switch to another intermediary.

Intensity of Market Coverage

LO 5 To identify the intensity of market coverage

In addition to deciding which marketing channels to use to distribute a product, marketers must determine the intensity of coverage that a product should get—that is, the number and kinds of outlets in which it will be sold. This decision depends on the characteristics of the product and the target market. To achieve the desired intensity of market coverage, distribution must correspond to behavior patterns of buyers. In Chapter 10, we divided consumer products into four categories—convenience products, shopping products, specialty products, and unsought products—according to how consumers make purchases. In considering products for purchase, consumers take into account replacement rate, product adjustment (services), duration of consumption, time required to find the product, and similar factors.[10] These variables directly affect the intensity of market coverage. As shown in Figure 14.5, the three major levels of market coverage are intensive, selective, and exclusive distribution.

figure 14.5

INTENSITY OF MARKET COVERAGE

Intensive
Convenience products such as Coke, Pringles, and Duracell batteries

Available in many retail outlets

Selective
Shopping products such as iPods, televisions, DVD players, and shoes

Available in some outlets

Exclusive
Specialty products such as haute couture, Mont Blanc pens, BMWs, and Fendi handbags

Available in very few outlets

---

intensive distribution
Using all available outlets to distribute a product

Intensive Distribution

Fig Newtons are widely available and distributed through intensive distribution.

© 2007 Kraft Foods

Packed with real fruit taste, it's...
The cookie that thinks it's a fruit.

Fig Newtons

Intensive Distribution

Intensive distribution uses all available outlets for distributing a product. Intensive distribution is appropriate for most convenience products such as bread, chewing gum, soft drinks, and newspapers. Convenience products have a high replacement rate, require almost no service, and are often bought based on price cues. To meet these demands, intensive distribution is necessary, and multiple channels may be used to sell through all possible outlets. For example, soft drinks, snacks, laundry detergent, and pain relievers are available at convenience stores, service stations, supermarkets, discount stores, and other types of retailers. To consumers, availability means a store is located nearby and minimum time is necessary to search for the product at the store. This ensures that consumers are provided with the greatest speed in obtaining the product, the quality they have come to expect of a certain convenience product, the flexibility to buy the product wherever it is convenient to them, and the lowest cost possible.

Sales may have a direct relationship to product availability. The successful sale of convenience products such as bread and milk at service stations or gasoline at convenience grocery stores illustrates that the availability of these products is more important than the nature of the outlet. Companies such as Procter & Gamble that produce consumer packaged items rely on intensive distribution for many of their products (for example, soaps, detergents, food and juice products, and personal-care products) because consumers want ready availability.

Selective Distribution

Selective distribution uses only some available outlets in an area to distribute a product. Selective distribution is appropriate for shopping products; durable goods such as televisions, stereos, and home computers usually fall into this category. These products are more expensive than convenience goods, and consumers are willing to spend more time visiting several retail outlets to compare prices, designs, styles, and other features.

Selective distribution is desirable when a special effort, such as customer service from a channel member, is important to customers. Shopping products require differentiation at the point of purchase. To motivate retailers to provide adequate pre-sale service, selective distribution and company-owned stores are often used. Many business products are sold on a selective basis to maintain control over the products—for example, in cases where dealers must offer services to buyers such as instructions about how to apply herbicides safely or the option to have the dealer apply the herbicide. Other examples include the launch of Apple's iPhone, distributed in AT&T and Apple retail stores in the United States, and music sold at Starbucks Coffee locations through selected labels such as Concord Music.

Exclusive Distribution

Exclusive distribution uses only one outlet in a relatively large geographic area. Exclusive distribution is suitable for products purchased infrequently, consumed over a long period of time, or requiring service or information to fit them to buyers' needs. It is also used for expensive, high-quality products, such as Porsche, BMW, and other luxury automobiles. It is not appropriate for convenience products and many shopping products.

Exclusive distribution is often used as an incentive to sellers when only a limited market is available for products. For example, like luxury automobiles, Patek Philippe watches, which may sell for $10,000 or more, are available in only a few select locations. A producer using exclusive distribution generally expects dealers to carry a complete inventory, send personnel for sales and service training, participate in promotional programs, and provide excellent customer service. Some products are appropriate for exclusive distribution when first introduced, but as competitors enter the market and the product moves through its life cycle, other types of market coverage and distribution channels often become necessary. A problem that can arise with exclusive distribution (and selective distribution) is that unauthorized resellers acquire and sell products, violating the agreement between a manufacturer and its exclusive authorized dealers. This has been a problem for Rolex, a manufacturer of luxury watches.

Strategic Issues in Marketing Channels

LO 6 To examine strategic issues in marketing channels, including leadership, cooperation, and conflict

To fulfill the potential of effective supply-chain management and to ensure customer satisfaction, marketing channels require a strategic focus on certain competitive priorities and the development of channel leadership, cooperation, and the management of channel conflict. They may also require consolidation of marketing channels through channel integration.

Competitive Priorities in Marketing Channels

Much evidence exists that supply chains can provide a competitive advantage for many marketers. As mentioned earlier, effective supply-chain management has been linked to a marketing orientation. Because supply-chain decisions cut across all functional areas of the business, it is a competitive priority. Building the most effective and efficient supply chain can sustain a business in a variety of competitive environments.

It is estimated that a significant supply-chain problem can reduce a firm's market value by more than 10 percent. Deloitte Touche Tohmatsu has reported that

selective distribution Using only some available outlets in an area to distribute a product

exclusive distribution Using a single outlet in a fairly large geographic area to distribute a product

YOU'VE NEVER FELT MORE ALIVE.
YOU'VE NEVER FELT MORE INSIGNIFICANT.

AMY ROOKER'S NATURE VALLEY. AMY ROOKER'S NATURE VALLEY BAR.
WHERE'S YOURS?™

THE ENERGY BAR NATURE INTENDED.®
wheresyours.com

Channel Leadership

Nature Valley provides channel leadership in the distribution of its products.

just 7 percent of companies today are managing their supply chains effectively; however, these companies are 73 percent more profitable than other firms. Many well-known firms, including Amazom.com, Dell, FedEx, Toyota, and Wal-Mart, owe much of their success to outmaneuvering rivals with unique supply-chain capabilities.

If supply-chain activities are not integrated, functions exist without coordination. As supply chains integrate functions, the reward is efficiency and effectiveness as well as a holistic view of the supply chain. Goal-driven supply chains, by direction of their firms, focus on the "competitive priorities" of speed, quality, cost, or flexibility as the performance objective. For example, before Dominos got into legal trouble for its 30-minute-or-free promise for pizza deliveries, speed was its main concern. The quality, cost, and the variety of toppings on the pizza were secondary to the time it took to get a hot pizza delivered to the customer's door. Other companies (e.g., Rolls Royce) focus on different competitive priorities, such as delivering top-notch quality products, where neither cost nor speed is an issue. Rolls Royce, however, still stresses certain flexibility in the product customization. Wal-Mart is the poster example of stressing low cost, often at the "cost" of speed, quality, and flexibility. Yet, some firms thrive on being flexible. For example, L.L. Bean provides almost endless flexibility, particularly in return policies. However, very few L.L. Bean stores exist, so customers may receive products at a slower speed than for other competitors. Cost is higher than the industry average, but their products are usually of high quality.

Channel Leadership, Cooperation, and Conflict

Each channel member performs a different role in the distribution system and agrees (implicitly or explicitly) to accept certain rights, responsibilities, rewards, and sanctions for nonconformity. Moreover, each channel member holds certain expectations of other channel members. Retailers, for instance, expect wholesalers to maintain adequate inventories and deliver goods on time. Wholesalers expect retailers to honor payment agreements and keep them informed of inventory needs.

Channel partnerships facilitate effective supply-chain management when partners agree on objectives, policies, and procedures for physical distribution efforts associated with the supplier's products. Such partnerships eliminate redundancies and reassign tasks for maximum systemwide efficiency.

One of the best-known partnerships is that between Wal-Mart and Procter & Gamble. Procter & Gamble locates some of its staff near Wal-Mart's purchasing department in Bentonville, Arkansas, to establish and maintain the supply chain. Sharing information through a cooperative information system, P&G monitors Wal-Mart's inventory and additional data to determine production and distribution plans for its products. The results are increased efficiency, decreased inventory costs, and greater satisfaction for the customers of both companies. In this section we discuss channel member behavior, including leadership, cooperation, and conflict, that marketers must understand to make effective channel decisions.

Channel Leadership. Many marketing channel decisions are determined by give-and-take among channel partners, with the idea that the overall channel ultimately will benefit. Some marketing channels, however, are organized and controlled by a single leader, or **channel captain** (also called *channel leader*). The channel captain may be a producer, wholesaler, or retailer. Channel captains may establish channel policies and coordinate development of the marketing mix. Wal-Mart, for example, dominates the supply chain for its retail stores by virtue of the magnitude of its resources (especially information management) and strong, nationwide customer base. To attain desired objectives, the captain must possess **channel power,** the ability to influence another channel member's goal achievement. The member that becomes the channel captain will accept the responsibilities and exercise the power associated with this role.

When a manufacturer's large-scale production efficiency demands that it increase sales volume, the manufacturer may exercise power by giving channel members financing, business advice, ordering assistance, advertising services, sales and service training, and support materials. For example, U.S. automakers provide these services to retail automobile dealerships. However, these manufacturers also place numerous requirements on their retail dealerships with respect to sales volume, sales and service training, and customer satisfaction.

Retailers may also function as channel captains. With the rise in power of national chain stores and private-brand merchandise, many large retailers such as Wal-Mart are taking a leadership role in the channel. Small retailers too may assume leadership roles when they gain strong customer loyalty in local or regional markets. These retailers control many brands and sometimes replace uncooperative producers. Increasingly, leading retailers are concentrating their buying power with fewer suppliers and, in the process, improving their marketing effectiveness and efficiency. Long-term commitments enable retailers to place smaller and more frequent orders as needed rather than waiting for large-volume discounts or placing huge orders and assuming the risks associated with carrying a larger inventory.

Wholesalers assume channel leadership roles as well, although they were more powerful decades ago, when many manufacturers and retailers were smaller, underfinanced, and widely scattered. Today wholesaler leaders may form voluntary chains with several retailers, which they supply with bulk buying or management services; these chains may also market their own brands. In return, the retailers shift most of their purchasing to the wholesaler leader. The Independent Grocers' Alliance (IGA) is one of the best-known wholesaler leaders in the United States. IGA's power is based on its expertise in advertising, pricing, and purchasing knowledge that it makes available to independent business owners. Other wholesaler leaders help retailers with store layouts, accounting, and inventory control.

Channel Cooperation. Channel cooperation is vital if each member is to gain something from other members. Cooperation enables retailers, wholesalers, suppliers, and logistics providers to speed up inventory replenishment, improve customer service, and cut the costs of bringing products to the consumer.[11] Without cooperation, neither overall channel goals nor individual member goals can be realized. All channel members must recognize that the success of one firm in the channel depends in part on other member firms. Thus, marketing channel members should make a coordinated effort to satisfy market requirements. Channel cooperation leads to greater trust among channel members and improves the overall functioning of the channel. It also leads to more satisfying relationships among channel members.

There are several ways to improve channel cooperation. If a marketing channel is viewed as a unified supply chain competing with other systems, individual members will be less likely to take actions that create disadvantages for other members. Similarly, channel members should agree to direct efforts toward common objectives so channel roles can be structured for maximum marketing effectiveness, which in turn can help members achieve individual objectives. A critical component in cooperation is a precise definition of each channel member's tasks. This provides a basis for reviewing the intermediaries' performance and helps reduce conflicts because each channel member knows exactly what is expected of it.

channel captain The dominant leader of a marketing channel or a supply channel

channel power The ability of one channel member to influence another member's goal achievement

Channel Conflict. Although all channel members work toward the same general goal—distributing products profitably and efficiently—members sometimes may disagree about the best methods for attaining this goal. However, if self-interest creates misunderstanding about role expectations, the end result is frustration and conflict for the whole channel. Consider what happened when the New England–based Hannaford Brothers supermarket chain introduced a new system that rated the nutritional content of every single product on the stores' shelves for the benefit of consumers looking for the healthiest products. Although Hannaford Brothers' executives insisted that they simply wanted to offer confused shoppers more guidance on finding healthful choices, many of its suppliers grumbled when the supermarket gave their products a lower-than-expected rating, especially those that were marketing products as "healthy" but that had significant salt or sugar content.[12] For individual organizations to function together, each channel member must clearly communicate and understand the role expectations. Communication difficulties are a potential form of channel conflict because ineffective communication leads to frustration, misunderstandings, and ill-coordinated strategies, jeopardizing further coordination.

The increased use of multiple channels of distribution, driven partly by new technology, has increased the potential for conflict between manufacturers and intermediaries. For example, Hewlett-Packard makes products available directly to consumers through its website, thereby competing directly with existing distributors and retailers, such as Best Buy and Circuit City. Channel conflicts also arise when intermediaries overemphasize competing products or diversify into product lines traditionally handled by other intermediaries. Sometimes conflict develops because producers strive to increase efficiency by circumventing intermediaries. Such conflict is occurring in marketing channels for computer software. A number of software-only stores are establishing direct relationships with software producers, bypassing wholesale distributors altogether.

When a producer that has traditionally used franchised dealers broadens its retailer base to include other types of retail outlets, considerable conflict can arise. When Goodyear intensified its market coverage by allowing Sears and Discount Tire to market Goodyear tires, its action antagonized 2,500 independent Goodyear dealers.

Although there is no single method for resolving conflict, partnerships can be reestablished if two conditions are met. First, the role of each channel member must be specified. To minimize misunderstanding, all members must be able to expect unambiguous, agreed-on performance levels from one another. Second, members of channel partnerships must institute certain measures of channel coordination, which requires leadership and benevolent exercise of control. To prevent channel conflict from arising, producers or other channel members may provide competing resellers with different brands, allocate markets among resellers, define policies for direct sales to avoid potential conflict over large accounts, negotiate territorial issues among regional distributors, and provide recognition to certain resellers for their importance in distributing to others.

Channel Integration

Channel members can either combine and control most activities or pass them on to another channel member. Channel functions may be transferred between intermediaries and to producers and even to customers. However, a channel member cannot eliminate supply-chain functions; unless buyers themselves perform the functions, they must pay for the labor and resources needed to perform them.

Various channel stages may be combined under the management of a channel captain either horizontally or vertically. Such integration may stabilize supply, reduce costs, and increase coordination of channel members.

Vertical Channel Integration. **Vertical channel integration** combines two or more stages of the channel under one management. This may occur when one member of a marketing channel purchases the operations of another member or simply performs the functions of another member, eliminating the need for that intermediary. For example, Smithfield Foods, a leading U.S. food processor, acquired Premium Standard Farms, Inc., the number two U.S. hog farmer.

vertical channel integration Combining two or more stages of the marketing channel under one management

Although the purchase may trigger antitrust concerns, it reflects a trend among large meat processors to grow and slaughter their own livestock instead of obtaining them from independent farmers.[13]

Unlike conventional channel systems, participants in vertical channel integration coordinate efforts to reach a desired target market. In this more progressive approach to distribution, channel members regard other members as extensions of their own operations. Vertically integrated channels are often more effective against competition because of increased bargaining power and the sharing of information and responsibilities. At one end of a vertically integrated channel, a manufacturer might provide advertising and training assistance, and the retailer at the other end might buy the manufacturer's products in large quantities and actively promote them.

Integration has been successfully institutionalized in marketing channels called **vertical marketing systems (VMSs),** in which a single channel member coordinates or manages channel activities to achieve efficient, low-cost distribution aimed at satisfying target market customers. Vertical integration brings most or all stages of the marketing channel under common control or ownership. The Limited, a retail clothing chain, uses a wholly owned subsidiary, Mast Industries, as its primary supply source. Radio Shack operates as a VMS, encompassing both wholesale and retail functions. Because efforts of individual channel members are combined in a VMS, marketing activities can be coordinated for maximum effectiveness and economy without duplication of services. VMSs are competitive, accounting for a share of retail sales in consumer goods.

Most vertical marketing systems take one of three forms: corporate, administered, or contractual. A *corporate VMS* combines all stages of the marketing channel, from producers to consumers, under a single owner. For example, the Limited established a corporate VMS that operates corporate-owned production facilities and retail stores. Supermarket chains that own food-processing plants and large retailers that purchase wholesaling and production facilities are other examples of corporate VMSs.

In an *administered VMS*, channel members are independent, but a high level of interorganizational management is achieved through informal coordination. Members of an administered VMS, for example, may adopt uniform accounting and ordering procedures and cooperate in promotional activities for the benefit of all partners. Although individual channel members maintain autonomy, as in conventional marketing channels, one channel member (such as a producer or large retailer) dominates the administered VMS so that distribution decisions take the whole system into account. Because of its size and power, Intel exercises a strong influence over distributors and manufacturers in its marketing channels, as do Kellogg (cereal) and Magnavox (televisions and other electronic products).

Under a *contractual VMS*, the most popular type of vertical marketing system, channel members are linked by legal agreements spelling out each member's rights and obligations. Franchise organizations, such as McDonald's and KFC, are contractual VMSs. Other contractual VMSs include wholesaler-sponsored groups, such as IGA (Independent Grocers' Alliance) stores, in which independent retailers band together under the contractual leadership of a wholesaler. Retailer-sponsored cooperatives, which own and operate their own wholesalers, are a third type of contractual VMS.

Horizontal Channel Integration. Combining organizations at the same level of operation under one management constitutes **horizontal channel integration.** An organization may integrate horizontally by merging with other organizations at the same level in the marketing channel. The owner of a dry-cleaning firm, for example, might buy and combine several other existing dry-cleaning establishments. Japan Tobacco, the world's third-largest cigarette maker, acquired Britain's Gallaher Group PLC, which owns several upscale cigarette brands and has a strong presence in Russia and Eastern Europe, for about $14.7 billion. The purchase boosted Japan Tobacco's global market share from 3 to 11 percent.[14] Horizontal integration may enable a firm to generate sufficient sales revenue to integrate vertically as well.

vertical marketing systems (VMSs) A marketing channel managed by a single channel member to achieve efficient, low-cost distribution aimed at satisfying target market customers

horizontal channel integration Combining organizations at the same level of operation under one management

Although horizontal integration permits efficiencies and economies of scale in purchasing, marketing research, advertising, and specialized personnel, it is not always the most effective method of improving distribution. Problems of size often follow, resulting in decreased flexibility, difficulties in coordination, and the need for additional marketing research and large-scale planning. Unless distribution functions for the various units can be performed more efficiently under unified management than under the previously separate managements, horizontal integration will neither reduce costs nor improve the competitive position of the integrating firm.

Physical Distribution in Supply-Chain Management

LO 7 To examine physical distribution as a part of supply-chain management

Physical distribution, also known as *logistics,* refers to the activities used to move products from producers to consumers and other end users. Physical distribution systems must meet the needs of both the supply chain and customers. Distribution activities are thus an important part of supply-chain planning and require the cooperation of all partners.

Within the marketing channel, physical distribution activities may be performed by a producer, a wholesaler, or a retailer, or they may be outsourced. In the context of distribution, **outsourcing** is the contracting of physical distribution tasks to third parties. Most physical distribution activities can be outsourced to third-party firms that have special expertise in areas such as warehousing, transportation, inventory management, and information technology. Some manufacturing firms, for example, outsource delivery services to Penske Truck Leasing, a joint venture between General Electric and Penske Corp. Penske Truck, in turn, has outsourced some of its own activities, including some scheduling, billing, and invoicing services, to employees and contractors in Mexico and India. Outsourcing has saved Penske $15 million and helped the company to improve efficiency and customer service.[15] Cooperative relationships with third-party organizations, such as trucking companies, warehouses, and data-service providers, can help to reduce marketing channel costs and boost service and customer satisfaction for all supply-chain partners. When choosing companies through which to outsource, marketers must be cautious and use efficient firms that help the outsourcing company provide excellent customer service. They need to recognize as well the importance of logistics functions such as warehousing and information technology in reducing physical distribution costs associated with outsourcing.[16]

Planning an efficient physical distribution system is crucial to developing an effective marketing strategy because it can decrease costs and increase customer satisfaction. Speed of delivery, flexibility, and quality of service are often as important to customers as costs. Companies that have the right goods, in the right place, at the right time, in the right quantity, and with the right support services are able to sell more than competitors that do not. Even when the demand for products is unpredictable, suppliers must be able to respond quickly to inventory needs. In such cases, physical distribution costs may be a minor consideration when compared with service, dependability, and timeliness.

Customer relationship management systems exploit the information from supply-chain partners' database systems to help logistics managers identify and root out inefficiencies in the supply chain for the benefit of all marketing channel members—from the producer to the ultimate consumer. Indeed, technology is playing a larger and larger role in physical distribution within marketing channels. It has transformed physical distribution by facilitating just-in-time delivery, precise inventory visibility, and instant shipment tracking capabilities, which help companies to avoid expensive mistakes, reduce costs, and even generate revenues. Information technology brings visibility to the supply chain by allowing all marketing channel members to see precisely where an item is within the supply chain at any time.[17]

Although physical distribution managers try to minimize the costs associated with order processing, inventory management, materials handling, warehousing, and transportation, decreasing the costs in one area often raises them in another. Figure 14.6 shows the percentage of total costs that physical distribution functions represent.

physical distribution Activities used to move products from producers to consumers and other end users

outsourcing The contracting of physical distribution tasks to third parties who do not have managerial authority within the marketing channel

figure 14.6   PROPORTIONAL COST OF EACH PHYSICAL DISTRIBUTION
FUNCTION AS A PERCENTAGE OF TOTAL DISTRIBUTION COSTS

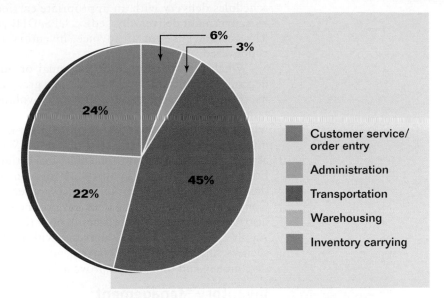

6%
3%
24%
22%
45%

Customer service/
order entry

Administration

Transportation

Warehousing

Inventory carrying

Source: From Davis Database, 2005. Reprinted by permission of Establish Inc./Herbert W. Davis and Company.

A total-cost approach to physical distribution enables managers to view physical distribution as a system rather than a collection of unrelated activities. This approach shifts the emphasis from lowering the separate costs of individual activities to minimizing overall distribution costs.

Physical distribution managers must be sensitive to the issue of cost tradeoffs. Higher costs in one functional area of a distribution system may be necessary to achieve lower costs in another. Tradeoffs are strategic decisions to combine (and recombine) resources for greatest cost-effectiveness. When distribution managers regard the system as a network of integrated functions, tradeoffs become useful tools in implementing a unified, cost-effective distribution strategy.

Another important goal of physical distribution involves **cycle time,** the time needed to complete a process. For example, reducing cycle time while maintaining or reducing costs and/or maintaining or increasing customer service is a winning combination in supply chains and ultimately leads to greater end-customer satisfaction.

In the rest of this section, we take a closer look at a variety of physical distribution activities, including order processing, inventory management, materials handling, warehousing, and transportation.

Order Processing

Order processing is the receipt and transmission of sales order information. Although management sometimes overlooks the importance of these activities, efficient order processing facilitates product flow. Computerized order processing provides a database for all supply-chain members to increase their productivity. When carried out quickly and accurately, order processing contributes to customer satisfaction, decreased costs and cycle time, and increased profits.

Order processing entails three main tasks: order entry, order handling, and order delivery. Order entry begins when customers or salespeople place purchase orders via telephone, snail mail, e-mail, or website. Electronic ordering is less time consuming than a manual, paper-based ordering system and reduces costs. In some companies, sales representatives receive and enter orders personally and also handle complaints, prepare progress reports, and forward sales order information.

Order handling involves several tasks. Once an order is entered, it is transmitted to a warehouse, where product availability is verified, and to the credit department, where prices, terms, and the customer's credit rating are checked. If the credit department approves the purchase, warehouse personnel (sometimes assisted by automated

cycle time The time needed to complete a process

order processing The receipt and transmission of sales order information

equipment) pick and assemble the order. If the requested product is not in stock, a production order is sent to the factory, or the customer is offered a substitute.

When the order has been assembled and packed for shipment, the warehouse schedules delivery with an appropriate carrier. If the customer pays for rush service, overnight delivery by FedEx, UPS, DHL, or another overnight carrier is used. The customer is sent an invoice, inventory records are adjusted, and the order is delivered.

Whether a company uses a manual or an electronic order-processing system depends on which method provides the greater speed and accuracy within cost limits. Manual processing suffices for small-volume orders and is more flexible in certain situations. Most companies, however, use **electronic data interchange (EDI)**, which uses computer technology to integrate order processing with production, inventory, accounting, and transportation. Within the supply chain, EDI functions as an information system that links marketing channel members and outsourcing firms together. It reduces paperwork for all members of the supply chain and allows them to share information on invoices, orders, payments, inquiries, and scheduling. Consequently, many companies have pushed their suppliers toward EDI to reduce distribution costs and cycle times. Krispy Kreme, for example, uses EDI to automate supply-chain and financial activities with both suppliers and wholesale customers such as supermarkets and convenience stores. The system helped the company to save money and time and improve information flows across its supply chain.[18]

Inventory Management

Inventory management involves developing and maintaining adequate assortments of products to meet customers' needs. It is a key component of any effective physical distribution system. Inventory decisions have a major impact on physical distribution costs and the level of customer service provided. When too few products are carried in inventory, the result is *stockouts*, or shortages of products, that, in turn, can result in brand switching, lower sales, and loss of customers. When too many products (or too many slow-moving products) are carried, costs increase, as do risks of product obsolescence, pilferage, and damage. The objective of inventory management is to minimize inventory costs while maintaining an adequate supply of goods to satisfy customers. To achieve this objective, marketers focus on two major issues: when to order and how much to order.

To determine when to order, a marketer calculates the *reorder point:* the inventory level that signals the need to place a new order. To calculate the reorder point, the marketer must know the order lead time, the usage rate, and the amount of safety stock required. The *order lead time* refers to the average time lapse between placing the order and receiving it. The *usage rate* is the rate at which a product's inventory is used or sold during a specific time period. *Safety stock* is the amount of extra inventory a firm keeps to guard against stockouts resulting from above-average usage rates and/or longer-than-expected lead times. The reorder point can be calculated using the following formula:

$$\text{Reorder point} = (\text{Order lead time} \times \text{Usage rate}) + \text{Safety stock}$$

Thus, if order lead time is 10 days, usage rate is 3 units per day, and safety stock is 20 units, the reorder point is 50 units.

Efficient inventory management with accurate reorder points is crucial for firms that use a **just-in-time (JIT)** approach, in which supplies arrive just as they are needed for use in production or for resale. When using JIT, companies maintain low inventory levels and purchase products and materials in small quantities whenever they need them. Usually there is no safety stock, and suppliers are expected to provide consistently high-quality products. JIT inventory management requires a high level of coordination between producers and suppliers, but it eliminates waste and reduces inventory costs significantly. This approach has been used successfully by many well-known firms, including Chrysler, Harley-Davidson, and Dell Computer, to reduce costs and boost customer satisfaction. When a JIT approach is used in a supply chain, suppliers often move close to their customers.

electronic data interchange (EDI) A computerized means of integrating order processing with production, inventory, accounting, and transportation

inventory management Developing and maintaining adequate assortments of products to meet customers' needs

just-in-time (JIT) An inventory-management approach in which supplies arrive just when needed for production or resale

Materials Handling

Materials handling, the physical handling of tangible goods, supplies, and resources, is an important factor in warehouse operations, as well as in transportation from points of production to points of consumption. Efficient procedures and techniques for materials handling minimize inventory management costs, reduce the number of times a good is handled, improve customer service, and increase customer satisfaction. Systems for packaging, labeling, loading, and movement must be coordinated to maximize cost reduction and customer satisfaction.

A growing number of firms are turning to radio waves to track materials tagged with radio frequency ID (RFID) through every phase of handling. Daisy Brand, for example, is using RFID to track its dairy products throughout the supply chain, which helps the firm recognize when a retailer has run out of product and needs to be replenished. The firm is also using data analyzed from its RFID program to help identify high-volume shopping times and manage promotions and new-product introductions.[19] The rise of RFID technology is especially pronounced in China, where it is used in transportation, cash replacement, and secure access cards. The system is even being used in China's national ID card system.[20]

Product characteristics often determine handling. For example, the characteristics of bulk liquids and gases determine how they can be moved and stored. Internal packaging is also an important consideration in materials handling; goods must be packaged correctly to prevent damage or breakage during handling and transportation. Most companies employ packaging consultants during the product design process to help them decide which packaging materials and methods will result in the most efficient handling.

Unit loading and containerization are two common methods used in materials handling. With *unit loading,* one or more boxes are placed on a pallet or skid; these units then can be loaded efficiently by mechanical means such as forklifts, trucks, or conveyer systems. *Containerization* is the consolidation of many items into a single, large container that is sealed at its point of origin and opened at its destination. Containers are usually 8 feet wide, 8 feet high, and 10 to 40 feet long. They can be conveniently stacked and shipped via train, barge, or ship. Once containers reach their destinations, wheel assemblies can be added to make them suitable for ground transportation. Because individual items are not handled in transit, containerization greatly increases efficiency and security in shipping.

Warehousing

Warehousing, the design and operation of facilities for storing and moving goods, is another important physical distribution function. Warehousing provides time utility by enabling firms to compensate for dissimilar production and consumption rates. When mass production creates a greater stock of goods than can be sold immediately, companies may warehouse the surplus until customers are ready to buy. Warehousing also helps to stabilize prices and the availability of seasonal items.

The choice of warehouse facilities is an important strategic consideration. The right type of warehouse allows a company to reduce transportation and inventory costs or improve service to customers. The wrong type of warehouse may drain company resources. Beyond deciding how many facilities to operate and where to locate them, a company must determine which type of warehouse is most appropriate. Warehouses fall into two general categories: private and public. In many cases a combination of private and public facilities provides the most flexible warehousing approach.

Companies operate **private warehouses** for shipping and storing their own products. A firm usually leases or purchases a private warehouse when its warehousing needs in a given geographic market are substantial and stable enough to warrant a long-term commitment to a fixed facility. Private warehouses are also appropriate for firms that require special handling and storage and that want control of warehouse design and operation. Retailers such as Sears and Radio Shack find it economical to integrate private warehousing with purchasing and distribution for their retail outlets. When sales volumes are fairly stable, ownership and control of a private warehouse may provide benefits such as property appreciation.

materials handling Physical handling of tangible goods, supplies, and resources

warehousing The design and operation of facilities for storing and moving goods

private warehouses Company-operated facilities for storing and shipping products

E-ntertainment MARKETING

Blue Bell Sweetens the Supply Chain

Blue Bell Creameries originated in 1907 as the Brenham Creamery Company, founded in Brenham, Texas. Prior to 1911, the company produced only butter. In 1911 the company began to hand-crank two gallons of ice cream each day. All of the major ingredients—milk, cream, eggs, fresh fruit—were purchased from local farmers and producers. The company's horse-drawn wagon allowed it to deliver ice cream to nearby areas. The creamery's ice cream quickly became a local favorite thanks to strong word-of-mouth communication. In 1930 the company changed its name to Blue Bell Creameries, after the native Texas bluebell wildflower. Nowadays, Blue Bell Creameries has achieved considerable success and has become a Texas icon, producing more than 50 ice cream flavors, frozen snacks, and a line of sugar-free/low-fat ice cream. The company distributes its products throughout the southern United States, and its products represent approximately 20 percent of all frozen products nationwide.

Despite its remarkable growth and status as a native favorite, Blue Bell recently had to face a capacity issue. Blue Bell is in charge of its own deliveries, allowing the company to maintain control throughout its supply chain. The main Blue Bell distribution center, located in Sylacauga, Alabama, needed to grow with the company. The center, which covers the majority of a 15-acre campus, employs 200 people who work two shifts to move ice cream from the production area to storage and then out to retail customers or smaller distribution centers. The company's problem was storage.

After considering several options, Blue Bell decided to focus on automated storage retrieval systems (ASRS) and ultimately chose Westfalia Technologies as its provider. To implement the changes, the project had to be broken down into two phases. First, Westfalia had to implement a pallet-conveying system to link the 400-foot distance between the production line and the new ASRS. The second phase consisted of building the ASRS itself. John Hinchey, Westfalia's vice president of sales, explained, "The system is nine levels high and comprises more than 7,000 pallet storage locations in 14,000 square feet of freezer space." The system is designed with two storage retrieval machines, providing a measure of redundancy: if one machine is down, the second can work instead, so the line never shuts down. The system is also designed to handle different pallet sizes, which allows Blue Bell to diversify its packaging sizes. To run the entire operation, Blue Bell employs Westfalia's Savanna.NET warehouse management system that "controls, tracks and records product movement from system entry to exit."

This system represents a big improvement, since before that, Blue Bell operated mostly manually. Kevin Wood, Blue Bell's general manager, says, "The system helped us reduce forklift traffic by 80 percent. . . . There is also less product damage and huge labor savings." In the future, the company plans to take further actions to enhance and improve the new system, such as wireless inventory solutions. All of these changes provide the product quality that consumers expect from the Blue Bell brand.[c]

Private warehouses, however, face fixed costs such as insurance, taxes, maintenance, and debt expense. They also limit flexibility when firms wish to move inventories to more strategic locations. Many private warehouses are being eliminated by direct links between producers and customers, reduced cycle times, and outsourcing to public warehouses.

Public warehouses lease storage space and related physical distribution facilities to other companies. They sometimes provide distribution services such as receiving, unloading, inspecting, and reshipping products; filling orders; providing financing; displaying products; and coordinating shipments. ODW, for example, offers a wide range of such services through its 3 million square feet of warehouse space at 11 facilities.[21] Public warehouses are especially useful to firms that have seasonal production or low-volume storage needs, have inventories that must be maintained in many locations, are testing or entering new markets, or own private warehouses but occasionally require additional storage space. Public warehouses also serve as collection points during product-recall programs. Whereas private warehouses have fixed costs, public warehouses offer variable (and often lower) costs because users rent space and purchase warehousing services only as needed.

Many public warehouses furnish security for products that are used as collateral for loans, a service provided at either the warehouse or the site of the owner's inventory. *Field public warehouses* are established by public warehouses at the owner's inventory location. The warehouser becomes custodian of the products and issues a receipt that can be used as collateral for a loan. Public warehouses also provide *bonded storage,* a warehousing arrangement in which imported or taxable products are not released until the products' owners pay U.S. customs duties, taxes, or other fees. Bonded warehouses enable firms to defer tax payments on such items until they are delivered to customers.

Distribution centers are large, centralized warehouses that receive goods from factories and suppliers, regroup them into orders, and ship them to customers quickly, the focus being on movement of goods rather than storage.[22] Distribution centers are specially designed for rapid flow of products. They are usually one-story buildings (to eliminate elevators) with access to transportation networks such as major highways and/or railway lines. Many distribution centers are highly automated, with computer-directed robots, forklifts, and hoists that collect and move products to loading docks. American Eagle Outfitters, for example, operates three distribution centers to serve the needs of its 913 U.S. and Canadian American Eagle Outfitter and Martin + Osa stores, which market apparel to the 15- to 25-year-old market, as well as a direct sales channel. Efficiency and creativity in distribution operations help the firm to keep up with a high volume of merchandise moving through the centers and to stay on top of busy holiday seasons.[23] Although some public warehouses offer such specialized services, most distribution centers are privately owned. They serve customers in regional markets and, in some cases, function as consolidation points for a company's branch warehouses.

Transportation

Transportation, the movement of products from where they are made to intermediaries and end users, is the most expensive physical distribution function. Because product availability and timely deliveries depend on transportation functions, transportation decisions directly affect customer service. A firm even may build its distribution and marketing strategy around a unique transportation system if that system can ensure on-time deliveries and thereby give the firm a competitive edge. Companies may build their own transportation fleets (private carriers) or outsource the transportation function to a common or contract carrier.

Transportation Modes. The basic transportation modes for moving physical goods are railroads, trucks, waterways, airways, and pipelines. Each has distinct advantages. Many companies adopt physical handling procedures that facilitate the use of two or more modes in combination. Table 14.3 shows the percentage of intercity freight carried by each transportation mode.

Railroads such as Union Pacific and Canadian National carry heavy, bulky freight that must be shipped long distances over land. Railroads commonly haul minerals, sand, lumber, chemicals, and farm products, as well as low-value manufactured goods and an increasing number of automobiles. They are especially efficient for transporting full carloads, which can be shipped at lower rates than smaller quantities because they require less handling. Many companies locate factories or warehouses near rail lines for convenient loading and unloading.

public warehouses Storage space and related physical distribution facilities that can be leased by companies

distribution centers Large, centralized warehouses that focus on moving rather than storing goods

transportation The movement of products from where they are made to intermediaries and end users

table 14.3   CHARACTERISTICS AND RATINGS OF TRANSPORTATION MODES BY SELECTION CRITERIA

	Railroads	Trucks	Pipelines	Waterways	Airplanes
Selection Criteria					
Cost	Moderate	High	Low	Very low	Very high
Speed	Average	Fast	Slow	Very slow	Very fast
Dependability	Average	High	High	Average	High
Load flexibility	High	Average	Very low	Very high	Low
Accessibility	High	Very high	Very limited	Limited	Average
Frequency	Low	High	Very high	Very low	Average
% Ton-Miles Transported	38.2	28.5	19.9	13.0	0.3
Products Carried	Coal, grain, lumber, heavy equipment, paper and pulp products, chemicals	Clothing, computers, books, groceries and produce, livestock	Oil, processed coal, natural gas	Chemicals, bauxite, grain, motor vehicles, agricultural implements	Flowers, food (highly perishable), technical instruments, emergency parts and equipment, overnight mail

Source: U.S. Bureau of Transportation Statistics, *National Transportation Statistics* (Washington, DC: U.S. Government Printing Office), July 2007, www.bts.gov/publications/national_transportation_statistics/html/table_01_46b.html.

Trucks provide the most flexible schedules and routes of all major transportation modes in the United States because they can go almost anywhere. Because trucks have a unique ability to move goods directly from factory or warehouse to customer, they are often used in conjunction with other forms of transport that cannot provide door-to-door deliveries. Trucks are more expensive and somewhat more vulnerable to bad weather than trains. They are also subject to size and weight restrictions on the products they carry. Trucks are sometimes criticized for high levels of loss and damage to freight and for delays caused by the rehandling of small shipments.

Waterways are the cheapest method of shipping heavy, low-value, nonperishable goods such as ore, coal, grain, and petroleum products. Water carriers offer considerable capacity. Powered by tugboats and towboats, barges that travel along intracoastal canals, inland rivers, and navigation systems can haul at least ten times the weight of one rail car, and oceangoing vessels can haul thousands of containers. More than 95 percent of international cargo is transported by water. However, many markets are inaccessible by water transportation unless supplemented by rail or truck. Droughts and floods also may create difficulties for users of inland waterway transportation. Nevertheless, the extreme fuel efficiency of water transportation and the continuing globalization of marketing likely will increase its use in the future.

Air transportation is the fastest but most expensive form of shipping. It is used most often for perishable goods; for high-value, low-bulk items; and for products that require quick delivery over long distances, such as emergency shipments. Some air carriers transport combinations of passengers, freight, and mail. Despite its expense, air transit can reduce warehousing and packaging costs and losses from theft and damage, thus helping to lower total costs (but truck transportation needed for pickup and final delivery adds to cost and transit time). Although air transport accounts for less than 1 percent of total ton-miles carried, its importance as a mode of transportation is growing. In fact, the success of many businesses is now based on the availability of overnight air delivery service provided by organizations such as UPS, FedEx, DHL, RPS Air, and the U.S. Postal Service. Amazon.com, for example, ships many of the products that are ordered online via UPS within one day.

Pipelines, the most automated transportation mode, usually belong to the shipper and carry the shipper's products. Most pipelines carry petroleum products or chemicals. The Trans-Alaska Pipeline, owned and operated by a consortium of oil companies that includes Exxon Mobil and BP-Amoco, transports crude oil from remote oil-drilling sites in central Alaska to shipping terminals on the coast. Slurry pipelines carry pulverized coal, grain, or wood chips suspended in water. Pipelines move products slowly but continuously and at relatively low cost. They are dependable and minimize the problems of product damage and theft. However, contents are subject to as much as 1 percent shrinkage, usually from evaporation. Pipelines also have been a concern to environmentalists, who fear installation and leaks could harm plants and animals.

Choosing Transportation Modes. Logistics managers select a transportation mode based on the combination of cost, speed, dependability, load flexibility, accessibility, and frequency that is most appropriate for their products and generates the desired level of customer service. Table 14.3 shows relative ratings of each transportation mode by these selection criteria.

Marketers compare alternative transportation modes to determine whether the benefits from a more expensive mode are worth the higher costs. Companies such as Accuship can assist marketers in analyzing various transportation options. This Internet firm's software gives corporate users, such as Coca-Cola and the Home Shopping Network, information about the speed and cost of different transportation modes and allows them to order shipping and then track shipments online. Accuship processes almost a million shipments every day.[24]

Coordinating Transportation. To take advantage of the benefits offered by various transportation modes and to compensate for deficiencies, marketers often combine and coordinate two or more modes. In recent years, **intermodal transportation,** as this integrated approach is sometimes called, has become easier because of new developments within the transportation industry. Several kinds of intermodal shipping are available. All combine the flexibility of trucking with the low cost or speed of other forms of transport. Containerization facilitates intermodal transportation by consolidating shipments into sealed containers for transport by *piggyback* (shipping that uses both truck trailers and railway flatcars), *fishyback* (truck trailers and water carriers), and *birdyback* (truck trailers and air carriers). As transportation costs have increased, intermodal shipping has gained popularity.

Specialized outsource agencies provide other forms of transport coordination. Known as **freight forwarders,** these firms combine shipments from several organizations into efficient lot sizes. Small loads (less than 500 pounds) are much more expensive to ship than full carloads or truckloads, which frequently require consolidation. Freight forwarders take small loads from various marketers, buy transport space from carriers, and arrange for goods to be delivered to buyers. Freight forwarders' profits come from the margin between the higher, less-than-carload rates they charge each marketer and the lower carload rates they themselves pay. Because large shipments require less handling, use of freight forwarders can speed delivery. Freight forwarders also can determine the most efficient carriers and routes and are useful for shipping goods to foreign markets. Some companies prefer to outsource their shipping to freight forwarders because the latter provide door-to-door service.

Another transportation innovation is the development of **megacarriers,** freight transportation companies that offer several shipment methods, including rail, truck, and air service. CSX, for example, has trains, barges, container ships, trucks, and pipelines, thus offering a multitude of transportation services. In addition, air carriers have increased their ground-transportation services. As they expand the range of transportation alternatives, carriers too put greater stress on customer service.

intermodal transportation Two or more transportation modes used in combination

freight forwarders Organizations that consolidate shipments from several firms into efficient lot sizes

megacarriers Freight transportation firms that provide several modes of shipment

Legal Issues in Channel Management

LO 8 To explore legal issues in channel management

The numerous federal, state, and local laws governing channel management are based on the general principle that the public is best served by protecting competition and free trade. Under the authority of such federal legislation as the Sherman Antitrust Act and the Federal Trade Commission Act, courts and regulatory agencies determine under what circumstances channel management practices violate this underlying principle and must be restricted. Although channel managers are not expected to be legal experts, they should be aware that attempts to control distribution functions may have legal repercussions. The following practices are among those frequently subject to legal restraint.

Dual Distribution

Earlier we noted that some companies may use dual distribution by using two or more marketing channels to distribute the same products to the same target market. Hewlett-Packard, for example, sells computers directly to consumers through a toll-free telephone line and a website, as well as through electronics retailers such as Best Buy. Courts do not consider this practice illegal when it promotes competition. A manufacturer can also legally open its own retail outlets. But the courts view as a threat to competition a manufacturer that uses company-owned outlets to dominate or drive out of business independent retailers or distributors that handle its products. In such cases, dual distribution violates the law. To avoid this interpretation, producers should use outlet prices that do not severely undercut independent retailers' prices.

Restricted Sales Territories

To tighten control over distribution of its products, a manufacturer may try to prohibit intermediaries from selling its products outside designated sales territories. Intermediaries themselves often favor this practice because it gives them exclusive territories, allowing them to avoid competition for the producer's brands within these territories. In recent years, the courts have adopted conflicting positions in regard to restricted sales territories. Although the courts have deemed restricted sales territories a restraint of trade among intermediaries handling the same brands (except for small or newly established companies), they have also held that exclusive territories can actually promote competition among dealers handling different brands. At present, the producer's intent in establishing restricted territories and the overall effect of doing so on the market must be evaluated for each individual case.

Tying Agreements

When a supplier (usually a manufacturer or franchiser) furnishes a product to a channel member with the stipulation that the channel member must purchase other products as well, a **tying agreement** exists. Suppliers may institute tying agreements to move weaker products along with more popular items, or a franchiser may tie purchase of equipment and supplies to the sale of franchises, justifying the policy as necessary for quality control and protection of the franchiser's reputation.

A related practice is *full-line forcing,* in which a supplier requires that channel members purchase the supplier's entire line to obtain any of the supplier's products. Manufacturers sometimes use full-line forcing to ensure that intermediaries accept new products and that a suitable range of products is available to customers.

The courts accept tying agreements when the supplier alone can provide products of a certain quality, when the intermediary is free to carry competing products as well, and when a company has just entered the market. Most other tying agreements are considered illegal.

Exclusive Dealing

When a manufacturer forbids an intermediary to carry products of competing manufacturers, the arrangement is called **exclusive dealing**. Manufacturers receive

tying agreement An agreement in which a supplier furnishes a product to a channel member with the stipulation that the channel member must purchase other products as well

exclusive dealing A situation in which a manufacturer forbids an intermediary to carry products of competing manufacturers

considerable market protection in an exclusive-dealing arrangement and may cut off shipments to intermediaries that violate the agreement.

The legality of an exclusive-dealing contract is generally determined by applying three tests. If the exclusive dealing blocks competitors from as much as 10 percent of the market, if the sales revenue involved is sizable, and if the manufacturer is much larger (and thus more intimidating) than the dealer, the arrangement is considered anticompetitive.[25] If dealers and customers in a given market have access to similar products or if the exclusive-dealing contract strengthens an otherwise weak competitor, the arrangement is allowed.

Refusal to Deal

For more than 75 years, the courts have held that producers have the right to choose channel members with which they will do business (and the right to reject others). Within existing distribution channels, however, suppliers may not legally refuse to deal with wholesalers or dealers merely because these wholesalers or dealers resist policies that are anticompetitive or in restraint of trade. Suppliers are further prohibited from organizing some channel members in refusal-to-deal actions against other members that choose not to comply with illegal policies.

SUMMARY

The distribution component of the marketing mix focuses on the decisions and activities involved in making products available to customers when and where they want to purchase them. An important function of distribution is the joint effort of all involved organizations to be part of creating an effective supply chain, which refers to all the activities associated with the flow and transformation of products from raw materials through to the end customer. Operations management is the total set of managerial activities used by an organization to transform resource inputs into products. Logistics management involves planning, implementation, and controlling the efficient and effective flow and storage of goods, services, and information from the point of origin to consumption in order to meet customers' needs and wants. Supply management in its broadest form refers to the processes that enable the progress of value from raw material to final customer and back to redesign and final disposition. Supply-chain management therefore refers to a set of approaches used to integrate the functions of operations management, logistics management, supply management, and marketing channel management so that products and services are produced and distributed in the right quantities, to the right locations, and at the right time. The supply chain includes all entities—shippers and other firms that facilitate distribution, as well as producers, wholesalers, and retailers—that distribute products and benefit from cooperative efforts.

A marketing channel, or channel of distribution, is a group of individuals and organizations that direct the flow of products from producers to customers. The major role of marketing channels is to make products available at the right time at the right place and in the right amounts. In most channels of distribution, producers and consumers are linked by marketing intermediaries. The two major types of intermediaries are retailers, which purchase products and resell them to ultimate consumers, and wholesalers, which buy and resell products to other wholesalers, retailers, and business customers.

Marketing channels serve many functions. They create time, place, and possession utilities by making products available when and where customers want them and providing customers with access to product use through sale or rental. Marketing intermediaries facilitate exchange efficiencies, often reducing the costs of exchanges by performing certain services and functions. Although some critics suggest eliminating wholesalers, the functions of the intermediaries in the marketing channel must be performed. As such, eliminating one or more intermediaries result in other organizations in the channel having to do more. Because intermediaries serve both producers and buyers, they reduce the total number of transactions that otherwise would be needed to move products from producer to the end customer.

Channels of distribution are broadly classified as channels for consumer products and channels for business products. Within these two broad categories, different channels are used for different products. Although consumer goods can move directly from producer to consumers, consumer channels that include wholesalers and retailers are usually more economical and knowledge efficient. Distribution of business products differs from that of consumer products in the types of channels used. A direct distribution channel is common in business marketing. Also used are channels containing industrial distributors, manufacturers' agents, and a combination of agents and distributors. Most producers have multiple or dual channels so the distribution system can be adjusted for various target markets.

Selecting an appropriate marketing channel is a crucial decision for supply-chain managers. To determine which channel is most appropriate, managers must think about customer characteristics, the type of organization, product attributes, competition, environmental forces, and the availability and characteristics of intermediaries. Careful consideration of these factors will assist a supply-chain manager in selecting the correct channel.

A marketing channel is managed such that products receive appropriate market coverage. In choosing intensive distribution, producers strive to make a product available to all possible dealers. In selective distribution, only some outlets in an area are chosen to distribute a product. Exclusive distribution usually gives a single dealer rights to sell a product in a large geographic area.

Each channel member performs a different role in the system and agrees to accept certain rights, responsibilities, rewards, and sanctions for nonconformance. Although many marketing channels are determined by consensus, some are organized and controlled by a single leader, or channel captain. A channel captain may be a producer, wholesaler, or retailer. A marketing channel functions most effectively when members cooperate; when they deviate from their roles, channel conflict can arise.

Integration of marketing channels brings various activities under one channel member's management. Vertical integration combines two or more stages of the channel under one management. The vertical marketing system (VMS) is managed centrally for the mutual benefit of all channel members. Vertical marketing systems may be corporate, administered, or contractual. Horizontal integration combines institutions at the same level of channel operation under a single management.

Physical distribution, or logistics, refers to the activities used to move products from producers to customers and other end users. These activities include order processing, inventory management, materials handling, warehousing, and transportation. An efficient physical distribution system is an important component of an overall marketing strategy because it can decrease costs and increase customer satisfaction. Within the marketing channel, physical distribution activities are often performed by a wholesaler, but they may also be performed by a producer or retailer or outsourced to a third party. Efficient physical distribution systems can decrease costs and transit time while increasing customer service.

Order processing is the receipt and transmission of sales order information. It consists of three main tasks—order entry, order handling, and order delivery—that may be done manually but are more often handled through electronic data interchange systems. Inventory management involves developing and maintaining adequate assortments of products to meet customers' needs. Logistics managers must strive to find the optimal level of inventory to satisfy customer needs while keeping costs down. Materials handling, the physical handling of products, is a crucial element in warehousing and transporting products. Warehousing involves the design and operation of facilities for storing and moving goods; such facilities may be privately owned or public. Transportation, the movement of products from where they are made to where they are purchased and used, is the most expensive physical distribution function. The basic modes of transporting goods include railroads, trucks, waterways, airways, and pipelines.

Federal, state, and local laws regulate channel management to protect competition and free trade. Courts may prohibit or permit a practice depending on whether it violates this underlying principle. Procompetitive legislation applies to distribution practices. Channel management practices frequently subject to legal restraint include dual distribution, restricted sales territories, tying agreements, exclusive dealing, and refusal to deal. When these practices strengthen weak competitors or increase competition among dealers, they may be permitted; in most other cases, when competition may be weakened considerably, they are deemed illegal.

IMPORTANT TERMS

Distribution, 388
Supply chain, 388
Operations
    management, 388
Logistics
    management, 388
Supply management, 388
Supply-chain
    management, 388
Marketing channel, 390
Marketing
    intermediaries, 390
Industrial distributor, 395

Dual distribution, 397
Strategic channel
    alliance, 397
Intensive
    distribution, 400
Selective
    distribution, 401
Exclusive
    distribution, 401
Channel captain, 403
Channel power, 403
Vertical channel
    integration, 404

Vertical marketing systems
    (VMSs), 405
Horizontal channel
    integration, 405
Physical
    distribution, 406
Outsourcing, 406
Cycle time, 407
Order processing, 407
Electronic data
    interchange (EDI), 408
Inventory
    management, 408

Just-in-time (JIT), 408
Materials handling, 409
Warehousing, 409
Private warehouses, 409
Public warehouses, 411
Distribution centers, 411
Transportation, 411
Intermodal
    transportation, 413
Freight forwarders, 413
Megacarriers, 413
Tying agreement, 414
Exclusive dealing, 414

DISCUSSION & REVIEW QUESTIONS

1. Define supply-chain management. Why is it important?

2. Describe the major functions of marketing channels. Why are these functions better accomplished through combined efforts of channel members?

3. List several reasons consumers often blame intermediaries for distribution inefficiencies.

4. Compare and contrast the four major types of marketing channels for consumer products. Through which type of channel is each of the following products most likely to be distributed?

   a. New automobiles

   b. Saltine crackers

   c. Cut-your-own Christmas trees

   d. New textbooks

   e. Sofas

   f. Soft drinks

5. Outline the four most common channels for business products. Describe the products or situations that lead marketers to choose each channel.

6. Describe an industrial distributor. What types of products are marketed through an industrial distributor?

7. Under what conditions is a producer most likely to use more than one marketing channel?

8. Identify and describe the factors that may influence marketing channel selection decisions.

9. Explain the differences among intensive, selective, and exclusive methods of distribution.

10. "Channel cooperation requires that members support the overall channel goals to achieve individual goals." Comment on this statement.

11. Explain the major characteristics of each of the three types of vertical marketing systems (VMSs): corporate, administered, and contractual.

12. Discuss the cost and service tradeoffs involved in developing a physical distribution system.

13. What are the main tasks involved in order processing?

14. Explain the tradeoffs that inventory managers face when they reorder products or supplies. How is the reorder point computed?

15. Explain the major differences between private and public warehouses. How do they differ from a distribution center?

16. Compare and contrast the five major transportation modes in terms of cost, speed, and dependability.

17. Under what conditions are tying agreements, exclusive dealing, and dual distribution judged illegal?

APPLICATION QUESTIONS

1. *Supply-chain management* involves long-term partnerships among channel members that are working together to reduce inefficiencies, costs, and redundancies and to develop innovative approaches to satisfy customers. Select one of the following companies and explain how supply-chain management could increase marketing productivity.

   a. Dell Computer

   b. FedEx

   c. Nike

   d. Taco Bell

2. Marketers can select from three major levels of marketing coverage when determining the number and kinds of outlets in which to sell a product: intensive, selective, or exclusive distribution. Characteristics of the product and its target market determine the intensity of coverage a product should receive. Indicate the intensity level best suited for the following products, and explain why it is appropriate.

   a. Personal computer

   b. Deodorant

   c. Canon digital cameras

   d. Nike athletic shoes

3. Describe the decision process you might go through if you were attempting to determine the most appropriate distribution channel for one of the following:

   a. Shotguns for hunters

   b. Women's lingerie

   c. Telephone systems for small businesses

   d. Toy trucks for 2-year-olds

4. Assume that you are responsible for the physical distribution of computers at a web-based company. What would you do to ensure product availability, timely delivery, and quality service for your customers?

INTERNET EXERCISE

Visit **www.cengage.com/marketing/pride-ferrell** for resources to help you master the material in this chapter, plus materials that will help you expand your marketing knowledge, including Internet exercise updates, ACE Self-Tests, hotlinks to companies featured in this chapter, and much more.

iSuppli

Distribution bottlenecks can be an expensive problem for any business. Trying to prevent such problems is iSuppli, an Internet supply-chain management tool that links all members of a supply chain from the supplier's system to the retailer's storefront system. Learn more about this innovative tool at **www.isuppli.com.**

1. Does iSuppli represent a new type of marketing channel? Why or why not?

2. Why would firms be cautious when deciding whether to use iSuppli?

3. Do you think iSuppli represents the future of supply-chain management? Why or why not?

developing your MARKETING PLAN

One of the key components in a successful marketing strategy is the plan for getting the products to your customer. To make the best decisions about where, when, and how your products will be made available to the customer, you need to know more about how these distribution decisions relate to other marketing mix elements in your marketing plan. To assist you in relating the information in this chapter to your marketing plan, consider the following issues:

1. Marketing intermediaries perform many activities. Using Table 14.2 as a guide, discuss the types of activities where a channel member could provide needed assistance.

2. Using Figure 14.2 (or 14.3 if your product is a business product), determine which of the channel distribution paths is most appropriate for your product. Given the nature of your product, could it be distributed through more than one of these paths?

3. Determine the level of distribution intensity that is appropriate for your product. Consider the characteristics of your target market(s), the product attributes, and environmental factors in your deliberation.

4. Discuss the physical functions that will be required for distributing your product, focusing on materials handling, warehousing, and transportation.

The information obtained from these questions should assist you in developing various aspects of your marketing plan found in the *Interactive Marketing Plan* exercise at **www.cengage.com/marketing/pride-ferrell.**

globalEDGE

1. Your firm is looking for competitive alternatives in its supply-chain management strategy. One method is to reduce costs by relocating the U.S.-based manufacturing of your food-processing division. The Competitive Alternatives website can assist with your analysis. Access this site by using the search term "competitive alternatives" at **http://globaledge.msu.edu/resourceDesk/.** Once you reach the Competitive Alternatives website, click on the Download tab and then download the International Report (Volume 1). Based on the results of relative costs in an analysis by industry and operation, to which country should you relocate your firm's operations based on information from the Competitive Alternatives website? Compare this with the results focused on particular cities in the same report. What are the five most promising cities listed? Does this change your decision on the relocation of your food-processing division.

2. Because conduct in international marketing channels typically involves the shipment of cargo around the world, managers must understand the different terms involved in the handling and delivery of "world cargo." Define the following terms: CFR, CIF, and CIP based on information from the World Cargo Alliance website. The information required can be accessed by using the search term "world cargo" at **http://globaledge.msu.edu/resourceDesk/.** In each of these three shipment conditions, which party is required to clear the goods under consideration for export?

video CASE 14.1

Netflix Gains Competitive Advantage Through a Unique Distribution System

Founded in 1997 by Reed Hastings and Marc Randolph, Netflix was originally nothing more than an online version of a traditional video rental store. Customers could visit the Netflix website and choose which items they wished to rent. Each rental cost $4, along with a $2 shipping fee, plus late fees, if applicable. This model was not very cost competitive or efficient compared to brick-and-mortar rental operations, so the company slowly transformed itself in order to gain a competitive advantage. The Netflix business model evolved into its current form around 1999 and has been focusing on technological advances and improving selection in order to stay on top of the video rental industry.

As with other rental companies, Netflix is membership based. What differs is that members subscribe to various packages based on the amount of movies they want to rent per month. Packages vary from two movies per month to four-at-a-time unlimited rentals. Members create a list of movies they would like to see in order of preference, and Netflix delivers them. Customers can keep the movie as long as they like with no late fees, but they are not sent a new one until the old one has been received at their local Netflix distribution center.

As the company became more popular, Netflix expanded its film and television show collection to include Blu-Ray disks. In order to stay ahead of the competition, Netflix added a Play Instantly feature, which allows subscribers to download movies from the Netflix website and watch them on their computer. This service gives people instant access to a wide selection of films. The additional benefit to the company is that it saves on shipping fees. However, many people have opted not to utilize this service, given low computer resolution or problems with the speed of Internet access.

In 2008, Netflix also began to offer a direct-to-television streaming box rental option. To gain access to more than 10,000 movies and television shows from the Netflix library, customers must purchase a box that hooks up to a television set. The box costs around $100 and streams video directly to television via high-speed Internet. Customers must sign up for a plan, but rather than wait for DVDs in the mail, they can watch them instantly on their televisions. Apple and Vudu offer similar products, but their boxes cost two to three times Netflix's price. Also in 2008, Netflix formed a partnership with Microsoft to stream movies through Xbox systems to the television.

Netflix has a number of competitive advantages over companies such as Movielink, Blockbuster, and Wal-Mart. First and foremost, Netflix offers more selections, including more independent and foreign films, documentaries, and television shows, than anyone else. Wal-Mart attempted to compete with Netflix starting in 2002, but by 2005 the company admitted that Netflix had won and bowed out of the race.

Blockbuster, a company that took some beatings as more consumers moved away from patronizing brick-and-mortar video stores, continues to be Netflix's toughest competitor. The company, which remains the largest in-store movie rental chain in the world, entered the online rental competition in 2004. Although Blockbuster originally tried to compete with Netflix on price, the two companies eventually settled on the same price point. The battle came to a head in 2006 when Netflix sued Blockbuster for infringing on two of its patents. The suit was settled a year later with undisclosed terms, but the competition remains fierce.

Netflix's rising popularity shows no sign of abating. Between 1997 and 2007, Netflix's customer base grew to an estimated 10 million subscribers. In 2007, the company posted revenues of over $1.5 billion. With ever-evolving technologies to take advantage of, the company firmly believes that there is still plenty of room to grow and plenty of brick-and-mortar customers to win over.[26]

Questions for Discussion

1. Describe Netflix's marketing strategy.
2. Why did Netflix's approach to distributing movies provide a competitive advantage over Blockbuster and Wal-Mart?
3. What technological innovations currently exist that might threaten Netflix's current distribution activities?

CASE 14.2

Grainger Wires the Channel for Business Products

Need an electric motor or a hard hat? W. W. Grainger has dozens for sale—among the many thousands of products showcased in its voluminous catalogs and on its website. Grainger is an industrial distributor offering virtually one-stop shopping for producer, government, and institutional markets seeking a wide range of maintenance, repair, and operating (MRO) supplies. With 600 distribution facilities spread across North America, the company can time shipments to arrive quickly when business customers place orders.

William W. Grainger founded the Illinois-based company in the 1920s as a wholesaler of electric motors. To build sales, Grainger mailed out postcards about his offerings and compiled a catalog titled *MotorBook*. In less than a decade, he was operating 15 U.S. sales branches to serve business customers from coast to coast. By 1949, he had expanded his branch network to 30 states.

Son David Grainger, now senior chairperson, continued the founder's expansion strategy. In the 1980s and 1990s, the company opened high-tech regional distribution centers in Kansas, Georgia, and Texas to supplement its Chicago-area facilities and slash fulfillment time for orders placed by customers around the country. Grainger also expanded its geographic reach by buying Acklands Ltd., a Canadian distributor of automotive and industrial safety products.

By the mid-1990s, Grainger was getting wired. Recognizing that the Internet could bring in many more business customers at a lower cost, management created **Grainger.com** as a comprehensive online catalog site. Over the years, the company continued to refine its web presence by posting informative resources, adding live-chat customer assistance, a virtual tour of the site for new customers, special international services, and web-only price promotions to bring customers back to the site again and again. Within the first three years of operation, annual Web sales grew from $3 million to $267 million as customers flocked to the online catalog, which features many more items than the 80,000 products shown in a typical printed Grainger catalog.

Not all of Grainger's Internet initiatives have been as successful, however. The company had high hopes for its Material Logic division covering three web-based distribution sites. **TotalMRO.com** was designed as an industrywide portal with catalogs from Grainger and competing distributors. **MROverstocks.com** was created as an auction site for discontinued or excess industrial products. **FindMRO.com** was designed as a search site for specialized and hard-to-find industrial products. After launching the three sites, Grainger tried to interest competing distributors and outside investors in buying a stake in Material Logic. The company had spent more than $100 million on its Web operations and sought outside funding to support its aggressive movement into electronic procurement. But when no one stepped forward to invest, Grainger quickly shut down the unprofitable division. At the same time, **FindMRO.com** was becoming popular, so it was merged into the existing **Grainger.com** operation.

Today Grainger sells nearly $6 billion worth of industrial products every year. Approximately 10 percent of total sales revenues come from the profitable **Grainger.com** site, and the percentage continues to rise as more customers switch from paper-based to electronic purchasing. Despite its Internet success, Grainger is not abandoning its branch system. In line with the changing demographics of its customer base, the company is reassessing the intensity of its market coverage in major metropolitan areas. It has closed two older branches, opened three new branches, expanded or relocated seven branches, and hired more sales staff. The company has also opened convenient on-site branches for two big customers, Florida State University and Langley Air Force Base. "Grainger's multi-channel model is what distinguishes us from our competition," the CEO emphasizes. "No other company has as broad a product line with tens of thousands of items immediately available all across the country."

Grainger is showing major customers such as the U.S. Postal Service how to better manage their supply chains and cut costs throughout the procurement process. It is also helping customers plan and budget for unexpected and infrequent MRO purchases. Customers often need parts right away to repair machines that break down without warning, but they want to minimize equipment downtime and the expense of storing all replacement parts on hand at all times. Grainger uses sophisticated software to analyze how often customers of similar sizes buy spare parts and related products and then suggests how individual businesses can find an appropriate balance of inventory and planned purchasing for these products.

To handle future volume more productively, Grainger is opening an additional nine automated distribution centers and implementing a new logistics network. The added efficiency will allow the company to lower its inventory investment by $100 million while profitably serving more customers. More efficiencies are ahead as the company, already the largest industrial distributor in North America, aggressively pursues higher market share and higher profits.[27]

Questions for Discussion

1. Why would a competing industrial distributor even consider investing in a portal designed by Grainger?
2. Is Grainger in a position to be a channel captain? Explain.
3. Why would a hospital buy from Grainger instead of buying directly from producers?

15 Retailing, Direct Marketing, and Wholesaling

LEARNING objectives

1 Understand the purpose and function of retailers in the marketing channel

2 Identify the major types of retailers

3 Explore strategic issues in retailing

4 Recognize the various forms of direct marketing and selling

5 Examine franchising and its benefits and weaknesses

6 Understand the nature and functions of wholesaling

7 Understand how wholesalers are classified

Organic Ice Cream: A Growing Niche Business

entrepreneurs IN ACTION

The seed was planted for Tara's Organic Ice Cream several years ago when friends gave Tara Esperanza a home ice cream maker. Many, many quarts of ice cream later, Esperanza achieved the balance, texture, and flavors she desired, along with feedback from friends. Her friends often told her that she should sell her ice cream, and so she did. Altogether she makes some 50 different flavors, which customers can buy in her retail shop in Santa Fe, New Mexico; pick up from some 20 different stores throughout Taos, Santa Fe, and Albuquerque; or even order it for home delivery. Friends have been instrumental in helping Esperanza create her unique flavors that include lemongrass, lavender, white pepper chocolate chip, and even garam masala.

In developing her business, Esperanza not only wanted her niche product to taste good, but she also wanted to emphasize her commitment to organic foods. She strongly believes in organic products and business and enjoys being an advocate for organic foods and the importance of organic products. Esperanza has grown her company more than 75 percent from one year to the next, and the company now has six employees. The growing company now delivers ice cream to Colorado, which Esperanza hopes will quadruple her business in the coming year.

As the only certified organic ice cream business in New Mexico, Esperanza buys dairy products from the California-based Straus Family Creamery, which uses a methane digester that converts methane from the cows into electricity for use on the farm. She strives to buy as many of the other ingredients as possible from New Mexico suppliers. By recognizing that organic ice cream was a niche market in New Mexico, Esperanza was able to launch her business and specialty product and wholesale the ice cream to small retail stores. Soon, she opened her own retail store and even developed online channels to sell her products. Esperanza learned quickly that you do not succeed without good distribution. She continues to sell to retailers and directly to consumers.[1]

Retailers such as Tara's Organic are the most visible and accessible marketing channel members to consumers. They are an important link in the marketing channel because they are both marketers for and customers of producers and wholesalers. They perform many supply-chain functions, such as buying, selling, grading, risk taking, and developing and maintaining information databases about customers. Retailers are in a strategic position to develop relationships with consumers and partnerships with producers and intermediaries in the marketing channel.

In this chapter we examine the nature of retailing, direct marketing, and wholesaling and their importance in supplying consumers with goods and services. First, we explore the major types of retail stores and consider strategic issues in retailing: location, retail positioning, store image, scrambled merchandising, and the wheel of retailing. Next, we discuss direct marketing, including catalog marketing, response marketing, telemarketing, television home shopping, and online retailing. We also explore direct selling and vending. Then we look at franchising, a retailing form that continues to grow in popularity. Finally, we examine the importance of wholesalers in marketing channels, including their functions and classifications.

retailing All transactions in which the buyer intends to consume the product through personal, family, or household use

retailer An organization that purchases products for the purpose of reselling them to ultimate consumers

Retailing

L O 1 Understand the purpose and function of retailers in the marketing channel

Retailing includes all transactions in which the buyer intends to consume the product through personal, family, or household use. Buyers in retail transactions are therefore the ultimate consumers. A **retailer** is an organization that purchases products for the purpose of reselling them to ultimate consumers. Although most retailers' sales are made directly to the consumer, nonretail transactions occur occasionally when retailers sell products to other businesses.

Retailing often takes place in stores or service establishments, but it also occurs through direct selling, direct marketing, and vending machines outside stores. Given the purchasing pattern trends of the last decade, there is a clear expectation that consumers will increasingly buy their goods and services online. Online shoppers prefer shopping on the Internet to avoid crowds, find lower prices, avoid the inconvenience of having to travel to stores, and have a wider selection of products.

Retailing is important to the national U.S. economy. Approximately 1.1 million retailers operate in the United States.[2] This number has remained relatively constant for the past 25 years, but sales volume has increased more than fourfold. Most personal income is spent in retail stores, and nearly one of every eight people employed in the United States works in a retail operation. Worldwide, retail sales are growing at an annual rate of about 8 percent (amounting to about US$12 trillion worldwide). In the future, the greatest potential for increases in retail sales is in emerging markets, with the so-called BRIC countries of Brazil, Russia, India, and China being the likely areas for retail expansion.[3]

Retailers add value, provide services, and assist in making product selections. They can enhance the value of products by making buyers' shopping experiences more convenient, as in home shopping. Through their locations, retailers can facilitate comparison shopping; for example, car dealerships often cluster in the same general vicinity, as do furniture stores. Product value is also enhanced when retailers offer services, such as technical advice, delivery, credit, and repair. Finally, retail sales personnel can demonstrate to customers how products can satisfy their needs or solve problems.

The value added by retailers is significant for both producers and end consumers. Retailers are the critical link between producers and end consumers because they provide the environment in which exchanges with

Importance of retailing in the U.S. economy

6.5% — Gross domestic product
13.3% — Employment
15.2% — All businesses

Source: U.S. Bureau of the Census, *Statistical Abstract of the United States, 2008* (Washington, DC: U.S. Government Printing Office, 2007), pp. 431, 496, 647, 650.

RESPONSIBLE marketing?

Starbucks Tries to Serve All Stakeholders

ISSUE: Is Starbucks doing enough to be socially responsible?

Starbucks is the largest coffee house chain in the world, with over 15,000 stores. Starbucks claims that "life happens over coffee" and has attempted to create a coffee culture that inspires customers to create a dialogue and discuss important concerns of the day. For example, the company listened to customers and moved from whole to 2 percent milk and eliminated ingredients that could create trans fats. Starbucks does much to support responsible and sustainable coffee purchasing and supports long-term relationships with coffee farmers. The company gives back to communities, supports diversity in hiring, and donates to community causes. Employee volunteerism is supported, and health care is provided for both full- and part-time employees. All employees receive stock options called Bean Stock. Annual reports use 100 percent recycled fibers, and certified renewable energy is used in their production to reduce cost and minimize the environmental footprint.

On the other hand, Starbucks has been accused of unfair competitive tactics in buying out small independent coffee retailers and saturating markets in its aggressive expansion. There is a concern that Starbucks dictates a pop culture of diminishing creativity and diversity in promoting high-calorie coffee drinks that can contribute to obesity. Although less than 10 percent of the coffee that Starbucks purchases is fair trade certified, Starbucks is the largest purchaser of fair trade coffee in North America. Starbucks promotes recycling, but its cups are made with only 10 percent recycled material. Starbucks was the first to use recycled material in direct contact with food, and a higher content is not allowed by the FDA. The company does use recycled material in cardboard cup sleeves, napkins, and cardboard carriers.[a]

ultimate consumers occur. Ultimate consumers benefit through retailers' performance of marketing functions that result in the availability of broader arrays of products that can satisfy the needs of consumers. Retailers play a major role in creating time, place, and possession utility and, in some cases, form utility.

Leading retailers such as Wal-Mart, Home Depot, Macy's, Staples, and Best Buy offer consumers a place to browse and compare merchandise to find just what they need. However, such traditional retailing is being challenged by direct marketing channels that provide home shopping through catalogs, television, and the Internet. "Bricks-and-mortar" retailers are responding to this change in the retail environment in various ways. Wal-Mart, for example, is offering more upscale merchandise such as plasma TVs and more fashionable apparel as well as more extended warranties on merchandise.[4] It also has established a website for online shopping and joined forces with fast-food giants McDonald's and KFC to attract consumers and offer them the added convenience of eating where they shop.

New store formats and advances in information technology are making the retail environment highly dynamic and competitive. Instant-messaging technology is enabling online retailers to converse in real time with customers so they do not click away to another site. For example, shoppers on the Lands' End website can click to chat, via keyboard, directly with a customer service representative about sizes, colors, or other product details. The key to success in retailing is to have a strong customer focus with a retail strategy that provides the level of service, product quality, and innovation that consumers desire. Partnerships among noncompeting retailers and other marketing channel members are providing new opportunities for retailers. For example, airports are leasing space to retailers such as Sharper Image, McDonald's, Sunglass Hut, and The Body Shop. Kroger and Nordstrom have developed joint co-branded credit cards that offer rebates to customers at participating stores.

Retailers are also finding global opportunities. For example, both McDonald's and The Gap, Inc., are now opening more international stores than domestic ones, a trend that is likely to continue for the foreseeable future. Starbucks has opened hundreds of stores in Japan and Southeast Asia. Increasingly, retailers from abroad, such as IKEA, Zara, and BP, are opening stores in the United States.

general-merchandise retailer A retail establishment that offers a variety of product lines that are stocked in considerable depth

Major Types of Retail Stores

LO 2 Identify the major types of retailers

Many types of retail stores exist. One way to classify them is by the breadth of products they offer. Two general categories include general-merchandise retailers and specialty retailers.

General-Merchandise Retailers

A retail establishment that offers a variety of product lines that are stocked in considerable depth is referred to as a **general-merchandise retailer.** The types of product

table 15.1	GENERAL-MERCHANDISE RETAILERS	
Type of Retailer	**Description**	**Examples**
Department store	Large organization offering a wide product mix and organized into separate departments	Macy's, Sears, JCPenney
Discount store	Self-service, general-merchandise store offering brand name and private brand products at low prices	Wal-Mart, Target, Kmart
Convenience store	Small self-service store offering narrow product assortment in convenient locations	7-Eleven, Circle K, Stripes
Supermarket	Self-service store offering complete line of food products and some nonfood products	Kroger, Albertson's, Winn-Dixie
Superstore	Giant outlet offering all food and nonfood products found in supermarkets, as well as most routinely purchased products	Wal-Mart Supercenters
Hypermarket	Combination supermarket and discount store; larger than a superstore	Carrefour
Warehouse club	Large-scale, members-only establishments combining cash-and-carry wholesaling with discount retailing	Sam's Club, Costco
Warehouse showroom	Facility in a large, low-cost building with large on-premises inventories and minimal service	IKEA

department stores Large retail organizations characterized by a wide product mix and organized into separate departments to facilitate marketing efforts and internal management

Department Store

Department stores like Macy's offer a wide variety of product lines and customer services.

"This Spring, it's all about the jacket. One is good, more is better."

Macy's Fashion Council

only at macy's
I·N·C International Concepts
Cropped jacket, $99;
Seamless tank, $20;
Pencil skirt, $79.

the magic of
★ macy's
macys.com

offerings, mixes of customer services, and operating styles of retailers in this category vary considerably. The primary types of general-merchandise retailers are department stores, discount stores, convenience stores, supermarkets, super-stores, hypermarkets, warehouse clubs, and warehouse showrooms (see Table 15.1).

Department Stores. Department stores are large retail organizations characterized by wide product mixes and staffs of at least 25 people. To facilitate marketing efforts and internal management in these stores, related product lines are organized into separate departments, such as cosmetics, housewares, apparel, home furnishings, and appliances, to facilitate marketing and internal management. Often each department functions as a self-contained business, and buyers for individual departments are fairly autonomous.

Department stores are distinctly service oriented. Their total product may include credit, delivery, personal assistance, merchandise returns, and a pleasant atmosphere. Although some so-called department stores are actually large, departmentalized specialty stores, most department stores are shopping stores. Consumers can compare price, quality, and service at one store with those at competing stores. Along with large discount stores, department stores are often considered retailing leaders in a community and are found in most places with populations of more than 50,000.

Typical department stores, such as Macy's, Sears, JCPenney, Dillard's, and Neiman Marcus, obtain a large proportion of sales from apparel, accessories, and cosmetics. Other products these stores carry include gift items, luggage, electronics, home accessories, and sports equipment. Some department stores offer such services as automobile insurance, hair care, income tax preparation, and travel and optical services. In some cases, space for these specialized services is leased out, with proprietors managing their own operations and paying rent to the store.

Discount Stores. In recent years, department stores have been losing sales to discount stores, especially Wal-Mart and Target. **Discount stores** are self-service general-merchandise outlets that regularly offer brand name and private brand products at low prices. Discounters accept lower margins than conventional retailers in exchange for high sales volume. To keep inventory turnover high, they carry a wide but carefully selected assortment of products, from appliances to housewares and clothing. Major discount establishments also offer food products, toys, automotive services, garden supplies, and sports equipment.

Wal-Mart and Target are the two largest discount stores. Wal-Mart has grown to 6,775 stores worldwide and brings in nearly $350 billion in sales annually.[5] Some discounters, such as Meijer, Inc., are regional organizations. Most of them operate in large (50,000 to 80,000 square feet), no-frills facilities. Discount stores usually offer everyday low prices rather than relying on sales events.

Discount retailing developed on a large scale in the early 1950s, when postwar production began catching up with consumer demand for appliances, home furnishings, and other hard goods. Discount stores were often cash-only operations in warehouse districts, offering goods at savings of 20 to 30 percent over conventional retailers. Facing increased competition from department stores and other discount stores, some discounters have improved store services, atmosphere, and location, raising prices and sometimes blurring the distinction between discount store and department store. Other discounters continue to focus on price alone.

Convenience Stores. A **convenience store** is a small self-service store that is open long hours and carries a narrow assortment of products, usually convenience items such as soft drinks and other beverages, snacks, newspapers, tobacco, and gasoline, as well as services such as automatic teller machines. The primary product offered by the "corner store" is convenience. 7-Eleven's director of processed foods says, "When consumers visit a 7-Eleven, they seek something that will solve their immediate need. They are in the mood for a consumable product and want it right now, and expect the convenience store to deliver it."[6]

According to the National Association of Convenience Stores, there are 145,119 convenience stores in the United States with 1.5 million employees. They are typically less than 5,000 square feet; open 24 hours a day, 7 days a week; and stock about 500 items. In addition to many national chains, there are many family-owned independent convenience stores in operation. The convenience store concept was developed in 1927 when Southland Ice in Dallas began stocking milk, eggs, and other products for customers who wanted to replenish their "ice boxes."[7] Southland eventually evolved into 7-Eleven, which now has 5,300 stores in the United States. Gasoline sales account for just one-third of the chain's total sales, which increasingly include upscale merchandise such as wine and high-end sandwiches and snacks.[8]

Supermarkets. **Supermarkets** are large self-service stores that carry a complete line of food products, as well as some nonfood products such as cosmetics and nonprescription drugs. Supermarkets are arranged in departments for maximum efficiency in stocking and handling products but have central checkout facilities. They offer lower prices than smaller neighborhood grocery stores, usually provide free parking, and also may cash checks.

Today, consumers make more than three-quarters of all grocery purchases in supermarkets. Even so, supermarkets' total share of the food market is declining because consumers now have widely varying food preferences and buying habits, and in many communities, shoppers can choose from several convenience stores, discount stores, and specialty food stores, as well as a wide variety of restaurants. Wal-Mart, for example, expects to generate in its "supermarket-type" stores more revenue than the

discount stores Self-service, general-merchandise stores that offer brand name and private brand products at low prices

convenience store A small self-service store that is open long hours and carries a narrow assortment of products, usually convenience items

supermarkets Large, self-service stores that carry a complete line of food products, along with some nonfood products

green MARKETING

Is There a Green Wal-Mart in the Future?

Almost everyone is familiar with Wal-Mart, the world's largest retailer and public corporation by revenue. It is the largest private employer in the world and the largest grocery retailer in the United States, with an estimated 20 percent of the retail grocery and consumables market. Wal-Mart has also been extremely successful in South America, China, Canada, and other regions of the world. Despite its success, the discount giant has been roundly criticized for its extensive foreign sourcing, low wages, gender discrimination, anti-union activities, and negative effect on existing stores in small communities. More recently Wal-Mart has been trying to make a difference in terms of eco-responsibility.

Wal-Mart has launched a green program to encourage sustainability of the world's fisheries, forests, and communities; slash energy use; reduce carbon emissions; recycle waste; and push its 60,000 suppliers to manufacture more products that do not harm the environment. Many believe that Wal-Mart is not pushing sustainability solely for the welfare of its stakeholders: company executives are recognizing that the company can boost profits by becoming more environmentally friendly. For example, Wal-Mart can earn millions of dollars by selling its trash to recycling centers and save hundreds of millions by cutting transportation costs. Wal-Mart, which operates the second-largest truck fleet in the United States, is now testing new hybrid engine prototypes. Its heavy-duty hybrid electric power system will be available in 2009 and should provide a 5 to 7 percent fuel saving versus comparable nonhybrids. The system captures energy generated by the diesel engine, recovers energy normally lost during braking, and stores energy in batteries.

The company is also attempting to reduce greenhouse gas emissions and waste resulting from the operation of Wal-Mart stores. Its goal is to reduce overall greenhouse gas emissions by 20 percent over the next eight years. The company is designing a store that will use 30 percent less energy and produce 30 percent less greenhouse gas emissions. Wal-Mart also announced that it is joining the Clinton Climate Initiative partnership to help create environmentally friendly cities across the United States and around the world. As a part of the partnership, Wal-Mart is committed to purchasing resources to lower prices on sustainable technologies such as energy-efficient systems, energy-efficient lighting, and clean energy products.

There will always be skeptics about Wal-Mart's intentions in going green, but its activities and behavior in the area of eco-responsibility presents an optimistic picture. Wal-Mart has the opportunity to provide leadership to other retailers and to prove that going green is not only the right thing to do for the environment, but it could also improve the bottom line.[b]

top three U.S. supermarket chains—Kroger, Albertson's, and Safeway—combined. To attract more customers, Albertson's plans to make grocery shopping quick and easy with new technology that will eliminate checkout lines.[9]

Superstores. Superstores, which originated in Europe, are giant retail outlets that carry not only food and nonfood products that are ordinarily found in supermarkets but also routinely purchased consumer products. Besides a complete food line, superstores sell housewares, hardware, small appliances, clothing, personal-care products, garden products, and tires—about four times as many items as supermarkets. Services available at superstores include dry cleaning, automotive repair, check cashing, bill paying, and snack bars.

superstores Giant retail outlets that carry food and nonfood products found in supermarkets, as well as most routinely purchased consumer products

hypermarkets Stores that combine supermarket and discount store shopping in one location

warehouse clubs Large-scale, members-only establishments that combine features of cash-and-carry wholesaling with discount retailing

Warehouse Club

Sam's Club is a warehouse club that markets many product lines. Most of Sam's Club product lines have limited depth.

Superstores combine features of discount stores and supermarkets. Examples include Wal-Mart Supercenters, some Kroger stores, and Super Kmart Centers. To cut handling and inventory costs, superstores use sophisticated operating techniques and often have tall shelving that displays entire assortments of products. Superstores can have an area of as much as 200,000 square feet (compared with 20,000 square feet in traditional supermarkets). Sales volume is two to three times that of supermarkets, partly because locations near good transportation networks help generate the in-store traffic needed for profitability.

Hypermarkets. **Hypermarkets** combine supermarket and discount store shopping in one location. Larger than superstores, they range from 225,000 to 325,000 square feet and offer 45,000 to 60,000 different types of low-priced products. They commonly allocate 40 to 50 percent of their space to grocery products and the remainder to general merchandise, including athletic shoes, designer jeans, and other apparel; refrigerators, televisions, and other appliances; housewares; cameras; toys; jewelry; hardware; and automotive supplies. Many lease space to noncompeting businesses such as banks, optical shops, and fast-food restaurants. All hypermarkets focus on low prices and vast selections.

Although Kmart, Wal-Mart, and Carrefour (a French retailer) have operated hypermarkets in the United States, most of these stores were unsuccessful and closed. Such stores may be too big for time-constrained U.S. shoppers. However, hypermarkets are more successful in Europe, South America, and Mexico, and more recently in the Middle East and India.

Warehouse Clubs. **Warehouse clubs,** a rapidly growing form of mass merchandising, are large-scale, members-only selling operations that combine cash-and-carry wholesaling with discount retailing. Sometimes called *buying clubs,* warehouse clubs offer the same types of products as discount stores but in a limited range of sizes and styles. Whereas most discount stores carry around 40,000 items, a warehouse club handles only 3,500 to 5,000 products, usually acknowledged brand leaders. Sam's Club stores, for example, stock about 4,000 items, with 1,400 available most of the time and the rest being onetime buys. Costco leads the warehouse club industry with sales of $64.4 billion. Sam's Club is second with nearly $40 billion in store sales. A third company, BJ's Wholesale Club, which operates in the Northeast and Florida, has a much smaller market.[10] All these establishments offer a broad product mix, including food, beverages, books, appliances, housewares, automotive parts, hardware, and furniture.

To keep prices lower than those of supermarkets and discount stores, warehouse clubs provide few services. They generally do not advertise, except through direct mail. Their facilities, often located in industrial areas, have concrete floors and aisles wide enough for forklifts. Merchandise is stacked on pallets or displayed on pipe racks. Customers must transport purchases themselves. Warehouse clubs appeal to many price-conscious consumers and small retailers unable to obtain wholesaling services from large distributors. The average

NOT READY *for them to* **LEAVE** *the* **NEST?**

Keep them under your wing by keeping them **well-prepared.** From class supplies and computers to dorm accessories and snacks, your local Sam's Club® has the items you need to send your student off to college. You'll not only score points with your child – you'll earn an A+ on your budget.

Not a Member? For a One-Day Guest Pass or to find a Club near you, visit **samsclub.com/college**.

warehouse club shopper has more education, a higher income, and a larger household than the average supermarket shopper.

Warehouse Showrooms. **Warehouse showrooms** are retail facilities with five basic characteristics: large, low-cost buildings; warehouse materials-handling technology; vertical merchandise displays; large on-premises inventories; and minimal services. IKEA, a Swedish company, sells furniture, household goods, and kitchen accessories in warehouse showrooms and through catalogs around the world, including China and Russia. These high-volume, low-overhead operations stress fewer personnel and services. Lower costs are possible because some marketing functions have been shifted to consumers, who must transport, finance, and perhaps store larger quantities of products. Most consumers carry away purchases in the manufacturer's carton, although stores will deliver for a fee.

Specialty Retailers

In contrast to general-merchandise retailers with their broad product mixes, specialty retailers emphasize narrow and deep assortments. Despite their name, specialty retailers do not sell specialty items (except when specialty goods complement the overall product mix). Instead, they offer substantial assortments in a few product lines. We examine three types of specialty retailers: traditional specialty retailers, category killers, and off-price retailers.

Traditional Specialty Store

Michaels is a specialty store that focuses on craft and home decorating products.

warehouse showrooms
Retail facilities in large, low-cost buildings with large on-premises inventories and minimal services

traditional specialty retailers Stores that carry a narrow product mix with deep product lines

Traditional Specialty Retailers. **Traditional specialty retailers** are stores that carry a narrow product mix with deep product lines. Sometimes called *limited-line retailers*, they may be referred to as *single-line retailers* if they carry unusual depth in one main product category. Specialty retailers commonly sell such shopping products as apparel, jewelry, sporting goods, fabrics, computers, and pet supplies. The Limited, Radio Shack, Hickory Farms, The Gap, and Foot Locker are examples of retailers offering limited product lines but great depth within those lines.

Although the number of chain specialty stores is increasing, many specialty stores are independently owned. Florists, bakery shops, coffee shops, pet stores, and bookstores are among the small, independent specialty retailers that appeal to local target markets, although these stores can be owned and managed by large corporations. Even if this kind of retailer adds a few supporting product lines, the store may still be classified as a specialty store.

Because they are usually small, specialty stores may have high costs in proportion to sales, and satisfying customers may require carrying some products with low turnover rates. However, these stores sometimes obtain lower prices from suppliers by purchasing limited lines of merchandise in large quantities. Successful specialty stores understand their customer types and know what products to carry, thus reducing the risk of unsold merchandise. Specialty stores usually offer better selections and more sales expertise than department stores, their main competitors. By capitalizing on fashion, service, personnel, atmosphere, and location, specialty retailers position

Breakfast in bed? No thanks.

Now you can have the kitchen you crave without paying specialty store prices. From our design specialists to our professional installers, cabinets to appliances, we have everything you need to complete your project. For your FREE kitchen design, visit your nearest Lowe's today.

LOWE'S
Let's Build Something Together

Category Killer

Some stores, like Lowe's, are referred to as category killers because of their enormous product mixes and low prices.

category killer A very large specialty store that concentrates on a major product category and competes on the basis of low prices and product availability

off-price retailers Stores that buy manufacturers' seconds, overruns, returns, and off-season merchandise for resale to consumers at deep discounts

themselves strategically to attract customers in specific market segments. Specialty stores may even become exclusive dealers in their markets for certain products. Through specialty stores, small-business owners provide unique services to match consumers' varied desires. For consumers dissatisfied with the impersonal nature of large retailers, the close, personal contact offered by a small specialty store can be a welcome change.

Category Killers Over the last 20 years, a new breed of specialty retailer, the category killer, has evolved. A **category killer** is a very large specialty store that concentrates on a major product category and competes on the basis of low prices and enormous product availability. These stores are referred to as category killers because they expand rapidly and gain sizable market shares, taking business away from smaller, high-cost retail outlets. Examples of category killers include Home Depot and Lowe's (home improvement chains); Staples, Office Depot, and OfficeMax (office-supply chains); Borders and Barnes & Noble (booksellers); Petco and PetSmart (pet-supply chains); and Best Buy and Circuit City (consumer electronics).

Off-Price Retailers **Off-price retailers** are stores that buy manufacturers' seconds, overruns, returns, and off-season production runs at below-wholesale prices for resale to consumers at deep discounts. Unlike true discount stores, which pay regular wholesale prices for goods and usually carry second-line brand names, off-price retailers offer limited lines of national-brand and designer merchandise, usually clothing, shoes, or housewares. The number of off-price retailers such as T.J. Maxx, Marshalls, Stein Mart, and Burlington Coat Factory has grown since the mid-1980s.

Off-price stores charge 20 to 50 percent less than do department stores for comparable merchandise but offer few customer services. They often feature community dressing rooms and central checkout counters. Some of these stores do not take returns or allow exchanges. Off-price stores may or may not sell goods with the original labels intact. They turn over their inventory 9 to 12 times a year, three times as often as traditional specialty stores. They compete with department stores for the same customers: price-conscious customers who are knowledgeable about brand names.

To ensure a regular flow of merchandise into their stores, off-price retailers establish long-term relationships with suppliers that can provide large quantities of goods at reduced prices. Manufacturers may approach retailers with samples, discontinued products, or items that have not sold well. Also, retailers may seek out manufacturers, offering to pay cash for goods produced during the manufacturers' off season. Although manufacturers benefit from such arrangements, they also risk alienating their specialty and department store customers. Department stores tolerate off-price stores as long as they do not advertise brand names, limit merchandise to lower-quality items, and are located away from the department stores. When off-price retailers obtain large stocks of in-season, top-quality merchandise, tension builds between department stores and manufacturers.

Strategic Issues in Retailing

LO ❸ Explore strategic issues in retailing

Whereas most business purchases are based on economic planning and necessity, consumer purchases may result from social and psychological influences. Because consumers shop for various reasons—to search for specific items, escape boredom, or learn about something new—retailers must do more than simply fill space with merchandise. They must make desired products available, create stimulating shopping environments, and develop marketing strategies that increase store patronage. In this section we discuss how store location, retail positioning, store image, category management, scrambled merchandising, and the wheel of retailing affect retailing objectives.

neighborhood shopping centers Shopping centers usually consisting of several small convenience and specialty stores

community shopping centers Shopping centers with one or two department stores, some specialty stores, and convenience stores

Location of Retail Stores

"Location, location, location" is a common saying among retailers (as well as realtors) because of its critical importance to success. At the same time, the retail location is the least flexible of the strategic retailing issues but is one of the most important because location dictates the limited geographic trading area from which a store draws its customers. Retailers consider various factors when evaluating potential locations, including location of the firm's target market within the trading area, kinds of products being sold, availability of public transportation, customer characteristics, and competitors' locations.

In choosing a location, a retailer evaluates the relative ease of movement to and from the site, including factors such as pedestrian and vehicular traffic, parking, and transportation. Retailers also evaluate the characteristics of the site itself: types of stores in the area; size, shape, and visibility of the lot or building under consideration; and rental, leasing, or ownership terms. Retailers look for compatibility with nearby retailers because stores that complement one another draw more customers for everyone.

Many retailers choose to locate in downtown central business districts, whereas others prefer sites within various types of planned shopping centers. Some retailers, including Toys 'R' Us, Wal-Mart, Home Depot, and many fast-food restaurants, opt for freestanding structures that are not connected to other buildings, but many chain stores are found in planned shopping centers and malls. Some retailers choose to locate in less orthodox settings. McDonald's, for example, has opened several stores inside hospitals, whereas Subway has franchise locations inside churches, laundromats, and hospitals.[11] Planned shopping centers include neighborhood, community, regional, superregional, lifestyle, and power shopping centers (Table 15.2).

Neighborhood shopping centers usually consist of several small convenience and specialty stores, such as small grocery stores, gas stations, and fast-food restaurants. Many of these retailers consider their target markets to be consumers who live within two to three miles of their stores, or ten minutes' driving time. Because most purchases are based on convenience or personal contact, there is usually little coordination of selling efforts within a neighborhood shopping center. Generally, product mixes consist of essential products, and depth of the product lines is limited.

Community shopping centers include one or two department stores and some specialty stores, as well as convenience stores. They draw consumers looking for shopping and specialty products not available in neighborhood shopping centers. Because these centers serve larger geographic areas, consumers must drive longer distances to community shopping centers than to neighborhood

Retail Location

McDonald's focuses on securing highly desirable, easy-to-enter and -exit locations in high-traffic areas.

What are our new Southwest Salad and our Caesar, Bacon Ranch, and Asian Salads made of? Up to 15 varieties of exotic lettuce and other premium ingredients like roasted tomatoes, edamame, mandarin oranges, almonds, poblano peppers, red peppers, fire-roasted corn, all white meat chicken breast and, of course, all natural Newman's Own® Dressings. See, we are as picky as you are. That's *What We're Made Of.*

i'm lovin' it

| table 15.2 | TYPES AND CHARACTERISTICS OF SHOPPING CENTERS |

Type	Concept	Open or Enclosed?	Acreage	Number of Anchors	Radius of Primary Trade Area (Miles)
Neighborhood center	Convenience	Open	3–15	1 or more	3
Community center	General merchandise, convenience	Open	10–40	2 or more	3–6
Regional center	General merchandise, fashion	Enclosed	40–100	2 or more	5–15
Superregional center	More variety than regional center	Enclosed	60–120	3 or more	5–25
Lifestyle center	Upscale specialty, dining, and entertainment, usually national chains	Open	10–40	0–2	8–12
Power center	Category-dominant anchors, a few smaller businesses	Open	25–80	3 or more	5–10
Outlet center	Manufacturers' outlet stores	Open	10–50	N/A	25–75

Source: Copyright © 2004 International Council of Shopping Centers, Inc., New York, New York. Published in [adapted from] "ICSC Shopping Center Definitions, Basic Configurations, and Types for the United States, " dated 8/19/2008, 2004. Reprinted with permission.

regional shopping center
A type of shopping center with the largest department stores, widest product mixes, and deepest product lines of all shopping centers

superregional shopping center A type of shopping center with the widest and deepest product mixes that attracts customers from many miles away

lifestyle shopping center A type of shopping center that is typically open air and features upscale specialty, dining, and entertainment stores

centers. Community shopping centers are planned and coordinated to attract shoppers. Special events, such as art exhibits, automobile shows, and sidewalk sales, stimulate traffic. Managers of community shopping centers look for tenants that complement the centers' total assortment of products. Such centers have wide product mixes and deep product lines.

Regional shopping centers usually have the largest department stores, widest product mixes, and deepest product lines of all shopping centers. Many shopping malls are regional shopping centers, although some are community shopping centers. With 150,000 or more consumers in their target market, regional shopping centers must have well-coordinated management and marketing activities. Target markets may include consumers traveling from a distance to find products and prices not available in their hometowns. Because of the expense of leasing space in regional shopping centers, tenants are more likely to be national chains than small, independent stores. Large centers usually advertise, have special events, furnish transportation to some consumer groups, maintain their own security forces, and carefully select the mix of stores. The largest of these centers, sometimes called **superregional shopping centers,** have the widest and deepest product mixes and attract customers from many miles away. Superregional centers often have special attractions beyond stores, such as skating rinks, amusement centers, or upscale restaurants. Mall of America, in the Minneapolis area, is the largest shopping mall in the United States with 520 stores, including Nordstrom and Bloomingdale's, and 50 restaurants. The shopping center also includes a walk-through aquarium, museum, theme parks, 14-screen movie theater, hotels, and many special events.[12]

With traditional mall sales declining, some shopping center developers are looking to new formats that differ significantly from traditional shopping centers. A **lifestyle shopping center** is typically an open-air shopping center that features upscale specialty, dining, and entertainment stores, usually owned by national chains. They are often located near affluent neighborhoods and may have fountains, benches, and other amenities that encourage "casual browsing." Indeed, architectural design is an important aspect of these "minicities," which may include urban streets or parks, and is intended to encourage consumer loyalty by creating a sense of place. Some lifestyle centers are designed to resemble traditional "Main Street" shopping centers or may have a central theme evidenced by architecture.[13]

Lifestyle Shopping Centers

Many lifestyle shopping centers consist of stores such as Eddie Bauer, Apple Store, Sharper Image, and Ann Taylor Lofts.

Some shopping center developers are bypassing the traditional department store anchor and combining off-price stores and small stores with category killers in **power shopping center** formats. These centers may be anchored by a store such as The Gap, Toys 'R' Us, Circuit City, PetSmart, and Home Depot. The number of power shopping centers is growing, resulting in a variety of formats vying for the same retail dollar.

Factory outlet malls feature discount and factory outlet stores carrying traditional manufacturer brands, such as Quicksilver, Liz Claiborne, Reebok, and Le Creuset. Some outlet centers feature upscale products. Manufacturers own these stores and make a special effort to avoid conflict with traditional retailers of their products. Manufacturers claim their stores are in noncompetitive locations; indeed, most factory outlet centers are located outside metropolitan areas. Not all factory outlets stock closeouts and irregulars, but most avoid comparison with discount houses. Factory outlet centers attract value-conscious customers seeking quality and major brand names. They operate in much the same way as regional shopping centers, but usually draw customers, some of whom may be tourists, from a larger shopping radius. Promotional activity is at the heart of these shopping centers. Craft and antique shows, contests, and special events attract a great deal of traffic.

Retail Positioning

The large variety of shopping centers and the expansion of product offerings by traditional stores have intensified retailing competition. Retail positioning is therefore an important consideration. **Retail positioning** involves identifying an unserved or underserved market segment and serving it through a strategy that distinguishes the retailer from others in the minds of those customers. For example, Payless Shoe-Source, a specialty store chain, has built a reputation for providing a wide variety of low-price shoes in a warehouse-like environment. The retailer is attempting to reposition itself as a purveyor of stylish and trendy shoes with a wider price range (going as high as $60) by expanding its merchandise mix and sprucing up its 4,500 stores. Targeting more women who are as interested in fashion as in low prices, Payless has even opened a New York design office to focus on original styles and has introduced a line of shoes designed by Laura Poretzky.[14] In recent years, a number of discount and specialty store chains have positioned themselves to appeal to time- and cash-strapped consumers with convenient locations and layouts as well as low prices. This strategy has helped them gain market share at the expense of large department stores.

Store Image. To attract customers, a retail store must project an image—a functional and psychological picture in the consumer's mind—that appeals to its target market. Store environment, merchandise quality, and service quality are key determinants of store image.

Atmospherics, the physical elements in a store's design that appeal to consumers' emotions and encourage buying, help to create an image and position a retailer. Barnes & Noble, for example, uses murals of authors and framed pictures of classic book covers to convey a literary image. Studies show that retailers can use different elements—music, color, and complexity of layout and merchandise presentation—to influence customer arousal based on their shopping motivation. Supermarkets, for example, should use cooler colors and simple layout and presentations because their customers tend to be task motivated, whereas specialty retailers may be able to use more complex layouts and brighter colors to stimulate their more recreationally motivated customers.[15]

power shopping center A type of shopping center that combines off-price stores with category killers

retail positioning Identifying an unserved or under-served market segment and serving it through a strategy that distinguishes the retailer from others in the minds of consumers in that segment

atmospherics The physical elements in a store's design that appeal to consumers' emotions and encourage buying

Exterior atmospheric elements include the appearance of the storefront, display windows, store entrances, and degree of traffic congestion. Exterior atmospherics are particularly important to new customers, who tend to judge an unfamiliar store by its outside appearance and may not enter if they feel intimidated by the building or inconvenienced by the parking lot.

Interior atmospheric elements include aesthetic considerations such as lighting, wall and floor coverings, dressing facilities, and store fixtures. Interior sensory elements contribute significantly to atmosphere. Color can attract shoppers to a retail display. Many fast-food restaurants use bright colors, such as red and yellow, because these have been shown to make customers feel hungrier and eat faster, which increases turnover. Sound is another important sensory component of atmosphere and may range from silence to subdued background music. Pottery Barn, for example, plays 1950s cocktail bar music, whereas JCPenney varies the music in its stores—even within departments—based on local demographics.[16] Many retailers employ scent, especially food aromas, to attract customers. Research suggests that consumer evaluations of a product are affected by scent, but only when the scent employed is congruent with the product.[17] In one study, 90 percent of surveyed consumers ranked cleanliness—particularly in supermarkets—as the most important atmospheric element in choosing a shopping destination. Lighting, temperature, and aisle width also were ranked highly. Active elements such as in-store televisions were rated among the least influential.[18]

Store Image

Sportsman's Warehouse utilizes atmospherics to create a rugged, outdoor feeling in its stores.

category management A retail strategy of managing groups of similar, often substitutable products produced by different manufacturers

scrambled merchandising The addition of unrelated product lines to an existing product mix, particularly fast-moving items that can be sold in volume

Category Management

Category management is a retail strategy of managing groups of similar, often substitutable products produced by different manufacturers. For example, supermarkets such as Safeway use category management to determine space for products such as cosmetics, cereals, and soups. An assortment of merchandise is both customer and strategically driven to improve performance. Category management developed in the food industry because supermarkets were concerned about highly competitive behavior among manufacturers.

Category management is a move toward a collaborative supply-chain initiative to enhance customer value. Successful category management requires the acquisition, analysis, and sharing of sales and consumer information between the retailer and manufacturer. Wal-Mart, for example, has developed strong supplier relationships with manufacturers such as Procter & Gamble. The development of information about demand, consumer behavior, and optimal allocations of products should be available from one source. Firms such as SAS provide software to manage data associated with each step of the category management decision cycle. The key is cooperative interaction between the manufacturers of category products and the retailer to create maximum success for all parties in the supply chain.

Scrambled Merchandising

When retailers add unrelated products and product lines—particularly fast-moving items that can be sold in volume—to an existing product mix, they are practicing **scrambled merchandising.** Retailers adopting this strategy hope to accomplish one or more of the following: (1) convert stores into one-stop shopping centers, (2) generate more traffic, (3) realize higher profit margins, and (4) increase impulse purchases. In scrambled merchandising, retailers must deal with diverse marketing channels. Scrambled merchandising also can blur a store's image in consumers' minds, making it more difficult for a retailer to succeed in today's highly competitive, saturated markets. Finally, scrambled merchandising intensifies competition among traditionally distinct types of stores and forces suppliers to adjust distribution systems to accommodate new channel members.

The Wheel of Retailing

As new types of retail businesses evolve, they strive to fill niches in a dynamic retailing environment. One hypothesis regarding the evolution and development of new types of retail stores is the **wheel of retailing.** According to this theory, new retailers enter the marketplace with low prices, margins, and status. Their low prices are usually the result of innovative cost-cutting procedures and soon attract imitators. Gradually, as these businesses attempt to broaden their customer base and increase sales, their operations and facilities become more elaborate and more expensive. They may move to more desirable locations, begin to carry higher- quality merchandise, or add services. Eventually they emerge at the high end of the price, cost, and service scales, competing with newer discount retailers following the same evolutionary process.[19]

Supermarkets, for example, have undergone many changes since their introduction in 1921. Initially they offered limited services and low food prices. Over time they developed a variety of new services, including free coffee, gourmet food sections, and children's play areas. Today supermarkets are being challenged by superstores, which offer more product choices and undercut supermarket prices.

Consider the evolution of department stores, discount stores, warehouse clubs, category killers, and online retailers. Department stores such as Sears started out as high-volume, low-cost merchants that compete with general stores and other small retailers. Discount stores developed later in response to rising expenses of services in department stores. Many discount outlets now appear to be following the wheel of retailing by offering more services, better locations, quality inventories, and therefore higher prices. Some discount stores are almost indistinguishable from department stores. In response have emerged category killers, such as PetSmart and Office Depot, which concentrate on a major product category and offer enormous product depth, in many cases at lower prices than discount stores. Even these retailers, however, seem to be following the wheel. Lowe's, a home improvement retailer, has added big-ticket items and more upscale brands, such as Laura Ashley.

The wheel of retailing, along with other changes in the marketing environment and in buying behavior itself, requires that retailers adjust to survive and compete. Consumers have less time than ever to shop. Shopping today centers on "needs fulfillment" and thus is more utilitarian and work oriented, a fact that many major retailing executives have noticed. As consumers have less time to shop and greater access to more sophisticated technology, retailing venues such as catalog retailing, television home shopping, and online retailing will take on greater importance. New retailers will evolve to capitalize on these opportunities, while those that cannot adapt will not survive.

wheel of retailing A hypothesis holding that new retailers usually enter the market as low-status, low-margin, low-price operators but eventually evolve into high-cost, high-price merchants

direct marketing The use of the telephone, Internet, and nonpersonal media to introduce products to customers, who can then purchase them via mail, telephone, or the Internet

Direct Marketing and Direct Selling

L O 4 Recognize the various forms of direct marketing and selling

Although retailers are the most visible members of the supply chain, many products are sold outside the confines of a retail store. Direct selling and direct marketing account for an increasing percentage of product sales. Products also may be sold in automatic vending machines, but these account for less than 2 percent of all retail sales.

Direct Marketing

Direct marketing is the use of the telephone, Internet, and nonpersonal media to communicate product and organizational information to customers, who can then purchase products via mail, telephone, or the Internet. Direct marketing is one type of nonstore retailing. Sales through direct marketing activities amount to $2 trillion per year.[20] In the auto industry alone, $77.8 billion in sales stemmed from the $8 billion spent on direct marketing campaigns in 2007.[21] **Nonstore retailing** is the selling of products outside the confines of a retail facility. This form of retailing accounts for an increasing percentage of total sales. Direct marketing can occur through catalog marketing, direct-response marketing, telemarketing, television home shopping, and online retailing.

Catalog Marketing. In **catalog marketing,** an organization provides a catalog from which customers make selections and place orders by mail, telephone, or the Internet. Catalog marketing began in 1872, when Montgomery Ward issued its first catalog to rural families. Today there are more than 7,000 catalog marketing companies in the United States, as well as several retail stores, such as JCPenney, that engage in catalog marketing. Some organizations, including Spiegel and JCPenney, offer a broad array of products spread over multiple product lines. Catalog companies such as Lands' End, Pottery Barn, and J. Crew offer considerable depth in just a few major lines of products. Still other catalog companies specialize in only a few products within a single line. Some catalog retailers—for instance, Cabela's, Crate & Barrel, and The Sharper Image—have stores in major metropolitan areas.

The advantages of catalog retailing include efficiency and convenience for customers. The retailer benefits by being able to locate in remote, low cost areas, save on expensive store fixtures; and reduce both personal selling and store operating expenses. On the other hand, catalog retailing is inflexible, provides limited service, and is most effective for a selected set of products.

Direct-Response Marketing. **Direct-response marketing** occurs when a retailer advertises a product and makes it available through mail or telephone orders. Generally, a purchase may use a credit card, but other forms of payment may be permitted. Examples of direct-response marketing include a television commercial offering exercise machines, cosmetics or household cleaning products available through a toll-free number, and a newspaper or magazine advertisement for a series of children's books available by filling out the form in the ad or calling a toll-free number. Direct-response marketing is also conducted by sending letters, samples, brochures, or booklets to prospects on a mailing list and asking that they order the advertised products by mail or telephone. In general, products must be priced above $20 to justify the advertising and distribution costs associated with direct-response marketing.

Telemarketing. A number of organizations use the telephone to strengthen the effectiveness of traditional marketing methods. **Telemarketing** is the performance of marketing-related activities by telephone. Some organizations use a prescreened list of prospective clients. Telemarketing can help to generate sales leads, improve customer service, speed up payments on past-due accounts, raise funds for nonprofit organizations, and gather marketing data.

Currently, the laws and regulations regarding telemarketing, although in a state of flux, are becoming more restrictive. In 2003 Congress implemented a national do-not-call registry for consumers who do not wish to receive telemarketing calls. By 2007, more than 145 million phone numbers in the United States had been listed on the registry.[22] The national registry is enforced by the Federal Trade Commission and the Federal Communications Commission, and companies are subject to a fine of up to $11,000 for each call made to a consumer listed on the national do-not-call registry.[23] Since the registry went into effect, the two federal agencies have collected $16 million in penalties and $8 million in restitution from violators.[24] Certain exceptions apply to do-not-call lists. A company still can use telemarketing to communicate with existing customers. In addition, charitable, political, and telephone survey organizations are not restricted by the national registry.

Television Home Shopping. **Television home shopping** presents products to television viewers, encouraging them to order through toll-free numbers and pay with credit cards. The Home Shopping Network in Florida originated and popularized this format. The most popular products sold through television home shopping are jewelry (40 percent of total sales), clothing, housewares, and electronics. Home shopping channels have grown so rapidly in recent years that more than 60 percent

nonstore retailing The selling of products outside the confines of a retail facility

catalog marketing A type of marketing in which an organization provides a catalog from which customers make selections and place orders by mail, telephone, or the Internet

direct-response marketing A type of marketing in which a retailer advertises a product and makes it available through mail or telephone orders

telemarketing The performance of marketing-related activities by telephone

television home shopping A form of selling in which products are presented to television viewers, who can buy them by calling a toll-free number and paying with a credit card

Online Retailing

ebay Motors is an online retailer offering a variety of vehicles.

of U.S. households have access to home shopping programs. Home Shopping Network and QVC are two of the largest home shopping networks. Approximately 60 percent of home shopping sales revenues come from repeat purchasers.

The television home shopping format offers several benefits. Products can be demonstrated easily, and an adequate amount of time can be spent showing the product so viewers are well informed. The length of time a product is shown depends not only on the time required for doing demonstrations but also on whether the product is selling. Once the calls peak and begin to decline, a new product is shown. Other benefits are that customers can shop at their convenience and from the comfort of their homes.

Online Retailing. **Online retailing** makes products available to buyers through computer connections. The phenomenal growth of Internet use and online information services such as AOL has created new retailing opportunities. Many retailers have set up websites to disseminate information about their companies and products. Although many retailers with websites use them primarily to promote products, a number of companies, including Barnes & Noble, REI, Lands' End, and OfficeMax, sell goods online. However, the number of companies selling online and in stores is growing dramatically as consumers demand multiple channels to obtain the goods and services they desire.

Consumers can purchase hard-to-find items, such as Pez candy dispensers and Elvis memorabilia, on eBay. They can buy upscale items for their dogs at **SitStay.com,** a Web retailer specializing in high-end dog supplies that carries a carefully screened selection of 1,500 products. Banks and brokerage firms have established websites to give customers direct access to manage their accounts and enable them to trade online. Forrester Research projects that online retail sales in the United States will climb to $335 billion by 2012, up from $175 billion in 2007.[25] With advances in computer technology continuing and consumers ever more pressed for time, online retailing will continue to escalate.

Although online retailing represents a major retailing venue, security remains an issue. In a recent survey conducted by the Business Software Alliance, about 75 percent of Internet users expressed concerns about shopping online. The major issues are identity theft and credit card theft.

Direct Selling

Direct selling is the marketing of products to ultimate consumers through face-to-face sales presentations at home or in the workplace. Traditionally called *door-to-door selling,* direct selling in the United States began with peddlers more than a century ago and has since grown into a sizable industry of several hundred firms. Although direct sellers historically used a cold-canvass, door-to-door approach for finding prospects, many companies today, such as Kirby, Amway, Mary Kay, and Avon, use other approaches. They initially identify customers through the mail, telephone, Internet, or shopping-mall intercepts and then set up appointments.

Although the majority of direct selling takes place on an individual, or person-to-person, basis, it sometimes also includes the use of a group, or "party," plan. With a party plan, a consumer acts as a host and invites friends and associates to view merchandise in a group setting, where a salesperson demonstrates products. The congenial party atmosphere helps to overcome customers' reluctance and encourages them

online retailing Retailing that makes products available to buyers through computer connections

direct selling Marketing products to ultimate consumers through face-to-face sales presentations at home or in the workplace

to buy. Tupperware and Mary Kay were the pioneers of this selling technique, paving the way for companies such as Pampered Chef to grow from a basement business into a corporation that brings in more than $700 million in revenues annually.[26]

Direct selling has both benefits and limitations. It gives the marketer an opportunity to demonstrate the product in an environment—usually customers' homes—where it most likely would be used. The door-to-door seller can give the customer personal attention, and the product can be presented to the customer at a convenient time and location. Personal attention to the customer is the foundation on which some direct sellers, such as Mary Kay, have built their businesses. Because commissions for salespeople are so high, ranging from 30 to 50 percent of the sales price, and great effort is required to isolate promising prospects, overall costs of direct selling make it the most expensive form of retailing. Furthermore, some customers view direct selling negatively, owing to unscrupulous and fraudulent practices used by some direct sellers in the past. Some communities even have local ordinances that control or, in some cases, prohibit direct selling. Despite these negative views held by some individuals, direct selling is still alive and well, bringing in revenues of $32 billion a year.[27]

Automatic Vending

Automatic vending is the use of machines to dispense products. It accounts for less than 2 percent of all retail sales. Video game machines provide an entertainment service, and most banks offer automatic teller machines (ATMs), which dispense cash and perform other services.

Automatic vending is one of the most impersonal forms of retailing. Small, standardized, routinely purchased products (e.g., chewing gum, candy, newspapers, cigarettes, soft drinks, coffee) can be sold in machines because consumers usually buy them at the nearest available location. Machines in areas of heavy traffic provide efficient and continuous service to consumers. Such high-volume areas may have more diverse product availability—for example, hot and cold sandwiches, and even upscale merchandise. ZoomSystems, for example, operates vending machines that market iPod cell phones in airports and Macy's department stores. Some new airport vending machines dispense digital cameras and designer cosmetics—and they accept credit cards.[28]

Because vending machines need only a small amount of space and no sales personnel, this retailing method has some advantages over stores. The advantages are partly offset, however, by the high costs of equipment and frequent servicing and repairs.

Franchising

L O 5 Examine franchising and its benefits and weaknesses

automatic vending The use of machines to dispense products

franchising An arrangement in which a supplier (franchiser) grants a dealer (franchisee) the right to sell products in exchange for some type of consideration

Franchising is an arrangement in which a supplier, or franchiser, grants a dealer, or franchisee, the right to sell products in exchange for some type of consideration. The franchiser may receive some percentage of total sales in exchange for furnishing equipment, buildings, management know-how, and marketing assistance to the franchisee. The franchisee supplies labor and capital, operates the franchised business, and agrees to abide by the provisions of the franchise agreement. Table 15.3 lists the leading U.S. franchises, types of products, and startup costs.

Because of changes in the international marketplace, shifting employment options in the United States, the expanding U.S. service economy, and corporate interest in more joint-venture activity, franchising is increasing rapidly. Franchising companies and their franchisees account for an estimated $1.5 trillion in annual U.S. retail sales from 760,000 franchised small businesses and employ nearly 18 million people.[29]

Major Types of Retail Franchises

Retail franchise arrangements fall into three general categories. In one arrangement, a manufacturer authorizes a number of retail stores to sell a certain brand name item. This franchise arrangement, one of the oldest forms, is common in sales of cars and trucks, farm equipment, shoes, paint, earth-moving equipment, and petroleum. In the second type of retail franchise, a producer licenses distributors to sell a given product to retailers. This arrangement is common in the soft-drink industry. Most national manufacturers of soft-drink syrups, including Coca-Cola, Dr Pepper, and

table 15.3   TOP U.S. FRANCHISERS AND THEIR STARTUP COSTS

Rank*	Franchise	Description	Number of Franchise Outlets Worldwide	Startup Costs
1	7-Eleven	Convenience stores	30,642	Varies
2	Subway	Sandwiches, salads	29,186	$76,100–$227,800
3	Dunkin' Donuts	Doughnuts, baked goods	7,376	Varies
4	Pizza Hut	Pizza	8,559	$1.1 million–$1.7 million
5	McDonald's	Hamburgers, chicken, salads	23,099	$506,000–$1.6 million
6	Sonic Drive-In Restaurants	Drive-in restaurants	2,655	$820,000–$2.3 million
7	KFC Corp.	Chicken	10,987	$1.1 million–$1.7 million
8	InterContinental Hotels Group	Hotels	3,289	Varies
9	Domino's Pizza LLC	Pizza, breadsticks, buffalo wings	7,945	$118,500–$460,300
10	RE/MAX International Inc.	Real estate	6,973	$35,000–$191,000
11	UPS Stores, Mail Boxes Etc.	Postal, business, and communication services	5,900	$170,800–$279,400
12	Ace Hardware	Hardware and home improvement	4,457	$400,000–$1 million
13	Jani-King	Commercial cleaning	12,699	$11,300–$34,100
14	Jiffy Lube	Fast oil change	1,950	$214,000–$273,000
15	Arby's	Sandwiches, chicken, salads	2,513	$336,500–$2.4 million
16	Baskin-Robbins	Ice cream, frozen yogurt, frozen beverages	5,835	$156,900–$560,400
17	Circle K	Convenience stores	3,842	$161,000–$1.3 million
18	Kumon Math & Reading Centers	Supplemental education	25,916	$30,400–$110,300
19	Great Clips Inc.	Hair salons	2,600	$106,900–$197,700
20	Bonus Building Care	Commercial cleaning	1,774	$7,800–$13,400

*Ranking is based primarily on financial strength and stability, growth rate, size of the system, number of years in business, startup costs, litigation, percentage of terminations, and whether the company provides financing.

Source: "Franchise 500® 2008 Rankings," www.entrepreneur.com/franchises/rankings/franchise500-115608/2008.html (accessed Feb. 12, 2008).

PepsiCo, grant franchises to bottlers, which in turn serve retailers. In the third type of retail franchise, a franchiser supplies brand names, techniques, or other services instead of complete products. The franchiser may provide certain production and distribution services, but its primary role in the arrangement is careful development and control of marketing strategies. This approach to franchising is very common today and is used by such organizations as Holiday Inn, AAMCO, McDonald's, Dairy Queen, KFC, and H&R Block.

Advantages and Disadvantages of Franchising

Franchising offers several advantages to both the franchisee and the franchiser. It enables a franchisee to start a business with limited capital and benefit from the business experience of others. Moreover, nationally advertised franchises, such as ServiceMaster and Burger King, are often assured of customers as soon as they open. If business problems arise, the franchisee can obtain guidance and advice from the franchiser at little or no cost. Franchised outlets are generally more successful than independently owned businesses. Fewer than 10 percent of franchised retail businesses fail during the first two years of operation, compared to approximately 50 percent of independent retail businesses. Also, the franchisee receives materials to use in local advertising and can benefit from national promotional campaigns sponsored by the franchiser.

Through franchise arrangements, the franchiser gains fast and selective product distribution without incurring the high cost of constructing and operating its own outlets. The franchiser therefore has more capital for expanding production and advertising. It can also ensure, through the franchise agreement, that outlets are maintained and operated according to its own standards. Some franchisers, however,

E-ntertainment MARKETING

Celebrities Want a Bite of Fatburger

In 1952, Lovie Yancey opened a three-stool hamburger stand in Los Angeles and called it Mr. Fatburger. That tiny location has now grown into Fatburger Corporation, based in Santa Monica, California, which operates and franchises more than 90 hamburger restaurants in 14 U.S. states, Canada, and China. Known as "the last great hamburger stand," Fatburger has become an African American cultural icon, with retro 1950s-style diners with jazz, rhythm and blues, and classic soul on the jukebox. In 1990, Yancey sold a majority of Fatburger to an investment group but retained ownership of the original Los Angeles location, which

was frequented from the start by celebrities like Redd Foxx and Ray Charles.

Fatburger has been immortalized over the years in a string of songs, movies, and TV shows, including the sitcom *Sanford and Son,* the film *The Fast and the Furious,* and the Ice Cube single "It Was a Good Day." Montel Williams owns five Fatburgers in Denver, Kanye West has the Chicago area, and Queen Latifah has a branch in Miami. "I grew up hanging out at Fatburger," says Latifah. "So it's pretty cool to now own one." One of the biggest investments was made in 2000 by Magic Johnson, who sponsored a $5.3 million management buyout with help from celebrity friends Janet Jackson, David Spade, Cher, and Darren Starr, the creator of the HBO series *Sex and the City.* Other celebrities keep lining up at the door for franchises. In 2006, Orlando Brown, who played for the Baltimore Ravens, signed on for restaurants around the D.C. area. The same year two members of the hip-hop group The Roots bought a franchise in Philadelphia. Grammy-winning artist and producer Pharrell Williams brought the chain to China in late 2007, with plans to add more than 20 additional Chinese locations by 2010.

One caution when aligning a business with celebrities was exemplified when Magic Johnson decided to take steps to lessen his involvement with the chain after three years with Fatburger. He sold a majority of his share, retaining a minority, nonvoting interest. Much of the difference between the two parties was related to brand loyalty: "We prefer to control our own brand," said CEO Keith Warlick. "Magic Johnson is a brand itself, and with celebrity groups, their interest is controlling their brand."[c]

permit their franchisees to modify their menus, hours, or other operating elements to better match their target market's needs. For example, Wings Over, a buffalo-style chicken wing franchise, has permitted menu variations to match local tastes and allowed some franchisees located near colleges and universities to open at 4 p.m. and close at 3 a.m.[30] The franchiser benefits from the fact that the franchisee, being a sole proprietor in most cases, is likely to be very highly motivated to succeed. Success of the franchise means more sales, which translate into higher income for the franchiser.

Franchise arrangements also have several drawbacks. The franchiser can dictate many aspects of the business: decor, menu, design of employees' uniforms, types of signs, hours of operation, and numerous details of business operations. In addition, franchisees must pay to use the franchiser's name, products, and assistance. Usually there is a onetime franchise fee and continuing royalty and advertising fees, often collected as a percentage of sales. For example, Subway requires franchisees to come up with $70,000 to $220,000 in startup costs. Franchisees often must work very hard, putting in 10- to 12-hour days six or seven days a week. In some cases, franchise agreements are not uniform; one franchisee may pay more than another for the same services. Finally, the franchiser gives up a certain amount of control when entering into a franchise agreement. Consequently individual establishments may not be operated exactly according to the franchiser's standards.

Wholesaling

L O 6 Understand the nature and functions of wholesaling

Wholesaling refers to all transactions in which products are bought for resale, for making other products, or for general business operations. It does not include exchanges with ultimate consumers. A **wholesaler** is an individual or organization that sells products that are bought for resale, for making other products, or for general business operations. In other words, wholesalers buy products and resell them to reseller, government, and institutional users. For example, Sysco, the nation's number one food-service distributor, supplies restaurants, hotels, schools, industrial caterers, and hospitals with everything from frozen and fresh food and paper products to medical and cleaning supplies. There are more than 429,500 wholesaling establishments in the United States,[31] and more than half of all products sold in this country pass through these firms.

Table 15.4 lists the major activities wholesalers perform, but individual wholesalers may perform more or fewer functions than those in the table. Distribution of all goods requires wholesaling activities whether or not a wholesaling firm is involved. Wholesaling activities are not limited to goods; service companies, such as financial institutions, also use active wholesale networks. For example, some banks buy loans in bulk from other financial institutions as well as making loans to their own retail customers.

Wholesalers may engage in many supply-chain management activities, including warehousing, shipping and product handling, inventory control, information system management and data processing, risk taking, financing, budgeting, and even marketing research and promotion. Regardless of whether there is a wholesaling firm involved in the supply chain, all product distribution requires the performance of these activities. In addition to bearing the primary responsibility for the physical distribution of products from manufacturers to retailers, wholesalers may establish information systems that help producers and retailers better manage the supply chain from producer to customer. Many wholesalers are using information technology and the Internet to allow their employees, customers, and suppliers to share information between intermediaries and facilitating agencies such as trucking companies and warehouse firms. Other firms are making their databases and marketing information systems available to their supply-chain partners to facilitate order processing, shipping, and product development and to share information about changing market conditions and customer desires. As a result, some wholesalers play a key role in supply-chain management decisions.

wholesaling Transactions in which products are bought for resale, for making other products, or for general business operations

wholesaler An individual or organization that sells products that are bought for resale, for making other products, or for general business operations

table 15.4	MAJOR WHOLESALING FUNCTIONS
Supply-chain management	Creating long-term partnerships among channel members
Promotion	Providing a sales force, advertising, sales promotion, and publicity
Warehousing, shipping, and product handling	Receiving, storing, and stock keeping Packaging Shipping outgoing orders Materials handling Arranging and making local and long-distance shipments
Inventory control and data processing	Processing orders Controlling physical inventory Recording transactions Tracking sales data for financial analysis
Risk taking	Assuming responsibility for theft, product obsolescence, and excess inventories
Financing and budgeting	Extending credit Borrowing Making capital investments Forecasting cash flow
Marketing research and information systems	Providing information about markets Conducting research studies Managing computer networks to facilitate exchanges and relationships

Services Provided by Wholesalers

Wholesalers provide essential services to both producers and retailers. By initiating sales contacts with a producer and selling diverse products to retailers, wholesalers serve as an extension of the producer's sales force. Wholesalers also provide financial assistance. They often pay for transporting goods; they reduce a producer's warehousing expenses and inventory investment by holding goods in inventory; they extend credit and assume losses from buyers who turn out to be poor credit risks; and when they buy a producer's entire output and pay promptly or in cash, they are a source of working capital. Wholesalers also serve as conduits for information within the marketing channel, keeping producers up to date on market developments and passing along the manufacturers' promotional plans to other intermediaries. Using wholesalers therefore gives producers a distinct advantage because the specialized services wholesalers perform allow producers to concentrate on developing and manufacturing products that match customers' needs and wants.

Wholesalers support retailers by assisting with marketing strategy, especially the distribution component. Wholesalers also help retailers to select inventory. They are often specialists on market conditions and experts at negotiating final purchases. In industries in which obtaining supplies is important, skilled buying is indispensable. For example, Atlanta-based Genuine Parts Company (GPC), the nation's top automotive parts wholesaler, has more than 70 years of experience in the auto parts business, which helps it serve its customers effectively. GPC supplies more than 300,000 replacement parts (from 150 different suppliers) to 1,325 NAPA Auto Parts stores.[32] Effective wholesalers make an effort to understand the businesses of their customers. They can reduce a retailer's burden of looking for and coordinating supply sources. If the wholesaler purchases for several different buyers, expenses can be shared by all customers. Furthermore, whereas a manufacturer's salesperson offers retailers only a few products at a time, independent wholesalers always have a wide range of products available. Thus, through partnerships, wholesalers and retailers can forge successful relationships for the benefit of customers.

The distinction between services performed by wholesalers and those provided by other businesses has blurred in recent years. Changes in the competitive nature of business, especially the growth of strong retail chains like Wal-Mart, Home Depot, and Best Buy, are changing supply-chain relationships. In many product categories, such as electronics, furniture, and even food products, retailers have discovered that they can deal directly with producers, performing wholesaling activities themselves at a lower cost. An increasing number of retailers are relying on computer technology to expedite ordering, delivery, and handling of goods. Technology is thus allowing retailers to take over many wholesaling functions. However, when a wholesaler is eliminated from a marketing channel, wholesaling activities still have to be performed by a member of the supply chain, whether a producer, retailer, or facilitating agency. These wholesaling activities are critical components of supply-chain management.

Types of Wholesalers

L O 7 Understand how wholesalers are classified

Wholesalers are classified according to several criteria. Whether a wholesaler is independently owned or owned by a producer influences how it is classified. Wholesalers also can be grouped according to whether they take title to (own) the products they handle. The range of services provided is another criterion used for classification. Finally, wholesalers are classified according to the breadth and depth of their product lines. Using these criteria, we discuss three general types of wholesaling establishments: merchant wholesalers, agents and brokers, and manufacturers' sales branches and offices.

Merchant Wholesalers. **Merchant wholesalers** are independently owned businesses that take title to goods, assume risks associated with ownership, and generally buy and resell products to other wholesalers, business customers, or retailers. A producer is likely to rely on merchant wholesalers when selling directly to customers would be economically unfeasible. Merchant wholesalers are also useful for providing market coverage, making sales contacts, storing inventory, handling orders, collecting market information, and furnishing customer support. Some merchant wholesalers are even involved in packaging and developing private brands to help retail customers be competitive. Merchant wholesalers go by various names, including *wholesaler, jobber, distributor, assembler, exporter,* and *importer.* They fall into one of two broad categories: full-service and limited-service (see Figure 15.1).

Full-service wholesalers perform the widest possible range of wholesaling functions. Customers rely on them for product availability, suitable assortments, breaking large quantities into smaller ones, financial assistance, and technical advice and service. Universal Corporation, the world's largest buyer and processor of leaf tobacco, is an example of a full-service wholesaler. Based in Richmond, Virginia, the firm buys, processes, resells, and ships tobacco and provides financing for its customers, which

merchant wholesalers
Independently owned businesses that take title to goods, assume ownership risks, and buy and resell products to other wholesalers, business customers, or retailers

full-service wholesalers
Merchant wholesalers that perform the widest range of wholesaling functions

figure 15.1

TYPES OF MERCHANT WHOLESALERS

Merchant wholesalers
Take title, assume risk, and buy and resell products to other wholesalers, to retailers, or to other business customers

Full-service wholesalers
▸ General-merchandise
▸ Limited-line
▸ Specialty-line

Limited-service wholesalers
▸ Cash-and-carry
▸ Truck
▸ Drop shipper
▸ Mail-order

include cigarette manufacturers such as Philip Morris (which accounts for a significant portion of Universal's sales). Universal is also involved in sales of lumber, building products, and other agricultural products and has operations in 35 countries.[33] Full-service wholesalers handle either consumer or business products and provide numerous marketing services to their customers. Many large grocery wholesalers help retailers with store design, site selection, personnel training, financing, merchandising, advertising, coupon redemption, and scanning. Although full-service wholesalers often earn higher gross margins than other wholesalers, their operating expenses are also higher because they perform a wider range of functions.

Full-service wholesalers are categorized as general-merchandise, general-line, and specialty-line wholesalers and as rack jobbers. **General-merchandise wholesalers** carry a wide product mix but offer limited depth within product lines. They deal in products such as drugs, nonperishable foods, cosmetics, detergents, and tobacco. **General-line wholesalers** carry only a few product lines, such as groceries, lighting fixtures, or oil-well-drilling equipment, but offer an extensive assortment of products within those lines. Bergen Brunswig Corporation, for example, is a general-line wholesaler of pharmaceuticals and health and beauty aids.

General-line wholesalers provide a range of services similar to those of general-merchandise wholesalers. **Specialty-line wholesalers** offer the narrowest range of products, usually a single product line or a few items within a product line. Red River Commodities, Inc., for example, is the leading importer (specialty-line wholesaler) of nuts, seeds, and dried fruits in the United States.[34] **Rack jobbers** are full-service, specialty-line wholesalers that own and maintain display racks in supermarkets, drugstores, and discount and variety stores. They set up displays, mark merchandise, stock shelves, and keep billing and inventory records; retailers need furnish only space. Rack jobbers specialize in nonfood items with high profit margins, such as health and beauty aids, books, magazines, hosiery, and greeting cards.

Limited-service wholesalers provide fewer marketing services than do full-service wholesalers and specialize in just a few functions. Producers perform the remaining functions or pass them on to customers or to other intermediaries. Limited-service wholesalers take title to merchandise but often do not deliver merchandise, grant credit, provide marketing information, store inventory, or plan ahead for customers' future needs. Because they offer restricted services, limited-service wholesalers are compensated with lower rates and have smaller profit margins than full-service wholesalers. The decision about whether to use a limited-service or a full-service wholesaler depends on the structure of the marketing channel and the need to manage the supply chain to provide competitive advantage. Although certain types of limited-service wholesalers are few in number, they are important in the distribution of products such as specialty foods, perishable items, construction materials, and coal. Table 15.5 summarizes the

general-merchandise wholesalers Full-service wholesalers with a wide product mix but limited depth within product lines

general-line wholesalers Full-service wholesalers that carry only a few product lines but many products within those lines

specialty-line wholesalers Full-service wholesalers that carry only a single product line or a few items within a product line

rack jobbers Full-service, specialty-line wholesalers that own and maintain display racks in stores

limited-service wholesalers Merchant wholesalers that provide some services and specialize in a few functions

table 15.5 SERVICES THAT LIMITED-SERVICE WHOLESALERS PROVIDE				
	Cash-and-Carry	Truck	Drop Shipper	Mail-Order
Physical possession of merchandise	Yes	Yes	No	Yes
Personal sales calls on customers	No	Yes	No	No
Information about market conditions	No	Some	Yes	Yes
Advice to customers	No	Some	Yes	No
Stocking and maintenance of merchandise in customers' stores	No	No	No	No
Credit to customers	No	No	Yes	Some
Delivery of merchandise to customers	No	Yes	No	No

services provided by four typical limited-service wholesalers: cash-and-carry wholesalers, truck wholesalers, drop shippers, and mail-order wholesalers.

Cash-and-carry wholesalers are intermediaries whose customers—usually small businesses—pay cash and furnish transportation. Cash-and-carry wholesalers usually handle a limited line of products with a high turnover rate, such as groceries, building materials, and electrical or office supplies. Many small retailers whose accounts are refused by other wholesalers survive because of cash-and-carry wholesalers. **Truck wholesalers,** sometimes called *truck jobbers,* transport a limited line of products directly to customers for on-the-spot inspection and selection. They are often small operators who own and drive their own trucks. They usually have regular routes, calling on retailers and other institutions to determine their needs. **Drop shippers,** also known as *desk jobbers,* take title to products and negotiate sales but never take actual possession of products. They forward orders from retailers, business buyers, or other wholesalers to manufacturers and arrange for carload shipments of items to be delivered directly from producers to these customers. They assume responsibility for products during the entire transaction, including the costs of any unsold goods. **Mail-order wholesalers** use catalogs instead of sales forces to sell products to retail and business buyers. Wholesale mail-order houses generally feature cosmetics, specialty foods, sporting goods, office supplies, and automotive parts. Mail-order wholesaling enables buyers to choose and order particular catalog items for delivery through United Parcel Service, the U.S. Postal Service, or other carriers. This is a convenient and effective method of selling small items to customers in remote areas that other wholesalers might find unprofitable to serve. The Internet has provided an opportunity for mail-order wholesalers to sell products over their own websites and have the products shipped by the manufacturers.

Agents and Brokers. Agents and brokers negotiate purchases and expedite sales but do not take title to products (see Figure 15.2). Sometimes called *functional middlemen,* they perform a limited number of services in exchange for a commission, which generally is based on the product's selling price. **Agents** represent either buyers or sellers on a permanent basis, whereas **brokers** are intermediaries that buyers or sellers employ temporarily.

Although agents and brokers perform even fewer functions than limited-service wholesalers, they are usually specialists in particular products or types of customers and can provide valuable sales expertise. They know their markets well and often form long-lasting associations with customers. Agents and brokers enable manufacturers to expand sales when resources are limited, to benefit from the services of a

cash-and-carry wholesalers Limited-service wholesalers whose customers pay cash and furnish transportation

truck wholesalers Limited-service wholesalers that transport products directly to customers for inspection and selection

drop shippers Limited-service wholesalers that take title to goods and negotiate sales but never actually take possession of products

mail-order wholesalers Limited-service wholesalers that sell products through catalogs

agents Intermediaries that represent either buyers or sellers on a permanent basis

brokers Intermediaries that bring buyers and sellers together temporarily

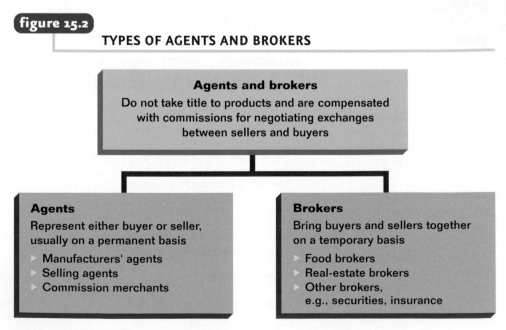

figure 15.2

TYPES OF AGENTS AND BROKERS

Agents and brokers
Do not take title to products and are compensated with commissions for negotiating exchanges between sellers and buyers

Agents
Represent either buyer or seller, usually on a permanent basis
▸ Manufacturers' agents
▸ Selling agents
▸ Commission merchants

Brokers
Bring buyers and sellers together on a temporary basis
▸ Food brokers
▸ Real-estate brokers
▸ Other brokers, e.g., securities, insurance

table 15.6	SERVICES THAT AGENTS AND BROKERS PROVIDE			
	Manufacturers' Agents	**Selling Agents**	**Commission Merchants**	**Brokers**
Physical possession of merchandise	Some	Some	Yes	No
Long-term relationship with buyers or sellers	Yes	Yes	Yes	No
Representation of competing product lines	No	No	Yes	Yes
Limited geographic territory	Yes	No	No	No
Credit to customers	No	Yes	Some	No
Delivery of merchandise to customers	Some	Yes	Yes	No

trained sales force, and to hold down personal selling costs. Table 15.6 summarizes the services provided by agents and brokers.

Manufacturers' agents, which account for more than half of all agent wholesalers, are independent intermediaries that represent two or more sellers and usually offer customers complete product lines. They sell and take orders year-round, much as a manufacturer's sales force does. Restricted to a particular territory, a manufacturer's agent handles noncompeting and complementary products. The relationship between the agent and the manufacturer is governed by written contracts that outline territories, selling price, order handling, and terms of sale relating to delivery, service, and warranties. Manufacturers' agents have little or no control over producers' pricing and marketing policies. They do not extend credit and may be unable to provide technical advice. Manufacturers' agents are commonly used in sales of apparel, machinery and equipment, steel, furniture, automotive products, electrical goods, and certain food items.

Selling agents market either all of a specified product line or a manufacturer's entire output. They perform every wholesaling activity except taking title to products. Selling agents usually assume the sales function for several producers simultaneously and are used often in place of marketing departments. In fact, selling agents are used most often by small producers or by manufacturers that have difficulty maintaining a marketing department because of seasonal production or other factors. In contrast to manufacturers' agents, selling agents generally have no territorial limits and have complete authority over prices, promotion, and distribution. To avoid conflicts of interest, selling agents represent noncompeting product lines. They play a key role in advertising, marketing research, and credit policies of the sellers they represent, at times even advising on product development and packaging.

Commission merchants receive goods on consignment from local sellers and negotiate sales in large, central markets. Sometimes called *factor merchants,* these agents have broad powers regarding prices and terms of sale. They specialize in obtaining the best price possible under market conditions. Most often found in agricultural marketing, commission merchants take possession of truckloads of commodities, arrange for necessary grading or storage, and transport the commodities to auction or markets where they are sold. When sales are completed, the agents deduct commission and the expense of making the sale and then turn over profits to the producer. Commission merchants also offer planning assistance and sometimes extend credit but usually do not provide promotional support.

A broker's primary purpose is to bring buyers and sellers together. Thus brokers perform fewer functions than other intermediaries. They are not involved in financing or physical possession, have no authority to set prices, and assume almost no risks. Instead, they offer customers specialized knowledge of a particular commodity and a network of established contacts. Brokers are especially useful to sellers of

manufacturers' agents Independent intermediaries that represent two or more sellers and usually offers customers complete product lines

selling agents Intermediaries that market a whole product line or a manufacturer's entire output

commission merchants Agents that receive goods on consignment from local sellers and negotiate sales in large, central markets

certain types of products, such as supermarket products and real estate. Food brokers, for example, sell food and general merchandise to retailer-owned and merchant wholesalers, grocery chains, food processors, and business buyers.

Manufacturers' Sales Branches and Offices. Sometimes called *manufacturers' wholesalers,* manufacturers' sales branches and offices resemble merchant wholesalers' operations. **Sales branches** are manufacturer-owned intermediaries that sell products and provide support services to the manufacturer's sales force. Situated away from the manufacturing plant, they are usually located where large customers are concentrated and demand is high. They offer credit, deliver goods, give promotional assistance, and furnish other services. Customers include retailers, business buyers, and other wholesalers. Manufacturers of electrical supplies, such as Westinghouse Electric, and of plumbing supplies, such as American Standard, often have branch operations. They are also common in the lumber and automotive parts industries.

Sales offices are manufacturer-owned operations that provide services normally associated with agents. Like sales branches, they are located away from manufacturing plants, but unlike sales branches, they carry no inventory. A manufacturer's sales office (or branch) may sell products that enhance the manufacturer's own product line.

Manufacturers may set up these branches or offices to reach their customers more effectively by performing wholesaling functions themselves. A manufacturer also may set up such a facility when specialized wholesaling services are not available through existing intermediaries. A manufacturer's performance of wholesaling and physical distribution activities through its sales branch or office may strengthen supply-chain efficiency. In some situations, though, a manufacturer may bypass its sales office or branches entirely—for example, if the producer decides to serve large retailer customers directly.

sales branches Manufacturer-owned intermediaries that sell products and provide support services to the manufacturer's sales force

sales offices Manufacturer-owned operations that provide services normally associated with agents

SUMMARY

Retailing includes all transactions in which buyers intend to consume products through personal, family, or household use. Retailers, organizations that sell products primarily to ultimate consumers, are important links in the marketing channel because they are both marketers for and customers of wholesalers and producers. Retailers add value, provide services, and assist in making product selections.

Retail stores can be classified according to the breadth of products offered. Two broad categories are general-merchandise retailers and specialty retailers. The primary types of general-merchandise retailers include department stores, discount stores, supermarkets, superstores, hypermarkets, warehouse clubs, and warehouse and catalog showrooms. Department stores are large retail organizations employing at least 25 people and characterized by wide product mixes of considerable depth for most product lines. Their products are organized into separate departments that function like self-contained businesses. Discount stores are self-service, low-price, general-merchandise outlets. A convenience store is a small self-service store that is open long hours and carries a narrow assortment of products, usually convenience items. Supermarkets are large, self-service food stores that also carry some nonfood products. Superstores are giant retail outlets that carry all the products found in supermarkets and most consumer products purchased on a routine basis. Hypermarkets offer supermarket and discount store shopping at one location. Warehouse clubs are large-scale, members-only discount operations. Warehouse and catalog showrooms are low-cost operations characterized by warehouse methods of materials handling and display, large inventories, and minimal services.

Specialty retailers offer substantial assortments in a few product lines. They include traditional specialty retailers, which carry narrow product mixes with deep product lines; off-price retailers, which sell brand name manufacturers' seconds and production overruns at deep discounts; and category killers, large specialty stores that concentrate on a major product category and compete on the basis of low prices and enormous product availability.

To increase sales and store patronage, retailers must consider strategic issues. Location determines the trading area from which a store draws its customers and should be evaluated carefully. When evaluating potential sites, retailers take into account a variety of factors, including the location of the firm's target market within the trading area, kinds of products sold, availability of public transportation, customer characteristics, and competitors' locations. Retailers can choose among several types of locations, including freestanding structures, traditional business districts, or shopping centers. The major types of shopping centers are neighborhood shopping centers, community shopping centers, regional shopping centers, superregional shopping centers, lifestyle shopping centers, power shopping centers, and outlet shopping centers.

Retail positioning involves identifying an unserved or underserved market segment and serving it through a strategy that distinguishes the retailer from others in those customers' minds. Store image, which various customers perceive differently, derives not only from atmospherics but also from location, products offered, customer services, prices, promotion, and the store's overall reputation. Atmospherics refers to the physical elements of a store's design that can be adjusted to appeal to consumers' emotions and thus induce them to buy. Category management is a retail strategy of managing groups of similar, often substitutable products produced by different manufacturers. Scrambled merchandising adds unrelated product lines to an existing product mix and is being used by a growing number of stores to generate sales. The wheel of retailing hypothesis holds that new retail institutions start out as low-status, low-margin, and low-price operations. As they develop, they increase services and prices, and eventually become vulnerable to newer organizations, which enter the market and repeat the cycle.

Direct marketing is the use of the telephone, Internet, and nonpersonal media to communicate product and organizational information to customers, who can then purchase products via mail, telephone, or the Internet. Direct marketing is a type of nonstore retailing, the selling of goods or services outside the confines of a retail facility. Forms of direct marketing include catalog marketing, direct-response marketing, telemarketing, television home shopping, and online retailing. Two other types of nonstore retailing are direct selling and automatic vending. Direct selling is the marketing of products to ultimate consumers through face-to-face sales presentations at home or in the workplace. Automatic vending is the use of machines to dispense products.

Franchising is an arrangement in which a supplier grants a dealer the right to sell products in exchange for some type of consideration. Retail franchises are of three general types. A manufacturer may authorize a number of retail stores to sell a certain brand name item; a producer may license distributors to sell a given product to retailers; or a franchiser may supply brand names, techniques, or other services instead of a complete product. Franchise arrangements have a number of advantages and disadvantages over traditional business forms, and their use is increasing.

Wholesaling consists of all transactions in which products are bought for resale, for making other products, or for general business operations. Wholesalers are individuals or organizations that facilitate and expedite exchanges that are primarily wholesale transactions.

For producers, wholesalers are a source of financial assistance and information; by performing specialized accumulation and allocation functions, they allow producers to concentrate on manufacturing products. Wholesalers provide retailers with buying expertise, wide product lines, efficient distribution, and warehousing and storage.

Merchant wholesalers are independently owned businesses that take title to goods and assume ownership risks. They are either full-service wholesalers, offering the widest possible range of wholesaling functions, or limited-service wholesalers, providing only some marketing services and specializing in a few functions. Full-service merchant wholesalers include general-merchandise wholesalers, which offer a wide but relatively shallow product mix; general-line wholesalers, which offer extensive assortments within a few product lines; specialty-line wholesalers, which carry only a single product line or a few items within a line; and rack jobbers, which own and service display racks in supermarkets and other stores. Limited-service merchant wholesalers include cash-and-carry wholesalers, which sell to small businesses, require payment in cash, and do not deliver; truck wholesalers, which sell a limited line of products from their own trucks directly to customers; drop shippers, which own goods and negotiate sales but never take possession of products; and mail-order wholesalers, which sell to retail and business buyers through direct-mail catalogs.

Agents and brokers, sometimes called functional middlemen, negotiate purchases and expedite sales in exchange for a commission, but they do not take title to products. Usually specializing in certain products, they can provide valuable sales expertise. Whereas agents represent buyers or sellers on a permanent basis, brokers are intermediaries that buyers and sellers employ on a temporary basis to negotiate exchanges. Manufacturers' agents offer customers the complete product lines of two or more sellers. Selling agents market a complete product line or a producer's entire output and perform every wholesaling function except taking title to products. Commission merchants are agents that receive goods on consignment from local sellers and negotiate sales in large, central markets.

Manufacturers' sales branches and offices are owned by manufacturers. Sales branches sell products and provide support services for the manufacturer's sales force in a given location. Sales offices carry no inventory and function much as agents do.

IMPORTANT TERMS

DISCUSSION & REVIEW QUESTIONS

1. What value is added to a product by retailers? What value is added by retailers for producers and for ultimate consumers?

2. What are the major differences between discount stores and department stores?

3. In what ways are traditional specialty stores and off-price retailers similar? How do they differ?

4. What major issues should be considered when determining a retail site location?

5. Describe the three major types of traditional shopping centers. Give an example of each type in your area.

6. Discuss the major factors that help to determine a retail store's image. How does atmosphere add value to products sold in a store?

7. In what ways does the use of scrambled merchandising affect a store's image?

8. How is door-to-door selling a form of retailing? Some consumers believe that direct-response orders bypass the retailer. Is this true?

9. If you were opening a retail business, would you prefer to open an independent store or own a store under a franchise arrangement? Explain your preference.

10. What services do wholesalers provide to producers and retailers?

11. What is the difference between a full-service merchant wholesaler and a limited-service merchant wholesaler?

12. Drop shippers take title to products but do not accept physical possession of them, whereas commission merchants take physical possession of products but do not accept title. Defend the logic of classifying drop shippers as wholesale merchants and commission merchants as agents.

13. Why are manufacturers' sales offices and branches classified as wholesalers? Which independent wholesalers are replaced by manufacturers' sales branches? By sales offices?

APPLICATION QUESTIONS

1. Juanita wants to open a small retail store that specializes in high-quality, high-priced children's clothing. What types of competitors should she be concerned about in this competitive retail environment? Why?

2. Location of retail outlets is an issue in strategic planning. What initial steps would you recommend to Juanita (see Marketing Application 1) when she considers a location for her store?

3. Visit a retail store you shop in regularly or one in which you would like to shop. Identify the store, and describe its atmospherics. Be specific about both exterior and interior elements, and indicate how the store is being positioned through its use of atmospherics.

4. Contact a local retailer you patronize, and ask the store manager to describe the store's relationship with one of its wholesalers. Using your text as a guide, identify the distribution activities performed by the wholesaler. Are any of these activities shared by both the retailer and the wholesaler? How do these activities benefit the retailer? How do they benefit you as a consumer?

INTERNET EXERCISE

Visit **www.cengage.com/marketing/pride-ferrell** for resources to help you master the material in this chapter, plus materials that will help you expand your marketing knowledge, including Internet exercise updates, ACE Self-Tests, hotlinks to companies featured in this chapter, and much more.

Walmart.com

Wal-Mart provides a website where customers can shop for products, search for a nearby store, and even preorder new products. The website lets browsers see what is on sale and view company information. Access Wal-Mart's website at **www.walmart.com.**

1. How does Wal-Mart attempt to position itself on its website?

2. Compare the atmospherics of Wal-Mart's website to the atmospherics of a traditional Wal-Mart store. Are they consistent? If not, should they be?

3. Read the "Wal-Mart Story" on the website. Relate the firm's history to the wheel of retailing concept.

developing your MARKETING PLAN

Distribution decisions in the marketing plan entail the movement of your product from the producer until it reaches the final consumer. An understanding of how and where your customer prefers to purchase products is critical to the development of the marketing plan. As you apply the information in this chapter to your plan, focus on the following issues:

1. Considering your product's attributes and your target market's (or markets') buying behavior, will your product likely be sold to the ultimate customer or to another member of the marketing channel?

2. If your product will be sold to the ultimate customer, what type of retailing establishment is most suitable to your product? Consider the product's characteristics and your target market's buying behavior. Refer to Table 15.1 for retailer types.

3. Discuss how the characteristics of the retail establishment, such as location, store image, and scrambled merchandising, have an impact on the consumer's perception of your product.

4. Are direct marketing or direct selling methods appropriate for your product and target market?

5. If your product will be sold to another member in the marketing channel, discuss whether a merchant wholesaler, agent, or broker is most suitable as your channel customer.

   The information obtained from these questions should assist you in developing various aspects of your marketing plan found in the *Interactive Marketing Plan* exercise at **www.cengage.com/marketing/pride-ferrell.**

globalEDGE

1. You are an upper-level manager of a large retailing firm that currently is undertaking a primary initiative of international expansion. In your analysis on this topic, an important factor in choosing which markets to enter is the level of retail development in the countries targeted. Access the Global Retail Development Index website by using the search term "retail development" at **http://globaledge.msu.edu/ibrd.** What are four components that may assist in assessing the retail readiness of a country based on information provided by the Global Retail Development Index website? Can you name the top five emerging markets as ranked by an index on the topic? Are there any markets on your list that surprised you? Which three countries have the greatest market potential? Which market is the most stable?

2. Like many firms in your industry, your firm sources materials from abroad. The shipment of materials vital to the manufacturing process of a new line of high quality, water-resistant winter sweaters is currently missing. You had expected the shipment four weeks ago, but the tracking information you have is outdated. To determine whether your shipment entered the United States, you must consult with the Global Statistics website, which can be accessed by using the search term "global statistics" at **http://globaledge.msu.edu/ibrd.** Once you reach the Global Statistics website, click on the Charts link at the top right. Using this information, find the largest domestic container ports and seaports. This will direct your search and help you resolve the impending manufacturing emergency. Where will you be traveling to begin your investigation?

Eastern Mountain Sports Tries to Regain Its Retail Position

One of the original outdoor specialty retailers, Eastern Mountain Sports (EMS), was founded by two Massachusetts-based rock climbers, Alan McDonough and Roger Furst, in 1967. Their venture emerged out of frustration when trying to purchase suitable ice-climbing axes within the United States. They saw a market need and decided to fill it themselves. Shortly after opening their retail outlet, McDonough and Furst also opened the first mountain-climbing school in the United States, the Eastern Mountain Sports Rock Climbing School. From that first location, the school grew and now has five locations and eight East Coast satellite schools, making it not only the oldest but also the largest climbing school in the country. Since their foundation, the retail store and the school have worked hand-in-glove by teaching people how to be expert climbers and then selling them the gear they will need to pursue the sport.

McDonough and Furst were never committed to being businessmen, and after a decade of running EMS they sold it in 1979. Over the next 15 years, EMS changed owners several times before landing under the ownership of a management team led by Eastern Mountain Sports president and CEO Will Manzer in 2004.

With roughly 80 stores in 16 states, the turnover in ownership didn't stunt the company's growth but did have an impact on its original vision— equipping the extreme-sport enthusiast—and subsequently resulted in some financial turbulence. Under the various owners succeeding McDonough and Furst, EMS began to transition toward more mainstream gear, including items such as everyday backpacks. By 2003, the year Manzer took over, the company had become a "Gap with climbing ropes," as he described it. EMS had no real distinguishing characteristics and stocked the same equipment offered by numerous other chains. Manzer was determined to take the company back to its roots in order to regain a loyal customer base of climbers, hikers, bikers, and other extreme-lifestyle seekers. This maneuver has been considered risky by some, but the hope is that it will ultimately help EMS to regain a sharp focus of the company it once was and rediscover its original target market. Manzer hopes to differentiate the company from the competition by becoming the go-to place for the best gear. EMS is the company that will stock $1,400 sea kayaks with ergonomic foot contours and waterproof storage areas. It may sell only a few, but hardcore outdoor enthusiasts know that they can go to EMS and always find what they need.

While its bricks-and-mortar outlets are still popular as they allow consumers to try on and test out gear, get fitted, and talk to experts, EMS's online operations are becoming vital to the organization. The Internet is where top management expects much of EMS's retail growth will come from in the future, and the company has been taking measures to ensure that its website, on-line shopping, and customer service are top-notch. The company also uses business intelligence software to track consumer preferences to get a better idea of what consumers at each location would like and in what quantity. The software also allows for complete transparency and consistency of data throughout the company. Everyone from the CEO down to a store manager has access to the same data, making it easier to see which products and promotions are successful in order to better create successful promotions, store layouts, and stock decisions.

With high-tech software support and a renewed focus on target market, EMS's success has climbed despite increasingly difficult economic times. In fact, EMS has continued to expand steadily with new stores in the East and the Mid-Atlantic. New locations have extended product lines, including a revised design meant to appeal to young consumers and features like custom bike shops with 'round-the-clock technicians. Highlighting bike offerings is a strategy that is paying off in times when people are searching for cheap means of transportation. Given Manzer's renewed focus on core customers, and with high energy prices driving more people to seek alternative transportation, the future for EMS is bright and the potential is sky high.[35]

Questions for Discussion

1. What changes occurred at EMS that caused the company to lose its unique retail position?
2. Evaluate the current CEO's decision to take the company back to its roots.
3. How can the Internet be used to help EMS achieve a new marketing strategy?

CASE 15.2

Low Prices and Lots of Suprises at Costco

More than 20 years after Costco opened its first warehouse club store in Seattle, the company's philosophy can still be summed up as "pile 'em high, price 'em low." Costco stores are anything but fancy; in fact, the first store was located inside a warehouse. Yet nearly 50 million consumers and small-business owners pay $50 (fee may vary) annually so they can save on everything from mayonnaise, wine, and prescription medicines to handheld computers, truck-size snow tires, and fine art. In fact, customers never really know what products they will find each time they visit one of the 529 Costco warehouse stores around the world. Surprises are all part of the shopping experience at Costco.

"The art form of our business is intuition," says CEO James D. Sinegal. His buyers must choose carefully, because the typical Costco carries less than 10 percent of the number of products displayed in a Wal-Mart store. Moreover, Costco aims for a profit margin of no more than 14 percent, which means inventory must sell quickly. If products sell slowly, they will tie up precious cash that could be better spent on newer or more popular merchandise. Therefore, Costco's buyers watch for particularly hot products and product categories. When the chief electronics buyer noticed the cost of plasma-screen televisions dropping, for example, he took what he calls "an educated gamble" and placed a sizable order. The gamble paid off: the televisions, priced below $5,000, sold out quickly even before the year-end holiday shopping season.

Costco carries a broad and varied merchandise assortment, all priced low to move quickly. It sells 55,000 rotisserie chickens every day and $600 million worth of fine wines every year. It also sells 45 million hot dogs and 60,000 carats of diamonds annually. The hot dogs retail for $1.50 each, while a single piece of jewelry can retail for as much as $100,000. Well-known manufacturers' brands share shelf space with Kirkland Signature, Costco's private brand. Members may walk past stacks of best-selling books on the right and color printers on the left as they push their shopping carts down the aisle. This variety enhances the store's appeal, says the CEO: "Our customers do not drive 15 miles to save on a jar of peanut butter. They come for the treasure hunt." Among the treasures they might find: an $8,000 Suzuki grand piano, a $6,000 100-CD Wurlitzer jukebox, and a seven-carat diamond ring for $125,000. Such items now comprise 5 to 10 percent of Costco's sales.

Despite the low prices, Costco offers a generous return policy. Customers can return anything at any time. If dissatisfied with their membership, they can even get a full refund on that. The sole exception is computers, which cannot be brought back after six months. No receipt? No problem at Costco. Customers have ample opportunity to exchange or return items because they visit the stores frequently. Research shows that, on average, members visit Costco stores more than 11 times a year and spend $94 on each visit.

Costco's main competitor is Sam's Club, owned by Wal-Mart. Given Wal-Mart's buying power and channel leadership, Sam's Club can buy products at very low prices and get them to stores with unusual efficiency. Nonetheless, Costco tops Sam's Club in a number of ways. Each U.S. Costco store rings up, on average, $112 million worth of merchandise annually. By comparison, the average yearly sales of each U.S. Sam's Club store are $63 million. Whereas the average sales per square foot at Sam's Club is $497, Costco's equivalent figure is a whopping $797 per square foot. Although Sam's Club charges a lower membership fee, Costco's members are quite loyal, with a renewal rate of 86 percent. And they have a median income of $72,000 compared to Sam's customers, with a median income of $50,000.

In recent years, Costco has expanded by offering new services at low prices. For example, members can log on to the retailer's website (**www.costco.com**) and sign up for long-distance telephone service, apply for a mortgage, buy life insurance, or price a vacation trip. The company has also started a new chain of stores, Costco Home, which specializes in home furnishings. In warehouse retailing, however, Sam's Club remains the competitor to beat. Before Sam's Club opened stores in Canada, Costco prepared for the increased competition by remodeling some of its stores. And price wars sometimes break out when the two competitors battle for customers. The parent company of Sam's Club is by far the largest company in the world, but Costco is so adept at warehouse retailing that it continues to hold its own.[36]

Questions for Discussion

1. How do Costco's atmospherics support its retail positioning?
2. Analyze the retail strategy represented by the new Costco Home chain.
3. How is Costco's retail positioning likely to be affected by its target profit margin of 14 percent?

strategic CASE 6

Direct Selling Mistine Cosmetics in Thailand

Better Way (Thailand) Company Limited was founded in 1988 by Thailand's "king of direct selling," Dr. Amornthep Deerojanawong, and Boonyakiat Chokwatana. Dr. Amornthep had worked as a medical doctor at Avon in Thailand, where he got the idea to start his own Thai-based cosmetics company. The company has become highly successful in Thailand using direct selling to launch its Mistine cosmetic brand. Although Thai people were not very familiar with the direct selling of cosmetics, within six years Mistine had become the leader in the consumer cosmetics market in Thailand, a market worth an estimated 25 billion baht (approximately US$635 million) and growing at a rate of 5 to 10 percent annually.

Better Way began with fewer than 100 products. Today, the company markets more than 4,000 makeup, skin-care, fragrance, and personal-care products. In addition, the company operates one retail store on the outskirts of Bangkok. Its warehouse is considered the largest cosmetics depot in Southeast Asia, with 1,170 regular employees.

The company primarily targets women who have a high school, occupational certificate level, or high occupational certificate level of education and have a monthly income of about US$125–200, as well as working women who have a monthly income of about US$200–300. Mistine's core target market, which accounts for 70 to 80 percent of its total revenues, are housewives with low to medium incomes. The company is expanding its customer base by targeting working people, men, and vocational school students, especially working people who have high purchasing power. There are now more than 420,000 customers nationwide.

Mistine positions itself as an Asian company marketing products developed and formulated specifically for the Asian woman. They are designed to blend well with the Asian skin tone and complexion. They are also made to better suit the warmer, more humid climate of the Asian region so that the product stays on longer and looks fresher.

Mistine's Marketing Activities

Mistine products are manufactured by the best-quality cosmetics manufacturers all over the world. Additional support is provided by Kolmar Laboratories, the largest and most experienced cosmetics manufacturer in the United States. An experienced production team develops hundreds of new and unique products each year, with at least two to three new products launched each month.

Every Mistine product is thoroughly inspected and tested before being delivered to the warehouse. Customers can be assured that they will receive the highest-quality products, and, indeed, Mistine will replace or offer a full refund for any product for which a customer is not completely happy. "Our customer's satisfaction is what we care about the most" is one of Mistine's slogans, which helps it to maintain its leadership in a competitive market.

Direct selling companies normally depend on word of mouth to develop brand awareness, recruit salespersons, and encourage product purchases. Better Way decided to do things differently by being the first direct selling company in Thailand to use mass media advertising. The company's continuous and award-winning advertising campaigns have been executed to build brand image and positioning in the customers' minds. Many products are promoted by popular celebrities.

Sales Force Characteristics

Mistine's direct-sales system is a simple, single-level marketing (SLM) approach. The company recruits district managers who in turn recruit as many salespersons as they can manage. This approach meshes well with Thai culture and lifestyle. The benefit of this approach is that each salesperson earns full commission without having to share his or her earnings with others. Thus the more sales a salesperson makes, the more income he or she receives.

The company welcomes anyone—male or female—who has some free time on their hands and would like to earn money, make new friends, and develop their self-confidence to become a salesperson. Salespersons can plan their own schedules and routes in order to reach sales objectives and obtain rewards. If a salesperson achieves no sales within three selling periods, then he or she is automatically terminated. The annual turnover rate for the sales force is about 200 percent because, for most salespersons, selling Mistine products is a second job. Moreover, most of the salespersons do not have any sales experience. Although they receive up to 25–30 percent commission, if they are not determined and committed, they leave. Generally, about 70 percent are terminated within six selling periods.

Sales goals are set according to the sales promotion plans and advertising budget spent for a particular distribution period. The company offers major incentives, such as trips to Europe and gold jewelry, to all district managers who achieve sales goals.

With the belief that the salespersons can live without Mistine but Mistine cannot live without the salespersons, several programs have been launched to create employee loyalty to the company. Internal relationship programs such as the "Mistine Thank-You Concert" were organized in nine provinces around Thailand, aimed at gathering Mistine salespersons together as a family, as well as at showing that the company cares about and is responsible for its employees. The company also provides life insurance with coverage of US$50,000 for each salesperson, which is an unusual benefit in Thailand. Nonmonetary rewards and recognition incentives for salespersons include crystal trophies and photos in the Hall of Fame.

Improving Sales Performance

In direct sales, the length of a selling period is crucial and shapes business operations. Normally, direct selling companies operate three-week selling periods, totaling 18 periods within a year. Mistine, however, found that most salespersons do not actually start selling products to customers until the last week of a selling period, meaning that the first two weeks are essentially wasted. Consequently, management decided to reduce the selling period to two weeks, resulting in 26 selling periods per year. This dramatic change was implemented despite objections. Ultimately, sales increased by 80 percent over the previous year, and salespersons became more active in selling the products.

These impressive sales increases occurred because of the reduced selling cycles and the positive attitude fostered throughout the company toward salespersons. One motto that employees of all levels still pledge to this day is "We will make Mistine No. 1."

Growth and Expansion

Despite Mistine's great success with direct cosmetic sales, the company continues to strategize to maintain its market share amidst intense competition. To achieve its goals, the firm intends to continue recruiting new salespersons in order to increase sales and expand its marketing coverage area. It has increased its local promotion budget by 50 percent and developed 400 new-product items to maintain its leading position. After observing that the sales of men's personal-care products have been increasing in department stores, Better Way launched nine men's products, including shampoo, deodorant, day and night cream, and sun protection lotion.

The company has formed a strategic alliance with DTAC, a leading telecommunications service provider, under the name "Mistine Corporate Solution," or MCS, which enables Mistine salespersons to call the 24-hour Mistine Call Center for free when using the DTAC cellular phone network system. This innovative direct selling tool will help the salespersons in ordering products, requesting product information, and asking about promotions. This strategic alliance will help the

company cut costs of about US$25,000 per month on phone charges.

To penetrate the teenage market segment, Mistine partnered with RS Promotions and employed D2B, an RS Promotions "boy band" popular among Thai teens, to present Mistine's Pink Magic lipstick. The campaign helped boost sales to teens by as much as 10 percent.

Recently Mistine has an aggressive strategy in its products and marketing communication in both domestic and international markets. The company opened manufacturing sites in the Philippines and Vietnam. Mistine has successfully offered products in Cambodia, Laos, and Myanmar. The success is due to its affordable price, which matches the income of the people in those countries. Moreover, its advertising campaigns that use popular actresses who are well known to people in those countries support its sales. Mistine will be exporting its cosmetic products to distributors in Taiwan and to China within two to three years. Hungary and Russia are potential markets in the future.[37]

Questions for Discussion

1. Is it possible that having a retail outlet creates channel conflict? Explain.
2. From a customer's standpoint, what are the advantages or disadvantages of having a retail outlet? What about from the company's standpoint?
3. How would Mistine's use of mass media advertising influence the performance of its sales force?
4. Should Mistine's management expect to change marketing strategies when the company enters new international markets such as Hungary and Russia? Explain.
5. In what ways does the single-level direct selling approach affect its turnover rates? Explain.

part 7

Promotion Decisions

Part Seven focuses on communication with target market members and, at times, other groups. A specific marketing mix cannot satisfy people in a particular target market unless they are aware of the product and know where to find it. Some promotion decisions relate to a specific marketing mix; others are geared toward promoting the entire organization. **Chapter 16** discusses integrated marketing communications. It describes the communication process and the major promotional methods that can be included in promotion mixes. **Chapter 17** analyzes the major steps in developing an advertising campaign. It also explains what public relations is and how it can be used. **Chapter 18** deals with personal selling and the role it can play in a firm's promotional efforts. This chapter also explores the general characteristics of sales promotion and describes sales promotion techniques.

16 Integrated Marketing Communications

LEARNING objectives

❶ To describe the nature of integrated marketing communications

❷ To examine the process of communication

❸ To understand the role and objectives of promotion

❹ To explore the elements of the promotion mix

❺ To examine the selection of promotion mix elements

❻ To understand word-of-mouth communication and how it affects promotion

❼ To understand product placement promotions

❽ To examine criticisms and defenses of promotion

Comic Books Save the Day for Pivman

entrepreneurs IN ACTION

Andrew Sinkov became interested in comic books as an adult and now is in charge of marketing for CoreStreet, a Cambridge, Massachusetts, security software company that markets Pivman, a handheld computer system for emergency workers. Although not the most exciting technology product, the Pivman required a creative communications strategy to build good buzz or word-of-mouth hype about the product. Sometimes the best new idea for promotion involves going back to the past to finding something that will engage potential buyers. Sinkov observed that some marketers have turned to comics as a way to reach customers. Even Best Buy has a comic strip touting its Geek Squad computer support service, and Microsoft has a Web comic at enchantedoffice.com about how Office 2007 works. Although comics are not necessarily a trend, they can be effective when they stand out above the clutter of promotions and grab attention for the product.

The Pivman system consists of handheld devices and server software that allow authorized personnel to control access to any location by quickly authenticating and validating the identities and roles of individuals who want to enter the site. The system allows authorities to manage information on a very large number of individuals without affecting performance and without requiring a constant connection to a data source—as is sometimes the case in emergency situations such as homeland security incidents or natural disasters that require the support and cooperation of various federal, state, and local agencies, as well as private organizations. The Pivman system obtains individual identities and privileges from existing independent databases and then makes the data available to Pivman handhelds and other devices. Then, when someone presents her smart card, the information on it is validated and her access privileges are displayed to the person who is controlling access.

The Pivman comic explains how the device can be used in an emergency situation, ensuring potential customers thay they can easily understand the systems' real benefits. Sinkov found it easy to publish a Pivman comic for just $5,000. He found an artist on Craigslist and had the artist draw a 12-page comic book that explained technical information about the product and included characters for educational training. He then had 500 copies printed in four colors. The comic worked better than any other promotional tool the firm has employed: it proved so popular that within a few days another 10,000 copies were printed. In fact, CoreStreet's comic book is generating potential buyers at twice the rate of other marketing materials. The company was able to land part of a security contract with the city of Los Angeles, as well as obtaining many other customers through comic book buzz.[1]

Organizations such as CoreStreet employ a variety of promotional methods to communicate with their target markets. Providing information to customers and other stakeholders is vital to initiating and developing long-term relationships with them.

This chapter looks at the general dimensions of promotion. First, we discuss the nature of integrated marketing communications. Next, we analyze the meaning and process of communication. We then define and examine the role of promotion and explore some of the reasons promotion is used. Then we consider major promotional methods and the factors that influence marketers' decisions to use particular methods. Next, we explain the positive and negative effects of personal and electronic word-of-mouth communication. Finally, we examine criticisms and defenses of promotion.

The Nature of Integrated Marketing Communications

LO 1 To describe the nature of integrated marketing communications

Communication Channels

Adriano Goldschmied jeans uses magazine advertising to create the appropriate image for its designer jeans.

integrated marketing communications Coordination of promotion and other marketing efforts for maximum informational and persuasive impact

Integrated marketing communications refer to the coordination of promotion and other marketing efforts to ensure maximum informational and persuasive impact on customers. Coordinating multiple marketing tools to produce this synergistic effect requires a marketer to employ a broad perspective. A major goal of integrated marketing communications is to send a consistent message to customers. When United Airlines launched Ted, a Chicago-based discount carrier that catered to its own business customers' vacation needs, it employed a variety of tactics to introduce the new brand and reinforce its identity. For example, a fleet of orange trucks paraded throughout Chicago and appeared at special events, bringing fun activities and treats to get people to think that Ted's low fares would enable them to treat themselves to a vacation. In the "Random Acts of Ted" promotion, special representatives handed out small treats (e.g., glow sticks at a Fourth of July celebration, fans after a marathon). Fifteen-second television ads targeted specific Chicago neighborhoods with the simple low-fare message, and radio ads employed a humorous "man-on-the-street" approach. The startup's consistent message across many vehicles helped boost brand awareness, which quickly translated to full planes.[2] Indeed, research suggests that the use of such spokespersons results in more favorable brand images in integrated marketing communications.[3]

Because various units both inside and outside most companies have traditionally planned and implemented promotional efforts, customers have not always received consistent messages. Integrated marketing communications allow an organization to coordinate and manage its promotional efforts to transmit consistent messages. Integrated marketing communications also enable synchronization of promotion elements and can reduce overspending on elements that may produce a smaller return on investment.[4] Thus, this approach fosters not only long-term customer relationships but also the efficient use of promotional resources.

The concept of integrated marketing communications has been increasingly accepted for several reasons. Mass media advertising, a very popular promotional method in the past, is used less frequently today because of its high cost and lower effectiveness in reaching some target markets.[5] Marketers can now take advantage of more precisely targeted promotional tools, such as cable TV, direct mail, the Internet, special-interest magazines, CDs and DVDs, cell phones, and even iPods. Database marketing is also allowing marketers to more precisely target individual customers. Until recently, suppliers of marketing communications were specialists. Advertising agencies provided advertising campaigns, sales promotion companies provided sales promotion activities and materials, and public relations organizations engaged in publicity efforts. Today a number of promotion-related companies provide one-stop shopping for the client seeking advertising, sales promotion, and public relations, thus reducing coordination problems for the sponsoring company. Because the overall cost of marketing communications has risen significantly, upper management demands systematic evaluations of communication efforts and a reasonable return on investment.

The specific communication vehicles employed and the precision with which they are used are changing as both information technology and customer interests become increasingly dynamic. For example, companies can run short advertisements during broadcasts of TV shows and other videos that users can watch on their cell phones.[6] Some companies are even creating their own branded content to exploit the many vehicles through which consumers obtain information. Burger King, for example, produced a movie, *Above the King*, about a teenager who lives over a Burger King restaurant and befriends an aristocrat. The company also used its updated king mascot not only in television commercials but also in its own Xbox video games and in a MySpace profile.[7] Mars created an Internet show, "Instant Def," for its Snickers brand featuring hip-hop performers will.i.am, Fergie, Taboo, and apl.de.ap. Such branded content does not replace traditional advertising, but it gives marketers new, controlled avenues for reaching consumers who have more entertainment choices today than ever before.[8]

Today marketers and customers have almost unlimited access to data about each other. Integrating and customizing marketing communications while protecting customer privacy has become a major challenge. Through the Internet, companies can provide product information and services that are coordinated with traditional promotional activities. In fact, gathering information about goods and services is one of the main reasons people use the Internet. College students in particular say they are influenced by Internet ads when buying online or just researching product purchases.[9] The sharing of information and use of technology to facilitate communication between buyers and sellers are essential for successful customer relationship management.

Promotion and the Communication Process

LO 2 To examine the process of communication

Communication is essentially the transmission of information. For communication to take place, both the sender and receiver of information must share some common ground. They must have a common understanding of the symbols, words, and pictures used to transmit information. An individual transmitting the following message may believe he or she is communicating with you:

在工廠吾人製造化粧品,在商店吾人銷售希望。

However, communication has not taken place if you don't understand the language in which the message is written.[10] Thus, we define **communication** as a sharing of meaning.[11] Implicit in this definition is the notion of transmission of information because sharing necessitates transmission.

As Figure 16.1 shows, communication begins with a source. A **source** is a person, group, or organization with a meaning it attempts to share with an audience. A source could be a salesperson wishing to communicate a sales message or an organization wanting to send a message to thousands of customers through an advertisement. Developing a strategy can enhance the effectiveness of the source's communication. For example, a strategy in which a salesperson attempts to influence a customer's decision by eliminating competitive products from consideration has been found to be effective.[12] A **receiver** is the individual, group, or organization that decodes a coded message, and an *audience* is two or more receivers.

To transmit meaning, a source must convert the meaning into a series of signs or symbols representing ideas or concepts. This is called the **coding process,** or *encoding*.

communication A sharing of meaning through the transmission of information

source A person, group, or organization with a meaning it tries to share with a receiver or an audience

receiver The individual, group, or organization that decodes a coded message

coding process Converting meaning into a series of signs or symbols

figure 16.1

THE COMMUNICATION PROCESS

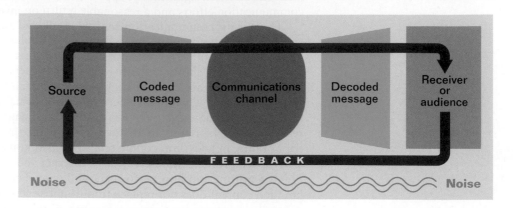

When coding meaning into a message, the source must consider certain characteristics of the receiver or audience. To share meaning, the source should use signs or symbols familiar to the receiver or audience. Research has shown that persuasive messages from a source are more effective when the appeal matches an individual's personality.[13] Marketers that understand this realize the importance of knowing their target market and ensuring that an advertisement, for example, uses language the target market understands. Thus, when General Mills advertises Cheerios, it does not mention all the ingredients used to make the cereal because some ingredients would have little meaning to consumers. Some notable problems have occurred in translating English advertisements into other languages to communicate with customers in global markets. For example, Coors's "Turn it loose" campaign was translated into Spanish as "Drink Coors and get diarrhea," and KFC's long-running slogan, "Finger lickin' good," was translated into Chinese as "Eat your fingers off." And Parker Pen was dismayed to learn that "Avoid embarrassment" (from a leaking pen) had been translated into "Avoid pregnancy" in Spanish.[14] Clearly it is important that people understand the language used in promotion.

When coding a meaning, a source needs to use signs or symbols that the receiver or audience uses to refer to the concepts the source intends to convey. Instead of technical jargon, explanatory language that helps consumers understand is more likely to result in positive attitudes and purchase intentions.[15] Marketers try to avoid signs or symbols that may have several meanings for an audience. For example, *soda* as a general term for soft drinks may not work well in national advertisements. Although in some parts of the United States the word means "soft drink," in other regions it may connote bicarbonate of soda, an ice cream drink, or something one mixes with Scotch whiskey.

To share a coded meaning with the receiver or audience, a source selects and uses a **communications channel,** the medium of transmission that carries the coded message from the source to the receiver or audience. Transmission media include ink on paper, air wave vibrations produced by vocal cords, chalk marks on a chalkboard, and electronically produced vibrations of air waves (in radio and television signals, for example). Table 16.1 summarizes the leading communications channels from which people obtain information and news.

When a source chooses an inappropriate communication channel, several problems may arise. The coded message may reach some receivers but the wrong ones. For example, dieters who adopt the Atkins low-carbohydrate diet are more likely to focus on communications that relate to their food concerns, such as "Eat Meat Not Wheat" T-shirts, QVC's Low-Carb Hour, and fast-food chain advertisements that communicate information about the carbohydrate content of menu items.[16] An advertiser that wants

communications channel
The medium of transmission that carries the coded message from the source to the receiver

table 16.1 WHERE PEOPLE GET THEIR NEWS AND INFORMATION

Survey respondents who say they . . . daily	%
Watch television	56.1
Use the Internet	53.3
Listen to the radio	34.3
Read print newspapers	33.5
Read print magazines	5.8

Source: Harris Interactive Inc., in Ron Alsop, "News, Ads Shape Corporate Images," *The Wall Street Journal,* Jan. 31, 2007, http://online.wsj.com.

to reach this group would need to take this information into account when choosing an appropriate communications channel. Coded messages may also reach intended receivers in incomplete form because the intensity of the transmission is weak. For example, radio and broadcast television signals are received effectively only over a limited range, which varies according to climactic conditions. Members of the target audience living on the fringe of the broadcast area may receive a weak signal; others well within the broadcast area may also receive an incomplete message if, for example, they listen to the radio while driving or studying.

In the **decoding process,** signs or symbols are converted into concepts and ideas. Seldom does a receiver decode exactly the same meaning the source coded. When the result of decoding differs from what was coded, noise exists. **Noise** is anything that reduces the clarity and accuracy of the communication; it has many sources and may affect any or all parts of the communication process. Noise sometimes arises within the communications channel itself. Radio static, poor or slow Internet connections, and laryngitis are sources of noise. Noise also occurs when a source uses signs or symbols that are unfamiliar to the receiver or have a meaning different from the one intended. Noise may also originate in the receiver; a receiver may be unaware of a coded message when perceptual processes block it out.

The receiver's response to a decoded message is **feedback** to the source. The source usually expects and normally receives feedback, although perhaps not immediately. During feedback, the receiver or audience is the source of a message directed toward the original source, which then becomes a receiver. Feedback is coded, sent through a communications channel, and decoded by the receiver, the source of the original communication. Thus, communication is a circular process, as indicated in Figure 16.1.

During face-to-face communication, such as occurs in personal selling and product sampling, verbal and nonverbal feedback can be immediate. Instant feedback lets communicators adjust messages quickly to improve the effectiveness of their communications. For example, when a salesperson realizes through feedback that a customer does not understand a sales presentation, the salesperson adapts the presentation to make it more meaningful to the customer. This may be why face-to-face sales presentations create higher behavioral intentions to purchase services than do telemarketing sales contacts.[17] In interpersonal communication, feedback occurs through talking, touching, smiling, nodding, eye movements, and other body movements and postures.

When mass communication such as advertising is used, feedback is often slow and difficult to recognize. Also, it may be several years before the effects of this promotion will be known. Feedback does exist for mass communication in the form of measures of changes in sales volume or in consumers' attitudes and awareness levels.

Each communication channel has a limit on the volume of information it can handle effectively. This limit, called **channel capacity,** is determined by the least efficient component of the communication process. Consider communications that depend on speech. An individual source can speak only so fast, and there is a limit to how much an individual receiver can take in aurally. Beyond that point, additional messages cannot be decoded; thus, meaning cannot be shared. Although a radio announcer can read several hundred words a minute, a one-minute advertising message should not exceed 150 words because most announcers cannot articulate words into understandable messages at a rate beyond 150 words per minute.

decoding process Converting signs or symbols into concepts and ideas

noise Anything that reduces a communication's clarity and accuracy

feedback The receiver's response to a decoded message

channel capacity The limit on the volume of information a communication channel can handle effectively

The Role and Objectives of Promotion

L O ❸ To understand the role and objectives of promotion

*E*VERYBODY WORRIES ABOUT THE COST OF FUEL. FALCON OWNERS WORRY 20-60% LESS.

The most efficient companies in twenty-six countries demand the most efficient large-cabin business jets and fuel is just one reason. Falcons not only match many smaller planes in fuel economy, high-tech design lets them use hundreds of small airports other wide-cabins can't. City-hopping, ocean-hopping, flying-more-people-to-more-places proves again: Less is more.

Visit us at: Falconjet.com
Or call: U.S. 201.541.4600 France +33.1.47.11.82.32

DASSAULT FALCON
ENGINEERED WITH PASSION

Objectives of Promotion

Marketers use ads to accomplish a wide variety of objectives. What are the objetives of this Dassault Falcon ad?

Promotion is communication that builds and maintains favorable relationships by informing and persuading one or more audiences to view an organization positively and to accept its products. Toward this end, many organizations spend considerable resources on promotion to build and enhance relationships with current and potential customers and other stakeholders. For example, Anheuser-Busch spent $247 million on advertising—particularly for its four core brands, Budweiser, Bud Light, Michelob, and Michelob Ultra—in just six months.[18] Marketers also indirectly facilitate favorable relationships by focusing information about company activities and products on interest groups (such as environmental and consumer groups), current and potential investors, regulatory agencies, and society in general. For example, some organizations promote responsible use of products criticized by society such as tobacco, alcohol, and violent movies. Companies sometimes promote programs that help selected groups. Yoplait, for instance, supports the Susan G. Komen Breast Cancer Research Foundation with its "Save Lids to Save Lives" campaign, which contributes 10 cents to the charity for every pink yogurt lid sent in by consumers.[19] Such cause-related marketing, as we discussed in Chapter 4, links the purchase of products to philanthropic efforts for one or more causes. By contributing to causes that its target markets support, cause-related marketing can help marketers boost sales and generate goodwill.

For maximum benefit from promotional efforts, marketers strive for proper planning, implementation, coordination, and control of communications. Effective management of integrated marketing communications is based on information about and feedback from customers and the marketing environment, often obtained from an organization's marketing information system (see Figure 16.2). How successfully marketers use promotion to maintain positive relationships depends to some extent on the quantity and quality of information the organization receives. Because customers derive information and opinions from many different sources, integrated marketing communications planning also takes into account informal methods of communication such as word of mouth and independent information sources on the Internet. Because promotion is communication that can be managed, we now analyze what communication is and how the communication process works.

Promotional objectives vary considerably from one organization to another and within organizations over time. Large firms with multiple promotional programs

promotion Communication to build and maintain relationships by informing and persuading one or more audiences

---

figure 16.2   **INFORMATION FLOWS ARE IMPORTANT IN INTEGRATED MARKETING COMMUNICATIONS**

Information about customers and marketing environment forces → Integrated marketing communications plan → Customers

F E E D B A C K

table 16.2 POSSIBLE OBJECTIVES OF PROMOTION	
Create awareness	Retain loyal customers
Stimulate demand	Facilitate reseller support
Encourage product trial	Combat competitive promotional efforts
Identify prospects	Reduce sales fluctuations

operating simultaneously may have quite varied promotional objectives. For the purpose of analysis, we focus on the eight promotional objectives shown in Table 16.2. Although the list is not exhaustive, one or more of these objectives underlie many promotional programs.

Create Awareness

A considerable amount of promotion efforts focus on creating awareness. For an organization that is introducing a new product or a line extension, making customers aware of the product is crucial to initiating the product adoption process. A marketer that has invested heavily in product development strives to create product awareness quickly to generate revenues to offset the high costs of product development and introduction. To create awareness of its new Sausage McSkillet breakfast burrito, for example, McDonald's ran television commercials in both English and Spanish highlighting the half-pound burrito's ingredients and portability while showing young people enjoying them at breakfast.[20]

Selective Demand

Vibram, whose founder developed the first rubber soles for shoes, creates awareness and demand for rubber soles for climbing shoes.

Creating awareness is important for existing products, too. Promotional efforts may aim to increase awareness of brands, product features, image-related issues (such as organizational size or socially responsive behavior), or operational characteristics (such as store hours, locations, and credit availability). Some promotional programs are unsuccessful because marketers fail to generate awareness of critical issues among a significant portion of target market members. For example, Chrysler Group effectively dropped an expensive campaign to launch its new Pacifica when sales failed to meet expectations. Chrysler wanted to target the new vehicle at younger, more affluent consumers. However, the company chose Celine Dion, the popular Canadian singer, to appear in television commercials for the campaign and only later discovered that she appeals to a much older audience, with an average age of 52.[21]

www.vibram.com

Grip obsesses us.

After more than seventy years of relentless, obsessive innovation, we're proud to introduce our most innovative climbing rubber yet.

© 2006 Vibram USA, Inc. All Rights Reserved.

vibram **XS GRIP**

Stimulate Demand

When an organization is the first to introduce an innovative product, it tries to stimulate **primary demand**—demand for a product category rather than for a specific brand of product—through **pioneer promotion.** Pioneer promotion informs potential customers about the product: what it is, what it does, how it can be used, and where it can be purchased. Because pioneer promotion is used in the introductory stage of the product life cycle, meaning there are no competing brands, it neither emphasizes brand names nor compares brands. When Apple introduced the iPod, for instance, it initially attempted to stimulate primary demand by emphasizing the benefits of music players in general rather than the benefits of its specific brand. Primary-demand stimulation is not just for new products. At times an industry trade association rather than a single firm uses promotional efforts to stimulate primary demand.

primary demand Demand for a product category rather than for a specific brand

pioneer promotion Promotion that informs consumers about a new product

selective demand Demand for a specific brand

To build **selective demand,** demand for a specific brand, a marketer employs promotional efforts that point out the strengths and benefits of a specific brand. Building selective demand also requires singling out attributes important to potential buyers. Selective demand can be stimulated by differentiating the product from competing brands in the minds of potential buyers. Selective demand can also be stimulated by increasing the number of product uses and promoting them through advertising campaigns, as well as through price discounts, free samples, coupons, consumer contests

E-ntertainment MARKETING

Lawdy Miss Clawdy Sweet Potatoes Are Good

The marketing of sweet potatoes faces many challenges, especially in developing effective promotion. Consumption of sweet potatoes has declined from 29.5 pounds per capita per year in the 1920s to around 4 pounds per capita today, trailing celery and several other less-popular vegetables. Given consumers' lack of interest, the sweet potato might as well be a turnip or a gourd despite its being high in fiber, vitamin A, and vitamin C. The image of the sweet potato is more of a poor man's food that was used to feed the Continental Army during the Revolutionary War. Today consumers are looking for more upscale foods that are considered fashionable and fun to eat.

Lloyd Price, a member of the Rock and Roll Hall of Fame, is trying to change the image of the humble sweet potato through his company's products. He used his most famous hit song "Lawdy Miss Clawdy" to brand his 16 sweet potato-based products in the Lawdy Miss Clawdy product line. His company, Lloyd Price Icon Food Brands Inc., sells sweet potato pies, pretzels, muffins, cheesecake on a stick, and even sweet potato cookies. Already stocked by Wal-Mart and a few other stores in southern states, the company is seeking wider distribution.

Price and other sweet potato aficionados believe that processing the nutritious orange vegetable into more convenient forms will boost its popularity beyond the Thanksgiving dinner table. About 75 percent of canned sweet potato sales come between Thanksgiving and New Year's, and 40 percent of the fresh crop is shipped during the last quarter of the year. Sales of sweet potato chips have more than doubled since 2003, according to Nielsen Co. To enhance awareness of and demand for the sweet potato, the Sweet Potato Commission introduced a sweet potato-shaped mascot named Spencer with a fuzzy orange costume, saucer-shaped eyes, and a nonstop grin. The commission even sponsored a stock car race called the Sweet Potato 300.

But Lloyd Price is trying to do what the Sweet Potato Commission has thus far failed to accomplish. He plans to take his rhythm and blues popularity and change the image of the sweet potato through word of mouth and traditional forms of advertising. He believes that his Lloyd Price Icon Food Brands and his Lawdy Miss Clawdy products will have an immediate impact on their targeted customers. The customers will react with feelings of warmth, affection, and a sense of belonging to these two brands, especially because of the Lloyd Price song that millions of fans worldwide have come to love. However, it remains to be seen if Price will be able to convince people to love sweet potatoes as much as they love the "Lawdy Miss Clawdy" song.[a]

and games, and sweepstakes. HP provides a coupon worth up to $50 when a consumer recycles computer hardware through the HP Recycling Services. This green marketing promotion protects the environment and stimulates the demand for HP products.[22] Promotions for large package sizes or multiple-product packages are directed at increasing consumption, which in turn can stimulate demand. In addition, selective demand can be stimulated by encouraging existing customers to use more of the product.

be positive. drink negative.

Encouraging Product Trial

Enviga encourages product trial by promoting the calorie-burning capability of its energy drink. Initial ads for the product included discounts and free coupons.

Encourage Product Trial

When attempting to move customers through the product adoption process, a marketer may successfully create awareness and interest, but customers may stall during the evaluation stage. In this case, certain types of promotion—such as free samples; coupons; test drives; or limited free-use offers, contests, and games—are employed to encourage product trial. Mars Snackfoods, for example, gave out product samples at college basketball games to promote its new Snickers Charged candy bar, which has 60 milligrams of caffeine to provide an energy boost as well as a sweet afternoon snack.[23] Whether a marketer's product is the first in a new product category, a new brand in an existing category, or simply an existing brand seeking customers, trial-inducing promotional efforts aim to make product trial convenient and low risk for potential customers.

Identify Prospects

Certain types of promotional efforts aim to identify customers who are interested in the firm's product and are most likely to buy it. A marketer may use a magazine advertisement with a direct-response information form, requesting the reader to complete and mail the form to receive additional information. Some advertisements have toll-free numbers to facilitate direct customer response. Customers who fill out information blanks or call the organization usually have higher interest in the product, which makes them likely sales prospects. The organization can respond with phone calls, follow-up letters, or personal contact by salespeople. Dun & Bradstreet, for example, offered a free article on customer relationship management to businesses that mailed in a card or called a toll-free number. This helped the consulting firm identify prospects to sell data used to develop and maintain customer relationships.

Retain Loyal Customers

Clearly, maintaining long-term customer relationships is a major goal of most marketers. Such relationships are quite valuable. Promotional efforts directed at customer retention can help an organization control its costs because the costs of retaining customers are usually considerably lower than those of acquiring new ones. Frequent-user programs, such as those sponsored by airlines, car rental agencies, and hotels, aim to reward loyal customers and encourage them to remain loyal. Regal Entertainment, for example, introduced the Regal Crown Club, a membership club for 10 million loyal moviegoers. Membership entitles consumers to earn points that can be used for free movies, popcorn, or beverages at a Regal Cinema.[24] Some organizations employ special offers that only their existing customers can use. To retain loyal customers, marketers not only advertise loyalty programs but also use reinforcement advertising, which assures current users they have made the right brand choice and tells them how to get the most satisfaction from the product.

Facilitate Reseller Support

Reseller support is a two-way street: producers generally want to provide support to resellers to maintain sound working relationships, and in turn they expect resellers to support their products. When a manufacturer advertises a product to consumers, resellers should view this promotion as a form of strong manufacturer support. In some instances, a producer agrees to pay a certain proportion of retailers' advertising expenses for promoting its products. When a manufacturer is introducing a new consumer brand in a highly competitive product category, it may be difficult to persuade supermarket managers to carry this brand. However, if the manufacturer promotes the new brand with free samples and coupon distribution in the retailer's area, a supermarket manager views these actions as strong support and is much more likely to handle the product. To encourage wholesalers and retailers to increase their inventories of its products, a manufacturer may provide them with special offers and buying allowances. In certain industries, a producer's salesperson may provide support to a wholesaler by working with the wholesaler's customers (retailers) in the presentation and promotion of the products. Strong relationships with resellers are important to a firm's ability to maintain a sustainable competitive advantage. The use of various promotional methods can help an organization achieve this goal.

Combat Competitive Promotional Efforts

At times a marketer's objective in using promotion is to offset or lessen the effect of a competitor's promotional program. This type of promotional activity does not necessarily increase the organization's sales or market share, but it may prevent a sales or market share loss. A combative promotional objective is used most often by firms in extremely competitive consumer markets, such as the fast-food and automobile industries. When some automakers began advertising their automobiles' ability to withstand collisions, as determined by crash tests conducted by various federal and private agencies, Volvo and other firms quickly launched their own safety ads to combat their competitors' advertising. Although these ads were trying to promote safety records, the companies were also trying to prevent market share loss in a very competitive market.

Reduce Sales Fluctuations

Demand for many products varies from one month to another because of such factors as climate, holidays, and seasons. A business, however, cannot operate at peak efficiency when sales fluctuate rapidly. Changes in sales volume translate into changes in production, inventory levels, personnel needs, and financial resources. When promotional techniques reduce fluctuations by generating sales during slow periods, a firm can use its resources more efficiently.

Promotional techniques are often designed to stimulate sales during sales slumps. For example, advertisements promoting price reduction of lawn-care equipment can increase sales during fall and winter months. During peak periods, a marketer may refrain from advertising to prevent stimulating sales to the point where the firm cannot handle all the demand. On occasion, a company advertises that customers can be better served by coming in on certain days. A pizza outlet, for example, might distribute coupons that are valid only Monday through Thursday because on Friday through Sunday the restaurant is extremely busy.

To achieve the major objectives of promotion discussed here, companies must develop appropriate promotional programs. In the next section, we consider the basic components of such programs: the promotion mix elements.

The Promotion Mix

© 2010 South-Western, Cengage Learning. ALL RIGHTS RESERVED.

L O 4 To explore the elements of the promotion mix

Several promotional methods can be used to communicate with individuals, groups, and organizations. When an organization combines specific methods to manage the integrated marketing communications for a particular product, that combination constitutes the promotion mix for that product. The four possible elements of a **promotion mix** are advertising, personal selling, public relations, and sales promotion (see Figure 16.3). For some products, firms use all four elements; for others, they use only two or three. In this section, we provide an overview of each promotion mix element; they are covered in greater detail in the next two chapters.

promotion mix A combination of promotional methods used to promote a specific product

Advertising

Advertising is a paid nonpersonal communication about an organization and its products transmitted to a target audience through mass media, including television,

figure 16.3

THE FOUR POSSIBLE ELEMENTS OF A PROMOTION MIX

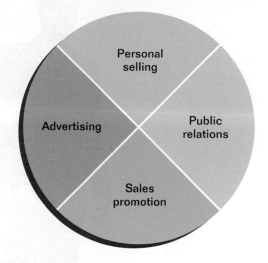

Personal selling

Advertising

Public relations

Sales promotion

Advertising as a Promotion Element

The Denver Zoo uses advertising and other promotional elements to encourage visits.

ADMIT ONE   DENVER ZOO   open every day of the year

2300 Steele Street,
Denver, CO 80205

When you support Denver Zoo, you provide aid to animals in the wild.

Denver Zoo is actively involved in animal conservation globally. Since 1997, we have participated in more than 300 animal conservation projects around the world and in the United States. To learn more, please visit denverzoo.org.

PRESERVATION INCLUDED WITH ADMISSION.

radio, the Internet, newspapers, magazines, video games, direct mail, outdoor displays, and signs on mass transit vehicles. Some companies even encourage consumers to get tattooed with their logos. Nearly 100 people have taken up an offer by Goodyear's Dunlop tire unit to get the company's flying-D logo tattooed somewhere on their body for a free set of tires. There's even a website, Leaseyourbody.com, that links advertisers with consumers who are willing to sport tattooed logos for money.[25] Individuals and organizations use advertising to promote goods, services, ideas, issues, and people. Being highly flexible, advertising can reach an extremely large target audience or focus on a small, precisely defined segment. For instance, Burger King's advertising focuses on a large audience of potential fast-food customers, ranging from children to adults, whereas advertising for Gulfstream jets aims at a much smaller and more specialized target market.

Advertising offers several benefits. It is extremely cost efficient when it reaches a vast number of people at a low cost per person. For example, the cost of a four-color, full-page advertisement in *Time* magazine is $241,350. Because the magazine reaches more than 3 million subscribers, the cost of reaching 1,000 subscribers is about $80.[26] Advertising also lets the source repeat the message several times. Southwest Airlines, for example, advertises on television, in magazines, and on outdoor displays. Advertising repetition has been found to be especially effective for brand name extensions beyond the original product category.[27] Furthermore, advertising a product a certain way can add to the product's value, and the visibility an organization gains from advertising can enhance its image. For example, research suggests that incorporating touchable elements that generate a positive sensory feedback in mail and print advertising can be a positive persuasive tool.[28] At times a firm tries to enhance its own or its product's image by including celebrity endorsers in advertisements. For example, the National Fluid Milk Processor Promotion Board's

Advertising Aimed at Prevention

This ad for "Changing Diabetes" focuses on creating awareness of the management and prevention of the disease.

"milk moustache" campaign has featured Beyoncé and Solange Knowles, David Beckham, the Fantastic Four, and the cast of *High School Musical*.[29]

Advertising has disadvantages as well. Even though the cost per person reached may be low, the absolute dollar outlay can be extremely high, especially for commercials during popular television shows. High costs can limit, and sometimes preclude, use of advertising in a promotion mix. Moreover, advertising rarely provides rapid feedback. Measuring its effect on sales is difficult, and it is ordinarily less persuasive than personal selling. In most instances, the time available to communicate a message to customers is limited to seconds, since people look at a print advertisement for only a few seconds and most broadcast commercials are 30 seconds or less. Of course, the use of infomercials can increase exposure time for viewers.

Personal Selling

Personal selling is a paid personal communication that seeks to inform customers and persuade them to purchase products in an exchange situation. The phrase *purchase products* is interpreted broadly to encompass acceptance of ideas and issues. Telemarketing, described in Chapter 15 as direct marketing over the telephone, relies heavily on personal selling. However, negative consumer attitudes and legislation restricting telemarketing have lessened its effectiveness as a personal selling technique.

Personal selling has both advantages and limitations when compared with advertising. Advertising is general communication aimed at a relatively large target audience, whereas personal selling involves more specific communication directed at one or several individuals. Reaching one person through personal selling costs considerably

STOP SELLING WHAT YOU HAVE.
START SELLING WHAT THEY NEED.

IBM helps major insurance companies develop flexible operations so they can offer clients personalized, dynamic services, and bring down processing costs at the same time. Start exceeding expectations at ibm.com/do/insurance STOP TALKING START DOING

Personal Selling

IBM offers business products that are sold directly to companies through a professional sales force.

kinesic communication
Communicating through the movement of head, eyes, arms, hands, legs, or torso

proxemic communication
Communicating by varying the physical distance in face-to-face interactions

tactile communication
Communicating through touching

more than through advertising, but personal selling efforts often have greater impact on customers. Personal selling also provides immediate feedback, allowing marketers to adjust their messages to improve communication. It helps them determine and respond to customers' information needs.

When a salesperson and a customer meet face to face, they use several types of interpersonal communication. The predominant communication form is language, both spoken and written. A salesperson and customer frequently use **kinesic communication,** or communication through the movement of head, eyes, arms, hands, legs, or torso. Winking, head nodding, hand gestures, and arm motions are forms of kinesic communication. A good salesperson often can evaluate a prospect's interest in a product or presentation by noting eye contact and head nodding. **Proxemic communication,** a less obvious form of communication used in personal selling situations, occurs when either person varies the physical distance separating them. When a customer backs away from a salesperson, for example, he or she may be displaying a lack of interest in the product or expressing dislike for the salesperson. Touching, or **tactile communication,** is also a form of communication, although less popular in the United States than in many other countries. Handshaking is a common form of tactile communication both in the United States and elsewhere.

Public Relations

Although many promotional activities focus on a firm's customers, other stakeholders—suppliers, employees, stockholders, the media, educators, potential investors, government officials, and society in general—are important to an organization as well. To communicate with customers and stakeholders, a company employs public relations. Public relations is a broad set of communication efforts used to create and maintain favorable relationships between an organization and its stakeholders. Maintaining a positive relationship with one or more stakeholders can affect a firm's current sales and profits, as well as its long-term survival.

Public relations uses a variety of tools, including annual reports, brochures, event sponsorship, and sponsorship of socially responsible programs aimed at protecting the environment or helping disadvantaged individuals. Nintendo, for example, is targeting older game players by hosting Super Bowl parties with men's magazines *Maxim* and *FHM,* as well as Spring Break parties and music tours, and it sponsored the Burton snowboarding championships.[30] Merrill Lynch sponsored a "Women of the World" art exhibit, which featured art by women artists from around the world, to help the financial services firm achieve its goal of targeting more affluent women.[31]

Other tools arise from the use of publicity, which is a component of public relations. Publicity is nonpersonal communication in news story form about an organization or its products, or both, transmitted through a mass medium at no charge. A few examples of publicity-based public relations tools are news releases, press conferences, and feature articles. To generate publicity, companies sometimes give away products to celebrities in the hope that the celebrity will be seen and photographed with the product and those photos will stimulate awareness and product trial among their fans. Meyers, a Swiss watch company, which has loaned watches to celebrities like Paris Hilton at the Sundance Film Festival and later auctioned off the returned timepieces for charity, says any resulting publicity from the effort can be worth as much as

$750,000.[32] Ordinarily public relations efforts are planned and implemented to be consistent with and support other elements of the promotion mix. Public relations efforts may be the responsibility of an individual or of a department within the organization, or the organization may hire an independent public relations agency.

Unpleasant situations and negative events, such as product tampering or an environmental disaster, may generate unfavorable public relations for an organization. For example, Wal-Mart responded to negative publicity due to news stories and lawsuits related to its hiring practices, union management, and aggressive expansion policies with a television ad campaign promoting the entrepreneurial vision of its founder, the savings it offers families, and its employee-benefit packages.[33] To minimize the damaging effects of unfavorable coverage, effective marketers have policies and procedures in place to help manage any public relations problems.

Public relations should not be viewed as a set of tools to be used only during crises. To get the most from public relations, an organization should have someone responsible for public relations either internally or externally, and should have an ongoing public relations program.

Sales Promotion

Sales promotion is an activity or material that acts as a direct inducement, offering added value or incentive for the product, to resellers, salespeople, or consumers. Examples include free samples, games, rebates, sweepstakes, contests, premiums, and coupons. To promote its new Call-10-Friends-for-Free plan, Alltel Wireless sponsored a "My Circle 500" sweepstakes asking subscribers to text a particular website to compete to win prizes, including an all-expenses-paid trip to the NASCAR Winston Cup.[34] *Sales promotion* should not be confused with *promotion;* sales promotion is just one part of the comprehensive area of promotion. Marketers spend more on sales promotion than on advertising, and sales promotion appears to be a faster-growing area than advertising. Coupons are especially important; Table 16.3 shows the product categories with the greatest distribution of coupons.

Generally, when companies employ advertising or personal selling, they depend on these activities continuously or cyclically. However, a marketer's use of sales promotion

table 16.3   **PRODUCT CATEGORIES WITH THE GREATEST DISTRIBUTION OF COUPONS**

Product Category	# Coupons Issued (in Millions)
1. Household cleaning	12.4
2. Pet food and treats	12.3
3. Rug and room deodorizers	10.8
4. Cross-category personal care	10.5
5. Snacks	7.2
6. Cold, allergy, flu care	6.7
7. Hair care	6.2
8. Vitamins	6.0
9. Dishwashing soap	5.5
10. Cereal	5.5

Source: Betsy Spethmann, "FSI Coupon Worth Reaches $300 Billion in 2006: MARX," *Promo,* Jan. 4, 2007, http://promomagazine.com/othertactics/news/fsi_coupon_worth_300_billion_010407/.

tends to be irregular. Many products are seasonal. A company such as Toro may offer more sales promotions in August than in the peak selling season of April or May, when more people buy tractors, lawn mowers, and other gardening equipment. Marketers frequently rely on sales promotion to improve the effectiveness of other promotion mix elements, especially advertising and personal selling. Decisions to cut sales promotion can have significant negative effects on a company. In fact, research suggests that about one-third of a gain in sales from a sales promotion occurs at the expense of other brands in the same category.[35]

An effective promotion mix requires the right combination of components. To see how such a mix is created, we now examine the factors and conditions affecting the selection of promotional methods that an organization uses for a particular product.

Selecting Promotion Mix Elements

L O ❺ To examine the selection of promotion mix elements

Marketers vary the composition of promotion mixes for many reasons. Although a promotion mix can include all four elements, frequently a marketer selects fewer than four. Many firms that market multiple product lines use several promotion mixes simultaneously.

Promotional Resources, Objectives, and Policies
The size of an organization's promotional budget affects the number and relative intensity of promotional methods included in a promotion mix. If a company's promotional budget is extremely limited, the firm is likely to rely on personal selling

Developing the Promotion Mix
Jamba Juice uses advertising with sales promotion to create trial of its new drinks.

because it is easier to measure a salesperson's contribution to sales than to measure the sales effectiveness of advertising. Businesses must have sizable promotional budgets to use regional or national advertising. Procter & Gamble, for example, spends $809 million a year on advertising in the United States.[36] Organizations with extensive promotional resources generally include more elements in their promotion mixes, but having more promotional dollars to spend does not necessarily mean using more promotional methods. Research indicates that resources spent on promotion activities have a positive influence on shareholder value.[37]

An organization's promotional objectives and policies also influence the types of promotion selected. If a company's objective is to create mass awareness of a new convenience good, such as a breakfast cereal, its promotion mix probably leans heavily toward advertising, sales promotion, and possibly public relations. For example, the Chinese firm Inner Mongolia Mengiu Milk Industry Co. advertises its dairy products during Chinese broadcasts of National Basketball Association games and reality shows, has participated in an NBA "Jam Van" road show that visited 17 Chinese cities, and donates cartons of milk to 500 Chinese elementary schools every day.[38] If a company hopes to educate consumers about the features of a durable good, such as a home appliance, its promotion mix may combine a moderate amount of advertising, possibly some sales promotion designed to attract customers to retail stores, and a great deal of personal selling because this method is an efficient way to inform customers about such products. If a firm's objective is to produce immediate sales of nondurable services, the promotion mix will probably stress advertising and sales promotion. For example, dry cleaners and carpet-cleaning firms are more likely to use advertising with a coupon or discount rather than personal selling.

Characteristics of the Target Market

Size, geographic distribution, and demographic characteristics of an organization's target market help dictate the methods to include in a product's promotion mix. To some degree, market size determines composition of the mix. If the size is limited, the promotion mix will probably emphasize personal selling, which can be very effective for reaching small numbers of people. Organizations selling to industrial markets and firms marketing products through only a few wholesalers frequently make personal selling the major component of their promotion mixes. When a product's market consists of millions of customers, organizations rely on advertising and sales promotion because these methods reach masses of people at a low cost per person.

Geographic distribution of a firm's customers also affects the choice of promotional methods. Personal selling is more feasible if a company's customers are concentrated in a small area than if they are dispersed across a vast region. When the company's customers are numerous and dispersed, advertising may be more practical.

Distribution of a target market's demographic characteristics, such as age, income, or education, may affect the types of promotional techniques a marketer selects, as well as the messages and images employed. The 2000 U.S. Census found that so-called traditional families—those composed of married couples with children—account for fewer than one-quarter of all U.S. households, down from 30 percent in 1980 and 45 percent in 1960. To reach the three-quarters of households consisting of single parents, unmarried couples, singles, and "empty nesters" (whose children have left home), more companies are modifying the images used in their promotions. Charles Schwab, for example, featured celebrity single mother Sarah Ferguson, the Duchess of York, in commercials for its financial services.

Characteristics of the Product

Generally promotion mixes for business products concentrate on personal selling, whereas advertising plays a major role in promoting consumer goods. This generalization should be treated cautiously, however. Marketers of business products use some advertising to promote products. Advertisements for computers, road-building equipment, and aircraft are fairly common, and some sales promotion is also used

We're living up to our name.

SunChips® snacks are now made with the help of solar energy in California.

As of April 22nd, one of our plants is using solar energy to help make SunChips® snacks. Not just because it's in our name, but because it's part of our vision for a healthy planet. It's a small step, but a step in the right direction.

live brightly

www.sunchips.com

Actual solar collectors at our SunChips plant in Modesto California.

Product Characteristics

Inexpensive, frequently purchased products, like snack foods, require significant levels of advertising.

occasionally to promote business products. Personal selling is used extensively for consumer durables, such as home appliances, automobiles, and houses, whereas consumer convenience items are promoted mainly through advertising and sales promotion. Public relations appears in promotion mixes for both business and consumer products.

Marketers of highly seasonal products often emphasize advertising, and sometimes sales promotion as well, because off-season sales generally will not support an extensive year-round sales force. Although most toy producers have sales forces to sell to resellers, many of these companies depend chiefly on advertising to promote their products.

A product's price also influences the composition of the promotion mix. High-priced products call for personal selling because consumers associate greater risk with the purchase of such products and usually want information from a salesperson. For low-priced convenience items, marketers use advertising rather than personal selling. Research suggests that consumers visiting a store specifically to purchase a product on sale are more likely to have read flyers and to have purchased other sale-priced products than consumers visiting the same store for other reasons.[39]

Another consideration in creating an effective promotion mix is the stage of the product life cycle. During the introduction stage, much advertising may be necessary for both business and consumer products to make potential users aware of them. For many products, personal selling and sales promotion are also helpful in this stage. In the growth and maturity stages, consumer services require heavy emphasis on advertising, whereas business products often call for a concentration of personal selling and some sales promotion. In the decline stage, marketers usually decrease all promotional activities, especially advertising.

Intensity of market coverage is still another factor affecting composition of the promotion mix. When products are marketed through intensive distribution, firms depend strongly on advertising and sales promotion. Many convenience products, such as lotions, cereals, and coffee, are promoted through samples, coupons, and money refunds. When marketers choose selective distribution, promotion mixes vary considerably. Items handled through exclusive distribution, such as expensive watches, furs, and high-quality furniture, typically require a significant amount of personal selling.

A product's use also affects the combination of promotional methods. Manufacturers of highly personal products, such as laxatives, nonprescription contraceptives, and feminine hygiene products, depend on advertising because many customers do not want to talk with salespeople about these products.

Costs and Availability of Promotional Methods

Costs of promotional methods are major factors to analyze when developing a promotion mix. National advertising and sales promotion require large expenditures. However, if these efforts succeed in reaching extremely large audiences, the cost per individual reached may be quite small, possibly a few pennies. Some forms of advertising are relatively inexpensive. Many small, local businesses advertise products through local newspapers, magazines, radio and television stations, outdoor displays, search engine result ads, and signs on mass transit vehicles.

Another consideration that marketers explore when formulating a promotion mix is availability of promotional techniques. Despite the tremendous number of media vehicles in the United States, a firm may find that no available advertising medium effectively reaches a certain target market. The problem of media availability becomes more pronounced when marketers advertise in foreign countries. Some media, such as television, simply may not be available, or advertising on television may be illegal. In China, the State Administration for Radio, Film, and Television banned a Nike commercial that featured basketball star LeBron James besting a kung fu master and a pair of dragons in a video game. In recent years, the agency has cracked down on U.S. and Japanese advertisements that fail to "uphold national dignity and interest, and respect the motherland's culture."[40] Available media may not be open to certain types of advertisements. In some countries, advertisers are forbidden to make brand comparisons on television. Other promotional methods also have limitations. For instance, a firm may wish to increase its sales force but be unable to find qualified personnel.

Push and Pull Channel Policies

Another element that marketers consider when planning a promotion mix is whether to use a push policy or a pull policy. With a **push policy,** the producer promotes the product only to the next institution down the marketing channel. In a marketing channel with wholesalers and retailers, the producer promotes to the wholesaler because in this case, the wholesaler is the channel member just below the producer (see Figure 16.4). Each channel member in turn promotes to the next channel member. A push policy normally stresses personal selling. Sometimes sales promotion and advertising are used in conjunction with personal selling to push the products down through the channel.

As Figure 16.4 shows, a firm that uses a **pull policy** promotes directly to consumers to develop strong consumer demand for its products. It does so primarily through advertising and sales promotion. Because consumers are persuaded to seek the products in retail stores, retailers in turn go to wholesalers or the producers to buy the products. This policy is intended to pull the goods down through the channel by creating demand at the consumer level. Consumers are told that if the stores don't have it, ask them to get it.

Push and pull policies are not mutually exclusive. At times an organization uses both simultaneously.

push policy Promoting a product only to the next institution down the marketing channel

pull policy Promoting a product directly to consumers to develop strong consumer demand that pulls products through the marketing channel

figure 16.4 **COMPARISON OF PUSH AND PULL PROMOTIONAL STRATEGIES**

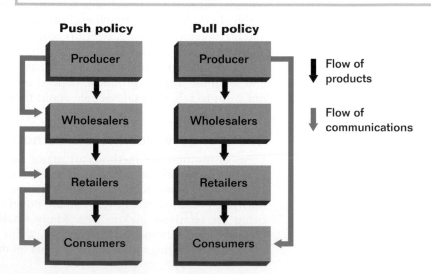

The Growing Importance of Word-of-Mouth Communications

L O 6 To understand word-of-mouth communication and how it affects promotion

snapshot

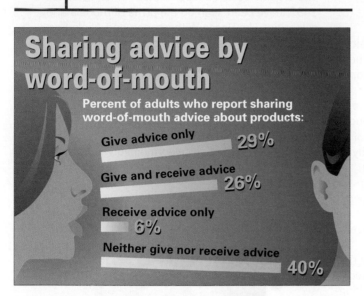

Sharing advice by word-of-mouth

Percent of adults who report sharing word-of-mouth advice about products:

Give advice only **29%**

Give and receive advice **26%**

Receive advice only **6%**

Neither give nor receive advice **40%**

Source: Forrester Research NACTAS Benchmark Survey, in Joan Voight, "Who Generates Buzz," *AdWeek*, Nov. 26, 2007, www.adweek.com/aw/news/article_display.jsp?vnu_content_id=100 3676225.

word-of-mouth communication Personal informal exchanges of communication that customers share with one another about products, brands, and companies

buzz marketing An attempt to incite publicity and public excitement surrounding a product through a creative event

When making decisions about the composition of promotion mixes, marketers should recognize that commercial messages, whether from advertising, personal selling, sales promotion, or public relations, are limited in the extent to which they can inform and persuade customers and move them closer to making purchases. Depending on the type of customers and the products involved, buyers to some extent rely on word-of-mouth communication from personal sources such as family members and friends. **Word-of-mouth communication** is personal, informal exchanges of communication that customers share with one another about products, brands, and companies.[41] Most customers are likely to be influenced by friends and family members when they make purchases. Word-of-mouth communication is very important when people are selecting restaurants and entertainment, and automotive, medical, legal, banking, and personal services such as hair care. Research has identified a link between word-of-mouth communication and new-customer acquisition when there is customer involvement and satisfaction.[42] Effective marketers who understand the importance of word-of-mouth communication attempt to identify opinion leaders and encourage them to try their products in the hope they will spread favorable word about them. Apple Computer, for example, has long relied on its nearly cult consumer following to spread by word of mouth their satisfaction with Apple products such as PowerBooks, iPods, and iPhones.

In addition, customers are increasingly going online for information and opinions about goods and services as well as about the companies. Electronic word of mouth is communicating about products through websites, blogs, e-mail, or online forums. Users can go to a number of consumer-oriented websites, such as epinions.com and Consumer Review.com. At these sites, they can learn about other consumers' feelings toward and experiences with specific products; some sites even encourage consumers to rate products they have tried. Users can also search within product categories and compare consumers' viewpoints on various brands and models. Not surprisingly, research has identified credibility as the most important attribute of a ratings website and found that reducing risk and saving search effort to be the primary motives for using such sites.[43] Buyers can peruse Internet-based newsgroups, forums, and blogs to find word-of-mouth information. A consumer looking for a new cell phone service, for example, might inquire in forums about other participants' experiences and level of satisfaction to gain more information before making a purchase decision. A study by Forrester and Intelliseek found that more than 90 percent of consumers trust such recommendations they get from other consumers.[44]

Electronic word of mouth is particularly important to consumers staying abreast of trends. At Facebook.com, a feature called The Pulse tracks trends relating to each school. Students, for instance, can see which band is the most popular on their campus and how it compares to all schools. At "social news" websites like Digg.com, Reddit.com, and Del.icio.us, trend-setting consumers can share bookmarks of their favorite websites or Internet stories. These sites have become so influential in introducing consumers to new products and shaping their views about them that marketers are increasingly monitoring them to identify new trends; some firms have even attempted to influence users' votes on their favorite items.[45]

Buzz marketing is an attempt to incite publicity and public excitement surrounding a product through a creative event. For example, NYC Marketing, the marketing arm of New York City, gave celebrities such as Nich Lachey and Liv Tyler new but seemingly

green MARKETING

I Am Not a Plastic Bag or Maybe I Am a Plastic Bag

Grocery shopping is becoming eco-responsible with designer totes to carry groceries home. The problem the totes address is the billions of plastic bags consumed in the world. Last year the United States used 88.5 billion plastic bags, and less than 1 percent of them were recycled. Production of those bags consumed 12 million barrels of oil. Looking at it another way, an American family of four consumes about 1,460 plastic bags each year. When you consider it takes 1,000 years for a plastic bag to decompose, it is no wonder that people are looking for greener alternatives.

One such person is Anya Hindmarch, who developed a stylish canvas tote for carrying groceries home that is embroidered with the phrase "I am not a plastic bag." The buzz surrounding these limited-edition $15 totes resulted in people standing in long lines in front of department stores and exclusive boutiques to obtain one. Anita Ahuja, also known as the "bag lady," is pulling plastic bags out of the garbage to create a tote called "I am a plastic bag" because the bags are made out of polyethylene. Ahuja employs downtrodden garbage pickers to collect the plastic bags in New Delhi, India, to produce her popular tote. Her products are now showing up in stores in the United Kingdom, France, and the United States, including chains like Whole Foods. Ahuja is donating some of her profits to charity and is also getting involved in Parisian fashion.

As countries around the globe debate whether to tax or ban the use of petroleum-based products like plastic grocery bags, other fashion designers are finding their own eco-friendly solutions. Stella McCartney, the British designer and daughter of Paul McCartney, has created a canvas shopper as a part of an organic clothing line sold in her shops. The organic cotton shopper totes, which retail for $495, have been seen on the arms of models and celebrities like Reese Witherspoon and Alicia Silverstone, and the resulting publicity has prompted more sales. Hermès has joined the scene by adding a $960 tote to the chic brand's famous silk scarves. The Louis Vuitton canvas tote retails for an unbelievable $1,740. These high-end fashionable totes are driving the sales of lower-priced totes and helping to fight the war against plastic bags. The key promotional driver of sales is celebrity involvement and word of mouth that makes it cool to carry a tote.[b]

frayed caps with the logo for its sanitation department, which are available for sale online and in city souvenir shops. The tactic worked, and the caps quickly became a must-have fashion item in a line that has in the past included NYPD and NYFD T-shirts and hats.[46]

Buzz marketing works best as a part of an integrated marketing communication program that also uses advertising, personal selling, sales promotion, and publicity. However, marketers should also take care that buzz marketing campaigns do not violate any laws or have the potential to be misconstrued and cause undue alarm. Consider that after a buzz effort to promote the Cartoon Network's "Aqua Teen Hunger Force" show, using electronic devices with flashing lights, caused a widespread terrorism scare in Boston, the performance artists that had been hired to implement the campaign were arrested and charged with disorderly conduct and creating a hoax in such a way as to cause panic. Turner Broadcasting, the corporate parent of the Cartoon Network, ultimately apologized for the incident and agreed to make restitution to the city for the expenses of responding to the apparent bomb threat.[47]

Viral marketing is a strategy to get consumers to share a marketer's message, often through e-mail or online video, in a way that spreads dramatically and quickly.

viral marketing A strategy to get consumers to share a marketer's message, often through e-mail or online video, in a way that spreads dramatically and quickly

RESPONSIBLE marketing?

Using Guerilla Marketing to Create Buzz: To Regulate or Not to Regulate?

ISSUE: Companies are using more invasive forms of sales promotion. Should marketers be more heavily regulated in this area?

Marketers are getting more aggressive in their promotion tactics. Many marketers use "guerilla" and buzz marketing activities to penetrate the clutter and reach consumers. Two companies were perhaps too aggressive in their promotion tactics. The Cartoon Network dropped electronic advertisements for its then upcoming movie *Aqua Teen Hunger Force* in several major markets across the country. Turner Broadcasting Systems never anticipated the response they received in Boston. The devices were dropped from the air and fell on highways, bridges, subway stations, and the Charles River. Witnesses thought Boston was experiencing some sort of terrorist attack. Police and fire squads were mobilized, traffic was disrupted, and general panic ensued. Turner Broadcasting apologized for the misunderstanding and paid $1 million to reimburse federal, state, and local agencies for the cost of the increased mobilization to thwart an alleged terrorism plot and an additional $1 million in goodwill funds for emergency response agencies.

Around this same time, Dr Pepper was promoting a national contest with a top prize of $1 million. It had created a sales promotion where participants could listen for clues and try to find coins that were hidden in cities all over the country. In Boston, a Dr Pepper coin was hidden in the Old Granary Burial Ground cemetery, where Paul Revere and many historic figures are buried. Contestants were told to bring implements to the cemetery to dig up the coin. Needless to say, the outcry was immediate and deafening.

Do you think that marketers should have to receive approval from cities or counties before engaging in these types of tactics to create buzz or publicity? What might be the effect on marketers of such a regulation?

Burger King, for example, created the "Subservient Chicken" website, where visitors can control a person in a chicken suit by typing in commands. Viral communications resulted in nearly 52 million visitors to the website in less than a year.[48] OfficeMax created 20 holiday websites to promote its stores as a gift-shopping destination. One of the sites, "ElfYourself," where users could create their own e-card with their own photo, resulted in 9.5 million elves with faces from users' uploaded photos. It garnered 36 million hits in just five weeks and also resulted in significant publicity in the form of news stories.[49] It is important to realize, however, that it is the public that determines whether something is interesting enough to "go viral."

Word of mouth, no matter how it is transmitted, is not effective in all product categories. It seems to be most effective for new-to-market and more expensive products. Despite the obvious benefits of positive word of mouth, marketers must also recognize the potential dangers of negative word of mouth. This is particularly important in dealing with online platforms that can reach more people and encourage consumers to "gang up" on a company or product. For example, music giant Sony BMG received negative press over a protest campaign that moved from online to the front of its office building. Sony had stopped production on the third album of its artist Fiona Apple after it decided the record was not radio-friendly. A copy of the album was mysteriously "leaked" on the Internet and soon became one of the most downloaded items online. Fans organized at websites and online forums to create petitions and mail apples to Sony's executives every day for several months. Sony agreed to release the album to stores after members of the online campaign picketed Sony's offices in New York and the story reached the mainstream media.[50]

Product Placement

LO 7 To understand product placement promotions

product placement The strategic location of products or product promotions within entertainment media content to reach the product's target market

A growing technique for reaching consumers is the selective placement of products within the context of television programs viewed by the target market. **Product placement** is a form of advertising that strategically locates products or product promotions within entertainment media to reach the product's target markets. The hit NBC show *The Office*, for example, has integrated products from Hewlett-Packard and Staples within storylines. Such product placement has become more important due to the increasing fragmentation of television viewers who have ever expanding viewing options and technology that can screen advertisements (e.g., digital video recorders such as TiVo). Research indicates that 60 to 80 percent of digital video recorder users skip over the commercials when they replay programming.[51]

In-program product placements have been successful in reaching consumers as they are being entertained rather than in the competitive commercial break time periods. For example, the NBC hit comedy show *30 Rock* has included numerous product placements, including rather obvious placements for Verizon's wireless service and Snapple beverages.[52] Reality programming in particular has been a natural fit for product placements because of the close interchange between the participants and the product (e.g., Sears and *Extreme Makeover Home Edition;* Levi's; Burger King; Marquis Jet; and Dove and *The Apprentice;* Coca-Cola and *American Idol*). For example, the MTV reality show *Gamekillers,* which is about young men's quests to charm women, is not only sponsored by the Unilever deodorant product Axe but also features the product in subtle ways.[53]

Product placement is not limited to U.S. television shows. The European Parliament recently greenlighted limited use of product placement, only during certain types of programs and only if consumers were informed at the beginning of the segment that companies had paid to have their products displayed. In general, the notion of product placement has not been favorably viewed in Europe and has been particularly controversial in the United Kingdom. However, British viewers have already been exposed to product placement within shows that have been imported from the United States, including *Desperate Housewives, The OC,* and *American Idol.*[54]

Criticisms and Defenses of Promotion

LO 8 To examine criticisms and defenses of promotion

Even though promotional activities can help customers make informed purchasing decisions, social scientists, consumer groups, government agencies, and members of society in general have long criticized promotion. There are two main reasons for such criticism: promotion does have flaws, and it is a highly visible business activity that pervades our daily lives. Although complaints about too much promotional activity are almost universal, a number of more specific criticisms have been lodged. In this section, we discuss some of the criticisms and defenses of promotion.

Is Promotion Deceptive?

One common criticism of promotion is that it is deceptive and unethical. During the nineteenth and early twentieth centuries, much promotion was blatantly deceptive. Although no longer widespread, some deceptive promotion still occurs. For example, T-Mobile paid $135,000 to the city of New York to settle a lawsuit accusing the company of misleading and confusing consumers with deceptive cell phone advertisements.[55] Questionable weight loss claims are made about various exercise devices and diet programs. Some promotions are unintentionally deceiving; for instance, when advertising to children, it is easy to mislead them because they are more naive than adults and less able to separate fantasy from reality. A promotion may also mislead some receivers because words can have diverse meanings for different people. However, not all promotion should be condemned because a small portion is flawed. Laws, government regulation, and industry self-regulation have helped decrease deceptive promotion.

Does Promotion Increase Prices?

Promotion is also criticized for raising prices, but in fact it often tends to lower them. The ultimate purpose of promotion is to stimulate demand. If it does, the business should be able to produce and market products in larger quantities and thus reduce per-unit production and marketing costs, which can result in lower prices. For example, as demand for flat-screen TVs and MP3 players has increased, their prices have dropped. When promotion fails to stimulate demand, the price of the promoted product increases because promotion costs must be added to other costs. Promotion also helps keep prices lower by facilitating price competition. When firms advertise prices, their prices tend to remain lower than when they are not promoting prices. Gasoline pricing illustrates how promotion fosters price competition. Service stations with the highest prices seldom have highly visible price signs.

Does Promotion Create Needs?

Some critics of promotion claim that it manipulates consumers by persuading them to buy products they do not need, hence creating "artificial" needs. In his theory of motivation, Abraham Maslow (discussed in Chapter 7) indicates that an individual tries to satisfy five levels of needs: physiological needs, such as hunger, thirst, and sex; safety needs; needs for love and affection; needs for self-esteem and respect from others; and self-actualization needs, that is, the need to realize one's potential. When needs are viewed in this context, it is difficult to demonstrate that promotion creates them. If there were no promotional activities, people would still have needs for food, water, sex, safety, love, affection, self-esteem, respect from others, and self actualization.

Although promotion may not create needs, it does capitalize on them (which may be why some critics believe promotion creates needs). Many marketers base their appeals on these needs. For example, several mouthwash, toothpaste, and perfume advertisements associate these products with needs for love, affection, and respect. These advertisers rely on human needs in their messages, but they do not create the needs.

Does Promotion Encourage Materialism?

Another frequent criticism of promotion is that it leads to materialism. The purpose of promoting goods is to persuade people to buy them; thus, if promotion works, consumers will want to buy more and more things. Marketers assert that values are instilled in the home and that promotion does not change people into materialistic consumers. However, the behavior of today's children and teenagers contradicts this view; many insist on high-priced, brand name apparel such as Gucci, Coach, Ralph Lauren, and Hummer.

Does Promotion Help Customers Without Costing Too Much?

Every year firms spend billions of dollars for promotion. The question is whether promotion helps customers enough to be worth the cost. Consumers do benefit because promotion informs them about product uses, features, advantages, prices, and locations where they can buy the products. Consumers thus gain more knowledge about available products and can make more intelligent buying decisions. Promotion also informs consumers about services—for instance, health care, educational programs, and day care—as well as about important social, political, and health-related issues. For example, several organizations, such as the California Department of Health Services, inform people about the health hazards associated with tobacco use.

Should Potentially Harmful Products Be Promoted?

Finally, some critics of promotion, including consumer groups and government officials, suggest that certain products should not be promoted at all. Primary targets are products associated with violence and other possibly unhealthy activities, such as handguns, alcohol, and tobacco. Cigarette advertisements, for example, promote smoking, a behavior proven to be harmful and even deadly. Tobacco companies, which spend billions on promotion, have countered criticism of their advertising by pointing out that advertisements for red meat and coffee are not censured even though these products may also cause health problems. Those who defend such promotion assert that as long as it is legal to sell a product, promoting that product should be allowed.

SUMMARY

Integrated marketing communications is the coordination of promotion and other marketing efforts to ensure maximum informational and persuasive impact on customers.

Communication is a sharing of meaning. The communication process involves several steps. First, the source translates meaning into code, a process known as coding or encoding. The source should employ signs or symbols familiar to the receiver or audience. The coded message is sent through a communications channel to the receiver or audience. The receiver or audience then decodes the message and usually supplies feedback to the source. When the decoded message differs from the encoded one, a condition called noise exists.

Promotion is communication to build and maintain relationships by informing and persuading one or more audiences. Although promotional objectives vary from one organization to another and within organizations over time, eight primary objectives underlie many promotional programs. Promotion aims to create awareness of a new product, a new brand, or an existing product; to stimulate primary and selective demand; to encourage product trial through the use of free samples, coupons, limited free-use offers, contests, and games; to identify prospects; to retain loyal customers; to facilitate reseller support; to combat competitive promotional efforts; and to reduce sales fluctuations.

The promotion mix for a product may include four major promotional methods: advertising, personal selling, public relations, and sales promotion. Advertising is paid nonpersonal communication about an organization and its products transmitted to a target audience through a mass medium. Personal selling is paid personal communication that attempts to inform customers and persuade them to purchase products in an exchange situation. Public relations is a broad set of communication efforts used to create and maintain favorable relationships between an organization and its stakeholders. Sales promotion is an activity or material that acts as a direct inducement, offering added value or incentive for the product, to resellers, salespeople, or consumers.

The promotional methods used in a product's promotion mix are determined by the organization's promotional resources, objectives, and policies; characteristics of the target market; characteristics of the product; and cost and availability of promotional methods. Marketers also consider whether to use a push policy or a pull policy. With a push policy, the producer promotes the product only to the next institution down the marketing channel. Normally, a push policy stresses personal selling. Firms that use a pull policy promote directly to consumers, with the intention of developing strong consumer demand for the products. Once consumers are persuaded to seek the products in retail stores, retailers go to wholesalers or the producer to buy the products.

Most customers are likely to be influenced by friends and family members when making purchases. Word-of-mouth communication is personal, informal exchanges of communication that customers share with one another about products, brands, and companies. Customers may also choose to go online to find electronic word of mouth about products or companies. Buzz marketing is an attempt to incite publicity and public excitement surrounding a product through a creative event. Viral marketing is a strategy to get consumers to share a marketer's message, often through e-mail or online video, in a way that spreads dramatically and quickly. A related concept, product placement is the strategic location of products or product promotions within television program content to reach the product's target market.

Promotional activities can help consumers make informed purchasing decisions, but they have also evoked many criticisms. Promotion has been accused of deception. Although some deceiving or misleading promotions do exist, laws, government regulation, and industry self-regulation minimize deceptive promotion. Promotion has been blamed for increasing prices, but it usually tends to lower them. When demand is high, production and marketing costs decrease, which can result in lower prices. Moreover, promotion helps keep prices lower by facilitating price competition. Other criticisms of promotional activity are that it manipulates consumers into buying products they do not need, that it leads to a more materialistic society, and that consumers do not benefit sufficiently from promotional activity to justify its high cost. Finally, some critics of promotion suggest that potentially harmful products, especially those associated with violence, sex, and unhealthy activities, should not be promoted at all.

IMPORTANT TERMS

Integrated marketing
    communications, 460
Communication, 461
Source, 461
Receiver, 461
Coding process, 461
Communications channel,
    462

Decoding process, 463
Noise, 463
Feedback, 463
Channel capacity, 463
Promotion, 464
Primary demand, 465
Pioneer promotion, 465
Selective demand, 465

Promotion mix, 468
Kinesic communication,
    471
Proxemic communication,
    471
Tactile communication,
    471
Push policy, 476

Pull policy, 476
Word-of-mouth
    communication, 477
Buzz marketing, 477
Viral marketing, 478
Product placement, 479

DISCUSSION & REVIEW QUESTIONS

1. What does the term *integrated marketing communications* mean?

2. Define *communication* and describe the communication process. Is it possible to communicate without using all the elements in the communication process? If so, which elements can be omitted?

3. Identify several causes of noise. How can a source reduce noise?

4. What is the major task of promotion? Do firms ever use promotion to accomplish this task and fail? If so, give several examples.

5. Describe the possible objectives of promotion and discuss the circumstances under which each objective might be used.

6. Identify and briefly describe the four promotional methods an organization can use in its promotion mix.

7. What forms of interpersonal communication besides language can be used in personal selling?

8. How do target market characteristics determine which promotional methods to include in a promotion mix? Assume a company is planning to promote a cereal to both adults and children. Along what major dimensions would these two promotional efforts have to differ from each other?

9. How can a product's characteristics affect the composition of its promotion mix?

10. Evaluate the following statement: "Appropriate advertising media are always available if a company can afford them."

11. Explain the difference between a pull policy and a push policy. Under what conditions should each policy be used?

12. In which ways can word-of-mouth communication influence the effectiveness of a promotion mix for a product?

13. Which criticisms of promotion do you believe are the most valid? Why?

14. Should organizations be allowed to promote offensive, violent, sexual, or unhealthy products that can be legally sold and purchased? Support your answer.

APPLICATION QUESTIONS

1. The overall objective of promotion is to stimulate demand for a product. Through television advertising, the American Dairy Association promotes the benefits of drinking milk, a campaign that aims to stimulate primary demand. Advertisements for a specific brand of milk focus on stimulating selective demand. Identify two television commercials, one aimed at stimulating primary demand and one aimed at stimulating selective demand. Describe each commercial and discuss how each attempts to achieve its objective.

2. Developing a promotion mix is contingent on many factors, including the type of product and the product's attributes. Which of the four promotional methods—advertising, personal selling, public relations, or sales promotion—would you emphasize if you were developing the promotion mix for the following products? Explain your answers.

a. Washing machine
b. Cereal
c. Halloween candy
d. Compact disc

3. Suppose marketers at Falcon International Corporation have come to you for recommendations on how to promote their products. They want to develop a comprehensive promotional campaign and have a generous budget with which to implement their plans. What questions would you ask them, and what would you suggest they consider before developing a promotional program?

4. Marketers must consider whether to use a push or a pull policy when deciding on a promotion mix (see Figure 16.4). Identify a product for which marketers should use each policy and a third product that might best be promoted using a mix of the two policies. Explain your answers.

INTERNET EXERCISE

Visit **www.cengage.com/marketing/pride-ferrell** for resources to help you master the material in this chapter, plus materials that will help you expand your marketing knowledge, including Internet exercise updates, ACE Self-Tests, hotlinks to companies featured in this chapter, and much more.

MySpace Is the Music Place

MySpace is not just for friends. It is also a unique promotional platform for musical artists, especially unsigned and independent artists. By creating a MySpace page, musicians can share their songs, post important dates, or even blog. MySpace music pages are different from record company websites because they feel more personal. Artists also take advantage of MySpace's viral nature by allowing other MySpace members to post their pictures, songs, and music videos on their own MySpace profile pages. Visit the website at **http://music.myspace.com,** and look for your favorite artist or explore a new one.

1. Who is the target market for members?
2. What is being promoted to these individuals?
3. What are the promotional objectives of this website?
4. Is word-of-mouth communication occurring at this website? Explain.

developing your MARKETING PLAN

A vital component of a successful marketing strategy is the company's plan for communication to its stakeholders. One segment of the communication plan is included in the marketing mix as the promotional element. A clear understanding of the role that promotion plays, as well as the various methods of promotion, is important in developing the promotional plan. The following questions should assist you in relating the information in this chapter to several decisions in your marketing plan.

1. Review the communication process in Figure 16.1. Identify the various players in the communication process for promotion of your product.

2. What are your objectives for promotion? Use Table 16.2 as a guide in answering this question.

3. Which of the four elements of the promotional mix are most appropriate for accomplishing your objectives? Discuss the advantages and disadvantages of each.

4. What role should word-of-mouth communications, buzz marketing, or product placement play in your promotional plan?

The information obtained from these questions should assist you in developing various aspects of your marketing plan found in the *Interactive Marketing Plan* exercise at **www.cengage.com/marketing/pride-ferrell.**

globalEDGE

1. Personalized marketing messages are important to appeal to the particular needs of individual customers. Due to the rapid globalization of your firm, you must determine which markets are more accepting of personalized messages to maximize the effect of your promotional campaign. Use the search term "Hofstede scores" at **http://globaledge.msu.edu/ibrd** to reach the Geert Hofstede Resource Center. Go to the link for Hofstede Scores, and then you can highlight all the scores and download them into a spreadsheet for analysis. Using Hofstede's scores, what are the top ten countries on this scale? Does this simplify or complicate the development of your firm's personalized marketing strategy?

2. The readiness of a global market's infrastructure is important for any integrated marketing communications campaign to communicate a similar message across different media (e.g., newspaper, magazine, radio, television, Internet) in an effective manner. One report that may be useful here is the Global Information Technology Report, which can be accessed by using the search term "global information technology" at **http://globaledge.msu.edu/ibrd.** Once there, find the most recent report. What are the ten markets with the most equipped infrastructures? Are there any surprises among the markets listed? What regions are represented in your report?

video CASE 16.1

The Toledo Mud Hens Make Marketing Fun

Since their dismal beginnings in 1896 when they played near a swamp (earning the name Mud Hens in honor of the coots inhabiting the marshy land), the Triple-A Toledo Mud Hens have become one of the most successful minor league baseball teams in the country, and their games some of the best attended. How did they leverage their climb from such a murky start? In a word: marketing. With their two slogans, "Toledo's Family Fun Park" and "Experience the Joy of Mudville," the Mud Hens harness the twin themes of family and history. These days the Mud Hens are the Triple-A affiliate of the major league team the Detroit Tigers. Because the Tigers do all of the hiring and firing of players, trainers, and medical staff, the Mud Hens' home office can focus all of its energy on improving the image and profitability of the Mud Hens enterprise.

The Mud Hens do not have the star power of the major league teams (aside from their popular bird mascots, Muddy and Muddonna), so marketers must seek another way to promote the games. They advertise the games as wholesome, affordable family fun—an alternative to bowling or going to the movies. People of all ages can come to the games and socialize, while watching potential up-and-coming baseball stars develop into mature athletes. Because there is no star paraphernalia to sell, most of the marketing attention is paid to promoting Mud Hens merchandise, like T-shirts and hats, and food and beverage sales. In fact, the team has been the league leader in ballpark merchandise sales since 2000 and ranks second in the minor league for overall merchandise sales. The on-premise Swampshop offers 50 styles of T-shirts and 60 styles of baseball caps in all sizes. Truly avid fans can shop online from anywhere in the world as well.

The league's continued sales and revenue growth stand in contrast to an overall downturn in attendance and purchases at minor league baseball games. This statistic attests to the strength of the Mud Hens' marketing strategy. They market directly to advance ticket buyers in order to target those people who are apt to buy tickets early, buy in quantity, and spend cash at the games. Other marketing channels are the more traditional radio, television, and print media. The Mud Hens enjoy an especially close relationship with local newspapers, where a prominent story about the team is almost guaranteed whenever the Mud Hens have a home game.

When the team decided to build the new Fifth Third Field in downtown Toledo, they knew that the move would generate additional excitement about the team. To accommodate and encourage increased spending at games, planners mapped out a huge 3,000-square-foot Swampshop to comfortably accommodate all consumers. The move to the downtown area has dramatically increased overall attendance rates, which have doubled. All of these strategic maneuvers are part of integrated marketing communications, which entails coordinating promotional and marketing efforts so as to have maximum impact on customers.

Clearly, the Toledo Mud Hens know their market, because they are consistently one of the high revenue generators in the minor leagues. Because the Tigers take care of most of the administrative tasks, the Mud Hens' staff can focus nearly all of their efforts on successfully using the promotion mix (advertising, personal selling, public relations, and promotion) and buzz to get people flocking to the park. The promise of affordable, wholesome family fun has clearly struck a chord with people in this working-class section of Ohio. Games have also been a big hit with corporate season ticket holders as a way to reward employees or to provide a congenial atmosphere for meeting with clients.

The Mud Hens go beyond mere marketing, however, and this is one of the keys to the organization's success. The team has become an integral part of the community—through direct marketing and regular media coverage, but also through charitable endeavors. Because the marketing focus is so much on family fun, community, and socializing, the organization does its best to give back to the community that so avidly supports them. The organization engages in educational and community outreach through various programs such as Muddy's Knothole Club, which provides tickets to underprivileged kids; regular fundraisers and auctions; and donations to local charities. Even pro-bono activities such as these can be part of a well-managed, integrated marketing communications strategy because they increase goodwill toward the organization and encourage people to attend games.[56]

Questions for Discussion

1. How do the Toledo Mud Hens use integrated marketing communications to promote their enterprise?
2. How do the Mud Hens identify and market to their target audience?
3. Suggest how the Mud Hens can gain publicity in order to maintain and increase attendance?

CASE 16.2

One Tough Mother at Columbia Sportswear

Eighty-four-year-old Gert Boyle is "one tough mother." Not only is she the chairman of the board for Columbia Sportswear, but she is also its spokeswoman. Gert assumed control of Columbia Sportswear 35 years ago after her husband Neil passed away. Gert reported for duty a mere four days after Neil's death to take the reins of the growing company—a company that has flourished under her tough leadership.

Founded by Paul and Marie Lamfrom (Gert Boyle's parents) in 1938, Columbia Sportswear Company is a global leader in the design, sourcing, marketing, and distribution of active outdoor apparel and footwear. The $1.36 billion company employs more than 2,700 people and distributes and sells products in 80 countries to more than 13,000 retailers internationally. As one of the largest outerwear brands in the world and the leading seller of skiwear in the United States, the company has developed an international reputation for quality, performance, functionality, and value.

Columbia Sportswear has worked hard over the years to develop its image of offering high-quality products. It promotes itself and its products through event sponsorships, print and television advertising, and a strong public relations program. It is actively involved in event marketing. For example, the company signed up to be the official apparel sponsor of Jeep's "King of the Mountain" series, proclaimed as the richest and most prestigious professional snow racing series in the world. For its involvement, Columbia Sportswear outfitted the event staff and volunteers, as well as VIPs attending the event. Other sponsorships include events such as the Mt. Baker Banked Slalom snowboarding competition, which draws world-class snowboarders; the annual World Superpipe Championships; and the Ski Mountaineering Competition in Korea.

The company has used many approaches to promote the quality of its products. Their greatest success however, is a campaign featuring Gert and her son, Tim Boyle. This positioning is an outgrowth of the relationship that has existed between Gert and Tim since they began running the company together. According to people who know them, Tim and his mother have argued from the beginning about how to run Columbia Sportswear. A director of the company says, "Tim and Gert are a lot like the Jack Lemmon and Walter Matthau characters in *The Odd Couple*. They complain all the time, and yet they cherish each other."

Over 20 years ago, Borders, Perrin & Norrander, the company's former advertising agency, came up with an idea to use the well-known relationship between Gert and her son to develop an identity for the company—an identity beyond technical claims about product quality. They developed an ad campaign that portrays Gert as "one tough mother," who uses her son to demonstrate that Columbia Sportswear clothes will protect whoever wears them under any weather conditions. In the many spots, Gert appears as a hard-driving mother who refuses to accept anything but the highest quality of products, for both her son and her company. The ads were so successful at positioning and promoting Columbia Sportswear's products that Gert and Tim became the company's ad staples.

Showing Gert put her son through a series of catastrophic tests to demonstrate the durability of the company's products did not only communicate product quality, but it also established an identity in the customers' minds. In one commercial, Gert drives an SUV with Tim strapped on top through a series of severe weather situations to show that his clothing is protecting him. The ending scene is a close-up of the jacket he is wearing with the tagline "Tested Tough." This theme is continued throughout a series of commercials that depict Tim in a number of cold-weather survival situations, such as being dropped on the top of a snow-covered mountain by a helicopter piloted by Gert, being under the ice in a hockey arena (staying alive with a breathing tube), and being covered by snow with Gert driving the snowplow. In all cases, Tim is unharmed and Gert is unconcerned—all because he is wearing Columbia outerwear.

Columbia Sportswear's signature spot shows Gert in a biker bar. The audio track says, "In a world of rugged individuals, only one is the toughest mother of them all. Mother Gert Boyle—maker of tough mother jeans." There is a close-up of Gert with a tattoo on her bicep that reads "Born to Nag," and the spot ends with a product shot of Columbia jeans. These irreverent and memorable ads appear to be working. Since their inception, Columbia Sportswear has carved out a 50 percent market share in its category. Now that's one tough mother![57]

Questions for Discussion

1. Identify the key objectives of Columbia Sportswear's promotion program. Are the objectives the same or different for its advertising and for its event sponsorships?
2. Does Columbia Sportswear use integrated marketing communications? What suggestions, if any, would you make to strengthen the coordination of Columbia's promotion activities?
3. Describe the characteristics of Columbia's target market. Are they the same for advertising and event sponsorships? Explain.

17 Advertising and Public Relations

LEARNING objectives

❶ To describe the nature and types of advertising

❷ To explore the major steps in developing an advertising campaign

❸ To identify who is responsible for developing advertising campaigns

❹ To examine the tools used in public relations

❺ To analyze how public relations is used and evaluated

Womenkind: An Advertising Agency for Women

Experts estimate that the majority of purchasing power in the United States is in the hands of women. With so many advertisements portraying women as either sex objects or mothers, it is important to determine how this large target market views advertising compared to how men look at it. Jerry Judge, a former executive of the Lowe agency, decided to create a new company, Womenkind, to address the development of effective advertising targeted at women and to avoid ads developed by men who think they understand women. The new agency provides a variety of advertising and other marketing services to companies whose emphasis is on targeting women. The agency also donates 5 percent of profits to causes that help disadvantaged women.

To develop the know-how to accomplish its objectives, Judge employs 60 female creative types, from copywriters to directors. Most of these women are freelancers who participate on a project basis rather than as full-time employees of the agency. The company has also assembled a group of small-business owners, mothers, and activists who will function as a focus group and communicate via a password-protected website as well as regular lunches, salons, and phone conversations.

Judge's new entrepreneurial venture has already attracted attention from major marketers such as Procter & Gamble, whose ads more often target more women than men. To better understand women, the company has developed online focus-group interviewing methods and created a research project called WomIntuition. The main function of this research is to measure the difference between men and women when they view an ad.

Creating the advertising message is a function of many factors including gender, choice of media, and the appropriate copy. Womenkind provides a new opportunity for marketers to send the right message to women.[1]

Both large organizations and small companies use conventional and online promotional efforts such as advertising to change their corporate images, launch new products, or promote current brands. In this chapter, we explore several dimensions of advertising and public relations. First, we focus on the nature and types of advertising. Next, we examine the major steps in developing an advertising campaign and describe who is responsible for developing such campaigns. We then discuss the nature of public relations and how it is used. We examine various public relations tools and ways to evaluate the effectiveness of public relations. Finally, we focus on how companies deal with unfavorable public relations.

The Nature and Types of Advertising

L O 1 To describe the nature and types of advertising

Advertising permeates our daily lives. At times, we view it positively; at other times, we avoid it. Some advertising informs, persuades, or entertains us; some bores, annoys, or even offends us.

As mentioned in Chapter 16, **advertising** is a paid form of nonpersonal communication that is transmitted to a target audience through mass media, such as television, radio, the Internet, newspapers, magazines, direct mail, outdoor displays, and signs on mass transit vehicles. McDonald's is even advertising Happy Meals on elementary students' report cards, although the initiative is proving controversial.[2] Organizations use advertising to reach a variety of audiences ranging from small, specific groups, such as stamp collectors in Idaho, to extremely large groups, such as all athletic-shoe purchasers in the United States.

When asked to name major advertisers, most people immediately mention business organizations. However, many nonbusiness organizations, including governments, churches, universities, and charitable organizations, employ advertising to communicate with stakeholders. For example, the United Kingdom's government spends more than $350 million a year on advertising to advise, influence, or gently chastise its citizens.[3] In 2006, the U.S. government was the twenty-ninth-largest advertiser in the country, spending approximately $1.1 billion on advertising.[4] Although we analyze advertising in the context of business organizations here, much of the material applies to all types of organizations. For example, the state of Texas developed a $22 million advertising campaign that included cable television commercials and magazine and website ads to show off the state's diversity of unique attractions and encourage leisure travelers and seniors to visit the Lone Star State. The campaign also includes new trip-planning tools on the state's tourism website, **www.TravelTex.com.**[5]

Advertising is used to promote goods, services, ideas, images, issues, people, and anything else advertisers want to publicize or foster. Depending on what is being promoted, advertising can be classified as institutional or product advertising. **Institutional advertising** promotes organizational images, ideas, and political issues. It can be used to create or maintain an organizational image. Institutional advertisements may deal with broad image issues, such as organizational strength or the friendliness of employees. They may also aim to create a more favorable view of the organization in the eyes of noncustomer groups such as shareholders, consumer advocacy groups, potential shareholders, or the general public. When a company promotes its position on a public issue—for instance, a tax increase, abortion, gun control, or international trade coalitions—institutional advertising is referred to as **advocacy advertising**. Institutional advertising may be used to promote socially approved behavior such as recycling and moderation in consuming alcoholic beverages. Philip Morris, for example, has run television advertisements encouraging parents to talk to their children about not smoking. Research has identified a number of themes that advertisers can use to increase the effectiveness of antismoking messages for adolescents.[6] This type of advertising not only has social benefits but also helps build an organization's image.

Product advertising promotes the uses, features, and benefits of products. There are two types of product advertising: pioneer and competitive. **Pioneer advertising** focuses on stimulating demand for a product category (rather than a specific brand)

advertising Paid nonpersonal communication about an organization and its products transmitted to a target audience through mass media

institutional advertising Advertising that promotes organizational images, ideas, and political issues

advocacy advertising Advertising that promotes a company's position on a public issue

product advertising Advertising that promotes the uses, features, and benefits of products

pioneer advertising Advertising that tries to stimulate demand for a product category rather than a specific brand by informing potential buyers about the product

by informing potential customers about the product's features, uses, and benefits. This type of advertising is employed when the product is in the introductory stage of the product life cycle. **Competitive advertising** attempts to stimulate demand for a specific brand by promoting the brand's features, uses, and advantages, sometimes through indirect or direct comparisons with competing brands. Advertising effects on sales must reflect competitors' advertising activities. The type of competitive environment will determine the most effective industry approach.

To make direct product comparisons, marketers use a form of competitive advertising called **comparative advertising,** which compares the sponsored brand with one or more identified competing brands on the basis of one or more product characteristics. Quizno's, for example, used comparative advertising to promote the value and size of its cheesesteak sandwich as compared to that offered by rival Subway.[7] Often the brands that are promoted through comparative advertisements have low market shares and are compared with competitors that have the highest market shares in the product category. Product categories that commonly use comparative advertising include soft drinks, toothpaste, pain relievers, foods, tires, automobiles, and detergents. Under the provisions of the 1988 Trademark Law Revision Act, marketers using comparative advertisements in the United States must not misrepresent the qualities or characteristics of competing products. Other countries may have laws that are stricter or less strict with regard to comparative advertising.

Other forms of competitive advertising include reminder and reinforcement advertising. **Reminder advertising** tells customers that an established brand is still around and still offers certain characteristics, uses, and advantages. **Reinforcement advertising** assures current users they have made the right brand choice and tells them how to get the most satisfaction from that brand.

Developing an Advertising Campaign

LO 2 To explore the major steps in developing an advertising campaign

An **advertising campaign** involves designing a series of advertisements and placing them in various advertising media to reach a particular target audience. As Figure 17.1 shows, the major steps in creating an advertising campaign are (1) identifying and analyzing the target audience, (2) defining the advertising objectives, (3) creating the advertising platform, (4) determining the advertising appropriation, (5) developing the media plan,

competitive advertising Tries to stimulate demand for a specific brand by promoting its features, uses, and advantages relative to competing brands

comparative advertising Compares the sponsored brand with one or more identified brands on the basis of one or more product characteristics

reminder advertising Advertising used to remind consumers about an established brand's uses, characteristics, and benefits

reinforcement advertising Advertising that assures users they chose the right brand and tells them how to get the most satisfaction from it

advertising campaign The creation and execution of a series of advertisements to communicate with a particular target audience

figure 17.1   GENERAL STEPS IN DEVELOPING AND IMPLEMENTING AN ADVERTISING CAMPAIGN

8 Evaluate advertising effectiveness

7 Execute campaign

6 Create advertising message

5 Develop media plan

4 Determine advertising appropriation

3 Create advertising platform

2 Define advertising objectives

1 Identify and analyze target audience

SOME THINGS ARE SUPPOSED TO BE WRINKLED AND SLIGHTLY SMELLY.
YOUR CLOTHES AREN'T ONE OF THEM.

LG's High Capacity SteamWasher," an established leader in the industry, does more than wash your clothes. Being one of the largest and most energy efficient machines available, the LG SteamWasher™ features steam technology that will revolutionize the way you do your laundry. Our unique SteamFresh™ Cycle reduces wrinkles* and freshens clothing without using water, and our SteamWash™ Performance System adds steam to wash cycles to brighten and sanitize your laundry. That's better laundry in less time and most importantly, less time spent at the ironing board.

Surprising As...Fresh As...Innovative as LG.

GOODBUYAWARDS* 2007 POPULAR SCIENCES 2006 AWARD WINNER

©2006 LG Electronics, Inc. Englewood Cliffs, NJ. LG Design is a trademark of LG Electronics, Inc. *Results may vary by fabric. Steam simulated above.

LG Life's Good

www.LGusa.com

Target Audience

LG produces a front-loading, high-efficiency steam washer. Who is the target audience for this ad?

target audience The group of people at whom advertisements are aimed

(6) creating the advertising message, (7) executing the campaign, and (8) evaluating advertising effectiveness. The number of steps and the exact order in which they are carried out may vary according to the organization's resources, the nature of its product, and the type of target audience to be reached. Nevertheless, these general guidelines for developing an advertising campaign are appropriate for all types of organizations.

Identifying and Analyzing the Target Audience

The **target audience** is the group of people at whom advertisements are aimed. Advertisements for Barbie cereal are targeted toward young girls who play with Barbie dolls, whereas those for Special K cereal are directed at health-conscious adults. Identifying and analyzing the target audience are critical processes; the information yielded helps determine other steps in developing the campaign. The target audience may include everyone in the firm's target market. Marketers may, however, direct a campaign at only a portion of the target market. For example, American Airlines, after recognizing that a growing percentage of its passengers were Hispanic, is now targeting them with a multimedia Spanish-language campaign with the theme *"No importa cual sea tu destino, nosotros te llevamos"* ("It doesn't matter what your destiny is, we will take you there"). The campaign features vignettes that show Latinos reconnecting with the people and the places they want to see.[8]

Advertisers research and analyze advertising targets to establish an information base for a campaign. Information commonly needed includes location and geographic distribution of the target group; the distribution of demographic factors, such as age, income, race, gender, and education; lifestyle information; and consumer attitudes regarding purchase and use of both the advertiser's products and competing products. The exact kinds of information an organization finds useful depend on the type of product being advertised, the characteristics of the target audience, and the type and amount of competition. Generally, the more an advertiser knows about the target audience, the more likely the firm is to develop an effective advertising campaign. When the advertising target is not precisely identified and properly analyzed, the campaign may fail, as illustrated in the boxed feature.

Defining the Advertising Objectives

The advertiser's next step is to determine what the firm hopes to accomplish with the campaign. Because advertising objectives guide campaign development, advertisers should define objectives carefully. Advertising objectives should be stated clearly, precisely, and in measurable terms. Precision and measurability allow advertisers to evaluate advertising success at the end of the campaign in terms of whether objectives have been met. To provide precision and measurability, advertising objectives should contain benchmarks and indicate how far the advertiser wishes to move from these standards. If the goal is to increase sales, the advertiser should state the current sales level (the benchmark) and the amount of sales increase sought through advertising. An advertising objective should also specify a time frame so that advertisers know exactly how long they have to accomplish the objective. An advertiser with average monthly sales of $450,000 (the benchmark) might set the following objective: "Our primary advertising objective is to increase average monthly sales from $450,000 to $540,000 within 12 months."

If an advertiser defines objectives on the basis of sales, the objectives focus on increasing absolute dollar sales or unit sales, increasing sales by a certain percentage, or increasing the firm's market share. Even though an advertiser's long-run goal is to increase sales, not all campaigns are designed to produce immediate sales. Some campaigns aim to increase product or brand awareness, make consumers' attitudes more favorable, or heighten consumers' knowledge of product features. If the goal is to increase product awareness, the objectives are stated in terms of communication. A specific communication objective might be to increase product feature awareness from 0 to 40 percent in the target audience by the end of six months.

Creating the Advertising Platform

Before launching a political campaign, party leaders develop a political platform stating major issues that are the basis of the campaign. Like a political platform, an **advertising platform** consists of the basic issues or selling points that an advertiser wishes to include in the advertising campaign. New Balance, for example, launched a campaign that mocks professional athletes while reminding its 25- to 49-year-old target market about the joys of competing for fun and the love of sports.[9] A single advertisement in an advertising campaign may contain one or several issues from the platform. Although the platform sets forth the basic issues, it does not indicate how to present them.

An advertising platform should consist of issues important to customers. One of the best ways to determine those issues is to survey customers about what they consider most important in the selection and use of the product involved. Selling features must not only be important to customers, they should also be strongly competitive features of the advertised brand. For example, New Balance's "Love or Money" campaign stemmed in part from Internet research that found that many people have

advertising platform Basic issues or selling points to be included in an advertising campaign

Advertising Platform

An advertising platform normally contains multiple appeals as this Reebok ad displays.

RESPONSIBLE marketing?

> **Pfizer: Advertising or Advertising Puffery?**
>
> **ISSUE:** Is advertising puffery acceptable when marketing a cholesterol-lowering drug?

Amid criticism, Pfizer Inc. pulled advertisements that featured Robert Jarvik as its endorser for Lipitor. Pfizer stopped the print and television ads after a congressional regulatory committee launched a probe into Dr. Jarvik's credentials and the ethics of celebrity drug endorsements. The information conveyed in the Lipitor ad is truthful: Lipitor lowers bad cholesterol. But does it matter if Dr. Jarvik, although the creator of the artificial heart, is not a practicing MD or an authority on cholesterol-lowering drugs? Puffery is defined by the FTC as "exaggerations reasonably to be expected of a seller" where "truth or falsity cannot be precisely determined." According to the Better Business Bureau's Code of Advertising, "Subjective claims are not subject to test of their truth or accuracy." Consumers, however, feel that Pfizer's should focus more on objective scientific data and less on producing subjective, emotional advertising for Lipitor.[a]

become disturbed by the behavior of well-known professional athletes, some of whom receive millions of dollars a year in endorsements from New Balance's competitors.[10]

Although research is the most effective method for determining what issues to include in an advertising platform, it is expensive. Therefore, an advertising platform is most commonly based on opinions of personnel within the firm and of individuals in the advertising agency, if an agency is used. This trial-and-error approach generally leads to some successes and some failures.

Because the advertising platform is a base on which to build the advertising message, marketers should analyze this stage carefully. A campaign can be perfect in terms of selection and analysis of its target audience, statement of its objectives, media strategy, and the form of its message. But the campaign will ultimately fail if the advertisements communicate information that consumers do not deem important when selecting and using the product.

Determining the Advertising Appropriation

The **advertising appropriation** is the total amount of money a marketer allocates for advertising for a specific time period. New Balance, for example, spent about $21 million on its "Love or Money" campaign.[11] It is difficult to determine how much to spend on advertising for a specific period because the potential effects of advertising are so difficult to measure precisely.

Many factors affect a firm's decision about how much to appropriate for advertising. Geographic size of the market and the distribution of buyers within the market have a great bearing on this decision. As Table 17.1 shows, both the type of product advertised and the firm's sales volume relative to competitors' sales volumes also play parts in determining what proportion of revenue to spend on advertising. Advertising appropriations for business products are usually quite small relative to product sales, whereas consumer convenience items, such as soft drinks, soaps, and cosmetics, generally have large advertising expenditures relative to sales.

Of the many techniques used to determine the advertising appropriation, one of the most logical is the **objective-and-task approach.** Using this approach, marketers determine the objectives a campaign is to achieve and then attempt to list the tasks required to accomplish them. The costs of the tasks are calculated and added to arrive at the total appropriation. This approach has one main problem: marketers sometimes have trouble accurately estimating the level of effort needed to attain certain objectives. A coffee marketer, for example, may find it extremely difficult to determine how much of an increase in national television advertising is needed to raise a brand's market share from 8 to 10 percent.

In the more widely used **percent-of-sales approach,** marketers simply multiply the firm's past sales, plus a factor for planned sales growth or decline, by a standard percentage based on both what the firm traditionally spends on advertising and the industry average. This approach, too, has a major flaw: it is based on the incorrect assumption that sales create advertising rather than the reverse. A marketer using this approach during declining sales will reduce the amount spent on advertising, but such a reduction may further diminish sales. Though illogical, this technique has been favored because it is easy to use.

Another way to determine advertising appropriation is the **competition-matching approach.** Marketers following this approach try to match their major competitors' appropriations in absolute dollars or to allocate the same percentage of sales for

advertising appropriation The advertising budget for a specific time period

objective-and-task approach Budgeting for an advertising campaign by first determining its objectives and then calculating the cost of all the tasks needed to attain them

percent-of-sales approach Budgeting for an advertising campaign by multiplying the firm's past and expected sales by a standard percentage

competition-matching approach Determining an advertising budget by trying to match competitors' advertising outlays

table 17.1	TWENTY LEADING NATIONAL ADVERTISERS		
Organization	U.S. Advertising Expenditures ($ millions)	U.S. Revenues ($ millions)	Advertising Expenditures as % of Revenues
1. Procter & Gamble	5,230.1	31,946.0	16.4%
2. AT&T	3,207.3	118,928.0	2.7%
3. Verizon Communications	3,016.1	89,504.0	3.4%
4. General Motors	3,010.1	100,545.0	3.0%
5. Time Warner	2,926.1	38,256.0	7.6%
6. Ford Motor	2,525.2	80,874.0	3.1%
7. GlaxoSmithKline	2,456.9	18,563.0	13.2%
8. Johnson & Johnson	2,408.8	32,444.0	7.4%
9. Walt Disney	2,293.3	27,286.0	8.4%
10. Unilever	2,245.8	18,372.0	12.2%
11. Sprint Nextel	1,903.2	40,146.0	4.7%
12. General Electric	1,791.3	86,200.0	2.1%
13. Toyota Motor	1,757.9	79,909.0	2.2%
14. Chrysler	1,739.4		
15. Sony	1,736.8	18,841.0	9.2%
16. L'Oreal	1,632.3	8,268.0	19.7%
17. Sears Holdings	1,627.8	45,101.0	3.6%
18. Kraft Foods	1,508.0	21,543.0	7.0%
19. Bank of America	1,491.3	59,731.0	2.5%
20. Nissan Motor	1,422.9	34,752.0	4.1%

Source: "100 Leading National Advertisers," *Advertising Age,* http://adage.com/datacenter/article?article_id= 127791 (accessed Sept. 22, 2008).

advertising that their competitors do. Although a marketer should be aware of what competitors spend on advertising, this technique should not be used alone because the firm's competitors probably have different advertising objectives and different resources available for advertising. Many companies and advertising agencies review competitive spending on a quarterly basis, comparing competitors' dollar expenditures on print, radio, and television with their own spending levels. Competitive tracking of this nature occurs at both the national and regional levels.

At times marketers use the **arbitrary approach,** which usually means a high-level executive in the firm states how much to spend on advertising for a certain period. The arbitrary approach often leads to underspending or overspending. Although hardly a scientific budgeting technique, it is expedient.

Deciding how large the advertising appropriation should be is critical. If the appropriation is set too low, the campaign cannot achieve its full potential. When too much money is appropriated, overspending results and financial resources are wasted.

arbitrary approach Budgeting for an advertising campaign as specified by a high-level executive in the firm

snapshot

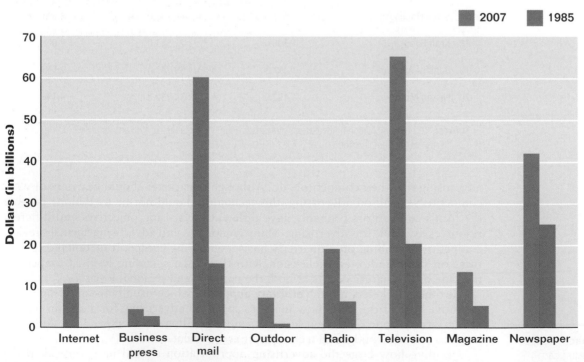

Top Super Bowl
advertisers, 1988–2007

1. Anheuser-Busch
2. Pepsi
3. General Motors
4. Time Warner
5. Walt Disney

Source: TNS Media Intelligence.

media plan A plan that specifies the media vehicles to be used and the schedule for running advertisements

Developing the Media Plan

As Figure 17.2 shows, advertisers spend tremendous amounts on advertising media. These amounts have grown rapidly during the past two decades. To derive maximum results from media expenditures, marketers must develop effective media plans. A **media plan** sets forth the exact media vehicles to be used (specific magazines, television stations, newspapers, and so forth) and the dates and times the advertisements will appear. The plan determines how many people in the target audience will be exposed to the message. Table 17.2 lists the leading sources of food information for consumers, which would help food marketers determine where to allocate their advertising. It also determines, to some degree, the effects of the message on those individuals. Media planning is a complex task requiring thorough analysis of the target audience. Sophisticated computer models have been developed to attempt to maximize the effectiveness of media plans.

To formulate a media plan, the planners select the media for the campaign and prepare a time schedule for each medium. The media planner's primary goal is to reach the largest number of people in the advertising target that the budget will allow. A secondary goal is to achieve the appropriate message reach and frequency for the target audience while staying within budget. *Reach* refers to the percentage of consumers in the target audience actually exposed to a particular advertisement in a stated period. *Frequency* is the number of times these targeted consumers are exposed to the advertisement.

figure 17.2

ADVERTISING SPENDING BY MEDIA CATEGORY: 1985 VS. 2007

■ 2007   ■ 1985

Dollars (in billions)

Internet · Business press · Direct mail · Outdoor · Radio · Television · Magazine · Newspaper

Sources: "Ad Spending Totals by Media," *Advertising Age,* June 25, 2007, p. S-15; Robert J. Coen, "Coen: Little Ad Growth," *Advertising Age,* May 6, 1991, pp. 1, 16.

table 17.2   WHERE SHOPPERS GET INFORMATION ABOUT FOOD

Category	Visits from Search Engines (Percent)
Newspaper food section	53
Website about food	17
Cable TV food channel	14
Food magazine	12
Food section of magazine	5

Source: Gallup & Robinson, in "Food Shoppers Have Strong Appetite for Newspaper Food Sections," *Advertising Age,* Jan. 1, 2007.

Media planners begin with broad decisions but eventually make very specific ones. They first decide which kinds of media to use: radio, television, the Internet, newspapers, magazines, direct mail, outdoor displays, or signs on mass transit vehicles. Internet advertising in particular is growing, with companies spending nearly $5 billion to run ads alongside Internet searches in sites like Yahoo! and Google, an amount projected to grow to nearly $8 billion by 2010.[12] Indeed, experts project that Internet ad spending will surpass that spent on radio advertising within a year or so.[13] Media planners assess different formats and approaches to determine which are most effective. Some media plans are highly focused and use just one medium. The media plans of manufacturers of consumer packaged goods can be quite complex and dynamic.

Media planners take many factors into account when devising a media plan. They analyze location and demographic characteristics of consumers in the target audience because people's tastes in media differ according to demographic groups and locations. There are radio stations especially for teenagers, magazines for men ages 18 to 34, and television cable channels aimed at women in various age groups. Media planners also consider the sizes and types of audiences that specific media reach. Miller Brewing Company, for example, has been cutting back on traditional media advertising, such as network television, in favor of local media advertising, product placement, and promotional events, such as the Miller Genuine Draft "The Craft" concert series. Rival Anheuser-Busch is also cutting back on traditional ad spending.[14] Declining broadcast television ratings have led many companies to explore alternative media, including not only cable television and Internet advertising but also ads on cell phones and product placements in video games. Several data services collect and periodically provide information about circulations and audiences of various media.

The content of the message sometimes affects media choice. Print media can be used more effectively than broadcast media to present complex issues or numerous details in single advertisements. If an advertiser wants to promote beautiful colors, patterns, or textures, media offering high-quality color reproduction, such as magazines or television, should be used instead of newspapers. For example, food can be effectively promoted in full-color magazine advertisements but far less effectively in black and white.

The cost of media is an important but troublesome consideration. Planners try to obtain the best coverage possible for each dollar spent. However, there is no accurate way to compare the cost and impact of a television commercial with the cost and impact of a newspaper advertisement. A **cost comparison indicator** lets an advertiser compare the costs of several vehicles within a specific medium (such as two magazines) in relation to the number of people each vehicle reaches. The *cost per thousand (CPM)* is the cost comparison indicator for magazines; it shows the cost of exposing 1,000 people to a one-page advertisement.

Figure 17.2 shows that the extent to which each medium is used varies and how it has changed since 1985. For example, the proportion of total advertising dollars spent on television has risen since 1985 and surpassed that spent on newspapers. Media are selected by weighing the various advantages and disadvantages of each (see Table 17.3).

Like media selection decisions, media scheduling decisions are affected by numerous factors, such as target audience characteristics, product attributes, product seasonality, customer media behavior, and size of the advertising budget. There are three general types of media schedules: continuous, flighting, and pulsing. When a *continuous* schedule is used, advertising runs at a constant level with little variation throughout the campaign period. With a *flighting* schedule, advertisements run for set periods

cost comparison indicator
A means of comparing the costs of advertising vehicles in a specific medium in relation to the number of people reached

table 17.3 ADVANTAGES AND DISADVANTAGES OF MAJOR MEDIA CLASSES

Medium	Advantages	Disadvantages
Newspapers	Reaches large audience; purchased to be read; geographic flexibility; short lead time; frequent publication; favorable for cooperative advertising; merchandising services	Not selective for socioeconomic groups or target market; short life; limited reproduction capabilities; large advertising volume limits exposure to any one advertisement
Magazines	Demographic selectivity; good reproduction; long life; prestige; geographic selectivity when regional issues are available; read in leisurely manner	High costs; 30–90-day average lead time; high level of competition; limited reach; communicates less frequently
Direct mail	Little wasted circulation; highly selective; circulation controlled by advertiser; few distractions; personal; stimulates actions; use of novelty; relatively easy to measure performance; hidden from competitors	Very expensive; lacks editorial content to attract readers; often thrown away unread as junk mail; criticized as invasion of privacy; consumers must choose to read the ad
Radio	Reaches 95 percent of consumers; highly mobile and flexible; very low relative costs; ad can be changed quickly; high level of geographic and demographic selectivity; encourages use of imagination	Lacks visual imagery; short life of message; listeners' attention limited because of other activities; market fragmentation; difficult buying procedures; limited media and audience research
Television	Reaches large audiences; high frequency available; dual impact of audio and video; highly visible; high prestige; geographic and demographic selectivity; difficult to ignore	Very expensive; highly perishable message; size of audience not guaranteed; amount of prime time limited; lack of selectivity in target market
Internet	Immediate response; potential to reach a precisely targeted audience; ability to track customers and build databases; highly interactive medium	Costs of precise targeting are high; inappropriate ad placement; effects difficult to measure; concerns about security and privacy
Yellow Pages	Wide availability; action and product category oriented; low relative costs; ad frequency and longevity; nonintrusive	Market fragmentation; extremely localized; slow updating; lack of creativity; long lead times; requires large space to be noticed
Outdoor	Allows for frequent repetition; low cost; message can be placed close to point of sale; geographic selectivity; operable 24 hours a day; high creativity and effectiveness	Message must be short and simple; no demographic selectivity; seldom attracts readers' full attention; criticized as traffic hazard and blight on countryside; much wasted coverage; limited capabilities

Sources: William F. Arens, *Contemporary Advertising* (Burr Ridge, IL: Irwin/McGraw-Hill, 2007); George E. Belch and Michael Belch, *Advertising and Promotion* (Burr Ridge, IL: Irwin/McGraw-Hill, 2006).

of time, alternating with periods in which no ads run. For example, an advertising campaign might have an ad run for two weeks, then suspend it for two weeks, and then run it again for two weeks. A *pulsing* schedule combines continuous and flighting schedules: during the entire campaign, a certain portion of advertising runs continuously, and during specific time periods of the campaign, additional advertising is used to intensify the level of communication with the target audience.

Creating the Advertising Message

The basic content and form of an advertising message are a function of several factors. A product's features, uses, and benefits affect the content of the message. Characteristics of the people in the target audience—gender, age, education, race, income, occupation, lifestyle, and other attributes—influence both content and form. For example, gender affects how people respond to advertising claims that use hedging words such as *may* and *probably* and pledging words such as *definitely* and *absolutely*. Researchers have found that women respond negatively to both types of claims, but pledging claims have little effect on men.[15] When Procter & Gamble

E-ntertainment MARKETING

Nielsen Gets Students to Play the Ratings Game

Most of us have heard of the Nielsen television ratings system, but few of us really understand how it works. Now that Nielsen is including away-from-home college students, it is time for a crash course. Nielsen uses a national panel consisting of 10,000 households to determine the country's viewing habits. Before 1987, people who resided in the randomly chosen households agreed to record in paper diaries the programs they watched on TV. Today, people in surveyed households press a button on an electronic "people meter" device installed by Nielsen each time they begin to watch a show. Once Nielsen receives this data, it estimates audience size to the nearest thousand and breaks down the data by demographics. For years the Nielsen system has been widely criticized. One regularly cited flaw has been the fact that college students who live in dorms have not been counted. However, Nielsen recently asked currently surveyed households to include viewing data from members who are living on college campuses. Of those who fall into this category, about one-third have agreed to take part in the survey. This means that the 130 participating college students will have a significant impact on Nielsen's description of the overall viewing habits of people age 18 to 24.

As a result of Nielsen's inclusion of away-from-home college students, ratings for several television shows and networks have jumped dramatically. Comedy Central in particular has seen a huge jump in ratings. Its *Drawn Together* cartoon boasted a 60 percent ratings increase among men age 18 to 24. *South Park, The Daily Show with John Stewart,* and *The Colbert Report* are also said to have large college audiences. ABC's *Grey's Anatomy* and CW's *Gilmore Girls* are also popular; their ratings have jumped more than 50 percent among those age 18 to 24.

Nielsen ratings are of critical importance to both networks and advertisers. Simply put, advertisers invest in those shows through which they can reach the greatest number of viewers in their target markets. Networks hope that higher ratings for shows that are popular with the 18-to-24 demographic translate into more money from advertisers targeting the college crowd. Although the addition of surveying on-campus college students appears to be a step forward for Nielsen, some still contend that the entire ratings system needs a major overhaul. Some experts assert that the sample size is simply too small to accurately represent viewing habits. Others worry that Nielsen's system doesn't account for those viewing television outside the home or dorm. People regularly view TV in less traditional locations: sports bars, hotel rooms, gyms, airport lounges, and so on. And, people are increasingly viewing their favorite shows on their computers, iPods, and cell phones. Although Nielsen executives do not feel its system is highly flawed, they do agree that it needs updating. They are currently working to develop portable people meters and to implement devices that will identify audio signals of radio and television programs without requiring an individual to press a button. The Nielsen system has yet to enter the twenty-first century, but it is taking the right steps to get there.[b]

promotes Crest toothpaste to children, the company emphasizes daily brushing and cavity control. When marketing Crest to adults, P&G stresses tartar and plaque control. To communicate effectively, advertisers use words, symbols, and illustrations that are meaningful, familiar, and appealing to people in the target audience.

An advertising campaign's objectives and platform also affect the content and form of its messages. If a firm's advertising objectives involve large sales increases, the message may include hard-hitting, high-impact language and symbols. When campaign objectives aim to increase brand awareness, the message may use much repetition of the brand name and words and illustrations associated with it. Thus, the advertising platform is the foundation on which campaign messages are built.

Choice of media obviously influences the content and form of the message. Effective outdoor displays and short broadcast spot announcements require concise, simple messages. Magazine and newspaper advertisements can include considerable detail and long explanations. Because several kinds of media offer geographic selectivity, a precise message can be tailored to a particular geographic section of the target audience. Some magazine publishers produce **regional issues,** in which advertisements and editorial content of copies appearing in one geographic area differ from those appearing in other areas. As Figure 17.3 shows, *Time* magazine publishes eight regional issues. A company advertising in *Time* might decide to use one message in the New England region and another in the rest of the nation. A company may also choose to advertise in only one region. Such geographic selectivity lets a firm use the same message in different regions at different times.

Copy. **Copy** is the verbal portion of an advertisement and may include headlines, subheadlines, body copy, and signature. Not all advertising contains all of these copy elements. Even handwritten notes on direct-mail advertising that say, "Try this. It works!" seem to increase requests for free samples.[16] The headline is critical because often it is the only part of the copy that people read. It should attract readers' attention and create enough interest to make them want to read the body copy. The subheadline, if there is one, links the headline to the body copy and sometimes serves to explain the headline.

Body copy for most advertisements consists of an introductory statement or paragraph, several explanatory paragraphs, and a closing paragraph. Some copywriters have adopted guidelines for developing body copy systematically: (1) identify a specific desire or problem, (2) recommend the product as the best way to satisfy that desire or solve that problem, (3) state product benefits and indicate why the product is best for the buyer's particular situation, (4) substantiate advertising claims, and (5) ask the buyer to take action. When substantiating claims, it is important to present the substantiation in a credible manner. The proof of claims should help strengthen both the image of the product and company integrity. Typeface selection can help advertisers create a desired impression using fonts that are engaging, reassuring, or very prominent.[17]

The signature identifies the advertisement's sponsor. It may contain several elements, including the firm's trademark, logo, name, and address. The signature should be attractive, legible, distinctive, and easy to identify in a variety of sizes.

Because radio listeners often are not fully "tuned in" mentally to what they're hearing on the radio, radio copy should be informal and conversational to attract listeners' attention. Radio messages are highly perishable and should consist of short, familiar terms, which increase their impact. The length should not require a rate of speech exceeding approximately two and one-half words per second.

In television copy, the audio material must not overpower the visual material, and vice versa. However, a

regional issues Versions of a magazine that differ across geographic regions

copy The verbal portion of advertisements

figure 17.3

GEOGRAPHIC DIVISIONS FOR TIME REGIONAL ISSUES

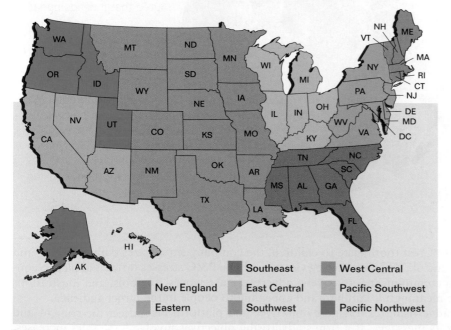

Legend:
- Southeast
- West Central
- New England
- East Central
- Pacific Southwest
- Eastern
- Southwest
- Pacific Northwest

Source: *Time* Magazine. © 2006 Time Inc. Reprinted by permission.

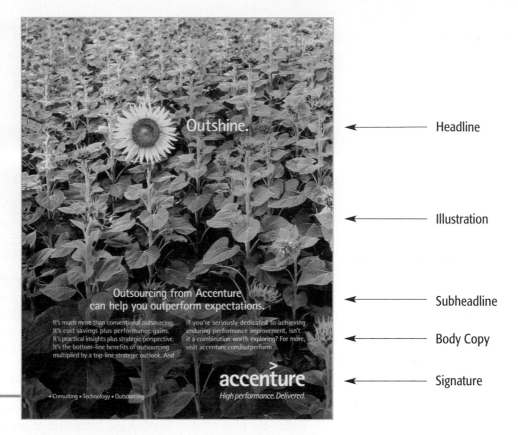

← Headline

← Illustration

← Subheadline

← Body Copy

← Signature

Components of a Print Ad

This Accenture ad shows all of the major components of a print ad.

storyboard A blueprint that combines copy and visual material to show the sequence of major scenes in a commercial

artwork An advertisement's illustrations and layout

illustrations Photos, drawings, graphs, charts, and tables used to spark audience interest in an advertisement

layout The physical arrangement of an advertisement's illustration and copy

television message should make optimal use of its visual portion, which can be very effective for product demonstrations. Copy for a television commercial is sometimes initially written in parallel script form. Video is described in the left column and audio in the right. When the parallel script is approved, the copywriter and artist combine copy with visual material by using a **storyboard,** which depicts a series of miniature television screens showing the sequence of major scenes in the commercial. Beneath each screen is a description of the audio portion to be used with that video segment. Technical personnel use the storyboard as a blueprint when producing the commercial.

Artwork. **Artwork** consists of an advertisement's illustrations and layout. **Illustrations** are often photographs but can also be drawings, graphs, charts, and tables. Illustrations are used to draw attention, encourage audiences to read or listen to the copy, communicate an idea quickly, or communicate ideas that are difficult to express. Illustrations can be more important in capturing attention than text or brand elements, independent of size.[18] They are especially important because consumers tend to recall the visual portions of advertisements better than the verbal portions. Advertisers use a variety of illustration techniques. They may show the product alone, in a setting, or in use, or show the results of the product's use. Illustrations can also take the form of comparisons, contrasts, diagrams, and testimonials.

The **layout** of an advertisement is the physical arrangement of the illustration and the copy (headline, subheadline, body copy, and signature). These elements can be arranged in many ways. The final layout is the result of several stages of layout preparation. As it moves through these stages, the layout promotes an exchange of ideas among people developing the advertising campaign and provides instructions for production personnel.

Executing the Campaign

Execution of an advertising campaign requires extensive planning and coordination because many tasks must be completed on time and several people and firms are involved. Production companies, research organizations, media firms, printers,

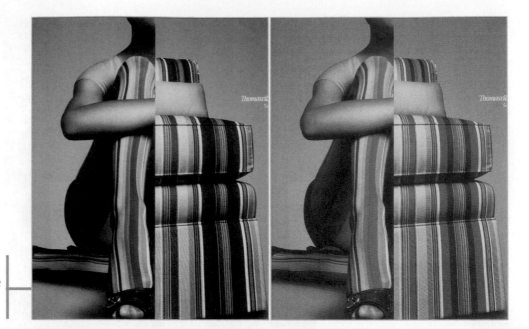

Black-and-White vs. Color
This ad highlights the importance of using color when advertising certain products.

photoengravers, and commercial artists are just a few of the people and firms contributing to a campaign.

Implementation requires detailed schedules to ensure that various phases of the work are done on time. Advertising management personnel must evaluate the quality of the work and take corrective action when necessary. Wendy's, for example, pulled the plug on its "That's Right" promotion campaign after it failed to generate sales. The short-lived campaign, which featured characters wearing pigtailed red-haired wigs, like the chain's mascot, who declared, "I deserve a hot juicy burger," attracted attention as well as controversy. The company quickly launched a more positive food-focused campaign with an animated Wendy's character and the tag line "Waaaay Better than Fast Food. It's Wendy's."[19] In some instances, changes are made during the campaign so it meets objectives more effectively. Sometimes one firm develops a campaign and another executes it.

Evaluating Advertising Effectiveness

A variety of ways exist to test the effectiveness of advertising. They include measuring achievement of advertising objectives; assessing effectiveness of copy, illustrations, or layouts; and evaluating certain media.

Advertising can be evaluated before, during, and after the campaign. An evaluation performed before the campaign begins is called a **pretest.** A pretest usually attempts to evaluate the effectiveness of one or more elements of the message. To pretest advertisements, marketers sometimes use a **consumer jury,** a panel of existing or potential buyers of the advertised product. Jurors judge one or several dimensions of two or more advertisements. Such tests are based on the belief that consumers are more likely than advertising experts to know what influences them. Companies can also solicit the assistance of marketing research firms such as Information Resources Inc. (IRI) to help assess ads.

To measure advertising effectiveness during a campaign, marketers usually rely on "inquiries." In a campaign's initial stages, an advertiser may use several advertisements simultaneously, each containing a coupon, form, or toll-free phone number through which potential customers can request information. The advertiser records the number of inquiries returned from each type of advertisement. If an advertiser receives 78,528 inquiries from advertisement A, 37,072 from advertisement B, and 47,932 from advertisement C, advertisement A is judged superior to advertisements B and C. Internet advertisers can also assess how many people "clicked" on an ad to obtain more product information.

Evaluation of advertising effectiveness after the campaign is called a **posttest.** Advertising objectives often determine what kind of posttest is appropriate. If the

pretest Evaluation of advertisements performed before a campaign begins

consumer jury A panel of a product's existing or potential buyers who pretest ads

posttest Evaluation of advertising effectiveness after the campaign

Evaluating Ad Effectiveness
Dove tests the effectiveness of its advertising in developing magazine ads for its ice cream and its chocolate bars.

objectives focus on communication—to increase awareness of product features or brands or to create more favorable customer attitudes—the posttest should measure changes in these dimensions. Advertisers sometimes use consumer surveys or experiments to evaluate a campaign based on communication objectives. These methods are costly, however.

For campaign objectives stated in terms of sales, advertisers should determine the change in sales or market share attributable to the campaign. For example, after a tourism campaign by the state of Utah—with the slogan "Utah: Life Elevated"— tourist spending in the state increased by nearly 8 percent to almost $6 billion.[20] However, changes in sales or market share brought about by advertising cannot be measured precisely; many factors independent of advertisements affect a firm's sales and market share. Competitors' actions, regulatory actions, and changes in economic conditions, consumer preferences, and weather are only a few factors that might enhance or diminish a company's sales or market share. By using data about past and current sales and advertising expenditures, advertisers can make gross estimates of the effects of a campaign on sales or market share.

Because it is difficult to determine the direct effects of advertising on sales, many advertisers evaluate print advertisements according to how well consumers can remember them. The marketers of HeadOn, an analgesic, used endless repetition to help consumers recall their product and gain rapid sales growth, from $1.9 million to $6.5 million in just one year.[21] Research indicates that ads that play on the theme of social desirability are more memorable when viewed in the presence of other people.[22]

Posttest methods based on memory include recognition and recall tests. Such tests are usually performed by research organizations through surveys. In a **recognition test,** respondents are shown the actual advertisement and asked whether they recognize it. If they do, the interviewer asks additional questions to determine how much of the advertisement each respondent read. When recall is evaluated, respondents are not shown the actual advertisement but instead are asked about what they have seen or heard recently. For Internet advertising, research suggests that the longer a person is exposed to a website containing a banner advertisement, the more likely he or she is to recall the ad.[23]

Recall can be measured through either unaided or aided recall methods. In an **unaided recall test,** respondents identify advertisements they have seen recently but are not shown any clues to help them remember. A similar procedure is used with an **aided recall test,** but respondents are shown a list of products, brands, company names, or trademarks to jog their memories. For example, the long-running national youth anti-drug media campaign by the Office of National Drug Control Policy has

recognition test A posttest in which respondents are shown the actual ad and asked if they recognize it

unaided recall test A posttest in which respondents are asked to identify advertisements they have seen recently but are not given any recall clues

aided recall test A posttest that asks respondents to identify recent ads and provides clues to jog their memories

nearly 70 percent recognition and recall among youth and 55 percent among parents.[24] Several research organizations, such as Daniel Starch, provide research services that test recognition and recall of advertisements.

The major justification for using recognition and recall methods is that people are more likely to buy a product if they can remember an advertisement about it than if they cannot. However, recalling an advertisement does not necessarily lead to buying the product or brand advertised. Researchers also use a sophisticated technique called *single-source data* to help evaluate advertisements. With this technique, individuals' behaviors are tracked from television sets to checkout counters. Monitors are placed in preselected homes, and microcomputers record when the television set is on and which station is being viewed. At the supermarket checkout, the individual in the sample household presents an identification card. Checkers then record the purchases by scanner, and data are sent to the research facility. Some single-source data companies provide sample households with scanning equipment for use at home to record purchases after returning from shopping trips. Single-source data provide information that links exposure to advertisements with purchase behavior.

Who Develops the Advertising Campaign?

LO 3 To identify who is responsible for developing advertising campaigns

An advertising campaign may be handled by an individual or by a few people within the firm, by the firm's own advertising department, or by an advertising agency.

In very small firms, one or two individuals are responsible for advertising (and for many other activities as well). Usually these individuals depend heavily on personnel at local newspapers and broadcast stations for copywriting, artwork, and advice about scheduling media.

In certain large businesses, especially large retail organizations, advertising departments create and implement advertising campaigns. Depending on the size of the advertising program, an advertising department may consist of a few multiskilled individuals or a sizable number of specialists such as copywriters, artists, media buyers, and technical production coordinators. Advertising departments sometimes obtain the services of independent research organizations and hire freelance specialists when a particular project requires it.

Many firms employ an advertising agency to develop advertising campaigns. The U.S. Army, for example, contracted with McCann Worldgroup to create an advertising campaign with the theme "Army strong." The recruiting campaign, expected to cost $1.35 billion over five years, included videos on YouTube, a website (goarmy.com), and a profile on MySpace.[25] When an organization uses an advertising agency, the firm and the agency usually develop the advertising campaign jointly. How much each participates in the campaign's total development depends on the working relationship between the firm and the agency. Ordinarily a firm relies on the agency for copywriting, artwork, technical production, and formulation of the media plan.

Advertising agencies assist businesses in several ways. An agency, especially a large one, can supply the services of highly skilled specialists—not only copywriters, artists, and production coordinators but also media experts, researchers, and legal advisers. Agency personnel often have broad advertising experience and are usually more objective than a firm's employees about the organization's products.

Because an agency traditionally receives most of its compensation from a 15 percent commission paid by the media from which it makes purchases, firms can obtain some agency services at low or moderate costs. If an agency contracts for $400,000 of television time for a firm, it receives a commission of $60,000 from the television station. Although the traditional compensation method for agencies is changing and now includes other factors, media commissions still offset some costs of using an agency. Table 17.4 lists some of the leading U.S. ad agencies. Like advertising, public relations can be a vital element in a promotion mix. We turn to this topic next.

table 17.4	LEADING AD AGENCIES—TRADITIONAL AND MEDIA SPECIALISTS		
Traditional Agencies	**Percent Billings**	**Media Specialists**	**Percent Billings**
1. JWT	4.3	1. OMD Worldwide	7.6
4. BBDO Worldwide	4.3	2. MindShare	7.5
2. McCann Erickson Worldwide	4.3	3. Starcom USA	6.2
3. Leo Burnett Worldwide	3.0	4. Mediedge:cia	5.2
5. Ogilvy & Mather Worldwide	2.8	5. Zenith Media USA	5.1

Source: *Advertising Age,* Dec. 31, 2007, pp. 48–52.

public relations Communication efforts used to create and maintain favorable relations between an organization and its stakeholders

Public Relations

LO 4 To examine the tools used in public relations

Public relations is a broad set of communication efforts used to create and maintain favorable relationships between an organization and its stakeholders. PepsiCo, for example, publishes a newspaper insert called *Disfrútalo* that not only introduces Spanish-speaking mothers to Pepsi products but also strives to build relationships through coupons, tips, and useful information to help Hispanic moms transition to life in the United States.[26] An organization communicates with various stakeholders, both internal and external, and public relations efforts can be directed toward any and all of them. A firm's stakeholders can include customers, suppliers, employees, stockholders, the media, educators, potential investors, government officials, and society in general.

Public relations can be used to promote people, places, ideas, activities, and even countries. It is often used by nonprofit organizations to achieve their goals. Public relations focuses on enhancing the image of the total organization. Assessing public attitudes and creating a favorable image are no less important than direct promotion of the organization's products. Because the public's attitudes toward a firm are likely to affect the sales of its products, it is very important for firms to maintain positive public perceptions. In addition, employee morale is strengthened if the public perceives the firm positively.[27] Although public relations can make people aware of a company's products, brands, or activities, it can also create specific company images, such as innovativeness or dependability. Companies such as Green Mountain Coffee Roasters, Patagonia, Sustainable Harvest, and Honest Tea have reputations for being socially

Annual Reports

Annual reports, when appropriately designed, can generate favorable public relations.

Ben & Jerry's Global Free Cone Day!
Scoop-Shop Only Flavor & Social Mission Campaigns Highlight Annual Event on April 29th

BURLINGTON, Vt.--(BUSINESS WIRE)--As Ben & Jerry's celebrates its 30th anniversary across the globe, the socially-minded ice cream maker, with the fun and funky flavors, asks what better way to share the love? They're giving it away.

No, this is not one of those internet pranks that makes you send ten emails to your friends for a free pair jeans. This is as plain and simple as vanilla. "Jerry and Ben started their first Free Cone Day as a thank you to their customers," said Debra Heintz, Retail Operations Director. "It's cool," added Heintz with full pun intended, "we get to continue the peace, love and FREE ice cream tradition every year across the world. **Free Cone Day is Tuesday, April 29th, 2008**.

Certainly you can try one of your old favorites such as the legend-dairy classic Cherry Garcia, Phish Food or Chocolate Fudge Brownie. However, if you're looking for a little something new to tickle your ice cream funny-bone the company is introducing a few brand new flavors to bring joy to your belly and soul.

- **Imagine Whirled Peace™** – Continuing in a long lineage of rock and roll flavors, we're honored to introduce Imagine Whirled Peace. John Lennon imagined a world without war, and asked us all to "Give Peace a Chance." We're proud to partner with Peace One Day to act globally and take one step closer to making our planet one of peace and love. Imagine Whirled Peace is a tongue-pleasing concoction of caramel and sweet cream ice creams mixed with fudge peace signs and toffee.

- **Coconut Seven Layer Bar** – What can we say, except we know you'll go coconuts for our latest and greatest flavor, based on the popular dessert: coconut ice cream with coconut & fudge flakes, walnuts & swirls of graham cracker & butterscotch. This is a treat solely for our Scoop Shop fans, as it is the only place in the world that you can get this flavor!

- **ONE Cheesecake Brownie™** - This top-testing new flavor is a decadent cheesecake ice cream with cheesecake brownie chunks. The amazing thing is the taste is only the half of it! We're partnering with ONE.org to "make poverty history." To find out all the campaign info, visit ONE.org/benjerry.

Press Release

Press releases are often used to spread news about a company or its products.

LO 5 To analyze how public relations is used and evaluated

publicity A news story type of communication about an organization and/or its products transmitted through a mass medium at no charge

news release A short piece of copy publicizing an event or a product

responsible not only because they engage in socially responsible behavior but because their actions are reported through news stories and other public relations efforts. By getting the media to report on a firm's accomplishments, public relations helps the company maintain positive public visibility. Some firms use public relations for a single purpose; others use it for several purposes.

Public Relations Tools

Companies use a variety of public relations tools to convey messages and create images. Public relations professionals prepare written materials, such as brochures, newsletters, company magazines, news releases, websites, blogs, and annual reports that reach and influence their various stakeholders. Procter & Gamble, for example, created a social-networking website called Capessa, where women—who are major consumers of P&G products—can discuss issues such as health, work, weight loss, pregnancy, and personal problems.[28]

Public relations personnel also create corporate identity materials, such as logos, business cards, stationery, and signs that make firms immediately recognizable. Speeches are another public relations tool. Because what a company executive says publicly at meetings or to the media can affect the organization's image, the speech must convey the desired message clearly. Event sponsorship, in which a company pays for part or all of a special event, such as a benefit concert or a tennis tournament, is another public relations tool. Examples are Home Depot's sponsorship of NASCAR and the U.S. Olympic team. Sponsoring special events can be an effective means of increasing company or brand recognition with relatively minimal investment. Event sponsorship can gain companies considerable amounts of free media coverage. An organization tries to ensure that its product and the sponsored event target a similar audience and that the two are easily associated in customers' minds. For example, corporate sponsors of professional beach volleyball, such as McDonald's, Nissan, and Budweiser, benefited from more than 1 billion media impressions during a single season.[29] Public relations personnel also organize unique events to "create news" about the company. These may include grand openings with celebrities, prizes, hot-air balloon rides, and other attractions that appeal to a firm's publics.

Publicity is a part of public relations. **Publicity** is communication in news story form about the organization, its products, or both, transmitted through a mass medium at no charge. For example, after Apple chairman Steve Jobs announced that the company would introduce a revolutionary new mobile phone, the iPhone, the story was covered in newspapers and television news shows throughout the world for months afterward. Although public relations has a larger, more comprehensive communication function than publicity, publicity is a very important aspect of public relations. Publicity can be used to provide information about goods or services; to announce expansions, acquisitions, research, or new-product launches; or to enhance a company's image.

The most common publicity-based public relations tool is the **news release,** sometimes called a *press release,* which is usually a single page of typewritten copy containing fewer than 300 words and describing a company event or product. A news release gives the firm's or agency's name, address, phone number, and contact person. Automakers and other manufacturers sometimes use news releases when introducing new products or making significant announcements. When Whole Foods Market announced its plan to eliminate environmentally unfriendly plastic grocery bags from all of its stores, making it the first U.S. supermarket chain to do so, it sent out news releases to newspapers, magazines, television contacts, and suppliers, which garnered considerable publicity in the form of magazine and newspaper articles and television coverage about its plan, as well as its new 99-cent reusable shopping bags.[30] As Table 17.5 shows, news releases tackle a multitude of specific issues. A **feature article** is a manuscript of up to 3,000 words prepared for a specific publication. A **captioned photograph** is a photograph with a brief description explaining its contents. Captioned photographs are effective for illustrating new or improved products with highly visible features.

There are several other kinds of publicity-based public relations tools. A **press conference** is a meeting called to announce major news events. Media personnel are invited to a press conference and are usually supplied with written materials and photographs. Letters to the editor and editorials are sometimes prepared and sent to newspapers and magazines. Videos and audiotapes may be distributed to broadcast stations in the hope they will be aired.

Publicity-based public relations tools offer several advantages, including credibility, news value, significant word-of-mouth communications, and a perception of media endorsement. The public may consider news coverage more truthful and credible than an advertisement because the media are not paid to provide the information. In addition, stories regarding a new-product introduction or a new environmentally responsible company policy, for example, are handled as news items and are likely to receive notice. Finally, the cost of publicity is low compared with the cost of advertising.[31]

Publicity-based public relations tools have some limitations. Media personnel must judge company messages to be newsworthy if the messages are to be published or broadcast at all. Consequently messages must be timely, interesting, accurate, and in the public interest. It may take a great deal of time and effort to convince media personnel of the news value of publicity releases, and many communications fail to

table 17.5   POSSIBLE ISSUES FOR PUBLICITY RELEASES

Changes in marketing personnel	Packaging changes
Support of a social cause	New products
Improved warranties	New slogan
Reports on industry conditions	Research developments
New uses for established products	Company's history and development
Product endorsements	Employment, production, and sales records
Quality awards	Award of contracts
Company name changes	Opening of new markets
Interviews with company officials	Improvements in financial position
Improved distribution policies	Opening of an exhibit
International business efforts	History of a brand
Athletic event sponsorship	Winners of company contests
Visits by celebrities	Logo changes
Reports on new discoveries	Speeches of top management
Innovative marketing activities	Merit awards
Economic forecasts	Anniversary of inventions

feature article A manuscript of up to 3,000 words prepared for a specific publication

captioned photograph A photograph with a brief description of its contents

press conference A meeting used to announce major news events

qualify. Although public relations personnel usually encourage the media to air publicity releases at certain times, they control neither the content nor the timing of the communication. Media personnel alter length and content of publicity releases to fit publishers' or broadcasters' requirements and may even delete the parts of messages that company personnel view as most important. Furthermore, media personnel use publicity releases in time slots or positions most convenient for them. Thus, messages sometimes appear in locations or at times that may not reach the firm's target audiences. Although these limitations can be frustrating, properly managed publicity-based public relations tools offer an organization substantial benefits.

green MARKETING

Would You Like to Buy a Recycled Toothbrush?

Although many eco-responsible entrepreneurs are looking at new products based on recycling technology, probably the last thing you would think about being recycled is your toothbrush. As it turns out, Eric Hudson, who sends product samples to movie sets, learned that Will Ferrell's character in the movie *Stranger Than Fiction* would be using a recycled toothbrush manufactured by Recycline. This company, which has been recognized as one of *Inc.* magazine's "50 green entrepreneurial companies," markets the Preserve line of toothbrushes, tongue cleaners, and razors from recycled materials such as yogurt cups. In the last year, the company has seen its sales jump 45 percent based on public relations, especially publicity.

Whereas public relations is used to maintain a favorable image of a product, including a positive attitude of the organization with stakeholders, publicity is the communication about the organization and its products that gets transmitted through a mass medium at no charge. With this in mind, Hudson's marketing firm took advantage of the Will Ferrell film to boost sales at select Target stores, which had just recently introduced the Preserve line. Articles in newspapers, trade publications, and the movie itself promoted the product. The company even offered free toothbrushes and movie tickets to volunteers who passed out postcards that read "meet Harold Crick's toothbrush" (Ferrell's character). The cards directed moviegoers to visit their nearest Target store to buy the toothbrush.

Good public relations, and especially publicity, helps create word-of-mouth communication. Because of growing consumer interest in green products, publicity about an interesting recycled product can travel fast. As in this case, Recycline also plans to use this type of promotional opportunity for its line of kitchen products, which it has introduced in Whole Foods stores. Recycline executives hope that their firm becomes the name that consumers think of for high-quality, innovative, and environmentally friendly personal-care products that can be used with comfort, performance, style, and conscience. The green product platform will be used in all promotional activities.[c]

Evaluating Public Relations Effectiveness

Because of the potential benefits of good public relations, it is essential that organizations evaluate the effectiveness of their public relations campaigns. Research can be conducted to determine how well a firm is communicating its messages or image to its target audiences. *Environmental monitoring* identifies changes in public opinion affecting an organization. A *public relations audit* is used to assess an organization's image among the public or to evaluate the effect of a specific public relations program. A *communications audit* may include a content analysis of messages, a readability study, or a readership survey. If an organization wants to measure the extent to which stakeholders view it as being socially responsible, it can conduct a *social audit*.

One approach to measuring the effectiveness of publicity-based public relations is to count the number of exposures in the media. To determine which releases are published in print media and how often, an organization can hire a clipping service, a firm that clips and sends news releases to client companies. To measure the effectiveness of television coverage, a firm can enclose a card with its publicity releases requesting that the television station record its name and the dates when the news item is broadcast (although station personnel do not always comply). Some television and radio tracking services exist, but they are quite costly.

Counting the number of media exposures does not reveal how many people have actually read or heard the company's message or what they thought about the message afterward. However, measuring changes in product awareness, knowledge, and attitudes resulting from the publicity campaign helps yield this information. To assess these changes, companies must measure these levels before and after public relations campaigns. Although precise measures are difficult to obtain, a firm's marketers should attempt to assess the impact of public relations efforts on the organization's sales. For example, critics' reviews of films can affect the films' box office performance. Interestingly, negative reviews (publicity) harm revenue more than positive reviews help revenue in the early weeks of a film's release.[32]

Dealing with Unfavorable Public Relations

Thus far, we have discussed public relations as a planned element of the promotion mix. However, companies may have to deal with unexpected and unfavorable publicity resulting from an unsafe product, an accident resulting from product use, controversial actions of employees, or some other negative event or situation. For example, an airline that experiences a plane crash faces a very tragic and distressing situation. Charges of anticompetitive behavior against Microsoft have raised public concern and generated unfavorable public relations for that organization. The public's image of the Body Shop as a socially responsible company diminished considerably when it was reported that the company's actions were less socially responsible than its promotion promised. Many companies have experienced unfavorable publicity connected to contamination issues, such as salmonella in peanut butter, lead in toys, and industrial compounds in pet foods. Unfavorable coverage can have quick and dramatic effects. For example, after JetBlue, a low-cost airline, left nine planes full of passengers stranded for six hours or more while waiting for a weather break during an ice storm, many negative news stories appeared on TV, in print, and online, and the company's stock plummeted. Some angry passengers even posted videos to YouTube, and others posted their stories online.[33] As it did with JetBlue, a single negative event that generates public relations can wipe out a company's favorable image and destroy positive customer attitudes established through years of expensive advertising campaigns and other promotional efforts. Moreover, today's mass media, including online services and the Internet, disseminate information faster than ever before, and bad news generally receives considerable media attention.

To protect its image, an organization needs to prevent unfavorable public relations or at least lessen its effect if it occurs. First and foremost, the organization should try to prevent negative incidents and events through safety programs, inspections, and effective quality control procedures. Experts insist that sending consistent brand messages and images throughout all communications at all times can help a brand maintain its strength even during a crisis.[34] However, because negative events can befall even the most cautious firms, an organization should have plans in place to handle them when they do occur. Firms need to establish policies and procedures for reducing the adverse impact of news coverage of a crisis or controversy. In most cases, organizations should expedite news coverage of negative events rather than try to discourage or block them. If news coverage is suppressed, rumors and other misinformation may replace facts.

An unfavorable event can easily balloon into serious problems or public issues and become very damaging. By being forthright with the press and public and taking prompt action, a firm may be able to convince the public of its honest attempts to deal with the situation, and news personnel may be more willing to help explain complex issues to the public. Dealing effectively with a negative event allows an organization to lessen, if not eliminate, the unfavorable impact on its image. Consider that after news reports about JetBlue leaving passengers stranded on runways for hours, the company offered the passengers full refunds and vouchers for free flights in the future. It also ran apologetic ads and issued press releases to communicate with affected stakeholders. JetBlue founder and CEO David Neeleman, who said he was "humiliated and mortified" by the incident, immediately implemented plans to add and train staff to remedy communications and operations issues that contributed to the crisis. He also pledged to enact a customer bill of rights that would penalize the airline and reward passengers should such a fiasco happen again.[35] Experts generally advise companies that are dealing with negative publicity to respond quickly and honestly to the situation and to keep the lines of communications with all stakeholders open.

SUMMARY

Advertising is a paid form of nonpersonal communication transmitted to consumers through mass media such as television, radio, the Internet, newspapers, magazines, direct mail, outdoor displays, and signs on mass transit vehicles. Both business and nonbusiness organizations use advertising. Institutional advertising promotes organizational images, ideas, and political issues. When a company promotes its position on a public issue such as taxation, institutional advertising is referred to as advocacy advertising. Product advertising promotes uses, features, and benefits of products. The two types of product advertising are pioneer advertising, which focuses on stimulating demand for a product category rather than a specific brand, and competitive advertising, which attempts to stimulate demand for a specific brand by indicating the brand's features, uses, and advantages. To make direct product comparisons, marketers use comparative advertising, which compares two or more brands. Two other forms of competitive advertising are reminder advertising, which reminds customers about an established brand's uses, characteristics, and benefits, and reinforcement advertising, which assures current users they have made the right brand choice.

Although marketers may vary in how they develop advertising campaigns, they should follow a general pattern. First, they must identify and analyze the target audience, the group of people at whom advertisements are aimed. Second, they should establish what they want the

campaign to accomplish by defining advertising objectives. Objectives should be clear, precise, and presented in measurable terms. Third, marketers must create the advertising platform, which contains basic issues to be presented in the campaign. Advertising platforms should consist of issues important to consumers. Fourth, advertisers must decide how much money to spend on the campaign; they arrive at this decision through the objective-and-task approach, percent-of-sales approach, competition-matching approach, or arbitrary approach.

Advertisers must then develop a media plan by selecting and scheduling media to use in the campaign. Some factors affecting the media plan are location and demographic characteristics of the target audience, content of the message, and cost of the various media. The basic content and form of the advertising message are affected by product features, uses, and benefits; characteristics of the people in the target audience; the campaign's objectives and platform; and the choice of media. Advertisers use copy and artwork to create the message. The execution of an advertising campaign requires extensive planning and coordination.

Finally, advertisers must devise one or more methods for evaluating advertisement effectiveness. Pretests are evaluations performed before the campaign begins; posttests are conducted after the campaign. Two types of posttests are a recognition test, in which respondents are shown the actual advertisement and asked whether they recognize it, and a recall test. In aided recall tests, respondents are shown a list of products, brands, company names, or trademarks to jog their memories. In unaided tests, no clues are given.

Advertising campaigns can be developed by personnel within the firm or in conjunction with advertising agencies. A campaign created by the firm's personnel may be developed by one or more individuals or by an advertising department within the firm. Use of an advertising agency may be advantageous because an agency provides highly skilled, objective specialists with broad experience in advertising at low to moderate costs to the firm.

Public relations is a broad set of communication efforts used to create and maintain favorable relationships between an organization and its stakeholders. Public relations can be used to promote people, places, ideas, activities, and countries, and to create and maintain a positive company image. Some firms use public relations for a single purpose; others use it for several purposes. Public relations tools include written materials, such as brochures, newsletters, and annual reports; corporate identity materials, such as business cards and signs;

speeches; event sponsorships; and special events. Publicity is communication in news story form about an organization, its products, or both, transmitted through a mass medium at no charge. Publicity-based public relations tools include news releases, feature articles, captioned photographs, and press conferences. Problems that organizations confront in using publicity-based public relations include reluctance of media personnel to print or air releases and lack of control over timing and content of messages.

To evaluate the effectiveness of their public relations programs, companies conduct research to determine how well their messages are reaching their audiences. Environmental monitoring, public relations audits, and counting the number of media exposures are all means of evaluating public relations effectiveness. Organizations should avoid negative public relations by taking steps to prevent negative events that result in unfavorable publicity. To diminish the impact of unfavorable public relations, organizations should institute policies and procedures for dealing with news personnel and the public when negative events occur.

IMPORTANT TERMS

Advertising, 490
Institutional
    advertising, 490
Advocacy
    advertising, 490
Product advertising, 490
Pioneer advertising, 490
Competitive
    advertising, 491
Comparative
    advertising, 491
Reminder
    advertising, 491

Reinforcement
    advertising, 491
Advertising campaign, 491
Target audience, 492
Advertising platform, 493
Advertising
    appropriation, 494
Objective-and-task
    approach, 494
Percent-of-sales
    approach, 494
Competition-matching
    approach, 494

Arbitrary
    approach, 495
Media plan, 496
Cost comparison
    indicator, 497
Regional issues, 500
Copy, 500
Storyboard, 501
Artwork, 501
Illustrations, 501
Layout, 501
Pretest, 502
Consumer jury, 502

Posttest, 502
Recognition test, 503
Unaided recall test, 503
Aided recall test, 503
Public relations, 505
Publicity, 506
News release, 506
Feature article, 507
Captioned
    photograph, 507
Press conference, 507

DISCUSSION & REVIEW QUESTIONS

1. What is the difference between institutional and product advertising?
2. What is the difference between competitive advertising and comparative advertising?
3. What are the major steps in creating an advertising campaign?
4. What is a target audience? How does a marketer analyze the target audience after identifying it?
5. Why is it necessary to define advertising objectives?
6. What is an advertising platform, and how is it used?

7. What factors affect the size of an advertising budget? What techniques are used to determine an advertising budget?
8. Describe the steps in developing a media plan.
9. What is the function of copy in an advertising message?
10. Discuss several ways to posttest the effectiveness of advertising.
11. What role does an advertising agency play in developing an advertising campaign?

12. What is public relations? Whom can an organization reach through public relations?

13. How do organizations use public relations tools? Give several examples you have observed recently.

14. Explain the problems and limitations associated with publicity-based public relations.

15. In what ways is the effectiveness of public relations evaluated?

16. What are some sources of negative public relations? How should an organization deal with unfavorable public relations?

APPLICATION QUESTIONS

1. An organization must define its objectives carefully when developing an advertising campaign. Which of the following advertising objectives would be most useful for a company, and why?

   a. The organization will spend $1 million to move from second in market share to market leader.

   b. The organization wants to increase sales from $1.2 million to $1.5 million this year to gain the lead in market share.

   c. The advertising objective is to gain as much market share as possible within the next 12 months.

   d. The advertising objective is to increase sales by 15 percent.

2. Copy, the verbal portion of advertising, is used to move readers through a persuasive sequence called AIDA: attention, interest, desire, and action. To achieve this, some copywriters have adopted guidelines for developing advertising copy. Select a print ad and identify how it (1) identifies a specific problem, (2) recommends the product as the best solution to the problem, (3) states the product's advantages and benefits, (4) substantiates the ad's claims, and (5) asks the reader to take action.

3. Advertisers use several types of publicity mechanisms. Look through some recent newspapers and magazines or use an Internet search engine and identify a news release, a feature article, or a captioned photograph used to publicize a product. Describe the type of product.

4. Negative public relations can harm an organization's marketing efforts if not dealt with properly. Identify a company that was recently the target of negative public relations. Describe the situation and discuss the company's response. What did marketers at this company do well? What, if anything, would you recommend that they change about their response?

INTERNET EXERCISE

Visit **www.cengage.com/marketing/pride-ferrell** for resources to help you master the material in this chapter, plus materials that will help you expand your marketing knowledge, including Internet exercise updates, ACE Self-Tests, hotlinks to companies featured in this chapter, and much more.

LEGO Company

LEGO Company has been making toys since 1932 and has become one of the most recognized brand names in the toy industry. With the company motto "Only the best is good enough," it is no surprise that LEGO Company has developed an exciting and interactive website. See how the company promotes LEGO products and encourages consumer involvement with the brand by visiting **www.lego.com.**

1. Which type of advertising is LEGO Company using on its website?

2. What target audience is LEGO attempting to reach through its website?

3. Identify the advertising objectives LEGO is attempting to achieve through its website.

developing your MARKETING PLAN

Determining the message that advertising is to communicate to the customer is an important part of developing a marketing strategy. A sound understanding of the various types of advertising and different forms of media is essential in selecting the appropriate methods for communicating the message. These decisions form a critical segment of the marketing plan. To assist you in relating the information in this chapter to the development of your marketing plan, consider the following issues:

1. What class and type of advertising would be most appropriate for your product?

2. Discuss the different methods for determining the advertising appropriation.

3. Using Table 17.3 as a guide, evaluate the different types of media and determine which would be most effective in meeting your promotional objectives (from Chapter 16).

4. What methods would you use to evaluate the effectiveness of your advertising campaign?

5. Review Table 17.5 and discuss possible uses for publicity in your promotional plan.

The information obtained from these questions should assist you in developing various aspects of your marketing plan found in the *Interactive Marketing Plan* exercise at **www.cengage.com/marketing/pride-ferrell.**

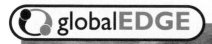

1. An essential component of advertising and public relations in marketing is a firm's ability to impart information to the most advanced consumers in a fast and efficient manner. To better focus your firm's communications worldwide in technologically savvy regions, you have been asked to survey the state of mobile technology by examining a report found on the GSM World website. Access this report by using either the search term "mobile" or "GSM" at **http://globaledge.msu.edu/ibrd.** At the GSM World website, go to the Media Centre option on the side and then click on GSM Statistics. Find the most recent quarterly report. What are the three most technologically savvy regions in the world? What does GSM represent?

2. Your firm is planning to begin advertising a new line of products exclusively to women. However, before doing so, you must determine which markets to use to guide the design as well as where to implement the testing of the product and advertising concepts. Access the NationMaster.com's Gender Development Index using the search term "compare various statistics" at **http://globaledge.msu.edu/ibrd.** Once there, under the Facts & Statistics heading, select the People category in the drop-down box to the right and the subcategory of Gender Development Index to download this data into a spreadsheet for analysis. Based on information in the Gender Development Index, establish the five countries you will target for the advertising and public relations campaign. What types of complications might you encounter in the transition from testing to mass marketing your product? Is there a country you may want to enter first once design and testing are completed?

video CASE 17.1

Vans Leverages Athletes in Its Advertising Platform

For most people, surfing and skateboarding come to mind immediately when they think of southern California culture. For forty years Vans has embodied the California lifestyle and remains one of the preeminent skater-shoe companies. Founded in Los Angeles in 1966 by Paul Van Doren, his brother Steve, and Belgian investor Serge D'Elia, Vans quickly became a staple in southern California. Starting with a few versions of the traditional lace-up deck shoe sold out of a factory, the style of shoe became popular almost immediately. Vans rapidly increased its level of popularity by customizing shoes in all different fabrics and designs. The Van Dorens secured their local customized shoe

business by selling plaid shoes to Catholic schools and sneakers with school colors to high school athletes. But, when the checkered slip-on was donned by Sean Penn and his surfer buddies in the film *Fast Times at Ridgemont High,* skaters all over the country were demanding their own pairs of Vans. The shoes went from local wear to iconic symbol in just a few years.

Contrary to many corporate success stories, the Vans company never spent much money on advertising. Paul Van Doren knew that he offered a superior product, and he relied on word of mouth to popularize the high-quality, extremely durable shoes. The most marketing Van Doren did at first was to have his children canvas their neighborhood with flyers. At all early Vans stores, signs encouraged customers to "tell a friend about Vans." For years, Van Doren focused mostly on the manufacturing aspect of the company so that even with a minimal amount of advertising, popularity grew because Vans were, quite simply, quality shoes. It wasn't until the late 1980s and early 1990s, when manufacturing was taken overseas, that Vans turned its attention to marketing.

One of Vans's earliest forays into promotion came about by chance. As skateboarders began to discover Vans shoes, the company responded by creating styles more amenable to skating. With their skater following growing, Vans paid a few top skaters a few hundred dollars apiece to wear their shoes at skating events. In 1989, Vans produced its first signature skateboarding shoe, the Steve Caballero shoe. Since then, Vans has partnered with numerous athletes such as Geoff Rowley, who has the best-selling signature Vans shoe to date, and Johnny Layton. As skateboarding culture has continued to flourish over the decades, Vans's connection to the scene has remained strong.

Vans's two-man marketing and promotional team focuses on spreading interest in Vans by doing its best to remain plugged into the youth culture and by fueling teenage interest in Vans products. To this end, the company advertises through print, online, TV, and sporting and music events. Currently, the key to Vans's marketing strategy is developing advertising partnerships with athletes, artists, and media outlets. People immersed in this culture want to own Vans products. Vans is not just a shoe; it is a lifestyle.

Young extreme-sports athletes, like skaters and surfers, remain Vans's most important customer base. In 1995, Vans hosted its first Triple Crown event. The Triple Crown spotlights skateboarding, surfing, snowboarding, BMX, FMX, and wakeboarding. Tony Hawk won the skateboarding competition that first year and has since become a household name. Also in 1995, Vans launched its first annual Warped Tour, blending skating with music through concerts and competitions. These types of events allow Vans to build brand recognition, cement its integral place in the skating lifestyle, and connect with customers via giveaways and promotions such as designing custom shoes.

In addition to events, Vans connects with its audience through magazine advertisements, television, and the Internet, especially to attract young female consumers, who represent a growing part of the Vans consumer base. In the past, the company has partnered with magazines such as *Teen Vogue* and *CosmoGirl* to reach the female demographic. In addition, the company works with some of television's action-sports networks and hosts a weekly show, *Vans Off the Wall Hour*, on FSN. Although it is over forty years old, Vans still connects with youth culture as well as ever—and shows no signs of slowing down.[36]

Questions for Discussion

1. Evaluate Vans's early word-of-mouth marketing strategy.
2. Why were the early Vans advertising activities related to skateboard shoes so successful?
3. How does Vans continue to capture its target market?

CASE 17.2

Restylane Wants to Reach the "Hottest Mom in America"

More and more Americans are searching for the perfect remedy that will turn back time on their skin. This quest for younger skin now represents a $12 billion-a-year industry. One of the many players in this industry is Medicis Pharmaceutical Corporation. Founded in 1988, Medicis now sells Restylane, the number one injectable dermal filler in the world, with more than 1.4 million treatments in the United States alone. Restylane is a natural cosmetic filler that works by adding volume to problem areas to smooth facial wrinkles and folds. The procedure for injecting the filler is quick, and the results last about six months.

Companies in the pharmaceutical cosmetics industry see great potential for growth in the market. More than 25 million American women age 30 and older can afford treatments such as Restylane or the popular Botox. In fact, for some cosmetic procedures, Restylane can be a suitable alternative to Botox, which has had a controversial history. In January 2008, Public Citizen, a national nonprofit organization, petitioned the Food and Drug Administration to follow the lead of the European Union in requiring stronger warnings about Botox and similar drugs that employ the botulinum toxin, the same bacteria found in botulism. In some cases, injections have led to serious adverse reactions, including death.

Public Citizen urged the FDA to require "black box" warnings, the strongest made by the agency, on Botox and Myobloc, a similar drug. This negative pressure on Botox creates a market opportunity for Restylane, which is made from hyaluronic acid, a substance that occurs naturally in the body. Many doctors view Restylane as a safe alternative for temporary wrinkle relief. To reach out to these potential customers, several companies in the industry, including Medicis, have begun aggressive promotion campaigns.

Medicis's advertising campaign remains the most unconventional to date. In addition to targeting dermatologists and plastic surgeons through public relations, direct mail, and industry conferences, the company is reaching out directly to customers using an original advertising campaign including viral elements. On the Internet, the company distributed a web video featuring a birthday party for a 50-year-old woman whose son is making an amateur video during the party. When he goes to interview one of his friends, he finds the 20-something smooching his mom on the sofa. The video ends with the line "Restylane Cosmetic Filler, Age Disgracefully." The web video uses humor, and because it is presented as "homemade," the public is likely to view it as just another funny video rather than the paid commercial it actually is.

Medicis also took a different approach for its broad advertising campaign for Restylane. In addition to using the Internet, blogs, and television spots, Medicis produced its own television show, *Hottest Mom in America*. The contest targets suburban moms to find "a woman who is in tune with her family, involved in her community, and in touch with her femininity," according to a letter sent by Medicis to its customers. The winner of Medicis's contest receives a college scholarship for her child and becomes an official Restylane spokeswoman. Recognizing that a heavy-handed promotional strategy might turn off viewers and potential customers, the company decided not to push the treatment within the show. Physicians who specialize in facial rejuvenation will advise and most likely perform treatments on the contestant during the show. Participating doctors could mention Restylane as a possible treatment, although they are also free to recommend treatments that are not sold by Medicis, the company says.

The company has not yet signed a television deal, so it is unclear when or where the show will air. Medicis says that it will produce at least 13 episodes, which will be hosted by model Niki Taylor. The company has filmed in-person auditions for the "hottest mom" in six U.S. cities and is soliciting more via online video submissions. A big selling point for the show to be picked up by a network is that networks would not have to pay for early marketing of the show because Medicis is bankrolling an initiative to build buzz around contest auditions. Alternatively, the show could end up on a niche cable channel geared to women. Medicis might be left with no other option than to pay for airtime, making the reality show in effect an infomercial, a form of advertising that often airs on late-night cable television.

With these tactics, Medicis, like other companies in the industry, is implementing an original and targeted advertising campaign to reach the many potential customers who wish to eliminate wrinkles.[37]

Questions for Discussion

1. Describe Medicis's advertising platform.
2. What other media vehicles and strategies could Medicis employ to create an integrated marketing communications campaign?
3. What public relations tools should the company use to help potential buyers become aware of Restylane?

18 Personal Selling and Sales Promotion

LEARNING objectives

1. To understand the major purposes of personal selling
2. To describe the basic steps in the personal selling process
3. To identify the types of sales force personnel
4. To recognize new types of personal selling
5. To understand sales management decisions and activities
6. To explain what sales promotion activities are and how they are used
7. To explore specific consumer sales promotion methods
8. To explore trade sales promotion methods

Selling Celebrities

Personal selling involves paid personal communication to encourage customers to buy products in exchange situations. A product can be the image and market desirability of a celebrity. John P. Caponigro has developed a sports management firm that uses old-fashioned personal selling to enhance the career of sports celebrities whether they are Indy 500 drivers or Detroit Pistons star players. Today's sports agents, like Tom Cruise's character in the movie *Jerry Maguire,* become a celebrity player's personal contact and key marketer. To achieve his clients' goals, Caponigro must be relentless in his personal communications with companies, and sports and marketing sponsorship agencies. He says that negotiating a player's contract amounts to only about 1 percent of the work; 99 percent of an athlete's representation should involve maximizing his or her value through sponsorships, endorsements, licensing, and, most importantly, post–playing career development. Former Detroit Piston Joe Dumars serves as the prototype of how Caponigro can help a player achieve success off the field. Dumars acknowledged the influence Caponigro has had on his postplaying career. Their relationship goes back 20 years and has maximized Dumars's celebrity value in business and promotional licensing.

Racing legend Mario Andretti, his son Michael Andretti, and his grandson Marco Andretti are all represented by Caponigro's Sports Management Network. Andretti, arguably the greatest racecar driver of all time, is routinely solicited by would-be representatives, but Andretti always says, "No . . . I'm not interested." Andretti maintains ownership in Andretti Green Racing and oversees ventures such as the Andretti Winery in Napa Valley, California, and the Mario Andretti Driving School in Las Vegas. Caponigro and Andretti met when Caponigro started working for Championship Auto Racing Teams, Inc. (CART), in the early 1980s when Andretti was racing for CART. Caponigro eventually took over the reins of CART but later left the firm. Soon afterward, he started his own Sports Management Network and focused his energies on the emerging sports and entertainment industry. Sports Management Network has continued to grow and tailor its service offerings within sports and entertainment. It also provides specialized marketing expertise and experience to corporations and communication agencies in a consulting capacity.

By building long-term relationships and avoiding onetime contract negotiations, Caponigro mastered personal selling and sales promotion of celebrities. His five "keys" to winning client endorsements are (1) be a marketable personality, (2) establish positive relationships, (3) it is okay to start small, (4) realize that endorsements can take many forms, and (5) be true to the endorsement.[1]

For many organizations, such as Sports Management Network, targeting customers with appropriate personal selling techniques and messages can play a major role in maintaining long-term, satisfying customer relationships, which in turn contribute to the company's success. As we saw in Chapter 16, personal selling and sales promotion are two possible elements in a promotion mix. Personal selling is sometimes a company's sole promotional tool, and it is becoming more professional and sophisticated, with sales personnel acting more as consultants and advisers.

In this chapter, we focus on personal selling and sales promotion. We first consider the purposes of personal selling and then examine its basic steps. Next, we look at types of salespeople and how they are selected. After taking a look at several new types of personal selling, we discuss major sales force management decisions, including setting objectives for the sales force and determining its size; recruiting, selecting, training, compensating, and motivating salespeople; managing sales territories; and controlling and evaluating sales force performance. Then we examine several characteristics of sales promotion, reasons for using sales promotion, and sales promotion methods available for use in a promotion mix.

The Nature of Personal Selling

personal selling Paid personal communication that attempts to inform customers and persuade them to buy products in an exchange situation

LO 1 To understand the major purposes of personal selling

Personal selling is paid personal communication that attempts to inform customers and persuade them to purchase products in an exchange situation. For example, a Hewlett-Packard (HP) salesperson describing the benefits of the company's servers, PCs, and printers to a small-business customer is engaging in personal selling. Likewise, a volunteer manning a petition-signing booth for a social or political cause uses personal selling to inform passersby about the issues and to persuade them to change their views or become involved. Personal selling gives marketers the greatest freedom to adjust a message to satisfy customers' information needs. It is the most precise of all promotion methods, enabling marketers to focus on the most promising sales prospects. Other promotion mix elements are aimed at groups of people, some of whom may not be prospective customers. However, personal selling is generally the most expensive element in the promotion mix. The average cost of a sales call is more than $400.[2]

Millions of people, including increasing numbers of women, earn their living through personal selling. Sales careers can offer high income, a great deal of freedom, a high level of training, and a high degree of job satisfaction. Although the public may harbor negative perceptions of personal selling, unfavorable stereotypes of salespeople are changing thanks to the efforts of major corporations, professional sales associations, and academic institutions. Research indicates that personal selling will continue to gain respect as professional sales associations develop and enforce ethical codes of conduct.[3]

Personal selling goals vary from one firm to another. However, they usually involve finding prospects, persuading prospects to buy, and keeping customers satisfied. Identifying potential buyers interested in the organization's products is critical. Because most potential buyers seek information before making purchases, salespeople can ascertain prospects' informational needs and then provide

BECOME A STATE FARM AGENT.

As a successful State Farm agent, you'll be your own boss — running your own insurance and financial services business, winning the trust of your customers, and making a name for yourself within the community.

It won't be easy, but you'll have the backing of a Fortune 500® company. And it could be the most challenging, most rewarding thing you've ever done.

Visit statefarm.com/careers or call 1-866-405-9813.

GROW. LEAD. SUCCEED.

STATE FARM INSURANCE

An Equal Opportunity Employer

LIKE A GOOD NEIGHBOR, STATE FARM IS THERE.®

Nature of Personal Selling
State Farm provides professional sales career opportunities to serve local communities.

relevant information. To do so, sales personnel must be well trained regarding both their products and the selling process in general.

Salespeople must be aware of their competitors. They must monitor the development of new products and keep abreast of competitors' sales efforts in their sales territories, how often and when the competition calls on their accounts, and what the competition is saying about their product in relation to its own. Salespeople must emphasize the benefits their products provide, especially when competitors' products do not offer those specific benefits.

Few businesses survive solely on profits from onetime customers. For long-run survival, most marketers depend on repeat sales, and thus need to keep their customers satisfied. In addition, satisfied customers provide favorable word-of-mouth communications, thus attracting new customers. Although the whole organization is responsible for achieving customer satisfaction, much of the burden falls on salespeople because they are almost always closer to customers than anyone else in the company and often provide buyers with information and service after the sale. Indeed, research shows that a firm's marketing orientation has a positive influence on salespeople's attitudes, commitment, and influence on customer purchasing intentions.[4] Such contact gives salespeople an opportunity to generate additional sales and offers them a good vantage point for evaluating the strengths and weaknesses of the company's products and other marketing mix components. Their observations help develop and maintain a marketing mix that better satisfies both the firm and its customers.

Elements of the Personal Selling Process

LO 2 To describe the basic steps in the personal selling process

The specific activities involved in the selling process vary among salespeople, selling situations, and cultures. No two salespeople use exactly the same selling methods. Nonetheless, many salespeople move through a general selling process. This process consists of seven steps, outlined in Figure 18.1: prospecting, preapproach, approach, making the presentation, overcoming objections, closing the sale, and following up.

figure 18.1

GENERAL STEPS IN THE PERSONAL SELLING PROCESS

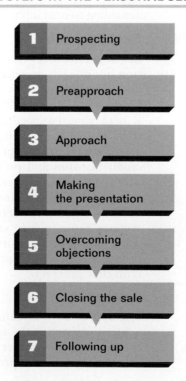

1 Prospecting

2 Preapproach

3 Approach

4 Making the presentation

5 Overcoming objections

6 Closing the sale

7 Following up

Your wish of growing sales is my command.

Get 100 FREE sales leads or mailing labels *and your wish will come true!*

Salesgenie.com ™
Unlimited Sales Leads
a service of infoUSA®

5711 S. 86th Circle • Omaha, NE 68127

SPECIAL $150 $250/month
LIMITED TIME OFFER
Go to: www.Salesgenie.com/sel
or call Rob Martin
at 1-866-313-4318

Prospecting

Salesgenie.com provides customized databases containing potential sales prospects.

Prospecting

Developing a list of potential customers is called **prospecting**. Salespeople seek names of prospects from company sales records, trade shows, commercial databases, newspaper announcements (of marriages, births, deaths, and so on), public records, telephone directories, trade association directories, and many other sources. Sales personnel also use responses to traditional and online advertisements that encourage interested persons to send in information request forms. Seminars and meetings targeted at particular types of clients, such as attorneys or accountants, may also produce leads.

Most salespeople prefer to use referrals—recommendations from current customers—to find prospects. Obtaining referrals requires that the salesperson have a good relationship with the current customer and therefore must have performed well before asking the customer for help. As might be expected, a customer's trust in and satisfaction with a salesperson influences his or her willingness to provide referrals.[5] Research shows that 1 referral is as valuable as 12 cold calls. Also, 80 percent of clients are willing to give referrals, but only 20 percent are ever asked. Among the advantages of using referrals are more highly qualified sales leads, greater sales rates, and larger initial transactions. Some companies even award discounts off future purchases to customers who refer new prospects to their salespeople. Consistent activity is critical to successful prospecting. Salespeople must actively search the customer base for qualified prospects that fit the target market profile. After developing the prospect list, a salesperson evaluates whether each prospect is able, willing, and authorized to buy the product. Based on this evaluation, prospects are ranked according to desirability or potential.

Preapproach

Before contacting acceptable prospects, a salesperson finds and analyzes information about each prospect's specific product needs, current use of brands, feelings about available brands, and personal characteristics. In short, salespeople need to know what potential buyers and decision makers consider most important and why they need a specific product.[6] The most successful salespeople are thorough in their *preapproach*, which involves identifying key decision makers, reviewing account histories and problems, contacting other clients for information, assessing credit histories and problems, preparing sales presentations, identifying product needs, and obtaining relevant literature. Marketers are increasingly using information technology and customer relationship management systems to comb through databases and thus identify their most profitable products and customers. CRM systems can also help sales departments manage leads, track customers, forecast sales, and assess performance. A salesperson with a lot of information about a prospect is better equipped to develop a presentation that precisely communicates with that prospect.

Approach

The **approach**—the manner in which a salesperson contacts a potential customer— is a critical step in the sales process. In more than 80 percent of initial sales calls, the purpose is to gather information about the buyer's needs and objectives. Creating a favorable impression and building rapport with prospective clients are

prospecting Developing a list of potential customers

approach The manner in which a salesperson contacts a potential customer

important tasks in the approach because the prospect's first impressions of the salesperson are usually lasting ones. During the initial visit, the salesperson strives to develop a relationship rather than just push a product. Indeed, coming across as a "salesperson" may not be the best approach because some people are put off by strong selling tactics. The salesperson may have to call on a prospect several times before the product is considered. The approach must be designed to deliver value to targeted customers. If the sales approach is inappropriate, the salesperson's efforts are likely to have poor results.

One type of approach is based on referrals: the salesperson approaches the prospect and explains that an acquaintance, an associate, or a relative suggested the call. The salesperson who uses the "cold canvass" approach calls on potential customers without prior consent. Repeat contact is another common approach: when making the contact, the salesperson mentions a previous meeting. The exact type of approach depends on the salesperson's preferences, the product being sold, the firm's resources, and the prospect's characteristics.

Making the Presentation

During the sales presentation, the salesperson must attract and hold the prospect's attention, stimulate interest, and spark a desire for the product. Research indicates that salespeople who carefully monitor the selling situation and adapt their presentations to meet the needs of prospects are associated with effective sales performance.[7] Salespeople should match their influencing tactics—such as information exchange, recommendations, threats, promises, ingratiation, and inspirational appeals—to their prospects. Different types of buyers respond to different tactics, but most respond well to information exchange and recommendations, and virtually no prospects respond to threats.[8] The salesperson should have the prospect touch, hold, or use the product. If possible, the salesperson should demonstrate the product or invite the prospect to use it. Automobile salespeople, for example, typically invite potential buyers to test-drive the vehicle that interests them. Audiovisual equipment and software may also enhance the presentation.

During the presentation, the salesperson must not only talk, but also listen. Non-verbal modes of communication are especially beneficial in building trust during the presentation.[9] The sales presentation gives the salesperson the greatest opportunity to determine the prospect's specific needs by listening to questions and comments and observing responses. Even though the salesperson plans the presentation in advance, she or he must be able to adjust the message to meet the prospect's informational needs. Research demonstrates that adapting the message in response to the customer's needs generally enhances performance, particularly in new-task or modified rebuy purchase situations.[10]

Overcoming Objections

An effective salesperson usually seeks out a prospect's objections in order to address them. If they are not apparent, the salesperson cannot deal with them, and the prospect may not buy. One of the best ways to overcome objections is to anticipate and counter them before the prospect raises them. However, this approach can be risky because the salesperson may mention objections that the prospect would not have raised. If possible, the salesperson should handle objections as they arise. They can also be addressed at the end of the presentation.

Closing the Sale

Closing is the stage in the personal selling process when the salesperson asks the prospect to buy the product. During the presentation, the salesperson may use a *trial close* by asking questions that assume the prospect will buy. The salesperson might ask the potential customer about financial terms, desired colors or sizes, or delivery arrangements. Reactions to such questions usually indicate how close the prospect is to buying. Properly asked questions may allow prospects to uncover their own problems and identify solutions themselves. One questioning approach uses broad questions

closing The stage in the personal selling process when the salesperson asks the prospect to buy the product

E-ntertainment MARKETING

Celebrities Go Green and Help Close the Sale

Consumers are becoming more favorable toward green products, but salespeople still have to work hard to sell these products. Environmentally friendly products are desired by about 20 percent of the U.S. market, but the real opportunity is getting the mass market to view green products as an advantage. Celebrities are taking a leadership role by purchasing green products and creating the opportunity for salespeople to use them as role models in their sales presentations. Will Ferrell, one of the world's most famous comedians, may be funny in his movies, but he is very serious about the environment. He is an active member of the National Resources Defense Council and was the first celebrity to buy the BMW L7, a luxury car that runs on hydrogen. Even Governor Arnold Schwarzenegger runs his Hummer on biofuel. All cars in the Indy Racing League switched to ethanol, and every Indy race promotes the environmental benefits of ethanol.

Consider a salesperson who is selling products based on renewable power such as solar and wind.

Although the purchase of these technologies may help prevent global warming, most consumers are more interested in their being a good economic investment. Even when selling the top-selling Toyota Prius hybrid, a salesperson must convince the buyer that spending an extra $3,500 for an electronic powertrain is worth the cost. Celebrities are doing their part to help promote the cause of eco-friendly cars. Leonardo DiCaprio, Tom Hanks, and Cameron Diaz all drive a Prius—even going so far as to show up at awards ceremonies in their eco-friendly vehicles. Sometimes, when a salesperson presents the environmental benefits of a particular product, she still must face the challenge that some consumers believe that green products do not perform as well as more conventional ones. Therefore, a salesperson must focus on each product's benefits, performance, and economy features. However, the glamour lent to going green by celebrity endorsements has helped to increase the popularity of these products.

Even Whirlpool, a company that has released a variety of energy-saving appliances, utilizes the international selling power of Australian celebrity chef Benjamin Christie. When Whirlpool Corp. promotes its Duet line of front-loading washing machines, salespeople can promote the washers' potential energy and water savings. Although some buyers may view the machines as a way to do something positive for the natural environment, others buy them to save money. The salesperson therefore must understand the customer and be careful to position the eco-responsible products to match their desires and concerns.[a]

(*what, how, why*) to probe or gather information and focused questions (*who, when, where*) to clarify and close the sale. A trial close allows prospects to indicate indirectly that they will buy the product without having to say those sometimes difficult words, "I'll take it."

A salesperson should try to close at several points during the presentation because the prospect may be ready to buy. An attempt to close the sale may result in objections. Thus, closing can uncover hidden objections, which the salesperson can then address. One closing strategy involves asking the potential customer to place a low-risk tryout order.

Following Up

After a successful closing, the salesperson must follow up the sale. In the follow-up stage, the salesperson determines whether the order was delivered on time and installed properly, if installation was required. He or she should contact the customer to learn if any problems or questions regarding the product have arisen. The follow-up stage is also used to determine customers' future product needs.

Types of Salespeople

L O ❸ To identify the types of sales force personnel

To develop a sales force, a marketing manager decides what kind of salesperson will sell the firm's products most effectively. Most business organizations use several different kinds of sales personnel. Based on the functions performed, salespeople can be classified into three groups: order getters, order takers, and support personnel. One salesperson can, and often does, perform all three functions.

Order Getters

To obtain orders, a salesperson informs prospects and persuades them to buy the product. The **order getter's** job is to increase sales by selling to new customers and increasing sales to present customers. This task is sometimes called *creative selling*. It requires that salespeople recognize potential buyers' needs and give them necessary information. Order getting is frequently divided into two categories: current-customer sales and new-business sales.

Current-Customer Sales. Sales personnel who concentrate on current customers call on people and organizations that have purchased products from the firm before. These salespeople seek more sales from existing customers by following up previous sales. Current customers can also be sources of leads for new prospects.

New-Business Sales. Business organizations depend to some degree on sales to new customers. New-business sales personnel locate prospects and convert them into buyers. In many organizations, salespeople help generate new business, but organizations that sell real estate, insurance, appliances, heavy industrial machinery, and automobiles depend in large part on new-customer sales.

order getter A salesperson who sells to new customers and increases sales to current customers

Order Solicitation
OutStartSellingEdge.com provides background information that can be helpful in soliciting and closing sales.

Order Takers

Taking orders is a repetitive task salespeople perform to perpetuate long-lasting, satisfying customer relationships. **Order takers** primarily seek repeat sales, generating the bulk of many firms' total sales. One of their major objectives is to be certain that customers have sufficient product quantities where and when needed. Most order takers handle orders for standardized products that are purchased routinely and do not require extensive sales efforts. The role of order takers is changing, however, as the position moves more toward one that identifies and solves problems to better meet the needs of customers. There are two groups of order takers: inside order takers and field order takers.

Inside Order Takers. In many businesses, inside order takers, who work in sales offices, receive orders by mail, telephone, and the Internet. Certain producers, wholesalers, and retailers have sales personnel who sell from within the firm rather than in the field. Some inside order takers communicate with customers face to face; retail salespeople, for example, are classified as inside order takers. As more orders are placed through the Internet, the role of the inside order taker continues to change.

Field Order Takers. Salespeople who travel to customers are outside, or field, order takers. Often customers and field order takers develop interdependent relationships. The buyer relies on the salesperson to take orders periodically (and sometimes to deliver them), and the salesperson counts on the buyer to purchase a certain quantity of products periodically. Use of small computers has improved the field order taker's inventory and order-tracking capabilities.

Support Personnel

Support personnel facilitate selling but usually are not involved solely with making sales. They engage primarily in marketing industrial products, locating prospects, educating customers, building goodwill, and providing service after the sale. There are many kinds of sales support personnel; the three most common are missionary, trade, and technical salespeople.

Missionary Salespeople. **Missionary salespeople,** usually employed by manufacturers, assist the producer's customers in selling to their own customers. Missionary salespeople may call on retailers to inform and persuade them to buy the manufacturer's products. When they succeed, retailers purchase products from wholesalers, which are the producer's customers. Manufacturers of medical supplies and pharmaceuticals often use missionary salespeople, called *detail reps*, to promote their products to physicians, hospitals, and retail druggists.

Trade Salespeople. **Trade salespeople** are not strictly support personnel because they usually take orders as well. However, they direct much effort toward helping customers, especially retail stores, promote the product. They are likely to restock shelves, obtain more shelf space, set up displays, provide in-store demonstrations, and distribute samples to store customers. Food producers and processors commonly employ trade salespeople.

Technical Salespeople. **Technical salespeople** give technical assistance to the organization's current customers, advising them on product characteristics and applications, system designs, and installation procedures. Because this job is often highly technical, the salesperson usually has formal training in one of the physical sciences or in engineering. Technical sales personnel often sell technical industrial products such as computers, heavy equipment, and steel.

When hiring sales personnel, marketers seldom restrict themselves to a single category because most firms require different types of salespeople. Several factors dictate how many of each type a particular company should have. Product use, characteristics, complexity, and price influence the kind of sales personnel used, as do the number and characteristics of customers. The types of marketing channels and the intensity and type of advertising also affect the composition of a sales force.

order takers Salespeople who primarily seek repeat sales

support personnel Sales staff members who facilitate selling but usually are not involved solely with making sales

missionary salespeople Support salespeople, usually employed by a manufacturer, who assist the producer's customers in selling to their own customers

trade salespeople Salespeople involved mainly in helping a producer's customers promote a product

technical salespeople Support salespeople who give technical assistance to a firm's current customers

Selected Types of Selling

L O ④ To recognize new types of personal selling

Personal selling has become an increasingly complex process due in large part to rapid technological innovation. Most importantly, the focus of personal selling is shifting from selling a specific product to building long-term relationships with customers by finding solutions to their needs, problems, and challenges. As a result, the roles of salespeople are changing. Among the new philosophies for personal selling are team selling and relationship selling.

Team Selling

Many products, particularly expensive high-tech business products, have become so complex that a single salesperson can no longer be expert in every aspect of the product and purchase process. **Team selling,** which involves the salesperson joining with people from the firm's financial, engineering, and other functional areas, is appropriate for such products. The salesperson takes the lead in the personal selling process, but other members of the team bring their unique skills, knowledge, and resources to the process to help customers find solutions to their own business challenges. Selling teams may be created to address a particular short-term situation or they may be formal, ongoing teams. Team selling is advantageous in situations calling for detailed knowledge of new, complex, and dynamic technologies such as jet aircraft and medical equipment. It can be difficult, however, for highly competitive salespersons to adapt to a team selling environment.

Relationship Selling

Relationship selling, also known as consultative selling, involves building mutually beneficial long-term associations with a customer through regular communications over prolonged periods of time. Like team selling, it is especially used in business-to-business marketing. Relationship selling involves finding solutions to customers' needs by listening to them, gaining a detailed understanding of their organizations, understanding and caring about their needs and challenges, and providing support after the sale. Relationship selling efforts can be enhanced through sales automation technology tools that enhance interactive communication.[11] At Computer Discount Warehouse (CDW), relationship selling is based on helping customers succeed. Before recent hurricanes struck Florida, for example, some CDW account managers contacted clients in the paths of the storms and suggested computer backup storage and battery solutions that could help their businesses weather the storms with greater confidence.[12]

team selling The use of a team of experts from all functional areas of a firm, led by a salesperson, to conduct the personal selling process

relationship selling The building of mutually beneficial long-term associations with a customer through regular communications over prolonged periods of time

Managing the Sales Force

L O ⑤ To understand sales management decisions and activities

The sales force is directly responsible for generating one of an organization's primary inputs: sales revenue. Without adequate sales revenue, businesses cannot survive. In addition, a firm's reputation is often determined by the ethical conduct of its sales force. Indeed, a positive ethical climate, one component of corporate culture, has been linked with decreased role stress and turnover intention and improved job attitudes and job performance in sales.[13] The morale and ultimately the success of a firm's sales force depend in large part on adequate compensation, room for advancement, sufficient training, and management support—all key areas of sales management. Salespeople who are not satisfied with these elements may leave. Evaluating the input of salespeople is an important part of sales force management because of its strong bearing on a firm's success.

We explore eight general areas of sales management: establishing sales force objectives, determining sales force size, recruiting and selecting salespeople, training sales personnel, compensating salespeople, motivating salespeople, managing sales territories, and controlling and evaluating sales force performance.

Establishing Sales Force Objectives

To manage a sales force effectively, sales managers must develop sales objectives. Sales objectives tell salespeople what they are expected to accomplish during a specified time period. They give the sales force direction and purpose, and serve as standards for evaluating and controlling the performance of sales personnel. Sales objectives should be stated in precise, measurable terms and should specify the time period and geographic areas involved.

Sales objectives are usually developed for both the total sales force and individual salespeople. Objectives for the entire force are normally stated in terms of sales volume, market share, or profit. Volume objectives refer to dollar or unit sales. For example, the objective for an electric drill producer's sales force might be to sell $18 million worth of drills, or 600,000 drills annually. When sales goals are stated in terms of market share, they usually call for an increase in the proportion of the firm's sales relative to the total number of products sold by all businesses in that industry. When sales objectives are based on profit, they are generally stated in terms of dollar amounts or return on investment.

Sales objectives, or quotas, for individual salespeople are commonly stated in terms of dollar or unit sales volume. Other bases used for individual sales objectives include average order size, average number of calls per time period, and ratio of orders to calls.

Determining Sales Force Size

Sales force size is important because it influences the company's ability to generate sales and profits. Moreover, size of the sales force affects the compensation methods used, salespeople's morale, and overall sales force management. Sales force size must be adjusted periodically because a firm's marketing plans change along with markets and forces in the marketing environment. One danger in cutting back the size of the sales force to increase profits is that the sales organization may lose strength and resiliency, preventing it from rebounding when growth occurs or better market conditions prevail.

Several analytical methods can help determine optimal sales force size. One method involves determining how many sales calls per year are necessary for the organization to serve customers effectively and then dividing this total by the average number of sales calls a salesperson makes annually. A second method is based on marginal analysis, in which additional salespeople are added to the sales force until the cost of an additional salesperson equals the additional sales generated by that person. Although marketing managers may use one or several analytical methods, they normally temper decisions with subjective judgments.

Recruiting and Selecting Salespeople

To create and maintain an effective sales force, sales managers must recruit the right type of salespeople. In **recruiting,** the sales manager develops a list of qualified applicants for sales positions. Effective recruiting efforts are a vital part of implementing the strategic sales force plan and can help assure successful organizational performance.[14] Costs of hiring and training a salesperson are soaring, reaching more than $60,000 in some industries. Thus, recruiting errors are expensive.

To ensure that the recruiting process results in a pool of qualified applicants, a sales manager establishes a set of qualifications before beginning to recruit. Although marketers have tried for years to identify a set of traits characterizing effective salespeople, no set of generally accepted characteristics yet exists. Experts agree that good salespeople exhibit optimism, flexibility, self-motivation, empathy, and the ability to network and maintain long-term customer relationships. Today companies are increasingly seeking applicants capable of employing relationship-building and consultative approaches.[15]

Sales managers must determine what set of traits best fits their companies' particular sales tasks. Two activities help establish this set of required attributes. First, the sales manager should prepare a job description listing specific tasks salespeople are to perform. Second, the manager should analyze characteristics of the firm's successful salespeople, as well as those of ineffective sales personnel. From the job

recruiting Developing a list of qualified applicants for sales positions

Recruiting and Selecting Salespeople

Careerbuilder.com assists in recruiting the right sales professionals.

description and analysis of traits, the sales manager should be able to develop a set of specific requirements and be aware of potential weaknesses that could lead to failure.

A sales manager generally recruits applicants from several sources: departments within the firm, other firms, employment agencies, educational institutions, respondents to advertisements, and individuals recommended by current employees. The specific sources depend on the type of salesperson required and the manager's experiences with particular sources.

The process of recruiting and selecting salespeople varies considerably from one company to another. Companies intent on reducing sales force turnover are likely to have strict recruiting and selection procedures. State Farm Life Insurance, for example, strives to retain customers by having low sales force turnover. Applicants for the job of State Farm insurance agent must go through a yearlong series of interviews, tests, and visits with agents before finding out if they have been hired. Approximately 80 percent of State Farm agents are still employed four years after being hired, compared with an industry average of only 30 percent.

Sales management should design a selection procedure that satisfies the company's specific needs. Some organizations use the specialized services of other companies to hire sales personnel. The process should include steps that yield the information required to make accurate selection decisions. However, because each step incurs a certain amount of expense, there should be no more steps than necessary. Stages of the selection process should be sequenced so that the more expensive steps, such as a physical examination, occur near the end. Fewer people will then move through higher-cost stages.

Recruitment should not be sporadic; it should be a continuous activity aimed at reaching the best applicants. The selection process should systematically and effectively match applicants' characteristics and needs with the requirements of specific selling tasks. Finally, the selection process should ensure that new sales personnel are available where and when needed.

Training Sales Personnel

Many organizations have formal training programs; others depend on informal, on-the-job training. Some systematic training programs are quite extensive, whereas others are rather short and rudimentary. Whether the training program is complex or simple, developers must consider what to teach, whom to train, and how to train them.

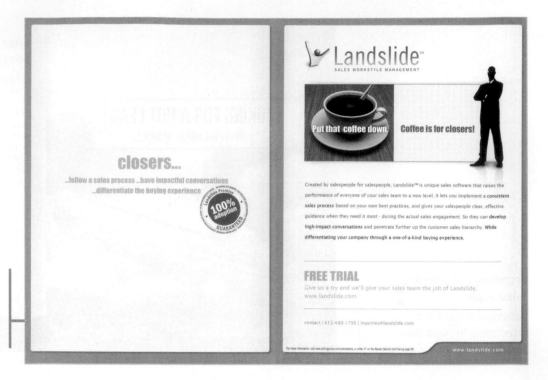

Training Sales Personnel
Landslide.com provides customized online sales training based on best practices in the industry.

A sales training program can concentrate on the company, its products, or selling methods. Training programs often cover all three. Such programs can be aimed at newly hired salespeople, experienced salespeople, or both. Training for experienced company salespeople usually emphasizes product information, although salespeople must also be informed about new selling techniques and changes in company plans, policies, and procedures. Honda, for example, designed a sales training program that involved going to 21 cities to train 7,500 sales associates about the automaker's entry-level auto, the Fit. The training program introduced sales reps not only to the features and benefits of the new car but also to the vehicle's target market: young buyers who are comfortable finding their own car information online.[16] Ordinarily, new sales personnel require comprehensive training, whereas experienced personnel need both refresher courses on established products and training regarding new-product information.

Sales training may be done in the field, at educational institutions, in company facilities, and/or online using web-based technology. For many companies, online training saves time and money, and helps salespeople learn about new products quickly. Some firms train new employees before assigning them to a specific sales position. Others put them into the field immediately, providing formal training only after they have gained some experience. Training programs for new personnel can be as short as several days or as long as three years; some are even longer. Sales training for experienced personnel is often scheduled when sales activities are not too demanding. Because experienced salespeople usually need periodic retraining, a firm's sales management must determine the frequency, sequencing, and duration of these efforts.

Sales managers, as well as other salespeople, often engage in sales training, whether daily on the job or periodically during sales meetings. Salespeople sometimes receive training from technical specialists within their own organizations. In addition, a number of outside companies specialize in providing sales training programs. Materials for sales training programs range from videos, texts, online materials, manuals, and cases to programmed learning devices and audio- and videocassettes. Lectures, demonstrations, simulation exercises, and on-the-job training can all be effective teaching methods. Self-directed learning to supplement traditional sales training has the potential to improve sales performance.[17] The choice of methods and materials for a particular sales training program depends on type and number of trainees, program content and complexity, length and location, size of the training budget, number of teachers, and teacher preferences.

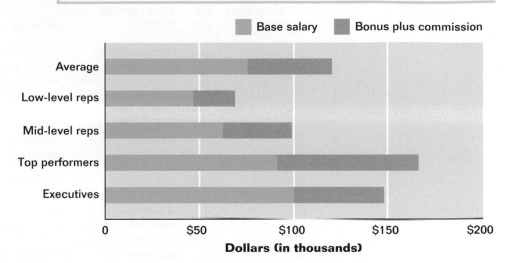

AVERAGE SALARIES FOR SALES REPRESENTATIVES

Source: From Joseph Kornik, "What's It All Worth?," *Sales and Marketing Management,* May 2007, p. 29.

Compensating Salespeople

To develop and maintain a highly productive sales force, a business must formulate and administer a compensation plan that attracts, motivates, and retains the most effective individuals. The plan should give sales management the desired level of control and provide sales personnel with acceptable levels of income, freedom, and incentive. It should be flexible, equitable, easy to administer, and easy to understand. Good compensation programs facilitate and encourage proper treatment of customers. Obviously it is quite difficult to incorporate all of these requirements into a single program.

Developers of compensation programs must determine the general level of compensation required and the most desirable method of calculating it. In analyzing the required compensation level, sales management must ascertain a salesperson's value to the company on the basis of the tasks and responsibilities associated with the sales position. Sales managers may consider a number of factors, including salaries of other types of personnel in the firm, competitors' compensation plans, costs of sales force turnover, and nonsalary selling expenses. The average low-level salesperson earns about $71,000 annually (including commissions and bonuses), whereas a high-level, high-performing salesperson can make as much as $162,000 a year, as shown in Figure 18.2.[18]

Sales compensation programs usually reimburse salespeople for selling expenses, provide some fringe benefits, and deliver the required compensation level. To achieve this, a firm may use one or more of three basic compensation methods: straight salary, straight commission, or a combination of the two. Table 18.1 lists the major characteristics, advantages, and disadvantages of each method. In a **straight salary compensation plan,** salespeople are paid a specified amount per time period, regardless of selling effort. This sum remains the same until they receive a pay increase or decrease. Although this method is easy to administer and affords salespeople financial security, it provides little incentive for them to boost selling efforts. In a **straight commission compensation plan,** salespeople's compensation is determined solely by sales for a given period. A commission may be based on a single percentage of sales or on a sliding scale involving several sales levels and percentage rates. Although this method motivates sales personnel to escalate their selling efforts, it offers them little financial security, and it can be difficult for sales managers to maintain control over the sales force. For these reasons, many firms offer a **combination compensation plan** in which salespeople receive a fixed salary plus a commission based on sales volume. Some combination programs require that a salesperson exceed a certain sales level before earning a commission; others offer commissions for any level of sales. This method is the most popular, as indicated in Table 18.1.

When selecting a compensation method, sales management weighs the advantages and disadvantages listed in the table. Research indicates that higher commissions are

straight salary compensation plan Paying salespeople a specific amount per time period, regardless of selling effort

straight commission compensation plan Paying salespeople according to the amount of their sales in a given time period

combination compensation plan Paying salespeople a fixed salary plus a commission based on sales volume

table 18.1		CHARACTERISTICS OF SALES FORCE COMPENSATION METHODS		
Compensation Method	**Use (%)***	**When Especially Useful**	**Advantages**	**Disadvantages**
Straight salary	17.5	Compensating new salespeople; firm moves into new sales territories that require developmental work; sales requiring lengthy presale and postsale services	Gives salespeople security; gives sales managers control over salespeople; easy to administer; yields more predictable selling expenses	Provides no incentive; necessitates closer supervision of salespeople; during sales declines, selling expenses remain constant
Straight commission	14.0	Highly aggressive selling is required; nonselling tasks are minimized; company uses contractors and part-timers	Provides maximum amount of incentive; by increasing commission rate, sales managers can encourage salespeople to sell certain items; selling expenses relate directly to sales resources	Salespeople have little financial security; sales managers have minimum control over sales force; may cause salespeople to give inadequate service to smaller accounts; selling costs less predictable
Combination	68.5	Sales territories have relatively similar sales potential; firm wishes to provide incentive but still control sales force activities	Provides certain level of financial security; provides some incentive; can move sales force efforts in profitable direction	Selling expenses less predictable; may be difficult to administer

*The figures are computed from *Dartnell's 30th Sales Force Compensation Survey,* Dartnell Corporation, Chicago, 1999.

Source: Charles Futrell, *Sales Management* (Ft. Worth: Dryden Press), 2001, pp. 307–316.

the most preferred reward, followed by pay increases.[19] For example, the Container Store, which markets do-it-yourself organizing and storage products, prefers to pay its sales staff salaries that are 50 to 100 percent higher than those offered by rivals instead of basing pay on commission plans.[20]

Motivating Salespeople

Although financial compensation is an important incentive, additional programs are necessary for motivating sales personnel. A sales manager should develop a systematic approach for motivating salespeople to be productive. Effective sales force motivation is achieved through an organized set of activities performed continuously by the company's sales management.

Sales personnel, like other people, join organizations to satisfy personal needs and achieve personal goals. Sales managers must identify those needs and goals and strive to create an organizational climate that allows each salesperson to fulfill them. Enjoyable working conditions, power and authority, job security, and opportunity to excel are effective motivators, as are company efforts to make sales jobs more productive and efficient. At the Container Store, for example, sales personnel receive hundreds of hours of training about the company's products every year so they can help customers solve organizational and storage problems.[21] Research has shown that a strong corporate culture leads to higher levels of job satisfaction and organizational commitment and lower levels of job stress.[22] Sales contests and other incentive programs can also be effective motivators. These can motivate salespeople to increase

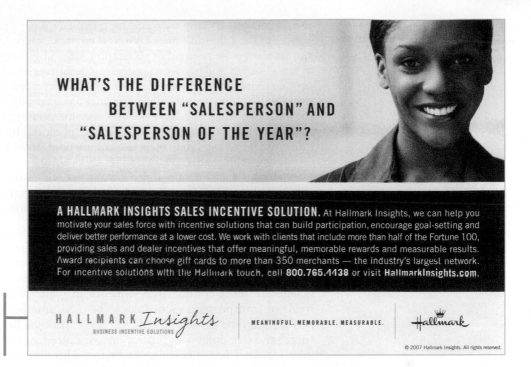

WHAT'S THE DIFFERENCE
BETWEEN "SALESPERSON" AND
"SALESPERSON OF THE YEAR"?

A HALLMARK INSIGHTS SALES INCENTIVE SOLUTION. At Hallmark Insights, we can help you motivate your sales force with incentive solutions that can build participation, encourage goal-setting and deliver better performance at a lower cost. We work with clients that include more than half of the Fortune 100, providing sales and dealer incentives that offer meaningful, memorable rewards and measurable results. Award recipients can choose gift cards to more than 350 merchants — the industry's largest network. For incentive solutions with the Hallmark touch, call **800.765.4138** or visit **HallmarkInsights.com.**

HALLMARK *Insights*
BUSINESS INCENTIVE SOLUTIONS

MEANINGFUL. MEMORABLE. MEASURABLE.

Hallmark

© 2007 Hallmark Insights. All rights reserved.

Motivating Salespeople

Hallmark Insights provides incentives to motivate the sales force.

sales or add new accounts, promote special items, achieve greater volume per sales call, and cover territories more thoroughly. However, companies need to understand salespersons' preferences when designing contests in order to make them effective in increasing sales.[23] Some companies find such contests powerful tools for motivating sales personnel to achieve company goals. In smaller firms lacking the resources for a formal incentive program, a simple but public "thank-you" from management at a sales meeting, along with a small-denomination gift card, can be rewarding.[24]

Properly designed incentive programs pay for themselves many times over, and sales managers are relying on incentives more than ever. Recognition programs that acknowledge outstanding performance with symbolic awards, such as plaques, can be very effective when carried out in a peer setting. The most common incentive offered by companies is cash, followed by gift cards and travel.[25] Travel reward programs can confer a high-profile honor, provide a unique experience that makes recipients feel special, and build camaraderie among award-winning salespeople. However, some recipients of travel awards may feel they already travel too much on the job. Cash rewards are easy to administer, are always appreciated by recipients, and appeal to all demographic groups. However, cash has no visible "trophy" value and provides few "bragging rights." The benefits of awarding merchandise are that the items have visible trophy value. In addition, recipients who are allowed to select the merchandise experience a sense of control, and merchandise awards can help build momentum for the sales force. The disadvantages of using merchandise are that employees may have lower perceived value of the merchandise and that the company may experience greater administrative problems. Some companies outsource their incentive programs to companies that specialize in the creation and management of such programs.

Managing Sales Territories

The effectiveness of a sales force that must travel to customers is somewhat influenced by management's decisions regarding sales territories. When deciding on territories, sales managers must consider size, shape, routing, and scheduling.

Creating Sales Territories. Several factors enter into the design of a sales territory's size and shape. First, sales managers must construct territories that allow sales potential to be measured. Sales territories often consist of several geographic units, such as census tracts, cities, counties, or states, for which market data are obtainable.

Sales managers usually try to create territories with similar sales potential or requiring about the same amount of work. If territories have equal sales potential, they will almost always be unequal in geographic size. Salespeople with larger territories have to work longer and harder to generate a certain sales volume. Conversely, if sales territories requiring equal amounts of work are created, sales potential for those territories will often vary. If sales personnel are partially or fully compensated through commissions, they will have unequal income potential. Many sales managers try to balance territorial workloads and earning potential by using differential commission rates. At times, sales managers use commercial programs to help them balance sales territories. Although a sales manager seeks equity when developing and maintaining sales territories, some inequities always prevail. A territory's size and shape should also help the sales force provide the best possible customer coverage and should minimize selling costs. Customer density and distribution are important factors.

Routing and Scheduling Salespeople. The geographic size and shape of a sales territory are the most important factors affecting the routing and scheduling of sales calls. Next in importance is the number and distribution of customers within the territory, followed by sales call frequency and duration. Those in charge of routing and scheduling must consider the sequence in which customers are called on, specific roads or transportation schedules to be used, number of calls to be made in a given period, and time of day the calls will occur. In some firms, salespeople plan their own routes and schedules with little or no assistance from the sales manager. In others, the sales manager is responsible. No matter who plans the routing and scheduling, the major goals should be to minimize salespeople's nonselling time (time spent traveling and waiting) and maximize their selling time. Planners should try to achieve these goals so that a salesperson's travel and lodging costs are held to a minimum.

Controlling and Evaluating Sales Force Performance

To control and evaluate sales force performance properly, sales management needs information. A sales manager cannot observe the field sales force daily and thus relies on salespeople's call reports, customer feedback, and invoices. Call reports identify the customers called on and present detailed information about interactions with those clients. Sales personnel often must file work schedules indicating where they plan to be during specific time periods. Data about a salesperson's interactions with customers and prospects can be included in the company's customer relationship management system. This information provides insights about the salesperson's performance.

Dimensions used to measure a salesperson's performance are determined largely by sales objectives, normally set by the sales manager. If an individual's sales objective is stated in terms of sales volume, that person should be evaluated on the basis of sales volume generated. Even if a salesperson is assigned a major objective, he or she is ordinarily expected to achieve several related objectives as well. Thus, salespeople are often judged along several dimensions. Sales managers evaluate many performance indicators, including average number of calls per day, average sales per customer, actual sales relative to sales potential, number of new-customer orders, average cost per call, and average gross profit per customer.

To evaluate a salesperson, a sales manager may compare one or more of these dimensions with predetermined performance standards. However, sales managers commonly compare a salesperson's performance with that of other employees operating under similar selling conditions, or the salesperson's current performance with past performance. Sometimes management judges factors that have less direct bearing on sales performance, such as personal appearance, product knowledge, and ethical standards. One concern is the tendency to reprimand top sellers less severely than poor performers for engaging in unethical selling practices.[26]

After evaluating salespeople, sales managers take any needed corrective action to improve sales force performance. They may adjust performance standards, provide additional training, or try other motivational methods. Corrective action may demand comprehensive changes in the sales force.

green MARKETING

Selling Green Homes

These days, almost everyone seems to be going green, including today's residential building industry. Among those promoting green building is EarthCraft House. Founded in 1999 by the Atlanta Home Builders Association and Southface, EarthCraft House is a residential green building program aiming to build comfortable homes that reduce utility costs and benefit the environment.

As of 2007, EarthCraft House has certified more than 4,000 single-family homes and 1,500 multi-family dwelling units within the Atlanta metropolitan area. Atlanta even boasts six entire EarthCraft communities. EarthCraft House has expanded beyond Georgia to South Carolina, Alabama, Tennessee, and Virginia. All are supported by local state agencies and home builders' associations. Similar organizations exist in Florida (Green Building Coalition) and North Carolina (Healthy Built Homes).

An EarthCraft house can be a newly constructed or a renovated house. To be certified by EarthCraft, a house must meet certain guidelines in energy efficiency, durability, indoor air quality, resource efficiency, waste management, and water conservation. EarthCraft houses reduce more than 1,100 pounds of greenhouse gas emissions each year, are built with as much recycled and quickly renewable materials as possible, and can conserve water and reduce storm water pollution. They have benefits beyond environmental sustainability, including health benefits and cost savings. An EarthCraft home can do away with mold and mildew and virtually obliterate airborne

dust, giving a family a healthier place to live than offered by conventional buildings. In addition to money saved through energy efficiency, two types of mortgage incentives exist to support ownership of EarthCraft houses. An energy mortgage can make it possible for a homebuyer to buy a higher-quality home due to the lower monthly operating costs of an energy-efficient home. Money saved in utility bills can offset higher monthly mortgage payments. The Energy Efficient Mortgage increases a buyer's new-home purchasing power. The Energy Improvement Mortgage can be used to finance energy-efficient upgrades on an existing home. All in all, EarthCraft and others predict that by 2010 about 10 percent of all homes will be green—up from 2 percent in 2006.

Despite their obvious benefits, EarthCraft-certified homes do not sell themselves automatically. Both personal selling and sales promotion efforts help reach potential buyers in a variety of environments. One way potential home buyers can find out about the EarthCraft housing program is through sponsors. These sponsors, called Grand Partners, include companies such as Georgia-Pacific, Home Depot, Whirlpool, John's Mansfield, Integrity Windows and Doors, and many others. These companies provide point-of-purchase materials and demonstrations in their stores or sales offices. Salespeople who want to see their products used in a green building explain the many reasons why a green house is good for society and how an Earth-Craft house can save a family a considerable amount of money over the long run. Additionally, homebuilder organizations such as the Greater Atlanta Homebuilders Association provide information about the EarthCraft house program on their websites. Home builders who have been certified to build EarthCraft houses can also be contacted to learn more about the program. It is up to the homebuilder to inform and persuade a potential buyer about the benefits of an EarthCraft home. Personal selling and sales promotion is a necessity for the EarthCraft house program to make a difference.[b]

The Nature of Sales Promotion

L O 6 To explain what sales promotion activities are and how they are used

Sales promotion is an activity or material, or both, that acts as a direct inducement, offering added value or incentive for the product, to resellers, salespeople, or consumers. It encompasses all promotional activities and materials other than personal selling, advertising, and public relations. Wendy's for example, teamed up with the Rhapsody online music service to promote its combo meals with a free downloadable song from Rhapsody. The code to download the free song is on the bottom of the combo meal's beverage cup.[27] In competitive markets, where products are very similar, sales promotion provides additional inducements that encourage product trial and purchase.

Marketers often use sales promotion to facilitate personal selling, advertising, or both. Companies also employ advertising and personal selling to support sales promotion activities. For example, marketers frequently use advertising to promote contests, free samples, and premiums. The most effective sales promotion efforts are highly interrelated with other promotional activities. Decisions regarding sales promotion often affect advertising and personal selling decisions, and vice versa.

Sales promotion can increase sales by providing extra purchasing incentives. Many opportunities exist to motivate consumers, resellers, and salespeople to take desired actions. Some kinds of sales promotion are designed specifically to stimulate resellers' demand and effectiveness, some are directed at increasing consumer demand, and some focus on both consumers and resellers. Some sales promotion efforts may result in consumer stockpiling of the promoted products, but research suggests that this is a positive outcome by boosting repeat purchases.[28] Regardless of the purpose, marketers must ensure that sales promotion objectives are consistent with the organization's overall objectives, as well as with its marketing and promotion objectives.

When deciding which sales promotion methods to use, marketers must consider several factors, particularly product characteristics (price, size, weight, costs, durability, uses, features, and hazards) and target market characteristics (age, gender, income, location, density, usage rate, and shopping patterns). How products are distributed and the number and types of resellers may determine the type of method used. The competitive and legal environment may also influence the choice.

sales promotion An activity and/or material intended to induce resellers or salespeople to sell a product or consumers to buy it

consumer sales promotion methods Sales promotion techniques that encourage consumers to patronize specific stores or try particular products

coupons Written price reductions used to encourage consumers to buy a specific product

The use of sales promotion has increased dramatically over the last 20 years, primarily at the expense of advertising. This shift in how promotional dollars are used has occurred for several reasons. Heightened concerns about value have made customers more responsive to promotional offers, especially price discounts and point-of-purchase displays. Thanks to their size and access to checkout scanner data, retailers have gained considerable power in the supply chain and are demanding greater promotional efforts from manufacturers to boost retail profits. Declines in brand loyalty have produced an environment in which sales promotions aimed at persuading customers to switch brands are more effective. Finally, the stronger emphasis placed on improving short-term performance results calls for greater use of sales promotion methods that yield quick (although perhaps short-lived) sales increases.[29]

In the remainder of this chapter, we examine several consumer and trade sales promotion methods, including what they entail and what goals they can help marketers achieve.

L O 7 To explore specific consumer sales promotion methods

Consumer Sales Promotion Methods

Consumer sales promotion methods encourage or stimulate consumers to patronize specific retail stores or try particular products. Consumer sales promotion methods initiated by retailers often aim to attract customers to specific locations, whereas those used by manufacturers generally introduce new products or promote established brands. In this section we discuss coupons, cents-off offers, money refunds and rebates, frequent-user incentives, point-of-purchase displays, demonstrations, free samples, premiums, consumer contests and games, and consumer sweepstakes.

Coupons. **Coupons** reduce a product's price and aim to prompt customers to try new or established products, increase sales volume quickly, attract repeat purchasers, or

introduce new package sizes or features. Savings are deducted from the purchase price. Coupons are the most widely used consumer sales promotion technique. Consumer packaged goods manufacturers distribute about 253 billion coupons, saving consumers an estimated $2.6 billion or about 11.5 percent of their grocery bill. At least 86 percent of all consumers use coupons.[30] Coupons redemption rates among Hispanics are higher, ranging from 6 to 24 percent.[31] Figures 18.3 and 18.4 show that consumers' incomes and ages have surprisingly little effect on coupon usage. Although some firms have tried to scale back their use of coupons and other sales promotion methods in favor of an everyday-low-price strategy, some groups of consumers have resisted these efforts, perhaps preferring the sense of achievement they experience from buying products on sale and/or with a coupon.[32]

For best results, coupons should be easily recognized and state the offer clearly. The nature of the product (seasonal demand for it, life cycle stage, frequency of purchase) is the prime consideration in setting up a coupon promotion. Paper coupons are distributed on and inside packages, through freestanding inserts, in print advertising, and through direct mail. Electronic coupons are distributed online, via in-store kiosks, through shelf dispensers in stores, and at checkout counters.[33] When deciding on the distribution method for coupons, marketers should consider strategies and objectives, redemption rates, availability, circulation, and exclusivity. The largest number of coupons distributed are for household cleaners, pet food and treats, and room-and-rug deodorizers. The coupon distribution and redemption arena has become very competitive. To avoid losing customers, many grocery stores will redeem any coupons offered by competitors. Also, to draw customers to their stores, grocers double and sometimes even triple the value of customers' coupons.

Coupons

Minute Maid offers coupons to promote product trial and to increase the quantity purchased.

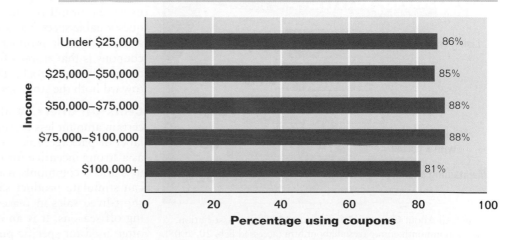

figure 18.3

EFFECT OF INCOME ON COUPON USAGE

Income	Percentage using coupons
Under $25,000	86%
$25,000–$50,000	85%
$50,000–$75,000	88%
$75,000–$100,000	88%
$100,000+	81%

Source: "All About Coupons," Promotion Marketing Association, www.coupon-month.com/pages/allabout.htm (accessed Feb. 20, 2008).

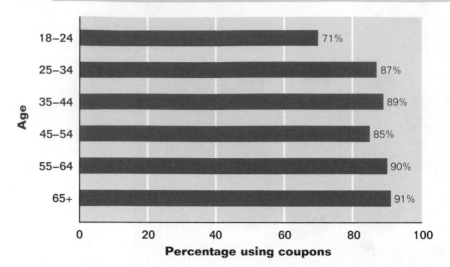

figure 18.4

EFFECT OF AGE ON COUPON USAGE

Age:
- 18–24: 71%
- 25–34: 87%
- 35–44: 89%
- 45–54: 85%
- 55–64: 90%
- 65+: 91%

Percentage using coupons (x-axis: 0, 20, 40, 60, 80, 100)

Source: "All About Coupons," Promotion Marketing Association, www.couponmonth.com/pages/allabout.htm (accessed Feb. 20, 2008).

cents-off offer A promotion that allows buyers to pay less than the regular price to encourage purchase

Coupons offer several advantages. Print advertisements with coupons are often more effective at generating brand awareness than are print ads without coupons. Generally, the larger the coupon's cash offer, the better the recognition generated. Coupons reward present product users, win back former users, and encourage purchases in larger quantities. Because they are returned, coupons also help a manufacturer determine whether it reached the intended target market. The advantages of using electronic coupons over paper coupons include lower cost per redemption, greater targeting ability, improved data-gathering capabilities, and greater experimentation capabilities to determine optimal face values and expiration cycles.[34]

Drawbacks of coupon use include fraud and misredemption, which can be expensive for manufacturers. The Coupon Information Council estimates that coupon fraud—including counterfeit Internet coupons as well as coupons cashed in under false retailer names—amounts to $500 million a year in the United States.[35] Another disadvantage, according to some experts, is that coupons are losing their value; because so many manufacturers offer them, consumers have learned not to buy without some incentive, whether a coupon, a rebate, or a refund. Furthermore, brand loyalty among heavy coupon users has diminished, and many consumers redeem coupons only for products they normally buy. It is believed that about three-fourths of coupons are redeemed by people already using the brand on the coupon. Thus, coupons have questionable success as an incentive for consumers to try a new brand or product. An additional problem with coupons is that stores often do not have enough of the coupon item in stock. This situation generates ill will toward both the store and the product.

Cents-Off Offers. With **cents-off offers,** buyers pay a certain amount less than the regular price shown on the label or package. Like coupons, this method can serve as a strong incentive for trying new or unfamiliar products and is commonly used in product introductions. It can stimulate product sales, multiple purchases, yield short-lived sales increases, and promote products during off seasons. It is an easy method to control and is often used for specific purposes. If used on an ongoing

snapshot

Percentage using coupons while . . .

- Living with parents — 10% OFF Expires Dec 31, 2010 — **51%**
- In college — 2 for 1 — **54%**
- Living on own — 20% OFF with purchase of $50 — **78%**
- Married or living with a partner — Buy one get one FREE — **88%**
- Maintaining a family — $5 OFF Store coupon — **92%**

Source: "All About Coupons," Promotion Marketing Association, www.couponmonth.com/pages/allabout.htm (accessed Feb. 20, 2008).

RESPONSIBLE marketing?

Saving with Internet Coupons

ISSUE: Are online coupons good for everyone?

Sales promotions that use coupons can stimulate consumer purchases. The real advantage of using coupons is developing loyalty repeat purchases. The Internet has provided an opportunity to obtain coupons and information that will allow discounts. The search for coupons and retailers who will accept them has involved into a science for some people. Entire websites, such as **www.coupons.com** or **www.coolsavings.com,** are devoted to the distribution of coupons and coupon codes, giving the consumer the ammunition he or she needs to get the lowest price on a product.

Internet sites such as Reesycakes.com post apparel discount codes that consumers can use to buy reduced-price merchandise. Shopstyle.com provides the opportunity to locate all the sites carrying the same item. A shopper can visit Reesycakes.com to match retailer coupons to desired merchandise that was located on Shopstyle.com. Once the information is acquired, the consumer can contact the retailer of choice to use the coupon. The game continues, and many wonder why retailers permit some consumers to bargain and search for discounts while other dedicated customers are paying full price. The answer is the nature of the highly competitive retail market. The bottom line is that a retailer can develop consumer loyalty by offering online coupons, and repeat sales support sales growth. It is much cheaper for a retailer to sell an item over the Internet than to have consumers phoning and inquiring about discounts and coupon acceptability. So those of us who do not wish to be "coupon rats" end up paying higher prices for the same product.[c]

basis, however, cents-off offers reduce the price for customers who would buy at the regular price and may also cheapen a product's image. In addition, the method often requires special handling by retailers who are responsible for giving the discount at the point of sale.

Money Refunds. With **money refunds,** consumers submit proof of purchase and are mailed a specific amount of money. Usually manufacturers demand multiple product purchases before consumers qualify for money refunds. Marketers employ money refunds as an alternative to coupons to stimulate sales. Money refunds, used primarily to promote trial use of a product, are relatively low in cost. However, they sometimes generate a low response rate, and thus have limited impact on sales.

Rebates. With **rebates,** the consumer is sent a specified amount of money for making a single product purchase. Rebates are generally given on more expensive products than money refunds and are used to encourage customers. Marketers also use rebates to reinforce brand loyalty, provide promotion buzz for salespeople, and advertise the product. On larger items, such as cars, rebates are often given at the point of sale. Most rebates, however, especially on smaller items, are given after the sale, usually through a mail-in process.

One problem with money refunds and rebates is that many people perceive the redemption process as too complicated. Only about 40 percent of individuals who purchase rebated products actually apply for the rebates.[36] Because of this, many marketers allow customers to apply for a rebate online, which eliminates the need for forms that may confuse customers and frustrate retailers. Consumers may also have negative perceptions of manufacturers' reasons for offering rebates. They may believe the products are untested or have not sold well. If these perceptions are not changed, rebate offers may actually degrade product image and desirability. On the other hand, rebates and low interest rates have been found to have a positive effect on car and truck sales.[37]

Frequent-User Incentives. Greeting cards aren't the only ones offered by Hallmark. To reward loyal customers, the company offers the Hallmark Gold Crown Card that allows frequent card buyers to accrue points that are redeemable for merchandise.[38] Many firms develop incentive programs to reward customers who engage in repeat (frequent) purchases. For example, most major airlines offer frequent-flier programs that reward customers who have flown a specified number of miles with free tickets for additional travel. Frequent-user incentives foster customer loyalty to a specific company or group of cooperating companies. They are favored by service businesses such as airlines, auto rental agencies, hotels, and local coffee shops. At Neiman Marcus, the InCircle Rewards program rewards loyal shoppers with dollar-for-dollar spent benefits, but they must spend $5,000 per year to be eligible. Indeed, research shows that 93 percent of consumers with household incomes above $100,000 participate in frequent-user programs, whereas only 58 percent of shoppers with incomes below $50,000 participate.[39] Frequent-user programs not only reward loyal customers but also generate data that can contribute significant information about customers that helps marketers foster desirable customer relationships.[40]

money refund A sales promotion technique that offers consumers a specified amount of money when they mail in a proof of purchase, usually for multiple product purchases

rebate A sales promotion technique in which a consumer receives a specified amount of money for making a single product purchase

TWO FUN CARDS FOR $108 OR —

SAVE $10 ON SINGLE-DAY ADMISSION

With two SeaWorld® San Diego Fun Cards get unlimited admission for all of 2008* for less than two full-priced single-day admissions. Or choose $10 off on single-day admission.

Experience seasonal park events like Spring into Night and Summer Nights. Plus don't miss the new Sesame Street 4-D movie premiering March 15 and the Sesame Street Bay of Play, an all-new play area coming your way in May.

Hurry, offers end April 30, 2008.
Visit SeaWorldSanDiego.com and enter Promo Code: SWCAAASpr08

*Not valid May 25, July 4 & 5 and Aug. 31, 2008. These offers also available at SeaWorld San Diego or call (800) 25-SHAMU press 14. Other restrictions may apply. Offers require AAA membership card for savings. Not valid with any other offers, promotions, discounts or Passport purchase. Price based on ages 10+. Limit three Fun Card two-packs per purchase. Limit six single-day admissions per purchase. © 2008 Busch Entertainment Corp. All rights reserved. ™/© 2008 Sesame Workshop.

SeaWorld
SeaWorldSanDiego.com

Show Your Card & Save®

Discount Offers

SeaWorld provides discounts on admission tickets to encourage multiple purchases.

point-of-purchase (P.O.P.) materials Signs, window displays, display racks, and similar devices used to attract customers

demonstration A sales promotion method a manufacturer uses temporarily to encourage trial use and purchase of a product or to show how a product works

free sample A sample of a product given out to encourage trial and purchase

premium An item offered free or at a minimal cost as a bonus for purchasing a product

Point-of-Purchase Materials and Demonstrations. **Point-of-purchase (P.O.P.) materials** include outdoor signs, window displays, counter pieces, display racks, and self-service cartons. Innovations in P.O.P. displays include sniff-teasers, which give off a product's aroma in the store as consumers walk within a radius of four feet, and computerized interactive displays. These items, often supplied by producers, attract attention, inform customers, and encourage retailers to carry particular products. A retailer is likely to use point-of-purchase materials if they are attractive, informative, well constructed, and in harmony with the store's image.

Demonstrations are excellent attention getters. Manufacturers offer them temporarily to encourage trial use and purchase of a product or to show how a product works. Because labor costs can be extremely high, demonstrations are not used widely. They can be highly effective for promoting certain types of products, such as appliances, cosmetics, and cleaning supplies. Even automobiles can be demonstrated, not only by a salesperson but also by the prospective buyer during a test drive. Cosmetics marketers, such as Merle Norman and Clinique, sometimes offer potential customers "makeovers" to demonstrate product benefits and proper application.

Free Samples. Marketers use **free samples** to stimulate trial of a product, increase sales volume in the early stages of a product's life cycle, and obtain desirable distribution. Schick, for example, gave away 200,000 Quattro for Women razors outside of office buildings in Chicago, New York, Philadelphia, and San Francisco.[41] Sampling is the most expensive sales promotion method because production and distribution—at local events, by mail or door-to-door delivery, online, in stores, and on packages—entail high costs. However, it can also be one of the most effective sales promotion methods: a survey by the Promotion Marketing Association's Product Sampling Council found that 92 percent of respondents said they would buy a new product they had sampled and liked. Nonetheless, sampling's expense remains a key reason why it is not used more often.[42]

Many consumers prefer to get their samples by mail. Other consumers like to sample new food products at supermarkets or to try samples of new recipes featuring foods they already like. In designing a free sample, marketers should consider factors such as seasonal demand for the product, market characteristics, and prior advertising. Free samples usually are inappropriate for slow-turnover products. Despite high costs, use of sampling is increasing. In a given year, almost three-fourths of consumer product companies may use sampling. Distribution of free samples through websites such as StartSampling.com and FreeSamples.com is growing.

Premiums. **Premiums** are items offered free or at a minimal cost as a bonus for purchasing a product. Like the prize in the Cracker Jack box, premiums are used to attract competitors' customers, introduce different sizes of established products, add variety to other promotional efforts, and stimulate consumer loyalty. Creativity is essential when using premiums; to stand out and achieve a significant number of redemptions, the premium must match both the target audience and the brand's image. Premiums must also be easily recognizable and desirable. Premiums are placed on or inside packages and can also be distributed by retailers or through the mail.

Examples include a service station giving a free carwash with a fill-up, a free toothbrush with a tube of toothpaste, and a free plastic storage box with the purchase of Kraft Cheese Singles.

Consumer Contests. In **consumer contests,** individuals compete for prizes based on their analytical or creative skills. This method can be used to generate retail traffic and frequency of exposure to promotional messages. Contestants are usually more highly involved in consumer contests than in games or sweepstakes, even though total participation may be lower. Contests may also be used in conjunction with other sales promotional methods, such as coupons. For example, Borders invited its Reward loyalty club members to submit essays about New Orleans to win a trip to the New Orleans Jazz & Heritage Festival.[43]

Consumer Games. In **consumer games,** individuals compete for prizes based primarily on chance—often by collecting game pieces such as bottle caps or a sticker on a carton of french fries. Because collecting multiple pieces may be necessary to win or increase an individual's chances of winning, the game stimulates repeated business. Development and management of consumer games is often outsourced to an independent public relations firm, which can help marketers to navigate federal and state laws that regulate games. Although games may stimulate sales temporarily, there is no evidence to suggest that they affect a company's long-term sales.

Marketers considering games should exercise care. Problems or errors may anger customers and could result in a lawsuit. McDonald's' wildly popular Monopoly game promotion, in which customers collect Monopoly real estate pieces on drink and french fry packages, has been tarnished by both fraud and lawsuits. After six successful years, McDonald's was forced to end the annual promotion when a crime ring, including employees of the promotional firm running the game, were convicted of stealing millions of dollars in winning game pieces. McDonald's later reintroduced the Monopoly game with heightened security. However, the Monopoly promotion is once again under scrutiny as it is the focus of a class-action lawsuit filed by Burger King franchisees, who claim their customers were lured away by the false promises of McDonald's' game.[44]

Sweepstakes. Entrants in a **consumer sweepstakes** submit their names for inclusion in a drawing for prizes. Kraft Foods, for example, sponsored a sweepstakes on packages of its Ritz, Wheat Thins, and Triscuit crackers adorned with photos of celebrity cook Rachel Ray. Participants looked for codes on the boxes to enter on a website to win prizes such as Rachel Ray cookware and cookbooks.[45] Sweepstakes are employed more often than consumer contests and tend to attract a greater number of participants. However, contestants are usually more involved in consumer contests and games than in sweepstakes, even though total participation may be lower. Contests, games, and sweepstakes may be used in conjunction with other sales promotion methods, such as coupons.

Trade Sales Promotion Methods

To encourage resellers, especially retailers, to carry their products and promote them effectively, producers use trade sales promotion methods. **Trade sales promotion methods** attempt to persuade wholesalers and retailers to carry a producer's products and market them more aggressively. Marketers use trade sales methods for many reasons, including countering the effect of lower-priced store brands, passing along a discount to a price-sensitive market segment, boosting brand exposure among target consumers, or providing additional incentives to move excess inventory or counteract competitors. Spending on trade sales promotion has grown in recent years to account for about 70 percent of a manufacturer's marketing budget, making it the second-largest manufacturer expense after the cost of goods.[46] These methods include buying allowances, buy-back allowances, scan-back allowances, merchandise allowances, cooperative advertising, dealer listings, free merchandise, dealer loaders, premium or push money, and sales contests.

consumer contests Sales promotion methods in which individuals compete for prizes based on their analytical or creative skills

consumer games Sales promotion methods in which individuals compete for prizes based primarily on chance

consumer sweepstakes A sales promotion in which entrants submit their names for inclusion in a drawing for prizes

trade sales promotion methods Methods intended to persuade wholesalers and retailers to carry a producer's products and market them aggressively

L O 8 To explore trade sales promotion methods

Trade Allowances. Many manufacturers offer trade allowances to encourage resellers to carry a product or stock more of it. One such trade allowance is a **buying allowance,** a temporary price reduction offered to resellers for purchasing specified quantities of a product. A soap producer, for example, might give retailers $1 for each case of soap purchased. Such offers provide an incentive for resellers to handle new products, achieve temporary price reductions, or stimulate purchase of items in larger-than-normal quantities. The buying allowance, which takes the form of money, yields profits to resellers and is simple and straightforward. There are no restrictions on how resellers use the money, which increases the method's effectiveness. One drawback of buying allowances is that customers may buy "forward"—that is, buy large amounts that keep them supplied for many months. Another problem is that competitors may match (or beat) the reduced price, which can lower profits for all sellers.

A **buy-back allowance** is a sum of money that a producer gives to a reseller for each unit the reseller buys after an initial promotional deal is over. This method is a secondary incentive in which the total amount of money resellers receive is proportional to their purchases during an initial consumer promotion, such as a coupon offer. Buy-back allowances foster cooperation during an initial sales promotion effort and stimulate repurchase afterward. The main disadvantage of this method is expense.

A **scan-back allowance** is a manufacturer's reward to retailers based on the number of pieces moved through the retailers' scanners during a specific time period. To participate in scan-back programs, retailers are usually expected to pass along savings to consumers through special pricing. Scan-backs are becoming widely used by manufacturers because they link trade spending directly to product movement at the retail level.

A **merchandise allowance** is a manufacturer's agreement to pay resellers certain amounts of money for providing promotional efforts such as advertising or point-of-purchase displays. This method is best suited to high-volume, high-profit, easily handled products. A drawback is that some retailers perform activities at a minimally acceptable level simply to obtain allowances. Before paying retailers, manufacturers usually verify their performance. Manufacturers hope that retailers' additional promotional efforts will yield substantial sales increases.

Cooperative Advertising and Dealer Listings. **Cooperative advertising** is an arrangement in which a manufacturer agrees to pay a certain amount of a retailer's media costs for advertising the manufacturer's products. The amount allowed is usually based on the quantities purchased. As with merchandise allowances, a retailer must show proof that advertisements did appear before the manufacturer pays the agreed-on portion of the advertising costs. These payments give retailers additional funds for advertising. Some retailers exploit cooperative-advertising agreements by crowding too many products into one advertisement. Not all available cooperative-advertising dollars are used. Some retailers cannot afford to advertise, while others can afford it but do not want to advertise. A large proportion of all cooperative-advertising dollars is spent on newspaper advertisements.

Dealer listings are advertisements promoting a product and identifying participating retailers that sell the product. Dealer listings can influence retailers to carry the product, build traffic at the retail level, and encourage consumers to buy the product at participating dealers.

Free Merchandise and Gifts. Manufacturers sometimes offer **free merchandise** to resellers that purchase a stated quantity of products. Occasionally free merchandise is used as payment for allowances provided through other sales promotion methods. To avoid handling and bookkeeping problems, the "free" merchandise usually takes the form of a reduced invoice.

A **dealer loader** is a gift to a retailer that purchases a specified quantity of merchandise. Dealer loaders are often used to obtain special display efforts from retailers by offering essential display parts as premiums. For example, a manufacturer might design a display that includes a sterling silver tray as a major component and give the

buying allowance A temporary price reduction to resellers for purchasing specified quantities of a product

buy-back allowance A sum of money given to a reseller for each unit bought after an initial promotion deal is over

scan-back allowance A manufacturer's reward to retailers based on the number of pieces scanned

merchandise allowance A manufacturer's agreement to pay resellers certain amounts of money for providing special promotional efforts, such as setting up and maintaining a display

cooperative advertising An arrangement in which a manufacturer agrees to pay a certain amount of a retailer's media costs for advertising the manufacturer's products

dealer listing An advertisement that promotes a product and identifies the names of participating retailers that sell the product

free merchandise A manufacturer's reward given to resellers that purchase a stated quantity of products

dealer loader A gift, often part of a display, given to a retailer that purchases a specified quantity of merchandise

tray to the retailer. Marketers use dealer loaders to obtain new distributors and to push larger quantities of goods.

Premium Money. **Premium money (or push money)** is additional compensation offered by the manufacturer to salespeople as an incentive to push a line of goods. This method is appropriate when personal selling is an important part of the marketing effort; it is not effective for promoting products sold through self-service. Premium money often helps a manufacturer obtain a commitment from the sales force, but it can be very expensive.

Sales Contest. A **sales contest** is designed to motivate distributors, retailers, and sales personnel by recognizing outstanding achievements. To be effective, this method must be equitable for all individuals involved. One advantage is that it can achieve participation at all distribution levels. Positive effects may be temporary, however, and prizes are usually expensive.

premium money (or push money) Extra compensation to salespeople for pushing a line of goods

sales contest A sales promotion method used to motivate distributors, retailers, and sales personnel through recognition of outstanding achievements

SUMMARY

Personal selling is the process of informing customers and persuading them to purchase products through paid personal communication in an exchange situation. The three general purposes of personal selling are finding prospects, persuading them to buy, and keeping customers satisfied.

Many salespeople, either consciously or unconsciously, move through a general selling process as they sell products. In prospecting, the salesperson develops a list of potential customers. Before contacting prospects, the salesperson conducts a preapproach that involves finding and analyzing information about prospects and their needs. The approach is the manner in which the salesperson contacts potential customers. During the sales presentation, the salesperson must attract and hold the prospect's attention to stimulate interest in and desire for the product. If possible, the salesperson should handle objections as they arise. During the closing, the salesperson asks the prospect to buy the product or products. After a successful closing, the salesperson must follow up the sale.

In developing a sales force, marketing managers consider which types of salespeople will sell the firm's products most effectively. The three classifications of salespeople are order getters, order takers, and support personnel. Order getters inform both current customers and new prospects and persuade them to buy. Order takers seek repeat sales and fall into two categories: inside order takers and field order takers. Sales support personnel facilitate selling, but their duties usually extend beyond making sales. The three types of support personnel are missionary, trade, and technical salespeople. The roles of salespeople are changing. Team selling involves the salesperson joining with people from the firm's financial, engineering, and other functional areas. Relationship selling involves building mutually beneficial long-term associations with a customer through regular communications over prolonged periods of time.

Sales force management is an important determinant of a firm's success because the sales force is directly responsible for generating the organization's sales revenue. Major decision areas and activities are establishing sales force objectives; determining sales force size; recruiting, selecting, training, compensating, and motivating salespeople; managing sales territories; and controlling and evaluating sales force performance.

Sales objectives should be stated in precise, measurable terms and specify the time period and geographic areas involved. The size of the sales force must be adjusted occasionally because a firm's marketing plans change along with markets and forces in the marketing environment.

Recruiting and selecting salespeople involve attracting and choosing the right type of salesperson to maintain an effective sales force. When developing a training program, managers must consider a variety of dimensions, such as who should be trained, what should be taught, and how training should occur. Compensation of salespeople involves formulating and administering a compensation plan that attracts, motivates, and retains the right types of salespeople. Motivated salespeople should translate into high productivity. Managing sales territories focuses on such factors as size, shape, routing, and scheduling. To control and evaluate sales force performance, sales managers use information obtained through salespeople's call reports, customer feedback, and invoices.

Sales promotion is an activity or a material (or both) that acts as a direct inducement, offering added value or incentive for the product to resellers, salespeople, or consumers. Marketers use sales promotion to identify and attract new customers, introduce new products, and increase reseller inventories. Sales promotion techniques fall into two general categories: consumer and trade. Consumer sales promotion methods encourage consumers to patronize specific stores or try a particular product. These sales promotion methods include coupons; cents-off offers; money refunds and rebates; frequent-user incentives; point-of-purchase displays; demonstrations; free samples and premiums; and consumer contests, games, and sweepstakes. Trade sales promotion techniques can motivate resellers to handle a manufacturer's products and market them aggressively. These sales promotion techniques include buying allowances, buy-back allowances, scan-back allowances, merchandise allowances, cooperative advertising, dealer listings, free merchandise, dealer loaders, premium (or push) money, and sales contests.

IMPORTANT TERMS

Personal selling, 518
Prospecting, 520
Approach, 520
Closing, 521
Order getter, 523
Order takers, 524
Support personnel, 524
Missionary salespeople, 524
Trade salespeople, 524
Technical salespeople, 524
Team selling, 525
Relationship selling, 525

Recruiting, 526
Straight salary compensation plan, 529
Straight commission compensation plan, 529
Combination compensation plan, 529
Sales promotion, 534
Consumer sales promotion methods, 534
Coupons, 534
Cents-off offer, 536
Money refund, 537

Rebate, 537
Point-of-purchase (P.O.P.) materials, 538
Demonstration, 538
Free sample, 538
Premium, 538
Consumer contests, 539
Consumer games, 539
Consumer sweepstakes, 539
Trade sales promotion methods, 539
Buying allowance, 540

Buy-back allowance, 540
Scan-back allowance, 540
Merchandise allowance, 540
Cooperative advertising, 540
Dealer listing, 540
Free merchandise, 540
Dealer loader, 540
Premium money (or push money), 541
Sales contest, 541

DISCUSSION & REVIEW QUESTIONS

1. What is personal selling? How does personal selling differ from other types of promotional activities?

2. What are the primary purposes of personal selling?

3. Identify the elements of the personal selling process. Must a salesperson include all these elements when selling a product to a customer? Why or why not?

4. How does a salesperson find and evaluate prospects? Do you consider any of these methods to be ethically questionable? Explain.

5. Are order getters more aggressive or creative than order takers? Why or why not?

6. Why are team selling and relationship selling becoming more prevalent?

7. Identify several characteristics of effective sales objectives.

8. How should a sales manager establish criteria for selecting sales personnel? What do you think are the general characteristics of a good salesperson?

9. What major issues or questions should management consider when developing a training program for the sales force?

10. Explain the major advantages and disadvantages of the three basic methods of compensating salespeople. In general, which method would you prefer? Why?

11. What major factors should be taken into account when designing the size and shape of a sales territory?

12. How does a sales manager, who cannot be with each salesperson in the field on a daily basis, control the performance of sales personnel?

13. What is sales promotion? Why is it used?

14. For each of the following, identify and describe three techniques and give several examples: (a) consumer sales promotion methods and (b) trade sales promotion methods.

15. What types of sales promotion methods have you observed recently? Comment on their effectiveness.

APPLICATION QUESTIONS

1. Briefly describe an experience you have had with a salesperson at a clothing store or an automobile dealership. Describe the steps the salesperson used. Did the salesperson skip any steps? What did the salesperson do well? Not so well? Would you describe the salesperson as an order getter, an order taker, or a support salesperson? Why? Did the salesperson perform more than one of these functions?

2. Leap Athletic Shoe, Inc., a newly formed company, is in the process of developing a sales strategy. Market research indicates sales management should segment the market into five regional territories. The sales potential for the North region is $1.2 million; for the West region, $1 million; for the Central region, $1.3 million; for the South Central region, $1.1 million; and for the Southeast region, $1 million. The firm wishes to maintain some control over the training and sales processes because of the unique features of its new product line, but Leap marketers realize the salespeople need to be fairly aggressive in their efforts to break into these markets. They would like to provide the incentive needed for the extra selling effort. What type of sales force compensation method would you recommend to Leap? Why?

3. Consumer sales promotions aim to increase sales of a particular retail store or product. Identify a familiar type of retail store or product. Recommend at least three sales promotion methods that could effectively promote the store or product. Explain why you would use these methods.

4. Producers use trade sales promotions to encourage resellers to promote their products more effectively. Identify which method or methods of sales promotion a producer might use in the following situations, and explain why the method would be appropriate.

   a. A golf ball manufacturer wants to encourage retailers to add a new type of golf ball to current product offerings.

   b. A life insurance company wants to increase sales of its universal life products, which have been lagging recently (the company has little control over sales activities).

   c. A light bulb manufacturer with an overproduction of 100-watt bulbs wants to encourage its grocery store chain resellers to increase their bulb inventories.

INTERNET EXERCISE

Visit **www.cengage.com/marketing/pride-ferrell** for resources to help you master the material in this chapter, plus materials that will help you expand your marketing knowledge, including Internet exercise updates, ACE Self-Tests, hotlinks to companies featured in this chapter, and much more.

TerrAlign

TerrAlign offers consulting services and software products designed to help a firm maximize control and deployment of its field sales representatives. Review its website at **www.terralign.com.**

1. Identify three features of TerrAlign software that are likely to benefit salespeople.

2. Identify three features of TerrAlign software that are likely to benefit sales managers.

3. Why might field sales professionals object to the use of software from TerrAlign?

developing your MARKETING PLAN

When developing its marketing strategy, a company must consider the different forms of communication that are necessary to reach a variety of customers. Several types of promotion may be required. Knowledge of the advantages and disadvantages of each promotional element is necessary when developing the marketing plan. Consider the information in this chapter when evaluating your promotional mix:

1. Review the various types of salespeople described in this chapter. Given your promotional objectives (from Chapter 16), do any of these types of salespeople have a place in your promotional plan?

2. Identify the resellers in your distribution channel. Discuss the role that trade sales promotions to these resellers could play in the development of your promotional plan.

3. Evaluate each type of consumer sales promotion as it relates to accomplishing your promotional objectives.

The information obtained from these questions should assist you in developing various aspects of your marketing plan found in the *Interactive Marketing Plan* exercise at **www.cengage.com/marketing/pride-ferrell.**

globalEDGE

1. Your firm has recently developed a revolutionary new chemical that is widely applicable, nearly cost-less, and does not harm the environment. However, before widespread production, you must identify the largest manufacturing companies worldwide that may be interested in your new product. The *Industry-Week*'s IW 1000 ranking should prove useful for this task. This can be found using the search term "largest manufacturing companies" at **http://globaledge .msu.edu/ibrd.** From there, follow the link to the IW 1000 Database and then choose the Chemicals industry as a choice criterion. What are the ten largest chemical companies as ranked by sales? Because your firm is based in the United States and focused on the domestic market, which companies are feasible to target for a comprehensive sales

strategy? If you were planning to enter a new market, which would it be?

2. Your Seattle-based maritime business is currently enjoying profitable conditions. Because your firm and national competitors have been catching an overabundance of fresh shrimp in recent weeks, you have noticed that the domestic market is currently saturated. You are unsure of the options that may exist internationally, so you decide to export through a local agent to assist in selling your products overseas. Find potential agents by using the search term "products overseas" at **http://globaledge .msu.edu/ibrd** to reach the FASonline website. Enter appropriate criteria. How many agents do you find that are near your offices when you search FASon-line's website? Which will you choose?

video **CASE 18.1**

IBM Sales Force Sells Solutions

In recent years, IBM has worked hard to reposition itself from a supplier of information technology hardware and software to a company that provides business solution services. In their own words, "We measure ourselves today by how well we help clients solve their biggest and most pressing problems." Obviously, successful problem solving leads to an increase in customers and an increase in goods and services sold.

Although IBM is still the world's largest provider of IT hardware and software, it regards this as the means to an end. The company relies heavily on its global sales force to make the transition from a goods to a solution services provider. The enormous task of changing the company's focus cannot be overstated.

Personal selling has always been a fundamental aspect of IBM's business philosophy and is one of the foundations of the company's success: IBM has customers in 174 countries who speak 165 languages. The company's sales force makes 18 billion client contacts a year and addresses 350,000 sales opportunities per day.

As in all organizations, IBM's change comes from the top. Last year Samuel J. Palmisano, IBM's chair, president, and chief executive officer, led a process of examining and redefining the company's core values. One of the first core values identified was "dedication to every client's success." From a sales perspective, this is achieved through consultative or solution selling, which

brings all of IBM's resources and expertise together to solve customer problems. This requires that the sales force thoroughly understand their customers' business environments and deliver the correct answers to their questions. As Palmisano points out, the company's business model has changed. It used to be "invent, build, and sell." Today it is "craft, solve, and deliver the solution."

Not surprisingly, solution selling has brought new challenges to the sales force. IBM believes that sales-people are not born, but trained. The company puts its salespeople through an extensive five-month training

program that encompasses three major areas of focus: IBM's commitment to its customers, techniques of collaborative selling, and techniques for gaining understanding of a company's resources and infrastructure. For large projects, salespeople often work in teams comprised of one sales leader and four to five sales specialists who have expertise relevant to the project.

For the most part, IBM salespeople use the Socratic method of selling. This involves asking open-ended questions to better understand their customers' problems, desires, and needs. As might be expected, solution (or pull) selling is more complex than product (or push) selling. The salesperson's role in solution selling is to gather information concerning the customer's business problem, provide a point of view, solve the problem (with the help of other team members), and determine the potential impact on the customer's business once the recommended solution is implemented.

The most accurate and important indicator of the success of the solutions service is customer reaction. An example of IBM achieving its sales objective of "insuring our clients are successful" is their Sales Connections Program. Actuate, an Independent Software Vendor (ISV) and IBM customer, used the Sales Connection website to express concerns about a customer dragging its feet on an applications deal. IBM discovered that the person Actuate was working with lacked the authority to close the deal. IBM provided Actuate with the correct contact person and the sale was quickly closed.

Another example is IBM's Software-as-a-Service program, which delivers software via the Internet. This eliminates the need for companies to buy, build, manage, and maintain applications that address areas such as accounting, human resources, customer relationship management, and enterprise resource planning. Companies benefit from this concept because they can reduce their operational costs and maintenance expenses, therefore increasing profits. In an effort to sell this service more broadly, an IBM sales team designed a sales incentive that awards a 10 percent referral fee and additional marketing incentives to IBM customers that submit leads resulting in business for IBM. The marketing incentives include direct mail, telemarketing, advertising, and technical resources to help businesses generate leads. This program enabled one of IBM's customers to generate 800 sales leads in one year.

With this kind of dedication, there is little doubt that IBM's solutions service will continue its success.[47]

Questions for Discussion

1. What are the advantages for IBM in selling solutions rather than goods?
2. Why is solution selling more complex than hardware and software selling? Identify the sales skills needed for each approach.
3. What are some ways that IBM can measure the effectiveness of its solutions or consultative selling?

CASE 18.2

Fraud Forces Sub Club Closing

With 21,000 outlets, Subway Restaurants is the fastest-growing fast-food chain. It is so successful that the number of sandwiches sold annually would wrap around the earth at least six times. Subway's success is based on high-quality food and loyal customers drawn by Subway's offerings of healthy sandwiches made to order and Sub Club stamps. Subway's Sub Club has been a staple of the chain for over 25 years and is one of the most popular frequent-user incentive programs ever. Under the Sub Club system, customers would be rewarded with a stamp when purchasing a six-inch sandwich (two stamps for a foot-long sandwich). After collecting eight stamps, the customer received a free six-inch sandwich. The stamps were dutifully collected by many loyal customers and helped increase Subway's repeat business. If the club was so popular with customers, why did Subway abruptly shut it down?

Aside from posting signs in its restaurants, Subway made no official announcements of its decision to end its 25-year program. The posted signs indicated only that the program was closing, without providing the reason for Subway's decision. Many loyal customers vented on blogs and online message boards over the sudden and mysterious demise of the club. Media soon began pointing to fraud as the culprit. It turns out that, armed with laser printers and photo-editing software, it was relatively easy for counterfeiters to reproduce the Sub Club card and stamps, and franchisees were redeeming these fake stamps and losing money. The imitation stamps were being distributed online, especially through eBay. (At one point, eBay had over 50 separate auctions of Sub Club stamps and cards.) The counterfeiters were selling the stamps in large quantities for thousands of dollars. Two Virginia Tech students were arrested for forging stamps when reported by the owner of a local Subway franchise.

Counterfeiting wasn't the only method of fraud. A portion of the Sub Club stamp auctions on eBay featured authentic stamps, some in quantities as large as an entire roll. These authentic stamps were being stolen by Subway employees. The stolen stamps hurt franchisees because they were redeemed without accompanying sales. Although Subway insists that the amount of money lost via stamp fraud was not significant, it is apparent that the problem was significant enough to end the Sub Club.

The Sub Club is not the only customer loyalty program to be targeted by counterfeiters. Cold Stone Creamery also had to discontinue its customer loyalty program due to counterfeiting. Its punch-card program rewarded customers with a free scoop of ice cream when their cards were completely punched.

Franchisees have been evaluating Sub Club alternatives, and some have been tested in certain markets. One is the plastic Subway Cash Card, which can be loaded with up to $100 for purchases at any Subway. In initial tests, customers bought more and completed purchases faster with the cards than with cash, and the program allows Subway to print targeted promotional offers on each cardholder's receipt. Subway has even established a website to make card management easier (**www.mysubwaycard.com**). Card holders can add money, check point totals, or order cards to be sent as gifts.

Another alternative that is being tested in 15 states is the Subway Rewards Card. In this program, customers receive one point for every dollar spent with the card. They can later redeem points for menu items such as a six-inch sub (50 points), soft drinks (20 points), a cookie (10 points), or a foot-long sandwich (75 points).

Subway continues to float ideas to replace its submerged Sub Club; surely a successful customer loyalty program will surface.[48]

Questions for Discussion

1. What is the major reason for Subway to have the Sub Club?
2. Given that Subway is a large, well-established organization with over 21,000 stores, does Subway need a customer loyalty program like the Sub Club?
3. If Subway wanted to restart the Sub Club, what recommendations would you make to avoid the problems that led to the Club being closed?

strategic CASE 7

T-Mobile Promotes with Celebrity Sidekicks

Look out, America, here comes Big Pink! With the purchase of U.S. wireless carrier Voice Stream Wireless, Germany's Deutsche Telekom became the first European company to cross the Atlantic and join the highly competitive U.S. wireless phone market. Deutsche Telekom envisioned becoming the world's first single-branded international cellular phone service. Operating as T-Mobil in Germany, it added an "e" for a more English-friendly calling card, and T-Mobile, in six different countries including the United States, was born.

Promoting a product in any market can be difficult, but T-Mobile was faced with the unique challenge of promoting its single brand in six different markets and across continents. Nikesh Arora, who heads up global marketing for T-Mobile, was up for the challenge: "On the marketing side, you need a one-brand approach, which means you have common products and common ways of representing the business. We have to make sure we have exciting offers for our customers in every market," says Arora. "I have to build a solid, sustainable, and differentiated brand." When developing the promotion strategy, Arora and his team decided to look at the positive: "We had to sit down and decide what is common across all of the markets and what the key strength of T-Mobile today is." To reach its goal of promoting a consistent brand image, T-Mobile uses a single advertising agency that handles all of its advertising in all six countries.

T-Mobile started out as a genuine underdog in the United States' already established wireless phone market, pitting itself against strong competitors such as Cingular, Verizon, Sprint, and NexTel. The company has more than met the challenge. T-Mobile is the fastest-growing wireless carrier in the United States, boasting as many as 1.4 million new subscribers per quarter and totaling over 268 million customers in the United States alone. How has T-Mobile become a major competitor in the U.S. wireless phone market? Effective promotion efforts have helped.

T-Mobile's Star-Studded Promotion Efforts

As an unknown European brand, T-Mobile had to seek ways to create a definitive brand image in the United States among brands that were already well established. To create a recognizable brand, T-Mobile hired Academy Award–winning actress Catherine Zeta-Jones. The highly recognizable Welsh-born actress has been instrumental in building the brand image in the United States by appearing in television, print, and radio ads. Because Zeta-Jones is so well known, customers not only noticed the company's ads but also remembered them. Although Zeta-Jones was the official spokesperson, she is not the only star behind T-Mobile's promotions. The company rolled out the red carpet when it introduced its high-end multimedia device, the Sidekick. T-Mobile used a long lineup of celebrities in television ads and promotional events. The television commercials featured rapper Snoop Dogg using his T-Mobile Sidekick to message a long series of celebrities—such as Paris Hilton, Wee Man from MTV's *Jackass,* Wayne Newton, and Burt Reynolds—for help in doing his laundry. The goal of the advertisement was not just to sell a lot of Sidekicks but to establish T-Mobile as a hip, young, and cool brand.

The company reinforces this message by sponsoring events such as ESPN's X Games and parties featuring hot musical acts such as the Black Eyed Peas and the Pussycat Dolls. T-Mobile has made sure that its Sidekick is photographed in the hands of Hollywood's hottest trend-setting stars, such as Beyoncé Knowles, Lindsay Lohan, Jessica Simpson, and Nicky and Paris Hilton. T-Mobile has also offered special editions of the Sidekick, partnered by hip clothing lines Juicy Couture and Lifted Research, luxury designer Diane von Furstenberg, and urban artist Mister Cartoon. The Juicy Couture Sidekick is baby pink with the designer brand's signature Scottie dogs emblazoned on the back. Juicy Couture also offers jewelry charms, velour wristlets, and trendy carrying cases customized for the T-Mobile Sidekick. The

Mister Cartoon Sidekick is decorated with the artist's drawings. T-Mobile also partners with NYC Peach, the company that decorated Paris Hilton's infamously hijacked Sidekick. NYC Peach will completely customize a Swarovski crystal design for T-Mobile Sidekicks.

T-Mobile doesn't rely on celebrities just for its Sidekick. It sponsors the T-Mobile All Access Concert Series featuring intimate venues with hot musical acts such as Kelly Clarkson, Gavin DeGraw, Simple Plan, and Good Charlotte. To cross-promote the tour, subscribers could download free ring tones of performances or wallpapers of the touring musicians.

T-Mobile also has a multiyear marketing partnership as Official Wireless Services Partner with the NBA and WNBA. This agreement allows T-Mobile to reach a wide market of basketball fans. T-Mobile is integrated into all NBA and WNBA broadcasts and events. It also offers special basketball-related content on its phones, such as participation in NBA All-Star balloting, MVP voting for the NBA All-Star Game and the championship finals, as well as the latest NBA-related news, statistics, and other fun features. T-Mobile is confident that this partnership will broaden its exposure and enhance its youth-targeted image.

Some of T-Mobile's ads poke fun at competitors. One commercial featured two grocery store employees locked in a walk-in freezer. Although suffering from hypothermia, they refuse to call for help because they are outside of their network and don't want to be charged roaming fees. Another ad features a series of parents angry at their children because of high cell phone coverages. To promote its flat-rate text-messaging plan, a T-Mobile ad shows a suspicious dad roaming the house hoping to catch his children sending text messages. These ads poke fun at common consumer complaints within the wireless phone industry and provide T-Mobile as the provider with a solution. These ads set T-Mobile apart as the company that understands the frustration of wireless bills and coverage charges.

T-Mobile's Customers "Get More" Customer Service

T-Mobile lacks some of the multimedia services offered by competitors such as iTunes and live TV. The company attributes its growth without multimedia to exceptional customer service. It ranked number one on J. D. Power & Associates' industry survey in "Overall Customer Satisfaction," "Customer Care," and "Call Quality." Its mission is not only to remain at the top of its industry in customer service but also to eventually become the most highly respected service company

across industries. To achieve this goal, T-Mobile's CEO Robert Dotson and Chief Marketing Officer Mike Butler visit a large number of T-Mobile stores every quarter. Butler says that the purpose of the visits is not to lecture employees but to learn from them: "We come away with a list of items we're going to address to help deliver better customer service in the future." Many of the ideas expressed by T-Mobile store employees have been incorporated by the company. One suggested change was to provide more detailed information to potential customers about service coverage. T-Mobile developed color-coded maps that allow potential customers to view the coverage in their area as specifically as at street level. "We would rather they went down the street to someone else than sign up with us and be unhappy," says Butler. T-Mobile even christened its headquarters as "T-Mobile Field Service," because it feels that the purpose of its headquarters is to assist field employees with the necessary tools to deliver outstanding customer service. Many of T-Mobile's ads focus on this dedication to customer service. It believes in a promise that every customer will get more service, more savings, and more features.

What's Ahead for T-Mobile?

Some industry analysts speculate that T-Mobile might be the next target of a buyout or that it will be unable to compete against the multimedia features being offered by other service providers. But T-Mobile remains optimistic and fully expects to continue growing by focusing on excellent customer service and more traditional cell phone features. T-Mobile is betting on the idea that cell phone users find chatting with friends and family more important than other features. Only time will tell if this strategy will pay off; but T-Mobile's track record indicates they might be right.[49]

Questions for Discussion

1. What kind of brand image does T-Mobile want to build through its celebrity-packed promotion efforts?
2. What celebrities should T-Mobile use in its advertisements? Why?
3. How would T-Mobile's choice of promotional partners, such as Juicy Couture and the NBA, attract or discourage customers from selecting T-Mobile's phone services?
4. In what ways is T-Mobile supporting its personal selling activities at the retail level?
5. T-Mobile promotes its highly rated customer service as a selling point. Do you think it is effective against competitors that promote high-tech multimedia features? Explain.

part 8

PRICING DECISIONS

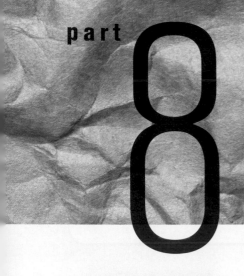

To provide a satisfying marketing mix, an organization must set a price that is acceptable to target market members. Pricing decisions can have numerous effects on other parts of the marketing mix. For example, price can influence how customers perceive the product, what types of marketing institutions are used to distribute the product, and how the product is promoted. **Chapter 19** discusses the importance of price and looks at some characteristics of price and nonprice competition. It explores fundamental concepts such as demand, elasticity, marginal analysis, and break-even analysis. Then the chapter examines the major factors that affect marketers' pricing decisions. **Chapter 20** discusses six major stages in the process marketers use to establish prices.

19 Pricing Concepts

Cell Phones Ring in Prices at Both Ends

Cell phone marketers are ringing in prices at both extremes of the market. From high-end, super-luxury models for status-conscious buyers to low-priced, entry-level phones for rising-income buyers in emerging nations, there's a cell phone for every place, pocket, and pocketbook.

Nokia, which dominates the global market for cell phones, has been selling designer cell phones through its Vertu division since 2002. Although Nokia's headquarters are in Finland, each phone is handcrafted in England using top-notch electronics plus gems and precious metals. With prices that range up to $370,000 for a diamond-encrusted model, Vertu phones have become must-have status symbols for celebrities such as Beyoncé Knowles and business leaders such as Donald Trump. Vertu phones are delivering healthy sales growth and hefty profit margins for their parent company, as well.

Meanwhile, Samsung Electronics has worked hard to increase its worldwide market share by launching ultra-low-price cell phones developed specifically for emerging markets in Southeast Asia and Africa. The South Korean company has already earned a solid reputation for quality with its higher-priced phones. The new lines of low-priced phones are intended to take some market share away from Nokia and help Samsung stay ahead of competitors such as the U.S.-based Motorola and South Korea's LG Electronics.

In contrast to Nokia's experience with its high-priced Vertu phones, Samsung's profit margins on the low-end lines could be disappointing—even despite a series of aggressive cost-cutting measures. Now, as Samsung continues its drive for higher unit sales and increased revenue, its marketers are closely monitoring the profit situation and making plans for difficult calls about marketing changes if results fall short of their expectations.[1]

The right price can mean the difference between success and failure for a marketer. It can influence potential buyers' perceptions of and response to a product, as it does for Nokia's Vertu phones, and it can determine whether a firm achieves profitability. Additionally, the right price can help boost demand for a new product and potentially discourage competitors from entering the market.

In this chapter, we focus first on the nature of price and its importance to marketers. We then consider some characteristics of price and nonprice competition. Next, we discuss several pricing-related concepts such as demand, elasticity, and break-even analysis. Then we examine in some detail the numerous factors that can influence pricing decisions. Finally, we discuss selected issues related to pricing products for business markets.

The Nature of Price

LO 1 To understand the nature and importance of price

The purpose of marketing is to facilitate satisfying exchange relationships between buyer and seller. **Price** is the value paid for a product in a marketing exchange. Many factors may influence the assessment of value, including time constraints, price levels, perceived quality, and motivations to use available information about prices.[2] In most marketing situations, the price is apparent to both buyer and seller. However, price does not always take the form of money paid. In fact, **barter,** the trading of products, is the oldest form of exchange. Money may or may not be involved. Barter among businesses accounts for about $9 billion in annual U.S. sales. Websites such as SwapThing.com and BarterYourServices.com may help facilitate B2B bartering.[3]

Buyers' interest in price stems from their expectations about the usefulness of a product or the satisfaction they may derive from it. Because consumers have limited resources, they must allocate those resources to obtain the products they most desire. They must decide whether the utility gained in an exchange is worth the buying power sacrificed. Almost anything of value—ideas, services, rights, and goods—can be assessed by a price. In our society, financial price is the measurement of value commonly used in exchanges.

Terms Used to Describe Price

Value can be expressed in different terms for different marketing situations. For instance, students pay *tuition* for a college education. Automobile insurance companies charge a *premium* for protection from the cost of injuries or repairs stemming from an automobile accident. An officer who stops you for speeding writes a ticket that requires you to pay a *fine*, and the lawyer you hire to defend you in traffic court charges a *fee*. Airlines and taxi cabs charge a *fare*. A *toll* is charged for the use of bridges or toll roads. *Rent* is paid for the use of equipment or an apartment. A *commission* is remitted to a broker for the sale of real estate. *Dues* are paid for membership in a club or group. A *deposit* is made to hold or lay away merchandise. *Tips* help pay food servers for their services. *Interest* is charged for a loan, and *taxes* are paid for government services. Although price may be expressed in a variety of ways, its purpose is to quantify and express the value of the items in a marketing exchange.

The Importance of Price to Marketers

As pointed out in Chapter 11, developing a product may be a lengthy process. It takes time to plan promotion and to communicate benefits. Distribution usually requires a long-term commitment to dealers that will handle the product. Often price is the only thing a marketer can change quickly to respond to changes in demand or to actions of competitors. Under certain circumstances, however, the price variable may be relatively inflexible.

Price is a key element in the marketing mix because it relates directly to the generation of total revenue. The following equation is an important one for the entire organization:

$$\text{Profit} = \text{Total Revenue} - \text{Total Costs}$$
$$\text{Profits} = (\text{Price} \times \text{Quantity Sold}) - \text{Total Costs}$$

price The value paid for a product in a marketing exchange

barter The trading of products

Price affects an organization's profits in several ways because it is a key component of the profit equation and can be a major determinant of quantities sold. For example, price is a top priority for Hewlett-Packard in gaining market share and improving financial performance.[4] Furthermore, total costs are influenced by quantities sold.

Because price has a psychological impact on customers, marketers can use it symbolically. By pricing high, they can emphasize the quality of a product and try to increase the prestige associated with its ownership. By lowering a price, marketers can emphasize a bargain and attract customers who go out of their way to save a small amount of money. Thus, as this chapter details, price can have strong effects on a firm's sales and profitability.

Price and Nonprice Competition

L O 2 To identify the characteristics of price and nonprice competition

The competitive environment strongly influences the marketing mix decisions associated with a product. Pricing decisions are often made according to the price or nonprice competitive situation in a particular market. Price competition exists when consumers have difficulty distinguishing competitive offerings and marketers emphasize low prices. Nonprice competition involves a focus on marketing mix elements other than price.

Price Competition

When engaging in **price competition,** a marketer emphasizes price as an issue and matches or beats competitors' prices. To compete effectively on a price basis, a firm should be the low-cost seller of the product. If all firms producing the same product charge the same price for it, the firm with the lowest costs is the most profitable. Firms that stress low price as a key marketing mix element tend to market standardized products. A seller competing on price may change prices frequently, or at least must be willing and able to do so. Consider that when Wal-Mart, Circuit City, and Amazon.com reduced the price of a Toshiba high-definition DVD player to $200, consumer interest rose. But when Wal-Mart slashed the price by another $100 for 48 hours, consumers snatched up 90,000 to 100,000 of the players. Best Buy also boosted sales when it dropped the price of a Sony Blu-ray DVD player, which uses a rival format for high-definition video, to $399.[5] Whenever competitors change their prices, the company usually responds quickly and aggressively.

price competition Emphasizing price as an issue and matching or beating competitors' prices

Price Competition

Consumer electronics stores compete on the basis of price.

Price competition gives marketers flexibility. They can alter prices to account for changes in their costs or respond to changes in demand for the product. If competitors try to gain market share by cutting prices, a company competing on a price basis can react quickly to such efforts. However, a major drawback of price competition is that competitors too have the flexibility to adjust prices. If they quickly match or beat a company's price cuts, a price war may ensue. For example, a price war has developed in the market for some generic prescription drugs. After Wal-Mart announced that it would offer many generic medicines for $4 in some markets, rival Target announced that it would offer $4 generics at every U.S. Target store with a pharmacy. Wal-Mart swiftly expanded its $4 generic program, and Kmart began offering some generic medicines at $15 for a 90-day supply. Some large regional supermarket chains such as Meijer and Giant Eagle also joined the price war.[6] Chronic price wars such as this one can substantially weaken organizations.

Nonprice Competition

nonprice competition
Emphasizing factors other than price to distinguish a product from competing brands

Nonprice competition occurs when a seller decides not to focus on price and instead emphasizes distinctive product features, service, product quality, promotion, packaging, or other factors to distinguish its product from competing brands. Thus, nonprice competition allows a company to increase its brand's unit sales through means other than changing the brand's price. Mars, for example, markets not only Snickers and M&Ms, but also has an upscale candy line called ethel's chocolates. With the tagline,

green MARKETING

Getting Wallets Ready for Eco-Friendly Paint

Painting it green costs more green, but a growing number of homeowners and builders are willing to pay a few dollars more for paints that are friendlier to the environment. That is good news for Benjamin Moore, which makes Aura house paint. Traditional paints release polluting volatile organic compounds (VOCs) while they dry, and their smell can offend sensitive noses. In contrast, low-VOC paints such as Aura do not smell as bad, release lower levels of polluting chemicals, and dry more quickly.

After investing $150 million to develop the Aura line, Benjamin Moore adopted a nonprice strategy and introduced it at a price of $55 a gallon, $15 more than the $40 per gallon of the company's other paints. Because customers expect pricey paint to do more than save the planet, Aura paints can be custom mixed in any color, dark or light, for good coverage in fewer coats. Another benefit is that Aura is more durable than ordinary paint and can withstand more scrubbing. Finally, new technology enables Benjamin Moore dealers to match Aura colors more accurately. As a result, customers who run out of paint before they run out of walls will find that the color in the next can of Aura precisely matches the color in the previous can.

Year by year, states are passing regulations to reduce pollution by mandating lower VOC levels in house paint. Aura is ahead of the curve in many states, and despite the higher price, sales are rising so quickly that the brand will soon make Benjamin Moore's bottom line a richer shade of green.[a]

"no mystery middles," ethel's chocolates competes on the basis of taste, attractive appearance, and hip packaging and thus has little need to engage in price competition.[7] A major advantage of nonprice competition is that a firm can build customer loyalty toward its brand. If customers prefer a brand because of nonprice factors, they may not be easily lured away by competing firms and brands. In contrast, when price is the primary reason customers buy a particular brand, a competitor is often able to attract those customers through price cuts.

Nonprice competition is effective only under certain conditions. A company must be able to distinguish its brand through unique product features, higher product quality, effective promotion, distinctive packaging, or excellent customer service. For example, Vermont Pure, a New England bottled-water producer, used superior service and customer-oriented delivery to compete against the bottled-water offerings of Coca-Cola, PepsiCo, and Nestlé. The firm's focus on the service aspects of bottled water helped boost its sales by 15 percent.[8] Buyers not only must be able to perceive these distinguishing characteristics but must also view them as important. The distinguishing features that set a particular brand apart from competitors should be difficult, if not impossible, for competitors to imitate. Finally, the firm must extensively promote the brand's distinguishing characteristics to establish its superiority and set it apart from competitors in the minds of buyers.

Even a marketer that is competing on a nonprice basis cannot ignore competitors' prices. It must be aware of them and sometimes be prepared to price its brand near or slightly above competing brands. Therefore, price remains a crucial marketing mix component even in environments that call for nonprice competition.

Analysis of Demand

LO 3 To explore demand curves and price elasticity of demand

Determining the demand for a product is the responsibility of marketing managers, who are aided in this task by marketing researchers and forecasters. Marketing research and forecasting techniques yield estimates of sales potential, or the quantity of a product that could be sold during a specific period. These estimates are helpful in establishing the relationship between a product's price and the quantity demanded.

The Demand Curve

For most products, the quantity demanded goes up as the price goes down, and the quantity demanded goes down as the price goes up. Intel, for example, knows that lowering prices boosts demand for its Pentium PC processors. Thus, an inverse relationship exists between price and quantity demanded. As long as the marketing environment and buyers' needs, ability (purchasing power), willingness, and authority to buy remain stable, this fundamental inverse relationship holds.

Figure 19.1 illustrates the effect of one variable, price, on the quantity demanded. The classic **demand curve** ($D1$) is a graph of the quantity of products expected to be sold at various prices if other factors remain constant.[9] It illustrates that as price falls, quantity demanded usually rises. Demand depends on other factors in the marketing mix, including product quality, promotion, and distribution. An improvement in any of these factors may cause a shift to, say, demand curve $D2$. In such a case, an increased quantity ($Q2$) will be sold at the same price (P).

Many types of demand exist, and not all conform to the classic demand curve shown in Figure 19.1. Prestige products, such as selected perfumes and jewelry, tend to sell better at high prices than at low ones. These products are desirable partly because their expense makes buyers feel elite. If the price fell drastically and many people owned these products, they would lose some of their appeal. The demand curve in Figure 19.2 shows the relationship between price and quantity demanded for prestige products. Quantity demanded is greater, not less, at higher prices. For a certain price range—from $P1$ to $P2$—the quantity demanded ($Q1$) goes up to $Q2$. After a certain point, however, raising the price backfires: if the price goes too high, the quantity demanded goes down. The figure shows that if price is raised from $P2$ to $P3$, quantity demanded goes back down from $Q2$ to $Q1$.

demand curve A graph of the quantity of products expected to be sold at various prices if other factors remain constant

figure 19.1 DEMAND CURVE ILLUSTRATING THE PRICE–QUANTITY RELATIONSHIP AND INCREASE IN DEMAND

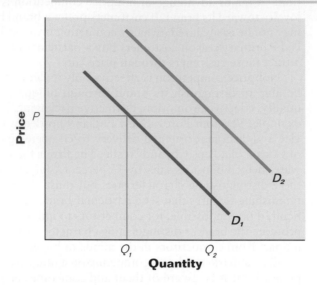

Demand Fluctuations

Changes in buyers' needs, variations in the effectiveness of other marketing mix variables, the presence of substitutes, and dynamic environmental factors can influence demand. Restaurants and utility companies experience large fluctuations in demand daily. Toy manufacturers, fireworks suppliers, and air-conditioning and heating contractors also face demand fluctuations because of the seasonal nature of their products. The demand for broadband services, beef, and flat-screen TVs has changed over the last few years. In the case of flat-screen plasma and LCD TVs, demand accelerated as prices dropped by as much as 50 percent.[10] In some cases, demand fluctuations are predictable. It is no surprise to restaurants and utility company managers that demand fluctuates. However, changes in demand for other products may be less predictable, leading to problems for some companies. Other organizations anticipate demand fluctuations and develop new products and prices to meet consumers' changing needs.

figure 19.2 DEMAND CURVE ILLUSTRATING THE RELATIONSHIP BETWEEN PRICE AND QUANTITY FOR PRESTIGE PRODUCTS

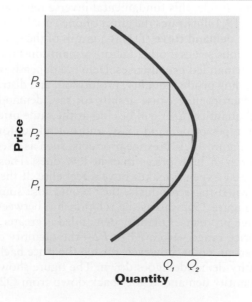

figure 19.3

ELASTICITY OF DEMAND

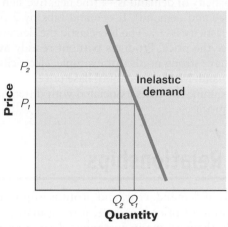

ELECTRICITY

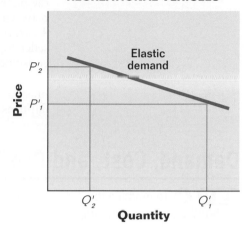

RECREATIONAL VEHICLES

Assessing Price Elasticity of Demand

Up to this point, we have seen how marketers identify the target market's evaluation of price and its ability to purchase and how they examine demand to learn whether price is related inversely or directly to quantity. The next step is to assess price elasticity of demand. **Price elasticity of demand** provides a measure of the sensitivity of demand to changes in price. It is formally defined as the percentage change in quantity demanded relative to a given percentage change in price (see Figure 19.3).[11] The percentage change in quantity demanded caused by a percentage change in price is much greater for elastic demand than for inelastic demand. For a product such as electricity, demand is relatively inelastic: when its price increases, say, from $P1$ to $P2$, quantity demanded goes down only a little, from $Q1$ to $Q2$. For products such as recreational vehicles, demand is relatively elastic: when price rises sharply, from $P1$ to $P2$, quantity demanded goes down a great deal, from $Q1$ to $Q2$.

price elasticity of demand
A measure of the sensitivity of demand to changes in price

If marketers can determine the price elasticity of demand, setting a price is much easier. By analyzing total revenues as prices change, marketers can determine whether a product is price elastic. Total revenue is price times quantity; thus, 10,000 rolls of wallpaper sold in one year at a price of $10 per roll equals $100,000 of total revenue. If demand is *elastic,* a change in price causes an opposite change in total revenue: an increase in price will decrease total revenue, and a decrease in price will increase total revenue. *Inelastic* demand results in a change in the same direction as total revenue: an increase in price will increase total revenue, and a decrease in price will decrease total revenue. Demand for gasoline, for example, is relatively inelastic—even when prices well exceed $3 per gallon—because people must still drive to work, run errands, shop, and engage in other behaviors that require fuel for their vehicles. Although higher gasoline prices have forced more consumers to change some behaviors in an effort to reduce the amount of gasoline they use, most have cut spending in other areas instead because they require a certain level of fuel for weekly activities such as commuting.[12] The following formula determines the price elasticity of demand:

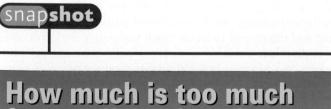

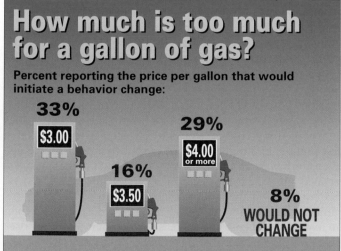

Source: Data from AAIA Survey.

$$\text{Price Elasticity of Demand} = \frac{(\% \text{ Change in Quantity Demanded})}{(\% \text{ Change in Price})}$$

For example, if demand falls by 8 percent when a seller raises the price by 2 percent, the price elasticity of demand is −4 (the negative sign indicating the inverse relationship between price and demand). If demand falls by 2 percent when price is increased by 4 percent, elasticity is $-\frac{1}{2}$. The less elastic the demand, the more beneficial it is for the seller to raise the price. Products without readily available substitutes and for which consumers have strong needs (for example, electricity or appendectomies) usually have inelastic demand. Marketers cannot base prices solely on elasticity considerations. They must also examine the costs associated with different sales volumes and evaluate what happens to profits.

Demand, Cost, and Profit Relationships

L O 4 To examine the relationships among demand, costs, and profits

The analysis of demand, cost, and profit is important because customers are becoming less tolerant of price increases, forcing manufacturers to find new ways to control costs. In the past, many customers desired premium brands and were willing to pay extra for those products. Today customers pass up certain brand names if they can pay less without sacrificing quality. To stay in business, a company must set prices that not only cover its costs but also meet customers' expectations. In this section, we explore two approaches to understanding demand, cost, and profit relationships: marginal analysis and break-even analysis.

Marginal Analysis

Marginal analysis examines what happens to a firm's costs and revenues when production (or sales volume) changes by one unit. Both production costs and revenues must be evaluated. To determine the costs of production, it is necessary to distinguish among several types of costs. **Fixed costs** do not vary with changes in the number of units produced or sold. For example, a wallpaper manufacturer's cost of renting a factory does not change because production increases from one to two shifts a day or because twice as much wallpaper is sold. Rent may go up, but not because the factory has doubled production or revenue. **Average fixed cost** is the fixed cost per unit produced and is calculated by dividing fixed costs by the number of units produced.

Variable costs vary directly with changes in the number of units produced or sold. The wages for a second shift and the cost of twice as much wallpaper are extra costs incurred when production is doubled. Variable costs are usually constant per unit; that is, twice as many workers and twice as much material produce twice as many rolls of wallpaper. **Average variable cost,** the variable cost per unit produced, is calculated by dividing the variable costs by the number of units produced.

Total cost is the sum of average fixed costs and average variable costs times the quantity produced. The **average total cost** is the sum of the average fixed cost and the average variable cost. **Marginal cost (MC)** is the extra cost a firm incurs when it produces one more unit of a product.

Table 19.1 illustrates various costs and their relationships. Notice that average fixed cost declines as output increases. Average variable cost follows a U shape, as does average total cost. Because average total cost continues to fall after average variable cost begins to rise, its lowest point is at a higher level of output than that of average variable cost. Average total cost is lowest at 5 units at a cost of $22.00, whereas average variable cost is lowest at 3 units at a cost of $11.67. As Figure 19.4 shows, marginal cost equals average total cost at the latter's lowest level. In Table 19.1, this occurs between 5 and 6 units of production. Average total cost decreases as long as marginal cost is less than average total cost and increases when marginal cost rises above average total cost.

Marginal revenue (MR) is the change in total revenue that occurs when a firm sells an additional unit of a product. Figure 19.5 depicts marginal revenue and a demand

fixed costs Costs that do not vary with changes in the number of units produced or sold

average fixed cost The fixed cost per unit produced

variable costs Costs that vary directly with changes in the number of units produced or sold

average variable cost The variable cost per unit produced

total cost The sum of average fixed and average variable costs times the quantity produced

average total cost The sum of the average fixed cost and the average variable cost

marginal cost (MC) The extra cost incurred by producing one more unit of a product

marginal revenue (MR) The change in total revenue resulting from the sale of an additional unit of a product

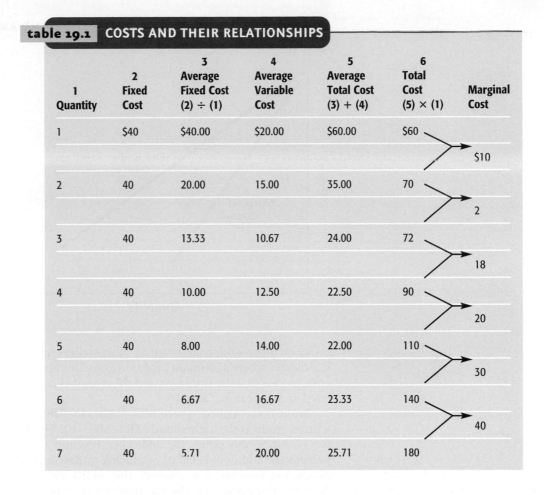

table 19.1 COSTS AND THEIR RELATIONSHIPS

1 Quantity	2 Fixed Cost	3 Average Fixed Cost (2) ÷ (1)	4 Average Variable Cost	5 Average Total Cost (3) + (4)	6 Total Cost (5) × (1)	Marginal Cost
1	$40	$40.00	$20.00	$60.00	$60	
						$10
2	40	20.00	15.00	35.00	70	
						2
3	40	13.33	10.67	24.00	72	
						18
4	40	10.00	12.50	22.50	90	
						20
5	40	8.00	14.00	22.00	110	
						30
6	40	6.67	16.67	23.33	140	
						40
7	40	5.71	20.00	25.71	180	

curve. Most firms in the United States face downward-sloping demand curves for their products; in other words, they must lower their prices to sell additional units. This situation means that each additional unit of product sold provides the firm with less revenue than the previous unit sold. MR then becomes less-than-average revenue, as Figure 19.5 shows. Eventually MR reaches zero, and the sale of additional units actually hurts the firm.

However, before the firm can determine whether a unit makes a profit, it must know its cost, as well as its revenue, because profit equals revenue minus cost. If MR is a unit's addition to revenue and MC is a unit's addition to cost, MR minus MC tells us whether the unit is profitable. Table 19.2 illustrates the relationships among

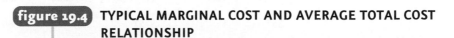

figure 19.4 TYPICAL MARGINAL COST AND AVERAGE TOTAL COST RELATIONSHIP

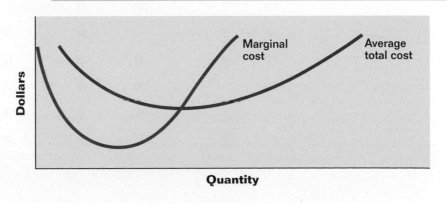

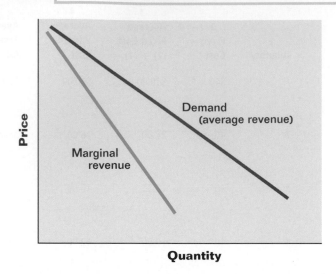

TYPICAL MARGINAL REVENUE AND AVERAGE REVENUE RELATIONSHIP

price, quantity sold, total revenue, marginal revenue, marginal cost, and total cost. It indicates where maximum profits are possible at various combinations of price and cost. Notice that the total cost and the marginal cost figures in Table 19.2 are calculated and appear in Table 19.1.

Profit is the highest where MC = MR. In Table 19.2, note that at a quantity of 4 units, profit is the highest and MR – MC = 0. The best price is $33, and the profit is $42. Up to this point, the additional revenue generated from an extra unit sold exceeds the additional cost of producing it. Beyond this point, the additional cost of producing another unit exceeds the additional revenue generated, and profits decrease. If the price were based on minimum average total cost—$22 (Table 19.1)—it would result in a lower profit of $40 (Table 19.2) for 5 units priced at $30 versus a profit of $42 for 4 units priced at $33.

table 19.2   **MARGINAL ANALYSIS METHOD FOR DETERMINING THE MOST PROFITABLE PRICE**

1 Price	2 Quantity Sold	3 Total Revenue (1) × (2)	4 Marginal Revenue	5 Marginal Cost	6 Total Cost	7 Profit Cost (3) − (6)
$57	1	$ 57	$57	$60	$ 60	$–3
50	2	100	43	10	70	30
38	3	114	14	2	72	42
33 *	**4**	**132**	**18**	**18**	**90**	**42**
30	5	150	18	20	110	40
27	6	162	12	30	140	22
25	7	175	13	40	180	–5

* Boldface indicates the best price-profit combination

figure 19.6 COMBINING THE MARGINAL COST AND MARGINAL REVENUE CONCEPTS FOR OPTIMAL PROFIT

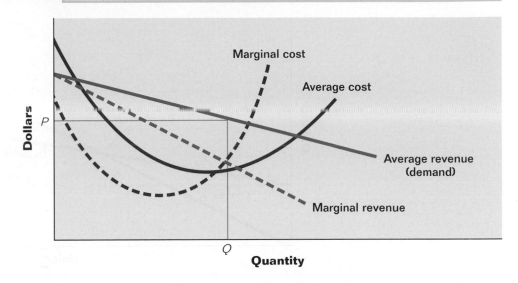

Graphically combining Figures 19.4 and 19.5 into Figure 19.6 shows that any unit for which MR exceeds MC adds to a firm's profits, and any unit for which MC exceeds MR subtracts from profits. The firm should produce at the point where MR equals MC because this is the most profitable level of production.

This discussion of marginal analysis may give the false impression that pricing can be highly precise. If revenue (demand) and cost (supply) remained constant, prices could be set for maximum profits. In practice, however, cost and revenue change frequently. The competitive tactics of other firms or government action can quickly undermine a company's expectations of revenue. Thus, marginal analysis is only a model from which to work. It offers little help in pricing new products before costs and revenues are established. On the other hand, in setting prices of existing products, especially in competitive situations, most marketers can benefit by understanding the relationship between marginal cost and marginal revenue.

Break-Even Analysis

The point at which the costs of producing a product equal the revenue made from selling the product is the **break-even point.** If the wallpaper manufacturer has total annual costs of $100,000 and sells $100,000 worth of wallpaper in the same year, the company has broken even.

Figure 19.7 illustrates the relationships among costs, revenue, profits, and losses involved in determining the break-even point. Knowing the number of units necessary to break even is important in setting the price. If a product priced at $100 per unit has an average variable cost of $60 per unit, the contribution to fixed costs is $40. If total fixed costs are $120,000, the break-even point in units is determined as follows:

$$\text{Break-Even Point} = \frac{\text{Fixed Costs}}{\text{Per-Unit Contribution to Fixed Costs}}$$

$$= \frac{\text{Fixed Costs}}{\text{Price} - \text{Variable Costs}}$$

$$= \frac{\$120,000}{\$40}$$

$$= 3,000 \text{ Units}$$

break-even point The point at which the costs of producing a product equal the revenue made from selling the product

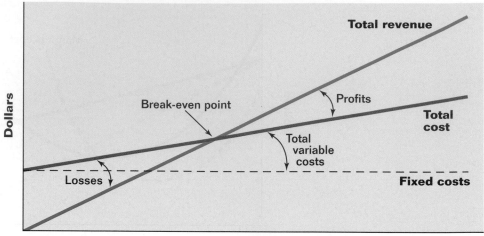

figure 19.7

DETERMINING THE BREAK-EVEN POINT

To calculate the break-even point in terms of dollar sales volume, the seller multiplies the break-even point in units by the price per unit. In the preceding example, the break-even point in terms of dollar sales volume is 3,000 (units) times $100, or $300,000.

To use break-even analysis effectively, a marketer should determine the break-even point for each of several alternative prices. This determination allows the marketer to compare the effects on total revenue, total costs, and the break-even point for each price under consideration. Although this comparative analysis may not tell the marketer exactly what price to charge, it will identify highly undesirable price alternatives that should definitely be avoided.

Break-even analysis is simple and straightforward. It does assume, however, that the quantity demanded is basically fixed (inelastic) and that the major task in setting prices is to recover costs. It focuses more on how to break even than on how to achieve a pricing objective, such as percentage of market share or return on investment. Nonetheless, marketing managers can use this concept to determine whether a product will achieve at least a break-even volume.

Factors That Affect Pricing Decisions

L O 5 To describe key factors that may influence marketers' pricing decisions

Pricing decisions can be complex because of the number of factors to consider. Frequently there is considerable uncertainty about the reactions to price among buyers, channel members, and competitors. Price is also an important consideration in marketing planning, market analysis, and sales forecasting. It is a major issue when assessing a brand's position relative to competing brands. Most factors that affect pricing decisions can be grouped into one of the eight categories shown in Figure 19.8. In this section, we explore how each of these groups of factors enters into price decision making.

Organizational and Marketing Objectives

Marketers should set prices that are consistent with the organization's goals and mission. For example, a retailer trying to position itself as value oriented may wish to set prices that are quite reasonable relative to product quality. In this case, a marketer would not want to set premium prices on products but would strive to price products in line with this overall organizational goal.

Pricing decisions should also be compatible with the firm's marketing objectives. For instance, suppose one of a producer's marketing objectives is a 12 percent

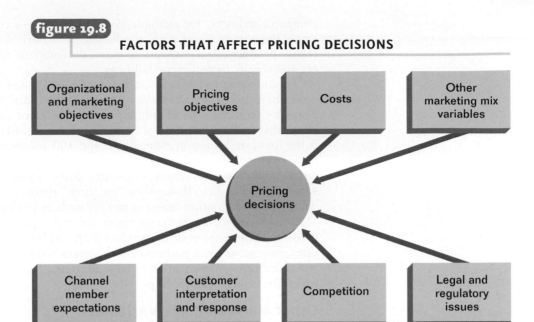

figure 19.8

FACTORS THAT AFFECT PRICING DECISIONS

increase in unit sales by the end of the following year. Assuming buyers are price sensitive, increasing the price or setting a price above the average market price would not be in line with this objective.

Types of Pricing Objectives

The types of pricing objectives a marketer uses obviously have considerable bearing on the determination of prices. For example, an organization that uses pricing to increase its market share would likely set the brand's price below those of competing brands of similar quality to attract competitors' customers. A marketer sometimes uses temporary price reductions in the hope of gaining market share. If a business needs to raise cash quickly, it will likely use temporary price reductions such as sales, rebates, and special discounts. We examine pricing objectives in more detail in the next chapter.

Costs

Clearly costs must be an issue when establishing price. A firm may temporarily sell products below cost to match competition, generate cash flow, or even increase market share, but in the long run it cannot survive by selling its products below cost. Even a firm that has a high-volume business cannot survive if each item is sold slightly below its cost. A marketer should be careful to analyze all costs so they can be included in the total cost associated with a product.

To maintain market share and revenue in an increasingly price-sensitive market, many marketers have concentrated on reducing costs. In the highly competitive

RESPONSIBLE marketing?

Credit Limits

ISSUE: Are credit card companies playing fair?

Some credit card companies lobby Congress for less regulation and for regulation that is more favorable to credit card issuers. Have regulatory changes led to questionable practices by some companies? Credit card companies can increase credit card interest rates even though the card holder has paid at least the minimum payments on time and has not been charged penalty payments. Credit card companies sometimes change a holder's billing cycle, which reduces the number of days between receiving the bill and the due date, hoping that the card holder does not notice the new due date and makes a "late payment" that results in both a late fee and a finance charge. Last year, a majority of all credit card holders in the United States paid at least one late fee. Credit card companies can also add penalties, such as for a late payment, which puts the balance on the card over the credit limit and incurs an over-the-limit fee.

Is it fair for a credit card company to shorten the billing cycle without notice and charge a late fee if the card holder fails to pay "on time"? Why should a credit card company be allowed to charge an over-the-limit penalty when the account is over its limit due to charges made only by the credit card company? Should a credit card company be permitted to increase a card holder's interest rate when the customer has paid according to the original contract?[b]

computer industry, for example, Sun Microsystems constantly looks for ways to lower the cost of developing, producing, and marketing computers, software, and related products. As a cost-cutting move, the company recently laid off 3,700 employees and shrunk its real estate holdings.[13]

Labor-saving technologies, a focus on quality, and efficient manufacturing processes have brought productivity gains that translate into reduced costs and lower prices for customers. In an industry ravaged by labor concerns and monetary losses, Southwest Airlines has managed to stay one step ahead of its larger rivals. Southwest is the low-fare leader on more of the top 100 routes in the United States than the three largest airlines—American, Delta, and United. One reason for the Texas-based airline's success is its ability to control costs. Southwest's per-seat mile costs are somewhat lower than those of its "big three" rivals. However, Southwest now faces competition from other low-cost airlines such as JetBlue.

Besides considering the costs associated with a particular product, marketers must take into account the costs the product shares with others in the product line. Products often share some costs, particularly the costs of research and development, production, and distribution. Most marketers view a product's cost as a minimum, or floor, below which the product cannot be priced.

Other Marketing Mix Variables

All marketing mix variables are highly interrelated. Pricing decisions can influence evaluations and activities associated with product, distribution, and promotion variables. A product's price frequently affects the demand for that item. A high price, for instance, may result in low unit sales, which in turn may lead to higher production costs per unit. Conversely, lower per-unit production costs may result from a low price. For many products, buyers associate better product quality with a high price and poorer product quality with a low price. This perceived price–quality relationship influences customers' overall image of products or brands. Sony, for example, prices its television sets higher than average to help communicate that Sony televisions are high-quality electronic products. Consumers recognize the Sony brand name, its reputation for quality, and the prestige associated with buying Sony products. Individuals who associate quality with a high price are likely to purchase products with well-established and recognizable brand names.[14]

The price of a product is linked to several dimensions of its distribution. Premium-priced products—a Bentley or Rolls-Royce automobile, for example—are often marketed through selective or exclusive distribution; lower-priced products in the same product category may be sold through intensive distribution. For example, Cross pens are distributed through selective distribution and Bic pens through intensive distribution. Moreover, an increase in physical distribution costs, such as shipping, may have to be passed on to customers. After fuel prices soared, many firms were forced to pass the cost on to their customers in the form of higher prices or fuel surcharges. Big Sky Airlines, for example, had to increase fares by 25 to 40 percent, and Briggs Distributing Company had to levy a fuel surcharge of $3 on every delivery of beer and other beverages to its retail customers.[15] When setting a price, the profit margins of marketing channel members, such as wholesalers and retailers, must also be considered. Channel members must be adequately compensated for the functions they perform.

Price may determine how a product is promoted. Bargain prices are often included in advertisements. Premium

Price Affects Promotion Decisions

Most fragrance advertisements do not include prices.

With Love...
HILARY DUFF
The fragrance
withlovehilaryduff.com

prices are less likely to be advertised, though they are sometimes included in advertisements for upscale items such as luxury cars or fine jewelry. Higher-priced products are more likely than lower-priced ones to require personal selling. Furthermore, the price structure can affect a salesperson's relationship with customers. A complex pricing structure takes longer to explain to customers, is more likely to confuse potential buyers, and may cause misunderstandings that result in long-term customer dissatisfaction. For example, the pricing structures of many airlines are complex and frequently confuse ticket sales agents and travelers alike.

Channel Member Expectations

When making price decisions, a producer must consider what members of the distribution channel expect. A channel member certainly expects to receive a profit for the functions it performs. The amount of profit expected depends on what the intermediary could make if it were handling a competing product instead. Also, the amount of time and the resources required to carry the product influence intermediaries' expectations.

Channel members often expect producers to give discounts for large orders and prompt payment. At times, resellers expect producers to provide several support activities such as sales training, service training, repair advisory service, cooperative advertising, sales promotions, and perhaps a program for returning unsold merchandise to the producer. These support activities clearly have associated costs that a producer must consider when determining prices.

Customers' Interpretation and Response

When making pricing decisions, marketers should address a vital question: How will our customers interpret our prices and respond to them? *Interpretation* in this context refers to what the price means or what it communicates to customers. Does the price mean "high quality" or "low quality," or "great deal," "fair price," or "rip-off"? Customer *response* refers to whether the price will move customers closer to purchase of the product and the degree to which the price enhances their satisfaction with the purchase experience and with the product after purchase.

Customers' interpretation of and response to a price are to some degree determined by their assessment of value, or what they receive compared with what they give up to make the purchase. In evaluating what they receive, customers consider product attributes, benefits, advantages, disadvantages, the probability of using the product, and possibly the status associated with the product. In assessing the cost of the product, customers likely will consider its price, the amount of time and effort required to obtain it, and perhaps the resources required to maintain it after purchase. Research shows that an increasing number of investors with at least $500,000 of assets to invest are using full-service brokers. This suggests that these customers view the costs of full-service brokerage services as more acceptable, given the return on their investments.[16]

At times, customers interpret a higher price as higher product quality. They are especially likely to make this price–quality association when they cannot judge the quality of the product themselves. This is not always the case, however; whether price is equated with quality depends on the types of customers and products involved. Obviously marketers that rely on customers making a price–quality association and that provide moderate- or low-quality products at high prices will be unable to build long-term customer relationships.

External Reference Price

Advertisements, like this one, provide information that customers use to establish or change their reference prices.

When interpreting and responding to prices, how do customers determine if the price is too high, too low, or about right? In general, they compare prices with internal or external reference prices. An **internal reference price** is a price developed in the buyer's mind through experience with the product. It reflects a belief that a product should cost approximately a certain amount. To arrive at an internal reference price, consumers may consider one or more values, including what they think the product "ought" to cost, the price usually charged for it, the last price they paid, the highest and lowest amounts they would be willing to pay, the price of the brand they usually buy, the average price of similar products, the expected future price, and the typical discounted price.[17] Research has found that less-confident consumers tend to have higher internal reference prices than consumers with greater confidence, and frequent buyers—perhaps because of their experience and confidence—are more likely to judge high prices unfairly.[18] As consumers, our experiences have given each of us internal reference prices for a number of products. For example, most of us have a reasonable idea of how much to pay for a six-pack of soft drinks, a loaf of bread, or a cup of coffee. For the product categories with which we have less experience, we rely more heavily on external reference prices. An **external reference price** is a comparison price provided by others, such as retailers or manufacturers. For example, a retailer in an advertisement might state, "While this product is sold for $100 elsewhere, our price is only $39.95." Research has found a negative association between price volatility and internal reference prices, whereas consumers' knowledge of prices

internal reference price A price developed in the buyer's mind through experience with the product

external reference price A comparison price provided by others

E-ntertainment MARKETING

Are Sports Going to the (Hot) Dogs?

Will baseball fans buy tickets for seats far from home plate if they get an all-you-can-eat buffet of hot dogs, nachos, and soft drinks? Typically, teams have difficulty selling many seats in sections where fans have to really strain to see whether a runner sliding into home plate is safe or out. The Los Angeles Dodgers used to address this problem by pricing the 3,000 right-field pavilion seats in Dodger Stadium below $10. Even then, the section rarely filled up unless a group or business bought a large block of tickets so its members could sit together.

Then the Dodgers decided to try something a little different. Instead of setting an ultra-low price for the pavilion seats, team marketers hiked the price to a minimum of $20 and added an all-you-can-eat incentive. Starting 90 minutes before the first pitch, fans with pavilion tickets could walk up to the concession stand below the right-field bleachers and get free Dodger Dogs, peanuts, popcorn, soft drinks, and more. They could come back for more until two hours into the game, when the endless buffet finally ended.

Thanks to this experiment with food-included pricing, the Dodgers filled all 3,000 pavilion seats during 8 of the team's first 18 home games in the 2007 season. And because ticket holders had to pay extra for parking and for candy, ice cream, beer, and souvenirs, this pricing plan drove the team's total revenue higher.[c]

and propensity to comparison shop has a positive influence on external reference prices.[19] Customers' perceptions of prices are also influenced by their expectations about future price increases, by what they paid for the product recently, and by what they would like to pay for the product. Other factors affecting customers' perceptions of whether the price is right include time or financial constraints, the costs associated with searching for lower-priced products, and expectations that products will go on sale.

Buyers' perceptions of a product relative to competing products may allow the firm to set a price that differs significantly from rivals' prices. If the product is deemed superior to most of the competition, a premium price may be feasible. However, even products with superior quality can be overpriced. Strong brand loyalty sometimes provides the opportunity to charge a premium price. On the other hand, if buyers view a product less than favorably (though not extremely negatively), a lower price may generate sales.

In the context of price, buyers can be characterized according to their degree of value consciousness, price consciousness, and prestige sensitivity. Marketers that understand these characteristics are better able to set pricing objectives and policies. **Value-conscious** consumers are concerned about both price and quality of a product.[20] These consumers may perceive value as quality per unit of price or as not only economic savings but also the additional gains expected from one product over a competitor's brand. The first view is appropriate for commodities such as bottled water, bananas, and gasoline. If a value-conscious consumer perceives the quality of gasoline to be the same for Exxon and Shell, he or she will go to the station with the lower price. For consumers looking not just for economic value but additional gains they expect from one brand over another, a product differentiation value could be associated with benefits and features that are believed to be unique.[21] For example, a BMW may be considered to be better than a Cadillac. To appeal to the value-conscious consumer, Nike, through its Exeter Brand Group, recently introduced the Tailwind line of footwear in Payless shoe stores. The shoes are priced from $19.99 to $34.99.[22] **Price-conscious** individuals strive to pay low prices.[23] They want the lowest prices and would respond to Wal-Mart's claim that "we sell for less." A price-conscious pet food buyer, for example, would probably purchase Wal-Mart's Ol' Roy brand because it is the lowest-priced dog food and satisfies a basic need. Research has found that bargain-hunting price-conscious consumers comprise just 1.2 percent of all shoppers and in general reduce profits by less than 1 percent.[24] **Prestige-sensitive** buyers focus on purchasing products that signify prominence and status.[25] For example, APO jeans, the most expensive blue jeans available at $4,000 a pair, feature gold, silver, or platinum rivets and diamonds instead of buttons.[26]

On the other hand, some consumers vary in their degree of value, price, and prestige consciousness. In some segments, consumers "trade up" to higher-status products in categories such as automobiles, home appliances, restaurants, and even pet food, yet remain price conscious regarding cleaning and grocery products. This trend has benefited marketers such as Starbucks, Sub-Zero, BMW, Whole Foods, and PETCO, which can charge premium prices for high-quality, prestige products, as well as Sam's Club and Costco, which offer basic household products at everyday low prices.[27] Indeed, it appears that a new "mass class" market is emerging in part due to technology and communication advances, the prevalence of designer goods, and the proliferation of counterfeit goods. As a result, more designers like Karl Lagerfeld are creating exclusive designer originals for upscale markets and less-expensive mass market goods for a much broader target audience.[28]

---

value conscious Concerned about price and quality of a product

price conscious Striving to pay low prices

prestige sensitive Drawn to products that signify prominence and status

---

Prestige Sensitivity

Prestige-sensitive customers are attracted to products like jewelry, which are associated with prominence and status.

Some popular cuts don't make the most of a diamond's brilliance. Randy Lapointe makes it his mission to talk you out of them.

Serious jewelers since 1897.

greenwich vail beaver creek palm beach betteridge.com | BETTERIDGE

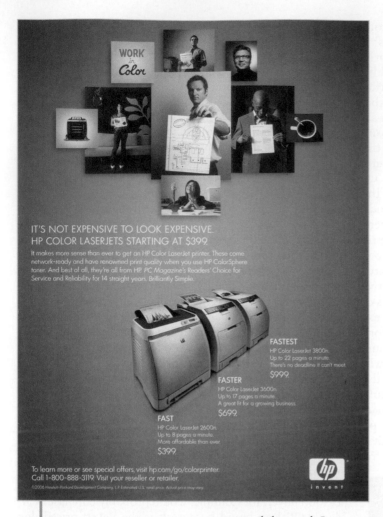

IT'S NOT EXPENSIVE TO LOOK EXPENSIVE.
HP COLOR LASERJETS STARTING AT $399.

It makes more sense than ever to get an HP Color LaserJet printer. These come network-ready and have renowned print quality when you use HP ColorSphere toner. And best of all, they're all from HP. PC Magazine's Readers' Choice for Service and Reliability for 14 straight years. Brilliantly Simple.

FASTEST
HP Color LaserJet 3800n.
Up to 22 pages a minute.
There's no deadline it can't meet.
$999.

FASTER
HP Color LaserJet 3600n.
Up to 17 pages a minute.
A great fit for a growing business.
$699.

FAST
HP Color LaserJet 2600n.
Up to 8 pages a minute.
More affordable than ever.
$399.

To learn more or see special offers, visit hp.com/go/colorprinter.
Call 1-800-888-3119. Visit your reseller or retailer.
©2006 Hewlett-Packard Development Company, L.P. Estimated U.S. retail price. Actual price may vary.

hp invent

Impact of Market Structure

The setting and changing of HP printer prices are affected by the fact that the printer industry is an oligopoly.

Competition

A marketer needs to know competitors' prices so it can adjust its own prices accordingly. This does not mean a company will necessarily match competitors' prices; it may set its price above or below theirs. However, for some organizations (such as airlines), matching competitors' prices is an important strategy for survival.

When adjusting prices, a marketer must assess how competitors will respond. Will competitors change their prices and, if so, will they raise or lower them? In Chapter 3, we described several types of competitive market structures. The structure that characterizes the industry to which a firm belongs affects the flexibility of price setting. For example, because of reduced pricing regulation, firms in the telecommunications industry have moved from a monopolistic market structure to an oligopolistic one, which has resulted in significant price competition.

When an organization operates as a monopoly and is unregulated, it can set whatever prices the market will bear. However, the company may not price the product at the highest-possible level to avoid government regulation or to penetrate a market by using a lower price. If the monopoly is regulated, it normally has less pricing flexibility; the regulatory body lets it set prices that generate a reasonable but not excessive return. A government-owned monopoly may price products below cost to make them accessible to people who otherwise could not afford them. Transit systems, for example, sometimes operate this way. However, government-owned monopolies sometimes charge higher prices to control demand. In some states with state-owned liquor stores, the price of liquor is higher than in states where liquor stores are not owned by a government body.

The automotive and airline industries exemplify oligopolies, in which only a few sellers operate and barriers to competitive entry are high. Companies in such industries can raise their prices in the hope that competitors will do the same. When an organization cuts its price to gain a competitive edge, other companies are likely to follow suit. Thus, very little advantage is gained through price cuts in an oligopolistic market structure.

A market structure characterized by monopolistic competition has numerous sellers with product offerings that are differentiated by physical characteristics, features, quality, and brand images. The distinguishing characteristics of its product may allow a company to set a different price than its competitors. However, firms in a monopolistic competitive market structure are likely to practice nonprice competition, discussed earlier in this chapter.

Under conditions of perfect competition, many sellers exist. Buyers view all sellers' products as the same. All firms sell their products at the going market price, and buyers will not pay more than that. This type of market structure, then, gives a marketer no flexibility in setting prices. Farming, as an industry, has some characteristics of perfect competition. Farmers sell their products at the going market price. At times, for example, corn, soybean, and wheat growers have had bumper crops and been forced to sell them at depressed market prices.

Legal and Regulatory Issues

As discussed in Chapter 3, legal and regulatory issues influence pricing decisions. To curb inflation, the federal government can invoke price controls, freeze prices at certain levels, or determine the rates at which firms may increase prices. In some states and many other countries, regulatory agencies set prices on such products as insurance, dairy products, and liquor.

Many regulations and laws affect pricing decisions and activities in the United States. The Sherman Antitrust Act prohibits conspiracies to control prices, and in interpreting the act, courts have ruled that price fixing among firms in an industry is illegal. Marketers must refrain from fixing prices by developing independent pricing policies and setting prices in ways that do not even hint at collusion. Both the Federal Trade Commission Act and the Wheeler-Lea Act prohibit deceptive pricing. Some other nations and trade agreements have similar prohibitions. The European Commission, for example, fined five rubber producers—Royal Dutch Shell PLC, Eni SpA, Dow Chemical Co., Unipetrol AS, and Trade-Stomil—a combined $682 million for fixing the price of rubber products. Bayer AG had been found guilty of the same charges but escaped a fine after blowing the whistle on the other companies to the European Union's trade watchdog.[29] The commission is also investigating allegations of price fixing in the global candy industry, asking numerous candy makers, including U.S.-based Hershey and Mars, to provide it with information on their pricing practices.[30] In establishing prices, marketers must guard against deceiving customers.

The Robinson-Patman Act has had a particularly strong impact on pricing decisions. For various reasons, marketers may wish to sell the same type of product at different prices. Provisions in the Robinson-Patman Act, as well as those in the Clayton Act, limit the use of such price differentials. **Price discrimination,** the practice of employing price differentials that tend to injure competition by giving one or more buyers a competitive advantage over other buyers, is prohibited by law. However, not all price differentials are discriminatory. A marketer can use price differentials if they do not hinder competition, if they result from differences in the costs of selling or transportation to various customers, or if they arise because the firm has had to cut its price to a particular buyer to meet competitors' prices. Airlines, for example, may charge different customers different prices for the same flights based on the availability of seats at the time of purchase. As a result, fliers sitting in adjacent seats may have paid vastly different fares because one passenger booked weeks ahead, whereas the other booked on the spur of the moment a few days before when only a few seats were still available.

Pricing for Business Markets

L O 6 To consider issues affecting the pricing of products for business markets

Business markets consist of individuals and organizations that purchase products for resale, for use in their own operations, or for producing other products. Establishing prices for this category of buyers sometimes differs from setting prices for consumers. Differences in the size of purchases, geographic factors, and transportation considerations require sellers to adjust prices. In this section, we discuss several issues unique to the pricing of business products, including discounts, geographic pricing, and transfer pricing.

Price Discounting

Producers commonly provide intermediaries with discounts, or reductions, from list prices. Although many types of discounts exist, they usually fall into one of five categories: trade, quantity, cash, seasonal, and allowance. Table 19.3 summarizes some reasons to use each type of discount and provides examples. Such discounts can be a significant factor in a marketing strategy. Consider that Simmons, the mattress manufacturer, had $95 million in allowances, incentives, and cash discounts, or more than 11 percent of its wholesale shipment volume, in 2005.[31]

Trade Discounts. A reduction off the list price given by a producer to an intermediary for performing certain functions is called a **trade, or functional, discount.** A trade discount is usually stated in terms of a percentage or series of percentages off the list price. Intermediaries are given trade discounts as compensation for performing various functions, such as selling, transporting, storing, final processing, and perhaps

price discrimination
Employing price differentials that injure competition by giving one or more buyers a competitive advantage

trade, or functional, discount A reduction off the list price a producer gives to an intermediary for performing certain functions

table 19.3 DISCOUNTS USED FOR BUSINESS MARKETS

Type	Reasons for Use	Examples
Trade (functional)	To attract and keep effective resellers by compensating them for performing certain functions, such as transportation, warehousing, selling, and providing credit	A college bookstore pays about one-third less for a new textbook than the retail price a student pays
Quantity	To encourage customers to buy large quantities when making purchases and, in the case of cumulative discounts, to encourage customer loyalty	Large department store chains purchase some women's apparel at lower prices than do individually owned specialty stores
Cash	To reduce expenses associated with accounts receivable and collection by encouraging prompt payment of accounts	Numerous companies serving business markets allow a 2 percent discount if an account is paid within 10 days
Seasonal	To allow a marketer to use resources more efficiently by stimulating sales during off-peak periods	Florida hotels provide companies holding national and regional sales meetings with deeply discounted accommodations during the summer months
Allowance	In the case of a trade-in allowance, to assist the buyer in making the purchase and potentially earn a profit on the resale of used equipment; in the case of a promotional allowance, to ensure that dealers participate in advertising and sales support programs	A farm equipment dealer takes a farmer's used tractor as a trade-in on a new one. Nabisco pays a promotional allowance to a supermarket for setting up and maintaining a large, end-of-aisle display for a two-week period

providing credit services. Although certain trade discounts are often a standard practice within an industry, discounts vary considerably among industries. It is important that a manufacturer provide a trade discount large enough to offset the intermediary's costs, plus a reasonable profit, to entice the reseller to carry the product.

Quantity Discounts. Deductions from list price that reflect the economies of purchasing in large quantities are called **quantity discounts.** Quantity discounts are used in many industries and pass on to the buyer cost savings gained through economies of scale.

Quantity discounts can be either cumulative or noncumulative. **Cumulative discounts** are quantity discounts aggregated over a stated time period. Purchases totaling $10,000 in a three-month period, for example, might entitle the buyer to a 5 percent, or $500, rebate. Such discounts are intended to reflect economies in selling and to encourage the buyer to purchase from one seller. **Noncumulative discounts** are onetime reductions in prices based on the number of units purchased, the dollar value of the order, or the product mix purchased. Like cumulative discounts, these discounts should reflect some economies in selling or trade functions.

Cash Discounts. A **cash discount,** or price reduction, is given to a buyer for prompt payment or cash payment. Accounts receivable are an expense and a collection problem for many organizations. A policy to encourage prompt payment is a popular practice and sometimes a major concern in setting prices.

Discounts are based on cash payments or cash paid within a stated time. For example, "2/10 net 30" means that a 2 percent discount will be allowed if the account is paid within 10 days. If the buyer does not make payment within the 10-day period, the entire balance is due within 30 days without a discount. If the account is not paid within 30 days, interest may be charged.

quantity discounts Deductions from the list price for purchasing in large quantities

cumulative discounts Quantity discounts aggregated over a stated time period

noncumulative discounts Onetime price reductions based on the number of units purchased, the dollar value of the order, or the product mix purchased

cash discounts Price reductions given to buyers for prompt payment or cash payment

Seasonal Discounts. A price reduction to buyers that purchase goods or services out of season is a **seasonal discount.** These discounts let the seller maintain steadier production during the year. For example, automobile rental agencies offer seasonal discounts in winter and early spring to encourage firms to use automobiles during the slow months of the automobile rental business.

Allowances. Another type of reduction from the list price is an **allowance,** a concession in price to achieve a desired goal. Trade-in allowances, for example, are price reductions granted for turning in a used item when purchasing a new one. Allowances help make the buyer better able to make the new purchase. This type of discount is popular in the aircraft industry. Another example is a promotional allowance, a price reduction granted to dealers for participating in advertising and sales support programs intended to increase sales of a particular item.

Geographic Pricing

Geographic pricing involves reductions for transportation costs or other costs associated with the physical distance between buyer and seller. Prices may be quoted as F.O.B. (free-on-board) factory or destination. An **F.O.B. factory** price indicates the price of the merchandise at the factory, before it is loaded onto the carrier, and thus excludes transportation costs. The buyer must pay for shipping. An **F.O.B. destination** price means the producer absorbs the costs of shipping the merchandise to the customer. This policy may be used to attract distant customers. Although F.O.B. pricing is an easy way to price products, it is sometimes difficult to administer, especially when a firm has a wide product mix or when customers are widely dispersed. Because customers will want to know about the most economical method of shipping, the seller must be informed about shipping rates.

seasonal discount A price reduction given to buyers for purchasing goods or services out of season

allowance A concession in price to achieve a desired goal

geographic pricing Reductions for transportation and other costs related to the physical distance between buyer and seller

F.O.B. factory The price of merchandise at the factory before shipment

F.O.B. destination A price indicating the producer is absorbing shipping costs

Pricing for Business Markets

LESCO offers lawn and garden retailers quantity discounts on large orders as well as attractive financing.

To avoid the problems involved in charging different prices to each customer, **uniform geographic pricing,** sometimes called *postage-stamp pricing,* may be used. The same price is charged to all customers regardless of geographic location, and the price is based on average shipping costs for all customers. Paper products and office equipment are often priced on a uniform basis.

Zone pricing sets uniform prices for each of several major geographic zones; as the transportation costs across zones increase, so do the prices. For example, a Florida manufacturer's prices may be higher for buyers on the Pacific Coast and in Canada than for buyers in Georgia.

Base-point pricing is a geographic pricing policy that includes the price at the factory, plus freight charges from the base point nearest the buyer. This approach to pricing has virtually been abandoned because of its questionable legal status. The policy resulted in all buyers paying freight charges from one location, such as Detroit or Pittsburgh, regardless of where the product was manufactured.

When the seller absorbs all or part of the actual freight costs, **freight absorption pricing** is being used. The seller might choose this method because it wishes to do business with a particular customer or to get more business; more business will cause the average cost to fall and counterbalance the extra freight cost. This strategy is used to improve market penetration and to retain a hold in an increasingly competitive market.

Transfer Pricing

Transfer pricing occurs when one unit in an organization sells a product to another unit. The price is determined by one of the following methods:

- *Actual full cost:* calculated by dividing all fixed and variable expenses for a period into the number of units produced

- *Standard full cost:* calculated based on what it would cost to produce the goods at full plant capacity

- *Cost plus investment:* calculated as full cost plus the cost of a portion of the selling unit's assets used for internal needs

- *Market-based cost:* calculated at the market price less a small discount to reflect the lack of sales effort and other expenses

The choice of transfer pricing method depends on the company's management strategy and the nature of the units' interaction. An organization must also ensure that transfer pricing is fair to all units involved in the transactions.

uniform geographic pricing Charging all customers the same price, regardless of geographic location

zone pricing Pricing based on transportation costs within major geographic zones

base-point pricing Geographic pricing that combines factory price and freight charges from the base point nearest the buyer

freight absorption pricing Absorption of all or part of actual freight costs by the seller

transfer pricing Prices charged in sales between an organization's units

SUMMARY

Price is the value paid for a product in a marketing exchange. Barter, the trading of products, is the oldest form of exchange. Price is a key element in the marketing mix because it relates directly to generation of total revenue. The profit factor can be determined mathematically by multiplying price by quantity sold to get total revenue and then subtracting total costs. Price is the only variable in the marketing mix that can be adjusted quickly and easily to respond to changes in the external environment.

A product offering can compete on either a price or a nonprice basis. Price competition emphasizes price as the product differential. Prices fluctuate frequently, and price competition among sellers is aggressive. Nonprice competition emphasizes product differentiation through distinctive features, service, product quality, or other factors. Establishing brand loyalty by using nonprice competition works best when the product can be physically differentiated and the customer can recognize these differences.

An organization must determine the demand for its product. The classic demand curve is a graph of the quantity of products expected to be sold at various prices if other factors hold constant. It illustrates that as price falls, the quantity demanded usually increases. However, for prestige products, there is a direct positive relationship between price and quantity demanded: demand increases as price increases. Next, price elasticity of demand, the percentage change in quantity demanded relative to a given percentage change in price, must be determined. If demand is elastic, a change in price causes an opposite change in total revenue. Inelastic demand results in a parallel change in total revenue when a product's price is changed.

Analysis of demand, cost, and profit relationships can be accomplished through marginal analysis or break-even analysis. Marginal analysis examines what happens to a firm's costs and revenues when production (or sales volume) is changed by one unit. Marginal analysis combines the demand curve with the firm's costs to develop a price that yields maximum profit. Fixed costs do not vary with changes in the number of units produced or sold; average fixed cost is the fixed cost per unit produced. Variable costs vary directly with changes in the number of units produced or sold. Average variable cost is the variable cost per unit produced. Total cost is the sum of average fixed cost and average variable cost times the quantity produced. The optimal price is the point at which marginal cost (the cost associated with producing one more unit of the product) equals marginal revenue (the change in total revenue that occurs when one additional unit of the product is sold). Marginal analysis is only a model; it offers little help in pricing new products before costs and revenues are established.

Break-even analysis, determining the number of units that must be sold to break even, is important in setting price. The point at which the costs of production equal the revenue from selling the product is the break-even point. To use break-even analysis effectively, a marketer should determine the break-even point for each of several alternative prices. This makes it possible to compare the effects on total revenue, total costs, and the break-even point for each price under consideration. However, this approach assumes the quantity demanded is basically fixed and the major task is to set prices to recover costs.

Eight factors enter into price decision making: organizational and marketing objectives, pricing objectives, costs, other marketing mix variables, channel member expectations, customer interpretation and response, competition, and legal and regulatory issues. When setting prices, marketers should make decisions consistent with the organization's goals and mission. Pricing objectives heavily influence price-setting decisions. Most marketers view a product's cost as the floor below which a product cannot be priced. Because of the interrelationship among the marketing mix variables, price can affect product, promotion, and distribution decisions. The revenue channel members expect for their functions must also be considered when making price decisions.

Buyers' perceptions of price vary. Some consumer segments are sensitive to price, but others may not be. Thus, before determining price, a marketer needs to be aware of its importance to the target market. Knowledge of the prices charged for competing brands is essential to allow the firm to adjust its prices relative to competitors'. Government regulations and legislation also influence pricing decisions. Several laws aim to enhance competition in the marketplace by outlawing price fixing and deceptive pricing. Legislation also restricts price differentials that can injure competition. Moreover, the government can invoke price controls to curb inflation.

Unlike consumers, business buyers purchase products for resale, for use in their own operations, or for producing other products. When adjusting prices, business sellers consider the size of the purchase, geographic factors, and transportation requirements. Producers commonly provide discounts off list prices to intermediaries. The categories of discounts include trade, quantity, cash, seasonal, and allowance. A trade discount is a price reduction for performing such functions as storing, transporting, final processing, or providing credit services. If an intermediary purchases in large enough quantities, the producer gives a quantity discount, which can be either cumulative or noncumulative. A cash discount is a price reduction for prompt payment or payment in cash. Buyers who purchase goods or services out of season may be granted a seasonal discount. An allowance, such as a trade-in allowance, is a concession in price to achieve a desired goal.

Geographic pricing involves reductions for transportation costs or other costs associated with the physical distance between buyer and seller. With an F.O.B. factory price, the buyer pays for shipping from the factory. An F.O.B. destination price means the producer pays for shipping; this is the easiest way to price products, but it is difficult to administer. When the seller charges a fixed average cost for transportation, it is using uniform geographic pricing. Zone prices are uniform within major geographic zones; they increase by zone as transportation costs increase. With base-point pricing, prices are adjusted for shipping expenses incurred by the seller from the base point nearest the buyer. Freight absorption pricing occurs when a seller absorbs all or part of the freight costs.

IMPORTANT TERMS

Price, 552
Barter, 552
Price competition, 553
Nonprice competition, 554
Demand curve, 555
Price elasticity of demand, 557
Fixed costs, 558
Average fixed cost, 558
Variable costs, 558
Average variable cost, 558

Total cost, 558
Average total cost, 558
Marginal cost (MC), 558
Marginal revenue (MR), 558
Break-even point, 561
Internal reference price, 566
External reference price, 566
Value conscious, 567
Price conscious, 567

Prestige sensitive, 567
Price discrimination, 569
Trade (functional) discount, 569
Quantity discounts, 570
Cumulative discounts, 570
Noncumulative discounts, 570
Cash discounts, 570
Seasonal discount, 571
Allowance, 571
Geographic pricing, 571

F.O.B. factory, 571
F.O.B. destination, 571
Uniform geographic pricing, 572
Zone pricing, 572
Base-point pricing, 572
Freight absorption pricing, 572
Transfer pricing, 572

DISCUSSION & REVIEW QUESTIONS

1. Why are pricing decisions important to an organization?

2. Compare and contrast price and nonprice competition. Describe the conditions under which each form works best.

3. Why do most demand curves demonstrate an inverse relationship between price and quantity?

4. List the characteristics of products that have inelastic demand, and give several examples of such products.

5. Explain why optimal profits should occur when marginal cost equals marginal revenue.

6. Chambers Company has just gathered estimates for conducting a break-even analysis for a new product. Variable costs are $7 a unit. The additional plant will cost $48,000. The new product will be charged $18,000 a year for its share of general overhead. Advertising expenditures will be $80,000, and $55,000 will be spent on distribution. If the product sells for $12, what is the break-even point in units? What is the break-even point in dollar sales volume?

7. In what ways do other marketing mix variables affect pricing decisions?

8. What types of expectations may channel members have about producers' prices? How might these expectations affect pricing decisions?

9. How do legal and regulatory forces influence pricing decisions?

10. Compare and contrast a trade discount and a quantity discount.

11. What is the reason for using the term *F.O.B.*?

12. What are the major methods used for transfer pricing?

APPLICATION QUESTIONS

1. Price competition is intense in the fast-food, air travel, and personal computer industries. Discuss a recent situation in which companies had to meet or beat a rival's price in a price-competitive industry. Did you benefit from this situation? Did it change your perception of the companies and/or their products?

2. Customers' interpretations and responses regarding a product and its price are an important influence on marketers' pricing decisions. Perceptions of price are affected by the degree to which a customer is value conscious, price conscious, or prestige sensi-

tive. Discuss how value consciousness, price consciousness, and prestige sensitivity influence the buying decision process for the following products:

a. A new house

b. Weekly groceries for a family of five

c. An airline ticket

d. A soft drink from a vending machine

INTERNET EXERCISE

Visit **www.cengage.com/marketing/pride-ferrell** for resources to help you master the material in this chapter, plus materials that will help you expand your marketing knowledge, including Internet Exercise updates, ACE Self-Tests, hotlinks to companies featured in this chapter, and much more.

Autosite

Autosite offers car buyers a free, comprehensive website to find the invoice prices for almost all car models. The browser can also access a listing of all the latest new-car rebates and incentives. Visit this site at **www.autosite.com.**

1. Find the lowest-priced Lexus available today, and examine its features. Which Lexus dealer is closest to you?

2. If you wanted to purchase this Lexus, what are the lowest monthly payments you could make over the longest time period?

3. Is this free site more credible than a "pay" site? Why or why not?

developing your MARKETING PLAN

The appropriate pricing of a product is an important factor in developing a successful marketing strategy. The price contributes to the profitability of the product and can deter competition from entering the market. A clear understanding of pricing concepts is essential in developing strategy and the marketing plan. Consider the information in this chapter when focusing on the following issues:

1. Does your company currently compete based on price or nonprice factors? Should your new product continue with this approach?

2. Discuss the level of elasticity of demand for your product. Is additional information needed for you to determine its elasticity?

3. At various price points, calculate the break-even point for sales of your product.

4. Using Figure 19.8 as a guide, discuss the various factors that affect the pricing of your product.

The information obtained from these questions should assist you in developing various aspects of your marketing plan found in the *Interactive Marketing Plan* exercise at **www.cengage.com/marketing/pride-ferrell.**

globalEDGE

1. A fundamental component of the price of newsprint in the world market is its supply and demand. At the national level, information can typically be gathered based on a country's imports and exports. Using the Food and Agriculture Organization (FAO) of the United Nations website as a resource devoted to food and agriculture, find Canadian, Mexican, and U.S. trade statistics concerning the newsprint industry. Use the search term "food and agriculture" at **http://globaledge.msu.edu/ibrd** to reach the FAOSTAT website, and then click on the Production link at the top. From the next page, choose ForeSTAT. Click on "newsprint" in the Commodity drop-down box, and then choose the most recent year available in the Year drop-down box. Then, holding down the CTRL key for multiple choices in the country information drop-down boxes, select Canada, Mexico, and the United States. Finally, in the Subject drop-down box, first choose "Import quantity" and then "Export quantity" to conduct separate searches to access the data. From the three countries surveyed, which could be said to increase the price of newsprint in the world market? Which might decrease its price?

2. Business strategists and economists sometimes use a consumer price index (CPI) in their decision models. In fact, some organizations perform a comparison across countries to inform the public of consumer pricing trends. A report titled "Consumer Price Indices (CPI) for OECD Countries" should prove helpful in answering this question. Access this report by using the search term "comparison across countries" at **http://globaledge.msu.edu/ibrd.** Once you reach the OECD web page, click on "View Long Abstract" for the link for Consumer Price Indices (CPI) for OECD Countries. What is a CPI generally used to measure?

Washburn Guitars Tunes Up Pricing Decisions

Chicago-based Washburn Guitars has been making guitars, banjos, and mandolins for every kind of music and every kind of budget since 1883. Whether they play blues or bluegrass, heavy metal or hard rock, musicians and music students buy Washburn instruments for their sound quality, solid craftsmanship, and good looks. Professionals especially appreciate the way Washburn guitars stand up to the wear and tear of lengthy concert tours.

Washburn offers six product lines: electric guitars, acoustic guitars, bass guitars, bluegrass instruments, classical guitars, and travel guitars. More than two dozen of its guitars are designated as "Signature" models designed by well-known musicians such as Dan Donegan of Disturbed, Scott Ian of Anthrax, Joe Trohman of Fall Out Boy, Nick Catanese of Black Label Society, Paul Stanley of Kiss, Nuno Bettencourt of Extreme, and Greg Tribbett of Mudvayne. These names add luster to the Washburn brand and enhance the perceived value of the specially designed Signature models.

In setting the manufacturers' suggested retail price for each product, the company has established four broad price points. At the low end, products that sell for $349 or less are entry level. Products that sell for $350 to $999 are intermediate level, and products that sell for $1,000 to $3,000 are professional level. At the high end, products that sell for more than $3,000 are collectors' level. At every level, Washburn promises that each of its instruments "represents the finest quality at the best possible price."

The guitars made in Washburn's U.S. factory are priced at $2,259 and up, reflecting the high cost of handcrafting. These guitars are perceived to be high quality and are therefore in high demand among professional musicians. In fact, Washburn has a six- to nine-month backlog of orders for its U.S.-made guitars. Its very highest-priced guitars—the few Signature models that sell for $5,000 or more—not only influence customers' perceptions of Washburn quality, they also attract attention and get people talking about the brand. Apart from the high-end models, Washburn's instru-

ments are machine manufactured outside the United States. This keeps both fixed and variable costs lower than in the U.S. factories. Although Washburn's variable costs go down as its manufacturing volume rises, the company has found that changing equipment to make different models takes time and adds to its costs.

Washburn sells its instruments through independent retailers in the United States, Canada, and several dozen countries worldwide. These stores receive quantity discounts for large orders and expect to earn a certain profit margin based on a percentage of the manufacturer's suggested retail price for each product. Although the stores now face intense price competition from online-only retailers that have lower fixed costs, Washburn insists that its authorized retailers not offer discounts below certain minimum prices. Stores that price Washburn products lower than the company's minimum receive a warning, and if they don't change their prices, they are removed from the list of authorized retailers and receive no more shipments.

Washburn's advertising campaigns include magazine and television commercials spotlighting the star quality of the performers and the particular Washburn guitars they prefer, without mentioning prices. Recent campaigns included podcasts that showed Washburn's skilled employees carefully crafting Signature guitars for Nick Catanese and other musicians. Washburn has a strong online presence, including a virtual catalog and a MySpace page with a company blog and information about selected products and the performers who use them. Even after more than 125 years in the music business, Washburn still keeps its marketing—including its pricing—as fresh as the newest number one hit song.[32]

Questions for Discussion

1. Is Washburn using price or nonprice competition? Explain your answer.
2. What effect do you think a manufacturer's suggested retail price is likely to have on customers who buy Washburn guitars from a local music store?
3. Which factors shown in Figure 19.8 are likely to have a major impact on pricing decisions at Washburn?

CASE 19.2

Amazon.com: Putting Price on the Same Page as Profit

Online retail pioneer Amazon.com has built a profitable $14.5 billion business by paying close attention to pricing details. Founded as a web-based bookstore with discount prices, Amazon has since expanded into dozens of product categories and countries. The company never stops investing in technology to upgrade its sites, systems, and offerings. Although hefty high-tech costs are a drag on profit margins, they are essential to Amazon's strategy of attracting customers and keeping them loyal by making the shopping experience easy, fast, and fun.

One hallmark of Amazon's pricing is its long-running offer of free shipping for orders of $25 or more. Because shoppers know they are saving money, they are more inclined to keep spending even after they reach the $25 order threshold to qualify for free shipping. Free shipping has helped Amazon build sales over the years, but it has also added to the company's costs and cut into profits. In the wake of Amazon's success with free shipping, L.L.Bean and others have tested free shipping with no minimum purchase requirement during some holiday periods. Yet making free shipping pay off is tricky, notes a marketing executive at L.L.Bean: "It is expensive to do and it is easy to lose a lot of money doing it."

Amazon is earning significant profits from serving as an online storefront for other merchants (and consumers) to sell their wares. Every time a customer buys something new or used from a seller participating in the Amazon Marketplace, Amazon collects a fee. The margins are especially attractive in this fast-growing part of the business because Amazon does not pay to buy or store any inventory, and the cost of posting items for others is extremely low now that the electronic storefront is up and running.

All-digital products like electronic books, music, and movies are also lucrative because they entail no inventory or shipping costs. This is why Amazon has developed the technology to move more aggressively into downloadable products in several ways. First, it opened a digital music store featuring more than 2 million songs, many priced lower than what Apple's iTunes—the leading online music store—charges for similar products.

Second, it opened a digital movie store that sells movies and television programs priced at about the same level as the DVD versions. Amazon has found that customers who do not want the hassle of going to a video store or placing an order and waiting for a DVD to arrive in the mail are willing to pay for the convenience of instant downloading and viewing. The Amazon Unbox site also rents many of these movies and programs and lets customers watch brief previews before they click to buy or rent.

Third, Amazon has introduced the Kindle reading device, a portable gadget that can wirelessly connect to the Internet and download an electronic book, newspaper, blog, or magazine in seconds. More than 90,000 books are ready for immediate downloads, with best-sellers priced at $9.99 and some classic books priced below $2. "Our vision is to have every book that has ever been in print available in less than 60 seconds," says Amazon founder Jeff Bezos.

Will Amazon's Kindle catch on? This type of product has been tried before by mighty competitors like Sony, Xerox, Barnes & Noble, and Philips Electronics, with little success. Moreover, Amazon initially priced the Kindle $100 higher than the Sony Reader. Even if the company is willing to accept a tiny profit margin on a high volume of download purchases, can the Kindle generate the kind of profitability Amazon needs to continue investing in new models and innovative technology?[33]

Questions for Discussion

1. Are Amazon's shipping costs variable or fixed? How is the company's profitability likely to be affected if customers do not buy more than $25 worth each time they shop?
2. Do you agree with Amazon's decision to price the Kindle higher than the Sony Reader? Explain your answer.
3. If millions of customers are willing to pay what iTunes charges for music, why would Amazon price the same products slightly lower?

20 Setting Prices

LEARNING objectives

❶ To describe the six major stages of the process used to establish prices

❷ To explore issues related to developing pricing objectives

❸ To understand the importance of identifying the target market's evaluation of price

❹ To examine how marketers analyze competitors' prices

❺ To describe the bases used for setting prices

❻ To explain the different types of pricing strategies

TerraCycle Turns Trash into Cash

How should a company price products made from trash? That's a big issue for New Jersey–based TerraCycle. Founded in 2001 by two Princeton University students, TerraCycle's first product was organic plant food made from worm castings, which is what worms leave behind as they gobble up food waste. TerraCycle's newest product line includes tote bags, umbrellas, backpacks, shower curtains, and other items made from recycled cookie wrappers, juice pouches, yogurt containers, soft-drink bottles, and other trash.

entrepreneurs IN ACTION

To get trash, the company has organized thousands of "brigades," local recycling programs sponsored by food and beverage firms like Stonyfield Farm, Coca-Cola, and Nabisco. Consumers who join a local brigade receive postage-paid collection bags to send bundles of wrappers or containers to TerraCycle. The sponsors donate a few cents per recycled wrapper or package to a school, nonprofit organization, or charity of the consumer's choice. So, not only do consumers feel good about keeping wrappers out of landfills, they know their brigade is supporting a worthy cause.

Because the recycling brigades are funded by corporate sponsors, TerraCycle avoids the kind of cost increases that would otherwise reduce profits. "We make a product out of garbage, so our raw-materials prices aren't going up," the CEO says. "Many other raw materials are linked to petroleum products, so everyone else's costs are going up."

As a result, TerraCycle can set highly competitive prices for its products and build profits while helping the environment. "We're able to retail at the store for the same price as a normal Hannah Montana backpack," he adds, "except ours is made from garbage collected by American kids. And each pouch represents a little donation—and parents are captured by this." Now TerraCycle's annual sales are headed past $15 million as the company expands its recycling brigades, designs new products, and gears up to turn more trash into cash.[1]

Because price has such a profound impact on a firm's success, finding the right pricing strategy is crucial. Marketers at TerraCycle are able to set very competitive prices because the costs of raw materials are low. Selecting a pricing strategy is one of the fundamental components of the process of setting prices.

In this chapter, we examine six stages of a process that marketers can use when setting prices. Figure 20.1 illustrates these stages. Stage 1 is the development of a pricing objective that is compatible with the organization's overall marketing objectives. Stage 2 entails assessing the target market's evaluation of price. Stage 3 involves evaluating competitors' prices, which helps determine the role of price in the marketing strategy. Stage 4 requires choosing a basis for setting prices. Stage 5 is the selection of a pricing strategy, or the guidelines for using price in the marketing mix. Stage 6, determining the final price, depends on environmental forces and marketers' understanding and use of a systematic approach to establishing prices. These stages are not rigid steps that all marketers must follow; rather, they are guidelines that provide a logical sequence for establishing prices.

(L O 1) To describe the six major stages of the process used to establish prices

Development of Pricing Objectives

(L O 2) To explore issues related to developing pricing objectives

The first step in setting prices is developing **pricing objectives**—goals that describe what a firm wants to achieve through pricing. Developing pricing objectives is an important task because pricing objectives form the basis for decisions about other stages of pricing. Thus, pricing objectives must be stated explicitly, and the statement should include the time frame for accomplishing them.

Marketers must ensure that pricing objectives are consistent with the firm's marketing and overall objectives because pricing objectives influence decisions in many functional areas, including finance, accounting, and production. A marketer can use both short- and long-term pricing objectives and can employ one or multiple pricing objectives. For instance, a firm may wish to increase market share by 18 percent over the next three years, achieve a 15 percent return on investment, and promote an image of quality in the marketplace.

In this section, we examine some of the pricing objectives companies might set for themselves. Table 20.1 shows the major pricing objectives and typical actions associated with them.

figure 20.1

STAGES FOR ESTABLISHING PRICES

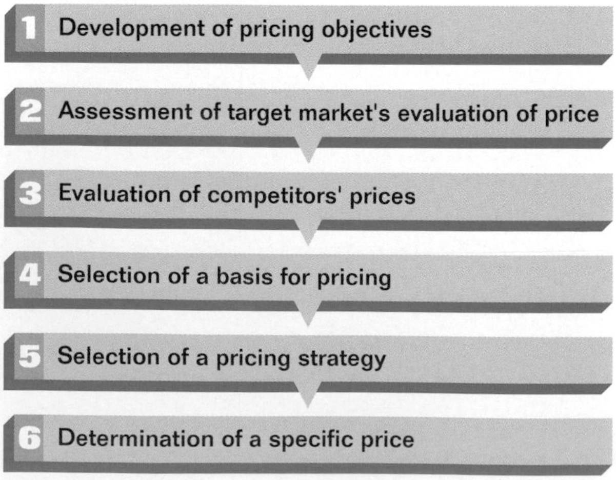

1 Development of pricing objectives

2 Assessment of target market's evaluation of price

3 Evaluation of competitors' prices

4 Selection of a basis for pricing

5 Selection of a pricing strategy

6 Determination of a specific price

pricing objectives Goals that describe what a firm wants to achieve through pricing

table 20.1	**PRICING OBJECTIVES AND TYPICAL ACTIONS TAKEN TO ACHIEVE THEM**

Objective	Possible Action
Survival	Adjust price levels so the firm can increase sales volume to match organizational expenses
Profit	Identify price and cost levels that allow the firm to maximize profit
Return on investment	Identify price levels that enable the firm to yield targeted ROI
Market share	Adjust price levels so the firm can maintain or increase sales relative to competitors' sales
Cash flow	Set price levels to encourage rapid sales
Status quo	Identify price levels that help stabilize demand and sales
Product quality	Set prices to recover research and development expenditures and establish a high-quality image

Survival

Survival is one of the most fundamental pricing objectives. Most organizations will tolerate setbacks such as short-run losses and internal upheaval if necessary for survival. For example, many builders like D.R. Horton and KB Homes slashed prices on brand-new homes by as much as six figures to stimulate sales during a severe housing slump and to slim down an expensive inventory of unsold homes.[2] Because price is a flexible variable, it is sometimes used to keep a company afloat by increasing sales volume to levels that match expenses. For example, a women's apparel retailer may run a three-day, 60-percent-off sale to generate enough cash to pay creditors, employees, and rent.

Profit

Although a business may claim that its objective is to maximize profits for its owners, the objective of profit maximization is rarely operational because its achievement is difficult to measure. Because of this difficulty, profit objectives tend to be set at levels that the owners and top-level decision makers view as satisfactory. Specific profit objectives may be stated in terms of either actual dollar amounts or a percentage of sales revenues. For example, when Procter & Gamble introduced the Gillette Fusion five-blade razor, it set a price 30 percent higher than its Mach 3 three-blade products. With an overall 72 percent market share, P&G hopes the Fusion family of shaving products will help boost profits.[3]

Return on Investment

Pricing to attain a specified rate of return on the company's investment is a profit-related pricing objective. Most pricing objectives based on return on investment (ROI) are achieved by trial and error because not all cost and revenue data needed to project the return on investment are available when setting prices. General Motors, for example, uses ROI pricing objectives. Many pharmaceutical companies also use ROI pricing objectives because of their great investment in research and development.

Market Share

Many firms establish pricing objectives to maintain or increase market share, a product's sales in relation to total industry sales. Toyota, for example, priced its Prius hybrid at a reasonable price that helped consumers afford the car and, in turn, built a strong market share in the hybrid category.[4] To maintain that market share, the company intends to slash both the size and the price of its next-generation Prius.[5] Many

green MARKETING

A Green House You Can Live In

From energy-generating solar panels to nature-friendly building materials, new homes are getting greener by the day. According to the National Association of Home Builders, nine out of ten home-builders now incorporate good-for-the-environ-ment features in new construc-tion. However, cutting-edge products such as solar panels and decking made from recycled plastics are often marketed using a price-skimming strategy. As a result, even people who want to own a green home hesitate when they see the price tag of these extra features.

For instance, the cost of installing solar panels to generate electricity when the sun shines can run $25,000 or more per home. This investment will pay for itself by drastically reducing the owner's energy costs in the long run. Yet of the 1 million new U.S. homes sold every year, fewer than 10,000 are equipped with solar panels. McStain Neighborhoods, a Colorado homebuilder that specializes in environmentally friendly hous-ing, has installed solar panels on only 3 of the nearly 2,000 homes it has sold in the past six years.

Little by little, prices are starting to move lower as more competitors enter the market. In addition, state- and federal government–sponsored incentives are making green home features more affordable for buy-ers. Finally, no matter how high the price tag, builders and buyers in many communities will soon have no choice but to go greener to com-ply with local building codes.[a]

firms recognize that high relative market shares often translate into higher profits. The Profit Impact of Market Strategies (PIMS) studies, conducted over the last 30 years, have shown that both market share and product quality heavily influence profitability. Thus, marketers often use an increase in market share as a primary pricing objective.

Maintaining or increasing market share need not depend on growth in industry sales. Remember that an organization can increase its market share even if sales for the total industry are flat or decreasing. On the other hand, a firm's sales volume may increase while its market share decreases if the overall market is growing.

Cash Flow

Some companies set prices so they can recover cash as quickly as possible. Financial managers understandably seek to quickly recover capital spent to develop products. This objective may have the support of a marketing manager who anticipates a short product life cycle. Although it may be acceptable in some situations, the use of cash flow and recovery as an objective oversimplifies the contribution of price to profits. If this pricing objective results in high prices, competitors with lower prices may gain a large share of the market.

Status Quo

In some cases, an organization is in a favorable position and, desiring nothing more, may set an objective of status quo. Status quo objectives can focus on several dimen-sions, such as maintaining a certain market share, meeting (but not beating) competitors' prices, achieving price stability, and maintaining a favorable public image. A status quo pricing objective can reduce a firm's risks by helping to stabilize

Product Quality
This ad for MicroCotton towels focuses on high product quality to support a higher price.

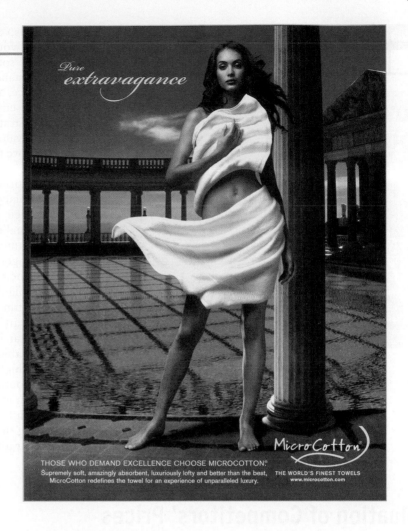

demand for its products. The use of status quo pricing objectives sometimes minimizes pricing as a competitive tool, leading to a climate of nonprice competition in an industry. Professionals such as accountants and attorneys often operate in such an environment.

Product Quality

A company may have the objective of leading its industry in product quality. This goal normally dictates a high price to cover the costs of achieving high product quality and, in some instances, the costs of research and development. For example, Bentley Motors uses premium prices to help signal the quality of its hand-made cars, which can cost from $176,000 to more than $263,000 depending on accessories and options.[6] As previously mentioned, the PIMS studies have shown that both product quality and market share are good indicators of profitability. The products and brands that customers perceive to be of high quality are more likely to survive in a competitive marketplace. High quality usually enables a marketer to charge higher prices for the product.

Assessment of the Target Market's Evaluation of Price

L O 3 To understand the importance of identifying the target market's evaluation of price

After developing pricing objectives, marketers next must assess the target market's evaluation of price. Despite the general assumption that price is a major issue for buyers, the importance of price depends on the type of product, the type of target market, and the purchase situation. For example, buyers are probably more sensitive to gasoline prices than to luggage prices. With respect to the type of target market, adults may have to pay more than children for certain products. The purchase

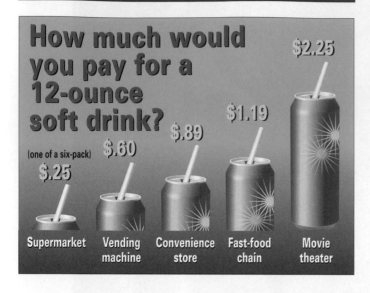

How much would you pay for a 12-ounce soft drink?

(one of a six-pack)

$.25 Supermarket
$.60 Vending machine
$.89 Convenience store
$1.19 Fast-food chain
$2.25 Movie theater

situation also affects the buyer's view of price. Most moviegoers would never pay in other situations the prices charged for soft drinks, popcorn, and candy at movie concession stands. By assessing the target market's evaluation of price, a marketer is in a better position to know how much emphasis to put on price in the overall marketing strategy. Information about the target market's price evaluation may also help a marketer determine how far above the competition the firm can set its prices.

Because some consumers today are seeking less-expensive products and shopping more selectively, some manufacturers and retailers are focusing on the value of their products. Value combines a product's price and quality attributes, which customers use to differentiate among competing brands. Consumers are looking for good deals on products that provide better value for their money. They may also view products that have highly desirable attributes, such as organic content or time-saving features, as having great value. Consumers are increasingly willing to pay a higher price for food that is convenient and time saving, as illustrated in Table 20.2. Companies that offer both low prices and high quality, such as Target and Best Buy, have altered consumers' expectations about how much quality they must sacrifice for low prices.[7] Even retail atmospherics can influence consumers' perceptions of price: the use of soft lights and colors has been found to have a positive influence on perception of price fairness.[8] Understanding the importance of a product to customers, as well as their expectations about quality and value, helps marketers correctly assess the target market's evaluation of price.

Evaluation of Competitors' Prices

(L O 4) To examine how marketers analyze competitors' prices

In most cases, marketers are in a better position to establish prices when they know the prices charged for competing brands, the third step in establishing prices. Discovering competitors' prices may be a regular function of marketing research. Some grocery and department stores, for example, have full-time comparative shoppers who systematically collect data on prices. Companies may also purchase price lists, sometimes weekly, from syndicated marketing research services.

Uncovering competitors' prices is not always easy, especially in producer and reseller markets. Competitors' price lists are often closely guarded. Even if a marketer has access to competitors' price lists, those lists may not reflect the actual prices at which competitive products are sold because those prices may be established through negotiation.

Knowing the prices of competing brands can be very important for a marketer. Competitors' prices and the marketing mix variables they emphasize partly determine how important price will be to customers. A marketer in an industry in which price competition prevails needs competitive price information to ensure its prices are the same as, or lower than, competitors' prices. In some instances, an organization's prices are designed to be slightly above competitors' prices to give its

table 20.2 **EXAMPLES OF PERCEPTIONS OF PRODUCT VALUE**

Basic, Cost-Effective Product	Expensive, Time-Saving Product
1 head romaine lettuce, $1.99	1 bag EarthGreens organic romaine hearts, $3.99
1 sandwich with Welch's jelly, Jif peanut butter, white bread, 46¢	1 Smucker's Uncrustables ready-made peanut butter and jelly sandwich, 82¢
24 oz. Clorox Liquid Bleach, roll of Viva paper towels, $2.69	1 package Clorox Disinfecting Wipes, $3.49

Source: "Stop Getting Eaten Alive by Grocery Bills," *Money,* January 2006, p. 34.

products an exclusive image. In contrast, another company may use price as a competitive tool and price its products below those of competitors. General Motors, for example, priced its Chevrolet Malibu $1,000 less than the top-selling Honda Accord in part because the redesigned car's standard features, fresh interior, and automatic transmission made it a competitive value.[9]

Selection of a Basis for Pricing

LO 5 To describe the bases used for setting prices

The fourth step involves selecting a basis for pricing: cost, demand, and/or competition. The selection of the basis to use is affected by the type of product, the market structure of the industry, the brand's market share position relative to competing brands, and customer characteristics. Although we discuss each basis separately in this section, an organization generally considers two or all three of these dimensions, even if one is the primary basis on which it determines prices. For example, if a company is using cost as a basis for setting prices, marketers in that firm are also aware of and concerned about competitors' prices. If a company is using demand as a basis for pricing, those making pricing decisions still must consider costs and competitors' prices. Indeed, cost is a factor in every pricing decision because it establishes a price minimum below which the firm will not be able to recoup its production and other costs; demand likewise sets an effective price maximum above which customers are unlikely to buy the product. Fairchild Semiconductor uses software to assess all three dimensions, as well as buying behavior, manufacturing capacity, inventories, and product life cycles, in setting prices for its 44,000 products.[10]

Cost-Based Pricing

With **cost-based pricing,** a dollar amount or percentage is added to the cost of the product. This approach thus involves calculations of desired profit margins. Cost-based pricing does not necessarily take into account the economic aspects of supply and demand, nor must it relate to just one pricing strategy or pricing objective. Cost-based pricing is straightforward and easy to implement. Two common forms of cost-based pricing are cost-plus and markup pricing.

Cost-Plus Pricing. With **cost-plus pricing,** the seller's costs are determined (usually during a project or after a project is completed), and then a specified dollar amount or percentage of the cost is added to the seller's cost to establish the price. Cost-plus pricing and competition-based pricing are in fact the most common bases for pricing services.[11] When production costs are difficult to predict, cost-plus pricing is appropriate. Projects involving custom-made equipment and commercial construction are often priced using this technique. The government frequently uses such cost-based pricing in granting defense contracts. One pitfall for the buyer is that the seller may increase costs to establish a larger profit base. Furthermore, some costs, such as overhead, may be difficult to determine. In periods of rapid inflation, cost-plus pricing is popular, especially when the producer must use raw materials that are fluctuating in price. In industries in which cost-plus pricing is common and sellers have similar costs, price competition may not be especially intense.

Markup Pricing. With **markup pricing,** commonly used by retailers, a product's price is derived by adding a predetermined percentage of the cost, called *markup,* to the cost of the product. Although the percentage markup in a retail store varies from one category of goods to another—35 percent of cost for hardware items and 100 percent of cost for greeting cards, for example—the same percentage is often used to determine the prices on items within a single product category, and the percentage markup may be largely standardized across an industry at the retail level. Using a rigid percentage markup for a specific product category reduces pricing to a routine task that can be performed quickly.

Markup can be stated as a percentage of the cost or as a percentage of the selling price. The following example illustrates how percentage markups are determined and points out the differences in the two methods. Assume a retailer purchases a can

cost-based pricing Adding a dollar amount or percentage to the cost of the product

cost-plus pricing Adding a specified dollar amount or percentage to the seller's cost

markup pricing Adding to the cost of the product a predetermined percentage of that cost

of tuna at 45 cents, adds 15 cents to the cost, and then prices the tuna at 60 cents. Here are the figures:

$$\text{Markup as Percentage of Cost} = \frac{\text{Markup}}{\text{Cost}}$$

$$= \frac{15}{45}$$

$$= 33.3\%$$

$$\text{Markup as Percentage of Selling Price} = \frac{\text{Markup}}{\text{Selling Price}}$$

$$= \frac{15}{60}$$

$$= 25.0\%$$

demand-based pricing
Pricing based on the level of demand for the product

competition-based pricing
Pricing influenced primarily by competitors' prices

Obviously, when discussing a percentage markup, it is important to know whether the markup is based on cost or selling price.

Markups normally reflect expectations about operating costs, risks, and stock turnovers. Wholesalers and manufacturers often suggest standard retail markups that are considered profitable. To the extent that retailers use similar markups for the same product category, price competition is reduced. In addition, using rigid markups is convenient and is the major reason retailers, which face numerous pricing decisions, favor this method.

Demand-Based Pricing

Demand-Based Pricing

Rental car companies often use demand-based pricing. When demand for rental cars in a specific location is low, then rental rates are low.

Marketers sometimes base prices on the level of demand for the product. When **demand-based pricing** is used, customers pay a higher price when demand for the product is strong and a lower price when demand is weak. For example, hotels that otherwise attract numerous travelers often offer reduced rates during lower-demand periods. Some long-distance telephone companies, such as Sprint and AT&T, also use demand-based pricing by charging peak and off-peak rates or offering free cell phone minutes during off-peak times. To use this pricing basis, a marketer must be able to estimate the amounts of a product consumers will demand at different prices. The marketer then chooses the price that generates the highest total revenue. Obviously the effectiveness of demand-based pricing depends on the marketer's ability to estimate demand accurately.

Compared with cost-based pricing, demand-based pricing places a firm in a better position to reach higher profit levels, assuming buyers value the product at levels sufficiently above the product's cost.

Competition-Based Pricing

With **competition-based pricing,** an organization considers costs to be secondary to competitors' prices. The importance of this method increases when competing products are relatively homogeneous and the organization is serving markets in which price is a key purchase consideration. A firm that uses competition-based pricing may choose to price below competitors' prices, above competitors' prices, or at the same level. Airlines use competition-based pricing, often charging identical fares on the same routes. Online travel

California is the land of sun, surf and savings.

Get a free upgrade plus up to 25% off your next Avis rental in California.

It's a great time to get out and explore California with valuable rental car savings from Avis. Simply make a reservation with **Avis Worldwide Discount (AWD) # D840400** and **coupon # UUWA021** and you'll get a **free upgrade plus savings of up to 25%** on your rental. These are big offers, but hey—it's a big state.

For more information and reservations, call Avis toll-free at **1-888-777-AVIS** or visit **avis.com**

Terms and Conditions: Coupon valid for a one time, one car group upgrade on an intermediate (group C) through a full-size four-door (group E) car. Maximum upgrade to premium (group G). The upgraded car is subject to vehicle availability at the time of rental and may not be available on some rates at some times. The savings of up to 25% applies to an Avis leisure weekly or weekend rate on an intermediate (group C) through full-size (group E) car and is applicable only to the time and mileage charges of the rental. Taxes, concession recovery fees, vehicle license fee, customer facility charges ($10/contract in CA) and fuel charges are extra. Optional items such as LDW ($27.99/day or less) fees and other surcharges may apply and are extra. Offer is available for U.S. and Canadian residents only for rentals at participating locations in the U.S. Offer may not be used in conjunction with any other coupon, promotion or offer. Weekend rate available Thursday noon; car must be returned by Monday 11:59 p.m., or higher rate will apply. **An advance reservation may be required.** Discount valid on rentals checked out no later between 1/1/07 and 12/31/08. Car rental return restrictions may apply. Offer subject to change without notice. Holiday and other blackout periods may apply. Renter must meet Avis age, driver and credit requirements. Minimum age may vary by location. An additional daily surcharge may apply for renters under 25 years old.

AVIS
We try harder.

services such as Orbitz, Expedia, and Priceline.com have also employed competition-based pricing. If you want to sell your home without the aid of a realtor, how do you determine the value of your home and thus a competitive asking price? One way is to turn to websites such as **www.zillow.com,** which offer estimates of your home's value based on its size and the sale of comparable homes in the area. While you may think your home is worth as much as a castle, if you set the asking price too high above comparable homes for sale, buyers will likely choose one with a lower price.

Although not all introductory marketing texts have exactly the same price, they do have similar prices. The price the bookstore paid to the publishing company for this textbook was determined on the basis of competitors' prices. Competition-based pricing can help a firm achieve the pricing objective of increasing sales or market share. Competition-based pricing may necessitate frequent price adjustments. For example, for many competitive airline routes, fares are adjusted often.

Selection of a Pricing Strategy

LO 6 To explain the different types of pricing strategies

After choosing a basis for pricing, the next step is to select a pricing strategy, an approach or a course of action designed to achieve pricing and marketing objectives. Generally pricing strategies help marketers solve the practical problems of establishing prices. Table 20.3 lists the most common pricing strategies, which we discuss in this section.

Differential Pricing

An important issue in pricing decisions is whether to use a single price or different prices for the same product. Using a single price has several benefits. A primary advantage is simplicity. A single price is easily understood by both employees and customers, and since many salespeople and customers dislike having to negotiate a price, it reduces the chance of an adversarial relationship developing between marketer and customer. The use of a single price does create some challenges, however. If the single price is too high, some potential customers may be unable to afford the product. If it is too low, the organization loses revenue from those customers who would have paid more had the price been higher.

Differential pricing means charging different prices to different buyers for the same quality and quantity of product. For differential pricing to be effective, the market must consist of multiple segments with different price sensitivities, and the method should be used in a way that avoids confusing or antagonizing customers. Customers who are paying the lower prices should not be able to resell the product to the individuals and organizations that are paying the higher prices, unless that is the seller's intention. Differential pricing can occur in several ways, including negotiated pricing, secondary-market discounting, periodic discounting, and random discounting.

differential pricing Charging different prices to different buyers for the same quality and quantity of product

negotiated pricing Establishing a final price through bargaining between seller and customer

Negotiated Pricing. **Negotiated pricing** occurs when the final price is established through bargaining between seller and customer. If you buy a house, for example, you are likely to negotiate the final price with the seller. Negotiated pricing occurs in a number of industries and at all levels of distribution. Cutler-Hammer/Eaton streamlined its contract-negotiations process for more than 90,000 products by reducing quote response times and implementing automatic acceptance of offers.[12] Even when there is a predetermined stated price or a price list,

table 20.3   COMMON PRICING STRATEGIES

Differential Pricing	**Psychological Pricing**
Negotiated pricing	Reference pricing
Secondary-market pricing	Bundle pricing
Periodic discounting	Multiple-unit pricing
Random discounting	Everyday low prices
	Odd-even pricing
New-Product Pricing	Prestige pricing
Price skimming	Customary pricing
Penetration pricing	
	Professional pricing
Product-Line Pricing	
Captive pricing	**Promotional Pricing**
Premium pricing	Price leaders
Bait pricing	Special-event pricing
Price lining	Comparison discounting

RESPONSIBLE marketing?

If you were to survey passengers on a specific flight and ask them how much they paid for their tickets, how many different prices would you get? Airlines use demand-based pricing, which means that different passengers pay different prices. Because they must fill every seat on the plane, the airlines use discount fares and overbooking. They would lose considerable revenue and be unable to make a profit if they offered discounted fares to all passengers. Instead, they provide a few discounted seats at several points prior to the flight to fill seats on the plane. They also hold a few expensive seats close to departure time for travelers who need to make last-minute travel changes and are willing to pay higher fares.

Should airlines be allowed to charge different prices to different customers for the same class of service? Is it fair for a passenger who booked several weeks in advance to pay a higher fare than a customer who bought a ticket only a few days in advance? Would it be more fair if an airline charged the same coach fare to all passengers, even if the average ticket price were somewhat higher than the current average ticket price?

manufacturers, wholesalers, and retailers may negotiate to establish the final sales price. Consumers commonly negotiate prices for houses, cars, and used equipment.

Secondary-Market Pricing. Secondary-market pricing means setting one price for the primary target market and a different price for another market. Often the price charged in the secondary market is lower. However, when the costs of serving a secondary market are higher than normal, secondary-market customers may have to pay a higher price. Examples of secondary markets include a geographically isolated domestic market, a market in a foreign country, and a segment willing to purchase a product during off-peak times. For example, some restaurants offer special "early-bird" prices during the early evening hours, movie theaters offer senior citizen and afternoon matinee discounts, and some textbooks and pharmaceutical products are sold for considerably less in certain foreign countries than in the United States. Secondary markets give an organization an opportunity to use excess capacity and stabilize the allocation of resources.

Periodic Discounting. Periodic discounting is the temporary reduction of prices on a patterned or systematic basis. Most retailers, for example, have annual holiday

secondary-market pricing Setting one price for the primary target market and a different price for another market

periodic discounting Temporary reduction of prices on a patterned or systematic basis

Random Discounting

UPS uses random discounting to attract customers to its UPS retail stores. By using random discounting, customers can't predict when discounts will be available.

sales. Some women's apparel stores have two seasonal sales each year: a winter sale in the last two weeks of January and a summer sale in the first two weeks of July. Automobile dealers regularly discount prices on current models in the fall, when the next year's models are introduced. From the marketer's point of view, a major problem with periodic discounting is that because the discounts follow a pattern, customers can predict when the reductions will occur and may delay their purchases until they can take advantage of the lower prices. Research suggests that placing a time limit on periodic discounts does not directly affect consumers' perceptions of the products' value or their search and purchase behavior.

Random Discounting. To alleviate the problem of customers knowing when discounting will occur, some organizations employ **random discounting;** that is, they temporarily reduce their prices on an unsystematic basis. When price reductions of a product occur randomly, current users of that brand are likely unable to predict when the reductions will occur and thus will not delay their purchases. However, in the automobile industry, with its increasing reliance on sales, rebates, and incentives such as 0 percent financing, random discounting has become nearly continuous discounting, and some analysts have warned that automakers will find it increasingly difficult to cease the generous incentives that consumers have come to expect. Marketers also use random discounting to attract new customers. For example, Lever Brothers may temporarily reduce the price of one of its bar soaps in the hope of attracting new customers.

Whether they use periodic discounting or random discounting, retailers often employ tensile pricing when putting products on sale. *Tensile pricing* refers to a broad statement about price reductions as opposed to detailing specific price discounts. Examples of tensile pricing would be statements such as "20 to 50 percent off," "up to 75 percent off," and "save 10 percent or more." Generally, using and advertising the tensile price that mentions only the maximum reduction (such as "up to 50 percent off") generates the highest customer response.[13]

New-Product Pricing

Setting the base price for a new product is a necessary part of formulating a marketing strategy. The base price is easily adjusted (in the absence of government price controls), and its establishment is one of the most fundamental decisions in the marketing mix. The base price can be set high to recover development costs quickly or provide a reference point for developing discount prices for different market segments. When a marketer sets base prices, it also considers how quickly competitors will enter the market, whether they will mount a strong campaign on entry, and what effect their entry will have on the development of primary demand. Two strategies used in new-product pricing are price skimming and penetration pricing.

Price Skimming. **Price skimming** means charging the highest possible price that buyers who most desire the product will pay. The Nokia N95 slider mobile phone, for example, has a starting price of $699, more than some laptop computers and $300 more than Apple's iPhone, but it offers a music player, a 5-megapixel camera with Zeiss lenses, removable memory cards, the ability to support wireless headphones, and the ability to connect to high-speed data networks.[14] This approach provides the most flexible introductory base price. Demand tends to be inelastic in the introductory stage of the product life cycle.

Price skimming can provide several benefits, especially when a product is in the introductory stage of its life cycle. A skimming policy can generate much-needed initial cash flows to help offset sizable development costs. Price skimming protects the marketer from problems that arise when the price is set too low to cover costs. When a firm introduces a product, its production capacity may be limited. A skimming price can help keep demand consistent with the firm's production capabilities. The use of a skimming price may attract competition into an industry because the high price makes that type of business appear quite lucrative. New-product prices should be based on both the value to the customer and competitive products.

random discounting Temporary reduction of prices on an unsystematic basis

price skimming Charging the highest possible price that buyers who most desire the product will pay

MEET DAD'S NEW GOLF BUDDY.

This Father's Day, when you give Dad a Gillette Fusion Power Phenom, you're not only giving him Gillette's best shave, you're giving him the chance to win a trip for two to play golf with Tiger Woods. Visit www.gillettechampions.com to find out more about the ultimate Father's Day gift.

gillettechampions.com

Gillette

The Best a Man Can Get™

Captive Pricing

The Gillette Turbo Fusion razor is inexpensive. To use this razor on a regular basis, customers must buy the replacement-blade cartridges. The annual cost of the replacement-blade cartridges is significant. Gillette is using captive pricing.

penetration pricing Setting prices below those of competing brands to penetrate a market and gain a significant market share quickly

Penetration Pricing. With **penetration pricing,** prices are set below those of competing brands to penetrate a market and gain a large market share quickly. Perhaps the ultimate penetration pricing strategy was implemented by the Arctic Monkeys. The U.K. rock band handed out free CDs of its music at early performances, and fans e-mailed the music to friends. The resulting viral effort led to a recording contract for the band, which boasts the fastest-selling debut album in British music history.[15] This approach is less flexible for a marketer than price skimming because it is more difficult to raise a penetration price than to lower or discount a skimming price. It is not unusual for a firm to use a penetration price after having skimmed the market with a higher price.

Penetration pricing can be especially beneficial when a marketer suspects that competitors could enter the market easily. If penetration pricing allows the marketer to gain a large market share quickly, competitors may be discouraged from entering the market. In addition, because the lower per-unit penetration price results in lower per-unit profit, the market may not appear to be especially lucrative to potential new entrants. Apple prices its iPod digital music players at penetration prices. Although retailers such as Best Buy and Circuit City earn very little profit on iPods, they benefit from selling iPod accessories. Many iPod buyers purchase at least two accessories, and the market for accessories such as speakers and covers is expected to double. Moreover, 40 percent of vehicles sold in the United States will offer some sort of iPod integration this year.[16]

Product-Line Pricing

Rather than considering products on an item-by-item basis when determining pricing strategies, some marketers employ product-line pricing. **Product-line pricing** means establishing and adjusting the prices of multiple products within a product line. When marketers use product-line pricing, their goal is to maximize profits for an entire product line rather than focusing on the profitability of an individual product. Product-line pricing can lend marketers flexibility in price setting. For example, marketers can set prices so that one product is quite profitable while another increases market share due to having a lower price than competing products.

Before setting prices for a product line, marketers evaluate the relationship among the products in the line. When products in a line are complementary, sales increases in one item raise demand for other items. For instance, desktop printers and toner cartridges are complementary products. When products in a line function as substitutes for one another, buyers of one product in the line are unlikely to purchase one of the other products in the same line. In this case, marketers must be sensitive to how a price change for one of the brands may affect the demand not only for that brand but also for the substitute brands. For example, if decision makers at Procter & Gamble were considering a price change for Tide detergent, they would be concerned about how the price change might influence sales of Cheer, Bold, and Gain.

When marketers employ product-line pricing, they have several strategies from which to choose. These include captive pricing, premium pricing, bait pricing, and price lining.

Captive Pricing. With **captive pricing,** the basic product in a product line is priced low, whereas items required to operate or enhance it are priced higher. Printer companies have used this pricing strategy: providing relatively low-cost, low-margin printers and selling ink cartridges to generate significant profits. Likewise, Sony set an introduction price for its PlayStation 3 video game console at $599—$240 below cost—with the anticipation of selling accessories and games to generate profits.[17]

Premium Pricing. **Premium pricing** is often used when a product line contains several versions of the same product; the highest-quality products or those with the most versatility are given the highest prices. Chevrolet, for example, set an initial price of $100,000 for its fastest, most powerful Corvette ZR1. The company expects the muscle car, with its hand-built 620-horsepower V8 engine, to compete with the performance of a Ferrari.[18] Other products in the line are priced to appeal to price-sensitive shoppers or to buyers who seek product-specific features.

Marketers that use a premium strategy often realize a significant portion of their profits from premium-priced products. Examples of product categories that commonly use premium pricing are small kitchen appliances, beer, ice cream, and cable television service.

Bait Pricing. To attract customers, marketers may put a low price on one item in the product line with the intention of selling a higher-priced item in the line; this strategy is known as **bait pricing.** For example, a computer retailer might advertise its lowest-priced computer model, hoping that when customers come to the store they will purchase a higher-priced one. This strategy can facilitate sales of a line's higher-priced products. As long as a retailer has sufficient quantities of the advertised low-priced model available for sale, this strategy is considered acceptable. In contrast, *bait and switch* is an activity in which retailers have no intention of selling the bait product; they use the low price merely to entice customers into the store to sell them higher-priced products. Bait and switch is considered unethical, and in some states it is illegal.

Price Lining. When an organization sets a limited number of prices for selected groups or lines of merchandise, it is using **price lining.** A retailer may have various styles and brands of similar-quality men's shirts that sell for $15 and another line of higher-quality shirts that sell for $22. Microsoft set different prices for different versions of its Vista operating system depending on features: the barebones Windows

product-line pricing Establishing and adjusting prices of multiple products within a product line

captive pricing Pricing the basic product in a product line low, while pricing related items higher

premium pricing Pricing the highest-quality or most versatile products higher than other models in the product line

bait pricing Pricing an item in a product line low with the intention of selling a higher-priced item in the line

price lining Setting a limited number of prices for selected groups or lines of merchandise

E-ntertainment MARKETING

The Pricing Game: Xbox vs. PlayStation vs. Wii

Microsoft raised eyebrows when it used captive pricing for its Xbox 360 video game system, seeking to profit from games and accessories. The Xbox did well for a time, particularly among buyers who like the *Halo* games, which were available exclusively for Xbox. When a manufacturing glitch caused many Xbox consoles to fail—some more than once— Microsoft repaired all broken units for free and, to reassure buyers, tripled the warranty period to three years. The company set aside $1 billion to cover these costs and also cut prices to boost sales. In all, Microsoft has so far lost an estimated $5 billion on consoles, paying a high price for staying in the game-console market.

Sony is also playing the captive-pricing game. Once the dominant player in consoles, Sony reportedly loses money on its PlayStation consoles but enjoys healthy profits on its popular games. However, when it launched the high-end PlayStation 3, buyers balked at the high price, despite new features such as a Blu-ray disc player. After losing market share to Microsoft and Nintendo for months, Sony slashed the console's price and sales rose sharply.

Meanwhile, Nintendo cannot keep up with demand for its Wii console, which has a handheld remote so users can play a video bowling game, for instance, by swinging the controller the way they would roll a bowling ball. This innovation helped Nintendo gain share against both the Xbox and the PlayStation 3 during the Wii's first year on the market—without resorting to price cutting.[b]

Vista Home Basic for $199; Windows Vista Home Premium, $239; Windows Vista Business, $299; and the feature-packed Windows Vista Ultimate for $399.[19] Price lining simplifies customers' decision making by holding constant one key variable in the final selection of style and brand within a line.

figure 20.2

PRICE LINING

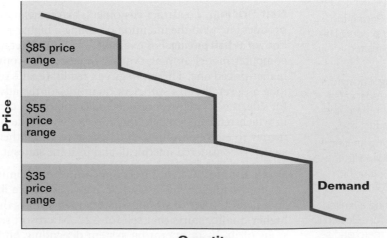

The basic assumption in price lining is that the demand for various groups or sets of products is inelastic. If the prices are attractive, customers will concentrate their purchases without responding to slight changes in price. Thus, a women's dress shop that carries dresses priced at $85, $55, and $35 may not attract many more sales with a drop to, say, $83, $53, and $33. The "space" between the price of $85 and $55, however, can stir changes in consumer response. With price lining, the demand curve looks like a series of steps, as shown in Figure 20.2.

Another type of price lining is subscription services. Cable or satellite TV subscribers choose different packages or groupings of channels with different prices. Likewise, subscribers to subscription DVD rental services such as Netflix can choose a membership price based on the number of DVDs they want to receive at one time.

Psychological Pricing

Learning the price of a product is not always a pleasant experience for customers. It is sometimes surprising (as at a movie concession stand) and sometimes downright horrifying; most of us have experienced some sort of "sticker shock." Research indicates that consumers are likely to have negative reactions to incomplete or unclear pricing information, especially when it is conveyed through misleading communications.[20] **Psychological pricing** attempts to influence a customer's perception of price to make a product's price more attractive. In this section, we consider several forms of psychological pricing: reference pricing, bundle pricing, multiple-unit pricing, everyday low prices (EDLP), odd-even pricing, customary pricing, and prestige pricing.

Reference Pricing. **Reference pricing** means pricing a product at a moderate level and displaying it next to a more expensive model or brand in the hope that the customer will use the higher price as an external reference price (i.e., a comparison price). Because of the comparison, the customer is expected to view the moderate price favorably. Reference pricing is based on the "isolation effect," meaning an alternative is less attractive when viewed by itself than when compared with other alternatives. When you go to Best Buy or Circuit City to buy a DVD player, a moderately priced DVD player may appear especially attractive because it offers most of the important attributes of the more expensive alternatives on display and at a lower price. It is not unusual for an organization's moderately priced private brands to be positioned alongside more expensive, better-known manufacturer brands. On the other hand, many private store brands are raising their prices in an effort to boost these products' image.[21]

Bundle Pricing. **Bundle pricing** is packaging together two or more products, usually complementary ones, to be sold at a single price. Many fast-food restaurants, for example, offer combination meals at a price that is lower than the combined prices of each item priced separately. Most telephone and cable television providers bundle local telephone service, broadband Internet access, and digital cable or satellite television for one monthly fee. To attract customers, the single bundled price is usually considerably less than the sum of the prices of the individual products. The opportunity to buy the bundled combination of products in a single transaction may be of value to the customer as well. Marketing research models suggest that marketers can develop heterogeneous bundles of products with optimal prices for different market segments.[22] Bundle pricing facilitates customer satisfaction and, when slow-moving products are bundled with those with a higher turnover, can help stimulate sales and increase revenues. It may also help foster customer loyalty and improve customer retention. Selling products as a package rather than individually may also result in cost savings. Bundle pricing is commonly used for banking and travel services, computers, and automobiles with option packages.

Some companies, however, are unbundling packages in favor of a more itemized approach sometimes called *à la carte pricing*. This approach gives customers the opportunity to pick and choose only the products they want without having to purchase additional products in the bundle that may not be right for their purposes.[23] Some television viewers, for example, have expressed a desire to subscribe to only their favorite cable channels rather than a predetermined package of

psychological pricing Pricing that attempts to influence a customer's perception of price to make a product's price more attractive

reference pricing Pricing a product at a moderate level and displaying it next to a more expensive model or brand

bundle pricing Packaging together two or more complementary products and selling them at a single price

You don't have to be royalty to afford this kind of magic.

$1600
(only $58 a day per person at a select Disney Value Resort)

Family of four, six nights, seven days including Theme Park tickets

Price based on two adults, one junior, one child, occupying one standard room, most nights during value, regular and summer seasons in 2007. The number of rooms allocated for this package may be limited. Tickets are for one Theme Park per day and must be used within 14 days of first use.

Endless magic, that's surprisingly affordable. It all begins the moment you realize a *Walt Disney World* vacation is within your reach. A family of four can enjoy six nights and seven days at a select Disney Value Resort for only $1600, including Theme Park tickets. That's about $58 a day per person. No matter your family's size or what time of year, there are *Walt Disney World* vacation packages to fit your budget.

To find out how affordable a *Walt Disney World* vacation can be, visit **Disneyworld.com/afford** or call **(407) 939-7715** or your local Travel Agent.

Walt Disney World

Walt Disney Travel Company CST# 1022229-50

Bundle Pricing

Price bundling is commonly used in the travel and tourism industry. Here, Walt Disney World promotes a package with a bundled price that includes lodging and park admission.

multiple-unit pricing Packaging together two or more identical products and selling them at a single price

everyday low prices (EDLP) Pricing products low on a consistent basis

channels. At online music services such as iTunes and Rhapsody, customers can pick and choose individual songs to download instead of buying a complete CD. Furthermore, with the help of the Internet, comparison shopping has become more convenient than ever, allowing customers to price items and create their own mixes. Nevertheless, bundle pricing continues to appeal to customers who prefer the convenience of a package.[24]

Multiple-Unit Pricing. Multiple-unit pricing occurs when two or more identical products are packaged together and sold at a single price. This normally results in a lower per-unit price than the price regularly charged. Multiple-unit pricing is commonly used for twin-packs of potato chips, 4-packs of light bulbs, and 6- and 12-packs of soft drinks. Customers benefit from the cost saving and convenience this pricing strategy affords. A company may use multiple-unit pricing to attract new customers to its brands and, in some instances, to increase consumption of them. When customers buy in larger quantities, their consumption of the product may increase. For example, multiple-unit pricing may encourage a customer to buy larger quantities of snacks, which are likely to be consumed in higher volume at the point of consumption simply because they are available. However, this is not true for all products. For instance, greater availability at the point of consumption of light bulbs, bar soap, and table salt is not likely to increase usage.

Discount stores and especially warehouse clubs, such as Sam's Club and Costco, are major users of multiple-unit pricing. For certain products in these stores, customers receive significant per-unit price reductions when they buy packages containing multiple units of the same product, such as an eight-pack of canned tuna fish.

Everyday Low Prices (EDLP). To reduce or eliminate the use of frequent short-term price reductions, some organizations use an approach referred to as **everyday low prices (EDLP).** With EDLP, a marketer sets a low price for its products on a consistent basis rather than setting higher prices and frequently discounting them. Everyday low prices, though not deeply discounted, are set far enough below competitors' prices to make customers feel confident they are receiving a fair price. EDLP is employed by retailers such as Wal-Mart and manufacturers such as Procter & Gamble. Indeed, Wal-Mart, which has already trademarked the phrase "Always Low Prices. Always," sought to trademark the acronym EDLP because of its extensive use of the practice. However, vociferous opposition from the National Grocers Association and Supervalue, a supermarket chain, as well as other firms ultimately led Wal-Mart to withdraw its trademark application.[25] A company that uses EDLP benefits from reduced losses from frequent markdowns, greater stability in sales, and decreased promotional costs. The furniture industry, where consumers' greatest concern seems to be price relative to quality, has taken a cue from Wal-Mart. Traditionally dominated by U.S. manufacturing, even long-standing U.S. companies such as Timberlake are now offering lower-priced furniture made overseas to compete more effectively.[26]

One of the major problems with EDLP is that customers can respond to it in several different ways. Over the last several years, many marketers have inadvertently "trained" customers to expect and seek out deeply discounted prices. In some product categories, such as apparel, finding the deepest discount has become almost a

Everyday Low Price

This grocery chain of neighborhood markets employs the everyday low prices pricing strategy.

national consumer sport. Thus, failure to provide deep discounts can be a problem for certain marketers. In some instances, customers simply do not believe everyday low prices are what marketers claim they are but are instead a marketing gimmick.

Odd-Even Pricing. Through **odd-even pricing**—ending the price with certain numbers—marketers try to influence buyers' perceptions of the price or the product. Odd pricing assumes more of a product will be sold at $99.95 than at $100. Theoretically, customers will think, or at least tell friends, that the product is a bargain—not $100, but $99 and change. Also, customers will supposedly think the store could have charged $100 but instead cut the price to the last cent, to $99.95. Some claim, too, that certain types of customers are more attracted by odd prices than by even ones. Research indicates that women are more likely to respond to odd-ending prices than men are.[27] However, research on the effect of odd-even prices has demonstrated conflicting results; one recent study found that odd prices that end in 5, 8, or 9 failed to trigger the threshold of consumer response.[28] Another study, however, found that consumers favor prices that end in 0 or 5 when they are making investment decisions.[29] Nonetheless, odd prices are far more common today than even prices.

Even prices are often used to give a product an exclusive or upscale image. An even price supposedly will influence a customer to view the product as being a high-quality, premium brand. A shirt maker, for example, may print on a premium shirt package a suggested retail price of $42.00 instead of $41.95; the even price of the shirt is used to enhance its upscale image.

Customary Pricing. With **customary pricing,** certain goods are priced primarily on the basis of tradition. Recent economic uncertainties have made most prices fluctuate fairly widely, but the classic example of the customary, or traditional, price is the price of a candy bar. For years, a candy bar cost 5 cents. A new candy bar would have had to be something very special to sell for more than a nickel. This price was so sacred that rather than change it, manufacturers increased or decreased the size of the candy bar itself as chocolate prices fluctuated. Today, of course, the nickel candy bar has disappeared. However, most candy bars still sell at a consistent, but obviously higher, price. Thus, customary pricing remains the standard for this market.

odd-even pricing Ending the price with certain numbers to influence buyers' perceptions of the price or product

customary pricing Pricing on the basis of tradition

Customary Pricing

Most candy bar manufacturers use a customary pricing strategy.

Prestige Pricing. With **prestige pricing,** prices are set at an artificially high level to convey prestige or a quality image. Prestige pricing is used especially when buyers associate a higher price with higher quality. Pharmacists report that some consumers complain when a prescription does not cost enough; apparently some consumers associate a drug's price with its potency. Research confirms that many consumers believe a more expensive medicine works better than a less costly one.[30]

Typical product categories in which selected products are prestige priced include perfumes, liquor, jewelry, and cars. Although appliances have not traditionally been prestige priced, upscale appliances have appeared in recent years to capitalize on the willingness of some consumer segments to "trade up" for high-quality products. These consumers do not mind paying extra for a Subzero refrigerator, a Viking commercial range, or a Whirlpool Duet washer and dryer because these products offer high quality as well as a level of prestige. If these producers lowered their prices dramatically, the new prices would be inconsistent with the perceived high-quality images of their products. From golf clubs to handbags, prestige products are selling at record levels. Consider some of the prestige products shown in Table 20.4 that were selected as the best by *Smart Money* magazine. For example, spending on pets has escalated to $36 billion a year, rivaling what some families spend on their children. Some consumers are willing to pay as much as $1,000 for designer dogs like the "puggle," a beagle-pug mix, for their nice dispositions, intelligence, and smaller sizes.[31]

table 20.4 | **SAMPLE PRESTIGE PRODUCT PRICES**

Mail-order beef	Neiman's Ranch Grass-Fed Prime Filet	$63/pound
Plasma TVs	Panasonic TH-50PZ750U 50"	$3,499
Winter Adventures	Week at Lake Placid Lodge's Owl's Head Cabin	$4,480/couple
Champagne	House of Salon's Salon Le Mesnil 1996	$350

Source: Kristen Bellstrom, "The Best of Everything," *Smart Money,* Nov. 13, 2007, www.smartmoney.com.

prestige pricing Setting prices at an artificially high level to convey prestige or a quality image

Professional Pricing

Professional pricing is used by people who have great skill or experience in a particular field. Professionals often believe their fees (prices) should not relate directly to the time and effort spent in specific cases; rather, a standard fee is charged regardless of the problems involved in performing the job. Some doctors' and lawyers' fees are prime examples, such as $75 for a checkup, $2,000 for an appendectomy, and $995 for a divorce. Other professionals set prices in other ways. Like other marketers, professionals have costs associated with facilities, labor, insurance, equipment, and supplies. Certainly costs are considered when setting professional prices.

The concept of professional pricing carries the idea that professionals have an ethical responsibility not to overcharge customers. In some situations, a seller can charge customers a high price and continue to sell many units of the product. Medicine offers several examples. If a person with diabetes requires one insulin treatment per day to survive, she or he will probably buy that treatment whether its price is $1 or $10. In fact, the patient will probably purchase the treatment even if the price rose. In these situations, sellers could charge exorbitant fees. Drug companies claim that despite their positions of strength in this regard, they charge ethical prices rather than what the market will bear.

Promotional Pricing

As an ingredient in the marketing mix, price is often coordinated with promotion. The two variables are sometimes so closely interrelated that the pricing policy is promotion oriented. Types of promotional pricing include price leaders, special-event pricing, and comparison discounting.

Price Leaders. Sometimes a firm prices a few products below the usual markup, near cost, or below cost, which results in prices known as **price leaders**. This type of pricing is used most often in supermarkets and restaurants to attract customers by giving them especially low prices on a few items. Management hopes that sales of regularly priced products will more than offset the reduced revenues from the price leaders.

Special-Event Pricing. To increase sales volume, many organizations coordinate price with advertising or sales promotions for seasonal or special situations. **Special-event pricing** involves advertised sales or price cutting linked to a holiday, a season, or an event. If the pricing objective is survival, special sales events may be designed to generate the necessary operating capital. Special-event pricing entails coordination of production, scheduling, storage, and physical distribution. Whenever a sales lag occurs, special-event pricing is an alternative that marketers should consider.

Comparison Discounting. **Comparison discounting** sets the price of a product at a specific level and simultaneously compares it with a higher price. The higher price may be the product's previous price, the price of a competing brand, the product's price at another retail outlet, or a manufacturer's suggested retail price. Customers may find comparative discounting informative, and it can have a significant impact on their purchases. However, overuse of comparison pricing may reduce customers' internal reference prices, meaning they no longer believe the higher price is the regular or normal price.[32]

Because this pricing strategy has occasionally led to deceptive pricing practices, the Federal Trade Commission has established guidelines for comparison discounting. If the higher price against which the comparison is made is the price formerly charged for the product, the seller must have made the previous price available to customers for a reasonable period of time. If the seller presents the higher price as the one charged by other retailers in the same trade area, it must be able to demonstrate that this claim is true. When the seller presents the higher price as the manufacturer's suggested retail price, the higher price must be similar to the price at which a reasonable proportion of the product was sold. Some manufacturers' suggested retail prices are so high that very few products are actually sold at those prices. In such cases, comparison discounting would be deceptive. An example of deceptive

professional pricing Fees set by people with great skill or experience in a particular field

price leaders A product priced below the usual markup, near cost, or below cost

special-event pricing Advertised sales or price cutting linked to a holiday, a season, or an event

comparison discounting Setting a price at a specific level and comparing it with a higher price

comparison discounting occurred when a major retailer put 93 percent of its power tools on sale, with discounts ranging from 10 to 40 percent. The retailer's frequent price reductions meant the tools sold at sale prices most of the year. Thus, comparisons with regular prices were deemed to be deceptive.

Determination of a Specific Price

A pricing strategy will yield a certain price, the final step in the process. However, this price may need refinement to make it consistent with circumstances as well as pricing practices in a particular market or industry. When Blockbuster eliminated late fees for movie rentals, it probably did not anticipate that revenue would fall by nearly 10 percent. Given increasing competition from online movie rental and pay-per-view services, the company will need to evaluate its overall marketing strategy—including pricing—in light of decreased profitability.[33]

Pricing strategies should help in setting a final price. If they are to do so, marketers must establish pricing objectives; have considerable knowledge about target market customers; and determine demand, price elasticity, costs, and competitive factors. Also, the way pricing is used in the marketing mix will affect the final price.

In the absence of government price controls, pricing remains a flexible and convenient way to adjust the marketing mix. In many situations, prices can be adjusted quickly—over a few days or even in minutes. Such flexibility is unique to this component of the marketing mix.

SUMMARY

The six stages in the process of setting prices are (1) developing pricing objectives, (2) assessing the target market's evaluation of price, (3) evaluating competitors' prices, (4) choosing a basis for pricing, (5) selecting a pricing strategy, and (6) determining a specific price. Setting pricing objectives is critical because pricing objectives form a foundation on which the decisions of subsequent stages are based. Organizations may use numerous pricing objectives, including short-term and long-term ones, and different objectives for different products and market segments. Pricing objectives are overall goals that describe the role of price in a firm's long-range plans. There are several major types of pricing objectives. The most fundamental pricing objective is the organization's survival. Price usually can be easily adjusted to increase sales volume or combat competition to help the organization stay alive. Profit objectives, which are usually stated in terms of sales dollar volume or percentage change, are normally set at a satisfactory level rather than at a level designed to maximize profits. A sales growth objective focuses on increasing the profit base by raising sales volume. Pricing for return on investment (ROI) has a specified profit as its objective. A pricing objective to maintain or increase market share links market position to success. Other types of pricing objectives include cash flow, status quo, and product quality. Assessing the target market's evaluation of price tells the marketer how much emphasis to place on price and may help determine how far above the competition the firm can set its prices. Understanding how important a product is to customers relative to other products, as

well as customers' expectations of quality, helps marketers correctly assess the target market's evaluation of price.

A marketer needs to be aware of the prices charged for competing brands. This allows the firm to keep its prices in line with competitors' prices when nonprice competition is used. If a company uses price as a competitive tool, it can price its brand below competing brands.

The three major dimensions on which prices can be based are cost, demand, and competition. When using cost-based pricing, the firm determines price by adding a dollar amount or percentage to the cost of the product. Two common cost-based pricing methods are cost-plus and markup pricing. Demand-based pricing is based on the level of demand for the product. To use this method, a marketer must be able to estimate the amounts of a product buyers will demand at different prices. Demand-based pricing results in a high price when demand for a product is strong and a low price when demand is weak. In the case of competition-based pricing, costs and revenues are secondary to competitors' prices.

A pricing strategy is an approach or a course of action designed to achieve pricing and marketing objectives. Pricing strategies help marketers solve the practical problems of establishing prices. The most common pricing strategies are differential pricing, new-product pricing, product-line pricing, psychological pricing, professional pricing, and promotional pricing.

When marketers employ differential pricing, they charge different buyers different prices for the same quality and quantity of products. Negotiated pricing, secondary-market discounting, periodic discounting, and random discounting are forms of differential pricing. With negotiated pricing, the final price is established through bargaining between seller and customer. Secondary-market pricing involves setting one price for the primary target market and a different price for another market; often the price charged in the secondary market is lower. Marketers employ periodic discounting when they temporarily lower their prices on a patterned or systematic basis; the reason for the reduction may be a seasonal change, a model-year change, or a holiday. Random discounting occurs on an unsystematic basis.

Two strategies used in new-product pricing are price skimming and penetration pricing. With price skimming, the organization charges the highest price that buyers who most desire the product will pay. A penetration price is a low price designed to penetrate a market and gain a significant market share quickly.

Product-line pricing establishes and adjusts the prices of multiple products within a product line. This strategy includes captive pricing, in which the marketer prices the basic product in a product line low and prices of related items higher; premium pricing, in which prices on higher-quality or more versatile products are set higher than those on other models in the product line; bait pricing, in which the marketer tries to attract customers by pricing an item in the product line low with the intention of selling a higher-priced item in the line; and price lining, in which the organization sets a limited number of prices for selected groups or lines of merchandise. Organizations that employ price lining assume the demand for various groups of products is inelastic.

Psychological pricing attempts to influence customers' perceptions of price to make a product's price more attractive. With reference pricing, marketers price a product at a moderate level and position it next to a more expensive model or brand. Bundle pricing is packaging together two or more complementary products and selling them at a single price. With multiple-unit pricing, two or more identical products are packaged together and sold at a single price. To reduce or eliminate use of frequent short-term price reductions, some organizations employ everyday low pricing (EDLP), setting a low price for products on a consistent basis. When employing odd-even pricing, marketers try to influence buyers' perceptions of the price or the product by ending the price with certain numbers. Customary pricing is based on traditional prices. With prestige pricing, prices are set at an artificially high level to convey prestige or a quality image.

Professional pricing is used by people who have great skill or experience in a particular field, therefore allowing them to set the price. This concept carries the idea that professionals have an ethical responsibility not to overcharge customers. As an ingredient in the marketing mix, price is often coordinated with promotion. The two variables are sometimes so closely interrelated that the pricing policy is promotion oriented. Promotional pricing includes price leaders, special-event pricing, and comparison discounting.

Price leaders are products priced below the usual markup, near cost, or below cost. Special-event pricing involves advertised sales or price cutting linked to a holiday, season, or event. Marketers that use a comparison discounting strategy price a product at a specific level and compare it with a higher price.

Once a price is determined by using one or more pricing strategies, it needs to be refined to a final price consistent with the pricing practices in a particular market or industry.

IMPORTANT TERMS

Pricing objectives, 580
Cost-based pricing, 585
Cost-plus pricing, 585
Markup pricing, 585
Demand-based pricing, 586
Competition-based pricing, 586
Differential pricing, 587

Negotiated pricing, 587
Secondary-market pricing, 588
Periodic discounting, 588
Random discounting, 589
Price skimming, 589
Penetration pricing, 590
Product-line pricing, 591
Captive pricing, 591

Premium pricing, 591
Bait pricing, 591
Price lining, 591
Psychological pricing, 593
Reference pricing, 593
Bundle pricing, 593
Multiple-unit pricing, 594
Everyday low prices (EDLP), 594

Odd-even pricing, 595
Customary pricing, 595
Prestige pricing, 596
Professional pricing, 597
Price leaders, 597
Special-event pricing, 597
Comparison discounting, 597

DISCUSSION & REVIEW QUESTIONS

1. Identify the six stages in the process of establishing prices.

2. How does a return on an investment pricing objective differ from an objective of increasing market share?

3. Why must marketing objectives and pricing objectives be considered when making pricing decisions?

4. Why should a marketer be aware of competitors' prices?

5. What are the benefits of cost-based pricing?

6. Under what conditions is cost-plus pricing most appropriate?

7. A retailer purchases a can of soup for 24 cents and sells it for 36 cents. Calculate the markup as a percentage of cost and as a percentage of selling price.

8. What is differential pricing? In what ways can it be achieved?

9. For what types of products would price skimming be most appropriate? For what types of products would penetration pricing be more effective?

10. Describe bundle pricing and give three examples using different industries.

11. What are the advantages and disadvantages of using everyday low prices?

12. Why do customers associate price with quality? When should prestige pricing be used?

13. Are price leaders a realistic approach to pricing? Explain your answer.

APPLICATION QUESTIONS

1. Price skimming and penetration pricing are strategies that are commonly used to set the base price of a new product. Which strategy is more appropriate for the following products? Explain.

   a. Short airline flights between cities in Florida

   b. A high-definition DVD player

   c. A backpack or book bag with a lifetime warranty

   d. Season tickets for a newly franchised NBA basketball team

2. Price lining is used to set a limited number of prices for selected lines of merchandise. Visit a few local retail stores to find examples of price lining. For what types of products and stores is this practice most common? For what types of products and stores is price lining not typical or feasible?

3. Professional pricing is used by people who have great skill in a particular field, such as doctors, lawyers, and business consultants. Find examples (advertisements, personal contacts) that reflect a professional pricing policy. How is the price established? Are there any restrictions on the services performed at that price?

4. Organizations often use multiple pricing objectives. Locate an organization that uses several pricing objectives, and discuss how this approach influences the company's marketing mix decisions. Are some objectives oriented toward the short term and others toward the long term? How does the marketing environment influence these objectives?

INTERNET EXERCISE

Visit **www.cengage.com/marketing/pride-ferrell** for resources to help you master the material in this chapter, plus materials that will help you expand your marketing knowledge, including Internet exercise updates, ACE Self-Tests, hotlinks to companies featured in this chapter, and much more.

T-Mobile

T-Mobile has attempted to position itself as a low-cost cellular phone service provider. A person can purchase a calling plan, a cellular phone, and phone accessories at its website. Visit the T-Mobile website at **www.t-mobile.com**.

1. Determine the various nationwide calling rates available in your city.

2. How many different calling plans are available in your area?

3. What type of pricing strategy is T-Mobile using on its rate plans in your area?

developing your MARKETING PLAN

Setting the right price for a product is a crucial part of marketing strategy. Price helps to establish a product's position in the mind of the consumer and can differentiate a product from its competition. Several decisions in the marketing plan will be affected by the pricing strategy that is selected. To assist you in relating the information in this chapter to the development of your marketing plan, focus on the following:

1. Using Table 20.1 as a guide, discuss each of the seven pricing objectives. Which pricing objectives will you use for your product? Consider the product life cycle, competition, and product positioning for your target market during your discussion.

2. Review the various types of pricing strategies in Table 20.3. Which of these is the most appropriate for your product?

3. Select a basis for pricing your product (cost, demand, and/or competition). How will you know when it is time to revise your pricing strategy?

The information obtained from these questions should assist you in developing various aspects of your marketing plan found in the *Interactive Marketing Plan* exercise at **www.cengage.com/marketing/pride-ferrell.**

1. Your firm may purchase raw materials from the Czech Republic. Initial estimates put the cost of your first shipment at 1 billion Czech koruna. Find out how much this is in U.S. dollars by using the search term "foreign exchange markets" at **http://globaledge .msu.edu/ibrd.** Once you reach the FX Street webpage, click on the Currency Converter. Using your abilities to navigate foreign exchange markets, how much is this amount in U.S. dollars?

2. You have been asked to make a comparison across countries to determine which countries have had the highest inflation over the past 12 months. This knowledge may help in projecting which countries' markets may not perform as well as expected due to rising costs and decreased consumer spending. This information can be found in the Consumer Price Indices (CPI) for OECD countries by using the search term "comparison across countries" at **http://globaledge.msu.edu/ibrd.** Once you reach the OECD web page, download the report titled "Consumer Price Indices (CPI) for OECD Countries" to find the three countries with the highest inflation for consumer prices.

The Smart Car: Tiny with a Price Tag to Match

Tiny car, tiny price tag, tiny gasoline bill. The Smart Car, made by Daimler's Mercedes Car Group in Hambach, France, first appeared on U.S. roads in 2008, just as prices at the gas pump were hitting record highs week after week. The timing could not have been better. Tired of emptying their wallets every time they filled their gas tanks, many U.S. drivers were thinking about downsizing from a big sport-utility vehicle or pickup truck to a smaller vehicle. But were they ready for a 106-inch-long car that seats only two people? Daimler was ready to find out.

The Smart Car had a good track record in other parts of the world. From 1998 to 2008, Daimler sold more than 900,000 Smart Cars in Europe, the Middle East, Asia, Australia, Mexico, and Canada. The car was cute, nimble, and unconventional—a good size for getting through crowded, narrow city streets and fitting into any tight parking spot. Not only was the purchase price highly affordable, but the excellent fuel efficiency made the car especially popular in countries where gas prices were generally high.

To bring the Smart Car to the United States, Daimler redesigned the body and engineering to meet U.S. safety standards. It added six inches to the car's length and included four air bags, an antilock braking system, a collapsing steering column, and other safety features. It also installed a fuel-saving 71-horsepower engine so that the Smart Car would go about 40 highway miles on a gallon of gasoline.

Daimler set the list price of the Smart Fortwo Pure model—the basic version of the two-seater—at $11,590. The list price of the Smart Fortwo Passion Coupe, equipped with more features, was $13,590. The list price of the Smart Fortwo Passion Cabriolet, a convertible with leather seats and additional features, was $16,590. Buyers had the option of ordering extras, such as a metallic-paint finish or an alarm system, for an additional fee. Keeping the list price as tiny as the car allowed Daimler to build market share quickly.

Rather than selling Smart Cars through its regular dealer network, Daimler contracted with the Penske Automotive Group to handle distribution and sales. In another unusual move, Daimler set up a website to let buyers reserve the model of their choice and choose from six interior colors and six exterior colors on the car body's removable panels. Three of the exterior colors were offered as part of the purchase price, while the three metallic exterior colors were offered at an extra cost. The $99 reservation fee was applied to the buyer's purchase price once the ordered model became available. By the time Smart Cars arrived in U.S. showrooms, 30,000 people had paid for reservations.

To build customer interest prior to the introduction, Daimler sent a number of Smart Cars on a 50-city U.S. tour. Nearly 50,000 members of the media and prospective car buyers took test drives. Although many reporters couldn't resist poking fun at the tiny car (*USA Today* called it a "breadbox on wheels"), they all noted its high fuel efficiency and low purchase price.

Soon, demand became so strong that even buyers who had reserved their cars well in advance had to wait months for delivery. A few U.S. customers who didn't want to wait paid as much as $39,000 for European Smart Cars adapted to meet U.S. safety and emissions standards. Down the road, as more auto manufacturers gear up to bring gas-sipping cars to U.S. markets, will the Smart Car maintain its popularity?[34]

Questions for Discussion

1. Why is bundle pricing appropriate for the various models of Smart Cars?
2. How is demand likely to affect dealers' willingness to negotiate prices with Smart Car buyers?
3. Imagine that Daimler is considering whether to sell unpainted Smart Cars and reduce the list price by $1,500. The Smart Car exterior consists of ten removable panels that can be easily painted. Buyers could paint their own panels, leave the panels unpainted, or pay the dealer an additional fee to personalize their cars by having the panels custom finished in almost any color or design. What are the advantages and disadvantages of this pricing idea?

CASE 20.2

Apple Hangs Up on High iPhone Price

Days before the first Apple iPhones went on sale, thousands of buyers lined up outside Apple stores, eager to try the new cell phone's large, user-friendly touch screen and multimedia capabilities. Like Apple's iconic iPod media player, instantly identifiable because of its sleek case and white ear buds, the stylish iPhone became a must-have status symbol for tech-savvy consumers across the United States. However, despite a major promotional campaign, widespread media coverage, many rave reviews, and a fast-growing customer base, the iPhone became the focus of criticism and controversy within two months of its release.

Apple has traditionally set high prices for its new products. One purpose of pricing in this way is to reinforce the brand's high-end positioning and special cachet. Another is to start recouping development costs and build profits from the very start of each product's life. This pricing strategy has worked with the company's Macintosh computers and its iPods, allowing the Apple to increase both revenues and profits year after year.

The iPhone was initially priced at $599, not including the cost of monthly phone service through an exclusive deal with AT&T. Two months later, in a break from its usual pattern, Apple abruptly slashed the iPhone's price by $200. Although electronic products often drop in price over time, they rarely sell for so much less so soon after introduction. This time, Apple had its eye on the year-end holidays, believing that setting a more affordable price during the fall would put the iPhone within reach of a larger number of gift-giving buyers. The company also saw an opportunity to close in on its goal of selling 10 million iPhones worldwide within 18 months of the product's launch.

Apple's pricing decision provoked angry protests from customers who protested that they had overpaid for a cutting-edge product that was going mainstream more quickly than expected. With Apple on the spot, CEO Steve Jobs quickly conceded that customers had a point. "Our early customers trusted us, and we must live up to that trust with our actions in moments like these,"

he said in a statement posted on Apple's website. To avoid alienating early buyers, the company offered a $100 Apple store credit to each customer who had purchased an iPhone before the price cut. Although this policy also drew criticism—because the credit had no value except toward the purchase of something from Apple—the pricing controversy lost steam after a few weeks.

Apple soon launched a series of new iPhone models with more features, more power, and a lower price than when the product was originally introduced. The iPhone has gone on to become an enormous success around the world, sparking excitement and prompting long lines at Apple stores in the United Kingdom, France, and other countries. Just as the iPod attracted many first-time Apple buyers, the iPhone's unique appeal has brought in new customers and given loyal customers another reason to buy from Apple.

The buzz from the iPhone and other new products has also boosted demand for Apple's line of Macintosh computers. In fact, the company gained enough market share to become the third-largest U.S. computer marketer, trailing only market leader Dell and Hewlett-Packard. Higher sales of Apple's entire product mix have resulted in record-setting company profits. Just as important, all these innovations have polished the Apple brand and added to its trend-setting image—which, in turn, allows the company to charge premium prices for its coveted products.[35]

Questions for Discussion

1. What was Apple's primary pricing objective when it introduced the iPhone? What was its primary objective in cutting the product's price just two months after introduction?
2. How much weight does Apple appear to have given to its evaluation of competitive pricing?
3. Do you agree with Apple's decision to switch away from price skimming after the iPhone's introduction? Defend your answer.

Tata Steers Into Ultra Affordable Cars

How can a car sell for less than $3,000? That's the price Tata Motors set for its new People's Car, a four-door, four-seat subcompact designed specifically for India. With a rear-mounted motor, this tiny car includes absolutely no extras—no radio, no reclining seats. What the People's Car does have, however, is an ultra-low price tag. And that is what makes it very attractive to millions of potential buyers in India. Now "someone who never even dreamed of a car finds it within reach," says Ravi Kant, the CEO/managing director of Tata Motors.

Racing to develop and market the world's cheapest car has been a challenge, even for a car manufacturer with as much experience as Mumbai-based Tata, which is India's largest automaker. The company began working on the People's Car in 2003 with the goal of creating a functional yet eye-pleasing design that would fit buyers' lifestyles and tight budgets and, at the same time, be profitable to manufacture and sell. The most essential ingredient was keeping costs in line to keep the car ultra-affordable.

Low Price, Low Costs

The first step in developing the People's Car was to establish an upper level for the car's price: roughly one lakh (100,000 Indian rupees), the equivalent of less than $3,000. To sell a car at this price, "you have to cut costs on everything—seats, materials, components—the whole package," says a Tata official. That's exactly what Tata did, using expertise gained from its years of marketing trucks, cars, and buses for markets in India, Europe, South America, Southeast Asia, and the Middle East. For instance, Tata sells its Indica compact car for $8,500 in eastern Europe.

The 33-horsepower engine of the People's Car may not win any races, but it can get the car to a top speed of about 80 miles per hour. Thanks to low-cost parts and manufacturing, the cost of each engine is only about $700. In contrast, an engine made in the West can cost twice as much. By shaving the cost of each part and component, streamlining assembly methods, and offering only a stripped-down basic model, Tata has been able to achieve its low-price goal.

What's Driving the Market?

India's healthy economy is propelling millions of consumers into the middle class and accelerating demand for affordable transportation. As many as 65 million people currently drive small motor scooters in India, often carrying family members on the back. Some of these drivers will be able to trade up to a new car if the price is right.

In fact, new-car sales are projected to double by 2013 to more than 3 million cars per year. Small wonder that Tata designed its People's Car with four doors to appeal to buyers who often have family members and friends riding along. Finally, India's population skews young, with a median age under 25. If Tata can attract young first-time buyers with a low-priced model and maintain their loyalty as they graduate to higher-priced cars in the years ahead, the company will profit in the long term.

Competition on the Roads of India

Competition is fierce at the low end of the car market. Maruti Suzuki India, which sells small cars starting at about $5,000, is the market leader. With its nationwide service network, high brand recognition, and new production facilities in the works, Maruti Suzuki is a formidable competitor.

Other rivals are also expanding to take advantage of this fast-growing segment of the market. Hyundai India, for instance, is opening a global center for small-car manufacturing and adding manufacturing space. Its Santro sedan, which offers both air conditioning and power steering as standard features, sells for about $6,300. Volkswagen is creating a new subcompact for India, even as its Skoda division introduces the low-priced Fabia model there.

Toyota is designing a no-frills car that will sell in India and other emerging nations for under $7,000. In the process, the company expects to develop new technology that will help it cut costs on other vehicles in its global product mix. Honda has a plant in India and is breaking ground for a second plant right now. Meanwhile, U.S. carmakers are looking at how they might enter the market in the near future.

Renault-Nissan, one of the most aggressive competitors that Tata will face, is just starting work on a car to be priced at or below $3,000. The company knows a lot about low-cost, low-priced cars, because since 2004, it has produced its popular $7,000 Logan four-door sedan in Romania and Russia. Nearly half a million Logans are already on the roads of Europe, and even though Renault-Nissan's two plants are operating at full capacity all day, every day, the firm is still struggling to meet ever-growing demand. To shave costs, Renault-Nissan limited the number of parts that go into the Logan and avoided expensive electronics. To speed development and eliminate the high costs of building prototypes, the company proceeded from digital design directly to production. This achievement alone saved $40 million and is one reason for CEO Carlos Ghosn's confidence that Renault-Nissan can succeed in the worldwide ultra-low-price segment. "With the Logan, we have the product and we have the lead," he says.

Environmental and Safety Concerns

As enthusiastic as Tata and other car manufacturers may be about marketing millions of tiny cars with tiny price tags, the car has generated both environmental and safety concerns. Some critics fear that broadening the base of car ownership will only add to the pollution problems in India's largest cities. Where national and local regulations do not require antipollution devices, manufacturers are unlikely to install them because of the added costs.

Safety is an issue because more cars on the road mean more traffic congestion and more opportunity for accidents. Cars made by Tata and its competitors comply with all of India's safety standards, but those standards do not require equipment such as air bags and antilock brakes. Safety advocates worry that people traveling in the smallest, lightest cars will be more vulnerable to serious injury if involved in a traffic accident. For now, the automakers are moving ahead as they monitor the issues and stay alert for possible changes in government regulations.

Getting in Gear

Can Tata score a big hit with the People's Car? Certainly the company has a long history of good marketing management and above-average profitability. Being based in India gives Tata the advantage of being close to its customers and understanding their needs. And Tata's engineers and designers have found creative ways of containing costs to keep the new car ultra-affordable. With competitors readying their own super-budget models, however, Tata will have to get in gear to keep the People's Car ahead of the pack.[36]

Questions for Discussion

1. Which factors seem to have the greatest influence on Tata's decision about pricing its People's Car? Explain.
2. What appear to be Tata's primary pricing objectives for the People's Car?
3. Assess the level of price competition in India's car industry. What are the implications for Tata's marketing?
4. Why must Tata pay close attention to legal and regulatory changes when planning and pricing future models of the People's Car?

Careers in Marketing

Changes in the Workplace

Between one-fourth and one-third of the civilian workforce in the United States is employed in marketing-related jobs. Although the field offers a multitude of diverse career opportunities, the number of positions in each area varies. For example, millions of workers are employed in many facets of sales, but relatively few people work in public relations and marketing research.

Many nonbusiness organizations now recognize that they perform marketing activities. For that reason, the number of marketing positions in government agencies, hospitals, charitable and religious groups, educational institutions, and similar organizations is increasing. Today's nonprofit organizations are competitive and better managed, with job growth rates often matching those of private-sector firms. Another area ripe with opportunities is the World Wide Web. The federal government makes more sales to consumers online than even Amazon.com. With so many businesses setting up websites, demand will rise for people who have the skills to develop and design marketing strategies for the Web.

Many workers outplaced from large corporations are choosing an entrepreneurial path, creating still more new opportunities for first-time job seekers. Even some individuals with secure managerial positions are leaving corporations and heading to smaller companies, toward greater responsibility and autonomy. The traditional career path used to be graduation from college, then a job with a large corporation, and a climb up the ladder to management. This pattern has changed, however. Today people are more likely to experience a career path of sideways "gigs" rather than sequential steps up a corporate ladder.

Career Choices Are Major Life Choices

Many people think career planning begins with an up-to-date résumé and a job interview.[1] In reality, it begins long before you prepare your résumé. It starts with *you* and what you want to become. In some ways, you have been preparing for a career ever since you started school. Everything you have experienced during your lifetime you can use as a resource to help you define your career goals. Since you will likely spend more time at work than at any other single place during your lifetime, it makes sense to spend that time doing something you enjoy. Unfortunately, some people just work at a *job* because they need money to survive. Other people choose a *career* because of their interests and talents or a commitment to a particular profession. Whether you arc looking for a job or a career, you should examine your priorities.

Personal Factors Influencing Career Choices

Before choosing a career, you need to consider what motivates you and what skills you can offer an employer. The following questions may help you define what you consider important in life:

1. *What types of activities do you enjoy?* Although most people know what they enjoy in a general way, a number of interest inventories exist. By helping you determine specific interests and activities, these inventories can help you land a job that will lead to a satisfying career. In some cases, it may be sufficient just to list the activities you enjoy, along with those you dislike. Watch for patterns that may influence your career choices.

2. *What do you do best?* All jobs and all careers require employees to be able to "do something." It is extremely important to assess what you do best. Be honest with yourself about your ability to succeed in a specific job. It may help to make a list of your strongest job-related skills. Also, try looking at your skills from an employer's perspective: What can you do that an employer would be willing to pay for?

3. *What kind of education will you need?* The amount of education you need is determined by the type of career you choose. In some careers, it is impossible to get an entry-level position without at least a college degree. Other careers may also require technical or hands-on skills. Generally, additional education increases your potential earning power.

4. *Where do you want to live?* Initially, some college graduates will want to move to a different part of the country before entering the job market, whereas others may prefer to reside close to home, friends, and relatives. In reality, successful job applicants must be willing to go where the jobs are. The location of an entry-level job may be influenced by the type of marketing career selected. For example, some of the largest advertising agencies are in New York, Chicago, and Los Angeles. Likewise, large marketing research organizations are based in metropolitan areas. On the other hand, sales positions and retail management jobs are available in medium-size as well as large cities.

Job Search Activities

When people begin to search for a job, they often first go online or turn to the classified ads in their local newspaper. Those ads are an important source of information about jobs in a particular area, but they are only one source. Many other sources can lead to employment and a satisfying career. Because there is a wealth of information about career planning, you should be selective in both the type and the amount of information you use to guide your job search.

In recent years the library, a traditional job-hunting tool, has been joined by the Internet. Both the library and the Internet are sources of everything from classified newspaper ads and government job listings to detailed information on individual companies and industries. You can use either resource to research an area of employment or a particular company that interests you. In addition, the Internet allows you to check electronic bulletin boards for current job information, exchange ideas with other job seekers through online discussion groups or e-mail, and get career advice from professional counselors. You can also create your own webpage to inform prospective employers about your qualifications. You may even have a job interview online. Many companies use their websites to post job openings, accept applications, and interview candidates.

As you start your job search, you may find the following websites helpful. (Addresses of additional career-related websites can be accessed through the Student Career Center at **www.cengage.com/marketing/pride-ferrell**.)

America's Job Bank: **www.ajb.dni.us**

This massive site contains information on nearly 250,000 jobs. Listings come from 1,800 state employment offices around the country and represent every line of work, from professional and technical to blue-collar, and from entry level on up.

CareerBuilder.com: **www.careerbuilder.com**

This site is one of the largest on the Internet, with more than 900,000 jobs to view. The site allows a job seeker to find jobs, post résumés, get advice and career resources, and obtain information on career fairs.

Hoover's Online: **www.hoovers.com**

Hoover's offers a variety of job search tools, including information on potential employers and links to sites that post job openings.

The Monster Board: **www.monster.com**

The Monster Board carries hundreds of job listings and offers links to related sites, such as company homepages and sites with information about job fairs.

Federal jobs: **http://usajobs.opm.gov**

If you are interested in working for a government agency, this site lists positions all across the country. You can limit your search to specific states or do a general cross-country search for job openings.

Other web addresses for job seekers include:

> **www.careers-in-marketing.com**
>
> **www.marketingjobs.com**
>
> **www.starthere.com/jobs**
>
> **www.careermag.com**
>
> **www.salary.com**

In addition to the library and the Internet, the following sources can be of great help when trying to find the "perfect job":

1. *Campus placement offices.* Colleges and universities have placement offices staffed by trained personnel specialists. In most cases, these offices serve as clearinghouses for career information. The staff may also be able to guide you in creating a résumé and preparing for a job interview.

2. *Professional sources and networks.* A network is a group of people—friends, relatives, and professionals—who are in a position to exchange information, including information about job openings. According to many job applicants, networking is one of the best sources of career information and job leads. Start with as many people as you can think of to establish your network. (The Internet can be very useful in this regard.) Contact these people and ask specific questions about job opportunities they are aware of. Also, ask each individual to introduce or refer you to someone else who may be able to help you in your job search.

3. *Private employment agencies.* Private employment agencies charge a fee for helping people find jobs. Typical fees can be as high as 15 to 20 percent of an employee's first-year salary. The fee may be paid by the employer or the employee. Like campus placement offices, private employment agencies provide career counseling, help create résumés, and provide preparation for job interviews. Before you use a private employment agency, be sure you understand the terms of any contract or agreement you sign. Above all, make sure you know who is responsible for paying the agency's fee.

4. *State employment agencies.* The local office of your state employment agency is a valuable source of information about job openings in your immediate area. Some job applicants are reluctant to use state agencies because most jobs available through them are for semiskilled or unskilled workers. From a practical standpoint, though, it can't hurt to consult state employment agencies. They will have information about some professional and managerial positions available in your area, and you will not be charged a fee if you obtain a job through one of these agencies.

Many graduates want a job immediately and are discouraged at the thought that an occupational search can take months. But people seeking entry-level jobs should expect their job search to take considerable time. Of course, the state of the economy and whether employers generally are hiring can shorten or extend a job search.

During a job search, you should use the same work habits that effective employees use on the job. Resist the temptation to "take the day off" from job hunting. Instead, make a master list of the activities you want to accomplish each day. If necessary, force yourself to make contacts, do job research, or schedule interviews that might lead to job opportunities. (In fact, many job applicants look at the job hunt as their actual job and "work" full time at it until they find the job they want.) Above all, realize that an occupational search requires patience and perseverance. According to many successful applicants, perseverance may be the job hunter's most valuable trait.

Planning and Preparation

The key to landing the job you want is planning and preparation—and planning begins with goals. In particular, it is important to determine your *personal* goals, decide on the role your career will play in reaching those goals, and then develop your *career* goals. Once you know where you are going, you can devise a feasible plan for getting there.

The time to begin planning is as early as possible. You must, of course, satisfy the educational requirements for the occupational area you desire. Early planning will give you the opportunity to do so. However, some of the people who will compete with you for the better jobs will also be fully prepared. Can you do more? Company recruiters say the following factors give job candidates a definite advantage.

■ *Work experience.* You can get valuable work experience in cooperative work/school programs, during summer vacations, or in part-time jobs during the school year. Experience in your chosen occupational area carries the most weight, but even unrelated work experience is useful.

■ *The ability to communicate well.* Verbal and written communication skills are increasingly important in all aspects of business. Yours will be tested in your letters to recruiters, in your résumé, and in interviews. You will use these same communication skills throughout your career.

■ *Clear and realistic job and career goals.* Recruiters feel most comfortable with candidates who know where they are headed and why they are applying for a specific job.

Again, starting early will allow you to establish well-defined goals, sharpen your communication skills (through elective courses, if necessary), and obtain solid work experience. To develop your own personal career plan, go to the **www.cengage.com/marketing/pride-ferrell** student site and access the Student Career Center. There you will find personal career plan worksheets.

The Résumé

An effective résumé is one of the keys to being considered for a good job. Because your résumé states your qualifications, experiences, education, and career goals, a potential employer can use it to assess your compatibility with the job requirements. The résumé should be accurate and current.

In preparing a résumé, it helps to think of it as an advertisement. Envision yourself as a product and the potential employers as your customer. To interest the customer in buying the product—hiring you—your résumé must communicate information about your qualities and indicate how you can satisfy the customer's needs—that is, how you can help the company achieve its objectives. The information in the résumé should persuade the organization to take a closer look at you by calling you in for an interview.

To be effective, the résumé should be targeted at a specific position, as Figure A.1 shows. This document is only one example of an acceptable résumé. The job target section is specific and leads directly to the applicant's qualifications for the job.

figure A.1

A RÉSUMÉ TARGETED AT A SPECIFIC POSITION

LORRAINE MILLER
2212 WEST WILLOW
PHOENIX, AZ 12345
(416) 862-9169

EDUCATION: B.A. Arizona State University, 2004, Marketing, achieved a 3.4 on a 4.0 scale throughout college

POSITION DESIRED: Product manager with an international firm providing future career development at the executive level

QUALIFICATIONS:

- Communicates well with individuals to achieve a common goal
- Handles tasks efficiently and in a timely manner
- Understands advertising sales, management, marketing research, packaging, pricing, distribution, and warehousing
- Coordinates many activities at one time
- Receives and carries out assigned tasks or directives
- Writes complete status or research reports

EXPERIENCES:

- Assistant Editor of college paper
- Treasurer of the American Marketing Association (student chapter)
- Internship with 3-Cs Advertising, Berkeley, CA
- Student Assistantship with Dr. Steve Green, Professor of Marketing, Arizona State University
- Solo cross-Canada canoe trek, summer 2003

WORK RECORD:

2003–Present	Blythe and Co., Inc.	
	—Junior Advertising Account Executive	
2001–2002	Student Assistant for Dr. Steve Green	
	—Research Assistant	
2000–2001	The Men	
	—Retail sales and consumer relations	
1998–2000	Farmer	
	—Helped operate relative's blueberry farm in Michigan for three summers	

In some cases, education is more important than unrelated work experience because it indicates the career direction you desire despite the work experience you have acquired thus far.

The qualifications section details capabilities—what the applicant can do—and also shows that the applicant has an understanding of the job's requirements. Skills and strengths that relate to the specific job should be emphasized. The achievement section ("Experiences" in Figure A.1) indicates success at accomplishing tasks or goals on the job and at school. The work experience section in Figure A.1 includes an unusual listing, which might pique the interviewer's interest: "helped operate relative's blueberry farm in Michigan for three summers." It tends to inspire rather than satisfy curiosity, thus inviting further inquiry.

Another type of résumé is the chronological résumé, which lists work experience and educational history in order by date. This type of résumé is useful for those just entering the job market because it helps highlight education and work experience.

Common suggestions for improving résumés include deleting useless or outdated information, improving organization, using professional printing and typing, listing duties (not accomplishments), maintaining grammatical perfection, and avoiding an overly elaborate or fancy format.[2] Keep in mind that the person who will look at your résumé may have to sift through hundreds in the course of the day in addition to handling other duties. Consequently it is important to keep your résumé short (one page is best, never more than two), concise, and neat. Moreover, you want your résumé to be distinctive so it will stand out from all the others.

In addition to having the proper format and content, a résumé should be easy to read. It is best to use only one or two kinds of type and plain, white paper. When sending a résumé to a large company, several copies may be made and distributed. Textured, gray, or colored paper may make a good impression on the first person who sees the résumé, but it will not reproduce well for the others, who will see only a poor copy. You should also proofread your résumé with care. Typos and misspellings will grab attention—the wrong kind.

Along with the résumé itself, always submit a cover letter. In the letter, you can include somewhat more information than in your résumé and convey a message that expresses your interest and enthusiasm about the organization and the job.

The Job Interview

In essence, your résumé and cover letter are an introduction. The deciding factor in the hiring process is the interview (or several interviews) with representatives of the firm. It is through the interview that the firm gets to know you and your qualifications. At the same time, the interview gives you a chance to learn about the firm.

Here again, preparation is the key to success. Research the firm before your first interview. Learn all you can about its products, its subsidiaries, the markets in which it operates, its history, the locations of its facilities, and so on. If possible, obtain and read the firm's most recent annual report. Be prepared to ask questions about the firm and the opportunities it offers. Interviewers welcome such questions. They expect you to be interested enough to spend some time thinking about your potential relationship with their organization.

Also, prepare to respond to questions the interviewer may ask. Table A.1 lists typical interview questions that job applicants often find difficult to answer. But don't expect interviewers to stick to the list given in the table or to the items appearing in your résumé. They will be interested in anything that helps them decide what kind of person and worker you are.

Make sure you are on time for your interview and are dressed and groomed in a businesslike manner. Interviewers take note of punctuality and appearance just as they do of other personal qualities. Bring a copy of your résumé, even if you already sent one to the firm. You may also want to bring a copy of your course transcript and letters of recommendation. If you plan to furnish interviewers with the names and addresses of references rather than with letters of recommendation, make sure you have your references' permission to do so.

Consider the interview itself as a two-way conversation rather than a question-and-answer session. Volunteer any information that is relevant to the interviewer's questions. If an important point is skipped in the discussion, don't hesitate to bring it up. Be yourself, but emphasize your strengths. Good eye contact and posture are

table A.1   INTERVIEW QUESTIONS JOB APPLICANTS OFTEN FIND DIFFICULT TO ANSWER

1. Tell me about yourself.
2. What do you know about our organization?
3. What can you do for us? Why should we hire you?
4. What qualifications do you have that make you feel you will be successful in your field?
5. What have you learned from the jobs you've held?
6. What are your special skills, and where did you acquire them?
7. Have you had any special accomplishments in your lifetime that you are particularly proud of?
8. Why did you leave your most recent job?
9. How do you spend your spare time? What are your hobbies?
10. What are your strengths and weaknesses?
11. Discuss five major accomplishments.
12. What kind of boss would you like? Why?
13. If you could spend a day with someone you've known or know of, who would it be?
14. What personality characteristics seem to rub you the wrong way?
15. How do you show your anger? What types of things make you angry?
16. With what type of person do you spend the majority of your time?

Source: Adapted from *The Ultimate Job Hunter's Guidebook,* 4th ed., by Susan D. Greene and Melanie C. L. Martel. Copyright © 2004 by Houghton Mifflin Company.

also important; they should come naturally if you take an active part in the interview. At the conclusion of the interview, thank the recruiter for taking the time to see you.

In most cases, the first interview is used to *screen* applicants, that is, choose those who are best qualified. These applicants are then given a second interview and perhaps a third, usually with one or more department heads. If the job requires relocation to a different area, applicants may be invited there for these later interviews.

After the interviewing process is complete, applicants are told when to expect a hiring decision.

After the Interview

Attention to common courtesy is important as a follow-up to your interview. You should send a brief note of thanks to the interviewer and give it as much care as you did your résumé and cover letter. A short, typewritten letter is preferred to a handwritten note or card, or an e-mail. Avoid not only typos, but also overconfident statements such as "I look forward to helping you make Universal Industries successful over the next decade." Even in the thank-you letter, it is important to show team spirit and professionalism, as well as to convey proper enthusiasm. Everything you say and do reflects on you as a candidate.

After the Hire

Clearly, performing well in a job has always been a crucial factor in keeping a position. In a tight economy and job market, however, a person's attitude, as well as his or her performance, counts greatly. People in their first jobs can commit costly political blunders by being insensitive to their environments. Politics in the business world

Source: Data from Robert Half Finance & Accounting survey. Margin of error: ±2.

includes how you react to your boss, how you react to your coworkers, and your general demeanor. Here are a few rules to live by.

1. *Don't bypass your boss.* One major blunder an employee can make is to go over the boss's head to resolve a problem. This is especially hazardous in a bureaucratic organization. You should become aware of the generally accepted chain of command and, when problems occur, follow that protocol, beginning with your immediate superior. No boss likes to look incompetent, and making him or her appear so is sure to hamper or even crush your budding career. However, there may be exceptions to this rule in emergency situations. It is wise to discuss with your supervisor what to do in an emergency, before an emergency occurs.[3]

2. *Don't criticize your boss.* Adhering to the old adage "praise in public and criticize in private" will keep you out of the line of retaliatory fire. A more sensible and productive alternative is to present the critical commentary to your boss in a diplomatic way during a private session.

3. *Don't show disloyalty.* If dissatisfied with the position, a new employee may start a fresh job search, within or outside the organization. However, it is not advisable to begin a publicized search within the company for another position unless you have held your current job for some time. Careful attention to the political climate in the organization should help you determine how soon to start a new job campaign and how public to make it. In any case, it is not a good idea to publicize that you are looking outside the company for a new position.

4. *Don't be a naysayer.* Employees are expected to become part of the organizational team and to work together with others. Behaviors to avoid, especially if you are a new employee, include being critical of others; refusing to support others' projects; always playing devil's advocate; refusing to help others when a crisis occurs; and complaining all the time, even about such matters as the poor quality of the food in the cafeteria, the crowded parking lot, or the temperature in the office.

5. *Learn to correct mistakes appropriately.* No one likes to admit having made a mistake, but one of the most important political skills you can acquire is minimizing the impact of a blunder. It is usually advantageous to correct the damage as soon as possible to avoid further problems. Some suggestions: be the first to break the bad news to your boss, avoid being defensive, stay poised and don't panic, and have solutions ready for fixing the blunder.[4]

Types of Marketing Careers

In considering marketing as a career, the first step is to evaluate broad categories of career opportunities in the areas of marketing research, sales, industrial buying, public relations, distribution management, product management, advertising, retail management, and direct marketing. Keep in mind that the categories described here are not all-inclusive and that each encompasses hundreds of marketing jobs.

Marketing Research

Clearly, marketing research and information systems are vital aspects of marketing decision making. Marketing researchers survey customers to determine their habits, preferences, and aspirations. The information about buyers and environmental forces that research and information systems provide improves a marketer's ability to understand the dynamics of the marketplace and therefore make effective decisions.

Marketing research firms are usually employed by a client organization such as a provider of goods or services, a nonbusiness organization, a research consulting firm, or an advertising agency. The activities performed include concept testing, product testing, package testing, advertising testing, test market research, and new-product research.

Marketing researchers gather and analyze data relating to specific problems. A researcher may be involved in one or several stages of research depending on the size of the project, the organization of the research unit, and the researcher's experience. Marketing research trainees in large organizations usually perform a considerable amount of clerical work, such as compiling secondary data from the firm's accounting and sales records and from periodicals, government publications, syndicated data services, the Internet, and unpublished sources. A junior analyst may edit and code questionnaires or tabulate survey results. Trainees may also participate in gathering primary data through mail and telephone surveys, personal interviews, and observation. As a marketing researcher gains experience, he or she may become involved in defining problems and developing research questions; designing research procedures; and analyzing, interpreting, and reporting findings. Exceptional personnel may assume responsibility for entire research projects.

Although most employers consider a bachelor's degree sufficient qualification for a marketing research trainee, many specialized positions require a graduate degree in business administration, statistics, or other related fields. Today trainees are more likely to have a marketing or statistics degree than a liberal arts degree. Courses in statistics, information technology, psychology, sociology, communications, economics, and technical writing are valuable preparation for a career in marketing research.

The Bureau of Labor Statistics indicates that marketing research provides abundant employment opportunities, especially for applicants with graduate training in marketing research, statistics, economics, and the social sciences. Generally, the value of information gathered by marketing information and research systems rises as competition increases, thus expanding opportunities for prospective marketing research personnel.

The major career paths in marketing research are with independent marketing research agencies/data suppliers and marketing research departments in advertising agencies and other businesses. In a company in which marketing research plays a key role, the researcher is often a member of the marketing strategy team. Surveying or interviewing customers is the heart of the marketing research firm's activities. A statistician selects the sample to be surveyed, analysts design the questionnaire and synthesize the gathered data into a final report, data processors tabulate the data, and the research director controls and coordinates all these activities so each project is completed to the client's satisfaction.

Salaries in marketing research depend on the type, size, and location of the firm, as well as the nature of the position. Overall, salaries of marketing researchers have increased slightly during the last few years. However, the specific position within the marketing research field determines the degree of fluctuation.[5] Generally, starting salaries are somewhat higher and promotions somewhat slower than in other occupations requiring similar training. The typical salary for a market analyst is $24,000 to $50,000; a marketing research director can earn $75,000 to $200,000.[6]

Sales

Millions of people earn a living through personal selling. Chapter 20 defines personal selling as paid personal communication that attempts to inform customers and persuade them to purchase products in an exchange situation. Although this definition describes the general nature of sales positions, individual selling jobs vary enormously with respect to the types of businesses and products involved, the educational background and skills required, and the specific activities sales personnel perform. Because the work is so varied, it offers numerous career opportunities for people with a wide range of qualifications, interests, and goals. The two types of career opportunities we discuss relate to business-to-business sales.

Sales Positions in Wholesaling. Wholesalers buy products intended for resale, for use in making other products, and for general business operations, and sell them directly to business markets. Wholesalers thus provide services to both retailers and producers. They can help match producers' products to retailers' needs and provide services that save producers time, money, and resources. Some activities a sales representative for a wholesaling firm is likely to perform include planning and negotiating transactions; assisting customers with sales, advertising, sales promotion, and publicity; facilitating transportation and storage; providing customers with inventory control and data processing assistance; establishing prices; and giving customers technical, managerial, and merchandising assistance.

The background needed by wholesale personnel depends on the nature of the product handled. A sales representative for a drug wholesaler, for example, needs extensive technical training and product knowledge, and may have a degree in chemistry, biology, or pharmacology. A wholesaler of standard office supplies, on the other hand, may find it more important that its sales staff be familiar with various brands, suppliers, and prices than have technical knowledge about the products. A person just entering the wholesaling field may begin as a sales trainee or hold a nonselling job that provides experience with inventory, prices, discounts, and the firm's customers. A college graduate usually enters a wholesaler's sales force directly. Competent salespeople also transfer from manufacturer and retail sales positions.

The number of sales positions in wholesaling is expected to grow about as rapidly as the average for all occupations. Earnings for wholesale personnel vary widely because commissions often make up a large proportion of their incomes.

Sales Positions in Manufacturing. A manufacturer's sales personnel sell the firm's products to wholesalers, retailers, and industrial buyers; they thus perform many of the same activities as a wholesaler's representatives. As in wholesaling, educational requirements for a sales position depend largely on the type and complexity of the products and markets. Manufacturers of nontechnical products usually hire college graduates who have a liberal arts or business degree and train them so they become knowledgeable about the firm's products, prices, and customers. Manufacturers of highly technical products generally prefer applicants who have degrees in fields associated with the particular industry and market.

Sales positions in manufacturing are expected to increase at an average rate. Manufacturers' sales personnel are well compensated and earn above-average salaries; most are paid a combination of salary and commission. Commissions vary according to the salesperson's efforts, abilities, and sales territory, as well as the type of products sold. Annual salary and/or commission for sales positions range from $63,511 to $78,348 for a sales manager and $30,000 to $52,000 for a field salesperson. A sales trainee would start at about $35,500 in business sales positions.[7]

Industrial Buying

Industrial buyers, or purchasing agents, are responsible for maintaining an adequate supply of the goods and services an organization requires for its operations. In general, industrial buyers purchase all items needed for direct use in producing other products and for use in day-to-day operations. Industrial buyers in large firms often specialize in purchasing a single, specific class of products—for example, all petroleum-based lubricants. In smaller organizations, buyers may be responsible for many different categories of purchases, including raw materials, component parts, office supplies, and operating services.

An industrial buyer's main job is to select suppliers that offer the best quality, service, and price. When the products to be purchased are standardized, buyers may base their purchasing decisions on suppliers' descriptions of their offerings in catalogs and trade journals. Buyers who purchase highly homogeneous products often meet with salespeople to examine samples and observe demonstrations. Sometimes buyers must inspect the actual product before purchasing it; in other cases, they invite suppliers to bid on large orders. Buyers who purchase equipment made to specifications often deal directly with manufacturers. After choosing a supplier and placing an order, an industrial buyer usually must trace the shipment to ensure ontime delivery. Sometimes the buyer is also responsible for receiving and inspecting an order and authorizing payment to the shipper.

Training requirements for a career in industrial buying relate to the needs of the firm and the types of products purchased. A manufacturer of heavy machinery may prefer an applicant who has a background in engineering. A service company, on the other hand, may recruit liberal arts majors. Although not generally required, a college degree is becoming increasingly important for industrial buyers who wish to advance to management positions.

Employment prospects for industrial buyers are expected to increase faster than average. Opportunities will be excellent for individuals with master's degrees in business administration or bachelor's degrees in engineering, science, or business administration. Companies that manufacture heavy equipment, computer equipment, and communications equipment will need buyers with technical backgrounds.

Public Relations

Public relations encompasses a broad set of communication activities designed to create and maintain favorable relationships between an organization and its stakeholders—customers, employees, stockholders, government officials, and society in general. Public relations specialists help clients create the image, issue, or message they wish to present and communicate it to the appropriate audience. According to the Public Relations Society of America, about 120,000 people work in public relations in the United States. Half the billings of the nation's 4,000 public relations agencies and firms come from Chicago and New York. The highest starting salaries are also found there. Communication is basic to all public relations programs. To communicate effectively, public relations practitioners must first gather data about the firm's stakeholders to assess their needs, identify problems, formulate recommendations, implement new plans, and evaluate current activities.

Public relations personnel disseminate large amounts of information to the organization's stakeholders. Written communication is the most versatile tool of public relations; thus, good writing skills are essential. Public relations practitioners must be adept at writing for a variety of media and audiences. It is not unusual for a person in public relations to prepare reports, news releases, speeches, broadcast scripts, technical manuals, employee publications, shareholder reports, and other communications aimed at both organizational personnel and external groups. In addition, a public relations practitioner needs a thorough knowledge of the production techniques used in preparing various communications. Public relations personnel also establish distribution channels for the organization's publicity. They must have a thorough understanding of the various media, their areas of specialization, the characteristics of their target audiences, and their policies regarding publicity. Anyone who hopes to succeed in public relations must develop close working relationships with numerous media personnel to enlist their interest in disseminating clients' communications.

A college education combined with writing or media-related experience is the best preparation for a career in public relations. Most beginners have a college degree in journalism, communications, or public relations, but some employers prefer a business background. Courses in journalism, business administration, marketing, creative writing, psychology, sociology, political science, economics, advertising, English, and public speaking are recommended. Some employers ask applicants to present a portfolio of published articles, scripts written for television or radio programs, slide presentations, and other work samples. Other agencies require written tests that include such tasks as writing sample press releases. Manufacturing firms, public utilities, transportation and insurance companies, and trade and professional associations are the largest employers of public relations personnel. In addition, sizable numbers of public relations personnel work for health-related organizations, government agencies, educational institutions, museums, and religious and service groups.

Although some larger companies provide extensive formal training for new personnel, most new public relations employees learn on the job. Beginners usually perform routine tasks such as maintaining files about company activities and searching secondary data sources for information to be used in publicity materials. More experienced employees write press releases, speeches, and articles, and help plan public relations campaigns.

Employment opportunities in public relations are expected to increase faster than the average for all occupations. One caveat is in order, however: competition for beginning jobs is keen. The prospects are best for applicants who have solid academic preparation and some media experience. Abilities that differentiate candidates, such as an understanding of information technology, are becoming increasingly important. Public relations account executives earn $30,000 to $45,000. Public relations agency managers earn in the $51,460 to $62,874 range.[8]

Distribution Management

A distribution manager arranges for transportation of goods within firms and through marketing channels. Transportation is an essential distribution activity that permits a firm to create time and place utility for its products. It is the distribution manager's job to analyze various transportation modes and select the combination that minimizes cost and transit time while providing acceptable levels of reliability, capability, accessibility, and security.

To accomplish this task, a distribution manager performs many activities. First, the individual must choose one or a combination of transportation modes from the five major modes available: railroads, trucks, waterways, airways, and pipelines. The distribution manager must then select the specific routes the goods will travel and the particular carriers to be used, weighing such factors as freight classifications and regulations, freight charges, time schedules, shipment sizes, and loss and damage ratios. In addition, this person may be responsible for preparing shipping documents, tracing shipments, handling loss and damage claims, keeping records of freight rates, and monitoring changes in government regulations and transportation technology.

Distribution management employs relatively few people and is expected to grow about as fast as the average for all occupations in the near future. Manufacturing firms are the largest employers of distribution managers, although some distribution managers work for wholesalers, retail stores, and consulting firms. Salaries of experienced distribution managers vary but generally are much higher than the average for all nonsupervisory personnel. Entry-level positions are diverse, ranging from inventory control and traffic scheduling to operations or distribution management. Inventory management is an area of great opportunity because of increasing global competition. While salaries in the distribution field vary depending on the position and information technology skill requirements, entry salaries start at about $40,000.[9]

Most employers of distribution managers prefer to hire graduates of technical programs or people who have completed courses in transportation, logistics, distribution management, economics, statistics, computer science, management, marketing, and commercial law. A successful distribution manager is adept at handling technical data and is able to interpret and communicate highly technical information.

Product Management

The product manager occupies a staff position and is responsible for the success or failure of a product line. Product managers coordinate most of the activities required to market a product. However, because they hold a staff position, they have relatively little actual authority over marketing personnel. Nevertheless, they take on a large amount of responsibility and typically are paid quite well relative to other marketing employees. Being a product manager can be rewarding both financially and psychologically, but it can also be frustrating because of the disparity between responsibility and authority.

A product manager should have a general knowledge of advertising, transportation modes, inventory control, selling and sales management, sales promotion, marketing research, packaging, pricing, and warehousing. The individual must be knowledgeable enough to communicate effectively with personnel in these functional areas and help assess alternatives when major decisions are being made.

Product managers usually need college training in an area of business administration. A master's degree is helpful, although a person usually does not become a product manager directly out of school. Frequently several years of selling and sales management experience are prerequisites for a product management position, which is often a major step in the career path of top-level marketing executives. Product managers can earn $60,000 to $120,000, while an assistant product manager starts at about $40,000.[10]

Advertising

Advertising pervades our daily lives. Business and nonbusiness organizations use advertising in many ways and for many reasons. Advertising clearly needs individuals with diverse skills to fill a variety of jobs. Creativity, imagination, artistic talent, and expertise in expression and persuasion are important for copywriters, artists, and account executives. Sales and managerial abilities are vital to the success of advertising managers, media buyers, and production managers. Research directors must have a solid understanding of research techniques and human behavior. A related occupation is an advertising salesperson, who sells newspaper, television, radio, or magazine advertising to advertisers.

Advertising professionals disagree on the most beneficial educational background for a career in advertising. Most employers prefer college graduates. Some employers seek individuals with degrees in advertising, journalism, or business; others prefer graduates with broad liberal arts backgrounds. Still other employers rank relevant work experience above educational background.

"Advertisers look for generalists," says a staff executive of the American Association of Advertising Agencies. "Thus, there are just as many economics or general liberal arts majors as M.B.A.'s." Common entry-level positions in an advertising agency are found in the traffic department, account service (account coordinator), or the media department (media assistant). Starting salaries in these positions are often quite low, but to gain experience in the advertising industry, employees must work their way up in the system. Assistant account executives start at $25,000, while a typical account executive earns $30,000 to $50,000. Copywriters earn $30,000 to $50,000 a year.[11]

A variety of organizations employ advertising personnel. Although advertising agencies are perhaps the most visible and glamorous employers, many manufacturing firms, retail stores, banks, utility companies, and professional and trade associations maintain advertising departments. Advertising jobs are also available with television and radio stations, newspapers, and magazines. Other businesses that employ advertising personnel include printers, art studios, letter shops, and package design firms. Specific advertising jobs include advertising manager, account executive, research director, copywriter, media specialist, and production manager.

About 59 percent of advertising employees are between 25 and 44 years of age compared to 51 percent of all workers in the U.S. economy. Employment opportunities in advertising are expected to increase faster than the average for all occupations through 2008.[12]

Retail Management

Although a career in retailing may begin in sales, there is more to retailing than simply selling. Many retail personnel occupy management positions. Besides managing the sales force, they focus on selecting and ordering merchandise, promotional activities, inventory control, customer credit operations, accounting, personnel, and store security.

Organization of retail stores varies. In many large department stores, retail management personnel rarely engage in actual selling to customers; these duties are performed by retail salespeople. Other types of retail organizations may require management personnel to perform selling activities from time to time.

Large retail stores offer a variety of management positions, including assistant buyers, buyers, department managers, section managers, store managers, division managers, regional managers, and vice president of merchandising. The following list describes the general duties of four of these positions; the precise nature of their duties may vary from one retail organization to another.

A section manager coordinates inventory and promotions and interacts with buyers, salespeople, and ultimate consumers. The manager performs merchandising, labor relations, and managerial activities, and usually works more than a 40-hour workweek.

The buyer's task is more focused. This fast-paced occupation involves much travel and pressure, and the need to be open-minded with respect to new, potentially successful items.

The regional manager coordinates the activities of several stores within a given area, usually monitoring and supporting sales, promotions, and general procedures.

The vice president of merchandising has a broad scope of managerial responsibility and reports to the organization's president.

Most retail organizations hire college graduates, put them through management training programs, and then place them directly in management positions. They frequently hire candidates with backgrounds in liberal arts or business administration. Sales positions and retail management positions offer the greatest employment opportunities for marketing students.

Retail management positions can be exciting and challenging. Competent, ambitious individuals often assume a great deal of responsibility very quickly and advance rapidly. However, a retail manager's job is physically demanding and sometimes entails long working hours. In addition, managers employed by large chain stores may be required to move frequently during their early years with the company. Nonetheless, positions in retail management often offer the chance to excel and gain promotion. Growth in retailing, which is expected to accompany the growth in population, is likely to create substantial opportunities during the next ten years. While a trainee may start in the $30,000 to $47,250 range, a store manager can earn from $50,000 to $200,000 depending on the size of the store.[13]

Direct Marketing

One of the more dynamic areas in marketing is direct marketing, in which the seller uses one or more direct media (telephone, online, mail, print, or television) to solicit a response. The telephone is a major vehicle for selling many consumer products. Telemarketing is direct selling to customers using a variety of technological improvements in telecommunications. Direct-mail catalogs appeal to such market segments as working women and people who find going to retail stores difficult or inconvenient. Newspapers and magazines offer great opportunity, particularly in special market segments. *Golf Digest,* for example, is obviously a good medium for selling golfing equipment. Cable television provides many opportunities for selling directly to consumers. Home shopping channels, for instance, have been very successful. The Internet offers numerous direct marketing opportunities.

The most important asset in direct marketing is experience. Employers often look to other industries to locate experienced professionals. This preference means that if you can get an entry-level position in direct marketing, you will have an advantage in developing a career.

Jobs in direct marketing include buyers, such as department store buyers, who select goods for catalog, telephone, or direct-mail sales. Catalog managers develop marketing strategies for each new catalog that goes into the mail. Research/mail list management involves developing lists of products that will sell in direct marketing and lists of names of consumers who are likely to respond to a direct-mail effort. Order fulfillment managers direct the shipment of products once they are sold. The effectiveness of direct marketing is enhanced by periodic analysis of advertising and communications at all phases of contact with the consumer. Direct marketing involves all aspects of marketing decision making. Most positions in direct marketing involve planning and market analysis. Some direct marketing jobs involve the use of databases that include customer information, sales history, and other tracking data. A database manager might receive a salary of $53,750 to $88,750. A telemarketing director in business-to-business sales could receive a salary of about $35,000.[14]

E-Marketing and Customer Relationship Management

Today only about 1.5 percent of all retail sales are conducted on the Internet.[15] Currently approximately one-half of all businesses order online. One characteristic of firms engaged in e-marketing is a renewed focus on relationship marketing by building customer loyalty and retaining customers—in other words, on customer relationship management (CRM). This focus on CRM is possible because of e-marketers' ability to target individual customers. This effort is enhanced over time as the customer invests more time and effort in "teaching" the firms what he or she wants.

Opportunities abound to combine information technology expertise with marketing knowledge. By providing an integrated communication system of websites, fax, telephone, and personal contacts, marketers can personalize customer relationships. Careers exist for individuals who can integrate the Internet as a touch point with customers as part of effective customer relationship management. Many Internet-only companies ("dot-coms") failed because they focused too heavily on brand awareness and did not understand the importance of an integrated marketing strategy.

The use of laptops, cellular phones, e-mail, voice mail, and other devices is necessary to maintain customer relationships and allow purchases on the Internet. A variety of jobs exist for marketers who have integrated technology into their work and job skills. Job titles include e-marketing manager, customer relationship manager, and e-services manager, as well as jobs in dot-coms.

Salaries in this rapidly growing area depend on technical expertise and experience. For example, a CRM customer service manager receives a salary in the $40,000 to $45,000 range. Database administrators earn salaries of approximately $70,500 to $90,000. With five years of experience in e-marketing, individuals responsible for online product offerings can earn from $50,000 to $85,000.

Financial Analysis in Marketing*

Our discussion in this book focuses more on fundamental concepts and decisions in marketing than on financial details. However, marketers must understand the basic components of financial analyses to be able to explain and defend their decisions. In fact, they must be familiar with certain financial analyses to reach good decisions in the first place. To control and evaluate marketing activities, they must understand the income statement and what it says about their organization's operations. They also need to be familiar with performance ratios, which compare current operating results with past results and with results in the industry at large. We examine the income statement and some performance ratios in the first part of this appendix. In the second part, we discuss price calculations as the basis for price adjustments. Marketers are likely to use all these areas of financial analysis at various times to support their decisions and make necessary adjustments in their operations.

The Income Statement

The income, or operating, statement presents the financial results of an organization's operations over a certain period. The statement summarizes revenues earned and expenses incurred by a profit center, whether a department, a brand, a product line, a division, or the entire firm. The income statement presents the firm's net profit or net loss for a month, quarter, or year.

Table B.1 (on p. A-18) is a simplified income statement for Stoneham Auto Supplies, a fictitious retail store. The owners, Rose Costa and Nick Schultz, see that net sales of $250,000 are decreased by the cost of goods sold and by other business expenses to yield a net income of $83,000. Of course, these figures are only highlights of the complete income statement, which appears in Table B.2 (on p. A-19).

The income statement can be used in several ways to improve the management of a business. First, it enables an owner or a manager to compare actual results with budgets for various parts of the statement. For example, Rose and Nick see that the total amount of merchandise sold (gross sales) is $260,000. Customers returned merchandise or received allowances (price reductions) totaling $10,000. Suppose the budgeted amount was only $9,000. By checking the tickets for sales returns and allowances, the owners can determine why these events occurred and whether the $10,000 figure could be lowered by adjusting the marketing mix.

After subtracting returns and allowances from gross sales, Rose and Nick can determine net sales, the amount the firm has available to pay its expenses. They are pleased with this figure because it is higher than their sales target of $240,000.

A major expense for most companies that sell goods (as opposed to services) is the cost of goods sold. For Stoneham Auto Supplies, it amounts to 18 percent of net sales. Other expenses are treated in various ways by different companies. In our example, they are broken down into standard categories of selling expenses, administrative expenses, and general expenses.

The income statement shows that for Stoneham Auto Supplies, the cost of goods sold was $45,000. This figure was derived in the following way. First, the statement

*We gratefully acknowledge the assistance of Jim L. Grimm, Professor Emeritus, Illinois State University, in writing this appendix.

table B.1   SIMPLIFIED INCOME STATEMENT FOR A RETAILER

Stoneham Auto Supplies
Income Statement for the Year Ended
December 31, 2008

Net Sales	$250,000
Cost of Goods Sold	45,000
Gross Margin	$205,000
Expenses	122,000
Net Income	$ 83,000

shows that merchandise in the amount of $51,000 was purchased during the year. In paying the invoices associated with these inventory additions, purchase (cash) discounts of $4,000 were earned, resulting in net purchases of $47,000. Special requests for selected merchandise throughout the year resulted in $2,000 in freight charges, which increased the net cost of delivered purchases to $49,000. When this amount is added to the beginning inventory of $48,000, the cost of goods available for sale during 2008 totals $97,000. However, the records indicate that the value of inventory at the end of the year was $52,000. Because this amount was not sold, the cost of goods that were sold during the year was $45,000.

Rose and Nick observe that the total value of their inventory increased by 8.3 percent during the year:

$$\frac{\$52,000 - \$48,000}{\$48,000} = \frac{\$4,000}{\$48,000} = \frac{1}{12} = .0833, \; or \; 8.33\%$$

Further analysis is needed to determine whether this increase is desirable or undesirable. (Note that the income statement provides no details concerning the composition of the inventory held on December 31; other records supply this information.) If Nick and Rose determine that inventory on December 31 is excessive, they can implement appropriate marketing action.

Gross margin is the difference between net sales and cost of goods sold. Gross margin reflects the markup on products and is the amount available to pay all other expenses and provide a return to the owners. Stoneham Auto Supplies had a gross margin of $205,000:

Net sales	$250,000
Cost of goods sold	45,000

Stoneham's expenses (other than cost of goods sold) during 2008 totaled $122,000. Observe that $53,000, or slightly more than 43 percent of the total, constituted direct selling expenses:

$$\frac{\$53,000 \; selling \; \text{expenses}}{\$122,000 \; total \; \text{expenses}} = .434, \; or \; 43\%$$

The business employs three salespeople (one full time) and pays competitive wages. The selling expenses are similar to those in the previous year, but Nick and Rose wonder whether more advertising is necessary because the value of inventory increased by more than 8 percent during the year.

The administrative and general expenses are essential for operating the business. A comparison of these expenses with trade statistics for similar businesses indicates that the figures are in line with industry amounts.

table B.2	INCOME STATEMENT FOR A RETAILER

Stoneham Auto Supplies
Income Statement for the Year Ended December 31, 2008

Gross Sales			**$260,000**
Less: Sales returns and allowances			$ 10,000
Net Sales			**$250,000**
Cost of Goods Sold			
Inventory, January 1, 2008 (at cost)		$48,000	
Purchases	$51,000		
Less: Purchase discounts	4,000		
Net purchases	$47,000		
Plus: Freight-in	2,000		
Net cost of delivered purchases		$49,000	
Cost of goods available for sale		$97,000	
Less: Inventory, December 31, 2008		$52,000	
Cost of goods sold			$ 45,000
Gross Margin			**$205,000**
Expenses			
Selling expenses			
Sales salaries and commissions	$32,000		
Advertising	16,000		
Sales promotions	3,000		
Delivery	2,000		
Total selling expenses		$53,000	
Administrative expenses			
Administrative salaries	$20,000		
Office salaries	20,000		
Office supplies	2,000		
Miscellaneous	1,000		
Total administrative expenses		$43,000	
General expenses			
Rent	$14,000		
Utilities	7,000		
Bad debts	1,000		
Miscellaneous (local taxes, insurance, interest, depreciation)	4,000		
Total general expenses		$26,000	
Total expenses			$ 122,000
Net Income			**$ 83,000**

Net income, or net profit, is the amount of gross margin remaining after deducting expenses. Stoneham Auto Supplies earned a net profit of $83,000 for the fiscal year ending December 31, 2008. Note that net income on this statement is figured before payment of state and federal income taxes.

table B.3   COST OF GOODS SOLD FOR A MANUFACTURER

ABC Manufacturing
Income Statement for the Year Ended December 31, 2008

Cost of Goods Sold				**$ 50,000**
Finished goods inventory January 1, 2008				
Cost of goods manufactured				
Work-in-process inventory, January 1, 2008			$ 20,000	
Raw materials inventory, January 1, 2008	$ 40,000			
Net cost of delivered purchases	$240,000			
Cost of goods available for use	$280,000			
Less: Raw materials inventory, December 31, 2008	$ 42,000			
Cost of goods placed in production		$238,000		
Direct labor		32,000		
Manufacturing overhead				
Indirect labor	$ 12,000			
Supervisory salaries	10,000			
Operating supplies	6,000			
Depreciation	12,000			
Utilities	$ 10,000			
Total manufacturing overhead		$ 50,000		
Total manufacturing costs			$320,000	
Total work-in-process			$340,000	
Less: Work-in-process inventory, December 31, 2008			$ 22,000	
Cost of Goods Manufactured				$ 318,000
				$ 368,000
Cost of Goods Available for Sale				48,000
Less: Finished goods inventory, December 31, 2008				
Cost of Goods Sold				**$320,000**

Income statements for intermediaries and for businesses that provide services follow the same general format as that shown for Stoneham Auto Supplies in Table B.2. The income statement for a manufacturer, however, differs somewhat in that "purchases" portion is replaced by "cost of goods manufactured." Table B.3 shows the entire Cost of Goods Sold section for a manufacturer, including cost of goods manufactured. In other respects, income statements for retailers and manufacturers are similar.

Performance Ratios

Rose and Nick's assessment of how well their business did during fiscal year 2008 can be improved through use of analytical ratios. Such ratios enable a manager to compare the results for the current year with data from previous years and industry statistics. However, comparisons of the current income statement with income statements and industry statistics from other years are not very meaningful because factors such as inflation are not accounted for when comparing dollar amounts. More useful comparisons can be made by converting these figures to a percentage of net sales, as this section shows.

The first analytical ratios we discuss, the operating ratios, are based on the net sales figure from the income statement.

Operating Ratios

Operating ratios express items on the income, or operating, statement as percentages of net sales. The first step is to convert the income statement into percentages of net sales, as illustrated in Table B.4. After making this conversion, the manager looks at several key operating ratios: two profitability ratios (the gross margin ratio and the net income ratio) and the operating expense ratio.

table B.4   INCOME STATEMENT COMPONENTS AS PERCENTAGE OF NET SALES

Stoneham Auto Supplies
Income Statement as a Percentage of Net Sales for the Year Ended December 31, 2008

		Percentage of Net Sales
Gross Sales		**103.8%**
Less: Sales returns and allowances		3.8
Net Sales		**100.0%**
Cost of Goods Sold		
Inventory, January 1, 2008 (at cost)		19.2%
Purchases	20.4%	
Less: Purchase discounts	1.6	
Net purchases	18.8%	
Plus: Freight-in	0.8	
Net cost of delivered purchases		19.6
Cost of goods available for sale		38.8%
Less: Inventory, December 31, 2008 (at cost)		20.8
Cost of goods sold		18.0
Gross Margin		82.0%
Expenses		
Selling expenses		
Sales salaries and commissions	12.8%	
Advertising	6.4	
Sales promotions	1.2	
Delivery	0.8	
Total selling expenses		21.2%
Administrative expenses		
Administrative salaries	8.0%	
Office salaries	8.0	
Office supplies	0.8	
Miscellaneous	0.4	
Total administrative expenses		17.2%
General expenses		
Rent	5.6%	
Utilities	2.8	
Bad debts	0.4	
Miscellaneous	1.6	
Total general expenses		10.4%
Total expenses		48.8
Net Income		**33.2%**

For Stoneham Auto Supplies, these ratios are determined as follows (see Tables B.2 and B.4 for supporting data):

$$\text{Gross Margin Ratio} = \frac{\text{Gross Margin}}{\text{Net Sales}} = \frac{\$205,000}{\$250,000} = 82\%$$

$$\text{Net Income Ratio} = \frac{\text{Net Income}}{\text{Net Sales}} = \frac{\$83,000}{\$250,000} = 33.2\%$$

$$\text{Operating Expense Ratio} = \frac{\text{Total Expenses}}{\text{Net Sales}} = \frac{\$122,000}{\$250,000} = 48.8\%$$

The gross margin ratio indicates the percentage of each sales dollar available to cover operating expenses and achieve profit objectives. The net income ratio indicates the percentage of each sales dollar that is classified as earnings (profit) before payment of income taxes. The operating expense ratio calculates the percentage of each dollar needed to cover operating expenses.

If Nick and Rose believe the operating expense ratio is higher than historical data and industry standards, they can analyze each operating expense ratio in Table B.4 to determine which expenses are too high and then take corrective action. After reviewing several key operating ratios, Nick and Rose, like many managers, will probably want to analyze all the items on the income statement. By doing so, they can determine whether the 8 percent increase in the value of their inventory was necessary.

Inventory Turnover Rate

The inventory turnover rate, or stock-turn rate, is an analytical ratio that can be used to answer the question "Is the inventory level appropriate for this business?" The inventory turnover rate indicates the number of times an inventory is sold (turns over) during one year. To be useful, this figure must be compared with historical turnover rates and industry rates.

The inventory turnover rate is computed (based on cost) as follows:

$$\text{Inventory Turnover} = \frac{\text{Cost of Goods Sold}}{\text{Average Inventory at Cost}}$$

Rose and Nick would calculate the turnover rate from Table B.2 as follows:

$$\frac{\text{Cost of Goods Sold}}{\text{Average Inventory at Cost}} = \frac{\$45,000}{\$50,000} = 0.9$$

Their inventory turnover is less than once per year (0.9 times). Industry averages for competitive firms are 2.8 times. This figure convinces Rose and Nick that their investment in inventory is too large and they need to reduce their inventory.

Return on Investment

Return on investment (ROI) is a ratio that indicates management's efficiency in generating sales and profits from the total amount invested in the firm. For Stoneham Auto Supplies, the ROI is 41.5 percent, which compares well with competing businesses.

We use figures from two different financial statements to arrive at ROI. The income statement, already discussed, gives us net income. The balance sheet, which states the firm's assets and liabilities at a given point in time, provides the figure for total assets (or investment) in the firm.

The basic formula for ROI is

$$\text{ROI} = \frac{\text{Net Income}}{\text{Total Investment}}$$

For Stoneham Auto Supplies, net income is $83,000 (see Table B.2). If total investment (taken from the balance sheet for December 31, 2008) is $200,000, then

$$\text{ROI} = \frac{\$83,000}{\$200,000} = 0.415, \text{ or } 41.5\%$$

The ROI formula can be expanded to isolate the impact of capital turnover and the operating income ratio separately. Capital turnover is a measure of net sales per dollar of investment; the ratio is figured by dividing net sales by total investment. For Stoneham Auto Supplies,

$$\text{Capital Turnover} = \frac{Net\ Sales}{Total\ Investment} = \frac{\$250,000}{\$200,000} = 1.25$$

ROI is equal to capital turnover times the net income ratio. The expanded formula for Stoneham Auto Supplies is

$$\text{ROI} = \frac{Net\ Sales}{Total\ Investment} \times \frac{Net\ Income}{Net\ Sales}$$

$$= \frac{\$250,000}{\$200,000} \times \frac{\$83,000}{\$250,000}$$

$$= (1.25)(33.2\%) = 41.5\%$$

Price Calculations

An important step in setting prices is selecting a basis for pricing, as discussed in Chapter 22. The systematic use of markups, markdowns, and various conversion formulas helps in calculating the selling price and evaluating the effects of various prices.

Markups

As discussed in the text, markup is the difference between the selling price and the cost of the item; that is, selling price equals cost plus markup. The markup must cover cost and contribute to profit; thus, markup is similar to gross margin on the income statement.

Markup can be calculated on either cost or selling price as follows:

$$\text{Markup as Percentage of Cost} = \frac{Amount\ Added\ to\ Cost}{Cost} = \frac{Dollar\ Markup}{Cost}$$

$$\text{Markup as Percentage of Selling Price} = \frac{Amount\ Added\ to\ Cost}{Selling\ Price} = \frac{Dollar\ Markup}{Selling\ Price}$$

Retailers tend to calculate the markup percentage on selling price.

To review the use of these markup formulas, assume an item costs $10 and the markup is $5:

$$\text{Selling Price} = \text{Cost} + \text{Markup}$$

$$\$15 = \$10 + \$5$$

Thus,

$$\text{Markup Percentage on Selling Price} = \frac{\$5}{\$10} = 50\%$$

$$\text{Markup Percentage on Selling Price} = \frac{\$5}{\$15} = 33\tfrac{1}{3}\%$$

It is necessary to know the base (cost or selling price) to use markup pricing effectively. Markup percentage on cost will always exceed markup percentage on price, given the same dollar markup, as long as selling price exceeds cost.

On occasion, we may need to convert markup on cost to markup on selling price, or vice versa. The conversion formulas are as follows:

$$\text{Markup Percentage on Selling Price} = \frac{Markup\ Percentage\ on\ Cost}{100\% + Markup\ Percentage\ on\ Cost}$$

$$\text{Markup Percentage on Cost} = \frac{\text{Markup Percentage on Selling Price}}{100\% - \text{Markup Percentage on Selling Price}}$$

For example, if the markup percentage on cost is $33\frac{1}{3}$ percent, the markup percentage on selling price is

$$\frac{33\frac{1}{3}\%}{100\% + 33\frac{1}{3}\%} = \frac{33\frac{1}{3}\%}{1.33\frac{1}{3}\%} = 25\%$$

If the markup percentage on selling price is 40 percent, the corresponding percentage on cost is as follows:

$$\frac{40\%}{100\% - 40\%} = \frac{40\%}{60\%} = 66\frac{2}{3}\%$$

Finally, we can show how to determine selling price if we know the cost of the item and the markup percentage on selling price. Assume an item costs $36 and the usual markup percentage on selling price is 40 percent. Remember that selling price equals markup plus cost. Thus, if

$$100\% = 40\% \text{ of Selling Price} + \text{Cost}$$

then,

$$60\% \text{ of Selling Price} = \text{Cost}$$

In our example, cost equals $36. Therefore,

$$0.6X = \$36$$
$$X = \frac{\$36}{0.6}$$
$$\text{Selling Price} = \$60$$

Alternatively, the markup percentage could be converted to a cost basis as follows:

$$\frac{40\%}{100\% - 40\%} = \frac{40\%}{60\%} = 66\frac{2}{3}\%$$

The selling price would then be computed as follows:

$$\text{Selling Price} = 66\frac{2}{3}\%(\text{Cost}) + \text{Cost}$$
$$= 66\frac{2}{3}\%(\$36) + \$36$$
$$= \$24 + \$36 = \$60$$

If you keep in mind the basic formula—selling price equals cost plus markup—you will find these calculations straightforward.

Markdowns

Markdowns are price reductions a retailer makes on merchandise. Markdowns may be useful on items that are damaged, priced too high, or selected for a special sales event. The income statement does not express markdowns directly because the change in price is made before the sale takes place. Therefore, separate records of markdowns would be needed to evaluate the performance of various buyers and departments.

The markdown ratio (percentage) is calculated as follows:

$$\text{Markdown Percentage} = \frac{\text{Dollar Markdowns}}{\text{Net Sales in Dollars}}$$

In analyzing their inventory, Nick and Rose discover three special automobile jacks that have gone unsold for several months. They decide to reduce the price of each item from $25 to $20. Subsequently these items are sold. The markdown percentage for these three items is

$$\text{Markdown Percentage} = \frac{3(\$5)}{3(\$20)} = \frac{\$15}{\$60} = 25\%$$

Net sales, however, include all units of this product sold during the period, not just those marked down. If ten of these items were already sold at $25 each, in addition to the three items sold at $20, the overall markdown percentage would be

$$\text{Markdown Percentage} = \frac{3(\$5)}{10(\$25) + 3(\$20)}$$

$$= \frac{\$15}{\$250 + \$60} = \frac{\$15}{\$310} = 4.8\%$$

Sales allowances are also a reduction in price. Thus, the markdown percentage should include any sales allowances. It would be computed as follows:

$$\text{Markdown Percentage} = \frac{\text{Dollar Markdowns} + \text{Dollar Allowances}}{\text{Net Sales in Dollars}}$$

Discussion and Review Questions

1. How does a manufacturer's income statement differ from a retailer's income statement?

2. Use the following information to answer questions a through c:

TEA COMPANY

Fiscal year ended June 30, 2009

Net sales	$500,000
Cost of goods sold	300,000
Net income	50,000
Average inventory at cost	100,000
Total assets (total investment)	200,000

a. What is the inventory turnover rate for TEA Company? From what sources will the marketing manager determine the significance of the inventory turnover rate?

b. What is the capital turnover ratio? What is the net income ratio? What is the return on investment (ROI)?

c. How many dollars of sales did each dollar of investment produce for TEA Company?

3. Product A has a markup percentage on cost of 40 percent. What is the markup percentage on selling price?

4. Product B has a markup percentage on selling price of 30 percent. What is the markup percentage on cost?

5. Product C has a cost of $60 and a usual markup percentage of 25 percent on selling price. What price should be placed on this item?

6. Apex Appliance Company sells 20 units of product Q for $100 each and 10 units for $80 each. What is the markdown percentage for product Q?

Sample Marketing Plan

This sample marketing plan for a hypothetical company illustrates how the marketing planning process described in Chapter 2 might be implemented. If you are asked to create a marketing plan, this model may be a helpful guide, along with the concepts in Chapter 2.

① The Executive Summary, one of the most frequently read components of a marketing plan, is a synopsis of the marketing plan. Although it does not provide detailed information, it does present an overview of the plan so readers can identify key issues pertaining to their roles in the planning and implementation processes. Although this is the first section in a marketing plan, it is usually written last.

② The Environmental Analysis presents information regarding the organization's current situation with respect to the marketing environment, the current target market(s), and the firm's current marketing objectives and performance.

③ This section of the environmental analysis considers relevant **external environmental forces** such as competitive, economic, political, legal and regulatory, technological, and sociocultural forces.

Star Software, Inc., Marketing Plan

① I. EXECUTIVE SUMMARY

Star Software, Inc., is a small, family-owned corporation in the first year of a transition from first-generation to second-generation leadership. Star Software sells custom-made calendar programs and related items to about 400 businesses, which use the software mainly for promotion. As Star's business is highly seasonal, its 18 employees face scheduling challenges, with greatest demand during October, November, and December. In other months, the equipment and staff are sometimes idle. A major challenge facing Star Software is how to increase profits and make better use of its resources during the off season.

An evaluation of the company's internal strengths and weaknesses and external opportunities and threats served as the foundation for this strategic analysis and marketing plan. The plan focuses on the company's growth strategy, suggesting ways it can build on existing customer relationships, and on the development of new products and/or services targeted to specific customer niches. Since Star Software markets a product used primarily as a promotional tool by its clients, it is currently considered a business-to-business marketer.

② II. ENVIRONMENTAL ANALYSIS

Founded as a commercial printing company, Star Software, Inc., has evolved into a marketer of high-quality, custom-made calendar software and related business-to-business specialty items. In the mid-1960s, Bob McLemore purchased the company and, through his full-time commitment, turned it into a very successful family-run operation. In the near future, McLemore's 37-year-old son, Jonathan, will take over as Star Software's president and allow the elder McLemore to scale back his involvement.

③ A. The Marketing Environment

1. *Competitive forces.* The competition in the specialty advertising industry is very strong on a local and regional basis, but somewhat weak nationally. Sales figures for the industry as a whole are difficult to obtain since very little business is conducted on a national scale.

   The competition within the calendar industry is strong in the paper segment and weak in the software-based segment. Currently paper calendars hold a dominant market share of approximately 65 percent; however, the software-based segment is growing rapidly. The 35 percent market share held by software-based calendars is divided among many different firms. Star Software, which holds 30 percent of the software-based calendar market, is the only company that markets a software-based calendar on a national basis. As software-based calendars become more popular, additional competition is expected to enter the market.

2. *Economic forces.* Nationwide, many companies have reduced their overall promotion budgets as they face the need to cut expenses. However, most of these reductions have occurred in the budgets for mass media advertising (television, magazines, newspapers). While overall promotion budgets are shrinking, many companies are diverting a larger percentage of their budgets to sales promotion and specialty advertising. This trend is expected to continue as a weak, slow-growth economy forces most companies to focus more on the "value" they receive from their promotion dollars. Specialty advertising, such as can be done with a software-based calendar, provides this value.

3. *Political forces.* There are no expected political influences or events that could affect the operations of Star Software.

4. *Legal and regulatory forces.* In recent years, more attention has been paid to "junk mail." A large percentage of specialty advertising products are distributed by mail, and some of these products are considered "junk." Although this label is attached to the type of products Star Software makes, the problem of junk mail falls on Star's clients and not on the company itself. While legislation may be introduced to curb the tide of advertising delivered through the mail, the fact that more companies are diverting their promotion dollars to specialty advertising indicates that most do not fear the potential for increased legislation.

5. *Technological forces.* A major emerging technological trend involves personal digital assistants (PDAs). A PDA is a handheld device, similar in size to a large calculator, that can store a wide variety of information, including personal notes, addresses, and a calendar. Some PDAs, such as the BlackBerry, can be loaded with a cell phone and walkie-talkie. The user can e-mail and schedule on the electronic calendar. As this trend continues, current software-based calendar products may have to be adapted to match the new technology.

6. *Sociocultural forces.* In today's society, consumers have less time for work or leisure. The hallmarks of today's successful products are convenience and ease of use. In short, if the product does not save time and is not easy to use, consumers will simply ignore it. Software-based calendars fit this consumer need quite well. A software-based calendar also fits in with other societal trends: a move to a paperless society, the need to automate repetitive tasks, and the growing dependence on computers, for example.

4 The analysis of current target markets assesses demographic, geographic, psychographic, and product usage characteristics of the target markets. It also assesses the current needs of each of the firm's target markets, anticipated changes in those needs, and how well the organization's current products are meeting those needs.

4 **B. Target Market(s)**

By focusing on commitment to service and quality, Star Software has effectively implemented a niche differentiation strategy in a somewhat diverse marketplace. Its ability to differentiate its product has contributed to superior annual returns. Its target market consists of manufacturers or manufacturing divisions of large corporations that move their products through dealers, distributors, or brokers. Its most profitable product is a software program for a PC-based calendar, which can be tailored to meet client needs by means of artwork, logos, and text. Clients use this calendar software as a promotional tool, providing a disk to their customers as an advertising premium. The calendar software is not produced for resale.

The calendar software began as an ancillary product to Star's commercial printing business. However, due to the proliferation of PCs and the growth in technology, the computer calendar soon became more profitable for Star than its wall and desktop paper calendars. This led to the sale of the commercial printing plant and equipment to employees. Star Software has maintained a long-term relationship with these former employees, who have added capabilities to reproduce computer disks and whose company serves as Star's primary supplier of finished goods. Star's staff focuses on further development and marketing of the software.

C. Current Marketing Objectives and Performance

Star Software's sales representatives call on potential clients and, using a template demonstration disk, help them create a calendar concept. Once the sale has been finalized, Star completes the concept, including design, copywriting, and customization of the demonstration disk. Specifications are then sent to the supplier, located about 1,000 miles away, where the disks are produced. Perhaps what most differentiates Star from its competitors is its high level of service. Disks can be shipped to any location the buyer specifies. Since product development and customization of this type can require significant amounts of time and effort, particularly during the product's first year, Star deliberately pursues a strategy of steady, managed growth. Star Software markets its products on a company-specific basis. It has an annual reorder rate of approximately 90 percent and an average customer-reorder relationship of about eight years. The first year in dealing with a new customer is the most stressful and time consuming for Star's salespeople and product developers. Subsequent years are faster and significantly more profitable.

A company must set marketing objectives, measure performance against those objectives, and then take corrective action if needed.

The company is currently debt free except for the mortgage on its facility. However, about 80 percent of its accounts receivable are billed during the last three months of the calendar year. Seasonal account billings, along with the added travel of Star's sales staff during the peak season, pose a special challenge to the company. The need for cash to fund operations in the meantime requires the company to borrow significant amounts of money to cover the period until customer billing occurs. Star Software's marketing objectives include increases in both revenues and profits of approximately 10 percent over the previous year. Revenues should exceed $4 million, and profits are expected to reach $1.3 million.

III. SWOT ANALYSIS

5 A. Strengths

1. Star Software's product differentiation strategy is the result of a strong marketing orientation, commitment to high quality, and customization of products and support services.

2. There is little turnover among employees, who are well compensated and liked by customers. The relatively small staff size promotes camaraderie with coworkers and clients, and fosters communication and quick response to clients' needs.

3. A long-term relationship with the primary supplier has resulted in shared knowledge of the product's requirements, adherence to quality standards, and a common vision throughout the development and production process.

4. The high percentage of reorder business suggests a satisfied customer base, as well as positive word-of-mouth communication, which generates some 30 percent of new business each year.

6 B. Weaknesses

1. The highly centralized management hierarchy (the McLemores) and lack of managerial backup may impede creativity and growth. Too few people hold too much knowledge.

2. Despite the successful, long-term relationship with the supplier, single-sourcing could make Star Software vulnerable in the event of a natural disaster, strike, or dissolution of the current supplier. Contingency plans for suppliers should be considered.

3. The seasonal nature of the product line creates bottlenecks in productivity and cash flow, places excessive stress on personnel, and strains the facilities.

4. Both the product line and the client base lack diversification. Dependence on current reorder rates could breed complacency, invite competition, or create a false sense of customer satisfaction. The development of a product that would make the software calendar obsolete would probably put Star out of business.

5. While the small size of the staff fosters camaraderie, it also impedes growth and new-business development.

6. Star Software is reactive rather than assertive in its marketing efforts because of its heavy reliance on positive word-of-mouth communication for obtaining new business.

7. Star's current facilities are crowded. There is little room for additional employees or new equipment.

7 Opportunities are favorable conditions in the environment that could yield rewards for an organization if acted on properly.

7 C. Opportunities

1. Advertising expenditures in the United States exceed $132 billion annually. More than $25 billion of this is spent on direct-mail advertising and another $20 billion on specialty advertising. Star Software's potential for growth is significant in this market.

2. Technological advances have not only freed up time for Americans and brought greater efficiency but have also increased the amount of stress in their fast-paced lives. Personal computers have become commonplace, and personal information managers have gained popularity.

3. As U.S. companies look for ways to develop customer relationships rather than just close sales, reminders of this relationship could come in the form of acceptable premiums or gifts that are useful to the customer.

4. Computer-based calendars are easily distributed nationally and globally. The globalization of business creates an opportunity to establish new client relationships in foreign markets.

8 Threats are conditions or barriers that may prevent the organization from reaching its objectives.

8 D. Threats

1. Reengineering, right-sizing, and outsourcing trends in management may alter traditional channel relationships with brokers, dealers, and distributors or eliminate them altogether.

2. Calendars are basically a generic product. The technology, knowledge, and equipment required to produce such an item, even a computer-based one, are minimal. The possible entry of new competitors is a significant threat.

3. Theft of trade secrets and software piracy through unauthorized copying are difficult to control.

4. Specialty advertising through promotional items relies on gadgetry and ideas that are new and different. As a result, product life cycles may be quite short.

5. Single-sourcing can be detrimental or even fatal to a company if the buyer supplier relationship is damaged or if the supplying company has financial difficulty.

6. Competition from traditional paper calendars and other promotional items is strong.

9 During the development of a marketing plan, marketers attempt to match internal strengths to external opportunities. In addition, they try to convert internal weaknesses into strengths and external threats into opportunities.

9 E. Matching Strengths to Opportunities/Converting Weaknesses and Threats

1. The acceptance of technological advances and the desire to control time create a potential need for a computer-based calendar.

2. Star Software has more opportunity for business growth during its peak season than it can presently handle because of resource (human and capital) constraints.

3. Star Software must modify its management hierarchy, empowering its employees through a more decentralized marketing organization.

4. Star Software should discuss future growth strategies with its supplier and develop contingency plans to deal with unforeseen events. Possible satellite facilities in other geographic locations should be explored.

5. Star Software should consider diversifying its product line to satisfy new market niches and develop nonseasonal products.

6. Star Software should consider surveying its current customers and its customers' clients to gain a better understanding of their changing needs and desires.

10 The development of marketing objectives is based on environmental analysis, SWOT analysis, the firm's overall corporate objectives, and the organization's resources. For each objective, this section should answer the question "What is the specific and measurable outcome and time frame for completing this objective?"

IV. MARKETING OBJECTIVES

Star Software, Inc., is in the business of helping other companies market their products and/or services. Besides formulating a marketing-oriented and customer-focused mission statement, Star Software should establish an objective to achieve cumulative growth in net profit of at least 50 percent over the next five years. At least half of this 50 percent growth should come from new, nonmanufacturing customers and from products that are nonseasonal or that are generally delivered in the off-peak period of the calendar cycle.

To accomplish its marketing objectives, Star Software should develop benchmarks to measure progress. Regular reviews of these objectives will provide feedback and possible corrective actions on a timely basis. The major marketing objective is to gain a better understanding of the needs and satisfaction of current customers. Since Star Software is benefiting from a 90 percent reorder rate, it must be satisfying its current customers. Star could use the knowledge of its successes with current clients to market to new customers. To capitalize on its success with current clients, the company should establish benchmarks to learn how it can improve the products it now offers through knowledge of clients' needs and specific opportunities for new-product offerings. These benchmarks should be determined through marketing research and Star's marketing information system.

Another objective should be to analyze the billing cycle Star now uses to determine if there are ways to bill accounts receivable in a more evenly distributed manner throughout the year. Alternatively, repeat customers might be willing to place orders at off-peak cycles in return for discounts or added customer services.

Star Software should also create new products that can use its current equipment, technology, and knowledge base. It should conduct simple research and analyses of similar products or product lines with an eye toward developing specialty advertising products that are software based but not necessarily calendar related.

11 The marketing plan clearly specifies and describes the target market(s) toward which the organization will aim its marketing efforts. The difference between this section and the earlier section covering target markets is that the earlier section deals with present target markets, whereas this section looks at future target markets.

12 Though the marketing mix section in this plan is abbreviated, this component should provide considerable details regarding each element of the marketing mix: product, price, distribution, and promotion.

11 V. MARKETING STRATEGIES

A. Target Market(s)

Target market 1: Large manufacturers or stand-alone manufacturing divisions of large corporations with extensive broker, dealer, or distributor networks

> Example: An agricultural chemical producer, such as Dow Chemical, distributes its products to numerous rural "feed and seed" dealers. Customizing calendars with Chicago Board of Trade futures or USDA agricultural report dates would be beneficial to these potential clients.

Target market 2: Nonmanufacturing, nonindustrial segments of the business-to-business market with extensive customer networks, such as banks, medical services, or financial planners

> Example: Various sporting goods manufacturers distribute to specialty shop dealers. Calendars could be customized to the particular sport, such as golf (with PGA, Virginia Slims, or other tour dates), running (with various national marathon dates), or bowling (with national tour dates).

Target market 3: Direct consumer markets for brands with successful licensing arrangements for consumer products, such as Coca-Cola

> Example: Products with major brand recognition and fan club membership, such as Harley-Davidson motorcycles or the Bloomington Gold Corvette Association, could provide additional markets for customized computer calendars. Environmental or political groups represent a nonprofit market. Brands with licensing agreements for consumer products could provide a market for consumer computer calendars in addition to the specialty advertising product, which would be marketed to manufacturers/dealers.

Target market 4: Industry associations that regularly hold or sponsor trade shows, meetings, conferences, or conventions

> Example: National associations, such as the National Dairy Association or the American Marketing Association, frequently host meetings or annual conventions. Customized calendars could be developed for any of these groups.

12 B. Marketing Mix

1. *Products.* Star Software markets not only calendar software but also the service of specialty advertising to its clients. Star's intangible attributes are its ability to meet or exceed customer expectations consistently, its speed in responding to customers' demands, and its anticipation of new-customer needs. Intangible attributes are difficult for competitors to copy, thereby giving Star Software a competitive advantage.

2. *Price.* Star Software provides a high-quality specialty advertising product customized to its clients' needs. The value of this product and service is reflected in its premium price. Star should be sensitive to the price elasticity of its product and overall consumer demand.

3. *Distribution.* Star Software uses direct marketing. Since its product is compact, lightweight, and nonperishable, it can be shipped from a central location direct to the client via UPS, FedEx, or the U.S. Postal Service. The fact that Star can ship to multiple locations for each customer is an asset in selling its products.

4. *Promotion.* Since 90 percent of Star's customers reorder each year, the bulk of promotional expenditures should focus on new-product offerings through direct-mail advertising and trade journals or specialty publications. Any remaining promotional dollars could be directed to personal selling (in the form of sales performance bonuses) of current and new products.

VI. MARKETING IMPLEMENTATION

13 This section of the marketing plan details how the firm will be organized—by functions, products, regions, or types of customers—to implement its marketing strategies. It also indicates where decision-making authority will rest within the marketing unit.

A. Marketing Organization

Because Star's current and future products require extensive customization to match clients' needs, it is necessary to organize the marketing function by customer groups. This will allow Star to focus its marketing efforts exclusively on the needs and specifications of each target customer segment. Star's marketing efforts will be organized around the following customer groups: (1) manufacturing group; (2) nonmanufacturing, business-to-business group; (3) consumer product licensing group; and (4) industry associations group. Each group will be headed by a sales manager who will report to the marketing director (these positions must be created). Each group will be responsible for marketing Star's products within that customer segment. In addition, each group will have full decision-making authority. This represents a shift from the current, highly centralized management hierarchy. Frontline salespeople will be empowered to make decisions that will better satisfy Star's clients.

These changes in marketing organization will enable Star Software to be more creative and flexible in meeting customers' needs. Likewise, these changes will overcome the current lack of diversification in Star's product lines and client base. Finally, this new marketing organization will give Star a better opportunity to monitor the activities of competitors.

14 This component of the marketing plan outlines the specific activities required to implement the marketing plan, who is responsible for performing these activities, and when these activities should be accomplished based on a specified schedule.

B. Activities, Responsibility, and Timetables for Completion

All implementation activities are to begin at the start of the next fiscal year on April 1. Unless specified, all activities are the responsibility of Star Software's next president, Jonathan McLemore.

- On April 1, create four sales manager positions and the position of marketing director. The marketing director will serve as project leader of a new business analysis team, to be composed of nine employees from a variety of positions within the company.

- By April 15, assign three members of the analysis team to each of the following projects: (1) research potential new-product offerings and clients, (2) analyze the current billing cycle and billing practices, and (3) design a customer survey project. The marketing director is responsible.

- By June 30, the three project groups will report the results of their analyses. The full business analysis team will review all recommendations.

- By July 31, develop a marketing information system to monitor client reorder patterns and customer satisfaction.

- By July 31, implement any changes in billing practices as recommended by the business analysis team.

- By July 31, make initial contact with new potential clients for the current product line. Each sales manager is responsible.

- By August 31, develop a plan for one new-product offering, along with an analysis of its potential customers. The business analysis team is responsible.

- By August 31, finalize a customer satisfaction survey for current clients. In addition, the company will contact those customers who did not reorder for the 2005 product year to discuss their concerns. The marketing director is responsible.

- By January, implement the customer satisfaction survey with a random sample of 20 percent of current clients who reordered for the 2005 product year. The marketing director is responsible.

- By February, implement a new-product offering, advertising to current customers and to a sample of potential clients. The business analysis team is responsible.

- By March, analyze and report the results of all customer satisfaction surveys and evaluate the new-product offering. The marketing director is responsible.

- Reestablish the objectives of the business analysis team for the next fiscal year. The marketing director is responsible.

VII. EVALUATION AND CONTROL

15 This section details how the results of the marketing plan will be measured and evaluated. The control portion of this section includes the types of actions the firm can take to reduce the differences between the planned and the actual performance.

A. Performance Standards and Financial Controls

A comparison of the financial expenditures with the plan goals will be included in the project report. The following performance standards and financial controls are suggested:

- The total budget for the billing analysis, new-product research, and the customer survey will be equal to 60 percent of the annual promotional budget for the coming year.

- The breakdown of the budget within the project will be a 20 percent allocation to the billing cycle study, a 30 percent allocation to the customer survey and marketing information system development, and a 50 percent allocation to new-business development and new-product implementation.

- Each project team is responsible for reporting all financial expenditures, including personnel salaries and direct expenses, for its segment of the project. A standardized reporting form will be developed and provided by the marketing director.

- The marketing director is responsible for adherence to the project budget and will report overages to the company president on a weekly basis. The marketing director is also responsible for any redirection of budget dollars as required for each project of the business analysis team.

- Any new-product offering will be evaluated on a quarterly basis to determine its profitability. Product development expenses will be distributed over a two-year period, by calendar quarters, and will be compared with gross income generated during the same period.

B. Monitoring Procedures

To analyze the effectiveness of Star Software's marketing plan, it is necessary to compare its actual performance with plan objectives. To facilitate this analysis, monitoring procedures should be developed for the various activities required to bring the marketing plan to fruition. These procedures include, but are not limited to, the following:

- A project management concept will be used to evaluate the implementation of the marketing plan by establishing time requirements, human resource needs, and financial or budgetary expenditures.

- A perpetual comparison of actual and planned activities will be conducted on a monthly basis for the first year and on a quarterly basis after the initial implementation phase. The business analysis team, including the marketing director, will report its comparison of actual and planned outcomes directly to the company president.

- Each project team is responsible for determining what changes must be made in procedures, product focus, or operations as a result of the studies conducted in its area.

accessory equipment Equipment that does not become part of the final physical product but is used in production or office activities (10)

advertising Paid nonpersonal communication about an organization and its products transmitted to a target audience through mass media (17)

advertising appropriation The advertising budget for a specific time period (17)

advertising campaign The creation and execution of a series of advertisements to communicate with a particular target audience (17)

advertising platform Basic issues or selling points to be included in an advertising campaign (17)

advocacy advertising Advertising that promotes a company's position on a public issue (17)

aesthetic modifications Changes relating to the sensory appeal of a product (11)

agents Intermediaries that represent either buyers or sellers on a permanent basis (15)

aided recall test A posttest that asks respondents to identify recent ads and provides clues to jog their memories (17)

allowance A concession in price to achieve a desired goal (19)

approach The manner in which a salesperson contacts a potential customer (18)

arbitrary approach Budgeting for an advertising campaign as specified by a high-level executive in the firm (17)

artwork An advertisement's illustrations and layout (17)

Asia-Pacific Economic Cooperation (APEC) An alliance that promotes open trade and economic and technical cooperation among member nations throughout the world (9)

atmospherics The physical elements in a store's design that appeal to consumers' emotions and encourage buying (15)

attitude An individual's enduring evaluation of feelings about and behavioral tendencies toward an object or idea (7)

attitude scale A means of measuring consumer attitudes by gauging the intensity of individuals' reactions to adjectives, phrases, or sentences about an object (7)

automatic vending The use of machines to dispense products (15)

average fixed cost The fixed cost per unit produced (19)

average total cost The sum of the average fixed cost and the average variable cost (19)

average variable cost The variable cost per unit produced (19)

bait pricing Pricing an item in a product line low with the intention of selling a higher-priced item in the line (20)

balance of trade The difference in value between a nation's exports and its imports (9)

barter The trading of products (19)

base-point pricing Geographic pricing that combines factory price and freight charges from the base point nearest the buyer (19)

benchmarking Comparing the quality of the firm's goods, services, or processes with that of its best-performing competitors (2)

benefit segmentation The division of a market according to benefits that consumers want from the product (6)

Better Business Bureau (BBB) A system of nongovernmental, independent, local regulatory agencies supported by local businesses that helps settle problems between customers and specific business firms (3)

blogs Web-based journals in which people can editorialize and interact with other Internet users (7)

brand A name, term, design, symbol, or other feature that identifies one marketer's product as distinct from those of other marketers (12)

brand competitors Firms that market products with similar features and benefits to the same customers at similar prices (3)

brand equity The marketing and financial value associated with a brand's strength in a market (12)

brand extension An organization uses one of its existing brands to brand a new product in a different product category (12)

brand insistence The degree of brand loyalty in which a customer strongly prefers a specific brand and will accept no substitute (12)

brand licensing An agreement whereby a company permits another organization to use its brand on other products for a licensing fee (12)

brand loyalty A customer's favorable attitude toward a specific brand (12)

brand manager The person responsible for a single brand (11)

brand mark The part of a brand that is not made up of words, such as a symbol or design (12)

brand name The part of a brand that can be spoken, including letters, words, and numbers (12)

brand preference The degree of brand loyalty in which a customer prefers one brand over competitive offerings (12)

brand recognition The degree of brand loyalty in which a customer is aware that a brand exists and views the brand as an alternative purchase if their preferred brand is unavailable (12)

breakdown approach Measuring company sales potential based on a general economic forecast for a specific period and the market potential derived from it (6)

break-even point The point at which the costs of producing a product equal the revenue made from selling the product (19)

brokers Intermediaries that bring buyers and sellers together temporarily (15)

buildup approach Measuring company sales potential by estimating how much of a product a potential buyer in a specific geographic area will purchase in a given period, multiplying the estimate by the number of potential buyers, and adding the totals of all the geographic areas considered (6)

bundle pricing Packaging together two or more complementary products and selling them at a single price (20)

business analysis Evaluating the potential impact of a product idea on the firm's sales, costs, and profits (11)

business (organizational) buying behavior The purchase behavior of producers, government units, institutions, and resellers (8)

business cycle A pattern of economic fluctuations that has four stages: prosperity, recession, depression, and recovery (3)

business market Individuals or groups that purchase a specific kind of product for resale, direct use in producing other products, or use in general daily operations (6)

business market Individuals, organizations, or groups that purchase a specific kind of product for resale, direct use in producing other products, or use in general daily operations (8)

business products Products bought to use in a firm's operations, to resell, or to make other products (10)

business services Intangible products that many organizations use in their operations (10)

buy-back allowance A sum of money given to a reseller for each unit bought after an initial promotion deal is over (18)

buying allowance A temporary price reduction to resellers for purchasing specified quantities of a product (18)

buying behavior The decision processes and actions of people involved in buying and using products (7)

buying center The people within an organization who make business purchase decisions (8)

buying power Resources, such as money, goods, and services, that can be traded in an exchange (3)

buzz marketing An attempt to incite publicity and public excitement surrounding a product through a creative event (16)

captioned photograph A photograph with a brief description of its contents (17)

captive pricing Pricing the basic product in a product line low, while pricing related items higher (20)

cash discount Price reductions given to buyers for prompt payment or cash payment (19)

cash-and-carry wholesalers A limited-service wholesaler whose customers pay cash and furnish transportation (15)

catalog marketing A type of marketing in which an organization provides a catalog from which customers make selections and place orders by mail, telephone, or the Internet (15)

category killer A very large specialty store that concentrates on a major product category and competes on the basis of low prices and product availability (15)

category management A retail strategy of managing groups of similar, often substitutable products produced by different manufacturers (15)

cause-related marketing The practice of linking products to a particular social cause on an ongoing or short-term basis (4)

centralized organization A structure in which top-level managers delegate little authority to lower levels (2)

cents-off offer A promotion that allows buyers to pay less than the regular price to encourage purchase (18)

channel capacity The limit on the volume of information a communication channel can handle effectively (16)

channel captain The dominant member of a marketing channel or supply chain (14)

channel power The ability of one channel member to influence another member's goal achievement (14)

client-based relationships Interactions that result in satisfied customers who use a service repeatedly over time (13)

client publics Direct consumers of a product of a nonbusiness organization (13)

closing The stage in the personal selling process when the salesperson asks the prospect to buy the product (18)

co-branding Using two or more brands on one product (12)

codes of conduct Formalized rules and standards that describe what the company expects of its employees (4)

coding process Converting meaning into a series of signs or symbols (16)

cognitive dissonance A buyer's doubts shortly after a purchase about whether the decision was the right one (7)

combination compensation plan Paying salespeople a fixed salary plus a commission based on sales volume (18)

commercialization Refining and finalizing plans and budgets for full-scale manufacturing and marketing of a product (11)

commission merchants Agents that receive goods on consignment from local sellers and negotiate sales in large, central markets (15)

Common Market of the Southern Cone (MERCOSUR) An alliance that promotes the free circulation of goods, services, and production factors, and has a common external tariff and commercial policy among member nations in South America (9)

communication A sharing of meaning through the transmission of information (16)

communications channel The medium of transmission that carries the coded message from the source to the receiver (16)

community shopping centers Shopping centers with one or two department stores, some specialty stores, and convenience stores (15)

company sales potential The maximum percentage of market potential that an individual firm within an industry can expect to obtain for a specific product (6)

comparative advertising Compares the sponsored brand with one or more identified brands on the basis of one or more product characteristics (17)

comparison discounting Setting a price at a specific level and comparing it with a higher price (20)

competition Other organizations that market products that are similar to or can be substituted for a marketer's products in the same geographic area (3)

competition-based pricing Pricing influenced primarily by competitors' prices (20)

competition-matching approach Determining an advertising budget by trying to match competitors' advertising outlays (17)

competitive advantage The result of a company's matching a core competency to opportunities it has discovered in the marketplace (2)

competitive advertising Tries to stimulate demand for a specific brand by promoting its features, uses, and advantages relative to competing brands (17)

component parts Items that become part of the physical product and are either finished items ready for assembly or items that need little processing before assembly (10)

concentrated targeting strategy A market segmentation strategy in which an organization targets a single market segment using one marketing mix (6)

concept testing Seeking a sample of potential buyers' responses to a product idea (11)

conclusive research Research designed to verify insights through objective procedures and to help marketers in making decisions (5)

consideration set A group of brands within a product category that a buyer views as alternatives for possible purchase (7)

consistency of quality The degree to which a product has the same level of quality over time (11)

consumer buying behavior   The decision processes and purchasing activities of people who purchase products for personal or household use and not for business purposes (7)

consumer buying decision process   A five-stage purchase decision process that includes problem recognition, information search, evaluation of alternatives, purchase, and postpurchase evaluation (7)

consumer contests   Sales promotion methods in which individuals compete for prizes based on their analytical or creative skills (18)

consumer games   Sales promotion methods in which individuals compete for prizes based primarily on chance (18)

consumerism   Organized efforts by individuals, groups, and organizations to protect consumers' rights (3)

consumer jury   A panel of a product's existing or potential buyers who pretest ads (17)

consumer market   Purchasers and household members who intend to consume or benefit from the purchased products and do not buy products to make profits (6)

consumer products   Products purchased to satisfy personal and family needs (10)

consumer sales promotion methods   Sales promotion techniques that encourage consumers to patronize specific stores or try particular products (18)

consumer socialization   The process through which a person acquires the knowledge and skills to function as a consumer (7)

consumer sweepstakes   A sales promotion in which entrants submit their names for inclusion in a drawing for prizes (18)

contract manufacturing   The practice of hiring a foreign firm to produce a designated volume of the domestic firm's product or a component of it to specification; the final product carries the domestic firm's name (9)

convenience products   Relatively inexpensive, frequently purchased items for which buyers exert minimal purchasing effort (10)

convenience store   A small self-service store that is open long hours and carries a narrow assortment of products, usually convenience items (15)

cooperative advertising   An arrangement in which a manufacturer agrees to pay a certain amount of a retailer's media costs for advertising the manufacturer's products (18)

copy   The verbal portion of advertisements (17)

core competencies   Things a firm does extremely well, which sometimes give it an advantage over its competition (2)

corporate strategy   A strategy that determines the means for utilizing resources in the various functional areas to reach the organization's goals (2)

cost-based pricing   Adding a dollar amount or percentage to the cost of the product (20)

cost comparison indicator   A means of comparing the costs of advertising vehicles in a specific medium in relation to the number of people reached (17)

cost-plus pricing   Adding a specified dollar amount or percentage to the seller's cost (20)

coupons   Written price reductions used to encourage consumers to buy a specific product (18)

credence qualities   Attributes that customers may be unable to evaluate even after purchasing and consuming a service (13)

cultural relativism   The concept that morality varies from one culture to another and that business practices are therefore differentially defined as right or wrong by particular cultures (9)

culture   The accumulation of values, knowledge, beliefs, customs, objects, and concepts of a society (7)

cumulative discounts   Quantity discounts aggregated over a stated time period (19)

customary pricing   Pricing on the basis of tradition (20)

customer advisory boards   Small groups of actual customers who serve as sounding boards for new-product ideas and offer insights into their feelings and attitudes toward a firm's products and other elements of marketing strategy (5)

customer-centric marketing   Developing collaborative relationships with customers based on focusing on their individual needs and concerns (1)

customer contact   The level of interaction between provider and customer needed to deliver the service (13)

customer forecasting survey   A survey of customers regarding the types and quantities of products they intend to buy during a specific period (6)

customer relationship management (CRM)   Using information about customers to create marketing strategies that develop and sustain desirable customer relationships (1)

customers   The purchasers of organizations' products; the focal point of all marketing activities (1)

customer services   Human or mechanical efforts or activities that add value to a product (11)

cycle analysis   An analysis of sales figures for a period of three to five years to ascertain whether sales fluctuate in a consistent, periodic manner (6)

cycle time   The time needed to complete a process (14)

database   A collection of information arranged for easy access and retrieval (5)

dealer listing   An advertisement that promotes a product and identifies the names of participating retailers that sell the product (18)

dealer loader   A gift, often part of a display, given to a retailer that purchases a specified quantity of merchandise (18)

decentralized organization   A structure in which decision-making authority is delegated as far down the chain of command as possible (2)

decline stage   The stage of a product's life cycle when sales fall rapidly (10)

decoding process   Converting signs or symbols into concepts and ideas (16)

Delphi technique   A procedure in which experts create initial forecasts, submit them to the company for averaging, and then refine the forecasts (6)

demand-based pricing   Pricing based on the level of demand for the product (20)

demand curve   A graph of the quantity of products expected to be sold at various prices if other factors remain constant (19)

demonstration   A sales promotion method a manufacturer uses temporarily to encourage trial use and purchase of a product or to show how a product works (18)

department stores   Large retail organizations characterized by a wide product mix and organized into separate departments to facilitate marketing efforts and internal management (15)

depression   A stage of the business cycle when unemployment is extremely high, wages are very low, total disposable income is at a minimum, and consumers lack confidence in the economy (3)

depth of product mix   The average number of different products offered in each product line (10)

derived demand   Demand for industrial products that stems from demand for consumer products (8)

descriptive research   Research conducted to clarify the characteristics of certain phenomena to solve a particular problem (5)

differential pricing   Charging different prices to different buyers for the same quality and quantity of product (20)

differentiated targeting strategy   A strategy in which an organization targets two or more segments by developing a marketing mix for each segment (6)

direct marketing   The use of the telephone, Internet, and nonpersonal media to introduce products to customers, who can then purchase them via mail, telephone, or the Internet (15)

direct ownership   A situation in which a company owns subsidiaries or other facilities overseas (9)

direct-response marketing   A type of marketing in which a retailer advertises a product and makes it available through mail or telephone orders (15)

direct selling   Marketing products to ultimate consumers through face-to-face sales presentations at home or in the workplace (15)

discount stores   Self-service, general merchandise stores that offer brand name and private-brand products at low prices (15)

discretionary income   Disposable income available for spending and saving after an individual has purchased the basic necessities of food, clothing, and shelter (3)

disposable income   After-tax income (3)

distribution   The decisions and activities that make products available to customers when and where they want to purchase them (14)

distribution centers   Large, centralized warehouses that focus on moving rather than storing goods (14)

drop shippers   A limited-service wholesaler that takes title to goods and negotiates sales but never actually takes possession of products (15)

dual distribution   The use of two or more marketing channels to distribute the same products to the same target market (14)

dumping   Selling products at unfairly low prices (9)

early adopters   People who adopt new products early, choose new products carefully, and are viewed as "the people to check with" by later adopters (10)

early majority   Individuals who adopt a new product just prior to the average person (10)

electronic data interchange (EDI)   A computerized means of integrating order processing with production, inventory, accounting, and transportation (14)

embargo   A government's suspension of trade in a particular product or with a given country (9)

empowerment   Giving customer contact employees authority and responsibility to make marketing decisions without seeking approval of their supervisors (2)

environmental analysis   The process of assessing and interpreting the information gathered through environmental scanning (3)

environmental scanning   The process of collecting information about forces in the marketing environment (3)

ethical issue   An identifiable problem, situation, or opportunity requiring a choice among several actions that must be evaluated as right or wrong, ethical or unethical (4)

European Union (EU)   An alliance that promotes trade among its member countries in Europe (9)

evaluative criteria   Objective and subjective product characteristics that are important to a buyer (7)

everyday low prices (EDLP)   Pricing products low on a consistent basis (20)

exchange controls   Government restrictions on the amount of a particular currency that can be bought or sold (9)

exchanges   The provision or transfer of goods, services, or ideas in return for something of value (1)

exclusive dealing   A situation in which a manufacturer forbids an intermediary to carry products of competing manufacturers (14)

exclusive distribution   Using a single outlet in a fairly large geographic area to distribute a product (14)

executive judgment   A sales forecasting method based on the intuition of one or more executives (6)

experience qualities   Attributes that can be assessed only during purchase and consumption of a service (13)

experimental research   Research that allows marketers to make causal inferences about relationships (5)

expert forecasting survey   Sales forecasts prepared by experts outside the firm, such as economists, management consultants, advertising executives, or college professors (6)

exploratory research   Research conducted to gather more information about a problem or to make a tentative hypothesis more specific (5)

exporting   The sale of products to foreign markets (9)

extended problem solving   A consumer problem-solving process employed when purchasing unfamiliar, expensive, or infrequently bought products (7)

external customers   Individuals who patronize a business—the familiar definition of "customers" (2)

external reference price   A comparison price provided by others (19)

external search   An information search in which buyers seek information from sources other than their memories (7)

family branding   Branding all of a firm's products with the same name or part of the name (12)

family packaging   Using similar packaging for all of a firm's products or packaging that has one common design element (12)

feature article   A manuscript of up to 3,000 words prepared for a specific publication (17)

Federal Trade Commission (FTC)   An agency that regulates a variety of business practices and curbs false advertising, misleading pricing, and deceptive packaging and labeling (3)

feedback   The receiver's response to a decoded message (16)

fixed costs   Costs that do not vary with changes in the number of units produced or sold (19)

F.O.B. destination   A price indicating the producer is absorbing shipping costs (19)

F.O.B. factory   The price of merchandise at the factory before shipment (19)

focus-group interview   An interview that is often conducted informally, without a structured questionnaire, in small groups of 8 to 12 people, to observe interaction when members are exposed to an idea or a concept (5)

franchising   A form of licensing in which a franchiser, in exchange for a financial commitment, grants a franchisee the right to market its product in accordance with the franchiser's standards (9)

franchising   An arrangement in which a supplier (franchiser) grants a dealer (franchisee) the right to sell products in exchange for some type of consideration (15)

free merchandise A manufacturer's reward given to resellers that purchase a stated quantity of products (18)

free sample A sample of a product given out to encourage trial and purchase (18)

freight absorption pricing Absorption of all or part of actual freight costs by the seller (19)

freight forwarders Organizations that consolidate shipments from several firms into efficient lot sizes (14)

full-service wholesalers Merchant wholesalers that perform the widest range of wholesaling functions (15)

functional modifications Changes affecting a product's versatility, effectiveness, convenience, or safety (11)

General Agreement on Tariffs and Trade (GATT) An agreement among nations to reduce worldwide tariffs and increase international trade (9)

general-line wholesalers A full-service wholesaler that carries only a few product lines but many products within those lines (15)

general merchandise retailer A retail establishment that offers a variety of product lines that are stocked in considerable depth (15)

general merchandise wholesalers Full-service wholesalers with a wide product mix but with limited depth within product lines (15)

general publics Indirect consumers of a product of a nonbusiness organization (13)

generic brand A brand indicating only the product category (12)

generic competitors Firms that provide very different products that solve the same problem or satisfy the same basic customer need (3)

geodemographic segmentation A method of market segmentation that clusters people in zip code areas and smaller neighborhood units based on lifestyle and demographic information (6)

geographic pricing Reductions for transportation and other costs related to the physical distance between buyer and seller (19)

globalization The development of marketing strategies that treat the entire world (or its major regions) as a single entity (9)

good A tangible physical entity (10)

government markets Federal, state, county, or local governments that buy goods and services to support their internal operations and provide products to their constituencies (8)

green marketing The specific development, pricing, promotion, and distribution of products that do not harm the natural environment (4)

gross domestic product (GDP) The market value of a nation's total output of goods and services for a given period; an overall measure of economic standing (9)

growth stage The product life cycle stage when sales rise rapidly, profits reach a peak, and then they start to decline (10)

heterogeneity Variation in quality (13)

heterogeneous market A market made up of individuals or organizations with diverse needs for products in a specific product class (6)

homogeneous market A market in which a large proportion of customers have similar needs for a product (6)

horizontal channel integration Combining organizations at the same level of operation under one management (14)

hypermarkets Stores that combine supermarket and discount store shopping in one location (15)

hypothesis An informed guess or assumption about a certain problem or set of circumstances (5)

idea A concept, philosophy, image, or issue (10)

idea generation Seeking product ideas to achieve organizational objectives (11)

illustrations Photos, drawings, graphs, charts, and tables used to spark audience interest in an advertisement (17)

importing The purchase of products from a foreign source (9)

import tariff A duty levied by a nation on goods bought outside its borders and brought into the country (9)

impulse buying An unplanned buying behavior resulting from a powerful urge to buy something immediately (7)

income For an individual, the amount of money received through wages, rents, investments, pensions, and subsidy payments for a given period (3)

individual branding A branding policy in which each product is given a different name (12)

industrial distributor An independent business organization that takes title to industrial products and carries inventories (14)

inelastic demand Demand that is not significantly altered by a price increase or decrease (8)

information inputs Sensations received through sight, taste, hearing, smell, and touch (7)

in-home (door-to-door) interview A personal interview that takes place in the respondent's home (5)

innovators First adopters of new products (10)

input-output data Information that identifies what types of industries purchase the products of a particular industry (8)

inseparability The quality of being produced and consumed at the same time (13)

installations Facilities and nonportable major equipment (10)

institutional advertising Advertising that promotes organizational images, ideas, and political issues (17)

institutional markets Organizations with charitable, educational, community, or other nonbusiness goals (8)

intangibility The characteristic that a service is not physical and cannot be perceived by the senses (13)

integrated marketing communications Coordination of promotion and other marketing efforts for maximum informational and persuasive impact (16)

intended strategy The strategy the organization decided on during the planning phase, and wants to use (2)

intensive distribution Using all available outlets to distribute a product (14)

intermodal transportation Two or more transportation modes used in combination (14)

internal customers The company's employees (2)

internal marketing A management philosophy that coordinates internal exchanges between the organization and its employees to achieve successful external exchanges between the organization and its customers (2)

internal reference price A price developed in the buyer's mind through experience with the product (19)

internal search An information search in which buyers search their memories for information about products that might solve their problem (7)

international marketing Developing and performing marketing activities across national boundaries (9)

introduction stage   The initial stage of a product's life cycle; its first appearance in the marketplace when sales start at zero and profits are negative (10)

inventory management   Developing and maintaining adequate assortments of products to meet customers' needs (14)

joint demand   Demand involving the use of two or more items in combination to produce a product (8)

joint venture   A partnership between a domestic firm and a foreign firm or government (9)

just-in-time (JIT)   An inventory-management approach in which supplies arrive just when needed for production or resale (14)

kinesic communication   Communicating through the movement of head, eyes, arms, hands, legs, or torso (16)

labeling   Providing identifying, promotional, or other information on package labels (12)

laggards   The last adopters, who distrust new products (10)

late majority   Skeptics who adopt new products when they feel it is necessary (10)

layout   The physical arrangement of an advertisement's illustration and copy (17)

learning   Changes in an individual's thought processes and behavior caused by information and experience (7)

level of involvement   An individual's degree of interest in a product and the importance of the product for that person (7)

level of quality   The amount of quality a product possesses (11)

licensing   An alternative to direct investment that requires a licensee to pay commissions or royalties on sales or supplies used in manufacturing (9)

lifestyle   An individual's pattern of living expressed through activities, interests, and opinions (7)

lifestyle shopping centers   A type of shopping center that is typically open air and features upscale specialty, dining, and entertainment stores (15)

limited problem solving   A consumer problem-solving process used when purchasing products occasionally or needing information about an unfamiliar brand in a familiar product category (7)

limited-service wholesalers   A merchant wholesaler that provides some services and specializes in a few functions (15)

line extension   Development of a product that is closely related to existing products in the line but is designed specifically to meet different customer needs (11)

logistics management   Planning, implementing, and controlling the efficient and effective flow and storage of products and information from the point of origin to consumption to meet customers' needs and wants (14)

mail-order wholesalers   Limited-service wholesalers that sell products through catalogs (15)

mail survey   A research method in which respondents answer a questionnaire sent through the mail (5)

manufacturer brand   A brand initiated by producers to ensure that producers are identified with their products at the point of purchase (12)

manufacturers' agents   Independent intermediaries that represent two or more sellers and usually offer customers complete product lines (15)

marginal cost (MC)   The extra cost incurred by producing one more unit of a product (19)

marginal revenue (MR)   The change in total revenue resulting from the sale of an additional unit of a product (19)

market   A group of individuals and/or organizations that have needs for products in a product class and have the ability, willingness, and authority to purchase those products (2)

market density   The number of potential customers within a unit of land area (6)

market growth/market share matrix   A helpful business tool, based on the philosophy that a product's market growth rate and its market share are important considerations in determining its marketing strategy (2)

marketing   The process of creating, distributing, promoting, and pricing goods, services, and ideas to facilitate satisfying exchange relationships with customers and develop and maintain favorable relationships with stakeholders in a dynamic environment (1)

marketing channel   A group of individuals and organizations that direct the flow of products from producers to customers within the supply chain (14)

marketing citizenship   The adoption of a strategic focus for fulfilling the economic, legal, ethical, and philanthropic social responsibilities expected by stakeholders (4)

marketing concept   A philosophy that an organization should try to provide products that satisfy customers' needs through a coordinated set of activities that also allows the organization to achieve its goals (1)

marketing control process   Establishing performance standards, evaluating actual performance by comparing it with established standards, and reducing the differences between desired and actual performance (2)

marketing decision support system (MDSS)   Customized computer software that aids marketing managers in decision making (5)

marketing environment   The competitive, economic, political, legal and regulatory, technological, and sociocultural forces that surround the customer and affect the marketing mix (1)

marketing ethics   Principles and standards that define acceptable marketing conduct as determined by various stakeholders (4)

marketing implementation   The process of putting marketing strategies into action (2)

marketing information system (MIS)   A framework for managing and structuring information gathered regularly from sources inside and outside the organization (5)

marketing intermediaries   Middlemen that link producers to other intermediaries or ultimate consumers through contractual arrangements or through the purchase and resale of products (14)

marketing management   The process of planning, organizing, implementing, and controlling marketing activities to facilitate exchanges effectively and efficiently (1)

marketing mix   Four marketing activities—product, distribution, promotion, and pricing—that a firm can control to meet the needs of customers within its target markets (1)

marketing objective   A statement of what is to be accomplished through marketing activities (2)

marketing orientation   An organizationwide commitment to researching and responding to customer needs (1)

marketing plan   A written document that specifies the activities to be performed to implement and control the organization's marketing activities (2)

marketing planning The systematic process of assessing marketing opportunities and resources, determining marketing objectives, defining marketing strategies, and establishing guidelines for implementation and control of the marketing program (2)

marketing research The systematic design, collection, interpretation, and reporting of information to help marketers solve specific marketing problems or take advantage of marketing opportunities (5)

marketing strategy A plan of action for identifying and analyzing a target market and developing a marketing mix to meet the needs of that market (2)

market manager The person responsible for managing the marketing activities that serve a particular group of customers (11)

market opportunity A combination of circumstances and timing that permits an organization to take action to reach a particular target market (2)

market potential The total amount of a product that customers will purchase within a specified period at a specific level of industrywide marketing activity (6)

market segment Individuals, groups, or organizations sharing one or more similar characteristics that cause them to have similar product needs (6)

market segmentation The process of dividing a total market into groups with relatively similar product needs to design a marketing mix that matches those needs (6)

market share The percentage of a market that actually buys a specific product from a particular company (2)

market test Making a product available to buyers in one or more test areas and measuring purchases and consumer responses to marketing efforts (6)

markup pricing Adding to the cost of the product a predetermined percentage of that cost (20)

Maslow's hierarchy of needs The five levels of needs that humans seek to satisfy, from most to least important (7)

materials handling Physical handling of tangible goods, supplies, and resources (14)

maturity stage The stage of a product's life cycle when the sales curve peaks and starts to decline, and profits continue to fall (10)

media plan A plan that specifies the media vehicles to be used and the schedule for running advertisements (17)

megacarriers Freight transportation firms that provide several modes of shipment (14)

merchandise allowance A manufacturer's agreement to pay resellers certain amounts of money for providing special promotional efforts, such as setting up and maintaining a display (18)

merchant wholesalers An independently owned business that takes title to goods, assumes ownership risks, and buys and resells products to other wholesalers, business customers, or retailers (15)

micromarketing An approach to market segmentation in which organizations focus precise marketing efforts on very small geographic markets (6)

missionary salespeople Support salespeople, usually employed by a manufacturer, who assist the producer's customers in selling to their own customers (18)

mission statement A long-term view, or vision, of what the organization wants to become (2)

modified rebuy purchase A new-task purchase that is changed on subsequent orders or when the requirements of a straight rebuy purchase are modified (8)

money refund A sales promotion technique that offers consumers a specified amount of money when they mail in a proof of purchase, usually for multiple product purchases (18)

monopolistic competition A competitive structure in which a firm has many potential competitors and tries to develop a marketing strategy to differentiate its product (3)

monopoly A competitive structure in which an organization offers a product that has no close substitutes, making that organization the sole source of supply (3)

motive An internal energizing force that directs a person's behavior toward satisfying needs or achieving goals (7)

MRO supplies Maintenance, repair, and operating items that facilitate production and operations but do not become part of the finished product (10)

multinational enterprise A firm that has operations or subsidiaries in many countries (9)

multiple sourcing An organization's decision to use several suppliers (8)

multiple-unit pricing Packaging together two or more identical products and selling them at a single price (20)

National Advertising Review Board (NARB) A self-regulatory unit that considers challenges to issues raised by the National Advertising Division (an arm of the Council of Better Business Bureaus) about an advertisement (3)

negotiated pricing Establishing a final price through bargaining between seller and customer (20)

neighborhood shopping centers Shopping centers usually consisting of several small convenience and specialty stores (15)

new-product development process A seven-phase process for introducing products: idea generation, screening, concept testing, business analysis, product development, test marketing, and commercialization (11)

news release A short piece of copy publicizing an event or a product (17)

new-task purchase An initial purchase by an organization of an item to be used to perform a new job or solve a new problem (8)

noise Anything that reduces a communication's clarity and accuracy (16)

noncumulative discounts Onetime price reductions based on the number of units purchased, the dollar value of the order, or the product mix purchased (19)

nonprice competition Emphasizing factors other than price to distinguish a product from competing brands (19)

nonprobability sampling A sampling technique in which there is no way to calculate the likelihood that a specific element of the population being studied will be chosen (5)

nonprofit marketing Marketing activities conducted to achieve some goal other than ordinary business goals such as profit, market share, or return on investment (13)

nonstore retailing The selling of products outside the confines of a retail facility (15)

North American Free Trade Agreement (NAFTA) An alliance that merges Canada, Mexico, and the United States into a single market (9)

North American Industry Classification System (NAICS) An industry classification system that generates comparable statistics among the United States, Canada, and Mexico (8)

objective-and-task approach Budgeting for an advertising campaign by first determining its objectives and then calculating the cost of all the tasks needed to attain them (17)

odd-even pricing Ending the price with certain numbers to influence buyers' perceptions of the price or product (20)

off-price retailers Stores that buy manufacturers' seconds, overruns, returns, and off-season merchandise for resale to consumers at deep discounts (15)

offshore outsourcing The practice of contracting with an organization to perform some or all business functions in a country other than the country in which the product or service will be sold (9)

offshoring The practice of moving a business process that was done domestically at the local factory to a foreign country, regardless of whether the production accomplished in the foreign country is performed by the local company (e.g., in a wholly owned subsidiary) or a third party (9)

oligopoly A competitive structure in which a few sellers control the supply of a large proportion of a product (3)

online retailing Retailing that makes products available to buyers through computer connections (15)

online survey A research method in which respondents answer a questionnaire via e-mail or on a website (5)

on-site computer interview A variation of the shopping mall intercept interview in which respondents complete a self-administered questionnaire displayed on a computer monitor (5)

operations management The total set of managerial activities used by an organization to transform resource inputs into products (14)

opinion leader A member of an informal group who provides information about a specific topic to other group members (7)

opportunity cost The value of the benefit given up by choosing one alternative over another (13)

order getter A salesperson who sells to new customers and increases sales to current customers (18)

order processing The receipt and transmission of sales order information (14)

order takers Salespeople who primarily seek repeat sales (18)

organizational (corporate) culture A set of values, beliefs, goals, norms, and rituals that members of an organization share (4)

outsourcing The practice of contracting noncore operations with an organization that specializes in that operation (9)

outsourcing The contracting of physical distribution tasks to third parties who do not have managerial authority within the marketing channel (14)

patronage motives Motives that influence where a person purchases products on a regular basis (7)

penetration pricing Setting prices below those of competing brands to penetrate a market and gain a significant market share quickly (20)

percent-of-sales approach Budgeting for an advertising campaign by multiplying the firm's past and expected sales by a standard percentage (17)

perception The process of selecting, organizing, and interpreting information inputs to produce meaning (7)

performance standard An expected level of performance against which actual performance can be compared (2)

periodic discounting Temporary reduction of prices on a patterned or systematic basis (20)

perishability The inability of unused service capacity to be stored for future use (13)

personal interview survey A research method in which participants respond to survey questions face-to-face (5)

personality A set of internal traits and distinct behavioral tendencies that result in consistent patterns of behavior in certain situations (7)

personal selling Paid personal communication that attempts to inform customers and persuade them to buy products in an exchange situation (18)

physical distribution Activities used to move products from producers to consumers and other end users (14)

pioneer advertising Advertising that tries to stimulate demand for a product category rather than a specific brand by informing potential buyers about the product (17)

pioneer promotion Promotion that informs consumers about a new product (16)

point-of-purchase (P.O.P.) materials Signs, window displays, display racks, and similar devices used to attract customers (18)

population All the elements, units, or individuals of interest to researchers for a specific study (5)

posttest Evaluation of advertising effectiveness after the campaign (17)

power shopping center A type of shopping center that combines off-price stores with category killers (15)

premium An item offered free or at a minimal cost as a bonus for purchasing a product (18)

premium money (or push money) Extra compensation to salespeople for pushing a line of goods (18)

premium pricing Pricing the highest-quality or most versatile products higher than other models in the product line (20)

press conference A meeting used to announce major news events (17)

prestige pricing Setting prices at an artificially high level to convey prestige or a quality image (20)

prestige sensitive Drawn to products that signify prominence and status (19)

pretest Evaluation of advertisements performed before a campaign begins (17)

price The value paid for a product in a marketing exchange (19)

price competition Emphasizing price as an issue and matching or beating competitors' prices (19)

price conscious Striving to pay low prices (19)

price discrimination Employing price differentials that injure competition by giving one or more buyers a competitive advantage (19)

price elasticity of demand A measure of the sensitivity of demand to changes in price (19)

price leaders A product priced below the usual markup, near cost, or below cost (20)

price lining Setting a limited number of prices for selected groups or lines of merchandise (20)

price skimming Charging the highest possible price that buyers who most desire the product will pay (20)

pricing objectives Goals that describe what a firm wants to achieve through pricing (20)

primary data Data observed and recorded or collected directly from respondents (5)

primary demand Demand for a product category rather than for a specific brand (16)

private distributor brand A brand initiated and owned by a reseller (12)

private warehouses Company-operated facilities for storing and shipping products (14)

probability sampling A type of sampling in which every element in the population being studied has a known chance of being selected for study (5)

process materials Materials that are used directly in the production of other products but are not readily identifiable (10)

producer markets Individuals and business organizations that purchase products to make profits by using them to produce other products or using them in their operations (8)

product adoption process The five-stage process of buyer acceptance of a product: awareness, interest, evaluation, trial, and adoption (10)

product advertising Advertising that promotes the uses, features, and benefits of products (17)

product competitors Firms that compete in the same product class but market products with different features, benefits, and prices (3)

product deletion Eliminating a product from the product mix when it no longer satisfies a sufficient number of customers (11)

product design How a product is conceived, planned, and produced (11)

product development Determining if producing a product is technically feasible and cost effective (11)

product differentiation Creating and designing products so that customers perceive them as different from competing products (11)

product features Specific design characteristics that allow a product to perform certain tasks (11)

product item A specific version of a product that can be designated as a distinct offering among a firm's products (10)

product life cycle The progression of a product through four stages: introduction, growth, maturity, and decline (10)

product line A group of closely related product items viewed as a unit because of marketing, technical, or end-use considerations (10)

product-line pricing Establishing and adjusting prices of multiple products within a product line (20)

product manager The person within an organization who is responsible for a product, a product line, or several distinct products that make up a group (11)

product mix The composite, or total, group of products that an organization makes available to customers (10)

product modification Changes in one or more characteristics of a product (11)

product placement The strategic location of products or product promotions within entertainment media content to reach the product's target market (16)

product positioning Creating and maintaining a certain concept of a product in customers' minds (6)

products Goods, services, or ideas (1)

professional pricing Fees set by people with great skill or experience in a particular field (20)

promotion Communication to build and maintain relationships by informing and persuading one or more audiences (16)

promotion mix A combination of promotional methods used to promote a specific product (16)

prospecting Developing a list of potential customers (18)

prosperity A stage of the business cycle characterized by low unemployment and relatively high total income, which together ensure high buying power (provided the inflation rate stays low) (3)

proxemic communication Communicating by varying the physical distance in face-to-face interactions (16)

psychological influences Factors that in part determine people's general behavior, thus influencing their behavior as consumers (7)

psychological pricing Pricing that attempts to influence a customer's perception of price to make a product's price more attractive (20)

publicity A news story type of communication about an organization and/or its products transmitted through a mass medium at no charge (17)

public relations Communication efforts used to create and maintain favorable relations between an organization and its stakeholders (17)

public warehouses Storage space and related physical distribution facilities that can be leased by companies (14)

pull policy Promoting a product directly to consumers to develop strong consumer demand that pulls products through the marketing channel (16)

pure competition A market structure characterized by an extremely large number of sellers, none strong enough to significantly influence price or supply (3)

push policy Promoting a product only to the next institution down the marketing channel (16)

quality The overall characteristics of a product that allow it to perform as expected in satisfying customer needs (11)

quality modifications Changes relating to a product's dependability and durability (11)

quantity discounts Deductions from the list price for purchasing in large quantities (19)

quota A limit on the amount of goods an importing country will accept for certain product categories in a specific period of time (9)

quota sampling A nonprobability sampling technique in which researchers divide the population into groups and then arbitrarily choose participants from each group (5)

rack jobbers Full-service specialty-line wholesalers that own and maintain display racks in stores (15)

random discounting Temporary reduction of prices on an unsystematic basis (20)

random factor analysis An analysis attempting to attribute erratic sales variations to random, nonrecurrent events (6)

random sampling A form of probability sampling in which all units in a population have an equal chance of appearing in the sample, and the various events that can occur have an equal or known chance of taking place (5)

raw materials Basic natural materials that become part of a physical product (10)

realized strategy The strategy that actually takes place (2)

rebate A sales promotion technique in which a consumer receives a specified amount of money for making a single product purchase (18)

receiver The individual, group, or organization that decodes a coded message (16)

recession A stage of the business cycle during which unemployment rises and total buying power declines, stifling both consumer and business spending (3)

reciprocity An arrangement unique to business marketing in which two organizations agree to buy from each other (8)

recognition test A posttest in which respondents are shown the actual ad and asked if they recognize it (17)

recovery A stage of the business cycle in which the economy moves from recession or depression toward prosperity (3)

recruiting Developing a list of qualified applicants for sales positions (18)

reference group A group that a person identifies with so strongly that he or she adopts the values, attitudes, and behavior of group members (7)

reference pricing Pricing a product at a moderate level and displaying it next to a more expensive model or brand (20)

regional issues Versions of a magazine that differ across geographic regions (17)

regional shopping center A type of shopping center with the largest department stores, widest product mixes, and deepest product lines of all shopping centers (15)

regression analysis A method of predicting sales based on finding a relationship between past sales and one or more independent variables, such as population or income (6)

reinforcement advertising Advertising that assures users they chose the right brand and tells them how to get the most satisfaction from it (17)

relationship marketing Establishing long-term, mutually satisfying buyer-seller relationships (1)

relationship selling The building of mutually beneficial long-term associations with a customer through regular communications over prolonged periods of time (18)

reliability A condition that exists when a research technique produces almost identical results in repeated trials (5)

reminder advertising Advertising used to remind consumers about an established brand's uses, characteristics, and benefits (17)

research design An overall plan for obtaining the information needed to address a research problem or issue (5)

reseller markets Intermediaries that buy finished goods and resell them for a profit (8)

retailer An organization that purchases products for the purpose of reselling them to ultimate consumers (15)

retailing All transactions in which the buyer intends to consume the product through personal, family, or household use (15)

retail positioning Identifying an unserved or underserved market segment and serving it through a strategy that distinguishes the retailer from others in the minds of consumers in that segment (15)

role Actions and activities that a person in a particular position is supposed to perform based on expectations of the individual and surrounding persons (7)

routinized response behavior A consumer problem-solving process used when buying frequently purchased, low-cost items that require very little search-and-decision effort (7)

sales branches Manufacturer-owned intermediaries that sell products and provide support services to the manufacturer's sales force (15)

sales contest A sales promotion method used to motivate distributors, retailers, and sales personnel through recognition of outstanding achievements (18)

sales force forecasting survey A survey of a firm's sales force regarding anticipated sales in their territories for a specified period (6)

sales forecast The amount of a product a company expects to sell during a specific period at a specified level of marketing activities (6)

sales offices Manufacturer-owned operations that provide services normally associated with agents (15)

sales promotion An activity and/or material intended to induce resellers or salespeople to sell a product or consumers to buy it (18)

sample A limited number of units chosen to represent the characteristics of a total population (5)

sampling The process of selecting representative units from a total population (5)

scan-back allowance A manufacturer's reward to retailers based on the number of pieces scanned (18)

scrambled merchandising The addition of unrelated product lines to an existing product mix, particularly fast-moving items that can be sold in volume (15)

screening Selecting the ideas with the greatest potential for further review (11)

search qualities Tangible attributes that can be judged before the purchase of a product (13)

seasonal analysis An analysis of daily, weekly, or monthly sales figures to evaluate the degree to which seasonal factors influence sales (6)

seasonal discount A price reduction given to buyers for purchasing goods or services out of season (19)

secondary data Data compiled both inside and outside the organization for some purpose other than the current investigation (5)

secondary-market pricing Setting one price for the primary target market and a different price for another market (20)

segmentation variables Characteristics of individuals, groups, or organizations used to divide a market into segments (6)

selective demand Demand for a specific brand (16)

selective distortion An individual's changing or twisting of information that is inconsistent with personal feelings or beliefs (7)

selective distribution Using only some available outlets in an area to distribute a product (14)

selective exposure The process by which some inputs are selected to reach awareness and others are not (7)

selective retention Remembering information inputs that support personal feelings and beliefs and forgetting inputs that do not (7)

self-concept A perception or view of oneself (7)

selling agents Intermediaries that market a whole product line or a manufacturer's entire output (15)

service An intangible result of the application of human and mechanical efforts to people or objects (10)

service quality Customers' perception of how well a service meets or exceeds their expectations (13)

shopping mall intercept interviews A research method that involves interviewing a percentage of individuals passing by "intercept" points in a mall (5)

shopping products Items for which buyers are willing to expend considerable effort in planning and making purchases (10)

single-source data Information provided by a single marketing research firm (5)

situational influences Influences that result from circumstances, time, and location that affect the consumer buying decision process (7)

social class An open group of individuals with similar social rank (7)

social influences The forces other people exert on one's buying behavior (7)

social networks Web-based services that allow members to share personal profiles that include blogs, pictures, audios, and videos (7)

social responsibility An organization's obligation to maximize its positive impact and minimize its negative impact on society (4)

sociocultural forces The influences in a society and its culture(s) that change people's attitudes, beliefs, norms, customs, and lifestyles (3)

sole sourcing An organization's decision to use only one supplier (8)

source A person, group, or organization with a meaning it tries to share with a receiver or an audience (16)

special-event pricing Advertised sales or price cutting linked to a holiday, a season, or an event (20)

specialty-line wholesalers Full-service wholesalers that carry only a single product line or a few items within a product line (15)

specialty products Items with unique characteristics that buyers are willing to expend considerable effort to obtain (10)

stakeholders Constituents who have a "stake," or claim, in some aspect of a company's products, operations, markets, industry, and outcomes (1)

statistical interpretation Analysis of what is typical and what deviates from the average (5)

storyboard A blueprint that combines copy and visual material to show the sequence of major scenes in a commercial (17)

straight commission compensation plan Paying salespeople according to the amount of their sales in a given time period (18)

straight rebuy purchase A routine purchase of the same products under approximately the same terms of sale by a business buyer (8)

straight salary compensation plan Paying salespeople a specific amount per time period, regardless of selling effort (18)

strategic alliances A partnership that is formed to create a competitive advantage on a worldwide basis (9)

strategic business unit (SBU) A division, product line, or other profit center within the parent company (2)

strategic channel alliance An agreement whereby the products of one organization are distributed through the marketing channels of another (14)

strategic philanthropy The synergistic use of organizational core competencies and resources to address key stakeholders' interests and achieve both organizational and social benefits (4)

strategic planning The process of establishing an organizational mission and formulating goals, corporate strategy, marketing objectives, marketing strategy, and a marketing plan (2)

strategic windows Temporary periods of optimal fit between the key requirements of a market and the particular capabilities of a firm competing in that market (2)

stratified sampling A type of probability sampling in which the population is divided into groups with a common attribute and a random sample is chosen within each group (5)

styling The physical appearance of a product (11)

subculture A group of individuals whose characteristics, values, and behavioral patterns are similar within the group and different from those of people in the surrounding culture (7)

supermarkets Large, self-service stores that carry a complete line of food products, along with some nonfood products (15)

superregional shopping center A type of shopping center with the widest and deepest product mixes that attracts customers from many miles away (15)

superstores Giant retail outlets that carry food and nonfood products found in supermarkets, as well as most routinely purchased consumer products (15)

supply chain All the activities associated with the flow and transformation of products from raw materials through to the end customer (14)

supply management In its broadest form, refers to the processes that enable the progress of value from raw material to final customer and back to redesign and final disposition (14)

supply-chain management A set of approaches used to integrate the functions of operations management, logistics management, supply management, and marketing channel management so products are produced and distributed in the right quantities, to the right locations, and at the right time (14)

support personnel Sales staff members who facilitate selling but usually are not involved solely with making sales (18)

sustainable competitive advantage An advantage that the competition cannot copy (2)

SWOT analysis Assessment of an organization's strengths, weaknesses, opportunities, and threats (2)

tactile communication Communicating through touching (16)

target audience The group of people at whom advertisements are aimed (17)

target market The group of customers on which marketing efforts are focused (1)

target public A collective of individuals who have an interest in or concern about an organization, product, or social cause (13)

team selling The use of a team of experts from all functional areas of a firm, led by a salesperson, to conduct the personal selling process (18)

technical salespeople Support salespeople who give technical assistance to a firm's current customers (18)

technology The application of knowledge and tools to solve problems and perform tasks more efficiently (3)

telemarketing The performance of marketing-related activities by telephone (15)

telephone depth interview An interview that combines the traditional focus group's ability to probe with the confidentiality provided by telephone surveys (5)

telephone survey A research method in which respondents' answers to a questionnaire are recorded by an interviewer on the phone (5)

television home shopping A form of selling in which products are presented to television viewers, who can buy them by calling a toll-free number and paying with a credit card (15)

test marketing A limited introduction of a product in geographic areas chosen to represent the intended market (11)

time series analysis A forecasting method that uses historical sales data to discover patterns in the firm's sales over time and generally involves trend, cycle, seasonal, and random factor analyses (6)

total budget competitors Firms that compete for the limited financial resources of the same customers (3)

total cost The sum of average fixed and average variable costs times the quantity produced (19)

total quality management (TQM) A philosophy that uniform commitment to quality in all areas of the organization will promote a culture that meets customers' perceptions of quality (2)

trade name The full legal name of an organization (12)

trade sales promotion methods Methods intended to persuade wholesalers and retailers to carry a producer's products and market them aggressively (18)

trade salespeople Salespeople involved mainly in helping a producer's customers promote a product (18)

trade, or functional, discount A reduction off the list price a producer gives to an intermediary for performing certain functions (19)

trademark A legal designation of exclusive use of a brand (12)

trading company A company that links buyers and sellers in different countries (9)

traditional specialty retailers Stores that carry a narrow product mix with deep product lines (15)

transfer pricing Prices charged in sales between an organization's units (19)

transportation The movement of products from where they are made to intermediaries and end users (14)

trend analysis An analysis that focuses on aggregate sales data over a period of many years to determine general trends in annual sales (6)

truck wholesalers A limited-service wholesaler that transports products directly to customers for inspection and selection (15)

tying agreement An agreement in which a supplier furnishes a product to a channel member with the stipulation that the channel member must purchase other products as well (14)

unaided recall test A posttest in which respondents are asked to identify advertisements they have seen recently but are not given any recall clues (17)

undifferentiated targeting strategy A strategy in which an organization designs a single marketing mix and directs it at the entire market for a particular product (6)

uniform geographic pricing Charging all customers the same price, regardless of geographic location (19)

universal product code (UPC) A series of electronically readable lines identifying a product and containing inventory and pricing information (12)

unsought products Products purchased to solve a sudden problem, products of which customers are unaware, and products that people do not necessarily think of buying (10)

validity A condition that exists when a research method measures what it is supposed to measure (5)

value A customer's subjective assessment of benefits relative to costs in determining the worth of a product (1)

value analysis An evaluation of each component of a potential purchase (8)

value conscious Concerned about price and quality of a product (19)

variable costs Costs that vary directly with changes in the number of units produced or sold (19)

vendor analysis A formal, systematic evaluation of current and potential vendors (8)

venture team A cross-functional group that creates entirely new products that may be aimed at new markets (11)

vertical channel integration Combining two or more stages of the marketing channel under one management (14)

vertical marketing system (VMS) A marketing channel managed by a single channel member to achieve efficient, low-cost distribution aimed at satisfying target market customers (14)

viral marketing A strategy to get consumers to share a marketer's message, often through e-mail or online video, in a way that spreads dramatically and quickly (16)

warehouse clubs Large-scale, members-only establishments that combine features of cash-and-carry wholesaling with discount retailing (15)

warehouse showrooms Retail facilities in large, low-cost buildings with large on-premises inventories and minimal services (15)

warehousing The design and operation of facilities for storing and moving goods (14)

wealth The accumulation of past income, natural resources, and financial resources (3)

wheel of retailing A hypothesis holding that new retailers usually enter the market as low-status, low-margin, low-price operators but eventually evolve into high-cost, high-price merchants (15)

wholesaler An individual or organization that sells products that are bought for resale, for making other products, or for general business operations (15)

wholesaling Transactions in which products are bought for resale, for making other products, or for general business operations (15)

width of product mix The number of product lines a company offers (10)

wikis Software that create an interface that enables users to add or edit the content of some types of websites (also called wikipages) (7)

willingness to spend An inclination to buy because of expected satisfaction from a product, influenced by the ability to buy and numerous psychological and social forces (3)

word-of-mouth communication Personal informal exchanges of communication that customers share with one another about products, brands, and companies (16)

World Trade Organization (WTO) An entity that promotes free trade among member nations by eliminating trade barriers and educating individuals, companies, and governments about trade rules around the world (9)

zone pricing Pricing based on transportation costs within major geographic zones (19)

Chapter 1

1. "About Leatherman History," Leatherman, www.leatherman.com/about-leatherman/history/default.asp (accessed Jan. 2, 2008); "About Leatherman Founder," Leatherman, www.leatherman.com/about-leatherman/founders/default.asp (accessed Jan. 2, 2008); Fawn Fitter, "Outdoing the Swiss Army Knife," *Fortune Small Business,* July 25, 2007, http://money.cnn.com/magazines/fsb/fsb_archive/2007/07/01/100123045/index.htm; Shelly Strom, "Leatherman Learns Patent Lesson the Hard Way," *Portland Business Journal,* Apr. 12, 2002, www.bizjournals.com/portland/stories/2002/04/15/focus4.html.

2. Lisa M. Keefe, "Marketing Defined," *Marketing News,* Jan. 15, 2008, p. 28.

3. Michael Lev-Ram, "A Smartphone's BFF: Teens and Tweens," *Business 2.0,* Aug. 24, 2007, www.cnnmoney.com.

4. "Nike Unveils Shoe for Native Americans," CNNMoney, Sept. 26, 2007, www.cnn.com.

5. "Launch Week Also Marks Debut of Cross Promo Ads," *USA Today,* Sept. 23, 2007, www.usatoday.com/; G. Chambers Williams III, "2008 Nissan Rogue," *Ft. Worth Star-Telegram,* Aug. 31, 2007, www.star-telegram.com/chambers_williams/story/219830.html.

6. Bruce Horovitz, "Marketers Take a Close Look at Your Daily Routines," *USA Today,* Apr. 29, 2007, www.usatoday.com.

7. Chris Isidore, "Brand It Like Beckham," CNNMoney, July 6, 2007, www.cnnmoney.com.

8. Kelly K. Spors, "Beyond Flowers: New Funeral Options Proliferate," *The Wall Street Journal,* Oct. 19, 2005, p. D2, http://online.wsj.com/.

9. Bruce Horovitz, "Something Else to Check Out at Library: Starbucks," *USA Today,* Sept. 27, 2007, www.usatoday.com.

10. Mike Beirne, "Kibbles 'n Bits Freshens Poochie Smooches," *Brandweek,* Sept. 11, 2006, www.brandweek.com/.

11. Above the Influence, Office of National Drug Control Policy, http://abovetheinfluence.com/ (accessed Jan. 2, 2008).

12. David Kirkpatrick, "The $100 (well, almost) Laptop Is Here," *Fortune,* Oct. 5, 2007, www.cnnmoney.com.

13. Anita Hamilton, "Forget Morton's," *Time,* Sept. 14, 2007, p. 64.

14. Ta-Nehisi Coates, "Hip-Hop's Down Beat," *Time,* Aug. 27, 2007, pp. 6–9.

15. Joseph B. White, "Detroit Finally Learns Tough Lesson," *The Wall Street Journal,* Sept. 11, 2006, http://online.wsj.com.

16. "Dunkin' Donuts Slimming Down," *Brandweek,* Aug. 27, 2007, www.brandweek.com/; Rory J. Thompson, "Burger King Joins Healthy Food Initiative," *Brandweek,* Sept. 12, 2007, www.brandweek.com/.

17. Ajay K. Kohli and Bernard J. Jaworski, "Market Orientation: The Construct, Research Propositions, and Managerial Implications," *Journal of Marketing,* Apr. 1990, pp. 1–18; O. C. Ferrell, "Business Ethics and Customer Stakeholders," *Academy of Management Executive* 18 (May 2004): 126–129.

18. John Brodie, "The Many Faces of Ralph Lauren," *Fortune,* September 5, 2007, www.cnnmoney.com.

19. Eugene W. Anderson, Claes Fornell, and Sanal K. Mazvancheryl, "Customer Satisfaction and Shareholder Value," *Journal of Marketing* 68 (Oct. 2004): 172–185.

20. Xeuming Luo and Christian Homburg, "Neglected Outcomes of Customer Satisfaction," *Journal of Marketing* 70 (Apr. 2007).

21. Kohli and Jaworski, "Market Orientation."

22. Kwaku Atuahene-Gima, "Resolving the Capability-Rigidity Paradox in New Product Innovation," *Journal of Marketing* 69 (Oct. 2005): 61–83.

23. Gary F. Gebhardt, Gregory S. Carpenter, and John F. Sherry, Jr., "Creating a Marketing Orientation," *Journal of Marketing* 70 (Oct. 2006), www.marketingpower.com.

24. Sunil Gupta, Donald R. Lehmann, and Jennifer Ames Stuart, "Valuing Customers," *Journal of Marketing Research* 41 (Feb. 2004): 7–18.

25. Horovitz, "Marketers Take a Close Look at Your Daily Routines."

26. Gary McWilliams, "Wal-Mart Era Wanes Amid Big Shifts in Retail," *The Wall Street Journal,* Oct. 3, 2007, p. A1, http://online.wsj.com.

27. Alan Grant and Leonard Schlesinger, "Realize Your Customers' Full Profit Potential," *Harvard Business Review,* Sept./Oct. 1995, p. 59; Peter C. Verhoef, "Understanding the Effect of Customer Relationship Management Efforts on Customer Retention and Customer Share Development," *Journal of Marketing,* Oct. 2003, p. 30.

28. Jagdish N. Sheth and Rajendras Sisodia, "More Than Ever Before, Marketing Is Under Fire to Account for What It Spends," *Marketing Management,* Fall 1995, pp. 13–14.

29. Stephen L. Vargo and Robert F. Lusch, "Evolving to a New Dominant Logic for Marketing," *Journal of Marketing* 68 (Jan. 2004): 1–17.

30. Matthew Boyle, "Best Buy's Giant Gamble," *Fortune,* Mar. 29, 2006, http://money.cnn.com.

31. Lynette Ryals and Adrian Payne, "Customer Relationship Management in Financial Services: Towards Information-Enabled Relationship Marketing," *Journal of Strategic Marketing,* Mar. 2001, p. 3.

32. Mya Frazier, James Tenser, and Tricia Despres, "Retail Lesson: Small Programs Best," *Advertising Age,* Mar. 20, 2006, pp. S-2– S-3.

33. Roland T. Rust, Katherine N. Lemon, and Valaric A. Zeithaml, "Return on Marketing: Using Customer Equity to Focus Marketing Strategy," *Journal of Marketing* 68 (Jan. 2004): 109–127.

34. V. Kumar and Morris George, "Measuring and Maximizing Customer Equity: A Critical Analysis," *Journal of the Academy of Marketing Science* 35 (2007): 157–171.

35. Ryals and Payne, "Customer Relationship Management in Financial Services," pp. 3–27.

36. Rajneesh Suri, Chiranjeev Kohli, and Kent B. Monroe, "The Effects of Perceived Scarcity on Consumers' Processing of Price Information," *Journal of the Academy of Marketing Science* 35 (2007): 89–100.

37. Natalie Mizik and Robert Jacobson, "Trading Off Between Value Creation and Value Appropriation: The Financial Implications of Shifts in Strategic Emphasis," *Journal of Marketing,* Jan. 2003, pp. 63–76.

38. Kathryn Kranhold, "GE to Pare Manufacture of Traditional Light Bulbs," *The Wall Street Journal,* Oct. 4, 2007, http://online.wsj.com.

39. O. C. Ferrell and Michael Hartline, *Marketing Strategy* (Mason, OH: South-Western, 2008), p. 104.

40. "Kids' Food Pyramid Launched," CNN, Sept. 28, 2005, http://www.cnn.com/.

41. "U.S. Charitable Giving Reaches $295.02 Billion in 2006, Giving USA Foundation, press release, June 25, 2007, www.aafrc.org/press_releases/gusa/20070625.pdf.

42. Steve Lohr, "Is IBM's Lenovo Proposal a Threat to National Security?" *The New York Times,* Jan. 31, 2005, www.nytimes.com.

43. Kelly Geyskens, Mario Pandlelaere, Siegfried Dewitte, and Luk Warlop, "The Backdoor to Overconsumption: The Effect of Associating 'Low-Fat' Food with Health References," *Journal of Public Policy & Marketing* 26 (Spring 2007): 118–125.

44. Andrew LaVallee, "Now, Virtual Fashion," *The Wall Street Journal,* September 22, 2006, p. B1, http://online.wsj.com; Gavin O'Malley, "Virtual Worlds: The Latest Fashion," *Advertising Age,* July 10, 2006, pp. 3+.

45. "Southwest Airlines Fact Sheet," Southwest Airlines, www.iflyswa.com/about_swa/press/factsheet.html (accessed Jan. 2, 2008).

46. Matt Richtel and Bob Tedeschi, "Online Sales Lose Steam," *The New York Times,* June 17, 2007, www.nytimes.com.

47. "A Perfect Fit: Staples and Kids in Need," *Chain Store Age,* Oct. 2005, p. 78.

48. Pete Engardio, with Kerry Capell, John Carey, and Kenji Hall, "Beyond the Green Corporation," *BusinessWeek,* Jan. 9, 2007, pp. 50–64.

49. James Poniewozik, "Green Screens," *Time,* Aug. 27, 2007, p. 62.

50. Sources: *Method,* http://www.methodhome.com (accessed July 15, 2008); Mark Borden, Bill Breen, Jeff Chu, Josh Dean, Rebecca Fannin, Amy Feldman, Charles Fishman, Paul Hochman, David Kushner, Mark Lacter, Robert Levine, David Lidsky, Ellen McGirt, Danielle Sacks, Chuck Salter, Elizabeth Svoboda, and Linda Tischler, "The World's Most Innovative Companies," *Fast Company,* March 2008, http://www.fastcompany.com/magazine/123/the-worlds-most-innovative-companies.html?page=1%2C3 (accessed July 15, 2008); Sarah Van Schagen, "Fighting Dirty," *Grist,* March 14, 2008, http://www.grist.org/feature/2008/03/14/index.html?source=rss (accessed July 15, 2008); Rob Walker, "Consumed: Method," *The New York Times,* February 29, 2004, http://www.nytimes.com/2004/02/29/magazine/29CONSUMED.html?ex=1393390800&en=3eb2d28743ce2e85&ei=5007&partner=USERLAND (accessed July 15, 2008).

51. Groupe Danone, www.danone.com (accessed Jan. 2, 2008); "Group Danone," Hoover's Fact Sheet, www.hoovers.com/danone/—ID__41774—/free-co-factsheet.xhtml (accessed Jan. 2, 2008); Lorraine Heller, "Danone Canada Launches DHA Yoghurt for Brain Health," June 3, 2006, Dairy reporter.com, www.dairyreporter.com/news/printNewsBis.asp?id=66238; Sally McGrane, "Danone Cuts Out the Cookies," *Time,* Oct. 29, 2007, p. Global 1.

Feature box references

a. John Gaudiosi, "Why Wii Won," *Business 2.0,* May 2007, pp. 25–37; Simon Carless, "Breaking: Nintendo Announces New Revolution name—Wii," *Gamasutra,* Apr. 27, 2006, www.gamasutra.com/php-bin/news_index.php?story=9075; "What is Wii?" Nintendo, http://wii.nintendo.com/whatiswii_index.jsp (accessed Jan. 2, 2008).

b. "Ford, McDonald's, IBM, Abbott, Time Inc. to Share Sustainability Strategies," Environmental Leader, http://www.environmentalleader.com/2007/07/17/ford-mcdonalds-ibm-abbott-time-inc-to-share-sustainability-strategies/, July 17, 2007 (accessed Mar. 17, 2008).
"When Business Tackles Climate Change," Corporate Climate Response Conference, http://www.greenpowerconferences.com/corporateclimateresponse/index.html (accessed Mar. 17, 2008). "Subscription-Based Sustainability Reporting Database Launches," www.environmentalleader.com, March 1, 2007 (accessed Mar. 25, 2008); http://www.environmentalleader.com/2007/03/01/subscription-based-sustainability-reporting-database-launches/ (accessed Mar. 17, 2008).

c. Sidra Durst, "Greening the Concrete Jungle," *Business 2.0,* Apr. 2007, p. 40; "EPA: Heat Island Effect," Environmental Protection Agency, www.epa.gov/hiri/strategies/greenroofs.html (accessed Jan. 2, 2008); "Green Roof and Wall Benefits," G-Sky, www.g-sky.com/Benefits_Default.aspx (accessed Jan. 2, 2008); John Heilmann, "Growing Green Buildings," *Business 2.0,* Nov. 2006, pp. 46–48; Kent Hoover, "Governments Pushing Developers to Go Green—by Law," *New Mexico Business Weekly,* July 20–26, 2007, p. 8.

Chapter 2

1. Diane Anderson, "When Crocs Attack," *Business 2.0,* Nov. 2006, pp. 51–53; Crocs 2006 Annual Report; "Crocs, Inc. Enters Into Definitive Agreement to Acquire Bite Footwear," Crocs, press release, July 30, 2007, www.crocs.com/company/press/; "Crocs, Inc. Launches Unique Footwear Line for Fashion Conscious Women," Crocs, press release, June 5, 2007, www.youbycrocs.com/pressrelease.pdf; Jennifer Huget, "Not Such a Croc, Might a Fad Shoe's Health Claims Stand?" *The Washington Post,* Aug. 1, 2006, p. HE01, www.washingtonpost.com/wp-dyn/content/article/2006/07/31/AR2006073100890.html.

2. O. C. Ferrell and Michael Hartline, *Marketing Strategy* (Mason, OH: South-Western, 2008), p. 10.

3. Christian Homburg, Karley Krohmer, and John P. Workman, Jr., "A Strategy Implementation Perspective of Market Orientation," *Journal of Business Research* 57 (2004): 1331–1340.

4. Ferrell and Hartline, *Marketing Strategy.*

5. Abraham Lustgarten, "iPod," in "Breakaway Brands," *Fortune,* Oct. 31, 2005, pp. 154–156.

6. J. Chris White, P. Rajan Varadarajan, and Peter A. Dacin, "Market Situation Interpretation and Response: The Role of Cognitive Style, Organizational Culture, and Information Use," *Journal of Marketing,* July 2003, pp. 63–79.

7. Ferrell and Hartline, *Marketing Strategy,* p. 51.

8. Graham J. Hooley, Gordon E. Greenley, John W. Cadogan, and John Fahy, "The Performance Impact of Marketing Resources," *Journal of Business Research* 58 (2005): 18–27.

9. Jeff May, "Wal-Mart's Drug Discounts Grow," *The Star-Ledger,* Sept. 28, 2007, www.nj.com/business/ledger/index.ssf?/base/business-7/119095480745080.xml&coll=1.

10. Emily Bryson York, "Nestle, Pepsi and Coke Face Their Waterloo," *Advertising Age,* Oct. 8, 2007, www.adage.com.

11. Derek F. Abell, "Strategic Windows," *Journal of Marketing,* July 1978, p. 21.

12. "eBay Fast Facts," eBay, http://news.ebay.com/fastfacts_ebay_marketplace.cfm (accessed Jan. 2, 2008); David Comiskey, "Study Shows eBay's Small Business Appeal," E-Commerce Guide, Aug. 18, 2005, www.ecommerce-guide.com/news/research/article.php/3528416.

13. Catherine Holahan, "Will Less Be More for AOL?" *BusinessWeek Online,* July 31, 2006, www.businessweek.com.

14. Gina Chon, "Chrysler Challenge: Burnish Image," *The Wall Street Journal,* Aug. 24, 2007, p. B3.

15. Ibid.

16. Douglas Bowman and Hubert Gatignon, "Determinants of Competitor Response Time to a New Product Introduction," *Journal of Marketing Research,* Feb. 1995, pp. 42–53.

17. "Designed to Grow," 2007 Annual Report, Procter & Gamble, p. 5.

18. "Our Mission," *Celestial Seasonings,* www.celestialseasonings.com/whoweare/corporatehistory/mission.php (accessed Sept. 28, 2007).

19. Cláudia Simões, Sally Dibb, and Raymond P. Fisk, "Managing Corporate Identity," *Journal of the Academy of Marketing Science* 33 (Apr. 2005): 154–168.

20. "Johnson Controls Launches New Brand to Support Focus on Comfort, Safety and Sustainability," CNNMoney, Sept. 30, 2007, www.cnn.com.

21. Laurence G. Weinzimmer, Edward U. Bond III, Mark B. Houston, and Paul C. Nystrom, "Relating Marketing Expertise on the Top Management Team and Strategic Market Aggressiveness to Financial Performance and Shareholder Value," *Journal of Strategic Marketing*, June 2003, pp. 133–159.

22. Kevin J. O'Brien, "Nokia Buys Software Maker for $8.1 Billion," *The New York Times*, Oct. 1, 2007, www.nytimes.com.

23. Thomas Ritter and Hans Georg Gemünden, "The Impact of a Company's Business Strategy on Its Technological Competence, Network Competence and Innovation Success," *Journal of Business Research* 57 (2004): 548–556.

24. Stanley F. Slater, G. Tomas M. Hult, and Eric M. Olson, "On the Importance of Matching Strategic Behavior and Target Market Selection to Business Strategy in High-Tech Markets," *Journal of the Academy of Marketing Science* 35 (2007): 5–17.

25. Jean L. Johnson, Ruby Pui-Wan Lee, Amit Saini, and Bianca Grohmann, "Market-Focused Flexibility: Conceptual Advances and an Integrative Model," *Journal of the Academy of Marketing Science* 31 (2003): 74–89.

26. Daisuke Wakabayashi, "Microsoft Rolls out New Zunes to Take on iPod," *The Washington Post*, Oct. 2, 2007, www.washingtonpost.com/.

27. Robert D. Buzzell, "The PIMS Program of Strategy Research: A Retrospective Appraisal," *Journal of Business Research* 57 (2004): 478–483.

28. George S. Day, "Diagnosing the Product Portfolio," *Journal of Marketing*, Apr. 1977, pp. 30–31.

29. "Designed to Grow," pp. 4–5.

30. Isabelle Maignan, O. C. Ferrell, and Linda Ferrell, "A Stakeholder Model for Implementing Social Responsibility in Marketing," *European Journal of Marketing* 39 (Sept./Oct. 2005): 956–977.

31. Coca-Cola 2004 Annual Report, www2.coca-cola.com/investors/annualandotherreports/2004/pdf/Coca-Cola_10-K_Item_01.pdf (accessed Oct. 2, 2007).

32. M. Fry and Michael J. Polonsky, "Examining the Unintended Consequences of Marketing," *Journal of Business Research* 57 (2005): 1303–1306.

33. Maignan, Ferrell, and Ferrell, "A Stakeholder Model for Implementing Social Responsibility in Marketing."

34. G. Tomas, M. Hult, David W. Cravens, and Jagdish Sheth, "Competitive Advantage in the Global Marketplace: A Focus on Marketing Strategy," *Journal of Business Research*, Jan. 2001, pp. 1–3.

35. Kwaku Atuahene-Gima and Janet Y. Murray, "Antecedents and Outcomes of Marketing Strategy Comprehensiveness," *Journal of Marketing* 68 (Oct. 2004): 33–46.

36. Marc Graser, "Toyota Hits Touch Points as It Hawks Yaris to Youth," *Advertising Age*, May 1, 2006, p. 28.

37. Christian Homburg, John P. Workman, and Ove Jensen, "Fundamental Changes in Marketing Organization: The Movement Toward a Customer-Focused Organizational Structure," *Journal of the Academy of Marketing Science*, Fall 2000, pp. 459–478.

38. Jack Neff, "Tissues Fit for the Toilet," *Advertising Age*, Nov. 27, 2006, pp. 3+.

39. Rajdeep Grewal and Patriya Tansuhaj, "The Chain of Effects from Brand Trust and Brand Affect to Brand Performance: The Role of Brand Loyalty," *Journal of Marketing*, Apr. 2001, pp. 67–80.

40. Steve Watkins, "Marketing Basics: The Four P's Are as Relevant Today as Ever," *Investor's Business Daily*, Feb. 4, 2002, p. A1.

41. Bent Dreyer and Kjell Grønhaug, "Uncertainty, Flexibility, and Sustained Competitive Advantage," *Journal of Business Research* 57 (2004): 484–494.

42. Anuradha Kher, "Time-Share Your Pet," *Business 2.0*, Sept. 2007, p. 27.

43. Hemant C. Sashittat and Avan R. Jassawalla, "Marketing Implementation in Smaller Organizations: Definition, Framework, and Propositional Inventory," *Journal of the Academy of Marketing Science*, Winter 2001, pp. 50–69.

44. Ferrell and Hartline, *Marketing Strategy*, p. 257.

45. "You Won't Want Fries with That?" *BusinessWeek*, Feb. 19, 2007, p. 12.

46. Colin Beasty, "Market Focus: Sports and Entertainment—CRM Scores for Sports Franchises," *Destination CRM*, Oct. 1, 2007, www.destinationcrm.com/articles/default.asp?ArticleID=7229.

47. Robert W. Palmatier, Lisa K. Scheer, and Jan-Benedict E. M. Steenkamp, "Customer Loyalty to Whom? Managing the Benefits and Risks of Salesperson-Owned Loyalty," *Journal of Marketing Research* XLIV (May 2007), www.marketingpower.com.

48. V. Kumar, "Customer Relationship Management," custom module for William M. Pride and O. C. Ferrell, *Marketing*, 14th ed. (Boston: Houghton Mifflin, 2006), www.prideferrell.com.

49. Chezy Ofir and Itamar Simonson, "The Effect of Stating Expectations on Customer Satisfaction and Shopping Experience," *Journal of Marketing Research* XLIV (Feb. 2007), www.marketingpower.com.

50. V. Kumar, J. Andrew Peterson, and Robert P. Leone, "The Power of Customer Advocacy," in Jean L. Johnson and John Hulland (eds.), *2006: AMA Winter Educators' Conference*, published in *Marketing Theory and Applications* 17 (Winter 2006): 81–82.

51. Adapted from Nigel F. Piercy, *Market-Led Change* (Newton, MA: Butterworth, Heinemann, 1992), pp. 374–385.

52. Ian N. Lings, "Internal Market Orientation: Construct and Consequences," *Journal of Business Research* 57 (2004): 405–413.

53. Betsy Spethmann, "Internal Affairs," *Promo*, Mar. 1, 2006, http://promomagazine.com.

54. Michelle Kessler, "Fridays Go from Casual to E-Mail Free," *USA Today*, Oct. 5–7, 2007, p. 1A.

55. Kee-hung Lee and T. C. Edwin Cheng, "Effects of Quality Management and Marketing on Organizational Performance," *Journal of Business Research* 58 (2005): 446–456; Wuthichai Sittimalakorn and Susan Hart, "Market Orientation Versus Quality Orientation: Sources of Superior Business Performance," *Journal of Strategic Marketing* 12 (Dec. 2004): 243–253.

56. Philip B. Crosby, *Quality Is Free: The Art of Making Quality Certain* (New York: McGraw-Hill, 1979), pp. 9–10.

57. Piercy, *Market-Led Change*.

58. Douglas W. Vorhies and Neil A. Morgan, "Benchmarketing Marketing Capabilities for Sustainable Competitive Advantage," *Journal of Marketing* 69 (Jan. 2005): 80–94.

59. Kenneth W. Thomas and Betty A. Velthouse, "Cognitive Elements of Empowerment: An 'Interpretive' Model of Intrinsic Task Motivation," *Academy of Management Review*, Oct. 1990, pp. 666–681.

60. Ferrell and Hartline, *Marketing Strategy*.

61. Rohit Deshpande and Frederick E. Webster, Jr., "Organizational Culture and Marketing: Defining the Research Agenda," *Journal of Marketing*, Jan. 1989, pp. 3–15.

62. Eric M. Olson, Stanley F. Slater, and G. Tomas Hult, "The Performance Implications of Fit Among Business Strategy, Marketing Organization Structure, and Strategic Behavior," *Journal of Marketing* 69 (July 2005): 49–65.

63. Bernard J. Jaworski, "Toward a Theory of Marketing Control: Environmental Context, Control Types, and Consequences," *Journal of Marketing*, July 1988, pp. 23–39.

64. "Toyota Sets Sales Goal May Pass GM," *The Los Angeles Times*, Dec. 26, 2007, www.latimes.com/business/la-fi-toyota26dec26,1,7590657.story?coll=la-headlines-business.

65. "Drop-In Customers Report Greater Satisfaction with Dealer Service than Customers Who Make Appointments," J. D. Powers & Associates, press release, July 19, 2007, www.jdpower.com/corporate/news/releases/pressrelease.aspx?ID=2007112.

66. Cliff Edwards, "HDTV Makers Pile on the Extras," *Business-Week Online*, Oct. 4, 2007, www.businessweek.com.

67. Sources: "100 Best Corporate Citizens 2007," *Business Ethics*, www.business-ethics.com/node/75 (accessed Jan. 2, 2008); "200 Best Small Companies in America," *Forbes*, Oct. 11, 2007, www.forbes.com/2007/10/11/best-small-companies-biz-07200best-cz_jg_cs_1011bestsmall_land.html; Green Mountain Coffee, www.greenmountaincoffee.com (accessed Jan. 2, 2008); Green Mountain Coffee Annual Report 10-K; "Green Mountain Coffee Roasters," Hoover's Online, www.hoovers.com/green-mountain-coffee/—ID__45721—/free-co-factsheet.xhtml (accessed Jan. 2, 2008).

68. Sources: "Greg Brenneman, Chairman and Chief Executive Officer, Burger King Corporation," Burger King Corporation, www.bk.com/CompanyInfo/bk_corporation/executive_team/brenneman.aspx (accessed Jan. 31, 2006); Burger King, www.bk.com/ (accessed Jan. 2, 2008); Bruce Horovitz, "Burger King of Cool?" *USA Today*, Feb. 7, 2007, www.usatoday.com/money/industries/food/2007-02-06-burger-king-usat_x.htm; Bruce Horovitz, "CEO Turns the Flame Up," *USA Today*, May 23, 2005, p. 3B; Kate MacArthur, "Franchisees Turn on Crispin's King," *Advertising Age*, Oct. 24, 2005, pp. 1, 42; Elaine Walker, "Whopper of a Recovery?" *The Kansas City Star*, Sept. 24, 2005, pp. C-1, C-2.

69. Sources: Kate MacArthur, "Visa, FedEx Pony Up For Future Fund," *Advertising Age*, Nov. 14, 2005, pp. 1, 37; Ellen Florian Kratz, "For FedEx, It was Time to Deliver," *Fortune*, Oct. 3, 2005, p. 65; "Pass the Parcel," *Economist*, Feb. 11, 2006, p. 61; Robert W. Mooman, "The IT Traffic Solution," *Air Transport World*, Sept. 2005, p. 58; Patricia Sellers, "Bigger and BIGGER," *Fortune*, Sept. 5, 2005, pp. 104–107; "BW50: Delivering the Goods at FedEx," *BusinessWeek Online*, June 13, 2005, www.businessweek.com; "DHL/Airborne Deal Could Shake Up U.S. Express Market," *Logistics Management*, Apr. 1, 2003, www.manufacturing.net; FedEx Corporation, www.fedex.com (accessed Jan. 2, 2008); "FedEx to Buy Kinko's for $2.4B," CNNMoney, Dec. 30, 2003, http://money.cnn.com; "FedEx Ground Opens 'Super Hub,'" *Transportation & Distribution*, Nov. 2000, pp. 12–13; Kristin S. Krause, "Handling the Holiday Crush," *Traffic World*, Dec. 4, 2000, p. 33; Betsy McKay and Rick Brooks, "FedEx Will Buy Kinko's for $2.4 Billion in Cash," *The Wall Street Journal*, Dec. 30, 2003, http://online.wsj.com; Theo Mullen, "Delivery Wars Go High-Tech—FedEx Ground Sends Message with $80M Investment to Improve Package Tracking," *Internetweek*, Oct. 23, 2000, p. 18; Jayne O'Donnell, "FedEx–Postal Service Alliance Delivers Goods," *USA Today*, Jan. 11, 2001, www.usatoday.com/; "Post Office, FedEx to Work Together," *USA Today*, Jan. 10, 2001, www.usatoday.com/; Monica Roman, "FedEx Hitches Up a New Trucker," *BusinessWeek*, Nov. 27, 2000, p. 66; Marc L. Songini, "FedEx Expects CRM System to Deliver," *Computerworld*, Nov. 6, 2000, p. 10; "UPS Wants Fed Probe into DHL–Airborne Deal," *San Francisco Business Times*, Mar. 27, 2003, www.bizjournals.com.

Feature box references

a. Andrew Lavallee, "Friends Swap Twitters, and Frustration," *The Wall Street Journal*, Mar. 16, 2007, http://online.wsj.com/; Aita Hamilton, "Why Everyone's Talking about Twitter," *Time*, Mar. 27, 2007, www.time.com/; Clive Thompson, "Clive Thompson on How Twitter Creates a Social Sixth Sense," *Wired Magazine*, June 26, 2007, www.wired.com/techbiz/media/magazine/15-07/st_thompson; Twitter, www.twitter.com (accessed Jan. 2, 2008).

b. Ilana DeBare, "Ridding World of Plastic Forks," *San Francisco Chronicle*, Jan. 7, 2007, http://sfgate.com/cgi-bin/article.cgi?file5/chronicle/archive/2007/01/07/BUG8KNE27Q1.DTL&type5business; Excellent Packaging & Supply, www.excellentpackaging.com/pages/1/index.htm (accessed Jan. 2, 2008); "Excellent Packaging & Supply Introduces Spudware© Starch Utensils at ESPN X Games," *Food & Beverage News*, July 31, 2005, via www.prleap.com/pr/11753/; Melanie Haiken, "5 Spuds Steal the Plastics Market," *Business 2.0*, Mar. 2007, p. 28.

c. "McDonald's Green Initiatives Different for Individual Markets," Environmental Leader, http://www.environmental-leader.com/2007/12/23/mcdonalds-green-initiatives-different-for-individual-markets/, Dec. 23, 2007 (accessed Mar. 17, 2008); "McDonalds Gets A+ for Sustainability Reporting," http://www.mcdonalds.com/corp/values/robert_center_rating.html, Jan. 10, 2008 (accessed Mar. 17, 2008); Nichola Groom, "McDonald's Sees Restaurants as Green Laboratories," Reuters, Dec. 20, 2007, http://www.reuters.com/article/ousiv/idUSN2041601020071220?sp5true (accessed Mar. 24, 2008).

Chapter 3

1. Jonathan Dee, "All the News That's Fit to Print Out," *The New York Times*, July 1, 2007, www.nytimes.com/2007/07/01/magazine/01WIKIPEDIA-t.html?ex=1189828800&en=b2e607ab370a06f8&ei=5070; Tom McNichol, "Building a Wiki World," *Business 2.0*, Mar. 2007, pp. 102–108; Daniel Terdiman, "Growing Pains for Wikipedia," *News.com*, Dec. 7, 2005, www.news.com/2102-1025_3-5981119.html?tag=st.util.print.

2. Gina Chon, "Sales of SUVs Fall Sharply," *The Wall Street Journal*, Oct. 4, 2005, p. D1, http://online.wsj.com/.

3. "Carbonated Soft Drinks Suffer Setback in 2005, Beverage Marketing Corporation Reports," Beverage Marketing Corporation, press release, Apr. 2006, www.beveragemarketing.com/news2zz.htm.

4. O. C. Ferrell and Michael Hartline, *Marketing Strategy* (Mason, OH: South-Western, 2008), p. 58.

5. Eric Newman, "Jamba Juice Puts Squeeze on McD, BK for Breakfast," *Brandweek*, Oct. 15, 2007, www.brandweek.com/bw/news/recent_display.jsp?vnu_content_id=1003658335.

6. Ferrell and Hartline, *Marketing Strategy*.

7. Aron O'Cass and Liem Viet Ngo, "Balancing External Adaptation and Internal Effectiveness: Achieving Better Brand Performance," *Journal of Business Research* 60 (Jan. 2007): 11–20.

8. Rodolfo Vazquez, Maria Leticia Santos, and Luis Ignacio Álvarez, "Market Orientation, Innovation and Competitive Strategies in Industrial Firms," *Journal of Strategic Marketing*, Mar. 2001, pp. 69–90.

9. Eberhard Stickel, "Uncertainty Reduction in a Competitive Environment," *Journal of Business Research* 51 (2001): 169–177.

10. "Household Income Rises, Poverty Rate Declines, Number of Uninsured Up," U.S. Census Bureau, press release, Aug. 28, 2007, www.census.gov/Press-Release/www/releases/archives/income_wealth/010583.html.

11. Telis Demos, "Does Bling Beat the Market?" *Fortune*, Sept. 17, 2007, p. 77.

12. Lorrie Grant, "Scrimping to Splurge," *USA Today*, Jan. 28, 2005, p. 1B.

13. Julie Schmit, "USDA Revamps Recall Procedures," *USA Today*, Oct. 5, 2007, p. 1B.

14. Federal Election Commission, June 4, 2007 data, via The Center for Responsive Politics, www.opensecrets.org/orgs/list.asp? (accessed Jan. 8, 2008).

15. Nannette Byrnes, "Big Tobacco's Showdown in the West," *BusinessWeek,* Sept. 11, 2006, p. 38.

16. "British Airways PLC and Korean Air Lines Co. Ltd. Agree to Plead Guilty and Pay Criminal Fines Totaling $600 Million for Fixing Prices on Passenger and Cargo Flights," U.S. Department of Justice, press release, Aug. 1, 2007, www.usdoj.gov/atr/public/press_releases/2007/224928.htm.

17. "Bush Signs Mortgage Debt Forgiveness Act," Home Sales San Diego, Dec. 20, 2007, www.homesalessandiego.com/blog/bush-signs-mortgage-debt-forgiveness-act/.

18. "FTC Gets Money Back for Consumers Who Bought 'Pain-Relief' Adhesive Tape," Federal Trade Commission, press release, Sept. 18, 2007, www.ftc.gov/opa/2007/09/biotape.shtm.

19. "National Restaurant Company Settles FTC Charges for Deceptive Gift Card Sales," Federal Trade Commission, press release, Apr. 3, 2007, www.ftc.gov/opa/2007/04/darden.shtm.

20. Sarah Ellison, "Why Kraft Decided to Ban Some Food Ads to Children," *The Wall Street Journal*, Oct. 31, 2005, p. A1, http://online.wsj.com/.

21. Jeffrey Greenbaum, "Advertising Prescription Drugs?" *Shoot*, Oct. 7, 2005, p. 9.

22. Jonathan D. Epstein, "BBB Expels Two Contractors over Complaints; Two Collection Agencies Quit," *The Buffalo News*, Oct. 4, 2007, www.buffalonews.com/145/story/176621.html.

23. "P&G Takes Issue with McNeil Ad Claims for Tylenol Cold Product," National Advertising Division, press release, Aug. 1, 2007, www.nadreview.org.

24. "Panel Update," *NARB Quarterly 5* (Summer 2007), www.narbreview.org/quarterly/07summer.asp.

25. Chris Woodward, "Some Offices Opt for Cellphones Only," *USA Today*, Jan. 25, 2005, p. B1.

26. "New Subscribers to Telecom Services Continues Growing in 2005," Cellular-News.com, Oct. 5, 2005, www.cellularnews.com/story/12792.php.

27. Gwen Moran, "Top New Marketing Trends," MSNBC, Aug. 7, 2006, www.msnbc.msn.com/id/14231013/.

28. Bruce Horovitz, "More Takeout Orderers Are All Thumbs," *USA Today*, Jan. 3, 2008, www.usatoday.com/tech/webguide/internetlife/2008-01-03-text-ordering-food_N.htm.

29. Brent Schlender, "Dawn of the Web Potato," *Fortune*, Sept. 17, 2007, p. 52.

30. Debbie McAlister, Linda Ferrell, and O. C. Ferrell, *Business and Society* (Boston: Houghton Mifflin, 2005), p. 85.

31. Ibid.

32. Ibid.

33. Vladimir Zwass, "Electronic Commerce: Structures and Issues," *International Journal of Electronic Commerce*, Fall 2000, pp. 3–23.

34. U.S. Bureau of the Census, *Statistical Abstract of the United States, 2008* (Washington DC: Government Printing Office, 2007), p. 14.

35. Ibid., p. 53.

36. Ibid., p. 10.

37. Ibid., p. 45.

38. U.S. Bureau of the Census, "U.S. Interim Projections by Age, Sex, Race, and Hispanic Origin," Mar. 18, 2004, www.census.gov/ipc/www/usinterimproj/natprojtab01a.pdf.

39. Jeffrey M. Humphreys, "The Multicultural Economy 2007," *Georgia Business and Economic Conditions* 67 (Third Quarter, 2007), p. 7, www.selig.uga.edu/forecast/GBEC/GBEC0703Q.pdf.

40. Carlotta Mast, "Latino Liftoff," *ColoradoBiz*, Aug. 2007, www.cobizmag.com/articles.asp?id=1764.

41. William H. Redmond, "Intrusive Promotion as Market Failure: How Should Society Impact Marketing?" *Journal of Macromarketing* 25 (June 2005): 12–21.

42. Sources: CROPP Cooperative, www.farmers.coop; Organic Valley, www.organicvalley.coop.

43. Sources: "Company Information Overview," First Solar, www.firstsolar.com/company_overview.php (accessed Jan. 8, 2008); "High-Flying First Solar Takes Aim at Utility Market," Seeking Alpha, Dec. 26, 2007, http://seekingalpha.com/article/58374-high-flying-first-solar-takes-aim-at-utility-market; Michael Kanellos, "First Solar Stock: from $20 to $220 in a Year," Jan. 8, 2007, www.news.com/8301-11128_3-9813692-54.html.

Feature box references

a. "Barbie Blues for Toy-Maker Mattel," BBC, Oct. 17, 2005, http://news.bbc.co.uk/2/hi/business/4350846.stm; "Barbie Encyclopedia," Global Oneness Commitment, www.experiencefestival.com/a/Barbie/id/1926997 (accessed Jan. 3, 2008); "Bratz Topple Barbie from Top Spot," BBC, Sept. 9, 2004, http://news.bbc.co.uk/2/hi/business/3640958.stm; Christopher Palmeri, "Barbie Goes from Vinyl to Virtual," *BusinessWeek*, May 7, 2007, p. 68; "Ruth Handler: Marketing Toys," Who Made America, www.pbs.org/wgbh/theymadeamerica/whomade/handler_hi.html (accessed Jan. 3, 2008).

b. Chaniga Vorasarun, "Clean Machine: James Dyson Got Rich Taking Bags out of Vacuums. Now He Aims to Take Some Bugs out of Public Restrooms," *Forbes,* Mar. 24, 2008, pp. 98–99; "The Dyson Story: The Airblade Hand Dryer-Clean Home, Clean Hands," www.dyson.com/about/story/airblade.asp (accessed Mar. 17, 2008); Steve Hamm, "The Vacuum Man Takes On Wet Hands," *BusinessWeek,* July 2, 2007, www.businessweek.com/magazine/content/07_27/b4041063.htm?chan5search (accessed Mar. 24, 2008).

c. "10 Principals," Burning Man, www.burningman.com/whatisburningman/about_burningman/principles.html (accessed Jan. 3, 2008); "Frequently Asked Questions," Burning Man, www.burningman.com/whatisburningman/about_burningman/faq_what_is.html (accessed Jan. 3, 2008); "Green Man Pavillion," Burning Man, www.burningman.com/environment/pavilion_invitation.html (accessed Jan. 3, 2008); Chris Taylor, "Burning Man Grows Up," July 2007, *Business 2.0*, pp. 67–70; "What Is Burning Man?" Burning Man, www.burningman.com/whatisburningman/ (accessed Jan. 3, 2008).

Chapter 4

1. Sources: Anderson Cooper, "A Life Saver Called "Plumpy'nut," *60 Minutes,* CBS News, Oct. 21, 2007, www.cbsnews.com/stories/2007/10/19/60minutes/main3386661_page3.shtml; "Malnutrition, MSF Warns More Food Will Not Save Malnourished Children," Doctors Without Borders/Medicians Sans Frontieres, Oct. 10, 2007, www.doctorswithoutborders.org/news/malnutri-/; "Nutriset: Hope for Undernourished," Conscious Management Scandinavia, www.lots.mindo.com/EN/news.aspx?id=330 (accessed Jan. 9, 2008); "Plumpy'nut," Nutriset, www.nutriset.fr/index.php?option=com_content&task=view&id=30&Itemid=28 (accessed Jan. 9, 2008); "World Hunger Facts 2008," World Hunger Education Service, www.world-hunger.org/articles/Learn/world%20hunger%20facts%202002.htm (accessed Jan. 9, 2008).

2. Peter R. Darke and Robin J. B. Ritchie, "The Defensive Consumer: Advertising Deception, Defensive Processing, and Distrust," *Journal of Marketing Research* XLIV (Feb. 2007), www.marketingpower.com.

3. Isabelle Maignan and O. C. Ferrell, "Corporate Social Responsibility and Marketing: An Integrative Framework," *Journal of the Academy of Marketing Science* 32 (Jan. 2004): 3–19.

4. Indra Nooyi, "The Responsible Company," World in 2008 issue, *The Economist,* Mar. 31, 2008, p. 132.

5. Barry Meier, "Narcotic Maker Guilty of Deceit Over Marketing," *The New York Times,* May 11, 2007, www. nytimes.com.

6. "About Avon," Avon, www.avoncompany.com/about/ (accessed Jan. 9, 2008); "The Avon Breast Cancer Crusade," Avon, www.avoncompany.com/women/avoncrusade/index.html (accessed Jan. 9, 2008).

7. Isabelle Maignan and O. C. Ferrell, "Antecedents and Benefits of Corporate Citizenship: An Investigation of French Businesses," *Journal of Business Research* 51 (2001): 37–51.

8. Debbie McAlister, Linda Ferrell, and O. C. Ferrell, *Business and Society: A Strategic Approach to Social Responsibility* (Boston: Houghton Mifflin, 2005), pp. 38–40.

9. O. C. Ferrell, "Business Ethics and Customer Stakeholders," *Academy of Management Executive* 18 (May 2004): 126–129.

10. "2007 Corporate Citizenship Report," Pfizer, www.pfizer.com/files/corporate_citizenship/cr_report_2007.pdf (accessed Jan. 7, 2008).

11. Archie Carroll, "The Pyramid of Corporate Social Responsibility: Toward the Moral Management of Organizational Stakeholders," *Business Horizons,* July/Aug. 1991, p. 42.

12. William T. Neese, Linda Ferrell, and O. C. Ferrell, "An Analysis of Federal Mail and Wire Fraud Cases Related to Marketing," *Journal of Business Research* 58 (2005): 910–918.

13. "Procter & Gamble Sues Blue Cross Laboratories on Trademark Infringement Crusade," *Los Angeles Business,* Jan. 7, 2007, www.bizjournals.com/losangeles/stories/2008/01/07/daily8.html.

14. "U.S. Charitable Giving Reaches $295.02 Billion in 2006, Giving USA Foundation, press release, June 25, 2007, www.aafrc.org/press_releases/gusa/20070625.pdf.

15. Stacy Perman, "Scones and Social Responsibility," *Business-Week,* Aug. 21–28, 2006, p. 38.

16. "Iconic Campbell's Soup Can Changes Legendary Colors for Breast Cancer Awareness Month," The Campbell Soup Company, press release, Sept. 19, 2007, via http://home.businesswire.com/portal/site/google/index.jsp?ndmViewId=news_view&newsId=20070919005142&newsLang=en.

17. Marianne Wilson, "Doing Good Is More Than a Feel-Good Option," *Chain Store Age,* Oct. 2005, pp. 77+.

18. McAlister, Ferrell, and Ferrell, *Business and Society*, p. 335.

19. Ibid.

20. Mindy Fetterman, "Wal-Mart Grows 'Green' Strategies," *USA Today,* Sept. 25, 2006, www.usatoday.com.

21. Amanda Schupak, "An Inconvenient Paint," *Forbes,* Mar. 26, 2007, p. 70.

22. Peter Asmus, "17th Annual Business Ethics Awards," *Business Ethics,* Fall 2005, pp. 18–20.

23. "Welcome to Eco Options: Sustainbl Forestry," Home Depot, www6.homedepot.com/ecooptions/index.html? (accessed Jan. 7, 2008).

24. "Better Banana Project," Chiquita, www.chiquita.com/ chiquita/discover/owbetter.asp (accessed Jan. 7, 2008).

25. Paul Hawken and William McDonough, "Seven Steps to Doing Good Business," *Inc.*, Nov. 1993, pp. 79–90.

26. Jill Gabrielle Klein, N. Craig Smith, and Andrew John, "Why We Boycott: Consumer Motivations for Boycott Participation," *Journal of Marketing* 68 (July 2004): 92–109.

27. Christian Homburg and Andreas Fürst, "How Organizational Complaint Handling Drives Customer Loyalty: An Analysis of the Mechanistic and the Organic Approach," *Journal of Marketing* 69 (July 2005): 95–114.

28. Asmus, "17th Annual Business Ethics Awards," p. 20.

29. "Take Charge of Education," Target, http://target.com/target_ group/community_giving/take_charge_of_education.jhtml (accessed Jan. 7, 2008).

30. "Philanthropy," New Belgium Brewing Company, www.newbelgium.com/philanthropy.php (accessed Jan. 9, 2008).

31. McAlister, Ferrell, and Ferrell, *Business and Society*.

32. Thomas L. Carson, "Self-Interest and Business Ethics: Some Lessons of the Recent Corporate Scandals," *Journal of Business Ethics,* Apr. 2003, pp. 389–394.

33. "Multi-Year Study Finds 21% Increase in Americans Who Say Corporate Support of Social Issues Is Important in Building Trust," Cone, Inc., press release, Dec. 8, 2004, www.coneinc.com/Pages/pr_30.html.

34. Claudia Grisales, "Sony Settles with Texas Consumers," *The Austin American-Statesman,* Dec. 20, 2006, www.statesman.com; Mark Lisheron, "Texas Sues Sony Over Hidden Software That Can Hurt PCs," *The Austin American-Statesman,* Nov. 22, 2005, www.statesman.com; Ethan Smith, "Sony BMG Pulls Millions of CDs Amid Antipiracy-Software Flap," *The Wall Street Journal,* Nov. 17, 2005, p. D5, http://online.wsj.com/.

35. "Lawsuit Challenges Ruby on Tropican Name," *Business Courier of Cincinnati,* Oct. 17, 2007, www.bizjournals.com/cincinnati/stories/2007/10/15/daily40.html.

36. "Consumer Cries Foul over Kraft Dip," *The Austin American-Statesman,* Nov. 30, 2006, www.statesman.com.

37. Tim Barnett and Sean Valentine, "Issue Contingencies and Marketers' Recognition of Ethical Issues, Ethical Judgments and Behavioral Intentions," *Journal of Business Research* 57 (2004): 338–346.

38. Betsy Querna, "The Big Pill Pitch," *U.S. News & World Report,* June 6, 2005, pp. 52–53.

39. David E. Sprott, Kenneth C. Mannign, and Anthony D. Miyazaki, "Grocery Price Setting and Quantity Surcharges," *Journal of Marketing,* July 2003, pp. 34–46.

40. Stephen Taub, "SEC Probing Harley Statements," CFO.com, July 14, 2005, www.cfo.com/article.cfm/4173321/c_4173841?f=archives&origin=archive.

41. "Josephson Institute's Report Card on American Youth," Josephson Institute of Ethics, press release, Oct. 15, 2006, www.josephsoninstitute.org/pdf/ReportCard_press-release_2006-1015.pdf.

42. Peggy H. Cunningham and O. C. Ferrell, "The Influence of Role Stress on Unethical Behavior by Personnel Involved in the Marketing Research Process" (working paper, Queens University, Ontario, 2004), p. 35.

43. Joseph W. Weiss, *Business Ethics: A Managerial, Stakeholder Approach* (Belmont, CA: Wadsworth, 1994), p. 13.

44. O. C. Ferrell, Larry G. Gresham, and John Fraedrich, "A Synthesis of Ethical Decision Models for Marketing," *Journal of Macromarketing,* Fall 1989, pp. 58–59.

45. Ethics Resource Center, "The Ethics Resource Center's 2007 *National Business Ethics Survey: An Inside View of Private Sector Ethics*" (Washington, DC: Ethics Resource Center, 2007), pp. 1, 45.

46. Barry J. Babin, James S. Boles, and Donald P. Robin, "Representing the Perceived Ethical Work Climate Among Marketing Employees," *Journal of the Academy of Marketing Science* 28 (2000): 345–358.

47. Ferrell, Gresham, and Fraedrich, "A Synthesis of Ethical Decision Models for Marketing."

48. Lawrence B. Chonko and Shelby D. Hunt, "Ethics and Marketing Management: A Retrospective and Prospective Commentary," *Journal of Business Research* 50 (2000): 235–244.

49. Linda K. Trevino and Stuart Youngblood, "Bad Apples in Bad Barrels: A Causal Analysis of Ethical Decision Making Behavior," *Journal of Applied Psychology* 75 (1990): 378–385.

50. Ethics Resource Center, "The Ethics Resource Center's 2007 National Business Ethics Survey," p. 12.

51. Ethics Resource Center, "The Ethics Resource Center's 2007 National Business Ethics Survey," p. ix.

52. Gene R. Laczniak and Patrick E. Murphy, *Ethical Marketing Decisions: The Higher Road* (Boston: Allyn & Bacon, 1993), p. 14.

53. Marjorie Kelly, "Tyco's Ethical Makeover," *Business Ethics*, Summer 2005, pp. 14–19.

54. "Welcome to HCA Ethics and Compliance," HCA Healthcare, http://ec.hcahealthcare.com (accessed Jan. 7, 2008); O.C. Ferrell, John Fraedrich, and Linda Ferrell, *Business Ethics: Ethical Decision Making and Cases*, 6th ed. (Boston: Houghton Mifflin, 2005), pp. 407–424.

55. "Social Responsibility Statement," American Apparel & Footwear Association, www.apparelandfootwear.org/LegislativeTradeNews/SocialResponsibility.asp (accessed Jan. 7, 2008); "About WRAP," WorldwideResponsible Apparel Production, www.wrapapparel.org/modules.php?name=Content&pa=showpage&pid=3 (accessed Jan. 7, 2008).

56. James C. Hyatt, "Birth of the Ethics Industry," *Business Ethics*, Summer 2005, pp. 20–26.

57. Kelly, "Tyco's Ethical Makeover."

58. Jeff Leeds, "2 Are Fired at Clear Channel After a Misconduct Inquiry," *The New York Times*, Oct. 12, 2005, www.nytimes.com.

59. Sir Adrian Cadbury, "Ethical Managers Make Their Own Rules," *Harvard Business Review*, Sept./Oct. 1987, p. 33.

60. Caren Epstein, "Food Companies Marketing Products to People Living with Chronic Disease," *The [Fort Colllins] Coloradoan*, Nov. 13, 2005, p. E4.

61. Ferrell, Fraedrich, and Ferrell, *Business Ethics*, pp. 27–30.

62. Marjorie Kelly, "Holy Grail Found: Absolute, Definitive Proof that Responsible Companies Perform Better Financially," *Business Ethics,* Winter 2005, www.business-ethics.com/current_issue/winter_2005_holy_grail_article.html; Xueming Luo and C. B. Bhattacharya, "Corporate Social Responsibility, Customer Satisfaction, and Market Value," *Journal of Marketing* 70 (October 2006), www.marketingpower.com; Isabelle Maignan, O. C. Ferrell, and Linda Ferrell, "A Stakeholder Model for Implementing Social Responsibility in Marketing," *European Journal of Marketing* 39 (Sept./Oct. 2005): 956–977.

63. "Multi-Year Study Finds 21% Increase in Americans Who Say Corporate Support of Social Issues Is Important in Building Trust."

64. Maignan, Ferrell, and Ferrell, "A Stakeholder Model for Implementing Social Responsibility in Marketing."

65. Sources: Ben & Jerry's, www.benjerry.com (accessed July 11, 2008); Greyston Bakery, www.greystonbakery.com (accessed July 11, 2008).

66. Sources: "Animal Shelters to Receive Nearly $1.7 Million from PETCO Foundation," PETCO, press release, Apr. 11, 2007, www.petco.com/Content/PressRelease.aspx?PC=pr041107&Nav=146&=; Catherine Colbert, "PETCO Animal Supplies, Inc.," Hoovers, www.hoovers.com/petco/—ID__137426—/free-co-factsheet.xhtml (accessed January 4, 2008); Corporate Governance—Code of Ethics, PETCO, http://ir.petco.com/phoenix.zhtml?c=93935&p=irol-govConduct (accessed Jan. 4, 2008); "Fortune 500 2006," CNNMoney.com, http://money.cnn.com/magazines/fortune/fortune500/snapshots/2154.html (accessed Jan. 4, 2008); Michelle Higgins, "When the Dog's Hotel Is Better than Yours," *The Wall Street Journal*, June 30, 2004, p. D1; "Just Say No! Petco—the Place Where Pets Die," Kind Planet, www.kindplanet.org/petno.html; Ilene Lelchuk, "San Francisco Alleges Cruelty at 2 PETCOs," *San Francisco Chronicle*, June 19, 2002, www.anapsid.org/pettrade/petcocit2.html; "Lifestyle Trends Affect Pet Markets," *PET AGE*, Jan. 2006, www.petage.com/News010607.asp; Robert McMillan, "PETCO Settles Charge It Left Customer Data Exposed," NetworkWorld, Nov. 17, 2004, www.networkworld.com/news/2004/1117petcosettl.html; Chris Penttila, "Magic Markets," *Entrepreneur*, Sept. 2004, www.entrepreneur.com/article/0,4621,316866-2,00.html; "PETA and PETCO Announce Agreement," PETA, press release, Apr. 12, 2005, www.peta.org/feat/PETCOAgreement/default.asp; PETCO, www.petco.com (accessed Jan. 4, 2008); "PETCO Pays Fine to Settle Lawsuit," PETA Annual Review, 2004, www.peta.org/feat/annual_ review04/notToAbuse.asp; "PETCO Foundation to 'Round-up' Support for Spay/Neuter Programs," PETCO, press release, July 13, 2005, Forbes, www.forbes.com/prnewswire/feeds/prnewswire/2005/07/13/prnewswire200507131335PR_NEWS_B_WES_LA_LAW067.html; "PETCO Lawsuit—Mistreating Animals San Diego, CA," May 28, 2004, Pet-Abuse.com, www.pet-abuse.com/cases/2373/CA/US; "PETCO Looks to the Web to Enhance Multi-Channel Marketing," *Internet Retailer,* Jan. 16, 2006; "PETCO's Bad Business Is Bad for Animals," *PETA Animal Times*, Spring 2003, www.peta.org/living/at-spring2003/comp2.html; "PETCO Settles FTC Charges," Federal Trade Commission, November 17, 2004, www.ftc.gov/opa/2004/11/petco.htm; "PETCO Settles Suit Alleging Abuse, Overcharging," May 27, 2004, CBS News, www.anapsid.org/pettrade/petcocit2.html; "The Pet Market—Market Assessment 2005," Research and Markets, Apr. 2005, www.researchandmarkets.com/reports/c26485/; "Pet Portion Control," *Prevention*, Feb. 2006, p. 201; "Pet Store Scandal: PETA Uncovers Shocking Back-Room Secrets," *PETA Animal Times*, Summer 2000, www.peta.org/living/at-summer2000/petco.html; "Say No to PETCO," *PETA Animal Times*, Spring 2002, www.peta.org/living/at-spring2002/specialrep/; Julie Schmidt, "Pet Bird Buyers Asking Sellers about Avian Flu," *USA Today*, Nov. 28, 2005; Jessica Stannard-Freil, "Corporate Philanthropy: PR or legitimate News?" OnPhilanthropy, May 20, 2005, www.onphilanthropy.com/tren_comm/tc2005-05-20.html.

67. Reprinted Courtesy of Texas Instruments. Sources: www.ti.com (accessed Jan. 7, 2008), Texas Instruments Annual Report 10-K, Texas Instruments training materials available for employees in brochure format titled: "Designing for the Environment," "Working with Suppliers," "Workplace Safety," "TI, the Law and You. A Survival Guide for Changing Times." Texas Instruments Corporate Social Responsibility, www.ti.com/corp/docs/csr/index.shtml (accessed Feb. 8, 2006); Texas Instruments Ethics, www.ti.com/corp/docs/company/citizen/ethics/index.shtml (accessed Jan. 7, 2008); TI Code of Ethics, www.ti.com/corp/docs/investor/corpgov/valuesethicsconduct.pdf; "100 Best Corporate Citizens 2007," *Business Ethics,* Spring 2007, www.business-ethics.com/node/75; Thomas L. Friedman, "A Green Dream in Texas," *The New York Times*, Jan. 18, 2006; "TI Recognized as an Ethics Benchmark," www.ti.com/corp/docs/company/citizen/ethics/benchmark.shtml (accessed Jan. 4, 2008); "Texas Instruments: 100 Best Companies to Work For," *Fortune*, http://money.cnn.com/magazines/fortune/bestcompanies/2007/snapshots/87.html (accessed Jan. 4, 2008).

Feature box references

a. "Who Really Pays for CSR Initiatives," Environmental Leader, www.environmentalleader.com/2008/02/15/who-really-pays-for-csr-initiatives/, Feb. 15, 2008 (accessed Mar. 17, 2008);

"Global Fund," www.joinred.com, http://www.joinred.com/globalfund/ (accessed Mar. 25, 2008).

b. Reena Jana, "Green Threads for the Eco Chic," *Business-Week*, Sept. 27, 2006, www.businessweek.com/print/innovate/content/sep2006/id20060927_111136.htm; "Levi's Brand Launches 100% Organic Cotton Jeans," Levi Strauss & Co., press release, July 5, 2006, www.levistrauss.com/News/PressReleaseDetail.aspx?pid5784; Laura McClure, "Green Jeans," *Reader's Digest*, June 2007, p. 213; Laura Petrecca and Theresa Howard, "Eco-marketing a Hot Topic for Advertisers at Cannes," *USA Today*, June 22, 2007, www.usatoday.com/money/advertising/2007-06-22-cannes-green-usat_N.htm?csp534.

c. ABC, www.abc.com (accessed Oct. 29, 2007); "Extreme Makeover: Home Edition," All American Patriots, Oct. 17, 2007, www.allamericanpatriots.com/48735143_entertainment_extreme_makeover_home_edition_episode_oct_28; "Greening the Concrete Jungle," *Business 2.0*, Apr. 2007, p. 40.

Chapter 5

1. Sources iModerate, http://imoderate.com (accessed Jan. 9, 2008); Eric Peterson, "Tech Startup of the Month," *ColoradoBiz*, Aug. 2007, p. 20.

2. Anne L. Souchon, John W. Cadogan, David B. Procter, and Belinda Dewsnap, "Marketing Information Use and Organisational Performance: The Mediating Role of Responsiveness," *Journal of Strategic Marketing* 12 (Dec. 2004): 231–242.

3. "A Wake-up Call for Coffee," *BusinessWeek*, Oct. 22, 2007, p. 23.

4. Ellen Byron, "New Penney: Chain Goes for 'Missing Middle,'" *The Wall Street Journal*, Feb. 14, 2005, http://online.wsj.com/.

5. Catherine Arnold, "Self-Examination: Researchers Reveal State of MR in Survey," *Marketing News*, Feb. 1, 2005, pp. 55, 56.

6. Kenneth Chang, "Enlisting Science's Lessons to Entice More Shoppers to Spend More," *The New York Times*, Sept. 19, 2006, www.nytimes.com.

7. Jacquelyn S. Thomas, "A Methodology for Linking Customer Acquisition to Customer Retention," *Journal of Marketing Research*, May 2001, pp. 262–268.

8. Jamie Lareau, "Hummer's H3 Thrives in Slow SUV Market Despite Higher Gas Prices," *Auto Week*, Oct. 11, 2005, www.autoweek.com/news.cms?newsId=103335.

9. "Trading the Bleachers for the Couch," *BusinessWeek Online*, Aug. 22, 2005, www.businessweek.com.

10. A. Parasuraman, Dhruv Grewal, and R. Krishnan, *Marketing Research* (Boston: Houghton Mifflin, 2004), p. 63.

11. Ken Manning, O. C. Ferrell, and Linda Ferrell, "Consumer Expectations of Clearance vs. Sale Prices," University of Wyoming, working paper, 2008.

12. Parasuraman, Grewal, and Krishnan, *Marketing Research*, p. 64.

13. Brian T. Ratchford, Myung-Soo Lee, and Debabrata Talukdar, "The Impact of the Internet on Information Search for Automobiles," *Journal of Marketing Research*, May 2003, pp. 193–209.

14. Parasuraman, Grewal, and Krishnan, *Marketing Research*, p. 73.

15. Vikas Mittal and Wagner A. Kamakura, "Satisfaction, Repurchase Intent, and Repurchase Behavior: Investigating the Moderating Effects of Customer Characteristics," *Journal of Marketing Research*, Feb. 2001, pp. 131–142.

16. Haya El Nasser, "Census Bureau No Longer Waiting 10 Years for Data," *The [Fort Collins] Coloradoan*, Jan. 17, 2005, p. A2.

17. "Information Resources, Inc.," *Marketing News*, June 15, 2007, pp. H18–H19.

18. "External Secondary Market Research," CCH Business Owner's Toolkit, www.toolkit.com/small_business_guide/sbg.aspx?nid=P03_3011 (accessed Jan. 9, 2008).

19. Arnold, "Self-Examination."

20. Jack Neff, "Consumers Rebel Against Marketers' Endless Surveys," *Advertising Age*, Oct. 2, 2006, www.adage.com.

21. Ibid.

22. Randy Garner, "Post-It Note Persuasion: A Sticky Influence," *Journal of Consumer Psychology* 15 (2005): 230–237.

23. John Harwood and Shirley Leung, "Hang-Ups: Why Some Pollsters Got It So Wrong This Election Day," *The Wall Street Journal*, Nov. 8, 2003, pp. A1, A6.

24. Ibid.

25. Ibid.

26. Robert V. Kozinets, "The Field Behind the Screen: Using Netnography for Marketing Research in Online Communities," *Journal of Marketing Research* 39 (Feb. 2002): 61–72.

27. Glen L. Urban and John R. Hauser, "'Listening In' to Find and Explore New Combinations of Customer Needs," *Journal of Marketing* 68 (Apr. 2004): 72–87.

28. "Where the Stars Design the Cars," *Business 2.0*, July 2005, p. 32.

29. Daniel Gross, "Lies, Damn Lies, and Focus Groups," *Slate*, Oct. 10, 2003, http://slate.msn.com/id/2089677/.

30. Theodore T. Allen and Kristen M. Maybin, "Using Focus Group Data to Set New Product Prices," *Journal of Product and Brand Management*, Jan. 2004, pp. 15–24. Sean Geehan and Stacy Sheldon, "Connecting to Customers," *Marketing Management*, Nov./Dec. 2005, pp. 37–42.

31. Kenneth Hein, "KFC Cooks Up Moms Panel," *Brandweek*, Aug. 22, 2006, www.brandweek.com.

32. Barbara Allan, "The Benefits of Telephone Depth Sessions," *Quirk's Marketing Research Review*, Dec. 2000, www.quirks.com.

33. Jagdip Singh, Roy D. Howell, and Gary K. Rhoads, "Adaptive Designs for Likert-Type Data: An Approach for Implementing Marketing Surveys," *Journal of Marketing Research*, Aug. 1990, pp. 304–321.

34. Bas Donkers, Philip Hans Franses, and Peter C. Verhoef, "Selective Sampling for Binary Choice Models," *Journal of Marketing Research*, Nov. 2003, pp. 492–497.

35. Bruce Howard, "Marketers Take a Close Look at Your Daily Routines," *USA Today*, Apr. 29, 2007, www.usatoday.com.

36. Thomas T. Semon, "Determine Survey's Purpose for Best Results," *Marketing News*, Jan. 6, 2003, p. 7.

37. Eunkyu Lee, Michael Y. Hu, and Rex S. Toh, "Are Consumer Survey Results Distorted? Systematic Impact of Behavioral Frequency and Duration on Survey Response Errors," *Journal of Marketing Research*, Feb. 2000, pp. 125–133.

38. Judy Strauss and Donna J. Hill, "Consumer Complaints by E-mail: An Exploratory Investigation of Corporate Responses and Customer Reactions," *Journal of Interactive Marketing*, Winter 2001, pp. 63–73.

39. Kevin Kelleher, "66,207,986 Bottles of Beer on the Wall," *Business2.0*, Feb. 25, 2004, www.cnnmoney.com.

40. D. Aaker, V. Kumar, and G. Day, *Marketing Research*, 8th ed. (New York: Wiley & Sons, 2004).

41. Marlus Wübben and Florian von Wangenheim, "Predicting Customer Lifetime Duration and Future Purchase Levels: Simple Heuristics vs. Complex Models," in Jean L. Johnson and John Hulland, eds., *2006: AMA Winter Educators' Conference; Marketing Theory and Applications* 17 (Winter 2006): 83–84.

42. Thomas Mucha, "The Builder of Boomtown," *Business 2.0*, Sept. 2005, www.business2.com.

43. Noah Rubin Brier, John McManus, David Myron, and Christopher Reynolds, "'Zero-In' Heroes," *American Demographics*, Oct. 2004, pp. 36–45.

44. Laurence N. Goal, "High Technology Data Collection for Measurement and Testing," *Marketing Research*, Mar. 1992, pp. 29–38.

45. Philip Hans Franses, "How Nobel-Worthy Economics Relates to Databases," *Marketing News*, Mar. 12, 2001, p. 14.

46. Behrooz Noori and Mohammad Hossein Salimi, "A Decision-Support System for Business-to-Business Marketing," *Journal of Business & Industrial Marketing* 20 (2005): 226–236.

47. Amy Merrick, "New Population Data Will Help Marketers Pitch Their Products," *The Wall Street Journal*, Feb. 14, 2001, http://online.wsj.com/public/us.

48. Spencer E. Ante, "IBM," *BusinessWeek*, Nov. 24, 2003, p. 84.

49. Source: Reprinted with permission of The Marketing Research Association, P.O. Box 230, Rocky Hill, CT 06067–0230, 860–257–4008.

50. Carlos Denton, "Time Differentiates Latino Focus Groups," *Marketing News*, Mar. 15, 2004, p. 52.

51. "Top 25 Global Research Organizations: The Nielsen Co.," *Marketing News*, Aug. 15, 2007, p. H4.

52. Lambeth Hochwald, "Are You Smart Enough to Sell Globally?" *Sales & Marketing Management*, July 1998, pp. 52–56.

53. Ibid.

54. Sources: Steve Bassill, "How to Implement a Winning Segment Strategy," *Marketing Profs.com*, Feb. 21, 2006, www.marketingprofs.com/6/bassill1.asp; Lake Snell Perry Mermin & Associates, www.lakesnellperry.com (accessed Jan. 9, 2008); "Leading Democratic Polling Firm Celebrates 10th Anniversary with New Partner," Lake Snell Perry Mermin & Associates, press release, Mar. 11, 2005, www.lakesnellperry.com/new/Mermin0311.htm.

55. Sources: Best Buy, www.bestbuy.com (accessed Jan. 10, 2008); "Best Buy Case Study," Experian, www.Experian.com (accessed Jan. 10, 2008); Ariana Eunjung Chu, "In Retail Profiling for Profit; Best Buy Stores Cater to Specific Customer Types," *The Washington Post*, Aug. 17, 2005, p. A1; Stacey Collett, "Turning Data into Dollars," *Computer World*, Sept. 23, 2004, www.computerworld.com; *Fiscal 2005 Annual Report*, Best Buy; Gary McWilliams, "Minding the Store: Analyzing Customers, Best Buy Decides Not All Are Welcome," *The Wall Street Journal*, Nov. 8, 2004, http://online.wsj.com/; Ann Zimmerman, "Best Buy Courts Big Spenders," *The Wall Street Journal*, Nov. 7, 2007, p. B5. .

Feature box references

a. Sarah McBride, "Pirated Music Helps Radio Develop Playlists," *The Wall Street Journal*, July 12, 2007, pp. B1–B2; BigChampagne, www.bigchampagne.com/about.html (Jan. 9, 2008).

b. Allison Becker, "Recycling Efforts Falter in U.S." *The Atlanta Journal-Constitution*, Aug. 10, 2007, www.container-recycling.org/mediafold/newsarticles/plastic/2007/8-10-RecyclingEffortsFalter.htm; Pat Franklin, "Down the Drain: Plastic Water Bottles should no longer be a wasted resource," Container Recycling Institute, May/June 2006, www.container-recycling.org/mediafold/newsarticles/plastic/2006/5-WMW-DownDrain.htm; Betsy McKay, "Message in the Drink Bottle: Recycle," *The Wall Street Journal*, Aug. 30, 2007, pp. B1, B6; "Waste and Opportunity: U.S. Beverage Container Recycling Scorecard and Report," Container Recycling Institute, www.container-recycling.org/publications/reports/scorecard.htm (accessed Oct. 29, 2007).

c. "2007 World's Most Ethical Companies," *Ethisphere*, http://ethisphere.com/2007-worlds-most-ethical-companies/

(accessed Mar. 17, 2008); "Fortune's Most Admired Companies," www.haygroup.com/ww/Expertise/index.asp?id5906 (accessed Mar. 17, 2008); Cathy Planchard, "'World's Most Ethical Companies' Ranking Issued by *Ethisphere* Magazine," The Corporate Social Responsibility Newswire, May 8, 2007 (accessed Mar. 26, 2008), /www.csrwire.com/News/8413.html.

Chapter 6

1. Sources: Andrew Scott, "Natural Eats, Tasty Profits," *Fairfield County Business Journal*, July 25, 2005, pp. 1+; "Tasty Bite May Raise $12M to Fuel Growth," *The Economic Times*, July 8, 2006; Shivani Vora, "Curry in a Hurry," *Time*, Feb. 12, 2007, p. G10.

2. Marc Graser, "Toyota Hits Touch Points as It Hawks Yaris to Youth," *Advertising Age*, May 1, 2006, p. 28.

3. Marie Swift, "Niche Masters," *Financial Planning*, Sept. 2006, pp. 105–106.

4. Vanessa O'Connell, "Neiman Marcus's Cusp Tries for Younger Crowd," *The Wall Street Journal*, June 13, 2007, p. B1, http://online.wsj.com.

5. Suzanne Vranica, "In Haggar's Bold Ad Blitz, Middle-Aged Is the New Young," *The Wall Street Journal*, Nov. 6, 2006, p. B1, http://online.wsj.com.

6. Service Corporation International, www.hoovers.com/service-corporation-international/—ID_11341—/free-co-factsheet.xhtml (accessed Jan. 10, 2008).

7. Stephanie Kang, "Chasing Generation Y," *The Wall Street Journal*, Sept. 1, 2006, p. A11, http://online.wsj.com.

8. Brad Edomondson, "America, New & Improved," *Advertising Age*, Jan. 2, 2006, p. 34.

9. Constantine von Hoffman, "K-C Is Rolling Out Toilet Paper for Tykes," *Brandweek*, Mar. 13, 2006, p. 4, www.brandweek.com.

10. "Kids and Commercialism," Center for New American Dream, http://newdream.org/kids/facts.php (accessed Jan. 10, 2008).

11. U.S. Bureau of the Census, *Statistical Abstract of the United States*, 2008 (Washington, DC: Government Printing Office, 2007), p. 10.

12. Marvin Maties, "The New Product Game: Why Targeting Women Is Key," *Prepared Foods*, June 2003, p. 35.

13. "Dora the Explorer Leads Doll Revolution," CNN, Aug. 13, 2007, www.cnn.com.

14. Constantine von Hoffman, "For Some Marketers, Low Income Is Hot," *Brandweek*, Sept. 11, 2006, www.brandweek.com.

15. Jason Fields, "America's Families and Living Arrangements: 2003," *Current Population Reports*, U.S. Census Bureau (Washington, DC: Government Printing Office, 2003), pp. 20–553.

16. "About LifeStage Marketing," MicroMarketing, www.micromarketing.com/clients/index.html (accessed Jan. 10, 2008).

17. Ann Zimmerman, "To Boost Sales, Wal-Mart Drops One-Size Fits-All Approach," *The Wall Street Journal*, Sept. 7, 2006, p. A1, http://online.wsj.com.

18. Emily Bryson York, "Taco Bell, Starbucks Trot Out 'Light' Offerings for New Year," *Advertising Age*, Dec. 27, 2007, www.adage.com.

19. Joseph T. Plummer, "The Concept and Application of Life Style Segmentation," *Journal of Marketing*, Jan. 1974, p. 33.

20. SRI Consulting Business Intelligence, www.sric-bi.com/VALS (accessed Jan. 10, 2008).

21. "Energy Statistics," NationMaster, data from CIA June 14, 2007, www.nationmaster.com/graph/ene_ele_con_percap-energy-electricity-consumption-per-capita.

22. Stephanie Thompson, "Want that Perfect Body? Have Some More Dannon," *Advertising Age*, Sept. 25, 2006, p. 3+.

23. Philip Kotler, *Marketing Management: Analysis, Planning, Implementation, and Control*, 11th ed. (Englewood Cliffs, NJ: Prentice-Hall, 2003), p. 144.

24. Stephanie Thompson, "Pepsi Dons Disguise in Attempt to Seduce Whole Foods Devotees," *Advertising Age*, Nov. 9, 2006, www.adage.com.

25. Steve Miller, "Ford Rises to a (Driving) Challenge," *Brandweek*, Jan. 5, 2007, www.brandweek.com/bw/news/autos/article_display.jsp?vnu_content_id=1003528228.

26. "Want a Cause with That?" *Forbes*, Jan. 8, 2007, p. 83.

27. Charles W. Chase, Jr., "Selecting the Appropriate Forecasting Method," *Journal of Business Forecasting*, Fall 1997, pp. 2, 23, 28–29.

28. "ACNielsen Market Decisions: Controlled Market Testing," ACNielsen, http://us.acnielsen.com/products/rms_amd_controlledmktest.shtml (accessed Apr. 17, 2006).

29. Constantine von Hoffman, "P&G Plans to Shrink Line of Detergents," *Brandweek*, Oct. 16, 2006, p. 6, www.brandweek.com.

30. Sources: Jordan's Furniture, www.jordans.com (accessed Jan. 10, 2008); "Jordan's Makes Furniture Shopping a Fun Event," *Metro Report Boston*, July 2005, p. 30; Janet Groeber, "That's Entertainment," *Display & Design Ideas*, May 2005, p. 22; Bruce Mohl, "Jordan's Knows Cost of Victory Full Well," *Boston Globe*, Oct. 30, 2007, p. A13; "Three Customer-Centric Retailers," *Chain Store Age*, Oct. 2005, pp. 26–29.

31. Sources: Lisa Chamberlain, "A New Style of Hotel Where Work Meets Play," *The New York Times*, May 6, 2007, sec. 3, p. 28; Michelle Higgins, "Working at the Hotel? Corners Are Popular," *The New York Times*, Sept. 17, 2007, p. H7; Hyatt, www.hyatt.com (accessed Jan. 10, 2008); Susan Stellin, "Hotel as Lifestyle," *New York Times*, May 15, 2007, p. C10.

32. Sources: Jennifer Carofano, "The Turnaround Gunning for the No. 1 Spot in Athletic Footwear, Reebok Cranked Up the Heat in 2003," *Footwear News*, Dec. 8, 2003, p. 22; Polly Devaney, "Reebok Shoots from the Hip-Hop in Sneaker Wars," *Marketing Week*, July 31, 2003, p. 21; Rosemary Feitelberg, "Eve to Rap Up Reebok Classic," *Women's Wear Daily*, Mar. 20, 2003, p. 8; www.hoovers.com; Morag Cuddeford Jones, "Reebok Has Spring in Its Step," *Brand Strategy*, Oct. 2003, p. 9; David Lipke, "Reebok Targets Men with New NYC Store," *Daily News Record*, Oct. 27, 2003, p. 14; Wayne Niemi, "Chasing China: With Several Major Athletic Players Betting Big on China, the Sneaker Wars Are Heating Up," *Footwear News*, Dec. 15, 2003, p. 12; Elizabeth Olson, "Being Chased by the Big Boys," *The New York Times*, Nov. 27, 2003, p. C4; Joseph Pereira and Stephanie Kang, "Phat News: Rappers Choose Reebok Shoes," *The Wall Street Journal*, Nov. 14, 2003, p. B1; Reebok, www.rbk.com (accessed Jan. 24, 2006); Scott Van Voorhis, "Reebok Pitching Licensing Deal to MLB," *Boston Herald*, Jan. 15, 2004, p. 40.

Feature box references

a. Stuart Elliott, "Marketers Are Joining the Varsity," *The New York Times*, June 11, 2007, pp. C1, C4; Brian Steinberg, "Gimme an Ad! Brands Lure Cheerleaders," *The Wall Street Journal*, Apr. 19, 2007, p. B4.

b. Dan Alaimo, "'Green' Housewares Growing: Mintel," *Supermarket News*, Mar. 19, 2007, n.p.; Julie Gallagher, "Earth-Friendly Packaging May Have Grocers Seeing Green," *Supermarket News*, Jan. 15, 2007, n.p.; Phillip Hennessey, "Green Initiatives Are Hot," *Successful Meetings*, July 2007, p. 11; Jim Hanas, "A World Gone Green," *Advertising Age*, June 11, 2007, p. S-1.

c. "Tobacco Company Marketing to Kids," Campaign for Tobacco Free Kids, http://tobaccofreekids.org/research/factsheets/pdf/0008.pdf, Sept. 20, 2007 (accessed Mar. 27, 2008); "Surgeon General's Report—Reducing Tobacco Use," Centers for Disease Control and Prevention, http://cdc.gov/tobacco/data_statistics/sgr/sgr_2000/highlights/highlight_advertising.htm, Aug. 9, 2001 (accessed Mar. 28, 2008); "Tobacco Advertising," Globalink, http://globalink.org/factsheets/en/advertising.shtml, Mar. 23, 2008 (accessed Mar. 28, 2008).

Chapter 7

1. Facebook, www.facebook.com (Jan. 15, 2008); Steven Levy, "Facebook Grows Up," *Newsweek*, Aug. 20, 2007, pp. 41–46; Ellen McGirt, "Hacker. Dropout. CEO," *Fast Company*, May 2007, pp. 74–80; Brad Stone, "In Facebook, Investing in a Theory," *New York Times*, Oct. 4, 2007, pp. C1, C2.

2. Wayne D. Hoyer and Deborah J. MacInnis, *Consumer Behavior*, 3rd ed. (Boston: Houghton Mifflin, 2004), pp. 57–59.

3. Andrew D. Gershoff and Gita Venkataramani Johar, "Do You Know Me? Consumer Calibration of Friends' Knowledge," *Journal of Consumer Research* 32 (Mar. 2006): 496+.

4. Barbara Kiviat, "Why We Buy," *Time*, Aug. 27, 2007, pp. 50–51.

5. Russell W. Belk, "Situational Variables and Consumer Behavior," *Journal of Consumer Research*, Dec. 1975, pp. 157–164.

6. Nathan Novemsky, Ravi Dhar, Norbert Schwarz, and Itamar Simonson, "Preference Fluency in Choice," *Journal of Marketing Research* 44 (Aug. 2007): 347–356.

7. Victoria Murphy Barret, "The Digital Diamond District," *Forbes*, Oct. 25, 2007, www.forbes.com/.

8. Chien-Huang Lin, HsiuJu Rebecca Yen, and Shin-Chieh Chuang, "The Effects of Emotion and Need for Cognition on Consumer Choice Involving Risk," *Marketing Letters* 17 (Jan. 2006): 47–60.

9. Jeremy Caplan, "Scents and Sensibility," *Time*, Oct. 16, 2006, pp. 66–67.

10. Jaideep and Sengupta Rongrong Zhou, "Understanding Impulsive Eaters' Choice Behaviors: The Motivational Influence of Regulatory Focus," *Journal of Marketing Research* 44 (May 2007): 297–308.

11. "Scented Hotel Rooms? Hampton Says Nonsense!" Hampton Hotels, press release, Oct. 2007, http://hospitality-1st.com/PressNews/Hampton-102307.html.

12. Laura Q. Hughes and Alice Z. Cuneo, "Lowe's Retools Image in Push Toward Women," *Advertising Age*, Feb. 26, 2001, www.adage.com; Amy Tsao, "Retooling Home Improvement," *BusinessWeek Online*, Feb. 14, 2005, www.businessweek.com/bwdaily/dnflash/feb2005/nf20050214_3207_db_082.htm.

13. SRI Consulting Business Intelligence, www.sric-bi.com/VALS (accessed Jan. 15, 2008).

14. Maria Mooshil, "More Retailers Take Steps to Capture Women's Consumer Allegiance," *Chicago Tribune*, June 15, 2005, http://web.lexis-nexis.com/.

15. David B. Wooten, "From Labeling Possessions to Possessing Labels: Ridicule and Socialization Among Adolescents," *Journal of Consumer Research* 33 (Sept. 2006): 188+.

16. Christopher Hart and Pete Blackshaw, "Internet Inferno," *Marketing Management*, Jan./Feb. 2006, p. 21.

17. Donnel A. Briley and Jennifer L. Aaker, "When Does Culture Matter? Effects of Personal Knowledge on the Correction of Culture-Based Judgments," *Journal of Marketing Research* 33 (Aug. 2006), via marketingpower.com.

18. U.S. Bureau of the Census, "2006 American Community Survey Data Profile Highlights," http://factfinder.census.gov/servlet/ACSSAFFFacts?_sse=on (accessed Jan. 15, 2008).

19. Jeffrey M. Humphreys, "The Multicultural Economy 2007," *Georgia Business and Economic Conditions* 67 (Third Quarter 2007), www.selig.uga.edu/forecast/GBEC/GBEC073Q.pdf.

20. Lisa Sanders, "How to Target Blacks? First, You Gotta Spend," *Advertising Age,* July 3, 2006, p. 19.
21. Sanders, "How to Target Blacks?"; Ann Zimmerman, "To Boost Sales, Wal-Mart Drops One-Size Fits-All Approach," *The Wall Street Journal,* Sept. 7, 2006, p. A1, http://online.wsj.com.
22. "Target Dreams in Color for King Day and Beyond," Target, press release, Jan. 11, 2007, http://news.target.com/phoenix.zhtml?c=196187&p=irol-newsArticle&ID=949530.
23. U.S. Bureau of the Census, "2006 American Community Survey Data Profile Highlights."
24. Humphreys, "The Multicultural Economy 2007."
25. Mindy Fetterman, "Stores Embrace Hispanic Tradition of 3 Kings Day," *USA Today,* Jan. 1, 2008, www.usatoday.com/money/industries/retail/2008-01-01-three-kings-day_N.htm.
26. Della de laFuente, "American Takes Latinos Home for the Holidays," *Brandweek,* Nov. 19, 2007, www.brandweek.com/bw/news/leisuretrav/article_display.jsp?vnu_content_id=1003674048.
27. U.S. Bureau of the Census, "2006 American Community Survey Data Profile Highlights"; Christina Hoag, "Asian-Americans Are Fastest Growing Group," *Miami Herald,* Apr. 7, 2003.
28. "The 'Invisible' Market," *Brandweek,* Feb. 1, 2006, www.brandweek.com.
29. Wendy Pedrero, "Changing Travel One Step at a Time: Michelle Peluso: CEO, Travelocity," *Latino Leaders,* Feb-Mar. 2008, pp. 14+; Marty Gast, "Travelocity.com: A Glimpse Through History," *Travel News,* Dec. 23, 2003, www.breakingtravelnews.com/article.php?story5200312222211110443&mode5print; Josh Roberts, "Travelocity, Expedia Aim to Prove Their Differences," *USA Today,* May 11, 2005, www.usatoday.com/travel/deals/inside/2005-05-11-column_x.htm; Travelocity, www.travelocity.com.
30. Sources: AutoTrader.com, www.autotrader.com (accessed Nov. 1, 2007); Ralph Kisiel, "AutoTrader Tops in Dealer Survey, *Automotive News,* Sept. 17, 2007, p. 24; "AutoTrader.com Continues Summer Marketing Blitz with Television Buy," *PR Newswire,* June 30, 2003, www.prnewswire.com; "AutoTrader.com Gears Up for One-of-a-Kind Interactive Online Gaming Experience," AutoTrader, news release, Aug. 2, 2001, www.autotrader.com; "AutoTrader.com Ranks Highest in Overall Satisfaction Among Both New and Used Vehicle Services in J. D. Power and Associates Study," AutoTrader.com, press release, Sept. 12, 2007, www.autotrader.com/about/pressroom/media/press-release_detail.jsp?contentid=25848; "How to Translate a TV Ad into an Online Promotion," MarketingSherpa.com, Nov. 1, 2001, www.emarketingtoher.com; Steve Jarvis, "Pedal to the Cyber-Metal," *Marketing News,* Jan. 21, 2002, pp. 6–7; GregoryJordan, "Online, Used Car Lots That Cover the Nation," *The New York Times,* Oct. 22, 2003, p. G13 ; Chaz Osburn, "AutoTrader Adds Online Auction Listings," *Automotive News,* Jan. 13, 2003, p. 28.

Feature box references

a. "Arm Teens with Good Credit Skills," *The Wall Street Journal,* http://online.wsj.com/article/SB120139461017220029.html, Jan. 27, 2008 (accessed Mar. 31, 2008); "Credit Cards: Increased Complexity in Rates and Fees Heightens Need for More Effective Disclosures to Consumers," Government Accountability Office, http://gao.gov/new.items/d06929.pdf, Jan. 9, 2006 (accessed Mar. 31, 2008).
b. Micheline Maynard, "Toyota Hybrid Makes a Statement, and That Sells," *The New York Times,* July 4, 2007, pp. A1, A11; John K. Teahen, Jr., "Hybrids Aren't Taking Auto World by Storm," *Automotive News,* Sept. 17, 2007, p. 20.
c. Phil Gallo, "'School' Stays Cool as Showdown Looms," *Daily Variety,* Sept. 13, 2007, p. 3; Andrew Hampp, "'HSM2' Has Wal-Mart Dancing," *Advertising Age,* Aug. 27, 2007, p. 4; Merissa Marr, "Can 'High School' Last Forever?" *The Wall Street Journal,* Aug. 17, 2007, p. B1; Dorothy Pomerantz, "Bop to the Top," *Forbes,* Aug. 13, 2007, p. 44.

Chapter 8

1. Sources: Maha Atal, "Sustaining the Dream," *BusinessWeek,* Oct. 15, 2007, p. 60; Kristen Gerencher, "Treadmill Desks Let Employees Feel the Burn," *Boston Globe,* Mar. 26, 2006, n.p.; Reena Jana, "Exercise More than Just Your Options," *BusinessWeek,* Oct. 29, 2007, p. 24; "Making the Tough Call," *Inc.,* Nov. 2007, pp. 36+; Katherine Yung, "Steelcase's Think Chair One Example of Commitment to the Environment," *Detroit Free Press,* Aug. 5, 2007, n.p.
2. "STP: Segmentation, Targeting, Positioning," American Marketing Association, www.marketingpower.com/content1488C381S3.php (accessed Jan. 15, 2008).
3. Ibid.
4. Matt Kelly, "Consortium Finds a Happy Ending," *eWeek,* Sept. 19, 2005, pp. C1, C4.
5. Michael D. Hutt and Thomas W. Speh, *Business Marketing Management* (Mason, OH: Thomson/South-Western, 2004), p. 93.
6. U.S. Bureau of the Census, *Statistical Abstract of the United States, 2008* (Washington DC: Government Printing Office, 2007), p. 649.
7. Ibid., pp. 649, 651.
8. Ibid., p. 307.
9. Ibid., p. 263.
10. "Identix Wins the U.S. Department of State Facial Recognition Solicitation," *Business Wire,* Sept. 29, 2004.
11. Das Narayandas and V. Kasturi Rangan, "Building and Sustaining Buyer-Seller Relationships in Mature Industrial Markets," *Journal of Marketing,* July 2004, p. 63.
12. Alex R. Zablah, Wesley J. Johnston, and Danny N. Bellenger, "Transforming Partner Relationships through Technological Innovation," *Journal of Business & Industrial Marketing* 20 (Aug. 2005): 355–363.
13. Lisa Harrington, "Right Moves," *Inbound Logistics,* Nov. 2005, pp. 37–40.
14. Leonidas C. Leonidou, "Industrial Buyers' Influence Strategies: Buying Situation Differences," *Journal of Business & Industrial Marketing* 20 (Jan. 2005): 33–42.
15. Joseph O'Reilly, "A Ready-Mix Transport Solution," *Inbound Logistics,* Nov. 2005, pp. 70–71.
16. Jeffrey Burt, "Gateway Eyes Small Businesses," *eWeek,* Sept. 5, 2005, www.eweek.com.
17. Frederick E. Webster, Jr., and Yoram Wind, "A General Model for Understanding Organizational Buyer Behavior," *Marketing Management,* Winter/Spring 1996, pp. 52–57.
18. Laura Heller, *DSN Retailing Today,* Jan. 10, 2005, pp. 13–14.
19. George S. Day and Katrina J. Bens, "Capitalizing on the Internet Opportunity," *Journal of Business & Industrial Marketing* 20 (2005): 160–168.
20. Steve Hamm, "GM's Way or the Highway," *BusinessWeek,* Dec. 19, 2005, pp. 48–49.
21. Niklas Myhr and Robert E. Spekman, "Collaborative Supply-Chain Partnerships Built upon Trust and Electronically Mediated Mediated Exchange," *Journal of Business & Industrial Marketing* 20 (2005): 179–186.
22. "Development of NAICS," U.S. Census Bureau, www.census.gov/epcd/www/naicsdev.htm (accessed Jan. 15, 2008).
23. Sources: Lisa McLaughlin, "Tea's Got a Brand New Bag," *Time,* Mar. 27, 2008, www.time.com; "Numi Organic Tea,"

Beverage Industry, Nov. 2007, p. 10; "Numi Organic Tea," *Beverage Industry,* June 2007, p. 13; Crystal Detamore-Rodman, "A Perfect Match?" *Entrepreneur,* Oct. 2003, pp. 60+; www.numitea.com.

24. Sources: Don Muret, "Target's Chase Field Rebranding Hits Mark," *Sports Business Journal,* Oct. 8, 2007, p. 4; "Targeted Branding," *Contract,* Aug. 24, 2007, n.p.; www.targetcommercialinteriors.com; Ann Zimmerman, "Designs on a New Market Niche," *The Wall Street Journal,* Oct. 4, 2007, p. B1.

Feature box references

a. "Lead Paint Prompts Mattel to Recall 967,000 Toys," *The New York Times,* http://nytimes.com/2007/08/02/business/02toy.html?ex51343707200&en51f7a6cb6a8627d6e&ei55088&partner5rssnyt&emc5rss, Aug. 2, 2007 (accessed Apr. 9, 2008); "Made in China: Perspectives on the Global Manufacturing Giant," *Inbound Logistics,* http://inboundlogistics.com/articles/features/0308_feature02.shtml, Mar. 1, 2008 (accessed Apr. 9, 2008).

b. Tom Chesshyre, "Paper Chase: Travel News," *The [London] Times,* Mar. 31, 2007, p. 22; Ann Keeton, "American Air Sets Plan to Show Its Green Side," *The Wall Street Journal,* July 18, 2007; Daniel Michaels and Susan Carey, "Airlines Feel Pressure as Pollution Fight Takes Off," *The Wall Street Journal,* Dec. 12, 2006, p. A6.

c. Maggie Rauch, "Virtual Reality: How IBM Uses Web 2.0 to Grow Its Brand, from Wikis to Viral Video to Second Life," *Sales and Marketing Management,* Jan.–Feb. 2007, pp. 18+; Charlotte Woolard, "Virtual Events Keep Down Costs," *B to B,* Apr. 23, 2007, p. 31.

Chapter 9

1. Sources: BraBaby, www.brababy.com/about.html?article=2994 (accessed Jan. 21, 2008); Jonathan Cheng, "A Small Firm Takes on Chinese Pirates," *The Wall Street Journal,* July 5, 2007, p. B3.

2. "The Arab World Wants Its MTV," *BusinessWeek,* Oct. 22, 2007, pp. 79–81; Johnnie L. Roberts, "World Tour," *Newsweek,* June 6, 2005, pp. 34–35.

3. "Company Profile," Starbucks, Aug. 2007, www.starbucks.com/aboutus/Company_Profile.pdf; "Latest Counts of Wal-Mart," Wal-Mart.com, www.wal-martchina.com/english/news/stat.htm (accessed Jan. 21, 2008).

4. David Kiley, "Jack's Global Splash," *BusinessWeek,* Oct. 22, 2007, p. 24.

5. "About CIBERs," CIBERweb, http://ciberweb.msu.edu/about.asp (accessed Jan. 21, 2008).

6. Gary A. Knight and S. Tamer Cavusgil, "Innovation, Organizational Capabilities, and the Born-Global Firm," *Journal of International Business Studies,* Mar. 2004, pp. 124–141.

7. Janet Adamy, "As Burgers Boom in Russia, McDonald's Touts Discipline," *The Wall Street Journal,* Oct. 16, 2007, pp. A1, A17.

8. Gordon Fairclough and Janet Adamy, "Sex, Skin, Fireworks, Licked Fingers—It's a Quarter Pounder Ad in China," *The Wall Street Journal,* Sept. 21, 2006, p. B1, http://online.wsj.com; "What Made McDonald's Click in India?" Hindustan Times.com, Sept. 7, 2006, via http://content.msn.co.in/Lifestyle/Work/LifeStyleHT_070906_1906.htm.

9. Anton Piësch, "Speaking in Tongues," *Inc.,* June 2003, p. 50.

10. "Product Pitfalls Proliferate in Global Cultural Maze," *The Wall Street Journal,* May 14, 2001, p. B11.

11. Jeffrey G. Blodgett, Long-Chuan Lu, Gregory M. Rose, and Scott J. Vitell, "Ethical Sensitivity to Stakeholder Interests: A Cross-Cultural Comparison," *Journal of the Academy of Marketing Science* 29, no. 2 (2001): 190–202.

12. Thomas G. Brashear, Elzbieta Lepkowska-White, and Cristian Chelariu, "An Empirical Test of Antecedents and Consequences of Salesperson Job Satisfaction Among Polish Retail Salespeople," *Journal of Business Research,* Dec. 2003, pp. 971–978.

13. Sadrudin A. Ahmed and Alain D'Astous, "Moderating Effects of Nationality on Country-of-Origin Perceptions: English-Speaking Thailand Versus French-Speaking Canada," *Journal of Business Research* 60 (Mar. 2007), pp. 240–248; George Balabanis and Adamantios Diamantopoulos, "Domestic Country Bias, Country-of-Origin Effects, and Consumer Ethnocentrism: A Multidimensional Unfolding Approach," *Journal of the Academy of Marketing Science,* Jan. 2004, pp. 80–95; Harri T. Luomala, "Exploring the Role of Food Origin as a Source of Meanings for Consumers and as a Determinant of Consumers' Actual Food Choices," *Journal of Business Research* 60 (Feb. 2007), pp. 122–129; Durdana Ozretic-Dosen, Vatroslav Skare, and Zoran Krupka, "Assessments of Country of Origin and Brand Cues in Evaluating a Croatian, Western and Eastern European Food Product," *Journal of Business Research* 60 (Feb. 2007), pp. 130–136.

14. Ming-Huel Hsieh, Shan-Ling Pan, and Rudy Setiono, "Product-, Corporate-, and Country-Image Dimensions and Purchase Behavior: A Multicountry Analysis," *Journal of the Academy of Marketing Science,* July 2004, pp. 251–270.

15. Janet Adamy, "Eyeing a Billion Tea Drinkers, Starbucks Pours It On in China," *The Wall Street Journal,* Nov. 29, 2006, p. A1, http://online.wsj.com.

16. CIA, *The World Fact Book,* https://www.cia.gov/library/publications/the-world-factbook/index.html (accessed Jan. 28, 2008).

17. CIA, *The World Fact Book;* U.S. Bureau of the Census, *Statistical Abstract of the United States, 2008* (Washington, DC: Government Printing Office, 2007), pp. 825–827, 837.

18. Deborah Ball, "Cadbury's New Bubble-Gum Battle," *The Wall Street Journal,* Oct. 4, 2007, p. A8, http://online.wsj.com.

19. American Marketing Association, Code of Ethics, www.marketingpower.com/content435.php (accessed Jan. 21, 2008).

20. "Will the New Congress Shift Gears on Free Trade?" *The Wall Street Journal,* Nov. 18–19, 2006, p. A7.

21. Ibid.

22. "U.S. Trade in Goods and Services," U.S. Bureau of the Census, Foreign Trade Statistics, June 8, 2007, www.census.gov/foreign-trade/statistics/historical/gands.pdf.

23. Charles R. Taylor, George R. Franke, and Michael L. Maynard, "Attitudes Toward Direct Marketing and Its Regulation: A Comparison of the United States and Japan," *Journal of Public Policy & Marketing,* Fall 2000, pp. 228–237.

24. Frederik Balfour, "Fakes!" *BusinessWeek,* Feb. 7, 2005, pp. 54–64.

25. "Major U.S. Film Companies File Lawsuit in China," *Forbes,* Sept. 13, 2006, www.forbes.com/home/feeds/afx/2006/09/13/afx3012637.html.

26. This section adapted from O.C. Ferrell, John Fraedrich, and Linda Ferrell, *Business Ethics: Ethical Decision Making and Cases,* 7th ed. (Boston: Houghton Mifflin, 2008), pp. 260–290.

27. Dave Izraeli and Mark S. Schwartz, "What We Can Learn from the Federal Sentencing Guidelines for Organizational Ethics," *Journal of Business Ethics,* July 1998, pp. 9–10.

28. Business for Social Responsibility, www.bsr.org (accessed Jan. 21, 2008).

29. Charles Forelle, "Microsoft Defeat in Europe Court Rewrites Rules," *The Wall Street Journal,* Sept. 17, 2007, pp. A1, A10.

30. This Is Systembolaget, www.systembolaget.se/Applikationer/Knappar/InEnglish/Swedish_alcohol_re.htm (accessed Jan. 21, 2008).

31. CIA, *The World Fact Book.*

32. Click Z Network, "Euro Teens Respond to Online Advertising," Feb. 23, 2006, www.clickz.com/stats/sectors/demographics/article.php/3586966.

33. Ting Shi, "A Gas Pump for 300 Million Phones," *Business 2.0*, June 2005, p. 78.

34. Louisa Kasdon Sidell, "The Economics of Inclusion," *Continental*, Apr. 2001, pp. 64–67.

35. U.S. Bureau of the Census, *Statistical Abstract of the United States, 2008*, pp. 825–827, 837; "NAFTA: A Decade of Success," Office of the United States Trade Representative, July 1, 2004, http://ustr.gov/Document_Library/Fact_Sheets/2004/NAFTA_A_Decade_of_Success.html.

36. CIA, *The World Fact Book*.

37. "Trade with Canada: 2006," U.S. Bureau of the Census, www.census.gov/foreign-trade/balance/c1220.html (accessed Jan. 28, 2008).

38. William C. Symonds, "Meanwhile, to the North, NAFTA Is a Smash," *BusinessWeek*, Feb. 27, 1995, p. 66.

39. "Will the New Congress Shift Gears on Free Trade?" *The Wall Street Journal*, Nov. 18 2006, http://online.wsj.com.

40. CIA, *The World Fact Book*; "Trade with Mexico: 2006," U.S. Bureau of the Census, www.census.gov/foreign-trade/balance/c2010.html#2006 (accessed Jan. 28, 2008); U.S. Bureau of the Census, *Statistical Abstract*, p. 802.

41. globalEDGE, Country Insights, http://globaledge.msu.edu (accessed Jan. 8, 2007).

42. "Exxon Mobil Expected to File 40 mln USD NAFTA Suit Against Canada in November," CNNMoney, Oct. 16, 2007, www.cnnmoney.com.

43. "The European Union at a Glance," Europa (European Union online), http://europa.eu.int/abc/index_en.htm (accessed Jan. 28, 2008).

44. Ibid.

45. Gateway to the European Union, http://europa.eu.int/index_en.htm (accessed Mar. 28, 2006).

46. "Common Market of the South (MERCOSUR): Agri-Food Regional Profile Statistical Overview," Agriculture and Agri-food Canada, Mar. 2005, http://atn-riae.agr.ca/latin/3947_e.htm; "Profile: Mercosur—Common Market of the South," BBC News, Dec. 15, 2006, http://news.bbc.co.uk/2/hi/americas/5195834. stm.

47. "About APEC," Asian Pacific Economic Cooperation, www.apecsec.org.sg/apec/about_apec.html (accessed Jan. 28, 2008).

48. Asian Pacific Economic Cooperation, www.apec.org/content/apec/about_apec/achievements_and_benefits.html (accessed Jan. 28, 2008).

49. Xin Zhiming, "Year-on-Year Inflation Likely to Be 4.5%," *China Daily*, Nov. 9, 2007, www.chinadaily.com.cn/bizchina/2007-11/09/content_6242599.htm.

50. Janet Adamy, "One U.S. Chain's Unlikely Goal: Pitching Chinese Food in China," *The Wall Street Journal*, Oct. 20, 2006, p. A1, http://online.wsj.com.

51. World Trade Organization, www.wto.org/index.htm (accessed Jan. 28, 2008).

52. "What Is the WTO?" World Trade Organization, www.wto.org/english/thewto_e/whatis_e/whatis_e.htm (accessed Jan. 28, 2008).

53. Leigh Thomas, "E.U., U.S., Canada Haul China Before WTO over Auto Parts Dispute," Yahoo! News, Sept. 15, 2006, http://news.yahoo.com/s/afp/20060915/bs_afp/euuscanadachinawto_060915221834.

54. Jan Johanson and Finn Wiedersheim-Paul, "The Internationalization of the Firm," *Journal of Management Studies*, Oct. 1975, pp. 305–322; Jan Johanson and Jan-Erik Vahlne, "The Internationalization Process of the Firm—A Model of Knowledge Development and Increasing Foreign Commitments," *Journal*

of International Business Studies, Spring/Summer 1977, pp. 23–32; S. Tamer Cavusgil and John R. Nevin, "Internal Determinants of Export Marketing Behavior: An Empirical Investigation," *Journal of Marketing Research*, Feb. 1981, pp. 114–119.

55. Pradeep Tyagi, "Export Behavior of Small Business Firms in Developing Economies: Evidence from the Indian Market," *Marketing Management Journal*, Fall/Winter 2000, pp. 12–20.

56. Berrin Dosoglu-Guner, "How Do Exporters and Non-Exporters View Their 'Country of Origin' Image Abroad?" *Marketing Management Journal*, Fall/Winter 2000, pp. 21–27.

57. Farok J. Contractor and Sumit K. Kundu, "Franchising Versus Company-Run Operations: Model Choice in the Global Hotel Sector," *Journal of International Marketing*, Nov. 1997, pp. 28–53.

58. "Tribune Outsourcing Customer Service, Cutting 250 Jobs," *USA Today*, Aug. 28, 2006, www.usatoday.com/money/media/2006-08-28-tribune-cuts_x.htm.

59. Katie Hafner, "EBay Is Expected to Close Its Auction Site in China," *The New York Times*, Dec. 19, 2006, www.nytimes.com.

60. Margreet F. Boersma, Peter J. Buckley, and Pervez N. Ghauri, "Trust in International Joint Venture Relationships," *Journal of Business Research*, Dec. 2003, pp. 1031–1042.

61. "What We're About," NUMMI, www.nummi.com/co_info.php (accessed Jan. 28, 2008).

62. William Q. Judge and Joel A. Ryman, "The Shared Leadership Challenge in Strategic Alliances: Lessons from the U.S. Health-care Industry," *Academy of Management Executive*, May 2001, pp. 71–79.

63. Ibid.

64. Loretta Chao, "Claiborne to Bring Juicy Apparel Line to China Market," *The Wall Street Journal*, Sept. 20, 2006, p. A20, http://online.wsj.com.

65. Jan Johanson and Finn Wiedersheim-Paul, "The Internationalization of the Firm," *Journal of Management Studies*, Oct. 1975, pp. 305–322; Jan Johanson and Jan-Erik Vahlne, "The Internationalization Process of the Firm—A Model of Knowledge Development and Increasing Foreign Commitments," *Journal of International Business Studies*, Spring/Summer 1977, pp. 23–32; D. Naidler, M. Gerstein, and R. Shaw, *Organization Architecture* (San Francisco: Jossey-Bass, 1992).

66. "Export Department," Clipsal, www.clipsal.com.au/trade/about_us/Export (accessed Jan. 28, 2008).

67. Theodore Levitt, "The Globalization of Markets," *Harvard Business Review*, May/June 1983, p. 92.

68. Deborah Owens, Timothy Wilkinson, and Bruce Keillor, "A Comparison of Product Attributes in a Cross-Cultural/Cross-National Context," *Marketing Management Journal*, Fall/Winter 2000, pp. 1–11.

69. "Dunkin' Donuts Coming to Mainland China," *USA Today*, Jan. 25, 2008, www.usatoday.com.

70. Anil K. Gupta and Vijay Govindarajan, "Converting Global Presence into Global Competitive Advantage," *Academy of Management Executive*, May 2001, pp. 45–58.

71. Sources: "About IDG," International Data Group, www.idg.com/www/home.nsf/AboutIDGForm?OpenForm&region_WW (accessed Apr. 13, 2006); Sam Perkins and Neal Thornberry, "Corporate Entrepreneurship for Dummies," Harvard Business School Publishing (Case BAB114).

72. Sources: Rekha Balu, "Hop Faster, Energizer Bunny: Rayovac Batteries Roll On," *The Wall Street Journal*, June 15, 1999, p. B4; "Battle of the Blades Draws Corporate Blood," "For Mighty Gillette, These Are the Faces of War," *The New York Times*, Oct. 12, 2003, sec. 3, p. 1; The Gillette Company, www.pg.com/en_US/gillette/index.jhtml (accessed Jan.29, 2008); Gillette 1999–2005 Annual Reports, www.pg.com/

investors/annualreports.jhtml (accessed June 2, 2006); "Gillette's Edge," *BusinessWeek*, Jan. 19, 1998, pp. 70–77; "Gillette, Schick End Legal War, but Battle in Market Rages On," *The Boston Globe,* Feb. 17, 2006, www.boston.com/business/healthcare/articles/2006/02/17/gillette_schick_end_legal_war_but_battle_in_market_rages_on; "Wal-Mart Selling Its Own Brand of Alkaline Batteries," *The Wall Street Journal*, Dec. 10, 1999, pp. C4–C5. Don Roy, Middle Tennessee State University; Michael D. Hartline, Florida State University; and G. Tomas M. Hult, Michigan State University, assisted in the development of these case materials.

73. Janet Adamy, "Steady Diet: As Burgers Boom in Russia, McDonald's Touts Discipline," *The Wall Street Journal*, Oct. 16, 2007, p. A1; Michael Bush, "Quality Control," *PR Week (US)*, Oct. 22, 2007, http://www.prweekus.com/Quality-control/article/58038/; Stuart Elliott, "Straight A's, with a Burger as a Prize," *The New York Times*, Dec. 6, 2007, p. C4; Richard Gibson, "Franchisees Balk at Dollar Menu," *The Wall Street Journal*, Nov. 14, 2007; "McDonald's China Strategy," *Los Angeles Times*, Sept. 17, 2007, p. C4; McDonald's, www.mcdonalds.com (accessed Jan. 28, 2008).

Feature box references

a. Matthew Knight "Plastic Bags Fly into Environmental Storm," CNN.com, http://edition.cnn.com/2007/TECH/11/14/fsummit.climate.plasticbags/index.html, Nov. 16, 2007 (accessed Mar. 17, 2008); "Whole Foods Market to Sack Disposable Plastic Grocery Bags," www.wholefoodsmarket.com/cgi-bin/print10pt.cgi?url5/pressroom/pr_01-22-08.html, Jan. 22, 2008 (accessed Mar. 17, 2008); "Diamant Corporation Furthers National Consumer Awareness Efforts as British Prime Minister Gordon Brown Announces Tougher Measures to Dramatically Reduce the Society's Dependence on Single-Use Plastic Bags," CNNmoney.com, money.cnn.com/news/newsfeeds/articles/marketwire/0379140.htm, Mar. 25, 2008 (accessed Mar. 25, 2008).

b. Tier (Technology and Infrastructure for Emerging Regions), http://tier.cs.berkeley.edu/wiki/Wireless (accessed Jan. 21, 2008); Michael Zhao, "60-Mile Wi-Fi," *Forbes*, Apr. 9, 2007, pp. 76–78.

c. Stephen Ebert, "First Look: The 3 Skypephone," Absolute Gadget, Oct. 30, 2007, www.absolutegadget.com/20071030878/reviews/phones/first-look-the-3-skypephone/Page-2.html; Bruce Meyerson, "Skype Takes Its Show on the Road," *BusinessWeek,* Oct. 29, 2007 p. 38; Skype, www.skype.com/ (accessed Jan. 21, 2008).

Chapter 10

1. Sources: Laura Lorber, "Small Business Link: How Online Marketing Videos Became a Hit in Their Own Right," *The Wall Street Journal*, July 2, 2007, p. B4; Marianne Kolbasuk McGee, "YouTube Videos Stir Up New Sales For 'Will It Blend' Maker," *Information Week*, Sept. 27, 2007, www.informationweek.com; Samantha Murphy, "Blend-Worth Technology: Companies Take Online Videos to the Next Level," *Chain Store Age*, July 2007, p. 82.

2. Jay Boehmer, "Three Hotel Chains Introduce Select Service Prototypes," *Business Travel News*, Oct. 17, 2005, pp. 10–34.

3. "Company Fact Sheet," Starbucks, Aug. 2007, www.starbucks.com/aboutus/Company_Profile.pdf.

4. Debbie Howell, "HEB Plus! Is at It Again—Turning Heads with a NEW GM Line," *DSN Retailing Today*, Dec. 19, 2005, pp. 3+.

5. Steve Hargreaves, "Calming Ethanol-Crazed Corn Prices," CNNMoney, Jan. 30, 2007, http://money.cnn.com/.

6. Joann Muller, "Parts for the Sensitive Car," *Forbes*, Nov. 28, 2005, pp. 204–208.

7. Ellen Byron, "Aiming to Clean Up, P&G Courts Business Customers," *The Wall Street Journal*, Jan. 26, 2007, http://online.wsj.com.

8. Barry Janoff, "Reebok Sees Dollars, Scents in New Kool-Aid Line," *Brandweek,* Jan. 29, 2008, www.brandweek.com/bw/news/apparelretail/article_display.jsp?vnu_content_id=1003703357.

9. William P. Putsis, Jr., and Barry L. Bayus, "An Empirical Analysis of Firms' Product Line Decisions," *Journal of Marketing Research,* Feb. 2001, pp. 110–118.

10. Muller, "Parts for the Sensitive Car."

11. Deborah Ball, "Snack Attack: As Chocolate Sags, Cadbury Gambles on a Piece of Gum," *The Wall Street Journal*, Jan. 12, 2006, p. A1, http://online.wsj.com/.

12. Miguel Helft, "LeapFrog Hopes for Next Hit with Interactive Reading Toy," *The New York Times*, Jan. 28, 2008, www.nytimes.com.

13. "Birds Eye Lines Seek to Inspire Consumers," *Frozen Food Age*, May 2006, p. 12.

14. Brian A. Lukas and O. C. Ferrell, "The Effect of Market Orientation on Product Innovation," *Journal of the Academy of Marketing Science,* Feb. 2000, pp. 239–247.

15. Michael D. Johnson, Andreas Herrmann, and Frank Huber, "Evolution of Loyalty Intentions," *Journal of Marketing* 70 (Apr. 2006), via www.marketingpower.com.

16. "Who Is Dr. Gadget?" The Dettman Group, www.doctorgadget.com/Who_Is_Dr._Gadget.html (accessed Jan. 30, 2008).

17. Elizabeth Esfahani, "Finding the Sweet Spot," *Business 2.0*, Nov. 2005, www.business2.com.

18. James R. Healey and Jayne O'Donnell, "Popularity of Crossovers Leaves SUVs in Dust," *USA Today*, Dec. 8, 2005, pp. 1B, 3B.

19. O. C. Ferrell and Michael Hartline, *Marketing Strategy* (Mason, OH: South-Western, 2008), pp. 172–173.

20. "Coke Blak Goes Black," *BevNet*, Aug. 31, 2007, www.bevnet.com/news/2007/08-31-2007-Blak_coca-cola.asp.

21. Adam Horowitz, Mark Athitakis, Mark Lasswell, and Owen Thomas, "101 Dumbest Moments in Business," *Business 2.0*, Jan./Feb. 2005, pp. 103–112.

22. Dennis K. Berman and Ellen Byron, "P&G Sells Sure Deodorant Label to Private Firm Innovative Brands," *The Wall Street Journal*, Sept. 26, 2006, p. B2, http://online.wsj.com.

23. Adapted from Everett M. Rogers, *Diffusion of Innovations* (New York: Macmillan, 1962), pp. 81–86.

24. Arch G. Woodside and Wim Biemans, "Managing Relationships, Networks, and Complexity in Innovation, Diffusion, and Adoption Processes," *Journal of Business & Industrial Marketing* 20 (July 2005): 335–338.

25. Ibid., pp. 247–250.

26. Horowitz, Athitakis, Lasswell, and Thomas, "101 Dumbest Moments in Business."

27. Susan Casey, "Object-Oriented: Everything I Ever Needed to Know About Business I Learned in the Frozen Food Aisle," *eCompany,* Oct. 2000, www.ecompany.com.

28. Louis Lavelle, "What Campbell's New Chief Needs to Know," *BusinessWeek,* June 25, 2001, p. 60.

29. Sources: "100 Best Corporate Citizens 2007," *Business Ethics,* Spring 2007, www.business-ethics.com/node/75; "Brewing Up a Strong Starbucks Alternative," MSNBC, Feb. 5, 2006, www.msnbc.msn.com/id/4163701/; "Coke, Illycaffe Announce Ready-to-drink Coffee Venture," *Gourmet Retailer,* Oct. 19, 2007; "Company Fact Sheet," Starbucks, Aug. 2007, www.starbucks.com/aboutus/Company_Profile.pdf; Judith Crown, "Coffee Gets Hotter at McDonald's," *BusinessWeek Online,* Jan. 9, 2008, www.businessweek.com/bwdaily/dnflash/content/jan2008/db2008019_036171.htm; "'Fortune 100 Best Companies to Work for 2007," *Fortune,*

http://money.cnn.com/magazines/fortune/bestcompanies/2007/snapshots/16.html (accessed Jan. 30, 2008); "In Rare Flop, Starbucks Scraps Chocolate Drink," MSNBC, Feb. 10, 2006, www.msnbc.msn.com/id/11274445/; Matt Richtel, "At Starbucks, Songs of Instant Gratification," *The New York Times*, Oct. 1, 2007, p. C1; Starbucks, www.starbucks.com (accessed Jan. 30, 2008); Emily Bryson York, "'Fired Up' Shultz Gives Peek at Starbucks Turnaround Plan," *Advertising Age*, Jan. 30, 2008, www.adage.com.

30. Sources: "Dell at a Glance," Dell, www1.us.dell.com/content/topics/global.aspx/corp/background/en/facts?c=us&l=en&s=corp&~section=000&~ck=mn (accessed Jan. 30, 2008); Heather Green, "Consumer Electronics: Free-Falling Prices and Rocketing Sales," *Business Week*, Jan. 12, 2004, pp. 99–101; Jeff Jarvis, "Dell Learns to Listen," *BusinessWeek*, Oct. 29, 2007, p. 118; Bolaji Ojo, "Equipped with Hard Drive," *EBN*, Oct. 27, 2003, p. 2; "Staples Will Sell Dell Computers," *Nashville Business Journal*, Oct. 24, 2007, www.nashville.bizjournals.com; Cathy Booth Thomas, "Dell Wants Your Home," *Time*, Oct. 6, 2003, pp. 48–50; Cynthia L. Webb, "Battle of the Consumer Electronics Giants," *The Washington Post*, Sept. 26, 2003, www.washingtonpost.com.

Feature box references

a. Bruce Geiselman, "Aisle 7 for Eco Options," *Waste News*, Apr. 30, 2007, p. 35; Home Depot, www.homedepot.com; "Home Depot Hammers Out Eco Options ID Program," *Brandweek*, Apr. 23, 2007, p. 5; Clifford Krauss, "Can They Really Call the Chainsaw Eco-Friendly?" *The New York Times*, June 25, 2007, p. A1.

b. "Thoughts on Music," Apple Inc.—Steve Jobs, www.apple.com/hotnews/thoughtsonmusic/, Feb. 6, 2007 (accessed Apr. 3, 2008); "iTunes Stores Sales Going Strong," MacWorld, www.macworld.com/article/54775/2007/01/sales/html, Jan. 9, 2007 (accessed Apr. 3, 2008).

c. Brooks Barnes, "Web Playgrounds of the Very Young," *The New York Times*, Dec. 31, 2007, www.nytimes.com; Brian Hindo, "Toys with a Second Life," *BusinessWeek*, Dec. 31, 2007–Jan. 7, 2007, p. 91; "Move Over, Beanie Babies, Webkinz Are Coming to a Store—and Virtual World—Near You," knowledge@.wharton.upenn.edu/article.cf?articleid51805#; Bob Tedeschi, "Fuzzy Critters with High Prices Offer Lessons in New Concepts," *The New York Times*, Mar. 26, 2007, p. C4.

Chapter 11

1. Sources: Reena Jana, "Pure Digital Flips the Script," *BusinessWeek*, Apr. 28, 2008, pp. 76–78; David Pogue, "Camcorder Brings Zen to the Shoot," *The New York Times*, Mar. 20, 2008, p. C1; Jefferson Graham, "Fun Flip Wows Camcorder Crowd with Ease of Use, Low Price," *USA Today*, Sept. 12, 2007, p. 5B.

2. Mary Jane Credeur, "Coke Poured Out 1,000 New Products in 2005," *USA Today*, Dec. 8, 2005, p. B5.

3. Vanessa L. Facenda, "In Search of More Growth, P&G's Febreze Hits the Road," *Brandweek*, Aug. 6, 2007, www.brandweek.com.

4. Steven Gray, "Hormel Struggles to Add Upscale Foods Without Alienating Lovers of Its Spam," *The Wall Street Journal*, Nov. 29, 2006, p. B1, http://online.wsj.com.

5. Kate MacArthur, "Drink Your Fruits, Veggies: Water's the New Fitness Fad," *Advertising Age*, Jan. 3, 2005, p. 4.

6. Chung K. Kim, Anne M. Lavack, and Margo Smith, "Consumer Evaluation of Vertical Brand Extensions and Core Brands," *Journal of Business Research*, Mar. 2001, pp. 211–222.

7. Maria Sääksjärvi and Minttu Lampinen, "Consumer Perceived Risk in Successive Product Generations," *European Journal of Innovation Management* 8 (June 2005): 145–156.

8. Jean Halliday, "Bet Your Luxury Car Can't Do This," *Advertising Age*, Nov. 13, 2006, www.adage.com.

9. Arik Hesseldahl, "The Paperless Map Is the Killer App," *BusinessWeek*, Nov. 26, 2007, pp. 71–72.

10. Jeff Sabatini, "An SUV with Sports-Car Envy," *The Wall Street Journal*, Dec. 1, 2006, p. W11C, http://online.wsj.com.

11. Frank Franzak and Dennis Pitta, "New Product Development at Eastern Spice & Flavorings," *Journal of Product & Brand Management* 14 (2005): 462–467.

12. Gray, "Hormel Struggles to Add Upscale Foods Without Alienating Lovers of Its Spam."

13. Chris Isidore, "Toyota Catches GM in Global Sales," CNNMoney, Jan. 23, 2008, http://money.cnn.com/; Scott Sprinzen and Robert Schulz, "Running on Empty in Detroit," *BusinessWeek Online*, Dec. 9, 2005, www.businessweek.com.

14. Kate Macarthur, "Coke, Nestlé Offer a Workout in a Can," *Advertising Age*, Oct. 16, 2006, p. 8.

15. "Making Headway with Helmets," *BusinessWeek*, Jan. 15, 2007, p. 75.

16. Lee G. Cooper, "Strategic Marketing Planning for Radically New Products," *Journal of Marketing*, Jan. 2000, pp. 1–16.

17. "Generating New Product Ideas: An Initial Investigation of the Role of Market Information and Organizational Characteristics," *Journal of the Academy of Marketing Science*, Jan. 2001, pp. 89–101.

18. Janet Adamy, "For McDonald's It's a Wrap," *The Wall Street Journal*, Jan. 30, 2007, p. B1, http://online.wsj.com.

19. "A. G. Lafley: Procter & Gamble," *BusinessWeek*, Dec. 19, 2005, p. 62.

20. "Inside a White-Hot Idea Factory" *BusinessWeek*, Jan. 15, 2007, pp. 72–73.

21. Stephen J. Carson, "When to Give Up Control of Outsourced New Product Development," *Journal of Marketing* 71 (Jan. 2007): 49–66.

22. Jack Gordon and Bill Vernick, "What All Brands, CEOs Must Know About Developing Great New Products," *Cost Engineering* 47 (Nov. 2005): 8–9.

23. Dennis A. Pitta and Danielle Fowler, "Online Consumer Communities and Their Value to New Product Developers," *Journal of Product & Brand Management* 14 (2005): 283–291.

24. Jathon Sapsford, "Honda Caters to Japan's Pet Population Boom," *The Wall Street Journal*, Oct. 5, 2005, p. B1, http://online.wsj.com/public/us.

25. Deborah Ball, "As Chocolate Sags, Cadbury Gambles on a Piece of Gum," *The Wall Street Journal*, Jan. 12, 2006, p. A1, http://online.wsj.com/public/us.

26. Jack Neff, "P&G Begins Slow Test of Probiotic Supplements," *Advertising Age*, Dec. 12, 2007, www.adage.com.

27. Alexander E. Reppel, Isabelle Szmigin, and Thorsten Gruber, "The iPod Phenomenon: Identifying a Market Leader's Secrets through Qualitative Marketing Research," *Journal of Product & Brand Management* 15 (2006): 239–249.

28. "P&G Ends Test of Impress Plastic Wrap," *Advertising Age*, July 18, 2001, www.adage.com.

29. Lisa Sanders, "Berlin Cameron Wins Heineken Light Beer Ad Campaign," *Advertising Age*, Dec. 27, 2005, www.adage.com.

30. Jack Neff, "Swiffer by Another Name," *Advertising Age*, Apr. 11, 2005, p. 11.

31. Bruce Horovitz, "CEO Turns the Flame Up," *USA Today*, May 23, 2005, p. 3B; Kate MacArthur, "What's Eating Burger King," *Advertising Age*, Jan. 26, 2004, pp. 1, 30.

32. Adapted from Michael Levy and Barton A. Weitz, *Retailing Management* (Burr Ridge, IL: Irwin/McGraw-Hill, 2001), p. 585.

33. Sidra Durst, "How Zappos Became No. 1 in Online Shoes," *Business 2.0,* Jan. 15, 2007, http://money.cnn.com/.

34. Stephanie Kang and Suzanne Vranica, "Condé Nast to Shutter House & Garden," *The Wall Street Journal,* Nov. 6, 2007, pp. B1, B10.

35. Stephanie Thompson, "Mars to Scale Back M-Azing Brand," *Advertising Age,* Oct. 26, 2006, www.adage.com.

36. Pavel Strach and André M. Everett, "Brand Corrosion: Mass-Marketing's Threat to Luxury Automobile Brands after Merger and Acquisition," *Journal of Product & Brand Management* 15 (2006): 106–120.

37. Rajesh Sethi, "New Product Quality and Product Development Teams," *Journal of Marketing,* Apr. 2000, pp. 1–14.

38. Sources: Rick Barrett, "A Home for Harley's Heritage," *Milwaukee Journal-Sentinel,* June 29, 2008, www.journalsentinel.com; Matthew Goodman, "Harley-Davidson Chief Jim Ziemer Is Not Enjoying an Easy Ride," *The Sunday Times,* June 29, 2008, business.timesonline.co.uk; Jacqueline Mitchell, "Ten Auto Gifts for Dad," *Forbes,* June 5, 2008, forbes.com; www.harley-davidson.com.

39. Sources: Paul Betts, "Coke Aims to Give Pepsi a Roasting in Cold Coffee War," *Financial Times,* Oct. 17, 2007, p. 16; Kenji Hall, "Fad Marketing's Balancing Act," *BusinessWeek,* Aug. 6, 2007, p. 42; "Pepsi Tries Cucumber Flavor in Japan," *USA Today,* June 13, 2007, www.usatoday.com/money/industries/food/2007-06-13-pepsi-cucumber_N.htm; "Suntory to Increase Pepsi Nex Bottle Can Production," *AsiaPulse News,* Aug. 7, 2007, n.p.

Feature box references

a. Peter Burrows, "Nabbing Video Pirates: Who Needs Google?" *BusinessWeek,* Oct. 16, 2007, www.businessweek.com; Jonathan Cohen, "Britney Spears Reveals 'Blackout' Track List," *Billboard,* Oct. 12, 2007, www.billboard.com; John Horn, "'Spider-Man 3's' First Conquest: Film Pirates," *Los Angeles Times,* May 4, 2007, p. E1; Merissa Marr and Sarah McBride, "Studios Begin Hunt Over Pirated Movies," *The Wall Street Journal,* June 22, 2007, p. B3.

b. Vanessa L. Facenda, "A Guide to the Small Green Health and Beauty Brands: Marketers Once Considered Niche Are Getting Exposure, Distribution in Mainstream Venues," *Brandweek,* Aug. 6, 2007, p. 16; Julie Naughton, "At Carol's Daughter, the Family Continues to Grow," *WWD,* July 27, 2007, p. 5; "New Leaf Paper Releases 100% Post-Consumer Waste Sakura Line," *Energy Resource,* May 1, 2007; Kemi Osukoya, "Small Firms See Big Potential in Going Green," *The Wall Street Journal,* June 12, 2007, p. B4.

c. "Airborne settles suit over false claims," NPR, http://npr.org/templates/story/story.php?storyId-587937907, Jan. 6, 2008 (accessed Mar. 26, 2008); "Cold Remedy Airborne Settles Lawsuit," WebMD, http://webmd.com/cold-and-flu/news/20080304/cold-remedy-airborne-settles-lawsuit, Mar. 4, 2008 (accessed Mar. 28, 2008); "Airborne Settles Lawsuit," Inc.com, http://inc.com/news/articles/2008/03/airborne.html, Mar. 7, 2008 (accessed Mar. 28, 2008).

Chapter 12

1. Sources: Debra D. Bass, "Founder of Spanx Reshapes Foundation Wear," *St. Louis Post-Dispatch,* Mar. 27, 2007, www.stltoday.com; Walt Belcher, "Clearwater Native Judges 'American Inventor,'" *Tampa Tribune,* June 6, 2007, www.tampatrib.com; Spanx, www.spanx.com (accessed Feb. 5, 2008); "Spanx Banks on Its Mission," *Apparel,* Aug. 2007, pp. 5ff.

2. "Dictionary of Marketing Terms," American Marketing Association, www.marketingpower.com/mg-dictionary.php (accessed Feb. 5, 2008).

3. Warren Church, "Investment in Brand Pays Large Dividends," *Marketing News,* Nov. 15, 2006, p. 21.

4. Bethany McLean, "Classic Rock," *Fortune,* Nov. 12, 2007, pp. 35–40.

5. U.S. Bureau of the Census, *Statistical Abstract of the United States, 2008* (Washington, DC: Government Printing Office, 2007), p. 507.

6. Theresa Howard, "Marketers Use Brands to Help Holiday Shoppers," *USA Today,* Nov. 21, 2007, www.usatoday.com.

7. C. D. Simms and P. Trott, "The Perception of the BMW Mini Brand: The Importance of Historical Associations and the Development of a Model," *Journal of Product & Brand Management* 15 (2006): 228–238.

8. Douglas B. Holt, *How Brands Become Icons: The Principles of Cultural Branding* (Boston: Harvard Business School Press, 2004).

9. Nigel Hollis, "Branding Unmasked," *Marketing Research,* Fall 2005, pp. 24–29.

10. Don E. Schultz, "The Loyalty Paradox," *Marketing Management,* Sept./Oct. 2005, pp. 10–11.

11. David A. Aaker, *Managing Brand Equity: Capitalizing on the Value of a Brand Name* (New York: Free Press, 1991), pp. 16–17.

12. Dennis K. Berman and Ellen Byron, "P&G Sells Sure Deodorant Label to Private Firm Innovative Brands," *The Wall Street Journal,* Sept. 26, 2006, p. B2, http://online.wsj.com; "Procter & Gamble Sells Sure Deodorant to Innovative," *Deseret News,* Sept. 27, 2006, via www.findarticles.com.

13. Joel Rubinson, "Framework for Growth," *Marketing Research,* Summer 2005, pp. 15–16.

14. "Store Brands Achieving New Heights of Consumer Popularity and Growth," Private Label Manufacturer's Association, http://plma.com/storeBrands/sbt08.html (accessed Feb. 5, 2008).

15. Janet Adamy, "New Food, New Look," *The Wall Street Journal,* Nov. 21, 2005, p. R8, http://online.wsj.com/.

16. Marcel Corstjens and Rajiv Lal, "Building Store Loyalty Through Store Brands," *Journal of Marketing Research,* Aug. 2000, pp. 281–291.

17. Edmund J. Pazella, "Why 'Generic' Is Becoming the Prescription Drug Brand of Choice," *Employee Benefit Plan Review,* Nov. 2006, p. 29.

18. Chiranjeev S. Kohli, Katrin R. Harich, and Lance Leuthesser, "Creating Brand Identity: A Study of Evaluation of New Brand Names," *Journal of Business Research* 58 (2005): 1506–1515.

19. Dionne Searcey, "Bye, Cingular, in AT&T Rebranding," *The Wall Street Journal,* Jan. 12, 2007, p. B3, http://online.wsj.com.

20. Jay Boehmer, "Three Hotel Chains Introduce Select-Service Prototypes," *Business Travel News,* Oct. 17, 2005, via Business Source Premier.

21. Kitty Bean Yancey, "Could You Name a New Hotel Chain?" *USA Today,* Sept. 22, 2006, p. 11D.

22. Allison Fass, "Animal House," *Forbes,* Feb. 12, 2007, pp. 72–75.

23. Dorothy Cohen, "Trademark Strategy," *Journal of Marketing,* Jan. 1986, p. 63.

24. U.S. Trademark Association, "Trademark Stylesheet," no. 1A.

25. Dan Weeks, "Bacardi to Defend 'Vigorously' in Havana Club Lawsuit," *Caribbean Net News,* Aug. 17, 2006, www.caribbeannetnews.com/cgi-script/csArticles/articles/000028/002823.htm.

26. Stephanie Thompson, "Kellogg Has Megabrand Ambitions for Special K," *Advertising Age,* Nov. 6, 2006, p. 6.

27. Devon Del Vecchio and Daniel C. Smith, "Brand-Extension Price Premiums: The Effects of Perceived Fit and Extension Product Category Risk," *Journal of Marketing Science* 33 (Apr. 2005): 184–196.

28. Vicki R. Lane, "The Impact of Ad Repetition and Ad Content on Consumer Perceptions of Incongruent Extensions," *Journal of Marketing,* Apr. 2000, pp. 80–91.

29. Shantini Munthree, Geoff Bick, and Russell Abratt, "A Framework for Brand Revitalization," *Journal of Product & Brand Management* 15 (2006): 157–167.

30. Chris Pullig, Carolyn J. Simmons, and Richard G. Netemeyer, "Brand Dilution: When Do New Brands Hurt Existing Brands?" *Journal of Marketing* 70 (Apr. 2006).

31. Michael Lev-Ram, "This $310,000 Phone Blings, then Rings," CNNMoney, Dec. 20, 2006, http://money.cnn.com.

32. "Kohl's Inks Exclusive Deal for Tony Hawk Footwear," *Los Angeles Business,* Jan. 29, 2007, http://losangeles.bizjournals.com/losangeles/stories/2007/01/29/daily38.html?surround=lfn.

33. Jeff Falk, "Splish, Splash—Packaging Takes a Bath," *Global Cosmetic Industry,* Dec. 2005, pp. 44+.

34. Thomas J. Madden, Kelly Hewett, and Martin S. Roth, "Managing Images in Different Cultures: A Cross-National Study of Color Meanings and Preferences," *Journal of International Marketing,* Winter 2000, p. 90.

35. "Will Healthy Options = Healthy Sales? "*Packaging Digest,* July 2007, pp. 28–33.

36. Joel Dresang, "Making Bacon Pop," *Milwaukee Journal-Sentinel,* Nov. 17, 2007, www.jsonline.com/story/index.aspx?id=687166.

37. Deborah Ball, "The Perils of Packaging: Nestlé Aims for Easier Openings," *The Wall Street Journal,* Nov. 17, 2005, p. B1, http://online.wsj.com.

38. Valerie Folkes and Shashi Matta, ''The Effect of Package Shape on Consumers' Judgment of Product Volume: Attention as a Mental Contaminant," *Journal of Consumer Research,* Sept. 2004, p. 390.

39. Ball, "The Perils of Packaging."

40. "Looking for that Label," *Prepared Foods,* Sept. 2006, p. 38.

41. Federal Trade Commission, www.ftc.gov (accessed Nov. 21, 2007).

42. Sources: Peter Asmus, "Goodbye Coal, Hello Wind," *Business Ethics,* July/Aug. 1999, pp. 10–11; Robert Baun, "New Belgium Hits Top 5 Among U.S. Specialty Brewers," *The [Fort Collins] Coloradoan,* Feb. 21, 2002, p. 09; Robert Baun, "What's in a Name? Ask the Makers of Fat Tire," *The [Fort Collins] Coloradoan,* Oct. 8, 2000, pp. E1, E3; Jeff Cioletti, "Earth's Brewer," *Beverage World,* Oct. 15, 2007, pp. 22+; Robert F. Dwyer and John F. Tanner, Jr., *Business Marketing* (Burr Ridge, IL: Irwin/McGraw-Hill, 1999), p. 104; "Four Businesses Honored with Prestigious International Award for Outstanding Marketplace Ethics," Better Business Bureau, press release, Sept. 23, 2002, www.bbb.org/alerts/2002torch-winners.asp; Julie Gordon, "Lebesch Balances Interests in Business, Community," *The [Fort Collins] Coloradoan,* Feb. 26, 2003; Del I. Hawkins, Roger J. Best, and Kenneth A. Coney, *Consumer Behavior: Building Marketing Strategy,* 8th ed. (Burr Ridge, IL: Irwin/McGraw-Hill, 2001); David Kemp, Tour Connoisseur, New Belgium Brewing Company, personal interview by Nikole Haiar, Nov. 21, 2000; New Belgium Brewing Company, Ft. Collins, CO, www.newbelgium.com (accessed Feb. 5, 2008); New Belgium Brewing Company Tour by Nikole Haiar, Nov. 20, 2000; "New Belgium Brewing Wins Ethics Award," *Denver Business Journal,* Jan. 2, 2003, http://denver.bizjournals.com/denver/stories/2002/12/30/daily21.html; Dan Rabin, "New Belgium Pours It on for Bike Riders," *Celebrator Beer News,* Aug./Sept. 1998, www.celebrator.com/9808/rabin.html; Lisa Sanders, "This Beer Will Reduce Your Anxiety," *Advertising Age,* Jan. 17, 2005, p. 25; Bryan Simpson, "New Belgium Brewing: Brand Building Through Advertising and Public Relations," http://college.hmco.com/instructors/catalog/misc/new_belgium_brewing.pdf (accessed Feb. 5, 2008).

43. Sources: Anthony Bianco, "The New King Cole," *Business-Week,* Oct. 29, 2007, pp. 63–68; "Iconix Licensing Pact," *MMR,* Sept. 10, 2007, p. 2; Cheryl Lu-Lien Tan, "Iconix Plans to Announce Overseas Licensing Deals," *The Wall Street Journal,* Nov. 6, 2007, p. B8.

Feature box references

a. Roger Fillion, "Only Elite Club Allowed to Sell Big League Gear," *Rocky Mountain News,* Oct. 23, 2007, www.rockymountainnews.com; Paul Grimaldi, "The Business of Baseball," *Providence [Rhode Island] Journal,* Oct. 27, 2007, www.projo.com; "The Ticker: Adidas Group," *Boston Herald,* Nov. 10, 2007, www.bostonherald.com.

b. Amy Cortese, "Friend of Nature? Let's See Those Shoes," *The New York Times,* Mar. 7, 2007, p. H5; Claudia H. Deutsch, "Seeking a Joint Effort for Greener Athletic Shoes," *The New York Times,* Sept. 29, 2007, p. C2.

Chapter 13

1. Sources: Cirque du Soleil, www.cirquedusoleil.com (accessed Feb. 6, 2008); Douglas Belkin, "Talent Scouts for Cirque du Soleil Walk a Tightrope," *The Wall Street Journal,* Sept. 8, 2007, p. A1; Forrest Glenn Spencer, "It's One Big Circus," *Information Outlook,* Oct. 2007, pp. 22–23.

2. Leonard L. Berry and A. Parasuraman, *Marketing Services: Competing through Quality* (New York: Free Press, 1991), p. 5.

3. Michael Levy and Barton A. Weitz, *Retailing Management* (Burr Ridge, IL: Irwin/McGraw-Hill, 2001), p. 585.

4. Michelle Conlin, "Call Centers in the Rec Room," *Business-Week,* Jan. 23, 2006, www.businessweek.com.

5. Matthew Maier, "Building the Next Google," *Business 2.0,* Nov. 1, 2005, p. 117.

6. Raymond P. Fisk, Stephen J. Grove, and Joby John, *Interactive Services Marketing* (Boston: Houghton Mifflin, 2003), p. 25.

7. Fisk, Grove, and John, *Interactive Services Marketing,* p. 59.

8. The information in this section is based on K. Douglas Hoffman and John E. G. Bateson, *Services Marketing: Concepts, Strategies, and Cases,* 3rd ed. (Cincinnati: Thomson/South-Western, 2006); Valarie A. Zeithaml, A. Parasuraman, and Leonard L. Berry, *Delivering Quality Service: Balancing Customer Perceptions and Expectations* (New York: Free Press, 1990).

9. Michael K. Brady, Brian L. Bourdeau, and Julia Heskel, "The Importance of Brand Cues in Intangible Service Industries: An Application to Investment Services," *Journal of Services Marketing* 19 (Oct. 2005): 401–410.

10. Don E. Schultz, "Lost in Transition," *Marketing Management,* Mar./Apr. 2007, pp. 10–11.

11. Jeremy J. Sierra and Shaun McQuitty, "Service Providers and Customers: Social Exchange Theory and Service Loyalty," *Journal of Services Marketing* 19 (Oct. 2005): 392–400.

12. Steve Sizoo, Richard Plank, Wilifried Iskat, and Hendrick Serrie, "The Effect of Intercultural Sensitivity on Employee Performance in Cross-Cultural Service Encounters," *Journal of Services Marketing* 29 (June 2005): 245–255.

13. J. Paul Peter and James H. Donnelly, *A Preface to Marketing Management* (Burr Ridge, IL: Irwin/McGraw-Hill, 2003), p. 212.

14. Sabin Im, Charlotte H. Mason, and Mark B. Houston, "Does Innate Consumer Innovativeness Relate to New Product/Service Adoption Behavior? The Intervening Role of Social Learning via Vicarious Innovativeness," *Journal of the Academy of Marketing Science* 35 (2007): 63–75.

15. Sarah Nassauer, "Eliminating the Human Element," *The Wall Street Journal,* Nov. 14, 2006, p. D7, http://online.wsj.com.

16. Robert Moore, Melissa L. Moore, and Michael Capella, "The Impact of Customer-to-Customer Interactions in a High

Personal Contact Service Setting," *Journal of Services Marketing* 19 (July 2005): 482–491.

17. Michael D. Hartline and O. C. Ferrell, "Service Quality Implementation: The Effects of Organizational Socialization and Managerial Actions of Customer Contact Employee Behavior," *Marketing Science Institute Report*, no. 93–122 (Cambridge, MA: Marketing Science Institute, 1993).

18. "Company Fact Sheet," Starbucks, Aug. 2007, www.starbucks.com/aboutus/Company_Profile.pdf.

19. "Progressive Car Insurance Adds Pet Coverage," MSNBC, Nov. 12, 2007, http://msnbc.msn.com/id/21741410/.

20. Fisk, Grove, and John, *Interactive Services Marketing*, p. 56.

21. Ibid., p. 91.

22. "Flying the Friendly Skies? Delta Gives Air Etiquette Tips," CNN, Dec. 12, 2007, www.cnn.com/2007/TRAVEL/12/12/air.etiquette.ap/index.html.

23. Greg Lindsay, "Flight Plan," *Fast Company*, May 2007, pp. 100–107.

24. Laura Petrecca, "More Marketers Target Baby Boomers' Eyes, Wallets," *USA Today*, Feb. 25, 2007, www.usatoday.com.

25. International Smart Tan Network, http://saloncertification.com/basic/index.php (accessed Feb. 6, 2008).

26. Lesley Kump, "Teaching the Teachers," *Forbes*, Dec. 12, 2005, p. 121.

27. Ahmed Taher and Hanan El Basha, "Heterogeneity of Consumer Demand: Opportunities for Pricing of Services," *Journal of Product & Brand Management* 15 (May 2006): 331–340.

28. *Florian v. Wangenheim* and Tomás Bayón, "Behavioral Consequences of Overbooking Service Capacity," *Journal of Marketing* 71 (Oct. 2007): 36–47.

29. Zeithaml, Parasuraman, and Berry, *Delivering Quality Service*.

30. Dayana Yochim, "'Customer Rage' Is on the Rise," *The Motley Fool*, Nov. 3, 2005, via AOL.

31. John Gountas and Sandra Gountas, "Personality Orientations, Emotional States, Customer Satisfaction, and Intention to Repurchase," *Journal of Business Research* 60 (Jan. 2007): 72–75.

32. Valarie A. Zeithaml, "How Consumer Evaluation Processes Differ between Goods and Services," in *Marketing of Services*, ed. James H. Donnelly and William R. George (Chicago: American Marketing Association, 1981), pp. 186–190.

33. A. Parasuraman, Leonard L. Berry, and Valarie A. Zeithaml, "An Empirical Examination of Relationships in an Extended Service Quality Model," *Marketing Science Institute Working Paper Series*, no. 90–112 (Cambridge, MA: Marketing Science Institute, 1990), p. 29.

34. Chana R. Schoenberger, "Will Work with Food," *Forbes*, Sept. 18, 2006, pp. 92+.

35. Anja Reimer and Richard Kuehn, "The Impact of Servicescape on Quality Perception," *European Journal of Marketing* 39 (Jan. 2005): 785–808.

36. Valarie A. Zeithaml, Leonard L. Berry, and A. Parasuraman, "Communication and Control Processes in the Delivery of Service Quality," *Journal of Marketing*, Apr. 1988, pp. 35–48.

37. Valarie A. Zeithaml, Leonard L. Berry, and A. Parasuraman, "The Nature and Determinants of Customer Expectations of Service," *Journal of the Academy of Marketing Science*, Winter 1993, pp. 1–12.

38. John F. Milliman, Eric M. Olson, and Stanley F. Slater, "'Courting Excellence,'" *Marketing Management*, Mar./Apr. 2007, pp. 14–17.

39. Jose Martinez, "Voting Campaign Launched," *The [Sacramento State University] State Hornet*, Nov. 27, 2007, http://media.www.statehornet.com/media/storage/paper1146/news/2007/11/28/News/Voting.Campaign.Launched-3117720.shtml.

40. Philip Kotler, *Marketing for Nonprofit Organizations*, 2nd ed. (Englewood Cliffs, NJ: Prentice-Hall, 1982), p. 37.

41. Ibid.

42. Eric Newman, "March of Dimes Repositions Brand to Broaden Appeal," *Brandweek*, Jan. 16, 2008, www.brandweek.com/bw/news/pharmaceutical/article_display.jsp?vnu_content_id=1003696958.

43. Linda Formichelli, "A Delicate Balance," *Deliver*, Sept. 2007, pp. 8–9.

44. Sources: Lewis Lazare, "Why Southwest Soars as Other Airlines Sag," *Chicago Sun-Times*, June 20, 2008, www.suntimes.com; Trebor Banstetter, "Southwest's Boss Shuns Fees, Aims for More Fliers," *Fort Worth Star-Telegram*, June 2, 2008, www.dfw.com; Evan Smith, "Texas Monthly Talks: Evan Smith Sits Down with Herb Kelleher," *Texas Monthly*, June 2008, pp. 78+; Del Quentin Wilber, "Groundings Prompt FAA Safety Overhaul," *The Washington Post*, April 19, 2008, p. D1; "Southwest Airlines Traffic Up 7% in May," *Orlando Business Journal*, June 4, 2008, orlando.bizjournals.com/Orlando/stories/2008/06/02/daily25.html; "Southwest Air," *Business Civic Leadership Center*, U.S.Chamber of Commerce, 2005, www.uschamber.com/bclc/profiles/southwest.htm; www.southwest.com.

45. Sources: "About Allstate," "The Allstate Corporation at a Glance," Allstate Insurance Company, www.allstate.com/about/pagerender.asp?page=allstate_at_a_glance.htm (accessed Feb. 6, 2008); "Allstate CEO: Firms Should Be Politically Active," *USA Today*, July 18, 2005, www.usatoday.com/money/companies/management/2005-07-18-allstate_x.htm; Katherine Burger, "Walking the Walk," *Insurance & Technology*, Nov. 2007, pp. 27+; "Community Commitment," "The Allstate Foundation," Allstate Insurance Company, www.allstate.com/Community/PageRender.asp?Page=foundation.html (accessed Feb. 6, 2008); Darla Martin Tucker, "Employers Take Action after Wildfire Losses," *Business Press (San Bernardino, CA)*, Nov. 5, 2007, n.p.; "Years Like 2004 Bring Out the Best in Allstate," The Allstate Corporation Summary Annual Report 2004, pp. 5–9.

46. Sources: Anne Eisenberg, "When a Greeting Card Becomes a Photo Album," *The New York Times*, Oct. 14, 2007, p. BU4; Jefferson Graham, "At Holidays, Net Photo Business Cranks Up," *USA Today*, Dec. 22, 2006, p. 4B; Miguel Helft, "A Dot-Com Survivor's Long Road," *The New York Times*, Oct. 30, 2006, p. C1; Jeff Housenbold, "A Photographic Vision," *Newsweek*, Oct. 1, 2007, p. E4; "Nickelodeon and Shutterfly to Create New Character-Customized Digital Photo Products," *Wireless News*, Nov. 14, 2007, n.p.; "Olson Eyes Shutterfly Opportunities," *Brandweek*, Aug. 6, 2007, p. 40; Shutterfly, www.shutterfly.com (Feb. 6, 2008); "Shutterfly Goes East," *Digital Imaging Digest*, Feb. 2007, n.p.; "Shutterfly Joins Deloitte's 2007 Technology Fast 50 & Fast 500," *Wireless News*, Nov. 27, 2007, www.10meters.com.

Feature box references

a. Michael Carolan, "Blackstone Runs the Figures; Wax Ones, That Is, As It Pays $2 Billion for the Tussauds Empire," *The Wall Street Journal*, Mar. 6, 2007, p. C3; Penni Crabtree, "Legoland to Grow Again," *San Diego Union-Tribune*, Nov. 7, 2007, www.signonsandiego.com; "Merlin Outlines Three Key Reasons Behind Its Gardaland Purchase," *Leisure Report*, Dec. 2006, p. 10; "Roll Up, Roll Up," *The Economist*, July 7, 2007, p. 66.

b. "BBB Reports Nearly One in Five Adult Americans' Trust in Business Decreased in Past Year," Better Business Bureau, http://sev.prnewswire.com/banking-financial-services/20071109/DC0684008112007-1.html, Nov. 8, 2007 (accessed April 2, 2008); "Consumer Reports Survey Discovers People Hate Cell Phone Companies," *The Consumerist,* http://consumerist.com/consumer/notag/consumer-reports-survey-discovers-people-hate-cell-phone-companies-331041.php, Dec. 6, 2007 (accessed Apr. 9, 2008).

c. Jeffrey Ball, "The Carbon-Neutral Vacation," *The Wall Street Journal,* July 28, 2007, p. P1; Donna Hogan, "Hotels Thinking 'Green,'" *(Mesa, Arizona) Tribune,* Aug. 19, 2007, www.eastvalleytribune.com.

Chapter 14

1. "Cryo-Trans, Martin-Brower Announce Rail Transportation Milestone," *Refrigerated and Frozen Foods,* www.refrigeratedfrozenfood.com/article2.php?ida=21871 (accessed Feb. 12, 2008); Lillian Kafka, "For Rail-Sent Fries, Supersized Benefits," MHW Group, white paper, November 1, 2006, www.mhwgroup.com/Documentation/Manassas%20Rail%20Article.doc; Amanda Loudin, "Freezing Transport Costs in Their Tracks," *Inbound Logistics,* Jan. 2007, pp. 251–254, www.inboundlogistics.com/articles/casebook/casebook0107.shtml.

2. Kenneth Karel Boyer, Markham T. Frolich, G. Tomas, and M. Hult, *Extending the Supply Chain* (New York: AMACOM, 2005).

3. Ricky W. Griffin, *Principles of Management* (Boston: Houghton Mifflin, 2007), p. 400.

4. Lisa Harrington, "Getting Service Parts Logistics Up to Speed," *Inbound Logistics,* Nov. 2006, www.inboundlogistics.com/articles/features/1106_feature02.shtml.

5. *The Supply Chain Management Spending Report, 2006–2007* (AMR Research).

6. Soonhong Min, John Mentzer, and Robert T. Ladd, "A Market Orientation in Supply Chain Management," *Journal of the Academy of Marketing Science* 35 (2007): 507–522.

7. Anthony J. Dukes, Esther Gal-Or, and Kannan Srinivasan, "Channel Bargaining with Retailer Asymmetry," *Journal of Marketing Research* 43 (Feb. 2006).

8. Stewart Scharf, "Grainger: Tooled Up for Growth," *Business Week,* Apr. 25, 2006, p. 8.

9. "Ocean Spray and PepsiCo Form Strategic Alliance," Ocean Spray, press release, July 13, 2006, www.oceanspray.com/news/pr/pressrelease104.aspx.

10. Leo Aspinwall, "The Marketing Characteristics of Goods," in *Four Marketing Theories* (Boulder, CO: University of Colorado Press, 1961), pp. 27–32.

11. Wroe Alderson, *Dynamic Marketing Behavior* (Homewood, IL: Irwin, 1965), p. 239.

12. Andrew Martin, "The Package May Say Healthy, but This Grocer Begs to Differ," *The New York Times,* Nov. 6, 2006, www.nytimes.com.

13. Scott Kilman, "Smithfield to Buy Hog Farmer Premium Standard," *The Wall Street Journal,* Sept. 19, 2006, p. A12, http://online.wsj.com.

14. Hans Greimel, "Japan Tobacco Buying Gallaher for $14.7B," *BusinessWeek Online,* Dec. 15, 2006, www.businessweek.com/; Andrew Morse and Jason Singer, "Japan Returns to Global Stage as an Acquirer," *The Wall Street Journal,* Dec. 16, 2006, p. A1, http://online.wsj.com.

15. Pete Engardio, with Michael Arndt and Dean Foust, "The Future of Outsourcing," *BusinessWeek,* Jan. 30, 2006, pp. 50–58.

16. Vicki O'Meara, "Take a Deep Breath Before Diving into Global Outsourcing," *Inbound Logistics,* Sept. 2007, p. 36.

17. Lee Pender, "The Basic Links of SCM," Supply Chain Management Research Center, www.cio.com/research/scm/edit/020501_basic.html (accessed Feb. 12, 2007).

18. Merrill Douglas, "From Doughnuts to Dollars," *Inbound Logistics,* Nov. 2006, pp. 85–87.

19. Claire Swedberg, "Daisy Brand Benefits from RFID Analytics," *RFIDJournal,* Jan. 18, 2008, www.rfidjournal.com/article/articleview/3860/1/1/.

20. "RFID Eying Bright Future," *Inbound Logistics,* Sept. 2007, pp. 25–26.

21. Amanda Loudin, "Giving Voice to Warehouse Productivity," *Inbound Logistics,* Nov. 2006, pp. 81–83.

22. Anne T. Coughlan, Erin Anderson, Louis W. Stern, and Adel I. El-Ansary, *Marketing Channels* (Upper Saddle River, NJ: Prentice-Hall, 2001), p. 510.

23. Merrill Douglas, "Taking an Eagle's-Eye View," *Inbound Logistics,* July 2007, pp. 20–22.

24. Accuship, www.accuship.com/ (accessed Jan. 23, 2008).

25. Anne T. Coughlan, Erin Anderson, Louis W. Stern, and Adel I. El-Ansary, *Marketing Channels* (Upper Saddle River, NJ: Prentice-Hall, 2001), pp. 368–369.

26. Sources: *Netflix,* www.netflix.com (accessed July 17, 2008); Associated Press Staff Writer, "Movie rental giant Netflix rolls out is post-postal plan," *New York Daily News,* May 21, 2008, www.nydailynews.com/money/2008/05/21/2008-05-21_movie_rental_giant_netflix_rolls_out_its-1.html (accessed July 17, 2008); Associated Press Staff Writer, "Microsoft's Xbox 360 to stream Netflix movies," *New York Daily News,* July 14, 2008, www.nydailynews.com/money/2008/07/14/2008-07-14_microsofts_xbox_360_to_stream_netflix_mo.html (accessed July 17, 2008).

27. Sources: Alan Earls, "Valuing Exchanges," *Industrial Distribution,* Sept. 2000, p. E15; Victoria Fraza, "Grainger Branches Out," *Industrial Distribution,* Nov. 2003, p. 18; "Grainger at a Glance," W. W. Grainger, http://pressroom.grainger.com/phoenix.zhtml?c=194987&p=irol-factsheet (accessed Feb. 8, 2008); "Grainger Retreats, Closes Material Logic," *Industrial Distribution,* June 2001, p. 19; "Grainger Sets Growth Course by Expanding Market Presence," *PR Newswire,* Oct. 9, 2003, www.prnewswire.com; "Grainger Spruces Up Branches; Now Has Retail Look and Feel," *Purchasing,* July 14, 2005, pp. 121–125; "Grainger Takes New Look at Unplanned MRO Purchases," *Purchasing,* Sept. 1, 2005, pp. 53–55; James P. Miller, "Firm to Close Its Troubled Chicago-Area 'E-Procurement' Business," *Chicago Tribune,* Apr. 24, 2001, www.chicago.tribune.com; "Top Distributor Talks Business," *Industrial Distribution,* June 1, 2003, p. 46; "W. W. Grainger," Hoover's Online, www.hoovers.com (accessed Feb. 8, 2008).

Feature box references

a. Jennifer Alsever, "Wind Power the Home Edition," *Business 2.0,* Jan/Feb 2007; Southwest Windpower, www.windenergy.com/index_wind.htm (accessed Feb. 1, 2008); Skystream 3.7, Southwest Windpower, www.skystreamenergy.com/skystream/product-info/ (accessed Feb. 1, 2008); Skystream 3.7 factsheet, Southwest Windpower, www.skystreamenergy.com/documents/datasheets/skystream_%203.7t_datasheet.pdf (accessed Feb. 1, 2008).

b. Daniel Fisher, "A Dirty Game," *Forbes,* Mar. 10, 2008, pp. 38–40; Jim Rogers, "Point of View: A New Model for Energy Efficiency," *The News & Observer,* Feb. 19, 2008 (accessed Mar. 26, 2008 at www.newsobserver.com/print/tuesday/opinion/story/951188.html); "Greenwashing," *The Dictionary of Sustainable Management,* www.sustainabilitydictionary.com/g/greenwashing.php (accessed Mar. 26, 2008).

c. "Blue Bell Creameries' Sweet Success: Ice Cream Manufacturer Improves Inventory Visibility & Lot Control with ClearOrbit," *Business Wire,* July 11, 2007, www.allbusiness.com/services/

business-services/4520976-1.html; "Blue Bell Creameries L.P.," www.referenceforbusiness.com/history2/63/Blue-Bell-Creameries-L-P.html (accessed Feb. 4, 2008); Amanda Loudin, "Blue Bell Creameries Licks Its Storage Shortage," *Inbound Logistics,* Oct. 2007, pp. 77, 79.

Chapter 15

1. Laura Paskus, "Owner Won't Melt under Stress of Ice Cream Niche Business," *New Mexico Business Weekly,* July 27–August 2, 2007, p. 15; Bob Quick, "Ice-Cream Dreams," *The New Mexican,* May 10, 2005, www.freenewmexican .com/news/13589.html; "Tara's Gets Organic in New Mexico," *Ice Cream Reporter,* Oct. 20, 2005, www.allbusiness.com/ manufacturing/food-manufacturing-dairy-product-ice-cream/ 592756-1.html; Tara's Organic Ice Cream, www.tarasorganic .com/ (accessed Jan. 21, 2008).

2. U.S. Bureau of the Census, *Statistical Abstract of the United States, 2008* (Washington, DC: U.S. Government Printing Office, 2007), pp. 649, 651.

3. "Growth Retail Markets Worldwide 2007," Planet Retail, Apr. 2007, www.planetretail.net.

4. Ann Zimmerman and Kris Hudson, "Looking Upscale, Wal-Mart Begins a Big Makeover," *The Wall Street Journal,* Sept. 17, 2005, p. A1, http://online.wsj.com; Robert Berner, "Watch Out, Best Buy and Circuit City," *Business Week,* Nov. 21, 2005, pp. 46–48.

5. Wal-Mart Fact Sheet, Hoover's Online, www.hoovers.com/ wal-mart/—ID__11600—/free-co-factsheet.xhtml (accessed Jan. 18, 2008).

6. "Testing Ground, Why the Convenience Channel Is the Ideal Environment to Spur Consumer Trial," *Stagnito's New Products Magazine,* May 2005, p. 38.

7. National Association of Convenience Stores, Sept. 2007, www.nacsonline.com/NACS/Resource/PRToolkit/FactSheets/ prtk_fact_nacs.htm.

8. Elizabeth Esfahani, "7-Eleven Gets Sophisticated," *Business 2.0,* Jan./Feb. 2005, pp. 93–100.

9. Stanley Holmes, "The Jack Welch of the Meat Aisle; Former GE Exec Larry Johnston Brings High-Tech to Troubled Albertson's," *Business Week,* Jan. 24, 2005, p. 60.

10. Sam's Club Fact Sheet, Costco Wholesale Corporation Fact Sheet, B.J.'s Wholesale Club Fact Sheet, Hoover's Online, www.hoovers.com/free (accessed Jan. 18, 2008).

11. Janet Adamy, "For Subway, Every Nook and Cranny on the Planet Is Possible Site for a Franchise," *The Wall Street Journal,* Sept. 1, 2006, p. A11, http://online.wsj.com.

12. Mall of America, www.mallofamerica.com/ (accessed Jan. 18, 2008).

13. Kurt Blumenau, "Are Target, Best Buy Really Upscale? Owners of 'Lifestyle' Shopping Centers Still Signing Retail Tenants," *The [Allentown, Pennsylvania] Morning Call,* May 29, 2005, via LexisNexis; Debra Hazel, "Wide-Open Spaces," *Chain Store Age,* Nov. 2005, p. 120; "ICSC Shopping Center Definitions," International Council of Shopping Centers, http://icsc.org/srch/lib/USDefinitions.pdf (accessed Jan. 24, 2008); Greg Lindsay, "Say Goodbye to the Mall," *Advertising Age,* Oct. 2, 2006, p. 13.

14. Stephanie Kang, "After a Slump, Payless Tries on Fashion for Size," *The Wall Street Journal,* Feb. 10, 2007, p. A1, http://online.wsj.com.

15. Velitchka D. Kaltcheva and Barton A. Weitz, "When Should a Retailer Create an Exciting Store Environment?" *Journal of Marketing* 70 (Jan. 2006).

16. Mindy Fetterman and Jayne O'Donnell, "Just Browsing at the Mall? That's What You Think," *USA Today,* Sept. 1, 2006, http://usatoday.com.

17. Anick Bosmans, "Scents and Sensibility: When Do (In)Congruent Ambient Scents Influence Product Evaluations?" *Journal of Marketing* 70 (July 2006).

18. "Store Atmospherics Provide Competitive Edge," *Chain Store Age,* Dec. 2005, p. 74.

19. Stephen Brown, "The Wheel of Retailing: Past and Future," *Journal of Retailing,* Summer 1990, pp. 143–149.

20. "Direct Marketing Expenditures Account for 50% of Total Advertising Expenditures, DMA's 2007 'Power of Direct Marketing' Report Reveals," Direct Marketing Association, press release, Oct. 16, 2007, www.the-dma.org/cgi/disppressrelease?article=1015.

21. "Direct Marketing an $8 Billion Auto Industry Driver," *Brandweek,* Jan. 28, 2008, www.brandweek.com/bw/ news/recent_display.jsp?vnu_content_id=1003702944.

22. "Current Do Not Call Registrations," Federal Trade Commission, Oct. 5, 2007, www.ftc.gov/bcp/edu/microsites/donotcall/ pdfs/DNC-Registrations-10-05-20071.pdf.

23. "National Do-Not-Call Registry," Federal Trade Commission, https://www.donotcall.gov/ (accessed Jan. 18, 2008).

24 "FTC Announces Law Enforcement Crackdown on Do Not Call Violators," Federal Trade Commission, press release, Nov. 7, 2007, www.ftc.gov/opa/2007/11/dncpress.shtm.

25. Sucharita Mulpuru, "US eCommerce Forecast: 2008 to 2012," Forrester Research, Jan. 18, 2008, www.forrester.com/ Research/Document/Excerpt/0,7211,41592,00.html.

26. Lucinda Hahn, "Pampered Life," *Chicago Tribune,* Jan. 18, 2005, p. 1.

27. "Fact Sheet: U.S. Direct Selling in 2006," *Direct Selling Association,* www.dsa.org/pubs/numbers/ 06gofactsheet.pdf (accessed Jan. 18, 2008).

28 "Vending Machines Go Luxe," *Business Week,* Jan. 28, 2008, p. 17.

29. International Franchise Association, www.franchise.org (accessed Jan. 18, 2008).

30. Raymund Flandez, "New Franchise Idea: Fewer Rules, More Difference," *The Wall Street Journal,* Sept. 18, 2007, http:// online.wsj.com.

31. U.S. Bureau of the Census, *Statistical Abstract of the United States, 2008,* p. 647.

32. "Genuine Parts Company," Hoover's Online, www.hoovers .com/genuine-parts/—ID__10646—/free-co-factsheet.xhtml (accessed Jan. 18, 2008).

33. "Universal Corporation," Hoover's Online, www.hoovers.com/ universal-corporation/—ID__11564—/free-co-factsheet.xhtml (accessed Jan. 18, 2008).

34. "Red River Commodities, Inc.," Hoover's Online, www.hoovers .com/red-river-commodities/—ID__127954—/free-co-factsheet .xhtml (accessed Jan. 18, 2008); Red River Commodities, Inc., www.redriv.com (accessed Jan. 18, 2008).

35. Sources: Lucas Conley, "Climbing Back Up the Mountain," *Fast Company Magazine,* Issue 93, April 2005; Eastern Mountain Sports Climbing School, www.emsclimb.com; Drew Robb, "Eastern Mountain Sports: Getting Smarter with Each Sale," *Computer World,* Sept. 18, 2006, www.computerworld.com/action/article.do?command= viewArticleBasic&articleId=112778 (accessed July 15, 2008); Staff Writer, "JDA announces new software for softlines retailers," *Business Services Industry,* Aug. 7, 1996, http://findarticles.com/p/articles/mi_m0EIN/is_1996_August_ 7/ai_18568223 (accessed July 15, 2008); Lynette Carpiet, "EMS Expands in Northeast," *Bicycle Retailer and Industry News,* May 1, 2008, Volume 17, Issue 7.

36. Sources: "The Costco Way," *Business Week,* Apr. 12, 2004, www.businessweek.com/magazine/content/04_15/b3878084_ mz021.htm; Doug Desjardins, "Costco Comps Up 7%, Despite 4Q Lag," *DSN Retailing Today,* Oct. 27, 2003, p. 8;

Doug Desjardins, "Costco Home to Expand in '04," *DSN Retailing Today,* Dec. 15, 2003, p. 8; John Helyar, "The Only Company Wal-Mart Fears," *Fortune,* Nov. 24, 2003, p. 158; Kris Hudson, "Warehouses Go Luxe," *The Wall Street Journal,* Nov. 11, 2005, p. B1, http://online.wsj.com/public/us; "Investor Relations: Company Profile," Costco, http://phx.corporate-ir.net/phoenix.zhtml?c=83830&p=irol-homeprofile (accessed Jan. 25, 2008).

37. Sources: Better Way (Thailand) Company, www.mistine.co.th; Grammy Entertainment Public Company, www.gmmgrammy.com; RS Promotion Public Company, www.rs-promotion.co.th; Total Access Communication Public Company, www.dtac.co.th; "Mistine," Superbrands International, Nov. 24, 2004, www.superbrandsinternational.com/thailand/vol1/images/member/pdf/Mistine_TH20041229.pdf; Jaturong Kobkaew, *King of Direct Sales* (Bangkok: Thai Public Relations and Publishing, 2002); Anuwat Dharamadhaj, "How Direct Selling Is Regulated and Managed in Different Markets in Thailand," 2002, www.hkdsa.org.hk/symposium/anuwatppt.pdf; "U*Star and GMM Grammy Artists," Krungthep Turakij, Oct. 2, 2004, www.bangkokbiznews.com; "Branding for Direct Selling," *Business Thai,* Dec. 12, 2003, http://bcm.arip.co.th; "Direct Selling," *Marketeer,* Sept. 2003, p. 62; "U*Star to the Market," GoToManager, Sept. 13, 2003, www.gotomanager.com; "Direct Selling War," Krungthep Turakij, Mar. 24, 2003, www.bangkokbiznews.com; "Big Five Direct Sellers," *Business Thai,* Oct. 12, 2001, http://bcm.arip.co.th; MK621 Competitive Strategies in Marketing; Reports on Thailand Direct Selling from MIM Class 16, Thammasat University, 2004; MIM Class 17, Thammasat University, 2005, prepared this case under the direction of Dr. O. C. Ferrell, Colorado State University, and Dr. Linda Ferrell, University of Wyoming, as the basis for classroom discussion.

Feature box references

a. Starbucks Corporation 2007 Annual Report, Mar. 2008. http://media.corporate-ir.net/media_files/irol/99/99518/2007AR.pdf (accessed Mar. 17, 2008); Bruce Horovitz, "Starbucks Aims Beyond Lattes to Extend Brand to Films, Music and Books," *USA Today,* May 19, 2006, pp. A1, A2; Neil Merrett, "Starbucks Trims Fat to Meet Dairy Demands," Dairyreporter.Com, June 5, 2007, http://dairyreporter.com/news/ng.asp?id577070-starbucks-milk-low-fat-obesity (accessed Mar. 17, 2008).

b. Mindy Fetterman, "Wal-Mart Grows 'Green' Strategies," *USA Today,* Sept. 25, 2006, www.usatoday.com/money/industries/retail/2006-09-24-wal-mart-cover-usat_x.htm; "Renewable Energy," Wal-Mart, http://walmartstores.com/GlobalWMStoresWeb/navigate.do?catg5347 (accessed Feb. 14, 2008); Justin Thomas, "Wal-Mart Creates Its Own Electricity Company, Eyes Wind Power," *The Dallas Morning News,* Jan. 29, 2007; "Wal-Mart & Its Hybrid Trucks," *Energy Smart,* Mar. 19, 2007, http://energysmart.wordpress.com/2007/03/19/wal-mart-its-hybrid-trucks/.

c. Christine, "Fatburger's Market Entry Strategy in China," The China Business Network, Nov. 15, 2007, http://thechinabusinessnetwork.com/Hospitality-and-F-B/Fatburger-s-Market-Entry-Strategy-In-China.html; "Fatburger Corporation," bNet, via http://findarticles.com/p/articles/mi_gx5202/is_1993/ai_n19122231/pg_1 (accessed Feb. 14, 2008); Dennis McLellan, "Lovie Yancey, 96," *The Los Angeles Times,* Feb. 2, 2008, www.latimes.com/features/food.

Chapter 16

1. Sources: CoreStreet, www.corestreet.com/solutions/prod_tech/id/ (accessed Feb. 12, 2008); Monica Heger, "Super Marketing," *Business 2.0,* Mar. 2007, p. 44; Microsoft Office comic strip, www.enchantedoffice.com/ (accessed Feb. 12, 2008); "Pivman: For First Response," www.corestreet.com/about/library/other/pivman_comic-lores.pdf (accessed Feb. 12, 2008).

2. Martin Wodarz, "Paint the Town Ted: Launching an Airline Using IMC Principles," *Journal of Integrated Marketing Communications,* 2006, pp. 28–33.

3. Judith A. Garretson and Scot Burton, "The Role of Spokespersons as Advertisement and Package Cues in Integrated Marketing Communications," *Journal of Marketing* 69 (Oct. 2005): 118–135.

4. Prasad A. Naik and Kalyon Raman, "Understanding the Impact of Synergy in Multimedia Communications," *Journal of Marketing Research,* Nov. 2003, pp. 375–388.

5. Ibid.

6. Paul Davidson, "Free TV Shows May Air on Cell Phones," Cincinannati.com, Nov. 8, 2007, http://cincinnati.gns.gannetonline.com/apps/pbcs.dll/article?AID=/20071108/TECH01/703080773/1001/TECH.

7. Allison Fass, "A Kingdom Seeks Magic," *Forbes,* Oct. 16, 2006, pp. 68–70.

8. Louise Story, "Programmed to Sell," *The New York Times,* Nov. 10, 2006, pp. C1, C4.

9. Enid Burns, "Online Ads Influence Collegiate Set," ClickZ, Feb. 10, 2006, www.clickz.com/stats/sectors/demographics/article.php/3584441.

10. In case you do not read Chinese, the message, prepared by Chih Kang Wang, says, "In the factory we make cosmetics, and in the store we sell hope."

11. Terence A. Shimp, *Advertising, Promotion, and Supplemental Aspects of Integrated Marketing Communications* (Cincinnati: South-Western, 2003), p. 81.

12. Judy A. Wagner, Noreen M. Klein, and Janet E. Keith, "Selling Strategies: The Effects of Suggesting a Decision Structure to Novice and Expert Buyers," *Journal of the Academy of Marketing Science* 29, no. 3 (2001): 289–306.

13. Salvador Ruiz and María Sicilia, "The Impact of Cognitive and/or Affective Processing Styles on Consumer Response to Advertising Appeals," *Journal of Business Research* 57 (2004): 657–664.

14. Anton Piësch, "Speaking in Tongues," *Inc.,* June 2003, p. 50.

15. Samuel D. Bradley III and Robert Meeds, "The Effects of Sentence-Level Context, Prior Word Knowledge, and Need for Cognition on Information Processing of Technical Language in Print Ads," *Journal of Consumer Psychology* 14, no. 3 (2004): 291–302.

16. Mathew Boyle, "Atkins World," *Fortune,* Jan. 12, 2004, pp. 94–96.

17. David M. Szymanski, "Modality and Offering Effects in Sales Presentations for a Good Versus a Service," *Journal of the Academy of Marketing Science* 29, no. 2 (2001): 179–189.

18. "Report: Anheuser-Busch to Boost TV Ad Spending by $100M," *The Business Journal of Milwaukee,* Nov. 19, 2007, www.bizjournals.com/milwaukee/stories/2007/11/19/daily3.html.

19. "Yoplait Is Committed to Fighting Breast Cancer!" Yoplait, www.yoplait.com/breastcancer_commitment.aspx (accessed Feb. 13, 2008).

20. Emily Bryson York, "McDonald's Introduces Half-Pound Breakfast Burrito," *Advertising Age,* Nov. 27, 2007, www.adage.com.

21. "Inside Chrysler's Celine Dion Advertising Disaster," *Advertising Age,* Nov. 24, 2003, www.adage.com/news.cms?news ID_39262; Thomas Mucha, "Why the Caveman Loves the Pitchman," *Business 2.0,* Apr. 2005, p. 39.

22. "Bennigan's Celebrates 30th Anniversary with Irish Bash," *Promo,* Jan. 12, 2006, http://promomagazine.com/eventmarketing/bennigans_30anniversary_011206/.

23. Amy Johannes, "Mars Pushes Caffeinated Snickers via College Sampling," *Promo*, Jan. 29, 2008, http://promomagazine.com/sampling/mar_pushes_caffeinated_snickers_college_0129/.

24. Amy Johannes, "Regal Entertainment Group Loyalty Club Hits 10 Million Members," *Promo*, Nov. 28, 2007, http://promomagazine.com/incentives/regal_entertainment_loyalty/.

25. Vinnee Tong, "Tattoos, Once a Symbol of Rebellion, Now Are Advertising Cars, Tires, Energy Drinks," *The Austin American-Statesman*, Nov. 27, 2007, www.statesman.com.

26. "2007 U.S. National Edition Rates," *Time*, www.time.com/time/mediakit/1/us/timemagazine/rates/national/index.html (accessed Dec. 4, 2007).

27. Vicki R. Lane, "The Impact of Ad Repetition and Ad Content on Consumer Perceptions of Incongruent Extensions," *Journal of Marketing*, Apr. 2000, pp. 80–91.

28. Joann Peck and Jennifer Wiggins, "It Just Feels Good: Customers' Affective Response to Touch and Its Influence in Persuasion," *Journal of Marketing* 70 (Oct. 2006).

29. "Got Milk," National Fluid Milk Processor Promotion Board, www.milknewsroom.com/index.htm (accessed Feb. 13, 2008).

30. Beth Snyder Bulik, "Nintendo 'Maximi'-izes to Lure Older Generation of Gamers," *Advertising Age*, Feb. 7, 2005, p. 8.

31. Colleen DeBaise, "To Draw Women Investors, Firms Appeal to Senses," *Marketing News*, Feb. 15, 2005, p. 14.

32. Kiri Blakely, "Secrets of Celebrity Swag Season," *Forbes*, Feb. 12, 2008, www.forbes.com/business/2008/02/11/hollywood-celebrity-retailing-biz-media_cz_kb_0212swag.html.

33. Mya Frazier, "Wal-Mart Looks to Refurbish Image with Political-Style Ads," *Advertising Age*, Jan. 8, 2007, http://adage.com/article?article_id=114179.

34. "Alltel Sweeps Promotes Friends Calling Feature," *Promo Magazine*, Feb. 16, 2007, http://promomagazine.com/news/alltel_friends_calling_features_021607/.

35. Harald J. Van Heerde, Sachin Gupta, and Dick R. Wittink, "Is 75% of the Sales Promotion Bump Due to Brand Switching? No, Only 33% Is," *Journal of Marketing Research*, Nov. 2003, pp. 481–491.

36. Suzanne Vranica, "At MTV, a New Show that Pushes Deodorant," *The Wall Street Journal*, Sept. 13, 2007, p. A1, http://online.wsj.com.

37. Xueming Luo and Naveen Donthu, "Marketing's Credibility: A Longitudinal Investigation of Marketing Communications Productivity and Shareholder Value," *Journal of Marketing* 70 (Oct. 2006).

38. Normandy Madden, "How a Chinese Dairy Plans to Become a Global Brand," *Advertising Age*, Jan. 29, 2007, p. 31.

39. Rockney G. Walters and Maqbul Jamil, "Exploring the Relationships Between Shopping Trip Type, Purchases of Products on Promotion, and Shopping Basket Profit," *Journal of Business Research* 56 (2003): 17–29.

40. Geoffrey A. Fowler, "China Bans Nike's LeBron Ad as Offensive to Nation's Dignity," *The Wall Street Journal*, Dec. 7, 2004, http://online.wsj.com/.

41. John Eaton, "e-Word-of-Mouth Marketing," Teaching Module, Houghton Mifflin Company, 2006.

42. *Florian v. Wangenheim* and Tomás Bayón, "The Chain from Customer Satisfaction via Word-of-Mouth Referrals to New Customer Acquisition," *Journal of the Academy of Marketing Science* 35 (June 2007): 233–249.

43. Pratibha A. Dabholkar, "Factors Influencing Consumer Choice of a 'Rating Web Site': An Experimental Investigation of an Online Interactive Decision Aid," *Journal of Marketing Theory and Practice* 14 (Fall 2006): 259–273.

44. "The New Realities of a Low-Trust World," *Advertising Age*, February 13, 2006, www.adage.com.

45. Jamin Warren and John Jurgensen, "The Wizards of Buzz," *The Wall Street Journal*, Feb. 10–11, 2007, pp. P1, P4.

46. Sarah Kugler, "Hats Off to NY Fashion," *Houston Chronicle*, Jan. 9, 2007, www.chron.com/disp/story.mpl/life/4458016.html.

47. Pam Belluck, "Company Will Pay Boston After Scare Over Ads," *The New York Times*, Feb. 2, 2007, www.nytimes.com.

48. Allison Fass, "A Kingdom Seeks Magic," *Forbes*, Oct. 16, 2006, pp. 68–70.

49. Kenneth Hein, "Putting the 'I' in Viral Makes Web Ads Infections," *Brandweek*, Dec. 3, 2007, www.brandweek.com/bw/news/recent_display.jsp?vnu_content_id=1003680009; T. L. Stanley, "Eat That, Subservient Chicken: OfficeMax Site Draws 36M," *Advertising Age*, Jan. 29, 2007, pp. 4, 35.

50. Scott D. Lewis, "Fiona Apple vs. Sony," *The Oregonian*, Apr. 15, 2005, p. D1.

51. Lynna Goch, "The Place to Be," *Best's Review*, Feb. 2005, pp. 64–65.

52. Gail Schiller, "'30 Rock' Rolls Ads into Story Lines," Reuters UK, Nov. 28, 2007, http://uk.reuters.com/article/entertainmentNews/idUKN2833828120071128.

53. Vranica, "At MTV, a New Show that Pushes Deodorant."

54. Emma Hall, "Product Placement Faces Wary Welcome in Britain," *Advertising Age*, Jan. 8, 2007, p. 27.

55. "T-Mobile Pays $135,000 to Settle City's Lawsuit for Deceptive Ads," New York City Department of Consumer Affairs, press release, Dec. 14, 2005, www.nyc.gov/html/dca/html/pr2005/pr_121405.shtml.

56. Sources: *The Toledo Mud Hens*, www.mudhens.com (accessed July 14, 2008); *The Detroit Tigers*, http://tigers.mlb.com (accessed July 14, 2008).

57. Sources: "Columbia Sportswear Named Official Apparel Sponsor of Jeep Ski/Snowboard Series," The Auto Channel, Dec. 1, 2005, www.theautochannel.com/news/2005/12/01/153912. html; Erica Iacono, "Corporate Case Study—Columbia Sportswear Speaks to Many with One Voice," *PR Week*, Jan. 16, 2006; George Anders, "Drama's Profitable at Sportswear Maker—Columbia Run by Mother and Son," *The Seattle Times*, Oct. 12, 2005; Columbia Sportswear Press Release, *Columbia Sportswear Company Announces Butler, Shine, Stern & Partners as Advertising Agency of Record*, Apr. 21, 2008, http://columbia.com/who/press_release.aspx?type=c&id=178 (accessed May 23, 2008); Columbia Sportswear, www.columbia.com (accessed May 23, 2008).

Feature box references

a. "American Entertainment Icon Lloyd Price and His New Food Brand Lawdy Miss Clawdy 'Sweet Potato Cookies,' An Original Lloyd Price Recipe," Lloyd Price Icon Food Brands Press Release, http://blacknews.com/pr/lawdymissclawdycookies101.html (accessed Feb. 15, 2008); Lawdy Miss Clawdy, www.lawdymissclawdy.com/iconbrands.htm (accessed Feb. 15, 2008); Robert Tomsho, "The Sweet Potato Is Everybody's Friend, But a Fleeting One," *The Wall Street Journal*, Nov. 21, 2007, pp. A1, A16.

b. Megha Bahree, "Bag Lady," *Forbes*, Nov. 26, 2007, pp. 109–110, http://members.forbes.com/forbes/2007/1126/109.html (accessed Feb. 15, 2008); Lisa McLaughlin, "Paper, Plastic or Prada?" *Time*, Aug. 13, 2007, pp. 49–51.

c. Raja Mishra and John R. Ellement, "Marketing Treasure Hunt Trips in Historic Graveyard," *Boston Globe Online*, http://boston.com/news/local/articles/2007/02/23/marketing_treasure_hunt_trips_in_historic_graveyard, Feb. 23, 2007 (accessed Mar. 17, 2008); Katie Zezima, "Boston Reaches Settlement in Bomb Scare," *New York Times Online*, http://nytimes.com/2007/02/05/us/05cnd-hoax.html, Feb. 5, 2007, (accessed Mar. 17, 2008); Paul R. La Monica, "'Aqua Teen' Movie Tries Not to Bomb," CNNMoney.com, http://money.cnn.com/2007/04/05/news/companies/aquateen/index.htm (accessed Mar. 24, 2008).

Chapter 17

1. Sources: Susan Gunelius, "Womenkind Uses Women to Create Ads," *Brand Curve,* Nov. 21, 2007, www.brandcurve.com/womenkind-uses-women-to-create-ads/; Andrew McMains, "Womenkind Opens Doors," *AdWeek,* Nov. 16, 2007, www.adweek.com/aw/national/article_display.jsp?vnu_content_id=1003673910; Susanne Vranica, "Ads Made for Women, by Women," *The Wall Street Journal,* Nov. 21, 2007, p. B3.
2. Kenneth Hein, "McDonald's Blasted for Advertising on Report Cards," *BrandWeek,* Dec. 6, 2007, www.brandweek.com/bw/news/recent_display.jsp?vnu_content_id=1003681819&imw=Y.
3. Aaron O. Patrick, "U.K. Spends Millions Nagging Its Citizens," *The Wall Street Journal,* Jan. 24, 2006, p. B1, http://online.wsj.com/public/us.
4. "100 Leading National Advertisers," *Advertising Age,* June 25, 2007, p. S-4.
5. "Texas Tourism Debuts New Advertising Campaign with TM Advertising," Fox Business, Feb. 11, 2008, www.foxbusiness.com/article/texas-tourism-debuts-new-advertising-campaign-tm-advertising_474179_1.html.
6. Cornelia Pechmann, Guangzhi Zhao, Marvin E. Goldberg, and Elen Thomas Reibling, "What to Convey in Antismoking Advertisements for Adolescents: The Use of Protection Motivation Theory to Identify Effective Message Themes," *Journal of Marketing,* Apr. 2003, pp. 1–18.
7. Kate Macarthur, "Quiznos Launches 'Aggressive' Ad Effort Against Subway," *Advertising Age,* Sept. 20, 2006, www.adage.com.
8. Della de Lafuente, "American Takes Latinos Home for the Holidays," *Brandweek,* Nov. 19, 2007, www.brandweek.com/bw/news/leisuretrav/article_display.jsp?vnu_content_id=1003674048.
9. Joe Pereira, "New Balance Sneaker Ads Jab at Pro Athletes' Pretentions," *The Wall Street Journal,* Mar. 10, 2005, p. B1.
10. Ibid.
11. Ibid.
12. "U.S. Search Marketing Spending to 2010," *Advertising Age, Special Marketing Fact Pack,* Nov. 6, 2006, p. 6.
13. "Internet to Top Radio in Ad Spending, Forecaster Says," *USA Today,* Dec. 3, 2007, www.usatoday.com.
14. Jeremy Mullman, "Big Brewers Gut Ad Spend, Sell More Bear," *Advertising Age,* Sept. 24, 2007, www.adage.com.
15. Ilona A. Berney-Reddish and Charles S. Areni, "Sex Differences in Responses to Probability Markers in Advertising Claims," *Journal of Advertising* 35 (Summer 2006): 7–17.
16. Daniel J. Howard and Roger A. Kerin, "The Effects of Personalized Product Recommendations on Advertisement Response Rates: The 'Try This. It Works!' Technique," *Journal of Consumer Psychology* 14, no. 3 (2004): 271–279.
17. Pamela W. Henderson, Joan L. Giese, and Joseph A. Cote, "Impression Management Using Typeface Design," *Journal of Marketing* 68 (Oct. 2004): 60–72.
18. Rik Pieters and Michel Wedel, "Attention Capture and Transfer in Advertising: Brand, Pictorial, and Text-Size Effects," *Journal of Marketing* 68 (Apr. 2004): 36–50.
19. Eric Newman, "Wendy's Flips Its Wig," *Brandweek,* Jan. 28, 2008, www.brandweek.com/bw/search/article_display.jsp?vnu_content_id=1003702918.
20. Brock Vergakis, "Utah Tourism Spike Stifles Critics of Campaign," *Marketing News,* Feb. 1, 2007, p. 16.
21. Mya Frazier, "This Ad Will Give You a Headache, but It Sells," *Advertising Age,* Sept. 24, 2007, www.adage.com.
22. Stefano Puntoni and Nader T. Tavassoli, "Social Context and Advertising Memory," *Journal of Marketing Research* XLIV (May 2007).
23. Peter J. Danaher and Guy W. Mullarkey, "Factors Affecting Online Advertising Recall: A Study of Students," *Journal of Advertising Research* 43 (2003): 252–267.
24. "Media Campaign Fact Sheets," Office of National Drug Control Policy, www.mediacampaign.org/newsroom/factsheets/accomplishments.html (accessed Feb. 18, 2008).
25. Stuart Elliott, "Army's New Battle Cry Aims at Potential Recruits," *The New York Times,* Nov. 9, 2006, www.nytimes.com.
26. "Martha Bermudez: Senior Marketing Manager Pepsi-Cola North America," *Advertising Age,* Jan. 29, 2007, p. C10.
27. George E. Belch and Michael A. Belch, *Advertising and Promotion* (Burr Ridge, IL: Irwin/McGraw-Hill, 2004), p. 570.
28. Lisa Cornwell, "P&G Launches Two Social Networking Sites," *Marketing News,* Feb. 1, 2007, p. 21.
29. Deborah L. Vence, "Serves Them Right," *Marketing News,* Feb. 1, 2005, pp. 13, 16.
30. "Whole Foods Market to Sack Disposable Plastic Grocery Bags by Earth Day," Whole Foods Markets, press release, Jan. 22, 2008, www.wholefoodsmarket.com/pressroom/pr_01-22-08.html.
31. Belch and Belch, *Advertising and Promotion,* pp. 580–581.
32. Suman Basuroy, Subimal Chatterjee, and S. Abraham Ravid, "How Critical Are Critical Reviews? The Box Office Effects of Film Critics, Star Power, and Budgets," *Journal of Marketing,* Oct. 2003, pp. 103–117.
33. Jeff Bailey, "JetBlue's CEO Is 'Mortified' After Fliers Are Stranded," *The New York Times,* Feb. 19, 2007, www.nytimes.com/; Brian Quinton, "Sticky Situations," *Promo,* Oct. 1, 2007, http://promomagazine.com/mag/marketing_sticky_situations/; Rich Thomaselli, "Management's Misjudgment Gives JetBlue a Black Eye," *Advertising Age,* Feb. 19, 2007, www.adage.com.
34. Deborah L. Vence, "Stand Guard: In Bad Times, An Ongoing Strategy Keeps Image Intact," *Marketing News,* Nov. 15, 2006, p. 15.
35. Bailey, "JetBlue's CEO Is 'Mortified' After Fliers Are Stranded"; Quinton, "Sticky Situations"; Thomaselli, "Management's Misjudgment Gives JetBlue a Black Eye."
36. Sources: Vans Shoes, www.vans.com (accessed July 16, 2008); Jason Lee, "The History of Vans," *Sneaker Freaker,* http://www.sneakerfreaker.com/feature/history-of-vans/1/ (accessed July 16, 2008); Vans: 40 Years of Originality, www.vans40.com (accessed July 17, 2008).
37. Sources: Ken Alltucker, "Wrinkle Wars Fought Through Ads, on Internet," *Marketing News,* May 1, 2007, p. 25; Medicis Pharmaceutical Corporation, www.medicis.com/ (accessed Feb. 8, 2008); "Restylane Perlane Juvederm," MichaelLawMD, www.michaellawmd.com/restylane.html (accessed Feb. 19, 2008); "Restylane Treatment in Houston," Facial Center for Plastic Surgery, www.houstonfaces.com/houston-restylane-treatments.asp (accessed Feb. 19, 2008); "Stricter Warnings Needed for Botox, Myobloc Injections," Public Citizen, press release, Jan. 24, 2008, www.citizen.org/pressroom/release.cfm?ID=2593; Hema Sundaram, "Can Revance—or Reloxin—Revamp the Wrinkle War?" HealthCentral.com, Jan. 17, 2008, www.healthcentral.com/skin-care/c/75934/19292/revamp-war/1/; "Wrinkle Treatment Gets a New Line," BuzzNation, www.brandedentertainment.tv/branded-entertainment-wrinkle_treatment_gets_a_new_line.html (accessed Feb. 10, 2008).

Feature box references

a. Avery Johnson, "Pfizer Will Pull Some Lipitor Ads in Wake of Probe," *The Wall Street Journal,* Feb. 26, 2008, p. B5, http://online.wsj.com/article/SB120396972593291395.html; Vanessa Aristide, "Pfizer Voluntarily Withdraws Lipitor

Advertising Featuring Dr. Robert Jarvik," Pfizer press release, Feb. 25, 2008, http://pfizer.com/news/press_releases/pfizer_press_releases.jsp?rssUrl5http://mediaroom.pfizer.com/portal/site/pfizer/index.jsp?ndmViewId5news_view&ndmConfigId51010794&newsId520080225006247&newsLang5en; FTC, *Better Living, Inc.* et al., 54 F.T.C. 648 (1957), aff'd, 259 F.2d 271 (3rd Cir. 1958); BBB, http://us.bbb.org/WWW-Root/SitePage.aspx?site5113&id58e20ba59-acb8-4dcf-a1e2-0cc3ab9cfbb4 (Section 14).

b. Carl Bialik, "Nielsen's New College Numbers," *The Wall Street Journal,* Feb. 9, 2007, http://wsj.com; "Nielsen Begins Including College Students Away From Home in Its National People Meter Sample," Nielsen Media Research, press release, Jan. 29, 2007, www.nielsen.com/media/pr_070129_a.html; Louise Story, "At Last, Television Ratings Go to College," *The New York Times,* Jan. 29, 2007, www.nytimes.com/.

c. Recycline, www.recycline.com/ (accessed Feb. 18, 2008); "Recycline: Sitting on Mainstream's Doorstep," Sustainable Is Good, Mar. 21, 2007, www.sustainableisgood.com/blog/2007/03/recycline_produ.html; Nitasha Tiku, "Making the Most of a Brush With Fame," *Inc.,* Aug. 2007, p. 19.

Chapter 18

1. Sources: John Sitkiewicz and Brian Walters, "Agent Évocateur," *DBusinessmag.com,* July/Aug. 2007, pp. 58–61; Sports Management Network, www.sportsmanagementnetwork.com/ (accessed Feb. 19, 2008).

2. "Research and Markets: The Cost of the Average Sales Call Today is More Than 400 Dollars," *M2 Presswire,* Feb. 28, 2006.

3. Jon M. Hawes, Anne K. Rich, and Scott M. Widmier, "Assessing the Development of the Sales Profession," *Journal of Personal Selling & Sales Management* 24 (Winter 2004): 27–37.

4. Eli Jones, Paul Busch, and Peter Dacin, "Firm Market Orientation and Salesperson Customer Orientation: Interpersonal and Intrapersonal Influence on Customer Service and Retention in Business-to-Business Buyer–Seller Relationships," *Journal of Business Research* 56 (2003): 323–340.

5. Julie T. Johnson, Hiram C. Barksdale, Jr., and James S. Boles, "Factors Associated with Customer Willingness to Refer Leads to Salespeople," *Journal of Business Research* 56 (2003): 257–263.

6. Bob Donath, "Tap Sales 'Hot Buttons' to Stay Competitive," *Marketing News,* Mar. 1, 2005, p. 8.

7. Ralph W. Giacobbe, Donald W. Jackson, Jr., Lawrence A. Crosby, and Claudia M. Bridges, "A Contingency Approach to Adaptive Selling Behavior and Sales Performance: Selling Situations and Salesperson Characteristics," *Journal of Personal Selling & Sales Management* 26 (Spring 2006): 115–142.

8. Richard G. McFarland, Goutam N. Challagalla, and Tasadduq A. Shervani, "Influence Tactics for Effective Adaptive Selling," *Journal of Marketing* 70 (Oct. 2006).

9. John Andy Wood, "NLP Revisted: Nonverbal Communications and Signals of Trustworthiness," *Journal of Personal Selling & Sales Management* 26 (Spring 2006): 198–204.

10. Stephen S. Porter, Joshua L. Wiener, and Gary L. Frankwick, "The Moderating Effect of Selling Situation on the Adaptive Selling Strategy—Selling Effectiveness Relationship," *Journal of Business Research* 56 (2003): 275–281.

11. Gary K. Hunter and William D. Perreault, Jr., "Making Sales Technology Effective," *Journal of Marketing* 71 (January 2007): 16–34.

12. Chuck Salter, "The Soft Sell," *Fast Company,* Jan. 2005, pp. 72+.

13. Fernando Jaramillo, Jay Prakash Mulki, and Paul Solomon, "The Role of Ethical Climate on Salesperson's Role Stress, Job Attitudes, Turnover Intention, and Job Performance," *Journal of Personal Selling & Sales Management* 26 (Summer 2006): 272–282.

14. Michael A. Wiles and Rosann L. Spiro, "Research Notes: Attracting Graduates to Sales Positions and the Role of Recruiter Knowledge: A Reexamination," *Journal of Personal Selling & Sales Management* 24 (Winter 2004): 39–48.

15. Greg W. Marshall, Daniel J. Goebel, and William C. Moncrief, "Hiring for Success at the Buyer–Seller Interface," *Journal of Business Research* 56 (2003): 247–255.

16. Jacqueline Durett, "Road Warriors: Making Honda a Fit for Gen-Y," *Sales & Marketing Management,* Sept. 2006, pp. 46–48.

17. Andrew B. Artis and Eric G. Harris, "Self-Directed Learning and Sales Force Performance: An Integrated Framework," *Journal of Personal Selling & Sales Management* 27 (Winter 2007).

18. Joseph Kornik, "What's It All Worth?" *Sales and Marketing Management,* May 2007, p. 29.

19. Tara Burnthorne Lopez, Christopher D. Hopkins, and Mary Anne Raymond, "Reward Preferences of Salespeople: How Do Commissions Rate?" *Journal of Personal Selling & Sales Management* 26 (Fall 2006): 381–390.

20. Kirk Shinkle, "All of Your People Are Salesmen: Do They Know? Are They Ready?" *Investor's Business Daily,* Feb. 6, 2002, p. A1.

21. Ibid.

22. John W. Barnes, Donald W. Jackson, Jr., Michael D. Hutt, and Ajith Kumar, "The Role of Culture Strength in Shaping Salesforce Outcomes," *Journal of Personal Selling & Sales Management* 26 (Summer 2006): 255–270.

23. William H. Murphy, Peter A. Dacin, and Neil M. Ford, "Sales Contest Effectiveness: An Examination of Sales Contest Design Preferences of Field Sales Forces," *Journal of the Academy of Marketing Science* 32, no. 2 (2004): 127–143.

24. Eilene Zimmerman, "Motivation on Any Budget," *Sales & Marketing Management,* Jan. 2004, pp. 37, 38.

25. Patricia Odell, "Motivating the Masses," *Promo,* Sept. 1, 2005, http://promomagazine.com.

26. Joseph A. Bellizzi and Ronald W. Hasty, "Supervising Unethical Sales Force Behavior: How Strong Is the Tendency to Treat Top Sales Performers Leniently?" *Journal of Business Ethics,* Apr. 2003, pp. 337–351.

27. Amy Johannes, "Wendy's to Give Away 100 Million Songs," *Promo,* Nov. 14, 2007, http://promomagazine.com/entertainmentmarketing/news/wendys_give_away_songs/.

28. Kusum L. Ailawadi, Karen Gedenk, Christian Lutzky, and Scott A. Neslin, "Decomposition of the Sales Impact of Promotion-Induced Stockpiling," *Journal of Marketing Research* XLIV (August 2007).

29. George E. Belch and Michael A. Belch, *Advertising and Promotion* (Burr Ridge, IL: Irwin/McGraw-Hill, 2004), pp. 514–522.

30. "All About Coupons," Coupon Council, www.couponmonth.com/pages/allabout.htm (accessed Feb. 22, 2008); "Savings for All Ages: Stats Show Young Adults Embracing Coupon Usage," Coupon Council, press release, Sept. 6, 2007, www.couponmonth.com/pages/news.htm; Betsy Spethmann, "FSI Coupon Worth Reaches $300 Billion in 2006: MARX," *Promo,* Jan. 4, 2007, http://promomagazine.com/othertactics/news/fsi_coupon_worth_300_billion_010407/.

31. Shelly Lipton, "Coupon Redención," *Promo,* May 1, 2007, http://promomagazine.com/coupons/marketing_coupon_redencin/.

32. Judith A. Garretson and Scot Burton, "Highly Coupon and Sale Prone Consumers: Benefits Beyond Price Savings," *Journal of Advertising Research* 43 (2003): 162–172.

33. Arthur L. Porter, "Direct Mail's Lessons for Electronic Couponers," *Marketing Management Journal,* Spring/Summer 2000, pp. 107–115.

34. Ibid.

35. Karen Holt, "Coupon Crimes," *Promo,* Apr. 1, 2004, http://promomagazine.com/mag/marketing_coupon_crimes/.

36. Brian Grow, "The Great Rebate Runaround," *BusinessWeek,* Dec. 5, 2005, pp. 34–37.

37. Richard F. Beltramini and Patricia S. Chapman, "Do Customers Believe in Automobile Industry Rebate Incentives?" *Journal of Advertising Research* 43 (2003): 16–24.

38. "Getting to Know You," *Chain Store Age,* Nov. 2005, p. 51.

39. Mya Frazier, James Tenser, and Tricia Despres, "Retail Lesson: Small Programs Best," *Advertising Age,* Mar. 20, 2006, pp. S2–S3.

40. David Rosen, "Can't Beat Loyalty," *Promo,* Feb. 1, 2008, http://promomagazine.com/othertactics/marketing_cant_beat_loyalty/.

41. Betsy Spethmann, "Schick Revved Quattro with Sampling," *Promo,* Dec. 26, 2005, http://promomagazine.com/sampling/schick_sampling_122705/.

42. "Secret Weapon?" *Promo,* Dec. 1, 2007, http://promomagazine.com/sampling/secret_weapon_trial_purchase_study/.

43. Amy Johannes, "Borders Launches Contests for Reward Members," *Promo,* Feb. 7, 2007, http://promomagazine.com/contests/borders_contests_reward_members_020707/.

44. Amy Garber, "BK Franchisees File Class Action Suit Against McD," *Nation's Restaurant News,* Aug. 29, 2005, p. 1.

45. Amy Johannes, "Kraft Puts Rachel Ray on 62 Million Nabisco Boxes," *Promo,* Dec. 4, 2007, http://promomagazine.com/retail/kraft_rachel_ray_nabisco_sweepstakes/.

46. Miguel I. Gomez, Vithala R. Rao, and Edward W. McLaughlin, "Empirical Analysis of Budget and Allocation of Trade Promotions in the U.S. Supermarket Economy," *Journal of Marketing Research* XLIV (Aug. 2007).

47. Sources: "IBM Steps Up Efforts to Drive the Adoption of Software as a Service—Offers Broadest Range of Resources Enabling Business Partners to Transition to Rapid Delivery Model," *Market Wire,* Feb. 23, 2006, www.marketwire.com/mw/release_html_b1?release_id=110803; Dan Neel, "IBM Connects the Partner Dots," *Computer Reseller News,* Nov. 7, 2005; IBM, www.ibm.com (accessed Feb. 22, 2008); Video Interviews with IBM employees: Dan Pelino, Greg Pushalla, Karen Lowe, Monica Chambers (accessed Feb. 28, 2006).

48. Sources: "Sinking the Sub Club," *Snopes,* June 2, 2005, www.snopes.com; Amy Johannes, "Subway Phases Out Sandwich Promo," *Promo,* June 6, 2005; "Subway Slated to Roll Out Massive Gift Card Program," *Nation's Restaurant News,* July 11, 2005, p. 60; Cara Baruzzi, "Counterfeit 'Sub Club' Cards Force Subway to Cancel Promotion," *New Haven Register,* June 3, 2005, www.nhregister.com; My Subway Card, www.mysubwaycard.com (accessed Feb. 22, 2008); Jacob Ogles, "Fraud Sinks Subway's Club," *Wired News,* Sept. 25, 2005, www.wired.com; Scott Leamon, "Police Accuse Pair of College Students with Forging Subway Sub Club Stamps," WSLS News Channel 10, Oct. 22, 2004, www.wsls.com (accessed May 5, 2006).

49. Sources: Michael Lev-Ram, "Does the Sidekick Still Have Punch?" *Business 2.0,* May 9, 2007, http://money.cnn.com/2007/05/03/technology/sidekicksurvive.biz2/index.htm; Michal Lev-Ram, "This $310,000 Phone Blings, Then Rings," *Business 2.0,* Dec. 20, 2006, http://money.cnn.com/2006/12/13/magazines/business2/special_phones.biz2/index.htm;

Li Yuan, "Cellphone Accessories Enter Realm of Couture," *The Wall Street Journal,* Mar. 1, 2006, p. D5; Brad Stone, "More Fun For Your Mobile; Forget Mere Ringtones. 'Mobile Media' Have Arrived," *Newsweek,* Nov. 14, 2005, p. 36; Bob Garfield, "T-Mobile Spots Succeed Because They Ring True," *Advertising Age,* Aug. 22, 2005, p. 57; Alice Z. Cuneo, "T-Mobile's Novel Sell: Great Cell Service," *Advertising Age,* Nov. 28, 2005, p. 12; Matt Richtel and Ken Belson, "Yes, T-Mobile Is Profitable, But What to Do With It?" *The New York Times,* July, 11, 2005, C5 p. 6; "T-Mobile Heats Up Hollywood's Elite With the Debut of the New Limited Edition Versions of the T-Mobile Sidekick II," *PR Newswire,* Oct. 19, 2005; "T Mobile Inks Broad Marketing Partnership with NBA and WNBA," *Business Wire,* Oct. 3, 2005; "T-Mobile Brings Today's Hottest Artists Up Close and Personal," *PR Newswire US,* July 27, 2005, www.prnewswire.com; "The Ideas Behind The Big Pink T," *Global Telecom Business,* Jan.–Feb. 2004, p. 40; "Deutsche Telekom AG: T-Mobile USA Posts Gain of 1.4 Million New Subscribers," *The Wall Street Journal,* Jan. 27, 2006, p. 1; Alice Z. Cuneo, "T-Mobile Sprinkles Stardust on Sidekick II," *Advertising Age,* Nov. 22, 2004, p. 6; Kelly Hill, "T-Mobile USA Tops J.D. Power Customer Care Survey," *RCR Wireless News,* Jan. 30, 2006, p. 3; Dan Meyer, "Can T-Mobile USA Make It Alone?" *RCR Wireless News,* Apr. 18, 2005, p. 1; T-Mobile USA, www.t-mobile.com (accessed Feb. 22, 2008).

Feature box references

a. Brian Hindo, "Monsanto: Winning the Ground War," *BusinessWeek,* Dec. 17, 2007, pp. 37–39; Allison Linn, "Experts: It's Not Easy Selling Green," MSNBC, Dec. 17, 2007, www.msnbc.msm/id/18297361/print/1/displaymode/1098/; Bruce Upbin, "Greenhouse Stocks," *Forbes,* Dec. 24, 2007, pp. 64–66.

b. Earthcraft House, www.earthcrafthouse.com (accessed Feb. 20, 2008); "Earthcraft House Program," Greater Atlanta Home Builders Association, www.atlantahomebuilders.com/education/earthcraft.cfm (accessed Feb. 20, 2008); Laura Judy, "Green from the Ground Up," *Atlanta Home Improvement,* Jan. 2006, www.homeimprovementmag.com/Articles/2006/06Jan_ground_up.html; Melanie Lindner, "Living Green: EarthCraft House," *Atlanta Intown,* Jan. 2007, www.atlantaintownpaper.com/features/EarthCraftHouseJAN07.php.

c. Cheryl Lu-Lien Tan, "Haggelling 2.0," *The Wall Street Journal,* June 23–24, 2007, pp. P1, P3; "Haggling," Haggle Point, www.hagglepoint.com/about.html (accessed Mar. 17, 2008); Dan Sewell, "Grocers Clip Digital Coupons," *USA Today,* Jan. 14, 2008, http://usatoday.com/tech/products/services/2008-01-14-grocer-digital-coupons_n.htm.

Chapter 19

1. Sources: Andrea Chalupa, "Extravagant Electronics," *Portfolio.com,* Dec. 14, 2007, www.portfolio.com; "Marketing Society Awards for Excellence: International Brand Development," *Marketing,* June 20, 2007, p. 12; "Samsung Accused of Heavy Cost-Cutting," *UPI NewsTrack,* June 5, 2007, n.p.; "Samsung and LG Hear the Call for Low-End Mobiles," *Financial Times,* Mar. 26, 2007, p. 21; "Vertu Rings Till for British-Made Luxury Goods," *PC Magazine Online,* July 16, 2007, www.pcmag.com; John Walko, "Q3 Cell Phone Stats," *Electronic Engineering Times,* Dec. 3, 2007, p. 8.

2. Rajneesh Suri and Kent B. Monroe, "The Effects of Time Constraints on Consumers' Judgments of Prices and Products," *Journal of Consumer Research,* June 2003, p. 92.

3. Kelly K. Spors, "Trade You a Laptop? Online Sites Promote the Art of the Barter," *The Wall Street Journal*, Nov. 14, 2006, p. B1, http://online.wsj.com.

4. "Hewlett-Packard," case study, Professional Pricing Society, www.pricingsociety.com/Page5024.aspx (accessed Mar. 3, 2008).

5. Yukari Iwatani Kane and Sarah McBride, "Latest Cut in DVD-Player Duel: Prices," *The Wall Street Journal*, Nov. 23, 2007, pp. B1, B2.

6. Pallavi Gogoi, "Drug Wars at the Big-Box Stores," *BusinessWeek*, May 24, 2007, www.businessweek.com.

7. Lauren Young, "Candy's Getting Dandy," *BusinessWeek*, Feb. 13, 2006, pp. 88–89.

8. Frank Byrt, "Vermont Pure Seeks to Deliver Higher Margins by Shifting Focus," *The Wall Street Journal*, Feb. 16, 2005, p. 1.

9. *Dictionary of Marketing Terms*, American Marketing Association, www.marketingpower.com/mg-dictionary.php (accessed Mar. 3, 2008).

10. Gary McWilliams and Evan Ramstad, "Where the TV Bargains Are," *The Wall Street Journal*, Jan. 17, 2006, p. D1, http://online.wsj.com/.

11. *Dictionary of Marketing Terms*.

12. Elwin Green, "Gas Prices Aren't Slowing U.S. Motorists," *Pittsburgh Post-Gazette*, Nov. 25, 2007, www.post-gazette.com/pg/07329/836591-28.stm.

13. Nicole C. Wong, "Sun Turning Around to See Profits Ahead," *The Mercury News*, Feb. 6, 2007, www.mercurynews.com/mld/mercurynews/news/16637931.htm.

14. Donald Lichtenstein, Nancy M. Ridgway, and Richard G. Netemeyer, "Price Perceptions and Consumer Shopping Behavior: A Field Study," *Journal of Marketing Research*, May 1993, pp. 234–245.

15. Linda Halstad-Acharya, "Stuck in a Sea of Surcharges: Fuel Prices Abate, But the Add-Ons Keep Coming On," *Billings Gazette*, Jan. 27, 2007, www.billingsgazette.net/articles/2007/01/27/news/local/25-stuck.txt.

16. "Investing," *BusinessWeek*, Feb. 13, 2006, p. 90.

17. Russell S. Winer, *Pricing* (Cambridge, MA: Marketing Science Institute, 2005), p. 20.

18. Manoj Thomas and Geeta Menon, "Internal Reference Prices and Price Expectations," *Journal of Marketing Research* XLIV (Aug. 2007).

19. Tong Yin and Audhesh K. Paswan, "Antecedents to Consumer Reference Price Orientation: An Exploratory Investigation," *Journal of Product & Brand Management* 16 (April 2007): 269–279.

20. Lichtenstein, Ridgway, and Netemeyer, "Price Perceptions and Consumer Shopping Behavior."

21. Gerald E. Smith and Thomas T. Nagle, "A Question of Value," *Marketing Management*, July/Aug. 2005, pp. 39–40.

22. Helen Walters, "Nike's New Downmarket Strategy," *BusinessWeek Online*, Feb. 27, 2007, www.businessweek.com.

23. Lichtenstein, Ridgway, and Netemeyer, "Price Perceptions and Consumer Shopping Behavior."

24. "Where Have All the Tightwads Gone?" *BusinessWeek*, Oct. 15, 2007, p. 16.

25. Lichtenstein, Ridgway, and Netemeyer.

26. Hitha Prabhakar, "The World's Most Expensive Jeans," *Forbes*, Dec. 8, 2006, www.forbes.com/lifestyle/2006/12/07/expensive-jeans-denim-forbeslife-cx_hp_1208expensivejeans.html.

27. Lorrie Grant, "Scrimping to Splurge," *USA Today*, Jan. 28, 2005, p. 1B; Linda Tischler, "The Price Is Right," *Fast Company*, Nov. 2003, p. 83.

28. Diane Brady, "Best Ideas," *BusinessWeek*, Dec. 19, 2005, p. 80.

29. "Six Guilty in Synthetic Rubber Pricing Fixing," *The Tire Review*, Nov. 29, 2006, www.tirereview.com/default.aspx?type=wm&module=4&id=2&state=DisplayFullText&item=6752.

30. Marc Levy, "Europe Studies Candy Prices of Hershey, Mars," *USA Today*, Feb. 19, 2008, www.usatoday.com/money/industries/food/2008-02-19-candy-price-fixing_N.htm.

31. David Perry, "Simmons Sets Fast Pace in Allowances Category," *Furniture Today*, July 10, 2006, p. 36.

32. Sources: Washburn Guitar website, www.washburn.com; Washburn Guitar video.

33. Sources: "Amazon Launches Digital Music Store," *The Wall Street Journal*, Sept. 25, 2007, www.wsj.com; Mylene Mangalindan and Jeffrey A. Trachtenberg, "IPod of E-Book Readers? Amazon Taps Apple Strategy," *The Wall Street Journal*, Nov. 20, 2007, p. B1; Mylene Mangalindan, "Online Retailers Plan More Perks for the Holidays," *The Wall Street Journal*, Nov. 13, 2007, p. D1; Mylene Mangalindan, "Amazon's Latest Thriller: Growth," *The Wall Street Journal*, Oct. 24, 2007, p. A3; Brad Stone, "Amazon Says Profit Jumped in Quarter," *The New York Times*, Oct. 24, 2007, p. C3; Bob Tedeschi, "Nothing Says 'Buy' Like 'Free Shipping,'" *The New York Times*, Oct. 8, 2007, p. C8.

Feature box references

a. Theresa Sullivan Barger, "Paint Free of Fumes, Pollution," *Hartford Courant*, June 29, 2007, p. H1; Jim Edwards, "Dowdy Paint Gets Polish—and the Price Doubles," *Brandweek*, Jan. 29, 2007, p. 12; Amanda Schupak, "An Inconvenient Paint," *Forbes*, Mar. 26, 2007, p. 70.

b. "Finance/Credit Companies: Long-Term Contribution Trends," OpenSecrets.org, http://opensecrets.org/industries/indus.asp?Ind5F06, Mar. 3, 2008 (accessed Apr. 7, 2008); "Plastic Money's Predatory Lenders," The Nader Page, http://nader.org/interest/070303.html, July 3, 2003 (accessed Apr. 7, 2008).

c. Patt Morrison, "8,000 Dodger Dogs Going, Going, Gone," *Los Angeles Times*, Apr. 12, 2007, p. A21; Adam Thompson and Jon Weinbach, "Free Eats Sell Bad Ballpark Seats," *The Wall Street Journal*, May 16, 2007, p. B1.

Chapter 20

1. Sources: Gwendolyn Bounds, "TerraCycle Fashions a New Life for Old Wrappers," *The Wall Street Journal*, July 1, 2008, p. B5; Arden Dale, "Green Products Gain from New Price Equation," *The Wall Street Journal*, June 24, 2008, p. B7; Christopher Shulgan, "The Worm Wrangler," *Maclean's*, June 4, 2007, pp. 34+; www.terracycle.com.

2. Mara der Hovanesian and Christopher Palmeri, "That Sinking Feeling," *BusinessWeek*, Oct. 15, 2007, pp. 32–36.

3. William C. Symonds and Robert Bernes, "Gillette's New Edge," *BusinessWeek Online*, Feb. 6, 2006.

4. Kevin Schweitzer, "Hybrid Potential Limited Only by Price," *Chicago Tribune*, Feb. 11, 2005, p. 10.

5. Chang-Ran Kim, "Toyota to Halve Hybrid Price, Size for Next Prius," Reuters, Oct. 25, 2007, www.reuters.com/article/marketsNews/idUKT13140520071025?rpc=44&pageNumber=1&sp=true.

6. "New Bentley Pricing," Automotive.com, www.automotive.com/new-cars/pricing/01/bentley/index.html (accessed Mar. 5, 2008).

7. Robert J. Frank, Jeffrey P. George, and Laxman Narasimhan, "When Your Competitor Delivers More for Less," *McKinsey Quarterly*, www.Mckinseyquarterly.com (accessed Dec. 20, 2007).

8. Barry J. Babin, David M. Hardesty, and Tracy A. Suter, "Color and Shopping Intentions: The Intervening Effect of Price Fairness and Perceived Affect," *Journal of Business Research*, July 2003, pp. 541–551.

9. Alex Taylor III, "The Black Art of Auto Pricing," *Fortune*, Dec. 3, 2007, www.cnnmoney.com.

10. "Fairchild Dynamic Pricing Team," Professional Pricing Society, case study, www.pricingsociety.com/Page5023.aspx (accessed Mar. 5, 2008).

11. George J. Avlonitis and Kostis A. Indounas, "Pricing Objectives and Pricing Methods in the Services Sector," *Journal of Services Marketing* 19 (Jan. 2005): 47–57.

12. "Cutler-Hammer/Eaton Corporation," case study, Professional Pricing Society, www.pricingsociety.com/Page5022 .aspx (accessed Mar. 5, 2008).

13. Marla Royne Stafford and Thomas F. Stafford, "The Effectiveness of Tensile Pricing Tactics in the Advertising of Services," *Journal of Advertising*, Summer 2000, pp. 45–56.

14. Jonathan Sidener, "Feature-Rich Cell Phones Are All the Rate This Holiday Season, and Expected to Give the iPhone Stiff Competition," *San Diego Union-Tribune*, Dec. 9, 2007, www.signonsandiego.com/news/tech/20071209-9999-lz1b9phones.html.

15. "Arctic Monkeys Play on Web Hype," CNNMoney, Feb. 2, 2006, www.cnnmoney.com.

16. Amanda Cantrell, "iPod Add-Ons: Boombox Purses, and More," CNNMoney, Jan. 12, 2006, www.cnnmoney.com.

17. Lee Gomes, "A Peek Under PlayStation 3's Hood Shows Sony Is Selling Units at a Loss," *The Wall Street Journal*, Nov. 21, 2006, http://online.wsj.com.

18. Mark Phelan, "$100,000 Corvette Supercar Aims to Best Exotic Rivals," *USA Today*, Dec. 20, 2007, http://www.usatoday .com/money/autos/2007-12-20-corvette-zr1_N.htm.

19. Mike Ricciuti, "Microsoft Sets Vista Prices, Expands Testing," Cinet, Sept. 5, 2006, http://news.com.com/2100-1016_ 3-6112260.html.

20. Simona Romani, "Price Misleading Advertising: Effects on Trustworthiness Toward the Source of Information and Willingness to Buy," *Journal of Product & Brand Management* 15 (2006): 130–138.

21. Daniel A. Sheinin and Janet Wagner, "Pricing Store Brands across Categories and Retailers," *Journal of Product & Brand Management* 12 (Apr. 2003): 201–220.

22. Jaihak Chung and Vithala R. Rao, "A General Choice Model for Bundles with Multiple-Category Products: Application to Market Segmentation and Optimal Pricing for Bundles," *Journal of Marketing Research*, May 2003, pp. 115–130.

23. George Mannes, "The Urge to Unbundle," *Fast Company*, Feb. 2005, pp. 23–25.

24. Mannes, "The Urge to Unbundle."

25. Kris Hudson, "Competing Retailers Dispute Wal-Mart Trademark Request," *The Wall Street Journal*, Nov. 7, 2006, http://online.wsj.com; "NGA Stops Wal-Mart's EDLP Trademark Plan," *Frozen Food Age*, Apr. 4, 2007, http://archives .frozenfoodage.com/publication/article.jsp?id=319&pubId=1.

26. "'Made in USA' Means Little to Furniture Buyers," MSNBC, Feb. 10, 2006, www.msnbc.com.

27. Christine Harris and Jeffery Bray, "Price Endings and Consumer Segmentation," *Journal of Product & Brand Management* 16 (Mar. 2007): 200–205.

28. Ralk Wagner and Kai-Stefan Beinke, "Identifying Patterns of Customer Response to Price Endings," *Journal of Product & Brand Management* 15 (May 2006): 341–351.

29. Sajeev Varki, Sanjiv Sabherwal, Albert Della Bitta, and Keith M. Moore, "Price-End Biases in Financial Products," *Journal of Product & Brand Management* 15 (June 2006): 394–401.

30. Rita Rubin, "Placebo Tests 'Costlier is Better' Notion," *USA Today*, Mar. 4, 2008, www.usatoday.com/news/health/2008-03-04-placebo-effect_N.htm.

31. "Best Ideas," *BusinessWeek*, Dec. 19, 2005, pp. 76–77.

32. Bruce L. Alford and Brian T. Engelland, "Advertised Reference Price Effects on Consumer Price Estimates, Value Perception, and Search Intention," *Journal of Business Research*, May 2000, pp. 93–100.

33. "Blockbuster Plans to Eliminate 300 Jobs," *BusinessWeek Online*, Feb. 8, 2006.

34. Sources: Steve Miller, "Vroom for Two," *Brandweek*, June 2, 2008, pp. 20+; Bill Marsh, "Welcome, Little Smart Car, to the Big American Road," *The New York Times*, Jan. 6, 2008, sec. 4, p. 3; Chris Woodyard, "America Crazy about Breadbox on Wheels Called Smart Car," *USA Today*, Nov. 11, 2007, www.usatoday.com/money/autos/2007-11-11-smart-car_N.htm; Royal Ford, "Smallest Car, Biggest Market," *Boston Globe*, Dec. 6, 2007, p. E1.

35. Sources: Alice Z. Cuneo, "iPhone: Steve Jobs," *Advertising Age*, Nov. 12, 2007, p. S13; Katie Hafner and Brad Stone, "iPhone Owners Crying Foul Over Price Cut," *The New York Times*, Sept. 7, 2007, pp. C1, C7; Yukari Iwatani Kane and Nick Wingfield, "For Apple iPhone, Japan Could Be the Next Big Test," *The Wall Street Journal*, Dec. 19, 2007, p. B1; Brad Kenney, "Apple's iPhone: IW's IT Product of the Year," *Industry Week*, Dec. 2007, pp. 47+; Josh Krist, "The Painful Cost of First-on-the-Block Bragging Rights," *PC World*, Dec. 2007, pp. 53+; Alex Markels, "Apple's Mac Sales Are Surging," *U.S. News & World Report*, Sept. 26, 2007, n.p.; Jon Swartz, "iPhone Helps Apple Earn Juicy Profit," *USA Today*, Oct. 23, 2007, p. 1B.

36. Sources: Gail Edmondson, "The Race to Build Really Cheap Cars," *BusinessWeek*, Apr. 23, 2007, pp. 44–48; John Murphy, "Suzuki Sets the Pace in India," *The Wall Street Journal*, Dec. 13, 2007, p. C5; "Our Companies," Tata Motors, www.tata.com/tata_motors/index.htm (accessed Mar. 6, 2008); Steven Cole Smith, "Will Consumers Say Tata to Used Cars?" *Orlando Sentinel*, Nov. 16, 2007, www.orlandosentinel.com; Heather Timmons, "India's Automaker of Many Faces May Land Jaguar," *The New York Times*, Dec. 18, 2007, p. C3; Heather Timmons, "In India, a $2,500 Pace Car," *The New York Times*, Oct. 12, 2007, pp. C1, C4.

Feature box references

a. "Green as Houses: Environmentalism and Building," *The Economist*, Sept. 15, 2007, p. 42; Christopher Palmeri, "Green Homes: The Price Still Isn't Right," *BusinessWeek*, Feb. 12, 2007, p. 67.

b. N'Gai Croal, "Beware the Red Rings of Death," *Newsweek*, July 16, 2007, p. 10; "Japan: Microsoft Cuts Price of Xbox 360," *The New York Times*, Oct. 23, 2007, p. C7; Yukari Iwatani Kane and Nick Wingfield, "Nintendo Plays It a Wii Bit Cautious," *The Wall Street Journal*, Dec. 7, 2007, p. B1; Yukari Iwatani Kane, "Sony Price Cut Helps Its PS3 Gain Traction," *The Wall Street Journal*, Nov. 26, 2007, p. B4; Matt Richtel, "Xbox 360 Out of Order? For Loyalists, No Worries," *The New York Times*, Aug. 13, 2007, pp. C1, C7.

Chapter 1 p. 6: WireImage/Getty; p. 7 left: © 2007 Pepsico; p. 7 right: © 2007 The Coca-Cola Company; p. 8: Courtesy Petzl; p. 12: Courtesy Survey Sampling International; p. 16: newscom.com; p. 19 left: Photo © American Indian College Fund. All rights reserved.; p. 19 right: National Multiple Sclerosis Society, Join the Movement PSA campaign; p. 20 left: Apple Corporation; p. 20 right: Goodby, Silverstein & Partners; p. 22: © Corbis; p. 27: Courtesy Method.

Chapter 2 p. 30: AFP/Getty Images; p. 33: Burger King Brands, Inc.; p. 34: Courtesy Continental Airlines; p. 35: Courtesy twitter.com; p. 36 left: Courtesy Boca Foods; p. 36 right: Courtesy the Beef Checkoff Program; p. 40: Boeing Images; p. 43: Courtesy L.L.Bean; p. 44: Courtesy Southwest Airlines; p. 46: Getty Images; p. 49: Courtesy Samsung International; p. 57: Getty Images; p. 58: © MedioImages/Corbis.

Chapter 3 p. 62: Courtesy Wikipedia; p. 65 bottom left: Courtesy Subaru; p. 65 bottom right: Courtesy Honda Motor Company of America; p. 67 left: Courtesy IKEA; p. 67 right: Courtesy Lowe's; p. 68: www.barbie-dressupgames.com; p. 71 left: Courtesy Tag Heuer; p. 71 right: Courtesy Omega; p. 75: Courtesy American Spirit; p. 78: Sustainable Forestry Initiative; p. 80: Courtesy BASF and Ed James; p. 82 left: Courtesy Nestlé Purina Pet Care; p. 82 right: Courtesy Merial; p. 84: © cameragirl@burningman.com; p. 90: Lester Lefkowitz/Getty Images.

Chapter 4 p. 92: AP/Wide World; p. 94: Courtesy Home Depot; p. 97: Courtesy Shell RealEnergy; p. 100: © Andy Atchison/Corbis; p. 101 left: Courtesy Hertz; p. 101 right: U.S. EPA Climate Leaders Program; p. 103: Courtesy Atreus Homes and Communities; p. 108: Courtesy Simple Shoes; p. 110: Courtesy PETA; p. 114: Courtesy Susan G. Komen for the Cure®; p. 116: Courtesy FINCA International; p. 120: AP/Wide World.

Chapter 5 p. 127 top: Digital Vision/Getty; p. 127 bottom: Hugh Johnson/Getty Images; p. 128: Digital Vision/Getty; p. 131: Courtesy Irwin Research; p. 133: Dream Pictures/Getty Images; p. 135: Courtesy M/A/R/C Research, created by Avrea Foster; p. 136: Nicki Nikoni/Getty Images; p. 140: Courtesy Infosurv, Inc.; p. 146: Courtesy Market Strategies; p. 147: Courtesy ReRez; p. 149: Courtesy Western Wats.

Chapter 6 p. 158: Hugh Johnson/Getty Images; p. 164: Courtesy VISA USA; p. 165 left: Courtesy Procter & Gamble Company; p. 165 right: Courtesy Unilever United States, Inc.; p. 166 left: Courtesy Geico Insurance; p. 166 right: © 2007 Pepsico; p. 168: Zia Soleil/Getty Images; p. 171: Courtesy Garmin; p. 173: © Virgo Productions/zefa/Corbis; p. 178: Courtesy Levi Strauss & Co.; p. 180: Hershey Corporation; p. 189: Getty Images.

Chapter 7 p. 192: © Jerry Arcieri/Corbis; p. 196: Courtesy Kao Brands Company; p. 197: Courtesy Avis Budget Group; p. 203: Courtesy Unilever United States, Inc.; p. 204: The Nature Conservancy; p. 205: Courtesy The Stride Rite Corporation; p. 207: AP/Wide World; p. 209: AP/Wide World; p. 211: © Fox Interactive Media; p. 213: Courtesy scifen; p. 219: Image Source/Getty Images.

Chapter 8 p. 222: Tetra Images/Getty Images; p. 226: Courtesy BASF; p. 229: Courtesy CDW; p. 230: © George Hall/Corbis; p. 231: Courtesy Volvo Construction Equipment; p. 232: Courtesy Accenture; p. 233: Courtesy Intel; p. 235: Courtesy Sprint; p. 236: Poulides/Thatcher/Stone/Getty Images; p. 243: Dan Mandelkorn.

Chapter 9 p. 244: AP Photo/Greg Baker; p. 246: Kraft Foods; p. 247: Courtesy Cadbury Adams USA, Ltd.; p. 251: Cargill; p. 254: Courtesy Verizon Wireless; p. 255: © Peter Beck/Corbis; p. 258: PRNewsFoto/China8; p. 261: PRNewswire/PepsiCola North America; p. 264: © Martin Ruetschi/Keystone/Corbis; p. 270: PRNewsFoto/PepsiCola Company; p. 274: PRNewsFoto; p. 278: Getty Images.

Chapter 10 p. 280: Courtesy BlendTec; p. 282: Courtesy Houston Museum of Natural History; p. 284: Digital Vision/Getty Images; p. 285 bottom left: Courtesy Dreyer's Grand Ice Cream; p. 285 bottom right: Courtesy Marriott International; p. 287: Courtesy Rolex Watch USA Inc.; p. 288: Courtesy New Holland Construction/Kobelco; p. 289 left: Courtesy Mad Rock Climbing; p. 289 right:

Courtesy Hilton Hotels Corporation; p. 290: © 2008 Suzanne Smith; p. 292: Courtesy Apple Computer, Inc.; p. 302: PRNewswire.

Chapter 11 p. 304: © Tim Pannell/Corbis; p. 307: Courtesy General Mills; p. 308: Courtesy Jeep/Chrysler LLC; p. 310: PRNewswire; p. 314: AP/Wide World; p. 316: © Peter Adams/zefa/Corbis; p. 317: Vertu.com; p. 319: Courtesy Cort; p. 324: Morguefile.

Chapter 12 p. 326: Jupiter Images; p. 329: Courtesy Target Stores; p. 330: © 2007 Procter & Gamble; p. 332: Courtesy Bayer HealthCare LLC; p. 333: Courtesy Banana Republic; p. 336: © 2008 Susan Holtz; p. 339: © 2008 Susan Holtz; p. 340: © Neal Preston/Corbis; p. 343: © 2008 Susan Holtz; p. 346: Getty Images; p. 353: PrNewswire.

Chapter 13 p. 354: AP/Wide World; p. 357: Courtesy camelotthethemepark .co.uk; p. 359: Digital/Getty Images; p. 361: © 2008 Union Bank of California; p. 362: Courtesy Scripps Health; p. 365: © 2007 Mail Boxes Etc.; p. 366: Courtesy Verizon Wireless; p. 367: Courtesy ftd.com; p. 368: Courtesy Best Buy; p. 371: © 2008 Automobile Club of Southern California. All rights reserved.; p. 372: Digital Vision/Getty Images; p. 374: PRNewswire; p. 380: RF Corbis.

Chapter 14 p. 386: Courtesy MHW Group; p. 389 left: © 2007 YRC Logistics, Inc. All rights reserved.; p. 389 right: Courtesy Averitt Express; p. 391: Courtesy Lynden; p. 394: © Buddy Hayes/Corbis; p. 396: Courtesy Starbucks; p. 400: © 2007 Kraft Foods; p. 402: Courtesy General Mills; p. 410: DK Stock/Getty Images; p. 419: RF Corbis.

Chapter 15 p. 422: © amanaimages/Corbis; p. 426: Courtesy Macy's; p. 428: Time & Life Pictures/Getty Images; p. 429: Courtesy Sam's Club; p. 430: Courtesy Michael's; p. 431: Courtesy Lowe's; p. 432: © 2007 McDonald's. All rights reserved.; p. 434: AP Photo/Jerry S. Mendoza; p. 435: Courtesy Sportsman's Warehouse; p. 438: © 2007 eBay, Inc.; p. 441: Courtesy Fatburger; p. 452: AP/Wide World; p. 455: Digital Vision/Getty Images.

Chapter 16 p. 458: Stock Illustration Source/Getty Imges; p. 460: Courtesy Adriano Goldschmied; p. 464: Courtesy Dassault Falcon; p. 465: Courtesy Vibram USA Inc.; p. 466: Getty Images; p. 467: © 2007 The Coca Cola Company; p. 469: Courtesy Denver Zoo; p. 470: Courtesy www.DiabetesAware.com; p. 471: © IBM Corporation 2007. All rights reserved.; p. 473: © 2007 Jamba Juice Company; p. 475: Frito-Lay North America, Inc. © 2007; p. 478: Digital Vision/Getty Images; p. 486: Courtesy Columbia Sportswear.

Chapter 17 p. 488: © Henning v. Holleben/bilderlounge/Corbis; p. 492: © 2006 LG Electronics, Inc.; p. 493: © 2006 Reebok International; p. 499: Sean Murphy/Getty Images; p. 501: Courtesy Accenture; p. 502: © 2007 Thomasville; p. 503 left and right: ®2006 Mars, Incorporated. All rights reserved Masterfoods USA Newsroom; p. 505: Courtesy Dover Motorsports Inc.; p. 506: Courtesy Ben & Jerry's; p. 508: Stone/Getty Images; p. 515: © Solus-Veer/Corbis.

Chapter 18 p. 516: AP/Wide World; p. 518: Courtesy State Farm Insurance; p. 520: Courtesy infoUSA; p. 522: © Thom Lang/Corbis; p. 523: Courtesy OutStart SellingEdge.com; p. 527: Courtesy careerbuilder .com; p. 528: Courtesy landslide.com; p. 531: © 2007 Hallmark Insights. All rights reserved.; p. 533: © 2007 Atreus Homes & Communities; p. 535: © 2007 The Coca-Cola Company; p. 538: Courtesy Sea World, San Diego; p. 544: AP Photo/Adrian Bimmer.

Chapter 19 p. 550: The Image Bank/Getty Images; p. 553: Courtesy Best Buy; p. 554: Photonica/Getty Images; p. 564: © 2006 Elizabeth Arden, Inc. Hilary Duff™ is a trademark of Rafter H. Entertainment, Inc., and is used with permission, p. 565: © 2007 PSSW; p. 566: © Richard Ransier/Corbis; p. 567: Agency: klein+byers ny, Photographer: Nigel Parry, cpi; p. 568: © 2006 Hewlett-Packard Development Company, L.P.; p. 571: Courtesy Lesco Professional Turf Products; p. 576: Market Wire.

Chapter 20 p. 578: AP/Wide World/Andy Wong; p. 582: © Grand Tour/Corbis; p. 583: © 2000-2008 MicroCotton.com. All rights reserved.; p. 586: Courtesy Avis Rent A Car System, LLC; p. 588: Courtesy UPS Store; p. 590: Courtesy Procter & Gamble; p. 592: Joan Joannides/Alamy; p. 594: Courtesy Walt Disney Travel Company; p. 595: Courtesy Fresh & Easy Neighborhood Market Inc.; p. 596: PRNewswire; p. 603: © Simon Jarratt/Corbis.

Aaker, D., 331n, N8
Aaker, David A., N16
Aaker, Jennifer L., N10
Abell, Derek F., N2
Abratt, Russell, N17
Adamy, Janet, N12–N16, N20
Ahmed, Sadrudin A., N12
Ahuja, Anita, 478
Ailawadi, Kusum L., N24
Alaimo, Dan, N10
Alderson, Wroe, N19
Alford, Bruce L., N27
Allan, Barbara, N8
Allen, Theodore T., N8
Alltucker, Ken, N23
Alsever, Jennifer, N19
Álvarez, Luis Ignacio, N4
Anders, George, N22
Anderson, Diane, N2
Anderson, Erin, N19
Anderson, Eugene W., N1
Andretti, Marco, 517
Andretti, Mario, 517
Andretti, Michael, 517
Angelou, Maya, 215
Ante, Spencer E., N9
Apple, Fiona, 479
Arctic Monkeys, 590
Areni, Charles S., N23
Arens, William F., 498n
Aristide, Vanessa, N23
Arndt, Michael, N19
Arnold, Catherine, N8
Arora, Nikesh, 547
Artis, Andrew B., N24
Asmus, Peter, N6, N17
Aspinwall, Leo, N19
Atal, Maha, N11
Athitakis, Mark, N14
Atuahene-Gima, Kwaku, N1, N3
Avlonitis, George J., N27

Babin, Barry J., N6, N26
Bahree, Megha, N22
Bailey, Jeff, N23
Balabanis, George, N12
Balfour, Frederik, N12
Ball, Deborah, N12, N14, N15, N17
Ball, Jeffrey, N19
Balu, Rekha, N13
Banstetter, Trebor, N18
Barger, Theresa Sullivan, N26
Barksdale, Hiram C., Jr., N24
Barnes, Brooks, N15
Barnes, John W., N24
Barnett, Tim, N6
Barret, Victoria Murphy, N10
Barrett, Rick, N16
Baruzzi, Cara, N25
Bass, Debra D., N16
Bassill, Steve, N9
Basuroy, Suman, N23
Bateson, John E. G., 363n, N17
Baun, Robert, N17
Bayón, Tomás, N18, N22
Bayus, Barry L., N14
Beasty, Colin, N3
Becker, Allison, N9
Beckham, David, 8
Beinke, Kai-Stefan, N27
Beirne, Mike, N1
Belch, George E., 498n, N23, N24
Belch, Michael A., 498n, N23, N24

Belcher, Walt, N16
Belk, Russell W., N10
Belkin, Douglas, N17
Bellenger, Danny N., N11
Bellizzi, Joseph A., N24
Bellstrom, Kristen, 596n
Belluck, Pam, N22
Belson, Ken, N25
Beltramini, Richard F., N25
Benensen, Joel, 129
Bens, Katrina J., N11
Berman, Dennis K., N14, N16
Berner, Robert, N20
Bernes, Robert, N26
Berney-Reddish, Ilona A., N23
Berry, Leonard L., 363n, 369n, 370n, N17, N18
Best, Roger J., N17
Bettencourt, Nuno, 576
Betts, Paul, N16
Bezos, Jeff, 63, 577
Bhattacharya, C. B., N7
Bialik, Carl, N24
Bianco, Anthony, N17
Bick, Geoff, N17
Biemans, Wim, N14
Blackshaw, Pete, N10
Blackwell, Roger D., 212n
Blakely, Kiri, N22
Blakely, Sara, 327
Blodgett, Jeffrey G., N12
Blumenau, Kurt, N20
Boehmer, Jay, N14, N16
Boersma, Margreet F., N13
Bolaji, Ojo, N15
Boles, James S., N6, N24
Bolton, Lisa, 290
Bond, Edward U., III, N3
Borden, Mark, N2
Bosmans, Anick, N20
Bounds, Gwendolyn, N26
Bourdeau, Brian L., N17
Bowman, Douglas, N2
Boyer, Kenneth Karel, N19
Boyle, Gert, 486–487
Boyle, Matthew, N1, N21
Boyle, Tim, 486
Bradley, Samuel D., III, N21
Brady, Diane, N26
Brady, Michael K., N17
Brashear, Thomas G., N12
Bray, Jeffery, N27
Breen, Bill, N2
Brenneman, Greg, 57
Brewer, Eric, 255
Bridges, Claudia M., N24
Brier, Noah Rubin, N9
Briley, Donnel A., N10
Brodie, John, N1
Bronczek, Dave, 59
Brooks, Rick, N4
Brown, Orlando, 441
Brown, Stephen, N20
Buckley, Peter J., N13
Bulik, Beth Snyder, N22
Burger, Katherine, N18
Burns, Enid, N21
Burrows, Peter, N16
Burt, Jeffrey, N11
Burton, Scot, N21, N25
Busch, Paul, N24
Bush, Michael, N14
Butler, Mike, 548

Buzzell, Robert D., N3
Byrnes, Nannette, N5
Byron, Ellen, N8, N14, N16
Byrt, Frank, N26

Caballero, Steve, 514
Cadbury, Sir Adrian, N7
Cadogan, John W., N2, N8
Cantrell, Amanda, N27
Capell, Kerry, N2
Capella, Michael, N17
Caplan, Jeremy, N10
Caponigro, John P., 517
Carey, John, N2
Carey, Susan, N12
Carless, Simon, N2
Carofano, Jennifer, N10
Carolan, Michael, N18
Carpenter, Gregory S., N1
Carpiet, Lynette, N20
Carroll, Archie, 96n, N6
Carson, Stephen J., N15
Carson, Thomas L., N6
Carter, Sandy, 236
Casey, Susan, N14
Catanese, Nick, 576
Cavusgil, S. Tamer, N12, N13
Cescau, Patrick, 22
Challagalla, Goutam N., N24
Chalupa, Andrea, N25
Chamberlain, Lisa, N10
Chambers, Monica, N25
Chang, Kenneth, N8
Chao, Loretta, N13
Chapman, Patricia S., N25
Charles, Ray, 441
Chase, Charles W., Jr., N10
Chatterjee, Subimal, N23
Chelariu, Cristian, N12
Cheng, Jonathan, N12
Cheng, T. C. Edwin, N3
Cher, 441
Chesshyre, Tom, N12
Chidsey, John W., 57
Chih Kang Wang, N21
Chokwatana, Boonyakiat, 454
Chon, Gina, N2, N4
Chonko, Lawrence B., N6
Christie, Benjamin, 522
Chu, Ariana Eunjung, N9
Chu, Jeff, N2
Chuang, Shin-Chieh, N10
Chung, Jaihak, N27
Church, Warren, N16
Cioletti, Jeff, N17
Clinton, Bill, 129
Coates, Ta-Nehisi, N1
Cohen, Ben, 119
Cohen, Dorothy, N16
Cohen, Jonathan, N16
Colbert, Catherine, N7
Coldplay, 9
Cole, Neil, 352
Cole, Steven, 370
Coleman, Richard P., 211
Collett, Stacey, N9
Comiskey, David, N2
Coney, Kenneth A., N17
Conley, Lucas, N20
Conlin, Michelle, N17
Contractor, Farok J., N13
Cooper, Anderson, N5
Cooper, Lee G., N15

Halstad-Acharya, Linda, N26
Hamilton, Anita, 35, N1, N4
Hamm, Steve, N5, N11
Hampp, Andrew, N11
Hanas, Jim, N10
Hanks, Tom, 522
Hardesty, David M., N26
Hargreaves, Steve, N14
Harich, Katrin R., N16
Harrington, Lisa, N11, N19
Harris, Christine, N27
Harris, Eric G., N24
Hart, Christopher, N10
Hart, Susan, N3
Hartline, Michael, 32n, N1–N4, N14, N18
Harvey, Larry, 84
Harwood, John, N8
Hastings, Reed, 419
Hasty, Ronald W., N24
Hauser, John R., N8
Hawes, Jon M., N24
Hawk, Tony, 514
Hawken, Paul, N6
Hawkins, Del I., N17
Hazel, Debra, N20
Healey, James R., N14
Heger, Monica, N21
Heilmann, John, N2
Hein, Kenneth, N8, N22, N23
Helft, Miguel, N14, N18
Heller, Laura, N11
Heller, Lorraine, N2
Helyar, John, N21
Henderson, Pamela W., N23
Hennessey, Phillip, N10
Herrmann, Andreas, N14
Heskel, Julia, N17
Hesseldahl, Arik, N15
Hewett, Kelly, N17
Higgins, Michelle, N7, N10
Hill, Donna J., N8
Hill, Kelly, N25
Hilton, Paris, 471, 547
Hinchey, John, 410
Hindmarch, Anya, 478
Hindo, Brian, N15, N25
Hoag, Christina, N11
Hochman, Paul, N2
Hochwald, Lambeth, N9
Hoffman, K. Douglas, 363n, N17
Hogan, Donna, N19
Holahan, Catherine, N2
Hollis, Nigel, N16
Holmes, Stanley, N20
Holt, David, 351
Holt, Douglas B., N16
Holt, Karen, N25
Homburg, Christian, N1–N3, N6
Hooley, Graham J., N2
Hoover, Kent, N2
Hopkins, Christopher D., N24
Hopper, Dennis, 365
Horn, John, N16
Horovitz, Bruce, N1, N4, N5, N15, N21
Horowitz, Adam, N14
Housenbold, Jeff, 382, N18
Houston, Mark B., N3, N17
Hovanesian, Mara der, N26
Howard, Bruce, N8
Howard, Daniel J., N23
Howard, Theresa, N8, N16
Howell, Debbie, N14
Howell, Roy D., N8
Hoyer, Wayne D., N10
Hsieh, Ming-Huel, N12
Hu, Michael Y., N8
Huber, Frank, N14
Hudson, Eric, 508

Hudson, Kris, N20, N21, N27
Huget, Jennifer, N2
Hughes, Laura Q., N10
Hulland, John, N3, N8
Hult, G. Tomas M., N3, N14, N19
Humphreys, Jeffrey M., 214n, N5, N11
Hunt, Shelby D., N6
Hunter, Gary K., N24
Hutt, Michael D., N11, N24
Hyatt, James C., N7

Iacono, Erica, N22
Ian, Scott, 576
Im, Sabin, N17
Indounas, Kostis A., N27
Isidore, Chris, N1, N15
Iskat, Wilifried, N17
Izraeli, Dave, N12

Jackson, Donald W., Jr., N24
Jackson, Janet, 441
Jacobson, Robert, N1
James, Jerry, 84
James, LeBron, 476
Jamil, Maqbul, N22
Jana, Reena, N8, N11, N15
Janoff, Barry, N14
Jaramillo, Fernando, N24
Jarvik, Robert, 494
Jarvis, Jeff, 211, N15
Jarvis, Ron, 284
Jarvis, Steve, N11
Jassawalla, Avan R., N3
Jaworski, Bernard J., N1, N3
Jensen, Ove, N3
Jobs, Steve, 286, 506, 603, N15
Johannes, Amy, N22, N24, N25
Johanson, Jan, N13
Johar, Gita Venkataramani, N10
John, Andrew, N6, N18
John, Joby, N17
Johnson, Avery, N23
Johnson, Jean L., N3
Johnson, Julie T., N24
Johnson, Magic, 441
Johnson, Michael D., N14
Johnston, Wesley J., N11
Jones, Eli, N24
Jones, Morag Cuddeford, N10
Jordan, Gregory, N11
Jordan, Kim, 350
Jordan, Michael, 189
Judge, Jerry, 489
Judge, William Q., N13
Judy, Laura, N25
Jurgensen, John, N22

Kafka, Lillian, N19
Kaltcheva, Velitchka D., N20
Kamakura, Wagner A., N8
Kane, Yukari Iwatani, N26, N27
Kanellos, Michael, N5
Kang, Stephanie, N9, N10, N15, N20
Kant, Ravi, 604
Keefe, Lisa M., N1
Keeton, Ann, N12
Keillor, Bruce, N13
Keith, Janet E., N21
Kelleher, Kevin, N8
Kelly, Marjorie, N7
Kelly, Matt, N11
Kemp, David, N17
Kennedy, John F., 103
Kenney, Brad, N27
Kerin, Roger A., N23
Kessler, Gladys, 177
Kessler, Michelle, N3
Keyes, Alicia, 282

Kher, Anuradha, N3
Kiley, David, N12
Kilman, Scott, N19
Kim, Chang-Ram, N26
Kim, Chung K., N15
Kirkpatrick, David, N1
Kisiel, Ralph, N11
Kiviat, Barbara, N10
Klein, Jill Gabrielle, N6
Klein, Noreen M., N21
Knight, Gary A., N12
Knight, Matthew, N14
Kobkaew, Jaturong, N21
Kohli, Ajay K., N1
Kohli, Chiranjeev, N1, N16
Koop, C. Everett, 123
Kornik, Joseph, N24
Kotler, Philip, N9, N18
Kozinets, Robert V., N8
Kranhold, Kathryn, N1
Kratz, Ellen Florian, N4
Krause, Kristin S., N4
Krauss, Clifford, N15
Krishnan, R., 134n, N8
Krist, Josh, N27
Krohmer, Karley, N2
Krupka, Zoran, N12
Kuehn, Richard, N18
Kugler, Sarah, N22
Kumar, Ajith, N24
Kumar, V., N1, N3, N8
Kump, Leslie, N18
Kundu, Sumit K., N13
Kushner, David, N2

Lacter, Mark, N2
Laczniak, Gene R., N7
Ladd, Robert T., N19
Lafley, A. G., N15
Lagerfeld, Karl, 567
Lal, Rajiv, N16
Laliberté, Guy, 355
Lamfrom, Marie, 486
Lamfrom, Paul, 486
La Monica, Paul R., N22
Lampinen, Minttu, N15
Lane, Vicki R., N17, N22
Langert, Bob, 50
Lareau, Jamie, N8
Lasswell, Mark, N14
Lavack, Anne M., N15
LaVallee, Andrew, N2, N4
Lavelle, Louis, N14
Layton, Johnny, 514
Lazare, Lewis, N18
Leamon, Scott, N25
Leatherman, Tim, 3
Lebesch, Jeff, 350–351
Lee, Eunkyu, N8
Lee, Jason, N23
Lee, Kee-hung, N3
Lee, Ruby Pui-Wan, N3
Leeds, Jeff, N7
Lehmann, Donald R., N1
Lelchuk, Ilene, N7
Lemon, Katherine N., N1
Leone, Robert P., N3
Leonidou, Leonidas C., N11
Lepkowska-White, Elzbieta, N12
Lescanne, Michael, 93
Leung, Shirley, N8
Leuthesser, Lance, N16
Levine, Robert, N2
Levitt, Theodore, N13
Lev-Ram, Michael, N1, N17, N25
Levy, Marc, N26
Levy, Michael, N15, N17
Levy, Steven, N10